MW00991352

A History of the Roman People

"This new edition of *A History of the Roman People* presents a clear, reliable, and accessible survey of the ancient Roman world. The political narrative of the growth and transformation of the Roman Empire is described in fluid and engaging fashion, and social, cultural, and economic topics receive appropriate contextualization. Ancient sources are helpfully introduced at the beginning of chapters, and charming boxes on topics such as poisoning, latrines, and publishing provide colorful detail. This remarkable textbook should be the standard introduction to the Roman world."

—*Carolynn Roncaglia,* Santa Clara University, USA

A History of the Roman People offers students a comprehensive, up-to-date, readable introduction to the whole span of Roman history. Richly illustrated, this fully updated volume takes readers through the mists of Roman prehistory and a survey of the peoples of pre-Roman Italy to a balanced, thoughtful account of the complexities of the Roman Republic, its evolution into a full-fledged empire, and its ultimate decline. This latest edition enhances the political narrative with explorations of elements of daily life in the Roman world.

New features in this edition include:

- Addition of boxes that expand on interesting elements of Roman culture mentioned only in passing in the main text. The visual arrangement of the text helps students bear in mind what is supplemental to the central narrative
- Increased emphasis on the contributions of women to Roman society and in religious matters
- Incorporation of recent archaeological finds and current debates

A History of the Roman People is an excellent introduction for those with no background in Roman history. Its clear, accessible language makes it perfect for undergraduate readers in courses on Roman history and Roman culture. More experienced students wanting to expand their knowledge will also find it a rich resource for the full sweep of Roman antiquity.

Celia E. Schultz is Professor of Classical Studies at the University of Michigan, USA, where she is currently Director of the Interdepartmental Program in Greek and Roman History.

Allen M. Ward is Emeritus Professor of History at the University of Connecticut, USA.

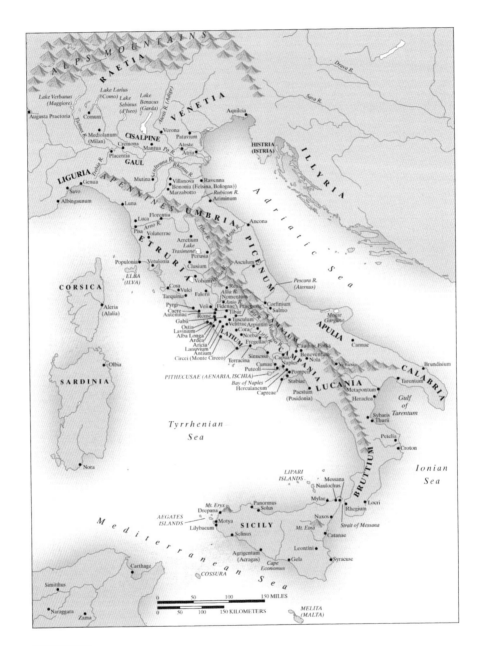

ANCIENT ITALY

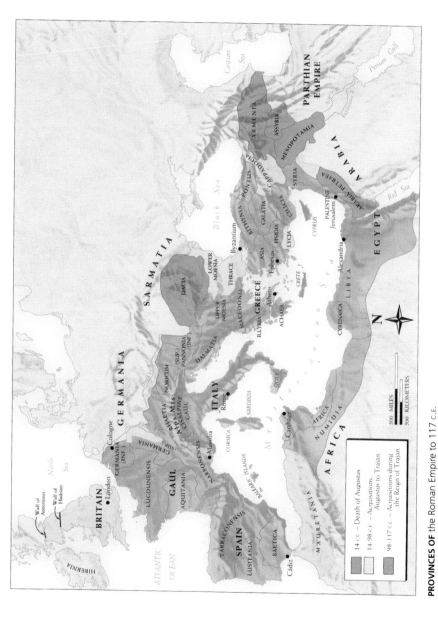

PROVINCES OF the Roman Empire to 117 C.E.

A History of the Roman People

Seventh edition

CELIA E. SCHULTZ AND ALLEN M. WARD

Routledge
Taylor & Francis Group

NEW YORK AND LONDON

Seventh edition published 2019
and by Routledge
52 Vanderbilt Avenue, New York, NY 10017

by Routledge
2 Park Square, Milton Park, Abingdon, Oxon, OX14 4RN

Routledge is an imprint of the Taylor & Francis Group, an informa business

First edition published by Prentice Hall 1962
Sixth edition published by Pearson Education, Inc. 2014

British Library Cataloguing-in-Publication Data
A catalogue record for this book is available from the British Library

Libray of Congress Cataloging-in-Publication Data
Names: Schultz, Celia E., author. | Ward, Allen Mason, 1942-author.
Title: A history of the Roman people/Celia E. Schultz and Allen M. Ward.
Description: Seventh edition. | Abingdon, Oxon; New York, NY: Routledge,
2019. | Includes bibliographical references and index.
Identifiers: LCCN 2018046786 (print) | LCCN 2019003862 (ebook) |
ISBN 9781315192314 (ebook) | ISBN 9781351754712 (web pdf) |
ISBN 9781351754705 (epub) | ISBN 9781351754699 (mobi/kindle) |
ISBN 9781138708891 | ISBN 9781138708891 (hardback; alk. paper) |
ISBN 9781138724693 (pbk.; alk. paper) | ISBN 9781315192314 (ebook)
Subjects: LCSH: Rome–History.
Classification: LCC DG209 (ebook) | LCC DG209 .W33 2019 (print) |
DDC 937–dc23
LC record available at https://lccn.loc.gov/2018046786

ISBN: 978-1-138-70889-1 (hbk)
ISBN: 978-1-138-72469-3 (pbk)
ISBN: 978-1-315-19231-4 (ebk)

Typeset in Bembo and Frutiger
by Deanta Global Publishing Services, Chennai, India

Contents

Figures

Preface

It is humbling to have been given charge of so excellent an account of Roman history as Allen Ward's sixth edition of *A History of the Roman People*, which built even further upon the strong foundation established by Fritz Heichelheim and Cedric Yeo. It has been a daunting task to improve upon it. Beyond the integration of some of the most recent advances in the field of Roman studies (both historical and archaeological) for which *A History of the Roman People* is well known, the most significant change in this latest edition is the inclusion of sidebars that expand on references in the main text to elements of Roman society and culture that are not often included in a political and military narrative. Members of Roman society outside the political elite receive increased attention here, and the presentation of religious matters in particular has been updated. I have decided not to include snippets of ancient texts, whether literary or epigraphical. They would be a poor substitute for having students read whole documents, and each instructor will have his or her own preferences for what to include and which translation to assign. The extensive bibliography that concluded the sixth edition has been considerably trimmed and redistributed as "Suggested reading" for each individual chapter. Given the overwhelming volume of publications that could be added to the list for any given chapter, I have followed Professor Ward's lead in focusing almost exclusively on single-authored monographs in English. Although Professor Ward had hoped to be able to offer the sixth edition of *A History of the Roman People* in two volumes (one for the Republic and one for the Empire, both containing the chapters that cover the triumviral period through to the death of Augustus), that will have to wait until the eighth.

I am grateful to Allen Ward for entrusting me with this project and for his sage advice as I have worked through it. I hope he is pleased with the results. Invaluable assistance in navigating the complexities of bringing this book to light came from

Amy Davis-Poynter, Lizzi Risch, and Louise Peterken at Routledge and Rachel Cook at Deanta Global. I have strived to incorporate the very helpful suggestions of outside evaluators Jilana Ordman of Lake Forest College and Benedictine College, Frank Russell at Transylvania University, George Pesely at Austin Peay State University, Andrea Vianello of Saint Joseph's College of Maine, and two anonymous reviewers. I am indebted to Michael Woo, whose eagle eye has kept me from numerous errors and whose queries have led me to clarify and sharpen the prose of this edition. Elina Salminen, Molly Shaub, James Faulkner, and Brittany Hardy completed the index in record time. Any errors that remain are entirely my own.

I owe the greatest thanks to my teachers, Paul B. Harvey, Jr. at the Pennsylvania State University and Darby Scott at Bryn Mawr College, for showing me what it means to be a Roman historian and for setting high standards for research. Their lessons have stuck with me. Read carefully. Set aside your prejudices so that you can hear what the sources have to say; it might not be what you expect. Do not cut corners: always go check the reference for yourself, and never, ever rely on a translation not your own. Be thorough: make sure there are "no dogs barking in the night." The key piece of information is often found where you least expect it. Write clearly and eschew obfuscation. Perhaps the most important lesson was that there is joy to be had in discovery and satisfaction to be achieved in the construction of a really good argument. Also, risotto, salad, and a glass of wine make a very pleasant dinner.

Celia E. Schultz
Ann Arbor, Michigan

CHAPTER 1

Roman history
Its geographic and human foundations

INTRODUCTION TO ROMAN HISTORY

When most people think of Rome, they envision the Rome of Julius Caesar and the Roman Empire that succeeded him. That is the Rome entertainingly, but not always accurately, portrayed in shows and films like the HBO series *Rome*, the Masterpiece Theater production of *I, Claudius*, or famous Hollywood sword-and-sandal epics like *Cleopatra, Ben Hur, Quo Vadis, The Fall of the Roman Empire*, and *Gladiator*. Prior to Caesar, however, the history of Rome extends back from the Republic to foundations laid in prehistoric Italy. The prehistoric foundations will be outlined briefly in this chapter. Subsequent chapters will cover the full scope of Roman history from the beginnings of the city of Rome in primitive villages on some hills beside the Tiber River to the disintegration of the Roman Empire about 1300 to 1400 years later.

To understand this whole complex history, it is necessary to begin with its geographic, demographic, and ethnic context. That context shaped the development of Rome from a collection of prehistoric villages to the urban republic whose citizens and allies embraced all the peoples of Italy. That accomplishment gave the Romans the resources and outlook that helped them conquer a vast overseas empire. They eventually united the greater part of western Europe, much of the ancient Near East, and most of North Africa, whose free inhabitants became a single entity, the *populus Romanus*, the Roman people. This expansion, however, eventually carried Roman power so far beyond its advantageous Italian base that it could no longer maintain the cohesion achieved at its height. It eventually disintegrated in the face of both internal and external pressures.

GEOGRAPHY

Given our modern day ability to control our environment through technology, it is easy to overlook the importance of geographic factors in historical developments. Also, modern historians rightly wish to avoid the simplistic fallacies of geographic determinism, that is, the notion that the course of development for any particular society is largely determined by its physical location. Nevertheless, geography and the physical environment are important in shaping the course of human events and should not be ignored in trying to explain the past. For example, the reason why Italy, unlike Crete and mainland Greece, did not reach a high level of civilization in the Bronze Age is that the latter were closer to the even earlier centers of civilization in the Near East and Egypt. It simply took longer for the influence of older civilizations to spread farther west to Italy. Nevertheless, once Italy had achieved an internal level of development on par with that of the older centers of civilization in the eastern Mediterranean basin, a number of geographic factors contributed to its becoming the center of a Mediterranean-wide empire under the control of Rome.

Maritime orientation and advantages

Separated from the rest of Europe by the Alps to the north, Italy is naturally oriented toward the sea. The west coast has access to the Tyrrhenian Sea, the southeast coast overlooks the Ionian Sea, and the east coast from the "heel" of the peninsula's "boot" northward fronts the Adriatic. Italy juts out like a giant pier from the continental mass of Europe southeastward 750 miles into the middle of the Mediterranean proper. Also, the island of Sicily is separated from the "toe" of Italy by only the narrow Straits of Messana (Messena, Messina) and from North Africa by only ninety miles of water. Therefore, Italy and Sicily naturally dominate the sea lanes that link the eastern and western Mediterranean basins and the lands around them. Before the rise of greater powers to the north and west, the power that controlled Italy was in an ideal strategic and economic position for dominating the whole Mediterranean world.

Natural and human resources

Bounded by the Alps to the north and northwest and by the Apennines to the south, the northern part of Italy is a vast alluvial plain watered by the Po and Adige rivers. On the west coast, between the Apennines and the Tyrrhenian Sea, are the wide lowland plains of Etruria, Latium, and Campania. They are fertilized by a layer of volcanic ash and weathered lava ejected by the many volcanoes that had been active in earlier geologic times. The Arno, the Tiber, the Liris, and the Volturnus river systems provide them water. The fertile and well-watered plains of northern and western Italy are among the largest and best agricultural areas in the Mediterranean world. They supported dense populations and made Italy, in the words of the poet Vergil, the "mother of men." Manpower was the main source of ancient military might.

Ancient Italy also had other valuable resources. Although it was not rich by modern standards, it was for its time. Extensive forests provided abundant wood for fuel and timber for ships and buildings until they were overcut in the late first millennium B.C.E. The most abundant mineral resources were stone building materials: hard stones like marble, granite, basalt, and flint; softer, more easily worked types like sandstone and various kinds of tufa (cappellaccio, peperino, Grotta Oscura, and travertine); and volcanic pozzolana for making cement. Etruria not only possessed these resources but also was rich in valuable metals. It produced lead, zinc, copper, silver, and tin. On the off-shore island of Elba (Ilva), it controlled most of ancient Italy's iron ore.

No serious physical barriers to internal unity

Topography made it possible for a single, centrally located, and populous city to unite Italy and utilize its great resources and strategic position to expand in the wider Mediterranean. Although the Apennine Mountains cut through Italy in a great arc swinging out from the northwest, heading southeast along the Adriatic coast and then back to the southwest coast along the Tyrrhenian Sea, they are not a serious barrier to internal unity. On average, they are 4000 to 6000 feet high and are pierced by numerous passes. Moreover, most of Italy is easily accessible by water, the most efficient avenue of transport and communication in ancient times. With its long coasts and a width no greater than 150 miles south of the Po valley, much of Italy could be reached directly by ancient ships. Navigable rivers like the Po, Arno, Tiber, Liris, and Volturnus provided convenient water routes between the sea and the interior. The Tiber River, its tributaries, and their valleys were particularly helpful to Rome in uniting the peoples of central Italy under its control. After that, Rome had the resources to dominate the rest of Italy.

The site of Rome

As the Roman historian Livy noted, Rome occupied "a site uniquely adapted to the growth of a great city" (Book 5.45.5). Rome was centrally located in the fertile plains of western Italy fifteen miles from the mouth of the Tiber River on the northern edge of Latium. Here the Tiber River makes a big eastward bend and is slowed somewhat by Tiber Island midstream. Near this same spot, seven hills ranging from 200 feet to 700 feet above sea level rise near the east (left) bank of the river. They make the site easily defensible. The hills nearest the Tiber are the Capitoline, the Palatine, and the Aventine, which are separated from one another by intervening valleys. Farther to the east and enclosing the three foregoing hills in a kind of arc, stand the other four: the Quirinal, the Viminal, the Esquiline, and the Caelian. On those seven hills eventually stood the city of Rome. Two other hills across the river, the Janiculum and the Vatican, were ultimately incorporated, too.

Although the importance of the Tiber River for Rome's growth and success as a city can be exaggerated, it was great. Opposite the Tiber Island, the river's slowed current and gently inward-curving left bank provided an ideal landing place for ancient merchant ships and riverboats. The island also provided the first convenient ford and bridgehead nearest to the river's mouth. Sandbars at the Tiber's mouth and Rome's location some distance upstream protected the city from attack by large warships and sudden sea raids by smaller vessels. Eventually, Rome became Italy's largest river port as Greek, Phoenician, and Etruscan merchants took advantage of its ideal location for trade.

The Tiber River and its valley provided Rome with communications north into central Italy. Possession of the bridgehead nearest to the mouth of the Tiber also gave the Romans easy access to the coastal route between Etruria and the plains of Latium and Campania. Thus, Rome's geographic position in Italy made it the focal point of the natural communication routes running up, down, and across the peninsula. Even in early times, the Tiber and its valley were major routes for bringing salt from the coast into central Italy.

Control of crucial water and land routes for communications in Italy also permitted Rome's armies to strike in almost any direction at will with minimum expenditure of effort. The seven hills made possible the observation of enemy movements, and the proximity of the hills to one another facilitated the fusion of several village communities into a single city. Ultimately, it became the largest in area and population not only in Italy but also, perhaps, in the whole premodern world.

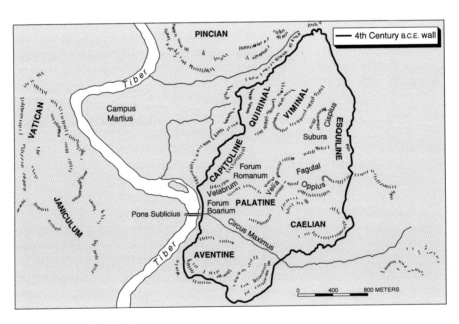

FIGURE 1.1 Site of ancient Rome

Strategically located for both defense and offense, Rome was a river port, bridge town, road center, and magnet of trade and population. It was thus favored by nature in ancient times to be the capital of a unified Italy. Then, given Italy's central location, natural resources, and large population, Rome became the seat of a Mediterranean empire.

THE PEOPLES AND CULTURES OF PRE-ROMAN ITALY

Demographic factors are another source of economic, social, political, military, and cultural strength. The population of Italy by the beginning of the Roman Republic (ca. 500 B.C.E.) was the product of a diverse ethnic and cultural heritage that stretched back thousands of years. Although later Roman myths and legends are not literally historical, they do reflect an understanding that the early Romans had heterogeneous origins. They stand in sharp contrast with the ethnically exclusive myths of origin embraced by ancient Greek city-states. Conflict and violence notwithstanding, the Romans were willing to assimilate other people. They united Italy into a strong federation based on a degree of equality and fairness unusual for ancient times.

From Paleolithic times to the end of the Bronze Age, 700,000 to 1000 B.C.E.

Human habitation in Italy goes back to at least 700,000 B.C.E. during the Lower Paleolithic period (2,500,000–200,000 B.C.E.). Numerous finds from the Upper Paleolithic period (40,000–10,000 B.C.E.) are associated with human beings of the present type, *Homo sapiens*. How much, if at all, groups from these periods contributed to the later population of Italy is not known, but from the Mesolithic (10,000–6000 B.C.E.) and the Neolithic (6000–2500 B.C.E.), there seems to have been a continuous development of peoples and cultures within Italy from both internal growth and external influences.

Changes occurred rapidly in early Neolithic times. Genetic evidence supports the theory that Neolithic farmers, building on the "Agricultural Revolution" that had originated in Southwest Asia, migrated from Anatolia and the Levant to the Balkans and then to Italy. In central Italy at Lake Bracciano, about twenty miles northwest of Rome, a large Neolithic village dated to ca. 5700 B.C.E. has been discovered under the present water level. It seems to have been settled by people who brought with them a fully developed Neolithic farming culture. Their large seaworthy canoes may indicate that they originally came some distance by sea, perhaps from previously settled southeastern Italy, which had large concentrations of Neolithic villages.

Painted Neolithic pottery from southern Italy has links eastward to Dalmatia and the Peloponnese and westward to Capri and the Lipari Islands. In northern Italy, there were people who produced small clay female figurines and dark, polished, square-mouthed pottery decorated with incised geometric designs. They had cultural links with people on the northeastern Adriatic coast and possibly eastern central Europe. People in northwestern Italy, however, had stronger connections with peoples of what is now western Switzerland and eastern France.

It is clear that there were flourishing internal and external trade networks during the middle and late Neolithic periods. Southeastern villages obtained obsidian from the Lipari Islands in the southwest. Stone axes of polished serpentine and jadeite came from both southwestern and northwestern Italy. In northern Italy, during the transition to the Bronze Age from around 2500 B.C.E. onward, artifacts first of copper and then of bronze have parallels with those from central Europe. Southern Italian copper and bronze goods from the same period have similarities with those from the Aegean. Material culture and the technology of metalworking advanced more rapidly in the Italian north. There, the trade in amber from northern Europe crossed the Alps into the Po valley on its way to the Aegean world via the Adriatic.

By ca. 1700 B.C.E., Bronze Age culture was flourishing throughout Italy. It can be seen in the substantial villages of the Peschiera and Terramara cultures in northern Italy. They were built on pilings beside Alpine lakes and in the Po valley. There are several contemporary sites in Campania in the vicinity of Mt. Vesuvius. One of them, near Nola, is a Bronze Age Pompeii. It is preserved to an amazing degree by the ash and mud that buried it during a massive eruption of Vesuvius ca. 1700 B.C.E. Another major site has been discovered at Poggiomarino on the Sarno River. It is ca. fifteen miles south of Nola and only six miles northeast of Pompeii. Settled ca. 1500 B.C.E., it was continuously inhabited during the rest of the Bronze Age and the early Iron Age. Then, it was overwhelmed by a flood ca. 500 B.C.E. and buried in mud. The houses were built on pilings, as at the Peschiera and Terramara sites and the even earlier Neolithic site at Lake Bracciano. The pilings were used to create artificial islets linked together by a sophisticated system of canals. The site seems to have been a center of manufacturing connected with the long-distance trade in high-status goods like bronze and Baltic amber.

Indo-European-speaking peoples and the late Bronze Age, 1300 to 1100 B.C.E.

The late Bronze Age seems to have witnessed the arrival of Indo-European-speaking peoples into Italy. The term *Indo-European* has no biological significance. It has replaced earlier labels like *Aryan*, *Indo-Aryan*, and *Indo-German*, which are associated with untenable nineteenth- and early-twentieth-century racist ideas. *Indo-European* is primarily a linguistic label used to identify the family of closely related languages that include Sanskrit in India, Persian, Armenian, the Slavic tongues, Greek, the Celtic dialects, the Germanic languages, English, Latin, and all the Latin-derived Romance languages.

Linguistic scholars have reconstructed a hypothetical Indo-European mother tongue from the common characteristics of these languages. It seems to have originated among people living between the Black and Caspian seas in what is now southern Russia. Probably in the third millennium B.C.E., various groups of Indo-European speakers began to migrate. Some headed south. Others went north and west. They resettled and intermingled—sometimes peacefully, sometimes violently—with the existing inhabitants of territories into which they migrated. Their language and culture became modified in ways that gradually distinguished them from other Indo-European-speaking groups. Eventually, some people from the new groups would undergo a similar process of physical and cultural assimilation and modification as they migrated to new regions. Thus, new Indo-European tongues arose.

The various Indo-European-speaking groups that evolved over time seem to have shared some other important cultural characteristics besides the linguistic. Words relating to weapons, horses, and cattle are prominent in their vocabularies, but there are few terms relating to farming and even fewer connected with seafaring. Probably, therefore, early Indo-European-speaking people originated as warlike, seminomadic pastoralists. They appear to have had a patriarchal social structure, often organized in tribal kinship groups. A king and his council usually provided leadership, but ultimate sovereignty often resided in an assembly of adult males. A polytheistic religion that prominently featured a patriarchal sky god also seems to have been common.

At the beginning of the late Bronze Age (ca. 1300 B.C.E.), the first Indo-European speakers to enter Italy may have crossed the Alps and mixed with the existing inhabitants of the Po valley. At the very least, major cultural changes took place that could be associated with an influx of Indo-European speakers: domestic horses and certain types of pottery appear for the first time in the archaeological record of Italy. Also, representations of chariots and four-wheeled wagons that many scholars associate with Indo-European culture were carved in Alpine rocks on the borders of northern Italy. As yet, however, no actual remains of such vehicles from that period have been found in Italy.

At the same time, the fairly uniform spread of what is called the *Apennine culture* throughout the Apennine range may reflect an influx of other Indo-European speakers. They could have come from the Balkans and entered Italy on the east and southeast coasts by way of the Ionian Sea. Their pottery is similar in style and decoration to that from the same period in Greece and the Balkans. On the other hand, the Apennine culture could also have grown out of the previous Bronze Age cultures and been influenced by trading contacts with Greece and the Balkans. The people of the Apennine culture and the other Bronze Age peoples of Italy had access to late Bronze Age trade goods, such as pottery and metalware that were brought from Greece by Mycenaean traders along the Italian coast. In fact, the stimulus of Mycenaean trade created a common style of bronze artifacts from central Europe, across Italy, and around the Aegean.

The spread of what is called the *Urnfield culture* from central Europe across the Alps into Italy around 1100 B.C.E. much more clearly represents an influx of Indo-European speakers than does the spread of the Apennine culture. This development probably was associated with the widespread disturbances and movements of peoples that characterized the late Bronze Age all over central Europe and the eastern half of the Mediterranean. The name *Urnfield* is taken from the distinctive practice of cremating the dead and placing their ashes in urns that were buried close together in cemeteries. These urns were all variations of a general design called *biconical* because they were tapered toward the top and bottom. The upper part was usually covered with a top shaped like a bowl or helmet.

The Indo-European Celtic languages evolved north of the Alps in association with the later stages of the Urnfield culture. The Italic Indo-European dialect group evolved south of the Alps in the areas where Urnfield material culture appears even later. Both groups have certain common linguistic elements that they do not share with other Indo-European languages. Therefore, it is hard to deny some significant influx of Indo-European-speaking people into Italy from north of the Alps. In the pre-digital age, people did not adopt significant elements of a new language through mere cultural contact nearly so readily as they adopted a new material culture to which they were exposed.

The *Urnfielders*, as they are called, spread rapidly from the Po valley to the southern limits of Italy. They seem at times to have taken over existing communities and at other times to have been assimilated into them. While Urnfield settlements were numerous, they in no way replaced or overwhelmed previous populations. Instead, they and the older inhabitants interacted to produce several distinctive local cultures and populations in the Iron Age.

Early Iron Age Italy, 1000 to 750 B.C.E.

In northeastern Italy, the Iron Age culture of the Atestines emerged around 950 B.C.E. It takes its name from the ancient town of Ateste (Este) ca. fifty-five miles northeast of Bologna. In much of the rest of Italy, the Villanovan culture marks the transition from the Bronze to the Iron Age during the tenth century B.C.E. in Italy. The term *Villanovan* does not signify any ethnic group. It comes from Villanova, a small hamlet five miles east of Bologna, where many of the artifacts typically associated with Villanovan culture were first discovered. The earliest examples of Villanovan culture have been found farther south, in southern Etruria and northern Latium, including the site of Rome. The peoples who produced the Villanovan culture probably evolved from interaction between those associated with the earlier Urnfield culture and various other peoples with whom they traded and intermingled.

The Villanovan culture carried on many of the traditions associated with the Urnfield culture. People continued to live in curved-sided huts made of wattle and daub on a frame of poles, cremated their dead, and buried their ashes in tall, biconical urns placed in round holes or rectangular stone-lined tombs. Various metal tools, weapons, and small ornaments, such as brooches, bracelets, and razors, were placed inside or around the tombs. In the South, the ashes of the dead were sometimes placed in hut-urns, which were miniature versions of the curved-sided huts used by the living.

Evidence of the kinds of cultural interactions that took place can be seen at or near southern Villanovan sites where some people did not cremate their dead but buried them in long, rectangular pits or trenches, *fossae* (sing. *fossa*), lined with stone. This tradition is probably derived from the Apennine culture that appeared earlier in this region. Nevertheless, to distinguish so-called Fossa people from Villanovans as different ethnic groups on the basis of their different burial practices is methodologically unsound.

FIGURE 1.2 A typical biconical cinerary urn for cremation burials in the Villanovan period.

THE PEOPLES OF ITALY, CA. 750 TO 400 B.C.E.

The various prehistoric cultures of Italy are known only from archaeological evidence. They eventually evolved into a number of distinctive groups identified in the written sources of Roman history and further understood through archaeological research. Numerous factors contributed to their evolution: first, specific local conditions; then, commercial contact with outsiders like the Phoenicians, Greeks, and emerging Celtic peoples north of the Alps; and, eventually, the heavy immigration of newer settlers, such as the Greeks in the South and the Celts in the North. The Romans themselves came into existence through this same process. The process would continue as the Romans interacted with and absorbed (often violently) the peoples identified in ancient historical sources. The names of these peoples will occur frequently in the next few chapters. It will be helpful to give a brief overview of them now (see map, p. 11).

Ligurians (Ligures)

The Ligurians were composed of several different subgroups. They inhabited the northwest corner of Italy bounded by the Alps, the Ticinus River, and the western flank of the Apennines down to the Arno River. Their linguistic affiliations are unclear. They were probably descended in large part from the early Neolithic inhabitants of the area. In their predominantly mountain terrain, most of the Ligurians never reached a high

9

level of development. In the second century B.C.E., they were often convenient targets for Roman commanders looking for easy triumphs. On the coast, however, several fine harbors like Genua (Genoa), Savo (Savona), and Albingaunum (Albegna) offered their inhabitants the chance to become skilled sailors and merchants and to establish prosperous communities.

Etruscans

To the east and south of the Ligurians were located people collectively known as *Etruscans*. Like their Greek contemporaries, they shared a common language and general culture but were politically fragmented and had many local differences. They spoke a non-Indo-European language. The words of surviving texts can be read because they are written in an alphabet borrowed from the Greeks. Yet these texts (long ones in particular) cannot be fully understood, because the language has no identifiable connection with any better-known language. The Etruscans were concentrated in Etruria, between the Arno and the Tiber rivers. Some extended north across the Apennines into the Po valley from the Rubicon River to Lake Maggiore. Others moved southward into Campania. They all developed a rich, powerful urban culture and will be treated more fully in the next chapter.

Veneti

In the northeast, bounded by the Atesis (Adige) River, the Alps, and the Adriatic eastward to Histria (Istria), were the Veneti. They eventually gave their name to Venice. They were descended from the Atestines, and were excellent metalworkers, horse-breeders, and merchants. Their language was an Indo-European dialect closely related to Latin but originally written in an alphabet borrowed directly from the Etruscans.

Gauls (Celts)

By the late fifth century B.C.E., the central part of the Po valley, between the Ligurians and the Veneti, had been heavily settled by Gauls (*Galli*). They overwhelmed the earlier Etruscan inhabitants and eventually caused the Romans to call this area *Cisalpine Gaul*, "Gaul this side of the Alps." The Gauls were a branch of the Indo-European Celts. The Celtic family of languages and the Italic dialects seem to share a common origin among the Indo-European-speaking people of the Urnfield culture of the late Bronze Age (p. 8). Spreading out from central Europe, the Celts had first moved west into France, the British Isles, and Spain. Then they moved south and east into Italy, the Balkans, and finally Asia Minor, where they became known as the *Galatians*.

Latins

On the west coast of central Italy south of the Tiber lies the fertile, well-watered plain of Latium, home of the Latins. They were another Indo-European-speaking

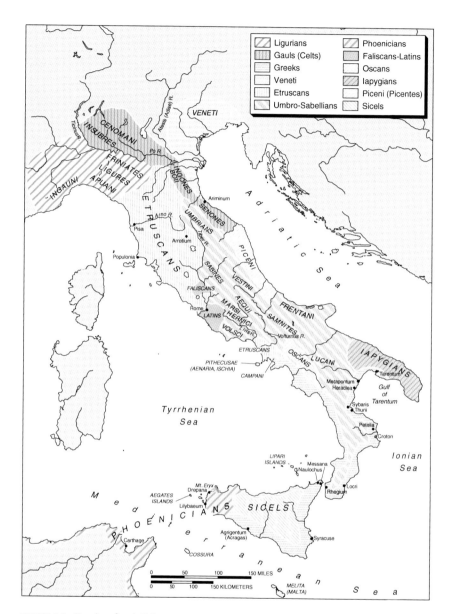

FIGURE 1.3 Peoples of early Italy.

group that had evolved out of the general spread of such speakers throughout most of Italy in the late Bronze and early Iron Ages. Their Italic dialect and that of the neighboring Faliscans to the north made up one of the two major Italic dialect–groups that predominated in the central Apennine region. The foothills of the Apennines in eastern Latium and the rolling central plain were ideal for herding and the cultivation of grain. Latium was well forested until late in the first millennium B.C.E. and provided an abundant supply of wood for building and fuel. Accordingly, the Latins grew in numbers and developed many prosperous individual towns—Alba Longa (destroyed ca. 600 B.C.E.), Antium, Ardea, Aricia, Cora, Lanuvium, Lavinium, Praeneste, Rome, Tibur, and Tusculum. Rome would eventually unite all of the Latins. Through Rome, their Italic dialect would become one of the most important languages in the world.

Umbro-Sabellians

Throughout the central Apennines, from the Rubicon in the North, where the mountains come close to the Adriatic at Ariminum (Rimini), and down through Campania and Lucania, dwelt various tribes of people called *Umbro-Sabellians*. They spoke related Italic dialects previously called *Osco-Umbrian* and now often referred to as *Sabellic*. Among these tribes were the Umbrians, Vestini, Frentani, Sabines, Aequi, Marsi, Volsci, Campani, Lucani, and Samnites. Although their family of Italic dialects was Indo-European, each dialect retained a large element of the non-Indo-European language spoken by earlier inhabitants of the region. The tribes represented by these dialects were primarily pastoralists and peasant farmers. They constantly needed more land to support their growing populations. The wealthier, more urbanized people of the neighboring plains, especially Latium and Campania, also often sought to expand their own territories. The result was frequent and bitter conflict. Thus, the external history of Rome during the early Republic (509–264 B.C.E.) revolves primarily around wars with neighboring tribes, particularly the Aequi, Marsi, Volsci, and Samnites.

FIGURE 1.4 Etrucsan bronze urn shaped like a hut, from Vulci (Lazio), seventh century B.C.E. Museo Nazionale Etrusco Di Villa Giulia (Rome).

Oscans and Iapygians

The Oscans originally dwelt in the part of Lucania around Campania. They were largely descendants of an earlier, non-Indo-European-speaking people. Sabellic speakers, particularly the Samnites, gradually moved into their territory and superimposed their Sabellic, Indo-European dialect. Even before that, however, the Oscans already may have been influenced by earlier Indo-European-speaking migrants.

Across the Apennines, along the lower Adriatic and around the Gulf of Tarentum, were several tribes known collectively as *Iapygians*. They had evolved in close cultural and commercial contact with Mycenaean and post-Mycenaean Greece. There may well have been some admixture of migrants from the Balkans, but certainty on this matter is impossible. The Messapii were one of these tribes. They gave their name to Massapian, the language of the Iapygians. It, too, was Indo-European but was not part of the two Italic dialect-groups.

Piceni (Picentes)

Various subgroups generally identified as Piceni or Picentes inhabited the mid-Adriatic coast north and south of Ancona between the Aesis and Pescara (Aternus) rivers. Their culture was not so uniform as once thought, but there are enough similarities to continue to treat them together. They had a long tradition of stock raising supplemented with hunting and fishing. From the ninth century B.C.E. onward, they maintained active trade networks: across the Adriatic, north and south along the Italian coast, and even west into Etruscan territory. The abundance of weapons found in early graves is compatible with their later reputation among the Romans as tough and warlike people. Linguistic evidence for the northern area is not clear, but the people in the southern region seem to have spoken a tongue firmly linked to the Sabellic dialects. A number of leading men from Picenum rose to prominence at Rome in the last century of the Republic, among whom was Pompey the Great, the most important man in the city and on the battlefield in the 60s B.C.E.

Greeks

All around the coast of southern Italy from the Bay of Naples to Tarentum, Greeks had established important colonies since the end of the ninth century B.C.E. Several were prosperous trading centers and exercised significant cultural and economic influence upon the other peoples in Italy. They will be discussed further in the next chapter.

THE GREATER PICTURE

Geographic and demographic factors greatly benefited the Romans. First, Rome's strategic location on the Tiber in west-central Italy enabled them to create a powerful city. Then, Italy, which was rich in natural resources, posed few serious topographical obstacles to control from Rome's central location. Also, by the fifth century B.C.E., Italy's land supported an extensive population of diverse ethno-linguistic groups.

Their disunified descendants were absorbed by the centrally located Romans through either peaceful alliance or, more often, violent conquest. By the end of the first century B.C.E., they had all become citizens of Rome, members of the *populus Romanus*. By the same time, Roman armies had used Italy's manpower, natural resources, and central location in the Mediterranean Sea to conquer a Mediterranean-wide empire.

SUGGESTED READING

Aldrete, G. *Floods of the Tiber in Ancient Rome.* Baltimore: John Hopkins, 2007.

Thommen, L. *An Environmental History of Ancient Greece and Rome.* Cambridge: Cambridge University Press, 2012.

CHAPTER 2

Phoenicians, Greeks, and Etruscans in pre-Roman Italy

Before Rome could unite Italy or create a Mediterranean-wide empire, the primitive villages from which it grew had to become a city and a state. The emergence in Italy of complex urban communities and organized states must be seen in the context of developments that began with the collapse of high Bronze Age civilizations in the eastern Mediterranean and the Aegean between 1200 and 1000 B.C.E. The first important developments took place on the coast of the Levant in several commercial cities inhabited by people known in English as the *Phoenicians*. They carried on much of what post-collapse trade remained in the eastern Mediterranean world. As peace and stability returned between 1000 and 800 B.C.E., an increase in population and commerce promoted the growth and spread of complex urban societies. They appeared among the Phoenicians first and then the Greeks, who were heavily influenced by contact with the Phoenicians and other Near Eastern people between 800 and 600 B.C.E.

By 800 B.C.E., Phoenician traders looking for metals like silver, copper, lead, tin, and iron were active along the west coast of Italy. They found significant sources in Etruria and on the island of Elba (Ilva). Greek traders soon joined the Phoenicians. Not long afterward, Greek settlers established numerous colonies in southern Italy and Sicily. Both the Phoenicians and the Greeks brought the native peoples of Italy into contact with the advanced cultures and economies of the eastern Mediterranean. That contact stimulated the growth of correspondingly complex societies in Italy, particularly in Etruria, Latium, and Campania. Its impact was strongest on those who inhabited the region of Etruria and came to be known in English as *Etruscans*.

THE PHOENICIANS

The Phoenicians were those whom the Greeks called *Phoinikes* and the Romans called *Poeni*. From the noun Poeni comes the Latin adjective *Punicus* (Punic) in reference to the Phoenicians who settled Carthage. They were descendants of the Canaanites described in the Hebrew Bible. During the second millennium B.C.E., the Canaanites inhabited the Syro-Palestinian coast of the Levant. It stretched from just above the city of Ugarit to the Egyptian frontier in the South, near the city of Gaza (see map, p. 17). The Canaanites spoke one of the Semitic languages, which include ancient Akkadian, Assyrian, and Amorite (Babylonian); biblical and modern Hebrew; and Arabic. Just as *Indo-European* and *Indo-European-speaking people* are cultural and linguistic terms with no biological or racial significance, so are *Semitic* and *Semitic-speaking people*. They merely indicate people who speak one of a number of linguistically similar languages.

Under Egyptian hegemony from 1900 to 1200 B.C.E., Canaanite ports prospered as vital entrepôts. They linked together Egypt, Crete, Cyprus, Mycenaean Greece, Anatolia, Syria–Palestine, and Mesopotamia in a vast network of international trade. Between 1500 and 1100 B.C.E., Canaanite traders benefited from the creation of a purely alphabetic form of writing instead of the cumbersome Egyptian hieroglyphic and Mesopotamian cuneiform writing systems. The Canaanite system was based on twenty-two consonantal signs. The names of the first two signs, *aleph* (*alpha* in Greek) and *bayt* or *bet* (*beta* in Greek), are the roots of the word *alphabet*. After the collapse of the Bronze Age in the eastern Mediterranean ca. 1200 B.C.E., the Canaanites' Phoenician descendants continued to write in what is now called the *Phoenician alphabet*. By the eighth century B.C.E., the Greeks had borrowed that alphabet and made certain modifications to represent vowels. This modified Phoenician alphabet, in turn, became the basis of all subsequent Western alphabets, including Rome's.

The cities identified as Phoenician occupied that part of old Canaanite territory roughly equal to modern Lebanon. They included Byblos, Sidon, and Tyre. Hemmed in by the Aramaeans, Israelites, and Philistines, the Phoenicians had little choice but to exploit their narrow hinterland and the sea. The fertile, well-watered river valleys provided enough food to sustain a critical mass of urban residents in the early part of the first millennium B.C.E. The mountains provided great forests of cedar, pine, and cypress for building ships and supplying foreign markets with timber. They also contained increasingly valuable deposits of iron, which the Phoenicians used to make ships' fittings or traded for other goods. The sea yielded fish that could be eaten or salted and exchanged in trade. The most valuable sea creature was the murex, a shellfish that secretes a purple dye when left to ferment in the sun. The Phoenicians used this dye to create expensive purple cloth. It was so eagerly sought as a mark of high status that it became the symbol of luxury and royalty throughout the ancient World and continues to be so today.

Phoenician ships brought back raw materials like cloth, leather, lead, copper, tin, silver, gold, glass, ebony, and ivory. Skilled craftsmen turned them into luxury goods. Those goods, as well as slaves acquired by purchase or capture, could be exchanged for food and more raw materials to support growing populations and thriving workshops.

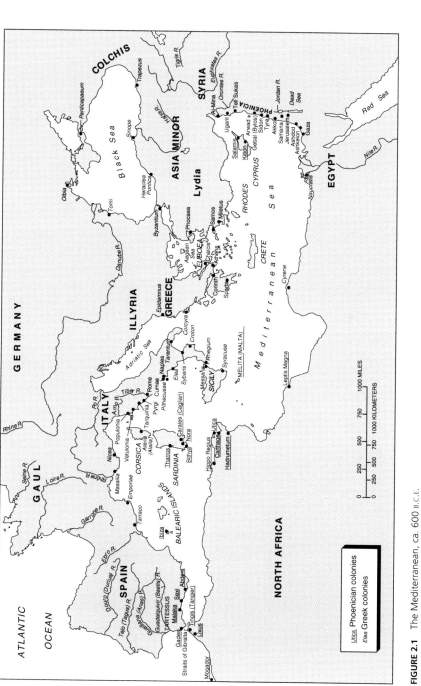

FIGURE 2.1 The Mediterranean, ca. 600 B.C.E.

The products of these workshops reflected the styles and tastes of the customers in their biggest markets, Egypt and Mesopotamia. They eventually inspired the "Orientalizing Period" in the art of the Greeks and Etruscans, with whom the Phoenicians also traded.

TYRE AND ITS COLONIES

By the early ninth century B.C.E., the Phoenician city of Tyre had emerged as the head of a combined kingdom of Sidon and Tyre and came to dominate the rest of the Phoenician cities. Tyre's location—just offshore on a small island—rendered it practically impregnable. Diplomacy and the establishment of commercial enclaves and trading posts during the ninth century made it powerful. First, Tyre gained control of trade in metals and slaves in much of the Near East. Then it exploited new sources of supply in Italy, Spain, and elsewhere in the western Mediterranean. These western sources became particularly important late in the ninth century as the struggles between the Aramaeans and the expanding Assyrian Empire blocked Tyre's access to metals from lands farther east.

To compensate, Tyre began establishing strategic Phoenician outposts to reinforce its maritime access to metals and to open up new sources in the West. It strengthened its position on the island of Cyprus, from which Near Eastern people had obtained copper for centuries. Tyre founded Citium (Kition) on the southeastern part of the island and established firm control over its valuable copper deposits. Tyrian colonies in the western Mediterranean opened up and controlled access to the rich metallic ores of Italy, Sardinia, Spain, and Morocco. Probably the oldest ones were Gadir (Gades, Cadiz), on the Atlantic coast of Spain just north of the Straits of Gibraltar; Lixus, south of the Straits on the Atlantic coast of Morocco; and Utica, in North Africa on the northwest shore of the Gulf of Tunis. During the eighth century B.C.E., a dense pattern of Phoenician settlements appeared on the south coast of Sardinia at sites such as Sulcis, Bithia, Nora, and Cagliari. Phoenicians also occupied Motya, Panormus (Palermo), and Solus (Solunto) on the western end of Sicily and the small island of Melita (Malta), between Sicily and North Africa.

The greatest of Tyre's colonies in the West was Carthage. The traditional date of its foundation is 814/813 B.C.E., but 750 B.C.E. has more archaeological support. Carthage was situated in North Africa just west of Cape Bon, at the head of the Gulf of Tunis. It had a fertile hinterland that supported a large population and produced surplus grain for trade. Its deep, well-protected harbors provided a safe halfway stop for ships bringing gold, silver, copper, and tin from Gades and other Atlantic ports back to Tyre. Carthage's own ships could easily trade with the rest of the western Mediterranean basin and block Tyre's competitors from entering through the narrow waters between North Africa and Sicily. Indeed, when Tyre went into decline after incurring the active hostility of Assyria and Babylon in the seventh century B.C.E., Carthage took control of Tyre's western colonies and trade. It became the primary competitor of first the Greeks and Etruscans and then the Romans for domination in the West for over 250 years.

Earlier, Phoenician traders and merchants had brought increased economic activity and the influences of the advanced Near Eastern cultures to the western coast of Italy.

They were searching for metals and slaves in return for wine, olive oil, and manufactured products. Thus, they helped to stimulate the growth of wealthy social elites and complex urban centers in Etruria, Latium, and Campania in the eighth and seventh centuries B.C.E. Under the leadership of Carthage in the sixth century, the Poeni, the Phoenicians' Punic descendants, even occupied trading posts on the coast of Etruria and established close relations with the Romans. The Greeks, of course, eventually surpassed the Phoenicians in terms of influence on Rome, but the Phoenician role in shaping the world that produced Rome and that Rome eventually took over should not be ignored.

GREEK COLONIZATION

About 825 B.C.E., Greeks from the island of Euboea took up residence beside Phoenician and other traders at the Syrian port of Al Mina, near the mouth of the Orontes River. Around 770–750 B.C.E., Euboean Greeks even established a commercial outpost on the island of Pithecusae (Ischia, Aenaria) off the coast of Italy in the Bay of Naples. Perhaps the Euboeans were even advised by Phoenician colleagues. A Phoenician presence at Pithecusae is supported by graves, pottery, and other artifacts excavated from the early settlement.

About a generation later, knowledge gained from Phoenician and Greek traders familiar with Italy and Sicily pointed the way for a flood of permanent Greek settlers. They hoped to gain strategic commercial outposts and find relief from a growing shortage of agricultural land and associated problems in their home cities. The colonists usually maintained sentimental, religious, and commercial ties with their mother cities. Still, each new colony became a completely independent city-state just like the autonomous mother cities in the Greek homeland. Therefore, the same divisiveness and lack of unity that characterized the mother cities also characterized their colonies.

Greek colonies in Italy

The chief sponsor of the Greek settlement of Pithecusae was the Euboean city of Chalcis. Its name means "copper" in Greek. It was a center of metalworking and had been trading and working with Phoenician merchants and metalworkers for over a century. The island of Pithecusae gave the first Greek settlers access to Italy's copper and a safe place to live. Along with the Chalcidians came some people from Eretria and two other neighboring Euboean towns, Cumae and Graia. A generation later, some Pithecusans, probably joined by newcomers from Euboea, moved across to the Italian mainland. They established Cumae, named for the town of Cumae in Euboea. Later, a little farther east on the bay, they founded a separate port town. When they outgrew those two places, they established another city, Naples (Neapolis, "New City"), to handle the overflow.

All of these towns left their marks on the Romans. It is probable that from Cumae, either directly or through Etruscan intermediaries, the Romans derived the Latin alphabet, in which the words of this book are written. Through Cumae, many Greek gods became familiar to neighboring Italic tribes—Herakles (Hercules), Apollo, Castor, and Polyduces (Pollux), for example. The oracle of the Sibyl at Cumae won great renown, and a collection of her supposed sayings, the *Sibylline Books*, was consulted for guidance at numerous crises in Roman history.

Although the Greeks called themselves *Hellenes*, the Romans called them *Greeks*, after the Graians (Graioi, Graei), whom they first met among Euboean settlements around the Bay of Naples. The port for Cumae became Puteoli (Pozzuoli), the most important trading port in Italy throughout most of Roman history. Naples became the most populous city in the rich district of Campania. It opposed Roman expansion there for many years. After the Romans took control of it, however, wealthy Romans built sumptuous seaside villas all around its bay. Many Romans, including Vergil, learned Greek literature and philosophy from Naples' poets and philosophers.

Numerous other Greek settlers soon followed the founders of Cumae. Greeks established so many cities in southern Italy and Sicily that the Romans called the whole area *Magna Graecia*, Great Greece. Attracted by fertile soil, Greeks from Achaea (a region in the northeast of the Peloponnese) settled on the western shore of the Gulf of Tarentum at Sybaris around 720 B.C.E. and Croton around 710 B.C.E. Sybaris was so famous for luxurious living that the term *sybarite* is still used to refer to a pleasure-loving person. Croton was the home of a series of famous athletes who competed and often won at the Olympic Games in Greece. To the north of Croton and Sybaris, the Spartans founded Taras (Tarentum, Taranto), also about 710 B.C.E. It became a great manufacturing center and gave its name to the whole gulf on which it was located. In 444/443 B.C.E., Athenians founded Thurii near the site once occupied by Sybaris, which Croton had destroyed during a bitter war in 510 B.C.E.

Sicily

Across from Italy, on the fertile island of Sicily, the Greeks founded even more cities than in Italy proper. There, they were the rivals of the Phoenicians, who settled on the western end (p. 17). The Greeks eventually occupied most of the rest of the island at the expense of the older, native inhabitants. The oldest of the Greek cities there, as in Italy proper, was established under the leadership of Chalcis. Founded about 730 B.C.E., it was named *Naxos* for some fellow settlers from the island of Naxos. It was located at the base of Mt. Aetna, where it guarded the Straits of Messana (Messena, Messina), between Sicily and Italy.

Dorian Greek cities predominated on the southeastern and southern coasts of Sicily. Of them, Syracuse, founded by Corinthian settlers around 730 B.C.E., was the most important. Syracuse grew even larger than Athens and rivaled it in wealth, power, and culture. Athens, with disastrous results for itself, attacked Syracuse in 415 B.C.E. during the Peloponnesian War. In the fifth, fourth, and early third centuries B.C.E., several powerful tyrants and kings ruled Syracuse. They vied with Punic Carthage and various Sicilian Greek cities for dominance in Sicily. Some even tried to take over Greek cities in Italy.

DECLINE OF THE GREEK CITIES IN ITALY AND SICILY

Greek city-states founded in Italy and Sicily achieved a high level of prosperity, culture, and political sophistication. Nevertheless, they failed to stop the Roman conquest of Italy in the fourth and third centuries B.C.E. The individual Italian and Sicilian Greek cities were unable to find a middle ground between uncooperative independence and predatory imperialism. Rather, they perpetuated the fierce independence and predatory rivalries of Greek city-states everywhere. Therefore, their alliances were weak and their empires unstable. While borrowing heavily from their artists, writers, and philosophers, the Romans ended their independence one by one.

THE ETRUSCANS

The Phoenicians and Greeks who traded and settled in Italy had an enormous impact on the social, economic, political, and cultural development of its native peoples, especially on those people known as *Etruscans*. The Greeks called them *Tyrsenoi* or *Tyrrhenoi*, and the Romans called them *Tusci* or *Etrusci*, but they seem to have called themselves *Rasenna*. The question of where the Etruscans originated has been generating speculation and controversy for at least 2500 years. According to Herodotus the earliest Greek writer of history (fifth century B.C.E.), the earliest Etruscans were Lydians who had migrated from Asia Minor to find a new homeland when their own was suffering from famine. About 450 years later, Dionysius of Halicarnassus (Herodotus' birthplace) took the opposite view in his *Roman Antiquities* (Book 1.25–30). He claimed that the Etruscans were native to Italy.

Despite sensationalistic claims, DNA research published in the early 2000s does not confirm Herodotus' account. Genetic links between both ancient and modern people and cattle in Tuscany and modern people and cattle in Turkey (ancient Anatolia, including Lydia) are not conclusive. They may merely reflect a much earlier spread of

FIGURE 2.2 Temple of Concordia, Acragas (Agrigentum), Sicily, fifth century B.C.E.

pre-Indo-European, Neolithic farmers from Anatolia to Italy, people whose descendants could have formed the bulk of the non-Indo-European-speaking population of ancient Etruria and whose genetic traces would remain in the modern populations of both Tuscany and Turkey.

Contemporary scholars also find no support for a modern theory that the Etruscans migrated from central Europe before 1000 B.C.E. and settled in the Po valley and later in Etruria. In fact, the most tenable modern hypothesis still is one that can be compared with Dionysius'. Extensive archaeological research indicates that Etruscan towns and cities evolved from villages that were part of the Villanovan culture during the late Bronze and early Iron Ages in Italy (p. 8).

This evolution began after the Phoenicians and Greeks started trading and settling along Italy's western shore. Most early Etruscan towns appear on or near earlier Villanovan sites without any radical break in the archaeological record to indicate an invasion of new people. For example, as at Tarquinia (Tarquinii), one of the earliest Etruscan cities, different styles of burial and the kinds of objects found in graves appear to result from progressive development: first, early Villanovan cremation and burial in simple urns; then either cremation and burial or inhumation (burial of the whole body) in trench graves (with more luxurious grave goods in each case); and finally, the general practice of inhumation in elaborately decorated and furnished rock-cut chamber tombs.

The early Orientalizing Period of Etruscan civilization in the late eighth and early seventh centuries B.C.E. shows many Near Eastern and Aegean influences in art, jewelry, dress, and weaponry. These influences were not limited to the Etruscans, but were part of a more general cultural development among the peoples of central Italy. They are rightly seen as the result of initial trade and contact with Phoenician and Greek intermediaries. There was no wholesale influx of outsiders. Although Greeks did begin to settle in Campania with the establishment of the colonies at Pithecusae (Aenaria, Ischia) and Cumae on the Bay of Naples around 770–750 B.C.E., they did not settle farther north nor even move into the interior of Campania. The indigenous communities already may have been numerous and well organized enough to resist Greek incursions.

Greek colonies were the primary vehicles of trade and contact. For example, the Etruscan alphabet quite clearly seems to have been borrowed from the Greek alphabet used at Cumae. There is no evidence of Etruscan literacy before contact with the Greeks, and the Greek colonies along the Bay of Naples remained resolutely Greek while sites elsewhere in Campania became Etruscan. There was no significant mixing of populations. A few individual Greeks and Phoenicians may have been resident in various early Etruscan cities and taken native wives. More than that cannot be said. Even in questionable historical legends, there is no hint of anything more than that for the Greeks. There is no evidence for any presence of Phoenician residents until the seventh century B.C.E.

By that time, evidence of small enclaves of Phoenician–Punic merchants and craftsmen begins to appear in the archaeological record from some of the port cities on the coast of Etruria. A major find from Pyrgi, the port city of Caere, comprises three gold-leaf tablets. Two have inscriptions in Etruscan and one in the Punic dialect of Phoenician. They refer to the dedication at Pyrgi of a temple to the Phoenician goddess

Astarte and date to ca. 500 B.C.E. That was long after the Etruscans had developed the characteristics that mark them as Etruscan.

THE LAND OF THE ETRUSCANS

Early Etruscan centers have been found at such places as Capua in Campania, Praeneste (Palestrina) in Latium, Veii and Volaterrae (Volterra) in Etruria, and Marzabotto and Felsina (Bononia, Bologna) in the Po valley. By 400 B.C.E., however, the expansion of other peoples had limited the Etruscans to a triangular area between the coast of the Tyrrhenian Sea, which still echoes their Greek name, and the Arno and Tiber rivers. Called *Etruria* in ancient times and *Tuscany* today, this region of Italy continues to recall the Etruscans' Roman name, *Tusci*.

Geographically, Etruria falls roughly into northern and southern halves. Northern Etruria possesses fertile river valleys, plains, and rolling sandstone or limestone hills with metal-bearing strata. The southern part is wilder and rougher, shaped by the actions of volcanoes, wind, and water. The soft, volcanic stone, called *tufa*, has been carved into deep valleys or gullies that are surmounted by peaks or small mesas, on which many of the earliest Etruscan cities are found.

At a time when village life predominated in the largest part of Italy, Etruscan sites had already become towns, and some of the towns were becoming cities that appear in the story of Rome and Italy. These cities were often built on or near Villanovan sites, sometimes on the coast or near it on a river—Caere (Cerveteri), Tarquinia (Tarquinii), Vulci, and Populonia (Populonium)—and sometimes inland—Volsinii (Orvieto), Clusium (Chiusi), Perusia (Perugia), Arretium (Arezzo), and Volaterrae (Volterra). They and some other major cities found a place in written history by fighting the Romans. Archaeologists sometimes find forgotten towns, some of them important.

Ancient sources say that the Etruscan people at their height were organized into a federation of twelve major cities. It is, however, not easy to list the twelve. The various sources do not agree on the names. Probably the membership changed as some cities rose in importance and others fell. Perhaps, more than one league existed. One of them may have been centered on a complex discovered in 1966 at Murlo, south of Siena. It was a rich and important site: large buildings have been found highly decorated with large terracotta (baked clay) statues and plaques depicting banquet scenes, a procession, a ritual scene, and a horse race. Substantial amounts of fancy pottery and even expensive jewelry have also been recovered. Later on, in Roman times, the city of Volsinii was said to have headed a league of twelve cities. When the Romans wiped out Volsinii in 264 B.C.E., they transferred its patron deity, Voltumnus, to Rome as the god Vertumnus—an early instance of the Romans' willingness to absorb powerful gods belonging to other peoples.

SOURCES FOR ETRUSCAN HISTORY

Most modern knowledge of the Etruscans is derived from the ruins of their cities and, more particularly, their tombs. Tombs of various sizes, shapes, and types—pit graves and trench tombs from Villanovan times, tumuli (great mushroom-shaped, grass-covered mounds with bases of hewn stone), circular stone vaults built into hill-sides, and corridor tombs cut out of rock—no matter whether they contain pottery, metal ware, furniture, jewelry, or wall paintings all help to reveal the cultural life of the Etruscan people.

Nearly 13,000 Etruscan inscriptions dating from the seventh century B.C.E. to the first century C.E. have been found. Only about a dozen contain more than thirty words. Most are only lists of proper names, religious formulae, dedications, or epitaphs. Because Etruscan is written in an alphabet borrowed from the Greeks, the texts can be transliterated, and much progress has been made in translating them. Because Etruscan is not related to any other known language, however, the longer, more complex texts cannot be fully translated or understood without a bilingual key (such as the Rosetta Stone provides for ancient Egyptian). Unfortunately, the Punic and Etruscan inscriptions on the Pyrgi tablets (discussed above, pp. 22–3) were not equivalent enough to each other or long enough for that purpose. Still, advances in understanding and deciphering the language are being made, particularly as new material is found. In 1992, the *Tabula Cortonensis*, a large bronze tablet from Cortona (near Lake Trasimene), came to light. Its forty lines of text have added to scholars' understanding of the meanings and grammatical forms or functions of Etruscan words. Useful social, religious, and cultural inferences also can be made from the stylistic and statistical patterns of words recurring in various inscriptions.

Unfortunately, surviving historical accounts of the Etruscans were all written by their Greek and Roman enemies. To the Greeks, the Etruscans, whatever their origins, are infamous as pirates and immoral lovers of luxury. Livy and later Latin historians describe a period of supposed Etruscan domination of Rome in the sixth century B.C.E. and concentrate mainly on Rome's wars with Etruscan cities. Cicero and other Roman writers also comment on Etruscan religion and its influences. The result is a biased and very incomplete historical record.

ETRUSCAN ECONOMIC LIFE

Etruscan civilization could not have existed without the natural wealth of its territory. The fertility of the soil and the mineral resources of the region were major economic assets (pp. 2–3). The Etruscans exploited them on a large scale through agriculture, mining, manufacturing, lumbering, and commerce.

The alluvial river valleys produced not only grain for domestic use and export but also flax for linen cloth and sails. Less fertile soils provided pasture for cattle, sheep, and horses. The hillsides supported vineyards and olive trees. As the population expanded, an ingenious system of drainage tunnels (*cuniculi*) and dams won new land by draining swamps and protected old areas by checking erosion.

The Etruscans energetically exploited the rich iron mines on the coastal island of Elba (Ilva) and the copper and tin deposits on the mainland. Many Etruscan cities exported finished iron and bronze wares, such as helmets, weapons, chariots, urns, candelabra, mirrors, and statues, in return for other raw materials and luxury goods.

They also made linen and woolen clothing, leather goods, fine gold jewelry, and pottery. Virgin forests of beech, oak, fir, and pine fueled the fires of Etruscan smelters; supplied wood for fine temples, houses, and furniture; and provided timber for warships and commerce.

Trade kept Etruscan Italy in close contact with the advanced urban cultures of the Mediterranean world. It led ultimately to the introduction of money and a standard coinage. The earliest coins found in Etruria were minted by Greek cities. After 480 B.C.E., Etruscan cities began to issue their own silver, bronze, and gold coins.

Etruscan foreign trade was mainly in luxury goods and high-priced wares. It enriched the trading and industrial classes and stimulated among the upper class a taste for elegance and splendor. That explains the Etruscans' reputation for excessive luxury among contemporary Greeks.

ETRUSCAN CITIES AND THEIR SOCIOPOLITICAL ORGANIZATION

In the late ninth and early eighth centuries B.C.E., competition among neighboring chiefdoms for control of resources and trade in high-status goods probably stimulated the earliest Etruscan state formation. By the end of the seventh century B.C.E., the Etruscans had developed several strong states, each centered on a rich and powerful city. For economic reasons, they located some cities within fertile valleys or near navigable streams; for military reasons, they built others on hilltops whose cliffs made them easily defensible. At first, they fortified their cities with wooden palisades or earthen ramparts and then with walls of masonry, often banked with earth.

Inside the walls, the Etruscans seem to have laid out some of their cities on a regular grid plan, as the Greeks had begun to do. In some cases, they appear to have centered the plan on two main streets intersecting at right angles, like the *cardo* and *decumanus* (main thoroughfares) of the later Roman military camp. The first monumental buildings to go up were temples for the gods and palaces for the kings. Then, as the population increased, side streets were paved, drains dug, and places for public entertainment built. These cities, as in Greece, were the political, military, religious, economic, and cultural centers of the various Etruscan states. As already noted, groups of cities formed themselves into leagues primarily for the joint celebration of religious festivals. The mutual jealousy of the member cities and their insistence on rights of sovereignty prevented the formation of any federal union that might have acted to repel the aggression of the Romans, who defeated them one by one. When events at last forced some cities to put up a united defense, it was too late.

Evidence from Etruscan inscriptions, Etruscan tombs, and later Greek and Roman writers reveals the broad outline of Etruscan political history. The executive power of each early Etruscan city-state was in the hands of a king. He was elected for life and assisted by a council of aristocratic chiefs. The king was the symbol of the state, commander-in-chief of the army, high priest of the state religion, and judge of his people. He wore purple robes and displayed other symbols of status and power. At least some kings had attendants who carried *fasces* (bundles of rods) and double-bitted axes, symbols of judicial, military, and religious authority. Later, lictors attended high public officials at Rome with these same symbols.

In many cities during the sixth or fifth century B.C.E., the nobles stripped the kings of their powers and set up republics governed by aristocratic senates and headed, as in Rome, by magistrates elected annually. The real power in the state was at all times in the hands of a small circle of landowning families. Having acquired or seized large tracts of the best land, they became a landed elite and enjoyed all the privileges of a warrior aristocracy and priestly class. In some cities, they were later forced to share power with a small group of wealthy outsiders who had won wealth and social standing through mining, craftsmanship, or commerce. The middle and lower classes consisted of small landowners, shopkeepers, petty traders, artisans, foreign immigrants, and the serfs or slaves of the wealthy.

WOMEN AND THE ETRUSCAN FAMILY

Women and the family played prominent roles in Etruscan life. Etruscans came to have two or three names corresponding to the Roman *praenomen*, *nomen* (*gentilicium*), and *cognomen* (pp. 60–1). The first indicated the individual, the second the family at large, and the third a particular branch of the family. Those who could afford the expense built large family tombs capable of holding many individuals. Epitaphs frequently recorded both the father and the mother of the deceased; the inclusion of a matronymic is distinctly Etruscan. Romans and Greeks only recorded their fathers' names. Tomb paintings and sarcophagi (coffins) often portrayed husbands and wives reclining or seated together in mutual respect and affection.

An Etruscan wife often appeared in public with her husband. She went to religious festivals with him, and, unlike her Greek counterpart, she reclined beside him at public banquets. The common practice of decorating women's hand mirrors with words

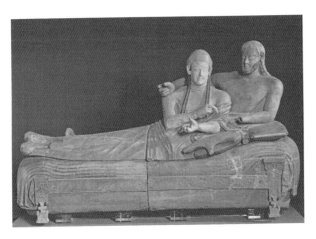

FIGURE 2.3 Clay sarcophagus from Cerveteri (Caere), Etruscan, sixth century B.C.E.

indicates a high degree of literacy among those who could afford these expensive items. Many Etruscan women also took a keen interest in sports, either as active participants or as spectators. Their presence at public games, where male athletes sometimes contended in the nude, was scandalous to the Greeks, who usually forbade their women to witness such exhibitions.

ETRUSCAN CULTURE AND RELIGION

Etruscan as a spoken language persisted as late as the second century C.E. Enough written material survived until the first century C.E. to enable the Emperor Claudius I (41–54 C.E.) to write an Etruscan history in twenty volumes. Nevertheless, all Etruscan literature is now lost. There probably were many works on religion and the practice of divination and, perhaps, annals of individual families and cities. There were also some rustic songs and liturgical chants. If the Etruscans composed poetry, dramas, or sophisticated works of philosophy, history, or rhetoric, no trace of them has been preserved or recovered.

Music and dancing brightened the lives of the Etruscans. They liked the flute, whose shrill strains accompanied all the activities of life—banquets, hunting expeditions, athletic events, sacrifices, funerals, and even the flogging of slaves. As flutists, trumpeters, and lyre players, they were renowned in Rome and throughout Greece. Tomb paintings, decorated bronze vessels, and painted pottery show them dancing at banquets, religious festivals, and funerals.

FIGURE 2.4 A wall painting (ca. 475 B.C.E.) in the Tomb of the Lionesses at Tarquinia showing a ritual dance.

FIGURE 2.5 A wall painting (ca. 500 B.C.E.) in the Tomb of the Augurs, showing wrestlers.

Sports

Tomb paintings also show that outdoor sports assumed an important place in Etruscan life. Because of their association with religion and rites for the dead, sports were serious affairs. To neglect them was considered a sacrilege. There were also sociological reasons for the popularity of games. The growth of cities, the expansion of industry and commerce, and the rise of a wealthy leisured class gave the time, opportunity, and money for indulgence in sports of all kinds. Hunting and fishing, which for prehistoric people had been a labor of necessity, became a form of recreation for the Etruscan rich. Next to hunting, riding and chariot racing were favorite sports.

Organized athletic competitions, such as were common in Greece, were especially popular. They gave upper-class youths a chance to display their skill and prowess; they served also as a source of entertainment for the masses. Most illuminating in this regard is the great painted frieze inside the *Tomb of the Chariots* at Tarquinia. It shows a vast stadium and a large number of spectators of both sexes applauding and cheering the charioteers, runners, boxers, wrestlers, and acrobats. Several paintings reveal the popularity of the equivalent of the Roman gladiatorial contest, which formed part of extravagant funeral games.

Religion

Many modern writers have asserted that the religion of the early Etruscans was pervaded with fear and gloom and dominated by a superstitious and authoritarian priesthood. Yet, wall paintings found in early tombs reveal that those who could afford such luxuries were joyous, life-accepting people. Like ancient Egyptians, they expected this life to continue in an afterlife.

Etruscans of all classes believed that the deities ruling the universe manifested themselves in every living thing: in human beings, in trees, in every flash of lightning, in lakes and streams, in the mountains and the sea. To penetrate the divine mysteries, to make the deities speak, to wrest from them their secrets called for elaborate ritual. Once discovered, divine will had to be obeyed and executed with meticulous care. As time went on, Etruscan religion does seem to have become more and more formal, theological, and legalistic in the struggle to guarantee the goodwill of powerful deities.

The Etruscan gods paralleled those of the Greeks and Romans. First among them was Tinia, who, like Zeus and Jupiter, spoke in thunder and hurled his lightning bolts across the sky. He executed the decrees of destiny. With him were associated two goddesses of Italic origin, Uni (Hera, Juno) and Menrva or Menerva (Athena, Minerva). Together, they formed a celestial triad whose temple (*kilth*) stood in every Etruscan city and on the Capitoline Hill at Rome.

The most striking aspect of Etruscan religion was the so-called *Disciplina Etrusca* (Etruscan Learning). It was an elaborate set of rules that aided the priests in the practice of divination. That entailed the study and interpretation of natural phenomena to forecast the future, know the will of the gods above, and turn away the wrath of the malignant spirits beyond the grave. There were several kinds of divination. The most important was hepatoscopy, the inspection of the livers from sheep and other animals slaughtered for sacrifice by special priests (*haruspices*). In fact, archaeologists have discovered several bronze and terracotta models of sheep's livers that may have been used for training priests. Thunder, lightning, and numerous other omens were also studied as tokens of the divine will (see Box 2.1). The flight of birds, which the Romans studied with scrupulous care before battles, elections, or other affairs of state, was of secondary importance to the Etruscans.

2.1 THE BRONTOSCOPIC CALENDAR

The longest extant Etruscan document is not preserved in the Etruscan language. The sixth-century C.E. Byzantine scholar John the Lydian translated into Greek an earlier Latin translation of an Etruscan brontoscopic calendar that was the work of P. Nigidius Figulus, one of the great Roman experts in divination who lived at the end of the Republic in the first century B.C.E. Cicero, a contemporary of Nigidius and the greatest orator of his day, referred to Nigidius as "the most learned and most venerable of all men"; Nigidius is known as the author of numerous works on natural history and religion, especially divination, all of which are now lost. Brontoscopy is the science of determining the will of the gods and predicting the future through the study of thunder, an important element in the *Disciplina Etrusca*. The calendar is arranged by twelve lunar months, beginning with June, and contains terse statements like "13 July: If it should thunder, very poisonous reptiles will appear," and "29 March: If it thunders, women will lay claim to a better reputation." The calendar reveals a society with many worries, most significantly diseases of man and beast, agricultural disasters, and civil unrest.

ETRUSCAN ART AND ARCHITECTURE

Early Etruscan art developed under the influence of ancient Near Eastern models as mediated by Phoenician and Greek merchants and craftsman. Later, Etruscan artists adopted aspects of archaic, classical, and Hellenistic Greek art. Still, Etruscan art is not merely derivative. It reveals its own lively spirit that sets it apart from its models. There is an emphasis on individual particulars rather than abstract types. It is full of movement, emotions, and the enjoyment of life.

Sculpture

Etruscan stone sculpture was not highly developed. Soft stone like limestone, travertine, and tufa were easily and often carelessly carved. Many examples come from graves and tombs. Some places marked graves with statues of sphinxes, lions, and rams. Others used squared pillars, *cippi* (sing. *cippus*), carved with vertical reliefs; still others used horseshoe-shaped slabs, *stelae* (sing. *stele* or *stela*), decorated with reliefs in horizontal bands. Stone funerary urns and caskets, *sarcophagi* (sing. *sarcophagus*), were also decorated with lively reliefs. Some featured half-length busts or complete standing, sitting, or reclining figures.

Terracotta was popular for votive plaques. Terracotta relief panels often sheathed the exposed wooden parts of temples and important buildings. Some workshops produced large terracotta sarcophagi in the shape of couches with full-sized figures of men and women reclining separately or together on them (p. 26, Figure 2.3). Archaic temples in southern Etruria exhibited large statues of deities on their roofs. One of the most famous is a standing Apollo from the Portonaccio temple at Veii (p. 36, Figure 2.11) Despite archaic Greek elements, it is characteristically Etruscan in the vigor of the god's stride and the tenseness of his muscular legs.

Many Etruscan cities produced bronze statuary. Small figures of deities, worshipers, warriors, and athletes were popular. A few magnificent large bronzes have also survived. It is disappointing that scientific analysis has now cast doubt on the Etruscan origin of the iconic Capitoline Wolf, which appears instead to have been crafted in the medieval period. Still, genuine works like the Chimaera of Arretium (fifth century B.C.E.) and the Mars of Todi (fourth century B.C.E.) are great achievements (pp. 32–2, Figures 2.7 and 2.8).

Painting

Etruscan painting is preserved on pottery and wall paintings from many tombs. The drawing is bold and incisive; the colors are bright and achieve fine effects through juxtaposition and contrast. The themes, usually taken from life, are developed with direct and uncompromising realism. They are often brutally frank. In the *Tomb of the Augurs* at Tarquinia (sixth century B.C.E.), one painting shows two wrestlers locked together in struggle (p. 28, Figure 2.5). Another depicts a burly, thickset man with a sack over his head as he tries to knock down a savage dog held on a leash by an opponent.

The festive side of life is a favorite theme in tomb paintings. In the *Tomb of the Lionesses*, men and women are depicted reclining at a banquet. Everybody is in high

FIGURE 2.6 The Capitoline Wolf (probably not a sixth-century B.C.E. Etruscan bronze, but apparently medieval [twin babes added in the Renaissance]).

spirits. In one scene, a massive bowl is wreathed with ivy, and musicians are playing. To the right of the bowl, a couple is performing a lively dance (p. 27, Figure 2.4).

Minor arts

From ca. 650 to 400 B.C.E., Etruscan potters produced black pottery known as *bucchero*. A very shiny, thin-walled variety called *bucchero sottile* copied Greek shapes and resembled more expensive bronze vessels. Pieces were often decorated with incised pictures or geometric designs. Some had stamped or molded reliefs. A heavier, less graceful, matte-finished, and more elaborately decorated *buchero* called *bucchero pesante* appeared at Clusium (Chiusi) around 500 B.C.E. Etruscan potters also imitated sixth-century

FIGURE 2.7 The Chimaera, fifth-century B.C.E. Etruscan bronze. (The Wounded Chimera of Bellerophon.)

FIGURE 2.8 Mars of Todi. Etruscan (fourth century B.C.E.). Bronze (Scala/Art Resource, NY).

B.C.E. Greek black-figure ware. They could not, however, compete with the excellent Attic red-figure pottery that flooded Etruria in the fifth century B.C.E.

Etruscan smiths were very skilled at making beautifully decorated bronze ware for daily use, such as tripods, basins, and candelabra. Fancy bronze containers and mirrors were elaborately engraved with domestic scenes, stories from Greek and Etruscan mythology, and religious rituals. Even more impressive are the products of Etruscan goldsmiths. Intricate gold bracelets, necklaces, pendants, earrings, and pins show amazing levels of craftsmanship and design.

Architecture

The remains of houses and cities in which people lived are scarce. Buildings were made largely of perishable wood and mud brick. Some cities were completely destroyed in ancient times. The rest have been continuously inhabited and rebuilt so that their ancient remnants are difficult to find or excavate. Cities of the dead, *necropoleis* (sing. *necropolis*), have fared much better. They were cemeteries outside the inhabited areas of ancient Etruscan cities. Their tombs were built of durable stone slabs or cut out of living rock.

By the late seventh century B.C.E., wealthy Etruscans were building large chamber tombs for family burials. In some places, large round or square tombs were topped with mounds to create round *tumuli* (sing. *tumulus*). At southern sites, tombs came to be carved out of solid tufa. Many chambers resembled the interior rooms of houses and contained furniture, tools, weapons, pottery, jewels, food, and walls painted or carved with scenes and articles of daily life. Tombs came to be lined up like houses on formal streets. Gradually, they began to resemble the outsides of houses, too.

Models found in early graves show that Etruscan houses in the eighth century B.C.E. were similar to the small oval huts of wattle and daub with thatched roofs common in Villanovan villages (p. 12, Figure 1.4). Rectangular houses with terracotta-tiled roofs and rear courtyards appeared during the sixth century, and *atrium* houses evolved by the fourth. An atrium house had an unroofed central court around which the living rooms were arranged. It might also have a walled colonnaded courtyard off the back (accompanying illustration).

Temples were a major feature of Etruscan architecture. They had the low, squat, top-heavy look of Italic temples in general (bottom of page). Often set on a hill, an Etruscan temple was also raised up on a stone base mounted in front by a broad flight of walled-in steps. The walls of the temple itself were built of mud brick. Wooden columns held up a deep porch in front. The solid walls of the cella (main chamber) were directly behind the porch. The cella, almost square in shape, was subdivided into three smaller chambers, one for each of a triad of gods. Each chamber had its own door at the front of the temple. Topping the whole structure was a long, low-pitched wooden roof protected by terracotta tiles. The wooden gable, ridge, and eaves were adorned and protected with brightly painted terracotta friezes and statuary of gods and mythical scenes.

THE ROLE OF THE ETRUSCANS IN ROMAN HISTORY

As will be seen, Roman art, architecture, and social life shared much with Etruscan civilization. These similarities are often explained as cultural "borrowing," particularly during a supposed period of Etruscan domination of Rome in the sixth century B.C.E. Indeed, sixth-century B.C.E. Roman archaeological remains look very much like what has been found from the same time in Etruria. The most recent research, however, indicates that Rome and the Etruscan cities were similar in this period not because of any externally imposed Etruscan takeover of Rome. Rather they shared in the development of a common central Italian culture. That culture was evolving from the interaction of native peoples with each other and with Phoenician and Greek traders and colonists.

THE FATE OF THE ETRUSCANS

By 600 B.C.E., the Etruscan cities had become the most powerful in Italy. In the Po valley, they battled the Ligurians on the west and expanded eastward to take advantage of trade coming into northern Italy through the Adriatic Sea. In fact, the Adriatic takes

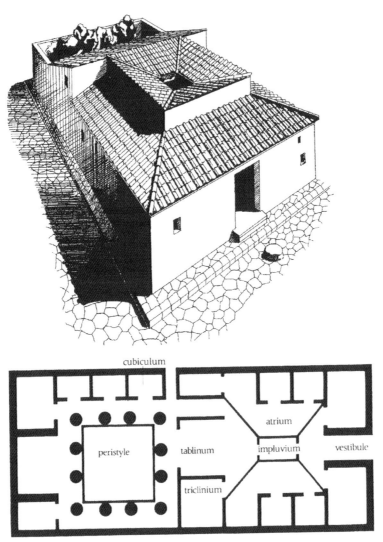

cubiculum

peristyle
tablinum
atrium
impluvium
vestibule
triclinium

FIGURE 2.9 Drawing and plan of a Roman atrium house with a peristyle and *hortus* (garden) off the back, drawing and plan of. From Nancy and Andrew Ramage, Roman Art, 2d ed., Upper Saddle River, Prentice Hall (Pearson), 1996. Reproduced with permission.

its name from Atria (Adria), a city originally founded by Greeks at the mouth of the Po and taken over by Etruscans in the fifth century B.C.E. Many rich and powerful independent cities had risen in Etruria. Some joined in one or more leagues for common religious celebrations, but they do not seem to have developed any strong common political or military institutions.

Etruscan expansion and conquests in new areas stemmed not so much from the concerted drive of any expanding state as from the uncoordinated efforts of individual war

FIGURE 2.10   Artist's reconstruction of Portonaccio temple at Veii.

chiefs and their retainers. On land, Etruscan warriors had begun to adopt the Greek hoplite style of warfare, in which soldiers wore metal helmets, breastplates, and greaves (shin guards) and fought in ranks instead of as individual "heroes." Etruscan seafarers had also adopted the latest advances in naval architecture. In 540 B.C.E., a combined Etruscan and Carthaginian fleet won a naval battle over the Phocaean Greeks near Corsica and forced them to withdraw to Massilia (Marseille), a powerful Phocaean colony on the southeast coast of what is now France. In 525/524 B.C.E., however, the Greek colony of Cumae, on the Bay of Naples, repulsed an Etruscan attack. In 504, Cumae and some Latin allies defeated an army of the Etruscan adventurer Lars Porsenna at Aricia, sixteen miles southeast of Rome. In 474 B.C.E., Cumae joined forces with the Greek tyrant Hieron I of Syracuse and won a great naval victory over an Etruscan fleet. From that point, the Etruscan cities' fate as independent states was sealed: the Gauls were moving into the Po valley, the Samnites began to take over Campania, the Romans soon started expanding into Etruria, and the Etruscan cities were too disunited to save themselves.

OVERVIEW

Rome originated in the context of wider developments in the Mediterranean and Italy. Phoenician explorers and traders reconnected post–Bronze-Age Italy with the greater Mediterranean world in the ninth century B.C.E. The Greeks soon followed. The Phoenicians, principally led by Tyre and Carthage, did not establish independent settlements in mainland Italy. The Greeks, however, planted so many colonies in southern Italy and Sicily that the two became known collectively as *Magna Graecia*, Great Greece.

Phoenician and Greek trade and contact stimulated the growth of both the cluster of native villages that became Rome and the communities that grew into the Etruscan

FIGURE 2.11 Apollo of Veii. Etruscan (ca. 500 B.C.E.). Painted terracotta. Height ca. 5 ft., 10 in. (1.8 m).

city-states. Significant mineral and agricultural resources enabled the Etruscan cities to prosper. They were ruled by kings or oligarchies. Their wealthy elites created a distinctive society, particularly in regard to the status of women. They also developed a fairly uniform culture that combined earlier native traditions with influences from the Phoenicians and Greeks. The cities even joined together in one or more leagues to celebrate common religious festivals and public events. Like the Greeks, however, they remained politically fragmented and engaged in bitter rivalries. The disunity of both the Greeks and the Etruscans in Italy contributed to their eventual takeover by the Romans.

SUGGESTED READING

Aubet, M. E. *The Phoenicians and the West: Politics, Colonies, and Trade.* Trans. M. Thurton. Cambridge and New York: Cambridge University Press, 1993.

Haynes, S. *Etruscan Civilization: A Cultural History.* Los Angeles: J. Paul Getty Museum, 2000.

Markoe, G. E. *Phoenicians.* Avon: British Museum Press, 2000.

Ridgway, D. *The First Western Greeks.* Cambridge and New York: Cambridge University Press, 1992.

CHAPTER 3

Early Rome to 500 B.C.E.

The stories of Rome's founding and the so-called Monarchy, or Regal Period, which ended ca. 500 B.C.E., present many problems for the modern historian. The traditional accounts found in ancient literary sources were not formed until hundreds of years after the events narrated therein. For example, an antiquarian named Marcus Terentius Varro in the late first century B.C.E. calculated the equivalent of April 21 753 B.C.E. as the date of Rome's founding. Moreover, the ancient literary sources do not always square either with each other or with the vast amount of physical evidence excavated by archaeologists since the late nineteenth century. Therefore, trying to construct a coherent and credible picture out of the disparate literary and archaeological evidence is a major challenge.

THE ANCIENT LITERARY TRADITION AND ITS SOURCES

The oldest extant literary accounts of any significance all come from the second half of the first century B.C.E. The first is the second book of Cicero's dialogue *De Re Publica* (ca. 50 B.C.E.). The most influential account is Book One of Livy's 142-book history of Rome, *Ab Urbe Condita* (ca. 25 B.C.E.). Later Imperial writers like Florus in the second century C.E. and Aurelius Victor, Eutropius, Festus, Orosius, and Julius Obsequens in the fourth and fifth centuries C.E. basically repeat Livy's account, which had become the dominant historical narrative. Poets of the Imperial Period, such as Vergil, Horace,

Ovid, and Propertius, are another important part of the literary tradition of Rome's early days.

Greek writers were also interested in Rome's beginnings. Among the most important sources are the first four books of the *Roman Antiquities* by the Greek author Dionysius of Halicarnassus (ca. 7 B.C.E.). Books Seven to Nine of the world history by Diodorus Siculus, a Greek from Sicily, are fragmentary but still important (ca. 30 B.C.E.). Plutarch was a Greek biographer and essayist in the late first or early second century C.E. He supplements the earlier historians, particularly in his "biographies" of the supposed early Roman kings Romulus and Numa Pompilius. Finally, Cassius Dio was a Bithynian Greek and high Roman official in the late second and early third centuries C.E. He covers early Rome in the first three books of his *Roman History*, but these books are preserved only in fragments.

It is important to remember that all of these ancient writers approached the writing of history as a branch of rhetoric. They wanted to entertain and morally instruct readers with memorable characters, exciting stories, and artful speeches. Also, their imagined view of the past was shaped by their own political concerns and experiences during the civil wars that destroyed the Roman Republic.

The sources of our sources

As the Roman literary tradition now exists, it rests on the mostly lost works of antiquarian researchers, earlier historians, and the writers of patriotic epics and drama. In the late third and early second centuries B.C.E., a number of historians (many of them called *annalists* because they narrated events on a year-by-year basis) and patriotic epic poets tried to present coherent versions of early Roman history (pp. 197–200). The annalists were mainly senatorial aristocrats, who were prone to exaggerating the roles of their own ancestors in historical events and who tended toward a pro-senatorial view of events and toward moralizing patriotism. These accounts are all lost but can be partially reconstructed from surviving later works, which ultimately depend on them. Also, during the second and first centuries B.C.E., antiquarian researchers preserved, and often misinterpreted, interesting or obscure facts about early Roman institutions, religion, life, and events. Their detailed and learned studies became raw material for other writers.

The data on which the poets, annalists, and antiquarians had to draw were not so scanty or worthless as many have assumed. Various traditional practices and oral sources preserved much authentic information, however imperfectly understood or distorted during transmission. Important families maintained wax images (*imagines*) and carved portraits of great ancestors. They sang or recited the exploits of the deceased during banquets, at funerals, and on military campaigns. Stories of major civic events were sometimes retold in dramatic performances. Some temples maintained their own archives of material, and some elements of ritual were maintained for hundreds of years. Archaic political institutions and practices were never completely abandoned. They were frequently overlaid with new ones as changed conditions required.

In addition to the raw materials available for history writing in Rome itself, Rome's Latin, Etruscan, and Greek neighbors had other customs, oral traditions, monuments, and records that Romans could utilize in reconstructing their early days. The earliest written accounts of Roman history were found in Greco-Sicilian historians like Timaeus (ca. 356–260 B.C.E.) and Philinus (ca. 250 B.C.E.). They were the models for early Roman accounts and preserved information from the traditions of the cities of *Magna Graecia*, which had had contacts with early Rome.

Although the Romans did not start writing literature until the middle of the third century B.C.E., literacy had a long history in Latium and Rome. The earliest known inscription written in a Greek alphabet was not found in Greece or the western Greek colonies, but in Latium. It appears on a small vase from a grave dated ca. 770 B.C.E. at Gabii. In Rome, the earliest known piece of writing is the possessive form of the Greek name *Ktektos* or *Kleiklos* on a Corinthian pot from a grave dated between ca. 730 and 625 B.C.E. The earliest public inscription yet found in Rome is the *Lapis Niger*, or Black Stone inscription, named for the black stone under which it was found in the Roman Forum (p. 48). It dates to some time in the sixth century B.C.E.

By 625 B.C.E., Rome had reached a significant level of urbanization. Some kinds of documentary records were needed. It is not likely that any records from that era were systematically maintained. Still, some information may have been kept on papyrus, cloth, or wood. Major items like laws, religious dedications, treaties, and commemorative inscriptions on public buildings were set up on durable stone or bronze. In the late first century B.C.E., school children were still memorizing the text of Rome's first law code, the Twelve Tables, which was compiled in the mid-fifth century B.C.E. (pp. 87–8).

Many have assumed that little of the documentation that existed before ca. 500 B.C.E. could have survived the sack of Rome by marauding Gauls ca. 390 B.C.E. Recent research, however, indicates that the devastation has been exaggerated. Records on durable materials like stone and bronze probably were largely unaffected. More perishable records were housed in buildings such as the temple of Saturn, the Capitol, and the Regia, where the *pontifex maximus* (Chief Pontiff) performed important duties and kept his archives during the Republic (p. 76). Those buildings remained intact. Records kept there may well have survived.

RECONSTRUCTING EARLY ROMAN HISTORY

For the period before 500 B.C.E., however, the surviving oral materials and written documentation were sufficient to construct the detailed picture our sources give us. No matter how much oral, monumental, and documentary material was available to later poets, historians, and antiquarians, its original context and meaning were not always clear to them, and they faced the task of making sense of information preserved haphazardly. Thus our authors filled in gaps as suited their own needs and circumstances, creating a foundation story that is far from historically accurate but that still contains valuable pieces of information that may ultimately rest on ancient oral traditions or documents and can help scholars make sense of raw archaeological data.

The traditional story of Rome's founding

The basic outline of the highly fictional traditional account of Rome's origin is as follows: the Trojan prince Aeneas, a hero from Homeric Greek epic, supposedly escaped the fall of Troy with his aged father, Anchises, and his young son, Ascanius (Iulus). After many years of wandering, he landed in Latium. There, he met the Greek hero Evander, who already had settled at the future site of Rome on the Palatine Hill. Aeneas also met Latinus, king of the Latins. He won the hand of Latinus' daughter, Lavinia, after a war with Turnus, the man to whom she was already engaged. Then he founded a city named Lavinium in his new wife's honor. Aeneas' son, Ascanius (Iulus), subsequently founded Alba Longa.

Much later, Numitor, the twelfth Alban king after Ascanius, had a daughter, Rhea Silvia (Ilia). Numitor's brother, Amulius, overthrew him and forced Rhea Silvia to join the Vestal Virgins. She became pregnant by the god Mars and bore two sons, Romulus and Remus. Amulius ordered them to be killed. They were set adrift on the Tiber and washed up on shore near the site of Rome. There, a she-wolf found them and suckled them. They were discovered by a shepherd, Faustulus, who raised them. Subsequently, they argued over founding a settlement near the site of their miraculous rescue. Romulus killed Remus and founded a settlement on the Palatine Hill. He populated it with men who were exiles and fugitives from all over Italy. Lacking wives, Romulus and his men carried off the women of a nearby Sabine village. The resultant war ended in a reconciliation of the two groups and an amalgamation under the joint rule of Romulus and Titus Tatius, the Sabine leader.

Deconstructing the traditional story

This highly fictional account reflects the combination of various Greek, Etruscan, Latin, and Roman legends. Greek settlers in Italy and Sicily wanted to link their area with the glorious epic traditions of their native land. The legendary wanderings of Odysseus in *The Odyssey* provided a handy link. One Greek story (ca. 600 B.C.E.) after the founding of Greek colonies on the Bay of Naples called Latinus a son of Circe and Odysseus and made him king of the Etruscans. The Greeks often did not distinguish between the Etruscans and the Latins. Latinus is obviously a manufactured eponym (a person for whom something is named or supposedly named) for Latium and the Latins. Later Greeks, perhaps as early as the sixth century B.C.E., may have added the story of Aeneas' journey to Italy. Aeneas quickly became associated with the Etruscans. They were the great foes of the Greeks in Italy, as the Trojans had been of the earlier Greeks in the Homeric epics.

The Etruscans eagerly adopted Aeneas as their own. Through him, they could have a past as ancient and glorious as that of their Greek rivals. Sixth-century B.C.E. votive statues of Aeneas carrying his father, Anchises, have been found at Veii. The same scene appears on seventeen vases found in Etruscan tombs of the late sixth and early fifth centuries B.C.E. Perhaps Roman kings of Etruscan origin during the sixth century B.C.E. popularized the links with the Greek epic tradition.

The story of the she-wolf in the legend of Rome's founding may have had an Etruscan origin. Although the most famous representation of the wolf, the great bronze she-wolf (with suckling twin boys added in the Renaissance) in modern Rome's Capitoline Museum, has now been identified on the basis of extensive scientific tests as a medieval piece, there are other images of her that are genuinely ancient. For example, a relief on an Etruscan grave stele dated ca. 400 B.C.E. from Felsina (Bologna) depicts what seems to be a she-wolf suckling a single baby boy, and an engraved Etruscan mirror dated ca. 340 B.C.E. displays a she-wolf nursing two infants.

The story that Romulus and Remus came from Alba Longa and founded Rome is part of the earliest Latin tradition. In the Regal Period, Alba Longa was Rome's chief rival for leadership of the other Latin towns. The story would have been useful propaganda to bolster Alba's claim to leadership. Archaeological evidence does show close connections between early Rome and Alba but cannot be used to prove any Alban origin for Rome.

Archaeological excavations have made clear that the site of Rome was inhabited long before the city's traditional founding in 753 B.C.E. Discoveries on the Palatine Hill and in the area of the Roman Forum that sits at its foot do not, despite some romantic interpretations, support the idea that Romulus and Remus were actual historical characters or that some other specific character founded Rome around that time. The characters Romulus and Remus look like two slightly different versions of the typical eponymous hero whose name is actually derived from the name of the city which he is supposed to have founded. Later Romans would have been familiar with such stories from the Greek settlers in southern Italy. In fact, one Greek legend claims that Rome was founded by Rhomus, another son of Odysseus and Circe.

One of the last elements to become part of the standard legend was the list of Alban kings. As Greek scholars and historians became more skilled, they became concerned with establishing precise chronologies. In the early part of the third century B.C.E., the Sicilian Greek Timaeus wrote the first comprehensive history of the western Greeks and events relevant to them. He equated the foundation date of Rome with that of Carthage, supposedly the equivalent of 814 B.C.E. About fifty years later, another Greek, Eratosthenes, established the standard date in antiquity for the fall of Troy, the equivalent of 1184 B.C.E. Clearly, even if Aeneas had existed, he could not have wandered 370 years (the time between the Trojan War and Eratosthenes' date for the founding of Rome) before getting to Italy. To plug the chronological gap, the ancients used the list of kings of Alba Longa, descended from Aeneas's son and going all the way down to Numitor, the grandfather of Romulus.

The rise of Greek city-states and its impact on Rome

It is clear that the traditional narrative of Rome's founding is completely unhistorical in its details. The idea that Rome originated with a specific act by a specific founder goes back to Classical and Hellenistic Greek historians who were trying to link Rome with their own "heroic" past. They also had in mind the examples of numerous Greek cities specifically established by founders as independent colonies in the Archaic Age and by kings as military outposts, centers of trade, or seats of royal administration in the

Hellenistic Age. Still, in a very general sense, those who created the ancient accounts of Rome's founding were right in considering Rome to be no different from the early Greek city-states and in placing its origin after the Trojan War of epic tradition at the end of what is now called the Bronze Age. The accumulation of archaeological evidence shows that Rome originated as part of the larger, unconscious process that produced city-states all over the Mediterranean world and even on the shores of the Black Sea between ca. 1000 and 600 B.C.E.

A city-state is characterized by a complex urban center containing a significant number of socially and economically differentiated inhabitants. It provides a central location for services such as health care, markets, defense, law enforcement, courts, large-scale communal worship or cultural events, education, and entertainment to both its inhabitants and those of a relatively compact dependent rural territory. Finally, it is controlled by a formally organized state apparatus (government).

At the end of the early Iron Age and the beginning of the archaic period (ca. 900–700 B.C.E.), Greeks, Phoenicians, and other Near Easterners took part in the expanding world of commerce and craft manufacturing. Those activities supported the growth of small villages and informal communities into formally organized urban centers in the Aegean. Although the Greeks borrowed many things from their neighbors, they developed their own distinctive social and political form of the city-state, the *polis* (pl., *poleis*). It was a self-governing community in which formal political power and rights were spread among a significant number of free inhabitants believed to be of common ancestry and legally recognized as citizens.

Initially, power in the Greek world had devolved into the hands of local chiefs and strongmen in the aftermath of the late Bronze Age. Later, as more formally organized urban or proto-urban communities emerged, some of the local leaders rose to positions of individual power as kings within the growing communities. These kings, however, were not rooted in a long tradition of dynastic monarchy. They were always limited in personal power. Rather, they depended on the cooperation and support of other important members of the community, who considered themselves to be more or less equal to any king. Often, powerful individuals even competed to become the next king. Usually, that competition led to the elimination of kingship altogether and the sharing of power among the heads of a community's leading families. They became an exclusive aristocracy and competed among themselves for election to positions of leadership in the community.

As many of these communities continued to grow, social and economic changes sparked internal conflicts. Sometimes, a particularly shrewd or ambitious man would take advantage of these conditions to gain enough popularity and armed support to seize personal control as a tyrant. His son or grandson, however, was usually overthrown. Subsequent periods of violence and compromise gradually placed more formal rights and political privileges in the hands of moderately well-to-do nonaristocrats. They had enough resources to serve in the heavily armed hoplite infantry, which became the main defense of the archaic and early classical *poleis*.

In Italy between ca. 750 and 300 B.C.E., Rome and other communities in Etruria, Latium, and Campania, neighbors to the Greeks of southern Italy and Sicily, followed a similar trajectory. Therefore, the development of Rome should be seen as part of the same process that made the *polis* the dominant type of state in the Classical Mediterranean world. That dominance was not supplanted until the rise of Hellenistic monarchies in the East. At the same time, Rome outgrew the territorial and demographic constraints of the traditional *polis* and became the dominant state first in Italy and then in the West.

Early Rome and Latium

Excavations indicate that the site of Rome has been continuously inhabited since between 1200 and 1000 B.C.E. It seems, however, that important changes leading ultimately to urbanization began around the middle of the eighth century B.C.E. Some ancient Roman religious institutions, rites, and monuments that still existed in later centuries may have had their origin in the mid-eighth century B.C.E. That may account for calculations like Varro's, which place the permanent settlement and foundation of Rome around the same time. Indeed, the archaeological evidence is compatible with the idea that small Iron Age villages found on some of the hills that Rome came to encompass began to expand and coalesce into a larger entity in that era.

Prior to the eighth century, the Indo-European-speaking villagers, who were similar to people who inhabited the rest of Latium, pursued simple lives as farmers and herders. Their lives are reflected in their graves and in later Roman legends, religious customs, and language. For example, Rome's legendary eponymous founder and his twin brother, Remus, allegedly were raised in a shepherd's cottage. The festival of the *Parilia* on April 21, the day on which Romulus supposedly founded Rome, celebrated a cleanup day for stalls and stables. In honor of *Tellus*, or Mother Earth—the goddess of the fruitfulness of animals as well as of crops—the early Romans twice annually celebrated the festival of the *Fordicidia*: they sacrificed a pregnant cow in the spring and a pregnant sow in early winter.

Because of this pastoral tradition, the Romans, like the other peoples of the ancient Mediterranean, sacrificed animals to their gods: goats, sheep, and cattle being the most popular offerings. Traces of the same background are evident in the name given to one of their city gates, the Mooing Gate (*Porta Mugonia*), as well as in the words *egregius* (meaning "out of the flock" and, therefore, "excellent") and *pecunia* (first meaning "wealth in flocks," but later "money" in general).

Even so, pastoralism could not have been pursued on a very large scale until the Romans had access to wider grazing lands and gained command of the trails to summer pastures in the Apennines. Perhaps standing behind the story of the Sabine women and the amalgamation with Latium's Sabine neighbors are later battles for those trails and treaties giving the Romans access to summer pastures in the mountains, the Sabines access to winter pastures in the lower Tiber valley, and both the right of intermarriage.

Meanwhile, the Iron Age villagers had other sources of livelihood. They fished; raised pigs and chickens; and planted gardens of turnips, peas, beans, lettuce, and cabbage. On small plots of land adjacent to their houses, they cultivated spelt, a hard kind of emmer wheat. Like durum, it was more suitable for making porridge than bread. People probably also gathered wild grapes and figs, which they either ate as fruit or brewed into wine.

They wore coarse, homespun clothing and used crude, handmade pottery fired without kilns. They seem to have imported little except some simple jewelry and bronze or iron tools. Their houses, like those associated with the Villanovan culture (p. 8), were round or elliptical huts with thatched roofs and wattle-and-daub walls supported by a framework of posts and poles. Smoke from the fireplace escaped through a hole in the roof, and a single large doorway served for additional lighting and ventilation. Foundations of such houses have been found on the Palatine Hill, in the Roman Forum, and at other sites in Latium.

1000 to 700 B.C.E.

The earliest graves at Rome are simple cremation burials found in the Forum. The oldest are dated between 1000 and 900 B.C.E., although late Bronze Age graves recently found near Ostia may cause the date to be revised upward. They and many similar burials have been found elsewhere in Latium and reflect the proto-Villanovan culture of the late Bronze Age shared by other people in Italy. From about 900 to about 830 B.C.E., cremation burials continued in the Forum. Along with them appear simple inhumation burials typical of the Latial culture that emerged in the early Iron Age throughout Latium. Around 830 B.C.E., a new cemetery with only inhumation burials was opened up on the Esquiline. Each male inhumation burial in both the Forum and Esquiline cemeteries between ca. 900 and 770 B.C.E. contained only two or three ordinary vases, a bronze *fibula* (a large safety pin, pl. *fibulae*), and, in contrast with later times, no weapons. A female burial usually contained a *fibula* and jewelry, mainly rings and glass or amber beads, along with spindle whorls and loom weights for spinning and weaving.

Clearly, no radical changes took place during this period, but evidence of population growth appears at the site of Rome and other places in Latium between 830 and 770 B.C.E. At Rome, dwellings spread from the Palatine to the Capitoline and Forum. The increased population and the habitation of the Forum probably necessitated the opening of the new burial ground on the Esquiline. By about 770 B.C.E., the growth of Rome and many other Latin communities had caught up with that of communities in Etruria. Both sets of communities were now poised to develop in tandem under the stimulus of increasing trade, particularly with the neighboring Greeks and Phoenicians, as is made clear by the discovery of Greek pottery (some bearing inscriptions in Greek) and Phoenician transport containers for wine, called *amphorae*, in Rome and the surrounding area. Early interaction with the wider Mediterranean world is also evidenced by the foundation of a cult of the Greek god Hercules, associated with trade, in the Forum Boarium. This may be due to the presence of Greek traders, or possibly even to Phoenician traders in Rome. The Phoenician god Melqart was equated with Hercules and was often the first deity to whom the Phoenicians would dedicate a temple in a new place.

The seventh century B.C.E.

The level of material culture in Rome and Latium changed enormously in the seventh century B.C.E. during the Orientalizing Period (p. 22). Princely tombs rivaling those of Etruria have been excavated south of Rome at Castel di Decima and Acqua Acetosa, Laurentina, and to the east at Praeneste. Graves at the first two sites contained men and women richly dressed with gold, silver, and bronze ornaments. Swords, lances, shields, and even chariots accompanied many of the men. At least one of the women at each site also had a chariot. The one at Acqua Acetosa, Laurentina, resembled a type found in Assyria. Some of the women had all the equipment for presiding over a sumptuous banquet—imported Greek pottery and Punic wine amphorae included. The tombs from Praeneste contained elaborate gold jewelry from workshops in Etruria, silver bowls with pseudo-Egyptian reliefs, bronze tripods from the Near East, bronze cauldrons decorated with oriental motifs like griffin heads, and many items carved from elephant ivory. The ivory could have originated only in Syria or Africa even if the carving was done by local craftsmen.

Parallels exist at Rome. One of the mid-seventh-century B.C.E. trench graves on the Esquiline contained a unit of armor and a chariot. A seventh-century B.C.E. grave in the Forum contained glass-paste beads, a bracelet of ivory, and a disc of amber from northern Europe. Others show that imports of expensive metalware and pottery from Etruria increased greatly after about 625 B.C.E.

During the seventh century B.C.E., the site of Rome acquired substantial private and public buildings similar to those appearing at the sites in central Italy and decorated in a similar style. Architectural remains excavated in the Forum show that by ca. 625 B.C.E., substantial houses were being built. They had stone walls made of square blocks of tufa and roofs of heavy terracotta tiles supported on wooden beams. The houses also had archaic terracotta decorations like those found on buildings from the same period in Etruria. At about the same time, the Forum received its first pavement and a formal drain, the *Cloaca Maxima*. Also, a new street was laid over a filled-in space between the northeast corner of the Palatine and the Velia.[1] Therefore, what had once been a loose collection of Iron Age hilltop villages by the Tiber had truly become the city of Rome.

The growth of separate villages into a significant town during the eighth and seventh centuries B.C.E. can be traced in some of the archaic Roman religious practices that survived into historical times. The religious festival of the Septimontium (Seven Hills or Enclosed Hills) seems to have originated in the establishment of a common religious festival by the communities on the Palatine, Esquiline, and Caelian hills. They actually embrace seven separate heights: the Esquiline and its three projections, the Oppius, the Cispius, and the Fagutal; the Palatine; the Velia; and the Caelian. Religious association seems to have led to a political union under the Palatine community prior to the later incorporation of the Quirinal.

Two ancient priesthoods, the Salii and the Luperci (p. 83), were each divided into two groups, one representing the Palatine and one the Quirinal. This practice may indicate that the priesthoods originally were common to two independent communities. According to Livy (Book 2.13), the combination of the Palatine and Quirinal communities resulted in what is known as *Roma Quadrata*, Rome of the Four Regions: the Palatine, Esquiline, Caelian, and Quirinal hills. These four regions also seem to fall generally within an early circuit of the *pomerium*.

The *pomerium* was the sacred boundary between the civil and the military spheres. This line did not necessarily correspond with the city's fortified walls or the zone of habitation. According to a legend, Romulus marked out the first *pomerium* when he founded Rome on the Palatine (p. 41). The eighth-century wall found on the Palatine may be such a sacred boundary even though it does not support the existence of Romulus. An extension of the *pomerium* traditionally ascribed to King Servius Tullius seems to correspond with Rome of the Four Regions.

THE EARLY ROMAN STATE

The combined archaeological and literary evidence indicates that not only the city but also the state that can be called Rome came into existence around 625 B.C.E. That was about when the Forum was paved and began to receive monumental shrines and temples. These projects required a greater coordination of labor and resources than an informal community could have commanded.

A state implies some kind of formal political institutions and practices that are collectively identified as its constitution. Rome never had a written constitution. As in Great Britain today, only a constantly growing and changing body of custom, precedent, and legislation determined what the "constitution" was at any historical moment. The archaic constitution of the Regal Period is unlikely to have been complex, but little is actually known about it. What can be said has to be deduced or inferred from archaeological evidence, comparison with monarchies in other societies at a similar stage of development, and the vestiges preserved in the Republic that followed.

The kings

According to tradition, Rome was ruled from its founding to 509 B.C.E. by seven kings (Titus Tatius, Romulus' brief Sabine colleague, being excluded). The first four were alternately Latin and Sabine: Romulus, Numa Pompilius, Tullus Hostilius, and Ancus Marcius. The last three were Tarquinius Priscus (Tarquin the Elder), Servius Tullius, and Tarquinius Superbus (Tarquin the Proud). The two Tarquins were always recognized as Etruscan, but the question of Servius' Latin or Etruscan origin is in doubt. The names notwithstanding, it is a reasonable assumption that early Rome came to be ruled by kings, and so, too, did other archaic Latin city-states, such as Aricia, Tusculum, and Lanuvium.

That kings ruled Rome in the sixth century B.C.E. is supported by two pieces of explicit archaeological evidence. The first, dated to the last quarter of the century, is part of a bucchero cup clearly inscribed with the word *rex*, king. Moreover, it was excavated at the site of the Regia, the King's House—the royal palace. The Regia's successive restorations and re-building on the same site in the Roman Forum can be traced back to a date even earlier than the traditional founding date of the city (p. 42).

The Romans believed that it was originally built by Romulus' successor, King Numa. It was next to the temple of Vesta and the house of the Vestal Virgins (p. 70). After the Monarchy, the Regia became the headquarters of the *pontifex maximus*, who assumed some of the religious functions of the old kings.

The second piece of evidence is the *Lapis Niger* (Black Stone) inscription on a block of Grotta Oscura tufa under the black pavement of the Forum. The inscription is dated to the late sixth century B.C.E. It contains the word *RECEI*, a form of the word *rex* (king). In later times, it was believed to mark the grave of one of the early kings.

That certain terms and titles related to kings were used during the Republic also indicates the existence of kings in an earlier stage of political development. In the Republic, an elective office might become vacant because of death, resignation, or the failure to hold elections on time. In that case, the senate would declare an *interregnum*, which literally meant "a period between kingships." Then, it would appoint an *interrex*, interim king, to hold an election for the office. From early in the Republic, the word *rex* was also used in the title of an important priest, the *rex sacrorum*, king of rites. His job was to carry on religious functions that probably belonged originally to the kings. His wife was called *regina sacrorum*, queen of rites, and she, too, had a prescribed set of religious duties.

While the existence of early Roman kings seems clear, the detailed accounts of the kings found in the literary sources must be rejected. First, as previously noted, the name of Romulus, Rome's supposed founder and first king, seems obviously to be a made-up eponym. Second, even with Romulus, there are not enough kings to cover the period from 753 to 509 B.C.E. They require improbably long reigns averaging thirty-five years. It is more probable that the earliest records went back to only ca. 625 B.C.E. Depending on the inclusion or exclusion of Titus Tatius, six or seven kings between ca. 625 and 509 B.C.E. would yield much more probable average reigns of seventeen to twenty years. On the other hand, there is no reason to reject the story that a man whose Roman name became Tarquinius successfully migrated to Rome from Tarquinia and eventually became king. The archaeological record shows that Greeks, Etruscans, and Phoenicians frequented the important trading center that was archaic Rome, and there is every reason to believe that a number settled there.

An apparently independent Etruscan tradition is depicted in the François Tomb near Vulci. It supports the existence of the Tarquins and antedates the earliest Roman historical speculations. What probably should be rejected, however, is the idea of a long-term Etruscan takeover of Rome. In the light of current archaeological evidence, it is much more probable that seventh-century B.C.E. Rome looked like an Etruscan city because both Rome and the contemporary "Etruscan" cities were part of a larger, central Italian cultural complex. A sharp distinction between the two is valid only later when the people who inhabited Rome had developed a clearly different culture from that which prevailed in those cities of Etruria with whom they later fought.

The nature of early Roman kingship

Like kingship in many early or "primitive" societies, the early Roman monarchy probably had religious origins and was not absolute or strictly hereditary. That king had important religious duties seems clear from the existence of the *rex sacrorum* during the Republic. The gods who guaranteed the welfare of the community would have been offended if they were not served by a king, as they always had been. The republican practice of appointing an *interrex*, interim king, when certain elected magistrates were lacking also supports the religious nature of early Roman kingship. First, the patricians in the senate, the *patres*, appointed one of themselves to be the *interrex*. They were the leading members of families who supplied Rome's public priests (p. 70). Second, the *interrex* held and passed on to subsequently elected magistrates the religious power of taking auspices (p. 69). Presumably, the *patres* had this power because their ancestors during the Monarchy had chosen who was to be king when the throne was empty. It is also significant that the chief priest of the Roman Republic, the *pontifex maximus*, had his headquarters in the Regia, the old royal residence.

With the spread of more and better weapons in Latium, as evidenced by seventh-century graves, Roman kingship probably acquired an increasingly military nature. The republican *interrex* preserved not only the auspices but also the *imperium*, the power of military command, in the absence of proper magistrates. During the later Monarchy, kings probably had to become war leaders to protect the community. Some may even have started as leaders of warrior bands who forced their way onto the throne or were chosen kings because of their military prowess. At some point, it seems to have become necessary that the appointment of a king had to be ratified by an early assembly of arms-bearing men, the *comitia curiata*.

As the leading religious and military authority in the early state, the king would have had broad powers in peace and war. He probably had the power to make war and negotiate treaties. His final word on public affairs most likely had the force of law. The power to enforce laws and even execute wrongdoers seems to have been represented by the *fasces* and double-headed ax, ancient royal symbols that were later carried in front of magistrates with *imperium* during the Republic (p. 79). Still, the king could not have functioned alone. He seems to have sought the advice and approval of others to ensure his legitimacy.

The senate

As the Republic evolved, the senate became the state's most powerful institution. Under the kings, however, it probably was just what its name implies, an advisory body of elders (*senes*, from which *senior* and *senile* derive) to the king. It would have only advised the kings in the Monarchy, just as it only advised the magistrates in the early Republic. It would have been a king's private council, appointed by him from among his friends and important members of the city's leading families. As in the Republic, the senate could not have legislated under the kings. It would have given advice only when summoned by the king. He would not have to accept its advice, but it would not have been politically wise for a king habitually to ignore or reject it, particularly on major issues. If he did, he would sooner or later incur the enmity of too many powerful men and might even lose his throne, as Roman tradition says the last Tarquin did.

The army and the earliest popular assembly, the *comitia curiata*

The king also would have had to consider the *populus*, the arms-bearing adult male citizens. They seem to have made up both the early army and the *comitia curiata* (Curiate Assembly), the original popular (derived from *populus*) assembly. The *comitia curiata* was based on the groups to which the adult arms-bearing men originally belonged for the purpose of military service. Originally, all citizens were divided up into three tribes (*tribus*, literally "by threes"): Ramnes, Tities, and Luceres. Each tribe probably represented a major district of the earliest city. Apparently, each tribe was subdivided into ten smaller districts called *curiae*, from which is derived *curiata*, for a total of thirty *curiae*. At some point, perhaps with the incorporation of the community on the Quirinal Hill into the early Roman state, the population was divided into four urban tribes and twenty-six rural districts, *pagi* (sing. *pagus*), or regions, *regiones* (sing. *regio*). After that, each tribe and district supplied one of the thirty *curiae* of the army. In assembly, all of the men associated with each *curia* would have mustered together just as they would if called up for active military duty.

The armed citizens who constituted this assembly theoretically had sovereign power (*maiestas*), and they took part in the inauguration of a new king. That seems evident from the vestigial *comitia curiata* that confirmed a magistrate's *imperium* in the Republic (p. 49). The Curiate Assembly may even have attended the king in the performance of some of his religious duties, confirmed the appointment of public priests, witnessed (if not approved) wills and adoptions, and dealt with other matters connected with private law. The assembly's main function during the Monarchy was to listen to and show approval or disapproval of proposals put forward by the king. A king was wise to seek the *comitia curiata*'s approval, if only to win the armed citizens' cooperation and willing consent to major changes in law and policy. Their opinion was particularly valuable in matters of war and peace.

The evolution of the army and a new popular assembly, the *comitia centuriata*

Before Rome had developed into a fully organized state, warfare, such as it was, probably involved warrior bands loyal to individual leaders. Such bands may have been the origin of certain clans, *gentes* (pp. 60–3). Even under the Monarchy and early Republic, individual clans sometimes conducted independent military operations. The creation of a formal state and the full urbanization of Rome in the last quarter of the seventh century B.C.E. paralleled and was integral to the spread of new arms, armor, and military tactics in central Italy at the same time. A similar pattern had occurred at the beginning of the seventh century B.C.E. in Greece. The old, heroic style of combat involved a few elite warriors backed up by a rather disorganized mass of retainers as seen in Homer. It gradually gave way to tactics based on the hoplite phalanx.

The classic hoplite phalanx was a formation in which heavily armed infantry troops advanced to the attack in a tightly ordered battle line several ranks deep. Each soldier carried a long spear for thrusting and a sword for close combat. He was protected by a *hoplon* (*clipeus* in Latin), a round shield smaller than earlier body shields. It was fastened to the left arm through a loop in the middle and a handgrip near the edge. A helmet, breastplate or corselet, and greaves (shin guards), all made of various materials such as leather, heavy linen, and metal, completed the panoply. Each man's right side was protected by the shield on his neighbor's left. So long as each man kept in formation, the hoplite phalanx was almost indestructible.

Evidence from graves shows that the Greek hoplite panoply was introduced into Italy in the late seventh century B.C.E. It spread rapidly among those who could afford it. How early and to what extent the Romans and others in Italy adopted the classic Greek phalanx of hoplite infantry is problematical. Ancient and modern reconstructions of the Roman army in the seventh and sixth centuries B.C.E. may too neatly reflect the formal organization and tactics of later Greek and Roman armies. The following reconstruction is offered with that caveat.

The formal field army that emerged in tandem with the evolving state was the legion, *legio*, literally a "selection" or "levy." It was drawn from all the able-bodied men who had the means to serve as cavalry or the Roman equivalent of hoplite heavy infantry. Collectively, those men may have been known as the *classis*, literally the "call-out" or "summoning."

It is supposed that each of the ten *curiae* from each of Rome's three original tribes provided the legion with a quota of ten to forty cavalry and one hundred heavy infantry from its members who met the qualifications for the *classis*. The resulting 3000 heavy infantry probably fought in a massed formation similar to the Greek phalanx. Men who could not meet the qualifications for the *classis* were thus *infra classem*, below the *classis*. They probably supplied more poorly armed auxiliary troops. They would have supported the heavy infantry as light infantry and skirmishers.

The infantrymen from each tribe seem to have been commanded by a tribal officer of the soldiers, *tribunus militum*. An analogous tribal officer of the cavalry, *tribunus celerum* (or *equitum*), seems to have commanded the cavalry supplied by each tribe. At the top, the supreme command belonged to the king or his appointee, the *magister populi*, master of the army. Next to the king or *magister populi* in rank was the commander of the whole cavalry, the *magister equitum* (master of the cavalry).

From the latter part of the sixth century B.C.E., the curiate organization of Roman manpower, now based on four urban tribes and twenty-six rural districts (*pagi*) or regions (*regiones*), became obsolete for military purposes. To align Rome's military manpower with its growing wealth and population, the legion's infantry was reorganized in accordance with the reforms ascribed to King Servius Tullius in the literary tradition (p. 77). All of the changes credited to Servius Tullius could not have happened at once and probably developed over a long period of time, coming into their classic form only well into the Republic. Still, it seems likely that Servius Tullius or someone like him increased the heavy infantry to 4000 men in forty units now called *centuries* (*centuriae*), hundreds, instead of *curiae*. Later, the heavy infantry expanded to 6000 men in sixty centuries. The officer in charge of each century naturally became known as a *centurion*.

Another part of the "Servian" reform was the consolidation of rural districts into larger geographical units to create rural tribes along with the four urban ones. As the state grew in population and territory during later periods, the number of urban tribes remained fixed at four, but new rural tribes were added until a limit of thirty-one rural tribes was reached. Each tribe contributed similarly armed men to groups from which the field army, the legion (*legio*), was drawn. These groups also came to be called *centuries*, because originally one hundred men taken from each group formed one of the centuries of the legion. Eventually, the whole adult male citizen body was organized into 193 centuries. Men were ranked by the value of their property and the type of military service they could afford to provide. If not by the end of the Monarchy, then in the early Republic, adult male citizens assembling by centuries became the *comitia centuriata* (Centuriate Assembly) and replaced the *comitia curiata* as Rome's primary popular assembly.

THE GENERAL PICTURE

Despite problems presented by the late literary accounts of Rome's early history and with the help of a growing body of archaeological evidence, historians can construct a general picture of Rome's origin and early growth as a city and a state. Beginning in the early to mid-eighth century B.C.E., a handful of small agricultural villages on a group of hills by the eastern bank of the lower Tiber River began to coalesce. They had evolved into a true city and state that can be called *Rome* by the last quarter of the seventh century B.C.E. Location on advantageous trade routes had greatly stimulated this development and created a thriving urban center in the same cultural context as that of contemporary Etruscan cities. By the end of the sixth century B.C.E., Rome had acquired a relatively sophisticated political and military organization. It was on par with the major archaic city-states of Greece and the rest of central Italy. Rome may well have been ruled by kings of Etruscan origin in the last part of the sixth century near the end of the Regal Period, but that does not mean it was controlled by some external Etruscan power. Indeed, it had become a significant force in its own right in Latium and southern Etruria.

NOTE

1 The Velia was once a low hill overlooking the southeast end of the Forum. It ran between the Palatine and the Esquiline (p. 4).

SUGGESTED READING

Cornell, T. J. *The Beginnings of Rome: Italy and Rome from the Bronze Age to the Punic Wars (c. 1000–264 b.c.)*. London and New York: Routledge, 1995.
Fulminante, F. *The Urbanization of Rome and Latium Vetus: From the Bronze Age to the Archaic Era*. Cambridge and New York: Cambridge University Press, 2014.
Smith, C. J. *Early Rome and Latium*. Oxford and New York: Oxford University Press, 1996.
Wiseman, T. P. *Clio's Cosmetics*. Leicester: Leicester University Press, 1979.

CHAPTER 4

Early Roman society, religion, and values

To understand Roman history, it is necessary to understand the nature of Roman personal and social relations and the religious and ethical frameworks within which they functioned.

THE PRINCIPLE OF HIERARCHY

An operative principle in all aspects of Roman life was hierarchy, the ranking of people or things from higher status, power, privilege, or value to lower. Inequality was an accepted condition of life in the Romans' view. Under ideal circumstances, those lower down in the hierarchy owed obedience to those above. In return, those above had a duty to benefit those lower down.

THE FAMILY

The Roman family was at the center of the hierarchical social and political system. Each family itself was hierarchically structured. A patriarch, called the *paterfamilias* (father of the family), stood at the top (pp. 54–5).

The English word *family* is used to translate the Latin word *familia*, from which it is derived. The Roman concept is not so wide ranging as the English concept in some respects and is more extensive in others. The Romans recognized different types of kinship connections that English often loosely lumps under the term *family*. There were three major classes of kin in descending order of closeness: agnates (*agnati*), cognates (*cognati*), and affines (*adfines/affines*). Agnates were those related by blood or adoption through a father and his male relatives up and down the line: for example, a father's brother or sister, a paternal grandfather, a brother or sister, a brother's children, a son, or a son's children. Cognates were those related by blood or adoption in general, but often were those specifically in the female line, the *maternum genus*: for example, a mother's brother or sister, a maternal grandfather, a sister's children, or a daughter's children. Affines were relatives by marriage more broadly conceived than the English term *in-laws* designates. For example, a Roman would be an affine not only to a mother-in-law, father-in-law, sister-in-law, or son-in-law but also to their parents. A stepparent, stepsibling, or stepgrandchild would also be an affine because of the relationship created by the marriage of a blood relation such as one's mother, father, or child.

Agnates were very important in Roman law for such things as determining one's *paterfamilias*, inheriting property, or choosing the guardian of a minor child in case of intestacy. Cognates and affines, however, were also highly valued and important. Along with agnates, they provided the dense networks of relations that could support one's position in the social and political hierarchy.

Somewhat confusingly, the term *cognates* was also used to refer to one's immediate family, the *domus* (house): one's parents, siblings, children, and siblings' children. The *familia* was closely associated with the *domus* but included much more. It was, rather, a hierarchical association of housemates: one's immediate family, clients (freeborn dependents), freed slaves (*liberti*), and slaves. Moreover, it included the spirits of deceased ancestors, the "greater ones" (*maiores*). They stood at the top of a generational hierarchy. Next were the living generations. Last were those yet unborn. The living had to serve the spirits of the dead, *Di Manes*, by maintaining the sacrifices and rituals of the family cult and following the *mos maiorum* (custom of the ancestors) with utmost respect. They also would seek to earn the respect of the unborn generations by enhancing the wealth and status of the family, of which the unborn would be the heirs.

The *familia* consisted of property as well as persons. It was an economic unit operating under self-given rules within the community's larger economic framework. It was also a system of defense, law, and government—a miniature state. In the earliest phase of Roman law, it was recognized as a closed, self-sufficient, self-contained association. Finally, the *familia* was a religious organization, a community of worship centered on the cult of the hearth and the cult of the dead.

THE *PATERFAMILIAS* AND *PATRIA POTESTAS*

The *paterfamilias*, the patriarchal head of the Roman family, controlled the children in the family's male, agnatic line. He continued to do so until he died or chose to release them from his control. He might have no children of his own; he might even be a bachelor. The only qualification was that he be subject to no authority save that of the state—that he be *sui iuris*. That is, he was legally independent and self-sufficient in dealing with other families and the state. In a legal sense, he was the family, and without him, there was no family or household.

The *paterfamilias'* power within his family was called *patria potestas* (father's power). It was almost absolute. The *paterfamilias* was the legal owner of all family property. Only he could lend, mortgage, or sell it or engage in contracts involving the family. He was also the source of law within the family. His orders were recognized by the state as having the force of law. His authority was based on ancestral custom, of which he was legally the sole judge and interpreter. He was the judge of the household. His rulings normally could not be set aside by any external authority. Unless he was declared insane, he could kill, mutilate, expel, or give into bondage his children or housemates and could break or dispose of the household property as he wished.

The *patria potestas* was not supposed to be despotic or tyrannical power. The father was supposed to consult other members of the family, especially the adult males and his wife, the *materfamilias*. Together they constituted the family council (*concilium*). Along with *patria potestas* came a duty to promote the welfare of the entire family, not destroy it by abuse. Religiously reinforced respect for and obedience to tradition usually tempered the exercise of paternal authority. It was not a brutal display of force, but a recognized distribution of the only justice that could be secured until the "moral imperative" of custom was replaced later by the "legal imperative" established by the state.

FIGURE 4.1   Junius Brutus, a Roman noble, with busts of his ancestors; lifesize marble, first century c.e.

Men within the family and marriage

Unless a *paterfamilias* became insane or mentally incompetent or voluntarily emancipated those under his *patria potestas*, his role as head of the family terminated only at his death. During his lifetime, his power extended to all of his descendants in the direct male line. In theory, an adult Roman man, his wife (if she were not still under the authority of her own *paterfamilias*), his children, and his dependents could be under the authority of his grandfather or even great-grandfather. In practice, the low average life expectancy in ancient times made that highly unlikely.

Inscribed burial stones, monuments, and other documents from the late Republic and early Empire, especially from Roman Egypt, indicate that the average life expectancy at birth for upper-class men was about thirty years, and that the majority of men who survived to adulthood and married did so for the first time in their mid- to late-twenties. Therefore, by the age of seventeen, more than half of the men documented would have lost their fathers. These ages may be even lower for the poorer classes, for whom some evidence suggests lower life expectancy and lower age at first marriage. Still, something less than 1 percent of the population may have reached eighty, and a few even attained one hundred.

A Roman boy could legally marry after he reached puberty, which came to be defined in law as fourteen years of age for males. That coincides with the usual practice of giving a boy his toga of manhood (*toga virilis*) in his fifteenth year. Still, there were many reasons for a man to put off marriage until his twenties or thirties. Beginning at age seventeen, citizens of middling wealth had to serve as many as six consecutive military campaigns in the infantry, and the wealthiest citizens had to serve ten in the cavalry. It took time for both small landholders and wealthy members of the elite to acquire the resources necessary to support an independent family and household. Sons of elite families needed to acquire the training and lower military and public offices that would show their promise as suitable mates for the daughters of other prominent families. Some who were still subject to the *patria potestas* of long-lived fathers might have preferred to wait until they were free of such control.

A *paterfamilias* might choose to emancipate a son from his *patria potestas*. To do so, he followed a procedure known as *emancipatio*. He sold the son three times to a cooperative third party, who freed the son after each "sale." The son then became *sui iuris* (independent). Any male, even a minor too young to father children, became a *paterfamilias* after the death of his own *paterfamilias*. A *paterfamilias* usually provided in his will that a minor child be provided with a *tutor* (guardian), who would protect the child in his place. If he did not, one of his close male agnates automatically assumed the role. For boys, guardianship ended when they reached fourteen.

Women within the family and marriage

Within the familial hierarchy, women and children were always subject to the power of some adult male. It was a world where labor was scarce and only a father's legitimate offspring, unless explicitly excluded in a will, had a guaranteed right to inherit the property on which a family's welfare depended. Men viewed the strict control of access to women's labor and power of reproduction as an absolute necessity. A law in the Twelve Tables, about 450 B.C.E. (pp. 87–8), specified that a woman was always to be in the position of a daughter or ward to some adult male: her father, her husband, or a *tutor* (guardian). Her *tutor* could be a close male relative among her father's or husband's agnates or someone named in her father's or husband's will.

A woman who had no living father and no husband who had acquired control over her was *sui iuris*, that is, independent, at least to a certain extent, despite having a *tutor*. She could not, however, buy or sell property or make contracts without the *tutor's* permission. The only exceptions were the Vestal Virgins (p. 70). During the Republic, they were free of both the *patria potestas* and the requirement of a *tutor*. Still, the Vestal Virgins were supervised by the *pontifex maximus*, Rome's male chief priest.

A husband acquired control over a wife and the property that came with her as a dowry through her transference to his *manus* (hand). He could acquire *manus* over his wife in three ways. The first was a complex religious marriage ceremony known as *confarreatio* involving the sacrifice to Jupiter of a special cake made from a variety of wheat called *far*. Except when it was required for certain priests, *confarreatio* was largely replaced over time by a simpler form of marriage with *manus* called *coemptio*. That involved the nominal sale of the bride by her *paterfamilias* or guardian to her husband. In the third form of marriage, which was like a common-law marriage, *manus* was established through *usus* (use). If a man and woman consented to live together as man and wife without interruption for a full year, the woman and her dowry automatically came under her husband's control. To avoid *manus* in this type of marriage and remain in the power of her father or guardian, a woman had to be absent from her husband's home for at least three consecutive nights every year.

If a wife remained in her father's power, whatever property she brought with her to her husband reverted to her father or father's male heirs upon her husband's death or the dissolution of the marriage. She could also inherit a share of her birth family's property upon her father's death. After that, however, she would need the approval of a guardian to dispose of her property by gift, sale, or will. If a woman passed into her husband's control through marriage with *manus*, her dowry became her husband's property. At first, her dowry had to be returned if her husband divorced her. Later, there had to be a premarital agreement for that to happen. If the husband died during the marriage, a wife could inherit a share of his property. Nevertheless, she would subsequently need the approval of a guardian to dispose of her property. A groom who was not independent needed the consent of his father or guardian for marriage, just as the bride always did. In early Rome, the couple's consent may not have been needed, but later it was required. Since girls could marry at twelve and many were fourteen to eighteen years old at first marriage, such consent would have been mostly nominal anyway.

Frequently, girls in their teens were married to men twice their age. Having reached the point where he could support a family, a husband was anxious to have children while he had enough time to raise them. Childbirth was dangerous enough before the medical advances of the last 150 years. It was even more dangerous for young mothers whose bodies were not fully matured. Infant mortality was high for the same reasons.

Therefore, if the population was to grow at all, women had to average five or six life-threatening births in their relatively short lives.

Although a wife in a marriage with *manus* was never legally free of some man's complete control, there were some compensations if she belonged to the propertied classes. Her position as *materfamilias* within a thriving household brought her honor in society and a significant role in the household economy. While her husband conducted business and public affairs outside the home, she was mistress within. She held the keys to the family storerooms and kept track of all that was brought in or disbursed. She supervised the slaves and dependents who processed food and fiber for the household. As the ideal good wife, she was expected to spin wool herself. She also looked after the raising of the children and served as a trusted advisor on matters affecting the family.

A wife's primary name was always the name of her birth family (p. 61): when she married, her name did not usually change. Marriages were arranged primarily to benefit both partners' families in terms of finances, social standing, and the production of children. A wife would have been keenly aware of the role that she played in promoting her family's interests. Through her children, relatives, social connections, and inherited property, she could help to advance her family's fortunes.

Although fairly common in later centuries, divorce in early Rome seems to have been rare and difficult because of the prevalence of marriage with *manus*. In marriage with *manus*, only the husband or his *paterfamilias* could initiate a divorce, and then only on very limited grounds. Such grounds seem to have been a wife's attempt to poison her husband or his children, adultery, and drunkenness. Even if premarital provisions had been made to send a divorced wife back with her dowry to her father, the husband kept any children. If a husband divorced a wife on other than permissible grounds, he was liable to loss of his property. In marriage without *manus*, a wife who was *sui iuris*, or her *paterfamilias* if she was not, could also initiate divorce, but any children still stayed with the husband.

Children and the family

Tombstones, mostly from the period of the Late Republic and later, attest to deep affection between parents and children, and archaeology has revealed that Roman children played with many of the same toys children play with today: rattles for babies, dolls, spinning tops, games, and balls. But Roman childhood was not all fun and games. In the hierarchical world of Rome, the needs and emotions of children were often sacrificed to the greater needs of the parents and the larger welfare of the family. Children, particularly males, were essential to provide labor and to perpetuate the agnatic family. One could not, however, risk raising too many children. The family property would be dangerously diminished if there were too many children to provide with dowries and inheritances. If there were no sons, then adopting one, usually from one's agnates, was favored. One of the hallmarks of Roman society is the ease with which they accepted adoption.

Given the fairly short life expectancy in ancient Rome, many children were deprived of one or both parents early in life. Widowed and divorced parents often remarried.

That meant many children had a stepparent, stepsiblings, and half-siblings. Orphans would be raised by their agnatic kin. Such relationships were not always loving: those relatives might resent their new wards, abuse them, or take advantage of them financially. Poor orphans and children of poor parents might end up simply abandoned or sold as slaves to be raised as thieves and prostitutes.

As noted above, unless a *paterfamilias* was insane or mentally incompetent, he could punish his children as he wished. He could sell them into slavery or even kill them. Like slaves, children could have a *peculium*, an amount of money for personal use, but their *paterfamilias* still had legal control over it. On the other hand, suits for actions committed by children still subject to *patria potestas* had to be brought against the *paterfamilias*. The authority of a *paterfamilias* over his children did not take precedence over their rights and duties as citizens or as soldiers. A *paterfamilias*, however, could use his power to punish adult children who did not live up to their civic obligations.

The family and the state

The hierarchical, authoritarian nature of the patriarchal Roman family shaped the early Roman State. Family life fostered obedience to authority and the willingness to do one's duty. On the civic level, the king and, later, the Republic's magistrates stood in a position of authority similar to that of the *paterfamilias*. They could expect the same kind of obedience from subordinates. As commanders in war, they had the right to execute anyone who refused to obey. Under normal circumstances, the obedience to authority fostered by the Roman family helped to hold in check the centrifugal forces that also existed within the state because of each family's pursuit of its own interests.

What concerned the families as a group, particularly the most powerful among them, was the state, the *res publica* (literally the "common wealth" or "common thing," "the community"). Its close connection with the fathers of the leading families is confirmed by the Latin word for country, *patria*. It comes from the adjective *patrius*, "belonging to the father." Roman religion and law are thought to be extensions of the religious and ethical practices of the families and fathers who made up and controlled the community.

The predominance of the family over the state never completely disappeared in Roman history. That can be seen in the dynastic ambitions of Roman emperors right up to the end of the Empire. The family was a living thing; the state was not. Citizens could be motivated to benefit the state not so much for the state's sake as for the honor, prestige, and glory gained for themselves and their families. Ancestral death masks and busts adorned the upper-class Roman home to remind the living of the standards to be met. The ancestors' approval and the chance to perpetuate oneself in the memory of future generations were powerful incentives to civic action. Yet in periods of crisis where the interests of the family seemed to be at variance with those of the state, there was always a great temptation to sacrifice the state's interests. Therefore, the state could become a battleground of competing interests among the powerful families that controlled it.

PATRONS AND CLIENTS

In early Rome, a man not protected by a powerful *paterfamilias* was at the mercy of those above him in the social hierarchy. He could make up for this deficiency by attaching himself as a client (*cliens*) to a more powerful man, a patron (*patronus*). The patron would protect him in many of the same ways that a father would. The etymological connection between the words *patronus* and *pater* (father) is obvious. The relationship between patron and client was strengthened by the religiously sanctioned concept of *fides*, faithfulness in performing one's obligations (p. 71). It was an offense against the gods for either a patron or a client, once having accepted their mutual relationship, to shirk their duties.

The attitudes behind the patron–client relationship also affected dealings between Rome and other states. It was always Roman policy to grant a treaty to others only from a position of strength and not accept one forced on Rome. Therefore, Rome assumed the superior position of a patron, not the inferior one of a client, nor even one of an equal partner. *Fides* obligated the Romans to abide by any treaty and look out for the interests of the other party. Conversely, the other party was expected to be a faithful client to its Roman patron in ways that often were not spelled out. Allies failing to understand this Roman attitude and thinking themselves not obligated beyond the letter of a treaty could quickly find themselves the object of unexpected Roman anger.

SLAVES AND FREEDMEN

The existence of slavery was never questioned in antiquity, least of all by the Romans. It seemed to be a logical part of a hierarchical order. Today, any slave system is intolerable. At least the early Roman system avoided some of the worst features of slavery. It was not based on anything like the modern misguided notion of race. The evils of chattel slavery did not arise until later, with the exploitation of masses of slaves in large agricultural or industrial operations. In early Rome, slaves probably were not numerous. Failure to pay off debts was often a cause for enslavement. Women and children captured in war were usually enslaved and put to work.

Slaves in early Rome were valuable, and they constituted an integral part of the family as they worked beside other members of the family at home or in the fields. They could reasonably look forward to at least informal manumission, a grant of freedom, after some years of faithful service. At that time, they became freedmen (*liberti*, sing. *libertus*) or freedwomen (*libertae*, sing. *liberta*). They could be required by the terms of their manumission to fulfill various obligations to their former masters. Slaves who were freed in formal legal procedures even became Roman citizens.

ROMAN NAMES AND THE *GENS*

All Roman citizens belonged to a larger, ostensibly genealogical group called a *gens* (pl. *gentes*), often translated as "clan." The name of one's *gens*, the *nomen gentilicium*, was a person's most important name. It was the second of the three names often borne by a male citizen. The first name (*praenomen*), was the personal name: oldest sons were named after their fathers. The last, or surname (*cognomen*), if there was one, indicated the branch of the *gens* to which one's male lineage belonged. In some cases a *cognomen* attached to a family for generations because of a particular physical trait of one individual. For example, Cicero, the famous orator and statesman, was named Marcus Tullius Cicero. Therefore, he belonged to the Ciceronian line of the Tullian *gens*. A *cicer* is Latin for "chickpea": the story is that a distant relative had a cleft on the end of his nose that looked like the legume. To take another example, although we often refer to Julius Caesar, Julius was not his first name. Caesar's *praenomen* was Gaius; Julius is his clan-name (*nomen*). His *cognomen*, Caesar, means "hairy"; given the Roman penchant for mocking the physical appearance of others and given the fact that the family had been called Caesar for generations, we are left to wonder if the men of the family were all, like the most famous Caesar, bald. In other instances, a *cognomen* only attached to an individual and not to the family as a whole. Originally, Caesar's eventual rival, Pompey, was named only Gnaeus Pompeius. He later acquired the *cognomen* Magnus ("the Great") because of his early military exploits. When a non-Roman or former slave received Roman citizenship, he adopted the *gentilicium* of the man who sponsored or freed him. Since the *nomen gentilicium* provided the crucial identification for a Roman, scholarly books or reference works in ancient history will usually list a Roman under his or her *gentilicium*. In this book, for example, the three aforementioned men are found in the index under "Tullius," "Julius," and "Pompeius," respectively.

Because the male family line was more important than the individual, fathers and sons often bore the same *praenomen* for generations, or two names might alternate between fathers and sons. If there were more than one son each generation, other sons would be named for other male agnates, such as a father's brothers. As a result, during the Republic, there were only about sixteen commonly used male first names, which were usually indicated by such easily recognized abbreviations as "L." for Lucius, "M." for Marcus, "P." for Publius, "Q." for Quintus, and "T." for Titus. Gaius and Gnaeus are abbreviated "C." and "Cn." because "g" and "c" were not distinguished in the earliest Roman alphabet.

Since women in early Rome counted even less as individuals than men, they usually had only one official name throughout the republican period—the female form of the father's *gentilicium*. Therefore, Cicero's daughter was named Tullia and Caesar's, Julia. If a father raised more than one daughter, their formal names were all the same. Hence, the three infamous sisters of P. Clodius, the even more infamous enemy of Cicero (pp. 270–1), were all named Clodia. They may have been distinguished informally at home as Prima, Secunda, and Tertia (Clodia the First, the Second, and the Third). Although women did not, as a rule, change their names after they married, they were sometimes referred to with a possessive form of their husbands' name, often the *cognomen* if he had one, after her own. Thus, the Clodia who married Q. Caecilius Metellus Celer is known in modern scholarship as Clodia Metelli (Metellus' Clodia) and her sister who married L. Licinius Lucullus is known as Clodia Luculli.

The origin of the *gens*

The origin of the *gens* as a genealogical group is hard to discover. Naming patterns in the rest of central Italy indicate the existence of similar groups among surrounding peoples. They may have had their roots in warrior bands where loyal followers adopted the name of their leader to promote solidarity. The existence of such bands is indicated in seventh-century B.C.E. burials where lower status graves are grouped around the princely graves of some wealthy warriors. The story of Attus Clausus (Atta Claudius, Appius Claudius) and his 4000 dependents receiving citizenship *en bloc* in the early Republic lends support to this theory. So does the *Lapis Satricanus*, an inscription from Satricum, south of Rome. It mentions a Publius Valerius, who may have been the leader of a band of warriors.

During the Monarchy, such warrior bands may have been incorporated into the Roman army as Rome expanded its territory under the kings. Those men who did not belong to such a band would have been assigned to one or had one created for them. Before the creation of separate rural tribes, Rome was divided into four urban tribes and twenty-six rural districts (*pagi*) or regions (*regiones*). The total of tribes and rural territories combined corresponds to the thirty *curiae* of the early Roman army (p. 50). Probably, each rural district was identified by the name of its biggest *gens*. Significantly, when the rural districts were initially grouped into fewer, larger tribes, each tribe seems to have taken its name from that of a *gens*.

Patrician and nonpatricians *gentes*

In keeping with the Roman passion for hierarchical distinction, at some point before the end of the Monarchy and the beginning of the Republic (ca. 500 B.C.E.), certain *gentes* seem to have become distinguished as patrician. The members of those *gentes,* the patricians, had more prestige and privileges than the members of the other *gentes*. The word *patrician* (*patricius*) is derived from the word for father, *pater* (pl. *patres*). In archaic Rome, the word *patres*, "fathers," also applied to the men who monopolized the important priesthoods, held the office of *interrex*, and elected kings. Eventually, as a special group within the senate, they claimed the sole right to approve or reject legislation during the early Republic.

Perhaps the original *patres* were the fathers of the families whose clans headed the early tribes and rural districts that constituted the territory of the early Roman State. The family cults that they maintained might then have been incorporated into the public cults of the early state and secured for their *gentes* the privilege of supplying public priests. Patricians became further divided into greater and lesser *gentes* (*patres maiorum gentium* and *patres minorum gentium*). Perhaps, some patrician *gentes* were designated as "greater" after giving their names to tribes later consolidated out of the original twenty-six rural districts. Unfortunately, much has to remain in the realm of learned conjecture and speculation.

As a result of later developments, the nonpatrician *gentes* came to be identified as *plebeian*. For the late Monarchy and the beginning of the Republic, it is best to refer to patricians and nonpatricians. What did not automatically distinguish patricians and nonpatricians was wealth. Many nonpatricians were as wealthy as patricians. The great majority was not. Neither did the distinction have any particular ethnic basis. Both patricians and nonpatricians were a mixture of Latin, Sabine, and Etruscan elements. Nor were all nonpatricians clients of patricians, although many probably were.

As Roman citizens, nonpatricians had the right to make commercial contracts, own real property, contract valid marriages, sue or be sued in court, and vote in the popular assemblies of the early state. They could not hold public priesthoods. A few outstanding nonpatricians did obtain high office and membership in the senate. Patricians trying to build up networks of useful supporters may have helped them, even to the point of establishing ties of marriage. Over time, however, the patricians tried to assert exclusive rights to political leadership as a privileged noble class in the face of aspiring nonpatricians. Eventually, the citizens as a whole rejected their claims (p. 83ff.).

CLASSES IN ROMAN SOCIETY

There were many other hierarchical distinctions in Roman society. They are very complex. Modern English terms like class, status, and rank often do not have the same meanings as their Latin cognates or analogs. The English word *class*, for example, comes from the Latin *classis*, which came to indicate a classification based on wealth in the Roman census. A male citizen's *classis*, or lack of one, in the census, determined the type of military service for which he was liable and the century to which he was assigned in the Centuriate Assembly. The Latin word *status* was used primarily in Roman law to indicate a person's legal standing within both the family and the civil community: whether he was free or unfree; a citizen or a noncitizen; an independent head of household (*sui iuris*) or still under the power of the head of a household (*alieni iuris*). In modern English usage, "status" is closely linked to the concept of classes—horizontally conceived socioeconomic groups ranging from lower to higher, who each have some sense of common life experience and shared political interest.

Some would say that such a concept is problematical in dealing with Roman society. It tended to be vertically organized in the hereditary hierarchical relationships of the family, *gens*, tribe, and community. Vertical, hierarchical relationships cut across all horizontal generational and economic divisions in the performance of common cultic and civic duties. Nevertheless, the Romans did have a word indicating a citizen's social and political rank. It is the word *ordo*, order (as in the English expression "the lower orders of society"). It can also be translated as rank or class in the sense of a broad horizontally conceived social group within which members have a certain self-conscious identity. Hence, in the field of Roman history, the English phrase *Struggle (Conflict) of the Orders* signifies a conflict that the ancient sources depict between two simplistically conceived classes in the early Republic—the rich patricians and the poor plebeians.

The problem is that the sources were projecting back onto the early Republic the kind of more clearly defined orders that existed in the later Republic. At least at the beginning of the Republic, the patrician *gentes* probably had not yet claimed to be an exclusive governing elite. The plebeians, the *plebs*, consisted of many nonpatricians of various socioeconomic levels from the general mass of citizens (probably the original meaning of *plebs*), who came to feel politically, socially, and/or economically disadvantaged and banded together to develop their own "plebeian" institutions and officials and press for the redress of their grievances.

THE OPENNESS OF EARLY ROMAN SOCIETY TO OUTSIDERS

Despite their penchant for creating hierarchical distinctions, the early Romans, unlike their Greek contemporaries, were remarkably willing to incorporate outsiders as citizens of their community. As Rome's power expanded throughout its history, the Romans came into contact with increasingly different peoples and their diverse cultures. Since the Romans did not subscribe to modern ideas of race, they tended to treat individuals of different national and ethnic origins, even people of color, as they would anyone else of the same social status.

That is not to say Romans were not prejudiced against people they perceived as different. They were just as guilty as anyone else of xenophobia, negative ethnic stereotyping, and cultural intolerance. On the other hand, when non-Romans acquired Roman culture in terms of language, dress, manners, and education, often through years of faithful service as allies, subjects, soldiers, or slaves, they could become fully integrated into Roman society as Roman citizens.

Rome's origin as a community created from several neighboring villages and as a cosmopolitan center of trade among Etruscans, Greeks, Phoenicians, Latins, and other Italic peoples is significant. It probably explains why the Romans, unlike the citizens of Greek *poleis*, did not look upon themselves as a community of kin and were able to be more inclusive than their Greek counterparts. As Rome expanded by treaty and conquest during the Monarchy and early Republic, it incorporated people from added territories into the citizen community. At the same time, the new citizens' gods were incorporated into the divine community, whose public cults constituted the state religion. By the end of the Monarchy, Rome had grown from a few square miles of territory within the radius of the Forum to about 300 square miles embracing the northwestern third of Latium. The constant incorporation of new citizens enabled the Roman army to keep pace with and fuel even more expansion. Taking over the cults and deities of newly incorporated citizens gave Romans the self-assured feeling of divine favor toward their actions. It also lessened the alienation of those who had been forced to join them.

EARLY ROMAN RELIGION

Rome could easily assimilate other people's gods because Roman religion was not based on any creed or dogma. We are familiar with religions that have a set of beliefs that lie at their core; this is termed orthodoxy. For the Romans, however, it was not belief that pleased the gods, but the proper forms of worship (called "orthopraxy") that ensured success in daily life. Religion played a central role in private and public life. A multiplicity of gods occupied a hierarchical position of superiority above both human beings and the state. It was the duty of the individual, the family, and the state to perform the sacrifices and rituals that the gods required. Thus, everyone would prosper. Anybody's gods could be enlisted in the effort: Roman religion was a polytheistic system that allowed for the admission of new gods who had proven themselves to be powerful. One result of this openness is that it is nearly impossible to recover an original Roman religion that is free from the influences of outside peoples, including not only the Greeks and the Etruscans but also Rome's Latin neighbors.

What we can recover of Roman religion in the earliest period suggests that it reflected a life centered on home, farm, and pasture. Household rituals centered around the family hearth, where the goddess Vesta was worshiped and which was festooned with garlands on certain festival days. Rituals were observed to ensure the health of the family, their flocks, and their crops. Other observances that seem to date to a very early time in Roman history appear to address more communal concerns, such as the festival of the Lupercalia in February during which semi-naked men ran a circuit through the city that might reflect an early boundary line. The focus of most religious activity was the maintenance of the Romans' relationship with the gods, to which they gave the name of *pax deorum* (literally, the peace of the gods).

Communicating with the gods

The Romans believed that they could communicate with the gods and that their gods could communicate with them. There is no reason to think that the ancient Romans had anything like a modern prayer book, but it is clear from their literature that they often prayed to the gods. Numerous dedications written on stone record the presentation of gifts at temples as thanks-offerings for help received or as requests for help in the future. The Romans could also communicate with their gods through sacrifice, the offering of vegetable produce or animal victims at an altar. The gods received a portion of the offering as a sign of honor intended to make them well-disposed to hearing their worshipers' request. Humans ate the rest at a meal after the ritual was over.

The gods communicated with the Romans in a number of ways. On rare occasions, sometimes commemorated in inscriptions carved in stone, gods appeared to individuals through dreams or waking visions. Sometimes the gods spoke through oracles, temples where a priest would reveal the god's answer to questions put to him. More commonly, however, the gods made their opinions known through divine signs, called *prodigia* (sing. *prodigium*) in Latin which comes into English as "prodigy." Prodigies usually took the form of events that violated the regular, natural order of things, such as a statue that sweated blood, a newborn baby shouting "Victory!", or two suns appearing the sky at once. Some normal celestial phenomena like lightning strikes, peals of thunder, and comets were thought to be divine signs as well (see the inset on p. 29). The gods also spoke to their worshipers through the flight and cry of certain types of birds and through the entrails of sacrificed animals, which would be inspected by trained officials before the meat was roasted. If, for example, the animal's liver was misshapen, dire events were about to unfold (see p. 69). When any of these signs were observed, the Romans quickly enacted whatever they determined was needed to restore balance in the *pax deorum*.

Gods and festivals of the house and fields

The spirits of the house were few. There was Janus, who was associated with the household's front door. He faced both in and out, letting in friends and shutting out enemies. At weddings, it was the custom for the bride to smear Janus' doorposts with wolf's fat and to be lifted over his threshold. At the birth of a child, the threshold was struck with an ax, a pestle, and a broom to repulse wild spirits from the outside. When someone died in the house, the corpse was carried out feet first, perhaps for fear that the ghost might find its way back in.

Inside the house was Vesta, linked to the family hearth whose fire gave warmth and cooked the daily meals. It is said that no image or statue of her was made in early times. Yet, she was the center of family life and worship. To her, the head of the house presented his bride or newborn child. Before her hearth stood the dining table, also a sacred object. On it was the salt dish and the sacred cake of salted grain baked by the women of the house. At dinner, the head of the family ceremoniously threw part of the cake into the fire. As Janus began the roll of deities invoked in family prayer, so Vesta ended it.

Not far from the fireplace was the pantry. Here dwelt a vague group of nameless deities collectively known as the *Penates*. With Vesta, they shared the offerings made at the fireplace because they guarded the food that Vesta cooked. In Latin literature, they were a synonym for home. So were the *Lares*, a group of deities whose origin is obscure. They were associated with both the home and the *compitum*, a place where roads cross. Each home and crossroads had a shrine for its *Lares*. The crossroads *Lares* were celebrated each autumn at the festival of the *Compitalia*. In honor of this holiday, plows were hung up as a sign that the season's work was done. Everybody, even slaves, joined in the feasting and fun.

The festival of the *Ambarvalia* was held toward the end of May. It secured divine favor for the growing and ripening crops. The farmer and his family, dressed in white with olive wreaths around their heads, solemnly drove a pig, a sheep, and a bull three times around the farm. The three animals were then killed in a sacrifice called the *suovetaurilia*, a name that included the words for the three animals. The victims were opened, examined for omens, and burned upon the altar fire. Then followed a long prayer asking for good weather and good crops from Mars, originally a god of agriculture.

Other spring festivals were the *Liberalia*, for Liber (god of wine); the *Cerialia*, for Ceres (goddess of grain); and the *Robigalia*. At the *Robigalia*, a red dog was sacrificed to avert Robigus, the red mildew, or "rust," that attacked wheat. Shepherds had their spring festivals, too. The *Parilia* was the feast of Pales, spirit of flocks and herds. It took place on April 21, just before the annual trek to summer pastures. At dawn, the herdsmen sprinkled the animals with water, swept out the stalls, and decorated the barns with green branches. Then they lit a bonfire of straw, brush, and other items, through which the flocks were driven and the shepherds leaped. After an offering of milk and cakes to Pales and a prayer for the health, safety, and increase of the flocks, the shepherds spent the rest of the day in sports, eating, and drinking. Later, the day of this festival was accepted as the anniversary of Rome's founding, because the young Romulus, the legendary founder, had been depicted as a shepherd. April 21 is still celebrated as the birthday of Rome in Italy today.

Two noteworthy festivals held in late summer or early fall are coupled with the names of Jupiter and Mars. The first was a wine festival, the *Vinalia Rustica*. It was held on August 19 in honor of Jupiter. After the sacrifice of a ewe lamb, Jupiter's high priest inaugurated the grape-picking season by cutting the first bunch of grapes. The other was the ritual of the October Horse when a chariot race was held to honor Mars. The right-hand horse of the winning team and a spear were sacrificed to Mars. The Vestal Virgins, Rome's most important priestesses, gathered blood from the horse's tail and preserved it for later use in another festival. The horse's head, cut off and decked with cakes, was fought over by the men from rival neighborhoods within the city. The winners were allowed to display it as a trophy.

Early outside influence

Rome's early interaction with other peoples in the Italian peninsula extended to religious matters as well as political and commercial concerns. The Etruscan goddesses Uni and Menrva and the Italic Juno and Menerva (the Roman Minerva) came to be identified with the Greek goddesses Hera and Athena. The Etruscan Tinia and Italic Jupiter took on some of the features of Zeus. A great temple to the Roman triad of Jupiter, Juno, and Minerva was built on the Capitoline Hill at the end of the Monarchy and the beginning of the Republic. It was designed and decorated in a style that incorporated many elements from contemporary Greek temples. Similar temples were appearing in contemporary Etruscan and Latin cities.

Jupiter and Mars

Jupiter (Iuppiter, *Deus Pater*) was Rome's supreme civic god. The first part of his name is etymologically the same as Zeus, his Greek counterpart. Each is associated with the sky, thunder, lightning, and rain. With the growth of political and urban life among the Latins and the Romans, Jupiter became the symbol of the Roman State, the giver of victory, and the spirit of law and justice. Rome similarly exalted Mars (Mavors, Mamars), who gave his name to the first month, *Martius* (March), of the early Roman calendar. Once an Italic protector of the farmer's fields and herds or the community's boundaries, Mars became the defender of the Roman State against its enemies.

Juno and Minerva

One of the most prominent cults in early Italy, not just in Rome, was that of Juno. She was worshiped particularly in Latium and southern Etruria. At Rome, there were many different temples for Juno in her various guises: Juno Regina, Juno Sospita, Juno Lucina, to name a few. On a few occasions in the historical period, the Romans managed to defeat their enemies in part by persuading an opponent's Juno to abandon her people and come to Rome. The Roman goddess Minerva is closely linked with the cult of Menerva in Falerii, a semi-Etruscan Faliscan town north of Rome, west of the Tiber. She may have been introduced by immigrant Faliscans skilled in the pottery and metal trades. Her early presence in Rome is clearly in line with the archaeological evidence of close commercial and industrial ties between Rome and south Etruria.

Other cults

The expansion of early Roman commercial contacts is likewise emphasized by the erection in the Cattle Market (Forum Boarium) of an altar to Hercules (the Phoenician Melqart; the Greek Herakles), the patron god of traders and merchants. The worship of Diana (identified with the Greek Artemis) was transferred from Aricia, where she was worshiped by the Romans and many other Latin towns, to the Aventine Hill—a sign of Roman dominance over their neighbors. Other goddesses also migrated to Rome. Fortuna was imported from Antium (Anzio). Venus was formerly worshiped as a goddess of gardens and orchards at Ardea. She became identified later with Aphrodite, the Greek goddess of love and beauty.

Of the deities just named, all, except Hercules, were indigenous to Italy, yet all of them were subject to the influence of the religious traditions of other people. Even Ceres, an ancient Italic goddess associated with agricultural fertility, did not escape the effects of this transforming influence. When a famine struck ca. 496 B.C.E., the Romans sought divine help. They vowed to build a temple on the Aventine, overlooking the grain market of the Forum Boarium. Three years later it was dedicated to Ceres, Libera, and Liber. They represented a triad of agricultural deities associated with grain and wine. They were identical in almost everything but name with the Greek triad of Demeter, Persephone, and Iacchus. Moreover, Greek artists decorated the temple with paintings.

In 492 B.C.E., Mercury also received a temple on the Aventine. Like both Hermes, to whom he was assimilated, and Herakles (the Greek name for Hercules), he was a god of traders and seems particularly connected with grain merchants from both Etruria and Greek cities in southern Italy. Seaborne imports from southern Italy seem to account for an early connection between Poseidon, the Greek god of the great open sea, and Italic Neptune. Neptune quickly received the trident and sea horses of Poseidon and all of the mythology associated with him.

Not long after 500 B.C.E., the worship of Apollo, the god of healing and prophecy, came from Cumae, the nearest and oldest Greek settlement on the Italian mainland. Despite his unlatinized name, Apollo became in later times one of the greatest gods of the Roman pantheon. Cumae was also the home of the Sibyl, Apollo's inspired priestess. Her oracle must have been known in early Rome. The earliest oracles in the *Sibylline Books* seem to have been made around 500 B.C.E., at the beginning of the Republic. These books were kept in the temple of Jupiter during the Republic and could be consulted only by a special college of two priests. They played a decisive role throughout the Republic in deciding which foreign gods could come to Rome. They also introduced new forms of worship, such as *lectisternia* (sing. *lectisternium*), ritual banquets for the gods. Statues of the gods in male/female pairs were publicly displayed reclining on couches before tables of food and drink.

Divination

Like other ancient peoples, the Romans believed in divination, that is, reading signs in the natural world in order to predict the future and to determine the will of the gods. That consists of interpreting sacred signs, such as thunder, lightning, the flights of birds, and the entrails of sacrificial animals to discern the will and intentions of the gods. In particular, hepatoscopy—inspecting the size, shape, texture, and color of a sacrificed animal's liver—was highly regarded. The neighboring Etruscans were so devoted to the practice of divination that the Romans called it the *Disciplina Etrusca*, the Etruscan Learning (p. 29). Roman aristocrats, whose families provided the public priests, often sent their sons to Etruscan cities to learn this valuable lore. The Etruscan priests who interpreted these signs were called *haruspices*. On critical occasions, the Romans would summon *haruspices* from Etruria for extra assurance that they understood the divine will.

Two important branches of divination were the taking of auspices (*auspicia*) and the conducting of auguries (*auguria*). Taking auspices involved ceremonies of divination for the limited purpose of determining if the time was right for a particular private or public action. The person taking the auspices looked for special signs in the flight and behavior of birds, the unusual behavior of animals, and heavenly phenomena like thunder and lightning. The same signs were sought in conducting auguries. The auguries determined if the gods were favorable to an action, to a place where an action was to occur, or to the person about to undertake it. Any man could take auspices, but only special priests called *augurs* could perform auguries (p. 83). Although, as was mentioned above (p. 65), the Romans sometimes received messages directly from their gods through dreams, waking visions, and oracles, they were less enamored of this type of divination (called natural divination) than were the Greeks and some other peoples of the ancient Mediterranean.

THE STATE, RELIGION, AND WAR

The emerging Roman State embraced and incorporated all the older and smaller social and religious communities such as the family, the *gens*, and the tribe. According to legend, Romulus had inaugurated the Roman State with religious ceremonies when he established the original *pomerium*. As the city grew and expanded, it was the responsibility of the state to extend the *pomerium* and provide for the common religious life of the community. Much of that came to be related to war.

Janus became the guardian of Rome's Sacred Gateway at the northeast corner of the Forum. Its doors were shut only in peacetime, probably because the early armies marched through this gate on their way to war. The sacred fire in the Temple of Vesta guaranteed the secure existence of the state. After her hearth was cleaned, it was relit on March 1. That was early Rome's New Year, the first day of the month named for Mars, the god of war. His altar in the Campus Martius was the symbol of the city's military power. When Roman armies returned in triumph, victorious generals led their triumphal processions up to the Temple of Jupiter on the Capitoline Hill.

The king and early priesthoods

The priestly role of the king first as head of state and then as *rex sacrorum* has been described in the previous chapter (pp. 48–9). The Vestal Virgins may have originated as the king's wife and daughters tending his sacred household hearth. Significantly, the later Temple of Vesta and its sacred public hearth were built over part of the Regia, the old royal palace.

Eventually, the number of Vestal Virgins became fixed at six. They were usually chosen between the ages of six and ten from senatorial families. They were required to serve a minimum of thirty years. After that, they could retire and even marry, although our sources tell us that few did. Their chief duties were to keep the sacred fire of Vesta's hearth burning to ensure the permanence of Rome and to prepare many items necessary for ritual observances throughout the year. They prepared the mix of salt and grain used in all public sacrifices. Any hint of a Vestal's sexual impurity caused great public concern for the welfare of the state. Those convicted of sexual impropriety were sentenced to death by being entombed alive.

Other important early priests and priestesses were the *flamen Dialis* or chief priest of Jupiter and his wife (the *flaminica Dialis*). There were two other major flamens (*flamines*), one for Mars and one for Quirinus, a very obscure deity associated with the origins of Rome who came to be known as the deified Romulus. Not much is known about these two flamens except that they and the *flamen Dialis* always had to be patricians even after others did not. The flamen of Mars obviously was associated with the rituals of war, and he officiated at the festival of the October Horse (p. 67). Twelve minor flamens each served a deity characteristic of a largely agrarian people—Ceres, Flora, and Pomona, for example, who respectively represented grain, flowering plants, and fruit trees.

Some other early priests were the three augurs, official diviners who interpreted signs from the gods, and three pontiffs, who seem to have acquired a general function as keepers of civil and religious records. Two priesthoods that also seem to have originated in the early Monarchy were related to war: the fetial priests (*fetiales*) were responsible for declaring war; the Salii performed war dances associated with Mars (p. 83).

THE VALUES OF EARLY ROMAN SOCIETY

The early Romans developed a deeply held set of values that explain much of their behavior. These values resonate in the moral vocabulary of modern Western nations. For example, the English words *virtue, prudence, temperance, fortitude, justice, piety, fidelity, chastity, constancy,* and *perseverance* stem from Latin roots. Many of the corresponding Latin concepts are important to the public and family life of the early Roman community. They became enshrined in what came to be called the *mos maiorum,* custom of the ancestors. Later Classical Roman writers are now the major sources for these concepts. In attempting to reform the behavior of their contemporaries, Roman writers frequently pointed out how much the heroes and deeds of the past exemplified the values they idealized. They could do so, however, only because those values were already part of the cultural heritage that their contemporaries shared with the past.

Virtue (*virtus*)

The Latin word *virtus* had a meaning somewhat different from that of its English derivative, virtue. The Latin root of *virtus* is *vir*, a man. *Virtus* signified the particular qualities associated with manliness. A man needed a strong body to support and protect his family and fight for the community. The need for every able-bodied armed man to fight in the army produced a warrior ethos that made military valor particularly salient in the Roman concept of virtue. The upper-class magistrates of the early Republic were primarily military officers who had to show bravery and leadership in battle. The welfare of the community depended upon ordinary citizens in the army. Every soldier had to execute commands obediently in coordination with his comrades to ensure the protection of all. He had to exercise great self-discipline in the heat of battle so as not to break ranks and deny the man on his left the protection of his shield. The idea that a good man subordinated his own narrow interest to those of his family, his comrades, and the state underlies four qualities that became particularly associated with Roman virtue in general: dutifulness, faith, gravity, and constancy.

Dutifulness (*pietas*)

Dutifulness (*pietas*) implied in the first place devotion to duty within the family group. It encompassed both a willing acceptance of parental authority and a concern for children. It further meant reverence for and devotion to the gods through action in the exact performance of all required religious rites and ceremonies. Piety toward the state connoted obedience to the laws; dutiful performance of civic duties in a manner consistent with justice, law, and established custom; and patriotic military service.

Faith (*fides*)

Fides meant "faith" in the sense of "trust." It was faithfulness in the performance of one's duties and obligations. It meant being true to one's word, paying one's debts, keeping sworn oaths, and performing obligations assumed by agreement with both gods and men. Based on religion and law, it was the foundation of religious, public, and private life. Violation of *fides* was an offense against both the gods and the community. A patron who broke faith with his client by abuse of his power was placed under a curse. A magistrate who broke faith by acts of injustice and oppression against the people gave the latter the right to rebel. Faith rooted in the social conscience was stronger than written law or statute as a force for holding all parts of the society together in a common relationship. Failure to uphold religious obligations would incur divine wrath.

Gravity (*gravitas*) and constancy (*constantia*)

Faith had to be supplemented by two other Roman virtues: gravity and constancy. The first meant absolute self-control—a dignified, serious, and unperturbed attitude toward both good and bad fortune. To cite some early extreme examples, no Roman was supposed to dance in public, nor were husbands and wives supposed to kiss each other outside of their own homes. The second virtue was constancy or perseverance, even under the most trying circumstances, in doing what seemed necessary and right until success was won.

Dignitas, auctoritas, and gloria

Those who exhibited the four qualities discussed above, especially in public life, acquired what came to be called *dignitas* (reputation for worth, honor, esteem) and *auctoritas* (prestige, respect). Particularly outstanding public or military achievements also earned glory (*gloria*)—praise and public adulation. Roman aristocrats highly valued *dignitas*, *auctoritas*, and *gloria*. They confirmed the leading role of their families in society. Individual leaders demonstrated virtue by successfully defending the community or increasing its resources through warfare and by duly performing their duties as patrons, priests, magistrates, and senators. Thus, they acquired the honor, prestige, and glory that set them apart from others and gave them the power to continue to lead. That power further enhanced their status and that of their families in competition with their aristocratic peers.

Modesty (*pudicitia*) and chastity (*castitas*)

The virtues expected of Roman women were less public than those expected of their husbands, fathers, brothers, and sons. Wives and daughters were expected to exhibit *pudicitia* (modesty) by dressing appropriately and tending the home. Ancient writers sometimes criticize women who dressed too stylishly or who danced too well. Young women were expected to maintain their virginal chastity (*castitas*) until they were married. Matronal chastity was highly prized, as is exemplified by the fact that certain religious honors were only available to women who had married once. The quintessential matronal virtues are summed up by an epitaph from the period of the Republic, now lost, for a woman named Claudia: she is praised for her beauty, her modest manner and pleasant conversation, her love for her husband, and the fact that she bore two children. The epitaph concludes with the statement, "She kept her house. She spun wool."

Shame (*pudor*) and disgrace (*infamia, ignominia*)

Failure to live up to the Roman moral code brought public disgrace (*infamia, ignominia*) and a feeling of shame (*pudor*) to both men and women. To avoid such shame was as important to a Roman as it was to display the virtues Roman society prized. For the Romans as a whole, with their warrior ethos, to conquer was the greatest glory for men; to be conquered, the greatest disgrace. For women, the greatest glory was to be recognized by the community for outstanding *pudicitia*; it was disgraceful for a woman's *castitas* to be questioned. It is worth noting that some of the virtues we extol today (generosity, kindness, fair-mindedness, religious piety and so on), while still valued by the Romans, were not so highly prized by them.

OVERVIEW AND SIGNIFICANCE

Rome's characteristic hierarchical social structure, centered on the authoritarian, patriarchal family and dominated by an aristocratic elite, had already taken shape. It also appears that the complex religious amalgam of reverence for ancestors and worship of multiple gods who could communicate with mortals—and the various rituals associated with this worship—had assumed the basic form it would continue to have well into the future. Along with these developments and growing out of them evolved the system of values that defined the Romans' view of themselves as individuals and as a people and made the winning of military glory a paramount ambition of public life.

Ultimately, Roman family life, religion, and morality fostered a conservative type of human being. The authoritarian, patriarchal family and the attitude of dependency inherent in clientage produced an obedience to authority that greatly benefited the aristocratic *gentes* who controlled the state. The reverence for ancestors and their customs, as enshrined in the words *mos maiorum*, worked against attempts at radical innovation among all classes, as did the sobriety and piety of the Roman ethical tradition. The resultant abhorrence of innovation is signified by the Roman term for revolution, *res novae* (new things). So concerned were the Romans to maintain their traditions that many archaic and obsolete practices, institutions, festivals, and offices continued to exist long after they had lost their original function. When innovations were made, the Romans were careful to cast them as preserving ancient custom, no matter how dubious the claim. For example, in religion, the ancient *Sibylline Books*, with their convenient ambiguities and even opportune forgeries, could justify the introduction of new deities and rituals from time to time. Even in politics, in a society where the vagaries of oral tradition often predominated over written records, "ancestral precedents" might be of as recent origin as an orator's latest speech. Therefore, Roman conservatism was saved from being stultifying. Change could occur while a deep sense of continuity— one of Rome's greatest strengths—prevailed.

SUGGESTED READING

Forsythe, G. A. *A Critical History of Early Rome: From Prehistory to the First Punic War.* Berkeley, Los Angeles, and London: University of California Press, 2005.

MacMullen, R. *The Earliest Romans: A Character Sketch.* Ann Arbor: University of Michigan Press, 2011.

Smith, C. J. *The Roman Clan: The Gens from Ancient Ideology to Modern Anthropology.* Cambridge: University of Cambridge Press, 2006.

CHAPTER 5

From tyrant kings to oligarchic republic, 509 to 287 B.C.E.

The period of Roman history known as the Republic extended from the end of the Monarchy about 500 (traditionally 509) B.C.E. until Augustus became the first Roman emperor (30–27 B.C.E.: the process took several years). The term "republic," from the Latin *res publica* (common wealth, public thing) has come to mean a certain form of political constitution. Although in a republic the people play a role in the governing of the state (mostly through the election of officials), a republic is not necessarily democratic: a republic need not be structured so that every citizen's vote is counted equally. Even so, a republic is fundamentally different from the form of government that exists under a king or an emperor.

To the Romans, the words *res publica* originally signified common property and public affairs, as opposed to private property and affairs. After Rome was ruled by an emperor who had assumed almost unlimited private control over what once had been common and public, *res publica* took on new meaning for Romans opposed to one-man rule. They associated *res publica* with the unwritten constitution that had evolved into its classic form through a complex mixture of custom, precedent, and legislation during the fifth and fourth centuries B.C.E. The Roman people always voted on magistrates and legislation, but the Roman Republic remained far from democratic: governmental institutions were structured to favor the wealthy and those few families that were members of the senatorial class. Still, the conduct of public affairs had come to be shared among those who constituted the senatorial aristocracy. They governed via laws and institutions that limited the arbitrary exercise of power. Also, for a considerable time, they showed at least minimal concern for the lower ranks of society.

The evolution of that system is not well documented. All one can hope to do is construct a reasonable outline of what must have been a complex process. In any such attempt, however, there is nothing that cannot be or has not been challenged.

This chapter outlines several crucial phases of the Republic's constitutional development. First is the transition from kingship to the earliest form of the Republic at the end of the sixth and beginning of the fifth century B.C.E. Second is the creation of more formal rights and institutions that benefited plebeian citizens during the rest of the fifth century. The third phase, mostly during the fourth century, saw the culmination of plebeian rights, traditionally by 287 B.C.E. It also included the creation of new officers to perform the increasingly complex functions of war and government.

Many of the constitutional developments that are the focus of this chapter took place under the pressure of Rome's almost constant wars with other peoples in Italy. Those wars and many of the changes accompanying them will appear in the next chapter. Here, it is necessary to keep in mind that the prize for plebeian leaders was access to the offices that conferred command of the wars. They were the major source of wealth, *dignitas*, *auctoritas*, and *gloria* in a state that was organized for war. At the same time, the ordinary plebeians, whose needs their leaders articulated, could not be ignored. They made up the bulk of the arms-bearing men, the *populus*, needed to fight the wars.

SOURCES OF INFORMATION FOR EARLY REPUBLICAN HISTORY

The sources for this and the following chapter are essentially the same as those discussed at length in Chapter 3 (pp. 38–40). The two most extensive accounts are in Livy (Books 2–10) and Dionysius of Halicarnassus (*Roman Antiquities*, Books 4–20). Significant fragments from Books 4 to 10 of Cassius Dio's *Roman History* survive for this period, and the Byzantine monk Zonaras presents a summary of the same material. Polybius, a major mid-second-century B.C.E. Greek historian who lived in Rome, treats the theory and development of the Roman constitution in Book 6 of his universal history of the Mediterranean world. Cicero devotes thirteen short chapters (25–37) to early developments in Book 2 of his *De Republica*. A few additional facts and important traditions are included in Plutarch's biographies of Camillus, Coriolanus, Publicola, and Pyrrhus and in Books 10 to 20 (11–20 fully preserved) of Diodorus Siculus' world history. The latter's most important contribution is his list of Roman consuls (the chief yearly magistrates) beginning with approximately 486 B.C.E.

Like the various annalists and historians on whose lost works they based their own, these writers were often guilty of rhetorically exaggerated embellishments and anachronistic interpretation. Again, the surviving works of antiquarian writers mentioned in Chapter 3 preserve many alternative accounts and additional pieces of information culled from religious rituals, linguistic research, oral traditions, previous writers (Roman and non-Roman), and the more extensive documentation such as laws, treaties, and family archives that once were available for this period. Moreover, helpful archaeological evidence and inscriptions become more abundant at this point.

THE *FASTI*

The most valuable inscriptions are those that preserve lists of the annual consuls, the consular *Fasti*. In many ancient states, years were not numbered in sequence from some special starting point but were named after one or more of the annual officials: in Athens, after the head archon; in Sparta, after the chief ephor; in Rome, after the consuls. All such officials are known as *eponymous* (naming) *magistrates*. Such a system made phenomenal demands upon the memory unless lists were at hand for business, legal, and official purposes. Eventually, many such lists must have been available to public officials, priests, and private individuals.

The oldest list of Roman magistrates probably originated in the brief annual records of officials and major public and religious events that Rome's chief priest, the pontifex maximus, began to keep in the earliest years of the Republic. During each year the information was written down on a whitewashed board. Apparently, it was transferred to linen rolls at the end of the year as a permanent record. For unknown reasons, the pontiffs stopped setting up the yearly boards in 130 B.C.E. The accumulated information seems to have been available to later annalists and historians. Nevertheless, the idea that P. Mucius Scaevola, pontifex maximus in 130 B.C.E., edited the records and published them in a lost work called the *Annales Maximi* now seems unfounded.

Even if all of the early material from the pontiffs' records had not survived until 130 B.C.E., parallel records and other copies of information from the pontifical records that had been made for public and private use probably would have filled many gaps. It was possible, therefore, for Emperor Augustus in 18 B.C.E. to order the creation of a marble inscription that listed the entire chief yearly magistrates and triumphal generals since 509 B.C.E. This inscription was originally set up in the Forum but is referred to as the *Capitoline Fasti* because it is now housed in the Capitoline Museum. The consular list, half complete, has fragments of no year earlier than 483 B.C.E. The surviving names are remarkably consistent with the *Fasti* preserved in the literary sources and on the fragments of other inscribed lists that have been found. All versions of the *Fasti*, therefore, seem to be based on a common stock of source material, whose consistency can be attributed to the existence of a stable and fixed tradition from the earliest days of the Republic. Various attempts to challenge the reliability of the *Fasti* have failed. Scholars generally agree that the *Fasti*'s basically sound chronology allows the beginning of the Roman Republic to be dated about 500 B.C.E.

FROM KINGSHIP TO REPUBLIC, CA. 510 TO CA. 490 B.C.E.

The transition from kingship to republic is one of the most disputed questions of Roman history. How that change actually took place will probably never be known. Still, Rome seems to have followed a pattern familiar from the contemporary Greek world. By 550 B.C.E., Rome had grown into a large and complex city comparable to the larger cities of archaic Greece at that time. The city itself covered about 660 acres and controlled a territory of about 300 square miles with a total population reasonably estimated to have been between 25,000 and 40,000. Similar cities in the contemporary Greek world had fallen under the domination of ambitious "popular" tyrants backed by armed followers (pp. 42–3). Rome, which was in close contact with the Greek world and shared similar social, economic, and political characteristics, most likely followed the same trend.

For example, the stories surrounding the name of Servius Tullius, the next-to-last king in Roman tradition, reflect a situation in which a military leader seized and maintained power with armed backing. Supposedly, King Tarquin the Elder had given Servius important military commands. That coincides with the tradition that he was called *Macstrna* in Etruscan. *Macstrna* seems to be the Etruscan equivalent of *magister*, which was an archaic Roman term for "commander," as in *magister populi*, commander of the army. Servius is said to have succeeded to the throne with the help of Tarquin's widow and an armed guard after Tarquin's assassination. The story continues with Tarquin's son, Tarquin the Proud (*Tarquinius Superbus*), assassinating Servius.

All of the beneficial "reforms" traditionally ascribed to Servius Tullius were probably not the work of a single individual, but rather they developed over a period of time during the late Monarchy and the early Republic. When stripped of anachronistic complexities, however, the military reforms attributed to Servius look like an attempt during the late Monarchy to create an army that owed allegiance to its leader alone. That would have reduced the power of the aristocratic *patres*, who previously had chosen the kings.

Under the new system, the rural citizens were organized into tribes just as the urban citizens were. The tribes represented geographic territories. They were dissociated from the *curiae*, whose members were hereditary on the basis of their *gentes*. Tribal membership was based on residence.

The tribes now supplied men for the centuries that made up a reorganized legionary field army (p. 52). Each century comprised similarly armed men chosen from across the geographic tribes. Every century would have represented a cross-section of all the tribes. Its men would not have been loyal to any one powerful local hereditary clan leader.

Rome's last kings seem to have acted in the same way as popular Greek tyrants did. Probably, they used the army to pursue a popular program of expansion that opened up more land for Romans, promoted trade, and brought in booty to support public works. Archaeological evidence shows a great deal of building activity at Rome in the late sixth century B.C.E. It also confirms that the great temple of Capitoline Jupiter ascribed to Rome's traditional last king, Tarquin the Proud, was begun right about the end of the Monarchy, as the literary sources claim. Furthermore, this Tarquin supposedly had taken over the neighboring territory of Gabii and was besieging Ardea when he was overthrown. According to Livy (Book 1.57–60), L. Junius Brutus, L. Tarquinius Collatinus, and their friend P. Valerius Poplicola (Publicola) overthrew him because his son had raped Collatinus' virtuous wife, Lucretia, and caused her suicide.

The final struggles

Brutus, Tarquinius Collatinus, and Poplicola all appear as founders of the Republic in the patriotic, romanticized, and compressed saga of the literary sources. More likely, they were all struggling to supplant Tarquin themselves. That would explain the story of Collatinus suddenly being forced into exile with other male Tarquins in the first year of the Republic. It would also account for the stories that Poplicola had monarchic ambitions, particularly if he were the "Publius Valerius," apparently the leader of a war band mentioned in the *Lapis Satricanus* (p. 62).

The Etruscan Lars Porsenna of Clusium is depicted besieging Rome as an ally of Tarquin and even temporarily conquering Rome in some stories. Perhaps, he was mainly a war chief taking advantage of the confusion to make himself king at Rome. Porsenna, however, seems to have overreached himself with further attacks in Latium and then to have withdrawn or been driven from Rome itself around 504 B.C.E. (The arrival of another possible war chief, Attus Clausus [Atta Claudius, Appius Claudius], and his alleged 4000 followers at Rome in 504 B.C.E. also may be connected with Porsenna's loss of power.) Tarquin supposedly attempted to recapture Rome with help from Latin allies. The heroes of the story successfully resisted him and established what came to be known as the Republic.

Archaeology does support the idea of a violent end to the Monarchy at the end of the sixth or beginning of the fifth century B.C.E. Sites that can be associated with kings and popular tyrants were destroyed about that time. Around 500 B.C.E., the Regia was burned down, as was the Comitium. The Regia, as the name implies, was the old royal palace, and the Comitium was the place of assembly where popular tyrants could have addressed the people. Whatever the precise details may be, the Roman tradition seems based on a sound historical core: around 500 B.C.E., rule by popular royal tyrants at Rome was abolished in a violent upheaval that led to the establishment of a republican constitution.

THE EARLY FORM OF THE REPUBLIC

Although the republican constitution had roots in the institutions that had existed under the Monarchy, its earliest form bears the stamp of conservative aristocrats, primarily—but not exclusively—leading families from the patrician *gentes* (pp. 62–3). Probably, they were attempting both to end the chaotic power struggles that had characterized the last decade of the sixth century B.C.E. and to restore power and privileges that popular royal tyrants had usurped from them. They created a system that would keep them in control. They also made it difficult for any one aristocrat to acquire too much power at the expense of the rest as they competed for military honor and glory in defending or expanding Roman territory and power in central Italy. It is also clear that certain families excelled in that competition. In the consular *Fasti* from 509 to 367 B.C.E., fifteen *gentes* each held the consulship from ten to thirty-four times. Fifty each held it only from one to three times.

The consulship

The *Fasti* (p. 76) indicate that dual yearly chief magistrates were a crucial feature of the Republic right from the start. At first, they may have been the old army commander, the *magister populi*, perhaps now known as the *praetor maximus* (chief commander), and either the commander of the cavalry (*magister celerum*, *magister equitum*) or a civil judge (*iudex*). In the first case, the two commanders could have checked each other's political ambitions. In the second case, one would have commanded the army in the field while the other oversaw affairs at home. For the sake of simplicity, however, this book will follow the later Romans and use the terms *consul* and *consulship* throughout, particularly because the term *praetor* became attached to another office in 367 B.C.E. (pp. 93–4).

One of the early consuls' chief duties was to command the army. Regardless of possible origins, nomenclature, and ceremonial distinctions, the two senior magistrates who eventually came to be known as consuls each had the earlier kings' power of military command (*imperium*). Furthermore, each had the full power to veto the other. In that way, the risk of one gaining too much power was reduced because each could check the other militarily and legally.

The consuls also shared other old royal powers and privileges. Besides commanding the legions, they acted as judges, summoned meetings of the *comitia centuriata* (p. 81), and placed legislative proposals before it. They even retained much of the old royal paraphernalia. Although only a purple hem distinguished their daily clothes, they wore the purple toga of the old kings at festivals and could be buried in it. They also sat on a portable ivory throne called a *curule chair* (*sella curulis*). Each was attended by twelve lictors carrying the symbols of power earlier associated with Etruscan kings. In the city, the lictors carried only *fasces*, bundles of rods symbolizing the power of punishment. Outside the city on military campaign, a double-headed ax was added to the *fasces* to symbolize the right of execution.

The office of dictator

At times, dire military or domestic crises made it imperative for one man to have sole power, as in the days of the kings. In that case, a magistrate with *imperium* (a consul, an *interrex*, or, after 367 B.C.E., a praetor) appointed a dictator, who received the sole power of the old *magister populi* for no more than six months. The dictator appointed as his subordinate a man with the old title of *magister equitum*. The consuls remained in office but were subordinate to him. His superior *imperium* was signified by his having twenty-four lictors to attend him.

Junior elected military officers

The tribunes of the cavalry, *tribuni celerum* (*equitum*), and the military tribunes, *tribuni militum* (p. 51), all from wealthy families, continued to be the highest junior officers in the early republican army. Because the number of heavy infantry reached 6000 before the legion was split into two smaller legions, the number of military tribunes in each legion became fixed at six. They were all elected until the number of legions exceeded four. After that, twenty-four military tribunes continued to be elected, whereas the consuls appointed those needed for additional legions.

The senate

Throughout the Republic, the senate technically remained what it had been for the kings, an advisory council of prominent and experienced men. Senators could officially meet only at the summons of a consul or some other holder of *imperium* (a dictator or *interrex*); later, a praetor (pp. 93–4) until the tribunes of the *plebs* (p. 85) obtained the right to convene the senate in the third century B.C.E.

The senate could not pass laws. A vote of the senate constituted only a decree, usually called a *senatus consultum* (abbreviated *S.C.*). Such a decree was simply advice to a magistrate and was not legally binding. A magistrate could legally enforce it, but he was also free to modify or reject it altogether. Later, when tribunes of the *plebs* could veto a decree of the senate, a vetoed decree was recorded as expressing the opinion of the senate, *senatus auctoritas*.

Despite lacking the official legislative power we might expect it to have, the senate usually controlled foreign affairs, including the assignment of military commands and, later, provincial governorships. It also controlled expenditures from the treasury and supervised the performance of public contracts. The various lawmaking bodies to be discussed later could, but rarely did, pass laws overriding decisions of the senate or interfering in something usually left to the senate's discretion.

Meetings of the senate had to take place within a mile of the city's gates in a public, consecrated place, like a temple. No matter whether the assembled senators were originally addressed as *patres conscripti* (enrolled *patres*) or *patres et conscripti* (*patres* and enrolled ones), many early senators probably were public priests called *patres*. The *patrum auctoritas* (sanction of the *patres*) and the practice of meeting in a sacred place (*templum*) assured that public actions approved by the senate were in accord with divine will. The Romans were careful to ensure that they acted only with divine approval. Filling that need helped secure a high degree of power and status for the patrician *gentes*, whose members had the hereditary right to hold the public priesthoods.

To the extent that public priesthoods were held for life, the *patres* may have constituted a core of permanent senators and given the senate a certain corporate identity. Other influential advisors in the senate besides the priestly *patres* may have been enrolled as *conscripti* each year by the consuls. They would have been lower magistrates, ex-magistrates, and trusted friends of the consuls. Since most of them would have come from the families eligible to supply the public priests, that is the patricians, the term *patres* probably came to include all senators, whether they held priesthoods or not. Even a few may have been enrolled from wealthy nonpatrician families who shared the same aristocratic outlook. That would explain the Roman historical tradition that all of the early republican magistrates and senators were from patrician *gentes*, even when modern research shows that they were not. As time went on, the aristocrats in the senate turned it into the major organ of government, by which they could dominate the state.

The *comitia centuriata* and *comitia curiata*

At the beginning of the Republic, the loyalty of the arms-bearing men who made up the *populus* was essential for the success of the new regime. Therefore, the *comitia centuriata*, the assembly of arms-bearing men organized into centuries, probably acquired at the start of the Republic the right to elect the chief magistrates and other officers above the rank of centurion. The *comitia centuriata* also heard the cases of citizens who exercised the right of appeal (*provocatio*) when they had been condemned on capital charges by the magistrates. Exactly when the *comitia centuriata* acquired that function is unclear. If there is any truth to the tradition that P. Valerius Poplicola (Publicola) had obtained the right of appeal for the people at the beginning of the Republic, it probably represents another attempt to secure the loyalty of the army. Under the royal tyrants, the centuriate organization may have already been used to approve formal decrees, declarations of war, and the acceptance of peace. It continued to do so as it became the early Republic's sovereign assembly.

The *comitia curiata* probably was in decline after the so-called Servian reforms under the Monarchy (pp. 51–2). In the Republic, it was reduced to a pro forma meeting of thirty lictors representing each of the thirty *curiae*. It ratified the election of magistrates with *imperium* through passage of a *lex curiata de imperio*. In addition, it was convened to witness wills, adoptions, and the appointment of public priests. As time went on, male Roman citizens were organized into other, parallel popular assemblies that also had electoral, legislative, and judicial powers.

Women never had the right to vote or hold political office. Except for the likely exclusion of patricians in one case, all male Roman citizens were members of all assemblies. In each assembly, voters were broken up in voting units in various ways, but the organization of each assembly was such that the votes of the wealthy counted more than those of the poor. No one was elected to an assembly, nor were assemblies like modern parliamentary bodies: no one pursued a political career in an assembly. The members did not formally debate issues. They merely voted on the candidates or bills presented by the appropriate officials who summoned them, or they acted as mass juries in judicial cases brought before them. Speeches and discussions concerning issues to be voted on in assemblies could take place previously in public meetings called *contiones* (sing. *contio*) summoned by elected officials.

THE PRIESTHOODS AND PRIESTLY COLLEGES

During the Republic, priestly colleges (boards of public priests organized for the correct performance of public rituals) played a major role in public life. During the early Republic, their membership was limited to men and women from patrician *gentes*. In a world in which the state could not act without divine approval (p. 69), the priests in charge of maintaining Rome's relationship with the gods exercised great power and influence.

There were four priestly colleges: pontiffs (*pontifices*), augurs (*augures*), fetials (*fetiales*), and duovirs, originally a board of two men (*duoviri*), for conducting sacrifices (*duoviri sacris faciundis*). In addition, there were various societies or associations (*sodalitates*) of lesser priests. Priests were not necessarily individuals of exceptional piety or believed to be endowed with special psychic or clairvoyant powers. The men chosen for such honors were people of learning, political experience, and high social rank who did not form any professional priestly class, even though they did have to come from certain *gentes*. Their wealth enabled them to perform their priestly duties without financial reward. Many had been magistrates before becoming priests; some were priests and magistrates simultaneously; and most were members of the senate. The women selected for some public priesthoods were chosen as part of a married couple (as in the case of the *rex* and *regina sacrorum* and the *flaminicae*, wives of the various priests known as *flamens*): they were required to have married with a particular archaic wedding ceremony and could not divorce. Other women were chose precisely because they had never been married. The young girls selected to serve for thirty years as priestesses of the goddess Vesta, called Vestal Virgins, came from the most prestigious families and had to be free of any physical defect. Unlike all other public priests who continued to live with their families, the Vestal Virgins left home to live in a large complex next to Vesta's temple in the Roman Forum. In that way, they were able to maintain the sacred fire in the temple twenty-four hours a day. The chief qualification for holding any of these priesthoods was the right pedigree. Less important was a deep knowledge of religious tradition, of divine law, and of correct ritual and ceremonial procedure.

The pontiffs

Originally, a pontiff (*pontifex*, literally a "bridgemaker") performed rituals and incantations believed to give permanence to the flimsy wooden bridges in early Latium. Under the kings, there were three pontiffs (*pontifices*), who also acted as religious advisors. From the birth of the Republic, the membership of the college grew. The *rex* and *regina sacrorum* and the twelves flamens and their wives became full members. The Vestal Virgins came to be included as well. Under the leadership of the chief pontiff (*pontifex maximus*), the college of pontiffs assumed a larger and larger role in public and private life. They were keepers of temple archives and prescribed the various rituals, prayers, chants, and litanies for use in public worship and sacrifice. They also supervised the dedication and the consecration of temples and altars, the burial of the dead, and the inheritance of religious duties. It was they who organized the calendar that fixed the dates of festivals and the days on which a magistrate might not sit in court.

The pontiffs were the custodians and interpreters of the sacred law governing both the religious and legal relations of the community to the gods. They alone knew the exact formulae applicable in all secular legal transactions and the proper forms employed in the making of vows. The *pontifex maximus*, judge and arbiter of things human and divine, had the power to convene and the right to preside over the Curiate Assembly, which passed laws on adoptions and wills. As guardians of the laws, whose precise wording had to be followed in legal proceedings, pontiffs held a monopoly on jurisprudence during the first two centuries of the Republic. They were neither judges nor regularly practicing lawyers. Their contribution arose from their functions as consultants and interpreters of religious, public, and private law.

The augurs

Originally made up of three patricians, the college of augurs (*augures*) gradually increased to sixteen members from both patrician and plebeian *gentes* by the end of the Republic. The augurs were solely responsible for conducting the auguries and were experts in the taking of auspices (p. 69). Private individuals could take auspices, and public officials did so regularly. Officials might be assisted by an augur, and they regularly consulted the augurs on questions concerning the correct taking of auspices. The augurs had the right to block public business, particularly in the popular assemblies, by announcing unfavorable signs sent by the gods.

The *fetials*

The fetial priests (*fetiales*) were a board of twenty priests who dealt with issues of peace and war. In the early Republic, they dealt directly with enemy counterparts in Italy and accepted treaties with a ritual exchange of curses calling down punishment on the first to break faith. If the Romans had a grievance with another people, a fetial went to the latter, stated the Roman case, and demanded satisfaction. If satisfaction was not given in thirty-three days, the fetial went to the enemy's border, declared war, and hurled a fire-hardened spear across the boundary. Even after that ritual was no longer practical, fetial law, which built up over the years, governed declarations of war.

Duovirs for making sacrifices (*duoviri sacris faciundis*)

A board originally of two men, later ten and then fifteen men (*decemviri* and *quinde-cemviri*), the duovirs had the special responsibility of protecting the *Sibylline Books* that Tarquin the Proud supposedly had brought from Cumae (p. 68). When ordered to do so by the senate, they consulted those sacred texts for guidance when unusual portents or disasters occurred. They were also responsible for overseeing foreign cults and rituals adopted in response to such occasions.

The sodalitates

There were three ancient associations (*sodalitates*) of lesser priests: the Salii, the Luperci, and the Arval Brothers (*fratres arvales*). The Salii, "Leaping Priests," performed archaic war dances in annual rituals associated with Mars. The Luperci, whose name comes from *lupus* (wolf), were religious officials responsible for the Lupercalia festival at which they ran partially naked along a ritual circuit through Rome, smacking bystanders with leather thongs as they went (p. 65). The twelve Arval Brothers were the ancient priests of Dea Dia, a goddess of agriculture. They maintained her sacred grove and, in conjunction with the Ambarvalia (p. 66), celebrated her festival in May with a special hymn.

THE DYNAMICS OF CHANGE, 509 TO 287 B.C.E.

By ca. 300 B.C.E., many of the priesthoods were no longer restricted to members of patrician *gentes*. The process whereby they were opened to individuals from *gentes* now specifically identified as plebeian appears in the annalistic sources as part of the so-called *Struggle (Conflict) of the Orders*. First, writers like Livy assumed that, from the beginning, Roman society was rigidly divided into two distinct orders or classes: the rich patrician aristocrats and the poor plebeian commoners, the *plebs*. Then, they wove together separate kinds and episodes of conflict during the early Republic into an overly schematized "Struggle (Conflict) of the Orders." As in any attempt to create a clear narrative, convenient labels and generalizations usually mask a much more complex reality.

For example, it was said that patrician *gentes* had an absolute monopoly of the chief magistracies and membership in the senate from the start of the Republic. No amount of convoluted argument, however, can explain away the fact that the *Fasti* show no absolute monopoly. Between 509 and 486 B.C.E., a number of solidly attested and unassailably nonpatrician names appear in the consular lists. From 485 to 470, however, there are none. Then, only a few appear from 469 until 445, the year when those identified as plebeians supposedly were specifically allowed to hold the new office of military tribune with consular power (p. 90).

The most logical explanation is that, at the beginning of the Republic, the sharp patrician-plebeian dichotomy reflected in the late sources is oversimplified. Even in earlier sources, informal usage may have simplistically lumped together as *patricians* all of those who governed the early Republic as priests, magistrates, and senators, whether or not they were from patrician *gentes*. Similarly, those who were not part of the governing elite, even if they were wealthy and influential within certain segments of society, came to be identified in the sources as members of the *plebs*. In later times, *plebs* did signify the poor lower order of Roman society, but originally it probably meant the undifferentiated mass of citizens in general.

Despite the oversimplifications and over-dramatizations of the ancient sources, tensions and discontented groups certainly existed within the young Republic. Some wealthy and ambitious nonpatricians managed to get elected to high office. Others would not have been able to make such a breakthrough and would have been resentful. Small farmers, day laborers, shopkeepers, and artisans did not have the means to qualify for the *classis*, which supplied the heavy infantry and cavalry and dominated the original *comitia centuriata*. They were effectively disenfranchised, even though they may have served in a rank below the *classis* (*infra classem*) as light-armed and support troops. Not only they but also probably some of those who marginally qualified as heavy infantry faced serious economic problems that aggravated social and political tensions.

Many farmers suffered losses in the constant attacks by surrounding peoples. The need to divide family land among heirs also must have meant that small proprietors, even those who were modestly well off, rapidly found their holdings too small to support them. Moreover, as time went on, large landowners began to monopolize access to public lands for themselves, at the expense of poorer citizens.

The expansion of the Persian Empire into the eastern Mediterranean in the late sixth and early fifth centuries B.C.E. probably disrupted the flow of goods to Italy from Greece and the Near East. That flow had helped Rome prosper and grow. Indeed, archaeological evidence seems to confirm a drop in Greek imports during the early fifth century. As trade contracted, the urban economy probably declined so that hard-ship ensued for the poorer segments of the population in the city.

Those who contracted loans from wealthier neighbors ran afoul of Rome's harsh laws of debt. Creditors could summarily seize a defaulting debtor's property, force him to work off his debts (a practice called *debt bondage*), sell him into slavery, or even kill him. The unsettled conditions also created periodic food shortages that posed severe hardship for the poor. Therefore, there were many people who had reason to protest and demand changes from those who governed, the so-called patricians.

GROWING PLEBEIAN IDENTITY AND RIGHTS, CA. 500 TO CA. 400 B.C.E.

During the first half of the fifth century, growing discontent and protests fueled the growth of a self-conscious nonpatrician group identified as the *plebs*. This group con-stituted an independent political force that expressed the will of the discontented. Moreover, the constant need for manpower and unity during the wars against outside enemies described in the next chapter often forced those in power, the patricians, to make concessions to the discontented. Probably some patricians even sided with some of the discontented to gain support for personal political purposes.

The Council of the Plebs (*concilium plebis*)

According to tradition, the first step in creating a self-conscious *plebs* took place in 494 B.C.E. during a war with Rome's Latin neighbors. The patricians had refused to curb the abusive practices of creditors during a debt crisis. Large numbers of aggrieved citi-zens departed from the city and refused military service. They then constituted them-selves as the Council of the Plebs, *concilium plebis*, and elected their own independent yearly plebeian officials to protect their interests. Thus, they operated outside the regu-lar apparatus controlled by those called patricians in the ancient sources. There is much that is problematical about this "First Secession of the *Plebs*," and 494 B.C.E. may be too early for the creation of a *concilium plebis* and elected plebeian officials. Nevertheless, they eventually did appear.

According to the traditional dating, there was serious plebeian agitation again in 471 in the face of attacks from the Aequi and the Volsci. The supposed upshot of this agitation was the reorganization of the original way in which the *concilium plebis* voted. Among the many problems is that no one really knows how or when the *plebs* first voted in a formal council. Still, at some point in the early Republic, if not in 471 B.C.E., the *concilium plebis* began to vote by a system based on the residence of citizens grouped in the geographic territories called *tribes* (p. 62). This system gave more weight to the rural voters on whom the demands for military service were greatest. There were four urban and twenty-one rural tribes in the fifth century B.C.E. Eventually, ten more rural tribes were added as Roman territory expanded. After that, the number of tribes remained fixed at thirty-five. New citizens outside of Rome were simply assigned to one of the thirty-one rural tribes no matter where in Rome's expanding territory they lived.

In an assembly of tribes, each tribe voted as a unit: that is to say, each tribe had one vote determined by the majority voting within it at a meeting. A simple majority of units, ultimately at least eighteen of thirty-five, was enough to win the vote. Thus, the rural tribes always outvoted the four urban tribes no matter how few rural voters showed up to vote at Rome, where all voting took place. Since many small farmers did not always have the time or the resources to go to Rome to vote, those who did show up had a large impact on the outcome. Most modern scholars agree that when the tribes met to vote as the *plebs*, patrician members of the tribes were excluded. Therefore, some modern scholars call the *plebs* meeting to vote by tribes the Plebeian Tribal Council (*concilium plebis tributum*). Since the term *concilium plebis tributum* has no ancient authority, this book will continue to use *concilium plebis*. An assembly of all citizens voting by tribes, the *comitia tributa*, apparently arose later than the first meeting of the *plebs* by tribes (p. 98).

Tribunes of the *plebs*

The new officials elected by the *concilium plebis* were the tribunes of the *plebs* (*tribuni plebis*). It seems most likely that, as their name implies, tribunes of the *plebs* originated as, or were patterned on, junior military officers like the tribunes of the soldiers or the tribunes of the cavalry (p. 51). Whatever the events surrounding their origin, tribunes historically played a major role in protecting ordinary citizens from excessive demands for military service. That would make sense if they originated as officers chosen by armed citizens from the lower ranks. The *plebs* considered the tribunes sacrosanct. If anyone violently attacked a tribune or interfered with the performance of his duties, that person would be considered accursed and could be killed with impunity. In that way, tribunes were encouraged to take the strongest possible stands on behalf of the *plebs*.

Probably there were only two plebeian tribunes each year at first, although the sources do not agree on this point. Only nonpatricians could be tribunes of the *plebs*. They were men of enough wealth to pursue unpaid political leadership. The well-to-do nonpatricians who held the tribunate or supported the *plebs* probably became identified as plebeians, too. Thus, the historical distinction between patrician and plebeian *gentes* probably emerged.

The early tribunes had two main powers. The first was the right of giving aid (*ius auxilii*). A tribune was supposed to protect the life, person, and interests of those who called upon him for help against a magistrate's arbitrary use of power. The second was the right of intercession (*intercessio*), the right to veto (*veto* means "I forbid" in Latin) any official act, even another tribune's, that he deemed detrimental to the *plebs*. Always on call, he had to keep his house open day and night and could never go outside the city limits.

Plebeian aediles

At some point, the *concilium plebis* also began to elect two plebeian aediles to assist the tribunes. They were originally caretakers of the temple of Ceres, the goddess of grain, on the Aventine, which was outside the walls of Rome at that time. Appropriately, a grain market and Greek trading center were near this site. Resident Greeks may have been a source of inspiration for popular political agitation. Contemporary Greek states were also experiencing popular upheavals, and one of the Greek artists who decorated the temple of Ceres was named Damophilus, which means "Friend of the People." Also, Ceres' connection with grain and the proximity of her temple to the grain market indicate that many of the *plebs* were concerned with having an adequate supply of food. Many of the aediles' later functions are linked with providing for the material well-being of the average person. They acted as police and supervised markets, weights and measures, public works, food and water supplies, and public games. They also became custodians of the plebeians' treasury and archives and, later, of senatorial decrees.

Plebiscita

The *concilium plebis* not only elected the plebeian tribunes and aediles but also could vote on motions placed before it by the tribunes. Such a vote constituted a plebiscite, "the sense of the *plebs*" (*plebiscitum*), but the patricians did not initially recognize plebiscites (*plebiscita*) as laws (*leges*). A suspect tradition says that as early as 456 B.C.E., a tribune named Icilius obtained a law granting land on the Aventine to the poor. Still, organized popular pressure could not easily be ignored. Eventually, *plebiscita* came to be recognized as laws binding on the whole community.

The Decemvirs and the laws of the Twelve Tables, 451 to 450 B.C.E.

One major source of popular discontent probably was the complete domination of the law, which was largely customary and unwritten, by the patricians, whose families supplied the public priests. Among these priests were the pontiffs, who exercised great control over determining what the law was and how it could be applied in particular situations. Around 452 B.C.E., as the story goes, during continuing conflicts with the Aequi and the Volsci, there were some unsuccessful attempts to pass a plebiscite restricting the powers of the consuls, who often executed the laws in ways that seemed unfair to the *plebs*. The tribunes suggested to the senate that a committee representing both parties be chosen to frame a just and equitable written body of laws. The senate turned down the suggestion of plebeian participation but did agree to set up a commission of ten men, *decemviri*, to codify the existing laws. The story that a group of senators first went to Athens to study the laws of Solon may be apocryphal, but many senators must have been aware of contemporary law codes in the Greek colonies of *Magna Graecia*.

The Decemviral Commission

Supposedly, at the end of 452 B.C.E. the regular consulship and tribunate were suspended. During 451 and 450 B.C.E., the Decemviral Commission, chaired by Appius Claudius, ran the government and codified the laws. Much of the story surrounding Appius Claudius and the commission is confused, contradictory, and overlaid with dramatic fictions. For example, the story that Appius lusted after Verginia, the beautiful daughter of an ordinary citizen, and that her father killed her to prevent her dishonor, seems entirely made up. It was used to brand Appius as a tyrant who forced the commission to adopt some laws that came to be seen as unfavorable to the *plebs*, such as the one banning intermarriage between patricians and plebeians.

The main purpose of that law may have been to guarantee a supply of men meeting the traditional requirements for public priests (*patres*). Still, that would also have reinforced the exclusivity of the patrician *gentes*. Another clause seemingly beneficial to the patricians said that bills against individuals or for imposing capital penalties had to be passed in the *comitia centuriata*, which tribunes could not convene.

The one generally accepted part of the account of the Decemviral Commission is that the Decemvirs did produce a codification of existing early Roman laws. Those laws were set up eventually, if not originally, on twelve bronze tablets in the Forum. This code was henceforth known as the Law of the Twelve Tables or, more simply, the Twelve Tables.

Style and content of the Twelve Tables

About one-third of the text of the Twelve Tables is preserved in quotations by later authors. The style is archaic, simple, brief, harsh, but legally clear and exact: Table I, "If he calls him to court, go he shall; if he doesn't, plaintiff will call witness, then will take him"; Table VII, "They will keep road repaired; if they don't cobble it, man may drive team where he wants to"; Table VIII, "If burglary be done at night, if (owner) kills him, he shall be killed by law; if by day, not, unless burglar defends himself with weapon."

Significance of the Twelve Tables

The laws of the Twelve Tables fixed in writing the preexisting law of custom passed down among a privileged group. These laws also were capable of meeting future needs through interpretation. Among the most important provisions were those that spelled out powers of the *paterfamilias*, guaranteed the right to property and testament, provided for the intervention of the state in civil disputes, abolished family revenge, and provided that no one could be put to death without a trial. The Twelve Tables also abolished torture as a means of obtaining evidence from free men. In short, the basic importance of the Twelve Tables was that they publicly established in principle the equality of all free citizens before the law.

The creation of a written code of laws at Rome shares clear parallels with the codification of laws at Athens in the time of Draco. Both codes represent similar attempts by conservative aristocratic elites to solidify their dominance in the face of social and economic crises typical of archaic city-states. Since they both primarily codified existing practices, however, they did not really get at the roots of nonaristocratic discontent. They merely sharpened the perception of grievances that would lead to even stronger challenges to the existing order as some leaders sought support from outside the ranks of those who had traditionally monopolized political power.

The Valerio-Horatian laws of 449 B.C.E.

L. Valerius Poplicola Potitus and M. Horatius Barbatus, the patrician consuls of
449 B.C.E., provide a case in point. Although not all of the laws ascribed to them
are authentic, they appear to have supported the *plebs* and their tribunes against an
attempt by the Decemvirs to continue in office. At least they gave official recognition
to the tribunate and the right of tribunes both to protect individual plebeians from
the harsh and arbitrary actions of the consuls and to propose plebiscites. Whether or
not they passed legislation giving plebiscites automatic recognition as laws, a plebiscite could become law if it received the approval of the *patres* in the senate, as comi-
tial acts did. That would explain the attested tribunician laws of 445, 442, and 367
(below and p. 91).

The creation of another popular assembly, the *comitia tributa,* occurred around
the same time. Modeled on the tribal organization of the *concilium plebis*, the *comitia
tributa* was an assembly of all citizens, including the patrician *gentes*, voting by tribes.
As in the *concilium plebis*, the rural tribes would have dominated the voting (p. 86).
Being large landowners registered in the rural tribes, the members of the patrician
gentes, who were only a small percentage of the population, may have had some
influence on the votes of the rural tribes through their clients. Nevertheless, such
influence probably could not have been decisive except when other, nonpatrician
large landowners were narrowly divided. Because the *comitia tributa* included all male
citizens, there was no question that measures passed by it and approved by the *patres*
were binding on all.

The quaestors

No more than two years after its creation, the *comitia tributa* began to elect two annual
patrician quaestors, originally mere appointed assistants to the consuls. Their number
was increased to four in 421 B.C.E. when the office was first thrown open to men from
plebeian *gentes*, but plebeian quaestors did not actually appear until 409 B.C.E. Although
their original function was to investigate murders, minor crimes against property also
came under their jurisdiction.

Two of the four quaestors accompanied the consuls to the battlefield, where they
served as quartermasters in charge of supplies and the payment of troops. The other
two remained in the city to serve as keepers of the public treasury and prosecutors of
tax delinquents. Since the public treasury was in the temple of Saturn, they were also
in charge of the official records and documents kept in that building.

Apparitores

The original quaestors probably were classed as *apparitores*—the scribes, secretaries, accountants, and other skilled appointees who aided the priests and magistrates
in the performance of their duties. Those posts were open to ordinary citizens and
conferred considerable prestige on their holders. Eventually, the *apparitores* received
a salary.

The *lex Canuleia*, 445 B.C.E.

According to the simplistic traditional account of the "Struggle (Conflict) of the Orders," the tribune C. Canuleius, taking advantage of the Valerio-Horatian law of 449 B.C.E., struck a blow for the plebeians by obtaining passage of a plebiscite, the *lex Canuleia*. It rescinded the recently adopted law against the intermarriage of *patres* and plebeians. The original purpose of the prohibition may have been to preserve the bloodlines required to hold certain priesthoods. Nevertheless, some ambitious individuals among both the patrician and the wealthier plebeian *gentes* may have seen the law as preventing politically advantageous marital alliances. Therefore, they may have worked together to overturn it by the *lex Canuleia*.

Military tribunes with consular power

Another milestone in the traditional accounts of the "Struggle (Conflict) of the Orders" occurred in 445 B.C.E. The patricians supposedly agreed to create as an alternative to the consulship a new office open to plebeians. The new officials were military tribunes who had consular power (*imperium consulare*). They differed from consuls because they could not celebrate triumphs and could not become senators after their year of office. They were equal in power to, and could veto, each other. One remained in the city during times of war to carry out civil functions, while the others took the field as commanders of legions. The senate decided whether to have consuls or military tribunes with consular power for a given year. The latter held office in only fifty of the years from 444 to 367 B.C.E.

No securely attested plebeian held the new office until 422 B.C.E. Others appear only rarely from 400 to 367 B.C.E. Therefore, it is difficult to see the establishment of military tribunes with consular power as part of a compromise in any "Struggle (Conflict) of the Orders." Rather, the previous situation seems to have continued: the occasional success of a wealthy nonpatrician either through favor directly with the voters or as an ally of some ambitious patrician.

The fact that from three to six military tribunes with consular power served in most of the years for which they are recorded may reflect incomplete records. More likely, it indicates that there was a need for two or more legions and their commanding officers in years during which Rome faced military threats from Ardea, Veii, the Aequi, the Volsci, and the Gauls (p. 100ff). Subsequently, new pressures culminated in the reforms of 367 B.C.E., which regularized the titles of and qualifications for various magistracies and organized them into the classic hierarchical *cursus honorum*, "course of offices" (p. 94). Until then, however, there probably was no formal provision allowing members of plebeian *gentes* to hold high office.

The censors

In 444 B.C.E., the censorship appeared, which patrician *gentes* seem to have monopolized until 351 B.C.E. (p. 94). Two censors were elected at irregular intervals by the *comitia centuriata*. They compiled the census (the official list of Roman citizens eligible for military service, voting, and taxation). In time, they were elected every five years for a period of eighteen months. Censors did not have the *imperium* or the right to the *fasces*, they could not call meetings of the people or the senate, nor could they nominate their own successors. They did, however, sit on the curule chair (*sella curulis*), the sign of a senior magistrate (p. 79). After 339, censors acquired the power of appointing senators and of removing them from the senate if they did not meet the standards of the Roman moral code. By putting a black mark opposite a man's name, the censors could reduce him to a lower census class, move him from a rural tribe to a city tribe, or take away his civil rights altogether for at least five years. Such power made censors even more prestigious than consuls.

The censors also became concerned with the spending of funds appropriated by the senate or released by the consuls. Control of contracts for public works, of the tax registers, and of the state revenues gave censors considerable power. They leased public lands, mines, salt works, and fishing rights as well as the collection of certain taxes to private contractors, *publicani* (publicans). The only kind of revenue that they did not control was war booty.

A NEW PERIOD OF REFORM, 367 TO 287 B.C.E.

Between approximately 400 and 370 B.C.E., a strenuous war against the Etruscan city of Veii, a disastrous invasion of the Gauls, and hostilities with neighboring Latin cities probably created the conditions that led to further reforms by 367 B.C.E. Supposedly, during ten contentious years in office, two plebeian tribunes, C. Licinius Stolo and L. Sextius Lateranus, proposed major reforms that were finally enacted into the so-called *Licinio-Sextian laws*. There are many problems with details in the existing account of the Licinio-Sextian laws, particularly the tribunes' ten-year tenure in office. Nevertheless, most scholars accept that three major reforms associated with the names of Licinius and Sextius became law around 367 B.C.E.

First, that military tribunes with consular power were abolished seems certain. No more appear after 367. The legislation probably specified that one of the restored consulships each year *could* be held by someone from a plebeian *gens*. That one *must* be held by a plebeian was probably not specified until a law of L. Genucius in 342 B.C.E. Second, some kind of restriction on the growing concentration of land in the hands of large proprietors also seems reasonable. Soon, large tracts of public land were acquired through Roman conquests in central Italy, and many thousands of small holdings were created for impoverished peasants. Third, there was some kind of attempt to deal with debt, a perennial source of discontent.

Attempts to help debtors continued. Laws restricted interest rates to probably 8.6 percent a year in 357 and 4 1/6 percent in 347. In 342, a law of Genucius impractically abolished lending at interest and soon became a dead letter. A much more practical move in 352 B.C.E. created a governmental board of five men who helped debtors in trouble by assuming mortgages that could be adequately secured—in many cases probably by the new allotments of land that were now being distributed. Finally, the *lex Poetilia* of either 326 or 313 B.C.E. so severely limited the circumstances whereby a person could be enslaved for debt that the practice soon disappeared.

Military changes and reform of the *Comitia Centuriata*

With the permanent establishment of two annual consulships, the Roman army probably consisted of a regular levy of two legions, one for each consul. Three things increased the number of men who could regularly meet the demand: the principle of pay for military service established during the war with Veii, the distribution of land occasioned by the Licinio-Sextian reforms, and provision of at least some equipment by the state. Men who formerly did not have the means to serve in the heavy infantry and were thus *infra classem* (below the *classis*) in the census could now do so.

These changes seem to be reflected in the *comitia centuriata*, which elected the magistrates above the rank of aedile and could pass legislation. Its membership was expanded to include centuries of the citizens who were previously *infra classem*. Centuries no longer supplied specific units of the field army, but all voters, whether or not they physically served, were now organized into groups still called centuries. These centuries were ranked in several census classes based on the type of military equipment that able-bodied men of their property valuation could have afforded before receiving pay and equipment.

In fact, the less wealthy citizens were still effectively disenfranchised in the *comitia centuriata*. The reform seems to represent an attempt (perhaps as a concession to certain patricians or the wealthy in general) to minimize the impact of all but the highest census class, the original *classis*, on the election of the highest magistrates and on any legislation placed before it. The crucial aspects of the *comitia centuriata* are the number of centuries in each class, the way in which votes were counted, and the practice of voting from the wealthiest centuries downward.

The first census class comprised eighteen centuries of men who were ranked as cavalry (*equites*) and eighty centuries (forty senior and forty junior) of men who were ranked as heavy infantry. Thus, the wealthiest voters had a total of ninety-eight centuries. There were twenty centuries each (half senior and half junior) for classes two through four (those who could have supplied some arms and armor), thirty (half senior and half junior) for the fifth class (those without armor), and five centuries for people below the minimum property assessment required for armed service (two for craftsmen, two for trumpeters, and one for the proletarians). The total of all centuries, therefore, was 193.

Each century voted as a unit. A simple majority of each century determined its one vote. The voting proceeded in hierarchical order from the highest class to the lowest. It started with the eighteen equestrian centuries of the first class and continued with the eighty first-class infantry centuries, then the twenty second-class centuries, and so on. Voting on legislative and judicial questions stopped once a simple majority of ninety-seven votes was reached. Therefore, the wealthiest centuries would determine the vote if a majority in each voted in the same way. Voting would not likely reach the fifth class unless the outcome of voting in the ninety-eight wealthiest centuries was closely split. In elections, where, presumably, all centuries voted, candidates favored by the first four classes would usually poll the most votes to fill available positions.

Accordingly, the hierarchical, unit-vote system was far from democratic, even for free males, the only ones allowed to vote. The rich, with their ninety-eight centuries, always had more votes than the lower census classes. The old could always outvote the young, because the seniors, though numerically fewer, had as many centuries as the juniors. Moreover, close votes within some centuries might mean that the outcome of the unit vote did not reflect the will of the majority in the total number of units voting. Similarly, in the Electoral College system for electing presidents of the United States, it is possible for a candidate to lose the total popular vote but win a majority of the Electoral College.

The creation of a new nobility

The Licinio-Sextian legislation of 367 B.C.E. formally opened up the consulship to wealthy members of plebeian *gentes*. Their circumstances permitted a career of unpaid public service. Such a moment was bound to come anyway because the old patrician families that had dominated the early Republic were inexorably dying out. The universal tendency of upper classes to have small families, many patricians' refusal to intermarry with plebeians even after the *lex Canuleia* of 445 B.C.E., and deaths in battle during the numerous wars with Rome's neighbors had severely reduced their ranks. For example, only twenty-nine of fifty-three patrician *gentes* recorded for the fifth century appear in the fourth century. Men from plebeian *gentes* frequently after 367 B.C.E. (and regularly after 342) held the consulship. As a result, a patricio-plebeian consular nobility replaced the old, exclusively patrician nobility within the ranks of the broader senatorial aristocracy. It comprised those families who had a consular ancestor in the male line. A man who was the first of his family to reach the consulship thereby ennobled his family and enjoyed the undying gratitude of succeeding generations.

Despite the formal opening of the consulship to wealthy men from plebeian *gentes* after 367 B.C.E., the hardline patricians did not immediately surrender all of their control. They still monopolized the censorship, for example. They even created new magistracies open only to themselves. Gradually, however, those positions and important religious offices were opened to men of plebeian *gentes*.

The new praetorship

The growing complexity of war and public business made it desirable to create a junior colleague of the consuls. In 367 B.C.E., the patrician-dominated senate, therefore, revived the ancient office of praetor and restricted it to members of patrician *gentes*. Originally, there was only one praetor. His full title was *praetor urbanus*. Like the consuls, he was elected annually by the Centuriate Assembly. He came to be seen as a junior colleague of the consuls. He possessed *imperium*, but it was less than theirs: they were allowed to command two or more legions; he could command only one legion and was accompanied by only six lictors with fasces. Still, he had the purple-bordered toga, the curule chair (*sella curulis*), and all the other insignia of a higher magistrate. In the absence of the consuls or if deputized by them, a praetor could summon meetings of the Centuriate Assembly or the senate and perform all the executive functions of a consul.

The praetor's ordinary duties may have been primarily the administration of justice within the city. That would have allowed the consuls to give their undivided attention to military and foreign affairs, and the patricians could still maintain internal control through the legal system. Eventually, however, men from plebeian *gentes* gained access to the praetorship, too.

Around 244 B.C.E., a second praetor was created, the *praetor inter peregrinos* (later, *praetor peregrinus*). His duties probably involved maintaining Roman authority among the foreign people (*inter peregrinos*) whom Rome had conquered in Italy and Sicily. Thenceforth, the praetorship took on the character of a separate magistracy independent of the consulship, and more praetors were added as the administrative needs of the state increased.

The curule aedileship

Another office, the curule aedileship, was also created in 367 to help with the expanding burdens of municipal administration. There were two curule aediles, so called because, unlike the two existing plebeian aediles, they had the right to the curule chair. The first curule aediles were patricians, but men from plebeian *gentes* were later eligible in alternate years. They were elected by the *comitia tributa*. Their functions were basically the same as those of the plebeian aediles (pp. 86–7).

The cursus honorum

The hierarchical course of offices (*cursus honorum*) that marked an aristocratic political career for centuries was now all in place: quaestor, aedile, praetor, consul, and censor, in ascending order. Because they were officers of the *plebs* only, not magistrates of the whole state, the tribunes of the *plebs* stood outside of this *cursus*. So, too, did the office of dictator, which was an emergency creation and not an expected part of a regular career.

After 367 B.C.E., offices not open to leaders from plebeian *gentes* soon yielded to their pressure. The dictatorship fell to a plebeian in 356; the censorship in 351. Then, in 339, the *lex Publilia* of the plebeian dictator Q. Publilius Philo provided that one censor had to be a plebeian. Finally, plebeians gained access to the praetorship in 337. To prevent any one person from monopolizing power in high offices, it was also made illegal for a magistrate to hold more than one curule office (an office that allowed the holder a curule chair: curule aedile, praetor, consul, censor) in any one year or the same curule office twice within ten years.

Promagistracies

As Roman affairs became more complicated, the yearly magistrates were not numerous enough to handle all of the administrative and military tasks required. In order to create officers with the requisite authority, therefore, the senate resorted to the creation of acting magistrates called *promagistrates*. The first use of this new device was at the siege of Naples in 327 B.C.E., at the start of the Second Samnite War (p. 108). It seemed advisable that the consul who started the siege remain in command after his normal year of office. Therefore, the senate voted to retain him in place of a consul, *pro consule*, when his consulship officially ended. A magistrate who had his power extended in this way was said to have been prorogued. Although prorogation was used sparingly at first, promagistrates became quite common, especially proconsuls and propraetors, as the empire grew.

Admission of plebeians to religious offices

Another legislative reform of 367 permitted plebeian *gentes* to a share in the responsibility of looking after and interpreting the *Sibylline Books*. This task had been an exclusive prerogative of the patrician *duoviri sacris faciundis* (p. 93). Some *duoviri* had used the *Sibylline Books* to block proposals for social, political, and economic reform. The college was expanded to a board of ten men (*decemviri*), five of whom had to be from plebeian *gentes*, to take charge of these books.

One of the last patrician bulwarks was control of the major priesthoods. In 300 B.C.E., the *lex Ogulnia* increased the pontiffs to eight and the augurs to nine. It required four pontiffs and five augurs to be plebeian. The only priests who still had to be patricians were the *rex sacrorum*; the flamens of Jupiter, Mars, and Quirinus; and the Salii, or Leaping Priests.

Lifetime senators and the senatorial aristocracy

By the end of the fourth century B.C.E., appointment to the senate conferred lifetime membership. Two hundred years of almost yearly warfare (see next chapter) had made clear the need for some permanent body to provide experienced and consistent guidance in the face of annually changing generals and high officials. Since the yearly consuls appointed many senators from the ranks of ex-consuls, there was already a shared identity between senators and consuls. That and an innate Roman respect for precedent probably favored the reappointment of senators year after year, even in the fifth century B.C.E. The *lex Ovinia* (dated between 339 and 318 B.C.E.), however, formalized the automatic admission of ex-magistrates to the senate for life.

Senators had to be worth at least 100,000 of Rome's basic monetary unit, the bronze *as*, which weighed one Roman pound (p. 115). The censors could remove from the senate anyone who fell below that limit or acted immorally. The censors could also add men whom they deemed worthy in order to keep up the number of senators, probably around 300 by this time.

Some men who had no senatorial ancestors but met the property requirement were elected to one of the lower magistracies of the *cursus honorum* and gained admission to the senate. Such a man was a "new man" (*novus homo*). As a wealthy landowner, however, his interests usually coincided with those of men from established senatorial families. His family now joined them as part of the hereditary senatorial aristocracy and usually shared their conservative outlook. Still, there were always some senators willing for one reason or another to help those nonaristocrats who were not satisfied with the status quo.

Removal of patrician control over law and voting

In 339 B.C.E., when the dictator Publilius Philo promulgated the law which said that one of the censors had to be from a plebeian *gens*, Rome was at war against former Latin allies (pp. 105–6), and the lower classes were angry over the unfair distribution of land. Against that background, Publilius Philo was able to obtain passage of one or two other laws that reduced patrician power. One, if genuine, affirmed that plebiscites were legally binding on all citizens. The other required that the *patres* give their sanction (*patrum auctoritas*) to bills before the assemblies started voting. In this way, the patricians had to state any objections beforehand. They could not find another excuse to block a bill after a vote had occurred.

During the Second Samnite War (p. 108), Appius Claudius Caecus, censor in 312 B.C.E., was a patrician who sought support among the lower social orders. That he enrolled sons of freedmen in the senate may be an exaggeration. It was radical enough that he registered lower-born urban citizens throughout the twenty-seven then-existing rural tribes instead of just the four urban ones, where an individual's vote carried less weight. This move was highly unpopular with other aristocrats. Therefore, in 304 B.C.E., the new censors reregistered them in only the four urban tribes.

This measure may well have been aimed at preventing the rise of social parvenus who would compete with the established patrician and plebeian families in the senate. In that very year, Cn. Flavius, the son of a freedman and supposed protégé of Appius Claudius, had been elected aedile and, therefore, qualified for admission to the senate. That may be the basis of the story that Appius enrolled the sons of freedmen. As aedile, Flavius made available for the first time in convenient form the procedures and official calendar necessary to give the average citizen better access to the courts. He even advertised his support of the lower classes by dedicating a shrine to the goddess Concordia (Harmony) in the Forum.

In 300 B.C.E., the consul M. Valerius Maximus obtained a law that guaranteed the right of appeal, *provocatio*, from a magistrate's sentence of death or whipping within the city. About 290, another law abolished the patricians' veto over the election of magistrates. It also required that they ratify the results of elections in advance.

Finally, in ca. 287 B.C.E., the aftermath of the long, tedious Samnite wars (pp. 104–5) apparently brought another crisis over debts, with the *plebs* seceding to the Janiculum Hill across the Tiber. According to the traditional view, the consuls appointed the plebeian Q. Hortensius as a dictator to deal with the situation. He supposedly obtained a law, the *lex Hortensia*, which specified that whatever the *plebs* had enacted bound the whole people. That principle, however, seems already evident in both 449 (p. 89) and 339. The "law" ascribed to Hortensius may be no more than a standard legal formula attached to some unknown plebiscites, or Hortensius may have been only a pontiff issuing some legal ruling. The latter view is consistent with evidence that he also modi-fied the Roman calendar, which the pontiffs controlled, to permit people to conduct legal business in Rome on market days. That measure would have been popular with small farmers from the countryside because those days would have been the most con-venient for them to be in Rome.

THE OLIGARCHIC REALITIES OF THE ROMAN REPUBLICAN CONSTITUTION AFTER 287 B.C.E.

Whatever the precise nature of the *lex Hortensia* might be, an analysis of known laws enacted from about 300 to the end of the Republic shows that tribunes introduced about half of them in the *concilium plebis*. Therefore, some historians have called the republican constitution that had evolved by ca. 287 B.C.E. truly democratic. Others, like the second-century B.C.E. Greek historian Polybius (p. 75), have called that constitution a mixture, a blend of the three "good" types of constitution defined by Greek theorists: monarchy, represented by the magistrates; aristocracy, repre-sented by the senate; and democracy, represented by the tribunes of the *plebs* and the popular assemblies. According to this theory, each branch balanced the other, so that one could not become more powerful at the expense of the other two. Both views are wrong.

The Republic was controlled by a powerful oligarchy. It was made up of those wealthy landowners from patrician and plebeian *gentes* who had held the office of consul. They constituted a consular nobility within the senate, whose lower-ranking members were also wealthy patrician and plebeian landowners from the highest census class. Moreover, they and their families were linked together by countless intermar-riages, adoptions, personal friendships, shared experiences, and business dealings.

In a society that was extremely hierarchical and conscious of rank and prestige, modern egalitarian ideals did not exist. It was naturally assumed that some men were better than others. Business in the senate, for example, was conducted along strict lines of seniority in rank. At each census, the censors designated one of the prestigious ex-consuls as the *princeps senatus*, first man of the senate. This man gave his opinions first in debate. Then the other senators gave their opinions in descending order of rank according to the highest office yet held: censor, consul, praetor, aedile, quaestor, and, after the eventual admission of tribunes, tribune. Usually, the current holders of each office were the first of their rank to speak, but in 82 B.C.E. the magistrates-elect received that honor. Debate seldom went beyond senators of praetorian rank before the topic was exhausted. At that point, the membership voted by dividing, walking to one side of the room or the other. The men of the lower ranks were called *pedarii* because the only way that they usually had to express themselves was with their feet, *pedes*, as they walked across the room.

Under this system, then, it is clear that senatorial debate would have been framed by the consular nobility and would have proceeded along lines laid down by the early speakers. That is especially true because most of the men of lower rank often had been elected to their magistracies through the help of consular nobles and looked to their continued goodwill for election to higher office. Therefore, they were most likely to side with their consular patrons on a particular issue to avoid giving offense.

For the same reason, magistrates during their brief year of office were not really independent of the noble-dominated senate. They depended for advice on the collective wisdom of the ex-magistrates who constituted the senate. They themselves were looking to become senators if they were not already. Those who already were senators hoped to advance in rank. Just to stand for election, candidates for the offices of the senatorial *cursus honorum* normally had to be of a certain age, be of the highest census class, and have their candidacies accepted in person in Rome by the existing magistrate presiding over the voting. Even the consuls were dependent on the senate for funds and for appointment to prestigious or lucrative military commands and, after the acquisition of an overseas empire, provincial governorships. Accordingly, there was great pressure to conform to the wishes of the powerful consulars in the senate, who formed a virtual oligarchy.

Some of the tribunes of the *plebs*, wealthy men from plebeian *gentes* who started out as protectors of the common citizens, became co-opted by this oligarchy. As the number of plebeian families who had held high office and joined the senate grew, many of the new tribunes tended to be young men from their ranks who were starting out on political careers. Naturally, most of them desired to cooperate with the consular nobles, who controlled the senate. They were willing to exercise their vetoes over fellow tribunes in the interest of powerful nobles. Although it is not clear when, tribunes eventually were admitted to the ranks of senators, even though they were not strictly part of the *cursus honorum*.

Finally, one must not confuse the strong element of popular sovereignty represented by the various popular assemblies with democracy. Assemblies could not even meet unless they were summoned by one of the tribunes or magistrates, all of whom came from the wealthy land-owning class. Moreover, that same class dominated the voting in these assemblies. During most of the Republic, of course, the *comitia curiata* was merely a pro forma carryover from the past, so that there was little need to influence it one way or another. The *comitia centuriata*, *comitia tributa*, and *concilium plebis* were different, however. They had exclusive rights to elect magistrates and pass legislation, and they had important judicial functions. As already explained, because of the unit-voting procedure, the 193 centuries of the *comitia centuriata* were dominated by the ninety-eight centuries belonging to men of the wealthiest census class, the large landowners (p. 92). The situation was hardly changed by a slight reform, sometime between 241 and 215 B.C.E. (probably 220 B.C.E.), that necessitated voting by the second-highest census class before a majority could be reached.

The unit-vote rule also stifled the vote of the ordinary citizen in the *comitia tributa* and *concilium plebis*. In both of these meetings, voting took place by tribe. After 241 B.C.E., the number of tribes in which all Roman citizens were enrolled became fixed at four urban and thirty-one rural. Obviously, the large numbers of landless urban dwellers, who had only four votes, were outweighed by the thirty-one votes of the rural tribes. Furthermore, since all voting had to be done at Rome, the small landowners in the rural tribes were at a great disadvantage in comparison with the wealthy landowners, who maintained houses in Rome or could afford to go to Rome to vote. Even if a small landowner did get to Rome to vote, he was probably a client of a neighboring large landowner who was his patron. He often would have voted as his patron wished (p. 60). Thus, wealthy landowners heavily influenced many voters in the rural tribes of the *comitia tributa* and *concilium plebis* at the same time that they dominated the *comitia centuriata*, the senate, and the magistracies, and served as priests who could block public business by religious means.

After the wealthy landowners from plebeian *gentes* had gained political equality with the patricians, the interests of all large landowners were essentially the same for a long time. Therefore, wealthy landowners outside the senate had little incentive to challenge the patricio-plebeian consular nobles who dominated it. Although debt probably continued to be a problem for many, the ordinary citizens had made some important gains over the preceding two centuries: removal of the threat of enslavement for debt, protection from the arbitrary use of magisterial power, a more open legal system, and some successful attempts to obtain land for those without it. These gains sufficed to make them willing to accept the rule of their "betters" in the socio-political hierarchy. It is not coincidental that in the phrase which came to stand for the Roman government, "The Senate and the Roman People" (*Senatus Populusque Romanus* [*S.P.Q.R.*]), the senate came first.

Consequently, for a long period, there was no serious challenge to the small group of consular nobles in the senate who exercised great influence over the affairs of state. That would come 150 years later, only after conditions had greatly changed. Even then, however, the popular will could not be legally expressed except through the election of tribunes and magistrates from the ranks of the highest census classes who were willing to promote popular legislation in the teeth of fierce and often successful opposition from the ranks of those peers whom they were challenging for political leadership.

SUGGESTED READING

Lintott, A. W. *The Constitution of the Roman Republic.* Oxford and New York: Oxford University Press, 1999.

Raaflaub, K. A., ed. *Social Struggles in Archaic Rome: New Perspectives on the Conflict of the Orders.* 2nd ed. Malden, MA, and Oxford: Blackwell Publishing, 2005.

Stewart, R. *Public Office in Early Rome.* Ann Arbor: University of Michigan Press, 1999.

CHAPTER 6

The Roman conquest of Italy and its impact, 509 to 264 B.C.E.

The previous chapter alluded to the wars that the Roman Republic faced at critical junctures in its constitutional development. These wars are important for several reasons. First, the officers and manpower arrangements of the army created to fight them were the bases of the magistracies and popular assemblies of the civil community. Second, the critical role of the infantry in these wars gave a large number of those citizens referred to as *plebeians* leverage in demanding rights and privileges from the reluctant patrician elite who initially dominated the community. Third, the need to maintain internal unity in the face of external threats prevented social and political tensions from destroying the community. Fourth, the Romans of the early Republic expanded their community by incorporating allies and defeated enemies into it. Each rise in the number of citizens and closely bound allies increased the Republic's military might and caused the desire to use it to expand even more. Therefore, Rome continued to expand until it had brought all of peninsular Italy under its control, with significant consequences for itself, Italy, and the wider Mediterranean world.

CONFLICTS WITH IMMEDIATE NEIGHBORS

The wars of the fifth century B.C.E. make up a large part of Livy's narrative from the beginning of Book 2 until well past the middle of Book 5. Many of them are probably glorified plundering raids or border skirmishes over the possession of small amounts of land. Such fights often occurred between Rome and its close neighbors: the Latins, Sabines, Hernici, Aequi, Volsci, and Etruscans (map, p. 11). Patriotic Roman historians, of course, claimed that Rome fought others only in self-defense. Hardly any nation ever believes that it is the aggressor, and even fewer admit it. The Romans were as often to blame as their neighbors, and for the same reasons.

The early Romans and other peoples of Italy were mostly subsistence farmers and pastoralists. Shortage of land was chronic as populations expanded. Moreover, since wealth and status were based on land, wealthy leaders wanted more land just as much as the common people did. The only way to obtain more for everyone in any community was to take it from another group.

Plunder, glory, prestige, and revenge were additional objects of war. Common soldiers and aristocratic leaders alike anticipated sharing what they could carry away in victory. Both would also want their shares of the glory and prestige accruing from successful armed exploits, which counted heavily in the warrior ethos of Rome and its neighbors.

Rome's first attackers after the overthrow of Tarquin supposedly were the Etruscan cities of Veii and Tarquinia (see map on p. i), which backed Tarquin's bid to regain his throne. After they were defeated, the Etruscan Lars Porsenna of Clusium mounted an attack (p. 78). Apparently, he succeeded in capturing the city, despite the heroic legend of Horatius preventing Rome's fall by single-handedly holding off the attackers at the Sublician Bridge (*Pons Sublicius*) until it could be destroyed.

Porsenna attempted to use Rome to expand his control of Latium. The Greeks of Cumae and some Latin allies defeated him at the Battle of Aricia in 504 B.C.E. Conflict between Rome and its Latin neighbors continued. That merely invited the neighboring hill tribes, such as the Sabines, the Aequi, and the Volsci, to encroach on both the Latins and the Romans. It may also have encouraged the poorer citizens and leading nonpatricians at Rome to press for more rights.

Faced with common enemies, the Romans and the Latin League—the modern designation for the loose organization Latin communities other than Rome—settled their differences in 493 B.C.E. The Roman Spurius Cassius negotiated the treaty, which bears his name, *foedus Cassianum*. Rome's position in the alliance was equal to that of the Latin League as a whole. The Romans contributed half the forces used for common defense; the League, the other half. Any spoils were to be split evenly—half to Rome and half to the members of the League. It also seems that the Romans always commanded the joint forces of the league. Roman power was bound to increase at the Latins' expense. Rome by itself could decide to summon the common army to suit its own needs. The League needed a reason satisfactory to individual members before it could do so. The single city of Rome enriched itself with half of any spoils. Several cities split the other half.

Skillful Roman diplomacy also gained another advantage. The territories of the Aequi and the Volsci were separated by that of the Hernici, who feared those tribes more than they feared Rome. Around 485 B.C.E., the Romans made a treaty with the Hernici similar to the *foedus Cassianum*. Thus, they isolated the Aequi and the Volsci from each other. That made it easier to defeat them in the long run. The principle evident here, divide and rule (*divide et impera*), aided Roman expansion for centuries.

Struggles with the Aequi and the Volsci

Having earlier seized Mount Algidus near Tusculum, southeast of Rome, the Aequi almost annihilated a Roman army in 458 B.C.E. According to tradition, the situation was so alarming that a delegation from the senate went to L. Quinctius Cincinnatus. He was plowing a field on his four-acre farm. At the delegation's insistence, he accepted the offer of a dictatorship and decisively defeated the Aequi. Afterward, he resigned his dictatorship, went back home, and yoked up his ox. Still, the Romans did not drive the Aequi off Mount Algidus until 431 B.C.E.

The Volsci were even more troublesome. According to Roman legend, a Roman patrician named Cn. Marcius Coriolanus, exiled through plebeian hostility, led a Volscian army toward Rome in 491 until his brave mother and wife persuaded him to turn back. Whatever the truth of the story, the Volsci did penetrate as far north as the Alban Mount. Not until the end of the fifth century did Rome and the Latin allies initially push the Volsci out of Latium and guard the border with a series of colonies.

While the Latin League and the Romans successfully fought the Aequi and the Volsci, the Sabines pressed Rome from the northeast. In 460 B.C.E., the Sabine Appius Herdonius even captured the Capitol in Rome. After a few days, Latin neighbors from Tusculum aided the Romans in crushing the Sabine forces. By 449 B.C.E., the Sabine threat had been eliminated.

The war with Veii

Roman aggression during the fifth century was directed particularly against the Etruscan city of Veii. Located about ten miles north of Rome on the Cremera River, a western tributary of the Tiber, Veii was large, rich, and well fortified. It was also Rome's chief rival for control of the lower Tiber valley and had a garrison across the Tiber at Fidenae. The Romans fought on and off during seventy years (495–ca. 426 B.C.E.) to secure control of Fidenae. Twenty years or more later, they attacked Veii itself. They finally captured it in 396 after a ten-year siege, according to Livy, whose epic account too neatly echoes the *Iliad*.

Whatever else may or may not have happened, the Roman dictator M. Furius Camillus defeated and destroyed Veii. The Romans sold some of its inhabitants as slaves, annexed its territory, and imposed Roman citizenship on the remaining free inhabitants. Thus, the Romans almost doubled the area of the *ager Romanus* (Roman territory) and increased the number of citizens available for military service.

THE GALLIC SACK OF ROME

A sudden catastrophe befell Rome a few years after the triumph over Veii. Around 390 B.C.E. (probably 387/386), the Gallic war chief Brennus and his terrifying band of fighters swept down from the Po valley. In Etruria, they struck the city of Clusium, located about seventy-five miles north of Rome. As they continued south, a Roman army tried to intercept them near the Allia River, a small tributary joining the Tiber from the east about eleven miles north of Rome. The half-naked, wildly shouting Gallic warriors routed the Romans, captured the city, and looted it.

In Livy's highly dramatized account, the Gauls razed virtually the entire city, but part of the Roman army held out on the Capitol until the Gauls negotiated a payment to depart. When a Roman complained that the Gauls were using rigged weights to calculate the negotiated payment, Brennus tossed his sword into the balance and shouted, "Woe to the conquered!" (Livy, Book 5.48.9). However unhistorical the story, those words sum up the bitter lesson that the Romans learned from the Gallic sack. In the future, they would do everything in their power to be the conquerors and not the conquered.

UP FROM DEFEAT

Livy relates the story that Camillus, the conqueror of Veii, gathered the remnants of Rome's shattered forces and marched into the Forum just in time to deprive the Gauls of their gold and restore Rome's honor (Livy, Book 5.49.1–7). That is clearly a patriotic fiction. On the other hand, the devastation suffered by Rome has been exaggerated: archaeologists have not been able to identify evidence for widespread destruction in Rome that can be dated to time the sack is supposed to have happened. The details of the literary accounts, too, contradict the image of complete ruin. Rome's population and most of its army had survived the debacle. Under Camillus' leadership, the Romans restored their city and reasserted their power. Having seen the strength of Veii's walls earlier, the Romans built similar ones of the same grayish-yellow tufa quarried near Veii at Grotto Oscura. The finished wall was about twelve feet thick and, in places, at least thirty high. It extended about six and a half miles around the city and even included the Aventine Hill. Mislabeled the *Wall of Servius Tullius*, parts of it still stand.

The Romans hastened to shore up their position diplomatically. They seem to have exchanged the private rights of citizenship with the Etruscan city of Caere. It had been an ally against Veii and gave refuge to the Vestal Virgins during the Gallic attack. Rome made a similar arrangement with the Greek colony of Massilia in southern Gaul. Massilia apparently helped the Romans pay the ransom that freed their city and may have sent experts to help build Rome's walls. In this way, Massilia could hope for Roman help against restless Gallic tribes that threatened it.

A year or so after the sack, Camillus defeated attacks by some Etruscan cities on Rome's northern border. In turn, the Romans attacked Etruscan Tarquinia and planted strategic colonies on its border. They also aggressively began to extend their control in Latium. They fought against the Volsci to the south in the Pomptine coastal region and the Aequi to the east in the interior.

Rome's treaties with the Latin League and the Hernici seem to have lapsed. Some of the Latin cities remained loyal to Rome. Others, fearful of its aggressive posture, sided with the Volsci. In 381 B.C.E., the Romans seized control of Latin Tusculum and forcibly absorbed its people into the ranks of Roman citizens, who were subject to taxation and military service. Tusculum thus became the first Roman community known as a *municipium* (pl. *municipia*), an internally self-governing local community whose citizens had all of the obligations of Roman citizens. This arrangement became one of the principal means by which Rome eventually united Italy.

By 376 B.C.E., the Romans clearly dominated Latium again. They lived in relative peace until 370, when they undertook a three-year siege of the Latin town of Velitrae. That may have given tribunes the leverage needed to obtain passage of the famous reforms associated with Licinius and Sextius (p. 91). In 362, Rome's need for more land, perhaps reflecting the conditions associated with the so-called Licinio-Sextian land reforms, led to conflict with the Hernici and the Latins again. In 358, facing new Gallic raids, Rome, the Hernici, and the Latin League revived their old treaties, perhaps on terms even more favorable to Rome. The Latin cities of Tibur and Praeneste, however, never part of the original Latin alliance with Rome, continued to resist Rome. They were not subdued until 354. At the same time, the neighboring Etruscan cities of Tarquinia, Falerii, and even Caere grew alarmed at the growth of Roman power. They embarked on unsuccessful wars that marked the beginning of Rome's extensive conquest of Italy outside of Latium.

INITIAL CONQUESTS IN CENTRAL ITALY

Starting around 350 B.C.E., the Romans began to conquer central Italy. The reforms attributed to Licinius and Sextius in 367 B.C.E. had preserved internal harmony as the Romans reasserted themselves after the Gallic sack. They also had created a government and army capable of handling and promoting Rome's growing power. The reorganized Roman state easily turned back a new Gallic invasion about 349 B.C.E. Then, in 348 according to Livy (Book 7.27.2), the Romans countered the growing hostility of their Latin and Greek neighbors by renegotiating an earlier treaty with Carthage. Polybius (Book 3.20.9–26.7) says that the original one was made in the first year of the Republic. Allegedly, the Carthaginians received a free hand to attack the Latin coast so long as they avoided Latin cities allied with Rome. They could keep only booty, not territory, from any Latin city not subject to Rome. The Carthaginians could trade in Rome. The Romans, it is said, agreed not to trade or found colonies in Sardinia or Libya and probably Carthaginian territory in Spain. They could trade in Carthaginian-controlled territory on Sicily and at Carthage itself. To counter the Gauls on land, the Romans had already signed an alliance with the warlike Samnite hill people in 354 B.C.E. Both alliances, however, eventually crumbled in the face of Rome's growing power.

The Samnites and Rome

The first to fail was the alliance with the nearby Samnites. For a long time, population pressure and the lack of resources in the Samnites' homeland had been forcing them to expand their territory at their neighbors' expense. Constant Samnite pressure behind the Volsci had long been forcing the latter to invade Latium and wage endless wars with the Romans. To the Greek cities like Tarentum (Taranto) in southern Italy, Samnite tribes had been a perennial menace.

Around 350 B.C.E., the Samnites seemed much stronger than the Romans. They had more than four times as much territory and twice the population, but Rome gradually acquired superiority in manpower and resources. At the same time, many of the Samnites who had expanded into Campania and Lucania were willing to safeguard their gains by allying with Rome against their kinsmen. Also, the Romans could exploit weak relations between the Samnite homeland and related tribes on its northern flank.

The Samnite homeland itself was divided among four main tribes. In wartime, they formed a loose confederacy liable to come apart when unity and cohesion were most required. The confederacy lacked a strong national government that might have enabled the Samnites to formulate a clear, long-range war policy. Their most brilliant victories failed to produce any permanent results.

The Samnites could and did give the Romans many painful lessons in mountain fighting. Romans learned that a solid infantry phalanx, though irresistible on level ground, was a distinct liability in mountainous terrain. After a while, the Romans mastered the secret of mountain fighting, but the Samnite slowness to copy Roman political and diplomatic methods spelled the difference between final victory and defeat in a long series of wars with Rome.

The First Samnite War, 343 to 341 B.C.E.

About 343 B.C.E., the Samnites attacked the Sidicini, a small group in Campania on the northern border of Capua. The Capuans became alarmed and appealed to Rome for help. Despite the treaty of 354 with the Samnites, the Romans readily helped because it made them allies of Italy's second biggest city and gave them a foothold in Campania. The war itself was not a serious one, and the battles recorded are undoubtedly fictitious. But the narrative of the war presents an early instance of a pattern that Rome would repeat many times over the course of the fourth and third centuries: Rome responded to a request for aid from a weaker power, even though that brought Rome into conflict with a more powerful rival. The peace terms of 341 B.C.E. indicate that neither the Romans nor the Samnites won a clear victory. The treaty granted the Samnites the right to occupy the Sidicini's territory and acknowledged the Roman alliance with Capua.

The Latin war of 340 to 338 B.C.

The Latin and Campanian allies of Rome regarded the treaty of 341 B.C.E. as a shameful betrayal of the Sidicini. Contrary to Rome's warnings, they took up arms when the Samnite occupation of the Sidicini's territory began about 340. For years, the Latins had been chafing against their Roman alliance. It seemed to them another form of domination. Since the Gauls were no longer a menace after 349, the Latins saw a chance to make their bid for freedom and independence by defending the Sidicini.

The Latins were already at war with Samnium. Their insubordination over the Sidicini now brought war with Rome. With the help of the now-friendly Samnites, the Romans were able to settle the Latin problem before the Samnites became hostile again. The war also created circumstances favorable to the legislation of the dictator Publilius Philo in 339 B.C.E. (p. 96).

By 338 B.C.E., the bitter conflict was over. The Campanians had already accepted the generous terms offered to them and had deserted their allies. The Latins and the Volsci, who had both joined them, were crushed soon afterward. The Volsci never rose up again, and the old Latin League was dissolved. From then on, the future of the Latins would be determined at Rome's pleasure.

THE ROMAN SYSTEM OF ALLIANCES AND CITIZEN COMMUNITIES

The dissolution of the Latin League in 338 B.C.E. marked the creation of a flexible, hierarchical system of alliances and citizen communities. That system helped Rome to unite all of Italy under its control (map, p. 114). From there it was able to extend its sway over the entire Mediterranean world.

Latin allies

Under the terms of the *foedus Cassianum* of 493 B.C.E., the Romans had agreed to share certain rights with their Latin allies. These rights were known collectively as the *ius Latii*, the "Right Belonging to Latium." In early times, it was customary among the Romans, Latins, and their neighbors to accept a migrant from one community as a citizen in his new community. Later, Rome imposed limits on this custom in order to ensure that each allied community could supply the number of soldiers stipulated in its treaty. There never was a formal right of migration (*ius migrationis, ius migrandi*) between Rome and its early Latin allies. The rights that the citizens of Rome and individual Latin communities shared by the *foedus Cassianum* were only two: the right of intermarriage (*conubium*) and the right to do business and make legally binding contracts (*commercium*). The children of mixed marriages could inherit the citizenship of either parent and the property of both. Citizens of one city doing business in the other could sue or be sued in the other city's courts and could enjoy the benefits of its laws of sale and of succession. All contracts could be enforced only in the courts of the place where they were originally drawn up.

After 338, the Latin League was destroyed. Certain Latin towns received individual treaties. They could continue sharing Latin rights with Rome, but not with each other or anyone else. Gradually, the Romans separated Latin rights from their ethnic restriction and granted them to favored allies regardless of ethnicity.

With Latin allies may also be grouped Latin colonies. They were communities created by Rome or jointly by Rome and its allies for defending strategic locations or to serve some political purpose. The settlers received the Latin rights and allotments of land on which to settle. Latin communities and Latin colonies were, strictly speaking, sovereign states allied to Rome. In that way, they were distinguished from *municipia*, which were communities of Roman citizens.

Municipia

The first *municipium* was the Latin town of Tusculum, whose independence the Romans had destroyed in 381 B.C.E. Its free inhabitants received full Roman citizenship ("citizenship with the highest legal right," *civitas optimo iure*). In 338, the Romans imposed a similar status on many of the former Latin allies. Later, they extended it to others as they saw fit. In a second class of *municipia*, inhabitants received all the duties and private rights of Roman citizenship, essentially the Latin rights, but not the right to vote (*civitas sine suffragio*). In both cases, municipal status allowed people control over strictly local affairs but always under the watchful supervision of a prefect sent out from Rome.

Colonies defined as Roman also can be classed as *municipia*. They had full Roman citizenship. They were founded primarily as garrisons to keep enemies in check. They were generally smaller than Latin colonies, about 300 families as opposed to between 2500 and 6000 families. From about 338 to 288, the Romans founded a number of Roman colonies. Several protected the Latin coast. Some occupied key points in Campania and Apulia to forge a ring of fortresses around Samnium. Others in Umbria and points north kept the Gauls at bay. Around 177 B.C.E., the distinction between Latin and Roman colonies was abandoned. Subsequent colonies had the size of Latin colonies and the full citizenship of Roman ones. Thereafter, all colonies became hard to distinguish from *municipia* with full citizenship.

Socii

The Romans also made a number of one-on-one defensive pacts with individual Greek and Italian city-states that felt threatened by neighboring peoples. Those alliances were with states considered partners (*socii*) with Rome. Each treaty differed according to circumstances. All *socii*, however, were commonly required to place their military forces at Rome's disposal and to leave the conduct of foreign affairs in its hands. In return, Rome agreed not to impose taxes upon them and to allow each allied city to raise and equip its own troops under native officers. Nevertheless, they would fight under the supreme allied command of a Roman general. Rome would also provide the allied troops with food and would share the spoils of war with them. Furthermore, all allied cities could enjoy some, if not all, of the private rights of Roman citizenship.

The Romans created these various types of alliances and citizen status primarily in response to particular circumstances. At first, turning allies into citizens was more of a punishment than a reward because it deprived people of their highly valued independence. Harsh terms were imposed on those who had been particularly hard to subdue. Gradually, however, a system emerged that was viewed as rewarding the progressive Romanization of allies with more and more rights. *Socii* might at some point hope to acquire Latin status and eventually be awarded an equal share in the public life of Rome with a grant of full Roman citizenship. This system was especially favorable to local aristocratic elites. In return for keeping their populations loyal, they could look forward to the day when they or their descendants could have successful political careers in the metropolis itself. Thus, the Romans were able to keep increasing their armies with dependable supplies of loyal manpower despite occasional setbacks.

RENEWED WAR AND CONQUESTS IN CENTRAL ITALY

Rome's system of colonies and alliances was not intended to provoke hostilities with the Samnites. Yet it effectively cut off Samnite expansion westward and was bound to cause friction. The Second (Great) Samnite War (327–304/303 B.C.E.) broke out when the two sides backed different factions in an internal dispute at Naples. This war led to the Third Samnite War (298–290 B.C.E.) and a series of conflicts that ended with the subjugation of the Etruscans, Umbrians, and Gauls who had sympathized with the Samnites.

Much of the military history of these wars is obscure. Most of the battles recorded by Roman annalists are unimportant even if they did take place. The most famous and important battle of the Second Samnite War took place in 321 B.C.E. The Samnites lured a Roman army into a trap at a pass called the Caudine Forks in the mountains between Campania and Apulia. The Romans had to surrender, give hostages, and agree not to renew the war. Stripped down to single garments, they were driven under a yoke consisting of two spears stuck in the ground and united at the top by a third, a humiliating symbol of complete subjugation and unconditional surrender. Clearly, the Romans needed to learn more about mountain fighting. After making adjustments, they found an excuse for repudiating the peace treaty in 316 and renewing the war.

Continued difficulties

Rome still faced great difficulties. A serious defeat in 315 B.C.E. almost cost the loyalty of its Campanian allies. Strategic alliances and the founding of Latin and Roman colonies managed to contain the Samnites. They hoped to counter by gaining support among the Etruscans and Gauls, but they were foiled. The Romans continued to create a broad buffer zone across central Italy. From it they were able to make devastating raids into the heart of Samnium. By this show of force they also compelled wavering Etruscan allies to renew and honor their treaties.

The man who is thought to have masterminded this astute military and diplomatic strategy was the censor of 312 B.C.E., Appius Claudius Caecus (p. 112). It was also his idea to link Rome with Capua by a highway, the *Via Appia*, over which troops could swiftly move in any kind of weather. In 311 B.C.E., to protect the coast of Latium, the Romans built a small fleet of twenty triremes (ships with three banks of one-man oars). In 306, they renewed the treaty of 348 with Carthage (p. 104), perhaps with a new clause keeping Carthaginian arms out of Italy and Roman arms out of Sicily.

In spite of these efforts, the Romans gained no clear victory. The peace that ended the Second Samnite War in 304/303 B.C.E. represented basically a draw. The Samnites lost none of their original territory, none of their independence, and none of their capacity to fight again.

Rome's eventual supremacy

On the other hand, the balance of power in central Italy had gradually shifted in favor of Rome by the time the Third Samnite War broke out in 298 B.C.E. After 338, Rome and its dependents controlled an area of approximately 3400 square miles and a population of some 484,000, as compared with about 4900 square miles and a population of 450,000 for the Samnites. The danger of Rome's increasing strength even persuaded some among the Etruscans, Umbrians, and Gauls to join the Samnites. In 295, combined forces of Gauls and Samnites fought the Romans at Sentinum in Umbria. There, so the story goes, the consul Publius Decius Mus inspired the Romans to victory by devoting himself to the gods and exposing himself to death at enemy hands. His death, self-sacrifice or not, made him a hero.

Still, Manius Curius Dentatus, consul of 290, really determined the fight for central Italy. He forced the Samnites to surrender and sue for peace. They were then granted the status of Roman allies (*socii*). In the same year, Dentatus found reasons to attack the long-dormant Sabines and impose citizenship without the right to vote, *civitas sine suffragio*.

Some Etruscans, Umbrians, and Gauls fought on, however. The Gauls asked for peace in 282. Etruscans and Umbrians continued to resist for a number of years but finally surrendered under moderate terms. Of the Etruscan cities, only Caere, the former friend turned foe, lost territory. It was punished by annexation, probably in 273, and received *civitas sine suffragio*.

THE PYRRHIC WARS AND THE CONQUEST OF PENINSULAR ITALY

The Romans had granted Etruscan and Umbrian opponents moderate peace terms because Rome was now faced with another serious crisis. Victory against the Samnites in central Italy had removed a powerful buffer between Rome and the most powerful Greek city-state in southern Italy, Tarentum (Taranto). East of the Apennines, the Tarentines had been fighting not only the Samnites but also the Bruttians and Lucanians. In so doing, they had called in a number of Greek military adventurers from across the Adriatic to help them. One was King Alexander of Epirus, uncle of Alexander the Great. Another was Cleonymus, brother to a king of Sparta. They had failed either to make Tarentum a stronger power or to carve out empires for themselves.

Nevertheless, there was an important legacy. Either with Alexander of Epirus between 334 and 331 or with Cleonymus between 303 and 301, the Romans had agreed to a treaty in which they promised not to send ships into the Gulf of Tarentum. After the defeat of the Samnites in 290 B.C.E., Rome's aristocratic leaders were less well disposed toward democratic Tarentum and its ambitions to be the leading southern Italian Greek city. For the Romans, it was convenient to think that the treaty was dead along with the man who had negotiated it on Tarentum's behalf. For the Tarentines, there was good reason to fear the growing power of Rome and to claim that a treaty limiting it was still valid.

The Tarentines were already upset because Rome had rejected their attempt to mediate between the two sides in the Second Samnite War and had established the colony of Venusia on their Apulian border after the Third Samnite War. In 285 B.C.E., the southern Italian Greek city of Thurii, near the southwestern corner of the Gulf of Tarentum, was under attack by the Lucanians. Thurii appealed to Rome for help rather than to its strong rival and neighbor, Tarentum. The aristocratic leaders of Thurii probably felt more comfortable dealing with their Roman counterparts. Many Thurians also would have seen an alliance with Rome as a way of tipping the regional balance of power in their favor at the expense of their rival Tarentum. The Romans answered Thurii's appeal, defeated the Lucanians, and stationed a small garrison in Thurii itself. Other Greek cities in Italy also asked for and received Roman protection.

These actions provoked Tarentum: the pattern of Rome behavior (answering a plea for help from a weaker power against of a genuine rival) once again brought Rome into a major military conflict. Therefore, in 282 B.C.E., when Roman ships entered the Gulf of Tarentum in violation of the earlier treaty, the Tarentines attacked without warning, sank four ships, and killed the commander. Then the Tarentines marched to Thurii, drove out the Roman garrison, and sacked the town. The Romans sent ambassadors to Tarentum to seek redress. They were refused a hearing. According to patriotic Roman writers, they were also publicly insulted in gross and humiliating ways, contrary to the conventions of interstate relations. The Tarentines called in another Epirote King, Pyrrhus, grandnephew of Alexander of Epirus. Although Epirus was only a small mountainous country in northwestern Greece, Pyrrhus had ambitions of being another Alexander the Great, his second cousin. The invitation from Tarentum presented a real opportunity to establish the empire that he craved.

In the spring of 280 B.C.E., Pyrrhus set sail for Italy with a large mercenary army that included twenty war elephants. The Romans had never seen elephants before, nor had they ever faced a professionally trained Hellenistic army. Flexible tactics developed during the previous century enabled the Romans to counter Pyrrhus' phalanx of spearmen at the Battle of Heraclea, but the elephants wreaked havoc. By the least sensational count, the Romans lost 7000 men, while Pyrrhus lost 4000 in a costly tactical victory.

Encouraged by the Romans' rebellious Oscan and Samnite allies, Pyrrhus tried to attack Rome itself. The loyalty of its Latin allies, however, stopped him at Praeneste, forty miles away. Urged by Appius Claudius Caecus, now blind (*caecus*) from age, the Romans refused Pyrrhus' offers of peace. Buoyed by a defensive alliance with the Carthaginians in 279 B.C.E., they brought him to battle again at Asculum (Ausculum, Ascoli Satriano) in Apulia. After another costly victory, Pyrrhus allegedly declared, "Another such victory and I am lost!" Such an outcome has been known ever since as a *Pyrrhic victory*.

Pyrrhus' Sicilian Venture and the fall of Tarentum, 278 to 272 B.C.E.

Stymied, Pyrrhus answered a call from the Greeks of Sicily in 278 B.C.E. to come to their aid against the Carthaginians, who were on the verge of conquering the whole island. He was obliged to leave half of his forces in Italy, however, because the Romans continued to resist. His initial, brilliant successes in Sicily were undone when his Greek allies deserted him and he was forced to return to Italy. He lost part of his fleet in a battle with the Carthaginian navy on the way back to Italy in 276. Continued Roman resistance in 275 caused Pyrrhus to withdraw most of his army to Greece. He left Tarentum a small garrison. The Romans, with continued naval support from Carthage, finally forced him to remove it in 272. He died attacking Argos in Greece later that year.

The victory over Pyrrhus served notice that Rome was now a major power in the Mediterranean world. Rome had already received recognition from Ptolemy II of Egypt, who had asked for a treaty of friendship in 273 B.C.E. Later, in 264, Rome's destruction of the rebellious Etruscan city of Volsinii (Orvieto) made clear that all of peninsular Italy was under its undisputed control, from Pisa and Ariminum (Rimini) in the North to Brundisium (Brindisi), Tarentum, and Rhegium (Reggio di Calabria) on the Straits of Messana, in the South. Within the same year, even the straits would not be able to restrain Rome's growing power (map, p. 114).

THE MANIPULAR ARMY

Rome's power rested in part on an army utilizing new tactical infantry units called maniples, *manipuli* (sing. *manipulus*). A maniple was literally "a handful." In the army, as opposed to the *comitia centuriata*, centuries were now groups of only sixty men recruited from the *assidui* (sing. *assiduus*), all those landowners able to serve after the state began to supply pay and equipment that offset the expenses of service. One or two of these new centuries made up each maniple.

This manipular army had evolved since the Gallic sack ca. 390 B.C.E. It is impossible to trace that evolution in specific detail. Its cumulative effect, however, can be seen probably by the middle of the third century B.C.E. It allowed the Romans to make much greater use of military-age manpower, operate more effectively in hilly terrain, and respond more readily to changing circumstances in the heat of battle.

Formation and size

The army no longer relied on heavily armed spearmen in a single mass formation like the Greek phalanx. The maniples were grouped in three separate lines according to age, experience, and equipment. Each line had ten maniples. Each maniple of the first two contained two sixty-man centuries. Each maniple of the third line had only one. Thus, the three lines had fifty centuries in thirty maniples for a total of 3000 men. In addition, forty light-armed skirmishers were administratively attached to each maniple for a total of 1200 men. With a complement of 300 cavalry, a legion equaled 4500 men. Each consul now regularly commanded two legions plus an equal number of allied infantry and a considerably larger number of allied cavalry.

Men and equipment

The first line of heavy infantry comprised the *hastati* (sing. *hastatus*). They were young unmarried men in their late teens and early twenties. If one was killed, the loss to the community was not great. If they survived, they gained skill and experience and became *principes* (sing. *princeps*), men in their late twenties and early thirties, who made up the second line. The smaller maniples in the third line contained the *triarii* (sing. *triarius*), the fewer grizzled veterans who survived into their late thirties and early forties. The *hastati* and *principes* carried light and heavy javelins. The *triarii* used sturdy thrusting spears. In all three lines of heavy infantry, each soldier carried a *scutum* (pl. *scuta*), a large, oval plywood shield with a rim, spine, and central boss of metal. He also had a thrusting sword and a metal helmet. Metal plates strapped to his chest and back or a tunic of chain mail protected his body.

The light-armed skirmishers were called *velites* (sing. *veles*). They were often the youngest recruits. They each carried three light javelins, a short sword, and a round wicker shield, a *parma* (pl. *parmae*) about three feet in diameter. They wore no body armor, only caps made of thick cloth or leather.

In battle

When the manipular army was drawn up for battle, the cavalry were stationed on the wings to protect the flanks of the heavy infantry from the opposing cavalry. The three lines of maniples were lined up behind a screen of the light-armed *velites*. The *velites* would often rush forth and try to disrupt the enemy's advance and then retreat before the *hastati* hurled their javelins. The maniples of each heavy infantry line were drawn up to form a checker-board pattern called a *quincunx*, the arrangement of five dots that represent the number five on dice. That pattern allowed great flexibility of maneuver. The maniples of *principes* and *triarii* in the second and third lines could cover the gaps in the line in front of them. The two centuries of each maniple of *hastati* and *principes* could be lined up one behind the other or beside each other to create a shorter or longer front. They could be maneuvered to create a solid front or to open up lanes when it was time for the *velites* or one of the first two heavy-infantry lines to retire to the rear and regroup behind the *triarii*. If the enemy reached the *triarii*, the battle was going badly for the Romans. Either the *triarii* dropped to one knee and thrust forth their spears to break the enemy advance while the regrouped maniples stood behind and hurled javelins, or the army tried to make an orderly retreat.

THE ECONOMIC, SOCIAL, AND CULTURAL IMPACT OF ROMAN EXPANSION IN ITALY BY 264 B.C.E.

The conquest of peninsular Italy made Rome Italy's leading state not only politically and militarily but also economically and culturally. After the Gallic sack, Rome's growth as a center of trade and manufacturing and as the largest city in Italy resumed. Between ca. 350 and 300 B.C.E., the urban population doubled from about 30,000 to around 60,000, and by 275 it probably surpassed 90,000.

Trade and manufacturing

To sustain such a large population, food already had to be imported from sources easily reached by water transport along the western Mediterranean coast. Evidence to that effect appears in the treaty that Rome made with Carthage in 348 B.C.E. and, according to Livy (Book 9.43.26), renewed in 306. To obtain what they wanted, the Romans had to agree not to found colonies in Sardinia or North Africa and not to trade in Carthaginian territory except through Carthage itself or its ports in Sicily. That provision presupposes Roman interest in such activities. Indeed, Diodorus Siculus (Book 15.27.4) reports that the Romans had sent a colony to Sardinia in 386, and archaeological evidence indicates that they founded Ostia between 380 and 350 B.C.E. to protect the mouth of the Tiber. Further archaeological evidence indicates that these moves were not just to provide physical security but reflect Rome's interest in securing maritime trade.

In the last decade or so of the fourth century, the Portus (the harbor facilities along the bend of the Tiber) and the market area (Forum Boarium) just behind it underwent major redevelopment and expansion. On the tip of Tiber Island, the healing god Aesculapius (Asclepius), himself a Greek import, became the object of a cult about the same time and received a major temple in 291. By the beginning of the third century, Rome had become a major manufacturer and exporter of pottery that has been found throughout the very regions from which Rome must have been drawing grain to support its burgeoning population.

Another major product of Roman workshops was high-quality bronzes. For example, the magnificently engraved Ficoroni Cista, a large, finely engraved bronze container with cast bronze figures for the feet and lid handle, was produced in Rome around 315 B.C.E. (Figure 6.2, p. 115). At the same time, major pieces of bronze statuary began to be cast and set up in temples and in public places around the city. Other workshops were producing furniture, terra-cotta sculptures, and large and small carved-stone monuments, such as funeral altars and sarcophagi.

Major construction projects

The wealth that poured into Rome from the conquest of central and southern Italy produced a major building boom. From 302 to 264 B.C.E., numerous temples arose in the city. In 312, the censor Appius Claudius Caecus had inaugurated not only the construction of Rome's first major paved road, the Appian Way, but also Rome's first aqueduct, which supplied clean water for Rome's growing population. In 272, an even bigger aqueduct, the Anio Vetus, was needed to keep up with demand.

Development of coinage

The public works and wars in the late fourth and early third centuries made it increasingly necessary for Rome to finance them with coined money. During the fifth and much of the fourth centuries B.C.E., irregular lumps of bronze, *aes rude*, were the measure of value in economic transactions. They took the place of the actual cattle or sheep from which *pecunia*, the Roman word for money, was derived. Later, rectangular pieces of cast bronze replaced the irregular lumps. The state guaranteed the purity of the bronze by a distinctive sign stamped into the metal. The stamped bronze was called *aes signatum*. It was not true coinage, because only its purity, not weight or value, was indicated by the stamp.

FIGURE 6.1 Italy about 256 B.C.E.

FIGURE 6.2 The Ficoroni Cista.

During the fourth century, Rome's fiscal needs, particularly pay for soldiers, increased. As early as 289 B.C.E., the Romans created a mint and a board of three moneyers, *triumviri* (*tresviri*) *monetales*, to run it. It was located on the Capitoline Hill in the temple of Juno Moneta. From it are ultimately derived the words "mint" and "money." Rome's first real coins were called *asses* (sing. *as*) or *aes grave* (heavy bronze). These coins were cast and circular in shape. They were issued in units of one Roman pound (*libra*) or fractions thereof, as indicated by a standard mark. The *libra* equaled twelve Roman ounces (*unciae*). The Roman ounce (*uncia*) was slightly less than the U.S. ounce *avoirdupois* (27.2875 grams versus 28.3850 grams). Therefore, the *libra* weighed 11.536 ounces *avoirdupois* (327.45 grams).

Gradually reduced in size, the bronze *as* remained the common coin used throughout the republican period. Nevertheless, as the Romans became more deeply involved with the Greeks of southern Italy, especially during the war with Pyrrhus, they found it necessary to mint silver coins comparable to the silver coins commonly used by the Greeks. Therefore, the earliest Roman silver coins were two-drachma pieces, didrachms, and were clearly modeled on the silver coinage of Campania.

The agricultural sector

The Roman conquest of Italy was already reshaping Italian agriculture by 264 B.C.E. From 338 to 264, the *ager Romanus* (Rome's own land) increased from about 2200 square miles to over 10,000, about 20 percent of peninsular Italy's surface area, with a total population estimated at 900,000. In the process, much land had been confiscated to make room for poor Roman farmers. The original owners were often left without anything, deported, enslaved, or killed. Between 20,000 and 30,000 Roman men received allotments from this land. Moreover, another 70,000 Romans and Latins received allotments in nineteen Latin colonies established on conquered land between 334 and 263.

Confiscating other peoples' land and enslaving them not only satisfied the land hunger of poor Romans but also allowed rich Romans to amass larger holdings and farm them with slaves. Indeed, the enslavement of numerous war captives during the fourth century may have created the conditions favorable to passing the *lex Poetilia* and the virtual elimination of debt slavery for Roman citizens (p. 85). That, in turn, may have stimulated greater demand for chattel slaves captured in war, but the trend toward large slave-run estates in parts of Italy began later than was once thought. Near Rome itself, however, a growing urban market approaching 100,000 people in 264 was already stimulating the kinds of specialized and commercialized agriculture in which the upper classes increasingly invested the profits of imperialism during the next 130 years.

Social developments

The expansion of Roman power brought many social changes at Rome and in defeated and allied communities. The citizen population of the countryside around Rome in Latium declined. Many small farmers sought better economic opportunities and amenities in the city itself. Others took up allotments of land confiscated from defeated communities elsewhere in Italy. People who were defeated and had their lands confiscated were often enslaved to work for Roman masters.

The urban population of Rome not only increased but also changed socially. Many slaves as well as citizens from the country swelled its ranks. Slaves served in the growing households of the urban elite, and they labored in workshops and the building trades. As the number of slaves grew, so did the number of freedmen, with significant political ramifications (p. 96). Also, ambitious members of local elites from the allied and municipal towns of Italy moved to Rome and sought to achieve social and political status as equals with Rome's leading families. They, in turn, strengthened ties between Roman elites and those of their home towns.

Social conflict and war produced changes in the lives of women as well as men. Most of the surviving evidence relates to upper-class women. It seems that in the context of events surrounding the *lex Publilia* of 339 B.C.E. (p. 96), a girl named Minucia became the first plebeian Vestal. Her subsequent trial and execution by being buried alive two years later may reflect continued resistance by some patricians to plebeian advancement. In 296 B.C.E. Verginia, the patrician wife of a plebeian who was serving his second consulship in that same year, was denied the right to participate in the cult of Pudicitia Patricia (Patrician Chastity). In retaliation, she founded a cult of Pudicitia Plebeia (Plebeian Chastity).

Impressive art and architecture

By 300 B.C.E., the growing wealth and power of the Roman elite were creating a market for high-quality arts and crafts, fine terracotta and bronze statuary, and elaborate fresco paintings. Proud aristocrats proclaimed their success in war by building temples vowed in return for victory and decorating them with the finest workmanship.

Upper-class Romans also decorated their private homes with Hellenized art and architectural motifs. Ever since the late sixth century, the wealthy had enjoyed substantial town houses built on stone foundations in the neighborhood of the Palatine. The basic plan was centered on the traditional Italic atrium open to the sky, where the open hearth would have been in earlier times (Figure 2.9, p. 34). Here would be the family's Lares (p. 66) and the funerary masks and busts (*imagines*) of famous ancestors. Across the atrium from the front door was the *tablinum*, an office for the family's records, where the master of the house conducted business. Off the other sides would be several rooms that might function as bedrooms (*cubicula*) or dining rooms (*triclinia*) as the seasons or need required. In the back would be kitchens, storerooms, and slaves' quarters.

Rome's new temples were conservative in that they still reflected the influence of an already archaic Greek style that was commonly used in central Italy (Figure 2.10, P. 35). In less-tradition-bound circumstances, however, the impact of Classical Greek art was becoming more and more evident by 300. The scene from the tale of the Argonauts engraved on the Ficoroni Cista (facing page) rivals anything in late Classical Greek art, as did the bronze statuary of the time.

Self-conscious upper-class Hellenism

Prior to ca. 300 B.C.E., the influence of Greek culture in Italy had been the natural and inevitable result of general contact by non-Greeks with Greek trade goods and colonists. By the time the Romans captured Tarentum in 272, however, the importation of Classical Greek culture was part of a self-conscious attempt by Roman aristocrats to appropriate the aristocratic Greek cultural heritage for themselves. Indeed, Romans expropriated Greek or Hellenized art wherever they found it as they conquered Italy and carted off local treasures to decorate Rome. Thus, in 264, the Roman conqueror of Volsinii brought back 2000 fine statues to erect in the Forum Boarium.

By the mid-fourth century B.C.E., Roman aristocrats even began to adopt Greek *cognomina* such as Philo (Lover), Sophus (Wise), and Philippus (Lover of Horses). The cults of the new temples that they built often resembled Hellenistic victory cults. Not content with only those signs of Hellenization, many Romans appropriated Greek literature, too.

In early Rome, literature in any significant sense of the word did not exist. Writing, like most everything else, was primarily for practical, mundane purposes such as keeping financial accounts, recording laws and treaties, noting important yearly secular and religious events, and preserving oracles and religious rituals. Beginning in the third century B.C.E., however, the Romans were increasingly influenced by the advanced literary culture of the Greeks, especially those living in southern Italy and Sicily.

Greek literature had a certain practical and social value for the Roman upper classes. Greek allowed for the formulation and expression of far more complex concepts and ideas than did early Latin. It could provide a model for expanding the expressiveness of Latin itself in an increasingly complex world. Greek orators had perfected the principles of persuasive rhetoric, which were very useful to Roman aristocrats in senatorial debates, speeches at trials, and addresses to Roman voters in the Forum. Furthermore, knowledge of Greek and the appreciation of Greek literature were marks of social distinction. They helped the upper classes set themselves apart from the lower and gave them the sense of their own superiority that all elites crave. Soon, there would be a demand for teachers of Greek. It was supplied in the form of educated Greek captives serving as tutors in the homes of the wealthy. Those who were later freed often set up grammar schools, where they dispensed their wisdom to the sons of aspiring nonaristocrats for a fee.

ROME'S RISE SURVEYED AND EXPLAINED

For about 250 years, the Romans of the early Republic waged wars of varying intensity in peninsular Italy. Allied with their Latin neighbors, they pushed back the surrounding land-hungry hill tribes. They overcame their Etruscan rivals. They survived the Gallic sack to rebuild Rome's defenses, government, and alliances and emerge more united and stronger than ever. Subsequent wars with the Latins and Samnites led to a stronger system of alliances and a better equipped and tactically organized army and left the Romans firmly in control of central Italy and Campania. Afterwards, they took on Pyrrhus and his elephants and eventually prevailed. By 264 B.C.E., they had established their dominion over all peninsular Italy. In the process, they reshaped Rome and Italy economically, socially, and culturally and brought them into the mainstream of the Hellenistic Mediterranean world.

Many have sought some particular reason for Rome's rise to dominance in peninsular Italy. There is, of course, no single cause or motive to explain it. Various factors, many of which Rome shared with its rivals, were at work. The crucial point is that none shared Rome's unique combination of them.

Veii and Rome started out with roughly the same advantages in size and central location in Italy. Rome was no different from many of its neighbors in regard to its hierarchical social structure, moral values, warrior ethos, and willingness to accept as members of the community immigrants from other communities. Its initial size, however, enabled it to become the dominant partner in defending its smaller Latin neighbors. It absorbed them into the Roman state as it used their resources to conquer rivals like Veii, absorb more peoples, and become bigger and more powerful still as it shared the spoils of conquest with those who remained loyal to it.

External pressure from hostile neighbors would have been a force for internal unity in other cities as well as Rome. Combining internal unity and size, however, made a big difference. Again, as in Rome's case, many other states probably had their origin in the *populus*, namely, the army and its officers, so that military service and citizenship were synonymous and civil offices grew out of military ones. Therefore, there is no reason to think that Romans started out any more bellicose or aggressive than many of their neighbors. They all lived in a world permeated with a warrior ethos and sought wealth, security, and glory through conquest. As Rome grew, however, it also had to become a state better organized for the wars that enabled it to grow bigger. Military and executive functions were more efficiently distributed among a growing number of magistrates, so that the censors, for example, kept a comprehensive registry of every adult male citizen according to where he lived and the type of military service that he could render. During the conquest of Italy, 9–16 percent of those citizens regularly saw military service in a given year, and as many as 25 percent in a major crisis, extraordinarily high numbers in a preindustrial society.

That was possible in part because reforms protected the basic rights and economic interests of those who served in the ranks. At the same time, the magistracies were opened up to all citizens wealthy enough to hold them and strive for the honor and glory that they bestowed. The senate became a reservoir of talent and experience made up of ex-magistrates who crafted the military and diplomatic policies that created Rome's powerful system of alliances.

Still, one cannot ignore the irrational factor of sheer luck, *Fortuna*, a potent goddess. She did, perhaps, bestow more favor on the Romans than others in Italy. They were lucky that their potentially strongest enemies, the highly developed Etruscan and Greek city-states, were both rent by jealousies and rivalries that prevented either group from mounting strongly unified opposition. How fortunate it was that the Gauls who sacked Rome around 390 were not in a position to occupy their conquest permanently and left before the Romans had lost heart. It was fortuitous that the brilliant military adventurers from Greece who sought Italian empires were less accomplished politically and diplomatically. It was even more fortuitous that the Greeks of Sicily kept Carthage at bay while the Romans took over Italy with occasional Carthaginian cooperativeness.

SUGGESTED READING

Bradley, G. *Ancient Umbria: State, Culture and Identity in Central Italy from the Iron Age to the Augustan Era.* Oxford: Oxford University Press, 2000.

David, J.-M. *The Roman Conquest of Italy.* Trans. A. Nevill. Corrected ed. Oxford and Malden, MA: Blackwell Publishing, 1997.

Eckstein, A. M. *Mediterranean Anarchy, Interstate War, and the Rise of Rome.* Berkeley, Los Angeles, and London: University of California Press, 2006.

Stek, T. D. *Cult Places and Cultural Change in Republican Italy: A Contextual Approach to Religious Aspects of Rural Society after the Roman Conquest.* Amsterdam: Amsterdam University Press, 2009.

CHAPTER 7

The First Punic War, northern Italy, and Illyrian pirates, 264 to 219 B.C.E.

This and the next four chapters cover the period between 264 and 133 B.C.E. when the Roman Republic was at its height in many ways. By 264, the internal social and political struggles of the early Republic had largely abated. To preserve unity, patrician leaders had gradually agreed to grant important men from plebeian *gentes* equal access to the social and political levers of power. The acquisition of booty and territory from conquered neighbors had helped to alleviate the economic distress of the poor. Therefore, between 264 and 133 B.C.E., the Roman political system remained basically stable under the control of the new patricio-plebeian consular nobility in the senate.

Yearly warfare had practically become a way of life during the early Republic. Citizens of all classes had become accustomed to the profits of war, and aristocratic leaders craved military glory and benefited politically from the popularity won in victorious campaigns. By 264 B.C.E., the Republic had expanded militarily and diplomatically into the unchallenged leader of peninsular Italy. Subsequently, the Romans fought a series of wars that carried their power beyond peninsular Italy and resulted in the acquisition of a Mediterranean-wide empire.

With this empire came an acceleration of the integration of Roman culture and Hellenistic Greek civilization. (The term *Hellenistic* is used to designate the distinctive phase of Greek civilization that flourished after the conquests of Alexander the Great [d. 323 B.C.E.], when many non-Greek peoples adopted numerous elements of

Classical Greek civilization.) In 264 B.C.E., Hellenistic influences permeated political, economic, and cultural life in much of the world from the Himalayan Mountains in the East to the Atlantic coast of Spain in the West. After 264, Roman culture, too, developed rapidly under the tutelage of Hellenistic Greeks. Their poetry, drama, history, rhetoric, philosophy, and art provided the models for Romans to produce a distinctive Greco-Roman civilization that characterized the Mediterranean world for the rest of antiquity.

Finally, the Republic's Imperial success precipitated social, economic, and political changes that set the stage for its own destruction during the century after 133 B.C.E. Although Rome's conquests provide an interesting narrative, their impacts on the nature of the Republic itself are also worth studying.

SOURCES FOR ROMAN HISTORY FROM 264 TO 133 B.C.E.

At this point in Roman history, there are, for the first time, fairly reliable written sources of information. The early annalistic writers used by Polybius, Livy, and others were contemporaries of this period. They had either personally witnessed the events of which they wrote or learned of them directly from those who had. Polybius himself had come to Rome in 168 B.C.E., almost a century after the outbreak of the First Punic War (264 B.C.E.). His brief account of that war and his detailed description of the Second Punic War and Rome's subsequent conquest of the Mediterranean world are quite reliable. Unfortunately, his work is intact only to the year 216 B.C.E. (Books 1–6) and preserved only in fragments—a term that scholars use to describe both passages of lost works preserved as quotations in other authors and bits of text preserved on damaged parchment and papyrus—down to its end with the events of 145/144 B.C.E. (Books 7–40). Livy, however, who extensively used Polybius as well as Roman annalists, is complete for the years 219 to 167 (Books 21–45). Some of the lost books of his history are known through summaries (called *Periochae*) and epitomes of Roman history written in the late Empire (p. 398).

For events from 167 to 133 B.C.E., we must rely on later and, in some instances, less reliable sources such as the brief account by Velleius Paterculus (early first century C.E.), whose sources are unclear. More reliable are the histories of several Greek writers who drew on earlier Roman material: Cassius Dio, Diodorus Siculus, and Appian. Also useful are the biographies of some of the most important Roman and Carthaginian figures of the period by Cornelius Nepos and Plutarch. The Greek geographer Strabo and the Greek traveler Pausanias also preserve some details.

With this period, for the first time, there are contemporary works of literature, such as the plays of Plautus and Terence, that help to illuminate the life and culture of the period (pp. 199–200). Contemporary coins not only illustrate economic history but also reveal much about the officials who issued them and the places, events, and concepts depicted on them. Inscriptions—texts carved in stone or metal or (more rarely) painted on walls and objects—are also more numerous in this period. They

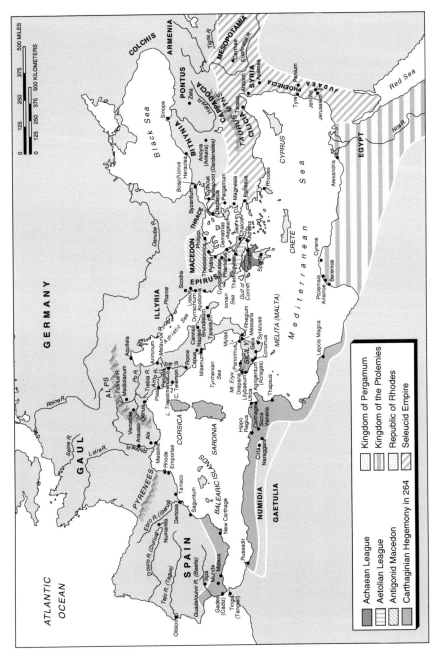

FIGURE 7.1 The Mediterranean world, ca. 264–200 B.C.E.

Achaean League
Aetolian League
Antigonid Macedon
Carthaginian Hegemony in 264
Kingdom of Pergamum
Kingdom of the Ptolemies
Republic of Rhodes
Seleucid Empire

preserve the texts of treaties and laws and the epitaphs that help to reconstruct the political relationships and careers of famous people and the daily lives of ordinary people. Finally, extensive archaeological excavations at Rome, Carthage, and hundreds of other sites around the Mediterranean reveal much about social, economic, political, and cultural trends.

A NEW CHAPTER IN ROME'S EXPANSION

The fateful year 264 B.C.E. emphatically punctuates the completion of Rome's control of peninsular Italy with the destruction of the rebellious Etruscan city of Volsinii (Orvieto). At the same time, it opens up a new chapter in the expansion of Rome's power with the start of the First Punic War. Like ever-widening ripples from a stone dropped in a quiet pool, Roman power had moved outward from its central location. It had already reached the southern tip of Italy when the Greek city of Rhegium (Reggio di Calabria) had accepted Rome's protection as an ally in 285. In 264, the ripple would spread across the three miles of water known as the Straits of Messana (Messina), which separate Rhegium from Sicily, where Punic Carthage was extending its sway.

CARTHAGE

By this time, Carthage had become a major Hellenistic power. It had never been conquered by Alexander the Great nor had it ever inherited any part of his conquests. Still, it had been extensively influenced by the Greeks through constant commercial contact and rivalry in the western Mediterranean, particularly on the strategically located island of Sicily. It was separated from Cape Bon, near Carthage, by only ninety miles of open water. The upper classes had adapted Greek models in government, agriculture, skilled crafts, architecture, dress, jewelry, art, metalware, and even language. Soon Carthage and Rome, which was rapidly rising in the same Hellenistic world, would become locked in a titanic struggle that would make Sicily Rome's first overseas conquest.

Phoenician Tyre had strategically located Carthage on the coast of North Africa where the Mediterranean Sea is at its narrowest. Therefore, Carthage was in an ideal position to dominate Phoenician trade between its eastern and western ends. Later, Carthage had settled its own colonists on the island of Melita (Malta), just below the southeast corner of Sicily. As a result, Carthage also held a strategic advantage over the Greeks, who were the Phoenicians' toughest commercial and colonial rivals in the western Mediterranean. Carthage could force the Greeks to access the west through only the dangerous narrow straits between Sicily and Italy.

When Tyre had weakened in the seventh and sixth centuries B.C.E., Carthage had become a power in its own right (pp. 18–9). To protect and expand their mercantile interests, the favorably situated Carthaginians created a navy second to none in the Mediterranean. Eventually, they incorporated former Phoenician colonies and other peoples in North Africa and the Iberian Peninsula into an empire that also included Sardinia, Corsica, parts of Sicily, and the Balearic Islands.

Carthaginian wealth and trade

Carthage controlled the richest mining resources of the western Mediterranean basin. Sardinia and Spain produced lead, zinc, copper, tin, iron, and silver. From Gades (Cadiz), on the Atlantic coast of Spain, the Carthaginians had access to tin from Cornwall and could sail south along the Atlantic coast of Morocco and perhaps down the West African shore as far as the mouth of the Senegal River to obtain gold, ivory, slaves, and war elephants.

By the third century, Carthage's workshops were turning out jewelry, ivory work, pottery, metal goods, and highly prized purple-dyed cloth in great quantities. An even greater source of wealth was the export of Carthaginian agricultural products: wine, olive oil, and various fruits like pomegranates and figures. Carthage did not have a monopoly on western sea lanes, but it was a formidable commercial force and eager to secure its advantage whenever it could.

Agriculture

The contribution that the Carthaginians made to scientific agriculture and especially to the unfortunate development of slave-worked plantations is usually ignored. They taught the Romans the technique of organizing large masses of slave labor on agricultural estates or plantations for the production of single marketable crops or staples. The slave trade and the use of slaves as farmhands and shop workers were well known in Greece and other ancient countries. Still, slave labor was never able to compete on a large scale with the labor of freeborn individuals in Greece, in the Seleucid Empire, or in Ptolemaic Egypt. The Carthaginians relied on Greek and Hellenistic treatises for the scientific cultivation of specific farm crops. On their own, they worked out a system for the large-scale use of slave labor.

Carthaginian government

As described by Aristotle in the fourth century B.C.E., Carthage was an aristocratic republic that had both democratic and oligarchic features. The details are not always clear, but four elements stand out: a popular assembly; a senate; a supreme court of 104 picked men; and elected officials, including generals and 2 annual chief magistrates called "judges" (*shophetim* in Punic and *suf(f)etes* in Latin). The popular assembly elected the generals and judges from a small group of wealthy commercial and landowning families who constituted a powerful oligarchy that also dominated the senate and supreme court. The senate, guided by an executive committee of thirty, and the judges presented questions to the assembly only if they could not agree. The supreme court kept the judges and generals in check.

The navy and army

Carthage, a seafaring city, manned its large navy with loyal citizens commanded by naval experts. Unlike Rome, however, Carthage did not have an extensive rural population of citizens from whom to recruit its armies. Therefore, the army contained few citizen troops. It was composed largely of conscripted natives of Libya, Sardinia, and Spain; troops hired from the allied but independent chiefs of what are now Algeria and Morocco; and mercenaries picked up in every part of the Mediterranean. It was difficult to maintain the army's loyalty when Carthaginian prestige or funds were low. Moreover, a successful general might be accused of dictatorial ambitions before the supreme court; an unsuccessful one might be nailed up on a cross to appease popular anger. The loss of experienced leadership could be critical at times.

SICILY AND THE OUTBREAK OF THE FIRST PUNIC WAR, 264 B.C.E.

Until 264 B.C.E., the western Greek cities of Italy and Sicily had been Carthage's major rivals in the western Mediterranean. For over 200 years, the Carthaginians and the Greeks of Sicily had been fighting for control of that rich and strategically located island. During that period, the Carthaginians had cultivated good relations with the Romans, as indicated by the various treaties that had regulated their commercial and state relations in 509(?), 348, 306, and 279 B.C.E. (pp. 112–3). In 279, they had even found a common interest in the war against Pyrrhus, who threatened Rome's interests in southern Italy and Carthage's in Sicily. Polybius, however, emphatically contradicting the pro-Carthaginian historian Philinus, denies that any treaty ever defined the two powers' respective interests so sharply that the Romans were barred from using arms anywhere in Sicily and the Carthaginians from anywhere in Italy (Book 3.26.1–7). Whether Polybius is right or wrong is largely irrelevant. Many Romans were aware that, treaty or no treaty, they would be in danger of provoking Carthage to war if they sent troops to Sicily in the situation that confronted them in 264.

The Mamertines

That situation resulted from the actions of the Mamertines, a group of Campanian mercenaries. They had once been hired to fight for Syracuse, the greatest Greek city founded in Sicily (p. 20). Later, in 289 B.C.E., they had deserted and seized the strategic town of Messana, in the northeastern corner of Sicily, on the straits that bear its name. The Mamertines had killed the men, taken their women, and had begun to plunder Syracusan territory periodically. Around 265, the Syracusan general Hiero inflicted a great defeat on the Mamertines. He won such popularity that he was able to make himself king at Syracuse as Hiero II. In 264, the remaining Mamertines, still in control of Messana, decided that they needed outside help to stave off any further attacks from Syracuse. One group appealed to the Carthaginians and another to the Romans. A Carthaginian commander who had a fleet nearby quickly responded to the first group's request. He garrisoned Messana's citadel with part of his forces, and Hiero refrained from taking any further action against the Mamertines.

Debate and the decision for war in Rome

Meanwhile, the Mamertines who had requested help from Rome had sparked a long and difficult debate in the Roman senate. Polybius mentions two countervailing views that could not be reconciled (Book 1.10.1–9). On one side, many argued that it was beneath the dignity of Rome to ally with the Mamertines. Their crimes at Messana had been equal to those of some allied Campanian soldiers whom Rome had recently punished at Rhegium (Reggio), just across the straits, in 270 B.C.E. Others were afraid that if Rome did not aid the Mamertines, Carthage would use Messana as a base for subduing Syracuse and the rest of Sicily that they did not already control. Since Carthage already held Sardinia, Corsica, and extensive territories in Spain and North Africa, adding all of Sicily would make the Carthaginians very powerful and danger-ous neighbors. Although Polybius does not say so, there were senators of Campanian origin who may have felt a kindred sympathy toward the Mamertines. Probably a number of senators argued that Rome needed to prevent the Carthaginians from gain-ing control of the Straits of Messana, or else they would be able to interfere with the shipping of Rome's southern Italian Greek allies, Carthage's traditional competitors. Still others may well have felt that without an adequate navy and already faced with a rebellion in Italy at Volsinii, Rome was in no position to risk a major overseas war with a great naval power like Carthage. Among the senators who would have risked war, there may have been those looking forward to winning glory and spoils in Sicily. Some opponents may have been concerned that such a war would enable an ambitious general to acquire political advantage over his peers in the senate. Many may have argued that Rome should finish the existing war against Volsinii first. In the end, a majority of senators did not approve aid for the Mamertines.

According to Polybius (Book I.11.1–3), however, the consuls, who were favorable toward aiding the Mamertines, brought up the matter before the voters (he does not specify in which assembly). With a second war to fight in their year of office, the consuls could each look forward to all of the advantages of a military victory. They pointed out to the voters the potential threat that Carthage would pose if it gained control of Sicily. Also, they reminded the voters of the rich spoils awaiting those of them who would end up fighting if it came to war with Carthage in Sicily. Those who served in the Roman army had become used to profiting from almost yearly warfare. Many would have remembered how Pyrrhus had tried to make use of Sicily against Rome only a dozen years before. Indeed, after almost continuous struggles with neighboring peoples in Italy, the Romans had developed an almost paranoid fear of powerful neighbors. Many voters may also have been mindful of Rome's need to protect the interests of allied Greek cities in southern Italy against their commercial rival Carthage.

Finally, although no ancient source mentions it, another consideration may have been a need to secure better access to supplies of grain for feeding Rome's rapidly growing urban population. Rome was already importing grain from places along the western Mediterranean coast, but treaties with Carthage limited Roman access to the richest western sources in Sardinia, Sicily, and North Africa. A desire to end that situa-tion also could have fostered a willingness among many Romans to go to war.

Appius Claudius Caudex invades Sicily

The consul Appius Claudius Caudex (a grandson of the famous censor of 312 B.C.E.) was appointed to assemble an army, cross over to Sicily, and place Messana under Roman protection. While Appius was preparing to transport his army from Rhegium to Messana, the pro-Roman Mamertines managed to induce the Carthaginian commander to withdraw his garrison. They urged Appius to cross over quickly and take his place. Perhaps the Carthaginian commander hoped that if he left Messana, the Romans would be content to remain in Italy. His superiors, however, were enraged at his failure to hold Messana. They crucified the man, stationed a fleet between Messana and the forces of Appius at Rhegium, and sent an army to retake Messana. Hiero II, allying himself with Carthage in this effort, brought up the Syracusan army and attacked Messana from his direction.

   At the same time, Appius made a daring night crossing from Italy to Sicily. He avoided the Carthaginian fleet and landed his forces at the harbor of Messana. His attempt to procure the withdrawal of either the Carthaginians or Hiero through negotiations failed. Therefore, acting boldly while his troops were still fresh and before his supplies ran out, Appius first attacked and defeated Hiero, who quickly withdrew to Syracuse. Then, on the next day, Appius turned against the Carthaginians and defeated them. The First Punic War had begun, with momentous consequences for the history of Rome, Carthage, and the whole Mediterranean world.

The Carthaginian view

The Carthaginians, although not prepared for a major war, had to risk fighting. Despite any legalistic interpretations that could have been given to existing treaties, the Romans appeared to be the aggressors. They had no previous interests in Sicily, whereas the Carthaginians had long been one of the dominant powers there. To have tolerated Roman interference would have made the Carthaginians appear weak and unwilling to protect their interests in a situation where justice seemed to be on their side. Moreover, to have negotiated any agreement based on Roman claims of a protectorate over the Mamertines would have left the Mamertines free to cause trouble in Sicily under the umbrella of Roman power. From the Carthaginian perspective, therefore, the Romans had to be opposed.

INITIAL CARTHAGINIAN SETBACKS, 263 AND 262 B.C.E.

Unfortunately for Carthage, most of its warships had been lying in storage ever since the Pyrrhic War. Ships had to be refitted; crews had to be recruited and trained. Meanwhile, Appius Claudius Caudex had laid siege to Carthage's ally Hiero II at Syracuse. Hiero was already alarmed that Carthaginian forces had not even been able to prevent Appius' main army from crossing the straits in 264. He was totally disillusioned when he did not receive the expected support against the Roman siege. Consequently, he negotiated a peace with the Roman consul who replaced Appius

Claudius Caudex in 263. The peace was to run for fifteen years, and Hiero agreed to help Rome against Carthage. Therefore, in 262, he aided the Romans in capturing the Carthaginian stronghold of Agrigentum (called Acragas by the Greeks, Agrigento in modern Italian).

EXPANSION OF THE WAR

After the fall of Agrigentum, the Romans saw the possibility of driving the Carthaginians out of Sicily altogether. The obstacle was the Carthaginian fleet. Once it was fully ready for action, it threatened to cut communications with Italy and starve the Roman army into surrender. It also raided Italian coastal cities. The Romans must already have realized that they needed to match the Carthaginian navy at all costs or else get out of the war.

Rome builds a new fleet, 261 B.C.E.

The small navy that had served Rome during the Second Samnite War and the war with Pyrrhus (pp. 109–11) probably had been abandoned. Even if it still did exist, it would not have been adequate for an overseas war. The navies of allied Greek city-states in Italy had transported the Roman armies to Sicily. Their light *triremes* had been sufficient before Carthage had mobilized its full naval power, which was based on the heavy *quinquereme*, heavy and strong warships manned by multiple units of five rowers spread across anywhere from one to three banks of oar and fronted with a great bronze beak used for ramming and sinking other ships.

Polybius tells the famous story that the Romans used a captured Carthaginian *quin-quereme* as a model and built one hundred *quinqueremes* along with twenty new *triremes* while new rowers trained in simulators on the shore (Book 1. 20.9–16). That they did it in sixty days from the cutting of the trees as Pliny the Elder claims (*Natural History* 16.192) seems impossible. It would have taken many months to cut and season timber; produce the ropes, sails, and fittings; and gather the number of skilled workers needed for such a large project.

It may be more accurate to say that the Romans assembled the ships in sixty days. The Carthaginian ship that they used as a model had been captured three years earlier. In the meantime, the Romans probably acquired raw materials and stockpiled various components prefabricated according to standard patterns based on the captured ship. When there were enough, the components could then be assembled quickly into complete ships.

To the bows of their new ships, the Romans added a device that the Athenians had tried during their disastrous expedition to Sicily (415–413 B.C.E.). It was a hinged gangplank raised upright by ropes and pulleys attached to the mast. After an enemy ship was rammed, this gangplank was dropped onto the disabled ship's deck. Roman marines would rush across to fight as they would on land. The end of the plank had a grappling spike, or beak, to hold on to the enemy ship so that it could not slip off the Roman ship's ram and escape. This spike gave the device its name, *corvus* (crow or raven). Although it served its purpose very well, it rendered Roman ships unstable in high seas when it was raised upright for transport.

A TITANIC STRUGGLE, 260 TO 241 B.C.E.

A war of titans commenced in 260 B.C.E., when the new Roman fleet defeated the Carthaginians in a great naval battle off Mylae, not far from Messana. The triumphant Romans erected a column decorated with the rams (*rostra*) of captured Carthaginian ships near the speaker's platform in the Forum. After failing to adapt to Roman tactics and losing another sea fight off Sardinia in 258, the commander of the Carthaginian fleet was crucified.

The Roman invasion of Africa, 256 to 255 B.C.E.

Having established sudden naval superiority, the Romans planned a massive invasion of Africa itself to end the war quickly. In 256, the Romans set sail with 250 warships, 80 transports, and about 100,000 men. They defeated another Carthaginian flotilla off Cape Ecnomus, on the south coast of Sicily, but new Carthaginian tactics began to counteract the *corvus*.

The Roman consul M. Atilius Regulus landed in Africa in the autumn of 256 B.C.E. He inflicted a minor defeat on the Carthaginians. Thinking that they were just about ready to give up, he offered them terms of peace so harsh that they were rejected. Though winter would have been the best season to fight in Africa, Regulus decided to wait until spring. Meanwhile, the Carthaginians had not been idle. They had engaged the services of Xanthippus, a Spartan strategist skilled in the use of the Macedonian phalanx and war elephants. New mercenaries were hired, and many Carthaginian citizens volunteered for service. All that winter, the work of preparation and training continued unabated.

In the spring of 255 B.C.E., Regulus advanced into the valley of the Bagradas but found the enemy already waiting for him. Here Xanthippus had drawn up his phalanx—elephants in front and cavalry on the wings. The Romans suffered a catastrophic defeat. Only 2000 men managed to escape. Regulus himself was taken prisoner along with 500 of his men. The dead probably numbered 10,000 or more.

A Roman armada sent to rescue survivors defeated another Carthaginian fleet and sailed off with the remnants of Regulus' army. As the Romans were approaching the shores of Sicily, a sudden squall caught the ships made top heavy by the *corvus*. All but 80 of 364 ships according to Polybius' account (Book 1.37.2) sank or crashed on the rocks with an estimated loss of 100,000 men. In 253, a similar disaster occurred.

The war in Sicily, 254 to 249 B.C.E.

After 255, Sicily and its surrounding waters remained the sole theater of military operations. Capturing Panormus (Palermo) in 254, the Romans drove the Carthaginians out of the island, except for two strongholds at the western tip—Lilybaeum and the naval base of Drepana (Trapani)—both of which they blockaded by land and sea. The Carthaginians concentrated their main effort on expanding their empire in Africa and stamping out native revolts in order to secure their resources at home. In 249, however, they regained the initiative against Rome.

Carthaginian success at sea, 249 to 247 B.C.E.

As the Romans had rebuilt their navy after the disasters of 255 and 253 B.C.E., they had abandoned the *corvus*. The Carthaginians had devised successful defensive tactics against it, while its height and weight made ships very vulnerable to storms at sea. In 249, the poor tactics of the consul Publius Claudius Pulcher (see Box 7.1) resulted in the loss of 93 out of 120 Roman ships off Drepana (Trapani). The version of events told by our ancient sources, however, blame not Claudius' ineptitude but his arrogance in angering the gods before the battle. A second Roman defeat soon followed Claudius' debacle: the other consul's enormous fleet was completely destroyed, partly by Carthaginian attack and partly by storm. For the next few years, the Carthaginians had undisputed mastery of the sea. They were now able to break the Roman blockade of Lilybaeum, cut communications between Rome and Sicily, and make new raids upon the Italian coast itself.

7.1 THE IMPORTANCE OF THE AUSPICES

The Romans believed that their success as a society was due to the fact they were beloved of the gods and that this was the result of their correct worship of them. The story our Roman sources report about the Battle of Drepana is a classic Roman illustration of what could happen when the gods were displeased.

Before setting off to battle, Publius Claudius Pulcher did what was required of every Roman commander: he took the auspices, that is, he consulted the gods to see if they were in favor of the action he planned. The Romans had numerous ways to do this (see p. 69); Claudius used one of the methods favored by commanders in the field. He ordered the sacred chickens to be let out of their crate. He hoped to see them gobble down the special meal that had been scattered on the ground for them—the best possible sign was if a chicken ate so fast that whole pieces of food dropped from its mouth and hit the ground. Unfortunately for Claudius, he received the worst sign: the birds would not eat. (Since he took the auspices on board his ship and since chickens are not seabirds, the animals were likely seasick.) In such circumstances, protocol dictated that Claudius wait twenty-four hours and then try consulting the gods again, but his anger and impatience got the better of him. He threw the uncooperative birds overboard, shouting "Since they will not eat, let them drink!" The near total loss of his fleet in battle later that day was thus divine retribution delivered through the Carthaginian fleet.

Hamilcar Barca and ultimate Carthaginian failure, 247 to 241 B.C.E.

Never had the picture looked brighter for the Carthaginians, especially after they had given the young Hamilcar Barca, the most brilliant general of the war, command of Sicily in 247 B.C.E. His lightning moves behind Roman lines and daring raids upon the Italian coast made him the terror of Rome. Well did he merit the name of *Barca*, Baraq (Barak, Barack) in Punic, which means "blitz" or "lightning."

Despite the brilliance of Hamilcar Barca and the amazing successes of the Carthaginian navy, Carthage lost the war. It was unable to deliver the final blow when Rome was staggering in defeat. Rome's ultimate victory was not wholly due to doggedness, perseverance, or moral qualities, as has often been suggested. Carthage was weakened by an internal division between the commercial magnates and the powerful landowning nobility.

A landowning group headed by Hanno the so-called Great had prospered with the conquest of territory in North Africa. To this group, the acquisition of vast territories of great agricultural productivity in Africa was more important than Sicily, the navy, and the war against Rome. It came into control of the Carthaginian government at the very moment when the Carthaginian navy and the generalship of Hamilcar Barca seemed about to win the war. That this new Carthaginian government was not interested in winning the war was clearly evident in 244 B.C.E. The entire Carthaginian navy was laid up and demobilized. Its crews, oarsmen, and marines were transferred from the navy to the army of African conquest.

Meanwhile, the Romans saw that their only chance for survival lay in the recovery of their naval power. They persuaded the wealthiest citizens to advance money for the construction of a navy by promising to repay them after victory. In 242, a fleet of 200 Roman ships appeared in Sicilian waters. In the following year, on a stormy morning near the Aegates Islands, it encountered a Carthaginian fleet of untrained crews and ships undermanned and weighted down with cargoes of grain and other supplies for the garrison at Lilybaeum. The result was a disaster for Carthage that cost it the war. The garrison at Lilybaeum could no longer be supplied. There was no alternative but to sue for peace.

Roman peace terms, 241 B.C.E.

The Carthaginian government empowered Hamilcar Barca to negotiate peace terms with the consul C. Lutatius Catulus, the victor of the recent naval battle. Both sides were exhausted. The Roman negotiators, well aware of the slim margin of victory, were disposed to make the terms relatively light. Carthage was to evacuate Lilybaeum, abandon all Sicily, return all prisoners, and pay an indemnity of 2200 talents (presumably silver) in twenty annual installments (a talent equals about twenty-five kilograms or sixty pounds). These terms seemed too lenient to the Roman voters, who had to ratify the treaty in the *comitia centuriata*. They increased the indemnity to 3200 talents to be paid in ten years. The Carthaginians were also required to surrender all islands between Sicily and Italy, keep their ships out of Italian waters, and discontinue recruiting mercenaries in Italy.

The impact of the First Punic War

As in all major wars, the victors and vanquished alike were profoundly affected and underwent significant changes. First of all, the war had exacted enormous tolls in men and matériel on both sides. Although casualty figures are often grossly inflated by ancient sources, Rome and Carthage each had lost hundreds of ships and tens of thousands of men. Thus, the lives and livelihoods of many parents, wives, and children were devastated, with lasting consequences for their communities and societies as a whole.

At the state level, Rome had gained its first provincial territory, Sicily. It also became a major naval and international power. Eventually, it was unable to remain uninvolved in the affairs of the wider Mediterranean world even if it had wanted to. Many Romans probably were suspicious of Carthage and feared that it might someday seek to even the score. Others had found their appetite for conquest whetted and wanted more.

The sea power of Carthage was broken, and its naval dominance of the western Mediterranean was ended for all time. Some Carthaginians resented their humiliating defeat and hoped someday to restore Carthaginian prestige abroad. Others continued to concentrate on the intensive agricultural development of the territory around Carthage. More immediately, however, Carthage suffered a major crisis because of its inability to pay the mercenary troops that made up the bulk of its army. The temptation to take advantage of this situation at Carthage's expense eventually proved too great for a number of Romans to resist.

THE TRUCELESS WAR AND ROMAN TRICKERY, 241 TO 238 B.C.E.

No sooner had the Carthaginians made peace with Rome at the end of the First Punic War than they had to fight their own mercenaries. Returning from Sicily, 20,000 mercenaries demanded their accumulated pay and the rewards promised to them by Hamilcar Barca. The Carthaginian government, then dominated by unsympathetic landlords such as Hanno the Great, refused. The mercenaries mutinied and were joined by the oppressed natives of Libya, the Libyphoenicians of the eastern part and the Numidians of the western. The mercenaries became masters of the open country, from which Carthage was isolated. It was a war without truces and was, therefore, known as the Truceless War. A similar revolt subsequently broke out in Sardinia.

Hanno assumed command of the army, but his "greatness" failed to achieve any military success. The situation deteriorated until Hamilcar Barca took command. Three years of the bloodiest fighting followed. Crucifixions and all manner of atrocities were committed on both sides until Hamilcar, finally with Hanno's cooperation, stamped out the revolt.

Carthage received the unexpected sympathy and help of Rome, which furnished it with supplies and denied them to its enemies. Rome permitted the Carthaginians to trade with Italy and even to recruit troops there. It also rejected appeals for alliance from the rebels of Utica and Sardinia. After the revolt against Carthage had been stamped out in Africa, however, a faction unsympathetic to Carthage gained the upper hand in the Roman senate. As Hamilcar was moving to reoccupy Sardinia in 238 B.C.E., this group, "contrary to all justice," in the words of the usually pro-Roman Polybius (Book 3.28.2), persuaded the senate to listen to the appeal of the Sardinian rebels, declare war on Carthage, rob Carthage of Sardinia, and demand an additional indemnity of 1200 talents.

Carthage gave in to Roman demands because it had no fleet and could not fight back. Losing Sardinia also meant that Carthage could no longer enforce any claim to neighboring Corsica, which the Romans invaded in 236. The natives of both Sardinia and Corsica fought ferociously against Roman occupation. Many continued to resist Roman authority long after the two islands were grouped together as the second Roman province in 227 B.C.E.

ROMAN CONQUESTS IN NORTHERN ITALY

Important Roman senators may have feared that, in the wrong hands, Sardinia and Corsica could be used to disrupt efforts to secure the northern frontier of Italy against the Gallic tribes of the Po valley. The Romans called that area *Gallia Cisalpina*, Cisalpine Gaul (Gaul This Side of the Alps). They had been fighting tribes from that region on and off since the time Brennus and his Gallic warriors had sacked Rome (pp. 102–3). Therefore, they always looked upon these people with fear and suspicion. There were two keys to holding the Gauls in check. One was Rome's stronghold at Ariminum (Rimini), a colony on the extreme southeastern corner of the Po valley. The other was the mountainous territory of Liguria in the southwest corner of continental Italy. Liguria blocked the western end of the Po valley and controlled the upper part of the route that ran north from Rome along the west coast of Italy. Still free of Roman control, Liguria would have to be conquered to secure the northern frontier against the Gauls or anyone else who might invade peninsular Italy from that direction.

In 241 B.C.E., before the formal end of the First Punic War, the Romans began laying the groundwork for their campaigns in the North by securing vital communications routes. They found an excuse to make war on the Faliscans, whose fifty-year treaty with Rome had run out two years before. The Faliscans' major stronghold, the fortified city of Falerii, was only about forty miles north of Rome. It was very close to the route of what would become the great Via Flaminia north from Rome through Umbria to the Adriatic coast and on to Ariminum. The Romans destroyed Falerii and moved its inhabitants to a less strategic spot three miles away. They also founded a colony at Spoletium in Umbria to protect the area through which they had to pass on the way to Ariminum.

At the same time, they began to build the great Via Aurelia northwest from Rome up the coast of Etruria to the colony of Cosa. Cosa was well fortified to protect both the land and sea routes to and from Liguria. Both of these routes could easily be attacked from the islands of Sardinia and Corsica. Northern Sardinia is only about 130 miles from the coast of Etruria, and the northern tip of Corsica is only about fifty miles from Populonia on the coast north of Cosa. Strategically minded Romans may well have feared that when they began the conquest of Liguria, the Ligurians would try to ally with the Carthaginians on Sardinia to harass Roman lines of supply and communication. Therefore, it scarcely seems coincidental that the consul Tiberius Sempronius Gracchus both led the Roman occupation of Sardinia and initiated the conquest of Liguria in 238 B.C.E.

In that same year, a Roman army based at Ariminum also started campaigning against the Gallic Boii at the eastern end of the Po valley. That campaign, in turn, provoked other Gauls, including transalpine tribes. Perhaps emboldened by the return of now-unemployed Gallic mercenaries who had served Carthage during the Truceless War, they joined with the Boii to attack the Romans at Ariminum in 236. Internal dissension among the Gauls led to their defeat. An uneasy truce during the next eleven years became even more uneasy in 232, when an ambitious tribune named C. Flaminius obtained passage of a law giving individual Roman settlers large amounts of land confiscated from the Boii fifty years earlier south of Ariminum.

THE PIRATES OF ILLYRIA, 229 AND 228 B.C.E.

Successful campaigns in Sardinia and Corsica in 231 B.C.E. and Liguria in 230 finally enabled the Romans to turn their attention to the festering problem of Illyrian pirates in the Adriatic. Previously, the maritime Greek cities of southern Italy had lost their independence, and Rome had become preoccupied with Carthage in western waters. In the meantime, the notorious pirates of Illyria, along the eastern coast of the Adriatic, had grown ever bolder. Queen Teuta, who had been expanding her Illyrian kingdom south to Epirus and the Gulf of Corinth, had been unable or unwilling to stop them. With the Greeks grown weak, pirates roved the seas at will, attacked not only Greek, but also Italian, ships and captured or killed their crews. Growing ever bolder, they ransacked towns along the Adriatic shores of southern Italy. The Romans were bound to protect the interests of their allies and could not tolerate attacks on Italy itself.

In 230 B.C.E., the Roman senate dispatched two envoys to lodge complaints with Queen Teuta. When pirates killed one of the envoys, the Romans responded swiftly. In the summer of 229 B.C.E., a fleet of 200 Roman ships appeared off the island of Corcyra (Corfu). Demetrius of Pharos, whom Teuta had charged with the defense of the island, betrayed her and surrendered to the Romans without a fight. The fleet then sailed north to support a large Roman army attacking the towns of Apollonia and Dyrrhachium (Durazzo). Teuta sued for peace in 228. She retained her crown on condition that she renounce her conquests in Greece, abandon all claims to islands and coastal towns captured by the Romans, and agree not to let more than two Illyrian ships at a time sail past Lissus, the modern Albanian town of Alessio. For his treachery, Demetrius received control of Pharos and some mainland towns.

RENEWED WAR WITH THE GAULS, 225 TO 220 B.C.E.

The Romans do not seem to have had any territorial goal in Illyria. They wanted to suppress piracy and establish friendly client relations with those rulers and communities in the region who were willing to keep the Adriatic safe for the ships of Rome and its allies. Of much more pressing concern to the Romans were the Gauls in northern Italy. Mutual fear, suspicion, and even hatred drove the actions of both as they tried to strengthen themselves against one another. By 225 B.C.E., each side had built up massive armies ready to strike. The Boii and three other Gallic tribes in the Po valley plus some allies from the Rhone valley across the Alps contributed to the Gallic army. To counter them, the Romans had stationed two large armies in the north. An army of two legions and an even larger number of allied troops waited at Ariminum under the command of L. Aemilius Papus. Another large force, mainly of allied troops, was positioned on the northern border of Etruria under the command of a praetor.

Leaving part of their forces to protect the Po valley, the Gauls struck first. They followed the route down through Etruria that Brennus had taken over 160 years earlier. The Roman praetor caught up with them near Clusium and fell into a trap. He suffered serious losses before he was rescued by Aemilius Papus, who had rushed south with the army from Ariminum. The Gauls decided to cut westward and retreat up the Via Aurelia with Papus in hot pursuit. Meanwhile, Rome's other consul, C. Atilius Regulus, who had been campaigning in Sardinia, landed his army at Pisa and marched south to intercept the fleeing Gauls. Trapped between the two Roman armies at Telamon, just north of Cosa, the Gauls fought furiously. They even managed to kill Regulus but ultimately were almost annihilated. Out of 50,000 Gauls, only 10,000 survived.

Subsequently, Aemilius Papus and then the consuls of 224 B.C.E. completely defeated the Boii in the Po valley. In 223, the consul C. Flaminius, who had obtained the law giving Gallic land to Roman settlers in 232 B.C.E., scored a major victory against the Insubrian Gauls. After more Roman victories in 222 and 221, all of Cisalpine Gaul was under Roman control. After being elected censor for 220, Flaminius initiated construction of the great paved road named for him, the Via Flaminia from Rome to Ariminum, and founded the colonies of Cremona and Placentia, which anchored Roman control of the central Po valley.

PIRATES AGAIN, 220 TO 219 B.C.E.

The hasty measures of 229 and 228 B.C.E. in Illyria had not solved the problem of Adriatic piracy. Demetrius of Pharos proved to be a very unreliable Roman client. Antigonus Doson, acting king of Macedon, disliked Roman interference in Balkan affairs. Conspiring with Doson, Demetrius stealthily extended his kingdom. After Teuta's death, he invaded the territories of those friendly to Rome, attacked Greek cities farther south, and made piratical raids far into the Aegean. The Romans could not overlook these activities. In 220, they launched a campaign to eliminate Demetrius and the pirates. They succeeded in driving out Demetrius, but events of 218 in Spain forced them to abandon any plans of dealing with the situation in Illyria more thoroughly. Meanwhile, Demetrius had fled to the court of Macedon's new king, the youthful Philip V. Whispering plots of revenge into the young king's ear, Demetrius remained there for several years.

ROME'S RISE AS A MEDITERRANEAN POWER SURVEYED

The Mamertines' requests for aid from both Rome and Carthage in 264 B.C.E. had pitted the two great republics of the western Mediterranean against each other and touched off the First Punic War. Rome turned itself into a major naval power to overcome Carthage's advantage at sea. It was able to use its massive reserves of manpower and matériel in Italy to overcome staggering losses and exhaust the will of the increasingly divided Carthaginians to carry on the fight by 241.

Immediately after that, Carthage was further weakened by the Truceless War with its mercenaries. At first, Rome cooperated with Carthage. In 238, the Romans put their own strategic, and perhaps financial, considerations uppermost when they turned on Carthage. They forced it to surrender Sardinia and pay an additional indemnity or face renewed war with them. While taking over Sardinia, and soon thereafter, Corsica, the Romans pursued their previously planned campaigns against the Ligurians and Gauls in northern Italy. In the same period, the Romans mounted brief expeditions to suppress Illyrian piracy (229–228 and 220–219 B.C.E.).

Thus in the space of forty-six years, Rome had risen from a regional power controlling peninsular Italy to a major Mediterranean power stretching from the foothills of the Alps on the north to a point in Sicily only ninety miles from North Africa on the south and from the islands of Sardinia and Corsica on the west to the shores of Illyria on the east. The events in Spain that demanded Rome's full attention in 218 B.C.E. would launch the Second Punic War with Carthage. That conflict would set Rome on the path to becoming the dominant power in the whole Mediterranean world.

SUGGESTED READING

Hoyos, D. *Mastering the West: Rome and Carthage at War. Ancient Warfare and Civilization*, Oxford and New York: Oxford University Press, 2015.

Hoyos, D. *Unplanned Wars: The Origins of the First and Second Punic Wars.* Berlin and New York: De Gruyter, 1997.

Rosenstein, N. *Rome and the Mediterranean, 290 to 146* b.c.e.: *The Imperial Republic.* Edinburgh: University of Edinburgh Press, 2012.

CHAPTER 8

War with Hannibal

The Second Punic War, 218 to 201 B.C.E.

After the First Punic War and Rome's takeover of Sardinia, the Romans were too involved with wars in Sardinia and Corsica, northern Italy, and Illyria to interfere in any serious way with what the Carthaginians were doing. In 220 B.C.E., however, with the two islands and northern Italy apparently secure, Carthaginian actions began to look more ominous, especially under the leadership of the charismatic general Hannibal in Spain. Relations between Rome and Carthage rapidly deteriorated. War between the two republics broke out once more in 218.

CARTHAGINIAN RECOVERY AFTER 238 B.C.E.

Shortly after the loss of Sardinia, Carthage made a strong recovery. Under the leadership of the Barcids (Hamilcar Barca, his son-in-law Hasdrubal, and his son Hannibal), the loss of the two islands was more than offset by conquests in Spain. During the First Punic War and, later, the Truceless War, Carthage had lost most of its Spanish possessions to native rebellions. Much of its western trade was taken over by the Greek colony of Massilia, which was located on the coast of Transalpine Gaul between northern Italy and northern Spain. In 237 B.C.E., Hamilcar landed in Spain at Cadiz. Then, by a judicious mixture of war and diplomacy, he founded a bigger and richer empire than Carthage had ever possessed.

Hamilcar Barca drowned while fleeing enemy horsemen in 229 B.C.E. His son-in-law Hasdrubal continued the work of empire building. He refounded the old city of

Mastia as New Carthage (Cartagena). It became the capital, the navy and army base, and the arsenal of the Carthaginian empire in Spain. All the important mining districts were now brought back under Carthaginian control. The mines of Spain helped the Barcids to produce annual revenues of between 2000 and 3000 talents, an enormous amount of money that enabled them to wield great power and influence in both Spain and Carthage.

Some Romans may have watched these developments with suspicion. They knew that the Barcids, who had been so successful against Rome in the First Punic War, controlled a growing empire in Spain, a small but modern navy, and a fine army. The latter was well equipped and undergoing intensive training in constant warfare against the Spanish tribes. On the other hand, before 220 B.C.E., most Romans were too busy with the wars in northern Italy to concentrate on far-away events in Spain. That could be left to their Greek friends in Massilia. It was closer to Spain, and its interests were more directly affected.

Long bound to Rome by ties of friendship, and probably a formal alliance by this time, Massilia shared a common enemy with Rome in the Gauls. Also, the expanding power of Rome's former Punic adversaries in Spain was threatening the trade that Massilia had expanded at Carthage's expense during the First Punic War. It was not unreasonable for the Massiliots to fear the consolidation of Carthaginian power in Spain. Carthage might then ally with tribes in neighboring Gaul to eliminate Massilia as a rival altogether. The Massiliots communicated their fears to Rome. The Romans would have understood how an alliance of Carthaginians and transalpine Gauls could have posed a serious danger to them in struggles with the Gauls on their side of the Alps. The Gallic tribes in the Po valley were becoming increasingly restless and may already have been seeking help from their transalpine cousins. Apparently, Roman emissaries went to Spain to investigate Carthaginian intentions in 231 B.C.E. and came back satisfied: Hamilcar explained that he was only trying to explore new sources of revenue to enable Carthage to finish paying its indemnity (presumably the one imposed in 238 B.C.E.) to Rome.

THE EBRO TREATY

Continued Carthaginian expansion in Spain under Hamilcar and then Hasdrubal evoked ever-louder complaints from Massilia. At last, in 226 B.C.E., when war with the Gauls of the Po valley and their transalpine allies was imminent, the Romans negotiated with Hasdrubal the famous Ebro Treaty. That treaty prohibited the Carthaginians from crossing the Ebro River with warlike intent but allowed them a free hand south of the river. Thus, the Carthaginians could operate unhindered in almost seven-eighths of the Iberian Peninsula. Massilia was guaranteed the security of its two coastal colonies lying between the Ebro and the Pyrenees and was not excluded from peaceful trade with Carthaginian Spain. The Romans could devote their entire attention to the Gauls on their side of the Alps. Massilia remained a strong check against those on the other side, who could expect no active help from Carthage.

HANNIBAL AND THE OUTBREAK OF THE SECOND PUNIC WAR

After Hasdrubal had brought almost the entire Iberian Peninsula south of the Ebro River under Carthaginian control, a disgruntled slave murdered him in 221 B.C.E. Hannibal, the eldest son of Hamilcar Barca, succeeded him. Polybius (Book 3.11.5–7) tells the romantic story, perhaps true, that Hamilcar, sacrificing at an altar before departing for Spain, consented to take along the nine-year-old Hannibal only after the latter took hold of the sacrifices and swore never to be well disposed to the Romans. Later authors said that Hannibal swore eternal hatred of Rome. That wording implies a more active hostility than does Polybius' version. It may represent postwar attempts to put all blame for the war on Hannibal and his family.

After the age of nine, Hannibal spent his entire life in the army. In ancient authors, he fits the stereotype of a good general: he ate with his men, dressed like them, and, covered only with a cloak, slept among them on the same hard ground. Whatever the details, Hannibal was an exceptional leader. For fifteen unbroken years, he commanded an army composed of Africans, Spaniards, Gauls, Phoenicians, and many other ethnic groups. They never once were known to mutiny or rebel. They followed him on long, fatiguing marches, across wide rivers, through swamps, and over the snow-capped Alps.

Upon succeeding Hasdrubal, Hannibal advanced northwest from the Carthaginian capital of Spain, New Carthage (Cartagena), toward what is now Salamanca. He conquered several tribes of the Upper Tagus and Douro rivers. Carthage now formally claimed all of Spain south of the Ebro, except Saguntum (Sagunto), a town perched on a rocky plateau overlooking the central eastern coast. It was a trading partner of Massilia and had become an ally of Rome sometime between 230 and 219 B.C.E. Since no mention was made of Saguntum in the Ebro Treaty of 226, Saguntum possibly became allied with Rome after 226, no doubt at the insistence of Massilia. In 219 B.C.E. Hannibal besieged Saguntum because of what he termed its unprovoked attacks on neighboring tribes subject to Carthage. After a desperate siege of eight months, the town fell. With its fall began the Second Punic War.

CAUSES OF THE SECOND PUNIC WAR

Although Polybius does make Barcid hatred of Rome one of the causes of the Second Punic War (Book 3.9.6–10.7), neither side seems actively to have brought it on. Between 238 and 219 B.C.E., both the Carthaginians and the Romans had adhered to the treaty of 241 and the Ebro Treaty of 226. The Romans' acceptance of an alliance of friendship with the city of Saguntum, south of the Ebro, had broached the letter of neither treaty. A step taken primarily to keep the goodwill of Massilia, it indicated no official Roman hostility toward Carthaginian activity in Spain. Still, some senators may well have thought that Saguntum could provide a strategic base of operations in any unanticipated conflict. At the time, Hannibal seems to have taken no immediate offense when Rome had ruled against a pro-Carthaginian faction in arbitrating a civil dispute at Saguntum. By not provoking Saguntum at that point, he avoided angering the Romans. After the war, the simplistic story that Hannibal and the Barcid family had been planning to attack Rome for a long time out of a bitter desire for revenge was a convenient fiction for both sides. The Romans favored it because it absolved them of any blame. Many Carthaginians promoted it because it allowed them to make the Barcids alone their scapegoats in dealing with the Roman victors.

Much more useful for understanding the outbreak of the Second Punic War, in 218 B.C.E., are the mutual fear and misunderstanding that forced the two parties into a corner and made them willing to support a new war when they reached an impasse in their relationship. Fear arose on both sides because Saguntum—encouraged by Massilia, Carthage's commercial rival in Spain—constantly complained to the Roman senate about Hannibal as he tried to advance his control up to the Ebro. In 220, probably to appease Saguntum and Massilia as well as to check up on Carthaginian intentions, the senate sent ambassadors to investigate the situation. It is unclear whether or not they pointed out to Hannibal that Saguntum enjoyed *fides* with Rome as Polybius claims (Book 3.15.5). In either case, Hannibal may well have feared that the Romans were now trying to use the Saguntines against Carthage, just as they had previously used the Mamertines on Sicily and the rebellious mercenaries on Sardinia. He immediately sent his assessment of the situation to the Carthaginian senate and asked for instructions. If his assessment was negative, the Carthaginian senate must have agreed, because his next act was to besiege Saguntum in early 219.

That the Romans had no immediate plans to use the Saguntine situation as a pretext for war against Carthage in Spain is clear. They were in the process of sending two consular armies in the opposite direction to deal with Demetrius of Pharos and the Illyrian pirates (p. 134). When news of Hannibal's attack on Saguntum reached Rome, the senate, preoccupied with Illyria, took no action. The fall of Saguntum in early 218, however, must have stirred up public opinion against Carthage: Roman prestige was badly damaged by the destruction of a city that had fruitlessly claimed the protection of Roman *fides*. An embassy of leading senators and the two consuls went to Carthage to demand the surrender of Hannibal unless the Carthaginians wanted war. Many may have expected Carthage to capitulate in view of its past actions.

The majority of Carthaginian senators, however, probably could not tolerate the humiliation of abandoning a commander whom they had supported. Resentment must already have existed over the way in which the Romans at the end of the First Punic War had imposed a treaty harsher than the one originally negotiated. Rome's perfidious seizure of Sardinia must have rankled even worse. Polybius makes it the principal cause of the war (Book 3.10.4). To give in meekly a third time now that Carthage was stronger would have been too much to bear, as Polybius indicates (Book 3.10.6). The Carthaginian senate chose war.

For numerous reasons, many Romans also favored war. There was probably a genuine fear, eagerly encouraged by Massilia, that the Carthaginians in Spain and the Celtic tribes in southern Gaul would eventually join against Rome. Also, as the *lex Claudia* of 218 reveals, a significant group of Romans now engaged in overseas trade (p. 170). With the revival of Carthage through expansion in Spain, Roman merchants and traders would have feared stronger competition and would have wanted to weaken Carthage once more. Finally, there were always ambitious aristocrats who sought to increase their prestige and power through successful military commands. Such men were the two consuls of 218, Publius Cornelius Scipio and Tiberius Sempronius Longus. Therefore, both sides accepted the challenge, and the Second Punic, or Hannibalic, War was on.

HANNIBAL'S WAR STRATEGY

Hannibal had a splendid army but not a big enough navy to assist it. Roman naval superiority was so great that Carthage could neither safely transport and supply large armies by sea nor prevent the Romans from establishing beachheads anywhere. The Romans' sea power permitted them to wage war on several fronts simultaneously and to invade Africa and Spain with several armies at the same time.

Hannibal's only strong base and source of manpower and supplies was Spain. He had only one really well-trained and reliable army. His sole chance of success lay in establishing a single front, preferably in Italy. So long as Rome was in danger, the Romans would concentrate the bulk of their forces in Italy. Only an invasion of Italy would enable him to seize the initiative. Only an invasion of Italy would render useless the great Roman navy.

By invading Italy, Hannibal also hoped to cut at the roots of Roman military power, which was potentially six or seven times that of Carthage. Only by wrecking Rome's system of alliances in Italy could he hope to paralyze and destroy that enormous war potential. Not coincidentally, the Gauls of northern Italy, only recently conquered, had revolted from Rome already and would rally around him. He hoped that Rome's allies in central and southern Italy also would quickly forsake their obligations and join him as their liberator.

ROMAN WAR PLANS

The Romans planned to wage an offensive war. Their naval superiority would enable them to seize and hold the initiative at once. They could choose the theater of military operations. The consul Publius Cornelius Scipio actually landed at Massilia with one army for the invasion of Spain; another army assembled in Sicily for the invasion of Africa. The decision to land at Massilia was theoretically good. From there, the Romans could either invade Spain or intercept Hannibal in Transalpine Gaul should he decide to invade northern Italy. They also could use Massilia's fleet for operations in Spanish waters.

HANNIBAL'S MARCH TO THE ALPS

Around the first of May in 218 B.C.E., Hannibal set out from New Carthage on the long march north to Italy. To protect his vital base in Spain, he left part of the Carthaginian army there under the command of his brother Hasdrubal (not to be confused with his dead brother-in-law). By late August or early September, he had crossed the Rhône on the way through Transalpine Gaul to the Alps. Scipio, who had been delayed by the revolts in Cisalpine Gaul, arrived at Massilia too late to intercept him. Wisely ordering his brother to lead the army into Spain, Scipio himself sailed back to Italy in order to lead the two legions in Cisalpine Gaul against Hannibal as he descended the Alps.

Scholars long debated where Hannibal crossed the Rhône and what route he took through the Alps. Now a combination of stratigraphic, geochemical, and microbiological evidence has lent strong support to the identification of the Col de la Traversette as the pass Hannibal took through the mountains. No matter which route he took, however, the journey would have been enormously difficult. His army is conservatively estimated to have included at the start about 30,000 infantry, 9000 cavalry, and at least 37 war elephants. To get it over the Alps under primitive conditions would have been a great feat even in summer. Hannibal did it at the start of the Alpine winter. His forces suffered great losses because of slippery trails, biting cold, and deep snows. Even worse were the sudden attacks of hostile mountain tribesmen. As he himself recorded on an inscription, only 20,000 infantry and 6000 cavalry reached the level plains of northern Italy in Cisalpine Gaul.[1] There, the Insubres and the Boii eagerly joined his army and made up for the lost men. After a short rest, his army met that of Scipio at the Ticinus River.

HANNIBAL'S EARLY VICTORIES, 218 AND 217 B.C.E.

The Battle of the Ticinus (218) was a minor cavalry skirmish, but Scipio was wounded. The result would have been more serious if Scipio's seventeen-year-old son, Publius Cornelius Scipio—the future Africanus, conqueror of Carthage, and victor over Hannibal—had not saved his father from capture. The father withdrew his army south of the Po, and the Romans recalled the other consul, Tiberius Sempronius Longus, from the planned invasion of Africa to reinforce Scipio. Hannibal's attempt to maintain a single front was succeeding.

The battle at the Trebia, 218 B.C.E.

By December of 218, the two consuls had taken up a strong position with 40,000 men on the eastern bank of the Trebia (Trebbia), a small southern tributary of the Po. Against the advice of the wounded Scipio, Sempronius was eager for battle. Hannibal easily tempted him into an ambush and annihilated three-quarters of the Roman army. The rich Po valley fell to Hannibal.

The loss of northern Italy infuriated those who had promoted the conquest and settlement of that region. They helped to elect Gaius Flaminius as consul for 217 B.C.E. He had subdued the Insubres and placed Cisalpine Gaul under Roman control in his consulship of 223 B.C.E. Gnaeus Servilius was the other consul. New legions were called into service. The new consuls were instructed to hold the line and, if possible, recover northern Italy.

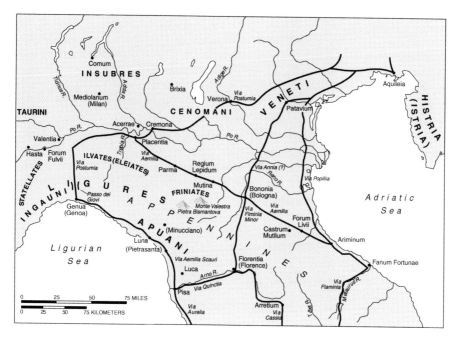

FIGURE 8.1 Northern Italy.

The Battle of Lake Trasimene, 217 B.C.E.

Always doing the unexpected, Hannibal invaded Etruria by a difficult, but unguarded, pass. Feigning a march against Rome itself, he lured Flaminius into a narrow spot between the hills and Lake Trasimene, near Perusia (Perugia). On a foggy morning, he ambushed the Roman army from the hills. Most of the 36,000 Romans were either killed or captured. Flaminius himself was slain. The same fate afterward befell 4000 cavalrymen whom Servilius had sent down the Flaminian Way, perhaps to support the legions at Trasimene.

The news of Trasimene filled Rome with fear of an imminent siege. The fear was groundless. Hannibal knew that the siege of a large fortified city without siege engines and a strong supply base would have been foolhardy. Also, the Romans still had field armies capable of intervening. Hannibal had another plan. He had invaded Italy in the hope of wrecking the Roman alliance system. Victorious battles were only a means to this end. So far they had produced satisfactory results only in the North and not in Etruria or central Italy. Hannibal decided to see what could be accomplished farther south.

FABIUS MAXIMUS, CUNCTATOR, 217 B.C.E.

The defeat at Trasimene, the fear of a siege, the daily meetings of the senate, the death of Flaminius (the people's idol), the eclipse of his faction in the senate, and the return of more conservative senators to power served to revive the dictatorship—an office defunct for thirty years—in the hands of Fabius Maximus (Quintus Fabius Maximus Verrucosus). He was a man of illustrious lineage and decidedly conservative views on politics and war. For some unclear reason, Fabius was not appointed by a magistrate with *imperium* (perhaps they were all in the field). He was elected directly by the Centuriate Assembly. Nor was he able to appoint his own master of the cavalry (*magister equitum*). Instead, the Centuriate Assembly saddled him with M. Minucius Rufus, a rash, impulsive, and headstrong person who always disagreed with Fabius' strategy.

Fabius' strategy included avoiding battles because the Roman cavalry was much inferior to Hannibal's. Fabius waited until Hannibal should inadvertently work himself into an impasse and be forced to fight under highly unfavorable conditions. Meanwhile, Fabius kept his army always on hilly terrain, where Hannibal could not use his superior cavalry to advantage. Fabius attempted to wear him down by constantly dogging his heels, hampering his movements, and preventing him from acquiring allies, feeding his army, or establishing bases. By this frustrating strategy, Fabius hoped to prevent Hannibal from destroying the Roman system of alliances.

Fabius' cautious strategy is to this day known as *Fabian*. In his own time, he gained the title *Cunctator*, "the Delayer." Minucius hated his caution, as did many others. The strategy of attrition is a naturally double-edged sword. It puts as hard a strain on the user as on the enemy. During the electoral campaigns of 217 B.C.E., popular speakers declared that Rome had not yet brought to bear its full force against Hannibal. They urged the election of men who would seek a speedy end to the war. After Fabius and Minucius duly stepped down from their posts, the newly elected consuls, Gaius Terentius Varro and Lucius Aemilius Paullus, expected to make short work of the wily Hannibal.

THE BATTLE OF CANNAE, 216 B.C.E.

The Roman commanders were overconfident in their superior numbers.[2] They marched south to engage Hannibal near Cannae, a small fortress town in Apulia. Having a smaller infantry force, Hannibal concentrated his Gallic and Spanish soldiers in the center and posted his heavily armed African veterans in echelon behind them, while his superior cavalry protected the wings. During the battle, Hannibal's center sagged inward. The Romans became trapped in a cramped pocket as they were outflanked by the Africans and cut off at the rear by Hannibal's victorious cavalry. Rome's loss was frightful. Only about 15,000 escaped death or capture. Many prominent men lay dead on the field with the consul Aemilius Paullus. Among those who survived were the consul Varro and two future Roman leaders, Marcus Claudius Marcellus and the young Publius Cornelius Scipio.

Marcellus and Scipio, along with about 10,000 of the other survivors, fled to Canusium. There, a wealthy woman named Busa provided them with clothes, money, and provisions at huge expense to herself. These supplies enabled the survivors to become a viable force for defending themselves and Canusium from the enemy. Later the senate honored Busa with a decree of thanks. The troops whom she saved, however, received no gratitude: Roman soldiers were supposed to win or die trying. The senate denied them their pay and sent them to fight in Sicily for as long as the war took. As for those who had surrendered to Hannibal, the senate refused his offer to return them for ransom. They were left to their fate.

FURTHER CARTHAGINIAN SUCCESSES

Never was the outlook brighter for Carthage than in the years between 216 and 212 B.C.E. The Roman allies were exhausted; some began to waver in their loyalty. Several towns in Apulia and most of Lucania and Bruttium went over to Hannibal. The big cities of Capua in Campania and Syracuse in Sicily revolted against their alliance with Rome and opened their gates to him. His capture of Tarentum in 213 was a major blow. Even some of the Latin towns and colonies began to complain about taxes and the terrific drain on their manpower and economies. More serious still, Philip V of Macedon, who was eager to drive the Romans from their bridgeheads in Illyria, had concluded a mutual assistance pact with Hannibal in 215 B.C.E.

THE ROMAN RECOVERY

After Cannae, the Romans returned to the Fabian strategy of attrition and the avoidance of set battles such as Cannae. They now began to concentrate on keeping their Italian allies loyal and winning back the cities that had gone over to Hannibal. The strategy was to prevent Hannibal from provisioning his army in Italy or obtaining reinforcements from Carthage. Meanwhile, the Romans vigorously prosecuted the war in Sicily, Illyria, and Spain. These tasks required the expenditure of enormous sums of money and manpower. A fleet of at least 200 ships had to be maintained. Twenty-five legions at home and abroad had to be fed and supplied.

With their enormous manpower and resources, the Romans not only checked Hannibal but also reconquered disloyal cities. Without an adequate navy to supply steady reinforcements from Carthage or Spain, Hannibal could not protect his Italian allies and keep an army in the field at the same time. He had to stand by helplessly and watch the Romans reconquer his new allies one by one. The Romans won back the Apulian cities and then laid siege to Capua. The fall of Capua in 211 B.C.E. restored all Campania to Roman control. Two years later, the Cunctator reoccupied Tarentum.

The siege of Syracuse

The year before Capua's defeat, Syracuse fell to M. Claudius Marcellus after a long siege. Syracuse had been able to defend itself with artillery and other devices invented by the renowned mathematician and physicist Archimedes. During the siege, Carthage gave Syracuse little effective support except for some feeble naval assistance. The city was finally betrayed from within. It was sacked after its capture, and its independence was destroyed. Its art treasures were shipped to Rome, and its greatest treasure,

Archimedes, was killed during the sack. After the capture of Agrigentum in 210 B.C.E., all Sicily fell under the Roman yoke once more.

THE FIRST MACEDONIAN WAR, 215 TO 205 B.C.E.

After allying with Hannibal, Philip V of Macedon attempted to seize the Roman protectorates and naval bases in Illyria and invade Italy with Carthaginian help. The Romans thwarted him with their superior naval power. They also created an anti-Macedonian coalition in Greece by an offensive alliance with the Aetolian League and other Greek states. Philip conducted four brilliant campaigns against the Greek coalition. Nevertheless, the Greek war kept Philip so occupied that he was unable to give Hannibal any effective assistance in Italy. A temporary stalemate in both Italy and the Balkans ensued. In 206, the Aetolians finally made a separate peace with Philip. The Romans were opposed to it but were forced to follow suit in 205 with the Peace of Phoenice.

THE WAR IN SPAIN, 218 TO 211 B.C.E.

Having failed to intercept Hannibal at the Rhône, the consul Publius Scipio had sent his brother Gnaeus to blockade Hannibal's brother Hasdrubal in Spain. After being defeated at the Trebia, Publius had joined Gnaeus and remained in command of Spain as proconsul. Together, the Scipios deprived Hannibal of any aid from Spain. They blocked the land routes, while the Roman navy, with aid from Massilia, controlled the sea. In 216 or 215, they actually defeated Hasdrubal near Dertosa, on the Ebro.

After that, many Spanish tribes went over to the Romans. The Carthaginian position further weakened when Hasdrubal was recalled to North Africa to suppress a revolt led by Syphax, an opportunist king of the Numidians. The capture of Saguntum in 212 was another blow. Then disaster struck the Romans. Hasdrubal returned in 211, recovered many of his Spanish allies, and mounted a three-pronged attack against the Romans. The Roman army was destroyed, and both Scipios perished.

SCIPIO AFRICANUS

The future Scipio Africanus, son and nephew of the slain Scipios, had been a military tribune who had survived Cannae and persuaded the other survivors to keep fighting. That plus his earlier rescue of his father at the Battle of the Ticinus had earned him a reputation for courage and leadership by the time he was elected a curule aedile for 213 B.C.E. In 210 B.C.E., the Romans were desperate to find a commander with the qualities needed to rescue the situation in Spain. The Centuriate Assembly, acting in conjunction with the senate, took an unprecedented step. Although Scipio was then only a private person, had held no rank higher than that of a curule aedile, and was a mere twenty-five years old, he was granted *imperium* and the rank of proconsul, and assigned to his father's old command.

In Spain, Scipio was careful to maintain the loyalty and harmony of his subordinate officers. He may have made some improvements to the Roman army. He is credited with its adoption of the well-tempered Spanish cut-and-thrust sword (the *gladius*) and the Spanish javelin. He probably required more drill and training than ever given to Roman legions in the past. His legions soon became efficient instruments of victory.

The conquest of Spain

After training his troops, Scipio boldly marched through enemy territory in 209 and captured the stronghold of New Carthage. The Carthaginian forces were too distant and spread out to oppose him. He was also able to take advantage of an unusual opportunity at New Carthage itself. The defenders had neglected the walls on the seaward side of the city, where the water usually was deep. A strong north wind, however, had pushed the water back enough for Roman soldiers to wade through and scale the walls. This piece of luck convinced Scipio's soldiers that he was divinely inspired, a belief that he eagerly encouraged. From then on they carried out his orders with blind faith.

With the capture of New Carthage, Scipio acquired a fine base, access to local silver mines, a number of ships, and immense quantities of booty, money, and weapons. He even liberated 10,000 Spaniards whom the Carthaginians had held hostage to ensure the loyalty of their compatriots. Scipio generously allowed the hostages to return home with a share of the booty. That act earned him much valuable goodwill among the Spanish tribes.

Hasdrubal escaped with most of his army after Scipio defeated him in 208. He then crossed the Alps to join Hannibal in Italy. With Hasdrubal gone, however, it was easier for Scipio to defeat the other Carthaginian generals in Spain, especially since they did not get on well with each other. Carthaginian power finally collapsed after the Battle of Ilipa in 206 B.C.E., in which Scipio proved himself a master of encircling tactics. Soon, the Romans claimed all of Spain as theirs. Even the ancient Phoenician colonies of Gades (Cadiz) and Malaga voluntarily became Roman allies.

THE BATTLE AT THE METAURUS AND THE DEATH OF HASDRUBAL, 207 B.C.E.

The years just before Hasdrubal's crossing of the Alps had not been good for Rome. With so many farmers in the army, agricultural production had declined. Many fertile districts had been repeatedly devastated. Famine was widespread. Had Rome not succeeded in obtaining some wheat from Egypt, the food problem would have been acute. Some of the Italian and Latin allies were so exhausted by the war that they refused to supply Rome with any more men or money.

If Hasdrubal had succeeded in effecting a junction with Hannibal's army, which was operating in Bruttium, Rome might have lost the war. Hannibal did move as far north as Apulia, but one of the consuls, Gaius Claudius Nero, barred further advance. The Romans intercepted Hasdrubal's message asking Hannibal to join him in Umbria. Claudius Nero left just enough troops to watch Hannibal and headed north against

Hasdrubal with the rest. Two Roman armies converged on Hasdrubal at the Metaurus River in 207. His army was destroyed, and he himself was slain. Several days later, his severed head was thrown into Hannibal's camp. Hannibal sadly withdrew to Bruttium.

Two other misfortunes for Hannibal followed. His brother Mago had escaped from Spain and landed at Genua (Genoa) with an army in 205 B.C.E. That same year, however, the Romans destroyed a Punic fleet bringing reinforcements and supplies to Hannibal. In 203, Mago was defeated and wounded. He withdrew to Genua, where he received orders from Carthage to set sail for home. During the voyage, he died.

THE END APPROACHES

In 206 B.C.E., Scipio, who had held only one office of the *cursus honorum*, had returned to Rome and had been elected a consul for 205. The senate debated how to end the war. Scipio wanted to invade Africa. He had already made a pact with Masinissa and Syphax, two petty kings of Numidia. Fabius Maximus, the Cunctator, leader of the senate, did not like the young upstart and his bold strategy. He vigorously opposed the African venture. Finally, Scipio obtained the command of two legions in Sicily, which included any remaining disgraced survivors of Cannae. The senate reluctantly granted permission to go to Africa, but not to draft troops. Scipio appealed directly to the people for volunteers for the African expedition. About 7000 enlisted. They, together with the two legions already in Sicily, made up the African expeditionary force. Fabius was certain that the expedition would fail. He did not take into account Scipio's extraordinary boldness, cunning, and charismatic leadership. Nor were those traits appreciated by the conservative-minded M. Porcius Cato (Cato the Elder). He had been praised for his efforts as a military tribune at the Battle of the Metaurus River. Then, as a quaestor for 204 B.C.E., he was assigned to Scipio in Sicily.[3]

In that year, Scipio landed near Utica in North Africa and immediately became involved in the quarrels of Syphax and Masinissa, both of whom were in love with Sophoniba (Sophonisba, Safonba'al), the beautiful daughter of Hasdrubal Gisco, the Carthaginian governor of Numidia. Syphax, the stronger of the two kings, won the hand of Sophoniba, deposed his rival, and allied himself with Carthage. Masinissa, now a king without love, land, or throne, found refuge in Scipio's camp.

Scipio had perfidiously entered into peace negotiations with Carthage and Syphax for the sole purpose of lulling their suspicions and learning the nature and disposition of their camps. One night, after learning what he wanted, he surrounded Syphax's camp and set it on fire. It was made of osiers and reeds. The fire spread fast. The Carthaginians, thinking that the fire was accidental, rushed out unarmed to help. Scipio then ambushed and destroyed both armies.

Masinissa then captured Syphax, returned to Numidia in triumph after winning back all that he had lost, and married Sophoniba. Scipio feared that Sophoniba might charm her husband into an alliance with Carthage. He insisted that she be turned over to him to parade in his Roman triumph. Masinissa did not dare to oppose Scipio but wished to spare Sophoniba humiliation as a captive. He provided her with a cup of poison. She proudly drank it.

The Carthaginians, imitating Scipio's guile, opened peace negotiations with him but recalled Hannibal (along with Mago) from Italy. After Hannibal's arrival in Africa, the peace talks suddenly ceased. The war continued until Scipio and Hannibal fought a great battle near Naraggara. It was a three-day march west of Zama, but Zama is the name conventionally given to the battle.

THE BATTLE OF ZAMA (NARAGGARA), 202 B.C.E.

Weak in cavalry, Hannibal hoped that his elephants would overcome the Roman legions. Scipio stationed the maniples of his battle lines directly behind each other. The light-armed *velites* were stationed between the gaps in the front line. They were to provoke the elephants to chase them down the lanes between the maniples. Some of the elephants panicked at the start of the battle and crashed into the cavalry of the Carthaginian left. Of the rest, some pursued the *velites*, and others turned and blundered into the cavalry of the Carthaginian right. The Roman cavalry wings were then able to drive off the Carthaginian cavalry and attack the flanks of Hannibal's infantry. They turned the battle in Rome's favor. Most of the Carthaginians were killed, but Hannibal escaped.

PEACE TERMS

Hannibal himself advised the Carthaginians to accept Scipio's unpalatable peace terms. In 201 B.C.E., Carthage was compelled to surrender all territories outside of Africa; to recognize the independence of Numidia and Masinissa's alliance with Rome; to agree not to wage war either outside of or within Africa without Roman permission; to reduce its fleet to ten light triremes or coastguard vessels; and to pay an indemnity of 10,000 talents, spread out in fifty yearly installments. The power of Carthage to challenge Rome was broken forever. Peace declared, Scipio returned to Rome and celebrated a magnificent triumph, which his rivals in the senate had petulantly tried to deny him. He also received the proud title of *Africanus*.

OVERVIEW AND REASONS FOR ROMAN SUCCESS

The Barcids had been able to restore Carthaginian fortunes through conquests in Spain from 237 to 221 B.C.E. They were not intent on a new war with Rome. The Romans were preoccupied with wars in Cisalpine Gaul and Illyria. Massilia, however, stoked Roman fears of a hostile alliance between the Carthaginians and Gauls. Roman worries were calmed by the Ebro Treaty of 226 B.C.E. In 218, however, Hannibal's destruction of Saguntum precipitated the Second Punic War. Hannibal's brilliant victories in Italy were not negated by lack of support at home. Carthage supported Hannibal and the war consistently to the best of its ability, which was limited by Roman naval superiority. Hannibal's failure in Italy was determined by Roman successes in Spain and the tenacity of Fabius Maximus, the Cunctator. Fabius' delaying tactics of harassment and attrition had utilized Rome's enormous reserves of manpower to frustrate Hannibal's main design of wrecking Rome's system of alliances. By delaying, Fabius saved the state (*cunctando restituit rem*, to quote Rome's first great poet, Ennius). Then, Scipio's guile and generalship defeated Hannibal and Carthage in Africa.

AFTERMATH AND THE FATE OF HANNIBAL

Hannibal revealed unusual talents as an administrator during his postwar career. After the war, the Carthaginian aristocracy tried to protect its wealth by corruption and by forcing the burden of paying the war indemnity onto the lower classes. The people turned to Hannibal, the popular war hero remembered for his fairness and good treatment of ordinary soldiers. They elected him *shophet*, judge, in 196 B.C.E.

Hannibal established a system of taxation based on income and ability to pay. He also made the government accountable to the people for its expenditures. Hannibal's financial administration was so efficient that in 191 B.C.E., only ten years after Zama, Carthage offered immediate payment of the forty remaining installments of its war indemnity. Rome refused the offer. Such a huge influx of revenue all at once would have been difficult to absorb. It seemed better to keep Carthage under continued obligation.

Carthage's commerce and industry revived as never before. Carthage again became one of the busiest ports of the Mediterranean. Nevertheless, Carthage soon lost the benefits of Hannibal's efficient administration. Powerful Romans became alarmed at Carthage's remarkable recovery. When Hannibal's political enemies accused him of planning another war, the Romans demanded his surrender as a war criminal. To save his life, Hannibal escaped from Carthage and took refuge in the East. Eventually, as the Romans added that part of the world to a then rapidly growing empire, they hounded him to death in 183 B.C.E. (p. 161). In the meantime, they focused their fears and resentments on King Philip V of Macedon.

NOTES

1 How many elephants survived he did not mention, but some did fight in his initial battles in Italy.
2 Estimates vary from 45,000 to 90,000 men. Somewhere around 50,000 seems reasonable. Hannibal had no more than 40,000, the equivalent of two fewer legions than the Romans probably had.
3 Some scholars date Cato's quaestorship to 205 B.C.E., but that is probably too early, and the story that Cato and Scipio quarreled openly in 204 B.C.E.. is probably an anachronistic reflection of their later public hostility.

SUGGESTED READING

Fronda, M. *Between Rome and Carthage: Southern Italy during the Second Punic War.* Cambridge: Cambridge University Press, 2010.

Garland, R. *Hannibal. Ancients in Action.* London: Bristol Classical Press, 2010.

CHAPTER 9

Roman imperialism East and West, 200 to 133 B.C.E.

The expansion of Roman power and territory up to the end of the First Punic War had been imperialistic to this extent: the Romans had sought to impose their will on others by force of arms or the establishment of alliances in which they were the dominant partners. Still, the Romans had not created what most people think of as an empire: a collection of separate or dependent territories subject to officials regularly appointed by a dominant external power to exercise supreme military and judicial authority over them. Nor had the Romans developed an attitude that they had a right to exercise such authority over anyone whom they chose.

A Roman magistrate's power to exercise supreme military and judicial authority and enforce obedience to it is summed up in the Latin word *imperium*. From it are derived *empire* and *imperialism* in English. *Imperium* was granted by a vote of an assembly representing the sovereignty of the Roman People and was the expression of the community's supreme authority over its individual members. With the acquisition of Sicily, Sardinia, and Corsica, the Romans had begun to extend the permanent operation of magisterial *imperium* over territories and people who had no hand in conferring it. Thus, they began to practice a more direct and explicit imperialism than they had exercised before. Eventually, they came to believe that they had a right to impose their *imperium* anywhere.

Still, the Romans had no consistent policy or program of overseas expansion. Their motives and actions follow a complex pattern similar to that which has been traced through their rise in Italy and their first two wars with Carthage. There is no single explanation for Roman expansion. Several factors operated at once. Sometimes one and sometimes another was more prominent. All interacted to reinforce each other.

PROVINCIAL GOVERNORS

The Romans first instituted direct rule over foreign territory when they created two permanent provinces in the western Mediterranean after the First Punic War. One comprised Sicily, the other Sardinia and Corsica. The Romans first attempted to govern Sicily by quaestors reporting to higher magistrates at Rome. Rome was too far away, however, and a quaestor did not have the power required to deal with such problems as defense and the maintenance of law and order. Only a magistrate possessing the *imperium*, such as a consul or a praetor, could do so. Accordingly, after 227 B.C.E., the Centuriate Assembly annually elected two additional praetors, one as governor of Sicily, the other for the combined province of Sardinia–Corsica. In 198, the Romans created two more praetors to govern the territories acquired in Spain at the end of the Second Punic War. After that, the primary meaning of the Latin word *provincia* (pl. *provinciae*) changed. It originally meant only the task to which a magistrate was assigned. Now, it became a defined territory governed by Roman officials.

The provincial edict

The Roman senate laid down the general principles concerning provincial administration. It left the details to be filled in by the praetor who governed a province. The usual term was only a year. On taking office, each newly elected praetor would publish an edict that set forth the rules and regulations which he intended to follow during his year in office. The edict also specifically stated the rules of procedure that he would apply in his administration of justice. These edicts varied little from year to year and were changed only under special conditions.

Duties and powers

The provincial praetor was assisted by one or more quaestors. They served as treasurers and receivers of revenues derived from taxes. Three *legati* (legates, lieutenants) of senatorial rank were appointed by the senate after nomination by the praetor. They acted as liaison officers between him and the senators. They also served as his advisors and often as his deputies. In addition, the praetor brought with him a number of comrades or young family friends. As members of his staff, they could gain insights into the workings of provincial administration. The remaining staff included clerks, secretaries, and household slaves. The praetor commanded the armed forces within the province, supervised the quaestors, and was responsible for the administration of justice in all civil and criminal cases involving Roman citizens. He also arbitrated disputes arising between the subject communities.

Inside the province, the powers of the praetor were practically absolute. There was no colleague of equal rank to oppose his decisions or acts, no plebeian tribune to interpose his veto in defense of private individuals, no senate to restrain his abuse of arbitrary power, and no popular assembly to pass laws that he had to obey. The provincials had neither the right of appeal nor legal guarantees to the rights of life, liberty, and property. Some cities had local liberties guaranteed in charters granted them by the Roman senate. Still, an unscrupulous governor could easily circumvent them. As the number of provinces grew, the Romans stopped creating more praetors. They began to appoint propraetors (officials with praetorian power) as governors of provinces. If particularly important military campaigns had to be conducted, even consuls or proconsuls (officials with consular power) became governors.

Theoretically, the provincials had the right to bring charges of misgovernment and extortion against a Roman governor after his term of office. During the second century B.C.E., such prosecutions were rare, however, and then only under the most unusual circumstances and for the most flagrant abuse. In time, the practically unlimited power of Roman provincial governors was dangerous to Rome's republican form of government. It depended on the willingness of individual members of the ruling aristocracy to respect the equal authority of their colleagues in times of conflict and disagreement. Men accustomed to almost royal independence abroad became impatient with republican restrictions at home.

ROMAN IMPERIALISM IN THE EAST

The Romans worked out a system of direct Imperial rule in the West. At the same time, they tried to assert their will in the eastern Mediterranean without acquiring permanent territorial possessions. Two local factors frustrated Roman efforts to establish a secure eastern frontier: the Imperial ambitions of kings descended from Alexander the Great's generals and the attempts of smaller powers to use Rome against them. Also, the Romans' own increasing arrogance, arbitrariness, and avaricious brutality promoted the chaos they abhorred. In the end, they could not avoid establishing permanent Imperial rule in the East, too.

The Hellenistic background

The empire created by Alexander the Great had originally embraced Macedon, Greece, most of Asia Minor, Egypt, and the entire ancient Near East, extending from the Mediterranean to central Asia and northern India. Alexander's death in 323 B.C.E. ushered in the Hellenistic Age. His empire soon fell apart in a struggle for power among his generals. None of them was able to establish himself as sole ruler and preserve its unity. By 275 B.C.E., three dynasties, descended from three of his generals (Antigonus the one-eyed, Ptolemy son of Lagus, and Seleucus Nicator), had established powerful kingdoms: Antigonid Macedon embraced Macedon and, from time to time, large parts of Greece; Ptolemaic, or Lagid, Egypt included Egypt, Cyrene, bridgeheads along the Red Sea and East Africa, Phoenicia, several islands in the Aegean, and some cities along the coast of Asia Minor and the Thracian Chersonese (Gallipoli Peninsula); Seleucid Syria laid claim to most of Persia's old empire, embracing the western and southern parts of Asia Minor, northern Syria, Mesopotamia, Persia, and, at one time, even northwestern India (Pakistan), Afghanistan, and Turkestan, in central Asia.

Among the minor Hellenistic states was Pergamum, in the northwest corner of Asia Minor. Under Attalus I and his successors in the second half of the third century B.C.E., Pergamum was enriched by agriculture and flourishing foreign trade. It blossomed as a center of art and literature and became a champion of Hellenism. Another important small state was the island republic of Rhodes, which lay off the southwestern tip of Asia Minor. Like Pergamum, it, too, was a brilliant cultural center. It owed its material prosperity to seaborne trade, which it guarded with a small but efficient navy.

In Greece, the once-powerful city-states of Thebes, Athens, and Sparta still maintained a precarious independence. There were also two political and military federations. One was the Aetolian League of small townships and rural communities along the north shore of the Gulf of Corinth. By 250 B.C.E. it controlled most of central Greece north of the Gulf. The other federation was the rival Achaean League. It included many minor cities of the Peloponnesus, but not Sparta, Elis, and Messene.

The existence of the small Hellenistic states depended upon the balance of power established among the three big kingdoms of Egypt, Syria, and Macedon between 277 and 225 B.C.E. If one of the major powers succeeded in expanding its influence and territory, the other two combined against it. Although none of the three liked this balance of power, it was the salvation of Pergamum, Rhodes, the Achaean and Aetolian leagues, and, toward the end of the century, even Egypt. When it was finally disturbed, Pergamum, Rhodes, the two Greek leagues, and Egypt repeatedly appealed to Rome to help restore the balance. They never dreamed that eventually all, both great and small, would become subject to Roman domination.

ANTIOCHUS III (THE GREAT) OF SYRIA AND PHILIP V OF MACEDON

While the Second Punic War was raging in the West, the balance of power was being disturbed in the East by two young monarchs, Antiochus III of Syria and Philip V of Macedon. As a youth of eighteen, Antiochus ascended the Seleucid throne in 223 B.C.E. The Seleucid Empire had already fallen into almost total disorder. By 205, however, he had completed the conquest of large areas of Asia Minor and had reconquered Armenia and northern Iran. He had even crossed the Hindu Kush Mountains into the valley of the Indus. There he received 150 valuable war elephants as a tribute. On his way back to Syria, he assumed the title of Antiochus the Great. His exploits were hailed throughout the Greek world as second only to those of Alexander.

In Macedon, Philip V was understandably apprehensive about the Roman attitude toward him at the end of the First Macedonian War (205 B.C.E., p. 146). To strengthen his position on the Adriatic coast vis-à-vis the Roman protectorates, he apparently acquired some additional Illyrian territory shortly after the war. In the winter of 203/202 B.C.E., Philip turned his attention eastward to an opportunity to restore Macedonian control over the Aegean. That had always been a major object of Antigonid ambitions in competition with the Ptolemies of Egypt. Egypt had enjoyed *amicitia* (friendship) with Rome since 273 B.C.E. during the war against Pyrrhus (pp. 109–11). It was now badly governed under the child-king Ptolemy V (Epiphanes).

In 203/202 B.C.E., Philip sought to acquire naval power by supporting the raids of Aetolian pirates in return for a share of their profits. He then used his share to build a fleet of his own. On the Greek mainland, he boldly strengthened his position wherever he could. He also reneged on his agreement to restore certain territories to the Aetolian League. The Aetolians asked the Romans to intervene in Greece again, but the latter refused. They were still occupied with Hannibal. Also, many Roman senators were resentful that the Aetolians had made a separate peace with Philip in 206 B.C.E.

Having acquired a fleet, however, Philip overplayed his hand. He was not content with attacking Egyptian possessions in the Aegean. He also attacked many free Greek cities, enslaved their populations, threatened the naval power of Rhodes, and seized control of the Black Sea trade lanes. The latter were of vital importance to the grain trade of both Rhodes and Athens. Rhodes declared war and persuaded Attalus I of Pergamum, an old friend of Rome, to do likewise. After a number of naval engagements, Attalus and the Rhodians concluded that they were unable to defeat Philip without outside help. They appealed to Rome and sent embassies to wait upon the senate in 201 B.C.E., only a year after it had rudely rebuffed the similar request of the Aetolians. Now, after the defeat of Hannibal, many senators were in a more receptive mood.

The Pergamene and Rhodian ambassadors did more than charge Philip with harming their states. They took full advantage of the hysterical atmosphere caused by the Hannibalic War and the bitter resentment engendered by Philip's opportunistic alliance with Hannibal after Cannae. They accused Philip of having made a secret pact with Antiochus III to carve up the foreign possessions of Egypt, which had aided Rome with food in the darkest days of the Hannibalic War. They even insinuated that the pact was ultimately aimed at Rome. Although this "pact" may have been a propagandistic lie to scare the Romans, it fell on open senatorial ears.

The Romans had used Greek allies during the First Macedonian War and used them badly. Roman prestige among those allies had suffered, and Philip had gotten off rather easily. Now was a chance to refurbish Rome's reputation by clipping Philip's wings in ways that would help Rome's friends, punish an enemy who had not suffered much before, and preserve the beneficial balance of power that Philip was now upsetting in the East. To show that they were serious, the senators voted to send an embassy of three men to make the rounds of the Greek East. They were to gain support for the conditions that the senate decreed Philip would have to accept to avoid war: he must not make war against any Greeks and must submit any disagreements with them to arbitration. In the elections for 200 B.C.E., P. Sulpicius Galba, who had commanded Roman forces in Greece during the First Macedonian War, succeeded in becoming consul for the second time. Macedon again was his assignment. The pattern of Roman expansion that was established in the fourth century in Italy and continued in the third century in Spain, Sicily, Corsica, and Sardinia was about to repeat again: the Romans' alliance with smaller states would bring them into conflict with a powerful rival, whom Rome would ultimately defeat and whose territory Rome would ultimately control.

THE SECOND MACEDONIAN WAR, 200 TO 196 B.C.E.

When Galba took office and proposed that the Centuriate Assembly declare war on Macedon, the proposal was rejected by those who controlled the top two classes of centuries: war-weary veterans and wealthy creditors to whom the state had not repaid money loaned to fight Hannibal. Philip, convinced that he had nothing to fear, ignored repeated warnings and attacked the Greeks more boldly. Now the senatorial leaders had to obtain a declaration of war at all costs. They placated the rich by paying off creditors with public land and mollified many veterans by exempting from service those who had served under Scipio. These measures and, perhaps, reports of Philip's stepped-up attacks were enough to obtain a declaration of war at a second vote of the *comitia*.

Motives and miscalculations

The last thing that Philip wanted was another war with Rome while he was expanding eastward. He probably thought that Roman interests in Greece were too slight and the Romans' exhaustion after the Second Punic War too great to make them choose war over peace if he called their bluff. Philip miscalculated. The Romans chose war, but not from any need for more land or alleged philhellenism (love of Greek culture). The Romans had shown no interest in keeping territory in Greece after the First Macedonian War, and they were conquering more than enough needed land in northern Italy and Spain. Moreover, Roman senators did not go to war out of love for someone else's culture. There were, however, many reasons why Roman leaders and even Roman voters would be willing to go to war once their immediate concerns were satisfied.

Those reasons aptly illustrate the general motives for Roman imperialism after the Second Punic War. As was so often the case, fear, pride, and revenge were at work. Although the Romans were not so greatly influenced by concern for markets and raw materials as modern imperial powers have been, economic motives also existed. Rome's maritime allies among the Greek cities of southern Italy and Sicily were very interested in eastern Mediterranean trade, which Philip was disrupting. At the beginning of the Second Punic War, the Romans had taken Malta, which Carthage had used to control maritime trade with the Levant and Egypt. During the war, access to grain from Egypt had become important for Rome. Also, as the *lex Claudia* of 218 shows (p. 170), many individual Romans were now involved in overseas trade. Such individuals would not have been reluctant to speak and vote in favor of a war that could improve their economic opportunities. Moreover, supplying Roman armies during a war could be a lucrative business.

In addition, the Greek East was the source of the most skilled and the best educated slaves. Galba had already profited handsomely from capturing slaves during the First Macedonian War. The Roman market for such slaves was growing rapidly. Another war with Macedon would also be the source of other valuable booty, which always attracted many Romans, noble and common. Furthermore, as the experience with Carthage had shown, rich states could be made to pay lucrative indemnities when defeated in war.

Overseas wars had also whetted aristocratic ambitions at Rome. The great military glory won by Scipio against Hannibal had given him preeminent *dignitas* and *auctoritas.* Publius Sulpicius Galba and those who would be eligible for consulships after him could hope to equal Scipio's exploits in another great overseas war. The huge armies involved in such wars also increased the numbers of ex-soldiers who could become useful clients in the political struggles of the Forum. Finally, the acquisition of rich and powerful friends abroad would increase the resources and prestige necessary for success in competition with other aristocrats. Those who advocated another war with Philip were probably not unmindful of those facts.

The first two years, 200 to 198 B.C.E.

The delay in gaining approval for the war meant that the campaigning season was almost over before Galba could assemble an army. Nevertheless, he went to Greece and established winter quarters to demonstrate Rome's commitment. In the course of the next year, Galba's good behavior and the Romans' determination persuaded the wary Aetolians to join in the new war. Athens, which Philip had earlier attacked, also joined. Other Greeks remained neutral and waited to see which horse they should back in an uncertain race.

Titus Quinctius Flamininus

In 198 B.C.E., the war took a dramatic turn with the arrival of the new consul Titus Quinctius Flamininus. Charismatic, cultured, and fluent in Greek, Flamininus electrified the Greek world with the slogan "Freedom and self-determination of all Greeks." With wider support, Flamininus maneuvered Philip from nearly all of Greece except the key fortresses of Demetrias in Thessaly, Chalcis in Euboea, and Corinth in the Peloponnesus. Philip, now confined to Thessaly, sought a peace conference with Flamininus. Although the two men understood and admired each other, the conference itself achieved nothing. It broke up over Philip's refusal to surrender the three fortresses, which he had inherited from his ancestors. Flamininus, however, was rewarded for his military success by being made a proconsul to continue the war.

The Battle of Cynoscephalae, 197 B.C.E.

The war was decided the next year at Cynoscephalae (Dog's Heads), a ridge of hills in Thessaly. The two armies were about equally matched. The right wing of the Macedonian army made a brilliant breakthrough on the Roman left, but the Roman right, augmented by a squadron of ten elephants, routed the Macedonian left before it could close ranks. The Romans gained the victory, however, because of a quick-thinking tribune. He detached some maniples from the rear of the successful Roman right and attacked the ponderous phalanx of the Macedonian right wing from behind. The greater tactical flexibility of the Roman manipular legion, not the elephants, proved decisive. Therefore, elephants did not become a permanent feature of Roman warfare.

Peace terms

Philip lost the Battle of Cynoscephalae and the war. He had no other army, Macedon was exposed to invasion, and peace had to be obtained at any price. The terms were better than expected. Flamininus and the majority of Roman senators did not want to destroy the Macedonian state (as the Aetolians demanded) now that Philip had been humbled. Macedon served as a buffer against the restless Balkan tribes to the north. Also, Philip might be a useful ally to Rome someday, perhaps more useful than the Aetolians.

Late in 197 B.C.E., Philip was compelled to recognize the freedom and independence of the Greeks; to withdraw all his garrisons from Greece, the Aegean, and Illyria; to surrender his fleet; to reduce his army to 5000 men; and to pay an indemnity of 1000 talents, half at once and the rest in ten annual installments. The infuriated Aetolians demanded the whole of Thessaly as their share of victory. Flamininus would concede them only Phocis and the western part of Thessaly. Even worse, he allowed Philip to make jokes at their expense during the peace negotiations.

Flamininus' proclamation of Greek freedom

In July of 196 B.C.E., Flamininus made a grand appearance at the Isthmian Games at Corinth. These games, like the Olympic Games, were one of the four quadrennial athletic and cultural festivals that attracted visitors from all over the Greek world. They would carry Flamininus' words back to their home cities. In the name of the Roman senate, Flamininus proclaimed the promised freedom and independence of the Greek states. They were to be subject to their own laws, without garrisons and without tribute. In joyous thanksgiving, Greek states struck gold coins imitating the famous gold *staters* of Alexander but bearing the portrait of Titus Flamininus. In some cities, he was even worshiped as a god. He was the first Roman to receive divine honors, a point not lost on other ambitious Roman aristocrats.

For a while, some of the Greeks, especially the pro-Roman aristocrats, enjoyed their newly proclaimed freedom enormously. As a Roman aristocrat, Flamininus understood and admired the aristocrats of Greece. He desired to perpetuate their domination of the masses. He knew little about the poor and cared less. He regarded their struggle for the cancellation of debts, the redistribution of land, and other social and economic reforms as subversive activity.

Aristocratic Greek friends even prevailed upon Flamininus to declare war on Sparta. King Nabis of Sparta had tried to increase the number of landholding citizens. They were needed to serve in an enlarged Spartan army and restore ancient Spartan glory. He had abolished debts, broken up large estates, distributed the land fairly, enfranchised the helots (Spartan serfs), and proclaimed liberty to captives and slaves. His kingdom had become a refuge to homeless exiles. Sparta had become a fairly strong power in a short time. It was, however, unable to resist the might of Rome. The victorious Flamininus reaped even greater glory, Roman soldiers carried off much plunder, and the Roman treasury received a hefty indemnity of 500 talents.

Flamininus and the Romans had no romantic notions about Greek freedom. Their concern was to keep Greece, with its strategic location and valuable manpower, politically fragmented and out of the hands of any strong power. Indeed, they expected that the various Greek states, as grateful clients, would follow Roman policy and preserve the status quo. They wanted hegemony, not the trouble and expense of direct rule. Unfortunately, there was always someone trying either to upset things within Greece or to take advantage of the Greeks from without.

THE AGGRESSIONS OF ANTIOCHUS III (THE GREAT), 196 TO 192 B.C.E.

No sooner had Flamininus pulled his legions out of Greece and celebrated a glorious triumph in Rome than the senate became alarmed at the activities of Antiochus III as he continued to reconstitute the empire of Seleucus I. While Philip had been occupied with fighting Rome, Antiochus had attacked and defeated the Egyptians at Panium in northern Palestine in 200 B.C.E. Seven years later, he concluded a marital alliance between his daughter, Cleopatra I, and the young Egyptian king, Ptolemy V. Then he began to annex the few free coastal cities like Ephesus still left in Asia Minor and Thrace.

The growth of Antiochus' power alarmed Pergamum. It had once formed part of the old Seleucid domains. Pergamum's new king, Eumenes II, decided to follow his father's example of appealing to Rome. In response to the appeals of Eumenes and some Greek cities in Asia Minor, the senate authorized Flamininus to negotiate with Antiochus in 196 B.C.E. Flamininus warned the king to keep his hands off the independent Greek cities in Asia Minor, not to cross the Hellespont (Dardanelles), and to evacuate all towns recently taken from Egypt. The king replied correctly that Flamininus had no right to speak on behalf of the Greek cities in Asia Minor. If, he said, the Romans would leave him alone, he would gladly leave them alone. The Romans were not yet ready to go to war. Still, influential men were laying the basis of future military action, which was eagerly anticipated and promoted by Scipio Africanus and his supporters.

Hannibal tries to help Antiochus

A year later (195 B.C.E.), Hannibal, forced into exile from Carthage (p. 150), arrived at Ephesus. In response to a question from Antiochus, Hannibal replied that the only chance for victory against Rome lay in the creation of a united front of all its enemies. Antiochus would have to come to terms with Philip V, with Egypt, with Pergamum—perhaps even make concessions. Antiochus thanked Hannibal for his sage advice and ignored it. He decided to ally himself instead with the little powers of Greece. That decision was extremely unwise.

159

THE WAR WITH ANTIOCHUS III (THE GREAT), 192 TO 188 B.C.E.

In Greece, the disgruntled Aetolians had become violently anti-Roman. In particular, the peace settlement of 197 B.C.E. restricted their favorite occupation, plundering their neighbors. They tried to enlist Philip's help in throwing off the hated Roman yoke. He, remembering how they had urged Flamininus to dismantle his kingdom, rejected their overtures. Antiochus was so ill advised as to accept their invitation. In 192 B.C.E., he landed in Greece with a force of 10,000 men and was promptly elected Aetolian commander in chief.

By such actions, Antiochus had triggered the responses that characterized Roman imperialism: fear, vengefulness, greed, and desire for glory. The Romans immediately made common cause with Philip against Antiochus. The Romans were now allied with Philip, Pergamum, Rhodes, the Achaean League, Numidia, and even Carthage. They easily defeated Antiochus at Thermopylae, a position historically impossible to hold (191 B.C.E.). One of those who contributed to the victory was Cato the Elder, who was serving again as a military tribune even after he had reached the consulship (p. 168). Antiochus managed to escape to Ephesus.

In view of the probable magnitude of further struggles with Antiochus, it would have been advantageous for Rome to elect Scipio Africanus, the greatest living Roman general, to the consulship. Unfortunately, Africanus had been consul in 194. He was not eligible for reelection until ten years later. The people elected his younger brother, Lucius Cornelius Scipio. They expected that Lucius would nominate Africanus as his legate and permit him to assume actual command. Lucius did just that. Early in 190 B.C.E., the Scipios sailed from Brundisium with a small army, took command of the larger army already in Greece, and began their march through Macedon to the Hellespont with Philip's active assistance.

The conquest of the East would have been impossible for the Romans without command of the sea. They secured it partly through their own tactical skill and the effective assistance of the Rhodian and Pergamene navies and partly through Antiochus' failure to utilize the talents of Hannibal effectively as a general and strategist. Hannibal had requested a fleet and an army to open up a second front against Rome in the West. Antiochus merely entrusted him with bringing naval reinforcements from Syria to the northern Aegean. A Rhodian fleet quickly defeated Hannibal. The Scipios' naval forces defeated Antiochus' main fleet a few weeks later. Having no naval opposition, the Roman army easily crossed the Hellespont.

Antiochus offers peace terms

In 190 B.C.E., Antiochus offered to abandon Thrace, break off relations with the Aetolian Greeks, and recognize the independence of the Greek cities in Asia Minor. In addition, Antiochus agreed to pay half the costs of the war. Six years earlier, Flamininus would have made peace with him had he merely agreed not to cross the Hellespont and not to attack the cities of Thrace. Now, his far more sweeping offers came too late.

Nothing would satisfy the ambitious Scipios short of the surrender of all Asia Minor north and west of the Taurus Mountains and payment of the entire costs of the war, terms that Antiochus rejected.

The Battle of Magnesia

The battle for Asia Minor took place near Magnesia ad Sipylum in 190 B.C.E. The Romans easily won despite the absence of the Scipios because of illness. Antiochus was hampered by poor generalship, poor equipment, and lack of coordination among the various units of his huge but ill-assorted army. At Magnesia, Antiochus lost the war, and the Seleucid Empire lost its power.

The peace treaty of Apamea, 188 B.C.E.

A peace treaty was finally worked out at Apamea in 188 B.C.E. The king was obliged to give up all his possessions in Asia Minor north of the Taurus Mountains and west of the Halys River, to surrender his navy, and to pay 15,000 talents, one of the largest indemnities exacted in ancient times. The Romans were not prepared to administer the vast territory that Antiochus surrendered in Asia Minor. They gave some of it to the Greek cities and the republic of Rhodes in return for their help. The lion's share went to Pergamum. Its original size was increased tenfold to an area almost equal to modern Great Britain's. The enlarged kingdom of Pergamum, writes Polybius, was now inferior to none.

The deaths of Antiochus III, Hannibal, Scipio Africanus, and Philip V

Antiochus III was assassinated after robbing a temple at Susa in 187 B.C.E. After Magnesia, Hannibal had escaped first to Crete and then to Bithynia, which was at war with Pergamum. He soon won a naval battle for his friend Prusias I of Bithynia, but Flamininus arrived in 183 B.C.E. and compelled Prusias to help him capture Hannibal. The still-defiant Carthaginian frustrated the plan by taking poison and dying as proudly as he had lived.

Earlier in the same year, Hannibal's greatest opponent, Scipio Africanus, also died under unhappy circumstances. Cato the Elder had never agreed with Scipio's aggressive overseas policy and unorthodox political career. He kept up relentless political and judicial attacks on Scipio, his family, and his friends. In 183 B.C.E., Africanus finally retired to his country estate and died a short time later.

Philip V had done comparatively well since his defeat at Cynoscephalae, although he did not reap many permanent advantages from his alliance with Rome against Antiochus. He received only a few paltry talents and the promise of a few towns in Thessaly—a promise that the Romans ultimately failed to keep. He did try, when it was almost too late, to cultivate good relations with the other Hellenistic states—Egypt,

Syria, and even Pergamum. He also changed the Macedonian constitution to permit the towns under his rule the right of local self-government. In that way, he could pose as the champion of the oppressed masses in Greece. At the same time, Philip set about building up the economic life of Macedon.

Philip's last days, however, were far from happy. He had put his son Demetrius to death on charges of treason, later found to be false. After learning the horrid truth, Philip was tortured with remorse. He could no longer sleep and fell an easy victim to illness. He died in 179 B.C.E., and his eldest son, Perseus, succeeded to the throne.

THE THIRD MACEDONIAN WAR, 171 TO 168/167 B.C.E.

The Third Macedonian War was caused partly by the reawakening power of Macedon, partly by the intrigues of Pergamum's King Eumenes II, and partly by the chaotic conditions in Greece after the dismal defeat of Antiochus and the Aetolians. Those factors gave convenient pretexts for war to ambitious aristocrats in the senate. They saw Macedon as their next opportune target after intervening wars in Spain and northern Italy had come to a close (pp. 165–8). Moreover, many senators were concerned that disorder in Greece provided tempting opportunities for the expansion of Macedonian power. After Flamininus' proclamation of Greek freedom at the Isthmian Games of 196, the Greeks thought that they were free to pursue their own interests and resume their old internal and interstate conflicts. The Romans had meant that they were free to live in peace in a world ordered to suit Rome's interests. Many Greeks, however, were not disposed to follow the lead of the Romans. They considered Romans barbarians, useful at times but still barbarians.

The first three years of the Third Macedonian War showed much incompetence on both sides. The Roman commanders made mistakes that a more resolute and daring enemy than King Perseus could have turned into disastrous defeats. Perseus' excessive caution and misguided hope that he could placate Rome without a humiliating capitulation prevented him from taking these opportunities.

Lucius Aemilius Paullus and the Battle of Pydna, 168 B.C.E.

Lucius Aemilius Paullus had been consul in 182 B.C.E. He accepted a second consulship in 168 only on the condition that his conduct of the war not be hampered by unsolicited and unwanted advice. He brought Perseus to a decisive battle at Pydna on the southeast coast of Macedon. This battle demonstrated once more, as did those at Cynoscephalae and Magnesia, that the phalanx was now a thoroughly obsolete battle formation.

Perseus escaped to the island of Samothrace but was captured a little later. In 167, Aemilius Paullus proudly displayed him along with other captives and huge amounts of booty in his triumphal procession. Rome profited so greatly from the confiscation of Perseus' treasury and the yearly tribute imposed on the Macedonians that all Roman citizens ceased to be subject to direct taxes. Imperialism could be lucrative.

ROME AND THE HELLENISTIC EAST AFTER PYDNA (168 B.C.E.)

No one in the Hellenistic East was able to mount effective resistance to Rome after Pydna. Those who tried to resist were summarily crushed. Those who did not only prolonged their decline.

Macedon and the Fourth Macedonian War, 149 to 148 B.C.E.

In Macedon, the Romans decided to try an experiment apparently modeled after the Greek leagues. They abolished the monarchy and replaced it with four independent republics—separate; partially disarmed; and deprived of the rights of alliance, intermarriage, or trade with each other. The Romans also made the royal mines and domains the property of the Roman state. They closed the royal gold and silver mines for ten years, forbade the export of timber, and exacted an annual tribute of hundred talents, half the amount of the land tax formerly paid to the kings.

The Macedonians resented their loss of unity. They had never regarded their monarchy as an oppressive evil. It was the symbol of their national unity. Hellenistic Macedon had more nearly resembled a nation than any other state in the ancient world. It was not a land of city-states like Greece or Italy; it was not a loose confederation of cities like the Achaean League; nor was it a multiethnic state held together solely by the king like the empire of the Seleucids. It was one people in ethnic background, language, religion, customs, and government. The Roman experiment violated the very nature and traditions of the Macedonian people.

It is little wonder, then, that within two decades the Roman experiment failed. Andriscus, an upstart pretender, probably the son of a cloth-maker, was able to convince the Macedonian people that he was the son of Perseus. They rallied around him. He restored the monarchy in 149 B.C.E., reunited the kingdom, and even overcame a small Roman army sent against him. After defeating him with a larger army, the Romans converted Macedon into the province of Macedonia in 148 B.C.E. Thus, they ended the political existence of Macedon for the rest of antiquity.

Greece and Epirus

The treatment of Macedon was mild compared with the punishment inflicted on others after Pydna. In Aetolia, the Romans lent troops to their supporters to carry out a purge of pro-democratic, pro-Macedonian activists. In Achaea, they deported to Italy 1000 of the leading citizens (including the historian Polybius). Their names were found among the papers that Perseus had neglected to destroy. For sixteen years, the Achaean hostages were kept interned without a trial or hearing. None was released until after 700 of them had died. In 167 B.C.E., the most horrible and revolting brutality was inflicted on Epirus. Rome had no legitimate complaint against it. Yet, seventy towns were destroyed, and 150,000 people were dragged off to the slave market, to the profit of Aemilius Paullus and his soldiers.

The worst was yet to come. In 146 B.C.E., Lucius Mummius arrived in Corinth to punish it for joining the Achaean League in a Greek rebellion against Rome. He turned his troops loose upon it, sacked it, and razed it to the ground. He massacred many of its inhabitants, sold many more as slaves, and shipped its priceless art treasures to Rome. Polybius' account of Mummius' soldiers using famous paintings as gaming tables did nothing to improve the Greeks' view of the Roman "barbarians."

After the destruction of Corinth, the Romans dissolved the Achaean League and most of the other Greek leagues. They destroyed the anti-Roman democracies and set up petty tyrants or aristocratic oligarchies in their place. Each city-state now had separate relations with Rome. The governor of Macedonia was empowered to intervene for settling disputes and preserving public order. In 27 B.C.E., Augustus finally made Greece a separate province (p. 371).

The Seleucids

Antiochus IV (Epiphanes), the third son of Antiochus III, came to the throne in 175 B.C.E. He tried to restore Seleucid fortunes, which had suffered badly after his father's disastrous war with Rome. In 168 B.C.E., he was about to take over Egypt. The Romans, freed by their victory at Pydna, intervened to save the throne of the Ptolemies, their longtime friends. The Roman envoy, C. Popillius Laenas, found Antiochus besieging Alexandria. He conveyed the senate's "request" that Antiochus withdraw from Egypt. When the king asked for time to consider, Popillius haughtily drew a circle around him in the sand and demanded a reply before he stepped out of it. Swallowing his pride, Antiochus prudently withdrew in the face of Roman might.

The Jewish revolt of the Maccabees, 164 to 161 B.C.E.

Antiochus IV had tried to turn Judea into a strongly Hellenized city-state as a buffer between Egypt and Syria. This program aroused some discontent among the Jews. Yet, no open revolt occurred until Antiochus tried to strengthen his position after being forced out of Egypt in 168. He not only stationed a garrison in Jerusalem but even converted the temple of the Judean god to the worship of Baal Shamin ("Lord of the Heavens"), a universal deity whom the Greeks identified with Olympian Zeus and Hellenized Jews with their singular god. Simultaneously, he revoked the decree of his father, Antiochus III, which had permitted the Jews to live and worship according to the Law of Moses.

A priestly landowner named Judas Maccabaeus and his brothers, Jonathan and Simon, aroused non-Hellenized Jews to rebellion. They gathered together an army and inflicted a series of defeats upon the king's troops. The Maccabees were aided by the death of Antiochus IV in Armenia late in 164 B.C.E. and by the subsequent disruption of the Seleucid Empire. They rooted out every last vestige of Seleucid rule in Jerusalem and restored the ancient temple state. In 161 B.C.E., the Romans saw a chance to erect a barrier to further Seleucid ambitions in Palestine and Egypt by recognizing the Jewish temple state as an ally.

Decline of the Ptolemies

From ca. 200 B.C.E. onward, the kingdom of the Ptolemies had been wracked by internal revolts and dynastic intrigues that kept it weak. Various Ptolemies maintained friendly relations with Rome to protect themselves from external enemies, as in 168 B.C.E. Eventually, Rome would intervene to prop up one favorite or another in the turmoil, often to the great profit of Roman politicians and moneylenders.

Rhodes

After Pydna, the hand of Rome fell heavily upon Rhodes. That old friend had made one mistake. Just before Pydna, it had tried to mediate between Rome and Perseus. It acted not so much out of sympathy toward Perseus as out of fear that Rome might become the unbalanced power in the eastern Mediterranean. Rome took offense at this attempted mediation. A praetor even proposed a declaration of war. It was defeated only after old Cato stood up and made a strong plea in defense of the Rhodians.

Although Rhodes humbly repented of its mistakes, it did not escape Roman vengeance. It was stripped of the territories given to it in Asia Minor after Magnesia, and the importation of vital shipbuilding timber from Macedon was prohibited. The island of Delos was given to Athens in 167/166 B.C.E. and made a customs-free port. The resulting competition from Delos reduced the income of Rhodes as a banking, shipping, and commercial center from about 166 talents annually to about 25. The loss of revenue from its Asiatic possessions and from harbor dues and banking crippled the finances of Rhodes. It had to reduce its navy and was no longer able to keep piracy in check in the eastern seas.

Pergamum

Eumenes II, king of Pergamum, who had done so much to place the Hellenistic world into the increasingly ruthless hands of the Romans, also incurred their wrath. Suspected of collusion with Perseus, he was punished by confiscation of territory and hounded by hostile Roman commissions sent to Asia Minor to gather evidence against him. Still, he had no other alternative than to remain subservient to Rome. When Eumenes died in 159 B.C.E., his brother and successor, Attalus II, followed the same policy. He also continued to promote Pergamum as a cultural and intellectual capital and maintained a Greek cultural offensive against the resurgence of native Near Eastern cultures. He was followed in 138 B.C.E. by Attalus III, whose parentage is uncertain. Like Louis XVI of France, he preferred his studies and hobbies to being a king. He did serious research in botany, zoology, medicine, scientific agriculture, and gardening. Having no direct heirs, he bequeathed his kingdom to the Roman People. His early death in 133 B.C.E. thereby closed the history of Pergamum as a separate state. It soon became the province of Asia, Rome's second eastern province.

ROMAN IMPERIALISM IN THE WEST, 200 TO 133 B.C.E.

After the Second Punic War, many of the same motives drove Roman imperialism in the West as in the East. In the West, however, the Romans often took a different approach to establishing control, particularly in northern Italy and Spain. There they actively sought territorial acquisition and gave land to thousands of veterans and settlers. In both northern Italy and Spain, people were still loosely organized in agrarian tribes. There were no large city-states or territorial monarchies that the Romans could manipulate to maintain hegemonic control. There was no sophisticated political elite whom they could co-opt and no shared body of concepts or values that could provide a basis for peaceful coexistence. Therefore, in those regions, the only way to achieve security, from the Roman point of view, was through outright conquest and direct rule.

NORTHERN ITALY

The Gallic tribes of northern Italy had periodically attacked Roman territory or sided with Rome's enemies ever since 390 B.C.E. Under the leadership of Gaius Flaminius just after the First Punic War, the Romans had begun to satisfy the need for both land and security. They systematically subdued the Cisalpine tribes and colonized the area that they called the "near side of the Po" (the *Cispadana*, as opposed to the *Transpadana*). This effort had been interrupted and undone by the war with Hannibal, whom the Gauls supported. As soon as the Romans were free of the Second Macedonian War, therefore, they began to settle the score with the Gauls of northern Italy. They founded colonies on both sides of the Po between 197 and 175 B.C.E. Small market towns and administrative centers rapidly sprang up as the many individual farmers who were encouraged to move north and take up land settled the area.

After the conquest and settlement of the central region of northern Italy, the Romans turned to the coastal areas. In 181 B.C.E., they founded a Latin colony at Aquileia, at the head of the Adriatic. It served as a springboard for the later conquest of Istria and the Dalmatian coast. During the late Republic and early Empire, Aquileia was one of the busiest shipping and commercial harbors of Italy (map, p. 114).

On the west coast, the conquest of the hardy but culturally backward Ligurian tribes was a long and difficult operation. There were several Roman defeats, some victories, and some notorious atrocities. By 172, the Romans had subdued both the Italian and what is now the French Riviera as far as the borders of Massilia. Roman and Latin colonies were planted on the northwest coast at places like Pisa. At the same time, 40,000 Ligurians were moved south to be settled on vacant public land near Beneventum in central Samnium (map, p. 114).

The building of many roads was equally important for the occupation and settlement of the North. After the final conquest of Cisalpine Liguria in 155 B.C.E., the wars ceased, and the use of the Latin language spread. Rome was rapidly consolidating its control over continental Italy.

SUCCESSES AND FAILURES IN SPAIN

The Romans had driven the Carthaginians from Spain in the Second Punic War. They stayed to prevent any other state from using it as a base for another attack on Italy. They were also influenced by tales of its fabulous mineral wealth and the remarkable fertility of its soil. They hoped to extract enough wealth from Spain to pay for the costs of its occupation, to recoup the staggering losses suffered from the Second Punic War, and perhaps to finance future wars as well.

The Romans encountered unexpected difficulties. Spain had no large self-governing states or kingdoms that could be held responsible for the collection of tribute or the maintenance of law and order. Also, the Carthaginians had claimed large areas in the interior and in the western part of the peninsula that they had never governed or even explored. The tribes living in these areas had long been in the habit of raiding the richer and more civilized parts of Spain now controlled by the Romans. To provide security for their recent gains, the Romans found it necessary to make further conquests.

Spain, however, was cut up by its mountains into thousands of small communities and as many separate clans. Communications among them were difficult. Access to them was practically impossible. The Romans could not conquer them in a few pitched battles, as they had conquered Macedon or Asia Minor. The Spaniards engaged in guerrilla warfare that Rome's conventional armies were ill equipped to counter.

Nearer and Farther Spain

For purposes of administration and defense, the senate decided in 197 B.C.E. to divide Roman Spain into two separate provinces known as *Nearer* and *Farther Spain* (*Hispania Citerior* and *Hispania Ulterior*). Normally, each was to be governed by a praetor but, in time of war and crisis, by a magistrate with consular power. The Mediterranean seaboard from the Pyrenees to a point slightly south of New Carthage (Cartagena) formed Nearer Spain. It was rich in silver mines but agriculturally somewhat poor. Farther Spain was roughly coextensive with modern Andalusia. It embraced the fertile Guadalquivir valley as far north as the silver-mining region of the Sierra Morena range. Neither province extended very far into the interior.

The costs of provincial administration and defense were defrayed by revenue derived from tribute and regular taxes. The tribute (*stipendium*) was imposed on all tribes, semi-urban communities, and a few municipalities such as Malaca (Malaga) and Gades (Cadiz). It sometimes consisted of farm products, such as wheat or barley, but more often of payments in silver or gold bullion or coin. Until 195 B.C.E., the amount of tribute varied from year to year according to the needs of the provincial government and the rapacity of the governor. As a rule, it was too high for primitive rural communities. It often provoked unrest and rebellion. The regular tax, on the other hand, was fairly low, being only one-twentieth of farm crops and payable in kind. All communities were required to furnish troops to the Roman army in addition to paying tribute and taxes.

In the year in which the two provinces were created, war broke out in each. The extortions and tyrannies of the Roman praetors were unbearable. The Romans, who had been welcomed as deliverers under Scipio, proved less tolerable than the Carthaginians had been. Even Gades and Malaca, finding themselves denied the promised status of allies, supported the inland tribes in the fight for independence.

Cato the Elder's pivotal governorship of Nearer Spain

As a praetor in 198, Cato the Elder had already earned a reputation for being an honest and effective provincial governor in Sardinia. Consul in 195, he was sent to restore order in Spain as governor of the nearer province (*Hispania Citerior*). With an army of 50,000 men, he was successful in stamping out the rebellion in his own province. He even subdued the region as far west as the headwaters of the Tagus. Still, his military achievements were not so outstanding or so permanent as his economic and administrative reforms. They applied to both provinces because he was the senior magistrate.

Cato did not reduce the tribute but set a fixed amount for each administrative district. Therefore, the people would know long in advance what they would have to pay. More important, he reopened the mines, which had been shut since the Carthaginian defeat. He placed most of them under public ownership and operation. They provided new income for the provincial administrations and employment for the poorer people living in New Carthage and other mining districts. Cato may also have anticipated Rome's need to finance the war brewing against Antiochus III (pp. 159–61).

Tiberius Sempronius Gracchus, 180 to 178 B.C.E.

Tiberius Sempronius Gracchus was another successful governor in Spain. He was the son-in-law of Scipio Africanus and father of the famous reforming tribunes Tiberius and Gaius Gracchus (see Chapter 12). As governor of Nearer Spain, he removed the causes of unrest. Founding many new towns and villages, he gave the peasants and workers in Nearer Spain good land for settlement. By 178, the people had become fairly content under the more enlightened policies of governors like Cato and Tiberius Gracchus. They remained relatively peaceful for over twenty years.

Revolt and the brutal Roman response, ca. 155 to 150 B.C.E.

Unfortunately, the corruption and outrages of many governors after Gracchus eventually became unbearable. The senate's efforts to check corrupt governors proved ineffectual despite the repeated appeals of the Spanish people. Frustration finally touched off a series of rebellions. They began in Farther Spain about 155 B.C.E. and spread to Nearer Spain in 153.

In 151 the consul L. Licinius Lucullus arrived to find that the rebellious tribes in Nearer Spain had come to terms with his predecessor. Eager for a triumph, he made an unjustified attack on a tribe that had not rebelled. The victims of his aggression agreed to terms and surrendered. Then, he treacherously massacred about 20,000 of their men. In the next year, with Lucullus' help and example, the governor of Farther Spain, Servius Sulpicius Galba induced some of the Lusitanians to surrender on generous terms. When they had laid down their arms, he massacred them. Cato the Elder, in 149, supported an effort to prosecute Galba. The effort failed.

THE THIRD PUNIC WAR, 149 TO 146 B.C.E.

While the Romans were trying to crush native resistance to their rule in the Iberian Peninsula, they tried to maintain indirect control over Carthage in North Africa. Their efforts led to the final and sorriest chapter in Rome's long history of conflict with that great city. Even after Zama, Carthage remained a busy industrial and shipping center. It controlled the trade between Africa and the Hellenistic world. With peace and order in North Africa, Carthage enjoyed a better market for its manufactured products than ever before. The crops grown on its farms and plantations were the envy of the Mediterranean world.

In an effort to please the Romans and cooperate with them, the Carthaginians had scrupulously observed all their treaty obligations. They had disavowed Hannibal and had supplied grain for the Roman armies on numerous occasions. They had helped Rome wage war against Philip V, Antiochus III, and Perseus by furnishing both military and naval assistance. Perhaps they would have remained on good terms had it not been for the ambitions and aggression of Masinissa. He unscrupulously expanded his kingdom of Numidia at the expense of the Carthaginians, whose hands were tied by their treaty with Rome.

Masinissa

The Romans had used Masinissa's small kingdom as a check on Carthage in the same way that they had used the smaller Hellenistic states to exercise indirect control over Macedon and the Seleucid Empire. The end result was also the same: the smaller power manipulated Rome and helped to precipitate a major war.

The treaty that ended the Second Punic War left Carthage in possession of many ports and trading posts along the African coast. Its home territory, however, was confined to what is now the northern half of Tunisia within frontiers known as the Phoenician Bounds. They enclosed an area of about 30,000 square miles. Masinissa, on the other hand, was permitted to occupy any land that either he or his ancestors had previously held. Another clause forbade Carthage to wage war without the consent of Rome. Masinissa, with Roman connivance, took full advantage of both clauses of the treaty.

One by one, Masinissa seized most of the Carthaginian coastal colonies. Not permitted to resist these aggressions by armed force, Carthage appealed to Rome, which sent commissions to arbitrate. These commissions sometimes decided in favor of Masinissa and sometimes left the dispute unsettled. By 154 B.C.E., Masinissa had whittled Carthage down to about 9000 square miles, one-third of its former area. In answer to an urgent Carthaginian appeal, the Romans sent out a boundary commission reportedly headed by Cato the Elder in 153 B.C.E. The commission left the matter undecided.

Before returning to Rome, the commissioners made an inspection tour in and around Carthage. The proud city—overflowing with wealth and luxury, teeming with fighting men, filled with arms and military supplies, and humming with busy shipyards—is said to have stirred in Cato an unreasonable hatred. The man who condemned Galba's brutal acts in Spain and had often opposed unjustified imperialistic adventures in the East demanded an unjust declaration of war against Carthage. Thereafter, he supposedly ended all his speeches, regardless of the subject, with the hysterical refrain *censeo Carthaginem esse delendam* ("In my opinion, Carthage must be destroyed!").

Motives for war

For some Romans like Cato, an irrational fear and hatred, not imperial expansion per se, may have been a motive for war against Carthage, their great enemy in two previous wars. Cato, as mentioned, had often opposed Imperial adventurism in the East. Again, however, economic considerations, though often denied, and the traditional aristocratic desire for glorious triumphs must not be underestimated. Cato, for example, had lucrative investments in shipping firms and companies engaged in foreign trade. (He used a dummy to get around the *lex Claudia* of 218 B.C.E., which forbade senators from engaging in foreign trade.) Carthaginians were the Romans' major foreign competitors in the West. Therefore, senators like Cato, probably with the support of many wealthy equestrians who had major interests in foreign trade, would have favored a new war against Carthage. Furthermore, only a short sail from Italy, Carthage was a major exporter of agricultural products to the huge Roman market. Many large senatorial and equestrian landowners could have been concerned about competition with the products of their own rural estates.

An even greater concern may well have been ensuring that Rome had unhindered access to sufficient food supplies. By 150 B.C.E., the population of the city had swollen to about 400,000. Food, particularly grain, from the easily accessible parts of Italy, southern Gaul, Sicily, and Sardinia probably was no longer enough to feed it. Having direct control over Carthage's highly productive hinterland would have been very desirable for ensuring that Rome's huge population could be fed.

Finally, in 152 B.C.E., Carthage had finished paying the huge indemnity imposed after the Second Punic War. The rich, fat goose was no longer going to lay golden eggs. Many Romans may have found it attractive to carve up the goose itself. Certainly, the general victorious in a war with Carthage would celebrate a magnificent triumph and contribute a vast hoard of plunder to the commonwealth.

There is no reason to doubt Polybius' statement that a majority in the Roman senate had been bent on war well before the event (Book 36.2.1). All that was lacking was a pretext that could decorously mask naked aggression. Such a pretext was conveniently provided as a result of Rome's tacit encouragement of Masinissa's unscrupulous seizures of Carthaginian territory. In Carthage, popular, anti-Roman leaders were exasperated by the aggressions of Masinissa and the indifference of Rome. They had seized power from pro-Roman oligarchs in 151 B.C.E. In 150, war broke out between Carthage and Masinissa with disastrous results for the Carthaginian army. Worse still, in waging war against Masinissa, the Carthaginians had violated the treaty of Zama. That gave Rome a convenient excuse for war.

Hearing that the Romans were preparing to send an army to Africa, the Carthaginians hastened to undo the mischief that they had done. They returned their pro-Roman oligarchs to power and executed popular leaders. Envoys from Rome arrived to investigate the situation. They obscured Roman intentions by vague replies when the Carthaginians asked how they could make amends. Meanwhile, the Roman senate, goaded by Cato, prepared for war, which the *comitia centuriata* finally declared in 149. The Carthaginians sent ambassadors to Rome to request peace terms. The ambassadors were told that Carthage would be permitted to retain its territory and independence. It had to hand over 300 noble hostages and carry out all future orders of the consuls. The consuls demanded the surrender of all arms and weapons. After the Carthaginians complied, the consuls grimly announced the senate's secret final terms: the Carthaginians must abandon and destroy their city and rebuild at least ten miles from the sea—a death sentence for people who made their living by commerce. The Romans probably calculated that Carthage would not submit willingly. It mattered little whether the city did or not. Either way, Rome would have a position of great superiority.

The siege of Carthage and rise of the younger Scipio Africanus

Beside themselves with fear and rage, the Carthaginians prepared to defend their beloved city. Supplies of food were hurriedly brought into the city from the surrounding countryside. People toiled day and night to make new weapons. Prisons were opened and slaves freed. Even temples were turned into workshops as the Carthaginians frantically prepared for a siege.

The siege lasted three years. Carthage was situated in an excellent defensive location. Its walls were enormously thick and strong. One of the junior Roman officers at the start of the siege was the man who became the younger Scipio Africanus, Publius Cornelius Scipio Aemelianus. He was the son of Aemilius Paullus and adopted grandson of the elder Scipio Africanus. In 148, he protected Rome's interests when the dying Masinissa asked him to arrange Numidia's future. He divided Numidia among the king's three sons to prevent a strong, united kingdom from taking the place of Carthage in North Africa. He returned to Rome in 147 B.C.E. to stand for election as curule aedile. He was only about thirty and ineligible for any higher office. A special law was passed clearing the way for his election as consul and placing him in command of the besieging army. The current commanders were criticized for incompetence and lack of discipline.

The young consul finally took Carthage by storm in the spring of 146 B.C.E. For six days and nights, the struggle raged inside the city from street to street, from house to house, until the old city was in flames. All survivors were enslaved, the site was cursed, and Carthage's territory became the province of Africa.[1]

According to the historian Polybius, who was there, Scipio wept at the final destruction of the once-magnificent city. He wept not for the suffering of the Carthaginians, which he was only too happy to inflict. Rather, he reflected that Rome might someday suffer a similar fate. At the time, however, Rome was invincible. Scipio had just conquered Rome's newest province. He would return home in glory as the new Scipio Africanus, Rome's most admired citizen.

THE VIRIATHIC AND NUMANTINE WARS IN SPAIN, 151 TO 133 B.C.E.

At the same time that Scipio was destroying Carthage, wars of resistance in the Spanish provinces were still raging. In Farther Spain (*Hispania Ulterior*), the Lusitanians found a skillful and inspiring leader by the name of Viriathus. He was a shepherd and a hunter who had escaped the massacre perpetrated by Galba (p. 168). He knew intimately the mountains, glens, and winding paths through which he led 10,000 guerrilla soldiers. For eight years, Viriathus and his followers held the Romans at bay and cut down one army after another.

In 141 B.C.E., Viriathus trapped a Roman army of 50,000 men. He spared them in return for a treaty respecting the freedom and independence of his people. The Romans cynically broke the treaty in the following year and renewed the war. The new Roman commander bribed two traitors to slit the throat of the sleeping Viriathus. The Lusitanians, left without a leader, submitted to Rome. Some of the captives were forced to go with Roman veterans to found a Latin colony at Valentia (Valencia). There they could not easily resist Roman authority again.

The siege of Numantia

Meanwhile, Viriathus had inspired an uprising of Celtiberian tribes in Nearer Spain (*Hispania Citerior*). The war was particularly fierce around the fortress town of Numantia. Even for its small garrison of about 4000 men, Numantia was easy to defend. It was on a hill at the junction of two rivers that flowed between deeply cut banks through thickly wooded valleys. The commander besieging Numantia in 137 B.C.E. was C. Hostilius Mancinus. His army of 20,000 was caught in an ambush by a much smaller Celtiberian force. Tiberius Sempronius Gracchus, son of the former governor of the same name, was a young officer among the Roman captives. Relying on the goodwill created by his father, Tiberius negotiated a treaty with the Numantines. This treaty saved a large Roman army from utter destruction. In the next year, after the men had been released on good faith, the senate, which had to approve Tiberius' treaty for it to be binding, refused to accept the terms and renewed the war. That act had major implications for Tiberius' later career as a popular tribune.

In 134 B.C.E., after several more defeats, the Romans sent to Spain the best general of the time, Scipio Aemilianus, the destroyer of Carthage. He had helped to block Tiberius' treaty in order to gain another opportunity to earn military glory and prestige. He revitalized the demoralized Roman army and surrounded Numantia with fortifications. During 133, he starved Numantia into unconditional surrender and set the town on fire. Thus, he earned a new triumph and an additional cognomen, *Numantinus*. He had made Rome supreme in the West.

OVERVIEW AND ASSESSMENT

After the First Punic War, Rome had developed a system of direct rule over Sicily and Sardinia–Corsica. The Romans had no desire to extend this system to the Hellenistic Greek East. During the Second Punic War, however, Philip V of Macedon had touched off the inconclusive First Macedonian War (215–205 B.C.E.). Afterward, Rome and the smaller Greek powers attempted to use each other to maintain a precarious balance of power among Macedon, Syria, and Egypt. That attempt resulted in three more Macedonian wars (200–196, 171–168, and 149–148 B.C.E.) and a war with Antiochus III of Syria (192–188 B.C.E.). Between 148 and 146, Rome made Macedon into a province and placed Greece under its governor's watchful eye. In the meantime, Syria slowly crumbled, dynastic struggles weakened Egypt, and Rome undercut the smaller powers when they showed any independence of action.

The Romans often pursued imperialism more directly in the West during this period. They successfully resumed the conquest of northern Italy. At the same time, they fought to subdue Spain after taking it from Carthage. Corrupt and oppressive governors often undid the work of responsible ones and drove Spanish tribes to long and bitter uprisings.

All the while, the Romans tried to check and weaken Carthage by favoring Masinissa's Numidian kingdom in North Africa. Driven to desperation, the Carthaginians went to war once more. Carthage finally fell to the troops of Scipio Aemilianus after a brutal siege from 149 to 146 B.C.E. The former territory of Carthage then became the Roman province of Africa.

Finally, the destruction of Numantia in Spain and the inheritance of Attalus' kingdom of Pergamum in Asia Minor in 133 B.C.E. terminated the remarkable period of a little less than seventy years during which Rome had acquired Imperial control over much of the Mediterranean world. By the end of that period, many Romans may well have believed that their *imperium* was, as Vergil later phrased it, *sine fine*, "without limit" (*Aeneid*, 1.279). Imposing Roman *imperium* was often a brutal process. Subjugating others, particularly those of different cultural backgrounds, often produces brutality. Such brutality certainly was not unprecedented in Roman history. The destructions of Alba Longa and Veii, for example, were prominently featured in patriotic, historical tradition. Nevertheless, the level of brutality that Roman commanders used against both highly civilized and less civilized peoples seem to have increased as Rome expanded abroad. Even the ancient historian Appian (Book 6.10.60) commented on the paradoxically barbarous brutality of the Romans, who later justified their imperialism by touting it as a civilizing force.

Many factors combined to increase the Romans' use of mass enslavements, wholesale massacres, and total destruction to subdue their adversaries: frustration that other people would not conform to Roman preconceptions of peace and order, Roman leaders' desire for glory, the need to keep abreast of political rivals in wealth, and the profits that accrued to Romans in general from successful wars. An increase in brutality against non-Romans, however, was not the only change produced by Rome's Imperial expansion. The changes produced in Rome's internal life were even greater and often equally lamentable. The following chapters will treat them in detail.

NOTE

1   Orosius (fifth century C.E.) exaggerated the ritual acts of cursing into the story that the whole city was sown with salt and plowed into oblivion. Actually, the ruins remained visible for generations afterward: in fact, Plutarch says that Marius once sat among them. They remained on such an immense scale that for centuries the old walls, temples, and other buildings were a quarry of ready-dressed stone. Far more thorough agents of demolition, therefore, than Scipio's soldiers were the builders of Roman Carthage, which was founded on the Punic site in 28 B.C.E., and the insatiable stone hunters of later centuries.

SUGGESTED READING

Champion. C. *Roman Imperialism: Readings and Sources*. Oxford: Blackwell, 2004.

Eckstein, A. M. *Rome Enters the Greek East: From Anarchy to Hierarchy in the Hellenistic Mediterranean*. Malden, MA: Wiley-Blackwell, 2008.

Gruen, E. S. *The Hellenistic World and the Coming of Rome*. Berkeley, Los Angeles, and London: University of California Press, 1984.

Harris, W. V. *War and Imperialism in Republican Rome, 327–70 B.C.* Oxford and New York: Oxford University Press, 1984.

CHAPTER 10

The transformation of Roman life, 264 to 133 B.C.E.

By intimidation and conquest, the Roman Republic had established its dominion over the Mediterranean world. Thus, it furthered the consolidation that began with Alexander the Great and continued under the Hellenistic monarchies. In less than a century and a half since the outbreak of the First Punic War, Rome had passed from city-state to empire. Zama (202 B.C.E.), Cynoscephalae (197 B.C.E.), Magnesia (190 B.C.E.), and Pydna (168 B.C.E.) mark Rome's triumphs on three continents. The Romans commanded obedience from many peoples. Vast streams of gold, silver, slaves, and other booty or tribute flowed into Roman hands. Roman cultural life became much more varied and sophisticated. At the same time, world conquest and expansion had begun to work revolutionary effects upon the economic, social, political, and ethical life of the Roman People. Those changes set the stage for the destruction of the Republic itself.

THE IMPACT OF WAR AND OVERSEAS EXPANSION ON SMALL FARMERS

The material and human losses suffered in the Second Punic War and subsequent wars of conquest were enormous. The prevailing view has been that those losses and the importation of cheap overseas grain, a great influx of slaves, and the rise of large, slave-worked villa estates had a disastrous result: they devastated the ranks of the small farmers who served in Roman and allied armies. New research paints a very different picture and explains the ultimate impoverishment of many small landholders by 133 B.C.E. in a surprisingly different way. First of all, large numbers of slaves were already in the rural labor force by 264 B.C.E. (p. 116). Even many of the relatively modest land-owners in the third census class appear to have owned at least one slave by the time of the Second Punic War. At that time, the senate required each member of this class to supply one slave to row in the navy. Men in the first and second classes had to supply more. The large numbers of slaves taken in the wars of the early second century B.C.E. probably did not much more than make up for the ones who had died or disappeared during the Second Punic War or who were freed for loyal service to Rome in the war.

Archaeological evidence indicates that the growth of large, slave-worked villa estates in the second century B.C.E. was both more limited and older than once thought. The trend toward such estates had already started in southern Etruria, northern Latium, and Campania during the third century B.C.E. It continued in the second century B.C.E., but the great growth was in the first century B.C.E. Moreover, these estates are often mis-named *latifundia* (sing. *latifundium*). That term came into use only in the first century C.E. It seems to refer to the practice of creating far-flung holdings that were too big to use slave labor efficiently and relied more on tenant farmers, *coloni* (sing. *colonus*).

The devastation of southern Italy in the Second Punic War was significant. Also, large tracts of public land (*ager publicus*) in that region were acquired through con-fiscations aimed at punishing those who had sided with Hannibal. This situation did encourage the growth of estates that specialized in stock-raising in areas like Apulia to provide meat for the growing Roman market. Nevertheless, small farmers survived in the region, too.

In the North, particularly in Cisalpine Gaul, the Romans also acquired huge tracts of *ager publicus*. Small allotments of public land were distributed to over 200,000 set-tlers and colonists from 201 to ca. 180 B.C.E. One of the reasons why such distributions ceased after ca. 180 is that it was hard to find new settlers. Many people preferred to find new opportunities in the booming economies of growing cities like Puteoli, Pompeii, Ostia, and especially Rome. According to one estimate, an average of 7000 freeborn citizens migrated from the countryside to Rome alone each year during the last two centuries B.C.E. That number was necessary to make up for the large excess of deaths over births in the urban population and still have enough left over for a net growth rate.

Nevertheless, there is no doubt that Rome's wars from 200 to 133 B.C.E. took a sig-nificant toll in deaths from the Roman and Italian population, primarily from families of small and medium-sized farmers. Solid statistics are lacking, but extrapolations from ancient casualty figures, the size of Roman armies in this period, and mortality rates from comparable premodern populations allow scholars to make reasonable deduc-tions. A good recent estimate places the excess deaths of young men from military service over those from natural mortality between ca. 279,000 and 320,000. Still, the population grew enough to keep up the steady migration to the cities. At the same time, except during unpopular wars in Spain toward the end of this period, Roman recruiters seem to have had little difficulty in finding *assidui*, men who owned enough property to qualify for service in the legions.

The view that the number of *assidui* was actually declining hinges on arguments that the minimum amount of land necessary for being an *assiduus* was progressively lowered during this period. These arguments are based on figures used to show that the monetary value of the minimum amount of land required progressively declined. It is not clear, however, in what chronological order these figures should be arranged. Even if they should be arranged progressively lower, they might not reflect a reduction in the amount of land required. They might reflect only the rising value of Rome's bronze coinage in periods when the amount of bronze for making coins was scarce because of wartime shortages. They might also reflect the falling value of land after large-scale Roman confiscations of land in Italy.

More important, except in times of extreme crisis, as in the Second Punic War after Cannae, the Romans drafted primarily young unmarried men ranging in age from seventeen to mid-twenties. These young men usually represented surplus rural labor. Their removal for extended periods of military service did not mean undue hardship for their birth families. For one thing, families did not have to grow food for those heavy-eating young men. Moreover, the pay that soldiers received and the bonuses and shares of booty awarded by victorious commanders were an economic benefit to their families.

Also, men usually did not marry until their late twenties or early thirties (p. 56). Military service in their earlier years did not take men away from wives and young families who would have needed their labor most. Many men would have finished their expected military service before they were ready to marry and start families of their own. Experienced soldiers who did marry before they had finished active military service were less likely to be killed in battle than their younger unmarried comrades. They would have been stationed as *principes* or *triarii* in the second and third lines of heavy infantry (pp. 111–12). The *principes* fought only after the younger *velites* and *hastati* had already weakened the enemy. The *triarii* were less likely to have to fight at all, and they made up only about 15 percent of the total infantry force.

Although it would have been cold comfort to those who lost loved ones, the deaths of largely unmarried young men in Rome's wars actually had a beneficial economic effect on the class of small farmers as a whole. Any remaining siblings would have inherited more family property. They then would have been better able to support themselves or to attract well-off spouses than they would have otherwise. Thus, newly formed families would have had more land at their disposal. Similarly, if the death of a soldier ultimately left a family with no direct heir, its land would pass to relatives. Their land would thereby have been increased to their benefit. Overall, ca. 300,000 extra male deaths because of wars meant that small family farms were less likely to be subdivided into units too small to support new families. Also, competition for access to public land to supplement small private holdings would have been less intense. As a result, the ability of Italy's small farmers to support themselves and their families improved and encouraged them to have bigger families.

In the period from 200 to 125 B.C.E., the number of freeborn citizens living in Rome seems to have increased by ca. 100,000. The census figures for freeborn men had increased by ca. 181,000 at the end of that period. Despite declines in some parts of Italy, the rural population as a whole was reproducing at a rate high enough to sustain losses incurred in war, supply a steady stream of migrants to Rome, and still show a significant growth in its own ranks. By the end of this period, however, such growth began to have negative consequences for small holders. The rural population had grown to the point where many small holdings were being subdivided into unacceptably small parcels. Also, enough *ager publicus* was no longer available in the face of increased demand to provide families with the extra land that they would have needed to produce enough to feed themselves. Therefore, they had to find other strategies than subsistence farming to survive. The emerging money economy encouraged some to grow high-value, labor-intensive crops on small plots near urban markets, or to earn wages as seasonal workers from larger landowners, or to seek economic opportunities as laborers or independent craftsmen in the growing cities.

COINAGE AND THE MONETIZATION OF THE ECONOMY

The wars from 264 to 133 B.C.E. were responsible for creating Rome's system of coinage and monetizing the economy of Italy. Rome needed to pay the hundreds of thousands of soldiers who served in these wars. The booty, indemnities, tribute, and mines acquired during imperial expansion provided the metals that ultimately permitted the creation of a stable silver and bronze coinage. Millions of silver and bronze coins of small size and modest value were paid to Roman and allied soldiers from throughout Italy. Thus, coins useful for everyday transactions came into wide circulation. They rapidly spread the use of money among the general populace. So also did the great sums spent on building projects and public works. This construction boom was fueled by the huge surpluses over and above military expenses that flowed into the Roman treasury and the hands of victorious generals.

Initially, the strains of the First and Second Punic wars caused a complete collapse of Rome's coinage around 212 B.C.E. A new system then emerged. The bronze *as* was reduced to two ounces, one-sixth (*sextans*) of a Roman pound. The didrachm, which had come to be called a "tenner," *denarius* (pl. *denarii*), because it was worth ten *asses*, was gradually reduced in weight to an official standard of seventy-two to a pound and sometimes as many as eighty. A half a *denarius* was a "fiver," *quinarius* (pl. *quinarii*), and a quarter of a *denarius* was a "half-again," *sestertius* (pl. *sestertii*), abbreviated HS. By 200 B.C.E., the *as* was down to only one ounce, and the *quinarius* and *sestertius* had disappeared. The *sestertius*, however, remained an abstract notion of value. In fact, like the dollar in the modern United States, it became the Republic's principal unit of account. In 187, the *denarius* was lightened so that eighty-four equaled a pound of silver. That kept new *denarii* equal in weight and intrinsic value to the millions of worn ones then in circulation. In 141 B.C.E., the bronze *asses* in circulation had become so worn that the value of the *denarius* was recalculated to equal sixteen *asses*. Four *asses* were now reckoned as a notional *sestertius*, and four notional *sestertii* equaled a *denarius*.

Large sums were sometimes expressed in terms of talents. One talent equaled 6000 *denarii* or 24,000 *sestertii*. To give some idea of what these monetary units were worth, a *denarius* was about the average daily wage of a hired laborer.

THE GROWTH OF TRADE, CITIES, INDUSTRY, AND COMMERCE

Rome's conquests and its political domination of the Mediterranean increasingly gave efficient slave-worked estates in Italy access to overseas markets. As early as 167 B.C.E., Italian wine and oil were exported to Delos and other places in the Greek East. The chief market for Italian farm products, however, was western and northern Europe. In Gaul, a six-gallon jug of wine cost as much as a slave. Exporting wine to Gaul must have been a very lucrative business, and it began surprisingly early. The remains of a Greek ship, which sank probably around 230 B.C.E., have been discovered among a group of islands south of Marseilles. It was laden with Campanian tableware and about 10,000 large jars of wine. Some of it was Greek, but most was red Latian produced on the Sabine hills.

In Italy, abundant supplies of grain came from overseas. They made possible the concentration of people in large urban centers with access to water transport, particularly Rome. Land once used to grow grain within short distances from the city now could be used to produce a great variety of higher-value items to be sold for cash in the increasingly monetized urban markets. Both villa estates and smaller farms could supply these markets with wine, olives, fresh fruits and vegetables, flowers, young meat animals, poultry, eggs, and cheese. Money from the sale of these products then could be used to purchase goods and services produced by the urban population.

Growth of the urban economy

Although agriculture always dominated the ancient economy, the rapid growth of Rome and other urban centers in Italy greatly expanded opportunities in small service businesses, handcrafts, and trades: wine bars, fast-food shops, butcher shops, barbershops, fulling and dyeing shops, bakeries, pottery making, metalworking, shoemaking, furniture making, carting, and the building trades. The construction of roads, bridges, aqueducts, sewers, temples and other public buildings, large private homes, apartment blocks (*insulae*), warehouses, and baths provided bigger opportunities for investors, builders, and suppliers. The manufacturing of bricks, roof tiles, and fine pottery became big business on rural estates near urban markets. Supplying timber, firewood, charcoal, and quarried stone was very profitable. So were shipbuilding; shipping; and the supplying of crates, baskets, and large clay amphorae as shipping containers.

Tax farming and other public contracts

Even more lucrative were public contracts for farming (collecting) taxes, supplying the legions, working state-owned mines, and building publicly financed projects. Companies formed to obtain and execute public contracts were unique in Roman business because they were allowed to incorporate as continuous legal entities. In order to raise working capital, the principal partners, *socii*, offered shares, *partes*, to the public. The company would then submit a bid to the censors for the right to farm a particular tax or carry out a particular project. In the case of farming the taxes, the highest bidder won. The profit would be the difference between what the company paid and the actual yield of the taxes collected. In the case of other contracts, the profit would be the difference between what the state paid the company and its actual costs. The work itself was beneath the dignity of the investors. It was left to slaves, freedmen, and laborers supervised by a hired manager, *magister*.

Naturally, there was a temptation for tax farmers to squeeze the taxpayers as much as they could and for other contractors to cut corners to increase profits. Some contractors committed outright fraud. One notorious case occurred during the Second Punic War when shippers had government insurance on ships and cargoes for supplying the army. One company loaded bogus cargoes on unseaworthy ships and made an insurance claim when they sank (Livy, Book 25.3).

Strengths and weaknesses of Roman business

The most highly developed areas of Roman business were financial operations. The huge influx of wealth turned Rome into the banking and moneylending center of the Mediterranean. Roman bankers became very sophisticated. Individuals could keep open accounts and use bankers' orders or letters of credit. In that way, payments could easily be made by bookkeeping entries. Coins, the only form of cash, would have been cumbersome and risky in large transactions.

Well-organized partnerships of investors often made loans to shipowners to finance their cargoes. More frequent and more profitable were loans to provincial taxpayers and whole cities that were hard pressed to pay their taxes or tribute. The official rate on such loans was usually limited to 12 percent; the actual rate could reach 24 or even 48 percent. Indeed, whole kingdoms sometimes became indebted to Roman moneylenders at these rates as client kings endeavored to pay for the support that secured their thrones.

By modern standards, the techniques of Roman business and manufacturing remained underdeveloped. The goal of many businessmen was not to reinvest their profits in ways to improve their productivity but in estates and villas. They wanted to live the lives of gentlemen on their rents and agricultural income. Some aspired to use their wealth and the leisure that it afforded to pursue public careers in their local communities. Others even tried to obtain senatorial office at Rome for themselves or their sons. Business was only a means to acquire land and the social status and political power that it conferred.

SOCIAL CHANGE AND DISCONTENT

Rome's wars of conquest and accompanying economic changes had major social consequences for both Romans and non-Romans in the third and second centuries B.C.E. Some people and groups benefited; many became discontented. Roman society became more complex as it was divided into more clearly identifiable classes with different needs and interests.

The provincials and other overseas people

Many inhabitants of the western provinces bitterly resented their loss of independence, the payment of taxes and tribute to Rome, and the depredations of corrupt Roman officials and financiers. Roman imperialism made life particularly difficult for the Greeks and other people of the Hellenistic East. Between 201 and 136 B.C.E., Greece, Egypt, Syria, and other parts of the Near East may have lost as much as 20–25 percent of their population. Houses fell into decay; large tracts of land lay fallow or were turned into pasture for want of labor. From 210 to 160 B.C.E., wages remained low. The prices of food, rent, and other necessities rose. In times of crop failure, food prices skyrocketed. Prices finally went down again because of the lack of buying power but not before the people had undergone intense suffering.

Still, there were those who benefited. Romans had always maintained control over conquered and allied people by supporting the power of local rulers and elites who were willing to cooperate in upholding Rome's interests. Cooperative foreign rulers and elites were able to maintain their wealth and power at the expense of others in their communities. In Roman social terms, they became clients of powerful Roman senators. Those senators tried to make sure that Rome looked after their foreign clients' interests. In return, the clients could provide valuable financial and even military support to Rome and the powerful senators who backed them.

The Italian allies

During the second century B.C.E., the Italian allies found their status more and more burdensome as Rome expanded overseas. Spending long years in wars overseas did not produce the same rewards for them as for Rome. First, Roman commanders began to give allied troops smaller shares of captured booty. Second, the indemnities and tribute imposed upon the conquered went to Rome alone. Roman commanders also imposed harsher discipline on allied soldiers. As Roman leaders became more and more secure at home and grew accustomed to dominance abroad, they became more high-handed in their treatment of their allies in Italy. At the least, they demanded free accommodations and entertainment when they traveled through allied territory. At the worst, they interfered in the allies' domestic affairs. For example, in 186 B.C.E., they tried to suppress the worship of Bacchus among the allies in southern Italy through the use of criminal trials and executions of cult members. In short, the Romans increasingly treated their allies in Italy as subjects. That eventually led many allies to demand Roman citizenship and its privileges. Ultimately they rebelled when the Romans obstinately refused to grant this just demand.

Slaves and freedmen

One of the most discontented and potentially dangerous groups comprised the large numbers of anonymous rural slaves. They worked in the fields, forests, and mines of great landlords and commercial operators throughout the Roman world. A huge influx of war captives in the middle of the second century B.C.E. had made such slaves plentiful and very cheap. They were treated like animals. When concentrated in groups, they were often chained up in underground prisons at night. Beatings were common; family life was denied them. Moreover, their only value was as the cheapest labor possible. They did not even have the hope of being allowed to purchase eventual freedom by retaining anything from the fruits of their labor. Not surprisingly, many slaves sought escape to become robbers and brigands. Some even raised serious revolts. Indeed, their ability to do so was considerable. They were numerous, their supervision was often poor, and many of them were former soldiers captured in war.

Slave revolts began breaking out all over the Roman world between 143 and 133 B.C.E. In Italy, a revolt apparently was suppressed in 143 with the crucifixion of 450 slaves. A bigger revolt involving about 4000 slaves seems to have broken out in 140. In 134, an uprising at the great slave market of Delos was put down by force of arms. So was another at the silver mines of Laurium, near Athens. Slave revolts are reported for both 134 and 133 in Italy. In Pergamum, the war of Aristonicus (alleged bastard son of Eumenes II) and his Stoic "Sunstate" against Rome (132–129 B.C.E.) was really a major revolt of slaves, proletarians, and soldiers (p. 230). Worst of all was the slave revolt in Sicily. Ordinary robbery and assault by slaves had swollen into full-scale war about 136 B.C.E. Its leader was a Syrian slave named Eunus. Vomiting fire and uttering oracles, he was able to persuade his 70,000 (some say 250,000) followers that he was Antiochus, the king of the Syrians. Only after several years of hard fighting, the murder of many landlords, and much damage to property were the Romans able to crush this revolt and extinguish its last sparks in 132 B.C.E.

Not all slaves were forced to work under harsh conditions in the countryside, in mines, and in quarries. Many trained, educated captives from the lands of the eastern Mediterranean had better lives in domestic service as bookkeepers, secretaries, doctors, tutors, cooks, butlers, waiters, maids, hairdressers, and footmen or as skilled craftsmen like potters, carpenters, masons, decorators, tailors, and jewelers. A vast retinue of such slaves was a mark of status. The wealthy often competed to impress their peers with the numbers they owned.

Although some masters were relatively kind and generous to slaves with whom they lived, total control over another person easily led to cruelty and abuse. Small infractions might provoke harsh punishment. If a slave murdered a master, no matter how cruel, all of his fellow slaves had to be put to death with him. Male and female slaves were always vulnerable to sexual exploitation and abuse by their owners. Because adultery was defined for a man only as sexual relations with another citizen's wife, it was commonly accepted that male and female slaves might served their master's pleasure.

The usual Roman practice of manumitting (freeing) loyal slaves who had long been part of the household continued. Also, many masters hired out skilled slaves and allowed them to keep part of their earnings as their *peculium*. When such a slave had accumulated a large enough *peculium*, he or she could often negotiate the purchase of freedom. A female slave might be granted freedom after producing a certain number of children. Large numbers of slaves were manumitted in wills after their owners died. In fact, manumission was so common that the state collected handsome revenues from a 5 percent tax on the value of formally manumitted slaves.

The masters who freed their slaves also had something to gain from their generosity. The prospect of freedom in return for faithful service encouraged slaves to be docile and work hard. Many wealthy Romans helped their skilled ex-slaves set up their own businesses in return for a share of the profits. At the very least, any ex-slave was expected to be a loyal client to his former master. For the dead slave owner, it meant that his tomb would be well cared for by his freedmen, that his memory would be kept green, and that his spirit would receive the proper ritual offerings. For the living, the increase of clients through manumission had important political implications: freedmen became voting citizens. Although freedmen (but not their sons) were barred from public office, freedmen clients could be very helpful to an office seeker as voters and political agents.

The political impact of freedmen citizens caused them problems. Lower-class, freeborn citizens resented the dilution of their voting power by the influx of freedmen into the tribes of voters. Many senators feared that their rivals might gain an advantage from having a large number of freedmen clients. Therefore, the issue of tribal enrollment for freedmen became a source of political controversy.

Customarily, freedmen had been enrolled in only the four urban tribes, where their impact was outweighed by the less populous but more numerous rural tribes dominated by landowners. Some censors, like the famous Appius Claudius Caecus (the Blind) in 312 B.C.E., had tried to strengthen their *clientela* by enrolling freedmen and other humble citizens in all of the tribes. Others had removed the freedmen from the rural tribes and confined them to the urban ones again. In 168 B.C.E., the censors restricted freedmen to only one urban tribe.

The rural and urban Roman plebs

Wealthy plebeian families achieved power and status after the reforms that ended the so-called Struggle of the Orders. Therefore, the term *plebeian* increasingly came to refer to the masses of Roman citizens who made up the census classes of small farmers and the urban poor. As previously noted, Rome's wars of conquest paradoxically benefited small farmers at first but eventually led to their distress as they became too numerous to be supported by available agricultural land (pp. 176–8). The rapid influx of rural migrants taking advantage of economic opportunities or looking for a more exciting life in the cities greatly increased the ranks of the urban poor. Despite the attractions of the growing urban economy, there were not always enough good opportunities for the newcomers, especially the unskilled.

Unemployment and underemployment caused hardship for many. Housing was in high demand and short supply. Rents were steep for even the worst accommodations. This situation encouraged overcrowding. That, in turn, produced serious health, sanitation, and safety problems. People lived in tightly packed rows of flimsy *tabernae*, one- or two-story buildings with timber frames and wicker walls open to the street except for shutters. In some neighborhoods, the *tabernae* were giving way to multistoried apartment blocks called *insulae*. Often they were hardly less flimsy than the *tabernae*. They sometimes collapsed, and many were firetraps. Without adequate fire protection, they burned in large numbers. The lack of any organized police force encouraged the growth of crime, which the hardships of life fostered. Consequently, the urban poor of Italy became increasingly discontented.

The situation became especially acute at Rome itself in the late second century B.C.E. The city's economy no longer rested on an adequate productive base. Its great growth during the first sixty years of the century had depended on the profits of overseas expansion. That had fueled a great construction boom in the city and created a mass market for labor, goods, and services. After the destruction of Carthage and Corinth in 146 B.C.E., however, there were no more profitable wars for some time. The drawn-out wars against relatively poor Spanish tribes probably did not even recover their own expenses. They disrupted the regular tribute, too. In 135 B.C.E., a slave rebellion in Sicily also required an expensive military effort. Whether or not there was a con-comitant decline in publicly and privately funded building activity and benefactions at Rome between 146 and 133 B.C.E. is debatable. Still, economic activity probably did not increase to the level needed to sustain the city's increased population, most likely 400,000 by 133 B.C.E.

The aristocratic senatorial order and the consular nobility

The aristocratic class or order (pp. 63–4) that dominated the social and political life of the middle and late Roman Republic was the senatorial order (*ordo senatorius*). It had emerged after the reforms of the fourth century B.C.E. It was made up of those wealthy patrician and plebeian landowning families whose direct male ancestors or current heads had obtained membership in the senate by appointment or by holding a qualifying elective office such as the quaestorship or aedileship. To hold a qualifying office or be a member of the senate, one needed to possess property equal in value to the minimum for enrollment in the first census class (400,000 HS in the late Republic). In practical terms, to reach the praetorship, consulship, or censorship, which distin-guished the highest ranks in the senate, one probably needed much more wealth than the minimum for membership.

Within the senatorial order, those patrician and plebeian families who counted a consul in their direct male lines constituted the nobles (*nobiles*, sing. *nobilis*) or the nobility (*nobilitas*), the most elite group in Roman society (p. 93). During the third and early second centuries B.C.E., this group of families had become more and more exclusive. The *nobiles* made political and marital alliances with each other to monopo-lize access to the consulship, keep control of the levers of power within the senate, and take advantage of the oligarchic bias in the Republic's institutional arrangements (p. 97). For example, 211 consuls were elected from 232 to 133 B.C.E. Ninety-one came from families representing only eleven *gentes* (pp. 60–1). Nineteen *gentes* supplied only one consul each. Seventeen of those were plebeian. Of those seventeen *gentes*, fourteen had no previous consuls, and eleven produced no more consuls in the remaining years of the Republic. Clearly, therefore, it was now difficult for members of nonconsular plebeian families to reach the consulship or, once they had, to keep their laurels fresh in competition with candidates from families of more entrenched patrician and plebeian *gentes*. This exclusivity of the *nobiles* angered ambitious members of the lower ranks of the senatorial aristocracy who also wished to become consuls.

The equestrian order

By 218 B.C.E., certain wealthy nonsenatorial families began to emerge as a separate upper class just below the senatorial order. Their male heads were enrolled in the first eighteen centuries of the first census class and constituted the *equites* (sing. *eques*), cavalrymen or knights (p. 92). Therefore, their families made up the *ordo equester*, the equestrian order or class. Sometimes, however, the term was informally stretched to include men of the first census class who were not enrolled in the eighteen equestrian centuries.

In the early Republic, the first eighteen centuries actually supplied the cavalry for the Roman army. Throughout the Republic, a man whom the censors enrolled in these centuries was given a cavalry horse and public funds for its upkeep even after the Romans stopped using citizens as cavalry. *Equites* were distinguished from senators by their dress. The latter wore a broad vertical band of purple, the *latus clavus*, on their tunics. *Equites* had only a narrow band, the *angustus clavus*, on theirs.

Often, however, the two orders overlapped. Senators' close male relatives—like brothers, sons, nephews, and cousins—who did not hold actual seats in the senate were enrolled in the equestrian centuries and wore the narrow band of purple. Many of the *equites* were as wealthy as some of the higher-ranking senators. Wealthy, individual local aristocrats (called *domi nobiles*) in Italy who had acquired Roman citizenship were enrolled in the equestrian centuries. These and other equestrians were often linked to senatorial families through ties of patronage and marriage.

The *equites* were not simply businessmen. Like senators, they were men of landed wealth. As such, *equites* and senators often had similar outlooks and interests, and both necessarily pursued business activities. In 218 B.C.E., however, the tribune Q. Claudius, probably with the support of C. Flaminius, sponsored the *lex Claudia* forbidding senators and their immediate families to engage in large-scale overseas commerce. Senators were also not allowed to participate in public contracts. Accordingly, equestrians came to dominate those activities. Sometimes they came into conflict with senators who did not share such business interests.

More seriously, ambitious *equites* who wanted to compete for the highest honors at Rome resented the attempts of the nobility in the senate to exclude them from the office of consul. Members of the great noble families might support an equestrian client for one of the lower offices of the *cursus honorum*. On the other hand, they greatly resented a *novus homo*, new man, who managed to be the first of his family to reach the consulship (see Box 10.1). Most equestrians probably were content with their rank. Still, many must have resented the slight implied to their *ordo* by the nobility's attitude toward those of them who wanted to achieve highest honors at Rome.

10.1 THE "NEW MAN" AT ROME

In the second century B.C.E., competition for the consulship was fierce, and the office was the almost exclusive property of men from a few elite senatorial families, whose wealth and powerful connections made them attractive to voters. Yet occasionally the office fell to a new man (*novus homo*), someone who was the first in his family to reach the highest office in Rome. M. Porcius Cato (p. 168), one of the most famous new men of the second century B.C.E., is a good illustration of how extraordinary a man had to be to break into the consular rank. Cato came from a wealthy family prominent in their hometown of Tusculum, which lies about fifteen miles southeast of Rome. Cato was a man of impeccable personal virtue and excelled in all the skills required of a magistrate—knowledge of the law, oratorical ability, and proven military valor—but it was not until his legal acumen and general popularity brought him to the attention of the patrician L. Valerius Flaccus, that a political career was an option. Valerius, whose ancestors had enjoyed political prominence for centuries, became Cato's patron, and the result was a long and especially close political partnership. With Valerius' support, Cato sought political office in Rome, and eventually the two men shared the consulship in 195 B.C.E. and the censorship in 184.

The *publicani*

Broadly speaking, all people involved in the business of public contracts were *publicani*, publicans. To the people in the provinces, the word *publican* meant "tax collector," that is, the contractors' agent or employee who actually collected the taxes for the companies of tax farmers. In Rome, however, the publicans were the wealthy principals and shareholders who put up the capital for and took the profits from companies engaged in public contracts. They came to be considered one of the orders of Roman society. They overlapped with the equestrian order because many of them were *equites* or met the property requirements for equestrian rank. Therefore, they had the level of wealth needed to finance the initial heavy expenses of public contracts. Senators, although legally barred from public contracts, often participated indirectly through loans to investors and the purchase of shares in the name of a friend or a client.

At times, however, *publicani* became embroiled in conflicts with the senate. They resented not only the attempts of honest senatorial magistrates and provincial governors to prevent illegal profiteering but also the schemes of corrupt ones to extort money from them. Even more frustrating were their unsuccessful attempts to use the courts to attack senators whom they disliked. The jurors were always senators and were often sympathetic to the accused. Therefore, the *publicani* eagerly supported attempts in the late second and during the first century B.C.E. to limit service on juries to nonsenators of the first census class. That class included many *equites* who were also *publicani* or investors in their operations.

The advancement of upper-class women

The role of upper-class Roman women becomes more conspicuous in the sources for the late third and second centuries B.C.E. One theme that runs throughout these accounts is the ostentatious display of wealth. For example, Aemilia, the wife of the elder Scipio Africanus, was notorious for such display. She died richer than her own brother, L. Aemilius Paullus Macedonicus, the victor at Pydna. In 215 B.C.E., during the Second Punic War, the *lex Oppia* limited how much expensive clothing and ornamentation a woman could wear in public. In 195 B.C.E., however, women protested in great numbers—a sign that there were already strong social networks among them in this early period. The law was repealed despite the conservative Cato's vehement objection. As a result of wartime casualties, many women came to possess great wealth as heiresses. In 169 B.C.E., a law was passed to restrict female inheritances, but its impact seems to have been limited.

As families became richer and their daughters' dowries and inheritances greater, fathers did not want to lose control of such wealth. Therefore, the old-fashioned marriage with *manus*, which transferred a wife to the complete control of her husband, became increasingly rare. Now, marriage contracts usually contained the stipulation that the dowry be returned to the wife's family if she predeceased her husband. In this way, a woman would live with a man who did not have legal supervision over her. The men who did have legal control over her, namely her male blood relatives or legal guardian, were physically separated from her, particularly if they were away on overseas service or business for long periods. As in the case of Busa after Cannae, such a situation allowed savvy and capable women much room to maneuver (p. 144). Often, they even had the approval and cooperation of fathers, husbands, and guardians. Wealthy and well-connected women could be useful partners in advancing mutual social, economic, and political interests.

The crisis of war also gave greater prominence to upper-class women's religious roles in the community. The Vestal Virgins were considered particularly important for ensuring divine favor through their chastity and were accorded important privileges along with their responsibilities. Elite families competed for the honor of having a daughter chosen to be a Vestal. Unfortunately, two Vestals, Opimia and Floronia, became scapegoats for the disaster at Cannae on the ground that they had been unchaste. Elite families' rivalries may well explain why these two were singled out. Condemned to death, one was buried alive, and the other committed suicide.

Upper-class women also played prominent parts in religious festivals and other rituals considered vital to the community. In 204 B.C.E., for example, the senate sought the protection of Cybele, the Great Mother, by bringing her from Asia Minor to Rome. Upper-class matrons came out to greet the ship bearing the black stone that embodied her. One of them was Claudia Quinta, perhaps a granddaughter of the famous censor Appius Claudius Caecus. Supposedly, when her fitness was doubted on the grounds of unchastity, she vindicated herself by single-handedly freeing the ship after it stuck in the riverbed.

The increased level of education among upper-class women also contributed to their prominence and influence. The growing wealth and sophistication of aristocratic families prompted them to acquire the most highly trained tutors for their children. The large staffs of domestic slaves meant that girls were not needed for household chores. Therefore, they were allowed to attend the lessons that might have been denied them in earlier times. Also, Roman aristocrats were now being exposed to the Hellenistic Greek model of the educated woman. Soon, a number of educated women were patronizing literary circles and running salons, as did aristocratic French women in the eighteenth century C.E.

One of the most famous Roman women of the late second century B.C.E. combines many of these characteristics and accomplishments. She was Cornelia, daughter of the elder Scipio Africanus and mother of the Gracchi (see Chapter 12). When her distinguished husband, the elder Tiberius Sempronius Gracchus, died, her wealth increased. Well educated under the influence of her philhellene father, she provided the best education possible for her daughter and two sons who, out of allegedly twelve children, survived to maturity. She was also well known as a patroness of writers and philosophers. Her own cultured letters were read for generations after her death. Her personal accomplishments, her wealth, and her politically valuable family connections made her a force in Roman aristocratic circles. She is even said to have received an offer of marriage from a king of Egypt (the rival brothers Ptolemy VI and Ptolemy VIII were both looking for Roman support to secure the throne). If so, she declined. She was much more interested in promoting her sons' careers at Rome, the new center of power in the Mediterranean.

POLITICAL DEVELOPMENTS

During the period of the Punic wars and the subsequent growth of Roman power, the consular families who had come to dominate the senate made sure that the opportunities for more families to acquire consular status were not created. Although Rome's imperial expansion greatly increased the need for high executives, the senate did not raise the number of annual consuls from the traditional two. Instead, it enlarged the number of praetors to six each year. It also greatly expanded the practice of proroguing (prolonging) a consul's or a praetor's military command or provincial governorship after his normal year in office. Magistrates whose terms of service were prorogued became promagistrates. Such men were able to use their extended terms to capitalize on the opportunities that their positions gave them to acquire clients and financial resources to further their domination of high offices. Moreover, the increase in praetorships meant that there were more eligible candidates—and consequently heightened competition—for the two annual consulships.

The result was a very unhealthy political situation for Rome. Unchecked by any challenges from without, oligarchic nobles often failed to deal with the pressing problems and discontent that accompanied imperial expansion. Instead, they competed with increasing intensity among themselves. They wanted dominance within the senate and the prizes of *gloria* (glory), *dignitas* (esteem), and *auctoritas* (prestige) that came with high office and military triumph. Simultaneously, the holding of high office helped a man to amass the resources of money and patronage needed to maintain or increase his family's advantage in competition with other nobles and lesser aristocrats for political and military advancement.

Political groupings

Political struggles within the senatorial order were not organized on the basis of formal political parties, organizations, and programs. There was no incentive to organize in such ways. The senate, a body of about 300 men with lifetime tenure, exercised great control over public affairs. Senators were not held directly accountable to the electorate or any other authority. Candidates for offices might well have different ideas concerning domestic issues or foreign affairs. Nevertheless, their electoral supporters were often organized on a highly personal basis of family connections, friendships, mutually advantageous coalitions, and patronage.

Some outstanding individuals might build up relatively stable factions of personal supporters that would last for some time. Others might last for only one electoral campaign. Members of a man's family or even *gens* might support his election to high office out of feelings of kinship or family pride. There are, however, not enough data to support the thesis that there were long-lasting factions of related families or otherwise allied groups who consistently supported fellow members for office and promoted concerted political programs in the senate.

Prosopography and Roman politics

An important tool for analyzing the highly personal politics of the Roman Republic is prosopography. This term comes from the Greek words meaning "writing about persons." It often involves the analysis of the social and geographic origins of individuals, their kinship networks, their personal friendships or associations, and their career paths. Those things can reveal social and political affiliations or affinities that are not explicitly documented in the ancient sources. Prosopography can also involve the analysis of biographical data from many individuals within a clearly identifiable group, such as Roman consuls. Those data can create valuable statistical profiles of that group.

The application of the prosopographical approach to Roman history has often been criticized for being limited mostly to studying the elite (who usually have left most of the information available) and for being applied too mechanically or simplistically: for example, "X was married to Y's cousin; therefore, X was a political supporter of Y." The undocumented behaviors or attitudes of a particular individual cannot be deduced from kinship relationships or other close affiliations and associations with people exhibiting the same or similar behaviors and attitudes. Nevertheless, the careful collection and interpretation of prosopographical information can be very useful for understanding a person's documented behavior or attitudes in a wider context. They reveal the commonalities that link the person to a wider group exhibiting the same or similar behaviors and attitudes. On the other hand, just because two or more people exhibit similar behaviors or attitudes, it is not legitimate to say that they constitute a group without other evidence of close associations. Where sufficient evidence exists for nonelite individuals, like freedmen or noncommissioned military officers, facts of their individual lives can yield useful statistical profiles of those groups. In Roman history, most such evidence comes from inscriptions. Unfortunately, inscriptional evidence does not become plentiful enough for nonelite individuals until the period of the Empire.

Attempts to check outstanding individuals

Many members of the nobility feared the rise of any outstanding individual. He might amass so much wealth, power, popularity, glory, prestige, and esteem that he would reduce the chances for them to compete for the same things on an equal basis. The social and financial rewards of political power increased with the power and wealth of Rome. Therefore, the temptation increased to violate the customary rules governing political behavior as men sought to secure competitive advantage. At the same time, those rewards included the means to violate traditional norms. Values and behavior necessary to preserve a republican form of government gradually began to disintegrate under the pressure. The way was imperceptibly opened for one man to overcome his competitors and dominate all in the manner of Hellenistic monarchs, whom Roman nobles had replaced as the masters of the Mediterranean world.

A good example of the process can be seen in the career of the elder P. Cornelius Scipio Africanus during the Second Punic War. After Scipio's father and uncle had been killed in Spain, the well-connected young Scipio obtained a proconsular command from the senate to continue the war there. He was only twenty-five, however, and had held no office beyond the aedileship. His successful prosecution of the war in Spain emboldened him to return to Rome and run for the consulship in 206 B.C.E. Still, he was far younger than normal and had never held the praetorship, normally a prerequisite for the consulship. Rival families and conservative-minded senators who objected to his unorthodox career opposed him. His popularity as a military hero and his promise to invade Africa if elected guaranteed his victory. Scipio's opponents sought to block him. They placed him in charge of the disgraced survivors of Cannae and denied him public funds. He used his popularity to raise enough funds and volunteers to man, equip, and train a first-rate army to invade North Africa in 204 B.C.E. Such power and independence in one man did not bode well for the Republic. Its stability depended upon adherence to the well-established political ground rules.

Other ambitious individuals soon followed Scipio's path and sought to equal or surpass his achievement. For example, T. Quinctius Flamininus had never been elected to any office beyond the junior one of military tribune. Still, he was made a propraetor in charge of Tarentum in 205 B.C.E. Not yet thirty, he was elected consul for 198 B.C.E. to prosecute the Second Macedonian War.

The extraordinarily rapid rise of such young men as Scipio and Flamininus was disturbing. Their rivals and leaders who saw unorthodox careers as a danger to the traditional Republic reacted vigorously. They procured laws to enforce what custom and tradition could no longer safeguard. For example, shortly after Flamininus was elected consul, the praetorship was made a prerequisite for the consulship in the *cursus honorum* (course of offices [p. 94]). That change probably was made to reduce the number of candidates for the two consulships each year. The number of praetors had increased from two to four at the end of the First Punic War to cope with administering new provinces. It was increased to six in 197 B.C.E. after the organization of the two Spanish provinces. Without this new prerequisite, fourteen former quaestors, aediles, and praetors would have been eligible to run for the two consulships. The chances that the voters would pass over an older man for a more popular younger one and the dangers of overheated electoral competition were too great for many senators to ignore.

In 180 B.C.E., the curule magistracies were systematically regulated by the *lex Villia Annalis*. It set minimum ages for holding the curule aedileship, the praetorship, and the consulship—probably thirty-six, thirty-nine, and forty-two, respectively. A minimum interval of two years between the end of one office and the holding of another was also required. The status of the quaestorship at this time is not clear. A minimum age of twenty-five may have been fixed for it. In any case, it became the normal, if not mandatory, first office of the senatorial *cursus honorum*. Finally, in 152 B.C.E. or soon after, a law was passed to forbid reelection to the consulship. Significantly, M. Claudius Marcellus had just been elected to his third consulship without waiting the required ten years after his second.

Still, the temptation to violate traditional political norms intensified with political competition. Between 181 and 131 B.C.E., several laws were passed to stop bribery and limit the control of patrons over voters in the assemblies. They required secret ballots and even instituted the death penalty for bribery. Two other laws attempted to limit the efforts of wealthy men to extend their private *clientelae* and impress voters with lavish entertainments and dinners. Nothing really worked.

When the prizes are large and the temptations correspondingly great, mere laws are not enough to restrain undesirable behavior. In Rome, the legal restraints on political behavior were especially weak. The Roman political system was not based on a written constitution that could be altered only after a lengthy process allowing due consideration and requiring the overwhelming approval of those responsible for making any changes. "Constitutional" matters were either merely customary or regulated by normal, ad hoc legislative acts like the *lex Villia Annalis*. All that an ambitious and popular leader had to do to circumvent such restraints was to procure a new law in his favor. For example, in 148 B.C.E. Scipio Aemilianus, the younger Africanus, obtained a special enactment to run for the consulship, although he met none of the conditions set by the *lex Villia Annalis*. Another special law also gave him the command against Carthage. That action breached the customary right of the senate to assign consuls to military commands. Finally, in 135 B.C.E. Scipio received an exemption from the law forbidding repetition of the consulship. That enabled him to take charge of the war against Numantia.

Other ambitious men dispensed with legality altogether. As provincial governors, they often exceeded their authority or disobeyed express senatorial decrees in order to win military laurels that would enhance their popularity at the polls. Individual governors were practically laws unto themselves in their provinces. Far from the watchful eyes of their senatorial colleagues, they enjoyed supreme judicial and military power in their provinces. The provincials were at their mercy. Governors usually held a particular province for only a year or two. They often had no interest in securing the long-term welfare of their charges. Too often they were interested in using their power to extort as much money as they could from hapless provincials. Thus, they would have the resources to advance their careers, pay off their debts, and maintain their status among competing peers back home. That is not to say that there were not many responsible and fair Roman governors who refused to put selfish interest above duty. Still, the bad ones were numerous enough to cause discontent in the provinces and concern among other senators.

The first permanent standing court (*quaestio perpetua*)

The problem had become acute in 149 B.C.E. with the failure to bring Servius Sulpicius Galba to justice for his crimes in Spain (p. 168). In that same year, a new law established Rome's first permanent jury court, the *quaestio perpetua de rebus repetundis*. It is doubtful, however, that it was intended to bring real relief to the provincials. It seems that only Roman citizens could bring suit in the court. A later reform was needed to make the extortion law a source of meaningful redress for provincials (p. 222). The law of 149 B.C.E. seems more an attempt to prevent ambitious individuals from misusing public service to acquire money for competing with their peers.

OVERVIEW AND ASSESSMENT

Imperial expansion transformed Rome's economic, social, and political life. Economically, small farmers as a whole benefited from the conquests of northern Italy and Spain and, paradoxically, even from the heavy casualties in the wars of the late third and early second centuries B.C.E. At the same time, it was easier for the wealthy to establish large slave-worked estates, especially in central and southern Italy. They and many small farmers began to produce commercially for Italy's rapidly growing cities. The latter grew from the influx of wealth from Rome's conquests and increased trade and commerce. The inflow of precious metals helped to create a stable monetary system, and the minting of millions of coins to pay soldiers helped to monetize the economy. Wealthy Romans increased their fortunes through war booty, overseas commerce, and lucrative public contracts.

Socially, imperial expansion benefited upper-class Romans, both men and women, and the provincial elites who cooperated with them. It also created numerous discontented social groups. Many provincials resented their loss of independence and felt oppressed by often corrupt and rapacious Roman governors and tax collectors. Even Rome's Italian allies came to feel abused. They did much of the fighting, but Rome kept most of victory's fruits and treated them more like subjects. Successful wars flooded Italy with slaves. While some skilled slaves came to work as household servants, tens of thousands ended up in far more dangerous and hostile conditions in mines, large workshops, and the fields of great estates. In the 140s and 130s B.C.E., several dangerous slave revolts broke out, particularly in Italy and Sicily. Even those slaves who eventually gained freedom and citizenship resented how the value of their votes was limited to the benefit of freeborn citizens. Many of the latter, particularly among the rural and urban plebs, faced desperate social and economic conditions by the late second century B.C.E. Wealthy nonsenators who made up the equestrian class resented the difficulties placed in the way of *equites* who sought to rise into the ranks of the consular nobility. Also, those engaged in public contracts as *publicani*, particularly the tax farmers, sometimes found that their economic interests brought them into conflict with the senatorial elite.

Politically, imperial expansion strained the Republic's system of government. The rewards that came from holding high office and commanding conquering armies greatly increased, and this in turn raised political competition among the leaders of noble or would-be-noble families in the senate to destructive levels. The expansion of the lower offices of the *cursus honorum* only intensified the competition for the two consulships at the top. Attempts to rein in ambitious individuals by legislating what had been traditional norms and by instituting punishments for those who violated them only produced greater efforts to evade them. At the same time, fear that someone might gain political advantage by sponsoring needed reforms prevented the senate from solving the problems that others could manipulate to their benefit. While Rome's empire grew, the competing oligarchs who controlled it became less and less able to solve the problems it created.

SUGGESTED READING

Brunt, P. A. *Italian Manpower, 225 B.C.–A. D. 14*. Oxford: Oxford University Press, 1971.

Rosenstein, N. *Imperatores Victi: Military Defeat and Aristocratic Competition in the Middle and Late Roman Republic*. Berkeley, Los Angeles, and Oxford: University of California Press, 1990.

Tan, J. *Power and Public Finance at Rome, 264–49 B.C. Oxford Studies in Early Empires*. New York: Oxford University Press, 2017.

CHAPTER 11

The great cultural synthesis, 264 to 133 B.C.E.

The aristocratic craze for things Greek accelerated during the period of overseas expansion. Wars on the Greek mainland and in Hellenistic kingdoms exposed the Romans to both the classicizing idealism of Attica and the emotional realism of the Hellenistic Greeks. Plundered paintings, statues, reliefs, and architectural pieces poured into Rome. Skilled Greek craftsmen and artists came to Italy as slaves or hired craftsmen. Many educated Greek slaves ended up as secretaries and tutors in elite Roman households. Enterprising Greek philosophers, poets, and publicists sought the patronage of rich and powerful Romans. Together, they combined Greek and native Italian influences to create a Greco-Roman classical culture that spread throughout the Mediterranean world.

ARCHITECTURE AND ART

Beginning around 264 B.C.E. with the construction of the *comitium*—a tiered, circular, stone place of public assembly in the Forum—the Romans began the process of remodeling under classical Greek influence. The design of the *comitium* probably came from Greeks in Sicily. In 263, it was adorned with a sundial pillaged (but never recalibrated) from a Sicilian city. In 221/220, Gaius Flaminius celebrated his Gallic triumph by opening up the Campus Martius (Mars' Field) to development. It was then outside the walls of the city along the great westward bend of the Tiber. There he built a new space for chariot racing and public meetings. Soon, other triumphant generals were adding temples modeled on Greek originals. They also constructed Hellenistic-style complexes to display the spoils of their victories over Hellenistic kings. Cato the Elder may have been the first to bring another type of Greek building to Rome. As censor in 184 B.C.E., he issued the contract to build in the Forum a small version of the type of Greek building known as a *basilica*. It was a rectangular covered building with interior supporting columns. People could use it for private or public business.

At first, the new Greek-style buildings were still constructed of wood on stone foundations. Expensive all-stone construction became more common after 150 B.C.E. One of Rome's earliest stone structures is a Greek-style round temple (*tholos*) built of plundered Greek marble. It still stands in the Forum Boarium. In 142, the first stone bridge across the Tiber appeared, the Pons Aemilius, part of which still remains.

Domestic architecture

Between 200 and 150, Greek influence had also modified domestic architecture. The simple atrium house now received additional amenities such as baths and gardens flanked by colonnaded walkways off the back. Greek-style fountains, pools, and statuary completed this pleasant setting where the members of well-to-do families could relax.

Innovations in construction

In 196, the first triumphal arch marked the blending of a distinctively Roman form with the Greek style of decoration. Even more important was the development of new construction techniques that allowed the Romans to combine massiveness of form with Greek elegance. The first was the development of molded concrete (*opus caementicium*): a mixture of mortar and small stones was packed into wooden forms that were stripped away once the mixture had set. Buildings could be made more quickly and with less skilled labor than by using dressed stone blocks. This type of construction was also more versatile because it made arches and vaults relatively simple to build. Thus, it was easy to provide strong but open supporting walls and vaulted ceilings that required no other support. The same advantages were available with baked bricks, which were fast coming into significant use. Soon the Romans were building to heights and expanses that the Greeks never imagined.

Sculpture and decoration

The tradition of Roman bronze sculpture and terracotta relief continued in the second century. By the second half of the century, however, Greek sculptors began to produce many neo-Attic marble statues and reliefs for Roman patrons. Greek artisans also produced frescoes and mosaics in the Hellenistic style to decorate both private and public buildings. By 133 B.C.E., therefore, the efforts of aristocratic Roman leaders had graced Rome with the best works of art that could be plundered or copied from the Greek world.

LITERATURE

Roman aristocrats used Greek art to proclaim their triumphs over the older culture that they were appropriating as a mark of social prestige. They also sought to harness the language, literature, and thought of the Greeks to their own patriotic and self-serving causes. Even Cato the Elder, who publicly scorned the "weak Greeklings" whom Rome had conquered, took the trouble to learn Greek.

First of all, Greek was the international language throughout the wider world of which Rome had become an important part. In order to deal with the leaders of Greece and the Hellenistic kingdoms as equals, it was necessary for Roman senators to understand and speak Greek. Second, there was a certain curiosity and a practical need on the part of the Romans. They wanted to find out more about the Greeks, whom they increasingly conquered and had to control. Third, despite their feelings of moral and military superiority, many Romans felt a certain amount of admiration for the accomplishments of an older, more refined culture. Wanting to imitate it is understandable. Still, they demonstrated a creative capacity to adapt existing forms to new cultural values.

The works of Livius Andronicus

Lucius Livius Andronicus was a Greek who had been enslaved at the fall of Tarentum in 272 B.C.E. (pp. 109–11). By the end of the First Punic War in 241, he had acquired his freedom and a reputation as a teacher and translator of Greek for eager Roman aristocrats. His life underscores how Roman culture was enriched by the incorporation of conquered and allied peoples into the Roman state. Just as with modern New York, London, or Paris, few of the great literary figures associated with ancient Rome were natives of the city itself.

One of Andronicus' earliest works was a Latin adaptation of a Greek epic poem, the *Odyssey*. Its meter is called *Saturnian*, an ancient native meter that the Romans later gave up in favor of forms used by the Greeks. Like English meter, Saturnian, is accentual, based on the stress and lack of stress on syllables within a word. The meter of ancient Greek poetry is quantitative, based on how long or how short a time it takes to say the syllables.

The *Odyssey* was a very good choice to adapt for Roman readers. Its description of travel in exotic lands appealed to Romans, whose horizons were just then extending beyond the narrow confines of Italy. Also, unlike the *Iliad*, it did not dwell on the Greek defeat of the Trojans, whom the Romans by now were claiming as their ancestors. Odysseus' wanderings and hardships even provided the models for those of Aeneas, who supposedly had led the Trojan refugees to Italy. Therefore, if not the first piece of Greek literature adapted to Latin, Andronicus' *Odyssey* was the first to attain wide popularity at Rome. It continued to be used as a school text for centuries. In the late first century B.C.E., the poet Horace once recalled having to memorize passages from it when he was a boy.

In 240 B.C.E., the aediles were planning the annual festival of the Roman Games, *Ludi Romani*. They wanted something special with which to celebrate the recent end

196

of the First Punic War. They asked Livius Andronicus to adapt a Greek tragedy and a Greek comedy for the Roman stage. He not only wrote the texts but also performed as the chief actor. His efforts aroused great enthusiasm and set the trend for Roman drama ever after.

The creativity of Roman literature

The fact that all subsequent Roman authors freely borrowed from the Greeks has often led people to charge that Roman literature is wholly derivative and not worthy of respect. That is not a legitimate view. The ancient Greek and Roman concept of creativity is different from the modern. For an ancient artist, the supreme challenge was to work within a given tradition in order to refine it and improve it, not to create something startlingly new. What the best Roman authors did was to adapt Greek literary forms to the expression of distinctively Roman themes and ideas. Much of Roman literature was intensely patriotic, even nationalistic, portraying the glories of Roman history and the values that distinguished Romans from other people.

Naevius (ca. 270 to 199 B.C.E.)

The first freeborn Roman citizen to achieve success as an author was Livius Andronicus' slightly younger contemporary Gnaeus Naevius. He grew up surrounded by Greek culture in Campania. He was proficient in tragedy, comedy, and epic. He continued to use the native Saturnian meter and was Rome's first nationalistic poet. He wrote the first important plays that dealt with events of Roman history rather than Greek mythology. He also wrote the first patriotic Roman epic. Appropriately enough, Naevius' subject was the First Punic War, in which he had served. Unfortunately, only a handful of fragments survive. From these, however, we can see that he wove in legends of Rome's founding by descendants of Aeneas. Thus, he provided Vergil (70–19 B.C.E.) with useful material for the *Aeneid*. In his plays, Naevius often made critical comments about contemporary political figures. His freedom of speech incurred the wrath of the powerful. He died, perhaps in exile, at Utica in North Africa. His difficulties with the powerful made later writers cautious about the use of personal invective on the Roman stage. That contrasts with the license of Greek Old Comedy, epitomized by the plays of Aristophanes (d. 386 B.C.E.).

Ennius (239 to 169 B.C.E.)

The heir of Naevius as a master of tragic, comic, and epic poetry was Quintus Ennius. The fortuitous circumstance of being a native Italian living near the Greek cities of southern Italy and under Roman domination made him trilingual, knowing Oscan, Greek, and Latin. His talent was equally diverse. He had a thorough understanding of Greek thought, a real ear and feeling for language, and a genuine admiration for Rome. That admiration impressed Cato the Elder. He brought Ennius to Rome in 204 B.C.E., after service together in the Roman army. At Rome, Ennius quickly became acquainted with other leading Romans, such as the elder Scipio Africanus, who acted as his patrons.

Ennius' tragedies were more admired than his comedies. They reveal the influence of Euripides (480s–407[?] B.C.E.) in their subjects, rational spirit, and critical liberalism. Ennius also wrote some philosophical books and a compendium of shorter poems. Its title, *Satura*, is the Latin root of the English *satire*. It indicated a miscellany containing personal comments on a variety of subjects in a variety of meters and contributed to the creation of the uniquely Roman genre of satire. Ennius' greatest achievement, however, was his patriotic epic poem entitled *Annales*. In eighteen books, it dealt with the tales of Rome's past and the history of the Second Punic War. Thus, Ennius carried on the process of integrating the legends of Rome's founding with real history. The poem's major innovation was the use of quantitative Greek-style meter instead of native Saturnian meter. In both respects, therefore, Ennius served as another of Vergil's major models.

SPECIALIZATION IN GENRES

As Roman authors became more skilled and experienced with various literary genres, it became more difficult for any one person to master them all. Some began to evidence special talents in particular fields. Even authors contemporary with Ennius started to specialize in one genre or another.

Pacuvius (ca. 220 to 130 B.C.E.) and Accius (170 to ca. 85 B.C.E.)

Marcus Pacuvius and Lucius Accius worked in all major poetic genres, but they concentrated their greatest efforts on tragedy. Pacuvius came from Brundisium. He was Ennius' nephew and shared Scipionic connections. Extensive fragments of his plays survive. They reveal good intellectual content, impressive characterization, and powerful language. Accius was born to freedmen parents at Pisaurum on the Adriatic north of Ancona. He had connections with the Junii Bruti. He seems to have shared Pacuvius' literary characteristics. Later, Horace and Quintilian counted him among Rome's greatest writers.

Lucilius (ca. 180 to 102 B.C.E.)

Gaius Lucilius was an Equestrian from Campania. In contrast to Pacuvius and Accius, he concentrated his attention on satire. That is Rome's most important contribution to the genres of Western literature. It grew out of a strong native tradition of poking fun at the faults of famous people during such events as triumphal celebrations and funeral processions. Lucilius really created the genre of satire in its modern sense: sharp, biting, witty commentary on the social and political life of various people and the times in general. As a close friend of the younger Scipio Africanus, Lucilius had access to many of the important men who looked to Scipio for leadership. As could be expected, he was particularly critical of Scipio's opponents. Although his Latin was not elegant, Lucilius had a natural, vigorous sense of humor. It was highly appreciated by the later satirists Horace and Martial and the critic Quintilian.

Plautus (ca. 254 to 184 b.c.e.) and Terence (ca. 195 to 159 b.c.e.)

Tragedy and comedy were the first literary genres to reach their highest stage of development at Rome. Unfortunately, the tragedians mentioned above are known only through fragmentary quotations and comments in later works. Roman comedy, however, is represented by a body of twenty-seven complete plays, twenty-one assigned to Titus Maccius Plautus and six belonging to Publius Terentius Afer. Few facts are known about the life of Plautus. Even his real name was unknown until 1815, when the oldest manuscript of his plays was discovered. He was an Umbrian from the Italian town of Sarsina.

A little more is known about Plautus' younger contemporary Terence, but the issue of his origin is a matter of dispute. According to the second-century c.e. biographer Suetonius, Terence had been born at Carthage and was a slave at Rome to a senator named Terentius Lucanus. Suetonius or his source may have inferred Terence's Carthaginian birth from his cognomen, *Afer* ("African"), which, however, was not usually applied to Carthaginians or even to Egyptians, but to people from other ethnic groups in North Africa. Terence is also called *fuscus*, "dark" or "swarthy," a descriptive word that Romans applied to individuals from all over the ancient world, from India, the Levant, and Asia Minor to even Gaul and Spain, but not to Black Africans. They were called Ethiopians (*Aethiopes*). It is likely, therefore, that Terence was not born a slave at Carthage but had been captured or bought as a child from one of Carthage's North African neighbors and brought to Rome, perhaps by a Carthaginian merchant.

Whatever the case, Terentius is said to have recognized the young man's intellectual gifts and set him free after giving him a good education. Terence's talents brought him to the attention of Scipio Aemilianus, the younger Africanus, who helped launch his career. Unfortunately, his talent was soon extinguished when he died during a trip to Greece in 159 b.c.e.

Both Plautus and Terence freely borrowed their plots, situations, and characters from writers of Greek New Comedy. They particularly favored Menander, Diphilus, and Philemon. Plautus, however, infused his plays more with the native comic traditions of Italy. Romans had not yet learned to despise those traditions, as they did when the influence of older Greek culture became even stronger in the latter two-thirds of the second century b.c.e. Despite the external trappings of urbane Greek New Comedy, Plautine comedy is basically farce inspired by native Italian farces and ribald poetry found in Etruria. It is rich in slapstick, fast-paced wordplay, and overtly satirical comment on matters of public concern. Those elements are lacking in the surviving examples of New Comedy, which was much more understated and philosophical in nature.

Terence, the younger author, reveals the greater impact of Hellenism on the younger generation of Romans in the second century b.c.e. He was patronized by aristocrats like Scipio Aemilianus, who had received a more thoroughly Greek education than their predecessors. Terence's plays are much more intellectual and refined and less farcical than the plays of Plautus. Terence's Latin reflects the speech of the educated upper class rather than the less polished, racier talk of the man in the street. His plays try to teach the psychological lessons of New Comedy. They make good literature but not such entertaining stage productions as those of Plautus. That is why Terence sometimes had trouble holding the attention of his audiences, as he sometimes complained. Moreover, it is significant that after Terence there are no more important writers of Roman comedy. The growing Hellenism of the educated elite prejudiced them against writing in a manner that would appeal to a mass audience. They turned to other forms of writing, while the average Roman enjoyed revivals of Plautus' and, occasionally, Terence's old plays. Their comedies have continued to inspire comic playwrights down to the present, as in the case of the 1962 musical-turned-film. *A Funny Thing Happened on the Way to the Forum.*

The plays of Plautus and Terence are important not only as major contributions to Western comic drama. They are also historical reflections of the great cultural, social, and economic changes that affected Rome with the acquisition of an empire. Obviously, the influence of Greek New Comedy on Roman authors mirrors the influence of Greek culture in general. Moreover, New Comedy appealed to the Romans precisely because of the parallels that they saw with their own times. The prominence of slave characters corresponds to the large presence of slavery in Roman society. Conflicts between fathers and sons often provide the plots. They are similar to the conflict between the more cosmopolitan younger generation of Romans like Scipio Aemilianus and Romans of the old school like Cato the Elder. Conflicts between husbands and wives emphasize the growing independence of upper-class women. The prominence of merchants, high-living young men, and gold-digging mistresses mirror the great influx of wealth that Rome was experiencing. The plays may have been set in Greece, but the topics were as much Roman as Greek.

PROSE LITERATURE

Roman prose took much longer to reach its highest development than did comedy. In fact, the first significant Roman prose authors were historians who wrote in Greek after the Second Punic War. Many of the early Roman historians are called *annalists*. Like the official records of the pontiffs, their works were organized on a year-by-year basis. The two earliest known historians, Quintus Fabius Pictor and Lucius Cincius Alimentus, were both Roman senators who had served in the Second Punic War. Fabius came from one of the most famous *gentes* in Roman history. He took special interest in the deeds of the Fabii and other great families. Alimentus was from one of the newer, plebeian aristocratic families. As is true of all the early annalists, their works are lost except for quotations and borrowings by later authors. The loss of Alimentus is particularly regrettable because he was captured by Hannibal's army and may have known Hannibal personally. His experience with the Carthaginians seems to be reflected in his reputation for being fair to both sides in the Punic wars. Fabius, on the other hand, was notoriously anti-Carthaginian and blamed the Second Punic War on the Barcids' hatred of Rome.

Two other senatorial annalists, Gaius Acilius and Aulus Postumius Albinus, appeared around 150 B.C.E. Acilius' intellectual interests are reflected in his role as interpreter for three Greek philosophers who represented Athens before the senate in 155 (pp. 202–3). Postumius had fought under Aemilius Paullus against Perseus and had extensive experience in the Greek East. They and their two predecessors all devoted much space to the period of the Monarchy and foundation of the Republic in order to construct a glorious past worthy of Rome's glorious present. They then emphasized Rome's recent greatness with lengthy treatments of the first two Punic wars.

Greek was the logical choice of language for Roman historians. First, the only models for writing prose history were Greek. It would have been easier to use existing Greek vocabulary and concepts than to create new ones in Latin. Second, the use of Greek made their works available to both Rome's educated elite and, more importantly, the Greeks. While Greeks were becoming more interested in Rome as Roman power grew, they seldom bothered to learn Latin. They considered it too crude and beneath their dignity. Also, Roman writers wanted to counteract the favorable view of Carthage that Greek audiences received from Greek accounts of the Punic wars.

Polybius (ca. 200 to ca. 118 B.C.E.)

The historian Polybius came to Rome as an Achaean Greek hostage after Pydna (p. 163). In many ways, he represents a continuation of the tradition of Roman historians writing in Greek for a Greek audience. Having obtained the friendship and patronage of Scipio Aemilianus, son of L. Aemilius Paullus, the victor at Pydna, he accompanied Scipio on military and diplomatic missions, including the Third Punic War. In this way, he developed intimate, firsthand knowledge of how Rome's aristocrats thought and acted. Similarly, he personally traveled over much of the Mediterranean world. He even retraced Hannibal's march over the Alps and undertook a voyage beyond the Pillars of Hercules down the West African coast.

Unfortunately, his account of that voyage is lost, but part of his forty-volume *Histories* survives, to the enormous benefit of today's historians. All of the first five books and a good part of Book 6 are extant. Later authors also preserve numerous excerpts from other books, but five are completely lost. Although he is not without bias, Polybius tries to provide the Greeks with a sophisticated and rigorously analytical explanation of how Rome came to dominate the Mediterranean world from ca. 220 to 167 B.C.E. He includes, however, a background discussion of the First Punic War and its aftermath. He also analyzes the effects of Rome's conquests on itself and others between 167 and the destruction of Carthage in 146 B.C.E. Although a rigorous intellectual, Polybius was no mere armchair historian. He practiced what he called *pragmatic history*: the careful analysis of documents, the interrogation of eyewitnesses, and the acquisition of first-hand geographical knowledge.

Cato the Elder (234 to 149 B.C.E.)

Marcus Porcius Cato the Elder was an older contemporary of Polybius. As in his architecture, so in his oratory and written works, he was willing to adopt what he found useful in Greek culture, while he was critical of what he saw as its dangers. He was the first Roman to compose an important history in Latin. It was entitled *Origines* (*The Origins*). It covered the early history of Italy and Rome as well as their recent past. For the recent period, he left out famous names and included parts of his own speeches. Thus, Cato deflated other prominent men and glorified himself. In one well-known episode, he underscored the omission of famous names by giving only the name of Surus, one of Hannibal's elephants. Cato made many important prose contributions other than his history of Rome. He wrote major works on law, medicine, and agriculture, the last of which, the *De Agricultura*, survives as the earliest extant work of Latin prose. It is a valuable source of information on Roman life and economic history in the second century B.C.E. Cato also published a book on rhetoric and was the first Roman to publish his own speeches.

Rhetoric

The publication of Cato's speeches and his work on rhetoric emphasize the growing importance of the art of rhetoric and rhetorical training. With the growth of Rome as a world power, the state needed officials and leaders capable of clearly expounding problems and policies in public meetings, in senatorial debates, and in dealings with foreign governments. The increased complexity of Roman life also meant more lawsuits. Therefore, a need arose for more trained advocates to plead them. Naturally, great Greek masters of oratory and rhetoric like Demosthenes, Isocrates, and Thucydides served as models for the formal practice of those arts at Rome.

Two of the most accomplished orators of the day were two of the most eager Hellenizers, Scipio Aemilianus and his Stoic friend Gaius Laelius. According to Cicero, Scipio had a reputation for solemnity, as befitted a great aristocrat. Laelius was a little softer and smoother but tended to be austere overall. Unfortunately, all of their works and those of their contemporaries are lost except for a few scraps quoted by later authors.

PHILOSOPHY

Hand in hand with history and oratory at Rome grew an interest in philosophy, which meant Greek philosophy. Philosophical systems were useful to the practical-minded Romans. They could provide the conceptual and logical structures for developing ideas in speech, could sharpen skill in debate, or could clothe personal and partisan purposes with high-sounding phrases. The formal study of philosophy at Rome also received a big boost in 155 B.C.E. Athens sent an embassy made up of the heads of three major philosophical schools: Critolaus the Peripatetic, Diogenes the Stoic, and Carneades, a Skeptic from the Platonic Academy. While waiting for an opportunity to address the senate, they gave a series of public lectures that aroused much interest.

Carneades made the greatest impression. As a Skeptic, he had no absolute dogmas or guides on ethical and intellectual questions. He substituted a system of probability and an eclectic spirit. He strove to combine the best aspects of all philosophical schools in order to improve the human condition. To show the weakness of absolute dogmas, he argued one side of a question one day and convinced the audience that he was right. Then, just as convincingly, he argued the other side on the following day. Cato the Elder was scandalized and expressed fear that this skeptical approach would undermine traditional Roman morals.

More compatible with traditional Roman values was the philosophy of Stoicism. The Stoics employed rigorously logical dialectical arguments. They believed in a divinely created world brotherhood and hierarchical order. They stressed duty, the upholding of established authority, and the natural rule of the wise. These ideas attracted Romans seeking to justify their growing empire to themselves and others. Panaetius of Rhodes popularized Stoic ideas at Rome. He lived for some time as a guest of Scipio Aemilianus and his famous friend Gaius Laelius. Famous for Stoic learning, Laelius came to be called *Sapiens*, "The Wise." Another Stoic, Blossius of Cumae, was the tutor of the tribunes Tiberius and Gaius Gracchus. He may have had some influence on the arguments used to justify their reforms to aid the poor in 133 and 123 B.C.E.

The philosophy of Epicureanism was less popular at Rome than the other schools. Epicureanism advocated for its followers to withdraw from public life, which the school's founder, Epicurus, had identified as a source of stress and anxiety. This, of course, clashed with a central Roman aristocratic value, and Epicurus' belief in gods that did not actually interfere in the human realm was contrary to traditional Roman thinking about the divine. Even so, by about 100 B.C.E., the philosophy had gained prominent followers among Rome's aristocrats, including some senators.

The Romans themselves made no notable original contributions to philosophy in this period. They had little patience with the intricacies and hairsplitting of philosophical controversies. They mostly received the established systems of the Greek schools, chose what suited their purposes, and applied it to their lives. For example, those who were concerned with law adopted the rigorous dialectic of the Stoics in order to give structure and order to Roman law.

LAW

The publication of Cn. Flavius' handbook on the wording of lawsuits and legal formulae in 304 (p. 96) had broken the pontiffs' monopoly on interpreting the civil law (*ius civile*). Afterward, a number of aristocrats became private students of the law. They obtained public recognition and gratitude as lawyers and legal interpreters known as "jurisconsults" (*iurisconsulti*). In 204 B.C.E., the jurisconsult Sextus Aelius Paetus Catus published a valuable, systematic legal work in three parts: the text of the Twelve Tables, various interpretations that had clarified and expanded the application of those laws over the years, and a detailed presentation of the various forms of lawsuits and their appropriate *formulae*. It became a classic that influenced Roman jurisprudence for centuries. The systematized exposition and interpretation of Roman law by aristocratic jurisconsults clearly reflected the influence of the Greek philosophy and rhetoric that were part of every Roman aristocrat's education. The spirit of Roman law, however, was always rooted in practical experience. Nowhere was that more visible than in the practical changes resulting in more efficient legal procedures as Roman society became more complex.

Civil procedure

The earliest procedure in civil cases was known as the *legis actio* because it was based on very specific statements of actionable deeds or occurrences called *legis actiones*. Under this procedure, both the plaintiff and the defendant had to appear before a pontiff or, after 367, a praetor. First, the plaintiff stated his case orally according to the precise wording of the appropriate *legis actio*. The defendant, whom the plaintiff could compel to appear, had to reply in the same way, as did the pontiff or praetor conducting the hearing. If the latter decided that there was a basis for a suit, he and the contending parties would appoint a mutually agreed-upon fellow citizen as judge. The judge would then hear the evidence and arguments in a separate proceeding and render a verdict. If the plaintiff won, he was responsible for enforcing compliance with the judgment. For example, he could handcuff his opponent for up to sixty days to compel him or his representative to pay a fine.

Because there were only five *legis actiones*, it became harder to find one that would fit a given complaint as life became more complex. Moreover, the prescribed oral statements were so cumbersome as to produce verbal slips that would cause cases to be rejected. The praetors began to create formulary procedures conducted in writing according to *formulae* published in their annual edicts. Like the *legis actio*, the formulary procedure involved an initial hearing and then a trial before a judge or panel of judges. Using a written formula, however, became much more popular during the third and second centuries. It was less subject to disqualifying slips. Also, praetors could modify the *formulae* or create new ones as new situations arose.

Criminal procedure

What the Romans called public law (*ius publicum*) dealt with criminal matters. The earliest ways of dealing with crimes continued to be widely used in the second century B.C.E. and beyond: personal revenge, raising a hue and cry among friends and neighbors to obtain rough and ready justice on the spot, or an informal "trial" before the accused's *paterfamilias*. A *paterfamilias* had the right to judge anyone who was legally subject to his *patria potestas*. He usually relied on ancestral custom (*mos maiorum*) and the advice of an informal council of friends to determine guilt and punishment.

In the more impersonal world of a large city, however, the private methods of dealing with crime were not always satisfactory. Sometime during the years 290 to 288, special minor magistrates called *triumviri capitales* were first appointed to deal with serious crimes like murder. They generally exercised jurisdiction over slaves and lower-class citizens. For members of the upper classes, who had power, money, and influence, there could be a trial before one of the higher magistrates with appeal to a popular assembly in capital cases. Cases prosecuted on appeal were usually handled by tribunes and sometimes by quaestors and aediles. In special cases of great interest to the governing class, the senate could set up special commissions to conduct trials.

As public life and politics became more complex, however, laws were passed to set up standing praetorian courts, *quaestiones perpetuae* (also called *iudicia publica*), to deal with major crimes. The first permanent *quaestio* was the extortion court (*de rebus repetundis*) established by L. Calpurnius Piso in 149 to hear cases against extortionate provincial governors (p. 192). During the first century, the permanent courts greatly increased in number. One of the major features of the courts was their use of juries made up of fifty senators chosen by lot. Later, the use of nonsenators on these juries would be a matter of great political controversy. As was the case in all courts, prosecution had to be initiated by the aggrieved party. There were no public prosecutors, and except for cases of capital punishment or a state fine, the winner of a criminal case also had to enforce the verdict himself.

RELIGION

While jurisprudence and legal procedure were becoming more systematic and efficient under the influence of Greek philosophy and practical experience, the role of Greek influence on the more spectacular events of the early second century B.C.E. is less clear. In 186 B.C.E., the senate passed a decree (a redaction of which is still extant) against the worship of the cult of Bacchus (the Greek god Dionysus, who was popular among the Etruscans to the north and the Greeks in southern Italy) and forbade, under penalty of death, more than five people to meet together for private worship in Rome or Italy without permission from a praetor. The text of the decree strongly implies that the Romans were concerned about the involvement of men—especially men of the political class—in the cult. A rather different picture emerges from Livy's account in Book 39 of his history, which describes the senate's panic about this foreign cult with its secret, orgiastic meetings where women and men, slave and free all worshiped together.

The senators also sought to restrain the overwrought emotionalism of the worship of Cybele, the Great Mother, which had been imported to Rome during the dark days of the Second Punic War (p. 187). The cult of the Great Mother centered on the death and resurrection of the god Attis, who was both her son and husband. The rites symbolized the annual death and rebirth of vegetation. Cybele's gorgeously clad eunuch priests led wild celebrations in her honor. They included riotous outdoor parades, ecstatic dances to the beat of drums and cymbals, and self-mutilations, even self-castrations, performed at the climax of religious fervor. Roman leaders were horrified and, despite the state's official sponsorship of the cult, denied Roman citizens the right to participate.

Expansion of traditional festivals and creation of the *epulones*

Traditional Roman religion was not immune to the desire for more intense religious activities in the exciting world of a great city. Therefore, partly in response to the needs of the people and partly as a result of increased wealth, the state greatly expanded the size and scope of religious festivals, *ludi*, at Rome. Circus races became a popular part of religious festivals. Gladiatorial combats arose in Etruria as funeral rites to supply departed spirits with blood and vitality. In 264 B.C.E., they were introduced at Rome. Dramatic performances, long associated with Greek religion, became part of Roman religious festivals when Livius Andronicus was hired to produce plays at the *Ludi Romani*, September games in honor of Jupiter, in 240 B.C.E. Other major festivals were the *Ludi Plebeii*, Plebeian Games, to honor Jupiter in November; the *Ludi Apollinares*, for Apollo, in July; and the *Ludi Megalenses* (in honor of the Great Mother), the *Ludi Cereales* (for Ceres), and the *Ludi Florales* (for Flora, the goddess of plants), all in April.

The increase in the size and number of religious festivals and games necessitated the creation of a new college of priests in 196 B.C.E. They were the *epulones* (sing. *epulo*), the banquet masters. They became responsible for holding the public religious banquets that accompanied many major festivals and events such as triumphs, state funerals, and special thanksgivings to the gods. The overall management of many major festivals was the responsibility of the aediles. As time went on, festivals brought them so much public recognition and popularity that they had an interest in expanding the number of days and events involved, often at their own expense.

New ideas and cults

The educated Roman elite did not abandon traditional religious practice. Nevertheless, they became more sophisticated in their religious views under the influence of Greek religion and philosophy. Many adopted the ideas of the Hellenistic thinker Euhemerus. He argued that the gods were simply extraordinary human beings who, like Hercules, had come to be worshiped for their great services to mankind. His work on the origin of the gods was so popular that Ennius translated it into Latin. It had a significant impact on the Roman aristocracy's ambition for fame and glory. It is even the underlying assumption behind the deification of Roman emperors later on. At the same time, the Greek-influenced personification of abstract concepts like hope, honor, and virtue as deities continued with the dedication of new temples to them.

EDUCATION

Expanded cultural and intellectual life created a need for more formal education at Rome. In the early days, everyone's education, such as it was, had centered on home and family. Slaves were not used as tutors. Mothers and other female relatives trained children at least until the age of seven. After that, girls remained under their mothers' tutelage to learn about household management. Boys accompanied their fathers into the fields and Forum to learn how to make a living and be good citizens. Fathers considered it one of their gravest duties to furnish precepts and examples from which their sons could learn their roles as citizens.

At about fifteen, a young male became a man and put on the *toga virilis*, toga of manhood. Soon, the young man left his father's personal care. A young aristocrat was often placed by his father in the hands of an old and distinguished friend for further training in public life. After a year or two, at about age seventeen, the young aristocrat entered military service. First, as a soldier in the ranks, he learned how to fight and obey orders. Then, he joined a general's staff to learn the techniques of command. After that, the young man apprenticed himself to another older man at Rome to complete his training in political life.

The purpose of this system was not only to provide a basic education in practical matters, but also to inculcate the rigid system of Roman moral values and service to the state as passed on in the ancestral customs, *mos maiorum*. This ideal is seen, for example, in the Roman attitude toward athletic training. The Hellenistic Greeks fostered athletics for health, beauty, and personal satisfaction in excelling through competition as much as for military training. Roman physical education still centered primarily on training for war.

In the third and second centuries, however, with the increasing interest in Greek culture, Romans began to adopt features of Greek education. Wealthy Romans began to use learned Greek slaves to take care of children and supervise the instruction of the young in Greek language and literature. Greek freedmen set up grammar schools to teach the children of those who could not afford slave tutors. At first, only Greek was taught. As Latin literature became established, Latin grammar schools appeared, too. In the second century, professional Greek philosophers were even coming to Rome to offer instruction at a higher level.

OVERVIEW AND PROSPECT

In every way, therefore, Rome's expansion into the wider Mediterranean world between 264 and 133 B.C.E. had intensified the interaction of Greek and Roman culture. Although Greek influence had been important since the arrival of the Greeks in Italy, it had never been so self-consciously cultivated as it was in this period. Roman leaders intentionally adorned their city with public buildings, monuments, and temples in the Greek style. They decorated public and private spaces with the best examples of Greek art taken as spoils of victory or copied for them by hired Greek craftsmen. The rich turned simple Italic atrium houses into complexes modeled on the houses of wealthy Hellenistic Greeks. At the same time, the Romans used new construction materials, particularly molded concrete and baked bricks, which allowed them to surpass the Greeks in the size and complexity of their structures with arches and vaults. By the last third of the second century B.C.E., Rome looked much more like a capitol city than it ever had before.

The Romans modeled their literature on that of the Greeks. The first known work of Latin literature was Livius Andronicus' translation of Homer's epic, the *Odyssey*. Later, Andronicus adapted Greek tragedies and comedies for performance at Roman religious festivals. Gnaeus Naevius used the Greek genres of epic, tragedy, and comedy to portray patriotic subjects in Latin literature. Quintus Ennius added to Naevius' legacy by adopting Greek quantitative meter in place of the native accentual Saturnian meter. Other authors like the comic playwrights Plautus and Terence specialized in particular genres.

The first Roman prose authors were aristocrats like Fabius Pictor and Cincius Alimentus. Writing in Greek, they produced annals, year-by-year accounts of Roman history, to advertise and justify Rome's achievements to the wider Hellenistic world. Not long after them, the Romanized Greek hostage Polybius wrote the greatest surviving Greek account of Roman history. Even the very nationalistic elder Cato learned to read Greek and adapt Greek prose models for his various writings in Latin.

Although Cato was skeptical of Greek philosophy, others eagerly adopted what they found useful from the Peripatetic, Academic Skeptic, and Stoic schools of Greek philosophy. Romans found Stoicism particularly compatible with their values and outlook. Epicureanism meshed less easily with traditional Roman values and beliefs.

Roman law and legal procedure developed in their own particularly Roman way. Nevertheless, the formal systemization and interpretation of Roman law owe much to the influence of Greek logic and rhetoric. Greek oratory and rhetoric also provided valuable guides for pleading cases in the permanent courts created to try major criminal cases in Rome's increasingly complex social and political life.

While Roman leaders curbed objectionable elements of Hellenistic cults like those of Dionysus (Bacchus) and Cybele (The Great Mother), they did not reject these deities. They also continued the deification of abstract concepts in the Greek manner. As early as Ennius, Romans were attracted to the Greek Euhemerus' theory that the gods originated as extraordinary human beings. In 240 B.C.E., the Greek practice of performing dramas at religious festivals was adopted in Rome. So many new festivals were created that Rome needed a new board of priests, the *epulones*, in 196 B.C.E. to oversee ritual banquets.

In the third and second centuries B.C.E., well-to-do and upper-class Romans began to distinguish themselves through more formal education. They bought or hired educated Greek tutors in language, literature, and thought for their children. More advanced students studied with professional Greek philosophers who found it profitable to set up shop in Rome.

During the next century, the Greco-Roman cultural synthesis would progress still further as the Romans became even more closely involved with their Greek subjects.

SUGGESTED READING

Feeney, D. *Beyond Greek: The Beginnings of Latin Literature.* Harvard: Harvard University Press, 2016.

Gruen, E. S. *Culture and National Identity in Republican Rome.* Ithaca: Cornell University Press, 1992.

CHAPTER 12

The Gracchi and the struggle over reforms, 133 to 121 B.C.E.

By 133 B.C.E., the changes resulting from the Punic wars and Rome's rapid expansion overseas were producing serious problems and discontent among a number of groups (pp. 180–5). At the same time, aristocratic political competition was intensifying (pp. 188–9). Tiberius Sempronius Gracchus and his brother Gaius tried to deal with some of these problems and advance themselves. They ushered in a century of increasingly violent political upheavals that helped eventually to destroy the Roman Republic. Therefore, the careers of these two men and the circumstances surrounding them constitute one of the most intensively studied subjects in Roman history.

SOURCES FOR THE PERIOD OF THE GRACCHI, 133 TO 121 B.C.E.

Sources for this crucial period are not nearly so extensive or reliable as for the preceding one. There is no extant contemporary source. Polybius lived through the Gracchan crisis, which colored the later stages of his writing, but he ended his history with the year 145/144 B.C.E. Posidonius' continuation of Polybius down to about 78 B.C.E. is lost (p. 334). Books 58 to 61 of Livy contained much valuable detail from contemporary or nearly contemporary sources. They, too, are lost, except for the brief summaries in the *Periochae* and the sparse outlines derived from Livy in the late Empire (p. 398). The few relevant fragments of Diodorus Siculus and Cassius Dio have little value, and Velleius

Paterculus' brief treatment has little to add. Two extensive accounts, Plutarch's biographies of Tiberius and Gaius and sections 7 to 26 in Book 1 of Appian's *Civil Wars*, make it possible to construct a reasonable analysis of the events.

MOUNTING PROBLEMS

By 133 B.C.E., many Romans must have sensed that serious problems needed to be addressed. Slave rebellions had been causing great difficulties since 143 B.C.E. There were shortages of grain in 140 and 138 at Rome. The government had to intervene. Worst of all from the point of view of Roman leaders, it was becoming harder to raise armies. By 133, whether or not the amount of actual property required for legionary service had been lowered, many Romans saw a crisis in the number of *assidui* (small landholders) available for military service. It now seems that the freeborn population did not fall but was actually increasing and dividing up a limited amount of available land into units too small for families. The number of Romans who registered for the census had dropped by 19,000, the equivalent of more than three legions, between 164/163 and 136/135. Men whose small inheritances did not meet the property requirement may not have bothered to register. Others who did meet the requirement may have wanted to avoid service by not registering. Levying troops for unpopular wars met stiff resistance on a number of occasions from 151 onward. In 134, Scipio Aemilianus was allowed to recruit only volunteers for service in Spain. Supposedly, a full-scale levy would have stripped Italy of manpower. Some people thought that the overall population was falling and that Romans needed to produce more children. Others sought to give more land to those who no longer had enough to support a family. The real problem may have been that Italy no longer had enough farmland for its population.

In 145 or, more probably, 140 B.C.E., Gaius Laelius, friend of Scipio Aemilianus (p. 206), had tried to relieve the situation by proposing a law to restore the provisions of the so-called Licinio-Sextian laws of 367. These laws supposedly limited to 500 *iugera* (about 320 acres) the amount of public land that an individual could hold. Laelius wished to confiscate the excess and resettle the needy on it. Whether he saw this proposal as a three-way solution for reducing the high urban population, replacing a portion of slave labor with small freeholders, and providing more *assidui* for legionary service is not known. Such goals were expressed for similar proposals later. Many fellow senators vehemently opposed Laelius. He decided to withdraw his proposal and avoid a difficult issue. In 133, however, the tribune Tiberius Sempronius Gracchus refused to avoid a confrontation under similar circumstances.

THE TRIBUNESHIP OF TIBERIUS GRACCHUS, 133 B.C.E.

The thirty-year-old Tiberius Gracchus took office as tribune of the people for 133 B.C.E. He bemoaned the impoverishment of Roman citizens and worried about the loss of recruits for Roman legions. Without consulting the senate, he immediately proposed a land-reform bill in the *concilium plebis*. His bill was designed to break up the large estates created out of public land and to divide them among landless Roman citizens. It had been drafted with the support of his father-in-law, Appius Claudius Pulcher, the "first man" (*princeps*) of the senate, and of two learned jurists, P. Licinius Crassus Dives Mucianus and P. Mucius Scaevola. Crassus was Gaius Gracchus' father-in-law; Scaevola was one of the consuls. The bill ordered the state to repossess holdings of public land in excess of 500 *iugera* (320 acres) plus an allowance of 250 *iugera* (160 acres) for each child. Those who held public land were to receive clear title to the amounts allowed. That land would be unencumbered by taxes or rent. Reimbursement would be made for any improvements (such as buildings or plantings) on the land to be repossessed. The repossessed land was to be assigned to landless citizens in lots varying in size, probably from fifteen up to thirty *iugera* (nine to eighteen acres). It would be subject to a nominal rent payable to the state. The allotments were inalienable and entailed against sale or transfer.

Although the bill was controversial and inflamed opinion against Tiberius in the senate, his initial failure to consult that body was neither illegal nor unprecedented. In 232 B.C.E., Gaius Flaminius had proposed his agrarian law without consulting the senate (p. 134). In 188, a tribunician bill to extend voting rights to some Latin towns was presented directly to the *concilium plebis*. Still, when the tribune Marcus Octavius vetoed Tiberius' bill, Tiberius agreed to submit it to the senate for debate. When the senate rejected it, he made the bill more attractive to the common people by making it less generous toward the large landholders. When he resubmitted it to the *concilium plebis*, Octavius seems to have violated "constitutional" custom by continuing to veto it. Temporary vetoes trying to force a compromise were normal; denying a fellow tribune permanently his right to put a proposal to the *concilium plebis* for a vote was not.

Neither law nor custom provided any clear guidance at such a "constitutional" impasse. To break it, Tiberius took an even more radical step. It would virtually nullify the power of veto. Arguing that Octavius was working against the interests of the *plebs* instead of for them as a tribune should, Tiberius called for a vote to remove Octavius from office. Tiberius needed eighteen of the thirty-five tribal votes. When the first seventeen tribes had voted against Octavius, Tiberius held up the voting for a moment to appeal to his colleague to change his mind. The latter remained obdurate. The voting resumed. Octavius was divested of his tribunate and forcibly removed from the tribunes' bench. Later, the land bill passed.

The implications of Tiberius' actions only aroused more opposition. By deposing a fellow tribune for exercising the veto, he had, in effect, removed one of the Republic's fundamental checks on the acquisition of excessive power. To many senators, even some not opposed to land reform, Tiberius appeared to have gone too far.

The Agrarian Commission

To carry out the provisions of the land act, Tiberius asked the people to appoint a commission of three members consisting of himself; his younger brother, Gaius; and his father-in-law, Appius Claudius. Such blatant packing of the commission, though probably not yet illegal, also may have disturbed many senators. The commission was later granted full judicial powers with *imperium* to determine which lands were public and which private, to repossess all public land not exempt by the law, and to distribute it to new settlers. Ample funds were required to pay the salaries of surveyors and other officials. They were also needed to help the settlers make a new start by providing them with housing, tools, work animals, seed, and even subsistence until their crops were harvested. Now Tiberius' opponents in the senate, which traditionally controlled appropriations, had a chance to stop him. They appropriated operating expenses of only a denarius and a half a day. Tiberius took another radical step to thwart them.

The Pergamene treasure

The late Attalus III of Pergamum had willed his personal fortune and kingdom to the Roman People (p. 165). This matter usually would have been handled in the senate. Yet, Tiberius, it is said, at once asked the people to make these funds available for the use of the commission. It is not completely certain whether such a threat to the senate's prerogatives in financial affairs was ever passed. Perhaps the mere proposal caused that body to open up the public treasury for the use of the commission. Thus thwarted, Tiberius' opponents began to threaten his life. To prepare the ground for violence, they circulated the rumor that he was planning to declare himself king (*rex*, i.e., tyrant) and had retained for that purpose the diadem, scepter, and royal vestments of the Pergamene kings.

Tiberius campaigns for a second term

To protect his legislation from annulment and to save himself from certain prosecution, Tiberius offered to run for a second term. That was contrary to recent custom but not illegal. The sovereign people could reelect him in spite of law or custom. They had similarly violated custom when they elected his maternal grandfather, the elder Scipio Africanus, to the supreme command during the Second Punic War. Tiberius frustrated and embittered his opponents by refusing to abide by traditional political rules. They were determined to stop him.

The first attempt to hold the election was broken up by a tribunician veto and bogus religious omens. The assembly reconvened in front of the Temple of Jupiter on the Capitoline Hill the next day. The spot could easily be blocked off. Tiberius' supporters assembled early and tried to keep out his opponents. The senate met in the nearby Temple of Fides (Faith) to decide what action to take. The cumulative effect of Tiberius' actions had raised fears, exploited by his personal enemies, that he was aiming to set up a *regnum* (tyranny). The majority of senators present invoked an ancient law under which he could be killed as a tyrant (*rex*).

The presiding consul, P. Mucius Scaevola, refused to take part in what he saw as unjustified murder. Tiberius' own first cousin, the *pontifex maximus* P. Cornelius Scipio Nasica Serapio, had no such scruples. He commanded those who wished to save the state to follow him. Scipio then turned his toga upside down and veiled his head with the purple hem in front and rushed out of the Temple of Fides. The change in his dress may would have communicated to others that Nasica was acting in some ritual capacity.

The exact nature of the ritual is still vigorously debated, but many scholars think that Scipio meant to turn Gracchus over to the wrath of the gods. As Scipio and his followers approached the voting, many of Tiberius' supporters fled. Using broken pieces of chairs and benches, Nasica and his followers clubbed to death Tiberius and 300 others. Then they threw the bodies into the Tiber.

P. Popillius Laenas and P. Rupilius, consuls in 132 B.C.E., set up a special court to try the Gracchan partisans. The more outspoken ones were executed. To forestall popular retribution in the backlash that followed Tiberius' death, Scipio Nasica was whisked away on a diplomatic mission to Pergamum for organizing Rome's new province, where he died.

TIBERIUS' MOTIVES

The struggle over Tiberius Gracchus' land bill has often been simplistically portrayed as a struggle between Tiberius, on the one hand, and the Roman senate, on the other: Tiberius appears as some kind of ideologically motivated, democratic liberal or radical reformer in the modern mold; the senate merely represents the corporate interest of a wealthy, landed oligarchy seeking to protect its financial interests without any regard for the social and economic problems of Rome. Such a view is untenable. Tiberius did not start out with some scheme of radical reform in mind. His reform was essentially a conservative one. It was designed to restore Roman military manpower, which had always depended on the class of smallholders, and to halt the spread of estates worked by slaves. Their increasing numbers posed a serious threat to internal peace and security, as witnessed by the slave revolts in Italy and Sicily from 143 to 132 B.C.E. (pp. 181–3).

Perhaps, Tiberius hoped that his law would stem further migration of poor rural citizens into the city and even attract back to the countryside some of those who had already gone to the city. Thus, the law might have helped to alleviate some of the unemployment and attendant sociopolitical stress existing in Rome itself. The flow of booty that had sustained economic growth at Rome had ceased with the sacks of Carthage and Corinth in 146. Since then, Rome's wars, mainly against poor tribesmen and slaves, had become an economic burden. The urban economy was heavily dependent on expenditures for publicly and privately funded construction projects. It probably was not growing enough to keep pace with population growth (p. 186).

Tiberius' reforms, therefore, were not based solely, or even primarily, on consideration of some abstract radical ideology. Still, it is quite possible that his education at the hands of Greek and Stoic teachers chosen by his mother (on whom, see p. 183) influenced his thinking and provided him with arguments to support the rightness and justice of his cause. Nor was Tiberius fighting the senate as an institution or seeking to destroy the primary role of the senatorial aristocracy in governmental affairs. Tiberius himself was a member of one of the consular families that dominated the senate. The senate was not a monolithic bloc opposed to Tiberius: it is often overlooked that powerful members of the senate worked on his initial reform bill.

Tiberius' initial actions must be viewed as part of the normal workings of the senatorial oligarchy. When some powerful and influential senators wanted to promote legislation that other senators opposed, it was not unusual for them to work through a friendly tribune. In return, he could hope to advance his career with their support in elections for higher offices. The crucial point is that Tiberius refused to follow the normal rules of republican politics by deposing a fellow tribune (albeit one who may have been going to an extreme himself), by usurping the senate's prerogatives in fiscal matters, and by violating the tribunes' customary practice of avoiding consecutive terms. Therefore, even many senators initially supporting his legislation abandoned or opposed him. The stability of the republican system depended on no one man having the kind of unfettered power that, as tribune, Tiberius seemed to be usurping, however laudable or understandable his motives.

Personal and factional conflicts

Tiberius Gracchus' determination to pursue agrarian reform in the face of bitter opposition from many of his fellow nobles cannot be understood without reference to the personalities, careers, alliances, and animosities of individual senatorial aristocrats. As expected of members of his class, Tiberius Gracchus was a politically ambitious young man. A number of factors made him particularly so. It was the duty of Tiberius, the oldest surviving son, to equal or surpass the achievements of his father and preserve the *dignitas* of the family. Tiberius' mother, Cornelia, was the daughter of the elder Scipio Africanus, victor over Hannibal. Ambitious for her sons, she is said to have urged them to live up to the glory of both sides of the family and make her known not only as the daughter of Africanus but also as the mother of the Gracchi. She obtained the accomplished rhetorician Diophanes of Mytilene and the respected Stoic philosopher Blossius of Cumae as their tutors. She also used her personal connections to promote their careers.

Cornelia's mother, Aemilia, was the sister of Lucius Aemilius Paullus, victor at Pydna. He was the natural father of Scipio Aemilianus, the younger Africanus, destroyer of Carthage. By blood, therefore, Scipio was Cornelia's first cousin. By law, having been adopted by Cornelia's brother, he was also her children's first cousin. Finally, he married her daughter Sempronia and thus became the brother-in-law of her sons, Tiberius and Gaius.

At first, the connections with Scipio Aemilianus served Tiberius well. As a youth, he had accompanied Scipio to Carthage and won his praise for valor. That would have impressed the voters when he ran for the quaestorship in 138. Nevertheless, there was ill-will between Tiberius' immediate family and Scipio over an issue of inheritance produced by their complex relationships. Also, the marriage of Sempronia, which probably had been designed to restore friendly relations, was an unhappy one and merely made matters worse. As so often happened in the Roman aristocracy, complex interrelationships that had arisen from close political cooperation between families in earlier generations led to personal animosities that embittered political differences and rivalries in later generations.

Probably two or three years after he returned from Carthage, Tiberius became betrothed to the daughter of Appius Claudius Pulcher, who happened to be Scipio's chief rival for preeminence within the nobility. In 137, Tiberius served as quaestor in Spain under C. Hostilius Mancinus, who was besieging Numantia. Mancinus' close relative, L. Hostilius Mancinus, was an enemy of Scipio. Mancinus and his whole army suffered the disgrace of being captured by the Numantines (p. 172). Tiberius, because of his father's reputation, was the only one with whom the Numantines would negotiate a treaty. He obtained the release of the whole Roman army and saved much precious manpower for Rome. It looked as if Tiberius would gain the kind of fame and honor that would advance his career.

Tiberius was bitterly disappointed. When he brought the treaty to the senate for ratification, Scipio Aemilianus strenuously opposed it and helped persuade a majority of senators to reject it. Furthermore, Mancinus, Tiberius, and the other officers were prosecuted for cowardice. Tiberius and the others secured an acquittal, but Mancinus was ordered stripped, bound in chains, and handed over to the Numantines. (The Numantines showed their contempt for Rome by sending him back.) Hostility to the Hostilii Mancini may well have been a factor in Scipio's actions. Even more important was his desire to keep the war going so that he could obtain the command and gain the glory of avenging Rome's disgrace with another great victory. He succeeded in 134 and 133 after obtaining exemption from the law forbidding second consulships. In fairness to Scipio, he did help Tiberius escape Mancinus' fate, and he took Tiberius' brother Gaius to Spain as an officer on his staff, but the whole episode had dealt a tremendous blow to Tiberius' prestige.

Running for the office of tribune in 134 B.C.E., Tiberius was desperate to find a means of saving his political career. Land reform was the perfect vehicle. It seemed to be a solution to some of Rome's pressing socioeconomic and military problems and was a very popular issue with a large bloc of voters in the rural tribes. Moreover, his father-in-law—Appius Claudius Pulcher—and Appius' powerful friends were backing land reform to gain popular support in rivalry with Scipio. Once Tiberius was elected and succeeded in obtaining a law for redistribution of land, they hoped that the recipients would become a grateful source of future votes in the rural tribes. The rural tribes, of course, were the key to the election of tribunes and passing of plebiscites in the *concilium plebis*. Also, the backing of a grateful Appius and his friends would help Tiberius gain election to the higher magistracies through the *comitia centuriata*. Significantly, Scipio Aemilianus' friend C. Laelius assisted the consuls P. Popillius Laenas and P. Rupilius, another friend of Scipio, in persecuting Tiberius' followers in 132.

Personal animosities and political maneuvering within the senatorial aristocracy, therefore, go a long way to explain the actions of Tiberius Gracchus, his major backers, and some of the leading opponents of his reform. Tiberius was certainly sincere in his desire to alleviate some of Rome's pressing problems through land reform. Moreover, he also may have honestly believed that there was more long-term danger to Rome's well-being if he bowed to the traditional obstructionist tactics of his opponents within the senate than if he mobilized the inherently sovereign power of the *concilium plebis* to overcome them. Nevertheless, for a politician, the most attractive reform is one that is not only just but also politically beneficial to the politician himself. Once embarked on reform, Tiberius could not give up in the face of powerful opponents. To have suffered a second political defeat after the rejection of the Numantine treaty may well have meant the end of his career within the senatorial elite. That is why, every time his opponents tried to use traditional legal means to stop him, Tiberius resorted to more and more untraditional practices to thwart them.

THE LAND COMMISSION AND ITS IMPACT

The land commission set up to administer the Sempronian land law was allowed to function even after its creator was slain. Again, therefore, it seems that much of the opposition to Tiberius in the senate was not based on ideological opposition to reform or narrow economic self-interest but on personal and larger political grounds. Because the man who would have reaped the most political benefits from the reform was now dead, it was no longer a threat to his rivals. Indeed, they now tried to reap for themselves the benefits of *gratia* (gratitude) among those who received land. One official, often identified as Popillius Laenas, actually boasted of what he had done to carry out the law. On a milestone in Lucania, it is inscribed that he was "the first to compel the shepherds to make way for the plowmen."

Also, once any perceived threat that Tiberius posed was gone, his brother and other supporters like M. Fulvius Flaccus and C. Papirius Carbo were allowed to serve on the land commission. Despite lawsuits and delaying tactics by those who possessed the land, within six years the commission may have settled over 75,000 men, an increase of 20 percent in the manpower available for military service. The Gracchan land law seems temporarily to have achieved the objective of strengthening the military power of Rome.

The work of the commission was hard and probably involved some injustice. After the passage of years and with the poor methods of keeping records in ancient times, it was seldom easy to determine what land was public. Probably, in some cases, the commissioners seized private property and in others confiscated the only good land that the occupiers possessed. The complaints must have been numerous and bitter.

ROME'S ALLIES AND THE DEATH OF SCIPIO

The grievances of Roman citizens probably were not given a sympathetic hearing, but those of the Latin and Italian allies could not have been brushed aside so easily. To have ignored the complaints of the allied states might have constituted a violation of their treaty rights with Rome, disturbed peaceful relations, and perhaps even invited revolt. To some allies, whether individuals or communities, Rome had assigned public lands by lease or by outright grant. In other cases, wealthy allied landowners simply had encroached on otherwise unoccupied Roman public land, as had wealthy Romans.

In either case, when the allies looked for a patron to champion their interests, they found one in Scipio Aemilianus, the destroyer of Carthage and Numantia. Realizing the value of their military help and anxious to extend his network of clients, he gladly consented to press their claims before the senate. He succeeded in having the judicial powers of the commissioners transferred to the consuls, at least as far as the Latin and Italian allies were concerned. If the consuls preferred to go on long campaigns to avoid involvement in irksome land disputes, the work of the commission would be brought to a standstill.

Scipio's meddling with the land problem in 129 B.C.E. did not help his popularity. In fact, his popularity had waned since 131 B.C.E., when he spoke out against a law proposed by the land commissioner Carbo, who was also a tribune that year. The bill was to legalize reelection to the tribuneship. In the course of the debate, Carbo asked him what he thought of the murder of Tiberius Gracchus. Scipio replied, "If Gracchus intended to seize the government, he has been justly slain." When the crowd greeted this remark with jeers and catcalls, Scipio roared, "I have never been scared by the shouts of the enemy in arms. Shall I be frightened by your outcries, you stepsons of Italy?" The bill in question failed, but Carbo did succeed in extending the secret ballot to legislative assemblies (see Box 12.1). That was detrimental to the politically entrenched nobles. At voting time, now, they could less easily hold accountable those on whom they had bestowed benefits.

12.1 THE SECRET BALLOT

Traditionally at elections and legislative assemblies, Roman citizens openly declared their votes in front of an official who recorded the vote in a record book. Anyone standing close by could hear the declaration, making it relatively easy for the powerful (patrons, commanders, landlords, etc.) to coerce or entice those dependent on them to vote in a particular way. In the new secret ballot system introduced to Roman voting assemblies over the course of the 130s B.C.E., voters posited a clay tablet, marked with "yes" or "no" (in the case of legislation) or the name of a candidate, into a basket. It is difficult to ascertain the precise ramifications of the secret ballot in Rome beyond giving voters some measure of independence, but it is unlikely to have eliminated electoral fraud. The introduction of the secret ballot in other societies has been shown to change one form of corruption for another. Under the new system at Rome, it would have been more difficult, if not impossible, to prove how an individual voted, so the use of bribes and threats to obtain a particular vote would be less useful than they had been in the past. Now less direct methods would have to do: the minds of voters could be turned by gifts of food and drink. Alternately, unfriendly voters could be persuaded to stay home, while supporters could be enticed to show up on voting day. Even so, the introduction of the secret ballot spurred important changes to the Roman political landscape and should be taken as a sign that, for the Romans, voting was a civic duty that was not taken for granted.

In May of 129 B.C.E., Scipio announced that he was going to make a speech about the Latin and Italian allies. It is not known whether he intended to talk about the granting of Roman citizenship. He went home early to work on his speech. The next morning he was found dead in bed. He may have died from natural causes. Rumor made him the victim of foul play by one of the Gracchans, perhaps aided by Sempronia, Scipio's wife and sister of Tiberius Gracchus. The truth cannot be known.

The Romans previously had been fairly generous in granting citizenship to upper-class individuals in the Latin and Italian towns. There had never been any widespread desire for Roman citizenship among the allied communities. Now, however, the activities of the Gracchan land commission seem to have brought into sharper focus the increasingly inequitable relationship between Roman citizens and the allies (p. 181). A number of Latins and Italians began to press more actively for citizenship. Their overt agitation in Rome made them quite unpopular. In 126, with senatorial approval, a tribune pushed a bill through the assembly to legalize their expulsion.

The land commissioner Fulvius Flaccus took up the cause of citizenship for the Italian allies. As consul in 125 B.C.E., he proposed the grant of citizenship to any of the allies that wanted it. Fulvius had to abandon his efforts when his opponents in the senate sent him off at the head of a consular army to help Massilia fight hostile neighbors in southern Gaul.

In the same year, 125 B.C.E., the allied town of Fregellae rose up in rebellion. What, if any, connection this event had with the question of Roman citizenship for the Italians is unclear. The events in Rome may simply have aggravated a particular local conflict among the Fregellans. At any rate, the revolt was crushed with the help of Fregellan "loyalists," who were rewarded. The rest were stripped of their property and the town was destroyed.

Although no other town revolted, the events at Fregellae may have heightened interest in the question of citizenship among other Italians. At Rome, feelings intensified: attempts were made to punish those who were suspected of having inspired and encouraged the revolt. Even the younger brother of Tiberius Gracchus, Gaius, who had just returned from a year as quaestor in Sardinia, was accused but was able to prove his innocence.

GAIUS GRACCHUS, TRIBUNE OF THE PLEBS, 123 TO 122 B.C.E.

The powers and capabilities of Gaius Gracchus were known and feared years before he became a tribune. Those who had opposed Tiberius considered Gaius a menace because of his influence over crowds and his membership in the land commission set up by his brother. In 124 B.C.E., despite hostility from powerful fellow nobles, he campaigned for the tribuneship with promises of reform and was elected for 123. Voters from the rural tribes poured into the city, as they had done ten years before to support his brother. In 123, they voted him into office again for 122 B.C.E., although he was not an official candidate at that time.

The motives of Gaius Gracchus in promoting reform were essentially those of his brother Tiberius, with two major additions. First, there was the desire to avenge the murder of his brother and repair the damage to his family's honor. Second, he wanted to build a far broader and more complex coalition of socioeconomic groups not normally powerful participants in the political process. He would gain an even broader base of political support than Tiberius had. That would help him win the offices necessary to repair his family's tattered *dignitas*.

The two years of the tribuneships of Gaius Gracchus were politically among the most memorable of the Roman Republic and perhaps the most crucial. The tribuneship had become an instrument controlled by the same small number of noble families that also dominated the senate. Gaius turned it into a powerful weapon by which an ambitious individual, usually from one of the same noble families, could effectively circumvent the control of his peers. A century later (in 23 B.C.E.), Emperor Augustus strengthened his position against opposition from nobles loyal to the old Republic by invoking not the powers of a consul but the power of a tribune (*tribunicia potestas*).

THE REFORMS OF GAIUS GRACCHUS

Upon taking office, Gaius Gracchus proceeded to stir the fury of the people against his brother's murderers, who had violated the sacrosanctity of a tribune. He also took aim at the procedure by which Popillius Laenas had condemned his brother's followers to death without appeal to the people. The *concilium plebis* responded by passing a bill that prohibited the senate from creating extraordinary tribunals to condemn political offenders without the right of appeal. Under a retroactive provision of this law, Popillius Laenas was condemned and exiled.

Revenged, Gaius Gracchus proposed a series of measures. He hoped to advance both his and the public's interests by organizing a coalition of the equestrian class, the proletarian city voters, and the small farmers. His program dealt intelligently and realistically with the social and economic problems generated by Imperial expansion. The most pressing problems concerned the spreading unemployment and slums, the periodic fluctuations in food prices, the decline of military strength and efficiency, the frequent slave revolts, the continuing challenges of provincial administration, and the disaffected allies.

Land and roads

To win over the farmers' vote and further meet their legitimate needs, Gaius revived and amplified his brother's legislation. He restored to the land commission the judicial powers that Scipio Aemilianus had persuaded the senate to remove. Most of the public land had by now been assigned, but he was able to benefit the farmers by an extensive road-building program that created a network of secondary roads linking farms with markets, villages with towns, and towns with Rome. These roads not only employed farmers as road builders but also permitted them to move their crops more easily and cheaply to markets and thus improved trade. Also, by facilitating travel to Rome and, therefore, attendance at assembly meetings, they promoted fuller participation in the affairs of government. The extraordinary speed with which this project was completed under Gaius' personal direction further increased the fears of many senators.

The Grain Law

To gain the political support of the city masses and relieve their real distress, Gaius persuaded the assembly to pass the famous *lex Frumentaria*, or Grain Law, which provided that the state should buy and import grain from overseas for sale to citizens residing in Rome. It was sold on demand in fixed monthly amounts at six and one-third *asses* per *modius* (about one-quarter of a bushel), a price roughly equivalent to one-half of an unskilled worker's daily wage. Sometimes this price was a little below the average market price in Rome, but it was often much higher than the market price, in which case there would be no demand for public grain until the market price rose again.

This law, the most severely criticized of all the Gracchan reforms, did not constitute a dole; it was passed solely to promote price stabilization for the benefit of the consumer, not, as now, for the producer. A considerable amount of the wheat consumed in Rome came in as tribute and cost the state only the expenses of transport, naval convoy, and storage. The Grain Law even provided for the construction of warehouses and wharves in Rome, a measure that would, intentionally or not, give employment to many while it implemented the subsidy for grain.

The Grain Law also had a more subtle purpose. It was designed to weaken the patronage of entrenched fellow nobles and increase that of Gaius by using public money. In periods of high food prices, candidates for high office had regularly bought votes by the provision or promise of cheap grain. The Grain Law helped to restore the independence of Roman citizens and rendered more effective Carbo's secret ballot law of 131 B.C.E. (p. 217). It also earned *gratia* for Gaius among the voters resident in Rome.

Military and monetary reform

Some other important laws also brought needed relief to poorer citizens and politically valuable gratitude to Gaius. The Military Law (*lex Militaris*) required the government to clothe and equip Roman soldiers without deductions from their pay, shortened the term of military service, and forbade the drafting of boys under the age of seventeen. This law was intended to improve army morale, always a concern of the Gracchi, and to win the political support of soldiers, allies, and voters with small incomes. Furthermore, in 122 B.C.E., the weight of the denarius was reduced. This measure not only meant that in real terms Roman citizens had to pay less in fixed rents and taxes but also significantly reduced the tribute of the Roman allies without special legislation.

New colonies

Gaius Gracchus' laws authorized commercial and agricultural colonies in Italy and across the sea. They were intended to relieve overpopulation in Rome and provide economic opportunities for farmers, traders, craftsmen, and small businessmen unable to make a living. The sites selected were Capua, Tarentum, and Carthage. The most ambitious of these projects was authorized by the *lex Rubria*, which a friend of Gaius proposed. It sanctioned the founding of Junonia near the cursed site of Carthage, where

6000 colonists drawn from Rome and the rest of Italy were to be settled on farms of 200 *iugera* (125 acres). Gaius went to Africa to supervise in person the initial stages of the settlement. His opponents, using propaganda and appealing to religious fears of the curse pronounced in 146 B.C.E., persuaded the voters to repeal the *lex Rubria*. Had the project succeeded, he would have created a colony of loyal supporters in the vital grain-growing area of North Africa. Here, too, he anticipated by almost a century the policy of Augustus.

Provincial taxes and jury service

In an effort to drive a wedge between the wealthy equestrian class and his senatorial rivals, Gaius appealed to the economic interests of important *equites*. Those *equites* who had significant interests in the operations of the *publicani*, particularly in tax collecting, were already irked by the senatorial aristocracy's control over finance and provincial administration. They were especially interested in the rich revenues of the new province of Asia. Its taxes were collected at a fixed rate directly by the senatorial governor. Gaius obtained passage of a law overturning this arrangement and directing instead that the taxes of Asia take the form of a tithe. Unlike the system employed in Sicily, where the tithe was auctioned and collected locally, the Gracchan law stipulated that the censors should auction the lucrative contracts for the tithes of Asia to companies of *publicani* in Rome for five-year terms. In that way, the money would come directly to the treasury in Rome, and the companies that won the contracts would then collect the taxes in the province.

The new system of taxation provided the Roman treasury with immediate funds and, theoretically at least, was less burdensome to the provincial taxpayers than fixed taxes. Payments would fluctuate with good or poor crops. It was also beneficial to the Roman tax collectors since clauses were added to protect them against losses from war and other calamities. It naturally benefited the rich men of the equestrian class, for the right to bid was open only to those owning property worth in excess of 400,000 *sestertii* (sesterces), the minimum equestrian census. Thus, Gaius' law increased the economic power of the wealthy equestrians. They, in turn, were expected to use some of their wealth to advance their benefactor's political career. At the same time, Gaius weakened the power of his rivals within the senatorial class.

An additional move that tended to divide the equestrians from Gaius' senatorial rivals within the nobility was the *lex Acilia*, sponsored by another of Gaius' supporters. It excluded senators, the relatives of senators, and all curule magistrates from the juries of the standing courts established by the *lex Calpurnia* of 149 B.C.E. to try provincial governors for extortion. The justification for the *lex Acilia* was the charge that senatorial juries acquitted governors commonly believed guilty. This law, therefore, transferred jury service from the senatorial class to the equestrian class. It dealt with a serious abuse and achieved its purpose of widening the breach between the *equites* and Gaius' rivals. Unfortunately, it also gave equestrian business interests the means to punish good governors for preventing the wholesale exploitation and plundering of the provinces by *publicani*.

The Extortion Law

At the same time, Gaius reformed the extortion law itself so that provincials could use it to seek real redress from unscrupulous governors. The unintended consequence was that bad governors wanted to extort even more wealth. They needed to have enough to fight prosecution and still have enough for other purposes. Also, the extortion court became a weapon in elite political competition. Men tried to destroy their rivals by supporting their prosecution for extortion. The penalty was loss of citizenship and exile.

The Italian question again

One of Gaius Gracchus' fellow tribunes in 122 was his old ally Fulvius Flaccus. Together they renewed Flaccus' ill-fated earlier attempt to procure citizenship, or at least some citizenship rights, for the allies in Italy. That bill was a good attempt to address the justified discontent of Rome's allies while it created more voters for Gaius and his friends. Unfortunately, it enabled those who opposed him for personal reasons or who genuinely thought that he was a demagogic threat to senatorial power to employ demagoguery against him.

LIVIUS DRUSUS

While Gaius was in Africa to lay the groundwork for the colony of Junonia, his enemies within the nobility went to work. Their agent was the tribune M. Livius Drusus. He pandered to the selfish interests of the Roman populace by pointing out that the benefits of citizenship would be diluted by extending it to greater numbers. His threat to veto the Gracchan bill extending citizenship to the Italians prevented it from being brought to a vote. It clearly would not pass. Livius then presented a bill to protect Italian soldiers from mistreatment by Roman army officers, which was an important advance, but a shabby substitute for the citizenship bill.

Livius subsequently introduced a bill to found twelve colonies in Italy, each to consist of 3000 colonists selected from the poorest class. The land was to be rent-free. He also proposed to end the payment of rent by settlers who had been allotted land under the law of Tiberius Gracchus. The proposal to found twelve colonies in Italy was never intended to be carried out. There was not enough public land left in Italy to permit so ambitious a scheme. After it had achieved its purpose of siphoning support from Gaius Gracchus, it was speedily dropped.

THE FALL AND DEATH OF GAIUS GRACCHUS

When Gaius returned from Africa, he discovered that Livius had succeeded in splitting the once-solid ranks of the city electorate, who had supported him. Too long had Gaius stayed in Africa; too late did he realize the extent of the alliance against him. His immense popularity had made him overconfident and forced his rivals into close cooperation against him. Fulvius Flaccus' refusal to be cowed over the proposed rights for the allies reinforced the opposition. Therefore, Gaius was defeated in his attempt to run for a third term. Only the *imperium* granted by the *lex Rubria* for founding Junonia stood in the way of enemies now resolved to take his life.

In 121 B.C.E., to remove the personal protection afforded by his *imperium*, they were hastening to bring about the annulment of the *lex Rubria*. No longer tribune, Gaius had neither the authority to summon the people nor the power to resist the threatened repeal. He still wished to avoid acts of violence. They might give his enemies the excuse for authorizing extreme measures against him. Nevertheless, the newly elected consul, Lucius Opimius, the destroyer of Fregellae and a vehement opponent of Gaius, deliberately provoked an incident between his armed supporters and those of Gaius. Then, Opimius' backers in the senate virtually declared martial law by passing what came to be known as a final decree of the senate, *Senatus Consultum Ultimum* (p. 228). Opimius organized an armed posse that killed many Gracchans, including Fulvius Flaccus. Gaius attempted to escape but, seeing the hopelessness of his position, ordered one of his slaves to kill him.

Thus died Gaius Gracchus. As tribune of the people two years in a row, he had temporarily broken the monopoly of power enjoyed by a small number of nobles who usually dominated the senate and the popular assemblies. He had concentrated in his hands many executive powers and functions. He had supervised the distribution of grain to the populace, changed the composition of juries, awarded contracts for and superintended the construction of highways, presided over meetings of the senate, supported and campaigned for candidates to the consulship, and converted the tribuneship into an office more powerful than the consulship itself. Some of his reforms were truly measures of enlightened statesmanship. Others were dictated by political calculation and must be described as frankly opportunistic. Most were combinations of both.

THE *POPULARIS* POLITICAL LEGACY OF THE GRACCHI

In death, the Gracchi became popular heroes. Statues were erected to them in public places, and the spots identified as where they had fallen became hallowed ground. Prayers and sacrifices were offered to them as to gods. Even the proudest noble, regardless of his private opinions, dared not speak of them in public except with respect. The common people gratefully remembered the benefactions that the Gracchi had tried to bestow upon them. The Gracchan strategy of gaining political advantage against fellow aristocrats by promoting such popular programs as land redistribution, colonization schemes, subsidized grain, and public works, particularly through the office of tribune, lived on. It became the hallmark of the *popularis* politician.

The careers of the Gracchi reveal a major reason why the reforms necessary for preserving the stability of the Roman Republic were extremely difficult to make. Reform, however altruistic or patriotically motivated, could not be separated from the highly personalized political competition within the Roman aristocracy. Laws always bore the name of the man who proposed them. Therefore, any law that brought about significant reform benefiting a large number of discontented people would bring the man who proposed it a large increase in supporters among the voters. Envy, jealousy, and political self-interest would cause many current or potential rivals for public office and esteem to resist the attempted reform with every weapon at their disposal—even including violence and eventually, as the competition intensified, civil war.

In addition, violence and murder reinforced themselves through vengeance. The victims of the violence employed by the opponents of Gaius Gracchus seethed in silence until they had an opportunity to retaliate. That, in turn, produced more retaliation and furthered the downward spiral to civil war. Overheated competition and the lust for revenge, therefore, created more and more instability. The republican system began to lurch from crisis to crisis without hope of a peaceful solution to its problems.

SUGGESTED READING

Dixon, S. *Cornelia, Mother of the Gracchi*. Oxford and New York: Routledge, 2007.
Stockton, D. *The Gracchi*. London: Oxford University Press, 1979.

CHAPTER 13

Destructive rivalries, Marius, and the Social War, 121 to 88 B.C.E.

The period from 121 to 88 B.C.E. marks the Roman Republic's progression from violent political rivalries and murder to the brink of civil war. The internal changes produced by overseas expansion plus the challenges of managing a Mediterranean-wide empire created greater opportunities for amassing preeminent popularity and power. The career of Gaius Marius perfectly illustrates the forces that were making the traditional Republic unsustainable in the context of its time.

SOURCES FOR THE PERIOD FROM 121 TO 88 B.C.E.

Just as for the Gracchi, the sources for this period are also in disarray. The brief summaries (*Periochae*) and epitomes of the relevant lost books of Livy provide only a bare outline, as does Velleius Paterculus. The fragments of Books 34–37 of Diodorus Siculus are valuable for the years from 111 to 88. The fragments of Books 26–29 in Cassius Dio are useful for events from 114 to 88.

The only lengthy extant sources are the *Jugurthine War* of the mid-first-century B.C.E. historian Sallust (p. 340); sections 27 to 54 of the first book on Rome's civil wars in Appian's history; and Plutarch's lives of Marius and Sulla, part of which are based on Sulla's *Memoirs*. Inscribed boundary stones, road markers, fragmentary inscriptions of laws, and excavations of colonial settlements help us to understand the process of land distribution after Gaius Gracchus. Cicero's speech *Pro Rabirio perduellionis* discusses the civil strife of 101 and 100 B.C.E. Indeed, Cicero knew many of the major figures from this period and made numerous references to them in his works, especially his philosophical dialogues and rhetorical treatises (pp. 339–40).

POPULARES AND *OPTIMATES*

In analyzing the political struggles marking the century of Roman history after the Gracchi, two labels are often applied to the protagonists. The label *populares* (sing. *popularis*) refers to those ambitious and even well-intentioned individuals who followed the Gracchi's example in two ways: utilizing the sovereign powers of the *concilium plebis* without senatorial approval; building public support by promoting reforms and policies benefiting significant discontented groups of voters or potential voters. In Roman political rhetoric, such people were called *populares* by more traditionally minded aristocrats or those whose current domination in the senate was guaranteed by the status quo. The latter kinds of leaders did not approve of seeking popularity among large groups of voters on public issues. Instead, they preferred to rely on the traditional political tools of family reputation, personal alliances with other aristocrats, and the marshaling of personal clients. They labeled themselves *optimates*, the best people, in contrast with the *populares*, whom they accused of using dangerously demagogic tactics. The *optimates* naturally disliked anyone who sought a base of power that they did not control. Many may honestly have feared that the actions of *populares* (rendered in English as "populists") would eventually produce a popular tyrant and destroy the Republic.

In no way did the labels *populares* and *optimates* represent anything like modern ideologically based institutional political parties. They do not even signify cohesive factions. Insofar as they mean anything, they broadly indicate two different types of political tactics: indeed, the career of a single individual could shift between optimate and populist positions (see Box 13.1). They can be applied only in the context of particular political conflicts between individuals or personal factions in the late Roman Republic. Both the social origins and the goals of *optimates* and *populares* were mostly identical. They almost always came from the senatorial aristocracy and sometimes from upwardly striving equestrian families allied with a powerful noble. Their goals were to retain or increase power and prestige in competition with their peers through the public service essential to the roles of aristocrats.

13.1 OPTIMATE AND *POPULARIS* IN A SINGLE CAREER

The career of Cn. Pompeius Magnus (Pompey the Great, pp. 253–4) illustrates how an individual Roman politician could shift from an alignment with the *optimates* to one with the *populares*—and back again—as it suited his pursuit of political and military preeminence.

At the beginning of his career, in the 80s B.C.E., Pompey aligned himself with Sulla and the *optimates* who sought to restore the dominance of the senate and to strip power from the tribunes of the plebs and the popular assemblies. Then, in the face of growing senatorial opposition to his desires for extraordinary magistracies and military commands, in the late 70s B.C.E. Pompey took up the populist cause of returning power to tribuneship (earlier stripped away by Sulla) as way to garner popularity with the people. He was then able over the next several years to bypass the senate's objections by having friendly tribunes put bills directly before the people to grant him power and lucrative military appointments. Eventually, Pompey entered into an alliance with two other *populares*, Caesar and Crassus, who were also popular with the people and the army and who were thwarted in their political aims by the senate. Over time, their union fell apart. After the death of Crassus, a civil war broke out between Caesar, who continued to defend popular interests, and Pompey, who found himself back with the optimates, once again the defender of senatorial preeminence.

Individual *optimates* were often just as much rivals with each other as they were with individual *populares*, and vice versa. Nor were *populares* always opposed to the dominant role of the senate in the Roman government. They themselves usually were members of the senate. They were looking for ways to establish their own dominance in the senate by utilizing the office of tribune of the *plebs* and other means of appealing to the mass of voters outside the senate. Many may also have been convinced of the rightness or justice of their positions as representing the popular will. In no way were they seeking to overthrow the power of the class to which they mostly belonged. They wished only to secure their individual preeminence in it.

Therefore, political conflicts in the late Roman Republic were not struggles between the senate as a monolithic institution and outside democratic leaders or reform groups. The question was what individual or group of personal allies would control the senate, which controlled Rome. Not even Julius Caesar, for example, ever sought to abolish the senate. In the civil war that Caesar precipitated at the end of the Republic, many senators supported him. He fought against those fellow senators who opposed him in the competition for glory and prestige, *dignitas*. Having beaten them, he merely packed the senate with his loyal supporters to ensure his personal domination.

The *optimates* let most of Gaius Gracchus' legislation operate once he was dead and could not benefit from it at their expense. They ceased regular grain distributions, but they changed neither the selection of jurors for the extortion courts nor the administration of provincial taxes. Except for the previously repealed *lex Rubria*, even the land laws and laws for the founding of colonies were only modified, not overthrown.

The *Senatus Consultum Ultimum*

The reign of terror following Gaius Gracchus' death seems to have silenced temporarily anyone who might have challenged the *optimates*. Opimius' acquittal in his trial for murder appeared to confirm the legality of the Ultimate Decree of the Senate, *Senatus Consultum Ultimum* (*S.C.U.*). That decree advised the consuls to take whatever steps they deemed necessary to preserve the safety of the state. It could be construed as a decree of martial law suspending normal "constitutional" procedures. The senate's right to issue such a decree, however, was not based on any legal statute or ancient customary practice.

Therefore, the question of the *S.C.U.*'s validity remained open and subject to the political passions of the moment. Popular politicians shunned it because of its origin as a weapon against the Gracchi and its lack of explicit legal sanction by a popular assembly. *Optimates* always considered it a perfectly acceptable weapon against those whom they considered threats to the established order during the late Republic. Because they were dominant at this point, their view temporarily prevailed. Even Popillius Laenas, who had been exiled by the people for killing the followers of Tiberius Gracchus, was now allowed to return to Rome. Nevertheless, many of the Gracchi's followers who had suffered at the hands of *optimates* wielding the *S.C.U.* nursed their resentment and waited for a popular issue to exploit against them.

POST-GRACCHAN LAND LEGISLATION

In the meantime, the *optimates* who dominated the senate pursued policies designed to protect their interests while satisfying those groups to whom the Gracchi had appealed. Three successive laws gradually modified the Gracchan land legislation to benefit all who had been affected. The first, probably in 121 B.C.E., permitted settlers to sell their allotments. That would have undermined any intent to guarantee a supply of men who met the property requirement for *assidui*. Still, it would have pleased many proprietors, who could have turned their allotments into cash. The second law (perhaps in 118 B.C.E.) would have pleased the Italian allies as well as Rome's small and large landholders. It abolished the land commission (whose work probably was already done), halted further division of *ager publicus* (public land) in Italy, and guaranteed, with a small rent, legal possession of lands already distributed. In 111 B.C.E., the third law benefited all of these groups: it abolished all rentals ordered by the second, declared as private property all public lands assigned by the Gracchan commission up to 320 acres, and guaranteed to colonies and municipalities secure tenure of lands already granted. It also forbade further encroachment and overgrazing on public pastures.

OTHER INTERNAL MATTERS

Scanty sources do not give a clear picture of other internal matters in the decade after Gaius Gracchus' death. There are, however, tantalizing hints of tension and chaos. For example, a number of aristocratic women seem to have been tried for poisoning their husbands. This was not the first time in Rome's history that a group of upper-class matrons was accused of this very crime. The repetition of such incidents (the first documented occurrence is 331 B.C.E., see Box 23.1, p. 427) may be a sign of female rebellion against unwanted marriages or perhaps women taking a political stance, as when Sempronia was rumored to have helped murder Scipio Aemilianus (p. 218). It is also entirely possible that the deaths were a result of some kind of epidemic, that the women were completely innocent, and that Rome, for reasons we cannot now recover, was gripped by baseless hysteria.

Conflicts over the role of women, *equites*, and even ordinary voters in public religious life may be seen in another episode from the year 114. First, a prodigy was reported: the virgin daughter of an *eques* was out riding a horse. A bolt of lightning struck her, blew off her clothes, and left her naked. Soothsayers interpreted the incident as a bad portent for Vestal Virgins and *equites*. Subsequently, charges of unchastity were leveled against three Vestals: Aemilia, Licinia, and Marcia. Here, as in the poisoning case discussed earlier, it is possible that the charges had some basis in fact, but it is equally possible that the women were innocent victims of political rivalries or widespread panic. The pontiffs, all aristocrats, condemned Aemilia to death but acquitted the other two. The outrage of ordinary citizens at this apparent cover-up by aristocratic priests enabled a tribune to obtain a plebiscite setting up a special secular prosecutor. All three Vestals were condemned and a number of men were also punished. The sources focus on the punishment of *equites*, although prominent aristocrats like the brothers of Aemilia and Licinia were also implicated. Mark Antony's grandfather, who had just risen from equestrian to senatorial rank, was accused of involvement and successfully defended himself.

THE IMPERIAL BACKGROUND TO DOMESTIC POLITICS

Domestic politics have to be understood in the wider context of events throughout Rome's empire. Different areas presented different problems and challenges. All helped to shape what happened in Rome.

Colonization and continued conquest in the West, 125 to 118 B.C.E.

The Gracchan program of land settlement in Italy was strongly reinforced both before and after the tribunates of Gaius by the conquest, colonization, and settlement of lands beyond the borders of Italy. Thousands of Roman settlers remained around Carthage after the formal abolition of the Roman colony. New settlements were made at Palma and Pollentia on the Spanish island of Majorca. Between 125 and 120, the Romans took over the coastal strip between the Alps and the Pyrenees, except for the small territory of Massilia (map, p. 368). It welcomed Rome's suppression of its restless neighbors.

This coastal strip became the province of Transalpine Gaul, later called Narbonese Gaul (*Gallia Narbonensis*), or simply the Province (hence, modern Provence). In 118, the Romans founded a citizen colony of discharged veterans at Narbo, which gave its name to *Gallia Narbonensis*. It was a strategic site on the Via Domitia, which linked the

Rhône valley to Spain. It not only provided commercial operators a trading center in southern Gaul but also gave small farmers from central Italy new lands to settle. Those who sold their Gracchan allotments in Italy could use the proceeds for a fresh start on bigger holdings in the rich transalpine province. In this way, the number of *assidui*, those qualified for military service, could be maintained, too.

Rome and the Greek East

After 133 B.C.E., the Romans tried to avoid direct involvement in the East beyond Macedonia and Thrace, Greece proper, and the newly acquired province of Asia. The governors of Macedonia supervised affairs in Greece. It remained calm enough for the Romans to remove previously imposed indemnities and restore some rights to leagues and cities. After the suppression of a minor revolt in Macedonia (ca. 140 B.C.E.), Roman governors were mainly occupied in fighting the Thracians and other tribes to the north and east in a series of campaigns from 135 to 101. As a result, Roman control spread toward the Hellespont.

In Asia, many refused to honor Attalus III's bequest of Pergamum to Rome. They mounted armed resistance under the leadership of Aristonicus, who claimed to be Attalus' illegitimate half-brother. Many of his followers came from the lower ranks of society (p. 182). Consequently, the propertied classes tended to favor Rome. The Romans also received aid from neighboring kings.

After a disastrous start, the Romans were finally victorious in 130 B.C.E. They sent a consul with a commission of ten senators to settle Asian affairs in 129. They granted large chunks of Attalus' kingdom to two friendly client kings, Ariarathes VI of Cappadocia and Mithridates V of Pontus. The failure to give a similar prize to Nicomedes II of Bithynia, however, set the stage for serious conflict in the future, particularly because of the widespread belief that Mithridates had given the Roman consul a large bribe. Still, the Romans reserved the richest part of the kingdom and its revenues for themselves. When Gaius Gracchus secured legislation turning over the collection of those revenues to the *publicani* (p. 221), he inadvertently opened up the province to greater corruption and exploitation. They fueled resentment and eventual rebellion against Roman rule. Between 127 and 87 B.C.E., however, Rome's military attention was focused elsewhere. The only significant military activity in Asia Minor consisted of naval operations against Cilician pirates (p. 236).

The Jugurthine War, 111 to 106 B.C.E.

The first great military problem that Rome faced after Gaius Gracchus' death was in North Africa. As in Asia Minor after 133 B.C.E., the Romans had not annexed large amounts of territory after the destruction of Carthage in 146 B.C.E. They had left large tracts of North Africa to the friendly kings of Numidia. These friendly relations ended with the outbreak of the Jugurthine War in 111. Moreover, this war finally gave the vengeful and ambitious in post-Gracchan Rome an issue to exploit in a *popularis* manner against the dominant *optimates* in the senate.

The war was named after Jugurtha, a grandson of Scipio Aemilianus' old Numidian ally Masinissa. Brave and quick witted, he had attracted Scipio's favor during his service in the war against Numantia. Scipio persuaded King Micipsa, son of Masinissa, to adopt Jugurtha. Trouble followed when Micipsa died in 118 B.C.E. He left Numidia jointly to Jugurtha and his own two natural sons. Soon Jugurtha moved against his adoptive brothers as he sought control of the whole kingdom. He was aided by the connivance of powerful Roman senators.

In 112 B.C.E., Jugurtha besieged one of his rivals in the city of Cirta (Constantine, Algeria), an important center of the North African grain trade. Many equestrian grain merchants and their Italian agents were trapped in the besieged city. They were massacred when it fell. This massacre and the disruption of Rome's grain supply incensed both the common people and the *equites*. Those issues could be exploited with *popularis* tactics. In 111, the tribune Gaius Memmius openly accused some senators of taking Jugurtha's bribes. He attacked the senatorial leaders so vigorously that they were shamed into asking for a declaration of war.

The commanding consul, however, made only a pretense of fighting. He quickly offered Jugurtha easy terms. Popular opinion was outraged. Memmius ordered an investigation. Another tribune blocked him. Jugurtha then procured the murder of a cousin who was living in Rome and trying to get help against him. Such a slap in the face to the Roman People could not be ignored. The senate repudiated the tainted peace and renewed the war in 110 B.C.E. Jugurtha defeated the Roman army in 109 and demanded another humiliating peace. The people were even more outraged. Another tribune put through a bill setting up a special court to try senators deemed responsible for the debacle. The jury was filled from the list of equestrian jurors established by Gaius Gracchus for the extortion court. Among those condemned for corruption and sent into exile was the infamous Lucius Opimius, who had used the *S.C.U.* to slay the followers of Gaius Gracchus.

Command of the war finally went to a competent general, Quintus Caecilius Metellus. Consul in 109, he came from the most powerful family in Rome at the time. He was incorruptible and an excellent disciplinarian. Unfortunately for him, however, the damage to the army's morale and preparedness could not be repaired overnight. Both the *equites* and the common people wanted speedy results. They accused Metellus of prolonging the war for his own glorification.

THE *POPULARIS* RISE OF GAIUS MARIUS, 157 TO 86 B.C.E.

Although fighting as one of Metellus' senior officers in Numidia, Gaius Marius was calculating and unscrupulous enough to exploit popular unrest back in Rome in a *popularis* manner. He urged the equestrian merchants in North Africa to write letters to their friends and agents at Rome in praise of him and in protest of Metellus' conduct of the war. The campaign was so successful that Marius won enough votes to be elected consul himself.

Born outside of Arpinum, a little town south of Rome, Marius was the son of a wealthy *eques*, not a poor peasant as Plutarch's biography claims. His ambition was to reach the consulship at Rome and ennoble his family. He was an excellent soldier and was popular among the rank-and-file. Even after he became their commander, he is said to have slept on the same hard ground as they did. They would remember him at election time. His rough and ready appearance and his use of common idiom also endeared him to the average man.

Marius had been with Scipio Aemilianus at the siege of Numantia. His courage, physical endurance, and military professionalism had earned Scipio's respect. Later, he became a client of the powerful Metelli. They helped him to become a tribune for 119 B.C.E. At that point, however, he deserted those patrons for the first time.

As tribune, Marius successfully proposed a bill to make it difficult for patrons to influence the votes of their clients. The Metelli and other nobles opposed it. Marius won further admiration from the common people by threatening to arrest the consuls, including Metellus' brother, for obstructing the popular will. Outraged, the Metelli helped to ensure Marius' defeat in a campaign for the aedileship. Marius managed with some difficulty and much bribery, however, to get elected to a praetorship in 115 B.C.E. After that, he was sent as a propraetor to Farther Spain, his first military command.

Marius' praetorship had admitted him into the upper ranks of the senate. His money and success had earned him a useful connection with the ancient patrician family of the Julii Caesares: he married the aunt of the future Julius Caesar. He also had been able to mend fences with his offended former patrons and get Quintus Metellus to give him a post in the war against Jugurtha. Even so, without any noble ancestors of his own, Marius would have found the consulship beyond his reach, except perhaps under the most unusual circumstances.

Marius campaigns for the consulship

At first, Metellus scornfully refused when Marius asked for leave to campaign for the consulship. Finally, to get rid of a disgruntled officer, Metellus granted him permission to go to Rome, where he was elected consul for 107 B.C.E. Marius, now the first of his family to reach the consulship, was a *novus homo*, "new man," resented deeply by the old nobility. To add insult to their injury, a plebiscite gave him the North African command against the will of Metellus' optimate allies in the senate.

Recruiting troops for service in North Africa, Marius tried to solve the problem of military manpower by accepting as volunteers all who were physically fit, regardless of property qualifications. Such a move had occasionally been resorted to in past emergencies. After Marius, it became a regular practice.

Inadvertently, this change had serious political consequences. More and more men of little or no property joined the legions. Commanders who were generous with booty or promised other material rewards like grants of land could often count on their loyalty. Successful generals could now more easily compete with their political rivals by mustering the votes of loyal veterans or using them to intimidate their opponents. The value of military commands was thereby raised. Therefore, the temptation to provoke some foreign military crisis to obtain one became great. More ominously, a successful military commander backed by an experienced and personally loyal army was in a greater position to resort to civil war.

Marius defeats Jugurtha

Marius' methodical warfare forced Jugurtha on the defensive by 106 B.C.E. Marius was ably assisted by his quaestor, the young noble and future dictator Lucius Cornelius Sulla, who later became his bitter enemy. In the meantime, Sulla captured Jugurtha by persuading Jugurtha's principal ally, King Bocchus of Mauretania, to betray him. The captured Jugurtha eventually was executed by strangulation in the dungeon of the Tullianum after appearing in Marius' triumph (104 B.C.E.). Numidia was safe at last for investment and exploitation by Marius' equestrian friends and relatives.

Rome, however, still faced a formidable series of foreign and domestic crises. First was the threat of attack from a number of migrating Germanic tribes. To fight them, the *comitia centuriata* elected Marius, now the most popular military hero, to five consecutive consulships (104–100 B.C.E.). Sometimes he was elected *in absentia* and always contrary to the law requiring a ten-year interval between repeated offices.

The war with the Cimbri and the Teutones, 105 to 101 B.C.E.

Driven south by overpopulation and coastal inundations, the Cimbri, Teutones, and other Germanic tribes had sought to settle in Transalpine Gaul. Often they offered to serve in Roman armies in return for land. Met with refusal, they smashed three Roman armies in 109, 106, and finally, at the Battle of Arausio (Orange), in 105 B.C.E. Even if the report of 80,000 Roman casualties is high, this last disaster left Italy open to invasion. Tribunes seized on popular fear and frustration at corruption and incompetence. They attacked prominent commanders and leading senators with prosecutions. They also promoted more laws to limit aristocratic influence over voters. Marius' "unconstitutional" five consecutive consulships reflect the impact of fear and popular pressure on the Centuriate Assembly in a period of extreme crisis.

Marius' impact on the Roman army

Although Marius was long thought to replace the maniple with the cohort as a tactical army unit in preparing to fight the Germans, the cohort appeared as far back as the elder Scipio Africanus' command in Spain (210 B.C.E.). Metellus, Marius' predecessor in North Africa, also employed it. Marius, however, seems to have made it the standard tactical unit. His legions each had 3000 to 5000 men in ten cohorts ranging from 300 to 500 heavy infantry. Each cohort had six centuries of sixty to eighty men. Cohorts were strong enough to fight separately but still numerous enough to deploy in various combinations. Without losing its flexibility, the legion acquired a new compactness and cohesion now symbolized by an identifying emblem carried on a standard topped by a silver eagle.

Marius' major innovation in weapons was to substitute a wooden pin for one of the iron rivets that held the head of a javelin onto its shaft. It would break upon impact and render the javelin useless for the enemy to hurl back. Marius also issued oblong shields (*scuta*) to the light-armed *velites*. As a result, the *velites* became more like the heavy infantry, and the distinction between the two soon disappeared.

Following Metellus' example, Marius emphasized hard training and standardization. Each soldier carried his own cooking kit, construction tools, tent, and rations for three days. Soldiers came to be called "Marius' mules" because of their weighty backpacks. By a combination of open recruitment, cohesive organization, and hard training, Marius made the legion an even more formidable military force. In time, it would also become an effective political weapon in the hands of ambitious generals. Ironically, one of those generals would be his old quaestor Sulla, whom he now seems to have sent to help the other consul, Q. Lutatius Catulus.

Defeat of the Germans

With his well-trained, cohort-based legions, Marius defeated one group of Germans in 102 B.C.E. before they could cross the Alps into Italy, where the Cimbri defeated Catulus. In 101, he himself crossed the Alps to join Catulus in defeating the Cimbri at Vercellae (probably near Turin). After that, a third group of Germans wisely retreated home without a fight. Marius was now an even bigger popular hero.

THE SLAVE REVOLT IN SICILY, 104 TO 100 B.C.E.

Had the Germans invaded Italy and set at liberty a million slaves or more, the consequences might have been similar to a revolt of the slaves in Sicily that took five years to suppress. In 104 B.C.E., Marius asked the Roman client–kings of Asia Minor to send troops to help defend Italy against the Germanic invaders. The kings replied that up to half their able-bodied subjects had been kidnapped and sold as slaves by pirates. Many of those slaves were in Sicily. Marius and the senate ordered the governor of Sicily to release slaves held illegally. After the release of several hundred persons, the governor allowed himself to be browbeaten by the landowners. He harshly ordered the rest of the slaves applying for freedom to go back to their masters. They did not go back. Instead, they took to the hills, and the slave revolt swelled into full-scale war. For four years (104–101 B.C.E.), the slaves had control of the country. Before the defeat of the Germans released enough troops to put down the rebellion, 100,000 lives had already been lost.

PIRACY IN THE EASTERN MEDITERRANEAN

Even before the suppression of the Sicilian slaves, Rome had to deal with piracy in the eastern Mediterranean. Ever since the destruction of Rhodes as a naval power, the pirates and slave traders of Cilicia and Crete had freely roamed the seas. Their kidnapping raids upon Syria and Asia Minor supplied the great slave market of Delos, where 10,000 slaves are said to have been sold daily. In 102 B.C.E., the praetor Marcus Antonius (grandfather of the famous Mark Antony [p. 229]) was commissioned to attack and destroy the chief pirate bases and strongholds in the eastern Mediterranean. After destroying many pirate hideouts, he annexed the coastal part of Cilicia as a Roman province and base of future operations against pirates. These measures may have checked, but did not destroy, the scourge of piracy, which the Romans' own actions and policies had helped to create.

THE POLITICAL FALL OF MARIUS

Just returned from glorious victories in 101 B.C.E., Marius was the object of adulation at Rome. He was seen as "another Camillus," a savior. He enjoyed the unfailing support of a devoted army and beheld a populace crying out for leadership. After five consulships, he wanted more.

Marius entered his sixth consulship in 100 B.C.E. Unfortunately for him, however, Rome was at peace. All of his jealous enemies in the senate now felt free to work against him. To overcome their opposition to legislation benefiting his veterans, equestrian supporters, and Italian clients, Marius had to rely on two opportunistic *populares*, Lucius Appuleius Saturninus and Gaius Servilius Glaucia. They, however, were prepared to go to greater political extremes than Marius wanted.

Lucius Appuleius Saturninus and Gaius Servilius Glaucia, 103 to 100 B.C.E.

Saturninus was an eloquent speaker, an able and ambitious noble whose career had suffered a serious setback. Therefore, he became an active supporter of Marius in an attempt to gain popularity and a position of strength against rivals. Saturninus entered his first tribuneship in 103 B.C.E. He sponsored a law assigning one hundred *iugera* (sixty-five acres) of land in Africa to each of Marius' African veterans. A colleague joined his opponents and attempted to veto the bill. After a shower of stones, the man promptly withdrew the veto. Saturninus had no patience with obstructive tactics or legal technicalities. Fists and stones were more effective than vetoes or signs from the gods.

In 103, Saturninus also introduced a law that made it a criminal offense to compromise, injure, or diminish the honor or dignity (*maiestas*) of the Roman People. By the very vagueness of the charge, this law would become dangerous to all as time went on. For his part, Saturninus used it to prosecute unpopular nobles and enhance his own power. For example, he prosecuted the unpopular ex-consul who had obtained passage of a law in 106 B.C.E. to give the extortion court back to senatorial jurors. In 101, Glaucia was tribune and obtained passage of a law that returned the extortion court to equestrian jurors.

In 100 B.C.E., during his second tribuneship, Saturninus embarked on a full program of social legislation. Glaucia, who was now a praetor, supported him. Saturninus' legislation included a grain law (possibly dating back to his tribunate of 103 B.C.E.). It restored the regular monthly distributions of subsidized grain that had been suspended after the death of Gaius Gracchus. Saturninus' second bill provided for the founding of veteran colonies in Sicily, Greece, Macedonia, and possibly Africa. A third bill, an agrarian law, assigned land once occupied by the Cimbri and Teutones in Gaul (possibly Transalpine Gaul) to Marius' veterans. Finally, Saturninus proposed a general mobilization of Roman forces against the Cilician pirates and against Mithridates VI of Pontus. That command was intended for Marius. To these laws, Saturninus appended a clause requiring all senators to take an oath of obedience within five days or face loss of their seats, exile, and a fine of twenty talents. In spite of vetoes, divine signs, and violence, the laws were passed.

Marius and the fall of Saturninus and Glaucia

All eyes were fixed on Marius to see if he would take the oath of obedience appended to the bill assigning land in Gaul to his veterans. At the last minute, he did take the oath to observe the law with the qualification "so far as it is legal." This express reservation turned the law into a farce. Senators who took the oath would be able to make the same reservation. Marius' blunder lay in his indecision. He wanted to cooperate with the popular leaders. At the same time, he did not like to offend the powerful senators who opposed Saturninus. Marius thus reveals what was typical of most *populares*. He was quite willing to seek popularity by opportunistic means in order to gain high office and status, but he shared the same basic aristocratic outlook as his foes. He had achieved political equality with his former noble opponents and rivals. Now, he instinctively cooperated with them in preserving the political status quo and hoped to gain their respect and acceptance.

Saturninus had lost the support of both the equestrian class and the city masses before the end of his second tribuneship. The *equites* disliked his radical and revolutionary methods. They feared that he might next attack the sanctity of private property. The city voters turned against him because of his new agrarian law. It granted too many benefits to Marius' veterans, many of whom were Italians: the interests of the people and the interests of the military were no longer the same thing. Hostile optimate senators and personal enemies were quick to take advantage of the situation to bring down *populares* like Saturninus and Glaucia.

Saturninus and Glaucia, determined to stay in office, campaigned successfully for the tribuneship and consulship, respectively. Glaucia, however, was in defiance of the Villian Law, which required a two-year interval between the offices of praetor and consul (p. 191). In order to rid himself of a possibly successful opponent, Glaucia hired thugs to kill the former tribune Gaius Memmius. The senate declared a state of emergency and ordered Marius to take action under the *S.C.U.*

Marius did not want to injure or destroy Saturninus, Glaucia, and the other popular politicians to whom he and his veterans owed so many benefits. He forced Saturninus and those who had taken refuge with him in the Capitol to surrender. To save their lives and follow the senate's orders at the same time, he locked them up in the senate house (*curia*). An angry mob of nobles and *equites* climbed up to the roof, ripped off tiles, and pelted the prisoners to death. Glaucia, too, was murdered, but sources differ on the exact circumstances. Marius, still distrusted and disliked by his old enemies among the nobles, was now despised by his former friends for failing to protect those who had supported him. He was obliged to look on helplessly as the senate declared the laws of Saturninus null and void. This action apparently ruined Marius' career and gave second thoughts to those who would seek political advantage through a *popularis* strategy. It is not surprising that Marius suddenly "remembered" that he had to go to the East to fulfill a vow. He may also have wanted to scout new opportunities for military glory against the growing power of King Mithridates VI of Pontus (p. 242).

A DECADE OF OPTIMATE DOMINATION

Those who had tried to gain an edge in aristocratic political competition as *populares* had fallen to violence and murder once more. For most of the 90s B.C.E., optimate traditionalists firmly controlled public affairs through the senate. They were largely successful in dealing with Rome's enemies and their own. They had already crushed the Sicilian slave rebellion in 100 B.C.E. In 93, they defeated a Spanish uprising. Then they successfully intervened in Asia Minor. Sulla, who had been elected praetor for 97 B.C.E., received a proconsular command in Cilicia to place the pro-Roman Ariobarzanes I on the throne of Cappadocia. Sulla's actions in the East, however, had serious implications for the future. They drew the hostile attention of both Mithridates VI of Pontus and the neighboring Parthian Empire. They also set the stage for the disastrous rivalry between Sulla and Marius for command of Rome's first war against Mithridates in 88 B.C.E.

Meanwhile, Marius had returned from Asia and tried to restore his political fortunes. He supported his veterans' demands for land and the Italian allies' demands for citizenship. The optimate leaders continued to refuse both. They even expelled Italians resident in Rome. Furthermore, they sponsored a law that made it more difficult for *populares* to utilize tribunician legislation. It required an interval of seventeen days between the promulgation and enactment of a tribunician bill. In that way, those whose power was guaranteed by the status quo would have enough time to marshal their opposition. As a result, serious problems and grievances continued to bubble beneath the surface and build up pressure for another eruption.

For example, in 92 B.C.E., the growing tension between the *equites* and the optimate-dominated senate manifested itself in the trial of P. Rutilius Rufus. He had married into the family of Gaius Gracchus' opponent M. Livius Drusus (p. 222). As a legate in Asia, Rufus had tried to curb the abuses of *publicani* collecting taxes there. Marius was Rufus' long-time rival and a supporter of tax-collecting companies. He encouraged Rufus' prosecution on a charge of extortion. Since Gaius Gracchus had staffed the extortion court with equestrian jurors tied to or sympathetic to the *publicani*, Rufus was unjustly convicted.

THE EXPLOSIVE REFORMS OF M. LIVIUS DRUSUS THE YOUNGER, 91 B.C.E.

Livius Drusus' son, M. Livius Drusus the Younger, was allied with some moderate optimates who favored reforms to relieve the worst of the grievances that could be exploited in a *popularis* manner. As a tribune in 91 B.C.E., the younger Drusus launched a series of reforms with three major components: (1) doubling the size of the senate by admitting 300 of the richest and most prominent members of the equestrian class (to remove the chief source of friction between senators and *equites*, he proposed to choose jurors for the standing criminal courts from this expanded senate); (2) providing the poor with subsidized grain and with land through allotments and the establishment of colonies; (3) granting citizenship to the Italian allies.

These proposals could never be acceptable to all of the powerful optimate aristocrats, all of the *equites*, or even all of the Roman poor and Italian allies. The first two proposals seem to have passed initially. Then, vigorous opposition from extreme oligarchs and those *equites* who would not have been admitted to the senate caused them to be overturned. Even some powerful Italian allies were against the younger Drusus' citizenship law. They would have had to give up public land and some control in their communities. Before Drusus was able to bring that proposal to a vote, he was stabbed to death by an unknown assassin.

THE ITALIAN, OR SOCIAL, WAR, 90 TO 88 B.C.E.

The demands by many of Rome's Italian allies for citizenship were just. The allies had fought side by side with Romans to win them glory and empire. The Romans, however, no longer shared the fruits of victory equally with them. Roman selfishness and political rivalries made it difficult to grant their just demands. There may also have been a principled impediment from the Roman point of view. Roman citizens already occupied more territory than that of any previous Mediterranean city-state. It was far beyond what Aristotle considered to be ideal for such a polity. Such a state's stability depended on face-to-face relationships among the leaders and the people, a sense of sharing a common life and purpose. How far could the Roman commonwealth, the *res publica*, be extended before it ceased to be?

The failure of Livius Drusus to reconcile competing interests and views over the matter of Italian citizenship resulted in a bloody uprising. It threatened to destroy Rome's supremacy in Italy and, therefore, the Mediterranean. Among the insurgents, the Marsi and the Samnites were the fiercest. Together with their allies, they declared their independence and set up a confederacy. Its capital was at Corfinium, renamed *Italia*, about seventy-five miles due east of Rome. The Italian confederacy raised an army of 100,000 men (no lack of manpower on this occasion!). Many were hardened soldiers trained in the tactics and discipline of the Roman army, as their officers had been.

Sections of Umbria and Etruria, the more Romanized Latins and Campanians, and the Greek coastal cities from Naples to Tarentum remained loyal to Rome. The overseas provinces could supply extra manpower and resources. Nevertheless, the Romans fared badly in the first months of the war. Some of their defeats arose from many sena-tors' hostility and spite toward Marius. When he volunteered his services, they merely assigned him as a legate to an incompetent commander.

Citizenship for the Italians and collapse of the revolt, 90 to 88 B.C.E.

Finally, late in 90 B.C.E., one of the consuls, Lucius Julius Caesar (cousin of the more famous Gaius Julius Caesar), did what would have avoided war in the first place. He returned to Rome and carried a bill called the *lex Julia* to confer citizenship on all Latins and Italians still loyal to Rome and to those who would at once lay down their arms. In 89, two tribunes, M. Plautius Silvanus and C. Papirius Carbo, put through a more comprehensive bill, the *lex Plautia Papiria*. It granted citizenship to all free per-sons resident in any allied community who would register before a Roman praetor within sixty days. A third law, the *lex Pompeia*, was proposed by the consul Gnaeus Pompeius Strabo. It extended citizenship to all free persons residing in Cisalpine Gaul south of the Po. It granted Latin rights to those living north of the river. The revolts began to collapse.

Strabo was a very good general and an opportunistic politician. He backed whatever side in Roman politics seemed most personally advantageous at the moment. His son, who became Pompey the Great, served on his staff with other future famous figures like Cicero and Catiline. The younger Pompey was militarily and politically much like Strabo but more personally charming. At one point, it was only the young Pompey's pleas that saved his father from death at the hands of mutinous soldiers. Strabo ended the war in the North by capturing Asculum. He was also said to have misappropriated the booty. In 88 B.C.E., Strabo was guilty of complicity in the murder of his cousin, the consul Q. Pompeius Rufus, who was supposed to take over Strabo's command. Thereupon, Strabo continued to fight until the Marsi and their allies were defeated in central Italy.

The other consul of 88 was Lucius Cornelius Sulla, Marius' old quaestor in the Jugurthine War and now a favorite of his enemies. Sulla and his staunch ally Quintus Caecilius Metellus (son of the commander whom Marius had double-crossed in the Jugurthine War) eventually ground down the Samnites in the South. In Campania, however, Sulla's army still had to besiege Nola.

THE AFTERMATH OF THE SOCIAL WAR

The war had exacted a heavy price for the failure to adopt Livius Drusus' proposal to grant citizenship to Rome's Italian allies. The human and property losses may have been almost as great as those inflicted by Hannibal. Food was scarce and prices high. Rich and poor were oppressed by debts that they had no means of paying. Rome was crowded with Italian refugees. The city praetor of 89 B.C.E., A. Sempronius Asellio, attempted to give the debtors some relief by issuing an edict that revived the fourth-century B.C.E. law prohibiting interest. He was killed by a mob of angry creditors.

The Social War had practically been a civil war. It pitted against each other communities that in some cases had been fighting side by side for 200 years. Its bitter fighting set a dangerous precedent for actual civil warfare in Italy and trained a generation of leaders willing to resort to it in pursuit of personal political goals. With the war almost over, there was a move to avert the logical impact of the huge extension of citizenship that ended it. The strategy adopted limited the voting power of the new citizens by enrolling them in only eight or ten of the thirty-five tribes of citizens. This ploy merely fueled more divisive struggles that rent the Republic in the following years.

Nevertheless, the war produced some positive long-term results for Rome. It added almost 500,000 new citizens to the census rolls. From the Po River to the Straits of Messana, all free men were now Romans. The many different ethnic elements would in time be united by their common Roman citizenship. Local self-government still continued. All communities and municipalities enjoyed the right to elect their own boards of four magistrates (*Quattuorviri*). Gradually, they would adopt Roman private and public law as well as a common Latin language. The enfranchisement of Italy south of the Po eventually led to national unification and the development of a common Latin culture, but not under a republican form of government.

SUGGESTED READING

Bispham, E. H. *From Asculum to Actium: The Municipalization of Italy from the Social War to Augustus*. Oxford: Oxford University Press, 2007.

Evans, R. *Gaius Marius: A Political Biography*. Pretoria: University of South Africa Press, 1994.

Kendall, S. *The Struggle for Roman Citizenship: Romans, Allies, and the Wars of 91–77 BCE. Gorgias Studies in Classical and Late Antiquity 2*. Piscataway, NJ: Gorgias Press, 2013.

Mouritsen, H. *Italian Unification. A Study in Ancient and Modern Historiography* (BICS Suppl. 70). London: Institute of Classical Studies, 1998.

CHAPTER 14

Civil war and Sulla's reactionary settlement, 88 to 78 B.C.E.

Although the Republic had weathered the foreign and domestic crises that had beset it since the time of the Gracchi, none of the basic problems had been solved. Political competition within the aristocracy continued to intensify. It politicized any attempts at necessary reform so that nothing could be accomplished without violence and the creation of further instability. At the same time, Rome's wars put more and more power in the hands of ambitious military leaders. Therefore, they were able to resort to ever-higher levels of violence in the pursuit of their personal goals. Finally, beginning in 88 B.C.E., the Republic was rocked by a series of civil wars that ultimately destroyed it.

SOURCES FOR THE YEARS, 88 TO 78 B.C.E.

As for the previous period, the only two major sources are Appian and Plutarch. Plutarch's lives of Marius and Sulla are particularly important. Pertinent information is also found in the early portions of his biographies of Sertorius, Lucullus, Pompey, Crassus, Caesar, and Cicero. Velleius Paterculus presents a summary in Book 2 of his *Histories*, and Books 77 to 90 of Livy are summarized in the *Periochae* and later epitomes. There are a few fragments from Cassius Dio and sizable fragments from Diodorus Siculus. There also survive some interesting fragments on the First Mithridatic War from the first-century C.E. Greek historian Memnon of Heraclea in Pontus. For the First Mithridatic War, some official documents of both Sulla and Mithridates have been preserved on inscriptions. For internal affairs, numerous references scattered throughout the works of Cicero make him a valuable contemporary witness.

MITHRIDATES VI EUPATOR (134 TO 63 B.C.E.)

Senatorial leaders had ended the Social War by granting citizenship to the Italians. They had been prompted not only by the adverse military situation in Italy but also by the aggressive actions of Mithridates VI, king of Pontus. Mithridates had taken advantage of several factors: the resentment that often-corrupt Roman rule had aroused in the eastern provinces, Rome's confrontations with Germanic invaders, and the disruptions caused by the Social War. His goal was to overthrow Roman rule in the eastern Mediterranean. He wanted an empire of his own on the model of Alexander the Great's. By 90 B.C.E., he had gained control of all but the western coast of the Black Sea and most of the interior of Asia Minor. At that time, however, the Romans were thoroughly aroused by his simultaneous seizures of Bithynia and Cappadocia. Therefore, the senate sent special envoys to compel Mithridates to withdraw from both kingdoms. They demanded that he recognize Ariobarzanes as the lawful king of Cappadocia and Nicomedes IV as king of Bithynia. That done, one of the envoys, Manius Aquillius, did a very foolish thing: he incited Nicomedes to raid Pontus. Aquillius hoped to obtain enough loot to reward the Romans for their intervention in Bithynia. He also may have wanted to stir up a war to benefit Marius, his old commander and colleague as consul in 101 B.C.E. Marius was now in Asia and looking for opportunities to restore his glory.

Mithridates makes war on Rome

Nicomedes invaded Pontus in 90 B.C.E. After several unheeded protests, Mithridates decided to strike. Quickly defeating Nicomedes, he swept the weak Roman forces aside and attacked Pergamum. He captured Aquillius and, it is said, paid him the money that he had demanded by pouring molten gold down his throat. During 89 and 88, many in Asia Minor welcomed Mithridates as a deliverer and a savior. They seized the chance to make the Romans pay dearly for the previous forty years. By prearrangement, they slaughtered many Italians, mostly tax agents, moneylenders, and merchants, although the figure of 80,000 given in the sources may be highly exaggerated. Mithridates' only setback, a major one, was the failure of his powerful fleet to capture Rome's loyal naval ally Rhodes.

Mithridates would not feel secure unless he added Greece to his dominions. He knew that the Romans were hated there almost as much as in Asia. Therefore, he had sent his agents to Athens and other cities to make his case. Meanwhile, his navy had descended on Delos. There he ordered the massacre of 20,000 Italian merchants and slave dealers. Athens overthrew its pro-Roman oligarchic government and made common cause with Mithridates. Late in 88 B.C.E., his general occupied Athens' main port, the Piraeus, and from that base conquered most of southern Greece. Meanwhile, another Pontic army was gathering to invade Macedonia and northern Greece. Such was the dangerous situation in the East as Rome slowly recovered from the ravages of the Social War.

THE RISE OF SULLA (138 TO 78 B.C.E.)

Marius and Sulla eagerly sought command of the war against Mithridates. Marius wanted to recover the popularity that he had enjoyed after the Jugurthine and Cimbrian wars but had later lost. Sulla was from an old patrician family that had not been prominent within the consular nobility for some time. He wanted the command because he believed that the war would be easily won and a source of power, fame, and fortune. For some time now, he had been promoting his career at Marius' expense: he claimed credit for bringing an end to the Jugurthine War because of his role in Jugurtha's capture (p. 233). He was closely allied with Marius' optimate enemies in the senate. They had assured his election to the consulship of 88 B.C.E. and an important command in the Social War. Marius had been forced to settle for a legateship. Now powerful friends procured Sulla the coveted command against Mithridates.

The tribuneship of P. Sulpicius, 88 B.C.E.

The question of the Mithridatic command might well have been settled had it not been for the political aims of the tribune P. Sulpicius. Sulpicius had been a close friend and admirer of Livius Drusus the Younger. He had strongly opposed the restriction of the newly enfranchised Italians to eight of the thirty-five tribes. An orator of remarkable power and an heir to immense wealth, Sulpicius was also a member of one of the most ancient and illustrious patrician families. Nevertheless, he had given up his patrician status in 89 B.C.E. to qualify for election as tribune.

As tribune of the people, Sulpicius made four proposals that seem to have been presented in one omnibus bill: (1) to enroll the new Italian citizens as well as freedmen (see sidebar) in all the thirty-five tribes, (2) to recall all exiles, (3) to exclude from the senate all members owing bills in excess of 2000 *denarii* (in order to prevent bribery and corruption), and (4) to replace Sulla with Marius in the command against Mithridates. The first proposal was the least acceptable and made it difficult for the bill to gain the support of enough tribes to be passed in the *concilium plebis*. The fourth provision represented a deal with Marius. In exchange for the command against Mithridates, Marius probably delivered the required number of tribes through the votes of his veterans. The bill became law, although not without considerable opposition and violence. Sulla had left his army at Nola and rushed to Rome. He used his power as consul to suspend public business. Exasperated, Sulpicius and his armed followers rioted. Ironically, Sulla escaped by taking refuge in the house of Marius. After Sulla had agreed to lift the suspension of public business, Marius, like an old soldier doing a good turn for another, allowed him to escape from his house with the expectation that he would go into exile.

Sulla's march on Rome

Instead, Sulla hastened to return to Campania and his army at Nola. He took part of the troops and marched on Rome. The increasingly bitter competition among ambitious politicians had led to outright civil war for the first time in the annals of the Roman

Republic. Significantly, only one of his aristocratic officers, L. Licinius Lucullus, was willing to accompany him. It is a great irony that this act was made possible in part by Marius' military career, which had increased the personal dependence of the soldiers on their commanders and weakened their loyalty to the state.

The common people of Rome resisted fiercely until Sulla started to set fire to their houses. Once in control, he obtained a senatorial decree declaring Marius, Sulpicius, and ten others to be enemies of the state. He then obtained passage of a law condemning them to death and putting a price on their heads. Marius fled and reached the coast of North Africa after some narrow escapes. Betrayed by a slave, Sulpicius seems to have been the only one executed, but Sulla had set a disastrous precedent for the future.

The victorious Sulla rescinded Sulpicius' legislation. Although he introduced a reasonable law for the relief of debtors by reducing the maximum rate of interest to 10 percent, he then made a number of reactionary changes to the "constitution." They were designed to make it impossible for anyone outside his group of optimate friends to challenge their dominant position within the senatorial aristocracy. Sulla made the Centuriate Assembly the primary legislative assembly by revoking the right of tribunes to introduce legislation in the *concilium plebis*. The Centuriate Assembly was also reorganized so that the ninety-eight wealthiest centuries had a clear majority once more. Another reactionary step was the requirement that magistrates consult the senate before introducing new legislation.

Sulla's attempt to interfere with the consular elections failed. He did, however, manage to extract a promise from one of the newly elected consuls, Lucius Cornelius Cinna, not to tamper with any constitutional changes already made. Such an agreement could not last. Still, it allowed Sulla to depart for the East to make war against Mithridates.

CINNA'S CONSULSHIP, 87 B.C.E.

Hardly had Sulla left Italy when Cinna attempted to annul Sulla's laws and reenact those of Sulpicius. The prospect of enrolling the Italians in all thirty-five tribes aroused the opposition of *optimates* like Gnaeus Octavius, Cinna's consular colleague. After some rioting and a massacre of Italians in the Forum, Octavius drove Cinna from the city, and the senate declared him a public enemy. In so doing, Cinna's enemies seriously blundered. They gave him the opportunity of appealing to the Italian voters and winning the support of the troops that Sulla had left at Nola. Cinna recalled Marius from Africa and, imitating Sulla's deadly example, marched on Rome.

MARIUS AND HIS REIGN OF TERROR

Recalled from Africa, the elderly Marius, now well over seventy, stormed Ostia, the seaport of Rome, cut off Rome's food supplies, and starved the city into surrender. Marius was embittered by the ingratitude and snubs of the nobles. Enraged by his recent experiences in Italy and North Africa, he wanted revenge. With his blessing, his followers struck down prominent enemies who had not fled. Their mutilated corpses littered the streets. Their severed heads, dripping blood, decorated the rostra. Their houses and property were confiscated and auctioned. Marius' outrages made even Cinna quail and finally stop them. In 86 B.C.E., Marius at last achieved his long-cherished ambition of a seventh consulship, but he did not long enjoy his victory. He fell ill and died a few days after taking office.

THE SIGNIFICANCE OF MARIUS

For a *novus homo*, Marius had made an unusually great impact on Roman history. His military service in defeating Jugurtha and in annihilating the threat of Germanic invasion made him a popular hero. Politically, however, his impact was largely negative. The problem was not with his opening military recruitment to the propertyless. That and its unforeseen political consequences would have happened anyway. Rather, the problem was that, as was the case with many of Marius' contemporaries, his only goal was to achieve the consulship and maintain the greatest prestige at Rome. He had no real program to deal with Rome's pressing problems. Therefore, he only made them worse and undermined faith in the political system. He was not the first to resort to outright civil war. Still, his willingness to follow Sulla's example in that case helped to set precedents for violence that greatly aided in the destruction of the Republic. Moreover, the reputation of Marius as a military hero and the popular policies of his associates left a problematic legacy among his veterans, the urban masses, and new Italian citizens. They formed a large body of people who could be manipulated by recalling his name in the increasingly bitter political struggles of the late Republic.

CINNA'S TIME (*CINNANUM TEMPUS*)

After Marius' sudden death in 86 B.C.E., Cinna was, in effect, left as a dictator. Foregoing elections, he appointed Lucius Valerius Flaccus as consul to replace Marius. For 85 and 84, he simply appointed himself and Gnaeus Papirius Carbo to the consulship. Cinna attempted, however, to secure his position by using power much more responsibly than Marius ever had. He overturned Sulla's reactionary laws and tried to satisfy many legitimate grievances of his own supporters. On the other hand, he disappointed the newly enfranchised Italians on the issue of their enrollment in all thirty-five tribes. Their just demand was not even partially met until the senate passed a decree during the maneuvering after Cinna's death in 84. It was not fully met until censors finally took office again in 70. Cinna's friend Flaccus, however, introduced a law that forgave debtors three-quarters of their obligations. Financial stability was protected by restoring the value of the coinage, which had been debased by corrupt moneyers (officials of the mint) and thrown into disarray during the recent upheavals.

Under Cinna, the senate and courts continued to function. Many nobles supported him. Those who did not support him prudently kept a low profile and waited to see what would happen with Sulla. Despite being stripped of the command against Mithridates, Sulla ignored Cinna's government and continued to press the war. Cinna attempted to come to an amicable agreement, but Sulla would have none of it. Instead,

Sulla went from victory to victory and assumed control of the East with all of its resources. Support began to shift toward him at Rome. Cinna was forced to take a harder stand. As he prepared for another disruptive civil war, mutinous soldiers suddenly killed him in 84 B.C.E.

SULLA AND THE EAST, 87 TO 84 B.C.E.

Sulla had invaded Greece in 87 B.C.E. and captured Athens in 86 after a winter-long siege. He showed the typical Roman love of Greek art by looting every painting, sculpture, and monument that he could put on a ship. During the summer, Sulla's experienced veterans from the Social War won hard-fought battles against two different Mithridatic armies and their superior cavalry. The first was at Chaeroneia; the second, at Orchomenus. Sulla then refused to surrender his command to the consul Flaccus, whom Cinna had sent to replace him. After some of Flaccus' troops defected to Sulla, Flaccus took the rest of his army to Asia to fight Mithridates. There, he was murdered by Flavius Fimbria, a mutinous legate. Fimbria seized command, defeated Mithridates' son, and marched on the stronghold of Pergamum. Mithridates, already facing revolts stirred up by his heavy taxation to support the war, decided to make a deal with Sulla. The latter lacked adequate naval forces and wanted to deny victory to Fimbria or avoid the union of Mithridates and Fimbria against him. Therefore, he came to terms.

The treaty was signed at Dardanus in the Troad in 85 B.C.E. Mithridates had to abandon his conquests in Asia Minor, surrender his best warships, and pay an indemnity of 2000 or 3000 talents. Nevertheless, remaining a "friend and ally" of Rome, he kept his kingdom of Pontus. Sulla imposed far harsher terms on the province of Asia: an indemnity of 20,000 talents; five years' back taxes; and pay, food, and lodging for his troops during the winter of 85–84. To raise the vast sums required, the province had to turn to Roman moneylenders and fell victim to a crushing burden of debt.

By these harsh actions and by subordinating many formally independent political entities within the boundaries of Rome's original province of Asia, Sulla foreshadowed later Roman rule in the East as a whole. At the time, however, he did nothing to change Rome's basically hegemonic imperial policy in the rest of the region. He restored Bithynia and Cappadocia to their former kings and gave Paphlagonia back to Bithynia. Galatia and Heraclea, never subject to Rome, retained the independence that they had recently won, while Rhodes regained its mainland territories. Southeast of the Meander River, he left it for others to reassert Roman control over native dynasts and pirates. What Sulla mainly did was create the conditions for more wars with Mithridates. In the meantime, as Sulla built up his forces in Greece for a civil war, negotiations for his peaceful return to Rome failed.

SULLA'S RETURN TO ITALY, 83 TO 82 B.C.E.

In the spring of 83 B.C.E., Sulla set sail for Italy. He left Flaccus' old army to serve as a permanent garrison in Asia under the command of Lucius Licinius Murena. When Sulla landed his own troops at Brundisium, he easily overpowered the two consular armies sent against him. In fact, one simply deserted to his side. The only anti-Sullan who might have been a match for him was Quintus Sertorius, who had fought under Marius. The nobles who had opposed Sulla scorned Sertorius for his equestrian origin and disliked him for his blunt criticism of their actions. Therefore, he had left Italy to take up the province of Nearer Spain, to which he had been assigned as praetor.

Sulla, on the other hand, acquired a number of effective supporters once he arrived in Italy. The first was Quintus Caecilius Metellus Pius. He came with a number of recruits from his hiding place in North Africa. Next, the young Marcus Licinius Crassus returned at the head of a small army from Spain. Gnaeus Pompeius (Pompey), the young son of Pompeius Strabo, was an even more valuable addition, both in the number of troops that he brought and in military skill. On his own initiative, he had raised three legions in Picenum. Despite his youth, upon reaching Sulla, Pompey was hailed with the flattering title of *Imperator* (Commander). After he had won several victories, Sulla somewhat facetiously called him *Magnus*, "the Great." The title stuck.

To bolster their tottering regime, Sulla's opponents elected two consuls for 82 B.C.E.: Cn. Papirius Carbo, Cinna's old consular colleague of 85 and 84, and Gaius Marius, son of the elder Marius. Their reputations enabled them to raise large numbers of recruits, but they proved to be inadequate generals against Sulla and his lieutenants. The younger Marius was besieged in Praeneste, where he eventually committed suicide or was killed. Carbo lost his nerve and fled to Africa. (Pompey later captured and executed him.) Nevertheless, thousands of Samnites rose up to fight Sulla, who still treated them as enemies from the Social War (pp. 238–9). Sulla met them late one day just outside Rome's Colline Gate. He was defeated on the left wing, which he personally commanded, but Marcus Crassus won a victory on the right in time to save the day.

SULLA'S REIGN OF TERROR, 82 B.C.E.

The bloody battle at the Colline Gate ended all effective resistance in Italy. Then began a reign of terror. Thousands suffered torture and death. Next door to the temple of Bellona, where Sulla was addressing a meeting of the senate, 6000 Samnite prisoners were brutally executed. Their only crime was that they lost a battle for what they believed was freedom and justice. The screams of the dying broke into his speech and distressed some of the senators to the point of fainting. Sulla grimly explained that only some criminals were being punished at his orders.

The proscriptions

To ruthlessness, Sulla added the method of proscription. To be proscribed meant to be put on a published list of people to be killed. Sulla and his henchmen listed some for political reasons, others to avenge private injuries, and still others for no reason except that they owned large and valuable properties. The proscribed, with prices set on their heads, were to be hunted down as outlaws and murdered. Sulla confiscated their property and revoked the citizenship of their children. Among the thousands he doomed to die were 90 senators, 15 men of consular rank, and 2600 *equites*. Their property was distributed among Sulla's supporters and veterans. As beneficiaries of his murders, they would, when required, rally around him or loyally support the oligarchy that he put in power. He secured additional supporters by freeing 10,000 slaves who had belonged to his victims. He also generously rewarded some freedmen. One, for example, was allowed to buy an estate worth about 1.5 million *denarii* for about 2500.

Unfortunately, the murder and spoliation of rich individuals failed to provide enough money or land for Sulla to redeem his promises of pay, pensions, and farms to his discharged veterans. He penalized communities suspected of having resisted his rise to power or of having supported his enemies. Their punishment was in proportion to the duration and strength of their resistance and opposition. Cities that had offered only mild opposition were required to pay fines, have their walls torn down, and surrender most, if not all, of their territory. Others, such as Praeneste in Latium or Florentia (Florence) in Etruria, which had resisted him long and stubbornly, were destroyed. Their inhabitants were sold into slavery. Sulla also turned the richest and most thickly populated districts of Samnium into a desolate waste. Such were the atrocities that resulted from the increasingly bitter rivalries within the Roman ruling elite.

SULLA'S DICTATORSHIP AND POLITICAL REFORMS

In 82 B.C.E., a few days before arriving in Rome, Sulla had demanded and secured from the Centuriate Assembly passage of a law, known as the *lex Valeria*. It appointed him dictator for an undefined period for the purpose of drafting laws and "reconstituting" the state. That appointment, confirming what had already been established by military force, formally revived the dictatorship (last held in 216 B.C.E.). It also legalized Sulla's subsequent murders, confiscations, and other atrocities. Unrestrained by law or custom, right of appeal, or tribunician veto, Sulla's dictatorship could be terminated only by his death or resignation. He had the power of life and death, and his *imperium* was absolute. With that *imperium*, Sulla wanted to revise the Republic in such a way that no one would be able to challenge the dominance of the senate as an institution or break its control by an oligarchy of his grateful optimate supporters who became consular nobles.

In 81 B.C.E., Sulla increased the membership of the senate to 600. Normally around 300, membership had been reduced by the civil war and the murderous activities of Marius and Sulla himself. The new members came from the first eighteen centuries of the Centuriate Assembly. They included the rich, landowning *equites* from the Italian municipalities. The main object of expanding the senate's membership was to make a larger number of persons available for jury service, which Sulla transferred from the *equites* to the senate. In expanding the membership of the senate and making senators alone eligible as jurors, Sulla was actually carrying out a proposal of Livius Drusus the Younger (p. 238). Of course, the new members would become grateful clients loyal to Sulla and those who had supported him in the civil war. Finally, Sulla abolished the position of *princeps senatus* to prevent any one man from having too much influence over the other senators.

Reform of the courts

In reforming the courts, Sulla went much further than Livius Drusus. He abolished ordinary trials before the popular assemblies and assigned them to a system of standing courts. Their juries were manned by senators. He raised the number of special jury courts for the trials of major crimes to seven: the *quaestio de repetundis*, dealing with extortion; *de maiestate*, with treason; *de ambitu*, with bribery in elections; *de falsis*, with forgery; *de peculatu*, with embezzlement of public property; *de sicariis et veneficis*, with murder; and *de vi publica*, with assault and battery. To provide enough judges to preside over these standing courts, he increased the number of praetors from six to eight. The reform of the courts was the greatest and the most permanent of Sulla's reforms. It clarified and recast the law dealing with serious crimes and laid the foundation of subsequent Roman criminal law (pp. 331–2).

Changes in the magistracies and the tribuneship

Sulla tried to regulate the system of officeholding and prevent the unorthodox careers that had increased political competition to destructive levels. He reenacted, in a considerably modified form, the *lex Villia Annalis* of 180 B.C.E. He prescribed a regular order of holding office (*cursus honorum*)—first the quaestorship, then the praetorship, and finally the consulship. He reaffirmed the rule prescribing an interval of ten years between successive consulships. His revised law advanced the minimum age probably to twenty-nine for the quaestorship, thirty-nine for the praetorship, and forty-two for the consulship. Finally, Sulla increased the number of quaestors from around ten to twenty. They became members of the senate automatically after their year of office. In that way, they would replace the average yearly vacancies that occurred in a senate of 500 to 600 members. Also, the censors would be less able to play favorites because they no longer controlled admission to the senate.

Changes were made in the tribuneship to destroy the effectiveness of that office and the temptation to use it in a *popularis* manner. Sulla crippled it most by disqualifying a tribune from holding any higher office, making the tribuneship unattractive to able and ambitious men. He limited the veto power of tribunes to the protection of personal rights and restricted or abolished their right to propose laws or prosecute cases before the *concilium plebis*.

Reorganization of the provinces

Before the time of Sulla, Rome had nine provinces, six in the West (Sicily, Sardinia-Corsica, Nearer Spain, Farther Spain, Africa Proconsularis, and Gallia Transalpina) and three in the East (Macedonia, Asia, and Cilicia). Cyrenaica, though accepted in 96 B.C.E. as a legacy from its king, Ptolemy Apion, was not formally organized as a province until 74 B.C.E. Sulla made Cisalpine Gaul the tenth province by detaching it from the rest of Italy. He sent a governor and a garrison to guard it against the raiders who periodically descended from the Alps.

Most important was the attempt to fortify the power of the senate even more and prevent ambitious governors from doing what he himself had done: seize control of the state. Sulla limited the independence of provincial governors through his law of *maiestas*: a governor could no longer initiate a war, leave his province (with or without his army), or enter a foreign kingdom without express authorization from the senate. A governor also had to leave his province within thirty days of his replacement's arrival. Sulla hoped thus to give the senate full control over the armed forces and limit the war-making potential of provincial commanders.

Sulla's consulship, abdication, and death

Sulla had fully reorganized the government to his own satisfaction. He had created a system designed to maintain the dominance that he and his allies had achieved. In 81 B.C.E., he stood for election as consul for 80. He probably resigned the dictatorship at the end of 81, or possibly earlier that year. After the consulship of 80, he retired to his country estate near Puteoli (Pozzuoli) in Campania. He hoped to pass the rest of his life there in ease, luxury, and pleasure. He did not enjoy himself long. After his death in 78 B.C.E., he was cremated at Rome during a magnificent funeral. Before his death, he had dictated an epitaph to be inscribed upon his tomb to the effect that no one had ever surpassed him in rewarding his friends with good, or his enemies with evil.

THE FAILURE OF SULLA

Sulla had named himself *Felix*, "Fortunate." He was even fortunate in death. He never saw the utter futility of much that he had done. He had worked to create a system that would produce a stable government for Rome under the oligarchic control of the optimate friends whom he had rewarded. They were to dominate the senate. The avenues that previously had allowed other ambitious members of the senatorial class to challenge the dominant leaders were to remain blocked. The governmental system that he tried to make permanent did have some admirable features, such as the reform of the courts, the admission of new senators from the equestrian class, and the rational ordering of the magistracies and provincial government. Yet, it was doomed to failure. It did nothing to solve Rome's basic social, economic, and political problems. Ambitious men who did not want to play the political game by his rules could exploit those problems in building bases of power to challenge the men whom he had left in control. No sooner had the ashes of his funeral pyre cooled than his whole carefully designed political superstructure began to collapse upon the sand beneath it.

First of all, his reforms of the magistracies actually intensified the competition for high office by increasing the number of quaestors and praetors. Previously, at least one-half of the quaestors could hope to reach the praetorship; one-third of the praetors could hope for consulships. Now, only two-fifths of the quaestors had a chance to become praetors; only one-fourth of the praetors were likely to become consuls. Therefore, the holders of lower offices had to intensify their efforts to reach the consulship. Second, the attempt to limit the war-making potential of provincial commanders was futile. An ambitious provincial commander determined to defy the senate could still do so with a loyal army, just as Sulla himself had done. There was little that senators could do except raise up another potentially dangerous commander against him.

Other safeguards that Sulla had created to check the destructive competition for personal preeminence that had led to civil war in the 80s were inadequate. In fact, they were part of the problem because they also restricted the rights and privileges of the *equites* and the common people. Ambitious politicians could gain popular support by advocating repeal of the safeguards that were supposed to keep them in check. Also, removing the *equites* from juries in the extortion court left no check on corrupt and abusive provincial governors. That only fueled discontent in the provinces, which provided more troubled waters in which the ambitious could fish.

Furthermore, Sulla had left a legacy of bitterness and hatred that created many enemies for the oligarchs who succeeded him. The bitterest enemies of these oligarchs were the sons, relations, and friends of the senators and wealthy *equites* who had suffered proscription, exile, or confiscation of their property. In the forests of Etruria roamed bands of once-peaceful and well-to-do farmers whose lands had been confiscated by Sulla for distribution among his veterans. In the city of Rome, the poor had been deprived of their subsidized grain. Of those *equites* who had not been killed, many had suffered financial ruin. All had been deprived of jury service in the courts.

As the years passed, no group was more frustrated and rebellious than Sulla's veterans. They had been given confiscated land but had no knowledge of farming or desire for the monotony of rural life. They were soon enmeshed in debt and were only too happy to support anyone who promised them personal gain without regard to political proprieties. It is not surprising, therefore, that the flawed fabric of Sulla's reforms soon began to fray.

SUGGESTED READING

Keaveney, A. *Sulla: The Last Republican.* 2nd ed. London and New York: Routledge, 2005.

Mayor, A. *The Poison King: The Life and Legend of Mithradates, Rome's Deadliest Enemy.* Princeton and Oxford: Princeton University Press, 2010.

CHAPTER 15

Personal ambitions

The failure of Sulla's optimate oligarchy, 78 to 60 B.C.E.

The oligarchic system that Sulla created to stabilize the Roman Republic only destabilized it further. His own example was a powerful incentive for ambitious men to circumvent the restraints that he tried to put in place. Sulla had alienated and embittered numerous groups within Roman society, and they were willing to support any leader who wanted to challenge Sulla's repressive system, even one who was originally a part of that system. In addition, the need to control an extensive overseas empire required the creation of extraordinary military commands. Sulla had vainly tried to eliminate them, lest one man achieve so much more power and prestige than his noble peers that he could dominate them. Throughout the 70s and 60s B.C.E., therefore, a series of domestic and foreign crises gave ambitious individuals opportunities to gain so much popularity, clientage, and military power that the senate became powerless to restrain them. These leaders opened up another round of upheavals and civil wars, which destroyed the Republic by 30 B.C.E.

SOURCES FOR ROMAN HISTORY FROM 78 TO 30 B.C.E.

The years from 78 to 30 B.C.E., which will be covered in this and the following four chapters, are among the best documented in Roman history. Cicero's voluminous writings provide much invaluable information by a keen observer and participant in events until his death in 43 B.C.E. (pp. 239–40). Cicero's correspondence also includes letters to him from other important participants or observers. The second largest group of contemporary works covers the conquest of Gaul and the civil war from 58 to 46 B.C.E.: Caesar's commentaries, namely, the *Gallic War* and the *Civil War*; other accounts by some of his officers, namely, the final book of the *Gallic War*, the *African War*, the *Alexandrian War*, and the *Spanish War*. Another valuable contemporary witness is Sallust. His *Histories*, covering the years from 78 to 67, is preserved only in fragments, but his account of Catiline's conspiracy (63 B.C.E.) is extant. Cornelius Nepos was another contemporary historian. Unfortunately, his biography of Cicero is lost, but his life of Cicero's devoted friend Atticus is extant. Other contemporary historians, orators, and antiquarians are preserved mainly in fragments.

The poems of Catullus (pp. 338–9) and the didactic epic *De Rerum Natura* (*On the Nature of Things*), by Lucretius (p. 339), help to reveal the atmosphere at the time of Caesar's rise. The *Eclogues and Georgics* of Vergil (pp. 394–5) do the same for the time of Caesar's heir, Octavian, the future Emperor Augustus. Fragments of a biography of Augustus' early life by the late-first-century B.C.E. writer Nicolaus of Damascus also survive. Most of Augustus' own official summary of his career, *Res Gestae Divi Augusti*, has been preserved because it was set up on stone inscriptions in various cities. The most complete version is the *Monumentum Ancyranum*, from Ankara in modern Turkey (p. 397).

Later writers also supply abundant material. The mid-first-century C.E. commentary by Asconius on some of Cicero's speeches, particularly some lost ones, is extremely valuable. The biographies of Caesar and Augustus by the early-second-century C.E. author Suetonius, who often quotes from contemporary writers and documents, are veritable gold mines. So, too, are Plutarch's biographies of many leading figures of the period, which are often based on contemporary sources like Asinius Pollio (p. 397). The relevant books of Livy survive only in the summaries of the *Periochae* and in the brief late Imperial histories, and the relevant books of Diodorus Siculus are lost except for some fragments. Nevertheless, there are extensive narrative sources. Appian's *Civil Wars* narrates the years 78 to 35. Beginning with events of 69 B.C.E., Cassius Dio is complete for the remaining years of this period. Also, Velleius Paterculus' narrative, though brief, is much fuller for this period than for earlier ones.

THE RISE OF POMPEY THE GREAT (106 TO 48 B.C.E.), 78 TO 71 B.C.E.

The rise of Pompey the Great, Gnaeus Pompeius Magnus, is a study in opportunism, much like the career of his father, Gnaeus Pompeius Strabo (p. 239). As Strabo's heir, Pompey was the largest landowner in the district of Picenum. Therefore, he had a large number of clients and vast personal resources. He was personally charming and seems to have inspired great loyalty and love in his children and most of his several wives. He was also extremely ambitious and missed no opportunity to use his resources to advance his personal career. In 85 B.C.E., Pompey successfully argued against a suit instituted to recover from his father's estate booty misappropriated during the Social War (pp. 238–9). It seems more than coincidental that he soon married Antistia, the daughter of the presiding judge. In 84, at the age of twenty-three, after Cinna had refused to grant him the recognition that he wanted, he raised a large private army and joined Sulla (p. 247). Later, he willingly divorced Antistia when Sulla wanted him to marry Aemilia. She was Sulla's pregnant stepdaughter and had to divorce her husband in order to marry Pompey. Sadly, she soon died in childbirth. Pompey then married Mucia Tertia. She was the third daughter of the famous jurist Q. Mucius Scaevola the Pontiff (p. 332) and half-sister of two Caecilii Metelli, whose powerful family had backed Sulla.

Pompey did not even protest when Sulla struck down before his very eyes former friends who had helped him in times of trouble. His zealous hunting of Sulla's enemies earned him the nickname *adulescentulus carnifex*, "teenage butcher." Then, when Sulla asked him to disband his army after killing Cn. Papirius Carbo and others in Sicily and North Africa (p. 247), he refused. Instead, he demanded that Sulla grant him a triumph, for which he was ineligible under Sulla's own laws. When Sulla balked, Pompey is said to have reminded him, not very subtly, that more men worship the rising than the setting sun. Sulla gave in to preserve harmony, an act that reinforced the perception of Pompey as *Magnus* (Great).

As a general, Pompey was not brilliant. His detractors said, with some justice, that his victories were prepared by others who had fought before him. Still, Pompey often succeeded where others had not. He planned methodically and seldom attacked unless he had secured an overwhelming numerical superiority. As a statesman, Pompey was somewhat inept and shortsighted. He spoke poorly and awkwardly at times and often fell back on silence because he could think of nothing to say. He had no ideology or political program. His main ambition was simply to be admired as the Republic's greatest hero and enjoy the political prestige that such heroes naturally acquired. There is no reason to think that he wanted to destroy the Republic that had produced him and was the source of the glory that he sought.

Pompey supports and abandons Marcus Aemilius Lepidus, 78 to 77 B.C.E.

As a renegade Marian, Marcus Aemilius Lepidus (ca. 120–77 B.C.E.) had supported Sulla in 83. He had increased his own wealth by buying property of the proscribed at cut rates. Afterward, as governor of Sicily, he shamelessly plundered the province. He narrowly escaped prosecution and lost Sulla's favor. Lepidus then sought support among the disaffected groups in society. Pompey, who felt little loyalty to the now-retired Sulla, backed Lepidus in the consular elections for 78 over Sulla's bitter objections. Pompey may well have calculated that Lepidus was likely to give him an opportunity to pose as the champion of the status quo even as he violated the rules aimed at preserving it. If so, he was not disappointed.

As consul, Lepidus opposed a state funeral for Sulla. He proposed the recall of all exiles, the resumption of cheap grain distributions to the poor, the return of all confiscated properties to the former owners, and the restoration of the powers of the tribunes. Pompey ostentatiously made sure that Sulla received a grand state funeral even though Sulla had pointedly cut him out of his will. Sulla' death and Lepidus' proposals encouraged men like Cinna's son, the young L. Cornelius Cinna, as well as Cinna's son-in-law and Marius' nephew, C. Julius Caesar, who had fled under Sulla, to return to Rome. Plots and conspiracies sprang up everywhere, but Caesar wisely stayed aloof.

Those who controlled the senate sought to get rid of Lepidus by sending him to suppress a rebellion of dispossessed farmers near Florence. Instead, Lepidus used the assignment as an opportunity to raise an even bigger rebellion of his own. Pompey enthusiastically accepted a command to help suppress the man whose election he had recently supported. Pompey defeated Lepidus, who fled to Sardinia and died there while trying to establish closer ties with the Marian holdout Sertorius in Spain.

Pompey obtains an irregular command against Sertorius in Spain, 76 to 71 B.C.E.

Quintus Sertorius (ca. 122–73 B.C.E.) was a serious foe of the Sullan regime. Whoever defeated him would be seen as an important member of the Roman nobility. Sertorius had fallen out with the anti-Sullan leaders in Italy before he could ennoble his family with a consulship (p. 247). Removing himself to Spain, he had fought to be the hero who would restore the anti-Sullan cause and return to long-sought honors at Rome. After some initial setbacks, he and a few other Roman officers loyal to him gained the support of the native peoples by treating them with dignity and justice. Using native Spanish troops, Sertorius had frustrated provincial governors sent out to fight him. He opposed only Sulla's government and always proclaimed loyalty to Rome. After Sulla's death, he was eager for reconciliation, but Sulla's political heirs were determined to continue the war, which had been under the command of Sulla's old ally Quintus Caecilius Metellus Pius since 79 B.C.E.

Metellus had not been able to make much progress against Sertorius by 77. Then Pompey the Great returned to Rome from mopping-up operations after defeating Lepidus. Pompey refused a senatorial order to disband his army and practically demanded to be sent to Spain to join Metellus, who had been asking for reinforcements against Sertorius. A number of senators objected to Pompey. Some of Metellus' friends may not have wanted to send him such an opportunistic colleague. To others, Pompey's assignment would have represented just the kind of irregular command that Sulla had tried to prevent. Such a major military operation required a grant of proconsular *imperium* and Pompey had not yet held even the lowest office of the *cursus honorum*. A majority, however, sided with the young military hero. Pompey received proconsular *imperium* and the chief command in Nearer Spain.

Pompey's arrival in Spain (76 B.C.E.) proved inauspicious: Sertorius defeated him twice with fewer men. On one occasion, only the timely arrival of old Metellus saved Pompey's army from annihilation. Pompey threatened to withdraw and leave the way open for Sertorius to march into Italy. That prospect brought reinforcements from the senate. Still, Pompey was able to end the war in 72/71 only after a traitor assassinated Sertorius in 74 or 73 B.C.E. Pompey then promptly executed the assassin. A less skillful tactician than Metellus, Pompey received public credit for ending the war. Ironically, but wisely, he followed Sertorius' example in victory and treated the Spanish people with great justice. His honorable peace terms restored prosperity to Spain, where the people long and gratefully remembered Pompey as their patron.

THE GREAT (THIRD) MITHRIDATIC WAR, 74/73 TO 63 B.C.E., AND LUCULLUS' BID FOR GLORY, 74 TO 66 B.C.E.

While Metellus and Pompey were fighting Sertorius in Spain, L. Licinius Lucullus (ca. 116–57 B.C.E.) saw his chance to achieve preeminence at the eastern end of the Mediterranean. Lucullus was the one officer to march on Rome with Sulla in 88 B.C.E. (p. 244). He came from an old aristocratic family that had fallen into obscurity. He had revived his family's fortunes through loyal service to Sulla against Marius and Marius' successors and in the first war against Mithridates (p. 242). Thus, he had entered the innermost circle of Sulla's political heirs and been rewarded with election to a consulship for 74. When a third war with Mithridates was imminent in 74, Lucullus contrived to obtain for himself the main command in the anticipated theater of operations.

Both sides had long expected war. Rome's humiliation at Mithridates' hands in 88 B.C.E. remained unavenged. The Roman senate had refused to ratify Sulla's easy peace terms after the first war. Then L. Licinius Murena, Sulla's ambitious legate in Asia, touched off the brief Second Mithridatic War in 83 and 82 by an unauthorized attack until Sulla recalled him. In late 75 or early 74 B.C.E., the childless king of Bithynia, Nicomedes IV, bequeathed his kingdom to the Roman People. The senate accordingly declared Bithynia a Roman province. This provoked Mithridates, who feared that Roman control of Bithynia would block navigation from the Black Sea to the Aegean.

Mithridates braced for war. He had already engaged exiled Roman officers who had supported Marius. They now tried to modernize Mithridates' army along Roman lines. Some had come from Sertorius, with whom Mithridates made an alliance. Mithridates also made alliances with his own son-in-law, Tigranes II of Armenia, and with the pirates of Crete and Cilicia. The pirates rebuilt the navy shattered in his first war with Rome.

At Rome, the other consul of 74, M. Aurelius Cotta, was not to be outdone by Lucullus. He successfully argued that he should be reassigned from his scheduled province to the new province of Bithynia. The senate also gave the praetor M. Antonius, father of the famous Mark Antony, an extraordinary commission to fight pirates all over the Mediterranean. Then, more fearful than ever of Mithridates, the senate assigned a fleet to Cotta and added another legion to Lucullus' command.

In the spring of 73, Mithridates struck first by attacking Cotta. The Third Mithridatic War was on in earnest. The other commanders bungled their operations in the war, but Lucullus scored a series of stunning victories. In 72, Mithridates finally fled in exile to the court of Tigranes.

Lucullus' legates (sub-commanders) completed the reduction of Pontus. Lucullus himself returned to the Roman province of Asia to relieve its cities of the crushing indemnity levied by Sulla and the extortionate loans that they had contracted with Roman moneylenders to pay it. Lucullus' relief measures rapidly restored the economic health of the province but infuriated the financiers at Rome. They worked for his downfall.

The downfall of Lucullus, 69 to 66 B.C.E.

When Tigranes refused to surrender Mithridates, Lucullus invaded Armenia in 69 and captured Tigranes' capital Tigranocerta. Lucullus, however, did not have authorization to attack Armenia, and agents of his political enemies undermined his efforts. One of them was his own brother-in-law, the young, ambitious, and unscrupulous Publius Clodius Pulcher (p. 270). Lucullus' iron discipline and refusal to permit indiscriminate plunder made it easy for Clodius to stir up a mutiny that forced Lucullus to withdraw from Armenia. That permitted Mithridates to seize the initiative once more. Early in the summer of 67, near Zela in south-central Pontus, Mithridates almost annihilated two legions commanded by Lucullus' legates.

Lucullus' failure to defeat Mithridates was not the only problem. To the consternation of many, his crossing of the Euphrates River to attack Armenia had invited the hostile attention of resurgent Iranian peoples led by the aggressive dynasty of Arsacid kings. They had taken over the Seleucids' eastern territories and created the Parthian Empire, which became Rome's chief rival in the East. Pompey subsequently intrigued to become the supreme military commander in the East and eventually succeeded in ending the war. Though denied a chance for final victory, Lucullus did eventually obtain the triumph that he claimed. Meanwhile, he found consolation in his wine cellar, his fishponds, and his cherry trees, but he seized every opportunity to oppose Pompey.[1]

CRASSUS SEEKS ADVANTAGE IN THE SLAVE WAR AGAINST SPARTACUS IN ITALY, 73 TO 71 B.C.E.

While Pompey and Lucullus were waging wars at either end of the Mediterranean, Marcus Licinius Crassus (ca. 115–53 B.C.E.) was trying to advance himself in Rome. For three generations his family had enjoyed great prominence among the nobility. His father, brother, and many of their friends had died while opposing Marius. Crassus was the only one left to uphold the family's honor. Like Pompey and Lucullus, he had started out as a Sullan partisan. He had even played the decisive role in Sulla's victory at the Colline Gate (p. 247). He, however, had fallen behind Pompey and Lucullus in the race for preeminence at Rome.

Accused of manipulating Sulla's proscriptions to benefit himself financially, Crassus had lost the crucial favor of Sulla and Sulla's political heirs. Moreover, despite his later reputation for great wealth, Crassus had begun his career with only a modest inheritance by the standards of the Roman nobility. Therefore, he had to build up his own financial resources and a network of useful supporters essential for success in the intense competition of Roman politics. His strategy was to take advantage of the opportunities for profit in the world of business and finance. He used his profits, along with traditional forms of patronage, to obligate as many people to him as possible. He was particularly attentive to the *publicani*, the *equites*, and the lower ranks of the senatorial aristocracy.

Crassus' financial operations earned him an unfair reputation for greed in ancient times. It was not considered proper for a Roman aristocrat, particularly a prominent member of the senate, to be so directly concerned with making money. Pompey actually became much richer than Crassus through the profits of war, an employment considered very honorable. Crassus, on the other hand, invested in profitable agricultural land, mines, and business loans. He maintained a large staff of highly trained slaves who could be rented out to those who needed temporary help. He also used them to repair and rebuild property that he bought at bargain prices as a result of the many fires in overcrowded and flimsily built Rome.

Many believe that Crassus maintained a private fire brigade (there was no public fire protection in the city) that would not put out a fire until the unfortunate owner agreed to sell his property to Crassus at a reduced rate. There is no ancient evidence for this story. It was not, however, unusual for wealthy men to maintain private fire brigades in their role as patrons of the less fortunate. Crassus may have done so, too, but it would not have been worth the ill will created to refuse to save a burning building before the owner sold.

Crassus was famous for his willingness to defend anyone in court, even though advocates could receive no fees. He often loaned money to people without interest. In that way, he earned the loyalty of many lesser-known members of the senate. As a result, Crassus had patiently advanced his career and had reached the praetorship in 73 B.C.E., a few years after he was first eligible. In that same year, a major slave revolt broke out. Although defeating slaves was not so glorious as conquering free peoples, this war proved to be unusually significant and was not already in the hands of a major figure. By the time Crassus took over, he had reason to hope that a victory would help advance him to the consulship.

It was probably late summer of 73 B.C.E., when Spartacus, a Thracian slave and gladiator, led a breakout of fellow gladiators from the barracks of a training school at Capua. They fortified themselves in the crater of Vesuvius and called upon all farm slaves to join them in a fight for freedom. Many thousands did, especially enslaved Gauls and Germans. Some slaves came already armed. The others soon obtained arms by buying them from pirates and unscrupulous traders or capturing them from the Roman armies sent to subdue them. Their force grew to at least 70,000 as they ranged over the country, broke open the slave prisons, and armed the slaves.

The slaves' rebellion was able to gain momentum because Rome's best soldiers were pinned down in Spain and Asia Minor. The Romans were now locked in a desperate struggle to maintain their power against a loosely coordinated uprising that spanned the whole Mediterranean. Earlier, Sertorius, Mithridates, and the Mediterranean pirates had taken some cooperative steps. Now the pirates were supplying arms and matériel to the rebellious slaves in Italy.

The government, which had thought the slave revolt would be easily quelled, soon learned that Spartacus commanded a large army and was a master strategist as well. Defeat followed defeat. After Spartacus had vanquished the armies of four praetors and two consuls, the senate, in desperation, appointed Crassus to take command. It assigned him six new legions, in addition to remnants of the four consular legions that Spartacus had shattered. Reputed once to have said that no man could be considered rich who could not finance a legion on his own, Crassus recruited even more troops with his own money.

After he had trained his men, Crassus pursued Spartacus to the southern part of Bruttium. Despite many difficulties, Crassus finally defeated the bulk of the slaves.

Spartacus was killed, his body unidentifiable amid the slaughter. Still, 5000 slaves escaped capture. Pompey, returning from Spain, encountered them in Etruria and destroyed them. This minor feat of arms enabled Pompey to claim credit for ending yet another war, much to Crassus' chagrin. Crassus, however, made a big show of crucifying 6000 captured slaves along the Appian Way.

THE CONSULSHIP OF POMPEY AND CRASSUS, 70 B.C.E.

Pompey and Crassus, both victors, marched to Rome and encamped their armies outside the gates. Each expected military honors; both wanted the consulship. Crassus, praetor in 73 B.C.E., was eligible for the office. Pompey was six years too young to be a consul and had not yet held any of the lower offices that the law required for a consular candidate. The senators could grant Pompey's demands only by violating the Sullan constitution, on which their power was based. Yet they could not reject the demands without the risk of having legions enter Rome. The hope of playing Crassus off against Pompey was equally vain. Although the two were political rivals, they realized that their hopes for consulships could be fulfilled only by cooperation at this point. To increase their popularity and put further pressure on their opponents in the senate, they supported popular demands for the restoration of full powers to the tribunes of the *plebs* and the placing of nonsenators on juries. They also seem to have favored the election of the first censors since 86 B.C.E. Pompey received a dispensation from the legal requirements, and both he and Crassus were elected consuls for 70 B.C.E.

The consulship of Pompey and Crassus completed the ruin of the Sullan constitution, which had been under attack for several years. The optimate leaders of the senate had made some concessions to popular pressure in the hope of defusing discontent. In 75, the consul Gaius Aurelius Cotta had carried a law permitting the tribunes to hold higher offices. The consuls of 73 B.C.E., a year of scarcity and high prices, had sponsored a bill to distribute five pecks of grain a month to 45,000 citizens at the price set by Gaius Gracchus. Pompey and Crassus now proposed and carried a law to restore to the tribunes all the powers taken away by Sulla. (Pompey hoped that tribunes with full powers would later help him to secure desirable commands. They did not disappoint him.) The tribunes of 70 proposed a law to restore citizenship to all who had fought under Lepidus and Sertorius. The new censors finally enrolled in all thirty-five tribes the Italians enfranchised at the end of the Social War (p. 239). They also ejected sixty-four of Sulla's partisans from the senate. Both moves would have benefited Crassus and Pompey.

Near the end of their historic consulship, an optimate praetor drafted and carried a law to break the senatorial monopoly of jury service and to draw jurors in equal numbers from the senate, the *equites*, and the *tribuni aerarii* ("tribunes of the treasury"), effectively ending fifty years of fighting over who could serve as jurors. About the *tribuni aerarii* almost nothing is known. They were probably inferior to the *equites* in rank, but, like the *equites*, belonged to the upper nonsenatorial census classes, which henceforth supplied two-thirds of the jurors. After Pompey and Crassus left office, they both resumed their rivalry. Each looked for further ways to enhance his fame and prestige so that he would be in a better position to exploit the next public crisis. Pompey never attended meetings of the senate, where he was most unwelcome. On his rare appearances in the Forum, he was always accompanied by a mass of clients and retainers, to the mingled awe and pride of the populace. Crassus worked diligently behind the scenes to increase his wealth and network of grateful friends on whom he could depend when the need arose. Also, the cooperation of Pompey and Crassus in office had provided other ambitious men opportunities to join the parade of political prominence.

CICERO GAINS FAME IN THE TRIAL OF VERRES, 70 B.C.E.

The issue of who should sit on juries, which Pompey and Crassus' consulship had brought to the fore, was underlined by the famous trial of Gaius Verres in 70 B.C.E. Yet another old supporter of Sulla, he had become a praetor for 74 B.C.E. and had received the governorship of Sicily for the following three years. As governor, he had cheated, blackmailed, plundered, and even murdered people, some of whom were clients of Pompey. In 70, injured Sicilians charged Verres with extortion. He assumed that Sulla's old supporters in the senate would procure his acquittal. So did many others, who saw this trial as a test of the integrity of senatorial jurors.

Powerful friends did rally to Verres' support. They persuaded Quintus Hortensius Hortalus, the most famous orator of the day, to defend him. They used the most ingenious tricks and dodges in a vain attempt to quash the indictment or postpone the trial until one of them could preside. They even tried to obtain a friendly prosecutor. At every turn, however, Marcus Tullius Cicero (106–43 B.C.E.), an eager young orator who had served as a quaestor in Sicily (75 B.C.E.), was there to meet them.

Cicero, the son of a prominent *eques*, had been born at Arpinum near the home of Marius, to whom he was related by marriage. Cicero had received a fine education; had traveled extensively; had studied philosophy and rhetoric in Athens, Asia, and Rhodes; and had trained himself for the Roman bar. He became one of the world's most renowned orators and greatest literary figures (pp. 339–40).

Throughout his life, Cicero unveiled the offenses and scandals of the optimate nobles who dominated the senate. Nevertheless, he never wholly lost faith in them or ceased to look up to them. His ideal was to join them and convince them to be true, impartial servants of the common good. In 80 B.C.E., he gained notice by defending, at considerable personal risk, a young man who was threatened by one of Sulla's corrupt freedmen. In 70, the trial of Verres gave him a chance to show genuine sympathy for the victims of corruption. He also did a political favor by protecting Pompey's Sicilian friends. At the same time, he bolstered his own clientele among the Sicilians and gained fame as an orator by beating Hortensius in a successful prosecution.

Cicero marshaled such a mass of damning evidence against Verres that the great Hortensius gave up the defense. Verres fled into exile to Massilia, where the mullets were delicious and the climate delightful—not a really harsh punishment for a man who had robbed the Sicilian people of millions and had even crucified a Roman citizen. That Verres was not acquitted, however, may have helped to make the subsequent compromise of sharing the seats on juries among the senators, *equites*, and *tribuni aerarii* acceptable to both Sulla's political heirs and to the majority of voters. Shortly thereafter, Cicero was elected aedile for 69 B.C.E. After the reform of the juries and the restoration of full tribunician powers, the Republic had, for the most part, been returned to its pre-Sullan state.

TRIBUNES MAKE THEIR MARKS AND POMPEY TAKES CONTROL OF THE EAST, 67 TO 62 B.C.E.

While Cicero won fame through the courts, other ambitious young men soon utilized the recently restored powers of the tribunes to gain favor and influence. In 67 B.C.E., the tribunes Gaius Cornelius and Aulus Gabinius were particularly active. The first law of the tribune Cornelius obliged praetors to administer justice according to the principles that they had laid down in their edicts on taking office. That enactment was supremely important. It laid the foundation of uniform law and equity throughout the provinces (p. 332). The second law imposed a fine and future exclusion from office for persons guilty of bribing the electorate. The third made it illegal for the senate to exempt individuals from the laws unless a quorum of 200 members was present. Of Cornelius' other proposals, later carried by Gabinius, the first forbade the lending of money to foreign and provincial envoys for the purpose of securing an audience with the senate by bribery; the second compelled the senate to give priority to the reception of embassies during its February meetings to protect Roman allies against dilatory political tactics. These excellent and salutary laws were enacted in spite of the violent opposition of many leading senators, who stood to lose significant financial and political advantages. They seemed to justify freeing tribunes from the restrictions imposed by Sulla.

Still, men like Cornelius and Gabinius were not simply public-spirited reformers. They were doing just what Sulla had feared. As competitors in senatorial politics, they were using the restored powers of the tribunes to get around the dominant senatorial leaders, just as the Gracchi and others had done earlier. Part of their strategy was to attract the favor of other powerful senators, like Pompey and Crassus, who also stood outside the group of Sulla's optimate political heirs, which dominated the senate.

Much of the legislation sponsored by Cornelius and Gabinius corrected abuses that had helped the optimate oligarchs to keep control in the face of rival *populares*. Gabinius was especially notable in promoting the interests of Pompey, who was intriguing to obtain command of the Third Mithridatic War at Lucullus' expense. One of the laws that he sponsored in 67 B.C.E. removed Lucullus from the command of Bithynia and Pontus and ended his role in the war. Gabinius' most famous service to Pompey is a law that dealt with the scourge of piracy in the Mediterranean. Previous attempts to suppress it had proved ineffective (pp. 234–5 and 256). The menace had recently reached dangerous proportions. Pirates had attacked large coastal cities in Italy itself and destroyed a large Roman fleet near Ostia. They so infested the waters around Sicily that grain ships supplying the city of Rome no longer ventured to sail. Food prices had risen, and the people, threatened with famine, resolved to clear the seas.

The bill that Gabinius laid before the voters in 67 B.C.E. provided for the appointment of a supreme commander over the waters and coasts of the Mediterranean basin for three years. He was to have consular rank and extraordinary authority. As finally enacted, the *lex Gabinia* placed enormous power in the hands of one man. His authority, superior to that of the provincial governors, extended over all coastal lands up to fifty Roman miles (ca. forty-five English miles, or seventy-five kilometers) from the sea. He could draw from the public treasury 6000 talents; raise a fleet up to 500 ships; if necessary, recruit an army of 120,000 infantry and 5000 cavalry; and appoint a staff of 24 sub-commanders (legates) of praetorian rank and 2 quaestors (see Box 15.1).

15.1 PROVINCIAL COMMANDS

Pompey's command against the pirates can be seen as the culmination of the evolution of the process by which Romans determined who would maintain control over their expanding empire. Traditionally, the prerogative to assign provincial commands (whether for a geographical region or, as in Pompey's case, a carefully defined task) resided with the senate, which assessed Rome's entire military situation each year and handed out (either by lot or by arrangement) provincial commands to the consuls and praetors who had just been elected. Sitting consuls were not above using their prestige and authority to lobby for particularly plum assignments: such commands could enhance a man's military glory and bestow upon him tremendous wealth. To curb this, in 123 or 122 B.C.E., the tribune Gaius Gracchus passed a law that either required or provided incentive for the senate to announce the consular provinces prior to the election of new magistrates.

In the year 107 B.C.E., Marius introduced a new mechanism for assigning provinces, and the consequences, whether intended or not, were far-reaching and destructive to the Republic itself. A tribune put legislation before the people that Marius should be given as his province the command of the war against Jugurtha, even though the senate had already decided to continue the proconsul Metellus in that role (see p. 232). Assigning provinces in this way not only hampered the senate's ability to plan for military needs across the empire, but also opened the door for ever-increasing competition among politicians to curry popular favor as a means to a desirable provincial assignment. Within a few decades, men like Pompey, Caesar, Octavian, and Antony took things one step further, using the popular assembly to create for themselves massive territorial assignments or extraordinary commands over the objection of their colleagues in the senate. The result was fewer commanders in charge of ever-larger armies that contributed to the downfall of the republican system.

The consul C. Calpurnius Piso and other senators strenuously opposed Gabinius' proposed law precisely because it gave so much power to one man. The populace rioted against the consul. One of the tribunes vetoed the bill. He withdrew his veto when threatened with the treatment that Tiberius Gracchus had once dealt out to Octavius (p. 211). The bill passed. After it became law, the majority of senators appointed

Pompey to take the command. They had little choice because there was no one else of equal competence. Although not expressly named in the *lex Gabinia*, he was the person whom Gabinius and the voters had in mind.[2] Gabinius, in turn, was amply rewarded for his efforts on Pompey's behalf: Pompey chose him as a legate in 66 and ensured that he would enjoy the rare achievement of reaching the consulship as a *novus homo* in 58.

Pompey's campaigns against the pirates, 67 B.C.E.

Pompey's excellent organizational skills and the vast concentration of ships, men, and supplies made available by the *lex Gabinia* enabled him to sweep the western Mediterranean clean of pirates in forty days. He owed his swift victory over the pirates not only to the overwhelming superiority of his armaments but also to his treatment of captives. Instead of following the usual Roman practice of crucifying or selling them into slavery, he adopted the more humane methods that he had used successfully in Spain: those who surrendered he resettled on farms or in villages in Asia Minor. Many of the basic social and economic causes of piracy were thus eliminated, and the resettled pirates later became some of Rome's most loyal and useful subjects. Some were among the first in the East to receive Roman citizenship. They, like many in Spain, also became loyal clients of Pompey. He would rely on their support when his preeminence was later challenged.

Pompey and the defeat of Mithridates, 66 to 64 B.C.E.

Pompey, however, was not satisfied with only the command against the pirates. He still wanted command of the whole Third Mithridatic War. In 66 B.C.E., Pompey's friends and enemies in the senate argued about giving him the appointment. Another tribune, Gaius Manilius, made a bid for popularity and Pompey's powerful favor. He proposed the *lex Manilia*, which appointed Pompey the supreme commander of all Roman forces in Asia Minor. Other ambitious young men sought to cash in on the situation, too. For example, Cicero delivered a speech, *Pro Lege Manilia*, on the law's behalf. The Council of the Plebs adopted the resolution amid wild enthusiasm. Pompey was the idol of the populace. Though many in the senate, especially the leading *optimates*, opposed the sweeping provisions of the law, no one dared to speak in public against his appointment.

Like a buzzard coming to enjoy another's kill, Pompey arrived to take over the command of forces in Asia Minor from Lucullus in 66. Despite recent reverses, Lucullus had already severely weakened the armies and destroyed the prestige of Mithridates and King Tigranes II of Armenia. With about twice as many men as Lucullus ever had and a navy cruising about in the Black Sea, Pompey overtook and destroyed the inferior forces of Mithridates. The latter fled first to Armenia and then, when refused haven by Tigranes, to the distant Caucasus.

Before pursuing Mithridates, Pompey invaded Armenia and forced Tigranes to become a subordinate ally of Rome. Then he set out after Mithridates but abandoned the chase at the Caucasus Mountains. After Pompey returned to administer the recently conquered territories, Mithridates made his way through the Caucasus to the

Crimea. There he planned a daring invasion of Italy via the Balkans and the eastern Alps, a grandiose idea carried out five centuries later by Attila the Hun. Worn out by taxation and conscription, Mithridates' subjects rebelled. Shut up in his palace, with all hope of escape or mercy gone, he murdered his wives and daughters and took his own life. His son Pharnaces II gave the body to Pompey, who buried it properly and gave Pharnaces the kingdom of Bosporus. Pompey earned Pharnaces' gratitude and enhanced his growing new reputation as a just and humane conqueror.

Pompey, Syria, and the Jews, 64/63 B.C.E.

News of Mithridates' death reached Pompey in Syria. He was fighting to stamp out the anarchy that had reigned there since Lucullus had driven out Tigranes II and restored Antiochus XIII to the decrepit throne of Seleucid Syria. Tyrants had seized control of the cities; robbers and pirates harassed the people. Pompey disposed of these nuisances and annexed Syria and Phoenicia as a Roman province.

Turning south into Palestine, Pompey found two brothers, Hyrcanus and Aristobulus, fighting over the Judean throne of the Maccabees. Each gave him presents and sought his favor. In Rome's interest, he took the side of the rather feeble Hyrcanus, who was supported by the Pharisees and the aggressive Nabataean Arab King Aretas. Pompey opposed Aristobulus, the more able brother, leader of the Sadducees. In the process, he had to capture the fortified Temple Mount in Jerusalem against Aristobulus' followers. By supporting Hyrcanus, Pompey, who knew nothing about Jewish theology, unwittingly contributed to the ultimate triumph of the Pharisees over the Sadducees.

The Sadducees, composed mainly of the rich landed aristocracy and of the priestly caste, were conservative fundamentalists. They accepted literally the text of the Written Law contained in the Torah, or first five books of the Bible. The Pharisees, too, accepted the Written Law but included a mass of interpretations and oral traditions handed down by the scribes. The Pharisaic rabbis or teachers later produced the great commentaries on the law known as the Mishna and the Talmud. In deciding in favor of Hyrcanus on purely political grounds, Pompey may have set the future course of Judaism. He also did little to foster Jewish–Roman relations: he took it upon himself to violate one of the Jews' most sacred prohibitions and see what was inside the Holy of Holies, the inner sanctum of the Temple at Jerusalem.

Pompey's arrangements in the East, 62 B.C.E.

Pompey, when the dust of his marches had settled, was the de facto overlord of a vast empire. It stretched south from the north shore of the Black Sea across all of Asia Minor and down the coast of the Levant to the border of Egypt, and eastward to the Caucasus Mountains and the northwest reaches of the Parthian Empire (see map on p. 369). On his own, without the customary senatorial commission, he organized this vast territory in a way that he thought would best serve Rome's interests. He did not establish direct control over much more than the coastal fringes of Asia Minor and Syria. They were the lands most accessible, urbanized, wealthy, and easily administered as provinces. The only new territorial acquisitions among them were the core of Mithridates' old kingdom of Pontus, the coastal plain of Cilicia, and the Syrian stump of the old Seleucid Empire. The latter was riven by dynastic rivalries and was easy prey for opportunistic neighbors.

Running counterclockwise from northern Asia Minor, Rome's easternmost provinces now were Bithynia-Pontus, which embraced much of Paphlagonia; Asia, which included the western coast of Asia Minor and much of Phrygia; Cilicia, which stretched along the southern coast of Asia Minor through Pamphylia as far as Lycia and extended north through Lycaonia and the Taurus Mountains to the border of Cappadocia; and Syria, which encompassed the territory between the Cilician Gates and the Euphrates to the north, as well as the fertile strip southward between the desert and the Mediterranean Sea through Phoenicia to Judea. Within these provinces, Greek and Hellenized cities generally provided local administration. Rome's permanent military presence included only two legions in Cilicia and two in Syria.

To shield the Roman provinces and govern the less developed areas beyond them, Pompey set up a network of dependent dynasts and client kings who would do Rome's bidding. In what had been the southern part of Syria (Palestine), for example, he attached the Hellenized cities outside of Judea to the new Roman province of Syria. Judea was reduced to a tribute-paying dependency of the Syrian province, under the local control of the High Priest Hyrcanus. He was called an *ethnarch*, a title that many Jews preferred to *king*. Previously, after the capture of the Temple in Jerusalem, one of Pompey's legates had forced the Nabataean Arabian kingdom across the Jordan River to recognize Roman supremacy. For over a century thereafter, the Nabataeans were an effective buffer on the eastern frontier.

Pompey's career typified Roman Republican imperialism in the East. Neither the senate nor individual generals desired territorial conquest. They all wanted to impose Rome's will with as little direct governance and as much profit as possible. They desired to punish those who affronted Rome's dignity by refusing to maintain the order that Rome sought or who took up arms against it. They were not particularly interested in providing new opportunities for the *publicani* and financiers to profit, although they saw the need to protect existing interests. Pompey, for example, did not extend the privileges of the *publicani* beyond collecting taxes in the new provinces. Even there, he did not give them so much as he could have.

Pompey's main incentives were the acquisition of personal glory and wealth, the greatest prerequisites for political preeminence in Rome. No other general had advertised as many conquests as Pompey did when he finally celebrated his magnificent triumph in September of 61. He contributed 20,000 talents of gold and silver directly to the Roman treasury and raised the annual revenues of the state from 50 million *denarii* a year to 135 million. He gave his officers and soldiers 96 million and still had enough loot left over for himself so that his land holdings were worth 50 million *denarii* a few years later.

ROME IN THE ABSENCE OF POMPEY

During Pompey's absence, Lucullus and other optimate opponents in the senate were bitter and resentful toward him. In 65 B.C.E., they prosecuted the former tribunes Cornelius and Manilius, who had favored him. Cicero, hoping for the goodwill of Pompey and his supporters in anticipation of running for consul in 64, successfully defended Cornelius but abandoned his defense of Manilius after violence had disrupted the proceedings. Nevertheless, Pompey's optimate foes had little ability to inflict real harm. Many Romans feared that Pompey would return like another Sulla and crush his enemies with his overwhelming military power. Among them was Crassus. He was doing everything in his power to build up a countervailing position of strength for dealing with Pompey. He did favors wherever he could and accepted help from anyone who would give it.

Julius Caesar becomes a player, 65 B.C.E.

One of those willing to help Crassus at times was the relatively impoverished thirty-five-year-old Gaius Julius Caesar (100–44 B.C.E.).[3] Caesar had been born into a family that was very ancient and patrician but for centuries had been politically obscure. He had a strong *popularis* lineage. His aunt Julia had been the wife of Marius. As a young man, he married Cornelia, daughter of Cinna, Marius' colleague and Sulla's enemy, and he refused to divorce her in the face of Sulla's command. He won the civic crown (*corona civica*) for saving the life of a fellow soldier in battle. He was willing to prosecute men of high standing as a young orator, and he took bold retribution against pirates who had seized him for ransom. Yet, it was his mother, Aurelia, who saved him from Sulla's proscription. Sulla is said to have warned then that in Caesar was many a Marius.

At the beginning of the climb up the *cursus honorum*, Caesar may have spoken in favor of restoring the tribunician powers in 70 B.C.E. During that year, he definitely took advantage of the Sullan regime's unpopularity and the common people's high regard for the dead Marius to get elected quaestor for 69. Sulla had banned the showing of Marius' images in public. Caesar boldly displayed them at the funerals of his aunt Julia, Marius' widow, and of his own wife, Cornelia. He even dared to extol the deeds of Marius and Cinna in public eulogies on these occasions. Later in the same year, he went to serve in Spain, where he set about to make a name for himself and build up a useful group of Spanish clients.

Still, a young man trying to make his way up with small financial resources had no hope of making a mark at Rome. He needed help from older, more powerful supporters. Even after Caesar married Sulla's granddaughter Pompeia in 67 B.C.E., he was suspect among many of Sulla's political heirs because of his background. He needed support from people outside of their circle. Caesar may have sought popularity in 67 and 66 by backing the tribunician bills favorable to Pompey, but there is nothing to indicate any close connection with him.[4] In the late 60s, however, there is some evidence that Caesar was working actively with Crassus as the latter maneuvered to strengthen his position.

The maneuverings of Crassus and Caesar, 65 B.C.E.

Crassus succeeded in becoming one of the censors for 65 and seems to have backed the election of two men as consuls for that year. A crisis arose when the two consuls-elect were convicted of bribery, and they were removed from office. According to Cicero, they then conspired with L. Sergius Catilina (Catiline) to murder their replacements on New Year's Day, 65 B.C.E. This supposed plot, known as the *First Catilinarian Conspiracy*, never existed. Cicero was merely twisting certain facts in a piece of campaign rhetoric a year later when Catiline was his electoral rival.

Having become an aedile in 65, Caesar won popularity by entertaining the populace at unprecedented expense. For the people's pleasure, he had the Forum lavishly decorated, exhibited 320 pairs of gladiators, and gave silver-tipped weapons to the criminals condemned to fighting lions in the arena. Early one morning, people entering the Forum saw the victory trophies and gleaming gold statues of Marius set up everywhere. Marius' old veterans gathered around, tears of pride streaming down their cheeks. Such efforts entailed huge debts, however, and Crassus later helped to save Caesar from creditors (p. 272).

Crassus' ultimate purpose in building a base of popular support was to be able to create an army and military command that would give him the same kind of political strength that Pompey enjoyed. One of the best Roman recruiting grounds was northern Italy. Using the power of censor, Crassus proposed to give full citizenship to the Transpadanes, the people of Cisalpine Gaul north of the Po, by enrolling them in all thirty-five voting tribes. Caesar had unsuccessfully advocated the same thing in 68 and must have backed it now. Crassus was vetoed by his fellow censor, Quintus Lutatius Catulus. That staunch optimate trusted neither Pompey nor Crassus. The impasse was so unbreakable that both Crassus and Catulus resigned. Even so, advocating citizenship for the Transpadanes won for Crassus and Caesar the continued gratitude of the people north of the Po. Caesar easily recruited soldiers there later.

One of Crassus' schemes earlier in 65 concerned Egypt. Ptolemy X (Alexander I) had bequeathed it to the Roman People in 88 B.C.E. Crassus drafted a bill declaring Egypt a province. That bill would have given someone (perhaps Crassus) the right to raise an army, the Roman populace a rich source of grain, and equestrian financial interests a store of untapped wealth. Nevertheless, it was foiled by the efforts of Catulus and, also, Cicero, who was then one of Pompey's staunchest advocates. Cicero did not want such a command to be available to someone who would then be a serious political rival to Pompey.

The elections of 64 B.C.E.

Crassus and Caesar continued to build their political bases by supporting candidates for election. In 64, they both seem to have backed Catiline and C. Antonius Hybrida, who were now running against Cicero for the consulship of 63 B.C.E. Catiline was already a man of some fame or, rather, notoriety. Although descended from an ancient and illustrious lineage, Catiline was (if the ancient accounts are to be believed) a scoundrel, a murderer, and a master of every known vice. He had supported Sulla, playing a notorious role in Sulla's bloody proscriptions.

After serving as propraetor in the province of Africa in 67, Catiline was accused of extortion and brought to trial in 65.[5] Bribery secured his acquittal. He went on to stand for the consulship in the elections of 64. At the last minute, however, Catiline alarmed the electorate by his violent behavior and his radical talk about the canceling of debts. Cicero won election with widespread equestrian support and ennobled his family as a *novus homo*. Antonius Hybrida, the other candidate, was a successful but poor second; Catiline, a close third. Cicero soon won the allegiance of Antonius by letting him take Macedonia as a consular province. It was far richer than the one that Antonius had originally drawn.

Popular legislation and actions in 63 B.C.E.

Crassus and Caesar seem to have been associated with a number of popular measures in 63 that would win favor with the voters and prove useful in dealing with Pompey. One of them was the proposed land law of the tribune P. Servillius Rullus. This law would have established a land commission that was to control the distribution of public land (which Pompey had promised his veterans), have access to Pompey's war booty, enroll troops, and occupy Egypt by force. Cicero curried favor with Pompey by portraying it as a plot aimed directly at him and helped to bring about its defeat.

Caesar mounted a popular attack on the *Senatus Consultum Ultimum* (*S.C.U.*) by prosecuting the elderly senator Rabirius for treason (*perduellio*). Thirty years earlier, acting under the banner of the *S.C.U.*, Rabirius had taken part in the shameful murder of the tribune Saturninus (pp. 236–7). Trying to preserve stability in a period of increasing tension, Cicero gave a speech in defense of Rabirius (*Pro Rabirio Perduellionis*). In the end, the trial was halted before the jury voted. No matter, Caesar had declared his hostility to a weapon that the optimate oligarchs had often used against popular challengers.

A friend obtained passage of a voting bill that made it easier for Caesar to get elected *pontifex maximus* against the steadfast optimate Catulus. Caesar also was elected praetor for 62, but Cicero blocked a proposal that he backed to let the sons of those proscribed by Sulla hold public office. Soon, Caesar's support of Catiline's failed bid for the consulship would bring suspicion that Caesar was involved in Catiline's rash actions in late 63 B.C.E.

The Catilinarian conspiracy, 63 B.C.E.

Catiline again ran for the consulship in the elections for 62 B.C.E. Initially, he probably still had the support of Crassus and Caesar. His rhetoric, however, was more radical and alarming than what they were prepared to support. His demands for a general scaling down of debts repelled creditors and investors. On the other hand, they had a strong attraction for debtors, ruined aristocrats, Sulla's veterans, and the sons of the persons whom Sulla had proscribed. The more support Catiline received from exiles and the less fortunate members of society, the more he caused the well-to-do and more privileged citizens to fear him as a public nuisance, if not a dangerous enemy. Cicero did his best to whip up the fear that Catiline, if elected, would resort to violence and revolution.

Upon losing the election, Catiline, frustrated and desperate, formed a conspiracy to overthrow the government. Rumors reached Cicero, and more definite information arrived through the cooperation of a certain Fulvia, mistress of one of Catiline's accomplices. Also, Crassus secretly visited Cicero and entrusted to him a number of compromising letters that he had received from the conspirators.

Still, Cicero's first denunciation of Catiline before the senate was based largely on surmises. Even when he reported that Catiline's lieutenant, Manlius, was busily recruiting an army of malcontents in Etruria to seize control of the government, his evidence was dismissed as incomplete. The senate refused to issue the *Senatus Consultum Ultimum* until news arrived in Rome the next day that Manlius had indeed recruited a substantial army in Etruria. Cicero was right.

Cicero refrained from using the emergency decree and waited instead for Catiline's next move. He learned more of Catiline's plans through Fulvia. Thus, he was able to discredit Catiline and lay a trap for his accomplices in Rome. Caesar, courting popularity, unsuccessfully called for the return of Pompey to save the state. The arrest and execution of five leading conspirators dealt a major blow to Catiline, who was now in Etruria. Two-thirds of his army melted away, but, in early 62, he died fighting in heroic style at the head of the remnant.

Caesar, Cato the Younger, and the S.C.U.

When the senate met to determine the fate of Catiline's five accomplices, Caesar was a praetor-elect for 62. He took another opportunity to earn popular favor by speaking out against the *S.C.U.* His eloquence almost persuaded a majority of the senators, even Cicero, to vote for life imprisonment instead of death. Then M. Porcius Cato the Younger (Uticensis) (95–46 B.C.E.), a stern Stoic, fierce optimate, and great-grandson of Cato the Elder, took the floor. He attacked the weakness and irresolution of his colleagues. So stinging were his words that a majority of the senators finally voted for the death penalty. That same day, the conspirators paid for their crimes in the gloomy prison of the Tullianum. Their political ghosts would come back to haunt Cicero.

Cicero's hopes for the future

In the meantime, Cicero of Arpinum had attained sudden glory. For delivering Rome from danger, he was voted a thanksgiving festival and given the title *Pater Patriae*, "Father of His Country." Without the support of a proud family name, great wealth, military talents, or a strong political following, he had entered the senate, reached the consulship, and ennobled his family. Unfortunately, in often proclaiming this proud achievement, he sometimes became tiresome even to his friends. Certainly, he was spurred by the slights that he suffered: he was admitted to the nobility but not accepted; admired for his eloquence but ridiculed for his self-adulation. The first *novus homo* consul since the death of Marius, Cicero could not have failed to be hurt by the aloofness of his colleagues, by their tacit assumption of superiority, and by their frequent rudeness.

It must have been difficult for so proud a man to accept such treatment. Nevertheless, Cicero was convinced that the preservation of the Republic depended on maintaining the supremacy of the senate. The ancient nobility would give the senate prestige and continuity with the past. New men—like Cicero himself—would bring to it energy, intelligence, and an awareness of present problems. Peace, stability, and freedom depended on the continued concord or harmony of the orders (*concordia ordinum*) between the senatorial aristocracy and the wealthy equestrian class. In a slightly expanded form, the harmony of the orders was an alliance of those whom Cicero saw as good, law-abiding citizens against revolutionary attacks on property and the status quo. He also insisted on the *consensus Italiae*, "mutual agreement of Italy." By this phrase, he meant that Rome should conduct its affairs in conformity with the interests and sentiments of Italy as a whole—that is, of local Italian notables, from whom Cicero himself had come.

Cicero's concept of the ideal state, one governed according to law, reflected the Republic's highest ideal of *libertas*. To the magistrates was to be allotted executive power; to the senate, authority; to the people, liberty. It was to be a state in which the people, undisturbed by social strife or civil war, might live and work in peace and security. Members of the privileged classes could freely compete to maintain their *dignitas* (rank, prestige, and honor) in service to the state. Such a state, Cicero believed, could be neither a monarchy nor a participatory democracy on the Athenian model: only a free aristocratic republic was flexible enough to incorporate talented and patriotic men from nonaristocratic circles into the governing elite. Cicero's vision is too narrow for today, but it was better than most of his contemporaries' views.

Clodius, the *Bona Dea*, and Caesar, 62 B.C.E.

Unfortunately, Publius Clodius (Claudius) Pulcher (ca. 92–52 B.C.E.), the man who had done so much to ruin Lucullus' career (p. 257), was about to become Cicero's bitter enemy. He would drive Cicero from public life when Cicero's services were needed most. Although Clodius chose the plebeian spelling of his name, he was a scion of the Appii Claudii, the great patrician noble house. He was the kind of rakish, unorthodox, over-privileged young aristocrat who, Cicero thought, threatened to undermine the people's respect for their aristocratic betters. Late in the year 62, Roman women were celebrating the annual festival of the *Bona Dea*, "Good Goddess", at the house of the *pontifex maximus*, Julius Caesar. Men were rigidly excluded from this all-female ritual. Clodius, however, disguised as a woman and alleged at the time to have been the lover of Caesar's wife, Pompeia, managed to enter the house. His presence was detected, and a scandal ensued. As a result, Caesar made his famous declaration, "Caesar's wife must be above suspicion," and divorced Pompeia.

Early in 61 B.C.E., personal enemies like Lucullus among the leading optimates maneuvered against Clodius in the senate. They managed to have Clodius brought to trial on a special charge of *incestum* (unchastity) because Vestal Virgins had been at the rites that he had defiled. Clodius stirred up the populace against the senate. When called as a witness, Caesar characteristically did the unexpected by refusing to testify. He was about to depart for a provincial governorship in Spain and did not want to make an enemy of a popular and powerful political figure. Cicero decided that he had to testify to uphold public religion and support the authority of the senate, on which he had relied in suppressing Catiline. Cicero flatly contradicted Clodius' attempt to establish an alibi. Conviction seemed certain. Bribes proved otherwise: the jurors voted for acquittal.

As praetor in 62, Caesar had tried to make sure that he would have the goodwill of Pompey and his friends after Pompey returned from Asia. Caesar wanted to deny his and Pompey's optimate foe Catulus the honor of restoring the temple of Capitoline Jupiter. He attempted to give that honor to the popular hero Pompey. Violence and passage of a *Senatus Consultum Ultimum* resulted in Caesar's temporary suspension from office. That forced Caesar to abandon support of a tribunician bill to recall Pompey immediately from Asia. Q. Caecilius Metellus Nepos—half-brother of Pompey's wife, Mucia—proposed the bill. It would have enabled Pompey to take credit for the suppression of Catiline and his remaining forces. The bill failed. Nevertheless, Pompey and his friends would have noted Caesar's initial support.

AFTER POMPEY'S RETURN, 62 TO 60 B.C.E.

Toward the end of 62 B.C.E., Pompeius Magnus, conqueror of the East, landed at Brundisium. To the relief and amazement of many, he at once disbanded his powerful army. With it he could have seized dictatorial power as Sulla had done. His action gives the lie to the monarchic ambition sometimes attributed to him at this stage of his career. This fiction is based on the literal and serious acceptance of *rex* (king) and *regnum* (kingship), two terms equivalent to "tyrant" and "tyranny" in the political invective that was freely and loosely hurled in the late Roman Republic. Even Cicero, because he was a *novus homo* from Arpinum, felt their sting. He was maliciously called "the first foreign *rex* at Rome since the Tarquins."

The opening days of the year 61 B.C.E. looked bright for the future of the Republic. In 63 and 62, the optimate generals Lucullus and Metellus Creticus had finally been allowed to celebrate triumphs that had long been delayed by popular opposition. At the same time, the senate had shown unexpected strength and resolution in dealing with the Catilinarian conspiracy. The equestrian class had, in Cicero, a vigorous and eloquent spokesman. His *concordia ordinum* seemed an answer to social and civil strife, although not a substitute for needed reforms. A truly hopeful sign was Pompey's dismissal of his army and his refusal to seize dictatorial power. Cicero might yet have saved the Republic if Pompey could have been induced to support the policy of *concordia*.

Unfortunately, the jealousy of Crassus, the hostility of the optimate leaders of the senate toward Pompey, Pompey's own ineptness, and Cicero's unconquerable vanity all contributed to the breakdown of the tenuous harmony. Residing outside Rome to await a triumph, Pompey met with the senate outside the *pomerium*. He anticipated being hailed as another Alexander. Crassus solemnly rose and pointedly ignored Pompey. Instead, he dramatically declared Cicero the savior of Rome. Cicero, his vanity flattered, promptly forgot all about Pompey and went on to speak at great length of his own illustrious deeds. Cicero had already alienated Pompey by earlier boasts and thereby lost his crucial support for the *concordia ordinum*. Now Cicero had completely shattered any hope of cooperation from Pompey in protecting the Republic.

Pompey's demands, finally presented to the senate in 60 B.C.E., were modest. He understandably wanted land for his veterans and ratification of his *acta*, or arrangements, made in the East. Personal enmities and fear of Pompey's eventual dominance aroused bitter opposition. Soon after returning from the East, Pompey had divorced Mucia because of her rumored infidelity. Her half-brother, Q. Caecilius Metellus Celer, vigorously opposed Pompey's requests. So, too, did Q. Caecilius Metellus Creticus. He had been consul in 69 B.C.E. and held a grudge because Pompey had interfered with his command in Crete during the pirate war in 67. Lucullus, emerging from his princely gardens, vindictive and rancorous, insisted on debating Pompey's proposals in detail, not *en bloc* as Pompey requested. Lucullus had the support of Crassus, who was Pompey's jealous rival, and Cato the Younger, who saw Pompey's power as a threat to the Republic.

Not one of the optimate leaders of the senate opposed Pompey's requests with more rancor than Cato. Narrow-minded and pedantic, yet honest and fearless, he was one of the few Stoics who lived by the philosophy they professed. Cato's moral courage soon gained him recognition as the spokesman of the optimate heirs of Sulla. His forceful character won him a power greater than that of any other member of the senate. Because of Cato's obstructive tactics, ratification of Pompey's *acta* was delayed.

After destroying the possibility of goodwill between Pompey and the optimate leaders of the senate, Cato proceeded to alienate Crassus and the equestrian financial interests. He blocked passage of a bill for the relief of tax-collecting companies that had optimistically bid too high for the taxes in Asia. They were now requesting a reduction of their contract payments to the treasury. Cicero, though he privately considered the petition outrageous and impudent, had nevertheless supported the bill in order to promote the *concordia ordinum*.

Cato further antagonized the *equites* by forcing passage of a bill that declared as criminal the acceptance of bribes by *equites* serving on juries (it had long been so for senators). Again, Cicero, as politicians so often must, betrayed one principle for the sake of another: although he thought the bill a fair measure, he opposed it as being detrimental to harmony.

Cato's next object of attack was Julius Caesar. After Crassus had stood surety with Caesar's creditors in 61 B.C.E., Caesar had been able to take up his provincial governorship in Spain. On return from Spain in 60, Caesar had requested the right to declare his candidacy for the upcoming consular election *in absentia*. He had been voted a triumph for some victories against native tribes. He had found an excuse to attack them in order to have enough loot to pay off his debts—100,000,000 HS (*sestertii*)—and campaign for the coveted consulship. It was legally impossible for him to hold a triumph and declare his candidacy in the time remaining before the election. A recent law compelled potential candidates to declare their intentions personally in the Forum to the magistrate in charge of the election. To do so, he would have to cross the *pomerium* before he could hold his triumph. If he did that, another law would require him to forfeit his triumph.

When Caesar learned that Cato opposed the petition, he decided to forego the triumph and stand for the consulship. Cato feared that Caesar might win the election and thereby be eligible for another army along with another province to loot. He persuaded the senate to assign the cattle paths and forests of Italy as the provinces for the consuls of 59 B.C.E. If Cato had deliberately set out to destroy the Republic, he could not have been more successful.

Cato and his allies ultimately drove Pompey, Crassus, and Caesar into a coalition that made each member more powerful than he could have been by himself. Then, with each aiming for supreme honors, the natural rivalries that were bound to reemerge resulted in the dictatorship of Julius Caesar. It paved the way for the Principate of Augustus, which ended the Republic forever. The natural ambitions and rivalries of Roman nobles had reduced republican politics to a vast game of musical chairs in which only one man would ultimately be left to dominate the rest.

NOTES

1   The botanical name for the cultivated cherry is *prunus lucullus* because Lucullus brought it back to Europe from Asia Minor.
2   So great was the confidence in his leadership that grain prices fell the very day he received the command.
3   Although some scholars have argued for 102 or 101 B.C.E. as the year of Caesar's birth, the traditional date of 100 B.C.E. is now commonly accepted. The day is usually given as July 13, but some authorities prefer July 12.
4   Pompeia's distant relationship to Pompey indicates no connection between Caesar and Pompey.
5   The prosecutor at the trial was Publius Clodius Pulcher, who had helped to undermine Lucullus in Asia Minor (p. 257). Cicero, though convinced of Catiline's guilt, had at first thought of defending him and even worked out a deal with Clodius but then dropped the idea.

SUGGESTED READING

Santangelo, F. *Sulla, the Elites and the Empire: A Study of Roman Policies in Italy and the Greek East. Impact of Empire 8*. Leiden and Boston: Brill, 2007.
Schiavone, A. *Spartacus. Revealing Antiquity, 19*. Cambridge, MA and London: Harvard University Press, 2013.
Seager, R. J. *Pompey: A Political Biography*. 2nd ed. Oxford: Blackwell, 2002.

CHAPTER 16

Caesar wins and is lost, 60 to 44 B.C.E.

The opposition of Cato and the extreme optimates to Caesar was not irrational, even if it was shortsighted. They saw that for an aristocratic republic to provide its leaders with the liberty (*libertas*) to compete for honors, there had to be a rough parity of resources among them. They also realized the need to abide by laws and customs that prevented any one leader from acquiring such great advantages that the rest could not compete meaningfully with him.

Pompey had aroused the fear and resentment of the same men. From the very beginning of his opportunistic career, he would not abide by the rules designed to restrain him. Then, when he had finally made clear that he was not willing to go so far as he had made his optimate foes fear, they were determined to cut him down to size. They wanted to demonstrate that he would not be allowed to win the aristocratic competition for honors by violating its rules.

Many sensed that Caesar was even more of a threat because he was smart, unconventional, and bold almost to the point of recklessness. He always tried to make the odds as favorable as possible, but at crucial moments he was not afraid to roll the dice. What could one make of a man who would give up a coveted triumph to meet a technicality in the election laws? He was unpredictable. Indeed, there was no telling what a man who incurred extravagant debts and was once called "every woman's husband and every man's wife" would do.

CAESAR WINS AND IS LOST

Certainly, his long-running affair with Cato's half-sister Servilia would not have endeared Caesar to the upright Cato. Rumors of affairs with numerous noble Roman wives must also have raised mistrust among many important men. It is no wonder that Caesar was convinced that Cato and a clique of powerful optimate nobles were personally trying to keep him from obtaining his full measure of *dignitas*. Refusing to give in and suffer the shame of being bested by them, Caesar trumped them at every turn. He failed, however, to appreciate the magnitude of the fear and envious dislike (*invidia*) that he was building up against himself.

Having surprised Cato and his other optimate enemies by foregoing a triumph to run for the consulship in 60 B.C.E., Caesar used every strategy, including bribery, to win. Caesar's optimate enemies, even the incorruptible Cato, decided to raise their own bribery fund to ensure the election of Cato's son-in-law M. Calpurnius Bibulus. Countering them, Caesar secured the aid of Crassus and Pompey. Just as Caesar, they, too, had been thwarted and injured by optimate enemies in the senate. In view of their long and intense rivalry, they probably remained independent of each other at first. They both, however, were happy to help a candidate who promised to be a consul favorable toward each of them. A friend of Pompey even cooperated with Caesar by supplying bribes and running for the other consular position. Thus supported, Caesar had little trouble winning election. Second place, however, went to Bibulus, and that posed problems.

CAESAR PARTNERS WITH POMPEY AND CRASSUS, 60 TO 58 B.C.E.

Caesar and his allies needed to strengthen their hand as much as possible after the election of Bibulus. Probably it was only then that Caesar persuaded Pompey and Crassus to cooperate together in creating the strong coalition that modern writers often call the *First Triumvirate*. Actually, it is inaccurate to refer to their coalition as a triumvirate. In Roman terms, a triumvirate denoted a legally constituted board of three men with some clearly defined authority. The later triumvirate of Octavian, Antony, and Lepidus, which is often called the *Second Triumvirate*, was such a board (p. 374). The informal coalition of Pompey, Crassus, and Caesar was never an official board. The three private dynasts swore that each would seek only those ends not objectionable to the other two. Their personal motivations were fairly clear: Pompey wanted land for his veterans and ratification of his *acta* in the East; Crassus desired a reduction of the Asian tax contracts in the interest of his equestrian friends; Caesar sought command of a province and an army along with the wealth and loyal veterans that they would provide.

At the start, Caesar was clearly less powerful than either Pompey or Crassus. He, however, had a certain long-term advantage. Pompey and Crassus could never completely forget their rivalry. Therefore, Caesar could maneuver between them. He soon strengthened his position by marrying his daughter, Julia, to Pompey and taking to wife Calpurnia, the daughter of Lucius Calpurnius Piso Caesoninus. Piso, along with Pompey's friend Aulus Gabinius (pp. 262–3), was elected consul for 58 B.C.E. Eventually, with the help of Pompey, Crassus, and others, Caesar obtained passage of legislation that enabled him over time to amass enough political, military, and financial power to surpass everyone.

Caesar's legislation as consul, 59 B.C.E.

Caesar's first task, however, was to make good on his promise to obtain legislation that would fill the needs of Pompey and Crassus. At the start of his term, Caesar was studiously polite both to the optimate-controlled senate and to his optimate colleague, Bibulus. He consulted them on all matters, accepted their suggestions and amendments, and proposed only moderate bills. When even his mildest bills were endlessly debated and obstructed in the senate, he soon resorted to more direct methods. He even had Cato, the leader of the opposition, arrested. Upon reflection, however, he apparently decided not to turn the righteous Cato into a martyr and had him set free.

Caesar then presented his land bill for the settlement of Pompey's veterans to the Centuriate Assembly. Bibulus, as the other consul, promptly vetoed it and declared all of the other days on which the assemblies could meet during the year to be feast days. He thereby cut off the last constitutional path of action for the three dynasts.

Disregarding this legal obstacle, Caesar presented his land bill to the assembly a second time. Three tribunes interposed vetoes. The crowd's murmur rose to an angry roar. Dramatically, Caesar halted the voting and asked Pompey what other action he was prepared to take. Pompey placed his hand on his hip and declared that he would not hesitate to draw his sword. Bibulus pushed his way forward, but before he could say a word, the angry mob broke his *fasces*. Then, someone dumped a basket of feces over his head. The assembly passed the bill, and Caesar declared it carried.[1]

The humiliated Bibulus retired from public life. He spent the rest of his term shut up in his home. Some wag acutely observed that, from then on, the names of the two consuls were no longer Bibulus and Caesar, but Julius and Caesar. Now unopposed, Caesar carried out the rest of his legislative program with speed and efficiency. The whole package is often referred to as the Julian laws. One of them provided for the distribution of Campanian public lands among 20,000 needy citizens. The only requirement was that each should have at least three children. There was a law that ratified *en bloc* all of Pompey's settlements in the East. Another bill remitted one-third of the payments that the tax collectors of Asia, Crassus' friends, had contracted to give the treasury.

Caesar also obtained passage of legislation favorable to himself. One law, proposed by a friendly tribune, granted him immediate proconsular *imperium* for five years over the provinces of Cisalpine Gaul and Illyricum and command of three legions stationed at Aquileia. Caesar began at once to recruit some soldiers and staff and held them in readiness outside the city. His opponents were powerless: no senator dared oppose any of Caesar's measures, for fear of incurring his wrath. Those who still attended meetings summoned by Caesar were considerate and polite. When Metellus Celer, governor-to-be of Transalpine Gaul, suddenly died, the senate, on Pompey's motion, assigned it to Caesar.

One of Caesar's early laws ordered the publication of the *Proceedings of the Senate* (*Acta Senatus* or *Commentarii Senatus*). Publishing the proceedings of the senate made its actions more transparent in general. It also exposed to the public the specific doings of Caesar's senatorial enemies. Caesar's most statesmanlike law in 59 B.C.E. was the *lex Julia de Repetundis*. It stringently regulated the administration of the provinces to control extortion and abuses of power in several ways: governors were forbidden, under pain of heavy penalty, to accept presents. They could not sell or withhold justice and had to put their official edicts on deposit—two copies in the provinces and one at Rome. Finally, they could not pass beyond the limits of their provinces without authorization. If adequately enforced, this excellent law would have protected the people of the provinces from oppression and promoted their well-being and prosperity. Still, it, too, had a partisan purpose. It would make it more difficult for Caesar's enemies to abuse the provinces in an attempt to obtain power and resources against him and would make the danger of prosecution greater if they did.

Getting rid of Cicero through Clodius, 58 B.C.E.

Before leaving for Gaul, Caesar wanted to make sure that his opponents in the senate would not venture to attack him by annulling the Julian laws of 59 B.C.E. Cicero, who had publicly excoriated Caesar and his partners, was a man who might successfully lead such an attack. In an effort to prevent Cicero from freely speaking his mind, Caesar offered him a remunerative position on the Land Commission. That offer being rejected, Caesar then invited Cicero to accompany him to Gaul as his legate. Cicero turned down this and other offers. Finally, Caesar decided to leave Cicero to the devices of Publius Clodius, Cicero's sworn enemy after the Bona Dea affair (pp. 270–1). Early in 59 B.C.E., Caesar, as *pontifex maximus*, and Pompey, as an augur, had presided over Clodius' adoption into a plebeian family. In that way, Clodius could become a tribune for 58. He could then be used to frighten Cicero into silence if necessary.

One of the first laws that Clodius carried as tribune abolished the use of bogus portents for the obstruction of legislation. Another of his laws provided for the distribution of free grain to the needy. Most notorious is the law that forbade offering fire and water to any person who had put Roman citizens to death without trial or appeal to the people. Being denied fire and water meant exile. The law was retroactive and clearly aimed at Cicero who had ordered the execution of the Catilinarian conspirators in 63. He had thought that the *Senatus Consultum Ultimum* the senate had given him would protect him from any prosecution for his actions. Now, he was stunned to find himself facing exile. He and his friends vainly pleaded with the consuls, Piso, Caesar's father-in-law, and Gabinius, Pompey's friend. They had once promised him protection, but Clodius had bought them off with political favors. Even Pompey, according to Plutarch, slipped out of his house when Cicero came to ask for help. His pleas denied, Cicero had no choice but to leave Italy. He was forbidden to live within 400 miles of Rome.

Clodius next disposed of Cato by a law assigning him to govern the distant island of Cyprus. Clodius dryly observed that Cato was the only man in Rome honest enough to administer the royal treasures inherited with that new province. Cato, not willing to break a duly constituted law, stoically complied. The removal of Caesar's two ablest opponents left Caesar's Julian laws safe from attack.

GAUL AND THE FOUNDATION OF CAESAR'S MIGHT, 58 TO 56 B.C.E.

Caesar now hurried north and took command of the legion stationed in Transalpine Gaul. It is often called either the *Province* or *Narbonese Gaul*. The eastern part is now Provence, in southeastern France. Caesar hoped to use his governorship of Transalpine Gaul to pursue great wars and conquests. They would earn him undying glory, a large following of loyal veterans, and huge financial resources from booty. At this time, Transalpine Gaul was ideally located for fulfilling these hopes. It bordered the rich and populous lands of the free Gallic tribes in Gallia Comata, "Long-Haired Gaul." The political situation both within and around their territory was in an unsettled state. That could give ample pretexts for the neighboring Roman commander to intervene "to protect the vital interests of Rome." Much of what is known of the war comes from Caesar's own compelling narrative *On the Gallic War* (*De Bello Gallico*), a masterpiece of propaganda and self-glorification (pp. 340–1). Thus, he tried to equal or surpass Pompey's military glory in the popular imagination.

The situation in Gallia Comata

According to Caesar, Gallia Comata was divided into three parts by the Aquitanians in the south, various Celtic tribes in the center, and the Belgians in the north, all with different languages, customs, and institutions. Primarily agricultural people, the vast majority lived in villages and small towns. There were some mining and manufacturing centers on major rivers and trade routes, and a few hilltop fortresses like Bibracte, Gergovia, and Alesia in the interior. The Gauls, as a whole, were politically weak and unstable. Their largest political unit was the tribal state (*civitas*), a loose confederation of more or less independent clans. There were nearly one hundred such states, and they often fought with each other. Also, they were unstable internally. Most had abolished monarchic rule about fifty years earlier and were rent by feuding noble factions.

Defeat of the Helvetians, 58 B.C.E.

When Caesar arrived in the Province in the spring of 58 B.C.E., the Helvetians (*Helvetii*) of western Switzerland were ready to set out on a long-projected trek west across Gaul to find a new home. Fleeing aggressive Germanic tribes under kings like Ariovistus, they had burned their homes and villages behind them and stood poised on the banks of the Rhodanus (Rhône).

Caesar claimed that the migration of the Helvetians would threaten the security of the Province by creating turmoil in free Gaul and would leave their old territory open as an avenue for German tribes to invade Italy. Adding some freshly recruited cohorts and some allied troops, Caesar rushed north with his legion. He met the Helvetii near modern Geneva, hastily constructed defenses, and refused to let them cross the Rhodanus into Gaul. The Helvetians turned to an alternate route. Caesar reacted with the speed and determination that became his hallmarks. He left his trusted legate Titus Labienus in charge and sped back across the Alps. He took command of the three legions at Aquileia and moved west to the area around modern Turin. There, he quickly recruited two more legions. Then, a forced march brought him back across the Alps to Labienus in seven days. They caught up with the Helvetii as the latter were crossing the Arar (Saône) into the territory of the Aeduii. After a series of minor skirmishes, the two armies clashed near Bibracte in a decisive battle during which the Romans all but destroyed the Helvetian army. Caesar compelled most of the survivors, about a third of the population, to return to their native homeland.

Ariovistus

There began almost immediately a procession of envoys from many states of central Gaul to Caesar. Some offered congratulations for his recent victory; others implored his aid against Ariovistus. That powerful German king had already reduced two states to vassalage. His aggressions were daily growing more menacing. Caesar at once began negotiations with the king. Ariovistus' alleged rudeness and arrogance provided a plausible pretext for war. A quick, bold attack ended in the utter rout and destruction of the Germans. Caesar, after quartering his legions for the winter, hastened back to Cisalpine Gaul to hold the November sessions of his gubernatorial court.

The Belgic War, 57 B.C.E.

Caesar's selection of eastern Gaul for winter quarters had aroused the fears and hostilities of the Belgians in northern Gaul. A letter from Labienus informed Caesar of their warlike preparations. Caesar recruited two more legions and sent them across the Alps at the end of winter. As soon as it was possible to begin military operations, Caesar joined his eight legions and confronted the Belgians. Again, speed and resolute action were decisive. The Belgian force was disunified, short of supplies, and torn by mutual jealousies. It broke up and dispersed after only one minor skirmish. Caesar could now subdue the Belgian states one by one, not without some dangerous and hard-fought battles.

Meanwhile, young Publius Crassus, Crassus's son, had been sent with one of Caesar's legions to western Gaul. He compelled all the tribes along the English Channel and the Atlantic seaboard to submit to Rome. Gaul seemed prostrate at the feet of the conqueror. Even the Germans beyond the Rhine sent hostages and promised to obey his orders. On receiving report of these triumphs, the senate decreed a public thanksgiving of fifteen days, an unprecedented length (see Box 16.1). Caesar was the darling of Rome. With a loyal army and the wealth of Gaul at his disposal, his enemies' only hope was a disruption of his partnership with Pompey and Crassus.

16.1 ROMAN THANKSGIVING

When good fortune fell upon the Roman state, most often in the form of a major military victory, the senate would order the observance of a thanksgiving ritual called a *supplicatio*. Public and private business was put on hold so that the men and women of Rome, dressed in their finest clothes and sometimes adorned with laurel wreaths, could visit temples and shrines throughout the city. There they offered prayers, sacrifices, incense, and libations in order to thank the gods for their favor. Traditionally, thanksgiving celebrations lasted two or three days; celebrations lasting four days were ordered on a handful of occasions. As with many other aspects of public life, however, this changed in the last decades of the Republic when the *supplicatio* became another way to honor the preeminent men of the day. In the years 63 and 62 B.C.E., in honor of Pompey's victories in the East, the senate voted *supplicationes* of ten and twelve days, respectively. They may have seemed excessive at the time, but those festivals pale in comparison to *supplicationes* voted in honor of Caesar's successes, among which were thanksgivings of fifteen days in the year 57, thirty days in 47, forty in the following year, and fifty in the year after that. Under the Empire, the *supplicatio* was reserved for celebrating the military victories and major life events of the emperor and his family.

DISORDER IN ROME AND A RENEWED PARTNERSHIP, 58 TO 56 B.C.E.

While Caesar was winning wealth, fame, and loyal veterans in Gaul, Rome itself became the scene of disorder and violence. The optimate-controlled senate was too weak to govern, Pompey the Great too inept. Clodius had, by his free-grain law, made himself the idol of the populace. His armed gangs ruled the streets. These gangs were organized through the *collegia* (sing. *collegium*), neighborhood associations and trade guilds to which the craftsmen and members of the urban plebs belonged (p. 325). The senate, fearing their potential for organized political violence, had banned them in 64 B.C.E. Upon becoming tribune, Clodius had obtained passage of a plebiscite to legalize them once more. Then he organized them into potent weapons of political violence.

No sooner had Caesar left for Gaul than Pompey and Crassus had begun to quarrel. The former, in order to restore his ebbing popularity and win the support of the nobility, began to agitate for the recall of Cicero from exile. Clodius incited a series of riots, temporarily drove Pompey from public life, and made him cower in his house. Crassus, who also had no wish to see Cicero return, enjoyed Pompey's discomfiture and kept Clodius supplied with funds.

Cicero's recall, 57 B.C.E.

As tribune, Clodius could veto every proposal for the return of Cicero. He continued to incite his followers to riot whenever such a bill came up before the assembly.

Pompey returned to the political arena during the summer of the Belgic War. He began to attend meetings in the Forum once more, usually escorted by a large group of followers. Many of them were veterans of his campaigns in the East. They were headed by the tribune T. Annius Milo. Pompey called upon Cicero's brother, Quintus Cicero, to guarantee that the orator, if permitted to return, would do nothing to upset either the rule of the three dynasts or the Julian laws. Pompey's efforts bore fruit. In the autumn, a bill for Cicero's return passed the *comitia centuriata* with uproarious acclaim. The success of the bill had depended somewhat on the victory of Milo and his followers during a bloody scuffle with the followers of Clodius. Cicero's return was met with thunderous applause from the watching throngs, who scattered flowers in his path.

Pompey wants an army

After Cicero's return, a sudden and dangerous shortage of grain frightened the optimate leaders of the senate. They agreed to place Pompey in charge of the food supply. Cicero even became one of his legates. Pompey was given command of a fleet to transport grain and was offered an army. He solemnly demurred in order not to appear too eager for what he really did want, an army to rival Caesar's. His enemies happily took him at his word. Pompey's friends were exasperated.

Soon, however, Pompey tried to seize a new opportunity to acquire an army. Ptolemy Auletes (the Fluteplayer), king of Egypt, had been driven from his throne by the citizens of Alexandria. He came to Rome and formally requested Roman military aid. Pompey hoped to undertake it. He and Ptolemy even resorted to having thugs murder and otherwise terrorize a delegation of Alexandrians who had come to counter Ptolemy's pleas. Unfortunately for Pompey, someone took the trouble to consult the books of the Sibyl and found that it was forbidden to use an army to restore a king of Egypt. The matter was dropped.

The Conference of Luca, 56 B.C.E.

Caesar was undoubtedly kept informed of the political situation in Rome through correspondence with Pompey, Crassus, and others. He knew that Cicero and Clodius (the latter with the connivance of Crassus) were both attacking the Julian laws of 59 B.C.E., though for different reasons. He knew from a visit by Crassus to his winter quarters at Ravenna in early April of 56 that Pompey, with Cicero's encouragement, was veering over to the *optimates*.

A few days earlier, Crassus and Cicero had both appeared in defense of Marcus Caelius Rufus, a former protégé of each. He was being prosecuted for involvement in the murder of some of the Alexandrian envoys who had opposed the restoration of Pompey's friend Ptolemy. Cicero, however, had stolen the show with a brilliantly scurrilous attack on Clodius and one of his sisters, who had supported the prosecution. Clodius was outraged. Milo was emboldened to confront him with violence. Now, if Cicero could persuade Cato and other optimates to turn to Pompey in the face of escalating violence and offer him extraordinary power, Pompey might agree to withdraw support from Caesar.

It was time for Caesar himself to act. He met with Pompey and probably also Crassus at Luca in mid-April of 56 to work out a new plan of cooperation. They agreed that Pompey and Crassus should stand for the consulship of 55 B.C.E., that Cicero's acid speech-making should be curbed, and that the mobs of Clodius and Milo should be restrained. Probably there were three other provisions: Caesar's proconsulship would be renewed for another five years. After 55, Pompey would govern Spain for five years. Crassus would similarly govern Syria and have the right to wage war against the Parthians.

CAESAR OVERCOMES CHALLENGES IN GAUL, 56 TO 52 B.C.E.

The initial conquest of Gaul had been relatively easy, but while Caesar was at Luca in 56 B.C.E., the situation had changed. When he returned to Gaul, he first had to put down a revolt of the seafaring Veneti. Then he was faced with two large German tribes that had migrated across the Rhine. Provoked, he claimed, by a treacherous attack during negotiations, he engaged in a merciless slaughter. In 55, he overawed the Germans east of the Rhine by an impressive feat of bridge building that permitted lightning raids into their territory. Then, in late summer, he amazed the Roman world with a showy crossing of the English Channel to invade Britain. It so flattered Roman pride that the senate decreed another public thanksgiving, this time for twenty days.

The hard fighting in Britain came with the spring of 54. Caesar mounted a full-scale invasion with a specially constructed fleet. Soon after he landed, however, a storm destroyed it. He had to fight for his life before finally defeating the British war king Cassivellaunus. After Caesar imposed terms that permitted him to repair his losses, he returned to Gaul. With his legions in winter camps, he went to Cisalpine Gaul. Northern Gallic rebellions in early 53 were serious and cost Caesar a legion. He recruited two new legions in Cisalpine Gaul, borrowed one from Pompey, and crushed the revolts. Over the following winter, disgruntled tribes plotted a coordinated revolt. They were led by the Gallic chief Vercingetorix. Caesar had to match him or be destroyed. In early 52, Caesar surprised Vercingetorix by marching reinforcements from Transalpine Gaul through deep mountain snows. Vercingetorix then resorted to guerrilla tactics and a scorched-earth strategy.

Putting all ten legions in the field, Caesar finally maneuvered Vercingetorix into the hilltop town of Alesia and defeated him in a desperate siege. While pockets of resistance remained, Caesar had regained supremacy in Gaul. When the last rebel stronghold, Uxellodunum, fell, Caesar cold-bloodedly cut both hands off every captive. Begging for food every day thereafter, the handless wretches provided a brutal object lesson to anyone contemplating further rebellion. Unchallenged master of Gaul at last, Caesar had firmly established the military and financial basis for realizing his ambition of being Rome's most powerful and influential man.

CAESAR'S PARTNERS STRIVE TO
KEEP UP, 56 TO 53 B.C.E.

From the Conference of Luca in 56 B.C.E., Crassus and Pompey had gained renewed strength, which promised to keep them on a par with Caesar. Both would again stand for consulships and command armies and provinces. Their enemies were stunned. Cicero, bound by Pompey to preserve the peace and remembering the pain of exile, turned quickly from invective to softer words of praise and thanksgiving.

Pompey fortifies himself in the West

In 55 B.C.E., with Pompey and Crassus as consuls, the tribune C. Trebonius carried a law (the *lex Trebonia*) assigning the consuls their provinces for five years, as apparently agreed upon at the Conference of Luca. Pompey received the two Spains but decided, perhaps on Caesar's advice, to remain in the vicinity of Rome to watch the course of events. At last, however, he could again recruit legions. He would send some under his legates to Spain and retain others in Italy. Never again would he make the mistake of disbanding them too soon, as he had after his return from the East in 62 B.C.E.

Crassus looks to the East

To achieve the position that he wanted in the West, Pompey had to make a major concession to Crassus in the East. Pompey had been the dominant force there ever since his victories over the pirates and Mithridates. As governor of Syria since 57 B.C.E., Pompey's ally Aulus Gabinius had looked after his interests in the region. Now, the *lex Trebonia* assigned Crassus the province of Syria with the right to make war as he saw fit. Parthia was not mentioned in the law, but it was an open secret that Crassus was preparing a war against that rival power on Rome's eastern frontier. Gabinius had already been planning such a war himself after suppressing a revolt in Judea that the Parthians may have helped spark.

In 55, Gabinius was starting to invade Parthia when Pompey, now consul, illegally instructed him to restore Ptolemy Auletes to the throne of Egypt. Auletes is said to have paid Gabinius 10,000 talents. After another intervention in Judea, Gabinius did not have time to resume his invasion of Parthia before Crassus replaced him as governor of Syria in 54. Gabinius, who was not happy to be replaced, immediately faced prosecution from Pompey's optimate enemies for his illegal acts on Pompey's behalf. Cicero had wanted to prosecute Gabinius, who had helped betray him to Clodius in 58. Nevertheless, Pompey and Caesar ultimately forced Cicero to defend him against a charge of extortion. While Crassus took Gabinius' place in Syria, Gabinius was convicted and fled into exile.[2]

The downfall of Crassus, 54 to 53 B.C.E.

Those who had attacked Gabinius also had fought hard to prevent Crassus from taking up the governorship of Syria. It was hardly reassuring that Crassus had not seen military service in almost twenty years. He further undermined public confidence when he ignored the announcement of dire portents as Pompey escorted him through hostile crowds upon his departure. He did not improve his reputation when he fattened his war chest by looting the Temple at Jerusalem and other rich shrines in his province over the winter of 54–53. During the campaigning season of 54, he had taken his fresh recruits across the Euphrates to scout out his route, establish supply depots, and get some training for a real war in the following year. Despite these precautions, neither Crassus nor his army was experienced or trained enough to deal with the tactics and stratagems of the Parthians. In the spring of 53, near the town of Carrhae, Crassus, his son Publius, and seven legions met destruction at the hands of mail-clad Parthian cavalry (*cataphracts*) and mounted Parthian archers. Crassus' grisly head was displayed at the Parthian Court during a performance of Euripides' *Bacchae*, with its equally grisly ending. The proud eagles of his legions now graced Parthian temples.

Avenging Crassus' ignominious defeat and recovering the lost standards would become the rallying cries for Roman military and diplomatic efforts in the East for two generations. About 10,000 Romans were captured. Some may have been forced to guard the Parthian frontier in Central Asia. Eventually, they may have escaped only to be captured by the Han emperor and settled in what is now Gansu Province in western China.

RIVALRY AND CIVIL WAR BETWEEN CAESAR AND POMPEY, 53 TO 48 B.C.E.

The death of Crassus was the second blow to the delicate political equilibrium that had existed after Luca. The first was the death of Julia, Pompey's wife and Caesar's only child. She had died during childbirth in 54; her baby a few days later. Both men had been devoted to Julia. The common people showed their appreciation of her political importance by forcing her public burial in the Campus Martius.

Caesar offered a new marital alliance: Pompey would marry Caesar's grandniece, who would have to divorce her current husband. Caesar would marry Pompey's daughter, who was already betrothed to Sulla's son Faustus. Pompey rejected the offer. Caesar's meteoric rise was threatening Pompey's prestige and power. As Pompey indicated by betrothing his daughter to Faustus Sulla, he was looking to maintain his preeminence with help from Caesar's optimate enemies in the senate. Pompey drew even closer to them in 52 B.C.E. by marrying Cornelia, widow of the younger Crassus killed at Carrhae and daughter of Sulla's co-consul in 80 B.C.E., a man of impeccable optimate pedigree.

Meanwhile, disorder, corruption, and electoral bribery were rampant in Rome. The year 53 B.C.E. had begun without consuls; the year 52, likewise. Violence and rioting made the streets unsafe. Milo was running for the consulship; Clodius, with Pompey's support, for the praetorship. The bribes were lavish. Blood flowed. The year expired without elections, without magistrates. Authority had broken down. Rome was in anarchy.

The death of Clodius and Pompey's sole consulship, 52 B.C.E.

Clodius was murdered on the Appian Way during a brawl between his retinue and Milo's. After his body was brought back to Rome, a mob seized his body in the Forum, carried it to the senate house, and burned the building as his funeral pyre. Most people agreed that only Pompey was capable of restoring order and should be given emergency powers. His friends proposed a dictatorship, but that was too much for many senators to accept. Cato and Bibulus came up with a compromise that saw Pompey elected sole consul for 52 B.C.E. In this way, he had great latitude for action but was still subject to tribunician veto and would be held accountable for his acts.

Pompey quickly obtained passage of several laws designed both to restore order and to weaken his rivals. The first was aimed at punishing the perpetrators of the recent violence, even Milo, his former ally. Milo was expendable now that Clodius was dead. He was also a rival of electoral candidates whom Pompey preferred to him. The second law attacked bribery. That it was retroactive to 70 B.C.E. troubled Caesar's friends. Caesar knew that his enemies were looking for chances to prosecute him.

Milo was prosecuted for the actions leading to Clodius' death; Cicero was only too happy to defend him. To make certain that no one disrupted the trial to help Milo, Pompey surrounded the court with armed troops. Cicero was so flustered at the sight that he forgot what he wanted to say. Milo, convicted, went into exile to Massilia.

While ensuring law and order and passing laws to deal with important problems, Pompey also strengthened his hand against both Caesar and the *optimates*. His law requiring a five-year interval between holding a magistracy and governing a province not only made bribery in elections less attractive, but also subjected Caesar to immediate replacement by an available ex-magistrate. That would leave Caesar without *imperium*, so that he could be prosecuted. It even meant that he had to rely on Pompey in order to keep his province. Influential men like Cicero and Bibulus who had not held governorships would now have to take up provincial commands. That would leave their optimate friends even more dependent on Pompey. Furthermore, Pompey had his own command in Spain extended for five years. Then, by obtaining a law making it harder to run for office *in absentia*, he made it more difficult for Caesar to run for consul under the protection of a governor's *imperium*. When Pompey then publicly (and illegally) exempted Caesar from this law, he made Caesar look even more dependent. Finally, the optimates were pleased by the election of Pompey's new father-in-law as his consular colleague for the last few months of 52.

The prelude to civil war, 51 to 50 B.C.E.

A series of complicated maneuvers followed in 51 B.C.E. Some of the *optimates* tried immediately to remove Caesar from his command. Caesar's money, however, ensured the election of one friendly consul and ten friendly tribunes for the year 50. Among Caesar's other useful supporters was Marcus Antonius (Mark Antony), son of a Julia (probably Caesar's second cousin, not sister). Antonius had served in Gaul and became a tribune-elect for 49. One of the tribunes in 50 was C. Scribonius Curio, an eloquent speaker and a master of intrigue. He had married Fulvia, the fiery widow of P. Clodius. Curio and the friendly consul blocked meaningful debate on the issue of provincial commands.

In the summer of 50 B.C.E., Pompey used the threat of war with Parthia to take two legions away from Caesar but then stationed them at Capua. In December, Curio blocked another move in the senate to strip Caesar of his command while letting Pompey keep his. Instead, Curio proposed that both Caesar and Pompey lay down their commands together. The senators voted 370 to 22 in favor. Despite this overwhelming vote, the die-hard optimates continued to work on Pompey and push for a confrontation. On the next day, the optimate consul, Marcellus, summoned a special meeting of the senate and proposed passage of the *Senatus Consultum Ultimum* against Caesar. When Curio vetoed the motion, Marcellus handed a sword to Pompey and commissioned him to lead the two legions at Capua against Caesar.

Caesar offered to resign his command if Pompey would resign too. The extremists, however, ignored his proposal, engineered his declaration as a public enemy, and obtained passage of the *Senatus Consultum Ultimum*. Marcus Antonius and Quintus Cassius were two of the new tribunes of 49 B.C.E. Having taken office on December 10 in 50 B.C.E., they vetoed the *S.C.U.* They found themselves censured and their very lives in danger. Fleeing the city with Curio, they went to join Caesar.

Caesar crosses the Rubicon, 50/49 B.C.E.

Meanwhile, Caesar had arrived in Cisalpine Gaul. He had one Roman legion there and some detachments of German and Gallic cavalry. Setting up his headquarters at Ravenna, he summoned two other legions from Gaul. Swift and decisive action tipped the balance in Caesar's favor as it had against the Gauls. When Caesar heard of the senate's action, he decided to act without further delay. Around January 10, 49 B.C.E., by the calendar then in use (really ca. November 20, 50 B.C.E.), he secretly sent a few picked men to infiltrate and seize Ariminum (Rimini). It was the first important city south of the Rubicon, which separated Cisalpine Gaul from Italy proper. That night, he distracted the rest of his officers with a banquet. Once the guests were engrossed in the festivities, he himself hastened toward Ariminum with a few confidants and a detachment of cavalry. When he reached the Rubicon, he paused to ponder the significance of what he was about to do. Then he resolutely quoted a saying from the popular Greek playwright Menander, "Let the die be cast." At dawn, he arrived at Ariminum to find that he had won the throw: Ariminum was safely in his grasp, to the complete surprise of his foes.

Caesar claimed to be acting in defense of the lawful rights of the tribunes. A more powerful appeal to his loyal veterans was the request that they help him to avenge his enemies' affronts to his own *dignitas*. Issues of legality were not unimportant, but the struggle for personal preeminence at Rome was paramount.

Caesar's decision to invade Italy with only one legion and in the dead of winter was a brilliantly calculated risk. Most of Pompey's troops were still untrained and their loyalty uncertain. The only two trained legions at Pompey's command would not forget their long service with Caesar in Gaul. Resistance to Caesar in Italy collapsed; panic gripped Pompey's followers, who fled Rome without even taking the money in the treasury. Pompey himself hastened to Brundisium with all the troops that he could still find. He embarked for Greece just before Caesar's arrival.

Caesar's swift conquest of Italy had been made possible by three things: his absolute and uncontested command of his current forces, the loyalty of his retired veterans from prior years of service in Gaul, and his generous treatment of both civilians and captured soldiers as he swept toward Rome. Still, the tasks ahead were daunting. Pompey had undisputed command of the sea. He could cut Rome off from the grain supplies of Sicily and North Africa and starve the city into submission. Pompey had many battle-hardened legions in Spain and could also draw upon the vast resources and manpower of the East, where he had made and unmade kings. With these forces, he could launch a two-pronged attack on Italy. And what if Gaul, recently conquered and weakly held, should raise up another Vercingetorix?

Before reaching Rome, Caesar stopped off to call on Cicero. He tried to persuade Cicero to support the new regime by lending it both dignity and prestige. Cicero, who could not reconcile his republican principles with Caesar and Caesar's supporters, refused. Much disappointed, Caesar went on his way. After much dithering on the matter, Cicero finally decided to join Pompey in Greece.

Caesar's *clementia*

Caesar had shown magnanimity and clemency (*clementia*) to his enemies thus far, and he would continue to do so—a calculated rejection of the destructive legacy that Sulla's vengeance had left from the previous civil war. *Clementia*, however, was a double-edged sword. To Caesar's benefit, it put those who received it under a tremendous obligation of gratitude (*gratia*). Recipients among proud nobles who considered themselves to be Caesar's equals, however, might chafe under their perceived subordination and might eventually find it intolerable.

Caesar reorganizes the government, 49 B.C.E.

Caesar entered Rome for the first time in nine years. At once, he set about reorganizing the government. Summoning all senators still in Rome, he invited their cooperation to avoid bloodshed. Some responded willingly, others less so. They did accept a law granting citizenship to the people living north of the Po, to whom Caesar owed much.

Caesar speedily arranged for the temporary administration of Rome and Italy. One of the praetors was M. Aemilius Lepidus, son of the rebel leader whom Pompey had defeated in 77 B.C.E. Caesar ordered him to take charge of affairs in the city. He made Marcus Antonius (Mark Antony) governor of Italy and commander-in-chief of all the armed forces there. He sent Curio to secure the grain supplies of Sicily and North Africa. Others went to Illyria to block a possible attempt by Pompey to invade Italy from the northeast. Caesar ordered the doors of the state treasury opened and unceremoniously removed the tribune who attempted to intervene.

So much for the rights of tribunes! Thus he assured the administration of Rome and the soundness of his finances. Then he set out for Spain, which was controlled by forces loyal to Pompey.

Caesar in Spain, 49 B.C.E.

Caesar first had to break the opposition of Massilia. It endangered the line of communication between Spain and Italy. It also might have been able to encourage the resurgence of rebellion in Gaul. Leaving part of his army to reduce the city by siege, Caesar hurried on to Spain. Within forty days, despite some initial difficulty, he had subdued the Pompeian forces there. On the way back, he accepted the surrender of Massilia. It now became virtually an imperial possession of Rome. If Curio had not been killed in North Africa by Pompey's loyal friend Juba, king of Numidia, Caesar's control of the West would have been absolute.

CAESAR'S DICTATORSHIPS AND FINAL VICTORY, 48 TO 45 B.C.E.

News of Caesar's victory in Spain aroused popular enthusiasm in Rome and greatly increased Caesar's power. A special law proposed by Lepidus made Caesar dictator for eleven days in December of 49 to conduct elections for 48. Caesar obtained both a second consulship and a neutral colleague to share it. Their most pressing problem was the relief of debtors and the revival of credit and business undermined by the civil war. Caesar obtained passage of a law that reduced debts and suspended interest payments for one year. In order to make money circulate more freely and encourage lending, he revived an old law forbidding the hoarding of more than 15,000 *denarii*.

Among Caesar's most important initiatives were the recall of persons exiled by Pompey and the restoration of civil rights to victims of Sulla's cruel proscriptions. Proposed by praetors or tribunes, these laws were duly passed in proper legislative assemblies. Most of those who benefited would become Caesar's staunch supporters; those who objected could not accuse him of unconstitutional acts.

The Battles of Dyrrhachium and Pharsalus, 48 B.C.E.

In a characteristic surprise move, Caesar crossed the Adriatic from Brundisium (Brindisi) during the winter in January 48 B.C.E. He landed south of the port of Dyrrhachium (Durrës, Durazzo), where he nearly met disaster. He had only half of his forces. His old enemy Bibulus, patrolling in Pompey's fleet, captured his ships as they returned for supplies and the rest of his men. Caesar resorted to negotiations, proposing that he and Pompey both disarm and let the senate and people work out the details of peace. In this way, neither would be surrendering to the other. Pompey could never accept, as Caesar probably realized. Pompey's *dignitas* had already suffered from what many saw as an ignominious retreat from Italy. He had to prove that he was not a coward, as he would have been branded if he had accepted an offer of peace from an opponent in Caesar's precarious military position.

Forced to fight at Dyrrhachium, Caesar was outflanked by Pompey's superior numbers. He retreated all the way to Pharsalus in central Thessaly. Italy lay open to Pompey. He pursued Caesar instead. Refreshed by Thessaly's grain harvest, Caesar's experienced veterans defeated the forces of the overconfident Pompey. Surveying the slaughter after the battle and referring to those who had wanted to prosecute him for his actions as consul and proconsul, Caesar is reported to have said, "They wanted this. Despite my very great achievements, I, Gaius Caesar, would have been found guilty if I had not summoned help from my army" (Suetonius, *Julius Caesar* 30.4). It was, however, his choice as much as theirs.

The death of Pompey, 48 B.C.E.

Cicero and others accepted Caesar's vaunted *clementia* and returned to Italy. Pompey fled to Egypt. He arrived at Alexandria in the midst of a civil war between Ptolemy XIII (sometimes numbered XII) and his famous sister, Cleopatra VII. Ptolemy's advisors, hoping to link their cause to Caesar's rising star, treacherously procured Pompey's murder. They cut off his head, pickled it in brine for a gift to Caesar, and left the body to rot on the shore.

Caesar in Egypt, 48 B.C.E.

When Caesar arrived three days later, he appeared with the dread *fasces* of a consul to show that Egypt was now subject to the authority of the Roman People. Presented with Pompey's head, he supposedly turned away in disgust and wept. Caesar made a point of reverently burying Pompey's head and ordering the execution of those who had murdered a leader of the Roman People.

Caesar's high-handed actions at Alexandria aroused the populace against him and made life uncomfortable for Roman soldiers. Caesar, captivated by the brilliant and charming Cleopatra, had peremptorily restored her to her throne. He had also demanded that the Egyptians pay a debt owed by her late father. The advisors of Ptolemy XIII ordered out the royal army. They kept Caesar under siege for several months. Having only one small legion, Caesar was unable to cope with an army of 20,000 men as well as with the mobs of Alexandria. He was in dire peril until the arrival of the two legions that he had earlier summoned. The last one to arrive had been hastily collected by Mithridates of Pergamum, reportedly one of the many bastard sons of old Mithridates VI of Pontus.

After Mithridates had reached the Nile, Caesar took command and crushed the Egyptian army. Ptolemy fled and was drowned in the Nile. The Alexandrians submitted. The crown passed to Cleopatra and another brother, Ptolemy XIV, who became her dynastic husband. In August of 47 B.C.E., Caesar left Egypt. Later that year or sometime in 46, Cleopatra bore a son. She said that he was Caesar's, and he was nicknamed Caesarion, "Little Caesar."

From Egypt, Caesar passed through Syria, Cilicia, and Cappadocia on his way to Pontus, where he now planned to settle accounts with Pharnaces II, another son of

Mithridates VI. Taking advantage of the civil war, Pharnaces had betrayed his Roman patrons; had overrun Colchis, Pontus, Lesser Armenia, and part of Cappadocia; and had defeated any opposing army led by one of Caesar's commanders. In a five-day campaign, Caesar tracked him down and annihilated his army at Zela. Pharnaces fled but was killed by one of his own governors. In a letter written to a friend, Caesar proclaimed this swift and decisive victory with the laconic *Veni, Vidi, Vici* (I came, I saw, I conquered). Rewarding Mithridates of Pergamum for his services in Egypt, Caesar gave him eastern Galatia in Asia Minor and Pharnaces' kingdom of Bosporus in the Crimea. After settling other affairs in Asia Minor, the conqueror hastened back to Italy.

Caesar in Italy, 47 B.C.E.

Already appointed dictator for a second time (48 B.C.E.), Caesar reached Italy in September of 47. After an absence of almost two years, he faced serious problems. Marcus Antonius (Mark Antony), master of the cavalry to Caesar the dictator, had let the dangerous problem of debt become a catalyst for murder and riot. Caelius Rufus and Milo were killed leading a revolt of the poor in 48. Mutinous soldiers were marching on Rome when Caesar arrived. The presence of the dictator immediately restored peace and order. He dealt so firmly, but so fairly, with the soldiers that they begged to be accepted back in his good graces. Without publicly disgracing Antonius, he chose the older, more politic Lepidus as his new master of the cavalry and instituted moderate debt relief.

The start of the African campaign, 47 B.C.E.

After Pharsalus, Cato had regrouped Pompey's shattered forces and taken them to Africa. Forced by a storm to land in the Cyrenaica, he led his army for hundreds of miles through the North African desert from Berenice (Benghazi) to Lepcis Magna (Tripoli). From there, he went to Utica, where he joined King Juba of Numidia and the Pompeian governor of Africa. After this astonishing military feat, Cato, ever mindful of higher rank, misguidedly resigned the command in favor of the inept Metellus Scipio, Pompey's father-in-law. Scipio was joined by Juba and Labienus, who had been Caesar's right-hand man in Gaul but ultimately had sided with his old family patron Pompey. In late December of 47, the outnumbered Caesar landed in Africa to challenge Scipio.

Thapsus and the death of Cato, 46 B.C.E.

Near Thapsus, in April of 46 B.C.E., Caesar lured the inept Scipio onto unfavorable ground and annihilated his army. When Cato heard the news, he saw the approaching end of the aristocratic liberty (*libertas*) that had characterized the Republic. Although he might have obtained Caesar's calculated pardon, he could not bring himself either to request or to receive it. He preferred freely, and contemptuously, to take his own life instead.

As Cato anticipated, his suicide took some of the glory from Caesar's victory. "O Cato," Caesar is said to have exclaimed, "I envy you your death; you denied me the chance to spare your life" (Plutarch, *Cato Minor* 72.2). Caesar, however, could not leave it at that. When Cicero wrote an encomium on Cato, Caesar lashed out against his dead enemy with a spiteful *Anticato* that impugned Cato's career and character. Thus, Caesar may have turned Cato into more of a martyr to the old Republic than Cato had already made himself.

Caesar's homecoming and triumph, 46 B.C.E.

The news of Thapsus had preceded Caesar's return to Rome. His followers rejoiced. Caesar had reached the pinnacle of preeminence for which he had been aiming. The senators decreed a thanksgiving of forty days and voted seventy-two lictors (three times the usual number) to attend him at his triumph. They awarded him a dictatorship renewable annually for ten years. He was appointed prefect of morals for three years, with powers of a censor. He also received the right to express his opinion in the senate first, so that every timid and self-seeking politician could take his cue. His statue, cast in bronze, was to stand on the Capitol opposite that of Jupiter himself. Caesar allegedly rejected many other religious and monarchical honors showered upon him. Some of them are of late report and fictitious, undoubtedly suggested by the history of later Caesarism.

Soon after his arrival at Rome in 46, Caesar celebrated his long-awaited triumphs. There were four, each celebrated on a different day, over the Gauls, Egyptians, Pharnaces, and Juba. There was no triumph over Pompey or Scipio: triumphing over Roman citizens would have crossed a line of propriety. Even so, the four triumphs constituted one of the grandest displays ever seen in Rome: gigantic parades; the distribution of millions of *denarii* among soldiers and civilians; 20,000 tables loaded with food and wine for the *plebs*; elaborate shows, games, and gladiatorial combats; a naval battle in an artificial lake; and a mock battle between two armies on Mars Field.

At about this time, Cleopatra, her son, and her brother-husband also arrived in Rome. They stayed at a villa in Caesar's gardens across the Tiber, to the scandal and dismay of many, especially republican traditionalists. Still, important men like Cicero, looking for influence or information, sought the queen's help. Nothing is said about Cleopatra's son. Caesar, however, set up a golden statue of Cleopatra herself next to the statue of Venus in his temple of Venus Genetrix (p. 293). No doubt, people reflected on the juxtaposition of a monarch whose father was a god in Egypt and the goddess Venus, whom Caesar claimed as his ancestor in Rome.

Munda, Caesar's final victory in Spain, 45 B.C.E.

One more campaign had to be fought. Late in 46 B.C.E., Caesar embarked for Spain with eight legions, where Pompey's two sons, Gnaeus and Sextus, plus Labienus, who had escaped from Africa, had raised a major revolt. Failing to draw the Pompeians into a battle by attacking their fortified towns, Caesar finally caught up with them at Munda (between Seville and Malaga). Caesar's men had to deliver their attack uphill. The battle was one of ferocious savagery. Fear and hate on both sides supplied energy to their desperate valor. Superior discipline and generalship at last gave Caesar the decision. Labienus died in battle, and Gnaeus Pompey was caught three weeks later and killed. Sextus lived to fight years later against Caesar's successors (pp. 307–10).

Caesar returned to Rome and celebrated another triumph in October of 45. This time, he did not scruple to celebrate a victory over fellow citizens. Many thought it unseemly and feared for the future.

CAESAR'S WORK OF RECONSTRUCTION

If by war Caesar had saved his life, honor, and dignity, he would now have to save the Roman state from chaos and ruin; heal its wounds; and give to it such peace, justice, and stability as it had not known for almost a century. Otherwise, the very source of his fame and glory would have been destroyed.

Caesar was now armed with the sacrosanctity of a tribune of the *plebs*, which the senate conferred upon him. He also enjoyed the powers of a censor and had an annually renewable dictatorship. With them, he undertook the task of transforming the Roman Republic and its empire into a centralized world state. Unlike Sulla, he did not attempt to resurrect the pre-Gracchan constitution. Events of the past hundred years had shown that it could not be maintained under circumstances quite different from those that had given it birth. What Caesar, with his customary daring and decisiveness, did not realize, however, was that many Romans did not yet recognize that fact or wish to be functionaries in a state controlled by him.

Before he even began his work of reform, Caesar had removed one fatal weakness of the late Republic: separate control of the civilian government and provincial armies. Caesar was both chief executive of the state and commander-in-chief of the army. He sought to prevent anyone from doing what he himself had done with the command of Gaul. The general effect of his reforms, while they reinforced his own supremacy over all, was to reduce the absolute dominance of the city of Rome and to integrate Rome with Italy and Italy with the rest of the empire.

Administrative reforms

The most important of Caesar's administrative reforms had to do with the senate and the magistracies. To eliminate the senate, an institution virtually synonymous with Rome, would have been beyond even Caesar's daring. It also would have destroyed the very body whose expertise and cooperation was needed to run Rome's vast empire. Instead, Caesar raised its membership from 600 to 900 and filled the extra seats with old friends, wealthy equestrians, and even Romanized provincials. To keep up the membership of this enlarged senate, he raised the number of quaestors from twenty to forty and of praetors from eight to sixteen. This change also provided more administrators for Rome and the provinces and allowed more of Caesar's friends to reach senatorial rank and high office quickly. Moreover, out of gratitude and loyalty toward Caesar, they were expected to look out for his interests. Similarly, in the process of expanding the number of officeholders, he assigned men their various offices for several years in advance. They were to administer affairs to his advantage while he went off to conquer the Parthians in the East.

Social and economic programs

Caesar reduced from 320,000 to 150,000 those who received free grain at Rome. Therefore, he needed to provide employment for or siphon away those cut off. Indeed, reducing Rome's overcrowded and volatile population (then approaching 700,000) was socially and politically desirable. Caesar also had to provide homes and land for his war veterans.

In Rome, Caesar began a major building program. It was not only to provide employment but also to make Rome the beautiful and magnificent capital of a great empire. It would also reinforce the image of Caesar as the most powerful man in it. The chief architectural achievements of the period were the Basilica Julia (a covered hall to house the law courts), new Rostra in the Forum, and a new forum, the Forum Julium. The latter had galleries all around it and a temple of Venus Genetrix in the center. Caesar also had plans for a new senate house, a large meeting place for the popular assemblies, a fine public library, a splendid theater, and an enormous temple of Mars. All would be visible symbols of his greatness at the expense of those structures associated with the old order.

Even more gigantic and self-aggrandizing were the projects planned for Italy: an artificial harbor near Ostia for seagoing ships (a project that later materialized as Portus under the Emperor Claudius), a road across the Apennines to the head of the Adriatic, and the draining of the malarial Fucine Lake and the Pomptine Marshes for agriculture (a feat often attempted later but never accomplished until modern times). To promote the economic recovery and internal security of Italy, Caesar compelled all wealthy citizens to invest half their capital in land. He also required that at least a third of the cowhands and shepherds employed on large estates be men of free birth. Of course, all of these reforms made Caesar even more powerful by creating goodwill among the population in general.

Colonization, Romanization, and the provinces

To provide employment outside of Rome, remove excess population from Rome, and find homes for a large number of war veterans, Caesar resumed the colonizing work of Gaius Gracchus outside Italy, but on a much larger scale. In all, he founded or planned no fewer than twenty colonies and provided homes in the provinces for at least 100,000 Roman citizens. Many of these colonies are famous cities today: in Spain, Hispalis (Seville) and Tarraco (Tarragona); in France, Arelate (Arles), Nemausus (Nîmes), Arausio (Orange), and Lugdunum (Lyons); in Africa, Cirta (Constantine, Algeria) and Carthage; in Greece, Corinth; in Switzerland, Geneva. Farther east, he founded colonies at Sinope and Heraclea on the Black Sea.

Following the example of Marius, Caesar granted citizenship to the soldiers whom he had recruited in the Province. He enfranchised doctors, teachers, librarians, and scholars who came to Rome from various provinces; he granted Roman or Latin status to many provincial towns in Gaul and Spain and to all the towns of Sicily. He also founded schools and public libraries in many towns of the western provinces, whence came some of Rome's greatest writers a century or so later. In the East, Caesar reduced the burden of taxation. As far as possible, he transferred the task of tax collection from the harsh and corrupt Roman *publicani* and their agents, hitherto the curse of provincial administration, to the municipal governments. In Asia and Sicily, he replaced the traditional tithe by a land tax of fixed amounts. To promote the commercial importance of a new colony on the destroyed site of Corinth, he planned a canal (not completed until the late nineteenth century C.E.) across the Isthmus of Corinth. His colonies and favorable treatment of the provinces not only were fair solutions to long-standing problems but also increased the reservoir of clients and goodwill available to support his rule throughout Rome's empire.

Coinage

Caesar laid the foundation for Rome's imperial coinage. His programs and policies required coinage on a massive scale that characterized the fiscal needs of an empire's administration. The booty from his triumphs in 46, particularly the Gallic loot, allowed him to coin more money than any previous *imperator*. His friend Aulus Hirtius, now a praetor, minted Rome's first long-lived gold coinage by issuing a new gold coin called the *aureus*, worth twenty-five silver *denarii*. The *aureus* became the most prestigious coin of the Roman Empire.

Putting large numbers of coins in circulation helped to pay for the imperial scope of Caesar's programs and policies. Coins displaying the titles and symbols associated with him were also an excellent way to advertise his greatness. Two years later, just before his death, Caesar even became the first living Roman to have his portrait bust on coins. That became the standard practice of Augustus and succeeding Roman emperors.

Reform of the calendar

The most lasting of Caesar's reforms was a new calendar. He no longer based it on the phases of the moon with a year of 355 days, but on the Egyptian solar calendar, with a year of 365 1/4 days beginning on January 1. The new calendar was worked out by the Greek astronomer Sosigenes of Alexandria. It is still in use, with a few minor corrections added in 1582 C.E. by Pope Gregory XIII. In honor of Julius Caesar, the senate decreed that the month of his birth, formerly called Quintilis (the "Fifth"), be renamed Julius (July).

Even calendrical reform directly benefited Caesar. The vagaries of the old calendar had given priests and magistrates many opportunities to delay and obstruct the actions of political rivals. The regularization of the calendar made it impossible for anyone to use such tactics against Caesar as Bibulus had done during their year as consuls.

THE ASSASSINATION OF JULIUS CAESAR, MARCH 15, 44 B.C.E.

About February 14, 44 B.C.E., Caesar obtained unprecedented power. By a decree of the subservient senate, he assumed the title *dictator perpetuus*, "dictator for life." This "reform" was totally incompatible with the old Republic and alarmed many friends and former foes who still valued the old traditions.

Caesar hoped that with stability and security assured by his sweeping reforms, he would be free to pursue a scheme of conquest that would make him even greater than Alexander the Great. The last acts of his military career were to be campaigns against the Dacians, who lived north of the lower reaches of the Danube, and against the Parthians in the East, who had defeated and destroyed the army of Crassus at Carrhae in 53 B.C.E.

Still, Caesar's successes had driven many senators to desperation, lest he eclipse them forever. Some had probably voted him excessive honors in the hope of arousing a violent reaction against him. If so, they succeeded. Over sixty senators, led by Gaius Cassius Longinus (ca. 85–42 B.C.E.) and Marcus Junius Brutus (ca. 85–42 B.C.E.), were incensed at his growing power and unfailing popularity with the people. They plotted to kill him. They struck at a meeting of the senate on the Ides (15th) of March, 44 B.C.E., three days before his scheduled departure for the East.

Some of the conspirators, like Brutus and Cassius, were former enemies on whom he had bestowed his *clementia*. Cassius was married to Brutus' younger sister and had supported Pompey in 49 and 48 B.C.E. Brutus was closely linked to Cato: he was the son of Servilia, Cato's half-sister; he had been raised in Cato's house; and he was the husband of Cato's daughter Porcia, the only woman active in the conspiracy. The majority of conspirators, however, were Caesar's old friends and officers.

According to a famous story, a seer had warned Caesar of a danger coming by the Ides of March; Caesar saw him again on the way to the fateful meeting and teased him that the Ides had come; the man replied that they had not gone. However that may be, the meeting was held, ironically enough, in an annex to the portico attached to Pompey's theater (p. 336). While Caesar took his seat, a number of the conspirators crowded around him as if to make petitions. When the first blow struck, he rose from his chair in surprise and anger, but his cries were of no avail. Bleeding from numerous wounds, Caesar died at the foot of Pompey's statue. He had beaten Pompey in the competition for preeminent *dignitas* at Rome, but his undisguised attempt to make his preeminence permanent had unleashed the forces of his own destruction.

THE QUESTION OF MONARCHY

There is abundant evidence that during the last two years of his life Caesar was planning to establish some kind of monarchy. He took, or allowed to be taken, a number of steps that exalted him above ordinary mortals. It was not enough that the month of his birth was renamed for him; many expensive statues of him also appeared. One showed him standing on a globe, symbol of the world, and another was placed in the temple of Rome's first king, the deified Romulus (Quirinus).

Caesar's assumption of the unprecedented lifetime dictatorship, heavily advertised on coins just before his death, made him a king in all but name. He received such royal honors along with this dictatorship as the right to wear, on public occasions, both a triumphal robe (which was derived from the robes of Etruscan kings) and a laurel crown. He also was allowed to use a gilded chair instead of the ordinary magistrate's curule chair. Finally, Caesar was voted his own special priest (*flamen*), and Marcus Antonius was appointed to the position.

As previously suggested, it may well be that some of these measures were prompted by Caesar's enemies in order to provoke a reaction against him. Nevertheless, he could have refused them if he had wanted to. It would seem, therefore, that he was assuming the position of a monarch with a penumbra of divine sanction, if not actually with divine status, and was trying to deny only the hated title *rex* (king/tyrant). Accordingly, he had rebuked a crowd for hailing him as *rex* earlier in 44. Similarly, on February 15 at the Lupercalia festival, he had ostentatiously refused a royal diadem offered him by Antonius. Instead, he had the crown sent to Jupiter, whom he called the only king of the Romans. He ordered it to be publicly recorded that he had refused a *regnum* (kingship/tyranny). He was happy at that point to have the substance of kingship without the invidious name.

One cannot say, however, that Caesar had been planning from an early point in his career to overthrow the Republic and establish a monarchy. There is no hint of any such plan in his own latest writing, the *De Bello Civili* (*On the Civil War*), probably written in 48 or 47 B.C.E. Before the civil war, Caesar was merely acting like any other Roman noble in his quest for preeminence *within* the Republic. Only after the civil war with Pompey did Caesar face the problem of simultaneously protecting the position that he had achieved and creating a stable government for Rome and the vast polyglot empire that it had become. Previously, Sulla's reforms had failed. Some form of monarchy was the logical alternative, and Caesar's quick mind always cut to the heart of the matter when confronted with a problem.

THE SIGNIFICANCE OF CAESAR

With a quick mind and unconventional daring, Caesar was unusually talented. Still, too much should not be made of Caesar's individual responsibility for the collapse of the Roman Republic. He was not a unique phenomenon, only the culmination of a long series of ambitious nobles who had striven for supreme *dignitas* and *auctoritas* at Rome. If he had not risen to challenge Pompey's preeminence, someone else would have, just as Pompey had challenged Sulla and his heirs. The timing and the particulars would have been different. In the end, however, one man would have established sole domination of some kind, as Caesar's heir did again under similar circumstances in the next generation. Those who wanted to reject the permanent rule of a dominant leader had to yield to those who fought to be the successor to Caesar's domination.

NOTES

1   The authors of the bill had foresightedly included a clause, similar to the unusual one inserted into the land bill of Saturninus in 100 B.C.E. It required all senators to swear obedience to the law. They all did, including Cato.
2   Caesar recalled him during the civil war with Pompey. He died from illness while serving in Illyria (47 B.C.E.).

SUGGESTED READING

Goldsworthy, A. *Caesar, Life of a Colossus*. New Haven and London: Yale University Press, 2006.

Stevenson, T. *Julius Caesar and the Transformation of the Roman Republic*. London and New York: Routledge, 2015.

Woolf, G. *Et Tu, Brute? A Short History of Political Murder*. Cambridge, MA: Harvard University Press, 2007.

CHAPTER 17

The last years of the Republic, 44 to 30 B.C.E.

The assassination of Caesar solved nothing. It merely set the stage for another destructive civil war. The conspirators and their friends hoped to wipe out all vestiges of Caesar the divinely sanctioned dictator and return to free republican aristocratic competition as equals. Many of Caesar's allies and relatives wanted to take up his fallen mantle and use his popularity with the masses to assert their own dominance.

MARCUS ANTONIUS TRIES TO TAKE CONTROL, 44 TO 43 B.C.E.

At Brutus' insistence, the conspirators had planned nothing but killing the "tyrant," Caesar. Brutus naively thought that the old free Republic would miraculously return to life afterward. Once the deed was done, however, the other senators panicked and stole away to their homes. The conspirators, becoming unsure of the public's reaction, retired to the Capitol, erected barricades, and planned their future moves. Marcus Antonius (ca. 83–30 B.C.E.), Caesar's relative (p. 285) and colleague in the consulship of 44, had been detained outside the chamber during the murder. He had quickly fled and hidden in fear that he might be the next victim. That night, sensing a chance to act, he improvised a bodyguard, came out of hiding, and persuaded Caesar's widow, Calpurnia, to hand over all of her husband's papers to him. In this way, he could claim to be the dead dictator's legitimate representative.

Antonius has often been portrayed as a boozing, boorish bully of the worst kind. Any possible faults, weaknesses, and early follies, however, have been exaggerated by the propaganda of his enemies, especially Cicero and Augustus. It shaped the "official" version of events reflected in most surviving sources. Antonius had many good qualities as a soldier, general, and politician. His shrewdness and diplomacy helped to avoid serious trouble in the hours and days immediately following Caesar's assassination.

M. Aemilius Lepidus had been outside the gates of Rome with a newly recruited legion. While Antonius was securing Caesar's papers, Lepidus prepared to besiege the conspirators on the Capitol. The next morning, Antonius, having sensibly persuaded Lepidus to refrain, took charge of his troops. They then conferred with others of Caesar's old officers and friends and established contact with the conspirators. Both sides also kept in communication with Cicero, the elder statesman. He had not been part of the conspiracy but had declared support for Caesar's murderers immediately after the killing.

The outcome of the various conferences was a meeting of the senate on March 17. Antonius presided. Many senators wanted Caesar condemned as a tyrant, his assassination approved as necessary and just, his body flung into the Tiber, and all his acts declared null and void. Antonius urged them to reject such extremes; argued that they owed to Caesar their public offices, provinces, and political futures; hinted at the danger of popular uprisings; and pleaded that they listen to the people howling outdoors for vengeance and the blood of the conspirators. The appeal to fear and self-interest prevailed. The senators voted to give all Caesar's acts the force of law and to proclaim an amnesty for the conspirators. That night, Antonius entertained Cassius, Brutus dined with Lepidus, and various other conspirators joined other Caesarians. The toasts that they drank seemed to proclaim more loudly than senatorial resolutions that peace and harmony prevailed.

On the next day, Antonius and Caesar's father-in-law, Calpurnius Piso, persuaded the senators to make public Caesar's will and grant him a state funeral. As many of the conspirators and their allies feared, publicizing Caesar's will before the funeral stirred up the lower classes against the assassins. With news of Caesar's murder spreading, the popular mood was turning ugly. More and more of his veterans and admirers among the rural plebs streamed into the city. When they learned how generously Caesar had provided for them and even one of his murderers (Decimus Junius Brutus), they became increasingly outraged at their patron's killers. Caesar's benefactions to the Roman People included turning his gardens across the Tiber into a public park and giving 300 sesterces in cash to each Roman citizen.

The will also made Antonius' position more difficult in the long run. The chief beneficiary was not Antonius, a relative who was named only a minor heir, but Gaius Octavius Thurinus (63 B.C.E.–14 C.E.), Caesar's grandnephew, the future Emperor Augustus. He was the son of C. Octavius, a senator born to a wealthy equestrian family, and of Atia, daughter of Caesar's second older sister.

As the will required, Octavius took his uncle's more distinguished name, Gaius Julius Caesar, but he did not follow the usual practice of adding to it the adjectival form of his former *nomen*, in this case *Octavianus* (Octavian). His enemies, however, sometimes used it in an attempt to deny him the magic of Caesar's name and remind people of his less impressive equestrian origin. Now, to avoid the confusion that he actively sought between himself and Caesar, historians call him Octavian for the period after March of 44 B.C.E. and before he received the title *Augustus* in 27 B.C.E.

March 20 was the day of Caesar's funeral. A recounting of Caesar's mighty deeds on behalf of the Roman People aroused the feelings of the crowd for its lost leader. Next, Antonius, as consul, delivered the traditional eulogy. It probably was not so high flown as the reconstructions by Dio, Appian, and Shakespeare. As he progressed, however, he seems to have stirred up people's passions with expression of his personal feelings for their hero. Then, with consummate showmanship at the very end, Antonius thrust aloft Caesar's bloodied toga on the point of a spear and displayed on a rotating platform a wax image of the corpse with its oozing wounds. The people went completely berserk and seized Caesar's bier. They surged toward the Capitol with the intention of interring him in the Temple of Jupiter. The authorities, however, turned them back. Returning to the Forum, they made a makeshift pyre near the Regia, Caesar's headquarters as *pontifex maximus*. There they cremated his corpse and kept vigil over the ashes far into the night. Unfortunately, they also vented their rage by literally dismembering the hapless tribune C. Helvius Cinna. A friend of Caesar, he had come to the Forum to pay his respects. The crowd confused him with Caesar's former brother-in-law, the praetor L. Cornelius Cinna, who had recently denounced Caesar and praised his assassins.

The Amatius affair

At this time, it seemed that Antonius would succeed Caesar. Although disappointed that he was not Caesar's principal heir, he profited much from possessing the dictator's private funds, papers, and rough drafts; much more, still, from his own skillful diplomacy and conciliatory spirit. Seeking to satisfy both friends and enemies of Caesar, he procured Caesar's old position as *pontifex maximus* for Lepidus and was not violent toward the conspirators. The common people, however, were not happy with Antonius' moderate course. A certain Amatius, apparently a wealthy man of Greek origin, had assumed the mantle of popular leadership. He convinced many people that he was actually a grandson of Marius and, therefore, a relative of Caesar. Having built up a considerable following, Amatius sponsored the creation of a monument, altar, and attendant cult to Caesar on the spot where he had been cremated in the Forum. Here the *plebs* settled disputes, swore oaths in Caesar's name, and threatened violence against the conspirators. Clearly, the Forum was not a safe place for the latter, nor was Rome. Antonius quietly allowed them to proceed to their allotted provinces. Cassius and Marcus Brutus did not go directly but lingered among the towns of Latium in a vain effort to recruit support for their cause.

To the extent that Amatius had helped drive the conspirators from public life in Rome, he had been helpful to Antonius. At that point, however, his growing influence among Caesar's veterans and the *plebs* was too great a threat to be tolerated. Indeed, that a "nobody" like Amatius should be wielding so much influence in the Forum must have offended all sides in the senate. Therefore, on April 13, with the senate's full support, Antonius had Amatius arrested and summarily executed. The unauthorized shrine for Caesar's worship was then destroyed.

Antonius further dissociated himself from the monarchic tendencies that Caesar had lately demonstrated. On his initiative, the office of dictator was forever abolished to assure the nobility that there would never be another Caesar. Then, with the senate concurring, Antonius took up the province of Macedonia and all the legions that Caesar had mobilized for his intended invasions of the Balkans and Parthia. Thus, Antonius had carefully steered between those who wanted to wipe out everything that Caesar had done and those who wanted to enshrine it in public worship. He had saved Rome from chaos after Caesar's death and seemed to be solidifying his position as Rome's preeminent leader.

Opposition from Cicero and Octavian

As consul and executor of Caesar's estate, Antonius tried to bolster his position by showing special favor to friends like Lepidus. For example, he betrothed his eldest daughter to Lepidus' son and obtained Lepidus' appointment as *pontifex maximus* to replace Caesar. He also spent Caesar's money for his own benefit. These actions disturbed men like Cicero, who wanted to guide the ship of state. They doubted his motives and worked against him. Even more, it was the unexpected challenge of Caesar's principal heir, Octavian, which prevented Antonius from smoothly consolidating his supremacy. Caesar had sent Octavian to Epirus to train for the projected Parthian war. Only eighteen and of a rather delicate constitution, Octavian boldly determined to return to Italy and take advantage of any opportunity that the sudden turn of events might offer. He immediately demanded his inheritance, much of which Antonius had already spent. Seriously underestimating the young man, Antonius contemptuously rebuffed him. More determined than ever, Octavian undermined loyalty to Antonius among Caesar's veterans. He played upon the magic of his new name and exploited their resentment of Antonius' leniency with Caesar's assassins.

Antonius tried to strengthen his position by obtaining passage of a law transferring command of Cisalpine and Transalpine Gaul from Decimus Brutus and Lepidus to himself for five years. Obviously, Antonius hoped to dominate Italy and Rome from this advantageous position, as Caesar once did. Many of Caesar's old officers and soldiers did not want to fight each other or lose the political advantages of a united front. Their pressure kept Antonius and Octavian from intensifying their feud.

Antonius' troubles still increased. His new provincial command aroused the fear and jealousy of Marcus Brutus and Gaius Cassius. In July, they demanded more significant provinces than Crete and Cyrene. His patience worn thin, Antonius refused their demands. He issued such strong threats that they abandoned Italy in order to recruit armies among Pompey's old centers of support in the East. Moreover, Pompey's son Sextus, who had escaped the Pompeian disasters in Africa and Spain, was now seizing control of western waters and raising another revolt in Spain. Meanwhile, Octavian had improved his standing as Caesar's champion. He borrowed enough money to celebrate games scheduled in honor of Caesar's victory at

Pharsalus, since no one else would do it. After a comet fortuitously appeared during the celebrations, Octavian successfully encouraged the popular belief that it was Caesar's soul ascending to heaven.

Antonius was getting worried. He began to resent Cicero's absence from the senate, which many interpreted as criticism of Antonius' actions. Indeed, Cicero did believe that the Republic was being subverted, a belief sharpened by his own lack of power. On September 1, 44 B.C.E., Antonius publicly criticized Cicero's failure to attend meetings of the senate. In reply, Cicero delivered a speech mildly critical but irritating enough to provoke the increasingly sensitive Antonius to an angry attack upon Cicero's past career. Cicero in turn wrote and published a very hostile but never-spoken second "speech." He branded Antonius as a tyrant, ruffian, drunkard, and coward, a man who flouted morality by kissing his wife in public! Likening his speeches to Demosthenes' famous orations against Philip of Macedon in fourth-century Athens, Cicero dubbed them *Philippics*. Twelve other extant *Philippics* followed, an eternal monument to Cicero's eloquence but filled with misinformation and misrepresentation.

Rome had become unbearable for Antonius. Down to Brundisium, he went to meet four legions summoned from Macedonia, his original province. He intended to send them north to drive Decimus Brutus out of Cisalpine Gaul. The latter had refused to hand it over to Antonius despite the recent law. Antonius' consular year (44 B.C.E.) was near its end. Should he delay, he might be left without a province or legions to command. Brutus and Cassius had proceeded to the East to take over rich provinces and their large armies. Cassius had defeated the governor of Syria and had driven him to suicide. Lepidus, now in Nearer Spain, was a shifty and suspect ally; Lucius Munatius Plancus, in Gallia Comata, and Gaius Asinius Pollio, in Farther Spain, were even less dependable. Even worse, Octavian had returned to Rome at the head of 3000 troops. Some of them were Antonius' former soldiers who had now declared their loyalty to Caesar's young heir. Octavius, however, soon alienated public opinion in a fiery speech against Antonius and turned to Cicero for help. Cicero eagerly embraced him as a weapon that he could discard after destroying Antonius.

The siege of Mutina, 44 to 43 B.C.E.

Antonius hastened north and trapped Decimus Brutus in Mutina (Modena). In January, the senate finally sent Decimus reinforcements under the two new consuls, Aulus Hirtius and Gaius Vibius Pansa, former comrades of Antonius under Caesar. At Cicero's insistence, the senate also sent the young Octavian, granted propraetorian power and senatorial rank. He was promised rich rewards: money and land for his legitimized troops; for himself, the right to stand for the consulship when he reached the age of thirty-three, ten years before the legal age.

The three enemy armies finally forced Antonius to abandon the siege of Mutina but could not prevent his retreat across the Alps into southern Gaul. There he hoped to gain the support of Lepidus and Plancus. Both consuls lost their lives at Mutina: Hirtius, killed in battle; Pansa, later dying of his wounds. Their deaths cleared the field for Octavian.

Cicero had high hopes after Mutina. The enemy was on the run. The armies of the Republic would shortly track him down. The entire East fell into the hands of Brutus and Cassius. Decimus Brutus still held Cisalpine Gaul, and Sextus Pompey was supreme at sea. Soon, Cicero and his friends would close the ring and dispose of Octavian, too. Then would come the day for the glorious restoration of the Republic—so Cicero believed. He was cruelly deceived.

Antonius' enemies miscalculate

After Mutina, the senate declared Antonius a public enemy. Upon Brutus and Cassius, it conferred superior command (*imperium maius*) over all Roman magistrates in the East. To Decimus Brutus, the dominant senators voted a triumph and supreme command over all the armies in Italy. To Sextus Pompey, they extended a vote of thanks and an extraordinary command over the Roman navy. For Octavian, however, they proposed only a minor triumph, *ovatio*, and an inferior command. Even that proposal they finally voted down. They also refused to reward his troops and repudiated the promised consulship. Through their own folly, they drove Octavian back into the arms of the other Caesarians.

Octavian seizes the initiative, July 43 B.C.E.

To punish the slights and studied disdain of senatorial leaders, Octavian marched on Rome with eight legions. Two legions were brought over from Africa to defend his senatorial enemies. The legions deserted to him. All resistance collapsed. Octavian, not yet twenty, entered Rome and obtained the election of himself and Quintus Pedius as suffect (substitute) consuls to fill out the deceased consuls' terms. Pedius was Caesar's nephew, his former legate, and heir to one-eighth of his estate.

Octavius' first act as consul was to rifle the treasury and pay each soldier 2500 *denarii*; the next was the passage of a law instituting a special court to try Caesar's murderers and Sextus Pompey. In order to claim patrician status, he also sought to make himself Caesar's adopted son by more than just a provision in Caesar's will. Tribunes loyal to Antonius had blocked a previous attempt in 44. Now, with Antonius out of Rome, Octavian went through a formal adoption ceremony that normally would have been valid only if Julius Caesar had been alive to participate. Soon, Octavian would be too powerful for people to quibble over technicalities. Now, however, he still needed allies. To obtain them, he had the decree against Antonius and Lepidus revoked. That done, he hastened north to see them.

Meanwhile, Antonius had been neither idle nor unsuccessful. His debacle at Mutina had brought out the best in him. After a hard and painful march into southern Gaul, he confronted Lepidus' far larger army. Antonius cleverly played upon the sympathies of Lepidus' men, many of whom had served with him under Caesar in Gaul. Begrimed, haggard, and thickly bearded, he stole into the camp of Lepidus and addressed the men. Thereafter, the two armies began gradually to fraternize. Soon, Antonius was in real command. He used the same tactics in approaching the army belonging to L. Munatius

Plancus, Caesar's former legate and the governor of Gallia Comata. Then, Decimus Brutus was deserted by his army. Brutus himself attempted to escape to Macedonia, but he was trapped and slain by a Gallic chief.

When Antonius and Lepidus returned to Cisalpine Gaul with twenty-six legions, they found Octavian already there with seventeen. Although they greatly outnumbered the young pretender, they did not try to fight him. They feared that their men might refuse to fight against one who bore Caesar's name. Lepidus arranged a conference instead.

THE TRIUMVIRATE OF OCTAVIAN, ANTONIUS, AND LEPIDUS, 43 TO 36 B.C.E.

After some preliminary negotiations, the three leaders met near Bologna. They agreed upon a joint effort. They would form themselves into a three-man executive committee with absolute powers for five years for the reconstruction of the Roman state (*tresviri rei publicae constituendae*). The *lex Titia* to that effect was carried by a friendly tribune on November 27, 43 B.C.E. In name, the consulship survived along with its traditional prestige, title, and conferment of nobility. In fact, its powers were greatly reduced. Octavian and Pedius agreed to resign the office. Two nonentities took their place. Also, to strengthen the alliance, Octavian married Antonius' step-daughter Claudia. She was the daughter of Antony's wife, Fulvia, whom he had married in either 47 or 46. Claudia's father was Fulvia's first husband, Publius Clodius. Fulvia's second husband, Curio, had died fighting for Caesar in 49 (p. 288).

Octavian was not the dominant member in the triumvirate. Antonius, who had one less legion than Octavian, insisted that he be given four more and Octavian only three. Thus Octavian was limited to parity with Antonius. They both took their additional legions from Lepidus. As for the provinces, Antonius secured Cisalpine Gaul and Gallia Comata. Lepidus obtained Transalpine Gaul and the two Spains. Octavian received a more modest and doubtful portion: North Africa and the islands of Sicily, Sardinia, and Corsica, all disputed and some already seized by the outlawed Sextus Pompey.

The proscriptions, 43 B.C.E.

A few days later, the triumvirs instituted a proscription as cold-blooded as that of Sulla. Among their victims were 130 senators and, if Appian is correct, 2000 *equites*. The excuse alleged was the avenging of Caesar's murder. The reality is different. The triumvirs needed money for their forty-three legions and for the inevitable campaign against Marcus Brutus and Gaius Cassius. They soon found that the confiscated wealth of their victims was insufficient for their needs. Therefore, they imposed a capital levy upon rich women, laid crushing taxes upon the propertied classes in Italy, and set aside the territories of eighteen of the richest cities in Italy for veteran settlements. The women, at least, protested vociferously and won a significant reduction of their impost (pp. 327–8).

In addition to the triumvirs' need for money was a desire to wipe out political enemies. Their most distinguished victim, at Antonius' insistence, was Cicero. Unlike some of the proscribed, he lingered until too late. Abandoning his final flight, Cicero calmly awaited his pursuers along a deserted road and was murdered on December 7, 43 B.C.E., a martyr to the cause of the dying Republic. The Rostra from which Cicero had so often spoken saw his head and at least the gesturing right hand nailed upon it. Fulvia, often a victim of Cicero's sharp tongue, is said to have taken vengeance later by ripping it out and sticking a hairpin through it.

The consolidation of power, 43 and 42 B.C.E.

To buttress their regime of terror and violence, of confiscation and proscription, the triumvirs packed the senate with men of nonsenatorial origin who would become their loyal clients. They made the consulship the reward of graft or crime and nominated several pairs of consuls in a single year. To the praetors, whom Caesar had increased to sixteen, they added fifty more.

The consuls of 42 were to be Lepidus and Caesar's old legate Munatius Plancus. Another legate and C. Antonius Hybrida became censors. Hybrida, Cicero's suspect consular colleague in 63, was Antonius' uncle and former father-in-law.

Formally taking office January 1, 42 B.C.E., the triumvirs compelled the senate and the magistrates to swear an oath to observe Caesar's acts. They also provided for building a temple to Caesar on the site of the altar set up by Amatius in the Forum. Caesar became a god of the Roman state under the name *Divus Julius*, the Deified Julius. Consequently, Octavian called himself *Divi Filius* ("Son of a God"). Antonius was appointed Caesar's special priest, *flamen*, but realized the old nobility's strong dislike of Caesar's deification. Hoping, perhaps, to deflect some of their anger to Octavian, he delayed being inaugurated until 40 B.C.E.

The Battle of Philippi, 42 B.C.E.

After crushing all resistance in Italy, the triumvirs made war on Brutus and Cassius. Those two had accumulated nineteen legions and had taken up a strong position at Philippi on the Via Egnatia in eastern Macedonia. Their navy dominated the Aegean Sea. Nevertheless, in the fall of 42, Antonius and Octavian, eluding enemy naval patrols, landed their forces. Brutus defeated the less-able Octavian, but Antonius defeated Cassius, who, unaware of Brutus' victory, committed suicide. Instead of letting winter and famine destroy the enemy, Brutus yielded to his impetuous officers and offered battle three weeks later. After a hard and bloody battle, Antonius' superior generalship prevailed. Brutus took his own life.

Antonius, the real victor, received the greatest share of Rome's empire. He took all of the East and the Gallic provinces in the West, although he later gave up Cisalpine Gaul. It was then merged with Italy proper. Lepidus, who was reported to have negotiated secretly with Sextus Pompey while Antonius and Octavian were at Philippi, now began to lose ground. He had to give Narbonese (Transalpine) Gaul to Antonius and the two Spains to Octavian. Still, they allowed him to save himself by conquering North Africa. Octavian returned to deal with problems in Italy and reconquer Sicily and Sardinia, which Sextus Pompey had seized.

Antonius and the East, 42 to 40 B.C.E.

Antonius went to the easternmost provinces to regulate their affairs and raise money promised to the legions. He extracted considerable money from the rich cities of Asia by arranging for nine years' tribute to be paid in two. He also set up or deposed kings as it seemed advantageous to himself and Rome. Finally, in 41, he came to Tarsus in Cilicia, to which he had summoned Cleopatra. She had returned to Egypt from Rome about the time when Brutus and Cassius fled. She needed to protect her kingdom: both the Caesarians and anti-Caesarians would be seeking its resources against each other. She had tried to placate both sides without committing herself openly to either in the struggle that had culminated at Phillipi. Now she needed to convince the chief victor that he could rely on her in the future. She appeared in a splendid barge with silvery oars and purple sails, herself decked out in gorgeous clothes and redolent with exquisite perfumes. It is easy to follow propaganda and legend and see Antonius hopelessly seduced by a sensuous foreign queen. Passion notwithstanding, however, both pursued rational political interests. Each had something to gain by cooperating with the other: Cleopatra, the support of Roman arms against her rivals; Antonius, Egyptian wealth to defray the costs of a projected war against Parthia and rivalry with Octavian. In the meantime (40 B.C.E.), Cleopatra bore him a set of twins (p. 311).

Octavian in Italy vs. Fulvia and L. Antonius, 42 to 41 B.C.E.

Octavian probably realized that Italy was still the key to ultimate control of Rome's empire, despite the problems that awaited him there. The eighteen cities previously earmarked for soldiers' settlement proved inadequate to meet the needs of the 100,000 demobilized veterans who returned with him. The evicted owners angrily protested. Expanded confiscations, including now as many as forty towns, further increased the groundswell of discontent. The populace of Rome was also in a disturbed and angry mood. Sextus Pompey still controlled the seas and began to shut off grain supplies. Discontent, confusion, insecurity, and want threatened the stability of the state. Soldiers and civilians were at each other's throats. At one point, Octavian himself almost suffered violence at the hands of a battling mob.

In 41 B.C.E., intrigue aggravated Octavian's situation. Both Fulvia, Antonius' firebrand wife, and his brother Lucius, one of the consuls, worked to ensure that Antonius' veterans did not forget him even as Octavian was making sure they received their land allotments. At the same time, Lucius was sympathetic to the plight of the displaced landowners. Although Fulvia at first disagreed with Lucius' decision to align the Antonian cause with those opposed to Octavian, (so the story goes) she was persuaded once it was pointed out that Antonius himself might return home from Egypt if war broke out.

The Perusine War, 40 B.C.E.

Despite the repeated efforts of senators and of soldiers on both sides, Octavian and Lucius took up arms. Although all parties wrote to Antonius, it is not clear what his reaction to events in Italy was. Octavian's loyal generals Marcus Vipsanius Agrippa and Quintus

Salvidienus besieged Lucius in the Etruscan hill town of Perusia (Perugia); Fulvia was elsewhere, frantically trying to persuade Antonius' legates to bring aide to Lucius. Two marched from Gaul and got close enough to Perusia that the besieged troops could see the fires in their camps, but Octavian's generals blocked the way. Eventually, starvation forced Lucius to surrender. Although Octavian ruthlessly executed all but one member of Perusia's town council, he spared the lives of Lucius and his troops, and of Fulvia and of Antonius's children. He sent Lucius as governor to Spain, where he soon died. He allowed Fulvia to leave Italy with the children and join her husband.

Because Antonius' remaining legate in the two transalpine Gallic provinces had now died, Octavian sent some of his victorious forces to seize them. The dead legate's son surrendered without a fight, and Agrippa was placed in charge. Now, militarily, Octavian was virtually in charge of all western provinces in Europe.

Still, it was not the end of troubles for Octavian. Pillage, fire, mass executions, and military control of provinces had neither solved his problems nor made him safe from danger. His actions served only to increase hatred and discontent in a land still seething with revolt and held in the grip of famine, turmoil, and despair. The hostile fleets of Sextus Pompey menaced Italy's coasts, assailed the provinces, and interrupted grain shipments.

The Pact of Brundisium, 40 B.C.E.

Octavian, in his extremity, sought accommodation with Sextus. He had divorced Claudia, Fulvia's daughter, in the build-up to the conflict that ended at Perusia. In her stead, he married Scribonia, about ten years older than he. Scribonia's brother was one of Sextus' important political allies and was the father of his wife. Apparently, Octavian was unaware that Sextus was making overtures to Antonius. The latter had been in Egypt while Octavian was fighting his brother and Fulvia. Antonius had learned that the Parthians had overrun Syria, Palestine, and parts of Asia Minor. Not yet prepared to fight the Parthians, Antonius sailed for Greece to confer with Fulvia once she left Italy. Fulvia, who died shortly after their reunion, persuaded him to receive envoys from Sextus Pompey and accept the proffered alliance. Only then did Antonius proceed to Italy to recruit legions for a war against the Parthians.

By previous agreement, Antonius and Octavian were to use Italy as a common recruiting ground. How worthless that agreement was Antonius discovered when he found Brundisium closed against him by Octavian's troops. Frustrated and angry, he besieged the city. Simultaneously, his republican ally, Sextus Pompey, also struck southern Italy. When Octavian appeared at Brundisium to oppose his colleague, Caesar's old legions refused to fight. They fraternized instead. There followed negotiations, conferences, and finally a new agreement known as the Pact of Brundisium, which renewed the triumvirate. A redistribution of provinces added Illyricum to the other provinces that Octavian controlled. Antonius received the East. Lepidus retained Africa. Italy was to remain, theoretically at least, a common recruiting ground for all three. To seal the pact, Antonius married Octavia, the freshly widowed sister of Octavian. The covenant between the two powerful rivals filled Italy with hopes of peace.

The hopes were premature. Sextus Pompey believed that Antonius had played him false. He threatened Rome with famine. Taxes, high prices, and food shortages provoked riots. The people clamored for bread and peace. When Antonius and Octavian prepared to attack Sextus, popular reaction forced them to negotiate with him. Sextus' mother, Pompey the Great's ex-wife Mucia, played a crucial role in setting up the negotiations.

The Treaty of Misenum, 39 B.C.E.

At Misenum (near Naples) in the autumn of 39 B.C.E., the triumvirs met with Sextus Pompey, argued, bargained, and banqueted. They agreed to let him retain Sicily and Sardinia, which he had already seized and gave him Corsica and the Peloponnesus as well. They also allowed him compensation for his father's confiscated lands and promised him a future augurate and consulship. In return, he agreed to end his blockade of Italy, supply Rome with grain, and halt his piracy on the high seas.

The position of Octavian was improving. The Roman populace and Caesar's veterans favored him. Moreover, time was on his side. Years of Antonius' absence in the East would cause his influence to wane in the West.

The predominance of Antonius, 39 to 37 B.C.E.

For the present, however, the West looked bright to Antonius. His influence was especially strong among the senatorial and equestrian orders, old-line republicans, and most men of property throughout Italy. Sextus Pompey would surely counter the growing power of Octavian—so thought Antonius as he and Octavia set out for Athens. He spent two winters enjoying domestic happiness and the culture of that old university town. From there, he directed Ventidius Bassus and Herod (client king of Judea since 40 B.C.E.) to drive out Parthian invaders from Syria, Palestine, and Asia Minor.

By not offering battle except from advantageous positions on high ground, Ventidius negated the Parthian strength in archers and cataphracts (mail-clad cavalry). He shattered the Parthian forces in three great battles and rolled them back to the Euphrates. There he wisely stopped. Antonius, however, made plans to subjugate the Parthians completely and avenge Crassus' defeat at Carrhae. In 37 B.C.E., Antonius sent another of his commanders to pacify Armenia, on Parthia's northern flank. New troubles in the West, however, compelled Antonius to postpone his invasion of Parthia.

Livia strengthens Octavian in the West, 39 and 38 B.C.E.

The Treaty of Misenum had brought Italy peace and a brief respite from piracy, shore raids, and famine. To Octavian, it meant even greater benefits: republican aristocrats of ancient lineage, allies worth his while to court and win, returned home. The peace was of short duration, however. Sextus Pompey was upset with Antonius' delay in handing over the Peloponnesus and generally felt slighted by the triumvirs. He resumed the blockade of Italy later in 39. War threatened again, and Pompey's ill-will grew when Octavian suddenly divorced Scribonia. For love and politics, Octavian promptly married Livia Drusilla (58 B.C.E.–29 C.E.). She was young, beautiful, rich, politically astute, and anxious to secure the future prominence of her family and her children. She was also hugely pregnant with her second son by her first husband, Tiberius Claudius Nero, who had fought against Octavian at Perusia. Now, both he and Livia decided to pin their families' futures on Octavian. By mutual consent, the two divorced in 39 B.C.E. Octavian obtained a ruling from the pontiffs that he and Livia could become betrothed right away. They married in January of 38, once Livia gave birth. Octavian had been so anxious to pursue an advantageous union with Livia that he had divorced Scribonia on the very day that she bore him his only child, Julia, whom he would later use in numerous dynastic marriages. Although Livia bore him no children (there was a still-birth), she became one of Octavian's most trusted advisors. He consulted her at every major turn for the rest of his life.

FIGURE 17.1 Livia, wife of Octavian and future empress.

Octavian's marriage to Livia and the noble connections that she secured through her connections to the Claudian *gens* through her father and her first husband helped to broaden Octavian's support among leading senators and to undermine that of Antonius. At the same time, Octavian's origin from an equestrian family of Italian background was an asset against the noble-born Antonius. Octavian cultivated friends among the *equites*, who had long resented the exclusivity of the old republican nobility. From this class came two of his most loyal and important supporters: the wealthy patron of the arts who helped to mold public opinion in his favor, Gaius Cilnius Maecenas, and the architect of many of his military victories, Marcus Vipsanius Agrippa. Moreover, Octavian won strong support in the countryside of Italy, from which Roman armies were recruited.

War with Sextus Pompey, 38 B.C.E.

In 38, Octavian determined to destroy Sextus Pompey once and for all. He scored an initial coup when Pompey's traitorous governor of Sardinia defected with his province. Nevertheless, a little later that year, Octavian attempted an invasion of Sicily. It was a fiasco. Pompey destroyed two of his fleets. These reverses compelled Octavian to recall the indispensable Agrippa from Gaul and to invoke the aid of Antonius. The latter was angry at Octavian for going to war contrary to his advice and for causing a delay in his own campaign against the Parthians. Still, he loyally left Athens with a large fleet and came to his aid.

The Treaty of Tarentum and defeat of Sextus Pompey, 37 and 36 B.C.E.

The two triumvirs, resentful and suspicious of each other, met at Tarentum in 37. Through the patient diplomacy of Maecenas and the influence of Octavia, they concluded the Treaty of Tarentum. It renewed their triumvirate, which had lapsed on December 31, 38 B.C.E., for another five years. Octavian betrothed his two-year-old daughter, Julia, to Antyllus, Antonius' older son by Fulvia. In exchange for the 120 ships that Antonius now contributed to the war against Sextus Pompey, Octavian promised 20,000 Roman soldiers for service in the East. Antonius never got them. In an amphibious attack on Sicily, Octavian suffered a crippling defeat, but Agrippa crushed Pompey in a great naval battle at Naulochus, near the Straits of Messana. Sextus barely escaped to Asia Minor.

The downfall of Lepidus, 36 B.C.E.

Octavian had already overcome one rival, and soon he would another. Lepidus had come to reclaim his province of Sicily with twenty-two legions. Hungry for glory, he insisted on accepting the surrender of the island in person. When Octavian objected, Lepidus ordered him out of the province. Bearing the magic name of Caesar, Octavian boldly entered the camp of Lepidus and persuaded his legions to desert. Then he stripped Lepidus of any real power and committed him to comfortable confinement at the lovely seaside town of Circeii in Latium. Lepidus, still *pontifex maximus*, wisely lived there peaceably for another twenty-four years.

The triumphant return of Octavian, 36 B.C.E.

Rome joyously welcomed home the victorious Octavian. He had ended civil wars in the West, restored the freedom of the seas, and liberated Rome from the danger of famine. Although he had helped crush the liberty of the old nobility, he now brought the blessing of strong, ordered government to a populace exhausted by civil war. For his part, he gave vague promises of a future restoration of the civil state (*res publica*). People heaped honors upon him, even adoration and divine epithets. Statues of him were placed in Italian temples; a golden one was set up in the Roman Forum, and he received the sacrosanctity of a plebeian tribune in addition to the military title of *Imperator Caesar*, which he had previously usurped.

ANTONIUS AND CLEOPATRA RULE THE EAST, 37 TO 32 B.C.E.

Antonius had been tricked into spending the better part of two years helping Octavian win mastery of the West while he gained nothing. In 37 B.C.E., he returned to the East, to which he henceforth committed himself fully in order to secure his independent power. Later that year, his commitment was strikingly symbolized by a public ceremony with Cleopatra at Antioch. That act was not a marriage in any Roman sense, and he did not divorce Octavia. She was too politically valuable, and her status as his legitimate wife was not threatened by his liaison with a noncitizen.

By becoming co-ruler of the only remaining independent successor state of Alexander the Great's empire, Antonius was able to lay legitimate claim to that empire, much of which the Parthians controlled. This relationship also allowed Antonius to manipulate popular religious ideas to his advantage. He had already sought favor with the Greeks by proclaiming himself to be Dionysus, the divine conqueror of Asia in Greek mythology. Now, for the Greeks, he and Cleopatra became the divine pair, Dionysus and Aphrodite. To the native Egyptians, they appeared as Osiris and Isis.

The religio-political significance of their relationship is also revealed by Antonius' public acknowledgment and renaming of the twins whom Cleopatra had previously borne to him. They became Alexander Helios (Sun) and Cleopatra Selene (Moon). The choice of Alexander as part of the boy's name clearly shows the attempt to lay legitimate claim to Alexander the Great's old empire. The names of Helios and Selene had powerful religious implications for his and Cleopatra's political positions. According to Greek belief, the Age of Gold was connected with the sun deity. In some Egyptian myths, Isis (the role claimed by Cleopatra) was mother of the sun. By the Greeks, she was equated with the moon. Finally, the Parthian king bore the title *Brother of the Sun and Moon*, who were powerful deities in the native religion. Accordingly, Antonius probably was identifying these potent Parthian symbols with himself in order to strengthen his anticipated position as king of conquered Parthia.

Reorganization of eastern territories

In the past, the client kingdoms of the East had owed allegiance not to Rome but to their patron, Pompey the Great. The Parthian invasion had clearly revealed the weakness of their relationship to Rome. Antonius did not disturb the provinces of Asia, Bithynia, and Roman Syria, but he assigned the rest of the eastern territories to four client kings. They were dependent on Rome yet strong enough by means of their heavily armed and mail-clad cavalry to guard their frontiers against invasion.

To Cleopatra, he gave part of Syria along the coast, Cyprus, and some cities in Cilicia, territories not more extensive than those given to others but immensely rich. Antonius firmly rejected her demand for Judea, the kingdom of Herod I, although he did give her Herod's valuable balsam gardens at Jericho. Cleopatra had now regained control over much of what Ptolemaic Egypt had ruled at its height under Ptolemy II Philadelphus (283–246 B.C.E.). She emphasized this point by naming the son whom she bore to Antonius in 36 B.C.E. Ptolemy Philadelphus.

The Parthian campaign and its aftermath, 36 to 35 B.C.E.

Antonius' strengthened ties to Cleopatra in 37 had greatly bolstered his position in the reorganized East as he prepared for his major invasion of Parthia. He was, however, neither subservient to her nor dependent upon the financial resources of Egypt at that point. He prepared his expedition with the resources of the Roman East and embarked upon it against the advice of Cleopatra in 36. He should have listened to her. The expedition was a disaster. King Artavasdes II of Armenia, pursuing his own interests, withdrew his support from Antonius at a critical point. Antonius lost his supplies and 20,000 men.

Despite his losses, Antonius was still strong in the East and the dominant partner in a divided empire. He also had considerable popular support remaining in Italy and an impressive following among the senators, including Caesarians, Pompeians, and such staunch republicans as Cn. Domitius Ahenobarbus, Cato's grandson L. Calpurnius Bibulus, and several other kinsmen of Cato and Brutus. Nevertheless, the defeat in Parthia and, as a result, his increasing dependence on Cleopatra's resources provided plenty of fuel for Octavian's propaganda machine. Octavian refused to send the four legions that he had promised in the Treaty of Tarentum (p. 310). Also, he returned only the 70 ships surviving from the 120 that Antonius had lent him against Sextus Pompey. Even Sextus tried to take advantage of Antonius' Parthian defeat by attacking Asia Minor, where he was finally captured and killed in 35.

The importance of Octavia, 35 to 32 B.C.E.

Octavia remained intensely loyal to Antonius, despite his liaison with Cleopatra. She set out with a large store of supplies and 2000 fresh troops to aid her husband in the spring of 35. At Athens, a message from Antonius ordered her to return to Rome but still send on the troops and supplies. It was a bitter blow. Yet, she quietly obeyed.

Antonius restored his tattered military laurels by conquering Armenia in 34. While Octavia dutifully looked after his interests in Rome, Antonius spent the winter of 33 and 32 with Cleopatra in Ephesus to reinforce his position in the East. Then he carried off King Artavasdes to Egypt and celebrated an extraordinary triumph at Alexandria. In a ceremony known as the Donations of Alexandria, he gave Cleopatra and her children additional territories and recognized Cleopatra as supreme overlord of all eastern client kingdoms. She soon asserted her authority by having Artavasdes executed.

THE APPROACH AND RENEWAL OF CIVIL WAR, 32 TO 30 B.C.E.

Meanwhile, the prospect of war loomed larger. Octavian had built up his forces and military reputation with a successful campaign in Illyricum. Several of his generals also earned triumphs in Spain and Africa. Still, it would not be easy for even so crafty a politician as Octavian to go to war against Antonius. The latter, with both consuls of 32 B.C.E. and half the senate on his side, was elected consul for 31. To prove Antonius a menace to Rome was difficult. Cleopatra, however, was more vulnerable. She was portrayed as a detestable foreign queen plotting to make herself empress of the world. Antonius was made to seem only her doting dupe.

The breach between the two triumvirs constantly widened. Each hurled recriminations against the other, charges of broken promises, family scandal, and private vices. Poets, orators, lampoonists, and pamphleteers entered the fray at the expense of truth and justice. Both protagonists, just like Pompey and Caesar, were too proud to tolerate the appearance of backing down before each other. Truth lies buried beneath a thick, hard crust of defamation, lies, and political mythology. Had Antonius instead of Octavian won the eventual civil war, the official characterizations of the protagonists would have been equally fraudulent but utterly different. Antonius would have been depicted as a sober statesman and a loving husband and father, not a sex-crazed slave of Cleopatra; the savior of the Republic, not a tyrant striving to subject the liberties of the Roman People to Eastern despotism.

Earlier, Antonius had sent the two friendly consuls of 32 B.C.E. dispatches requesting the senate's confirmation of all his acts in the East and his donations to Cleopatra and her children. He even promised, for propaganda purposes, to resign from the triumvirate and restore the Republic. Fearing serious repercussions from the first two items, the two consuls withheld the contents of the dispatch, but one roundly condemned Octavian in a bitter speech in the senate. A few weeks later, Octavian appeared before the senate with an armed bodyguard. He denounced Antonius and dismissed the senate. The consuls and perhaps more than 300 senators fled from Rome to Antonius at Ephesus.

The divorce of Octavia and the will of Antonius

By early summer, Antonius and Cleopatra had moved their huge armada across the Aegean to Athens. Antonius probably realized that if he was to have the support of the eastern populace and the forces they provided, he needed to show his full commitment to them. Finally, then, he sent Octavia a letter of divorce. Some of Antonius' allies had begun to have doubts as his cause became more and more dependent on the East and Cleopatra. Divorcing Octavia was the last straw for the ever-foresighted survivor L. Munatius Plancus. To ingratiate himself with Octavian, he brought a precious gift, the knowledge that Antonius had deposited his last will and testament with the Vestal Virgins. Octavian promptly and illegally extorted it from them. He read it at the next meeting of the senate. The will allegedly confirmed the legacies to Cleopatra's children, declared that her son Caesarion was a true son and successor of Julius Caesar, and provided for Antonius' burial beside Cleopatra in the Ptolemaic mausoleum at Alexandria. Genuine or fraudulently altered, the will gave Octavian his greatest propaganda victory.

Octavian declares war, 32 B.C.E.

Capitalizing on popular revulsion against Antonius, Octavian now resolved to mobilize the power of the West against the East. By various means, he contrived to secure an oath of personal allegiance from the municipalities first of Italy and then of the western provinces. Fortified by this somewhat spurious popular mandate, he obtained a declaration stripping Antonius of his current *imperium* and upcoming consulship for 31 B.C.E. Late in the fall of 32 B.C.E., to avoid the appearance of initiating another civil war of Roman against Roman, war was declared on Cleopatra. Octavian then spent the winter in preparation for a spring offensive.

Meanwhile, Antonius and Cleopatra had not been idle. Toward the end of 32 B.C.E., they set up camp at Actium, at the entrance to the Ambracian Gulf. There lay the main part of their fleet. Antonius seemed much stronger than his foe. He was an excellent general and commanded an army numerically equal in both infantry and cavalry to that of Octavian. He also had one of the biggest and strongest fleets the ancient world had yet seen. His weakness, however, overbalanced his strength. Although most legionaries admired Antonius as a man and soldier, they hated war against fellow citizens. His Roman officers detested Cleopatra and privately cursed Antonius for not being man enough to send her back to Egypt.

The Battle of Actium, September 2, 31 B.C.E.

Marcus Agrippa, Octavian's second in command, had set up a blockade that caused a severe famine and an outbreak of plague in Antonius' camp during the summer of 31. Antonius' commanders were divided and quarreling among themselves; his troops were paralyzed by treason and desertions. Apparently, he and Cleopatra decided to make a strategic retreat. While they took only the faster, oared ships and broke out of the bay, the rest of the army, it seems, was to retreat overland to Asia Minor. Cleopatra's squadron of sixty ships got clean away, and Antonius managed to follow with a few of his ships. The rest became too involved with those of Agrippa, who sailed out to block them. Antonius' men soon surrendered. Octavian's victory was so complete that he felt no immediate need to pursue the fugitives to Egypt. He turned his attention to mutinous legions in Italy instead and recrossed the Adriatic to appease their demands for land and money.

The last days of Antonius and Cleopatra, 30 B.C.E.

In the summer of 30 B.C.E., Octavian, now desperate for money, finally went to Egypt. The legions of Antonius put up only brief resistance. Alexandria surrendered. Cleopatra's son Caesarion and Antonius' son Antyllus were quickly murdered. Antonius committed suicide. A few days later, Cleopatra followed, arousing joy, relief, and even grudging admiration among Romans like the poet Horace (*Odes*, Book 1.37). Thus passed the last of the Ptolemies, a dynasty that had ruled Egypt for almost 300 years. Egypt became part of the Roman Empire. Octavian was now undisputed master of the Mediterranean World.

THE END OF THE REPUBLIC

After 30 B.C.E., the forms of the Republic's political institutions, which shared power among the citizen assemblies, collegiate magistracies, and senate of aristocratic equals, would still remain. In reality, power had become concentrated in the hands of one man, the total antithesis of republicanism. From 29 B.C.E. onward, Octavian would shrewdly manipulate those forms while turning himself into Augustus, Rome's first emperor, and ending the Republic forever.

Many reasons have been offered to explain why the Republic collapsed. Ancient authors like Sallust, Cicero, and Plutarch offered moral explanations that modern historians have often favored: having conquered most of the Mediterranean world, the Romans no longer had the fear of external enemies to restrain them; they lost their old virtues and self-discipline through the debilitating influences of the alien cultures to which they had become exposed; great wealth and power corrupted them. Some modern historians have seen the Republic's fall primarily as the work of Julius Caesar in supposedly single-minded pursuit of a long-planned monarchic design or mystical sense of destiny.

Others have seen the problem primarily in institutional terms: the institutions of a small agrarian-based city-state were inadequate for coping with the great problems that came with vast overseas expansion. Some, however, would argue that there can be no general explanation for the Republic's fall. It was essentially an accident: the Republic had weathered the upheavals from the Gracchi to Sulla; it had made the necessary adjustments to changed conditions while maintaining its basic character; it was functioning quite normally and would have continued to do so if two egotistical, stubborn, and miscalculating men had not chanced to precipitate the civil war that destroyed it.

None of these explanations is adequate. To a certain extent, all history is accident, but that does not mean that important general causes cannot be found. To understand how the Republic finally came to an end, one must look at the outbreak of the particular civil war that destroyed it in the context of general, long-term social, economic, political, and cultural developments (described in Chapters 10 and 18).

Those who emphasize the inadequacy of the old Republic's institutions for coping with the new problems of a vast empire have an important point. Institutions that arise from or are designed for a particular set of circumstances will eventually cease to function satisfactorily under radically altered circumstances. For example, the old eighteenth-century New England town-meeting form of government is totally impractical in twenty-first-century Boston. Old institutions may be modified and adapted up to a point and remain basically the same. Still, that process can be carried only so far before they are transformed into something quite different. After 400 years of change, the British monarchy of Queen Elizabeth II is not the same as that of Elizabeth I.

Similarly, after 200 years, the old Roman republican system had ceased to work. Minor modifications had not helped to preserve it. Increased numbers of lower magistrates increased the intensity of the competition for the annual consulships, which remained fixed at two. Annually elected consuls were not capable of waging long-term overseas wars and governing distant provinces in alien lands. Using practically independent promagistrates and extraordinary commanders, often with extended terms of duty, to handle these problems was dangerous. It gave individuals unprecedented amounts of economic, political, and military power. They could then overcome normal constraints and destroy the equilibrium within the ruling elite that had kept the old system in balance. The tremendous social and economic changes accompanying 200 years of imperialism had also greatly altered the composition of the popular assemblies. They became more susceptible to ambitious and/or idealistic manipulators pursuing personal advantage over their peers, the alleviation of legitimate grievances, or both. Sulla's attempt to restore the old system in the face of changed conditions had merely doomed it to failure.

Still, institutional inadequacies in the face of changed conditions do not wholly explain the fall of the Roman Republic. Institutions do not exist or function apart from the people who control them. The character, abilities, and behavioral patterns of the people who run vital institutions do have a bearing on how well those institutions function under given circumstances. For example, during the Great Depression, the American presidency was not an effective instrument of popular leadership under Herbert Hoover, but it was under Franklin Roosevelt, no matter how one judges the ultimate worth of his policies. Therefore, individual leaders like Julius Caesar are important. Although he was not pursuing any mystical sense of destiny or long-meditated monarchic ambitions, he did have particular personality traits such as self-assurance, decisiveness, and unconventionality that made him particularly successful in the political and military competition destroying the Republic.

Nevertheless, individual differences should not be overemphasized. Caesar was operating within a general cultural context. It shaped his thoughts and actions in ways that were typical of men like Pompey, Crassus, Catiline, Clodius, Cato, Curio, Brutus, Antonius, and Octavian. They were all deeply concerned with the personal *gloria*, *dignitas*, and *auctoritas* that were the most highly valued prizes of their era. In the early Roman Republic, the great emphasis on and competition for *gloria*, *dignitas*, and *auctoritas* produced generations of leaders who eagerly defended the state against hostile neighbors; expanded Roman territory to satisfy a land-hungry population; and ably served the state as priests, magistrates, and senators. So long as Rome expanded within the relatively narrow and homogeneous confines of Italy, there was little opportunity for aristocratic competition at Rome to get out of hand; the values that fueled it were reinforced; and the highly desired stability of the state was maintained. These same values then contributed to overseas expansion along with accompanying disruptive changes at home. Both developments made it possible for individual aristocrats to acquire disproportionate resources for competing with their peers. In eagerly seeking those resources in accordance with long-held values, Roman aristocrats raised their competition to levels destructive to the very Republic that they cherished.

SUGGESTED READING

Goldsworthy, A. *Antony and Cleopatra.* New Haven and London: Yale University Press, 2010.

Osgood, J. *Caesar's Legacy: Civil War and the Emergence of the Roman Empire.* Cambridge: Cambridge University Press, 2006.

Welch, K. *Magnus Pius: Sextus Pompeius and the Transformation of the Roman Republic. Roman culture in an age of civil war.* Swansea: Classical Press of Wales, 2012.

CHAPTER 18

Social, economic, and cultural life in the late Republic, ca. 133 to ca. 30 B.C.E.

The political turmoil that began with the Gracchi was matched by continued social, economic, and cultural ferment. In the countryside of Italy, the problems that had contributed to the Gracchan crisis were often made worse by the series of domestic wars inaugurated by the Social War in 90 B.C.E. The provinces suffered from the ravages of war, both civil and foreign, and from frequently inept or corrupt administration. In Rome and Italy, people's values and behavior changed as the old social fabric frayed. The *mos maiorum* lost its strength, the state's cults suffered neglect during civil upheavals, and new religious influences from the Hellenistic East gained in popularity. Nowhere, however, was change more evident than in art and literature. Creative, thoughtful individuals responded to the social, economic, and political turmoil with new attitudes, forms, and concepts that mark the late Republic as a period of great creativity as well as crisis.

LAND, VETERANS, AND RURAL LIFE

Whatever success Gracchan land-redistribution legislation may have had in the late 100s B.C.E., the problems that it sought to alleviate in Italy were just as bad throughout much of the first century B.C.E. The forces that had impoverished many small farmers earlier still existed, and facts do not support the thesis that, beginning with Marius, powerful generals largely solved the problem by enrolling landless men in their armies and providing them with land upon discharge. That land was often taken from other smallholders. Those who received it frequently, in turn, lost it from a combination of economic, demographic, and political factors. Large-scale, long-term settlements in the provinces had to wait until after 30 B.C.E. when the civil wars of the Republic finally ceased.

Until then, instead of receiving their own land to farm, a number of landless or indebted peasants became free tenants, *coloni*, on great estates. This trend is evident primarily in central and southern Italy, where the great estates were concentrated and where the danger of rebellion among large concentrations of slaves had been emphasized by the revolt of Spartacus. Some owners, therefore, found it safer and more productive to settle *coloni* as cultivators on part of their land in return for a yearly rent.

Despite all the problems facing small farmers, many did survive. In the rural districts of interior Italy, small independent farmers still concentrated primarily on the cultivation of grain, whose surplus production could be sold in nearby towns. Near large towns and cities, specialized production for urban markets remained profitable. The great estates continued to specialize in raising sheep, cattle, and pigs to supply wool, hides, and meat for urban markets and Roman armies, or in the growing of grapes for wine and olives for oil.

Wealthy landowners also began to experiment with more exotic crops for either profit or ostentatious display on their own tables. Many large estates were turned into hunting preserves to supply their owners with choice wild game, and seaside properties became famous for their ponds of eels, mullet, and other marine delicacies.

In the western provinces, landowners in Sicily and North Africa intensified the production of grain for export to the insatiable Roman market. Italian immigrants in Spain and southern Gaul were establishing olive groves, vineyards, and orchards that would eventually capture the provincial markets of the exporters in Italy. The rural economy in the eastern provinces, however, was severely depressed as a result of the devastation, confiscations, and indemnities resulting from the Mithridatic wars and the civil wars of the 40s and 30s.

INDUSTRY AND COMMERCE

Manufacturing and trade in the East had also been severely disrupted by the wars of the late Republic. Many Italian merchants and moneylenders in Asia Minor lost their wealth and their lives in the uprising spurred by Mithridates in 88 B.C.E. Delos, which the Romans had made a free port to undercut Rhodes in 167/166, never recovered from being sacked in 88 and 69. When commerce did revive between the Levant and Italy, it was largely in the hands of Syrian and Alexandrian traders, who maintained sizable establishments at Puteoli to serve Rome and Italy. Italians, however, dominated the western trade, particularly the export of grain from Africa and Sicily and the exchange of Italian wine, pottery, and metalwork across the Alps in return for silver and slaves.

Two of Italy's most important industries, the production of bronze goods and ceramic tableware, were concentrated respectively at Capua in Campania and Arretium in Etruria. Capua produced fine bronze cooking utensils, jugs, lamps, candelabra, and implements for the markets of Italy and northern Europe. Using molds, the Arretine potters specialized in the mass manufacture of red, highly glazed, embossed plates and bowls known as *terra sigillata*, or Samian ware. It enjoyed great popularity all over the western provinces, which eventually set up rival manufacturing centers of their own.

The copper mines of Etruria were becoming exhausted in terms of the prevailing techniques of exploitation, but the slack was more than taken up by production in Spain, where private contractors operated the mines on lease from the state. Tin, which was alloyed with copper to form bronze, was imported from Cornwall in the British Isles along a trade route that had been opened up by the father of Marcus Crassus during his governorship of Spain in 96 B.C.E.

Several factors limited economic growth: the low level of ancient technology in the production and transportation of goods, the extensive use of slave labor, and the extremely uneven distribution of wealth. They hampered development of large-scale industries and mass markets that would have provided high levels of steady, full-time employment for wage laborers. Rather, Rome and other large cities like Capua, Puteoli, and Brundisium were the domain of the *taberna* (home plus retail shop) or the *officina* (workshop) and small individual proprietors, both men and women (pp. 329–30). Helped by family members and a slave or two, the shopkeeper would carry on the retail sale of particular types of food, goods, or services or engage in the specialized production of goods on a handicraft basis. Goods might also be sold at retail on the premises or at wholesale in batches to a merchant who would consolidate them for bulk shipment elsewhere or peddle them individually in smaller towns that could not support a local retailer or producer.

Specific trades were often concentrated in certain streets or neighborhoods. At Rome, for example, there were the Street of the Sickle Makers and the Forum Vinarium, where the wine merchants gathered. In that way, it was easy for merchants and craftsmen to exchange information of mutual interest, receive materials, and be accessible to customers looking for what they sold or produced.

In Rome and Italy, the building trades flourished. Sulla, Pompey, and Caesar used the spoils of war to finance many public works in Rome. Wealthy nobles covered the Palatine with sumptuous townhouses. Elsewhere in the city, speculators put up huge blocks of flimsy, multistoried apartment buildings, *insulae*, to house a population probably nearing a million (if we include the outlying suburbs) by 30 B.C.E., despite attempts to reduce it.

Some of the lower-class freedmen or freeborn tradespeople and craftworkers could acquire significant wealth and property. People who produced or sold luxury goods for the wealthy in their *tabernae* and *officinae* were very successful. Some owned several shops in their specialties around the city of Rome. People who dealt in gold and silver jewelry, pearls, precious stones, perfumes, luxury furniture, and artwork were quite prosperous. One large-scale baker named M. Vergilius Eurysaces was so successful that

FIGURE 18.1 Pompeii, the Street of Abundance, with workshops and stores.

when he died, around 30 B.C.E., he left for himself and his wife, Atistia, one of the largest and most impressive funeral monuments still in existence from ancient Rome (see Figure 18.2). On it, the couple commemorated all aspects of commercial bread-making in a handsomely sculpted frieze. A freedman named Q. Caecilius Spendo, who specialized in making cheap clothes, built a tomb large enough to include eighteen of his own ex-slaves along with him and his wife.

Other than war, the business that still produced the biggest profits was finance, both public and private. The numerous annexations in Asia Minor greatly expanded the business of tax farming, which was carried on by companies of *publicani* (p. 186). Money lending was an important source of profits to wealthy financiers. Often, provincial cities needed to borrow money to pay the *publicani*, or client kings needed loans to stay solvent after paying huge sums to obtain Roman support for their thrones. With interest rates as high as 24 or 48 percent, even the greatest nobles were tempted to exploit this source of revenue. Pompey loaned some of the huge fortune that he had acquired in the East to Ariobarzanes II, whom he had confirmed as king of Cappadocia. In 52 B.C.E., Cicero was shocked to learn that Marcus Brutus was the Roman who indirectly pressured him to use his power as governor of Cilicia to force the Cypriot city of Salamis to make payment on an illegal loan at 48 percent interest.

On the other hand, there were many lenders, mostly well-to-do *equites*, who engaged in the more normal business of advancing money to merchants and shipowners to finance trade or to Roman aristocrats to finance their careers. One of these men was Cicero's confidant, publisher, and banker, T. Pomponius Atticus. Although they were heavily engaged in business, they shared the basic outlook of the landed aristocracy and used much of their profits to invest in land and live like gentlemen. For example, vast estates acquired in Epirus allowed Atticus to spend the turbulent years from 88 to 65 at Athens (hence his cognomen, Atticus), where he was safe from Rome's political storms. When he returned to Rome, he patronized the arts and literature from his

FIGURE 18.2 The funeral monument of M. Vergilius Eurysaces, a wholesale miller and baker of late Republic or early Augustan times. The various operations of milling and baking are depicted in the bas-reliefs at the top.

house on the Quirinal. He made so many important contacts that he was protected on all sides during the subsequent civil wars.

THE CONCENTRATION OF WEALTH

Atticus, with his great wealth, illustrates one of the striking features of the late Republic: the concentration of wealth in a few upper-class hands and the ever-widening gap between rich and poor. This trend had already been evident since at least the time of the Punic Wars. It was greatly accelerated by Marius' and Sulla's introduction of proscription. In times of civil war, those on the winning side, or at least not on the losing side, could acquire the property of proscribed individuals at a mere fraction of its normal value, either through favoritism or because the sudden increase in property for sale temporarily depressed prices. When property values rose with the return of normalcy, their net worth increased enormously. For example, Marcus Crassus had inherited a relatively modest fortune of 300 talents upon the deaths of his father and brother in the civil war of 87. After siding with Sulla in 83, however, he took advantage of Sulla's proscriptions in order to acquire valuable properties. Then, through shrewd management, he increased his wealth still further, so that his vast real-estate holdings alone were worth more than 7000 talents in 55 B.C.E.

The profits of war and imperial administration that accrued to the nobility were even greater. Despite his failure to defeat Mithridates totally, Lucullus had amassed enough wealth from Asia Minor to live like a king in numerous villas after his recall to Italy. He became so famous for his conspicuous consumption that the term *Lucullian* has come to characterize rich living. The wealth acquired by Pompey and Caesar during their respective conquests in the East and Gaul made them far wealthier than even Crassus. His only hope of matching them was to conquer the wealthy empire of Parthia.

Provincial governors often abused their power in order to amass personal fortunes to compete with their aristocratic rivals for high office and social status. Verres, the notorious governor of Sicily from 73 to 71 (pp. 260–1), was reported to have said that the illegal gains of his first year were to pay off the debts that he had incurred in running for his praetorship of 74, those of the second year were to bribe the jury to acquit him of his crimes, and those of the third were for himself. Significantly, the artworks that he had plundered from Sicily were said to have earned him a place on Antonius' proscription list in 43. Even an honest governor, such as Cicero had been in Cilicia in 52, was able to profit handsomely from office. In addition, though a man of relatively modest means among the Roman nobility, Cicero had prospered through inheritances, gifts, and favorable loans from other nobles whom he defended in court. He was able to buy a townhouse on the Palatine for 3.5 million sesterces and at least eight well-appointed country villas. He, too, of course, lost them along with his life in the proscriptions of 43.

LIFE FOR THE URBAN POOR

As an imperial city, Rome acquired a more and more diverse population through voluntary immigration and the importation of slaves from all over the Mediterranean world. Some ended up doing very well. Most joined the hundreds of thousands who toiled in anonymity. The luckier ones might have been able to afford to live in some of the better *insulae* that were being built with concrete, which had been introduced in the second century (p. 195). Still, even these *insulae* were often ill-lit, poorly ventilated, and unsanitary. In fact, overall health conditions in a large preindustrial city like Rome were such that it could not have expanded or even maintained the number of its inhabitants without a constant high level of immigration.

Although there were large numbers of artisans and shopkeepers, there were even more unskilled and semi-skilled people. They had to rely on occasional employment as day workers on construction projects, on the docks, and in odd jobs like porterage and message-carrying for the more fortunate. As clients of the rich, many of the poor were helped by gifts of food (*sportulae*) and occasional distributions of money (*congiaria*). Public festivals and triumphs could also produce helpful bonuses. Crassus, for example, feasted the whole city of Rome to celebrate his victory over Spartacus and gave each Roman citizen a three months' supply of grain. The public distribution of free grain to several hundred thousand Roman citizens also helped to keep prices reasonable for those who had to buy all of their grain. Since it was limited to adult men, however, it was not enough to sustain their families. The distribution of free grain was not based on need. Grain went to all of those who met basic citizenship and residency requirements, even the rich. Many poor inhabitants of Rome and Italy received no free grain. For them, hunger must have been a constant threat.

Fire, flood, and violence

Life in the cities, particularly Rome, was precarious in other ways, too. There was no public fire department to control the numerous fires that swept through crowded slums. There was no systematic effort to prevent the Tiber from flooding the low-lying, usually poor neighborhoods. Nor was there a police force to prevent the crime and violence that poverty and crowded conditions bred. Private associations might try to provide local protection. Some wealthy individuals earned popularity by maintaining private fire brigades, as Crassus is believed to have done and as did a certain Egnatius Rufus later. The rich surrounded themselves with private bodyguards when they traversed the city, especially at night. The poor had to rely mainly on their own efforts or those of family and friends to protect themselves or secure justice from those who committed crimes against them. The principle of self-help was still widely applied. There was no public prosecutor, and the courts, with their cumbersome procedures, were mainly for the rich (pp. 204–5).

Politically inspired violence also increased greatly in late republican Rome. The most notable examples, of course, are the civil wars and proscriptions, during which many thousands were killed. Increasingly, however, important trials, political meetings (*contiones*), elections, and legislative meetings of the assemblies were marred by violence. Rival politicians hired gangs to intimidate and harass each other (p. 280).

Public entertainments

As a result of elite political competition and the availability of greater resources, public entertainments at Rome became more numerous, more elaborate, and more violent during the late Republic. These entertainments were associated with various public religious festivals of the Roman year (pp. 66–7), special celebrations, and funerals. During the Republic, the aediles became responsible for presenting games, *ludi*, at major public festivals. There were two types: *ludi scaenici*, which involved the presentations of plays and pantomime dances accompanied by flutes, and *ludi circenses*, which consisted of chariot races in a circus built for that purpose. The aediles received some public funds but increasingly sought popularity for election to higher office by lavish additional expenditures of their own. They even provided such extras as exotic-beast hunts (*venationes*) and gladiatorial combats, which wealthy families often put on at the funerals of prominent members.

Supplying wild beasts and gladiators for entertainments at Rome required big operations. The hunting, trapping, shipping, and handling of wild beasts involved complicated networks of suppliers and agents. Enterprising men set up training schools, like the one from which Spartacus escaped (pp. 258–9), to turn promising slaves and volunteers into professional fighters whom they provided on contract for gladiatorial shows. Gladiators fought according to strict regulations regarding equipment and rules of combat. Contrary to modern belief, they did not usually fight to the death unless the sponsor was willing to pay a hefty premium for the privilege of wasting what were valuable professional athletes. Like modern athletes, they developed followings of loyal fans who often showered them with money that allowed them eventually to buy their freedom and retire as wealthy men if they lived long enough.

The same was true of the charioteers who raced in the *ludi circenses*. There were usually four competing in each race. In the late Republic, the people in charge of the games would hire the charioteers, the horses, and the chariots from four different groups organized for that purpose. The groups came to be known as factions (Latin, *factiones*), and each one distinguished itself by a special color—red, white, blue, or green. In a society where the urban poor often led idle and frustrating lives, the circus races aroused intense interest. Daredevil driving and deaths in spectacular crashes rivaled modern automobile races, and there was always the chance to make a little money by betting on the winner. The restless and bored attached themselves to individual factions, wearing their faction's distinctive color, cheered their favorites, and sometimes fought with each other in brawls.

Voluntary associations

To obtain some measure of protection and comfort in the violent, disease-ridden, and unpredictable world of the *tabernae* and *insulae*, the lower classes of Rome and other cities organized themselves into voluntary associations, *collegia* (briefly outlawed from 64 to 58 B.C.E. [p. 280]). People organized *collegia* based on their occupations, religious cults, or local neighborhoods (*vici*), districts (*pagi*), or hills (*montes*). They elected their own officers and pooled their modest resources to provide banquets and entertainments for themselves, ensure proper burial when they died, and protect their interests against the higher authorities if need be. Indeed, aristocrats campaigning for office courted their votes and hoped that the *collegia* would promote their campaigns.

SLAVES AND FREEDMEN

The kidnapping activities of pirates before 67 B.C.E., Pompey's conquests in the East, and Caesar's conquests in Gaul produced a continual flood of slaves. Overall, the lives of slaves did not change much over the course of the Republic. Roman masters, however, did learn from the dreadful uprisings of mistreated rural slaves in Sicily (104–99 B.C.E.) and under Spartacus in Italy (73–71 B.C.E.). Therefore, they improved the treatment or control of such slaves enough to prevent future outbreaks. Roman masters did sometimes free personal and domestic slaves, whom they frequently came to know and view as members of their own families, personal friends, and bedmates. A good example was Cicero's personal secretary Tiro. Tiro served Cicero faithfully as a freedman, invented

FIGURE 18.3 The funerary monument of the freedman A. Clodius Metrodorus, a doctor (medicus), flanked on the left by his son, Clodius Tertius (also a doctor), and on the right by his daughter, Clodia.

a system of shorthand (still extant) to handle his voluminous dictation, wrote a biography of him after his death, and helped to collect his correspondence for publication.

Many freedmen became successful and even wealthy in business. They often got their start with financial help from their former masters, with whom they shared their profits. Ironically, freedmen had larger profits to share after 118 B.C.E., when a law removed many other obligations that freedmen once owed their former masters. Nevertheless, many freeborn, upper-class Romans became very ambivalent toward freedmen. On the one hand, they enjoyed the profitable business associations with successful freedmen; on the other hand, they saw the success of freedmen as threats to their own social status. One result was the extremely negative upper-class stereotype of the boorish nouveau-riche freedman later epitomized by the character Trimalchio in Petronius' *Satyricon* (p. 479). Even lower-class freeborn citizens jealously guarded their privileges. Efforts to give freedmen membership in all the voting tribes were bitterly resisted and always failed.

ITALIANS AND PROVINCIALS

Unlike freedmen, the Italians, who had won the franchise as a result of the Social War, were able eventually to obtain equitable enrollment in the voting tribes (pp. 259–60). Still, for the average Italian, the difficulty of going to Rome to exercise the franchise regularly made the vote of little worth. For the local Italian landed aristocracy, who now became Roman *equites*, it was another matter, however. They joined the older *equites* in demanding a greater voice in public affairs. Sulla's addition of 300 *equites* to the senate did not appreciably alter the status of the rest. They continued to feel that the noble-dominated senate was not doing enough to protect their legal and financial interests. Men like Cicero (who came from the equestrian class), Pompey, Crassus, and Caesar, however, eagerly supported many equestrians. Their money, votes, and influence could be highly useful in the struggles of the Forum. Similarly, powerful Roman aristocrats courted wealthy provincials, provincial cities, and even entire provinces as clients. Their money, manpower, and material resources were great advantages in domestic struggles and foreign wars.

WOMEN IN THE LATE REPUBLIC

Upper-class women played a significant role in the intellectual and political life of the late Republic. To be sure, fathers did not send their daughters away to places like Athens or Rhodes for higher training as they did their sons (p. 331). Nevertheless, some accomplished and loving fathers, like Hortensius, Cicero, and the younger Cato, took great personal interest in educating their daughters beyond the ordinary level. Cicero lavished much attention on his daughter Tullia. While he was in exile, he became extremely distressed that her mother, Terentia, had arranged a marriage for her with a man whom he correctly thought was unworthy of her virtue and intelligence. Cicero was inconsolable over her death and even contemplated the establishment of a cult and shrine for her. Cato's daughter, Porcia, was like her father with respect to his outspoken republicanism. She supported her first husband, M. Calpurnius Bibulus, in his opposition to Caesar. She insisted that she participate with her second husband, Brutus, in the planning of Caesar's assassination. After her death, Cicero delivered a powerful eulogy for her.

In 42 B.C.E., Hortensia, the daughter of Cicero's oratorical rival Hortensius, appeared with a female delegation in the Forum to argue against the imposition of a special

FIGURE 18.4 Woman with a stylus and wax writing tablet; wall painting from Pompeii, 40–50 C.E.

tax on wealthy women to pay for the war against Brutus and Cassius (see Box 18.1). She gained public support and won her point. Pompey's last and most beloved wife, Cornelia, daughter of Metellus Scipio, earned praise because she was well read, could play the lyre, and, most significantly, was adept at geometry and philosophy. Nor can anyone ever forget Sallust's picture of the high-born, highly educated, and daring Sempronia, a conspirator with Catiline in 63 B.C.E. (*Bellum Catilinae*, 25) and possibly the mother of Caesar's assassin Decimus Brutus.

18.1 FEMALE NETWORKS

The episode of the confrontation over the triumvirs' proposed tax on the estates of wealthy women demonstrates that Roman women had their own social networks that ran alongside, and sometimes intersected with, the networks of which their husbands, sons, and fathers were part. This was not something new in the late 40s B.C.E.; rather, it is a phenomenon of which we can catch a glimpse every now and then in the literary sources going at least as far back as the late third century.

In 42 B.C.E., after organizing themselves as a group, the women first made their case to the closest female relatives of the men in charge: Fulvia, the wife of Antonius; Julia, his mother; and Octavia, the sister of Octavian. This was, clearly, proper protocol for voicing their opposition. Hortensia and her colleagues were well received by Julia and Octavia; Fulvia, demonstrating a striking independence from social pressure, rejected their overtures. Her rudeness, so the story goes, inflamed the other women so that, in the heat of the moment, they headed *en masse* to the Forum where they confronted the triumvirs. Antonius, Octavian, and Lepidus, affronted by the women's brazenness, ordered them removed from the forum. Hortensia's speech, however, had persuaded the crowd standing around the tribunal, so the people rushed to the women's defense. Ultimately, the women won a partial victory: the triumvirs did not cancel the tax, but they did restrict it to only the 400 wealthiest women in the city rather than the original 1400 who had been targeted.

Pompey's third wife, Mucia, also deserves mention. She did not disappear from public life after Pompey divorced her. She quickly married M. Aemilius Scaurus, Pompey's former quaestor and brother of Aemilia, Pompey's deceased second wife. Mucia thus remained connected to the world of elite politics. She actively promoted the fortunes of her three children by Pompey and the son whom she bore to Scaurus. She played a key role in arranging the negotiations for the Treaty of Misenum (p. 308). After the Battle of Actium, she secured a pardon for her son by Scaurus.

Terentia, Cicero's first wife, also should not be overlooked. She was a resourceful and influential person in her own right. She is said to have had a significant role in the bitter relations that Cicero had with Catiline and Clodius. While Cicero was in exile or abroad during his governorship or civil war, she handled his complicated finances, oversaw his various villas, managed her own considerable properties, protected his children, and promoted his cause even if she did not always win his approval. After their divorce, she continued to manage her investments and received at least one significant legacy from a wealthy banker. Although she did not have Cicero's depth of intellectual interests, she appreciated her learned slave Diocles enough to free him. He had been trained by Tyrannio of Amisus, who edited the rediscovered manuscripts of Aristotle (p. 330). As a freedman, Diocles established a school and probably shared its income with Terentia. St. Jerome's statement that Terentia later married the historian Sallust has been rightly challenged: his source probably meant that Sallust had married Cicero's much younger second wife, Publilia. Terentia, whom Cicero had divorced in 46 B.C.E., lived a very long life, dying only at age 103 (ca. 6 C.E.).

The need for powerful marriage alliances in the growing competition for power among the aristocracy of the rapidly expanding Roman Republic gave numerous upper-class Roman women opportunities to influence public affairs. As members of powerful aristocratic families, many of them pursued family or personal agendas and were willing to use marriages and sexual liaisons to advance them. Prime examples include Cornelia, Pompeia, and Calpurnia, Caesar's wives; Fulvia, wife of Clodius, Curio, and Marcus Antonius; Servilia, mistress of Julius Caesar and mother of Marcus Brutus; Octavia, wife of C. Claudius Marcellus and Marcus Antonius and sister of Octavian; Scribonia, Octavian's second wife; and Livia, Octavian's last wife.

The frequent charges of sexual misconduct are one of the most visible signs of the increased power and independence of upper-class women in the late Republic. While some woman like Cornelia, mother of the Gracchi, though quite independent, had held to the ideal of a virtuous Roman matron and widow, others became the target of gossip and scandal. Pompey divorced Mucia because she was alleged to have been unfaithful while he was fighting Mithridates. Caesar's second wife, Pompeia, was caught in the famous affair with P. Clodius (pp. 270–1). One of Clodius' three sisters (each named Clodia), the wife of Metellus Celer, was reputed to have been highly promiscuous. Among her lovers, many believe, were the poet Catullus and Cicero's friend M. Caelius Rufus (p. 281). Another of the sisters, Lucullus' ex-wife, was accused in sworn testimony of having had incestuous relations with Clodius while she was still married to Lucullus. Sallust claims that a number of talented and dissolute women besides Sempronia became involved in Catiline's conspiracy. The independent, intelligent, and unconventional aristocratic women of the late Republic have their counterparts in many of the women in later Imperial dynasties. Clearly, they also generated politically motivated invective regarding their characters as did powerful men.

Women of the lower classes

There were three major categories of lower-class Roman women: slaves, freedwomen, and poor freeborn women. Female slaves continued to make up a large percentage of the household workforce in such capacities as nurses, weavers, hairdressers, handmaidens, cooks, and housekeepers. The more there were and the more specialized their tasks, the greater their owner's prestige. Large numbers of female household slaves eventually gained freedom. Some stayed on as free retainers with their former owners, others practiced the trades that they had learned as slaves, and some rose to a comfortable status by good marriages, generous patrons, or hard work.

The most unfortunate group of female slaves was that of the prostitutes. Prostitution was extensive, and often the unwanted female children of slaves and poor citizens were sold by masters and parents to procurers who raised them for that purpose alone. In general, they had little to look forward to. Even if they obtained their freedom, they were not trained to do anything else and could have become worse off without an owner who had an interest in providing a minimum level of shelter, food, and physical security.

Ironically, the slaves and freedwomen of the aristocracy often had far greater opportunities in life than freeborn women of the poorer citizen classes. Girls were less valued than boys. With the added burden of a high incidence of death in childbirth, life for poor women was precarious indeed. They often worked the lowliest jobs: laundry work, spinning and weaving, turning grindstones at flour mills, working as butchers, and selling fish are frequently recorded. Inscriptions from Pompeii list some other occupations for women, such as dealer in beans, seller of nails, brickmaker, and even stonecutter. Many women worked as waitresses in taverns or servers at food counters, where they may also have engaged in prostitution on the side. The names of waitresses and prostitutes are found scribbled on numerous tavern walls, with references to their various virtues or vices, attractions or detractions as the case may be. For many unskilled poor women, prostitution was the only source of livelihood, and unlike slave prostitutes, who had at least the protection of a brothel, they had to practice their trade unprotected out of doors in the public archways, *fornices*, whence comes the word *fornicate*.

NEW WAVES OF HELLENIZATION

The First and Third Mithridatic wars sent two new surges of Hellenization over Roman arts and letters. In 88, Philo of Larissa, head of Plato's Academy in Athens, fled to Rome. He became the teacher of important political and intellectual leaders like Quintus Catulus and Cicero. When Sulla looted Athens in 86, he sent home fleets of ships loaded with the finest products of Greek artists, writers, and thinkers. Among them were the works of Aristotle and his successor as head of the Lyceum. These works had been damaged earlier and had not been widely known for some time. Their intellectual impact was extensive, particularly after Lucullus brought back the captive Greek scholar Tyrannio of Amisus during the Third Mithridatic War, who helped to amend and publish them.

At the end of the third war, Pompey brought back the Greek historian Theophanes of Mytilene and the medical library of Mithridates. Lucullus had already looted a large library of books from Pontus, which he housed in a complex of study rooms and colonnades where Greek intellectuals and interested Roman aristocrats met to study and debate. Indeed, Lucullus set the fashion for large private libraries such as Cicero created. Caesar had planned to outdo them all by building Rome's first public library and filling it with books from the famous library of the Ptolemies at Alexandria. This Roman mania for Greek libraries stimulated a tremendous demand for the copying and selling of books, which made Greek culture even more accessible to the Romans.

EDUCATION

By the first century B.C.E., Rome had developed a fairly extensive system of education. Its availability was limited by the ability to pay, since the state contributed no support. Primary schools (*ludi literarii*) were open to both boys and girls. There they learned the fundamentals of reading, writing, and arithmetic, often painfully, since corporal punishment was frequently applied. Between the ages of twelve and fifteen, girls and boys took different paths. A girl would often be married to an older man at about fourteen, and if she were not of the wealthy elite, formal education stopped. Roman boys moved on to the secondary level under the tutelage of a *grammaticus*, who taught them Greek and Latin language and literature. No Roman of the first century B.C.E. could be considered truly educated if he did not speak and write Greek as fluently as Latin and did not know the Classical Greek authors by heart.

Since the Romans had come to dominate Italy and the western Mediterranean by the first century B.C.E., it was essential for other people to know Latin. Therefore, schools of Latin, and even Greek for those who had real ambitions, were becoming common everywhere. They spread the Latin language and Greco-Roman culture widely and produced a remarkably uniform culture among the upper classes of Italy and the western provinces. As earlier, the masters of the primary and secondary schools were frequently freed slaves, like Terentia's Diocles, who had been tutors in the houses of the wealthy. Their pupils were often offspring of equestrian or prosperous lower-ranking fathers like those of Cicero, Vergil, and Horace, who had ambitions for their sons to enter Roman politics and rise in social standing.

The prevalence of private tutors among the aristocracy meant that aristocratic girls often received instruction at the secondary level along with their brothers. Sometimes they were even able to participate in the higher training of rhetoric and philosophy, if, as with Sempronia, sister of the Gracchi, their families brought men accomplished in these fields into their homes and supported them in return for instructing their children. Many sons of both aristocrats and nonaristocrats were sent to professional rhetoricians for instruction at the highest level. Frequently an upper-class young man capped his formal education with a tour to the great centers of Greek rhetoric and philosophy at Athens and Rhodes.

For a long time, Greek rhetoric dominated the higher curriculum. Right at the beginning of the first century, there was a movement to create a parallel course of professional instruction in Latin rhetoric. In 92, however, the censors banned teachers of Latin rhetoric, perhaps out of fear that rhetorical skills, the foundation of political success, might be made too accessible to the lower orders. Julius Caesar finally lifted the ban when he became dictator.

LAW AND THE LEGAL SYSTEM

Roman law continued to be shaped by private unpaid, learned, aristocratic jurists, the jurisconsults (pp. 203–4), but their role became less visible than it had been in earlier centuries. One reason was the establishment of the various permanent jury courts (*quaestiones*) under Sulla (p. 249). The praetors, by exercising their *imperium* as magistrates in charge of the courts, created law through their edicts granting relief to plaintiffs, issuing injunctions, and establishing procedural rules. As could anyone else involved in legal proceedings, praetors often consulted with the jurists before issuing their edicts. Praetors from one year tended to adopt the edicts of their predecessors. Over time, there grew up a body of praetorian law that supplemented the traditional civil law and specific statutes.

One of the major trends in the late Republic was a striving for fairness and equity, not just the strict application of the letter of the law. The jurists often resorted to the principle of good faith (*bona fides*) as a way of advancing equity. For the most part, this effort was a practical response to the increasing complexity of the Roman world rather than the mere borrowing of a concept from Greek law or philosophy, as has sometimes been argued. Nevertheless, as in the case of the Gracchan reforms, Greek law and philosophy may have helped to provide Roman jurists with a vocabulary and rationale for what they were doing or had done.

The same is true in the development of the famous *ius gentium* (law of nations) in the late Republic. Roman civil law and statutes did not always apply in cases where non-Romans were involved. That was increasingly the case with the expansion of Roman power. Therefore, the *praetor peregrinus* at Rome and the governors of provinces often incorporated into their edicts useful elements from the laws of other people. Greek philosophical concepts like the Stoic idea of a natural law (*ius naturale*) uniting all people supplied useful jargon and justification for what the Romans were doing, but they do not seem to have supplied any ideological motivation.

On the other hand, the principles of logic, debate, and rhetoric worked out earlier by Greeks were important for the rise of professional forensic orators. They began to take over from traditional jurisconsults in pleading cases before standing courts of nonspecialist judges and jurors. Orators, however, still relied on the expertise of learned jurists like two cousins from the Scaevola family. The older was Quintus Mucius Scaevola the Augur, consul in 117 B.C.E. He was the son-in-law of Scipio Aemilianus' famous friend Laelius. He was also the father-in-law of his own protégé L. Licinius Crassus. As a pupil of both Scaevola the Augur and L. Crassus, Cicero absorbed their idealism and moderation. The younger of the two Scaevolae was Quintus Mucius Scaevola the Pontiff, consul in 95 B.C.E. The greatest of all legal works published during the Republic was his *Civil Law (Ius Civile)*, the first systematic exposition of private law and a model for legal commentators down into the second century C.E.

THE RELIGIOUS WORLD OF THE LATE REPUBLIC

Religious life continued to be vibrant and varied throughout the late Republic. The cults and festivals of rural villagers and urban members of countless *collegia* and neighborhood associations continued to flourish. Worshipers frequented temples, leaving gifts for the gods alongside their prayers. The frequency with which augury, divination, and the reporting of omens were used by political rivals against each other shows just how seriously those things were taken. Indeed, the more one thought that he was on the side of the gods, the more convinced he would have been of finding favorable auguries, signs, and omens. Of course, an enemy, who often is equally convinced of his own rightness, will naturally claim that his opponent is a liar and a fraud.

If the state for which the great deities were chiefly responsible was not faring well and public cults were being neglected during destructive civil wars, it was not seen as a failure of religion. It was a failure of the leaders. They were always equally responsible for running the state and carrying out the religious duties that maintained the *pax deorum* (peace of the gods) vital to its welfare. That Julius Caesar had won the civil war with Pompey and was restoring peace and stability was proof to many of his divine favor and justified bestowing on him such honors as made him seem more than human.

In a manner, going all the way back to Hercules in the Forum Boarium (p. 206), Julius Caesar became just another in a long line of new deities whom the Roman state had officially welcomed into the Roman family of gods over the centuries. It was always wise to have as many gods as possible participate in the *pax deorum* that protected the state and fostered the growth of Roman power. As Rome had incorporated new people into the ranks of its Italian allies and overseas empire, so it had incorporated their gods. In times of crisis, the senate was even known to have sanctioned the adoption of a completely foreign deity, as was the case with the Great Mother (*Magna Mater*), Cybele, from Asia Minor during the Hannibalic War in 204 (p. 187).

Nevertheless, Roman authorities were leery of cultic practices and deities that seemed too un-Roman or appeared to promote political loyalties other than to Rome. The senate may have viewed Jewish immigrants, adherents of the Temple and high priest at Jerusalem, as being just like the Bacchic worshipers whom it suppressed in 186 (p. 205). However that may be, a senatorial decree of 139 ordered the expulsion of Jewish immigrants from Rome. Only after Pompey captured Jerusalem and established Roman hegemony in Judea during the Third Mithridatic War were the captives whom he brought back to Rome successful in establishing permanent synagogues there. Chaldean astrologers were particularly suspect because of the secret knowledge that they claimed to have and that might be used against established authority. Therefore, a law, probably of 67 B.C.E., expelled them, too. Similarly, when Roman relations with Cleopatra's Egypt were tense in the 50s and 40s, there were several attempts to destroy the increasingly popular worship of the paired Egyptian deities Isis and her consort, Serapis (Sarapis). The priests of Isis and Serapis were independent of the official Roman priesthoods. They fostered a personal attachment to the loving goddess Isis and her consort, who were closely associated with the Ptolemaic dynasty. Originally, she had been an ancient Egyptian nature goddess, but in Ptolemaic times she was transformed into a universal mother figure and savior of mankind.

The growth of Hellenized mystery cults like those of Isis and, later, Mithras (pp. 491–2) shows the spread of new religious forces in the Roman world, particularly in the large multiethnic, polyglot populations of cities like Rome. Traditional Roman religion still had great meaning for the Roman elite, who controlled it, and the native-born citizens, whom it served. Yet large numbers of willing and unwilling immigrants (slaves) from the eastern Mediterranean made up an increasingly large percentage of the urban population. They often found greater comfort in the mystery cults of their homelands. The conditions that had made them popular there were now being replicated in Rome and other large western cities. People who had been uprooted from the close-knit world of family, village, and local cults lived in a vast, dangerous, and unpredictable urban world made even more dangerous and unpredictable by partisan conflict and civil war. Sharing the mysteries of an initiation rite helped individuals stripped of previous associations create a new sense of community and belonging to one another. Moreover, deities like Isis, Mithras, and Cybele promised not only salvation in the next life, but also nurture and protection in this one through a personal connection with a powerful universal deity who was not limited to one city or territory. Such religions would find greater and greater appeal in the increasingly urbanized and cosmopolitan Roman world of the next two centuries.

GREEK PHILOSOPHY AND THE ROMAN ELITE

The removal of Greek philosophers and whole libraries of Greek philosophical writings to Rome and Italy during the first century B.C.E. stimulated the study of philosophy on a scale never seen before among the educated elite. There are those who say that this increased exposure to the rationalism of Greek philosophy undermined the ruling class' belief in traditional Roman religion. That was true, no doubt, in some individual instances. Many probably had no difficulty in separating their religion and its important public role from their private intellectual pursuits as gentlemen. After all, many highly trained physicists and biologists today practice religions whose literal scriptures are at variance with many of their scientific suppositions. Cicero, for example, who subjected major aspects of Roman religion to intellectual scrutiny in such works as *On the Nature of the Gods* and *On Divination*, was in no way willing to discard them, even if he did not accept them in every single particular. So, for example, in the dialogue *On the Nature of the Gods*, one of his speakers says that he still believes in the traditional religion even though he cannot find proofs that meet his standards as an adherent of the Academic school of philosophy.

Stoicism

Stoic philosophy had been modified in the late second and early first centuries B.C.E. by the pro-Roman Panaetius of Rhodes (p. 203) and Posidonius of Apamea. Their views appealed to Romans like Cato the Younger and Brutus, who saw support for traditional Roman morality in Stoic ethics. Panaetius emphasized the virtues characteristically ascribed to a Roman noble: magnanimity, benevolence, generosity, and public service. In 87 B.C.E., as a Rhodian ambassador to Rome, Posidonius had developed a dislike of Marius. Therefore, in his historical writings, he favored Marius' optimate enemies and their outlook, which further endeared his Stoic teachings to men like the younger Cato. Cicero and Pompey had both sat at his feet in Rhodes. Posidonius was so impressed with Pompey that he appended a favorable account of Pompey's wars to the fifty-two books of his continuation of Polybius.

Posidonius saw Rome's empire as the earthly reflection of the divine commonwealth of the supreme deity. Its mission was to bring civilization to less advanced people.

Statesmen who served this earthly commonwealth nobly would join philosophers in the heavenly commonwealth after death. Cicero adopted that idea in his *Republic* to inspire Roman nobles to lives of unselfish political service. Posidonius also believed that the human soul was of the same substance as the heavenly bodies, to which it returned after death. His scientific demonstration of the effect of the moon on earthly tides reinforced this idea and gave great impetus to astrology at Rome. The growing popularity of these ideas, therefore, made it less difficult to accept the notion that the comet seen soon after Caesar's death was his soul ascending to heaven.

Epicureanism

Not everyone at Rome was a Stoic in the late Republic. A number of prominent Romans, including both Caesar and his assassin, Cassius, adopted the skeptical, materialistic, and very un-Roman philosophy of Epicurus. He had argued that such gods as there were lived beyond this world and took no part in it: the gods were not concerned about whether humans worshiped them or not, nor were they interested in how humans lived their lives. Epicurus believed that the soul is made up entirely of atoms that disperse among the other atoms of the universe upon death. Therefore, he stressed that death is not to be feared because there is no afterlife of eternal punishment, and he advocated that people should shun the cares of marriage, parenthood, and politics to live quietly in enjoyment of life's true pleasures. Among the Romans, Epicureanism was popularized by Philodemus of Gadara. He came to Italy after the First Mithridatic War. Later, he lived at Herculaneum on the Bay of Naples near his patron L. Calpurnius Piso Caesoninus, Caesar's father-in-law. Charred papyrus rolls containing some of Philodemus' writings have been found in the remains of Piso's villa. It was destroyed 150 years later by the famous eruption of Vesuvius and has now been spectacularly replicated to house the J. Paul Getty Museum in Malibu, California.

Roman Epicureans were less restrained in taking their pleasures than Epicurus himself would have approved; yet the Epicurean ideal of a life of pleasant retirement in one's garden may help to explain why Sulla retired at the height of his power and why Lucullus, Caesar, and others lavished so much attention on their pleasure gardens.

The Peripatetics and the New Academy

The Aristotelian Peripatetic School and the New Academy of the Skeptic Carneades (pp. 203–4) were much less popular than other philosophical schools at Rome. Crassus, however, maintained the Peripatetic Alexander in his household. Cicero was greatly drawn to the Academic school, with its emphasis on the testing of ideas through rational inquiry and debate. Still, in general, Cicero was eclectic. He greatly favored Stoic ethics and attitudes but reveals Academic and Peripatetic influences, especially in his political thought (p. 339). Rather than creating new systems of philosophy, Cicero and other Roman philosophical writers adapted to the Roman context the ideas that they admired and found useful in the works of Greek thinkers.

ART AND ARCHITECTURE

Romans continued to admire Greek art. They created a large market for standardized reproductions of famous Greek bronze statues in marble and of famous Greek paintings in frescoes and mosaics on the walls and floors of affluent homes. Still, native Roman and Italic traditions in realistic portraiture and landscape scenes flourished and became more sophisticated in technique.

In architecture, Romans adopted the Hellenistic Greek articulation of different architectural elements into a symmetrical whole along a central axis. The best example in Italy is the Sanctuary of Fortuna Primigenia at Praeneste (see Figure 18.2), which Sulla reconstructed. Sulla's Tabularium (Record Office), carefully sited on the brow of the Capitoline just behind the Roman Forum and finished by Catulus in 78 B.C.E., gave a central backdrop to the Forum. Its colonnaded upper story provided a clear architectural link between the buildings of the Forum and those on the Capitoline to create an articulated whole (see the plan of Rome on p. 390). Rome's first permanent theater, built by Pompey in 55 B.C.E., was another carefully articulated stone complex. Unlike Greek theaters, which were built into solid hillsides, Pompey's was a freestanding semicircle with the stage and backdrop on the chord and the seats rising in tiers on the arc. A shrine to Venus Victrix stood on the center of the topmost tier. A colonnaded portico attached to the back wall of the stage provided shelter in case of rain and had an annex for meetings of the senate.

Caesar himself planned the Basilica Julia, across from the recently rebuilt Basilica Aemilia, to give greater definition to the Forum. In 46 B.C.E., Caesar built an entirely new and symmetrical forum known as the Forum Julium. It was a rectangle completely surrounded by a colonnade. Along the central longitudinal axis from back to front were a temple of Venus Genetrix, an equestrian statue of Caesar, and a fountain. This forum set the pattern for all subsequent *fora* built by the Roman emperors.

The Romans creatively began to combine different architectural elements and materials. They framed arched openings with half columns derived from the three traditional Greek orders—Doric, Ionic, and Corinthian as on the facades of the Sanctuary of Fortuna and Pompey's theater. Using arches and vaults made of brick and concrete allowed the Romans to build more complex and massive buildings than did the Greeks. The Romans made these buildings look more expensive by covering them with thin veneers of stone or with stucco painted to imitate stone.

LATE REPUBLICAN LITERATURE FROM THE GRACCHI TO SULLA

Many major works of Roman oratory, poetry, history, and philosophy appeared in the century from the Gracchi (133 B.C.E.) to the Battle of Actium (31 B.C.E.). Unfortunately, almost nothing from the first half of the century has survived. The only extant book from before the death of Sulla (78 B.C.E.) is an anonymous Latin textbook on oratory, the *Rhetorica ad Herennium* (*The Art of Rhetoric Addressed to Herennius*), which shows marked Gracchan and Marian sympathies.

FIGURE 18.5 Remains of the Sanctuary of Fortuna Primigenia at Praeneste. The careful symmetrical arrangement of different shapes and architectural elements along a central axis extending from the bottom to the top can still be discerned.

Orators and historical writers

The two most notable orators in the early first century B.C.E. were Marcus Antonius, grandfather of the triumvir with the same name, and Lucius Licinius Crassus, one of Cicero's teachers and a relative of Marcus Crassus. Once friends of Marius, both Antonius and Crassus joined the optimate opposition and perished during Marius' proscriptions in 87 B.C.E. Gaius Gracchus and P. Sulpicius, the famous popular tribune of 88, were early practitioners of the Asianic style of oratory that is said to have originated in Pergamum. It was a highly emotional style of oratory, which used histrionic gestures, florid verbosity, and musical cadences to overpower the audience's senses. The consummate practitioner was Cicero's older rival, Q. Hortensius. In reaction to Asianism, there arose the Atticist school. It valued a plain, direct, simple style like that of the famous Attic Greek orator Lysias.

From the second century onward, the writers of history followed the lead of Cato the Elder and wrote in Latin. They were more interested in presenting their views on important topics to fellow Romans than to Greeks. Many still took the annalistic approach, some from a pro-Gracchan, *popularis* perspective and others from an anti-Gracchan, optimate stance.

Closely related to oratory and history was the emergence of aristocratic autobiography and antiquarianism. In the partisan atmosphere after the Gracchi, important men wanted to condemn their enemies and cement their own place in history by writing commentaries (*commentarii*). The two rivals M. Aemilius Scaurus and P. Rutilius Rufus mutually recriminated each other. Marius' rivals Q. Lutatius Catulus and Sulla (using Greek) wrote accounts of their lives that reflected well on them and poorly on Marius. Marius' reputation in later centuries has suffered in part because he never wrote his own account of his accomplishments. Antiquarian scholarship (research into the origins of old institutions, customs, and traditions) was stimulated by patriotic pride in competition with the Greeks and by partisan politics as the proponents of different policies and practices sought precedents in the past.

Drama and poetry

By the end of the second century B.C.E., plays of tragedy and comedy that had already become classics (pp. 197–200) increasingly competed with other dramatic forms, including native Italic traditions of slapstick, farce, and mime. By Caesar's time, mimes dominated popular comedy. Their actors, male and female, appeared without masks and in plain shoes, did comic skits from daily life, sang and danced, and even put on stripteases. The skits might parody something from the high culture in the language of the street and include domestic quarrels or risqué love scenes without any sophisticated plot or point.

THE *NOVI POETAE*

Among the wealthy, cosmopolitan young aristocrats of the post-Sullan period were a number of poets who have come to be known as the *Novi Poetae* (New Poets) or Neoteric Poets from some references in the letters of Cicero, who disapproved of some aspects of their work but whose own poetry (which exists today only in fragment, see below) shares some important characteristics with it. They modeled their works on the personal and emotional writings of the early Greek lyric and elegiac poets like Sappho and Alcaeus or later Alexandrian love poets like Asclepiades. They also delighted in the learned, obscure, and exotic allusions to mythology, literature, and geography that characterized Alexandrian poets like Callimachus. They did not write for a large public but for themselves. That is why the works of all but one of them (including the epigrams of Cornificia, the only woman associated with them) have perished except for a choice line or two quoted by some grammarian or commentator on another work.

CATULLUS (CA. 85 TO CA. 54 B.C.E.)

The one New Poet whose work has survived, albeit in a single manuscript from his hometown, is Gaius Valerius Catullus of Verona. Little is known of his life. He was born about 85 and died around 54 B.C.E. He moved in the highest circles of the aristocracy. His participation in public life was limited to a year of service in 57 on the staff of Gaius Memmius, governor of Bithynia, and to some scurrilous poems about politically prominent people, particularly Caesar, with whom he was reconciled shortly before he died.

At some point, Catullus met a woman with whom he had a torrid love affair. He called her Lesbia. Many believe that she was really Clodia, one of the sisters of the notorious P. Clodius and wife of Metellus Celer, but her identity is in no way certain. Apparently, "Lesbia's" beauty and charm were equaled only by her promiscuity, as Catullus discovered to his bitter sorrow, which he expressed in a number of poems. He also expressed many other moods and emotions, such as grief in a touching lament for his dead brother, lightheartedness in a drinking song, reverence in a hymn to Diana, and ecstatic frenzy in a long poem on the god Attis. In all of his poems, Catullus shows himself to be a serious craftsman by being the first to adapt many Greek lyric meters to Latin poetry.

LUCRETIUS (CA. 94 TO CA. 55 B.C.E.)

One of the contemporary poets who did not share the outlook and focus of Catullus and other *Novi Poetae* was the Epicurean Titus Lucretius Carus. Even less is known about Lucretius than about Catullus. He was born about 94 and died probably in 55 B.C.E. His patron was Gaius Memmius, the same man whom Catullus served in Bithynia. A house excavated at Pompeii indicates that Lucretius' family may have lived in the area around the Bay of Naples, where Philodemus and other Epicurean philosophers were concentrated.

Lucretius' only known work, the *De Rerum Natura* (*On the Nature of Things*), is a didactic epic in six books of dactylic hexameter verse on Epicurean philosophy (p. 335). It is remarkable for the extraordinary beauty of the images it evokes, the elegance of its Latin, and the clarity and force of its argument. For Lucretius, reason, not religion, was the only safe guide to life. The only thing that he feared was passionate emotion because it clouds the reason and leads to extremes of behavior, the inevitable result of which is pain. By imparting Epicurus' views on the true nature of reality and death, Lucretius hoped to convince people that the competition for wealth, fame, and power to achieve immortality, or the frenetic search for pleasure to blot out the fear of death, are completely vain.

CICERO (106 TO 43 B.C.E.)

Many people forget that the orator Cicero was also a poet. Like the *Novi Poetae*, he experimented in a number of genres, but he preferred epic. The only poem of which much survives is an early didactic epic, the *Aratea*. It is a loose translation of the *Phaenomena*, a Hellenistic epic by the Stoic philosopher Aratus, who studied the stars and their effect on earthly life. We also have a substantial fragment of an original poem on the career of Marius. Cicero was well regarded as a poet, at least until he produced, late in his life, an epic on the events of 63 B.C.E., the year of his consulship, which was ridiculed for its pompous and self-congratulatory tone.

The study of poetry helped Cicero to become Rome's greatest orator: rhythm and vivid language are essential tools of the orator. Cicero also studied famous classical Greek orators, like Demosthenes, and trained with the best contemporary Latin and Greek masters, such as Lucius Crassus and Apollonius Molon. He alternated between the Attic and Asian Greek styles (p. 338) as the occasion demanded. He often used his oratorical skill to obfuscate and mislead when his case was weak or polemical, as, for political reasons, it often was. Nevertheless, the surviving published versions of his speeches bring to life the political history of the Late Roman Republic. His voluminous letters to Atticus and other friends do so even more.

Forced to abandon active politics twice, first under the so-called *First Triumvirate* and then during Caesar's dictatorship, Cicero tried to help himself and Rome by writing on philosophy and the art of oratory. His study of philosophy, particularly the Stoic, Peripatetic, and Academic Skeptic schools, had grounded him in logic and ethics. In Cicero's view, they were essential for making the orator into a statesman who could persuade his fellow citizens to adopt the right course. Like Lucretius, Cicero tried to prevent Roman aristocrats from ruining the Republic with their destructive rivalries for power and *dignitas*. Unlike Lucretius, however, Cicero argued in the *De Re Publica* that virtuous behavior on behalf of the state would be rewarded with a blessed after-life among the gods. Indeed, in other works, he expressly refuted Epicurean views of the gods and human happiness. He believed that men should be intensely involved in public affairs. A state guided by an enlightened leader of outstanding prestige, a *princeps civitatis* (First Man of the State), with a senate and citizenry performing their separate duties, would guarantee stability and happiness by reconciling individual freedom with social responsibility. He was clearly looking to Pompey to fill the leading role at one point but was sorely disappointed in the result. Ultimately, Octavian would play the part of *princeps civitatis* more effectively later (p. 346).

SALLUST (86 TO CA. 34 B.C.E.)

Like Cicero, the historian C. Sallustius Crispus, or Sallust, had come from a small Italian town, Amiternum in central Italy, and had started on a senatorial career. As a tribune in 52, he associated himself with Publius Clodius. When Clodius was murdered later that year, Sallust played a leading role in burning down the senate house at his funeral and opposing Cicero, who unsuccessfully defended Milo, Clodius' murderer, in court.

The optimate censor of 50 B.C.E., Appius Claudius Pulcher, Clodius' brother, expelled Sallust from the senate. Sallust sought to restore his position by serving Julius Caesar in the civil war against Pompey and Caesar's optimate enemies. His reward was election to the praetorship in 46 and governorship of the revamped province of Africa. He enriched himself scandalously at the provincials' expense and was tried for extortion. Caesar's influence seems to have saved him, but his political career came to an end.

Sallust retired from politics and for the rest of his life wrote historical monographs in the style of the Greek historian Thucydides and, with some hypocrisy, condemned the Roman nobility's ambition, corruption, and greed. By writing history, Sallust hoped to find the glory that he had failed to achieve in politics. He wrote three historical works: first, the *Bellum Catilinae* (*The War of Catiline*); second, the *Bellum Jugurthinum* (*The Jugurthine War*); and finally, the *Historiae* (*Histories*), whose five books covered events from 78 to 67 B.C.E. and may have been unfinished at his death. The first two works are extant, while only fragments of the *Histories* remain.

CAESAR (100 TO 44 B.C.E.)

Julius Caesar's success as a general and politician was based in no small part on being both an accomplished orator and a consummate literary stylist. His skills as a speaker and writer enabled him to win the loyalty and devotion of his troops, acquire votes, and create a positive public image to counter the accusations of his foes. Caesar favored the straightforward, lightly adorned Attic style.

By 50 B.C.E., Caesar had published the first seven books of *De Bello Gallico* (*On the Gallic War*). The eighth book was later written by his loyal legate Aulus Hirtius. The three books of *De Bello Civili* (*On the Civil War*) were probably written in late 48 or early 47 B.C.E. but were not published until after Caesar's death. The *De Bello Gallico*, other than presenting a descriptive military narrative, is a masterpiece of understated self-glorification and propaganda. It seems to have been read as dispatches from the front to the people of Rome to advertise the wealth and territory that Caesar was winning for them. These dispatches also justify his gratuitous conquests of the Gauls by calling up the memory of wrongs that the Romans and Caesar's own family had suffered in past generations and raising the specter of new Gallic hordes attacking Rome. *On the Civil War* is different. Because waging civil war was one of the worst of crimes in Roman society, he had to show extreme provocation: a small group of ultra-reactionaries had perversely driven him to defend his honor and dignity and the good name and best interests of the Roman People. The men are shown as cruel and vain, cowardly in battle and ignominious in defeat. There are no outrageously false statements in the account, but the truth may be said to have been tested for elasticity.

SCHOLARSHIP AND PATRIOTIC ANTIQUARIANISM

Many of Rome's greatest writers were being shaped by the events of this period and would blossom into maturity after the civil wars came to an end in 30 B.C.E. Arcane scholarship and antiquarian research were safer than other genres that might offer overt critique of those in power. Scholars and antiquarians often exhibit a nostalgic longing for a glorious past and a desire to gain control over the present through research and philosophy.

Marcus Terentius Varro (116 to 27 B.C.E.)

The best representative of such authors is Marcus Terentius Varro. He fought against Caesar at Pharsalus but was pardoned. Caesar admired his great learning in works on history, law, religion, philosophy, education, linguistics, biography, literary criticism, and agriculture. He even entrusted Varro with creating Rome's first great library, which was never finished. Varro's greatest work was probably the *Antiquities Human and Divine*. It contained a vast array of knowledge, as well as many errors. In this work, Varro fixed the canonical date for the supposed founding of Rome by Romulus as April 21, 753 B.C.E. Of his numerous writings, the only ones to survive in more than small fragments are his three valuable books on agriculture; six of his twenty-five books on the Latin language.

Atticus (110 to 32 B.C.E.) and Nepos (ca. 100 to ca. 24 B.C.E.)

Varro based part of his research in early Roman history on a now lost chronology of Rome produced by his and Cicero's old friend T. Pomponius Atticus (pp. 321–2). Cornelius Nepos, born about 100 B.C.E. in Cisalpine Gaul, was a friend of both Cicero and Atticus and also of Catullus. Nepos' main contribution was the popularization at

Rome of the Greek genre of biography. Before 32 B.C.E., Nepos published the first edition of his sixteen-volume *De Viris Illustribus* (*On Illustrious Men*). It contained short biographies of generals, statesmen, writers, and scholars, both Roman and non-Roman, in an easy-to-read style. Twenty-five biographies survive. Unfortunately, like most ancient biographers, Nepos was more interested in drawing moral lessons than in historical accuracy. His real contribution is his multicultural emphasis on Persians, Carthagians, and Greeks to show the Romans that they had no monopoly on talent and virtue.

THE CULTURAL LEGACY OF THE LATE REPUBLIC

Politically, those who were the last generation of the Roman Republic had not been able to preserve the traditional constitution. They did not meet the challenges produced by the acquisition of a vast empire and the great social and economic changes that had ensued. Culturally, however, they must be credited with great accomplishments. In art, architecture, rhetoric, literature, and scholarship, they were worthy successors to the Greeks of earlier generations. They had advanced the distinctive blending of Greek and native Italic traditions that was the hallmark of Roman culture to the point where the next generation of Roman artists, architects, writers, and thinkers could produce a new Golden Age. It would rival that of Classical Greece and become the dominant cultural force in Western Europe for centuries.

SUGGESTED READING

Rawson, E. *Intellectual Life in the Late Roman Republic*. Baltimore: Johns Hopkins University Press, 1985.

Wallace-Hadrill, A. *Rome's Cultural Revolution*. Cambridge: Cambridge University Press, 2008.

CHAPTER 19

The Principate of the early Roman Empire takes shape, 29 B.C.E. to 14 C.E.

Octavian, heir of Julius Caesar, had ended the Roman Republic's civil wars in 30 B.C.E. by disposing of Antony and Cleopatra in Egypt. After settling Roman affairs in the East, he returned to Rome in August of 29 B.C.E. and initiated what has come to be known as the Roman Empire. Referred to as Augustus after 27 B.C.E. (p. 348), Octavian eventually worked out a new kind of monarchy called the *Principate*, from the word *princeps*, which was frequently used to designate the man who also came to be called *Imperator* (Emperor). The title *princeps* was traditionally applied to highly respected Roman statesmen. As used by Augustus and his successors up until 282 C.E., *princeps* indicated that the emperor, although the acknowledged head of state, was only *primus inter pares* (first among equals) within the Roman nobility and that he governed in cooperation with them. The period after 282 C.E., however, is often called the Dominate because the emperors were undisguisedly autocratic and preferred to be called *dominus* (Lord, Master).

SOURCES FOR THE AUGUSTAN PRINCIPATE

Most of the information for the political history of Augustus' rule comes from Suetonius' biography of Augustus; books 52–56 of Dio's history; a portion of Velleius Paterculus' brief compendium; and monumental inscriptions containing Augustus' account of his own deeds, the *Res Gestae* (p. 397). Of great importance for provincial matters is a long Greek inscription known as the *Edicts of Cyrene*, which contains four edicts of Augustus and a senatorial decree. Numerous other inscriptions, abundant archaeological remains, documents on Egyptian papyri, coins, and the surviving works of the great authors from the Augustan Age (pp. 394–400) are rich sources for the social, economic, cultural, and intellectual life of the period. Unfortunately, Books 134 to 142 of Livy, who was a contemporary of Augustus and covered events down to 9 C.E., are lost and receive the briefest of all the summaries in the *Periochae*.

HOPES FOR PEACE

Octavian's return to Rome in the late summer of 29 B.C.E. brought the joy of victory and high hopes for peace. The senate had already approved his arrangements in the East. It had also ordered that the doors to the temple of Janus be closed for the first time since the end of the First Punic War over 200 years before, the mute but visible sign of peace on land and sea. Poets hailed the mighty conqueror. Then, on three successive days, Octavian celebrated triumphs for victories in Dalmatia, at Actium, and in Egypt. They all surpassed in pomp and splendor the triumphs of Julius Caesar and emphatically declared an end to conflict.

PROBLEMS TO BE FACED

Nevertheless, many problems and uncertainties remained. Despite the symbolic closing of Janus' portals, wars were still underway in Gaul, Spain, and North Africa. Imposing Rome's will in the provinces and creating stable frontier defenses were top priorities. The tribes massed beyond the Rhine and the Danube would eventually call for a firm policy of aggressive war (pp. 366–72). In the meantime, the Roman armies themselves were an even greater potential menace to internal peace and stability than any outsiders. Under the command of ambitious and ruthless generals, they could again turn and rend the state, as they had in the recent past. After Actium, Octavian had to find a way to retain supreme command over Rome's legions and reduce their number from seventy to thirty, a number sufficient for defense without bankrupting the treasury. At the same time, he had to find land on which to settle the demobilized veterans without unpopular confiscations of private property or higher taxes.

Furthermore, not all of the aristocrats would readily accept Octavian's supremacy. He needed to reconstruct the government to provide stable, centralized control over Rome and its empire without alienating the old governing class traditionally represented by the senate. Finally, he had to reassure the common people that he and his family were in charge and were looking after their interests, too.

OCTAVIAN'S ADVANTAGES

The sickly Octavian may have seemed doomed at the start. Nevertheless, he had many advantages in terms of money, popularity, military power, political allies, and a ruling class exhausted by years of civil war. He utilized them with the same willpower, ruthlessness, and political astuteness that he had demonstrated from the beginning of his arduous climb to power over the previous fifteen years.

He had returned from the East a popular idol, with such prestige and power as even Caesar had never possessed. East and West were bound to him by oaths of allegiance. He had supreme command of the biggest and best army in Roman history, as well as access to the revenues and resources of a rich and mighty empire. The confiscated treasures of the Ptolemies alone might have sufficed to provide what he needed: land and bonuses for his veterans, food and amusement for the Roman populace, and the revival of Italy's prosperity through the reduction of taxes and a vast program of public works.

Octavian had, in addition to his financial resources, an *auctoritas* (prestige and dignity) unique in Roman history. At first, the deified Julius Caesar, manifested by a comet (p. 302), had been called upon to aid Octavian in his struggle for power. That "divine" legacy would continue to support Caesar's Julian heir. Three days after Octavian's third triumph, two significant buildings were dedicated in Caesar's honor: a temple to the Divine Julius at the eastern end of the Forum and, at the northwest corner, a new senate house, named the *Curia Julia*, which Caesar had intended to replace the old senate house (p. 293). Thus, monuments to Octavian's "divine father" visibly embraced the heart of Roman civic life as Octavian himself set out to "restore" that life.

Octavian now had the added benefits of being a war hero and popular idol in his own right. He was the powerful source of patronage and favors as the leader of a victorious personal faction. The symbolism of a famous statue of Victory that he placed in the new senate house would not be lost on the assembled senators. The general public would daily see the *rostra* (beaks, rams) taken from enemy ships at Actium and mounted as a victory trophy in front of the new temple at the opposite end of the Forum.

Names and titles

One of Octavian's foremost assets was the name that he had adopted, Caesar. It continued to appear on his coins and later became a title borne by Roman emperors. In more recent centuries, it was assumed in linguistically altered form by the kaiser of Germany and the czar (tsar) of Russia. The senate had also granted Octavian the right to take as a permanent *praenomen* the old temporary republican title *imperator*. Troops had given it to their victorious commanders, who could use it until they had celebrated their triumphs. Octavian hoped that it would inspire the troops' loyalty. Although his immediate successors abandoned it, *imperator* became the standard title of all Roman rulers beginning with Vespasian (69–79 C.E.). It survives as *emperor* in English. Finally, although it was never officially bestowed, Octavian assumed the honorific republican title *princeps civitatis* (First Man of the State), a term usually shortened to *princeps*, from which are derived *principate* and *prince*. It originally signified an ex-consul who had been recognized as a person of great prestige and venerability, *auctoritas*. Cicero used it for his ideal leader (p. 340).

Honors and powers

Even before Octavian had returned from Egypt and the East, the senate and people had been outdoing themselves in voting him special honors, privileges, and titles that strengthened his position at Rome. He received such visible honors as triumphal arches, games, supplications, and statues. His birthday was declared a public holiday. In 30 B.C.E. the senate apparently had voted him the full power of a tribune (*tribunicia potestas*), although he may have refused it or utilized only the tribunician right to aid citizens. At the same time, he received the right to hear judicial appeals, the power to grant pardons in criminal cases tried in popular courts, and the right to raise men to patrician status. In 29, Octavian and his loyal subordinate Agrippa were made joint consuls for 28, and they were, or soon would be, granted the power of censors (*censoria potestas*).

THE EVOLVING CONSTITUTIONAL ARRANGEMENTS OF THE PRINCIPATE

Octavian was in a very difficult political and constitutional position in 29 B.C.E.: it was not clear exactly where he fit in the old republican arrangement of governmental powers and offices. He was still clearly in power, but on what basis? Whether the triumvirate had formally lapsed on December 31 of 33 or 32 B.C.E. does not matter very much. During the latter part of 32, Octavian justified his public acts by the oath of personal loyalty sworn to him by most of the inhabitants of Italy and many in the municipalities throughout the West. Such a purely personal and dangerously unorthodox position had been somewhat mitigated when he assumed one of the consulships for 31. As consul in that and each subsequent year, he had claimed precedence over his colleagues on the basis of the earlier personal oath and was accompanied by all twenty-four lictors, as dictators had been before the abolition of that office by Antonius.

To counteract criticism, Octavian had promised to give up his extraordinary position and restore the normal operation of the *res publica* when the civil war was over. By 28, it was time for Octavian to start making good on that promise—or at least appear to be doing so. If he did not, he could expect the same fate as Julius Caesar or at best some dangerous and difficult opposition. Fortunately, the term *res publica* (public business, commonwealth, state) was a somewhat flexible and loose concept that was not spelled out in any written constitution. It hardened into the present meaning of *Republic* only after historians could look back and compare what the Roman system of government had been like before Augustus' long rule and what it was like after. Indeed, until the end of the Latin-speaking emperors, the Roman state never ceased being called the *res publica*.

Initial steps

Octavian took the first visible step on the road to political reconstruction when he and Agrippa took office as consuls on January 1, 28 B.C.E. He surrendered twelve of his extraordinary twenty-four lictors. Handing them over to Agrippa, he indicated that equality had been restored to his consular colleague in accordance with normal republican practice. The next step was to use their recently granted censorial power to register citizens and revise the role of the senate. Revision of the senate was imperative if the claim to be restoring political normalcy was to have any credibility. The senate had been the centerpiece of the traditional *res publica* and the pride of the old nobility, whose goodwill and cooperation Octavian urgently needed.

To bolster respect for the senate, Octavian and Agrippa reduced its number from about 1000 to 800. They purged many of the outsiders whom Caesar and the triumvirs had appointed in reward for political services during the civil wars. They did not purge anyone on the basis of republicanism or lack of support in those wars. That would merely have aroused the hostility of those whom they wished to conciliate. With further reductions in 18 and 13 B.C.E., the senate ultimately returned to about 600, the number established by Sulla. Octavian, to show his honored position in the reformed senate, took the title *princeps senatus* (First Man of the Senate), an honor that censors had bestowed upon the most prestigious member of the senate in the days before Sulla.

Octavian had ensured that the number of senators would ultimately stabilize at 600 by reducing the number of quaestors to Sulla's twenty. He also tried to ensure the prestige of new senators by restricting the quaestorship to men at least twenty-five years old, of senatorial family and good moral character. They needed to have served in the military and to possess property worth at least 800,000 sesterces (later 1 million). Men of equestrian rank could also hold the quaestorship if they had held one or more of certain lower level magistracies. Octavian pleased traditionalists by cutting back the number of praetors from sixteen to ten. Finally, he lowered the minimum ages for the praetorship and consulship to thirty-two and thirty-five, respectively.

Octavian made admission into the equestrian order dependent, as before, on a minimum property valuation of 400,000 sesterces. To invigorate both the equestrian and senatorial orders with new blood, Octavian adopted Caesar's policy of admitting a few rich and aristocratic residents from the Italian *municipia* and even from the Roman colonies of Gaul and Spain. Future emperors would continue that policy on a much more extensive scale.

The arrangements of 27 B.C.E.

On January 13, 27 B.C.E., Octavian dramatically appeared before the senate and offered to surrender all his extraordinary powers. In grateful return, the majority of the senators, probably inspired by his close friends, officially bestowed upon him a huge provincial command. He received a grant of proconsular *imperium* for ten years over the large and geographically separated single province of the two Spains, Gaul, Syria, and Egypt, where most of the legions were stationed. As did Pompey during the pirate war, Octavian had the right to appoint legates of consular and praetorian rank and to make war and peace as he saw fit.

In this new division of power, the senate resumed control over Rome and Italy and over the provinces of Sicily, Sardinia and Corsica, Illyricum, Macedonia, Greece, Asia, Bithynia, Crete–Cyrene, and Africa. Octavian was to govern the imperial provinces through his own legates or deputies, whereas the senate controlled the senatorial provinces through proconsuls recruited from the ranks of ex-consuls and ex-praetors.[1] The *princeps*, who continued to be elected consul each year, probably maintained effective control over the governors of the senatorial provinces through either his *auctoritas* or the weight of his *imperium* as both consul and proconsul. He thus retained as much real power after his new arrangement as he had possessed before.

The crucial point is that his power was legitimate. It had been bestowed by a body having the recognized authority within the traditional *res publica* to do so, just as in the similar case of Pompey in 66 B.C.E. Such legitimacy distinguished the *res publica* from arbitrary personal rule, or *regnum*. In that very important sense, then, the *res publica* was restored.

Three days after Octavian's "surrender" of power, the senate met to honor the restorer of the legitimate government. A laurel wreath was to be placed above the doorposts of his house. A golden shield inscribed with his virtues of valor, clemency, justice, and piety was to be hung up in the senate. He received an even greater honor, the name *Augustus* (Revered), which had exalted connotations and religious associations. It had never before been given to a human being.

In turn, Augustus, as he shall now exclusively be called, exalted the senate and augmented its powers. He restored its control over public finance and, for a time at least, even the right of coining money in gold and silver. Although Augustus continued to recognize the popular assemblies as lawmaking bodies, he permitted the senate to issue decrees having the force of law without ratification by the people. Officially, the senate became a full partner in the government. Theoretically, it was even more: the ultimate source of the *princeps'* power. What it had granted it could also take away.

The arrangements of 23 B.C.E.

By 23 B.C.E., it had become clear that further adjustments to Augustus' position were necessary to preserve the consensus of support on which his *auctoritas* as *princeps* ultimately rested. In late 27 B.C.E., he had left Rome to take control of urgent military operations in his provinces of Gaul and Spain. He was gone almost two and a half years (p. 367). In 26, for example, he had tried to retain control of events in Rome by reviving the ancient office of prefect of the city. His appointee was Marcus Valerius Messalla Corvinus, a former partisan of Brutus and Cassius before he switched to Antonius and, finally, Augustus. The office had its roots in the pre-republican monarchy, however, and had fallen into disuse with the growth of the praetorship after 367 B.C.E. Messalla held the office for only six days before he resigned it as being improper, perhaps a sign that traditionalist nobles were beginning to grumble.

The lavish honors that Augustus' friends had continued to propose in the senate after he returned from Spain in early 24, as well as his unprecedented eleventh consulship in 23, surely aroused resentment among the old nobility. Unfortunately, no specific events of early 23 are clear. A famous trial at which Augustus' intervention provoked both criticism and a plot to assassinate him may belong anywhere from late 24 to early 22 B.C.E. With or without such a plot, rumblings of discontent with his political domination must not have escaped his ears by 23 B.C.E. The major irritant to the old nobles was

Augustus' continued tenure of the consulship. That was too reminiscent of Marius and Caesar, whose careers were not pleasing to traditionalists. Moreover, the consulship was the goal of every ambitious senator. By holding one of the two consulships year after year, Augustus was reducing by half those available to others.

Augustus was unable to take any action before he suddenly became gravely ill. Once he recovered, and after consulting with members of the senate, he resigned his consulship on July 1, 23 B.C.E. In return, he received anew (or possibly re-emphasized) the full tribunician power, *tribunicia potestas*, which he had been voted but had either refused or not fully utilized in 30. He had enjoyed tribunician sacrosanctity since 36. Now he made the full tribunician power the official legal foundation of his position. From 23 B.C.E. onward, he numbered the years of his principate by the number of years during which he had held the *tribunicia potestas* (abbreviated "T.P." on his coins). Legally, a patrician could not hold the tribunate. If Augustus became a tribune, it would either be illegal or he would have to negate his formal adoption as Caesar's son and become a plebeian again (p. 303). The tribunician power gave Augustus many important rights and privileges: he could propose legislation to the *concilium plebis*; convene meetings of the senate; and submit motions in writing to the senate, which took precedence over all other business. Nevertheless, he needed more powers to make up for the loss of the consulship. Augustus was allowed to retain the consular right to nominate candidates for office. Of course, he had the same prerogative as any high-ranking individual to endorse candidates after their candidacies had been accepted. Once elected, however, all incoming magistrates were required to swear that they would uphold all past and future public acts of Augustus. He also received the right to nominate jurors to the various standing courts, which gave him additional control over the administration of justice. Finally, his proconsular *imperium* was strengthened. He was allowed to retain it in the city, and it was made *maius* (greater) so that he could still override other provincial governors and exercise command over all legions if need be. This *imperium* was renewed at intervals of five or ten years in 18, 13, and 8 B.C.E. and 3 and 13 C.E.

Other adjustments were also made in 23 B.C.E. Augustus increased the number of praetors from ten to twelve, the two new ones being placed in charge of the city's treasury. To provide two additional governorships for the increased number of ex-praetors that would result, he transferred control of Gallia Narbonensis (Provence) and Cyprus to the senate. (Provinces annexed after 23 needed garrisons and were kept by him.) If not in 23, then sometime later, the senate acquired the right to hear appeals regarding the decisions of Roman officials in Italy and the provinces. Suits brought against senatorial governors by provincials simply for the restitution of allegedly misappropriated property were tried by a small ad hoc committee of fellow senators. Also, only the senate was allowed to try senators accused of political or criminal offenses. The ghost of Sulla would have been pleased!

Popular dissatisfaction

Although traditionalist nobles might have approved of the changes made in 23 B.C.E., the populace of Rome did not. In 22, a combination of flood and famine made life very difficult for ordinary citizens. They were not impressed by how the senate handled matters. They riotously demanded that Augustus be given a perpetual consulship or dictatorship and that he take up the censorship and curatorship of the grain supply, *cura annonae*. He refused the consulship, dictatorship, and censorship, but with his vast personal resources, he was able to alleviate the grain shortage within a few days. Also in 22, because it was less dignified for the senate to be summoned by a person with only tribunician power, Augustus accepted the consular right to summon the senate.

In the spring of 22, Augustus again departed to take care of matters in the provinces. The senate was left to handle affairs at Rome without him. The people, unhappy without Augustus clearly in charge, refused to elect two consuls for 21 unless he would become one. Forced to intervene, he refused to accept the other consulship but persuaded the people to accept his own personal nominee, a noble with good republican credentials. Much the same happened in 21, 20, and 19. Also in 19, Augustus' authority was challenged when candidates whom he had rejected for the quaestorship refused to withdraw. Then, a man named Egnatius Rufus illegally ran for the consulship right after his praetorship. He had become very popular by organizing a fire department for Rome at his own expense and by sponsoring splendid games as aedile. A majority of senators passed the *Senatus Consultum Ultimum* and begged Augustus to intervene again and restore order.

The arrangements of 19 B.C.E.

Augustus' return on October 12, 19 B.C.E., was declared a national holiday. He was voted further consular powers: perhaps now the right to appoint a prefect of the city in his absence, the use of twelve *fasces*, and the right to sit on a curule chair between the two annual consuls. It must have become clear to Augustus and many traditionalist nobles as well that he had given up too much in 23. Now he had regained everything of importance that he had lost in giving up the consulship. Although he still did not have the title of consul, he was in effect a permanent third consul. The nobles could now happily vie for the two annual consulships; the common people could be reassured that their hero was in control. After 19 B.C.E., the legions still remained under his *imperium*, and no one outside his family was allowed a triumph.

Minor alterations after 19 B.C.E.

The arrangements of 19 B.C.E. were the last major series of constitutional adjustments and changes in Augustus' power. Occasional alterations were made over the years, however. In 15 B.C.E., he acquired the sole right to coin gold and silver. In 12 B.C.E., after his old triumviral partner Lepidus died, Augustus was elected *pontifex maximus* in his place. That office gave him great prestige as head of the state religion. It was kept by all subsequent Roman emperors, even Christian ones, until Gratian (ca. 375 C.E.). In 8 B.C.E., the month Sextilis was renamed Augustus in honor of the month in which he had earned major victories in several different years. Further prestige accrued to Augustus in 2 B.C.E. The senate voted him the title *pater patriae* (Father of His Country), an honor formerly voted to Cicero after the suppression of the Catilinarian conspiracy (p. 269).

After 19 B.C.E., therefore, the form of the Augustan Principate was fairly well fixed, and the stability of the state seemed secure. Augustus himself was confident enough to celebrate the beginning of a new era with the holding of the Secular Games of 17 B.C.E. (see Box 19.1). As did many ancient peoples, the Romans believed that the history of the world moved in a cycle of epochs (*saecula*: hence the word *secular*). Each *saeculum* was often calculated at 100 or 110 years, and the tenth *saeculum* of the cycle was thought to inaugurate a new Golden Age. With a little prompting from Augustus, who was a member, the board of priests in charge of the *Sibylline Books* indicated that the tenth era of the current cycle was about to begin in 17 B.C.E. The celebration of magnificent festival games in honor of the event would give Augustus the perfect opportunity to advertise the end of the evil period of political chaos and civil war and the dawn of an era of peace and prosperity under his newly "restored" Republic. The message was clear: the wounds of civil war had now been healed; health had returned to the body politic. No more fitting symbol of that idea can be found than the fact that the most important religious element of the whole celebration, a joyous hymn to Apollo, was composed by Horace, a man who had once fought against Augustus at Philippi.

19.1 AUGUSTUS' SECULAR GAMES

We have more details of the Secular Games of 17 B.C.E. than we do for almost any other individual festival from the entire Roman world thanks to the preservation of a commemorative inscription that survives from the city of Rome. It includes the order of sacrifices and who performed them, as well as some of the prayers that were said. From this document, it is clear that Augustus extended the festival beyond the traditional three nights of sacrifices and theatrical performances that were the core of the observance as other sources report it had been performed in earlier instantiations (in 348, 249, and 146 B.C.E.). The new, grander version included many more days of sacrifices and other entertainments. Offerings of animal victims and cakes on different days or nights were accompanied by a chorus of boys and girls singing Horace's hymn, prayers offered by the matrons of the city, and the all-female celebration of *sellisternia* (religious banquets at which statues of goddesses were seated on chairs, *sellae* in Latin). After these solemn rituals were completed, the people could watch plays, equestrian performers, chariot races, and an animal hunt.

The Secular Games continued to be observed well into the Empire. The details of their last celebration, by the emperor Septimius Severus in the year 204 C.E., are preserved in a lengthy inscription similar to the one commemorating Augustus' celebration 220 years before.

THE NATURE OF THE PRINCIPATE

With the establishment of the Principate, Augustus had created a stable form of government that enabled the Roman Empire to enjoy a remarkable degree of peace and prosperity for two centuries. Generations of historians, therefore, have sought to determine what kind of government it was. In form, and that was important, the old system symbolized by the words *res publica* had been restored: the senate, the magistrates, and the Roman People continued to perform many of their old functions in the familiar way. Indeed, Augustus' many offices and powers almost invariably had precedents in the Republic. Nevertheless, it was the simultaneous and continuous possession of them that gave him more power than anyone in the Republic (except perhaps dictators) had ever held.

Having achieved great personal and official power, Augustus showed considerable respect to the senate as an institution and eagerly solicited its cooperation in running the Empire. Therefore, many have characterized the Principate as a dyarchy, an equal rule between *princeps* and senate. That, too, is wide of the mark: no matter how much he tried to disguise it or others were willing to overlook it, Augustus was the dominant force at Rome. Cassius Dio, a Greek from the eastern provinces who wrote a comprehensive history of Rome from the beginning to his own time under Septimius Severus and who was much less squeamish than a native Roman about monarchy, said simply that the Augustan Principate was a monarchy.

That judgment is closer to the truth but not wholly satisfactory. It needs refinement and qualification. Augustus' position certainly was monarchic, but it was not like that of the Persian, Hellenistic, or Parthian kings, who provided the standard models of monarchy in both Augustus' and Dio's day. Augustus and his successors did not hold their positions by right of dynastic succession (although, in practice, dynastic considerations were important). Their powers were not based on any absolute sovereignty of the ruler but on laws and decrees passed by the traditional sources of legitimate authority at Rome—the senate and the people. Gradually, as the traditions of the Republic faded further and further into the past, the force of these restraints weakened. Given the emperor's overwhelming constitutional powers, financial resources, and raw military force, the later emperors became absolute monarchs in every way.

In the first two centuries C.E., however, the Principate of Augustus and his successors was more like an elective constitutional monarchy. Their powers were bestowed and limited by laws not of their own making. The choice of a successor to the previous emperor had to be ratified by the senate, and his powers were voted anew. The senators could be compelled to give their votes by the threat of military force, but that shows that their votes still meant something. Moreover, if an emperor acted like an arbitrary despot, the traditions of the Republic were still strong enough to foster dangerous conspiracies against him. He might even suffer condemnation as a public enemy by a vote of the senate, as happened in the case of Nero (pp. 434–5). Sovereignty still lay in the hands of another institution.

In the last analysis, of course, the governmental system created by Augustus was uniquely itself. The man who had clawed his way to the top as a ruthless opportunist in civil war had created an enduring monument of statesmanship. He had performed a delicate political balancing act with consummate patience and skill as he bent and shifted to counteract the conflicting forces that would have toppled others from the tightrope of power. He created a constitutionally limited monarchy that was strong enough to ensure his own power and the stability of the state, while it preserved enough characteristics of the free Republic to satisfy many Romans' deep respect for the traditional constitutional forms and institutions that had been the focal point of their public lives for centuries. If politics is the art of the possible, then Augustus became one of its greatest masters.

THE CREATION OF A CENTRAL ADMINISTRATION

Under the Republic, both the city and the provinces had been administered rather haphazardly by the yearly magistrates and provincial promagistrates on short-term assignments. Theoretically, the whole senate, with its collective wisdom, was supposed to offer sound guidance and provide coherence. Nevertheless, the growing complexity of affairs in an empire of an estimated 50 to 70 million people did not allow the senate to give adequate attention to many problems. Senators often had not gained any more direct familiarity with problems during their short tenure of various offices and posts than those whom they were supposed to advise. Finally, communications to the provinces were slow, so that governors were often left to face crises on their own. In the past, this situation had helped to create emergencies that ambitious men could exploit for their own aggrandizement. Also, the republican practice of not paying high officials any salary greatly increased the temptation to engage in graft and corruption, which contributed to provincial unrest. Therefore, Augustus was anxious to institute administrative reforms.

Augustus did not so much replace the nonprofessionalized administrative system of the Republic's empire as organize and centralize it under his personal control. Although he systematized career paths and salaries of those who held important administrative posts, the extent to which he bureaucratized the system was minimal. The people who held the most prestigious civil and military posts were not trained, professional experts who devoted the majority of their working lives to their duties. They were still basically gentlemen who enhanced their social standing through conspicuous public service. They obtained their posts by patronage from the emperor. He evaluated them not on narrow professional qualifications but on generally meritorious qualities such as loyalty, character, and judgment. They also were responsible directly to him and not some bureaucratic chain of command.

Senators in imperial administration

After using his censorial power to rid the senate of those who did not meet his standards, Augustus had placed many of the rest in posts that bestowed great honor. Between 27 and 18 B.C.E., he had secured the appointment of a senatorial committee to assist him in preparing the agenda for meetings of the senate. This committee, often called the *Concilium Principis* (Council of the *Princeps*), consisted of the consuls, one representative from each of the other magistracies, and fifteen senators selected by lot. It changed every six months. As reorganized in 13 C.E. and reinforced by members of the imperial family and the equestrian order, the committee began to assume functions formerly belonging to the senate. Even then, it was not a true cabinet or privy council. Meeting more or less publicly, it was an administrative, not a policy-making, body.

This clumsy, rotating committee of the senate was abandoned by Augustus' successor. The real predecessor of the later imperial privy council consisted of topflight administrators, close friends of Augustus, high-ranking senators, legal experts, and other specialists, who met informally behind closed doors. They decided many questions: the policy of the government; the legislation to be presented at meetings of the senate and the popular assemblies; the candidates whom it might please Augustus to recommend at the coming elections; the next governor of such and such a province; and all matters pertaining to public finance, foreign affairs, law, religion, and the administration of the Empire.

Augustus reserved many of the most prestigious provinces, such as Asia and Africa, for senatorial governors. The prefect of the city (*praefectus urbi*), who had under his command the first police force in Rome's history—the three urban cohorts (*cohortes urbanae*)—was at first always a senator of consular rank (p. 364), as were the men in charge of the grain supply (until 6 C.E.), water supply, and flood control at Rome.

Equestrians in imperial administration

Augustus also drew many of his top-ranking administrators from the equestrian class. Its members welcomed the new recognition and status conferred. Many *equites* had acquired valuable experience, especially in the fields of finance, taxation, and commerce, which were vital to the smooth functioning of an empire. Augustus regarded *equites* as more reliable and less politically dangerous than senators because they were more dependent upon him for patronage and future advancement. Eventually, faithful service could advance an *eques* to membership in the senate. A newcomer obligated to Augustus could help keep that vital body loyal to him.

The careers open to equestrians were military, judicial, financial, and administrative. A young *eques* usually began his career as a prefect of an auxiliary cavalry squadron, advanced to tribune of a cohort or legion, then to prefect of a cohort. Experienced equestrian prefects frequently commanded legions on garrison duty, particularly in Egypt, a land generally forbidden to senators. After a year or two in the regular army, some *equites* became attorneys in the civil administration. Others frequently served as procurators (imperial agents) in the provinces.

In the imperial provinces, a procurator was both the manager of the emperor's private properties and the public tax collector and paymaster. In the senatorial provinces, he was officially only the manager of the emperor's private properties. In both cases, procurators also served as the eyes of the emperor. A procurator was often more powerful than even a governor of consular senatorial rank. A corrupt and rapacious governor had to be exceedingly wary of a procurator's reports, lest he be liable to stern reprimand at the end of his term.

As prefects, *equites* might also govern provinces, especially the more backward and turbulent ones, such as Raetia and Noricum north and east of the Alps, not to mention Egypt, the richest and most important province of all. Even the proudest senatorial governor might envy the eminence and power of its prefect. Second in power to the prefect of Egypt were the two prefects (also of equestrian rank) to whom Augustus had given joint command over the nine cohorts of his personal protectors, the Praetorian Guard, in 2 B.C.E. Two other prefectures, created around 6 C.E., were less important but often served as stepping-stones to higher office. One belonged to the commissioner of the grain supply (*praefectus annonae*), the other to the prefect of the *vigiles* (*praefectus vigilum*), a corps of seven cohorts, each consisting of 1000 former slaves, who patrolled the streets at night and guarded Rome against riot or fire (p. 364).

Slaves and freedmen in administration

The people who most resembled trained professionals were the countless slaves and freedmen whom an emperor employed directly or under consular senators or equestrian prefects in the real work of administration. They were essential to such vital operations as the grain supply (*cura annonae*), the grain dole (*frumentatio*), the water supply (*cura aquae*), control of the Tiber's floods (*cura riparum et alvei Tiberis*), the mint (*moneta*), and the Military Treasury (*aerarium militare* [p. 363]). They became the nucleus of the great body of imperial slave administrators and functionaries known as the *familia Caesaris* (the emperor's household). Basically, Augustus was using his slave household and his own freedmen to run the Roman Empire the way in which a great Roman senator or large landowner ran his far-flung estates and business interests.

Although slaves performed the more menial and obscure jobs, higher, salaried positions that required managerial talent and judgment went to the emperor's trusted freedmen. Many of them were shrewd and skillful ministers. They held positions equivalent to those secretary-ships in a modern government such as state, treasury, defense, war, and transportation. Acting as the emperor's agents, they soon came to exercise great influence over financial affairs: how much the emperor should spend on armaments, public works, games, and spectacles; the weight, fineness (purity), and numbers of gold or silver coins to be minted; the taxes or tribute that provinces must pay; the salaries that governors, prefects, procurators, and other appointed officials should receive. Finally, certain freedmen in high positions began to receive petitions and requests from every part of the Empire. The option of ignoring such petitions or bringing them to the emperor's notice put these freedmen functionaries in positions of real patronage and power. They could reach levels of privilege and prestige never available to freedmen under the Republic.

Operation of the popular assemblies

In directing the Roman administration, it was important for Augustus to influence the popular assemblies in their electoral and legislative functions. As did any prominent man, he had the right to canvass voters on behalf of candidates whom he favored. Through his consular *imperium*, he shared with the consuls the right to accept or reject men who wished to be candidates. These two rights, *commendatio* and *nominatio*, in combination with his great personal popularity and *auctoritas*, gave a major advantage to people whom he preferred.

Still, Augustus did not always get his way by these means, and he was reluctant to interfere too much in consular elections lest he offend the nobles. They continued to dominate the consulship for a number of years and often employed bribery and violence to do so. In 5 C.E., therefore, Augustus induced the consuls to propose the *lex Valeria Cornelia*. It altered the procedure for voting in the Centuriate Assembly, so that in elections ten centuries composed of the 600 senators and the 3000 *equites* enrolled as jurors voted first and indicated their preference for two consular candidates and twelve praetorian. The remaining centuries would then usually follow their lead in the rest of the voting. From that time on, the majority of *equites* in these ten centuries usually secured the election of "new men," who were much to Augustus' liking.

The common people were pleased with Augustus' attempts to influence the outcome of elections. They wanted him to have loyal magistrates and demanded to know whom he preferred. In 8 C.E., when he was no longer strong enough to canvass for candidates in person, he began to post lists of those candidates whom he commended to the voters.

Augustus' power to influence legislation was also great. By virtue of his *tribunicia potestas* or consular *imperium*, he could submit bills directly. Usually, however, he preferred to have friendly magistrates submit desired bills, as in the case of the *lex Valeria Cornelia*.

Administration of justice

Augustus introduced a number of changes to improve the administration of justice and make it more efficient through a series of laws in 18 and 17 B.C.E. First, he established two new standing criminal courts (*quaestiones perpetuae*) for the crimes of adultery (*de adulteriis*) and either the hoarding of or speculating in grain (*de annona*). He also increased the representation of *equites* on the jury panels and lowered the age requirement from thirty to twenty-five in order to increase the pool of jurors for the expanded court system. Several other laws, probably of 8 B.C.E., further classified the jurisdictions of the various courts so that there would be a comprehensive system embracing all common varieties of crimes.

In the realm of civil procedure, Augustus seems to have abolished the old *legis actiones* (p. 204) for all practical purposes in 17 B.C.E. That avoided duplication with the more popular formulary procedure and also the possibility that a party who was dissatisfied with a verdict under the formulary procedure would bring suit again under a *legis actio*. More important, however, was Augustus' adoption of a streamlined procedure known as *cognitio extraordinaria*, under which there was no two-stage process. The emperor or his appointee determined the suitability of the case and judged it in a single process. Another advance over the formulary procedure was that under *cognitio*, the judge could compel a defendant to answer a summons and could find him guilty by default if he failed to appear. Moreover, the judge did not have to wait for a complaint to be lodged by someone else but could launch an investigation of his own. Because lower judges were merely subordinates of a higher authority, defendants who were citizens had the right of appeal all the way to the emperor. The *cognitio* procedure gradually replaced both the *quaestiones perpetuae* in criminal cases and the formulary procedure in civil cases.

SOCIAL REFORMS

Augustus hoped to reinforce the peace and stability that he created with his constitutional and administrative arrangements by reforming Roman society. He tried to secure the restoration of political order by the renewal of a clear and fixed hierarchical social order that embraced the class structure, women, and the family. Also, by restoring stable family life, he hoped to regenerate the Roman and Italian freeborn population devastated by the bloodshed, confiscations, and chaos of civil war. A recent analysis of Roman census data and the frequency with which people hid and failed to recover hoards of coins in Italy during the first century B.C.E. reinforces the picture of a significant drop in the number of Roman citizens during internal disorders.

Slaves and freedmen

Augustus neither opposed slavery nor did anything to reduce its incidence or importance in Roman life. His frontier wars brought huge numbers of new slaves to Rome and Italy. They may have caused him to worry about the impact that the unregulated granting of freedom to many of those slaves would have had on the citizenry. He set limits on the percentages of masters' total slaves that could be freed in their wills, with one hundred individuals as the absolute maximum. He instituted a 5 percent tax on formal manumissions. Furthermore, he strictly regulated the practice of informal manumission and made it less financially attractive to masters who wanted to avoid the 5 percent tax on formal manumissions by freeing slaves informally. Previously, all property belonging to an informally freed slave upon his death had to go to his former master, but Augustus allowed such an informally freed ex-slave to dispose of his property as he wished in a will. Finally, he would not permit freedom for any slave who had been imprisoned for a crime or disgraceful deed.

At the same time, Augustus tried to promote relatively humane treatment of slaves. One of the duties of Augustus' newly established urban prefect was to look into complaints by slaves that they were being denied enough to eat. Of course, the actual treatment of slaves was not the Emperor's only concern. With the growing number of slaves and fewer chances of manumission, Augustus realized that slave owners would have to treat slaves decently if they were to avoid the kinds of massive revolts that had occurred in the late Republic.

Augustus encouraged and rewarded cooperative freed slaves. By the *lex Junia Norbana* (17 B.C.E.), those who were freed informally had their noncitizen status regularized as Junian Latins, with specific provisos for future full citizenship. An informally freed slave under the age of thirty could obtain citizenship by marrying any free Roman or Junian Latin woman and producing a child who was still alive after one year. A freedwoman who produced four children also received extra privileges similar to those given to citizen women who had borne three. On the other hand, Augustus banned freedwomen from marrying senators.

To compensate freedmen for being barred from the regular magistracies in Rome and the municipalities, Augustus created new posts just for them. In Rome, they served as *vicomagistri*, who worked with the *vigiles* in fighting fires and maintaining the night watch. They also had charge of the neighborhood festivals. In the municipal towns of Italy, freedmen made up the bulk of local boards of six called the *Seviri Augustales*, or simply *Augustales*, who had charge of the emperor's local cult and put on games for their fellow townspeople.

Popular benefactions

The great mass of exploitable common citizens that had built up at Rome since the second century B.C.E. had been a significant factor in the instability of the late Republic. Augustus had blunted their direct political power by effectively gaining control of the popular assemblies himself. On the other hand, he still had to cope with the potential that they represented for violence and disorder. To limit their numbers, he had contemplated eliminating the distribution of free grain in 2 B.C.E., but he decided against such a potentially provocative move. Instead, he reduced the number of people receiving free grain to 200,000 freeborn citizens by making about 120,000 freedmen ineligible. He also set up a more efficient system of procuring and distributing free grain and kept the retail price reasonable for all.[2] At his own expense, he also expanded the number of games and public entertainments, such as the increasingly popular gladiatorial contests.

Women and the family

Less effective were the attempts to control promiscuity and regulate marriage and family life. Two Julian laws of 18 B.C.E. and the *lex Papia Poppaea* of 9 C.E. were specifically designed to curb immorality, speed up the birthrate, and revive "ancient Roman virtue." These laws prohibited long engagements, regulated divorce, required all bachelors and spinsters to marry as soon as possible, and forced all widows under fifty and all widowers under sixty to marry within three years. Failure to comply carried penalties and disabilities: partial or complete ineligibility to receive legacies or hold public office and exclusion from public games and spectacles. Married persons who were childless, impotent, or sterile incurred similar disabilities, whereas those with three or more children could advance rapidly in their public careers and social life. For example, women who had borne three or more children were freed from guardianship.

The total effectiveness of the law, however, was somewhat diminished by the conferral of the special and fictitious "right of three children" (*ius trium liberorum*). Persons of influence might claim this right. Thus, the unmarried poets Vergil and Horace, Augustus himself with only one child, Empress Livia with two, and even the two bachelor consuls who lent their names to the *lex Papia Poppaea* did not have to comply with the provisions of the law.

The new laws made adultery a criminal as well as a private offense. A *paterfamilias* might kill adulterous women under his power along with their paramours; a husband could kill his wife's lover. A man who refused to divorce an adulterous wife or who knowingly married an adulteress was equally guilty before the law. Flagrant adulterers suffered penalties varying from fines and loss of property to banishment and even death.

RELIGIOUS REFORMS

To the Romans, the peaceful working of the state depended on maintaining the Peace of the Gods, *pax deorum*. To do that, it was necessary to perform all of the ancestral rites and ceremonies that the gods had ordained. Therefore, in 28 B.C.E., Augustus undertook the repair of many temples in Rome (eighty-two, according to his own statement). He also resurrected long-neglected ceremonies and priesthoods. In 27, for example, he reconstituted the ancient college of the Arval Brothers, who once led the people each year in the *Ambarvalia* (p. 66) at the end of May. Furthermore, Augustus revived the priesthood of the *Flamen Dialis* with all its old taboos (p. 70). It was a difficult undertaking. Many of the ancient priesthoods and rites had fallen into disuse during the disturbed conditions of the civil wars. The archaic language of ancient hymns and incantations was no longer understood. Much antiquarian research went into solving the questions that arose.

Augustus also created new temples and cults that would help shape a positive image of his rule. Accordingly, 29 B.C.E. witnessed the dedication of the new temples of the Divine Julius (in the old Forum) and of Apollo (on the Palatine), a fitting tribute because both gods were protectors of the Julian dynasty, givers of victory, and saviors of the state from civil war. In 2 B.C.E., Augustus erected a new temple of Mars the Avenger in the newly built Forum of Augustus. In 13 B.C.E. the senate voted to erect an altar of Augustan Peace (*Ara Pacis Augustae*). One of the sculptured panels of this superb monument shows Augustus and his family proceeding in solemn pomp to offer sacrifice. Another panel shows a goddess seated on a rock and holding two children and the fruits of the earth on her lap (p. 392, Figure 21.5). A companion panel depicts the armed goddess Roma, and a fourth portrays Aeneas piously sacrificing a sow to his household gods. Thus, the altar suggests peace and plenty, which flowed from the martial valor of Augustus and his pious devotion to the gods, on whose favor everything depended.

Augustus was able to push his religious program with more zeal and vigor after 12 B.C.E. when he succeeded Lepidus as *pontifex maximus*. By 7 B.C.E., he had the city divided into fourteen regions and the regions into wards or precincts (*vici*). The *vicomagistri*, or ward masters, officiated at the shrines dedicated to the worship of the *Lares Compitales*, now called the *Lares Augusti*, guardian spirits of the crossroads and household (p. 66). At each shrine, the *vicomagistri* also offered sacrifices to the Genius of Augustus, his guiding spirit, just as the genius of the *paterfamilias* was traditionally honored in the household worship of the Lares and Penates. Other gods also became "Augustan": when Augustus' stepson, Tiberius, refurbished the old temple to Concord in the Forum, the goddess was reconfigured as *Concordia Augusta* (Augustan Concord), and her cult changed from being a celebration of unity of Rome's upper and lower classes to a celebration of harmony with the imperial family. Romans could also worship Augustan Justice (*Iustitia Augusta*), Augustan Plenty (*Ops Augusta*), Mars Augustus and Diana Augusta. Some Italian cities, especially in the Greek South, actually erected temples to Augustus, but he did not encourage such overt expressions of divinity in Italy. He preferred to promote municipal cults of his genius and encourage their maintenance by the colleges of *Seviri Augustales*. These religious demonstrations were spontaneous enough, but they also subtly helped organize public opinion behind the government.

OVERVIEW AND ASSESSMENT

During the course of forty years, Augustus accomplished a radical reformation of Rome. Trying not to attempt too much too soon, but proceeding by gradual steps and building on precedents, he shaped a new form of government, the Principate. It blended the constitutional forms of the old Republic and the reality of one-man rule into a palatable constitutional monarchy for the Roman Empire. He created a complex administrative hierarchy that reserved many positions of highest status for the old senatorial aristocracy. At the same time, he brought the equestrians of Italy into positions of real power and made them a loyal part of the system, with chances of obtaining senatorial status. In some ways, slaves and freedmen were more restricted, but they, too, had important roles to play in an increasingly complex administrative system and could hope for enhanced status for themselves or their children through loyal service. The urban poor played a much more limited role in political life, but they were kept content with generous benefits. Attempts at restricting women and reforming personal morality did not turn out well. Still, Augustus gave renewed influence to the state religion and successfully promoted the cult of his genius as a way of fostering widespread loyalty to his imperial regime. Many would not care for that regime today. Most Romans, however, preferred it to chaos, civil wars, and failure to address crucial problems, which had characterized the last century of the aristocrats' free Republic, *libera res publica*.

NOTES

1 The so-called senatorial provinces were, according to Dio (53.12.2 and 53.13.1), generally peaceful and, unlike the imperial provinces, did not require a garrison of legionary troops. This distinction did not always hold, for the proconsuls of the senatorial provinces of Africa, Illyricum, and Macedonia had legionary troops under their command at various times during the early Principate.
2 The recipients of free grain were not limited to poor freeborn citizens. Rather, receiving free grain was a mark of status for *all* freeborn citizens, who were expected to show gratitude to their benefactor for it.

SUGGESTED READING

Eck, W. *The Age of Augustus*. 2nd ed. Translated by D. L. Schneider and R. Daniel. Malden. MA: Blackwell, 2007.

Levick, B. *Augustus: Image and Substance*. New York: Longman, 2010.

Richardson, J. S. *Augustan Rome 44 BC to AD 14: The Restoration of the Republic and The Establishment of the Empire. The Edinburgh History of Ancient Rome*. Edinburgh: Edinburgh University Press, 2012.

CHAPTER 20

Imperial stabilization under Augustus

While Augustus had been working out his unique governmental position and making extensive administrative and social reforms at Rome, he also had to secure the safety and stability of what can now be called the Roman Empire. Military and fiscal reforms and the establishment of defensible (but not static or permanent) provincial frontier zones were essential for this effort. Augustus' primary motive always was to secure the benefits of empire for Rome and Italy in a world safely structured around the unifying core of the Mediterranean Sea, *Mare Nostrum* (Our Sea), as the Romans justly called it. He wanted to be remembered as the bringer of peace, prosperity, and increased power to the Roman People. Although he preferred subtler and gentler means, Augustus had no qualms about ruthlessly crushing anyone or anything that stood in the way of that primary goal. Therefore, the process that created the *Pax Romana* (Roman Peace) was not always experienced as peaceful or benign by those who were to serve Rome's and Augustus' glory.

MILITARY REFORMS

In 27 B.C.E., to prevent the rise of powerful military commanders who could have undermined his own power and the peace that he earnestly wished to give the Roman Empire, Augustus had obtained for himself the provinces containing the most legions.

He placed them under the immediate command of his own loyal equestrian legates. Moreover, all soldiers were required to take an oath of personal allegiance to Augustus.

Reduced size of army

Augustus' first step in dealing with military problems, however, had been to reduce the sheer number of men under arms and provide them with their expected grants of land. Both of these steps were necessary to decrease the risk of civil disorder from unoccupied and disgruntled soldiers. They also reduced the crushing economic burden that the huge armies of the civil war placed upon the exhausted treasury. After Actium, Augustus had demobilized about 300,000 men and cut the number of legions from over sixty to perhaps twenty-eight (about 160,000 men).

He avoided the harsh confiscations that had accompanied his settlement of discharged veterans in 41 B.C.E. New colonies in Italy and throughout the Empire provided land for his veterans. They also helped to increase the security and Romanization of the surrounding areas. The vast wealth of Egypt gave Augustus the funds necessary to carry out this colonization scheme without increasing taxes or denying compensation to those whose land was used for colonial settlements.

A retirement system

Eventually, it became impractical to give all veterans land upon discharge. To have done so on a regular basis would have required a costly administrative system. Good land would have become prohibitively expensive as peace and stability encouraged the rapid growth of population once more. Outright confiscation would have revived rural unrest, and distributing cheap waste or marginal land would have left a dangerous number of disgruntled veterans.

Therefore, beginning in 13 C.E., Augustus began to reward many veterans with a system of monetary payments to provide them with financial security upon discharge. Praetorian guardsmen received grants of 5000 *denarii* and ordinary soldiers 3000, the equivalent of almost fifteen years' pay. That is far more money than the average person could have saved in a lifetime. Moreover, soldiers were encouraged, and later required, to save some of their pay in a fund kept at legionary headquarters. Spent wisely, their savings and discharge bonuses alone, on the average, would have supplied the daily needs of veterans for as long as they might expect to live after retiring at thirty-five or forty years of age. On the other hand, a retired veteran could invest his money in a small farm or open up a small shop to support himself in retirement. A higher paid centurion might even have enough from his bonus and savings to acquire equestrian status and pursue a career in higher offices after retirement. The auxiliary troops, however, did not fare as well. Because their bonus, if any, was small, their greatest reward was the diploma of citizenship.

During the years from 7 to 2 B.C.E., Augustus paid discharged veterans no less than 400 million sesterces from his own funds. Still, even his resources could not stand that kind of expense forever. Therefore, in 6 C.E. he shifted the burden to the state by setting up a special fund (*aerarium militare*). He contributed 170 million sesterces of his own money at the start. For the future, he funded it with the revenues from certain taxes (p. 365), as well as with gifts and legacies received from his subjects and clients.

Professionalization

Augustus created a permanent professional army commanded by men loyal to him and to Rome. Terms of service and rates of pay were regularized. Ordinary soldiers received 225 *denarii* a year and, at first, were required to serve sixteen years. Later, to relieve the strain on manpower and reduce the drain on retirement funds, the official term was raised to twenty years, but men might be kept in service even longer.

The backbone of the army was the corps of professional officers composed of the centurions. Under the Principate, they were the lowest commissioned officers and commanded the individual cohorts of the legions. They were often promoted from the ranks of the noncommissioned officers and received triple pay and bonuses. The ranks from military tribune on up were held by equestrians and younger members of the senatorial class in preparation for higher civilian careers. The highest officers were usually members of Augustus' family or were nobles of proven loyalty.

The individual legions were made permanent bodies with special numbers and titles. Through the use of identifying symbols for each legion, a soldier was encouraged to develop a strong loyalty to his unit and strive to enhance its reputation. Each legion tended to be stationed permanently in some sector of the frontier. Many important cities in Europe grew up around such legionary camps.

Legionary soldiers were recruited primarily from Roman citizens in Italy and heavily Romanized areas such as Spain and southern Gaul. In the East, freshly enfranchised natives were also used. Each Roman legion was accompanied by an equal number of auxiliary forces, particularly cavalry, from warlike peoples in the less developed parts of the Empire and from non-Roman allies. They often supplied whole units along with their native officers. Regular pay for auxiliaries was only seventy-five *denarii* a year, and their term of service was twenty-five years.

The combined total of legionary and auxiliary forces under Augustus was between 250,000 and 300,000 men, not too large an army for defending a frontier at least 4000 miles long. Of the twenty-eight legions, at least eight guarded the Rhineland and seven the Danubian region. Three legions were in Spain, four in Syria, two in Egypt, one in Macedonia, and one in Africa. The equivalent of two others were scattered in cohorts in Asia Minor, Judea, and Gaul.

The Praetorian Guard

In Italy itself, however, Augustus stationed the nine cohorts of the Praetorian Guard. They were specially recruited Roman citizens and were called the *Praetorian Guard* after the bodyguard of republican generals. Each cohort probably contained 500 (later 1000) men. Three were stationed near Rome and six others in outlying Italian towns. As privileged troops, the praetorians served for only sixteen years and received 375 *denarii* a year, with 5000 upon discharge. Many praetorians were promoted to legionary centurions.

The imperial Roman navy

The war with Sextus Pompey and the Battle of Actium clearly demonstrated the need for a sizable Roman navy. To suppress piracy, defend the shores of Italy, and escort grain transports and trading ships, Augustus created two main fleets, one based at Misenum on the Bay of Naples, the other at Ravenna on the Adriatic. He had other fleets also, especially at Alexandria and, for a time, at Forum Julii (Fréjus) in southern Gaul. The sailors were largely provincials from the Dalmatian coast but included some slaves and freedmen. They served under the command of prefects who were sometimes equestrians but more often freedmen. Auxiliary river flotillas patrolled the Nile, the Rhine, the Danube, and the major rivers of Gaul.

VIGILES AND *COHORTES URBANAE*

Augustus created the *vigiles* and *cohortes urbanae* to fight fires and maintain public order in Rome (p. 354). They were organized along military lines but were not considered part of the military. The *vigiles* consisted of seven cohorts 1000 men apiece, and each was in charge of two of the fourteen regions into which Augustus divided Rome. The three urban cohorts had 1000 to 1500 men each. The *vigiles* were recruited from freedmen and commanded by an equestrian prefect of the watch (*praefectus vigilum*). The *cohortes urbanae* were freeborn citizens commanded by the new prefect of the city (*praefectus urbi*), a senator of consular rank.

PROTECTION OF THE EMPEROR

The Praetorian Guard, the *vigiles*, and the urban cohorts not only preserved law and order in Rome and Italy but also were effective means of preventing or suppressing secret plots and rebellions against Augustus. Accompanying the establishment of these protections was Augustus' use of the Law of Treason (*maiestas*, p. 235). It was vague, flexible, and sweeping, encompassing all offenses from conspiracy against the state to insulting or even disrespecting the emperor in speech, writing, or deed. In light of Caesar's assassination, conspiracies such as that uncovered ca. 23 B.C.E. (p. 348), and the numerous civil wars of the previous century, Augustus was understandably anxious about plots against himself and the state. He was sensible and restrained in applying the law of *maiestas*. Yet, in the hands of insecure, inexperienced, and immature emperors, the law could be subject to deadly abuse. Sometimes, people acting as informers, *delatores* (sing. *delator*), would try to settle a grudge by accusing an enemy of plotting against an emperor. Indeed, there was an incentive for informers to prey upon an emperor's fears by accusing innocent people of *maiestas*. If someone whom a *delator* accused of *maiestas* was convicted, the *delator* received one-fourth of his property.

FISCAL REFORMS

Before the Principate of Augustus, the civil wars of the late Republic had depleted the funds of the old senate-controlled state treasury, the *aerarium Saturni*, and exhausted its revenues. The old system of tax collection, corrupt and inefficient at best, had completely broken down. The absence of any formal budget, regular estimate of tax receipts and expenditures, or census of taxable property made an already bad situation worse. Despite the urgent need for action, Augustus at first moved slowly and circumspectly. He wished to avoid in every way the suspicion of ruthlessly trampling upon the ancient prerogatives of the senate. In 28 B.C.E., he requested a transfer of control over the state treasury from inexperienced quaestors to ex-praetors selected by the senate. Their duties were given to two additional annual praetors after 23 B.C.E. Because Augustus' greater income enabled him to subsidize the state treasury, he soon acquired virtual control over all the finances of the state.

   He was content with informal control, however. After 27 B.C.E., he set up, for each imperial province, a separate account or chest called a *fiscus* (literally, "fig basket"), into which he deposited the tax receipts and revenues of the province for payment to the legions. The *fisci* not only helped him, as sole paymaster, to assume complete mastery of the armies. They also enabled him to take control over the administration of the Empire. Years later, Claudius united the several *fisci* into a single, central *fiscus*. It then became in fact and in law the main treasury of the Roman Empire and was administered separately from both the *aerarium Saturni* and the *aerarium militare*. Augustus had also continued the Republic's practice of maintaining a special sacred treasury, the *aerarium sanctius*, to provide financial reserves for military emergencies.

   Augustus had still another fund, the *patrimonium Caesaris*, of fabulous size, though not strictly a treasury. It consisted of Julius Caesar's private fortune, the confiscated properties of Antonius, the vast treasures of Cleopatra, the revenues from Augustus' private domains in the provinces, and the numerous legacies left him by wealthy Romans. (The legacies alone amounted to the huge sum of 1.4 billion sesterces.) The public treasuries and his enormous personal funds gave Augustus financial control over the entire administration of the Empire.

Taxation

To fund the *aerarium militare*, Augustus instituted a 5 percent tax on inheritances from well-off Roman citizens without close heirs and made use of a 1 percent tax on auctions. Another new tax, 2 or 4 percent on the sale of slaves, probably funded the *vigiles*. Augustus also levied a tax of as much as 25 percent on imports from outside the Empire and customs dues of 2 to 5 percent on the shipment of goods from one province to another. They were collected by tax contractors who paid the *aerarium Saturni* before collecting the taxes themselves. Augustus replaced the old provincial taxes of *stipendium* and tithe with a poll tax, called the *tributum capitis* (collected from all adults in some provinces and just adult males in others), and the *tributum soli*, a percentage of one's assessed property. Both taxes were determined by a periodic census and were deposited in the provincial *fisci* to cover the expense of imperial defense and administration.

The 5 percent tax on the manumission of slaves (p. 357) probably went into the special reserve treasury (*aerarium sanctius*).

PROVINCIAL REFORMS

The loyalty of the provinces required stable, efficient, and honest administration, with due regard for the provincials themselves. To ensure such administration, Augustus kept firm control over both imperial and senatorial governors. He strengthened the laws against extortion, and reformed the system of taxation by instituting a census of property at regular intervals. Subdividing or rearranging large provinces were other ways to achieve greater administrative efficiency and control. Augustus curbed the power of the tax-farming companies and gradually transferred the collection of direct taxes to quaestors and procurators assisted by local tax officials. Particularly in the East, those reforms made possible a rapid economic recovery and commercial expansion and helped Augustus win the loyalty of the provincial peoples.

The *princeps* respected local customs as much as possible. He also gave the provincials considerable rights of self-government. That encouraged the growth of urban communities out of villages, hamlets, and temple lands. Accordingly, he allowed the town councils (*curiae*) and the leagues (*consilia* or *koina*) of the provincial cities and tribes freedom of assembly and the right to express gratitude or homage and bring their grievances to the attention of the emperor or the senate.

Egypt was a special case. For millennia it had been the personal estate of its kings. To have imposed a new system might have been disruptive. Also, it was to Augustus' advantage simply to take the place of the ancient pharaohs and Hellenistic Ptolemies in order to keep Egypt's vast wealth and vital grain out of the hands of potential challengers. Therefore, he treated it as part of his personal domain and declared it off limits to Roman senators without special permission. He and his successors administered it through special prefects of equestrian rank.

To round out the conquest of the Mediterranean basin and expand imperial power to the most defensible geographic frontiers, Augustus added a number of new provinces and extended Roman control over other territories. By 14 C.E., there were twenty-eight provinces, ten of which were senatorial and eighteen imperial (map, pp. 368–9). From the Roman point of view, his policy was a great success and earned Augustus much prestige in a society that valued military prowess highly. It was not, however, always a pretty story in human terms. A century later, the historian Tacitus grasped the reality faced by the native peoples whose independence and homelands were destroyed in the process of creating the Roman Peace (*Pax Romana*). He has a native leader say of the Romans, "With false words they call robbery, murder, and rape 'empire' and where they have created an empty waste, 'peace'" (*Agricola*, 30.5).

CONQUESTS IN THE WEST

The policy of conquest was very evident in the West. There were still large areas near Italy that the Romans had not yet attempted to take over. It was necessary to do so, however, in order to protect Italy, the heart of the Empire, and secure efficient communications with the outlying territories. From 27 B.C.E. to 9 C.E., therefore, Augustus methodically rounded out imperial conquests in the West.

Spain and Gaul, 27 to 22 B.C.E.

Augustus personally led the fight against the Cantabrians and Asturians of northwestern Spain in 27, but his always-delicate health failed in 26, and he left in 24. Agrippa suppressed the rugged tribesmen years later through the brutal expedients of massacre and enslavement. In Gaul, Caesar's thorough victories left Augustus nothing more than minor campaigns in Aquitania and administrative reorganization. In 22 B.C.E., he transferred Gallia Narbonensis to the senate. He divided old Gallia Comata into three administrative parts: Aquitania, Lugdunensis, and Belgica, each under a separate legate subject to the governor, who had his headquarters in Lugdunum (Lyons).

The Alpine districts, 25 to 14 B.C.E.

Although the Roman Empire now extended from the Straits of Gibraltar to the Euphrates, the Alpine region had remained unsubdued and menaced Italy. In 25 B.C.E., a decisive victory and ruthless enslavement removed the menace. In the northern and eastern Alps, Roman armies subdued Raetia (eastern Switzerland, southern Bavaria, and western Tyrol) and Noricum (eastern Tyrol and western Austria) from 17 to 14 B.C.E. Those efforts were led by Augustus' stepsons, Tiberius Claudius Nero (Tiberius) and Nero Claudius Drusus (Drusus I). All the tribes near the headwaters of the Rhine and the Danube became Rome's subjects. The upper Danube then became Rome's northern frontier in the West.

Failure on the German frontier, 12 B.C.E. to 9 C.E.

Augustus' only failure on the frontiers was in Germany. Augustus wanted to cross the Rhine and push the frontier to the Elbe (Albis) and, later if possible, to the Vistula. The operations of Drusus I from 12 to 9 B.C.E. spectacularly accomplished the initial goal. Unfortunately, Drusus broke a leg by falling from a horse and later died of complications. Tiberius then handled matters effectively in Germany until he was called away to suppress a serious rebellion in Pannonia and Illyricum from 6 to 9 C.E. In 9 C.E., however, the German leader Arminius ambushed Quinctilius Varus and three legions in the Teutoburg Forest. Few escaped, and Varus committed suicide.

Although Augustus was unable to replace the three lost legions, he did not abandon an aggressive posture against the German tribes across the Rhine. Still, whether he intended to or not, the subsequent successful campaigns of Tiberius and Drusus' son Germanicus to avenge Rome's and his family's honor never resulted in the extension of Roman administrative control to the Elbe. Not extending such control posed serious strategic problems later. The Rhine–Danube frontier was 300 miles longer than an Elbe–Danube one would have been and required more men to defend. In addition,

FIGURE 20.1 The Roman Empire under the Principate. (Provincial Boundaries ca. 180 C.E.).

CARPATHIAN MTS

Vistula R.

Dniester R.

Dnieper R.

Don R.

Volga R.

Alani

Caspian Sea

DACIA

Olbia

Sea of Azov

Chersonesos

Black Sea

Porta Caucasica

CAUCASUS MOUNTAINS

UPPER MOESIA

LOWER MOESIA

Danube R.

Tomi

Sinope

Phasis

COLCHIS

Iberia (Tiflis)

Cyrus R.

THRACE

Trapezus

GREATER ARMENIA
(114–117 C.E.)

Artaxata

Araxes R.

MEDIA

MACEDONIA

Adrianopolis

Byzantium

Bosp(h)orus

Heraclea

Hieron

BITHYNIA

PONTUS

Paphlagonia

Halys R.

Lesser Armenia

Sophene

Tigranocerta

ASSYRIA

ATROPATENE

Thessalonica

Sea of Marmara

Ancyra

GALATIA

CAPPADOCIA

Commagene

Amida

Arbela

EPIRUS

Mysia

Phrygia

LYCAONIA

Edessa

Nisibis

Tigris R.

KINGDOM OF PARTHIA (PERSIA)

ACHAEA

Athens

Aegean Sea

Lydia

ASIA

Ephesus

PISIDIA

CILICIA

Carrhae

OSROENE

(116–117 C.E.)

MESOPOTAMIA

Ctesiphon

Euphrates R.

Corinth

Caria

LYCIA

PAMPHYLIA

Antioch

SYRIA

RHODES

CRETE

Orontes R.

CYPRUS

Palmyra

Sea

Damascus

Samaria

Syria Palestina

Jerusalem

Judea

Persian Gulf

Cyrene

Alexandria

ARABIA PETRAEA

Nabataeans

ARABIA

CYRENAICA

Wadi Natrun

Memphis

AEGYPTUS
(EGYPT)

Nile R.

Red Sea

Thebae

Syene

Berenice

the headwaters of the Rhine and the Danube created a triangular territory, the *Agri Decumates*, that would give attackers easy access to Italy and the western provinces if there were a breakthrough in that sector of the frontier.

Western North Africa

Caesar had enlarged Roman territory in western North Africa by the annexation of Numidia as the province of Africa Nova. Augustus was convinced that the enlarged territory was too difficult to defend. He consigned the western part of it to the kingdom of Mauretania (modern Algeria and Morocco). Upon Mauretania's vacant throne he placed Juba II of Numidia, who had married Cleopatra Selene (Moon), daughter of Antonius and Cleopatra. Augustus combined the rest of Africa Nova with the old Roman province to create an enlarged Africa Proconsularis with its capital at Carthage. Caesar had planned the refounding of Carthage as a colony for retired veterans, but it was Augustus who actually brought the plan to fruition. In addition, Augustus established at least nine other colonies in Africa Proconsularis to provide land for veterans and security for the province. He also fought at least five wars against the tribes on the southern frontiers. Between 21 B.C.E. and 6 C.E., Augustus' need to cultivate as much grain as possible in Africa to feed Rome's huge population and the tribes' need for open access to seasonal pasturage often led to conflict.

SOLIDIFYING CONTROL OF THE BALKANS, CRETE, AND CYRENE

The Balkan region (extending from Greece north to the middle Danube), Crete, and Cyrene formed a middle zone between the West and the rich provinces of the East. For the previous century, the Romans had concentrated on establishing their power in Asia Minor and the Levant. Now it was time to pay more attention to these intermediate territories, which sat astride the land and sea routes between the East and West.

The Danubian lands, 14 B.C.E. to 6 C.E.

Long overdue was the conquest of the Danubian lands in the northern Balkans. Illyricum (the modern republics of Bosnia, Croatia, and Macedonia; western Hungary; northern Serbia; and eastern Austria) was constantly disturbed by Pannonian and Dacian tribes. In addition, the Dalmatian coastal regions of Illyricum never had been completely pacified. In 13 B.C.E., Marcus Agrippa took over operations begun in the previous year against the Dalmatians and Pannonians. His heart failed during a harsh winter campaign, and Tiberius finished the task in four years of hard fighting from 12 to 9 B.C.E.

In the eastern Balkans, Thracian uprisings and Dacian invasions from across the Danube during 13 B.C.E. forced Augustus to act. Three years of fighting, from 12 to 10 B.C.E., eliminated the threat but depopulated Moesia (Serbia and northern Bulgaria) along the south bank of the Danube from Illyricum to the Black Sea. Eventually,

Roman armies rounded up 50,000 Dacians from across the Danube and settled them in the vacant territory.

By these conquests, Augustus moved the frontier of the Empire away from north-eastern Italy and greatly shortened communications between the vital Rhineland and the East. Moreover, although less economically valuable than many provinces, the Danubian lands soon proved to be the best recruiting grounds in the Empire. In later centuries, many of the emperors who fought to preserve the Empire from outside attacks came from this region.

Macedonia and Greece

In 27 B.C.E., Augustus separated Greece from Macedonia by creating the senatorial province of Achaea, apparently with Corinth as its capital. This new province included the Cycladic Islands, Aetolia, Acarnania, and part of Epirus. The island of Corcyra, Thessaly, Delphi, Athens, Sparta, and the League of Free Laconians remained technically autonomous.

Crete and Cyrene

The large island of Crete, despite its strategic location and the suppression of its pirates from 69 to 67 B.C.E., had remained independent during subsequent decades. It was not considered profitable enough for anyone to annex. Augustus finally ended this anomaly in 27 B.C.E. by combining Crete with Cyrene to create a proconsular province for a senator of praetorian rank. Cyrene and other prosperous Greek cities on the east coast of North Africa constituted a territory between Africa Proconsularis and Egypt. It had become a dependency of Egypt under the Ptolemies. Although the Romans had inherited the region from its Ptolemaic ruler in 96 B.C.E., they had done little with it until Augustus.

Holding the East

The problems presented by the East differed widely from those of the West. The eastern provinces were heirs to very old and advanced civilizations and were proud of their traditions. Many had been taken over only recently and were not yet fully reconciled to Roman rule. Beyond the eastern frontier lay the Parthian Empire, a vast polyglot state embracing an area of 1.2 million square miles from the Euphrates to the Aral Sea and beyond the Indus. Within recent memory, Parthia had inflicted three stinging defeats upon the Romans and was still considered a potential menace. As an organized state, however, it was capable of being dealt with through sophisticated diplomacy as well as force.

After Actium, an insistent clamor arose for a war of revenge against Parthia. Without openly defying the demands of public opinion and the patriotic sentiments of authors like Vergil and Horace, Augustus was reluctant to commit himself to a war with Parthia. Even if he could have defeated the Parthians in battle, it is doubtful that he could have committed the time, manpower, and resources to pacify and hold a large bloc of Parthian territory while there were more urgent matters that needed attention in the West. Augustus would try to strengthen Rome's position and neutralize Parthia by other methods.

Asia Minor and the Levant

In 27 B.C.E., Augustus made only minor adjustments to the provinces established by Pompey in Asia Minor and the Levant. The principal change was the reannexation of Cyprus, which Marcus Antonius had ceded to Cleopatra. Augustus left the provinces of Asia Minor to senatorial proconsuls, but he actively promoted the restoration of stability and prosperity. Ephesus and Pergamum were encouraged to mint large numbers of silver tetradrachms to aid commerce. Augustus himself gave money to restore cities damaged by Parthian attacks and natural disasters. He generously rewarded others for loyalty and honors bestowed upon him.

Client kingdoms

At first, Augustus continued the policy of Marcus Antonius, which was to maintain client kingdoms as buffer states between Parthia and the Roman provinces. After Actium, Augustus consigned large territories in Asia Minor (Galatia, Pisidia, Lycaonia, and most of Cilicia) to Amyntas the Galatian. He also gave eastern Pontus, Lesser Armenia, and the huge realm of Cappadocia to client kings. At the same time, he enlarged Judea, the kingdom of Herod I, the Great (37–4 B.C.E.). Eventually, all the client kingdoms became provinces. When Amyntas died in 25 B.C.E., Rome acquired the vast province of Galatia and Pamphylia. A decade after Herod's death, Augustus made Judea and Samaria an imperial province—or, rather, a subprovince attached to Syria and governed by prefects.

Armenia and Parthia

In only one kingdom, Armenia, had Roman influence deteriorated after the death of Antonius. Subdued and annexed as a province in 34 B.C.E., Armenia had slipped away from Roman control just before Actium. It had come under the brutal rule of King Artaxias II, who slew all Roman residents in Armenia. Augustus did not avenge their deaths. He made no effort to recover control of Armenia for over a decade, although it provided the best invasion routes from Parthia to Roman provinces in Asia Minor and Syria.

Meanwhile, he preferred intrigue and diplomacy to direct confrontation with Parthia. He gave refuge to Tiridates, a rival of the Parthian king Phraates IV. Tiridates turned over Phraates' kidnapped son for Augustus to use as a hostage. In 23 B.C.E., wanting to get back his son, Phraates agreed to return the battle standards and all surviving prisoners captured from the Romans at Carrhae (p. 284) or in subsequent Parthian victories. Phraates, however, had still not made the exchange by 20 B.C.E., when Artaxias of Armenia was killed. Augustus immediately sent in Tiberius with a

Roman army to place Tigranes III on the Armenian throne. Phraates, now fearful that Augustus might be able to use the army in Armenia to support Tiridates' seizure of the Parthian throne, handed over the promised prisoners and standards.

A rattle of the saber temporarily restored Roman prestige in the East and wiped away the stains upon Roman honor. Augustus, therefore, shrewdly declared a great victory and silenced further demands for war by advertising his success on coins with such slogans as *signis receptis* (the standards regained), *civibus et signis militaribus a Parthis recuperatis* (citizens and military standards recovered from the Parthians), and *Armenia recepta* (Armenia recaptured).

All was quiet in the East until the death of Tigranes in 1 B.C.E. A group of Armenians, aided and abetted by the Parthians, enthroned a king of their own choice without consulting Augustus. He at once sent out Gaius Caesar, his grandson/adopted son and heir apparent, armed with full proconsular *imperium* over the entire East. Gaius marched into Armenia at the head of a powerful army. This show of force compelled the Parthians to recognize Rome's preponderant interest in Armenia and accept a Roman appointee on the Armenian throne. The Armenians subsequently revolted but were suppressed after hard fighting. It was a costly victory, however. Gaius had suffered wounds that would not heal, and he died eighteen months later (4 C.E.).

Parthia, as well as Augustus, had reasons for avoiding war. Torn by the dissensions of rival claimants to the throne and continually menaced by Asian migrations, Parthia was in no position to attack. The Parthians willingly endured diplomatic defeat rather than risk military conflict. They calculated that their own diplomacy and intrigue might eventually succeed; overt aggression might fail and would surely be costly.

Both Parthia and Rome also had economic interests that would have been ruined by war. Peace along the Euphrates permitted the uninterrupted flow of the caravan trade that brought to each of them luxuries from India, Central Asia, and China. Under joint Parthian and Roman protection, Palmyra was rapidly becoming a large and prosperous caravan city with fine streets, parks, and public buildings. Other cities—Petra, Gerasa (Jerash), Philadelphia (Amman), and Damascus—were also beginning to enjoy the rich benefits of caravan trade.

Egypt and the Red Sea zone

Egypt, richest of all Augustan annexations and producer of one-third of the Roman annual grain supply (5 million bushels), remained relatively quiet except for some skirmishes on the Nubian border in upper Egypt. In 22 B.C.E., after three Roman campaigns in Nubia, the Nubian queen, Candace, agreed to fix the southern boundary of Egypt about sixty miles south of Syene (Aswan) and the First Cataract. It remained there for the next 300 years (map, p. 375).

About this time (25–24 B.C.E.), a Roman expedition, sent down to the Red Sea against the Sabaeans in Arabia near what is now Aden, sought to gain naval control of the Straits of Bab-el-Mandeb. Roman control would allow Alexandrian merchants to break the Sabaean monopoly on trade with India in precious stones, spices, cosmetics, and other commodities. The expedition failed, but it paved the way for more successful ones later.

ROAD BUILDING

The building of roads went hand in hand with conquest, frontier defense, and provincial communication. By 27 B.C.E., Augustus had completed the repair and reconstruction of the Italian roads (much neglected since the time of Gaius Gracchus)—especially the Flaminian Way, a vital artery of the Empire and the main thoroughfare between Rome and the North. After the conquest of the Alpine and Danubian regions, he began the construction of a road north from Tridentum (Trent) on the Adige in the Venetian Alps to Augusta Vindelicorum (Augsburg) on the Lech in Raetia. Other roads ran through the Alps between Italy and Gaul. The completion of this program brought Raetia and Noricum (modern Switzerland and parts of Austria and Bavaria), as well as Gaul, into close and rapid communication with Italy.

THE IMPERIAL POST (*CURSUS PUBLICUS*)

Road building made possible another Augustan achievement, the imperial postal service (*cursus publicus*). Much like that of ancient Persia, the Roman postal service carried official letters and dispatches and transported officials, senators, and other privileged persons. The expense of this service—relays of horses and carriages and the provision of hotel service for official guests—fell upon the towns located along the great highways. That was a burden on many towns, but it was essential to promote swift communication and the centralization of administration. Moreover, as did railroads in the second half of the nineteenth century and national highways in the first half of the twentieth, the routes used by the *cursus publicus* brought business and travelers to towns located along them.

COLONIZATION

Over the course of his long career, Augustus founded twenty-eight colonies in Italy and perhaps eighty in the provinces. The Italian colonies, mainly of veterans, were very loyal to the new regime. Augustus was not primarily interested in the commercial potential of colonies. He founded few, if any, civilian colonies outside of Italy. Most of his provincial colonies were for the settlement of veterans or served as fortresses or military outposts at strategic points to hold down and secure recently conquered territory in the Alps, Gaul, and Spain. As always, while veteran colonies acted as garrisons, they also helped to spread the use of the Latin language and Roman law among the conquered peoples. Thus, they became important agents of Romanization. In time, many large and prosperous communities grew out of veteran colonies. A number provided the original foundations of well-known modern cities: Barcelona (Barcino), Zaragoza (Caesaraugusta), and Merida (Emerita) in Spain; Vienne (Vienna), Nîmes (Nemausus), and Lyons (Lugdunum) in France; and Tangier (Tingis) in Morocco (map, pp. 378–9).

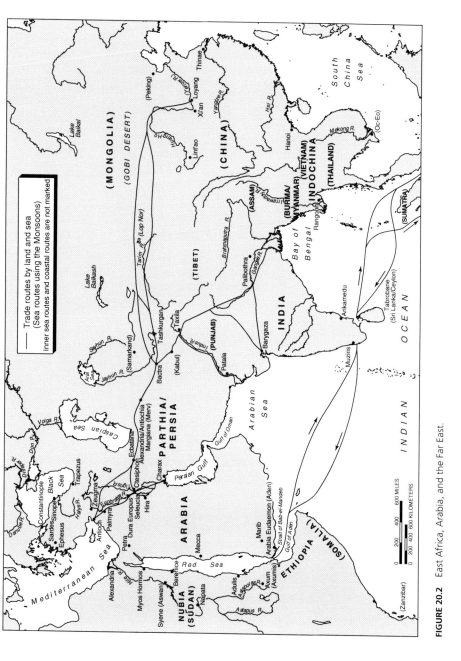

FIGURE 20.2   East Africa, Arabia, and the Far East.

URBANIZATION OF THE PROVINCES

Colonization probably should be seen as part of a long-term policy to promote urbanization and the growth of urban elites in general. The new cities would help to unify the Empire by the diffusion of Roman culture and would serve the central government as convenient administrative units for the collection of taxes and other useful functions. No doubt, too, Augustus realized that since the urban elites would owe their privileged position to the central government, they would in turn support the new imperial regime with vigor and enthusiasm.

GROWTH OF THE IMPERIAL CULT

The growth of emperor worship throughout the Empire was also useful in strengthening ties of loyalty to both Rome and the *princeps*. The people of the eastern provinces had long been used to worshiping their rulers as gods. When Augustus became ruler of the Roman world, many easterners began to establish cults for his worship. Augustus, however, was reluctant to be worshiped too directly. Whatever his personal feelings, it certainly would have entailed the political risk of alienating jealous or conservative nobles. Augustus insisted, therefore, that official provincial cults for his worship be linked with the goddess Roma. By 29 B.C.E., before he had received the title *Augustus*, temples of such cults already existed in the East. Later, with Augustus' encouragement, such cults appeared in the western provinces, too. Each cult included a yearly festival and periodic games managed by a high priest elected from among the leading aristocrats of the city or provincial assembly (*concilium, koinon*) that maintained it. In this way, the provincial elite became identified with, and loyal to, both Rome and the emperor. Thus, the cautious promotion of emperor worship built a basis for imperial unity that bridged the different local and ethnic traditions of a huge polyglot empire.

THE PROBLEM OF SUCCESSION

The problem of who would be the next *princeps* gave Augustus more difficulty than all the rest of the problems that he had faced. A smooth transfer of power would be essential for preserving the Principate and the stability of the Empire after his death. Legally and constitutionally, the choice of a successor was not his right, but that of the senate and the Roman People. Nevertheless, he feared that his failure to deal with the question beforehand might bring about a civil war after his death. Also, he naturally hoped to find a successor in his own family and of his own blood. Unfortunately, he had no sons and only one daughter, Julia, who had been married in 25 B.C.E. to his eighteen-year-old nephew M. Claudius Marcellus, Octavia's son by her first husband. Augustus assiduously promoted the political advancement of his son-in-law so that he would have accumulated the experience and prestige that would make him the natural one to succeed to the Principate.

Unfortunately, Marcellus was not old enough when Augustus fell gravely ill in 23 B.C.E. Therefore, the *princeps* gave his signet ring to Agrippa, his longtime friend, loyal aide and most successful general, to indicate that he should carry on in his place. If Augustus had died then, Agrippa probably would have acted as some kind of regent until Marcellus had matured into the position of *princeps*. Even when Augustus recovered, however, Agrippa shouldered a bigger share of the government thereafter.

First, Augustus gave Agrippa command over the imperial provinces and the task of strengthening the East against Parthia. Marcellus' sudden death later in 23, just after Agrippa's departure, fueled speculation, both ancient and modern, that Agrippa and/ or Livia had a hand in the death to benefit Agrippa or Livia's sons. That seems merely to reflect malicious gossip aimed at discrediting later emperors descended from them. Augustus certainly did not suspect them. Instead, he relied on Agrippa even more.

In 21 B.C.E., Augustus sent for Agrippa and prevailed upon him to divorce his wife and marry Julia. In 18 B.C.E., he obtained the extension of Agrippa's *imperium* over the senatorial provinces as well as the imperial ones and even had the tribunician power conferred on him for five years. Agrippa was now son-in-law, coregent, and heir-presumptive to the Augustan throne. Nor was that all: in 17 B.C.E., the *princeps* adopted, under the names of Gaius and Lucius Caesar, the two young sons of Julia and Agrippa. That would have settled the problem of succession not just for one, but for two generations to come.

When Agrippa died in 12 B.C.E., however, Lucius and Gaius were still too young. Augustus then turned to Livia's older son, Tiberius. Tiberius had served Augustus well on numerous military assignments and had held the consulship in 13 B.C.E. Augustus now made Tiberius divorce Vipsania, a child of Agrippa's first marriage, and marry Julia, the young widow of Marcellus and Agrippa. Julia bore Tiberius a son who died in infancy. Soon thereafter, the marriage soured. Supposedly, Julia turned to other lovers. If so, her motives may have been more dynastic than Dionysiac as she and Scribonia sought to promote Julia's sons by Agrippa ahead of Livia's son Tiberius in the line of succession to Augustus. Augustus had come to rely more and more on Tiberius after the latter's popular and talented younger brother, Drusus I, had died in 9 B.C.E. (p. 367). Tiberius, however, became frustrated and angry that Julia's inexperienced sons Gaius and Lucius seemed to receive advancement at his expense, despite his years of experience and hard work in loyal service to Augustus. In 6 B.C.E., therefore, he badgered Augustus to let him retire to Rhodes. Eventually, Augustus himself became disturbed enough by Julia's conduct to take action against her and important men associated with her. The latter included the younger son of Fulvia and Marcus Antonius, Iullus Antonius, who had received clemency, high office, and a marital alliance from Augustus. In 2 B.C.E., Augustus officially charged them with adultery, a crime that emperors often alleged to cover up more political reasons for prosecutions. Iullus was either executed or forced to commit suicide. Others, including Julia, were relegated (banished) to small islands. Scribonia showed her support for Julia by voluntarily going with her. Even Tiberius, as well as crowds of demonstrators, unsuccessfully interceded on Julia's behalf. The *princeps* would not relent, but in 4 C.E., he did permit her to move to Rhegium, where she eventually died (p. 406). One of her daughters by Agrippa, Julia the Younger, suffered banishment in 8 C.E. for similar reasons. At that time, the poet Ovid was somehow involved, and he, too, was forced into bleak exile.

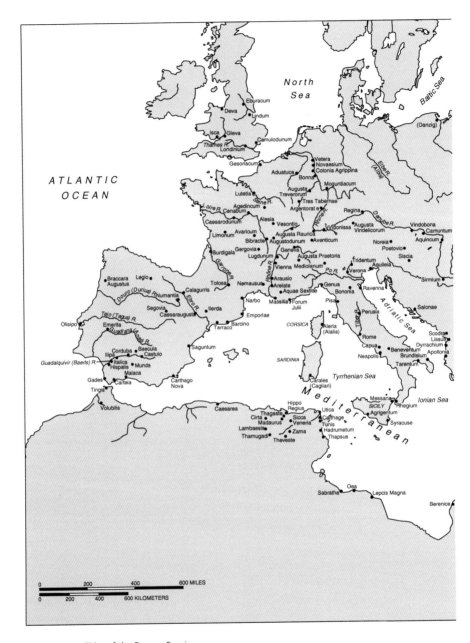

FIGURE 20.3 Cities of the Roman Empire.

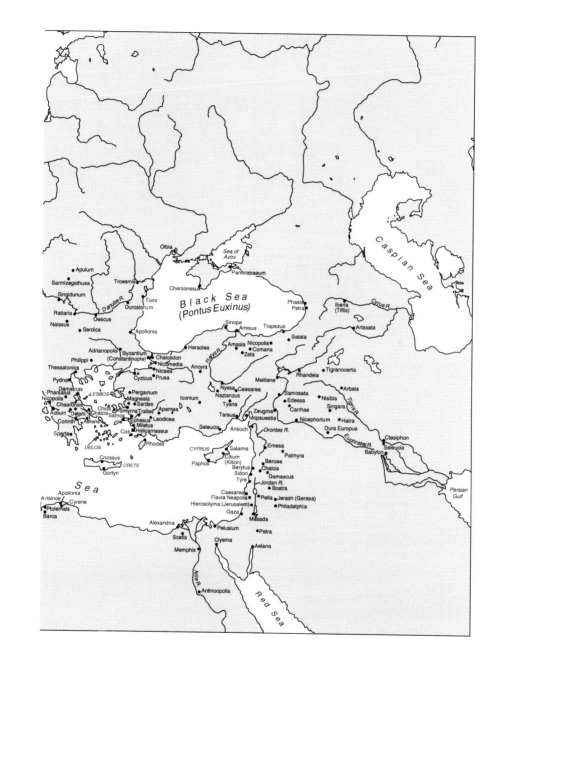

Apulum

Sarmizegethusa Troesmis Olbia

Singidunum Danube R. Tomi Chersonesus Sea of Azov

Ratiaria Oescus Durostorum Panticapaeum

Naissus Serdica Apollonia B l a c k S e a Phasis Iberia Cyrus R.

(Pontus Euxinus) Petra (Tiflis)

Sinope Amisus Trapezus Artaxata

Adrianopolis Byzantium Heraclea Amasia Nicopolis Satala

Philippi (Constantinople) Chalcedon Comana Tigranocerta

Thessalonica Nicomedia Ancyra Zela Rhandeia

Pydna Cyzicus Nicaea Prusa Melitene Arbela

Demetrias Pergamum Nyssa Caesarea Samosata Nisibis

Pharsalus Magnesia Nazianzus Edessa Singara

Nicopolis LESBOS Sardes Iconium Tyana Carrhae

Chaeronea Chios Smyrna Tralles Apamea Zeugma Nicephorium Hatra

Actium Delphi Chalcis Samos Laodicea Tarsus Mopsuestia Dura Europus

Corinth Ephesus Miletus Seleucia Antioch Orontes R. Ctesiphon

Sparta Athens Halicarnassus Cos Seleucia

DELOS Rhodes Babylon

Cnossus CYPRUS Salamis Emesa Palmyra

Gortyn CRETE Paphos Citium Beroea

(Kition) Berytus Chalcis

Sidon Damascus

S e a Tyre Jordan R. Bostra Persian

Apollonia Caesarea Pella Jerash (Gerasa) Gulf

Arsinoe Cyrene Flavia Neapolis Philadelphia

Ptolemais Hierosolyma (Jerusalem)

Barca Gaza

Masada

Alexandria Pelusium Petra

Scetis Clysma

Memphis Aelana

Nile R. Red S e a

Antinoopolis

C a s p i a n S e a

Helys R.

Tigris R.

Euphrates R.

The more Augustus sought to ensure his successor, the more many members of old senatorial families realized that he meant to establish a dynastic Principate that would not permit them to compete for being the leading man of Rome. Some hoped to make use of the rivalries and jealousies within the imperial family to promote a successor favorable to themselves. As time went on, Augustus began to take harsher measures against those deemed unsympathetic to his plans and wishes.

Fate always seemed to intervene on behalf of Tiberius' succession. In 2 C.E., Augustus reluctantly let Tiberius return after the attractions of Rhodes had worn off. Unfortunately, Lucius Caesar died on the way to Spain a little later that year, and Gaius Caesar died less than two years after that (p. 373). In grief and frustration, Augustus adopted Tiberius as his son in 4 C.E. and obtained a ten-year grant of the tribunician power for him, as well as a grant of *imperium* in the provinces. Over the years, Tiberius clearly acquired the position of a coregent as Augustus became older and frailer. In 13 C.E., when Tiberius' tribunician power was renewed along with another grant of *imperium* for both him and Augustus, there was no question that he was Augustus' equal partner. When Augustus died a year later, Tiberius was already in place, and the smooth succession for which Augustus had constantly labored automatically took place.

Still, in his attempt to secure the eventual succession of a member of his own family, the Julii, Augustus had complicated things for the future. At the same time that he had adopted Tiberius, he had also adopted Agrippa's posthumously born son by Julia, Agrippa Postumus, a move that he soon came to regret (p. 405). He had also required Tiberius to adopt Germanicus, son of Tiberius' own dead brother, Drusus I. Germanicus' mother, Antonia the younger, had given him the blood of Augustus' family because she was a child of the marriage between Augustus' sister, Octavia, and Marcus Antonius. The Julian family tie was further strengthened by having Germanicus marry Agrippina, another child of Julia and Agrippa. Tiberius' own son, Drusus II, who was not a blood relative to Augustus, received Germanicus' sister, widow of Gaius Caesar, as his wife. Those attempts to manipulate the succession in favor of Augustus' own Julian side of the imperial family created unfortunate tensions and rivalries in later generations of his Julio-Claudian dynasty.

THE DEATH OF AUGUSTUS

At last, after a political career of almost sixty years, on August 19 of 14 C.E., in the Campanian town of Nola, Augustus met a peaceful death (see Box 20.1). Nearly seventy-seven years old, he was ready, serene, cheerful; not plagued by doubt, guilt, or remorse, although there was much for which he could have been. Dying, he jokingly asked his assembled friends whether he had played out the farce of life well enough. Then he added a popular tag ending from Greek comedy: "Since it has been very well acted, give applause and send us off the stage with joy" (Suetonius, *Augustus* 99.1). A consummate actor, he had played his part well indeed. The ruthless and bloody dynast of the civil wars had skillfully assumed the role of statesman. The applauding Roman senators, most of whom owed their positions to him, willingly conferred the divinity that he had tactfully refused to claim outright while he was alive.

20.1 ROME'S FIRST IMPERIAL FUNERAL

The funeral of Rome's first emperor was elaborate and carefully choreographed. The event comprised all the traditional elements of an aristocratic funeral—procession, *imagines*, eulogy, and spectacle—but in grander dimensions than anything the city had seen before. Public business was suspended so that everyone, not just the imperial family, was free to mourn.

As Augustus' body was transported the long distance back to the capitol from the family estate where he died, the senators and equestrians who were granted the honor of carrying his body moved it only after dark to avoid the summer heat. During the daytime, the body lay in state in the towns where the procession paused.

The funeral itself began, not with the usual mourners' parade through the Forum, but with multiple processions that converged there. One brought a wax effigy of Augustus, dressed in triumphal garb, from the imperial palace, another carried an effigy of gold from the Curia Julia, and a third was brought in on a triumphal chariot. The usual parade of actors dressed as the deceased's most prominent ancestors was enhanced by the addition of images of great Romans of the past: Augustus' heritage and that of the Roman People were one and the same. After not one, but two eulogies were delivered, all the leading men of the city and their wives escorted the body to the Campus Martius. As the funeral pyre caught flame, an eagle was released to signal that Augustus' spirit had ascended to the gods above. Livia is said to have stayed by the pyre for five days and then moved his bones to his tomb.

SUGGESTED READING

Lintott, A. *Imperium Romanum: Politics and Administration*. London and New York: Routledge, 1993.

Garnsey, P. and R. Saller. *The Roman Empire: Economy, Society, and Culture*. 2nd ed. Berkeley: University of California Press, 2014.

CHAPTER 21

The impact of Augustus on Roman Imperial life and culture

The Augustan Age witnessed a quickening of economic life throughout the Mediterranean. The ending of civil wars, the suppression of piracy at sea and of banditry and lawlessness in Italy, and the construction of extensive roads in Italy and the provinces brought about a remarkable expansion of agriculture, industry, and commerce. At first, Italy benefited most from the new expansion. The East had not yet recovered from the effects of past wars and exploitation. The western provinces were still too young to take full advantage of the new order. Italy, therefore, continued to dominate the Mediterranean world not only politically but also economically and culturally.

THE POPULATION AND ECONOMIC IMPACT OF ROME

Disturbed conditions during the civil wars from 49 to 36 B.C.E. probably produced a temporary reduction in Rome's population, a large part of which was always very fluid and transient. Under the Augustan peace, the population rapidly rebounded. It probably reached a million as the *princeps* improved the attractiveness of Rome by restoring order, improving public amenities, providing for a steady supply of food, and inaugurating a building program that created much employment. In fact, Rome became the greatest metropolis of premodern Europe, if not the whole premodern world.

Within Italy and, therefore, the Empire, the great imperial metropolis drove economic and cultural developments. Until recently, Rome has been viewed in terms of the "consumer" or "parasite" model of the ancient city. According to this line of thinking, most large ancient cities produced little of economic value and served mainly their ruling elites. The ruling elite of a region's metropolitan center, it is said, inhibited the development of its hinterlands and subject territories. Surplus wealth was siphoned off in the form of rents, taxes, tribute, and spoils in order to support the metropolis as the physical embodiment of its elite's own greatness. Newer studies, however, based on more extensive archaeological research and comparisons with large cities in other premodern societies, have shown this model to be inadequate.

First, it underestimates the real value of a metropolis's central administration in suppressing intraregional conflicts and providing defense from external attack. Second, it ignores the impact of the market created by the metropolis' concentration of surplus wealth. That surplus financed the purchase and transportation of vast quantities of food, goods, and services from the hinterland and subject territories. Under Augustus and a relatively benign central administration, Rome gave the Mediterranean world a prolonged period of internal peace and freed its economy from the destructive conflicts and confiscations of earlier times. Moreover, Rome's legions freed subject cities and territories from the less efficient maintenance of their own individual armies. As a result, Rome's subjects had more wealth at their disposal to spur local economic growth, even after the deduction of Rome's taxes and tribute.

Furthermore, the taxes and tribute used to pay Roman armies on the frontier and build the transportation infrastructure that supported those armies were great stimuli to the economic growth of the frontier provinces. Finally, by subsidizing Rome as the Empire's metropolis, the wealth that flowed into the city also flowed out into the Italian hinterland, other parts of the Empire, and even beyond to purchase the foodstuffs, raw materials, services, manufactured goods, and luxuries that the city demanded. Those expenditures put more money in circulation, which created even more demand, which supported local and regional economic growth.

From the modern point of view, this economic growth can be considered less than ideal. Much of it was ultimately based on the politically derived purchasing power of the emperor and elite landowners. It was also limited by the lack of many significant technological developments. Profits often rested on the exploitation of slaves and were unevenly distributed in favor of those already privileged. Nevertheless, there was real economic growth, and many ordinary people benefited.

AGRICULTURE

After Actium, Augustus avoided the confiscations that had marked his attempts to settle veterans after Philippi (p. 383). The ranks of the small farmers stabilized throughout Italy. Augustus' upgraded road system and the growth of cities allowed more small farmers to specialize in high-value products for urban markets. By siphoning off the excess population of the countryside, growing cities also greatly reduced the small farmer's perennial problem of subdividing land into increasingly uneconomical units among heirs. Growing provincial cities and Rome's insatiable demand for food had an impact on provincial agriculture similar to that on Italian agriculture. More farmers produced for profitable markets rather than just for subsistence. Although part of Rome's need for grain was met through taxes in kind on provincial producers, the rest was acquired through purchase. Therefore, landowners in the grain-producing provinces of Sicily, Sardinia, North Africa, and Egypt profited from the enormous efforts to supply Rome and its armies. Similarly, along the Mediterranean coasts of Spain and Gaul and up the valley of the Rhône, vineyards and olive groves were beginning to produce large quantities of wine and oil for the lucrative Roman market.

AGRICULTURAL WEALTH AND URBANIZATION

In both Italy and the provinces, the larger landowners profited most from the commercialization and urbanization fostered by Rome, which they largely supported. The wealthy local landowners became the backbone and lifeblood of the curial class (*curiales*), the local aristocrats who filled the governing councils (*curiae*) of cities and municipalities all over the Empire. Like their counterparts in the Roman senatorial class, they dedicated a significant part of their agricultural profits to increase their status by building fine residences in the nearest significant city or town and by providing expensive benefactions, such as games, gifts of food, temples, theaters, schools, aqueducts, baths, fora (forums), and porticoes. These amenities attracted more population by making the growing cities and towns more appealing places to live and by creating employment in the building trades and the provision of goods and services to a growing population. Thus, in many places, there occurred an upward spiral of urban development fueled by the profits of local landowners. Some were part of an elaborate network funneling food and raw materials from their estates to Rome. Of course, some of the other growing cities were significant markets themselves and further enriched local landowners who also produced for them (map, pp. 378–9).

CITIES OF ITALY AND THE EMPIRE

Italian communities particularly well situated within the elaborate network of roads and waterways that funneled supplies to Rome had grown to be rather significant urban centers by the mid-first century C.E. For example, the crucial ports of Puteoli (Pozzuoli) and Ostia, where ships unloaded cargoes bound for Rome, reached populations of 30,000. Regional centers like Mediolanum (Milan), Patavium (Padua), and Capua had populations from 25,000 to as many as 40,000. About twenty-five other centers, including Verona, Cremona, Genua (Genoa), Beneventum, Pompeii, Brundisium, and Rhegium, could be classed as major cities, with populations between 5000 and 25,000.

On the other hand, being too close to Rome or another growing major center could cause decline. Many old cities of Etruria and Latium are good examples. The wealthy landowners in their territories generally concentrated their efforts on acquiring status in Rome itself. Formerly flourishing centers nearby withered and died. Nevertheless, many more places in Italy prospered.

Supplying Rome also stimulated urban growth around the Mediterranean as old centers were refounded or reinvigorated. Julius Caesar had refounded Corinth in 44 B.C.E. In 29 B.C.E., Augustus fulfilled Caesar's intention of refounding Carthage. Both were prime agricultural sites located on major maritime trade routes. As a result, they quickly grew to be major cities once more. The port of Alexandria flourished as never before and probably reached 500,000 in population. It was the collection point for the vital Egyptian grain shipped to Rome in great fleets. It was also the entrepôt for luxury goods that flowed to Rome and other cities from the upper Nile and the Red Sea (map, p. 375). In Gaul, Lugdunum (Lyons), founded in 43 B.C.E. near the confluence of the Rhône and the Saône, was the hub of the Gallic road system. From its island commercial center at the confluence of the two rivers, Gallic wine and other products were shipped downriver to Arelate (Arles). It grew tremendously under Augustus as a port where seagoing vessels picked up the cargoes from riverboats for shipment to Rome.

NON-AGRICULTURAL TRADE AND INDUSTRY

The production and transportation of raw materials and manufactured goods for the lucrative Roman market were also important factors in economic and urban growth under Augustus. Rome's network of roads and waterways encouraged centers of production to increase output. They shipped their products not only to Rome but also to distant markets, from Jutland (Denmark) to the Caucasus and from Britain to India (map, p. 387).

Textiles

Until the advent of power-driven, mechanized spinning and weaving, cloth was very expensive. It could be shipped long distances in the ancient world at a profit. Patavium (Padua, Padova), located in a major sheep-raising district north of the Po and not far from the Adriatic, became a great center for the production of woolen goods. Its output was so large that in Augustus' day it is reported to have supplied the huge demand for inexpensive clothing at Rome. Finer grades of woolen goods and purple dye, which was much in demand, came from Tarentum. Silk came from the Greek island of Cos (map, p. 379) and Alexandria supplied the Roman market with linen made from Egyptian flax.

The glass industry

The thriving glass industry had been revolutionized around 40 B.C.E. by the Syrian (or Egyptian) invention of the blowpipe. It made possible the production of not only beautiful goblets and bowls but even windowpanes. From the glass factories of Campania or of the Adriatic seaport of Aquileia came wares that found their way as far north as the Trondheim fjord in Norway and to the southernmost borders of Russia.

Arretine pottery

Manufacturers of red Samian ware, *terra sigillata*, at Arretium in Etruria and later at Puteoli had become highly successful. By the time of Augustus and Tiberius, they had achieved mass production and were exporting as far west as the British Midlands and as far east as modern Arikamedu near Pondicherry (ancient Poduke?) in southeastern India (p. 375). One Arretine operation had a mixing vat for 10,000 gallons of clay and required up to forty expert designers and a much larger number of mixers, potters, and furnacemen. Some manufacturers were now establishing branch operations in southern and eastern Gaul, in Spain, in Britain, and on the Danube.

The metal industries

Augustan Italy led the world in the manufacture of metalware. The chief centers of the iron industry were the two great seaports of Puteoli and Aquileia. The iron foundries of Puteoli smelted ores brought by sea from the island of Elba and, by a process of repeated forging, manufactured arms, farm implements, and carpenters' tools that were as hard as steel. Aquileia, with easy access to the rich iron mines of recently annexed Noricum, also manufactured excellent farm implements. They were sold throughout the fertile Cisalpina and exported to Dalmatia, the Danubian region, and even Germany.

For the manufacture of silverware (plates, trays, bowls, cups, and candelabra), the two leading centers were Capua and Tarentum (map, p. 378). Capua was also famous for bronze wares (statues, busts, lamp stands, tables, tripods, buckets, and kitchen pots and pans). Capuan manufacturers using perhaps thousands of workmen had evolved a specialization and division of labor usually associated with modern industry. The immense export trade of Capua to Britain, Germany, Scandinavia, and south Russia continued unabated until Gaul established workshops first at Lugdunum and, around 80 C.E., farther north in the Belgica and the Rhineland.

Building supplies and trades

The extensive building program of Augustus and the large sums spent on beautifying the Empire's capital stimulated the manufacture and extraction of building and plumbing materials—lead and terracotta pipes, bricks, roof tiles, cement, marble, and the so-called travertine, a cream-colored limestone quarried near Tibur. Some of these operations seem never to have developed large, systematized methods of production. Lead pipes, for instance, were made in small shops by the same people who also laid and connected them. On the other hand, the making of bricks and tiles reached a high degree of specialization especially on senatorial and imperial estates, which produced materials in large volumes for public works. Almost nothing, however, is known about the organization of the enterprises that made cement, a mixture of volcanic ash and lime, which was also in great demand.

The queen of building materials was marble. The Romans imported many varieties: the famous marbles of the Greek Aegean; the fine white, purple-veined varieties of Asia Minor; the serpentine and dark red porphyries of Egypt; and the beautiful,

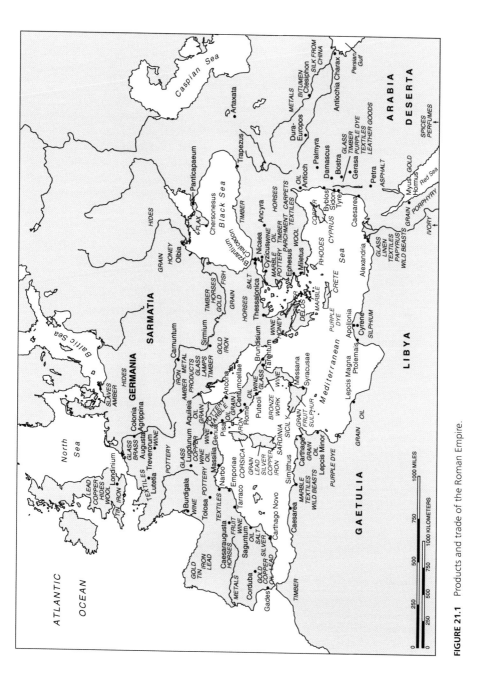

FIGURE 21.1 Products and trade of the Roman Empire.

gold-colored marble of Simitthu in Numidia. Also, in Augustus' time, they began to quarry marble in Italy: the renowned white Luna (Carrara) marble in Etruria and all those remarkable colored varieties of greens and yellows or mixed reds, browns, and whites found north of Liguria in the Italian Piedmont, in Liguria itself, and near Verona (front map).

THE ROMAN IMPERIAL COINAGE

The Augustan Age also witnessed new developments in the creation of a stable and abundant coinage that served ever-expanding fiscal and economic needs both within the Empire and far beyond its frontiers. Before Actium, the coinages of Italy and the Roman world had been in a confused and unreliable state as a result of inflation and disruption caused by war and civil strife. The huge amounts of gold and silver available to Augustus after his victory at Actium allowed him to reestablish the credibility of Roman coinage and issue an adequate supply from various mints. His principal gold coin, the *denarius aureus*, was virtually pure gold and was struck at a weight of forty to the Roman pound. It is usually known simply as the *aureus* to distinguish it from the more common *denarius* of silver, *denarius argentarius*. Augustus' silver *denarius* was 97.5 to 98 percent silver and was struck at eighty-four to the Roman pound (p. 115). Twenty-five silver *denarii* equaled one *aureus*. Each coin had its respective half, called a *quinarius*. The constant acquisition of more gold and silver through booty, mining, and trade allowed Augustus and most of his successors to maintain similar standards for almost 200 years. Civic and provincial coins were still produced, particularly in the East. All, however, were linked to the Roman *denarius*, which provided the standard of value.

Sometime after 23 B.C.E. (19 B.C.E.?), Augustus reopened the mint at Rome and instituted a college of three moneyers (*tresviri monetales*), officials who minted coins at the joint direction of the *princeps* and the senate. At that time, Augustus introduced a new series of token coins designed to meet the need for small denominations in daily transactions. He issued a *sestertius* (one-quarter of a silver *denarius*) and its half, the *dupondius*. They were minted in orichalcum, brass made of 75 percent copper, 20 percent zinc, and 5 percent tin. Pure copper went into the *as* (one-quarter of a *sestertius*) and the quarter *as*, called a *quadrans*. Although these coins were not intrinsically worth their official values, they were so well made and useful that they gained universal acceptance.

The Augustan coinage had an important propaganda or publicity value in addition to its purely economic function. It provided the newborn regime a flexible, subtle, and compelling method of influencing those who used it, particularly soldiers. They received enormous quantities of coins as pay and spent them all over the Empire. People would use and inevitably look at the coins, which could vaguely, yet effectively, suggest what the government wanted them to feel and believe. New coin types, appearing as frequently as modern commemorative stamps, kept the exalted figure of Augustus before the public eye in many forms.

As media of publicity and mass propaganda, the coins were more effective and malleable than the monumental arts. Even the most wonderful works of architecture and sculpture could not keep pace with new messages. Moreover, comparatively few of the Empire's 50 million to 70 million inhabitants ever saw the major monuments, whereas people everywhere daily used and handled the coins. Moreover, coins could depict monuments. Words on coins were also better vehicles than literary texts for advertising rapidly changing purposes, policies, and resolves of the government. Texts could not be reproduced and disseminated in great numbers so quickly as coins.

Architecture and art

First as Octavian, then as Augustus, the heir of Julius Caesar had an enormous influence on Roman art and architecture. He fostered the ultimate synthesis of Italic, Etruscan, and Greek traditions into an imperial style of Roman Classicism that was widely imitated in the provinces. At Rome, Augustus' refurbishment of eighty-two temples was a visible expression of his claim to have restored the *Res Publica* (p. 359). In addition, both Augustus and his faithful general and son-in-law, Marcus Agrippa, enhanced the city with useful public works, beautiful monuments, and magnificent new temples to earn gratitude from the populace and reinforce the themes and values that Augustus promoted. For buildings discussed below, see the plan of Rome on the facing page.

Next to Caesar's Forum Julium (map, p. 390), Augustus built the even more magnificent Forum Augustum, dedicated in 2 B.C.E. as a visible reminder of the pious vengeance that he had taken on Caesar's assassins. At the northeastern end, a great temple of Mars Ultor (Mars the Avenger) rose up on a high podium in the Italo-Etruscan manner. It had eight columns across the front, the same number as the Parthenon in Athens, but of the Corinthian, not the Doric, order. On the forum's long sides were parallel covered colonnades with semicircular projections, hemicycles, off the back at the ends near the temple. They linked the whole into a symmetrical Hellenistic complex. The colonnades and hemicycles displayed statues of republican heroes on one side and the men of the Julian *gens* on the other. Uniting the two, a large statue of Augustus himself stood in the center of the space in front of the temple.

In 28 B.C.E., Augustus commissioned Rome's first great building to be constructed entirely of gleaming white Luna (Carrara) marble, a temple to Apollo that sat next to his house (the Domus Augustus) on the Palatine. Augustus attributed his victory at Actium to Apollo's favor. This temple further linked Augustus and Apollo through their roles as patrons of the arts. Augustus attached two libraries, one Latin and one Greek, to the temple's precinct. Filled with Classical Greek sculpture and the busts of famous poets and orators, they also functioned as museums. Next to the temple, Augustus and Livia each maintained a relatively simple, republican-style home decorated with beautiful frescoes, some of which still survive, similar to those from the same period at Pompeii.

Under Augustus, the Forum Romanum acquired the appearance that marked it for centuries. He completed the Curia Julia, Caesar's new senate house (map, p. 390) and furnished it with a statue and altar of Victory that stood for centuries as assurances of Rome's imperial sway. He rebuilt the Basilica Aemilia after a fire in 14 B.C.E. Reconstruction after a fire also enabled him to enlarge the Basilica Julia. To the

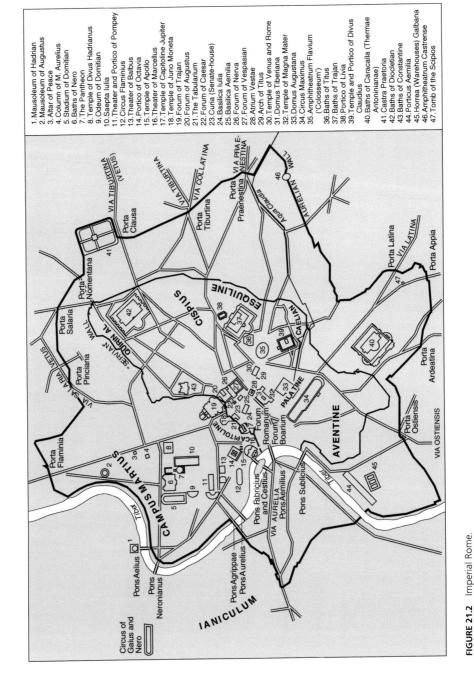

1. Mausoleum of Hadrian
2. Mausoleum of Augustus
3. Altar of Peace
4. Column of M. Aurelius
5. Stadium of Domitian
6. Baths of Nero
7. The Pantheon
8. Temple of Divus Hadrianus
9. Odeum of Domitian
10. Saepta Iulia
11. Theater and Portico of Pompey
12. Circus Flaminius
13. Theater of Balbus
14. Portico of Octavia
15. Temple of Apollo
16. Theater of Marcellus
17. Temple of Capitoline Jupiter
18. Temple of Juno Moneta
19. Forum of Trajan
20. Forum of Augustus
21. The Tabularium
22. Forum of Caesar
23. Curia (Senate-house)
24. Basilica Iulia
25. Basilica Aemilia
26. Forum of Nerva
27. Forum of Vespasian
28. Atrium Vestae
29. Arch of Titus
30. Temple of Venus and Rome
31. Domus Tiberiana
32. Temple of Magna Mater
33. Domus Augustana
34. Circus Maximus
35. Amphitheatrum Flavium (Colosseum')
36. Baths of Titus
37. Baths of Trajan
38. Portico of Livia
39. Temple and Portico of Divus Claudius
40. Baths of Caracalla (Thermae Antoninianae)
41. Castra Praetoria
42. Baths of Diocletian
43. Baths of Constantine
44. Porticus Aemilia
45. Horrea (Warehouses) Galbana
46. Amphitheatrum Castrense
47. Tomb of the Scipios

FIGURE 21.2 Imperial Rome.

northwest of the latter, the old temples of Concord and Saturn were remodeled in the imperial style. Close to those temples, he expanded the rostra (speakers' platform) recently built by Caesar. At the southeast end of the Forum, he erected a triple arch and the adjacent temple of his deified adoptive father, Divus Julius. The arch displayed the inscription now called the *Capitoline Fasti* (p. 76), and the façade of the temple portrayed three generations of Augustus' family.

Augustus built many monuments in the Campus Martius. At its northern limit, he placed his own imposing mausoleum (map, p. 390). Shaped like a mounded Etruscan tomb, it served the emperors and their families from the death of Octavia's son Marcellus in 23 B.C.E. to that of Emperor Nerva in 98 C.E. A little to the south, Augustus' architects marked out a huge sundial, the Horologium, in the pavement. A large obelisk, part of the spoils from his victory over Antonius and Cleopatra at Alexandria, formed the pointer. On Augustus' birthday, to remind people of the peace achieved by his victory, the obelisk's shadow aligned northeastward to intersect with the magnificent, new Altar of Augustan Peace (*Ara Pacis Augustae*).

The center of the Campus Martius contained benefactions by Agrippa: the original Pantheon ("Shrine of All the Gods"), a public park with a lake, and Rome's first major public baths. Other men, eager to be associated with the new era of peace and prosperity, also built impressive public buildings on the southern end of the Campus. Augustus himself built a theater in memory of Marcellus, much of which still stands (map, p. 390).

The Augustan peace fostered much similar building activity in Italian and provincial cities and towns. Examples abound in Gaul: the famous Roman temple at Nîmes (Nemausus), the so-called Maison Carrée (below, Figure 21.3); possibly the lofty Pont du Gard, which carried traffic and water to Nîmes on three tiers of majestic arches 160 feet above the river Gard (p. 392, Figure 21.4); and at Orange (Arausio), a triumphal arch and an immense theater, whose colonnade and central niche housed a colossal statue of Augustus.

FIGURE 21.3 La Maison Carrée at Nîmes, one of the most beautiful surviving Roman temples. It seems to have been erected in the early first century C.E. to commemorate Augustus' deceased adopted sons Gaius and Lucius.

FIGURE 21.4 Pont du Gard, Nîmes.

FIGURE 21.5 Sculptured relief from the Ara Pacis, with goddess and babies flanked by the East and West Winds and surrounded by symbols of peace and prosperity.

The serene and idealized realism of Attic Greek Classicism from the Golden Age of Pericles in the fifth century B.C.E. marked the Augustan style in art. It under-scored the arrival of a new Golden Age under Augustus. It is epitomized by the reliefs sculpted on the Ara Pacis (above, Figure 21.5) and by the impressive statue of Augustus set up at Livia's villa near Prima Porta (p. 393, Figure 21.6). The upper panels on two solid sides of the screen around the altar itself depict Augustus' family reverently taking part in a stately procession: perhaps the *supplicatio* (public thanks-giving) of 13 B.C.E., when the senate authorized the altar; perhaps the dedication of the altar in 9 B.C.E. The short upper panels flanking the entrances on the east and west sides portray the blessings and activities of peace: fruit, grain, cattle, a fecund young matron with two healthy babies, and the offering of a sacrifice. Augustus' statue from Prima Porta depicts a self-possessed and mature, yet youthful, commander in full parade dress. Reliefs carved on his cuirass show the Parthian king handing over to Tiberius the legionary standards that Crassus lost in 53 B.C.E., the final conquest of Spain and Gaul, the fertility of Mother Earth, and Jupiter's protective mantle over all. These monuments all advertise that peace and honor had been restored under the capable and pious leadership of Augustus and his family.

Similar, if not identical, ideas are conveyed in the same style by a marble altar from Roman Carthage with Roma seated on a heap of arms and contemplating an altar with a horn of plenty (*cornucopiae*), staff of peace (*caduceus*), and globe (*orbis terrarum*) resting upon it; by the exquisite Vienna cameo (*Gemma Augustea*) and the Grand Camée de France showing respectively a triumph of Tiberius and the ascension of Augustus into Heaven; by two silver cups from Boscoreale that portray the submission of the Germanic Sugambri to Augustus and Tiberius; and by a silver dish from Aquileia, which depicts the emperor surrounded by the four seasons and all the symbols of the fertility, plenty, and prosperity of the new Golden Age.

FIGURE 21.6 Statue of Augustus *Imperator* with sculptured breastplate (ca. 20 B.C.E.), from the Villa of Livia at Prima Porta.

393

Literature

The Augustan Age has often been called the Golden Age of Latin Literature. Already the political capital of the Mediterranean world, Rome was rapidly becoming the cultural center, attracting students, scholars, and writers from abroad. It offered themes for literary praise: a heroic past and a great and glorious present.

In the judgment of later generations, Roman writers acquired perfection in form and expression during the Principate of Augustus. Many writers and thinkers were also truly grateful that Augustus had brought an end to destructive civil war. They liked the policies that he designed to preserve the hard-won peace. Many of them were supported by Augustus himself or his close friend Gaius Cilnius Maecenas, a wealthy equestrian of Etruscan descent.

Unlike the age of Caesar, in which prose writers predominated (Cicero, Caesar, Sallust, Nepos, and Varro), the Augustan Age was notable for its poets (Vergil, Horace, Tibullus, Propertius, and Ovid). It was essentially an age of poetry. Even Livy's great history of Rome, *Ab Urbe Condita*, was no exception, for some critics have regarded it as an epic in prose form. Livy began where the *Aeneid* of Vergil left off.

VERGIL (70 TO 19 B.C.E.)

Publius Vergilius Maro, son of a well-to-do northern Italian farmer near Mantua, gave up a career in the courts to study philosophy with Siro the Epicurean at Naples. After Siro's death, he turned to poetry. In 38 or 37 B.C.E., he published his *Eclogues* (*Bucolics*), ten short pastoral poems in the style of the Hellenistic Greek poet Theocritus, poems idealizing country life and the loves and sorrows of shepherds. They were, however, more than pretty pastorals. The first and the ninth refer to the dispossession of small farmers to settle Octavian's veterans after Philippi. Both the fifth and ninth refer to the deification of Julius Caesar, while the fourth predicts the return of the Golden Age with the birth of a child. The sixth, reminiscent of Lucretius, expounds Epicurean philosophy, and the tenth is a tribute to fellow poet Cornelius Gallus (p. 396).

The *Eclogues* had brought Vergil to the attention of Maecenas. With Maecenas' support, Vergil began, and by 29 B.C.E. had completed, the four books of his *Georgics*. It is ostensibly a didactic poem on farming like the early Greek poet Hesiod's *Works and Days*. More than that, it is a hymn of praise to Italy's soil and sturdy farmers and to Augustus for restoring the peace so essential for prosperous agriculture and human happiness. As Augustus was returning to Rome from the east after the battle of Actium, he paused to rest a few days at the town of Atella. For his entertainment, Vergil read the *Georgics* to him.

After completing the *Georgics*, Vergil spent the next decade in writing his greatest work, the *Aeneid*. It is a national epic poem in twelve books. The first six correspond to Homer's *Odyssey*, the last six to the *Iliad*. The *Aeneid* begins the story of Rome with the burning of Troy and the legendary journey of the hero Aeneas to Latium. There, according to Vergil, it was fated that Rome would rise to become a great world empire and fulfill its glorious destiny under Augustus. Although Aeneas, the legendary ancestor of the Julian family, is nominally the hero, the real hero is Rome: its mission is to rule the world, to teach the nations the way of peace, to spare the vanquished, and to subdue the proud (Book 6.851–3). The fulfillment of this mission requires of all Roman heroes the virtues that made Rome great: courage, *pietas* (devotion to duty), constancy, and faithfulness. Vergil's emphasis upon these virtues was in line with the Augustan reformation of morals and the revival of ancient faith (*prisca fides*).

In contrast, Vergil, like Lucretius before him, condemns the lust (*cupido*) and blind emotion (*furor*) that he sees as the causes of prior civil strife. Those are the destructive forces that hinder Aeneas and the Trojans from fulfilling the glorious destiny decreed for Rome by Jupiter and that the virtuous hero Aeneas must overcome. Unfortunately, Vergil often portrays these evil forces in feminine terms, which help perpetuate the negative stereotype of women in Western literature.

On his deathbed, Vergil requested the burning of the *Aeneid*. He considered it not yet perfected. Augustus countermanded that request and ordered it published.

HORACE (65 TO 8 B.C.E.)

Another great poet of the age was Quintus Horatius Flaccus, son of a well-to-do freedman of Venusia in Apulia. His father sent him to school in Rome and later to higher studies at Athens. There, Horace met the conservative noble Brutus and fought for the Republic at Philippi. Afterward, penniless, he returned to Rome and got a job in a quaestor's office. Though boring, it gave him the time and means to write poetry.

By 35 B.C.E., he had composed some of his *Epodes*, bitter, pessimistic little poems in iambic meter (in imitation of the Greek poet Archilochus), and the first book of his *Satires*. He called his satires *Sermones* (informal "conversations"). They poke fun at the vices and follies of the capital. Despite being caustic, sometimes vulgar, and even obscene, Horace's early poems had enough style, wit, and cleverness to win the admiration of Vergil. He introduced Horace to Maecenas in 38 B.C.E. At first, Maecenas provided Horace an independent income and then, in 33 B.C.E., a sizable estate in the Sabine country near modern Tivoli.

In 30 B.C.E., Horace published his second book of *Satires*. There, he is more mellow and less caustic than in the first. Meanwhile, he had already begun, and for seven years thereafter continued to work on, his *Odes* (*Carmina*). The first three books appeared in 23 B.C.E. They comprised eighty-eight poems of varying lengths and meters. Horace derived most of the meters from Greek poets and adapted them to Roman lyric form.

Horace's fame rests chiefly on the *Odes*. He called them a monument "more durable than brass and loftier than the pyramids of Egyptian kings" (*Odes* 3.30.1–2). They touch, often lightly, on many subjects. That variety adds yet another charm to their artistry, compactness, pure diction, fastidious taste, and lightness. Some are so-called wisdom poems containing moral exhortations that he himself took seriously: "Be wise, pour out the wine, cut back long hope to suit a short time. While we are talking, envious time will have fled; seize the day [*carpe diem*]; trust tomorrow as little as possible" (*Odes* 1.11.6–8). Others discourse on friendship, the brevity of life, religion and philosophy, drinking wine, and making love, which for Horace was a lightly comic pastime, not an all-consuming passion as for Catullus. The long, more solemn, so-called Roman Odes (*Odes* 3.1–6) praise the virtues advocated by Augustus: moderation and frugality, valor and patriotism, justice, piety, and faith. In later years, Horace wrote two books of *Epistles*. They are sermons on morals, religion, and philosophy rather than real letters like Cicero's. The longest and most famous of these letters, the so-called *Art of Poetry* (*Ars Poetica*), sets forth the principles for writing poetry, especially tragedy. From it, Alexander Pope in the eighteenth century drew many of the principles versified in his *Essay on Criticism*.

THE LATIN ELEGISTS

The elegiac couplet consisting of a dactylic-hexameter line alternating with a pentameter had served in Greek and Latin literature a variety of purposes—drinking songs, patriotic and political poems, dirges, laments, epitaphs, votive dedications, epigrams, and love poetry. Following the innovations of Catullus (pp. 338–9), the first Roman to use the elegy extensively for love poetry was probably Gaius Cornelius Gallus (ca. 69–26 B.C.E.), who also served as governor of Egypt until he ran afoul of Augustus. His four books of *Amores* firmly established the subjective erotic elegy and were very popular among his contemporaries. Alas, until 1978, none of Gallus' poems was known to exist. Then, a piece of papyrus that contained one complete four-line poem and most of a second was discovered in Egypt.

Of Albius Tibullus (55–48 to 19 B.C.E.) little is known except that he belonged to the circle of poets around Marcus Valerius Messalla Corvinus, not only a member of the old nobility (p. 348) but also a literary patron and historian. Four books of poems appear under Tibullus' name in surviving manuscripts. Only two books, comprising sixteen elegies, are certainly his. Several of those elegies are addressed to Delia and to Nemesis—two fatal attractions. They alternately made him ecstatic and heartbroken but never prevented him from writing smooth, clear, and elegant verses.

Sulpicia (born ca. 50 B.C.E.) is the only woman whose poetry has survived from the Augustan Age. She was another member of Messalla's circle. Her six heartfelt poems to a lover named Cerinthus are included in the manuscripts of Tibullus. They show both her originality as a poet and her mastery of poetic forms normally associated with men.

Sextus Propertius (54–47 to ca. 15 B.C.E.) was another poet who enjoyed the patronage of Maecenas. His four books of elegies include patriotic themes and two poems in praise of Augustus, but he was never fully committed to the Augustan program. His early poems concentrate on his troubled relationship with a woman whom he calls Cynthia. Propertius, known for his innovative approach to Latin love elegy, shows great boldness and originality in his imagery, but obscure allusions and abrupt shifts in thought often make him difficult to understand.

Ovid (43 B.C.E. to 17–18 C.E.)

The most sensual and sophisticated of the elegists was Publius Ovidius Naso, Ovid. He came to Rome from Sulmo in the remote mountain region of Samnium. From a well-to-do equestrian family, he initially pursued a career in the courts but eventually devoted himself to poetry. He became the most prolific of the Augustan poets. He was friends with both Tibullus and Propertius, and Messalla helped his early career.

Ovid's earliest poems are highly polished love elegies, the *Amores*, in the manner of Tibullus. His *Heroides* (*Heroines*) is an original collection of poetic letters in which famous legendary women address their absent husbands or lovers. Two of his most famous works are the *Metamorphoses* (*Transformations*) and the *Fasti* (*Calendar*). The first is his only surviving work in epic meter; the second, like all the rest, is in elegiacs. The *Metamorphoses* provides much information about Greek mythology and has been the source of inspiration to countless poets, playwrights, novelists, and artists ever since. More than that, however, the *Metamorphoses* is an epic history of the world that culminates patriotically in the change of Julius Caesar from a man to a god. The *Fasti* was intended to describe the astronomical, historical, and religious events associated with each month of the year, one book per month. It nicely complemented Augustus' attempt to revive the many priesthoods and religious observances that had fallen into disuse. Unfortunately, the work is unfinished and covers only the first six months.

While the *Fasti* is compatible with Augustus' revival of defunct priesthoods and religious traditions, Ovid's *Ars Amatoria* (*Art of Love*) completely contradicts the moral reform that Augustus promoted. It is a salacious handbook, playfully didactic, that explains the arts of seduction and surveys all the known aspects of heterosexual experience, including rape to incest. Ovid attracted the attention of Augustus' fast-living granddaughter, Julia. For the details are unknown (although scholars have enjoyed speculating), Julia and Ovid were caught up in scandal and banished by the emperor.

Ovid spent the rest of his life at Tomi, a desolate place on the Black Sea near the mouth of the Danube. His last two books of poetry, the *Tristia* (*Sorrows*) and *Epistulae ex Ponto* (*Epistles from Pontus*), were written there. They are fruitless, often pathetic, pleas for permission to return to Rome.

LATIN PROSE WRITERS

The Latin prose writers of the Augustan Age have been less fortunate than the poets. None of the major historical writings has survived intact. Gaius Asinius Pollio (76 B.C.E.–5 C.E.) and the literary patron Marcus Valerius Messalla Corvinus (64 B.C.E.–8 C.E.) each wrote a major first-hand account of the civil wars. Both works are now lost, although the extant Greek writers Plutarch and Appian drew heavily on Pollio. Augustus wrote a valuable, but highly selective account of his own accomplishments (*Res Gestae*) in a clear and readable style. Much of it survives from Greek and Latin copies that were inscribed on public monuments in various cities of the Empire. The most complete is a large inscription at Ankyra (Ankara) in Turkey, the *Monumentum Ankyranum*. Augustus also wrote an autobiography, but it is no longer extant.

Livy (59 B.C.E. to 17 C.E.)

Titus Livius, or Livy, the supreme prose writer of the Augustan Age, came from Patavium (Padua) in Cisalpine Gaul. His *Ab Urbe Condita* (From the Founding of the City) contained 142 books on the history of Rome from its founding to the death of Drusus I in 9 B.C.E. Only Books 1 to 10 (from the legendary landing of Aeneas in Latium to 293 B.C.E.) and Books 21 to 45 (218–167 B.C.E.) are extant. The *Periochae*, short summaries or epitomes (written probably in the fourth century C.E.) indicate the contents of all the books except 136 and 137. Livy blended the styles of Cicero and Sallust with poetical phraseology and great dramatic skill to record the mighty deeds of earlier Romans as a divinely ordered march to world conquest. He denounced the vices of his own age; he wanted to show that Rome's rise to greatness had resulted from patriotism and traditional virtues.

Although his work is of great literary merit and reflects the attitudes of many upper-class Romans in Italy at the time, Livy has, from the modern point of view, numerous defects as an historian. He can be faulted, like most other ancient writers of history, for insufficiently critical use of sources, for failure to consult documents that were probably readily available to him, for his ignorance of economics and military tactics, and for failure to interpret primitive institutions in their proper social setting. Nevertheless, Livy succeeded in giving the world a compelling picture of Roman history and character as many Romans wanted to see them. That fact itself is of great significance for the modern historian.

Pompeius Trogus (ca. 50 B.C.E. to ca. 25 C.E.)

A quite different historian was Pompeius Trogus. Livy, writing from a patriotic Roman perspective, was not interested in other people except as enemies whom Rome conquered. Trogus wrote from the perspective of a provincial native, albeit a heavily Romanized one from Narbonese Gaul. Like Cornelius Nepos, he was much more interested in what Romans could learn from non-Romans than in glorifying an idealized Roman past. Out of the forty-four books of his *Philippic Histories* (*Historiae Philippicae*), only two focused on Rome. The bulk concentrated on Macedon and the great Hellenistic empires of Macedonian conquerors after Philip and Alexander. Others covered the Near East and Greece to the rise of Macedon. The rest treated Parthia, Spain, and Gaul to the time of Augustus. Unfortunately, the full text with much valuable information is lost, but a condensed version exists in an epitome made by Justin in the second or third century

THE IMPACT OF AUGUSTUS ON LATIN LITERATURE

In a society where writers depend on wealthy or powerful personal patrons, those patrons have a great impact on literary production. Directly, or indirectly through Maecenas, the impact of Augustus was great indeed. That is not to say he dictated what people wrote. Livy, for example, was no hack writing official history for Augustus. He wrote with a genuine patriotism that happened to coincide with Augustus' own needs and policies. The same can be said for Vergil, Horace, and Propertius, but that is what helped to attract the interest and patronage of Maecenas and Augustus. They in turn enabled the authors to concentrate on writing and ensured a public audience for, and the survival of, their works. Indeed, Augustus personally intervened to secure the publication of the *Aeneid* against Vergil's own stated wishes. This situation was not necessarily harmful, but it raises the question of how many talented writers, either through lack of connections or because of incompatible views, failed to find a powerful patron and disappeared.

The poet Cornelius Gallus committed suicide after incurring Augustus' official displeasure over the way in which he tactlessly publicized his own military accomplishments in Egypt. Gallus' disgrace, therefore, may help to account for the disappearance of his work except for a few lines (p. 396). Although official disgrace had no such effect on Ovid and his work, it did prevent him from finishing the *Fasti* and may well have denied the world better works than those bemoaning his exile and begging for release.

Augustus allowed writers a certain amount of political independence. Propertius, for example, often resisted Maecenas' request for more poems favorable to the *princeps*. Augustus even joked with Livy about the latter being sympathetic to Pompey. Still, he seems to have become less tolerant as people began to react against the increasing permanence of his new regime. Augustus was safely dead before Livy wrote about the sensitive events after Actium. It may not be coincidental that under Augustus' successors the summaries of the relevant books in the *Periochae* (134–142) give those events the shortest shrift of all. More ominously, in 8 or 12 C.E., the works of the rabidly Pompeian historian Titus Labienus were condemned to public burning, and he committed suicide. The books of the outspoken orator Cassius Severus were burned, too, and he was exiled.

GREEK WRITERS

Educated men from the Greek-speaking parts of the Empire continued to produce much literature for Greek audiences. Of special note are two who worked in Rome under Augustus. The first is Diodorus Siculus (the Sicilian). He wrote a history of the world in forty books from the earliest days to Caesar's conquest of Gaul. It is not a particularly distinguished work of history as such. Still, it is useful because it covers not only Greece and Rome but also Egypt, Mesopotamia, India, Scythia, Arabia, and North Africa, about which most ancient authors say little. Moreover, because Diodorus compiled his history from important earlier works now lost, he gives an indication of what they contained.

More important for the history of Rome and Italy is Dionysius of Halicarnassus, who taught Greek rhetoric at Rome from 30 to 8 B.C.E. In twenty books, his *Roman Antiquities* covered the history of Rome from its founding to the First Punic War. It preserves valuable material from lost Roman annalists and antiquarians on that period, the most poorly documented in Roman history, but the account is skewed by Dionysius' overarching argument that the Romans were originally Greeks.

Also important was Strabo (64–63 B.C.E. to 25 C.E.), a Greek from Pontus. His forty-seven books of history, exclusive of that covered by Polybius, are unfortunately lost, but his *Geography* in seventeen books survives. It covers the known world of the time. Although it is not always based on the best available mathematical, astronomical, and geographic research of the day, it presents in readable form much interesting geographical and historical information that would otherwise be lost.

SCHOLARLY AND TECHNICAL WRITINGS

Antiquarian scholarship, handbooks, and technical manuals of all types became increasingly popular from Augustus' time onward. Vitruvius' *De Architectura* became the standard handbook for Roman architects and exercised great influence on the Neoclassical architecture of the Renaissance and later Classical revivals. Verrius Flaccus, the tutor of Gaius and Lucius Caesar, compiled the earliest Latin dictionary, *De Verborum Significatu*, and Marcus Agrippa, who set up a large map of the Roman Empire in the Forum, wrote a detailed explanation of it in his *Commentaries*, which summarized the results of Greek geographic research and Roman surveying. A few years later, under Tiberius, Aulus Cornelius Celsus compiled an important encyclopedia whose section on medicine still survives as a valuable summary of earlier Greek medical knowledge.

Philology and literary scholarship

The works of Cicero, Vergil, and Horace became classics in their own lifetimes. They inspired a steady stream of philologists who analyzed their language and style and of scholarly commentators who dealt with literary and historical questions raised by their work. For example, Gaius Julius Hyginus supervised Augustus' great public library on the Palatine and published a famous series of commentaries on Vergil. His work has not survived, but it is the source of much material preserved in the works of later commentators.

LAW AND JURISPRUDENCE

The Augustan Age marks the beginning of the Classical period of Roman jurisprudence, which lasted until the reign of Diocletian. The old republican families of high pedigree and proud public achievement were gradually becoming extinct. New jurisconsults, or jurists, and legal experts from Italian and even provincial towns came to the fore. Many were professional consultants, writers, and teachers of law. Eventually, jurists became salaried officials of the imperial regime.

Responsa

Either Augustus or Tiberius may have first given select jurists the right to give *responsa* (responses to people seeking their legal opinions) that were reinforced by his own personal authority (*ius respondendi ex auctoritate principis*). Most praetors and judges respected and accepted these responses but were under no legal obligation to do so. Unauthorized jurists were still free to give responses and magistrates and judges to accept them, but the prestige of those with the *ius respondendi* made their opinions more widely respected and helped to produce greater uniformity. Official authorization of jurisconsults did not endure beyond the reign of Trajan (98–117 C.E.).

Traditions of jurisprudence

At the end of the Republic and beginning of the Principate, two traditions or schools of jurisprudence emerged. The older is often called *Sabinian* after the famous jurist Masurius Sabinus. The other tradition originated under Augustus even though it later received the name *Proculian* during Nero's reign. Apparently, they did not differ over fundamental questions such as the source or purpose of law but only in its application. The Sabinians tended to follow more particular, less systematic arguments in their legal opinions. The Proculians were willing to advance wider, more logically rigorous arguments but did not challenge existing legal principles and concepts.

THE AUGUSTAN ACHIEVEMENT

Law flourishes only in times of peace. Although Augustus started his career as another self-seeking leader in civil war, he made up for the destructiveness of his early years by earnestly trying to construct a better future for Rome. The restoration of peace and orderly government after Actium and the economic upsurge that followed laid the groundwork for a brilliant efflorescence of art, literature, and scholarship, which Augustus himself did much to inspire and encourage, albeit in ways beneficial to him.

SUGGESTED READING

Galinksy, K. *Augustan Culture: An Interpretive Introduction.* Princeton: Princeton University Press, 1996.

Severy, B. *Augustus and the Family at the Birth of the Roman Empire.* London: Routledge, 2010.

Zanker, P. *The Power of Images in the Age of Augustus.* Ann Arbor: University of Michigan Press, 1990.

CHAPTER 22

The first two Julio-Claudian Emperors

Tiberius and Gaius (Caligula), 14 to 41 C.E.

Augustus established the longest and most complex family of Roman emperors until the dynasty of Constantine and that of Valentinian and Theodosius in the fourth and fifth centuries C.E. The dynastic successors of Augustus are called the Julio-Claudians because of their connections with his Julian family and the Claudian family of his wife Livia. Of the four Julio-Claudian emperors, Augustus' immediate successor, Tiberius, son of Livia by her first husband, was the only one born without Julian ancestry. The other three, Gaius (popularly known as Caligula), Claudius, and Nero, were members of both families. The four reigns fall conveniently into two pairs, each of twenty-six-and-a-half years: Tiberius and Gaius (14–41 C.E.) and Claudius and Nero (41–68 C.E.).

In order to understand fully the characters of these important emperors and the intrigues and complexities of their reigns, it is necessary to keep in mind the intricate relationships of the Julio-Claudian family (chart on facing page). Augustus tenaciously sought a successor closely related to himself. His manipulation of marriages and adoptions created a confusing web of relationships as well as jealousies, rivalries, and intrigues that bedeviled and even warped those who managed to attain the office of *princeps* that he created.

SOURCES FOR THE JULIO-CLAUDIANS

Only two surviving ancient writers give significant accounts of the whole Julio-Claudian period: Suetonius, in his *Lives of the Twelve Caesars*, and Cassius Dio, in Books

57 to 63 of his *Roman History*. Both authors lived after the events described. Suetonius was born about 69 C.E., around the end of Nero's reign, and died about 140. As a child, he would have heard some firsthand information about the Julio-Claudians from his elders. Also, as Emperor Hadrian's secretary in charge of correspondence, he had access to archival documents, which he often quotes. Cassius Dio, a Greek aristocrat of Nicaea in Bithynia, was born about 150 C.E. He died around 235 after a distinguished senatorial career. As a high-ranking senator, Dio had access to much official information, too, but he seems to have made little use of it. Both he and Suetonius were dependent primarily upon earlier narrative accounts. Because the earlier writers were mainly senatorial aristocrats, who resented their loss of real power and privileges under the Principate, the works of Suetonius and Dio frequently reflect a bias against the Julio-Claudians. Moreover, both Suetonius and Dio enjoyed the sensational and the scandalous. Therefore, in their works, the plain, unvarnished truth often takes a back seat to the baseless rumors, damaging innuendoes, and malicious fabrications that they frequently found in other writers.

Other important literary sources exist for individual Julio-Claudian emperors. Velleius Paterculus was a loyal cavalry officer under Tiberius. He gives a highly favorable account of Tiberius' reign in the last part of the second book of his *History of Rome*. For Caligula, the Jewish historian Flavius Josephus, in his *Jewish Antiquities*, Books 18 and 19, and the Jewish scholar Philo of Alexandria, in his *Against Flaccus* and *Embassy to Gaius*, present valuable contemporary or nearly contemporary accounts of certain events. Book 19 of Josephus' *Jewish Antiquities* and Books 2 to 7 of his *History of the Jewish War* cover some events under Claudius and highlight the Jewish revolt under Nero. The philosopher Seneca the Younger, who had been exiled under Claudius, is believed to have written a scathing satire of that emperor, the *Apocolocyntosis* (*Pumpkinification*). The various philosophical and literary works of Seneca and the numerous nonhistorical writings of other authors reveal much about the social, economic, cultural, and even political history of the period (pp. 477–89).

A far more influential source than any of these works is found in the surviving books of the *Annals* of Tacitus. The *Annals* originally covered events from 14 to 69 C.E. Now, only Books 1 to 6 (with most of Book 5 missing), covering the reign of Tiberius, and Books 12 to 16, covering the reign of Nero to 66 C.E., survive. Tacitus, just as his modern admirer Edward Gibbon, has exercised a profound influence on historians of the Roman Empire because of a superb literary style combined with an intense personal viewpoint.

Still, a conscientious historian cannot uncritically accept what Tacitus says. He came from the ranks of conservative senators who resented the loss of independence and prestige that the senate suffered in the shadow of the emperors. Having experienced increasing despotism during the last years of Emperor Domitian (81–96 C.E.), he tended to interpret the actions of previous emperors accordingly. In fact, he became rather cynical and disillusioned about life in general.

Trained as an advocate in rhetoric and law, Tacitus believed that "the role of history is to make sure that virtues are not passed over in silence and that evil words and deeds have the fear of infamy among later generations" (*Annals* 3.65.1). It is often necessary,

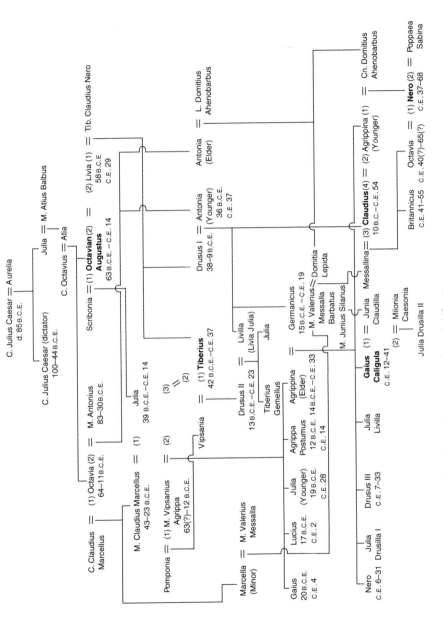

FIGURE 22.1 The Julio-Claudian dynasty (emperors are shown boldface).

therefore, that Tacitus' modern readers act the roles of both attorney and jury: the one to highlight evidence that Tacitus usually concedes as he rhetorically builds a case against it, the other to arrive at a balanced judgment.

Modern historians are aided by abundant archaeological research that has brought to light numerous coins, artifacts, monuments, inscriptions, and the remains of whole cities and towns from the period. This physical evidence illustrates the social, economic, and administrative developments that the ancient literary sources slight in favor of investigating the emperors' personalities, high politics, court intrigue, and wars. From the nonliterary evidence, it is possible to estimate what was happening to the more ordinary inhabitants of the Empire under their rulers, whose lives and deeds are the main focus of the literary sources.

TIBERIUS (14 TO 37 c.e.)

The full name of Tiberius was Tiberius Claudius Nero. At fifty-five, he was no longer a young man when he succeeded Augustus in 14 c.e. His lengthy experience in life was both a blessing and a curse. On the one hand, his long public service, first as a successful general on the frontiers and then as Augustus' virtual understudy for ten years, made him uniquely fitted to step into the role of *princeps*. On the other hand, his difficult personal experiences had left him ill-suited to the role he had to play. Born during civil war in 42 b.c.e., Tiberius had spent his first two years with his parents in fearful exile. The divorce of his mother, Livia, who was pregnant with his younger brother, Drusus I, and her hasty remarriage to Augustus also must have been stressful. Augustus appreciated the serious and cautious Tiberius but seems to have preferred Drusus I, a more jovial, appealing personality. As an adult, Tiberius was saddened and embittered by the forced divorce from his wife Vipsania (Agrippa's daughter) and disastrous marriage to Augustus' daughter (Agrippa's widow), Julia (p. 377).

Moreover, Augustus had made it clear in his will that he had chosen Tiberius as his successor only when there was no other choice. Even then, Augustus had tried to arrange that his sister Octavia's grandson Germanicus (son of Drusus I) would be preferred to Tiberius' own son once Tiberius died. Perhaps Tiberius was merely imitating Augustus' politic reluctance of 27 b.c.e. when he expressed hesitation over assuming the post of *princeps*. Still, he may have been genuinely ambivalent and lacking in self-confidence after his earlier experiences.

Agrippa Postumus, Julia, and Scribonia

The execution of Augustus' grandson/adopted son Agrippa Postumus soon followed Tiberius' accession. He was the only surviving son of Agrippa and Julia. He had become an angry, rebellious youth, and Augustus had banished him to an offshore island. It is not known who ordered the killing. Tacitus points to Tiberius and calls the execution the "first crime of the new principate" (*primum facinus novi principatus* [*Annals*, 1.6.1]). Nevertheless, there is a good reason why Augustus might have left instructions to execute Postumus: fear that he would be used for rallying opposition to Augustus' succession arrangements and that dangerous instability would ensue.

At this point, Julia had been divorced from Tiberius and had also been banished by Augustus (p. 377). Tiberius once tried to have her recalled. Now, probably he, Livia, and their advisors considered her dangerously useful to those who disliked Tiberius and would favor her son. Julia's mother, Scribonia, may have been one of them.

Before he became Augustus, Julia's father had humiliatingly divorced Scribonia in favor of Livia (p. 309). It would be natural for Scribonia to have wanted the imperial dynasty to descend from her through Julia's son, not from Livia through Tiberius or Drusus. Scribonia had voluntarily joined Julia in banishment. In 14 C.E., Tiberius cut off the funds that had supported Julia before Augustus' death. Soon thereafter, she died of starvation, perhaps intentionally to blacken the reputations of Tiberius and Livia. Unless Tiberius had forbidden Scribonia to help (the sources are silent), Julia would have had enough resources to keep herself alive had she wanted to.

Scribonia herself remained active. In 16 C.E., when she was probably about ninety, her grandnephew M. Scribonius Libo Drusus was accused of plotting against Tiberius. Perhaps not coincidentally, a freedman posing as Agrippa Postumus was then raising a rebellion in Italy and was about to march on Rome. Scribonia urged Libo Drusus not to avoid execution by committing suicide but to confront Tiberius in a trial. Her advice was not taken. To avoid stirring up more trouble, Tiberius did not investigate further. There is no record of Scribonia after that.

The mutiny of the legions

Shortly after Tiberius' accession, the legions stationed in Pannonia (Hungary) and the lower Rhineland mutinied. Tiberius sent his natural son, Drusus II, to Pannonia, where the mutiny was quickly suppressed. Germanicus, Tiberius' nephew and adopted son, soon restored order in the Rhineland, too.

GERMANICUS AND AGRIPPINA

Three major campaigns east of the Rhine from 14 to 16 C.E. gave Germanicus the chance to solidify his reputation as a worthy heir apparent. The last, a defeat of the German Arminius, made it possible to boast that Rome had avenged the defeat of Varus in the Teutoburg Forest (p. 367). Tacitus is unfair to Tiberius in claiming that he jealously prevented Germanicus from making permanent conquests across the Rhine. They probably agreed with Augustus' assessment that Rome did not yet have the manpower and resources to conquer and hold down a large piece of new territory there. Germanicus' campaigns were designed to destabilize and weaken the Germans, not conquer them permanently. It was a wise policy. Arminius and Maroboduus, king of the Marcomanni in what is now Bohemia, began to fight. Maroboduus lost his kingdom and fled to Italy. Arminius was assassinated. Bohemia became virtually a client kingdom of Rome.

Tiberius gave Germanicus a splendid triumph and sent him to the Near East with extraordinary powers in 17 C.E. Germanicus was to help cities damaged by earthquakes in Asia and superintend the annexation of the kingdoms of Cappadocia, Cilicia, and Commagene as imperial provinces.

At the same time, Tiberius appointed the experienced senator Cn. Calpurnius Piso as governor of Syria to assist the young Germanicus. The two did not get along. Without obtaining the required authorization from Tiberius, Germanicus left Syria and went to Egypt, where he helped to alleviate starvation in Alexandria by opening reserve granaries to relieve. The popularity this generated for Germanicus, combined with his failure to request permission to visit the province in the first place, disturbed Tiberius, who complained bitterly to the senate. That complaint encouraged Piso's disrespect for Germanicus. Upon returning to Syria, Germanicus found that Piso had contemptuously disobeyed all his orders. Germanicus' hostility caused Piso to abandon his post. Shortly after that, Germanicus became ill and accused Piso of attempting to kill him. Then, calling upon his wife and children to avenge his murder, he died.

Germanicus' wife was Agrippina the Elder, Augustus' granddaughter by Julia and Agrippa. She set out for Rome with her husband's ashes. Piso seized the opportunity to regain control of Syria by force. He was defeated and taken to Rome to face trial on charges that included poisoning Germanicus, stirring up civil war by trying to reenter the province of Syria after Germanicus' death, and corrupting military discipline. After the trial began, Piso committed suicide. Nevertheless, Tiberius requested that the prosecution continue, with Piso's sons acting for the defense. Piso was condemned posthumously. In the late 1980s, a well-preserved inscription of the senatorial decree announcing his punishments, the *Senatus Consultum de Cn. Pisone Patre*, was found in Spain.

Agrippina suspected Tiberius of complicity in Germanicus' death. She believed that he was jealous of Germanicus' popularity and wanted to clear the way for his own son, Drusus II, to succeed. Piso's suicide convinced others that he really was guilty of poisoning Germanicus. Piso probably was only trying to avoid execution so that his property would go to his heirs instead of being forfeited to the state. His friends in the senate, however, suspected that he had been made a scapegoat for Tiberius. Therefore, Tiberius had to contend with the hostility of Piso's influential family and friends and the suspicions of Agrippina for much of his reign. The children of Germanicus, who himself had shown a serious interest in Stoicism, became the hope of Stoic-inspired aristocrats who wanted to return to more republican principles.

LIVIA

Tiberius also had to contend with his mother, Livia. Always an important advisor to Augustus, she exemplified on a larger scale the great informal power that women of major aristocratic households often wielded. She attained even greater prominence after Augustus' death. In his will, she was accepted into the Julian *gens* and proclaimed *Augusta*.

Until her death at the age of eighty-six in 29 C.E., Livia sought to exercise influence commensurate with her status as virtual Empress of Rome. Through patronage, she had high standing with important cities and client kings. She seems to have supported Augustus' wishes that Tiberius' successor be from the line of her other son, Drusus I, that is, one of her great-grandsons via Germanicus and Agrippina the Elder. Their youngest son, Gaius (Caligula[1]), was raised in her house until she died. He even delivered the eulogy at her funeral.

Tiberius came to resent Livia. After she died, he even refused to execute her will, which, for example, included 50 million sesterces for Servius Sulpicius Galba, later the first non-Julio-Claudian emperor (pp. 438–9). Nor did Tiberius permit Livia's deification. The next two emperors respectively carried out those actions.

SEJANUS

A man whose attempts at self-aggrandizement made things worse for Tiberius was L. Aelius Seianus, usually called Sejanus in English. His father, an *eques*, had risen to be prefect of the Praetorian Guard. Sejanus eventually became his colleague. After the father's death, Sejanus made the Praetorian Guard his own base of power by persuading Tiberius to make him sole prefect. Then, he convinced Tiberius to concentrate all of the Guard's nine cohorts, hitherto partially dispersed in neighboring towns, into new barracks on the eastern outskirts of Rome. Acting as a loyal aide, Sejanus presented himself as the protector of Tiberius from the real or imagined plots that plagued him.

When Drusus II died suddenly in 23, Sejanus attempted to marry his widow, Livilla (Livia Julia, sister of Germanicus). Despite allegations that the two had murdered Drusus II, Sejanus may simply have taken advantage of what was a fortuitous death in hopes of maneuvering himself into some kind of imperial partnership with Livilla's young son, Tiberius' grandson, Tiberius Gemellus. Tiberius, however, refused to permit the marriage. In the meantime, Agrippina the Elder was doing everything that she could to advance the claims of her three sons by Germanicus: Nero (not the future emperor), Drusus III, and Gaius (Caligula).

In 26, Sejanus successfully urged Tiberius to enter semi-retirement on the island of Capreae (Capri) near Naples. At Rome, Sejanus used his power and influence as a praetorian prefect to drive Agrippina's highly placed friends into exile or procure their deaths by execution or suicide. After the death of Livia in 29, he apparently convinced Tiberius that Agrippina and her two adult sons were plotting against the throne. Agrippina and Nero were banished to desert islands, and Drusus III was cast into prison.

In early 31, the tide was flowing Sejanus' way. He became Tiberius' consular colleague for the first few months of the year. Tiberius consented to let Sejanus marry either Livilla or her daughter by Drusus II, the princess Julia. After their joint consulship, things turned against Sejanus. At the end of August in 30, a letter from Agrippina's mother-in-law, Antonia, the younger daughter of Marcus Antonius, may already have aroused in Tiberius some fear and suspicion of Sejanus. The murder or forced suicide of Agrippina's son Nero in prison later in 31 may have caused more concern. At any rate, Tiberius summoned Caligula, who had been living with Antonia since Livia's death, to Capri. With Tiberius Gemellus being too young, Caligula was the only remaining practicable alternative to Sejanus as Tiberius' successor. Tiberius now permitted him to put on his long-delayed toga of manhood in preparation for public life.

Sejanus took up his scheduled proconsular *imperium*. Also, he and his eldest son, Strabo, each received a priesthood. Sejanus may have sensed the ground shifting when Tiberius commended Caligula for one, too, and thereby indicated that he was becoming eligible for the throne. Still, Tiberius led Sejanus to believe that he would be granted the *tribunicia potestas* (tribunician power), a sure sign that he would be Tiberius' immediate successor. Then, in October of 31, Tiberius sprang a carefully laid trap. He sent the senate a letter which Sejanus believed would recommend him for receiving the *tribunicia potestas*. Naevius Sutorius Macro, prefect of the *vigiles*, delivered the letter. While Sejanus waited for it to be read in the senate, Macro, under Tiberius' orders, took command of the Praetorian Guard. The letter began with mild praise of Sejanus. Praise became criticism, criticism reproof, and reproof sharp denunciation and a peremptory order for arrest.

The senate at once voted condemnation and death. The populace hailed the fall of Sejanus, pulled down his statues, dragged his body through the streets, and flung it into the Tiber. Many of his friends and supporters became victims of the mob. The execution of his children soon followed. Still, nothing changed for Agrippina and Drusus III: Agrippina died in exile. Drusus III starved to death in prison.

THE LAW OF TREASON (*MAIESTAS*)

Stories that Sejanus and Livilla had murdered Drusus II only increased Tiberius' the fears and suspicions. As a result, the law of treason was increasingly used to prosecute suspected enemies. *Maiestas* had come to include not only high treason (*perduellio*) but also such things as arrogance, sacrilege, slander, extortion, adultery, incest, rape, and murder. *Maiestas* could even include consulting astrologers and soothsayers about the future health and welfare of the emperor.

Tiberius himself had the astrologer Thrasyllus of Rhodes as one of his principal advisors. He knew, however, that enemies could use the predictions of astrologers and popular prophets to stir up the masses or subvert the loyalty of the legions. Augustus, who also had appreciated Thrasyllus' skills, once ordered the destruction of 2000 prophetic books, forbade astrologers to predict when anyone would die, and made it illegal for anyone to consult astrologers in private. In 16 C.E., one of the bases for charging Scribonia's grandnephew M. Scribonius Libo Drusus with conspiring against Tiberius was that he consulted with astrologers, diviners, and magicians. Tiberius executed two of them and expelled all of their kind from Rome. Three years later, the suspicious emperor took similar action against Jews and the worshipers of Isis.

Tiberius and informers (*delatores*)

Private informers (*delatores*) eagerly accused people under the law of treason because the accuser would usually receive one-fourth of a convicted person's property. Unfortunately, *delatores* were necessary because the government's practical capacity to initiate investigations was limited. Tiberius has been accused of using informers' accusations of *maiestas* to institute a tyrannical reign of terror. Nevertheless, the number and successes of *delatores* often have been exaggerated at Tiberius' expense. Out of 106 known prosecutions for *maiestas*, only 35 succeeded. Often, Tiberius favored acquittal or disallowed convictions handed down in lower courts. There were also serious penalties for false and malicious accusations. Tiberius even exiled some unscrupulous *delatores*.

TIBERIUS AND THE SENATE: THE INCREASING POWER OF THE *PRINCEPS*

Nevertheless, the number of *delatores* and treason trials did increase in the latter part of Tiberius' reign. The increase embittered his already precarious relations with many senators. Indeed, the relationship between Tiberius and the senate reveals a serious paradox in the nature of the Augustan Principate, one that could not be resolved except in the direction of increased power for the *princeps*. Earnestly following Augustus' model, as he always tried to do, Tiberius attempted to make the senate a meaningful partner in governing the Empire. He styled himself as an equal citizen with the senators and refused such honors as the *praenomen* Imperator and the title *pater patriae*. If a worthy senator fell into such financial difficulties that his senatorial status was threatened, Tiberius provided money to remedy the problem. Before abandoning Rome for Capri, Tiberius had tried to attend all meetings of the senate. He encouraged freedom of speech and debate. At least once, he ended as a minority of one.

Tiberius also increased the powers and responsibilities of the senate. For example, he transferred to it the Centuriate Assembly's age-old function of electing the consuls and praetors. He made the senate a supreme court of justice, especially for the trial of influential persons accused of treason and for trials of both imperial and senatorial provincial governors accused of extortion and corruption. He also consulted the senate on all affairs of state. Yet, efforts to make the senators responsible partners in government did not really work. They knew that in the last analysis, Tiberius' powers as *princeps* were far greater than theirs. His very attempts to encourage senators to speak their minds freely only added to the suspicion that he was trying to set traps for those who did not like him.

An insoluble problem

It is easy to accuse many senators of servility. Tiberius himself is said to have often called them "men prepared for slavery" (Tacitus, *Annals* 3, 65.3). There was, however, no real incentive to counteract the pressures in that direction. A well-intentioned emperor like Tiberius could try to uphold the prestige of the senate or encourage the senators to take responsibility and act independently. Nevertheless, he could not give them the real power and rewards that conferred prestige and were incentives for assuming responsibility.

The office of *princeps* depended upon a monopoly of the highest powers, greatest military forces, and most strategic provinces—the very marks of prestige for which senators eagerly strove under the free Republic. If an emperor were to share them with other senators now, he would inevitably create rivals for himself. That was something a conscientious emperor could not risk, and an insecure or autocratic one would not tolerate. As a result, even under a respectful emperor, the tendency was for senators to abdicate the responsibilities that he was willing to let them have. Therefore, even a well-meaning emperor had to assume more direct responsibility himself. Thus, the senate was only weakened further and was even less able to resist the usurpations of a less politic *princeps*. Eventually, the power to flatter an emperor was all that the senate had left.

Stoic opponents

Of course, a significant number of senators resented this situation bitterly. They were descendants of the old republican nobility or were members of newer senatorial families from places like the conservative districts of northern Italy. They idealized the virtues of the old Republic. Their heroes were those who had opposed Caesar: men like Cato the Younger and the assassins Cassius and Brutus. They often professed the philosophy of Stoicism, which became associated at Rome with republican opposition to the Principate. When persecuted for their opposition, they frequently sought a martyr's death in suicide, their ultimate, though futile, act of protest.

The historian Cremutius Cordus was such an individual under Tiberius. He wrote a history of Rome in which he praised Brutus and called Cassius "the last of the Romans." As a result, in 25 C.E. he was prosecuted for *maiestas*. Tiberius attended the trial in the senate. His grim face showed that he disapproved of Cremutius' defense. Cremutius, therefore, gave up and starved himself to death. A majority of senators then sought favor with the emperor by ordering the aediles to confiscate all copies of Cremutius' history and burn them. Secretly, however, some saved copies that were published after Tiberius' death (see Box 22.1). They helped to inspire more such martyrs under later emperors.

22.1 PUBLISHING IN THE ROMAN WORLD

Publishing a book in the Roman world was a rather different process from what it is today. There were no publishing companies that could produce, advertise, and sell physical copies of new works and that would share the proceeds with the author. Most ancient authors were men of elevated social status who did not write for money: literature was generally a gentleman's pursuit. Once a writer finished dictating drafts of his new project to his slave secretary (*librarius*), he would have it copied by other highly trained slaves (his own or some on loan from someone else) and sent to a small number of friends whose opinions he valued. After the author had the opportunity in incorporate their comments and criticisms, he would arrange a *recitatio*, an event at which he or someone hired for the occasion would read the new work to an invited audience, who would offer suggestions for improvement. A work might go through several rounds of presentation and revision before reaching its final form. Once the author deemed it sufficiently polished, the work would again be copied and sent to its dedicatee and others who had asked for a copy of the final product. This last step was "publishing": this was the moment that the book was able to circulate among the reading public, and this was the moment that the author lost control of the text. Anyone in possession of a copy was free to have copies made for distribution. Bookshops seem mostly to have made on-demand copies of published works for their customers. There is no evidence that authors made any money directly from the sale of their work: for authors of less elevated status, literary fame could bring with it patronage that would support further artistic endeavors.

TIBERIUS THE ADMINISTRATOR

Any positive assessment of Tiberius rests chiefly on his ability in imperial administration. He followed the foreign policy of Augustus by relying on a combination of diplomacy and the cautious application of military force. For example, he pursued limited military goals in Germany and took pains to avoid involving Rome in a war with Parthia. The Augustan conquests in central Europe and the East required a pause for consolidation. By strengthening the defenses along the Rhine and other frontiers and by suppressing revolts in Gaul, Thrace, and North Africa, Tiberius kept the Empire largely at peace and at an unprecedented peak of prosperity.

To promote the material welfare of the provinces, he kept tribute and taxes to a minimum. By strict economy (e.g., the curtailment of expensive spectacles and ambitious building projects), he was able to halve the 1 percent tax on auctions and still build up a large surplus in the treasury. Unfortunately, his reduced spending on games, spectacles, and grandiose building projects made him unpopular among the common people of Rome. In an effort to procure a more honest and efficient collection of provincial taxes, he restricted the tax-farming companies to the collection of customs dues. To reduce provincial discontent, he severely punished all provincial governors guilty of extortion, floggings, confiscation of private property, or having a corrupt administration in general. Some of the governors found guilty of such injustices committed suicide rather than face the wrath of the emperor.

Tiberius appointed able and conscientious men to govern the imperial provinces. To inspire honest administration, he increased governors' salaries. He also lengthened their terms of office, perhaps as much out of necessity as by choice. In either case, governors became increasingly familiar with their duties and with local conditions. Many of the governors held office from five to ten years, some even longer. As a result of this policy, cases of extortion and corruption arose less frequently in the imperial provinces than in the senatorial ones, where governors normally held office for only one year. In both the imperial and senatorial provinces, Tiberius encouraged provincial assemblies (*concilia*, *koina*) to send delegates to Rome to lodge complaints before the emperor and the senate about the conduct of governors, legates, and procurators.

Policies such as promoting uniform silver coinage and building roads, bridges, and canals not only benefited soldiers and frontier defense but also promoted commerce and provincial prosperity. Increasing prosperity in the provinces, the efficient collection of taxes, and careful financial administration all contributed to increased revenues and a large surplus in the treasury. That surplus enabled the emperor to give prompt and liberal relief to disaster-stricken areas in both Italy and the provinces. Even after making these and other large grants from the treasury, Tiberius was able to leave behind a surplus of 2.7 billion sesterces (3.3 billion, according to some authorities).

TIBERIUS' LAST YEARS AND THE SUCCESSION

Tiberius spent the last ten years of his reign in almost continuous residence on the Isle of Capri. His preference for Capri led to malicious rumors that he spent his time in every vice and debauchery that a perverted mind could invent. Suetonius delighted in publicizing them, but they are highly exaggerated at best. Tiberius actually spent much of his time dealing with questions of state or in the company of scholars and artists.

One of the most serious questions of state in Tiberius' last years was that of a successor. The only dynastic choices left were Germanicus' son Gaius Caligula and Tiberius' own grandson, Tiberius Gemellus, son of Drusus II. Tiberius probably would have preferred Gemellus to be his sole immediate successor, but Gemellus, only sixteen, was still the less practical choice. Caligula was older by six or seven years and had already been made an augur, a pontiff, and a quaestor. He was connected to the families of Augustus and Caesar through both parents. Gemellus was connected only through his mother. Moreover, as the son of the popular Germanicus, Caligula enjoyed great support from the common people and the soldiers. It would have been too dangerous to pass over Caligula completely. Therefore, Tiberius made Gemellus and Caligula his joint heirs in 35 C.E.

In 37, Tiberius fell into a coma and died. It was rumored that when he had momentarily revived, the praetorian prefect Sutorius Macro had ordered him smothered in his bedclothes. The story was probably fabricated after Caligula turned out to be a ruler whom many saw as a murderous tyrant. It did receive circumstantial support: Macro had been the one who nominated Caligula to be sole *princeps* at a meeting of the senate right after Tiberius' death. The accommodating senators set aside Tiberius' will and declared Caligula his only heir. They also showed their disapproval of Tiberius' later years by refusing the deification granted Caesar and Augustus. On the other hand, they had great hopes for the last surviving son of the popular Germanicus. That their hopes were disappointed may help to explain the intense hostility toward Caligula in the sources.

GAIUS CALIGULA (37 TO 41 c.e.)

Sensationalistic ancient sources paint Caligula as a mad tyrant after a serious illness cut short a promising beginning to his reign. Modern historians have often accepted that picture to one degree or another. Some, however, have tried to penetrate beyond the hostility and rhetorical stereotyping of the sources to find more method and less madness in his actions, mean and vicious though he could be.

As a young child, Caligula had experienced his father's popularity and the heady fondness shown him by his father's troops. Then, his father's controversial death, his mother's distrust of Tiberius, and Sejanus' plottings against his family must have been traumatic. They certainly did nothing to build a trusting and magnanimous character. In his later teens, he lived with his grandmother Antonia in the constant companionship of three young Thracian princes; the young Herod Agrippa I, heir to the throne of Judea; and Ptolemy of Mauretania, the son of King Juba II and grandson of Marcus Antonius and Cleopatra. From them, some speculate, he may have acquired a more absolutist conception of monarchy than the position of *princeps* implied.

Certainly, as a relatively inexperienced youth of twenty-five, Caligula conceived of the office that he inherited more autocratically than did Augustus and Tiberius. Their long experience gave them a sense of how tightly they could hold the reins of power without provoking deadly hostility among powerful senators. Moreover, youth and inexperience probably made Caligula feel vulnerable to more mature and experienced senators who might believe that they were better qualified to rule than he. Not surprisingly, he soon began to assert his power, insist upon expressions of loyalty and deference, and strike down real or perceived threats to himself. To many in the senate and imperial household, he came to appear as a harsh tyrant. Their view, often vividly and maliciously embellished in the accounts that justified his assassination and legitimized his successor, is reflected in the literary sources.

A POPULAR *PRINCEPS* AT FIRST

After Tiberius' long, stern, and parsimonious reign, Caligula delighted the populace by distributing the legacies of Livia and Tiberius, by abolishing the 0.5 percent tax that still remained on auctions (p. 412), and by holding splendid spectacles, games, chariot races, and wild beast hunts. He even restored to the popular assemblies their ancient right of electing high magistrates, but that practice soon proved unworkable.

Caligula pleased the senate with his deference and courtesy and with his conciliatory attitude toward the nobility. He relieved the fear of those whom Tiberius had suspected of treason when he publicly burned Tiberius' private records, although he falsely denied having read them. He curbed the infamous *delatores*, recalled Tiberius' exiles, and piously interred the bones and ashes of his brother Nero and his mother, Agrippina the Elder, in the mausoleum of Augustus. He even adopted his cousin and former joint heir, Tiberius Gemellus, as his own son and heir, shared the consulship with his uncle Claudius, and had his three sisters honored throughout the Empire. He ensured the loyalty of the Praetorian Guard by doubling the 500 sesterces promised each guardsman in Tiberius' will. To cap it all, he stirred the patriotic fervor of all classes by announcing preparations for the conquest of Britain and Germany. In October of 37 C.E., however, a serious illness forced him to postpone this enterprise and prompted enormous public outpourings of anxiety and affection.

PROBLEMS IN THE PALACE

It is not necessary to see this illness as affecting Caligula's mind. It remained sharp and agile. Caligula had already shown his vindictive nature. For example, his ill-treatment of his grandmother Antonia, who tried to give him sound advice, seems to have led to her death. Still, Caligula's illness may have brought to the fore certain issues, such as a fear of being removed in favor of another should he fall sick again. At any rate, it was probably in late 37, right after his recovery, when he accused Tiberius Gemellus of conspiracy and forced him to commit suicide. In 38, he made Sutorius Macro, who had engineered his accession, do likewise. Also that year, he forced the suicide of the distinguished consular senator M. Junius Silanus, father of his deceased first wife, Junia Claudilla. Several others, members and partisans of the Claudian family, eventually fell, too. Caligula's uncle Claudius escaped only because he seemed to be a harmless dolt.

Tales of depravity and incest in the palace are part of the rhetoric surrounding the stereotype of a tyrant. In Caligula's case, they were probably inspired by how he controlled and used those close to him to reinforce his position and prevent the rise of rivals among his relatives and in-laws. For example, he took his sister Drusilla (Julia Drusilla I) away from her first husband and gave her to his close friend M. Aemilius Lepidus. That he gave his signet ring to Lepidus during his grave illness and had Drusilla deified after her death in September of 38 probably are the bases for stories of sexual relationships with them. Also, that he kept close to his two other sisters, Agrippina the Younger and Julia Livilla, most likely had to do with politics more than with lust or affection.

Caligula's first wife, Junia Claudilla, had died in childbirth, and the child did not survive. Caligula's next two marriages were capricious, short, and childless. In 39, he formally married his fourth wife, Milonia Caesonia, on the day she bore him a child, Julia Drusilla II, named after his dead sister. Now, the establishment of his direct line seemed assured. Therefore, he was even more ruthless in rooting out others with possible claims to the throne. Caesonia, to whom he seems to have been devoted, probably took an active part. Early in the fall of 39, Caligula marched north with a large force, charged the commander of the legions on the upper Rhine with conspiracy, and executed him. Caligula had also brought with him Lepidus, Livilla, and Agrippina, recently widowed and mother of the future Emperor Nero. Charging them, too, with plotting against him, he executed Lepidus, who was portrayed as Agrippina's lover, and exiled his two sisters.

TENSIONS WITH THE SENATE

By now, Caligula's relations with many senators were bad. The consuls of 39 had not even offered the customary prayers for him on his birthday (August 31). Sometime in late 39 or early 40, he removed the legion in Africa Proconsularis from the command of the senatorial proconsul L. Calpurnius Piso. About the same time, he gravely offended another member of this powerful family, Gaius Calpurnius Piso. He insisted on sleeping with Piso's wife, apparently a relative of Caligula's great-grandmother Livia, so that the paternity of her children would be doubtful.

It is not clear how much credence can be given to stories that Caligula forced individual senators to swear that they would lay down their lives for him and his sisters, to dress as slaves and wait upon his table, to trot beside his chariot in their togas, and even to kiss his feet in homage. Nevertheless, they reflect many senators' perception of their humiliation. It was reinforced by the reinstitution of slandering the emperor as a treasonable offense.

CALIGULA'S MILITARY OPERATIONS

After completing his purge on the upper Rhine, Caligula launched military operations that ancient sources ridicule with stories of faked battles and bogus captives. In fact, Caligula and the future Emperor Galba conducted several successful operations across the Rhine. They had the intended effect of reinforcing respect for Roman might among the free German tribes. True, in 40, Caligula's long-planned invasion of Britain in imitation of Julius Caesar's exploits became only a march to the Strait of Dover and the erection of a lighthouse 200 feet high at Gesoriacum (Boulogne). There are hints that a mutiny may have spoiled his plans. (Perhaps the story of his ordering the troops to gather seashells on the shore reflects some sort of punishment.) It is also possible that the political situation in Britain was no longer favorable, or money may simply have run out.

FISCAL PROBLEMS

Caligula had already spent enormous sums of money before he incurred the expense of raising two more legions for his operations in the North. The huge surplus that Tiberius had left in the treasury was gone. At the same time, abolition of the 0.5 percent tax on auctions had reduced revenues. In 40, Caligula needed to replenish the imperial coffers. To obtain new funds, he resorted to extraordinary taxes on foodstuffs, lawsuits, and the earnings of porters, panderers, and prostitutes. When auctioning off his exiled sisters' property and some of his own possessions did not suffice, he further alienated many senators by seizing their estates in Italy. He also confiscated the estates of wealthy landowners in Gaul. Finally, a desire to take over the revenues of Mauretania as well as to eliminate another close family member may explain why Caligula summoned his cousin Ptolemy to Gaul and then executed him.

CALIGULA'S FOREIGN AND PROVINCIAL POLICIES

The treatment of Ptolemy was quite at variance with Caligula's usual approach to foreign and provincial affairs. He generally favored the policies of Pompey and Marcus Antonius rather than those of Augustus and Tiberius. In the East, for example, he preferred client–kings with close ties to himself: Provincial governors might enter into conspiracies and create armies for rebellion against him. He abandoned the kingdom of Greater Armenia as a Roman sphere of influence and allowed Parthia to control it. In exchange, Parthia recognized Rome's interests in the East. Commagene, which Tiberius had annexed as a province, Caligula restored to its former king, Antiochus; he made his three young Thracian friends, who probably were his cousins, the respective client rulers of Thrace, Pontus and Bosp(h)orus, and Lesser Armenia; and he gave Herod Agrippa I control over some Jewish territory once ruled by the latter's grandfather Herod the Great.

CALIGULA'S RELIGIOUS POLICIES

Caligula's vigorous promotion of the imperial cult has often supported his depiction as a megalomaniacal madman trying to impose a divine Oriental monarchy on Rome. One may be skeptical of stories that he believed that his horse Incitatus was a reincarnation of Alexander the Great's Bucephalus, that he once wanted to make him a consul, and that he actually had him appointed high priest of his cult. Still, building on Roman practices and precedents, Caligula made up for not being able to call himself *divi filius* (Son of a God) after Tiberius' posthumous failure to be deified. He emphasized his own personal divine nature and that of close family members as a way of legitimizing and strengthening his rule. On the other hand, perhaps not wishing to risk Tiberius' fate, Caligula did violate Roman norms by insisting on being recognized as a living god and by building a temple to himself at Rome. Such honors would have been permissible in the provinces, but not in Rome.

Neither were his policies acceptable to the Jewish population. In Alexandria, where there was a large Jewish community, a Greek mob sacked the Jewish quarters and forced the survivors to eat pork in the theater during the celebration of Caligula's birthday. In 40, the Alexandrian Jews sent a delegation headed by the scholar Philo to Caligula but obtained no redress. Meanwhile, Caligula had instructed Petronius, his legate in Syria, to install his statue in the Temple at Jerusalem. The prudent delaying tactics of Petronius and the diplomacy of Herod Agrippa I avoided the implementation of this disastrous order. Caligula's death prevented further trouble.

CALIGULA'S ASSASSINATION

Caligula's brief, but controversial, career came to an abrupt end during the Palatine Games on January 24, 41 C.E. The first blow against Caligula was struck by Cassius Chaerea, a tribune of the Praetorian Guard. Caligula had often obscenely insulted him. With Chaerea were prominent members of the senate, administration, and army. Although Caligula had remained popular with the common people, he had alienated too many others whose support he needed to survive. To make sure that Caligula left no living legacy, the Praetorians mercilessly cut down Milonia Caesonia and dashed out the brains of Julia Drusilla II against the palace wall.

OVERVIEW AND PROSPECT

A long, distinguished career of service to Augustus had given Tiberius a thorough grasp of the Empire's military, diplomatic, administrative, and fiscal needs, which he satisfied very well. Unfortunately, his lack of Julian blood and a reserved personality always made him Augustus' second choice as a successor. His life had been complicated by Augustus' relentless manipulation of Julio-Claudian marriages and adoptions plus the imperious actions of his mother, Livia. The unfortunate circumstances surrounding the death of Tiberius' nephew Germanicus caused further problems. They spurred opposition to Tiberius and his line among powerful senators who disliked him and favored the children of Germanicus' widow, Agrippina the Elder.

A happier man may have managed relations with the senate better, but his earnest efforts to make the senate a meaningful partner in running the Empire were undercut by the paradoxical nature of the Principate itself. When the ambitious praetorian prefect Sejanus played upon Tiberius' fears of conspiracy and promised relief from his burdens, Tiberius' relations with the senate were embittered even more. Later, Tiberius awoke to the danger that Sejanus posed. He protected Agrippina's sole surviving son, Gaius Caligula, who eventually thwarted a joint succession with Tiberius' grandson and ruled alone.

Caligula had a warped and nasty personality, but he was not insane. His military and diplomatic policies followed previous precedents and kept the frontiers safe during his brief reign. Internally, however, his obsessive pursuit of personal security through exalting himself above all mortals, eliminating perceived threats, and buying popularity with the masses produced political and fiscal disaster. The result was his assassination in 41. Those who still preserved the traditions of the free Republic hoped to restore it, or some better semblance of it. The futility of such fantasies in the post-Augustan world was quickly brought home, however, by the circumstances surrounding the accession of the next Julio-Claudian.

NOTE

1 Literally, "Little Boot," a name bestowed on him as a child in the Rhineland by his father's soldiers because his mother, Agrippina, liked to dress him in the uniform of a legionary soldier, complete with little military boots, *caligulae*, the diminutive of *caligae*, leather military boots.

SUGGESTED READING

Barrett, A. A. (ed.). *Lives of the Caesars*. Malden, MA and Oxford: Blackwell, 2008.
Levick, B. *Tiberius the Politician*. 2nd ed. London: Routledge, 1999.
Winterling, A. *Caligula: A Biography*. Berkeley: University of California Press, 2011.

CHAPTER 23

Claudius, Nero, and the end of the Julio-Claudians, 41 to 68 C.E.

CLAUDIUS (41 TO 54 C.E.)

As the senators debated what to do after the assassination of Caligula (restore the Republic? Create a truly elective Principate?), their inability to control events was made painfully clear. The brother of Germanicus, Caligula's uncle Claudius (Tiberius Claudius Nero Germanicus), obtained the loyalty of the Praetorian Guard by promising each guardsman a gift of 15,000 sesterces. Although Tiberius and Caligula had given gifts of money to the Praetorian Guard after they became emperors, Claudius set a dangerous precedent by promising a reward for its support before he ascended to the Principate. When the guardsmen demanded that the senators confirm their choice, many protested. Claudius pointed out that with the Praetorian Guard behind him, the senators had no alternative.

Suetonius depicts Claudius' accession as pure farce: Ransacking the imperial palace after Caligula's assassination, some praetorian guardsmen happened to see two feet sticking out from under a curtain and discovered Claudius hiding in fright; instead of killing him, they carried him over to their barracks, where the guardsmen acclaimed him emperor. That is how one would expect a man whom hostile tradition depicted as a fool to become emperor. Josephus (*Jewish Antiquities*, Book 19.236–266) even adds that Herod Agrippa I played the pivotal role in persuading both Claudius to assume the purple and the senate not to oppose him. Claudius probably deserves more credit for shrewdly seizing the opportunity that Caligula's assassination presented to make himself emperor. Claudius was no fool, although he was an unlikely candidate for *princeps*.

Early life

All of his life, Claudius had to contend with serious physical and psychological handicaps: persistently poor health, physical deformity, slow mental development, social maladjustment, and timidity. A birth defect or an early illness apparently left him with a wobbly head, spindly legs, a gawky look, and a speech impediment that made him appear simpleminded. Often, his imperial relatives either felt ashamed of him and tried to keep him out of sight or made fun of him. Drinking and gambling provided relief, but also embarrassed the family.

In correspondence with Livia, however, Augustus acknowledged that Claudius did possess a good intellect. He encouraged its development by providing him with excellent teachers. Under their tutelage, Claudius became a philologist, an antiquarian, and an expert on Roman law and government. The famous historian Livy even encouraged him to write history, and he did. After learning to read Etruscan and Punic, Claudius wrote multivolume accounts (now lost) of Etruscan and Punic history based on original research.

Studying law and history is good training for a head of state. Moreover, Claudius was not without some public experience. He represented the imperial family among the *equites* and had presided over some of the major games. Under Augustus, he was made an augur and a priest of the imperial cult. Tiberius and Caligula gave him some distinctions. Even the senate occasionally decreed honors for him. Also, as a Julio-Claudian and brother of the popularly revered Germanicus, Claudius enjoyed the support of the army, the urban populace, the Italian upper class, and the people of the provinces.

As Augustus' grandnephew, Claudius was already the relative of a god. At the very end of his first year as *princeps*, he enhanced his divine pedigree even further. On January 17, 42, he obtained a senatorial decree declaring his grandmother Livia a goddess. Now he had deities on both sides of his family.

THE POLITICAL PHILOSOPHY AND POLICIES OF CLAUDIUS

From his study of Roman history and political institutions, Claudius had learned that Rome owed its greatness to a willingness to devise new institutions to meet new needs. Like Augustus, however, whose biography (lost) he also wrote, Claudius realized that change at Rome could not move too quickly and had to respect the past. No matter what he did, however, he could not avoid conflict with the senate.

Claudius and the senate

The main problem was that many senators resented how they had been forced to accept Claudius as *princeps*. Some questioned not only his legitimacy but also that of the hereditary principle. Others thought that they were better qualified by experience, birth, or both. As a result, powerful senators posed real or potential threats to Claudius' reign right from the start. In 42, the commander of two legions in Dalmatia, a descendant of Sulla and Pompey, unsuccessfully plotted with a number of senators to overthrow Claudius. The legions, however, remained loyal to the Emperor, and their commander either committed suicide or was murdered. His co-conspirators were quickly eliminated.

Afterward, Claudius often saw, or was persuaded to see, rivals and threats that had to be eliminated. They included several members of his own family. For example, his niece Julia Livilla, Caligula's sister, was executed shortly after Claudius recalled her from the banishment that Caligula had imposed (p. 416). She was the wife of a senator who had wanted to become emperor after Caligula's assassination. Even without her, he was ultimately deemed dangerous enough to be eliminated in 46. Another victim the next year was Pompeius Magnus, descendant of Caesar's great rival and husband of Claudius' own daughter, Antonia.

Claudius' attempts to win over many senators often failed. As in Tiberius' reign, the paradox inherent in the nature of the Principate itself strained the relations between senators and *princeps* and led to the continued weakening of the senate. After becoming *princeps*, Claudius earnestly sought the senate's collaboration by outward shows of deference. He returned to it the right to elect curule magistrates, which Caligula had removed. He even restored its control of Macedonia and Achaea, which Tiberius had made imperial provinces earlier. Nevertheless, Claudius could not forget that it was dangerous to let senators have too much independence. Taking up the office of censor, he purged the senate of some old members and added new ones in 47 and 48.

Nobles were affronted. No one, not even Augustus, had held the actual censorship for the past sixty-eight years. Moreover, some new senators were Claudius' provincial clients. They were rich and powerful chieftains from Gallia Comata whose families had received citizenship from Julius Caesar. Claudius defended his action before senatorial critics in a speech still preserved in an inscription. He pointed out how Rome had benefited throughout its history by incorporating outsiders. Now, the admission of Gallic senators gave leading Gauls political equality with Italian-born senators. They became loyal partners in Rome's world state and senatorial allies of Claudius.

To reduce the possibility of being challenged by a disgruntled or ambitious senator, Claudius weakened the senate's power over the armies and its own provinces. He transferred control of the Roman municipal treasury (*aerarium Saturni*) to two quaestors responsible to him and diverted revenues from several sources to a central imperial *fiscus*. Furthermore, he placed many vital services under his control: the grain supply, aqueducts, and flood control at Rome; roads, canals, and harbors throughout Italy.

Claudius also increased his power through the legal system. The number of trials that took place in the emperor's private court, *intra cubiculum principis*, grew at the expense of the magistrates, provincial governors, and the senate. Those who saw their powers diminished are probably behind some of the exaggerated stories in the ancient sources about Claudius' absentminded, arbitrary, and even capricious behavior as a judge. Others, however, may have appreciated that in hearing cases himself, Claudius spared senators the indignity that they had suffered under Tiberius and Caligula when they had to try their own colleagues for treason.

Systematized control

As Claudius sought greater security for himself, he needed more carefully organized loyal help. Therefore, he often replaced provincial prefects with more subordinate procurators. In Rome, he enlarged the privy council of trusted friends known as the *friends of Caesar (amici Caesaris)*. He gave even greater prominence to talented and loyal freedmen, whom he included in the council. Their duties were clearly designated by specific titles. Claudius thus created the framework for the bureaus or departments (*scrinia*; sing. *scrinium*) that marked more formally bureaucratic administration under later emperors.

Narcissus, Claudius' secretary for correspondence (*ab epistulis*), drafted all laws and decrees sent out around the Empire under the imperial seal. Callistus headed the department that examined petitions sent to the *princeps* from the provinces (*a libellis*) and had charge of the office handling judicial investigations and trials (*a cognitionibus*). Another important freedman was Pallas, whom Antonia, Claudius' mother, had freed. As head of the treasury department (*a rationibus*), he coordinated all the provincial *fisci* (p. 365) and the activities of the procurators. A fourth was Claudius Polybius, keeper of the records office and reference library (*a studiis*).

The equestrian and senatorial classes bitterly resented that these and other freedmen wielded great power in the government and frequently lined their own pockets at imperial expense. Ancient and modern writers, however, have often been too closely bound to a biased and hostile tradition when they depict Claudius as being under the thumb of his freedmen. Like other members of the court, however, they often were part of internal rivalries and pursued personal agendas.

FIGURE 23.1 Model of an apartment block at Ostia. (Scala/Art Resource, NY)

Popularity through public works and welfare

As did most of his predecessors, Claudius courted popularity through public works and relief measures. He forbade usurers to lend to teenage spendthrifts. He abolished sales taxes on food and relieved stricken communities of their tax burdens. Through his control of the imperial mint, he both prevented excessive inflation and met the expanding needs of trade and industry. Public works, such as aqueducts, highways, and canals, were an added economic stimulus all over the Empire.

A spectacular undertaking was Portus, an artificial harbor two miles north of Ostia, Rome's original port near the Tiber's mouth. Ostia lacked a harbor deep enough to accommodate large grain ships. Their cargoes had to be unloaded at Puteoli in Campania and hauled overland to Rome. At Portus, grain could easily be transferred to barges and shipped up the Tiber. Unfortunately, ships using Portus had to leave empty: Rome's exports were now insignificant in comparison with its immense imports. No sooner had Claudius diverted shipping from Puteoli (the outlet of a rich region exporting both agricultural and manufactured products) than the shipowners complained of losing money from a lack of return cargoes. To satisfy them and keep vital supplies moving into Rome, Claudius and his successors had to compensate them with special concessions such as insurance against shipwreck, tax exemptions, the waiving of inheritance laws, and grants of citizenship to those engaged in the grain-carrying service for six years.

FOREIGN POLICY AND IMPERIAL DEFENSE

The motives behind Claudius' aggressive foreign policy were complex. The security of the *princeps* greatly depended on the loyalty of the provincial armies. The best way to gain their loyalty was to command them personally and lead them in conquest. Claudius had not gained any military reputation. He needed to do so when he became emperor. The danger of his situation had become clear within his first year, when the commander of the legions in Dalmatia had revolted (p. 422).

As in other matters, Claudius desired to rationalize, systematize, and improve imperial defense. Besides restoring Macedonia and Achaea to the senate (p. 422), he annexed the kingdom of Thrace as an imperial province. This facilitated Roman intervention in Dacia (modern Romania), in the Crimean peninsula, and everywhere north of the Black Sea as far east as the Don. Claudius made the Black Sea almost a Roman lake.

In the Near East, Claudius' policy was at once vigorous and cautious. He fomented internal discord and rivalry in Parthia and reestablished the Roman protectorate over Armenia by reinstating a friendly client king. He rewarded his friend Herod Agrippa I by granting him the rest of his grandfather's old kingdom, including Judea. Upon the death of Agrippa, however, he reannexed Judea as a Roman province. His chief objectives were peace and Roman control over the eastern trade routes.

Early in his reign, Claudius had to suppress a revolt that Caligula had provoked in Mauretania by the murder of King Ptolemy (p. 417). After Roman generals crushed the rebels in two years of hard fighting, Claudius organized Mauretania into two imperial provinces: Mauretania Caesariensis in the east and Mauretania Tingitana (Tangier) in the northwest.

The conquest of Britain, 43 C.E.

The conquest of Britain reflects Claudius' need for military glory, popular acclaim, and money. There was wealth to be had in British minerals, timber, cattle, and slaves. Pretexts for an invasion were not lacking. Claudius had received pleas from lesser British chiefs who feared the expanding kingdom founded by Cunobelinus (the Cymbeline of Shakespeare) in the southeast. After Cunobelinus died (ca. 40 C.E.), his son Caratacus (Caractacus) had grown more powerful and had become the champion of Druidism. A strong British kingdom that promoted Druidism threatened Roman authority in Gaul, where Druids fostered Celtic unity and resistance to Roman rule. Augustus and Tiberius had suppressed the Gallic Druids on the grounds that they practiced savage and inhuman rites.

In 43, a Roman army landed in Kent. After quickly defeating the Britons, the troops awaited the arrival of Claudius. Under his official command, they soon defeated Caratacus and took his capital, Camulodunum (Colchester). In tribute to the swift victory, the senate voted Claudius a triumph and the proud name *Britannicus*. During the next eight years, his legates created a province extending from the borders of Wales in the southwest to the estuary of the Humber in the northeast near York (Eburacum).

COLONIZATION, URBANIZATION, AND ROMANIZATION IN THE PROVINCES

Along with conquest and imperial expansion went further colonization, urbanization, and the extension of Roman citizenship in the provinces. That process— begun by Julius Caesar, continued with restraint by Augustus, and slowed down by Tiberius—was resumed on a large scale by Claudius. Most colonies served at once as military bastions in conquered territory and islands of Roman citizenship. The conversion of rural and tribal communities into organized municipalities (*municipia*) served similar purposes.

CLAUDIUS' WIVES

One of the complicating factors of Claudius' reign was his marital life. Clearly, elite Roman marriages were fraught with political and dynastic significance. As women did in other important families, the women of Claudius' household wielded much informal power and influence. Claudius' first two wives were connected with Sejanus during Tiberius' reign. Plautia Urgulanilla, who also had connections with Livia, was divorced after some scandal. The connection of Aelia Paetina (mother of his daughter Antonia) to Sejanus might have been reason enough for Claudius to divorce her.

Claudius' marriage to his third wife, Valeria Messallina, was politically opportune for all parties. Through her parents, Domitia Lepida and Valerius Messalla Barbatus, Messallina was a great-granddaughter of Augustus' sister Octavia (p. 402). Therefore, her husband or children might lay claim to the throne. To Caligula, the disabled Claudius probably seemed a safe husband for her. Conversely, for Claudius the marriage put him in a strong position to succeed, should the chance arise. For Messallina, the union improved her chances of becoming Empress or Empress Mother. Claudius was close to fifty and Messallina about twenty (not the child bride often depicted) when they were married. She produced two children: a daughter, Octavia, and a son, Britannicus (named for Claudius' conquest of Britain). Ancient authors take pornographic delight in portraying Messallina as a voracious sexual predator consumed by lust and greed. To them, Claudius appears as a hopeless cuckold whom she used to obtain condemnation of certain senators on charges of treason to further her own ambitions. Actually, she and Claudius were often mutually seeking security.

For herself, Messallina needed to protect her own and her children's position at court. Probably that was the purpose of the affair that brought her downfall in 48. By that time, it may have become clear to her that her mother's sister-in-law, Claudius' niece Agrippina the Younger, was plotting with Claudius' influential freedman Pallas, Agrippina's alleged lover, to replace her as Claudius' wife. Then, Agrippina's son, L. Domitius Ahenobarbus (later known as Nero) by her deceased first husband (brother of Messallina's mother, Domitia Lepida) would be close in line for succession. While Claudius was away from Rome in 48, Messallina acquired a powerful protector when she publicly committed herself to the consul-elect Gaius Silius in a marriage ceremony. He had promised to adopt Britannicus. Therefore, if his apparent plan to replace Claudius with strong senatorial backing had worked, her young son, Britannicus, might have safely succeeded Messallina's new husband.

Whatever the case, important freedmen convinced Claudius that he faced an assassination plot by a treacherous wife. The executions of Silius and many associates quickly followed. Messallina forestalled execution by committing suicide. The freedman Pallas then successfully urged Claudius to marry Agrippina even though she was the daughter of Claudius' own brother Germanicus. By Roman law, such a marriage was incestuous. Therefore, Claudius had the law changed.

Like her mother, Agrippina the Elder, the younger Agrippina was eager to secure the throne for the family of Germanicus, of which she and her son were the only survivors. Claudius, on the other hand, was already fifty-eight years old and needed to provide the Empire with a suitable successor. His own son, Britannicus, was only seven. Agrippina's son was of the right lineage and, though only ten, could already begin training for succession. Claudius immediately betrothed his daughter Octavia to him. Originally, she had been betrothed to L. Junius Silanus, a great-great-grandson of Augustus. The combination of Silanus' lineage with Octavia's would have made him a strong rival to Agrippina's son. Thus Agrippina's allies in the senate engineered Silanus' expulsion from that body on a charge of incest with his sister. He committed suicide on the day that Agrippina married Claudius. In 50, Claudius adopted Agrippina's son and gave him the name Nero Claudius Caesar. The loyalty of the Praetorian Guard to the heir apparent was secured in 51 by the appointment of Agrippina's friend and her great-grandmother Livia's former procurator Sextus Afranius Burrus as praetorian prefect. The Stoic philosopher Seneca the Younger, whom Agrippina retrieved from exile by Claudius, was entrusted with Nero's education.

CLAUDIUS' DEATH AND THE SUCCESSION OF NERO (54 TO 68 c.e.)

Claudius died from an undetermined cause in 54. The story that Agrippina poisoned him with a bowl of mushrooms comes from her detractors and should be treated cautiously (see Box 23.1). That Agrippina benefited the most right after his death naturally raises suspicions. It is possible, however, that Claudius, with his tendency to overindulge in food and drink, accidentally choked to death.

23.1 POISONING

Romans from all levels of society are known to have, on occasion, administered poisons to romantic rivals, unwanted spouses, and relatives who might block an inheritance or get in the way of a business deal. Although our sources report numerous instances of men (including at least eight different emperors) murdering people in this way, poison had long been thought to be a woman's weapon of choice, probably because women were in charge of care-taking and food preparation: most poisons were administered through meals or as medicines. Indeed, in the earliest known case of a mass poisoning, in 331 B.C.E., a group of 170 matrons were convicted of poisoning their husbands. Two patrician women, who were among the accused, claimed that the potions were medicinal. The famous professional poisoners, both historical and literary, of the early Empire are all women: Canidia, Martina, and Locusta (who is said to have assisted Agrippina).

Agrippina's alleged assassination of Claudius was part of a long tradition of political poisonings. As early as 180 B.C.E., as part of the second mass poisoning case in five years, the wife of the consul of that year was convicted of her husband's murder: she was said to have killed him to advance her son, the consul's stepson, who was named consul in his place. The most famous case from the period of the Republic was the mysterious death of Scipio Aemilianus (p. 227). Rumors circulated that his mother-in-law, Cornelia, encouraged her daughter, Aemelianus' wife, to poison him to protect legislation advanced by her sons, Tiberius and Gaius Gracchus. In the Imperial period, accusations of poisoning were so rampant that professional food-tasters became sufficiently numerous in the city that they could organize themselves into a professional guild.

Agrippina, Seneca, and Burrus handled the succession smoothly. Nero visited the barracks of the Praetorian Guard and promised each man 15,000 sesterces. Then he effectively delivered to the senate a speech carefully prepared by Seneca. In it, Nero promised to respect senatorial powers and prerogatives. For Nero's benefit, the senate soon deified Claudius.

NERO SURVEYED

The principal ancient sources (Tacitus, Suetonius, and Dio) leave a generally negative impression of Nero, the same as in Caligula's case and for the same reasons (p. 414). Nero appears as a self-indulgent, extravagant megalomaniac. For example, the story of his "fiddling" (playing the lyre) while Rome burned is proverbial. Indeed, there is no doubt that he became self-indulgently obsessed with his artistic pursuits and chariot racing. His attempts to outshine all other aristocrats in Rome are politically understandable but were carried to megalomaniacal heights. That he was mean, vindictive, and cruel at times cannot be denied. Still, there were ancient accounts, now lost, that reflected a more positive, popular picture of Nero. The hostile extant sources perpetuate the one-sided views of his enemies and the succeeding Flavian dynasty.

Again, as they do with Caligula, the extant sources try to disguise the discrepancy between the favorable and hostile views by artificially dividing Nero's reign in two parts: (1) the good first five years, the so-called *quinquennium Neronis* ("Nero's five years"), when he was guided by the steady hands of Burrus and Seneca or restrained by the fear of his domineering mother; (2) the unfettered tyranny of the period after he murdered his mother and was no longer under the influence of Burrus and Seneca.

While there is some truth to this picture, it distorts and oversimplifies. The positive aspects of Nero's reign are not limited to its start. Nero and his advisors pursued positive policies throughout his career, particularly in regard to the common people at Rome, the governing of the provinces, and the management of foreign affairs. On the other hand, throughout his reign, the fear of rivals within the imperial family and the plottings of ambitious senators to succeed a childless emperor produced undeniable intrigue, conspiracy, and murder.

Good initial relations with the senate

At the start of his reign, Nero did seem to embrace the ideal of clemency set forth in Seneca's Stoic essay *De Clementia* (published in 55). He abandoned trials within the emperor's private chamber, which had made many senators hostile toward Claudius. He even provided annuities to assist impoverished senatorial families.

General foreign and provincial affairs

During much of Nero's reign, Rome successfully controlled the provinces and the frontiers. Trade also benefited from the continued suppression of piracy and mitigation of some oppressive taxes for many years. Nero himself once even proposed the total abolition of all indirect taxes and customs duties throughout the Empire. Responsible critics in the senate, however, pointed out such an act's dire consequences for the public finances. The idea was dropped. Provincial discontent with Roman tax-collectors remained high, and provincial governors were often prosecuted for extortion after their terms of office.

Armenia, 55 to 60 c.e.

Armenia, a problem since the days of Marcus Antonius, had bedeviled all of Nero's predecessors. Mountainous, with extremes of heat and cold, Armenia was hard to conquer and difficult to hold. Furthermore, so long as Parthia remained strong and was not constrained by a more secure Roman frontier, annexing Armenia was impossible. Neither Rome nor Parthia could allow the other to occupy it without loss of security and prestige.

The Armenian problem had arisen again at the end of Claudius' reign, when King Vologeses I of Parthia placed his brother, Tiridates I, on the Armenian throne. In 55, Nero sent out to the East Cn. Domitius Corbulo, one of the ablest generals of the century. By 60, Corbulo was able to place Tigranes V, a Roman client, on the Armenian throne and withdraw.

Military operations in Britain, 58 to 61 c.e.

In 58, Nero sent out C. Suetonius Paulinus, another able general, to continue the subjugation of Britain. Paulinus conquered the island of Mona (Anglesey), the main center of Druidism, but in 60 a dangerous rebellion broke out behind his lines among the Iceni and Trinovantes. The deceased king of the Iceni had willed his territory to the Roman People. Acting on behalf of moneylenders, such as Seneca, to whom the previous king had fallen into debt, Roman procurators confiscated farmlands and reduced the former owners to the level of serfs. They robbed the king's widow, Queen Boudicca (Boadicea), of her land, flogged her, and permitted the raping of her daughters. Allied with the Trinovantes, the outraged queen collected an army. She captured the Roman colony at Camulodunum (Colchester) and destroyed the Roman legion sent against her. She then marched on Londinium (London), where she reportedly caused the massacre of 70,000 Romans. Suetonius Paulinus defeated her army in battle by superior discipline and skill. The vanquished Boudicca took her own life. Once Paulinus had accomplished the immediate military task, Nero replaced him with other officials who were more suited to the peaceful work of reconstructing the province and mending relations with its inhabitants.

Armenia again, 61 to 66 c.e.

In 61, after Corbulo had left Armenia, Tigranes V attacked Adiabene (northern Assyria around Arbela), a powerful Parthian ally, and started a war that he could not finish. Parthia invaded Armenia in force. Nero sent another army to intervene, but the new commander proved incompetent. Vologeses badly defeated him in 62 and compelled the army's surrender. In 63, Corbulo again took command. He invaded Armenia with overwhelming force during 64. Soon, compromise suited both Rome and Parthia in the face of common threats from restless Alan tribes. Corbulo allowed Tiridates I to ascend the throne of Armenia again but insisted that he go to Rome and receive his crown at Nero's hands.

THE DARKER SIDE OF NERO'S EARLY REIGN

Clearly, the good aspects of Nero's reign were not limited to just his first five years. On the other hand, there was a darker side of murder and palace intrigue from the start. Under Claudius, Agrippina had already eliminated many whom she had viewed as threats: for example, Claudius' powerful freedman Callistus and her rival for influence with Nero, Domitia Lepida (his aunt, mother of Messallina, and grandmother of Octavia and Britannicus). Upon Claudius' death, Agrippina and her allies had forced his freedman Narcissus to commit suicide. Right after that, she allegedly contrived the murder of M. Junius Silanus. He was a brother of her earlier victim, L. Junius Silanus (p. 426), and would have been a rallying point for opposition to Nero. In 55, Nero became exasperated with his mother's objections to his love affair with Acte, one of Claudius' well-placed freedwomen (p. 502). Nero tried to undercut Agrippina by dismissing her strongest ally within the palace, the powerful freedman Pallas.

Supposedly, Agrippina threatened to back Nero's stepbrother, Britannicus, as the rightful heir to Claudius' throne and Nero forestalled her by poisoning him. The story is suspect, but the sudden death of Britannicus did put Nero in a stronger position as he tried to reduce his mother's influence. After a sudden reconciliation, Agrippina regained her prominence. Eventually, Nero acquired a new mistress, Poppaea Sabina, wife of M. Salvius Otho. The latter had enjoyed close ties with Livia and Tiberius. He also had aided Nero's affair with Acte and cooperated with him over Poppaea. In return, Otho became governor of Lusitania (Portugal). Later, he became emperor.

Nero's relations with his mother grew hostile once more. Finally, Tacitus records that in 59, supposedly egged on by Poppaea and aided by Otho, Nero enticed Agrippina onto a boat designed to collapse at sea and drown her in the Bay of Naples (*Annals* 14.3.1–9.5). The collapsible boat may be fictitious, but there was an attempt to drown Agrippina. She swam to safety and reached home. Nero then sought the help of Seneca and Burrus, who probably had not been privy to the plot. Nero feared that Agrippina would use the incident to stir up popular opinion against him and replace him with another protégé. Seneca and Burrus agreed to put out the story that she had been plotting to depose Nero. Burrus did not trust the praetorian guardsmen to finish what Nero had started. Sailors from the fleet at Misenum, whose commander had been in charge of the plot to drown Agrippina, went to her home and dispatched her with club and sword. At a meeting of the senate, most members happily believed the story concocted to justify Agrippina's murder. One, the renowned Stoic Thrasea Paetus, walked out in protest against what he saw as his colleagues' servile hypocrisy.

NERO ASSERTS HIMSELF

Nero had turned twenty-one at the end of 58. With his powerful mother out of the way, he was becoming more independent and self-assertive and less dependent upon the support of Seneca and Burrus. Burrus died in 62; claims by Suetonius and Dio that

Nero poisoned him are called "unproven" by Tacitus. Nero replaced him with Gaius Ofonius Tigellinus, prefect of the *Vigiles* and a friend of Seneca. Seneca himself, however, asked for permission to retire into private life. That would not seem unnatural for a man of sixty-five, but the decision may have been hastened by Nero's divorcing Octavia, a major guarantor of his claim to the throne, and marrying Poppaea.

First, Nero executed two previously exiled possible rivals: Rubellius Plautus, great-grandson of Tiberius, and Faustus Cornelius Sulla Felix, second husband of Claudius' daughter Antonia, son of Nero's late aunt Domitia Lepida's second marriage, and a direct descendant of the dictator Sulla, Augustus' sister, and Marcus Antonius. Then he divorced Octavia and exiled her to Campania. Shortly thereafter, when popular demonstrations erupted in her favor, the fearful Nero had her executed on trumped-up charges of plotting against him. Poppaea had encouraged Nero's hopes for an heir after their marriage when she produced a daughter in 63. The baby soon died, however, and Nero felt it necessary to eliminate another member of the Julian line, D. Junius Silanus Torquatus, a brother of Lucius and Marcus Junius Silanus. Also, with the loyal support of Tigellinus, Nero had resumed treason trials from 62 onward. All of these actions greatly alienated the senatorial elite.

GROWING HOSTILITY TOWARD NERO

The upper classes in general were scandalized by Nero's increasing attempts to gain popularity with public displays of his chariot-driving skills and his lavish expenditures on public entertainments of all kinds. Nero's genuine interest in the arts had helped to stimulate what is often referred to as the Silver Age, an important efflorescence of Roman cultural life after the Golden Age of Augustus that lasted until the time of Hadrian (pp. 478–80). Nevertheless, Roman aristocrats were never supposed to show more than a decorous private interest in such things as playing music, singing, and dancing, while racing chariots in public was definitely beneath their august dignity.

Nero and the Great Fire of Rome, 64 C.E.

One sizzling night in July of 64, after a long period of hot, dry weather, a fire broke out in the slums at the northeast end of the Circus Maximus. The fire raged for nine days and left more than half of Rome a blackened waste. Acres of flimsy apartment houses and some of Rome's most venerated temples and shrines went up in smoke. So did Nero's own palace, with its priceless collection of books, manuscripts, and works of art.

At the time, Nero had been staying at Antium (Anzio), about thirty-five miles south of Rome. He swiftly sped to the scene of the conflagration. In this crisis, Nero's good qualities shone. After a vain attempt to check the flames, he converted Mars' Field and his private gardens into shelters for the homeless and hastened the transport of grain supplies to feed the destitute. His energy in alleviating suffering, however, did not spare him from the malicious rumor that he had started the fire in order to acquire the glory of building a new and more beautiful Rome.

Rebuilding program

Although the accusation against Nero probably is false, it is true that he eagerly seized the opportunity to indulge his passion for aesthetic enjoyment and creative activity by rebuilding Rome. Much of what he did or approved to be done was good. Widened and straightened streets had pillared colonnades built on both sides of them to provide shade and lessen the danger of fire. The rebuilt sections of the city had many fountains and open squares. New houses had to have their facades and first stories built of fire-proof stone. They had to be separated by alleys and have rear gardens provided with fire buckets and supplies of water.

The Golden House

Nevertheless, the extravagance that Nero showed in rebuilding his own palace helped fuel the rumors that he was responsible for the fire. Not only was he trying to make a greater public impression than any of the great senatorial families could afford, but he also confiscated large areas where their homes once stood and forbade them to rebuild. Nero's new palace, the Golden House (Domus Aurea), rose on the cleared land. No expense was spared. It probably rivaled in cost and splendor the great palace of Louis XIV at Versailles. Its entrance court could accommodate a colossal statue over 100 (perhaps 120) feet high (commonly said to be of Nero but arguably of Helios, the Sun-god), and it had a portico with a triple colonnade a mile long. Together with colonnades, gardens, lakes, fields, and game parks, it occupied an area of ca. 125 acres between the Palatine and Esquiline hills.

Nero's persecution of early Christians

Nero revealed his worst side when he made Christians the scapegoats for the fire to stop the whispering against him. Tacitus tells the story in *Annals* 15.44 (written probably as late as 120, perhaps even 123):

> Therefore, to quell the rumor, Nero served up and most strikingly punished culprits who were hated for their abominations. The common people call them Christians. The one responsible for that name, Christus, had been executed by the procurator Pontius Pilate when Tiberius ruled. Having been temporarily suppressed, their pernicious superstition was breaking out again not only in Judea, the origin of that evil, but also in the city [of Rome], into which from everywhere all horrible and shameful things flow and are amplified. Therefore, those who confessed [to being Christians] were brought to trial first, and then, on their own evidence, large numbers were convicted, not so much on the charge of arson as for their hatred of humankind. Also, mockeries were heaped upon them as they perished, so that covered in the skins of wild beasts they died from the ravening of dogs, or, having been fixed on crosses in order to be set aflame, they also, when day was done, were burned for nighttime illumination.

Despite the prevailing prejudice expressed here, the vicious punishments that Nero inflicted produced a widespread reaction against him.

Disastrous fiscal and monetary policies

The huge sums spent on Nero's Golden House and the rebuilding of Rome overstrained imperial finances. Therefore, Nero and his advisors took a number of unpopular steps to reduce other expenses and increase revenues. They temporarily suspended distributions of grain. They even seem to have let the pay of some of the legions fall into arrears. Supposedly, like a stereotypical tyrant, Nero ordered magistrates to produce higher rates of convictions and confiscations of property in trials. Indeed, he is said to have executed the six largest landowners in Africa Proconsularis and thus gained possession of the rich Bragadas valley. In other provinces, increased demands for taxes and the confiscation of local temple treasures aroused great hostility, as happened in 66 over plundering the Temple at Jerusalem.

Such confiscations, however, did not yield enough precious metal to prevent the mint from debasing the coinage, which had remained quite stable since the time of Augustus. The *aureus* shrank in weight by 11 percent. It was now minted at forty-five instead of forty to a pound of gold. The *denarius* went from a standard of eighty-four to a pound of silver to ninety-six, and its silver content went from 98 to 93 percent. The total reduction in value of the *denarius* was more than 20 percent when the new standards were met; it could reach 25 percent during actual production. The mint also tried to discontinue copper *asses* in favor of lighter brass coins.

On the positive side, these changes may have brought Roman coinage even more closely in line with the local coinages of the Greek East to create a broadly uniform imperial standard. They may also have checked the drain of gold and silver to India and Southeast Asia by raising the prices of luxury imports and thereby discouraging their purchase. Roman coins stopped appearing in southern India shortly after 64. On the negative side, the changes undermined faith in the Roman currency and caused an increase in prices that was particularly hard on the poor. The cheap new brass coin intended for minor everyday transactions aroused such dissatisfaction that the mint had to return to copper for its small coins.

PLOTS AGAINST THE THRONE

Growing dissatisfaction with Nero led to the formation of serious plots against him in 65. The plotters appealed to traditional aristocratic values such as *libertas* and *dignitas* and the welfare of the *res publica*, but theirs was not a call for restoring the old Republic. They desired a more responsible *princeps*. The most serious candidate was Gaius Calpurnius Piso, the man whose first marriage Caligula had destroyed (p. 416) and a relative of the Piso who had quarreled with Germanicus (p. 407). Many *equites* as well as senators supported him, including the poet Lucan (Seneca's nephew) and several officers of the Praetorian Guard. When they were betrayed, the terrified Nero struck at the conspirators and many others whom he viewed as possible threats. Lucan and Seneca were forced to commit suicide.

The lack of an heir continued to make Nero feel vulnerable. The very irony, therefore, raises skepticism about the story that in a fit of rage not long after Piso's conspiracy, Nero killed his wife Poppaea, who was pregnant again, by kicking her in the stomach. Shortly after her death, Nero tried to persuade Claudius' daughter Antonia to marry him. Having had one husband killed by Claudius and another by Nero, she adamantly refused. Therefore, she was executed. Her execution brought more suspicion and death. One new victim was the son of M. Junius Silanus (p. 430). In 66, two senators who allegedly consulted astrologers about how long Nero would live committed suicide after being condemned for treason. So did Seneca's two brothers, as well as the famous Stoic Thrasea Paetus and a number of others, including Petronius, Nero's "arbiter of social graces" (p. 479). Meanwhile, Nero married Statilia Messallina, widow of one of his victims and descendant of the Augustan general and literary patron M. Valerius Messalla Corvinus.

PRELUDE TO A FALL

Neither fear of conspiracy nor the arduous tasks of government interrupted Nero's musical career. After elaborate preparations, Nero set out in the fall of 66 on a grand concert tour of Greece. The attempts to eliminate real or potential conspirators and the spectacle of Nero going off to public competitions in Greece only bred more discontent and conspiracy. As he was leaving Italy, an alleged plot was discovered at Beneventum. This time, the great general Domitius Corbulo was implicated. Nero summoned him to a meeting in Greece and forced him to commit suicide. Then, he did the same to the two brothers who commanded the armies of upper and lower Germany. Soon, there would be no one left to trust.

The concert tour, however, was a personal triumph, thanks to the shrewd cooperativeness of the Greeks. In 66 or 67, pleased with the Greeks' flattering reception and their vocal appreciation of his art, he proclaimed the liberation of Greece from the governor of Macedonia. His words, no doubt intentionally, echoed the speech of Titus Quinctius Flamininus in 196 B.C.E. (p. 158).

THE JEWISH REVOLT AND THE FALL OF NERO

In the meantime, a full-scale rebellion broke out in Judea among the Jewish inhabitants. Many had already been incensed by the plundering of the Temple's treasures in 66. The situation was further inflamed that year when Greeks attacked their Jewish neighbors in the city of Caesarea and were not punished by the Roman authorities. Protests in Jerusalem against Roman inaction quickly got out of hand when the Roman procurator, hoping to avoid further trouble, failed to crush the protesters quickly. The imperial legate of Syria, Cestus Gallus, then besieged Jerusalem. It was, however, late in the year. Gallus was not prepared for a long winter siege and suddenly retreated. The whole province then seized the chance to revolt.

Vespasian

Nero gave Titus Flavius Vespasianus (Vespasian) a special command to quell the uprising. In 67, Vespasian methodically set about retaking the countryside and drawing a tighter and tighter noose around Jerusalem. Many saw the inevitable success of this strategy and surrendered. Among them was the future historian Flavius Josephus, who had been placed in charge of the rebels in Galilee. Still, resistance was fierce, especially at Jerusalem and later Masada. Vespasian had several years of hard work ahead.

That was fortunate for him. Complete success at an early date might have proven fatal. Not interested in personally conducting military campaigns and visiting troops on the frontiers, Nero was perfectly happy to let others do that dirty work. On the other hand, he was afraid to let others have too much military success and popularity, as the recent fates of other generals attested.

The revolt of Vindex, 68 C.E.

Nero had planned to tour Asia Minor and Egypt. Bad news compelled him to cancel the trip and return to Rome from Greece in early 68: C. Julius Vindex, the governor of one of the Gallic provinces, was stirring up a revolt and raising a large army. By spring, Vindex also had the open support of two men who had been close to the old Empress Livia: Servius Sulpicius Galba, who had benefited handsomely from her will, governed Nearer Spain; M. Salvius Otho, Poppaea Sabina's compliant former husband, who governed Lusitania. North Africa and Rome itself were also seething with revolt. The rebellion received a sudden check when L. Verginius Rufus, the loyal governor of Upper Germany, led three legions into Gaul. Overwhelmed, Vindex committed suicide.

The final blow and the accession of Galba, 68 C.E.

Galba had sent agents to Rome to undermine the loyalty of the Praetorian Guard with a promise of 80,000 sesterces to each man. The guards succumbed to the bribe, deserted Nero, and backed Galba. Soon, other armies began to renounce their allegiance. The senate proclaimed Nero a public enemy and embraced Galba. Deserted, condemned, and not having the courage to do himself what he had often coldly ordered others to do, Nero persuaded a faithful freedman to plunge a sword into his throat. Reportedly, Acte saw to his decent burial.

AFTERWORD

The common people still loved Nero. His posthumous adoration and the flowers often placed by unknown hands on his tomb disturbed Galba. Otho, Galba's successor, exploited Nero's memory, as did Vitellius, who overthrew Otho. Years later, Emperor Domitian, who also preferred the more unfettered rule of a popular monarch instead of being a mere "first among equals" within the senate, revered Nero's memory and executed some of his surviving foes.

SUGGESTED READING

Champlin, E. *Nero*. Cambridge, MA: Harvard University Press, 2005.

Mason, S. *A History of the Jewish War, 66–74*. New York: Cambridge University Press, 2016.

Osgood, J. *Claudius Caesar: Image and Power in the Early Roman Empire*. Cambridge and New York: Cambridge University Press, 2011.

CHAPTER 24

The crisis of the Principate and recovery under the Flavians, 69 to 96 C.E.

Despite the murderous intrigues of the Julio-Claudians and those who challenged them for the imperial throne, under Claudius and Nero the Empire had been mostly well run. Nero, however, alienated the upper classes in Rome with his attempts to outshine all others. Worse trouble began after the great fire of 64, when his oppressive fiscal policies undermined his support in the provinces and the armies stationed there. Nero had failed to learn the lessons of Augustus' success: to gain at least the acquiescence, if not the willing cooperation, of powerful aristocrats, a *princeps* could not openly flaunt his power at the center of the Empire; he also had to cultivate assiduously the loyalty of the legions in the provinces to prevent challenges from the periphery.

   The lack of an heir only encouraged ambitious men to attempt replacing Nero as *princeps*. His death in 68 threatened the Empire with the same kind of destructive competition for preeminence that had destroyed the late Republic. The office of *princeps* became a revolving door through which four emperors passed in rapid succession as a result of assassination and civil war in 69. If the process had continued, the Roman Empire would have been irreparably damaged. Fortunately, Titus Flavius Vespasianus (Vespasian) was able to bring stability and calm.

SOURCES

The most important ancient source for the events of 69 and the Flavian emperors (Vespasian, Titus, and Domitian) is the historian Tacitus. His *Histories* covered the years from 69 to 96. Unfortunately, only the books that cover the years 69 and 70 survive. Tacitus also wrote the *Agricola*, a biography of his father-in-law, Cn. Julius Agricola, who governed Britain from 77 to 84; a discussion of the state of oratory during the Principate (*Dialogue on Oratory*); and a rather fanciful ethnographic account of the Germans (*Germania*). The *Jewish War* by the pro-Flavian historian Josephus is useful but, naturally, limited in scope. The only connected historical narrative is provided by Byzantine epitomes of Books 65 to 77 of Cassius Dio's history of Rome. Suetonius wrote extant biographies of the three emperors who followed Nero (Galba, Otho, and Vitellius), as well as of the three Flavians. Plutarch wrote two longer biographies of Galba and Otho.

Much valuable material can be extracted from the *Natural History* of Pliny the Elder, the *Letters* of Pliny the Younger, Quintillian's *Institutes of Oratory*, Frontinus' collection of military strategems (*Strategemata*) and his treatise on Rome's aqueducts (*De Aquis* [*De Aquaeductu*] *Urbis Romae*), and the poems of Statius, Martial, and Juvenal (pp. 481–4). Numerous official and private inscriptions, works of art, buildings, public works, fortifications, coins, and artifacts also supply useful information.

GALBA (68 TO 69 C.E.)

Servius Sulpicius Galba, the first to succeed Nero, fell in 69 after reigning only a few months. Although of an old aristocratic family connected with Livia, he showed little talent for practical politics as emperor. Before fully consolidating his power, he attempted two contradictory and impossible things: quickly balancing the budget and winning support from the armies. He alienated the Roman populace by cutting down the grain dole; the Praetorian Guard by failing to pay promised donatives; and the two armies on the Rhine, already hostile and sullen, by unwisely recalling the highly regarded commander in upper Germany, Verginius Rufus. The two armies mutinied and proclaimed the newly appointed commander in lower Germany, Aulus Vitellius, emperor of Rome.

Even then, Galba might have saved himself by adopting Verginius Rufus as heir and co-regent. He chose instead the aristocratic L. Calpurnius Piso Frugi Licinianus, whose main qualifications were his deep roots in the old aristocracy. He was a descendant of both Crassus (through adoption) and Pompey. His grandfather was Scribonia's grandnephew L. Scribonius Libo. His oldest brother was the Pompeius Magnus who had married Claudius' daughter Antonia and had been executed as a threat to Claudius and Messallina. His second-oldest brother had been executed under Nero, and his sister was married to the grandson of Germanicus' foe Cn. Calpurnius Piso. Unfortunately, he was totally devoid of popularity or of political and military experience. Piso's adoption turned Galba's former ally and would-be successor, Marcus Salvius Otho (the compliant ex-husband of Poppaea Sabina), into a dangerous enemy. Otho hurried off to the camp of the Praetorian Guard and by liberal promises of money persuaded its men to proclaim him emperor. They promptly murdered Galba and Piso.

OTHO (69 C.E.)

Supported by the Praetorian Guard and the Roman populace, Otho soon won recognition by the senate. No doubt, many senators were pleased by his execution of Nero's praetorian prefect Tigillinus, whom he conveniently blamed for Nero's murderous acts. On the other hand, Otho further ingratiated himself with the common people by emphasizing his close relationship with the still-popular dead emperor. He restored the fallen statues of Nero and Poppaea, married Nero's widow, Statilia Messallina, and took the name *Nero* for his own.

The armies on the Rhine, however, had already declared for Vitellius and were marching toward Italy. An early spring prevented Otho from blocking them at the Alpine passes. He managed to defeat part of the enemy forces. Then, fearing that he would be outflanked by the much larger main body if he delayed, he attacked it head on rather than wait for reinforcements. Defeated after a long, hard-fought battle and hoping to prevent further bloodshed, he terminated his short reign by suicide.

Significantly, Otho was the first emperor who did not have roots in the old aristocracy. The Julio-Claudians had recruited men like him in order to have a group of loyal followers to counterbalance champions of the old order in the senate: Otho's grandfather had been raised in Livia's household and reached the praetorship. Otho's father had been a very good friend of Tiberius and had received patrician status from Claudius. Otho's own close association with Nero, of course, had ensured his own rise in imperial service. With the end of the Julio-Claudians, there were no loyalties to prevent newcomers like Otho from attempting the throne themselves.

VITELLIUS (69 C.E.)

Vitellius was also a newcomer. His grandfather was one of Augustus' equestrian procurators. His father reached the consulship late in Tiberius' reign and twice under Claudius, with whom he was also censor. The father had also backed Agrippina the Younger, which turned out to be a wise move. It gave Vitellius the chance for friendly relations with Caligula, Claudius, and Nero, who advanced his career. Galba then appointed him commander in lower Germany in the mistaken belief that he was too lazy and decadent to pose a threat. Hostile sources portray him as one of the most inept and helpless emperors ever to disgrace the Roman throne. His failure to prevent looting and violence after victory is a black mark, but stories that he bankrupted the treasury by extravagant living during a reign of only seven months are not credible. His greatest significance is that he owed his elevation solely to legions from the frontier.

With Vitellius, the armies of the Rhine had already created one emperor. Now, those stationed in the East were about to create another—Vespasian (T. Flavius Vespasianus). He was a man of even more recent equestrian origin and the general whom Nero had sent to Judea in 66 to suppress the Jewish revolt (p. 434). Leaving his son Titus in charge of the siege of Jerusalem, Vespasian hastened to Egypt in order to prevent the shipment of grain to Rome. Meanwhile, the governor of Syria set off with his army to invade Italy on Vespasian's behalf. The Danubian armies did likewise and brutally sacked Cremona after defeating Vitellius' forces there.

Vespasian's brother Flavius Sabinus was already in Rome, where he was serving as prefect of the city. When Vitellius tried to surrender to Sabinus, Vitellius' soldiers refused and forced him to besiege Sabinus on the Capitoline. During the siege, fire destroyed the great temple of Jupiter Optimus Maximus, and Sabinus was captured and executed. Vespasian's younger son, Domitian, managed to escape Rome by disguising himself as a priest of Isis. When the Danubian troops arrived, they defeated the forces of Vitellius, killed him (December 20, 69), and rampaged through the city until Vespasian's Syrian legions appeared and restored order. The senate then chose Vespasian as the new emperor. He was able to gain permanent control and replace the defunct Julio-Claudian dynasty with his own Flavian family.

VESPASIAN (69 TO 79 c.e.)

The accession of Vespasian in the last days of 69 gave Rome a man who was able to end the civil wars and bloodlettings, just as Augustus had brought to an end the strife and anarchy of the dying Republic. Vespasian lacked the glamour and prestige of Julius Caesar's shrewd heir, and his reign was not quite as memorable. It did, nevertheless, usher in a new phase in the history of the Roman Empire and many of the policies typical of the second century.

Born in 9 c.e., Vespasian came from an equestrian family that lived near the hilltop town of Reate in the Sabine country. His grandfather had been an auctioneer; his father an imperial tax collector in Asia Minor and, after his retirement, a moneylender in the province of Raetia (southern Bavaria and eastern Switzerland). The father later returned to Italy, married into a family slightly above his own social station, and settled down on a medium-sized estate near Reate.

Young Vespasian had received a good enough education to be able to express his rather corny and at times slightly obscene humor even in Greek. His financial and military abilities had attracted attention in high places. His career received boosts at the imperial court from the advocacy of the powerful freedman Narcissus and the influential freedwoman Caenis, who became his mistress (p. 502). He received a number of important posts under Caligula, Claudius, and Nero. Vespasian's elder son, Titus, was even raised at court with Claudius' son, Britannicus. Vespasian suffered a setback after Agrippina the Younger, with whom he was on bad terms, came to the fore, but he rebounded under Nero after her death. Then, his failure to show proper appreciation of Nero's musical talents caused another setback. Vespasian still had advocates like Caenis, however, and Nero turned to him when someone competent was needed to suppress the Jewish revolt.

Coming to the throne in 69 at the age of sixty, bald, wrinkled, and tough, Vespasian had behind him much administrative and military experience. In one capacity or another, he had known Thrace, Spain, Gaul, Germany, Britain, Africa, Syria, and Egypt. He had the respect of the armies and could command their loyalty and obedience. He was also a tireless worker. Although he often took his time making up his mind on a specific course of action, he carried out his decisions with determination and steadfastness. Knowing the value of money, he gave Rome a sound fiscal policy and took endless pains in balancing the books. Such was the man who rescued Rome from the brink of financial and political disaster and made possible more than another century of internal peace and prosperity.

THE RESTORATION OF PEACE

Most urgent in 70 was the task of breaking the continued resistance of Vitellius' supporters in Gaul and Germany as well as crushing the revolt in Judea. In Gaul and Germany, Julius Civilis, a chief of the Germanic Batavi and a Roman citizen, had raised a revolt in favor of Vespasian against Vitellius. Apparently, Vespasian's attempts to compromise with Vitellius' defeated forces in 70 led to Civilis' disaffection and an attempt to combine with those still hostile to Vespasian. They constituted themselves as the Empire of the Gauls, *Imperium Galliarum*, probably to secure a base from which they could raise up their own candidate for Roman emperor and not, as is frequently claimed, to create an independent Gallic nation. The able Quintus Petilius Cerialis, son-in-law of Vespasian, destroyed their hopes in the spring of 70.

Capture of Jerusalem, 70 c.e., and Masada, 73 c.e.

Meanwhile, in the Jewish War, Vespasian's son Titus had stormed and captured Jerusalem. Neither side showed any mercy to the other. The slaughter was frightful. Large numbers of Jews who survived were sold into slavery. A relief on the Arch of Titus, completed by Titus' brother, Domitian, commemorates the capture and destruction of Jerusalem. It shows a triumphal procession bearing the spoils taken from the Temple—the seven-branched candlestick, the table of the shewbread, and other spoils. Not only did the depicted spoils finance this arch, but they also were used to erect the famous Flavian Amphitheater, better known as the Colosseum (p. 495). Finally, to demonstrate the inevitable punishment that awaited any resistance to Rome, three legions spent three years in crushing pockets of rebels. During the final six months, they built a huge earthen ramp to reach the fanatical defenders of Masada, a sheer rock fortress 1700 feet above the Dead Sea. When the Romans finally breached their walls, the defenders set fire to their buildings. Josephus says that all but two women and five children committed suicide (*Jewish War*, Book 7.389).

To reduce the chance of organized rebellion in the future, the Jewish council of the Sanhedrin and the office of high priest were abolished, the Temple was destroyed, and worship there was forbidden. Furthermore, the Jews were forbidden to seek converts, and the Jewish population of the whole Empire was forced to donate the tax formerly paid to the Temple at Jerusalem to Jupiter Capitolinus at Rome. All those born into

FIGURE 24.1   Relief from the Triumphal Arch of Titus (81 c.e.), depicting spoils from Jerusalem.

the Jewish faith, however, were still exempted from Caesar worship. Of the various Jewish factions, the Pharisees survived most successfully. They devoted themselves chiefly to the study of Jewish law. With Jerusalem destroyed, the small Christian sect was further cut off from its Jewish roots and began to take on an identity more of its own. That change helped its spread among non-Jews but soon caused problems over Caesar worship.

REFORM OF THE ARMY

The provincial soldiers' role in the havoc of 69 clearly indicated to Vespasian a need to reform the army. First, he disbanded the legions that had opposed him in Gaul and Germany. After creating two new ones, he seems to have maintained an army of twenty-nine legions, one more than under Nero. He stopped the practice of stationing some of the legionary and most of the auxiliary troops in the frontier regions from which they had been recruited. He feared that otherwise they were apt to sympathize with local leaders' political ambitions. To counteract such sympathies, he either formed new auxiliary units of mixed tribal and national origin or transferred units to frontiers far from their homelands and under the command of Italian officers. Finally, to reduce the chances of military coups by provincial commanders and provide for tighter defense at the same time, Vespasian tended to break up large concentrations of legions and space them out singly on the frontiers.

   Another problem was that the popularity of military service had been steadily declining among the population of Rome and Italy as peace and prosperity increased under the emperors. To take up the slack, Vespasian increased legionary recruitment from the more martial youth of Gaul and Spain, where military academies for the training of future Roman officers (*collegia iuvenum*) became ever more common. Thus Vespasian's military reforms were part of a process that Romanized the provinces and integrated them with Italy.

PROVINCIAL POLICY

Vespasian inaugurated a new age of municipalization in the Roman world. Completing the work of former centuries, he made Spain an integral part of the new imperial state by extending Latin rights to about 350 Spanish cities and towns. Dalmatia began to acquire a degree of urbanization and municipalization which it had not known before. Even the Danubian provinces began to receive Roman citizen colonies.

Vespasian did more to make the western provinces full partners in the government and administration of the Empire than simply using them for recruiting grounds or for granting Roman citizenship to grateful officeholders in the newly chartered *municipia*. He went beyond Claudius or any of his predecessors in employing the local aristocracy of Gaul and Spain in imperial administration. Becoming censor in 73, he even added members of the municipal aristocracy of southern Gaul and of Baetica in southwestern Spain to the rolls of the Roman senate. Previous purges and the recent civil war of 69 had depleted its ranks. By utilizing the talents and services of the Gallic and Spanish provincials, Vespasian gave them a stake in both defending the imperial frontiers and maintaining internal peace through loyal service to him. When the Flavian dynasty ended, however, members of their families would be in a position to seek the imperial purple for themselves.

Vespasian greatly strengthened the defenses of the northern frontiers by restoring to eight the number of legions serving along the Rhine in upper and lower Germany. Later, those two military commands, which had been attached to Gaul, became individual provinces. Along the Danubian frontier, Vespasian built numerous military roads and new stone fortresses. Moreover, he shortened the Rhine-Danube frontier by annexing the triangle of land called the *Agri Decumates*. It is now largely occupied by the Black Forest, between the upper reaches of the two rivers in what is today southwestern Germany and Switzerland (map, p. 368). Vespasian also sent three men of great renown to resume the conquest of Britain, which Claudius and Nero had left unfinished: Petilius Cerialis (71–74), who had vanquished Civilis in Germany; Julius Frontinus (74 to 77–78), who wrote the *Strategemata* and *On the Aqueducts*; and Cn. Julius Agricola (77–78 to 84), about whom Tacitus wrote the *Agricola*.

THE NEAR EAST

In the Near East (see end map and p. 379), Vespasian tried to remedy some of the fundamental weaknesses in his predecessors' defensive arrangements. He attempted to maintain peaceful relations with Parthia, even to the extent of resigning control, direct or nominal, over the kingdom of Greater Armenia. Still, he did not seek Parthia's friendship at the expense of Rome's own interests. His least friendly act toward the Parthians was his refusal to cooperate with them in repelling the Alans, a Sarmatian tribe living beyond the Caucasus. They had overrun Media Atropatene and Greater Armenia and were then a threat to the very existence of the Parthian state. Instead, he only helped the king of Iberia (modern Georgia) to occupy the Porta Caucasica (Dariel Pass), and he built a fortress near what is now Tblisi in 75. Some of Vespasian's other measures were also less than pleasing to the Parthian king. First, he strengthened Roman control over the great caravan city of Palmyra and made Judea a separate procuratorial province, with one full legion stationed at Jerusalem. He extended the province of Syria from the northern edge of the Lebanon mountain range eastward from Damascus to the upper reaches of the middle Euphrates. That required annexing the kingdom of Commagene, whose king he deposed. To the north, he created a huge province in Anatolia by adding Cappadocia and Lesser Armenia to the former province of Galatia. There he stationed two legions: one guarded the vital Euphrates crossing at Melitene; the other protected the important road junction of Satala, whence roads led to Trapezus (Trebizond) and other naval bases on the Black Sea. Thus, except at Zeugma and Samosata (now legionary strongholds), Vespasian diminished the responsibility of Syria for defending the Near East. Simultaneously, he created stronger bulwarks for protecting Rome's eastern provinces against Parthia.

VESPASIAN'S RELATIONS WITH THE SENATE

The senate had remained an influential sounding board of upper-class opinion. Still, it had been declining steadily as an independent organ of the government since the reign of Tiberius. Physically, it had been reduced to about 200 by the actions of Nero and the civil war of 68–69. The few remaining old families must have been annoyed when Vespasian held the censorship in 73: he removed some objectionable or recalcitrant senators and added 800 new ones to his own liking from Italy and the western provinces. Aside from enhancing Vespasian's personal security, the new members increased the pool of senatorial talent that he needed to administer the Empire. Of course, as often happens in such cases, some newcomers absorbed the values and traditions of the institution which they joined and defended its prerogatives against later emperors. Often their efforts were futile, but pushing senators too far could engender deadly hatred.

THE EXPANSION OF EXECUTIVE POWER

The weakening of the senate accompanied a steady concentration of powers and functions in the imperial executive and an increase in appointed officeholders. Their value as the sole means of preserving administrative continuity under rapidly changing emperors had come to light more clearly than ever before in 69. In appointing such officials, Vespasian made two important innovations: he replaced with equestrians many, but not all, of the freedmen who had held some of the highest positions under Claudius and Nero, and he appointed more and more Italians and provincials. Equestrians were less offensive to the senate than were freedmen, who had been offensive to the equestrians as well. Also, equestrians usually had considerable business and administrative experience and, often having greater private sources of income, were somewhat less tempted than freedmen to embezzle public funds. Men from the provinces and Italian municipalities brought with them knowledge of local conditions that must have been quite useful for administering a highly diversified empire.

FISCAL ADMINISTRATION

Vespasian's greatest claim to fame was his success in handling fiscal problems. He balanced the books and restored public finances, which had been thrown into chaos by Nero's extravagance and the civil wars of 69. He was personally frugal and financially experienced. He also had firm control over the armies, so that he did not need to buy their loyalty by expensive donatives. Using his powers as censor, Vespasian had a careful census taken of the financial resources of the Empire. He discovered that the provinces, after a century of peace and prosperity, were able to pay much more tribute than before. He assigned certain "free" cities and islands previously immune from taxation, such as Rhodes, Samos, and Byzantium, to provinces and forced them to pay taxes. He restored to the senate the province of Greece, to which Nero had granted freedom and immunity from taxes, and took back under imperial control the richer provinces of Sardinia and Corsica. He asserted the government's claim to land seized surreptitiously by private owners or occupied illegally by squatters. He even took back on behalf of the *Fiscus* many estates given by former emperors to their friends. Finally, he reorganized the revenues of the other imperial estates, especially those containing mines, quarries, fisheries, and forests. In short, no source of income, however unorthodox or unsavory (such as a tax on public latrines, see Box 24.1), was beneath Vespasian's notice.

24.1 LATRINES IN THE ROMAN WORLD

One common feature of Roman cities is the presence of latrines (Latin, *latrina*) in private homes and public spaces. Private toilets found in Roman homes were usually designed for one person at a time, although two-seat toilets have been found. Families often tucked toilets into corners near the kitchen or underneath stairwells. Most public toilets were accessible from the street through a door and were located next to bath or other industrial complexes in order to use water run-off from those enterprises to flush the sewer trench that ran under the bench toilet seats. A second, smaller gutter is often also present: presumably, this was used for washing the communal sponge stick, the Roman equivalent of toilet paper. Other items used for cleaning oneself were smooth stones, seashells, potsherds, and papyrus, though this last will have been much rarer given the expense. Basins for handwashing were also usually provided. Privacy was at a minimum in these large structures (one on the Aegean island of Kos could seat ninety): walls separating individual seats are rare, and it appears that men and women did not have separate facilities. Small windows set very high into the walls allowed for sunlight and fresh air to enter, and they at least protected the user from the prying eyes of passers-by. Decorations in most public restrooms were sparse: plaster walls and basic tile floors. In the second and third centuries C.E., however, there was a trend toward "luxury latrines" decorated with statues, mosaics, and wall-paintings.

FIGURE 24.2   Ostia, Schola di Traiano, four-seater latrine. From A. Koloski-Ostrow's *The Archaeology of Sanitation in Roman Italy; Toilets, Sewers, and Water Systems.* (University of North Carolina Press, 2015), p. 152, figure 38. Reproduced with permission.

PUBLIC EXPENDITURES

Despite a reputation for being tight with money, Vespasian spent freely on imperial armies; on roads, bridges, and fortifications in the provinces; on public buildings in Rome; and on literature and education. After repairing the damage wrought in Italy by the civil war of 69, he commemorated the end of the Jewish War by beginning major construction projects in Rome: the Forum of Vespasian, with the Temple of Peace in the center; the Arch of Titus; and the gigantic stone Flavian Amphiteater, or Colosseum (p. 495), a symbol of the might and majesty of Imperial Rome.[1] Another great architectural achievement of the reign was the completion of a new temple to Capitoline Jupiter in 71.

To encourage literature, Vespasian liberally subsidized poets and other writers. From public funds, he endowed schools and established a chair of literature and rhetoric at Rome. Marcus Fabius Quintilianus, the celebrated Spanish rhetorician, was its first holder (p. 483).

THE OPPOSITION TO VESPASIAN

Despite his conspicuous achievements and services to the Empire, Vespasian never fully escaped the opposition of leading senators and of the Stoic and Cynic philosophers. Many senators objected to his numerous consulships (by which he sought to enhance the nobility of his family), his assumption of the censorship, his practice of admitting municipal Italians and provincials into the senate, and his ill-concealed intention of founding a new dynasty by handing down the office of *princeps* to members of his own family. Nevertheless, the senatorial opposition was more bothersome than dangerous. Vespasian paid little attention to it. Far more irritating were the attacks of the Stoic and especially of the Cynic philosophers. They finally nettled him into ordering their expulsion from Rome. The continued attacks of the Stoic Helvidius Priscus, son-in-law of Thrasea Paetus (p. 434), ultimately resulted in Priscus' execution.

VESPASIAN'S DEATH, 79 c.e.

In the spring of 79, after a decade of rule, Vespasian caught a fever. Continuing to work, he soon became worse and died on June 23. The hour of death did not deprive him of his sense of humor. Reportedly, as he lay dying he muttered, "Dear me, I think I'm becoming a god!" (Suetonius, *Vespasian* 23.4).

Before his death, Vespasian had settled the question of his successor. He had carefully prepared his son Titus (named Titus Flavius Vespasianus after his father), to be his successor. Titus had held army commands, the proconsular *imperium*, and tribunician power. He had shared the censorship and seven consulships with his father. Vespasian had also appointed him sole prefect of the Praetorian Guard, a wise precaution that enabled Titus immediately to thwart Aulus Caecina's grab for the throne in 79.

TITUS (79 TO 81 c.e.)

After Vespasian's death, the senate at once conferred on Titus the usual honors and titles belonging to the *princeps*, although not without some qualms and misgivings. Titus was handsome, charming, genial, and generous enough, but allegedly, his moral conduct had not been of the best. He had associated rather freely with the wilder elements of Roman aristocratic society. A love affair with Julia Berenice, a sister of the Jewish king, Herod Agrippa II, even revived memories of M. Antonius and Cleopatra.

Once seated on the throne, however, Titus became the ideal *princeps*, eager to promote the welfare of his subjects and much beloved by the people. He recalled the philosophers exiled by his father and halted all treason trials. He rewarded unscrupulous informers (*delatores*) with public flogging and enslavement or exile to unhealthy islands. He sent away Berenice to avoid giving offense to conservative senators, and he entertained the people with splendid games and shows, to their amazement and delight.

Three catastrophes marred his brief but brilliant reign. In August of 79, Mt. Vesuvius violently erupted and destroyed the cities of Herculaneum, Stabiae, and Pompeii near the Bay of Naples. Next, a plague, like none ever seen before, descended on Campania. In Rome, another great fire broke out and raged for three days. These disasters, occurring as they did in rapid succession, severely tested the energy and philanthropy of Titus.

In September of 81, after a reign of twenty-six months, Titus contracted a fever, just as his father had, and died at the family's home. He was only forty-two. The Roman people mourned the death of their beloved ruler, and the senate showered him with posthumous praises and honors. Deification followed.

DOMITIAN (81 TO 96 c.e.)

The way was now open for Vespasian's younger son, Titus Flavius Domitianus, known as *Domitian*. Leaving his brother's deathbed, Domitian rode in haste to Rome, where he went to the barracks of the Praetorian Guard to be acclaimed emperor. The armies acquiesced; the senate approved. Neither had much choice. Vespasian had always made it clear that Domitian was to play a prominent role in the family. His cognomen, *Domitianus*, honored Nero's martyred general Domitius Corbulo, who had been popular with the senate and the people. In 70, the link had become even stronger when Domitian married Corbulo's daughter Domitia Longina, a significant force in her own right. Nevertheless, despite granting him seven honorific consulships, Vespasian had not entrusted him with early responsibilities comparable to Titus', nor had Titus. Domitian had busied himself by writing Greek verse and studying the *Acta* (*Deeds*) of Tiberius, whom he admired. Later, gossip predictably accused Domitian of poisoning Titus, but that is unfounded.

The autocrat in charge

Having been overshadowed by his older brother most of his life, Domitian lacked a certain amount of self-confidence. He compensated by being domineering and autocratic, behavior that offended many senators. Appearing before them in triumphal regalia, he looked like an *imperator* with the power to command. In nonmilitary attire, he would have been a *princeps* seeking advice. His twenty-four lictors, his ten more consulships, and his censorship-for-life (*censor perpetuus*) not only defied tradition but also revealed his intention of establishing a more autocratic monarchy. Particularly galling were his appointment of equestrians to his judicial *consilium* to sit in judgment of senators and his naming an *eques* proconsul of the senatorial province of Asia. Worse still, he outdid even Caligula and Nero by permitting and encouraging people to address him as *Lord and God* (*Dominus et Deus*).

Domitian advanced his claim to divinity as a defender of the *mos maiorum* and the gods who had made Rome great. He enforced the execution of Vestal Virgins for unchastity and in the case of one even revived the traditional punishment of entombing her alive. He restored the Pantheon (p. 391) and built or rebuilt other major temples. The greatest was a new temple to Jupiter Optimus Maximus on the Capitol. With columns of Pentelic marble, gold-plated doors, and roof tiles overlaid with gold leaf, it replaced the newly built temple that had burned in the fire under Titus. He also erected a high temple to Jupiter the Guardian (*Juppiter Custos*) and, with great significance for his own divinity, a beautiful new temple to the deified Vespasian.

Domitian was usually hostile to exotic foreign cults, particularly Judaism and Christianity, whose rigid monotheism clashed with traditional Roman religion and rituals and did not tolerate the deification of emperors. Under him, treason became linked with impiety, and participation in the imperial cult became a test of loyalty. He did, however, favor the Egyptian cult of Isis. He had escaped danger during the civil war of 69 by disguising himself as one of her acolytes. Therefore, he rebuilt the temple complex of Serapis and Isis, which had been gutted in the recent fire.

Domitian tried to earn favor with the Roman populace as well as with the gods. Three times he distributed donations (*congiaria*) to citizens resident in Rome, for a total of 225 *denarii* a head. He completed the Baths of Titus and rebuilt the Baths of Agrippa. For popular amusement, he organized splendid spectacles: wild beast hunts; mock sea and land battles; gladiatorial contests in the Colosseum, the building of which he completed (p. 495); and chariot races in the Circus Maximus. He built both the Stadium and the Odeum (Music Hall) in Mars' Field to encourage Greek-style competitions in both sports and literature.

At the same time, Domitian spent heavily on projects reflecting his power and leadership. He built many triumphal arches, the grand Domus August[i]ana palace on the Palatine (p. 390), and, on Mount Alba, a huge mansion overlooking the Alban Lake. In Italy, he constructed a road from Sinuessa to Cumae. In Britain, as well as along the Rhine and Danube, he established numerous fortresses and garrison camps. He raised the base pay of legionary solders from 225 to 300 *denarii* per annum and also fought several costly wars from 82 to 93.

Financial policies

Financing these expenditures earned Domitian a reputation for rapacity. His collection of taxes was rigorous, although he was liberal in some ways. He never accepted legacies from testators having five or more children. He canceled debts owed to the state for more than five years and, unlike Vespasian, gave clear title to occupiers of public land in Italy. To keep down expenses, he maintained only twenty-eight legions after 92 C.E. That he was able to pass on to his successors a fairly full treasury is quite surprising. He seems to have financed his wars by confiscating the property of wealthy persons condemned for treason, which did not improve his reputation.

WAR AND REBELLION, 82 TO 93 C.E.

Denied opportunities for military glory under his father and brother, Domitian eagerly sought to obtain it as emperor. In 82 and 83 he personally led a successful war against the German Chatti on the Rhine frontier. In 85, he shifted Rome's military focus to the Danube after Decebalus, the young and aggressive king of Dacia (roughly equivalent to modern Romania) had invaded the Roman province of Moesia, south of the Danube. The treason trials and confiscations used to pay for these wars seem to have spurred an unsuccessful conspiracy against Domitian in 87. The shift in focus to the Danube inspired a more serious plot by L. Antonius Saturninus, the governor of upper Germany and commander of two legions wintering in the double camp at Moguntiacum (Mainz). On January 1, 89, he seized his army's savings and payroll and bribed the troops to proclaim him emperor. To crush that revolt, Domitian at once sped north with his Praetorian Guard after he ordered Trajan (the future emperor) to bring up a legion from Spain. Both got there too late for the battle. The governor of lower Germany had suppressed the rebellion and killed Saturninus. Upon arriving, Domitian ruthlessly punished the officers and accomplices of Saturninus. He sent the severed head of Saturninus back to Rome, while he faced a new threat from the Quadi and the Marcomani in Pannonia.

The revolt of Saturninus had disrupted Domitian's conquest of Dacia. A Roman army had inflicted a great defeat on the Dacians in 88, so that in 89, both Domitian and Decebalus found it expedient to come to terms. Decebalus promised to surrender all Roman captives and accept the role of Roman client. In return, Domitian recognized him as the legitimate king of the Dacians, granted him an annual subsidy, and furnished him Roman engineers skilled in the art of building roads and fortresses.

The Dacian peace treaty was dictated by expediency. Many senators considered it an affront to Roman dignity. Still, it was of immense value to Rome. It turned Decebalus into a benevolent neutral, if not an active ally, when the Iazyges irrupted into Pannonia in 92 and badly mauled a Roman legion. It also helped Domitian isolate the hostile Marcomanni and Quadi: he added alliances with the Germanic tribes living to the north of them, with the Semnones east of the Elbe, and with the powerful Lugii of Silesia. Domitian was able to stabilize the Danubian frontier by concentrating nine or ten legions along the river in strongly fortified camps (to forestall chances of rebellion, however, there were no more double legionary camps). By 93, peace prevailed again along the entire Danubian frontier.

FEAR, PURGES, AND THE MURDER OF DOMITIAN, 89 TO 96 C.E.

The rebellion of Saturninus in 89 so upset Domitian that he began to imagine conspiracies forming against him everywhere. Spies and informers began to play upon his fears. In 89 and again in 95, he banished philosophers and astrologers from Rome. He also struck out most savagely against prominent senators and some able provincial governors. That he had no surviving children to succeed him increased his fear of such men. He attempted to bolster his position by adopting the sons of his cousin Flavius Clemens, who had married his own cousin and Domitian's niece, Flavia Domitilla. In 95 or 96, however, Domitian turned against Clemens and Domitilla. Clemens was executed and Domitilla exiled.

Fearing for their own lives, members of the court, possibly including the Empress Domitia Longina, entered into a conspiracy. Flavia Domitilla's devoted former butler, a certain Stephanus, pretended to have secret information about a conspiracy. Admitted to the emperor's bedroom, he handed Domitian a list of names. As Domitian read the list, Stephanus stabbed him in the groin. The wounded emperor shouted for his attendant to get the dagger that he always kept under his pillow, but its blade was gone. Stephanus and others, who rushed in to help him, finished the deed. While some of the chief conspirators were later punished (p. 454), Domitia Longina lived for at least another thirty years as a respected and wealthy widow managing her estates. Her adopted sons, who had been tutored by the famous rhetorician Quintillian, disappeared from view. Perhaps they wisely chose a quiescent life with Domitia, or with their birth-mother, if she returned from exile.

Domitian, like Caligula and Nero, had failed to learn the value of downplaying the inherent autocracy of the Principate and maintaining the goodwill of the senate. Nevertheless, he had kept a firm grip on the frontier legions. In so doing, he had protected the integrity and preserved the internal peace and prosperity of the Empire, the greatest legacy of the Flavian dynasty.

NOTE

1 The Colosseum owes its name not to its own size, but to the colossal statue that stood nearby. It was originally intended for the entrance court to Nero's Golden House (p. 432), but Vespasian erected it in the Sacred Way. Hadrian moved it near the Flavian Amphitheater to make way for his massive Temple of Venus and Rome (p. 496).

SUGGESTED READING

Jones, B. W. *The Emperor Domitian*. London and New York: Routledge, 1992.

Levick, B. Vespasian. 2nd ed. *Roman Imperial Biographies*. London and New York: Routledge, 2017.

Rutledge, S. H. *Imperial Inquisitions: Prosecutors and Informants from Tiberius to Domitian*. London: Routledge, 2001.

CHAPTER 25

The five "good" emperors of the second century, 96 to 180 C.E.

The death of Domitian in 96 marked the end of the Flavian dynasty, but the stability established by the Flavians endured. No destructive period of crisis and civil war followed, as had happened upon the death of Nero. The successful conspiracy against Domitian had originated not among provincial armies but within the imperial family and senatorial leadership at Rome. The senators elevated Marcus Cocceius Nerva, one of their own, but apparently not a conspirator, to be Domitian's successor. Sixty years old, childless, and long past his prime, he posed no threat of establishing another dynasty. Generous donatives, paid or promised, kept both the Praetorian Guard and the provincial armies temporarily satisfied and acquiescent. Thus, a peaceful transition was affected, and a new phase of the Principate was introduced.

The emperors Nerva, Trajan, Hadrian, Antoninus Pius, and Marcus Aurelius, from 96 to 180 C.E., are often called the "five good emperors." These five, compared with Domitian before them and Commodus after, conformed to the model established by those considered to be the best of the previous emperors: Augustus, Vespasian, and Titus. Like them, these five came to power as mature and experienced men who understood the problems that the *princeps* faced. For the most part, they realized that to retain power and govern effectively in a Roman context, they needed to maintain the goodwill of the senatorial elite and other propertied classes, secure the loyalty of the soldiers, and promote the basic welfare of the people whom they ruled.

They also enjoyed a considerable amount of good luck. Historians, particularly upper-class pagan ones, looking back from less happy times saw their reigns as a golden age of peace and prosperity. The influential eighteenth-century author of the *Decline and Fall of the Roman Empire*, Edward Gibbon, called it the period when the human race was most happy. Indeed, until the reign of Marcus Aurelius, there were no widespread natural disasters or massive military problems that would have stressed the Empire beyond its normal capacities to cope.

SOURCES

Only two sources, neither of first rank, provide connected accounts for all or most of this period. One is Cassius Dio. Books 67 to 72 of his history of Rome covered the reigns involved. They are preserved in only abbreviated form by two later Byzantine epitomes: a lengthy one now missing the reign of Antoninus Pius and the early years of Marcus Aurelius, and a shorter one based on the first. Biographies covering the years from 117 to 180 appear in a controversial collection known as the *Historia Augusta* and written probably about 395 C.E. It is generally agreed that the lives of Hadrian, Antoninus Pius, Marcus Aurelius, and Lucius Verus are based on a fairly good source and are trustworthy for the main historical outline. The lives of Lucius Aelius and Avidius Cassius are far less reliable and probably contain much sensationalistic fiction. Minor historical summaries and biographies can be found in several fourth-century epitomes (p. 632).

For the reigns of Nerva and Trajan, the contemporary letters of Pliny the Younger and his *Panegyric* (on Trajan) are very useful. The panegyric *To Rome* and the *Sacred Teachings* of the Greek rhetorician Aelius Aristides are useful for the period under Antoninus Pius. The *Letters* (*Epistulae*) of Marcus Aurelius' tutor Marcus Cornelius Fronto are a contemporary window into the period from Hadrian to Aurelius. Of course, Aurelius' own *Meditations* provide direct access to his interesting personality. Other literary and technical works and numerous Christian writings are also valuable for reconstructing the social, economic, and cultural milieu of the period, as are Jewish works like the Mishna, Midrash, and Talmud.

Monuments, such as the triumphal arch of Trajan at Beneventum and the columns of Trajan and Marcus Aurelius, present valuable historical information, as do numerous extant coins, inscriptions, and Egyptian papyri from this era. These latter three sources, along with archaeological excavations throughout the Empire, yield interesting data on the provinces. Finally, laws preserved in the *Corpus Iuris Civilis* (*Body of Civil Law*) shed light on the social and administrative developments under the "good" emperors.

NERVA (96 TO 98 c.e.)

Although Nerva's family contained several distinguished jurists, it was not an old one and had gained social acceptance only because his maternal uncle had married a woman of Julio-Claudian birth. Nerva himself had not won much distinction as a jurist or as a public speaker and had never governed a province or commanded an army. Being a safe and innocuous man willing to cooperate with any regime, he had been awarded two statues under Nero and had won two consulships, one under Vespasian and one under Domitian.

The senate regarded Nerva highly for many reasons during his short reign: his deference, his vow never to put to death a senator who was not condemned by a senatorial court, his restoration of the senate's administration of the grain dole, his suspension of the hated law of treason (*maiestas*), his recall of senatorial exiles, and his suppression of informers. On the other hand, when members of the Praetorian Guard besieged the palace and clamored for vengeance against Domitian's killers, Nerva meekly allowed them to kill their former prefect and several other conspirators. Furthermore, it became apparent early on that the unmartial Nerva needed strong military backing to check ambitious provincial commanders once they had a chance to reflect on the sudden turn of events with Domitian's assassination.

Therefore, the most important act of Nerva's brief rule was his adoption of Marcus Ulpius Traianus (Trajan) as son, heir, and co-regent. The very able and respected military governor of Upper Germany, Trajan was an excellent choice. A year after the adoption, Nerva died before his new son had even come to Rome. Thanks to Nerva's action, however, Trajan succeeded without incident.

TRAJAN (98 TO 117 C.E.)

Trajan, the first emperor of provincial origin, was born in Spain at Italica near Hispalis (Seville) in the rich province of Baetica. Vespasian had admitted his father into the senate and made him a patrician. In swift succession, his father had achieved the consulship, the Syrian command, the proconsulship of Asia, and numerous triumphal honors.

Trajan himself had enjoyed a long and distinguished military career under Vespasian and Domitian on the Rhine, the Danube, and the Euphrates; in Syria; and in Spain. As governor of Upper Germany during Nerva's reign, he had won the proud title of *Germanicus*. Under his own auspices, he would win still others: *Dacicus* and *Parthicus* (conqueror of the Dacians and the Parthians). After Nerva's death, two years spent in inspecting and strengthening defenses along the Rhine and the Danube preceded Trajan's long-awaited arrival in Rome.

A MODEL EMPEROR

At first, the senators had only grudgingly accepted Trajan, but his tact and respectfulness soon won them over. His was the attitude of the "Best Prince" (*Optimus Princeps*), a title bestowed as early as 100, stamped on the coinage in 105, but not officially assumed until 115. Centuries later, the Christian historian Eusebius recounted that the senate bestowed on every new emperor the supreme compliment: "Luckier than Augustus, better than Trajan" (*Felicior Augusto, melior Traiano*).

With a change in the composition of the senate, Trajan's provincial origin also helped him. As inscriptions and papyri show, the senate of Claudius and even Vespasian contained only a few members of provincial origin. Under Trajan, provincial senators came to make up slightly over 40 percent of the total, more and more of whom now came from the eastern provinces. Enjoying the support and affection of the senate, the people, the armies, and the provinces, Trajan was a successful and energetic emperor. He tried to give the Empire the best possible government, pursued many enlightened social and economic programs, and inaugurated many beneficial public works.

The *alimenta*: public assistance for children

The *alimenta* constituted a relief program to bolster the population of Italy by supporting children. Nerva may have instituted it. Trajan strongly promoted it. In the late first century C.E., viticulture and pottery manufacturing in central Italy were declining because of increased western provincial competition. The subsequent impoverishment of small farmers and craftsmen had a serious effect on their ability to raise children. One result was a decline of population in the affected parts of Italy that adversely affected recruitment for the army and for colonies, both of which helped to Romanize the provinces and promote imperial unity. Some wealthy individuals like Pliny the Younger had already set up private endowments to provide local relief. Following their lead, Nerva or Trajan created the publicly funded *alimenta* to subsidize the care and education of freeborn boys and girls deemed worthy, whether from poor or better-off families.

Under this plan, landowners in a given locality could each pledge so much land as collateral for a loan equal to about one-eighth of its value. They would agree to pay, apparently in perpetuity, about 5 percent interest a year on the amount of money received. The interest paid was put into a fund administered by imperial officials, who then distributed it. The loans themselves were of little use to smallholders, who did not have the collateral to obtain a meaningful amount of money. A large landowner, however, could pledge only part of his holdings and obtain a usable sum of money with only a small charge against future income.

Generosity to provinces and municipalities

The measures that Trajan took to improve conditions in the provinces were equally impressive. Roads, bridges, harbors, and aqueducts were built everywhere. Unfortunately, he also had to bail out the finances of many cities in Italy and the eastern provinces. They had overextended themselves by competing in the splendor of their buildings and public amenities or by borrowing to pay imperial taxes. Trajan, therefore, sent out men like Pliny the Younger as imperial agents or inspectors (*curatores* or *correctores*) to help municipalities solve their financial problems.

TRAJAN'S WARS

The treaty that Domitian had concluded with Decebalus in 89 had been expedient, but galling to Roman imperial pride. In 101, Trajan set out on an invasion of Dacia against King Decebalus but suffered a severe defeat. After several successful battles in 102, he finally occupied the capital city of Sarmizegetusa, where he stationed a permanent garrison. Decebalus surrendered unconditionally and agreed to become a Roman client once more. In 105, Decebalus broke the peace agreement. Trajan recruited two new legions, which raised Rome's total to thirty. He hastened to the lower Danube with thirteen and broke Dacian resistance in 106. After the suicide of Decebalus, Trajan annexed Dacia as a province and made Sarmizegethusa a colony (Ulpia Traiana). He settled numerous veterans and colonists from all over the Empire, ancestors of the present-day Romanians. Sadly for the Dacians, 50,000 war prisoners ended their days as slaves or gladiators.

The Parthian wars and provincial crises, 113 to 117 C.E.

After seven years of peace, Chosroes, the new Parthian king, provoked Trajan by deposing the king of Armenia without Rome's consent. Trajan's reaction was swift: he set sail for the East in the fall of 113. Within two years, he had captured one Parthian capital, Ctesiphon, and extended Rome's dominion from the headwaters of the Tigris and Euphrates to the Persian Gulf. Trade routes to the Far East were now within his grasp, and passage to India might have been his next move.

Trajan had extended the Empire to the farthest limits yet attained, but he had not adequately secured newly conquered territory behind him. Simultaneous revolts arose in Mesopotamia, Assyria, and even Armenia. Powerful Parthian armies reoccupied lost territory. Tribes along the northern frontiers took advantage of Trajan's preoccupation in the East: the Sarmatians and Roxolani along the Danube were again on the move; in Britain, Roman garrisons retreated from the borders of Scotland. The Jewish populations in Cyrenaica, Mesopotamia, Adiabene (northern Assyria around Arbela), Cyprus, and Egypt rose up in a rebellion that expressed their frustration with treatment by the Greek-speaking majority in many eastern cities.

FIGURE 25.1 Remains of the Temple of Trajan at Pergamum.

Trajan acted with resolution and promptness. Still, without help from his able marshal and comrade in arms Lusius Quietus the Moor, he would have failed to restore the rapidly deteriorating situation. Trajan himself pacified southern Mesopotamia by his capture and ruthless destruction of Seleucia on the Tigris, across from Ctesiphon. Quietus reconquered northern Mesopotamia. Later, as governor of Judea, he stamped out all Jewish riots in Palestine. Trajan's other marshals were less successful in suppressing the revolts in Cyrenaica, Cyprus, and Egypt. Nor was Trajan himself able to hold all of his Parthian conquests: in 116, he surrendered the province of southern Mesopotamia to a Parthian prince, nominally a Roman client, and lost the entire province of Assyria along with part of Greater Armenia.

THE DEATH OF TRAJAN, 117 c.e.

Three years of hard campaigning in the desert and the strain of recent months had overtaxed Trajan's strength. He was then past sixty and a heavy drinker. On the road back from Ctesiphon in 116, he became ill. During the winter at Antioch, where he was busily preparing for another campaign in Mesopotamia in the following spring, he grew steadily worse. Reluctantly, he abandoned his preparations. He set out for Rome and left Publius Aelius Hadrianus (Hadrian), governor of Syria, in command of the Near East at Antioch. At Selinus in Cilicia, he suffered a stroke and died a few days later (ca. August 8, 117).

THE EMPRESS PLOTINA

At this point, Trajan's wife, Pompeia Plotina, achieved a goal for which she had long worked. She had married Trajan when she was about fifteen but had not yet produced an heir when, about a decade later, Hadrian became ward of Trajan, his father's cousin and closest male relative. Plotina took a great interest in Hadrian and promoted his career. She was instrumental in obtaining his marriage to Trajan's grandniece Vibia Sabina. Plotina also secured his designation as one of the principal consuls for 118. As Trajan was dying (some said after he was dead) she arranged for his formal adoption of Hadrian as his successor.

THE EFFECTS OF TRAJAN'S WARS

Under Trajan, the Roman Empire reached the high tide of territorial expansion and prosperity. Nevertheless, the costs of Trajan's imperial expansion were high. He paid the price in health; the Empire, in manpower and resources. Moreover, Trajan had expanded the Empire beyond defensible limits. In the process, he had wholly or partially denied Rome the benefit of three strong buffer states: Dacia, Parthia, and Nabataean Arabia. Rome itself would later have to absorb and repel the mass invasions of the Goths and other Germans, the Alans, and Iranians. Impelled by the relentless pressure of the Huns from central Asia, they would break and burst through the brittle, overextended defenses of the Roman Empire on the Rhine, Danube, and Euphrates.

Undermining the defensive powers of the Dacians, Nabataeans, and Parthians spelled disaster for the Roman Empire of the future.

HADRIAN (117 TO 138 c.e.)

No sooner had news of Trajan's death reached Hadrian at Antioch than the armies of Syria acclaimed him as Rome's new emperor. Shortly thereafter, the senate officially confirmed the acclamation. The rumor that Hadrian owed his throne to a forged instrument of adoption carried little weight against acclamation by the army and the senate's ratification.

According to the *Historia Augusta*, Hadrian was born at Rome in 76. His mother was from Gades, Spain, and his father was a senator from Italica, the same Spanish town where Trajan was born. As Trajan's ward, he received an excellent education. Plotina, who was an admirer of Greek philosophy, may have encouraged his strong love of Greek art and philosophy. To that love, he owed his half-contemptuous nickname of *Graeculus* (Greekling). He became a man of refined artistic tastes, an intellectual with a keen, penetrating intelligence.

He had also pursued a long military and public career, and he had married Trajan's grandniece, Vibia Sabina, a strikingly beautiful but progressively frustrated woman, whom he probably would have divorced had it not been for his ambition. Hadrian was more at home hunting or on campaign with the army or touring the provinces than he was at Rome. Conventional home life did not satisfy him. He seems to have had his share of mistresses in his early years, but the great passion of his life was a handsome young Bithynian Greek named Antinous, whom he met on an eastern tour in 123. Such a relationship satisfied his innermost nature and was reinforced both by his love of Greek art and philosophy, which were heavily imbued with the homoeroticism of aristocratic Greek culture, and by his almost continuous service on active duty in the all-male society of the army.

THE EARLY YEARS OF HADRIAN'S PRINCIPATE

Hadrian inherited a difficult task that was not rendered easier by inevitable comparison with his illustrious predecessor, from whom he had, ironically, also inherited a legacy of revolts. The man who helped him quell those revolts was his trusted friend, Marcius Turbo, who replaced Lusius Quietus, Trajan's great Moorish marshal from Mauretania. Faced with revolts and needing to solidify his support back in Rome, Hadrian seems to have made a virtue out of necessity. He played the role of cautious Augustus to Trajan's conquering Caesar.[1] He abandoned all recent conquests east of the Euphrates, allowed Greater Armenia to revert to the status of a client kingdom, and made peace with Parthia. False rumors that he also planned to abandon Dacia showed that the new "Pax Augusta" did not please everyone—especially not Lusius Quietus and three former marshals. They had all admired Trajan's expansionism and disapproved of Hadrian's new frontier policy. The four were executed without Hadrian's sanction or knowledge, or so he averred. Revolt then broke out in Mauretania and had to be suppressed by Turbo.

Early in July of 118, Hadrian met with the senate. He promised the assembled dignitaries that henceforth no senator would be put to death without prior condemnation by a senatorial court. Hadrian tried to win favor on all sides with a magnificent triumph for Parthia's defeat, a large distribution of gifts, and a vast remission of debts and tax arrears. His success was limited, however. To the senate and people of Rome, he always remained something of an outsider. He spent much of his time looking after the provinces. Then, at the end of his reign, maneuverings to become his successor provoked a serious breach between him and many important senators.

HADRIAN'S TRAVELS

The year 121 found Hadrian in Gaul and the Rhineland. The next year, he went to Britain. There he inspected plans for the construction of his famous wall (see Box 25.1) from Solway Firth to the Tyne to keep marauding tribesmen of the North from raiding farmlands south of the Scottish border. On the way back from Britain, he passed through Gaul and spent the winter in Spain. In the spring of 123, he led a punitive expedition in North Africa against the Moors, who had been raiding Roman towns in Mauretania. There he received news that the Parthians had again broken the peace, and he set sail for Ephesus. His dramatic arrival in the Near East, backed by impressive troop concentrations, inspired Chosroes, the Parthian king, to negotiate rather than fight. The war over, Hadrian stayed on to hear petitions and complaints. He punished misgovernment of the provinces and arranged for many new construction projects.

25.1 LIFE ALONG HADRIAN'S WALL

Beginning in the 1970s and 1980s, excavations at a Roman military fort at Vindolanda, along Hadrian's Wall in northern England, have yielded well over 1000 writing tablets dated to 90–120 C.E. The tablets, mostly made of wood with a layer of wax for writing on, were used for daily correspondence, notes, and the like, and they offer an unparalleled glimpse into the daily lives of the people who lived at the fort: officers with their wives, children, and slaves, as well as the rank-and-file soldiers, brought together from Gaul, Germany, Spain, and the Balkans. The texts are an assortment of literary snippets, notes, personal correspondence, children's school exercises, soldiers' requests for leave, and military reports. They show us a community not only concerned with the business of the fort, such as work assignments, supply records, and assessments of the strength of the fort's forces, but also with birthday parties, care packages from home, and making sure there was good food to be had ("100 apples, if you can find nice ones").

In 128, Hadrian again visited North Africa. There he inspected the imperial estates and studied ways and means for more efficient economic exploitation. He spent the following winter in Athens, where he presided at games and festivals and codified laws. He also completed and dedicated a huge temple to Olympian Zeus, the Olympieion, which the Athenian tyrant Peisistratus had begun seven centuries before. In the suburbs of Athens, he built a new city, named Hadrianopolis. In it, he erected a pantheon, a stoa, a gymnasium, a library, and another great temple, the Panhellenion. He romantically dedicated the latter to an ancient ideal—Greek unity. In the spring of 129, he toured Asia Minor once more. Towns, temples, libraries, baths, and aqueducts sprang up wherever he went.

Unfortunately, in the next year, Hadrian displayed a singular lack of understanding at Jerusalem. There, he insisted on founding a Roman colony called *Aelia Capitolina*, and he erected a shrine to Jupiter Capitolinus on the site of the Jewish Temple. About the same time, he banned the Jewish ritual of circumcision. Thus, Hadrian eventually provoked one of the bloodiest Jewish rebellions in history.

Meanwhile, heedless of what he had done, Hadrian went to Egypt to reorganize its economic life and visit the monuments of its glorious past. While he was in Egypt, he was bereft of his beloved Antinous, who drowned in the Nile. In his honor, Hadrian founded a beautiful new city, Antinoopolis, on the east bank of the Nile near where the youth had drowned. After Antinous' death, Hadrian worshiped him as divine, built shrines and temples to him, struck coins bearing his likeness, and set up busts of him all over the Empire.

THE JEWISH REVOLT

Hadrian returned to Rome to learn that in the fall of 132 the Jews of Judea had now rebelled and were waging a guerrilla war against the Roman army. Led by a famous guerrilla strategist, Simon Bar Kokhba (Shim'on Ben [Bar] Cosiba in the Dead Sea Scrolls), the Jews captured Jerusalem, slaughtered an entire Roman legion, and, for a time, seemed about to drive the Romans out of Palestine. Hadrian hastened back to Syria, assembled reinforcements from the other provinces, and summoned the able Julius Severus from Britain to take command. Severus began systematically isolating strongholds and inhabited places in order to starve out the defenders. The Romans may have slaughtered as many as half a million people and enslaved as many more until the revolt was finally quelled in 135.

The surviving Jewish population of Jerusalem was forcibly removed, and Jews were forbidden to enter the city except on one officially designated day each year. The name of the city was formally changed to Aelia Capitolina and remained so until the days of Constantine (324–337). The name of Judea was changed to Syria Palestina. Jews there and throughout the Empire were still allowed to practice their ancestral religion and maintain their traditional schools and synagogues. Nevertheless, the vestiges of the national state that had been the focus of their aspirations for centuries were obliterated for 1800 years.

NEW DIRECTIONS UNDER HADRIAN

A man of ceaseless curiosity and innovative spirit, Hadrian instituted major changes in all aspects of Roman government and policy. His passion for perfection and efficiency is manifest in everything that he did. In many ways, the Roman Empire as an organized state came of age under his leadership.

Frontier defense

Hadrian's renunciation of Trajan's aggressive foreign wars and his surrender of some recent conquests did not constitute a neglect of frontier defense. He was the first emperor to erect large-scale fixed frontier defenses such as Hadrian's Wall in Britain. He extended fortifications for 345 miles in south Germany behind continuous lines of ditches and oakwood palisades nine feet high. These fortifications, with their garrisoned forts and watchtowers, not only protected the frontier from enemy raids and even mass attacks but also marked the frontier and served as checkpoints for the control of trade between the Roman and non-Roman worlds.

Reform of the army

Hadrian's reforms regarding discipline, recruitment, and tactics were of lasting importance to the army. To ensure discipline, Hadrian personally inspected army posts all over the Empire; watched soldiers drill, march, and maneuver; inspected equipment, dress, baggage, and mess kitchens; and ordered fatigue marches. Dressed as a common soldier, he marched along with the men, and carried his own knapsack. To no emperor were the armies more devoted, and under none were they more disciplined and efficient.

One of Hadrian's most important military reforms was the progressive removal of distinctions between the legions and the auxiliary corps (*auxilia*) with respect to training, equipment, and composition. For the first time, both consisted of Roman citizens and noncitizens recruited more and more in the frontier regions in which they were to serve. Many of the new recruits were soldiers' sons born near the permanent camps, and to them, Hadrian granted the right, hitherto withheld, of inheriting their fathers' property.

The traditional *auxilia*, which garrisoned the permanent forts strung out along the frontiers, were armed and organized like Roman legions. Especially in the German and Danubian provinces, in Britain, and in Mauretania, Hadrian began to levy many auxiliary units of a new type called *numeri*. They were small mobile corps, some of them light infantry, some cavalry, some mixed. Others consisted of mounted scouts known as *exploratores*. Although often commanded by Roman ex-centurions, the *numeri* retained their native languages, arms, and methods of fighting. They were used for patrolling, reconnaissance, and skirmishing.

Hadrian's greatest reform in battle tactics was the introduction of an improved form of the old Macedonian phalanx. In offensive operations, the *auxilia* would launch the initial attack, whereas the phalanx of the legions advanced later to deliver the final blow. If the enemy attacked first, the *auxilia* would take the brunt of the initial assault. The legions held in reserve in camps behind the frontier forts would then advance to destroy the exhausted forces of the enemy. Hadrian's tactics were to remain standard Roman practice, except for minor modifications, for over two centuries.

The provinces

Extensive travels and detailed reports from procurators and other agents afforded Hadrian an intimate knowledge of conditions in the provinces. No detail of provincial administration seemed too small for his personal attention, especially when it involved the defense of the weak against the strong, the poor against the rich (*humiliores* vs. *honestiores*; *tenuiores* vs. *potentiores*). Also, the urbanization of the Empire reached its peak under Hadrian, and the extension of Roman citizenship kept step with the diffusion of culture and civilization.

Hadrian even created the right of Greater Latinity (*Latium Maius*), which conferred citizenship on all decurions (*decuriones*, members of local town councils or senates), as well as local magistrates. This right was a device to reward local elites for loyalty and service to Rome and bind them and, therefore, their communities more tightly to the emperor who granted it. It also opened up careers in the imperial administration to new talent.

The reorganization of the Imperial administration

The growing administrative needs of the Empire, as well as Hadrian's passion for efficiency, led to further expansion and reorganization of the imperial administration. Gradually, operations were becoming more professional and bureaucratized. Hadrian insisted that holders of public office be able, well trained, and competent, as well as loyal to the emperor and devoted to the state. He paid them well and gave rewards for hard work, initiative, and efficiency.

Vespasian had reversed the policy of Claudius by employing *equites* more than freedmen in high administrative positions. Hadrian followed Vespasian's lead and appointed equestrians as directors of the four executive departments created by Claudius: imperial correspondence (*ab epistulis*), justice (*a libellis*), treasury (*a rationibus*), and the research and library service (*a studiis*). To enhance their prestige, he bestowed upon the holders of these offices such resounding titles as *vir egregius* (outstanding man), *vir perfectissimus* (most perfect man), and *vir eminentissimus* (most eminent man), which was held by the prefect of the Praetorian Guard. Gradations of salary also differentiated the various executive offices. Procurators, for example, received 60,000, 100,000, 200,000, or 300,000 sesterces per year, according to their rank. Four equestrian prefects commanded even higher salaries.

To the four governmental departments, Hadrian added two new ones of cabinet rank, both pointing not only to increased centralization but also to wider equestrian participation in public service. One of the new departments resulted from Hadrian's reform of the vitally important system of the imperial post and communications (*cursus publicus*). Formerly, it was a financial and administrative burden laid upon municipalities in Italy and the provinces. Hadrian lightened this burden by reorganizing the system as a state institution controlled by a central bureau in Rome and headed by an equestrian prefect of vehicles (*praefectus vehiculorum*).

The other new department resulted from overhauling the tax-collecting system, especially the collection of the 5 percent inheritance tax (*vicesima hereditatum*).

Hadrian, in line with policies set by Caesar, Augustus, and Tiberius, transferred it from tax-farming companies to a state agency presided over by an equestrian procurator. The procurator, assisted by numerous agents throughout the Empire, collected these and many other taxes, direct and indirect.

In creating a more professional, bureaucratic system, Hadrian departed from the policy of Augustus by separating the civil and military careers of equestrian officials and by appointing *equites* without prior military experience to civilian posts. Now, *equites* seeking high administrative positions had to begin their civilian careers by accepting such minor jobs as agents or attorneys of the treasury (*advocati fisci*), a newly created class of officials sent all over the Empire to prosecute cases of tax evasion and delinquency.

Hadrian's separation of civil and military careers was not completely beneficial. It deprived high government officials of military experience and control over the army. They were left helpless when confronted, as they would be in the third century, by a formidable group of army commanders. Those commanders often alienated the civilian elite, whose cooperation was necessary for maintaining control. In this instance, Hadrian's yearning for administrative efficiency proved injurious to the future stability of the state.

The growth of the Consilium Principis

Hadrian began the conversion of the *Consilium Principis*, an informal conclave (as opposed to the more formal *concilium*) of palace friends and advisors, such as Augustus and his successors had consulted, into a more permanent Imperial Council. It probably consisted of the heads of the various departments of the government, the chief prefects, and several distinguished jurists. Besides serving as the chief policy-making body of the Empire, it also acted as a supreme court. Its function was to hear cases involving senators and high-ranking officials and to advise and assist the emperor in the creation and interpretation of civil and criminal law.

Legal reforms

Of all the administrative reforms of Hadrian, the greatest and most enduring were in the field of law. One such reform gave the unanimous opinions (*responsa*) of distinguished jurists the force of law binding on judges trying similar cases. Only when the opinions conflicted could judges reach their own decisions. These responses later entered into the literature of Roman law and became enshrined at last in the *Digest* and *Code* of Justinian I (p. 675).

More important still was the editing and codification of the Praetorian Perpetual Edict. Ever since early republican times, each incoming urban praetor (*praetor urbanus*) had drawn up and posted edicts setting forth the laws and court procedure that he intended to follow during his year of office. The praetor for foreigners (*praetor peregrinus*) as well as the provincial governors had followed suit. The praetors normally retained the laws and procedures of their predecessors while adding new ones as need arose. Therefore, the edicts tended to perpetuate many obsolete rules, contradictions, and obscurities. Hadrian commissioned Salvius Julianus to draw up a permanent edict (*edictum perpetuum*) binding all present and future praetors without alteration or addition unless authorized by the emperor or by decree of the senate.

The statutes of the emperors (*constitutiones principum*) thereafter became increasingly important as sources of law. They consisted of each emperor's edicts (*edicta*), or proclamations issued by virtue of his *imperium*; his judicial decrees (*decreta*), or decisions; his re-scripts (*rescripta*), or responses to written inquiries on specific points of law; and his mandates (*mandata*), or administrative directives issued to officials subject to his orders.

To ease the crowded calendar of the praetors' courts in Rome and expedite the administration of justice in Italy, Hadrian divided the peninsula into four judicial districts, each presided over by a circuit judge of consular rank (*iuridicus consularis*) who tried cases of inheritance, trust, and guardianship and probably heard appeals from the municipal courts. The innovation was both salutary and necessary and not intended simply to reduce Italy to the status of a province, as many senators feared. At their insistence, Hadrian's successor, Antoninus Pius, unwisely abolished it. Marcus Aurelius had to revive it later.

Social policies

In accordance with prevailing Stoic philosophical principles, Hadrian made it illegal for a master to kill, torture, or castrate slaves; to sell them as gladiators; or to use them for any lewd or immoral purposes. He also deprived the *paterfamilias* of the power of life and death over his children and safeguarded the right of minors to inherit and own property. Continuing Nerva and Trajan's policy of using state funds for supporting the children of families in Italy, he appointed a superintendent of child welfare (*praefectus alimentorum*) to administer the distribution of alimentary funds. In education, he provided funds for secondary-school education in many municipalities of the Empire; endowed advanced rhetorical, philosophical, technical, and medical schools in both Rome and the provinces; and gave pensions to retired teachers.

THE LAST YEARS OF HADRIAN

During the Jewish War, Hadrian returned to Rome never to leave Italy again. He spent much time during his last years at his beautiful villa at Tibur (Tivoli) on the Anio River eighteen miles east of Rome. Still, he could not enjoy himself. The man who had traveled, seen, and done so much had lost all zest for life. Loneliness and despair plagued his mind; a progressive disease (coronary atherosclerosis) racked his body. As his illness grew worse and death seemed at hand, he turned his attention to the problem of choosing a successor. His first choice was his friend, Lucius Ceionius Commodus. Despite the opposition of many senators, Hadrian spent large sums of money to win the support of the soldiers and the people for adopting him as Lucius Aelius Caesar. The money was wasted, for Lucius died on the first day of 138. Hadrian next adopted a rich and virtuous senator, Titus Aurelius Antoninus. Then he required Antoninus to adopt two sons: the like-named seven-year-old son of the late Lucius Ceionius Commodus and Marcus Annius Verus, the seventeen-year-old nephew of Antoninus' wife, Annia Galeria Faustina. The younger boy took the name Lucius Aurelius Commodus. The older became Marcus Aurelius Verus. Marcus was already betrothed to the late Lucius' daughter and later became Emperor Marcus Aurelius. Many senators believed themselves to be more qualified as *princeps* than Antoninus and resented Hadrian's attempt to determine the succession for the next generation as well. After doing just that, Hadrian's last and only wish was to die in peace.

Death came, but not soon enough for him. Maddened by pain, he longed to take his life. He begged his doctor to give him a dose of poison; the doctor took one himself. He ordered a slave to stab him in the heart; the slave ran away. Finally, at Baiae near Naples on July 10, 138, nature granted his wish. His adopted son and heir, Antoninus, eventually had his body placed in a special mausoleum (now the Castel Sant' Angelo) at Rome. Against the opposition of the senate, he even secured Hadrian's deification. Another god now joined the Roman pantheon, and Antoninus won for himself the new surname of Pius.

ANTONINUS PIUS (138 TO 161 c.e.)

Antoninus Pius ushered in the dynasty of Antonine emperors (Antoninus through Commodus [130–192]). He was born and raised at Lanuvium, a famous old Latin town, but his grandfather had come from what was probably Plotina's home town, Nemausus (Nîmes), in southern Gaul. The grandfather had helped Vespasian become emperor and held the consulship under both Vespasian and Domitian. Now, as rich aristocrats, Antoninus' family owned numerous estates in Italy and valuable brickyards near Rome. Of all the estates, the one at Lorium, about ten miles west of Rome on the border of Etruria, pleased Antoninus most. Rome and its palaces and Hadrian's villa held little attraction for him.

Antoninus held all the offices of an unexceptional senatorial career. After his consulship in 120, he intended to retire to his country estates and enjoy himself. Instead, Hadrian made him a district judge of Italy and, in 135 and 136, proconsul of Asia, where he distinguished himself as an administrator. His expert knowledge of law and his skill in administration led to further appointments, none of which he solicited. Neither did they give him any experience as an imperial commander or familiarity with many provinces. Still, Hadrian made him a member of the Imperial Council and finally his successor and colleague.

FAUSTINA THE ELDER

Antoninus also owed much of his good fortune to his wife, Annia Galeria Faustina. Her mother, Rupilia Faustina, was the daughter of a consul and possibly half-sister of Hadrian's wife, Sabina. As did Trajan and Hadrian, Faustina's father, M. Annius Verus, belonged to an illustrious family from Spain. He was consul (once) under Nerva and both consul (twice) and Prefect of the City under Hadrian. Faustina's brother also held a consulship under Hadrian.

The senate honored Faustina with the title *Augusta* and authorized her portrait on coins as soon as Antoninus ascended the throne. She was particularly active in promoting the cult of Cybele and was deified immediately after her death (ca. 140). She received a major temple in the Forum and numerous gold and silver statues. When Antoninus created an endowment to benefit poor girls, the recipients were called "Faustina's girls." Of her four children, two boys and one girl died young. Her name lived on, however, with her daughter Faustina the Younger, whom she persuaded Marcus Aurelius to marry despite their betrothals to others (p. 468).

MAINTAINING THE STATUS QUO

Although Hadrian was a restless innovator, Antoninus Pius was a man who had always played it safe. He saw no need to tinker with Hadrian's smoothly running imperial machine. Maintenance was his specialty, and he was content to let the system run on its considerable inertia.

Antoninus and the senate

At the beginning of his reign, Antoninus frustrated the attempt of a number of senators to annul the edicts and acts (*acta*) of Hadrian, whose non-expansionistic, philhellenic, and cosmopolitan policies they had always disliked. In return, Antoninus agreed to abolish the four hated judgeships of Italy and to spare the lives of opposition senators proscribed by the dying Hadrian. Antoninus further improved his relations with the senate by his deferential attitude, by his attendance at meetings, by seeking its advice on policy, and by rendering financial assistance to insolvent senatorial families.

Public benefactions

Antoninus allotted Italy a generous share of the money earmarked for public works and social welfare. Nor did he entirely neglect the provinces. Under his reign of peace, the upper and middle classes prospered, although slaves and the poor continued to be exploited everywhere. Antoninus gave ready ear to the desires and petitions of the ruling classes of the cities of Greece and Asia Minor and some Aegean islands. He frequently reduced their taxes or canceled their debts and came to their aid when they were stricken by earthquake, fire, or flood. Furthermore, he spared them the heavy burden of the imperial retinue by staying at home.

Sound fiscal management

Before his death, despite his huge expenditures on charity and public works in Rome, Italy, and the provinces, Antoninus had succeeded, through sound fiscal management and personal frugality, in leaving behind in the treasury a surplus of 2 billion sesterces, the largest surplus since the death of Tiberius.

Contribution to Roman law

An even prouder achievement was his contribution to Roman law. Never had a Roman emperor surrounded himself with such an array of legal talent. Five jurists were members of the Imperial Council. Antoninus himself had an intimate knowledge of both the minutiae and the spirit of the law. He clarified the laws dealing with inheritance, the protection of the legal interests of minors, and the manumission of slaves. He increased penalties against masters who killed or mistreated their slaves, and he imposed a severe punishment on kidnapping, a frightful scourge in Italy and the provinces. Conversely, he reduced penalties for army deserters and released captives after ten years of hard labor in the mines; he permitted Jews the right of circumcision and restricted the persecution of Christians. Of more general interest was his ruling that a man must be considered innocent until proven guilty and that in cases where the opinions of the judges were evenly divided, the prisoner must receive the benefit of the doubt.

Foreign policy

Founded on the accomplishments of Trajan and Hadrian, Antoninus' prestige and influence as Emperor of Rome transcended the imperial frontiers. Embassies came to him from Bactria and India. He was known in central Asia and China. Eastern kings sought his advice, and a letter to the king of Parthia dissuaded an invasion of Armenia. He awarded thrones to some, enlarged the territories of others. Even the Quadi of Bohemia accepted his nominee as king.

Despite that, Rome's power was actually waning. The perception of Roman might rested solely on Trajan's military exploits and on Hadrian's indefatigable efforts to make the Roman army an efficient, battle-ready guardian of the frontiers. Antoninus, in his efforts to save money, allowed this military force to stagnate, although the nations beyond the frontiers—Germans, Huns, Iranians, and Arabs—were gradually acquiring better military capability by copying Roman arms and tactics. The superior equipment and training that had once made one Roman legionary a match for several Germans or Parthians was now no longer a Roman monopoly.

In the only two frontier zones—Britain and Germany—where Antoninus did exhibit energy or initiative, he was simply following Hadrian's policy. In Scotland, he pushed the frontier about seventy-five miles to the north and had a wall of turf and clay constructed between the firths of Forth and Clyde, a distance of some thirty-seven miles, about half the length of Hadrian's Wall between the Solway and the Tyne. In southwest Germany, he shortened the defensive frontier (limes) by pushing it forward from twenty to thirty miles and strengthened it with new stone forts and watchtowers.

THE LEGACY OF ANTONINUS

The defenses that Antoninus erected in Britain and Germany stood firm to the end of his reign, but not long after. The policy of relatively static defense and the failure to keep the army in top form had left the Empire poorly equipped to roll back the wave of massive assaults that broke after his death. Perhaps he dimly realized his mistake as he lay dying at Lorium in March 161. In his delirium, he talked fretfully about the Empire and all the lying kings who had betrayed him.

MARCUS AURELIUS (161 TO 180 c.e.)

As Hadrian had planned, Marcus Aurelius smoothly succeeded Antoninus Pius. He now took the name M. Aurelius Antoninus. He had been born in Rome in 121 of rich and illustrious Spanish parentage. He enjoyed all the educational advantages money, rank, and high favor could bestow. After his adoption by Antoninus Pius in 138, his betrothal to the daughter of the elder Lucius Ceionius Commodus was eventually broken so that he could marry Antoninus' daughter Faustina, his own first cousin, who had originally been betrothed to Lucius' son.[2] Faustina bore him at least fourteen children in thirty years of marriage, but only one son and five daughters reached adulthood.

His education and Stoicism

Marcus had been taught by the finest tutors whom Antoninus could find. He studied rhetoric under Cornelius Fronto (ca. 100–ca. 166), a famous rhetorician and advocate

FIGURE 25.2 Faustina the Younger, wife of Marcus Aurelius.

from Africa. The illustrious legal authority, L. Volusius Maecianus was his instructor in law. Herodes Atticus (ca. 101–177), a Greek sophist and rhetorician of incredible wealth, came from Athens to teach him Greek oratory. Marcus' favorite was the rhetorician Fronto, with whom he corresponded for many years. Fronto always urged Marcus to make rhetoric the primary focus of his studies. According to Fronto, training in rhetoric should produce a person not only learned in literature and effective in speech but also of high moral character. As a result, to Fronto's chagrin, Marcus developed a strong preference for studying philosophy, particularly the Stoicism of Epictetus (p. 489).

Written in Greek, one of the most well-known expressions of Stoicism is the *Meditations* (literally, *ta eis heauton*—"Things to Himself") of Marcus Aurelius. While encamped along the Danube during the Marcomannic wars (168–175, 178–180), Marcus spent his nights writing down his reflections—scattered, disjointed, and unaffected soliloquies or dialogues between himself and what is called the Universal Power. In the *Meditations*, he strongly reaffirmed the traditional Stoic virtues as the basis of morality, from which the spirit is propelled into both direct communion with the divine and unapprehensive resignation to its will.

Attitude toward Christians

Marcus Aurelius did not pursue a policy of persecuting Christians, but he did not prevent local officials from doing so. Like most pious pagan Romans of his time, however, he regarded the Christians as a depraved and superstitious sect and even an illicit and subversive organization dedicated to the overthrow of the Roman way of life. Otherwise, the willful and obstinate refusal of Christians to obey a magistrate's order to sacrifice to the gods of the state seemed incomprehensible. Indeed, it was contrary to the efforts of the emperors to restore ancient Roman culture and religion as a means of strengthening the Empire against the non-Romans from without and disintegration from within. The common people accused the Christians of atheism, incest, and even cannibalism and made them the scapegoats for the calamities that began to befall the Empire during Aurelius' reign. When angry mobs demanded vengeance, the officials were often sympathetic. For example, Justin Martyr (who adapted Platonic and Stoic philosophy to Jewish and Christian theology) died in Rome along with six companions in 165; twelve Christians died at Scyllium in Numidia in 180; and at Lugdunum and Vienna (Vienne) in Transalpine Gaul, numerous Christians were tortured to death in 177.

MARCUS AURELIUS AS EMPEROR AND SOLDIER

Marcus Aurelius was an able administrator and commander of armies. The first two years of his reign were filled with crises: a serious Tiber flood, an earthquake in Cyzicus, a famine in Galatia, a revolt in Britain, a German crossing of the Rhine, and an invasion of Armenia and Syria by the young Parthian king, Vologeses III. To help him meet these crises, Marcus had insisted at the start on appointing Lucius Aurelius Commodus, his adoptive brother (p. 465), as his colleague with the new name Lucius

Aurelius Verus. Many senators were opposed. They regarded Verus as a frivolous young man addicted to pleasure and self-indulgence. Aurelius prevailed, and Verus became his equal in honor, titulature, and power. Verus then went to the East to deal with the Parthian threat while Aurelius handled pressing problems in the West. In 164, the partnership was even more closely cemented by the marriage of Marcus' daughter Lucilla (Annia Aurelia Galeria Lucilla) to Verus. This division of responsibility between two equal colleagues at the start of a reign, not merely to indicate a successor near the end of a reign, would become an increasingly attractive solution to bearing the increasing burdens of imperial defense and administration. Eventually, this practice would become formalized, and the Empire would split in two.

The Parthian War and a plague, 161 to 165 c.e.

In the East, Verus cleverly combined pleasure with a thorough reorganization of the undisciplined and demoralized army of Syria and Cappadocia. He had as his subordinates two able generals. One was Statius Priscus. He invaded Armenia and captured and burned down its capital of Artaxata. The other was the Syrian-born Avidius Cassius. He whipped the Syrian army into shape, crossed the Euphrates, and invaded Mesopotamia. He rapidly captured several major centers, including Seleucia, which he burned to the ground.

Then two disasters suddenly struck. Soldiers returning from the ruins of Seleucia brought back a frightful plague. It forced the retreat of the victorious armies of the East and then infected Asia Minor, Egypt, Greece, and Italy. It destroyed as much as a third of the population in some places and finally decimated the armies guarding the frontiers along the Rhine and Danube. The defenses along the Danube had already been weakened by extensive troop withdrawals for service in the East. Now, hosts of Germans—the Marcomanni, the Quadi, and many others—sought to escape the slow but relentless pressure that had been building up against them from the steppes of Eurasia for centuries. They tried to breach the sparsely guarded frontiers in 167 and threatened the Danubian provinces of Raetia, Noricum, and Pannonia.

War along the Danube, 168 to 175 c.e.

Marcus Aurelius prepared to reinforce the Danubian frontier, but an outbreak of plague in Rome prevented him and Verus from launching their expedition before the spring of 168. After strengthening the frontier, they suffered an outbreak of plague in their winter quarters and had to return to Rome in early 169. On the way, Verus suffered a sudden stroke and died. Aurelius, now sole *princeps*, had to contend with several troubles. The main enemy—the Quadi, the Marcomanni, and the Sarmatian Iazyges—remained unsubdued and menacing. The Parthian king again invaded Armenia. In 169, the Chatti invaded the frontier regions of the upper Rhine, while the Chauci attacked the Belgic province.

In the fall of 169, Aurelius returned to the Danubian front after he had sold the gold vessels and artistic treasures of the imperial palace to finance his efforts. He was determined to destroy the Marcomanni, the Quadi, and the Iazyges one by one, finally annex their lands, and bring to pass the grand plan of Julius Caesar, which Augustus and Tiberius had been unable to complete. In 170, however, the Marcomanni and the Quadi defeated Aurelius, swept into Italy, and besieged Aquileia at the head of the Adriatic. Never since the Cimbric and Teutonic invasions in the days of Marius was Italy in greater danger from outside attack. Desperately, Marcus drafted slaves, gladiators, and brigands into the army; hired German and Scythian tribes to harass the enemy's rear; and blocked the Alpine passes and fortified the towns in the danger zone. His generals drove the invaders back to the Danube, where the booty-laden Marcomanni were defeated as they tried to cross.

In the meantime, the Moors attacked the shores of Mauretania and invaded the Spanish province of Baetica across the Straits of Gibraltar. The Costoboci of eastern Galicia joined forces with the Sarmatians, crossed the lower Danube, broke into Moesia, overran the Balkans, and invaded Greece as far south as Attica. While the other generals met those emergencies, Aurelius obtained temporary relief on the Danube by granting peace to the Marcomanni and the Quadi. They agreed to settle depopulated land within the Empire and serve in Roman armies.

Once the other emergencies had been met, Marcus Aurelius found pretexts to resume his campaigns against the Marcomanni, the Quadi, and the Iazyges. In 172, he crossed the Danube, attacked the Marcomanni first, then the Quadi, and finally the Iazyges. In 175, however, a revolt in the East forced him to grant terms before he could completely conquer their homelands. He concluded a peace with the proviso that they return all the Roman prisoners whom they had taken, make reparations for the damages that they had inflicted on the provinces, and evacuate a strip of territory ten miles wide running along the north bank of the Danube.

The usurpation of Avidius Cassius, 175 C.E.

A rumor that Aurelius had died may have prompted Faustina to look to Avidius Cassius, now governor of Syria, as a stand-in who could protect her young son, Commodus, until he could ascend the throne. In any case, Cassius proclaimed himself emperor and would not relent when he found out that Aurelius was alive. Marcus summoned Faustina and Commodus, to Sirmium (Mitrovica, Serbia) and prepared to set out with them to the East. Before his departure, a legionary showed up bearing the head of Cassius. The death of Cassius would seem to have removed the need for Marcus to leave, but he went anyway. Perhaps he desired to make a display of Roman power, receive expressions of loyalty, and remove disloyal officials from their posts. On his way through Asia Minor, he suffered the loss of Faustina, the wife whom he had loved for thirty years despite malicious rumors of her infidelity and any mistaken encouragement of Avidius Cassius.

After traversing Asia Minor, Syria, and Egypt, greeted everywhere by acclamations of loyalty, Marcus arrived in Rome in 176. He was a sad and lonely man, bereft of his wife and one of his best generals. He resolved never again to make a man governor of the province of his birth. To forestall any other potential usurpers, he at once recognized Commodus as his heir and successor. Then, Marcus celebrated his German and Sarmatian (over the Iazyges) triumphs. In the course of the celebration, he unveiled the famous equestrian statue of himself that now stands on the Roman Capitol (p. 498). Also, he laid the foundation stone of his column depicting the Second Marcomannic War, which still stands in the Piazza Colonna in Rome (p. 499).

Return to the Danube, 178 to 180 C.E.

Rumors of fresh troubles along the Danube caused the emperor to hasten north in 178. Leading his men himself, he crossed the Danube. After a long and strenuous campaign known as the Third Marcomannic War, he crushed the resistance of the Quadi and the Marcomanni. He established a new legionary camp on the Danube at Castra Regina (Regensburg in Bavaria) and proceeded to create two new provinces—Marcomannia and Sarmatia—by annexing a vast territory extending as far north as the Erzgebirge (a range of mountains on the border between the Czech Republic and Germany) and as far east as the Carpathian Mountains (eastern Romania). Thus, he hoped to shorten and strengthen the northern frontiers against future assaults. While engaged in this mighty task, Marcus Aurelius suddenly suffered a dangerous illness, possibly the plague. Rumors that he was poisoned are baseless. He died in camp on March 17, 180.

The most important result of the Danubian campaigns lay not in Aurelius' victories over Germanic and Sarmatian tribes, nor in his new provinces, which did not survive his death. It was the transplantation and settlement of thousands of Germans in the war-torn and plague-devastated provinces of Dacia, Moesia, Raetia, Pannonia, Dalmatia, Gaul, and even Italy. This measure not only temporarily relieved the pressure on the frontiers along the Rhine and the Danube, but significantly altered the ethnic composition of the Roman Empire.

THE QUESTION OF SUCCESSION

Those who have admired Marcus Aurelius' many fine qualities have often criticized him for designating his only living son, Commodus, as his successor and for abandoning the practice of adoption that had produced a series of remarkably able, dedicated, and well-regarded rulers from Trajan to Aurelius himself. Such critics are prejudiced by extremely hostile accounts of Commodus' reign. They forget that the practice of adoption was used by the first *princeps*. It was not any kind of theoretical alternative to dynastic succession. It was not a system based on the Stoic principle of choosing the most worthy individual regardless of birth. The practice of adoption was a reaffirmation of the dynastic principle.

Roman aristocrats had always resorted to adoption to maintain their families' existence in the absence of a natural heir. For various reasons, Nerva and his successors until Marcus Aurelius had lacked sons to succeed them. The dynastic principle, moreover, was so strongly favored by the soldiers and common people that Aurelius' four predecessors had felt it necessary to create sons where none existed. When it turned out that Aurelius had a natural heir, he had no choice but to proclaim him as his successor. Had he not, thousands would have supported Commodus, the first emperor "born in the purple" (i.e., during his father's reign), as having a superior claim to the throne. A disastrous civil war probably would have resulted. There is no reliable evidence, only later hostile rhetoric, that Aurelius had any doubts about Commodus' moral fitness to be emperor. He made Commodus his co-emperor in 177 to make sure that there would be no doubt about the succession. It became apparent only later that Commodus, a remarkably handsome youth, was totally different from his father in character and ideals.

PROBLEMS FOR THE FUTURE

Under the five "good" emperors, the second century C.E. appears to many as the golden age of the Roman Empire. So it was. Beneath the surface, however, were problems and trends that had negative implications for the third century and beyond.

Defense

Trajan's inability to hold on to his conquests in Mesopotamia and Hadrian's decision to adopt a more static defense indicate that the Empire had reached the limits of its power and that its resources were becoming stretched too thin for the defensive burdens that it had to bear. That point is driven home by the great difficulty that Marcus Aurelius had in trying to defend the frontiers simultaneously in the East and the West. The accident of plague certainly complicated his task, but the extreme measures that he had to take in mounting his last expeditions against the Germanic tribes indicate that the Empire had very little margin of safety when confronted with a major challenge on its frontiers.

Centralization of political power

The centralization of power in the hands of the emperor and his increasingly bureau-cratized servants accelerated as the problems of governance and defense became more complex. The very benevolence of the emperors naturally increased their power at the expense of the senate and magistrates at Rome and of the local councils (*curiae*) and officials of the provincial municipalities. Everyone came to rely on the emperor to solve all problems. In the third century, this situation ossified the imperial system and made it less responsive in times of crisis. Local regions came to feel remote from the central government and were willing to put regional interests above imperial interests, which undermined the unity of the Empire.

Increasing militarization

Despite their success as civilian administrators, it was chiefly as military men on the frontiers that Trajan, Hadrian, and Marcus Aurelius made their marks. The civilian side of life was becoming subordinate to the military. The civilian senate more and more became just another municipal council. To be sure, it was more prestigious than the others but in reality not more powerful. After the reign of Aurelius' son, the Roman senate had little impact on affairs outside of Rome and Italy in the third and subsequent centuries. It still formally ratified the accession of a new emperor, but the real choice increasingly lay in the hands of the provincial armies vital for the defense of a frequently besieged Empire. He who could control the soldiers could control the state; he who could not control them soon perished as the Empire of the third and early fourth centuries was transformed into an absolute, regimented military monarchy.

NOTES

1 He did not, however, adopt the magic legend of HADRIANVS AVGVSTVS on his coins until the year 123, which happened to be the 150th anniversary of the senate's conferral of the name *Augustus* upon Octavian.
2 Marriage between first cousins was usually frowned upon in Roman society, but it was not illegal. In this case, strong dynastic considerations obviously prevailed.

SUGGESTED READING

Grainger, J. D. *Nerva and the Roman Succession Crisis of AD 96–99*. London: Routledge, 2003.

Kulikowski, M. *The Triumph of Empire: The Roman World from Hadrian to Constantine*. Cambridge, MA: Harvard University Press, 2016.

Levick, B. M. *Faustina I and II: Imperial Women of the Golden Age. Women in Antiquity*. Oxford: Oxford University Press, 2014.

CHAPTER 26

Culture, society, and economy in the first two centuries c.e.

The first two centuries C.E. fully realized the potential created by Augustus' establishment of widespread peace within the Mediterranean core of the Roman Empire. Rome had become a giant magnet attracting trade and talent from every quarter and radiating its influence in all directions. The writers and artists of the Augustan Golden Age had created a common cultural frame of reference for the Empire's urbanized upper classes. Those classes shaped a remarkably uniform high imperial culture based on shared values and educational experience. They became an elite of imperial service. They were not bound by the parochial ties of language, tribe, or city, but the universal ideal of Rome as *the city*. It was the guarantor of civilized urban life against forces of destruction both within and without.

Indeed, the universal rule of Rome encouraged many to reject the old particularistic world of individual cities. Rome became their universal commonwealth. As its citizens, they lived under the care of a benevolent universal deity in the form of either the emperor himself or one of the savior gods popularized by various Eastern mystery cults.

Socially and economically, the Empire reached great heights. With Italy and the interior provinces enjoying unprecedented peace and prosperity and with threats on the frontiers usually contained, foreign and domestic trade flourished. There was enough surplus wealth to support a vigorous tradition of euergetism (the doing of good works).

The emperors and the upper classes ameliorated the plight of the poor. Those of moderate means found opportunities for economic and social advancement. At the same time, Stoic and Cynic philosophers popularized an enlightened spirit. That spirit was consonant with at least moderately improved conditions for women and the lower classes and with the integration of provincials as Roman citizens.

POST-AUGUSTAN LITERATURE

The late Republic and the reign of Augustus had produced a series of major Latin authors, who had used the great works of Greek literature as their models. The latter continued to be the foundation of traditional *paideia* (the training of youths) in the Greek East. In the West, they were now mediated through the classic Latin writings of Cicero, Caesar, Livy, Vergil, Horace, Propertius, Tibullus, and Ovid. Those authors had enshrined the values and ideals summed up in a later word, *Romanitas*. They now formed the basis of literary education in the West. Educated western provincials thus absorbed patriotic pride in the glories of Rome's past and espoused the ideals believed to have accounted for its greatness. As a result, the high culture of the imperial capital became indelibly etched on that of the western provinces.

The Latin language and its literature were also the western provincials' passport to the wider world of Rome itself and imperial service. Consequently, many of the leading figures in the world of Latin letters in the first two centuries C.E. no longer came from the old Roman aristocracy or from the municipalities of Italy. They sprang from the colonies and municipalities of Gaul, Spain, and North Africa. Such men were a constant source of fresh talent and gave Latin letters greater breadth and popularity than ever before.

The impact of rhetoric and politics

Latin authors of the first and second centuries C.E. often wrote in a highly rhetorical style different from the more restrained Classicism of the first century B.C.E. Rhetoric, the art of persuasive speech, had always been a large component of Greco-Roman education. Effective speaking was essential for success in the public life of Greek city-states and the Roman Republic. Rhetorical skills were needed more than ever in the Roman Empire. The greater number of law courts under the emperors and the greater number of cases generated by the more complex Empire required an army of lawyers trained to be as persuasive as possible. Countless petitions addressed to the emperor and his administrators required writers with rhetorical skill and polish. Emperors, provincial governors, military leaders, and local officials needed to communicate effectively with large audiences.

At the same time, it was politically dangerous to be too independent or original under an all-powerful emperor. He might view independent and original ideas as a threat to his own leadership. Flattery of the emperor and his agents was much safer. Therefore, the persuasive or argumentative declamations, *suasoriae* and *controversiae*, of the rhetorical schools became progressively artificial. Rhetoric increasingly concentrated on elaborate and exotic technique for its own sake. Sometimes, the constant striving for effect produced a turgid, twisted, and distorted kind of writing meant only to display one's verbal virtuosity in competition with others similarly trained. This trend was reinforced by the political need of the emperor and local elites to win popular favor by entertaining mass audiences with spectacles, games, and shows. Literary tastes now ran toward the more theatrical and emotional; the exotic, the grotesque, and the sensational became appealing subjects.

Of course, the idealized past of heroes and statesmen enshrined in many Classical authors was fundamentally incompatible with the autocracy that even the most restrained emperors found hard to mask. As the imperial monarchy became a permanent fixture under the Julio-Claudians, the contradiction between ideals and reality was difficult for some to overlook, particularly for traditionalists in the Roman senatorial class. Therefore, many of the Latin authors from that class during the first two centuries looked back in nostalgia or protest to the lost liberty of the Republic. They took refuge in the teachings of Stoicism symbolized by the great martyr to republican *libertas*, Cato the Younger. On the other hand, for authors who did not come from that class or were only recent arrivals, sometimes it was easier to overlook the contradiction between ideal and reality. Their writings were deferential to the emperors in whose service they rose to a prominence that they never could have attained under the old Republic.

POVERTY OF LITERATURE UNDER TIBERIUS AND CALIGULA

The stern and intrigue-ridden reign of Tiberius and Caligula's frightening suppression of real or imagined rivals stifled creativity and free expression in most fields of literature.

History and handbooks

There were few historians of note under those emperors. Velleius Paterculus (ca. 19 B.C.E.–ca. 32 B.C.E.), an equestrian military officer, wrote a brief history of Rome in a rhetorical style. Its importance is that it reflects the attitudes of his class. It is favorable toward Tiberius, with whom Velleius had served, and displays an unusual interest in Roman cultural history. Aulus Cremutius Cordus (d. 25 C.E.), on the other hand, wrote a traditional history of Rome's civil wars to at least 18 B.C.E. He reflected the attitudes of Stoic-inspired aristocrats who resented the emperor's monopoly of power and *dignitas*. Sejanus had Cordus tried for treason, his books were burned, and he committed suicide (p. 411).

Seneca the Elder—Lucius (or Marcus) Annaeus Seneca (ca. 55 B.C.E.–ca. 40 C.E.)—fared better, although his history of the same period is also lost. That is unfortunate because he came from Corduba in Spain, making him one of western provincials who were becoming prominent in early imperial Rome. What has survived of his writings is a handbook of rhetorical exercises (*controversiae* and *suasoriae*) culled from public declamations.

Practical handbooks were safe and popular. One of the most famous produced during Tiberius' reign was another compilation for use in rhetorical training, the *Nine Books of Memorable Deeds and Sayings* by Valerius Maximus. M. Gavius Apicius, a famous gourmet, even wrote a popular book on sauces. It is now lost. The extant book of recipes that goes by the name of Apicius is a fourth-century collection.

Poetry

Poetry fared almost as badly as prose under Tiberius, although he himself was a poet in the Alexandrian tradition. Unable, it seems, to reconcile the illusions of the Augustan Principate with its reality, Tiberius did not encourage celebratory, patriotic historical epic in the tradition of Vergil. With his interest in astronomy and astrology, however, he may have appreciated the only surviving pieces by his nephew and adopted son, Germanicus: two large fragments from translations of earlier Greek epics on astronomy and predicting the weather. Another scientific poem survives from this period, the *Astronomica* of Germanicus' contemporary Marcus Manilius. It covers the planets, the signs of the zodiac, the calculation of a horoscope, and the influence of the zodiacal signs at various points during their periods of dominance. It is very Stoic in its attempt to find a universal cosmic order.

Phaedrus (ca. 15 B.C.E. to ca. 50 C.E.)

The most interesting surviving author of the period is Gaius Julius Phaedrus or Phaeder. First of all, as a freed Thracian slave of Augustus, he represents a class whose voice is seldom heard in imperial Rome. Second, he introduced a whole new minor genre to Greco-Roman literature, the moralizing poetic fable in the tradition of Aesop. His tales are often thinly disguised criticisms of the powerful in his own day. Sejanus tried to silence him but failed.

THE BLOSSOMING OF THE SILVER AGE IN LITERATURE UNDER CLAUDIUS AND NERO

The period from 14 to 138 C.E. is often called the Silver Age in comparison with the Golden Age of Augustus. The Silver Age really blossomed under Claudius and Nero. It then surpassed the early years of Augustus in quantity of writing and, with one major break, in length of sustained activity. Claudius himself was a writer and historian of some accomplishment (p. 421). Ironically, under the influence of Messallina early in his reign, he banished Seneca the Elder's son, Lucius Annaeus Seneca (the Younger), an accomplished orator and devoted Stoic. This act must have cast a pall over free expression at Rome. In 49, however, at the prompting of Agrippina, Claudius recalled Seneca the Younger to tutor her young son, Nero. From that point until Seneca's fall from power under an increasingly fearful Nero, there was a great outburst of literary activity, especially among writers from Spain, many connected to Seneca's family.

Seneca the Younger (ca. 4 B.C.E. to 65 C.E.)

L. Annaeus Seneca, the most noted literary figure of the mid-first century C.E., was born to Seneca the Elder at Corduba, Spain, and came as a boy to Rome. He was one of Rome's most notable Stoic philosophers and a copious author of varied works: a spiteful burlesque on Claudius (*Apocolocyntosis*); a long treatise on natural science (*Quaestiones Naturales*); nine tragedies, typically Euripidean in plot and theme, in a highly rhetorical style; ten essays (misnamed *Dialogi*), containing a full exposition of Stoic philosophy; prose treatises; and 124 *Moral Epistles* (*Epistulae Morales*).

Lucan (39 to 65 C.E.)

Born in Corduba, M. Annaeus Lucanus (Lucan) was Seneca's nephew. His sole extant work is the *De Bello Civili* (often called *Pharsalia*), a violent and pessimistic epic poem in ten books, which narrates the war between Caesar and Pompey. It displays a strong republican bias, a deep hostility toward Caesar, and a rejection of Vergil's patriotic idealism. Suspected of complicity in Piso's conspiracy against Nero (pp. 433–4), both Lucan and Seneca the Younger were forced to commit suicide in 65.

Thrasea Paetus and Petronius (? to 66 C.E. for both)

Nero continued his persecution of Stoic critics in 66 by condemning to death Thrasea Paetus (P. Clodius Thrasea Paetus), who wrote a sympathetic biography of Cato the Younger. Others suspected of involvement with him were ordered to commit suicide. One of them was the Petronius whom Tacitus calls the "arbiter of social graces" (*elegantiae arbiter*) under Nero (p. 434). He is often identified with the Petronius who authored the witty and picaresque satirical novel *Satyricon* (or *Satyrica*). It combines humor with serious criticism of the times. In its world, the old Roman values are stood on their heads. Gross materialism and sensuality are the order of the day. Bad rhetoric runs riot. Everyone pretends to be what he is not. Beneath the laughter is the feeling that society has run amok.

Persius (34 to 62 C.E.) and Martial (ca. 40 to 104 C.E.)

Aulus Persius Flaccus and Marcus Valerius Martialis were both satirists who escaped Nero's purges. Persius may simply have died too soon. His six surviving hexameter poems, the *Satires*, are highly compressed, rather academic attacks on stereotypic human failings. On the other hand, Martial, a Spaniard from Bilbilis, in the twelve books of his *Epigrams*, attacks the shams and vices of real people. He was probably too young to attract much notice under Nero. He wrote mostly under the Flavians and eventually returned to Spain.

Curtius (ca. 20 to 80 C.E.)

Significantly, the most well-known historical work from Caligula to the Flavians was the *History of Alexander* by Quintus Curtius Rufus. It was more of an historical romance than serious history, which would have been dangerous. Curtius merely furthered the romanticized tales that had quickly obscured the real facts of Alexander's career after his death.

TECHNICAL WRITING AND SCHOLARSHIP

Research and writing on technical subjects were still much safer pursuits than poetry or history. For example, the *De Re Rustica* of Lucius Junius Moderatus Columella (ca. 10–70 C.E.), who came from Gades (Cadiz), is a practical guide for large-scale farmers. The earliest Roman geographical treatise that has survived belongs to Columella's contemporary and fellow Spaniard Pomponius Mela. Written in the archaizing style of Sallust, his *Description of Places* (*Chorographia*) starts at the Straits of Gibraltar, goes counterclockwise around the Mediterranean in three books, and ends up back at Gibraltar. Fantasy sometimes prevails over fact, but it indicates that Rome's acquisition of a large empire stimulated a desire to learn more about its lands and peoples.

Pliny the Elder, Gaius Plinius Secundus (ca. 23 to 79 C.E.)

Nowhere is the interest in conveying practical technical knowledge better epitomized than in the encyclopedic *Natural History* (*Historia Naturalis*) of Pliny the Elder. Pliny's Stoic-inspired goal was no less than to sum up the existing state of practical and scientific knowledge as a service to mankind. He died in the eruption of Vesuvius while he was combining intellectually curious observation with an attempt to rescue victims. Arranged topically in thirty-seven books, his immense work unscientifically but systematically compiles a vast array of information and misinformation on such subjects as geography, agriculture, anthropology, medicine, zoology, botany, and mineralogy. It is still useful because it preserves an enormous store of information that, correct or not, provides the modern historian with valuable raw material for fresh analysis.

Frontinus (ca. 30 to 104 C.E.)

A more technical and practically informed writer is Pliny's long-lived contemporary Sextus Julius Frontinus. His compilation of useful military stratagems culled from Greek and Roman history, the *Strategemata*, has survived. His more theoretical treatment of Greco-Roman warfare has not. Because military officers building camps, roads, and fortifications needed practical information on surveying, he wrote a treatise on that subject, too. Excerpts from it survive in a later compilation of writers known as the *Gromatici*, named from a Roman surveying instrument called a *groma*.

In 97, Emperor Nerva appointed Frontinus supervisor of Rome's water supply. To guide his successors and people dealing with the problems of water supply in other cities, Frontinus published all that he had found useful in his most famous and original work, the *De Aquis* (*De Aquae Ductu*) *Urbis Romae*. In two volumes, it gives an invaluable history of Rome's aqueducts and priceless technical information derived from personal experience, engineering reports, and public documents.

Artemidorus (late second century c.e.)

A far different kind of writer is Artemidorus, a Greek from Ephesus. He was very much interested in subjects that today would be associated with popular superstition or the occult. His *Interpretation of Dreams* records and explains dreams collected from people during his extensive travels. It provides a fascinating look at the popular anxieties and psychology of the time.

SCIENCE AND MEDICINE

Abstract science was not a forte of the Romans. The scientific work that did take place was carried on by the heirs of the Greek tradition in the East. Even they were primarily encyclopedists like Pliny the Elder and did little original work; instead, they tended to codify and compile the work of predecessors. Their summaries then became standard reference works that remained authoritative until the scientific revolution of the seventeenth and eighteenth centuries.

Ptolemy of Alexandria (mid-second century c.e.)

The most influential scientist of the first two centuries c.e. was the mathematician, astronomer, and geographer Ptolemy, Claudius Ptolemaeus. He expounded the geocentric theory of the universe in a thirteen-volume work known by the title of its Arabic translation, the *Almagest*. His complex theory of eccentric circles and epicycles to explain the observed motions of heavenly bodies in relation to the earth was mathematically very sophisticated. It dominated Arabic and Western astronomy until the Copernican revolution.

In his geographical writings, Ptolemy accepted the view of the Hellenistic scholar Eratosthenes on the spherical shape of the earth. He constructed a spherical projection with mathematically regular latitudes and longitudes. Ironically, however, he argued for Posidonius' much shorter circumference of the earth than the more accurate longer one of Eratosthenes. It was the belief in the spherical shape and short circumference of the earth that led Columbus to think that he could get to the Indies relatively quickly by sailing west.

Medical writers before Galen

A number of Greek and Roman physicians kept up the long-established tradition of medical writing. Under Claudius, the Roman Scribonius Largus produced a practical handbook of prescriptions for drugs and remedies that still exists under the title *Compositiones*. Largus is greatly surpassed, however, by his Greek contemporary Dioscorides Pedianus, who had traveled extensively as an army doctor. Dioscorides has left two works on drugs and remedies that became the standard reference in pharmacology for the rest of antiquity. Under Trajan and Hadrian, Soranus of Ephesus wrote twenty medical treatises in Greek, and many were translated into Latin. Of his surviving works, the most important are his gynecological writings. They provide a rare resource for studying women in relation to ancient medical theory and practice and often reveal male-biased misconceptions of female biology.

Galen (129 to ca. 200 c.e.)

The greatest physician and medical writer of antiquity was the Greek doctor Galen of Pergamum. He started out as a doctor for gladiators in Pergamum. Then he became Marcus Aurelius' court physician at Rome. He was both a theorist and a practitioner. Equally skilled in diagnosis and prognosis, he always sought to confirm his theories with practical experiments. Indeed, through careful dissection, he greatly advanced the physiological and anatomical knowledge of the day. His writings, now thirty printed volumes, were regarded as so authoritative that medical research in the West largely stagnated for the next thousand years.

PHILOLOGY AND LITERARY SCHOLARSHIP

Philological and literary criticism had begun to grow by the end of the first century B.C.E. It blossomed in the next two centuries as the recognized classics like Cicero, Vergil, Horace, and Ovid became the standard texts for Roman rhetorical education. Cicero's importance as a school text is seen in the extant commentaries that Asconius Pedianus wrote for his young sons on five speeches of Cicero. Asconius is particularly valuable because two of the speeches on which he wrote, *Pro Cornelio* and *In Toga Candida*, are lost. His comments help to reconstruct them.

Helenius Acron and Pomponius Porphyrio wrote school commentaries on Horace at the end of the second and beginning of the third centuries. Acron has been reworked by a later pseudo-Acron, but Porphyrio is intact. Both are indispensable for the study of Horace.

Sometime in the first century C.E., an author variously identified as *Dionysius* or *Longinus* (once wrongly identified with Cassius Longinus [p. 538]), wrote one of the most important pieces of literary criticism in the ancient world. Written in Greek and entitled *On the Sublime*, it is a highly original analysis of what makes a piece of literature great. It gets beyond the usual discussion of rhetoric and style and stresses the need for greatness of mind and feeling.

LACK OF GREAT LITERATURE UNDER THE FLAVIANS, 69 TO 96 c.e.

Nero's purge wiped out a whole generation of Roman writers just as it was reaching its prime. The political situation under the Flavians was not conducive to the emergence of a new one. Vespasian, Titus, and Domitian were not hostile to learning and literature, but they did not encourage the freedom of expression necessary for truly great literature. Vespasian set the tone when he banished the Stoic and Cynic philosophers from Rome and executed Helvidius Priscus (p. 447). Domitian reinforced it with similar banishments in 89 and 95 and ruthlessly employed informers to muzzle his critics (pp. 450–1).

Poetry

Only three poets other than Martial (p. 479) have survived. Silius Italicus (ca. 26–101 C.E.) wrote an uninspired epic, the *Punica*, in seventeen books on the Punic wars. Valerius Flaccus (?–ca. 90 C.E.) wrote a refined but unoriginal epic, the *Argonautica*, a rehash of Jason's expedition to find the Golden Fleece. Publius Papinius Statius (ca. 45–96 C.E.), the most talented of the three, was a professional writer patronized by Domitian. Two epics, the *Thebaid*, on the quarrel between Oedipus' sons, and the unfinished *Achilleid*, on Achilles, are extant. Statius' best work is the *Silvae*, thirty-two individual poems, many written to friends on special occasions.

Josephus (b. 37 or 38 C.E.)

The only important historian who published under the Flavians was their Jewish client Flavius Josephus. He was a captured Pharisee who allegedly prophesied that Vespasian would become emperor. He wrote the *Jewish War* to point out the futility of resisting Rome. Despite his pro-Roman outlook, however, he defended his people's faith and way of life to the gentiles in his twenty-volume *Jewish Antiquities*. He also wrote *Contra Apionem* against the anti-Semitic writings of the Alexandrian Greek Apion and defended his own career in an autobiography. His works all survive in Greek, but he wrote the original version of the *Jewish War* in Aramaic to reach Mesopotamian Jews.

Quintilian (ca. 33 to ca. 100 C.E.)

The central role of rhetoric in higher education resulted in a comprehensive handbook of rhetorical training by the Spaniard Marcus Fabius Quintilianus. He held Vespasian's first chair of rhetoric at Rome and tutored Domitian's heirs. His *Institutio Oratoria* (*Oratorical Education*) deals with all of the techniques of rhetoric and has influenced serious study of the subject ever since. It is also a source of important information on many other Greek and Latin authors.

RESURGENCE OF LITERATURE UNDER THE FIVE "GOOD" EMPERORS

The most important authors who came of age under the Flavians did not begin to publish their works until after the death of Domitian. His autocratic nature and constant fear of conspiracies after 88 made it dangerous to express thoughts openly on many subjects. On the other hand, the more relaxed atmosphere between the five succeeding emperors and the educated senatorial elite was more congenial to many writers.

Tacitus (ca. 55 to 120 c.e.) and Pliny the Younger (ca. 61 to ca. 114 c.e.)

The foremost author was Cornelius Tacitus, whose valuable historical works have been discussed above (p. 438). He also wrote the *Dialogue on Orators*, observations on earlier orators and how the lack of free institutions in his own day produced mere striving for rhetorical effect instead of real substance in contemporary orators. Nothing underscores Tacitus' point more clearly than the *Panegyric*, a speech of the younger Pliny, Gaius Plinius Caecilius Secundus, nephew of Pliny the Elder. It is full of flattery of Trajan and dares to offer advice only indirectly by safely criticizing the dead Domitian. The ten books of his *Letters*, however, are much better. In smooth, artistic prose, they are addressed to Trajan and numerous other important friends. They reveal an urbane, decent individual. He tried to live up to his responsibilities, avoid injustice, and do good where he could, as in endowing a school for boys and girls or refusing to accept anonymous denunciations of Christians.

Juvenal (ca. 55 to ca. 130 c.e.)

Little is known about Juvenal (Decimus Junius Juvenalis), who published he published sixteen *Satires* during the reigns of Trajan and Hadrian. They are vitriolic, misogynistic, and otherwise offensive attacks on vices and their practitioners. Juvenal was immensely popular in the Middle Ages because he titillated Christian moralists while confirming their view of pagan Roman decadence.

Suetonius (ca. 69 to ca. 135 c.e.)

Another writer who fascinated medieval Christians in the same way was Gaius Suetonius Tranquillus. He is often considered the last author of Latin's Silver Age. Friend of Pliny the Younger, he served Trajan and became Hadrian's private secretary and imperial librarian. He wrote on textual criticism, famous courtesans, illustrious men, literary figures, Greek and Roman games, and a variety of other topics. Nevertheless, most of those works are lost. His fame rests upon his major biographical work, the *Lives of the Twelve Caesars* (Julius Caesar to Domitian). These biographies, however, aim not so much at serious scholarship as at entertainment. Suetonius does preserve much valuable information from lost earlier sources, but his portraits must be treated cautiously. Rumor, gossip, and rhetorically embellished scandal are often included.

Fronto (ca. 100 to ca. 170 c.e.) and a new literary movement

Suetonius' fascination with the bizarre actions of past emperors and his research on obscure topics was symptomatic of his age. A general absorption in arcane and antiquarian subjects became a definite literary movement, almost a cult of antiquity, under the Antonines (Antoninus Pius through Commodus). A man who fostered this movement was Marcus Aurelius' tutor in rhetoric, M. Cornelius Fronto. Significantly, Fronto had been born at Cirta in North Africa, which soon replaced Spain as a provincial source of Roman writers.

Fronto's major interest lay in ransacking early Latin literature for archaic and uncommon words. He and his literary circle wanted to expand the rather limited vocabulary of the Classical writers like Cicero and Vergil. Fronto and his friends created what he called an *elocutio novella* (new elocution) to give greater point and variety to their expression.

Aulus Gellius (ca. 125 to ca. 175 C.E.)

The danger in Fronto's approach was that arcane archaisms and recondite research would become ends in themselves and irrelevant to the real world. A case in point is Fronto's cultured friend Aulus Gellius. Beginning as a student in Athens, he compiled interesting oddities culled from earlier writers and interspersed with accounts of conversations on a wide range of philological and antiquarian subjects. Called *Attic Nights* (*Noctes Atticae*) in honor of its origin, it is a valuable work to modern scholars because it preserves much important information from now-lost earlier works.

Apuleius (ca. 123 to ca. 180 C.E.)

Apuleius was a professional rhetorician and popular Middle Platonist philosopher in Roman Carthage. He published excerpts from his declamations in the *Florida*. In the encyclopedic spirit of the age, he also wrote widely on various subjects in such books as *Natural Questions*, *On Fish*, *On Trees*, *Astronomical Phenomena*, *Arithmetica*, and *On Proverbs*. Although he was inclined to show off, his interests were serious, as seen from his declamation *Concerning the God of Socrates*. His investigations into magic and theurgy eventually led to his prosecution for practicing forbidden magic after he married a wealthy older widow. That led to his two greatest works, the *Apology*, based on his successful self-defense in court, and the *Metamorphoses* (or *Golden Ass*), the only complete Latin novel to have survived.

In the novel, a certain Lucius is the victim of his own experiments in sex and magic. They turn him into an ass with human senses who suffers numerous comical and bawdy mishaps. Apuleius, however, has interspersed many additional elements from other stories to give it greater depth and to ridicule the magic and superstition of the age. In contrast, many argue, Apuleius describes the true power of pure faith in the saving grace of the goddess Isis through a moving scene of conversion at the end. To others, however, the ending may be a rather sexist spoof, another instance of Lucius' misplaced trust in a female who has all the answers.

Pausanias (fl. 150 C.E.)

The peace and prosperity of the first two centuries C.E. and the antiquarianism of the age encouraged travel and the viewing of historical places, monuments, and museums.

Therefore, travelogues and guidebooks were in great demand. Fortunately, one of the most valuable survives, the *Description of Greece* by Pausanias. He was a Greek geographer from Lydia in the mid-second century. Usually, he outlines the history and topography of cities and their surroundings and frequently includes information on their mythological lore, religious customs, social life, and native products. Pausanias is particularly interested in historic battle sites, patriotic monuments, and famous works of art and architecture. The accuracy of his descriptions has been very helpful in locating ancient sites and reconstructing what has been recovered.

RESURGENCE OF GREEK LITERATURE

It is significant that Pausanias was a Greek writer describing great monuments and locales in ancient Greece. The first two centuries C.E. saw a renewal of cultural activity and local pride in the Greek-speaking half of the Roman Empire. Greeks could reflect with pride that upper-class Romans continued to flock to the great Greek centers of culture to complete their education just as they had done during the late Republic. The vigorous philhellenism of emperors like Nero, Hadrian, and Marcus Aurelius recalled a sense of greatness to many Greeks. The return of prosperity to Greek cities under the imperial peace and the growing prominence of influential Greeks in imperial administration must have reinforced it. In fact, many significant Greek writers during this period were men who had successful careers in the Roman government.

Plutarch (ca. 45 to 120 C.E.)

An outstanding example of such a person is Plutarch (L.[?] Mestrius Plutarchus) of Chaeronea in Boeotia. Under Hadrian, Plutarch was procurator of Achaea. A large collection of miscellaneous ethical, rhetorical, and antiquarian essays (not all genuinely Plutarch's) is entitled *Moralia*. Plutarch's most famous work is the *Parallel Lives of Noble Greeks and Romans*. The overall theme of the *Lives* is that for every important figure of Roman history, a similar and equally important character appears in Greek history. Plutarch hoped to show that the Greeks were worthy partners of Rome in the great task of maintaining the Empire. Plutarch chose his material to highlight moral character, not present an objective or critical historical analysis.

Arrian (ca. 95 to 180 C.E.)

Another Greek writer who had served Rome was L. Flavius Arrianus, Arrian, from Nicomedia in Bithynia. Also a Roman citizen, he became a suffect consul in the early years of Hadrian and was governor of Cappadocia from 131 to 137. Retiring to the cultured life of Greece, he studied philosophy under Epictetus (p. 489). He presented a full account of Epictetus' Stoic teachings in his *Diatribes* (*Discourses*) and a synopsis in the *Enchiridion* (*Handbook*).

Of Arrian's extant historical works, the most important is his account of Alexander's war against Persia, the *Anabasis of Alexander*. It is the fullest and most soundly based account of Alexander that has survived. The loss of his *After Alexander* makes it much more difficult to reconstruct the history of Alexander's successors.

Appian (ca. 90 to 165 C.E.)

Appianus (Appian), a Greek from Alexandria and Arrian's contemporary, also obtained Roman citizenship. After a successful career at Rome, he wrote a universal history in Greek like Polybius' earlier work. His universal *Roman History* (*Romaika*) in twenty-four books began with the rise of Rome in Italy and then treated various ethnic groups and nations conquered by Rome. Books 13 to 17, however, form an interlude entitled *Civil Wars* on the period from the Gracchi to Actium. Appian often followed valuable, now-lost Greek and Latin sources.

Lucian (ca. 115 to ca. 185 C.E.)

The most original writer of this period was Lucian (Lucianus). He was a Hellenized Syrian from Samosata, who held a Roman administrative post in Egypt. He was a master of Classical Attic Greek and was deeply versed in its literature. Lucian's earlier works consist of rhetorical declamations and literary criticism, often laced with wit. Contrary to some claims, however, Lucian is probably not the author of a satirical novel entitled *Lucius* (or *The Ass*), based on the same original as Apuleius' *Golden Ass*. His most famous works are humorous, semipopular philosophical dialogues, such as his *Dialogues of the Dead*. They deflate human pride, pedantic philosophers, religious charlatans, and popular superstitions. He vigorously disliked all that was fatuous, foolish, or false.

THE SECOND SOPHISTIC

Lucian's interests and the range of his writings are too broad to be categorized easily. They must be seen in the context of a Greek literary movement known as the Second Sophistic. The Greek sophists of the fifth and fourth centuries B.C.E. had invented formal rhetoric. Hence, the professional rhetoricians of the second and third centuries C.E. were also called *sophists*. Many of them sought to revive the vocabulary and style of earlier Greek orators. Most of them were wealthy, cultured men proud of the Greek past and eager to promote the influence of their native cities within the Roman Empire. In their society, they were as popular and influential as modern celebrities. They cultivated relations with Roman aristocrats and were often favored by emperors. Their archaizing tendencies influenced Fronto. His *elocutio novella* represents a parallel movement in Latin.

A leading figure of the Second Sophistic was Aelius Aristides (ca. 120–189 C.E.). He delivered lectures and ceremonial speeches all over the Empire. There are fifty extant works ascribed to Aristides. In his panegyric address *To Rome*, he gives heartfelt thanks and praise for the peace and unity that Rome had brought to the Mediterranean world so that it had become, in effect, one city. His *Sacred Discourses* records dreams that he attributed to the healing god Asclepius. It provides a valuable look at practices associated with the cult of Asclepius (see Box 26.1) and the religious experience of an educated pagan.

26.1 INCUBATION CULTS

The Romans frequently sought aid or advice from their gods through prayers, offerings, and sacrifices. The gods often responded, sometimes through signs in the natural world (like lightning strikes or flooding rivers) and sometimes through direct appearances. Gods were thought to reveal themselves to mortals both in broad daylight and at night in dreams. While dream-epiphanies could happen no matter where the worshiper slept, sanctuaries belonging to certain gods, Asclepius most famous among them, offered a service called incubation (from the Latin *incubare*, "to lie in") where the worshiper could, after offering prayers and making a request, spend the night at the temple in hopes that the god would deliver advice or, in the case of Asclepius who specialized in medical matters, a cure in a dream. Inscriptions from numerous cult sites around the Roman world reveal that sometimes Asclepius would perform a medical procedure (even surgery) in the dream, and the worshiper would wake up cured. Other times, he would speak to the dreamer, delivering a prescription or a regimen of diet and exercise to be followed upon waking.

Dio Chrysostom (ca. 40 to ca. 115 C.E.)

The best representatives of the Second Sophistic were popular philosophical lecturers who earnestly communicated moral lessons to a wide audience. The most noteworthy is Dio Chrysostom (Golden-mouthed) from Prusa in Bithynia. His message was a mild blend of Stoicism and Cynicism that stressed honesty and simple virtues.

CHRISTIAN WRITERS

Chrysostom traveled the Empire and propagated what he believed were the best values of his civilization. Others were spreading a new religion. Although they and Chrysostom shared the values of their common Greco-Roman heritage, they would eventually transform that heritage into something quite different. Their best-known works are the four canonical Gospels ascribed to Matthew, Mark, Luke, and John and the missionary letters either written by the Apostle Paul or ascribed to him. They make up the bulk of the Christian New Testament. The Gospel writers sought to preserve the memory and message of Christ's life and teachings as they understood them. The Pauline letters form the intellectual foundation of much basic Christian theology.

Yet there were many other notable Christian writers. The most famous were Ignatius of Antioch (50–107 C.E.), the first great ecclesiastic and the father of Christian orthodoxy; Irenaeus of Lyons (ca. 130–202 C.E.), the powerful advocate of Christian unity, denunciator of heresy, and father of systematic theology; and Tatian "the Assyrian" (ca. 120–172 C.E.). The latter's *Life of Christ*, in Syriac, was a harmonized version of the four canonical Gospels. It was read in Syrian churches for almost three centuries. As Christians began to experience persecutions, Christian writers glorified and exalted the martyrs in works called *martyrologies* to inspire the living. The earliest such martyrology was the account of Polycarp's martyrdom at Smyrna (Izmir) on the coast of Asia Minor, probably in 155/156.

PHILOSOPHY

Hellenistic Greek philosophers like Panaetius and Posidonius had adapted Stoicism to the attitudes and needs of the Romans (pp. 334–5). Stoics, along with the Cynics, were the only philosophers to retain any vigor during the first two centuries C.E. Neither Greek nor Roman practitioners, however, broke any new ground in this period. Their efforts were directed mainly at popularizing and preaching the accepted doctrines of duty, self-control, and virtue as its own reward.

Seneca had expounded on numerous Stoic themes under Claudius and Nero (p. 479). Yet, his essays did not have so wide an impact in their day as the public lectures of his contemporary Gaius Musonius Rufus (ca. 30–ca. 100 C.E.). Rufus suffered banishment twice, first under Nero, after the abortive conspiracy of Piso (p. 433), and again under Vespasian's crackdown on Stoic opponents (p. 447). Many later Stoics were pupils of Rufus. The most notable was the lame Greek ex-slave Epictetus (55–135 C.E.). He suffered with Rufus under Nero and was banished by Domitian. During his exile, he taught at Nicopolis, across the Adriatic from Italy. He attracted a large following and heavily influenced Marcus Aurelius (p. 469). He did not write anything, but his teachings survive in Arrian's *Enchiridion* and *Diatribes*. He emphasized the benevolence of the Creator and the brotherhood of man. He believed that happiness depends on controlling one's own will and accepting whatever Divine Providence in its wisdom might require one to endure. These teachings of Epictetus and the *Meditations* of Marcus Aurelius have significantly influenced later Western ethical thought over many centuries.

GENERAL RELIGIOUS TRENDS

Stoicism, however, did not have such a widespread effect on the first and second centuries as did developments in religion. Augustus' renewal of traditional Roman cults, rituals, and festivals had greatly influenced the religious calendars of many other cities. Throughout the Empire, local cults were assimilated into parallel cults of the Roman pantheon. Thus, Roman paganism took on the appearance of an international religion. Each emperor took his duties as *pontifex maximus* seriously, and emperor worship grew steadily. Many people kept shrines of the emperor in their houses.

More significant was the impact of a centralized imperial state that increasingly controlled people's affairs. Individuals sought access to divine powers to achieve some sense of control over their lives and destinies. Oracles, omens, and portents were eagerly sought and studied. Astrology was popular within both the upper and lower classes.

Miracle workers who claimed to have access to divine powers found eager following. Under Nero and the Flavians, for example, the Cappadocian Apollonius of Tyana achieved great popularity as a sage and healer, so much so that Domitian banished him from Rome. After his death, he was worshiped with his own cult for a long time.

Under Antoninus Pius, another popular healer and purveyor of oracles was Alexander of Abonuteichos from Paphlagonia (Bithynia). He established a mystery cult that influenced a number of prominent Romans, including Fronto, the tutor of Marcus Aurelius. It, too, continued to exist after his death.

In a universal empire ruled by a powerful central monarch, the traditional local gods and cults were bound to seem diminished in power or not completely adequate. Moreover, the greater mobility of the population also weakened traditional religious ties among cosmopolitan urban populations. Therefore, gods that could claim some more universal power or appeal became prominent features of popular religion.

JUDAISM

One such deity who attracted considerable favorable attention in the cities of the early Empire was the god of the Jews. Pompey the Great had inadvertently aided the spread of Judaism to the western provinces in the late Republic (p. 333). There was occasional unwelcome attention from authorities in Rome itself, where foreign cults were often treated with suspicion. Still, Jewish communities grew and even attracted converts before the Jewish revolt from 66 to 70. Those unwilling to convert and undergo circumcision or observe other strictures of the Mosaic Law were called "God fearers." After 70, the destruction of the Temple, the elimination of the high priesthood, and the forced payment of the Temple tax to the pagan Jupiter Capitolinus permanently alienated many Jews. The disastrous revolts under Trajan and Hadrian resulted in severe restrictions on Judaism. The growth of Christianity (aided, ironically, by the earlier spread of Judaism) made the god of the Hebrew Covenant (Old Testament) more accessible to gentiles through the New Covenant (New Testament). Judaism then became limited largely to those born to it.

MYSTERY CULTS

Universalized mystery cults whose initiates received assurances of a better future became very popular. Among them were numerous Dionysiac cults. The initiation procedures of one such cult are vividly portrayed in a series of wall paintings at Pompeii in the Villa of the Mysteries. The cult of Demeter at the Athenian suburb of Eleusis attracted initiates from all over the Empire, one of whom was Emperor Hadrian.

Isis

Alongside traditional Greco-Roman mystery cults, Eastern mystery religions were growing with missionary zeal. The secret nature of their activities and the details of their beliefs (hence the label "mystery cults") and the complete victory of their

Christian rivals later on make information about them sketchy at best. Still, a few basic facts are known. Participants in the cult of Isis and her male counterpart, Serapis, followed a few simple rules of conduct and received promises of happiness in this world, if not the next. Worshippers also gained psychological satisfaction and a sense of community from direct participation in elaborate, emotionally charged rituals.

In 58 B.C.E., the senate had banned the worship of Isis from the city of Rome in the tense political atmosphere surrounding the issue of restoring Ptolemy Auletes to the throne of Egypt (p. 283). Her worshipers must have been back before 28 B.C.E., when Augustus banned Egyptian rites within the *pomerium*, Rome's sacred boundary. Tiberius banned the cult of Isis from the whole city in 19 C.E. Caligula, however, finally provided a public temple for her in the Campus Martius, and Domitian piously rebuilt it (p. 440). A major cult that had spread to every corner of the Empire could not be kept out of the center any longer.

Mithraism

Eventually, the Persian god Mithras also became popular in Rome. In Persian Zoroastrianism, Mithras was a god of light and truth. He aided Ahura-Mazda, the power of good, in an eternal struggle with Ahriman, the evil power. Mithras was closely associated with the sun god, an important ally of Ahura-Mazda, and he is sometimes identified as the sun. Among Mithras' divine accomplishments, the most celebrated was the capture and slaying of a bull. From its body sprang other useful forms of life. This death and birth are a central element in the Mithraic mysteries. The bull connects Mithraism with the zodiac and important astronomical phenomena. The most common type of Mithraic cult statue shows Mithras performing the tauroctony, the slaying of the bull.

In another common representation, perhaps associated with the celebration of his birth on December 25 near the winter solstice, Mithras emerges from a stone sphere or egg. The typical Mithraic temple, Mithraeum, was an artificial subterranean cave that may have symbolized death and the grave from which initiates were reborn to a better life. First, however, initiates had to be initiated with a bath in the blood of a sacrificed bull (the *taurobolium*) and complete certain ordeals. Among them seems to have been a simulated murder. Mithraism also involved a sacramental meal and imposed a strong moral code.

Archaeological evidence indicates that the Hellenized cult of Mithras found more favor in Ostia, Rome, and parts of the western provinces than in the eastern region where it originated. Restricted almost exclusively to men, the cult emphasized honesty, duty, and heroic valor in the face of evil and danger. It appealed particularly to merchants, skilled artisans, civil servants, soldiers, and sailors. It did not attract much following among either slaves or the elite classes of the Empire. Under the Flavians, Mithraism spread especially among the military camps and outposts along the Rhine and Danube. In the second and third centuries, western soldiers carried it to more scattered locations throughout the Empire.

Each Mithraeum usually represented a small self-governing group of only thirty to seventy-five men. Therefore, the numbers of initiates were always relatively small.

Mithraism's communal nature is seen in the lack of a professional Mithraic priesthood or any large institutional organization. Each initiate had to pass through seven stages or gates to reach the highest level of knowledge and spiritual awareness that would free him from the mundane forces that threatened his soul. Those in the higher stages mentored those below, and those who reached the highest stage became "fathers" who guided the particular group.

CHRISTIANITY

Christianity combined the appealing characteristics of many mystery religions: a loving, divine savior in Jesus, who overcame the forces of evil and death; a benevolent mother figure in the Virgin Mary; the promise of a blessed future; a sense of belonging to a special community in an era when local values and civic institutions were losing force in the face of a distant central government. In this third aspect, however, Christianity greatly surpassed the rest. The requirements of a strict moral code and, in keeping with its Jewish roots, the rejection of all other gods increased the Christians' sense of specialness. Furthermore, Christ's injunction to "love one another" resulted in charitable activities within Christian congregations that increased the feelings of fellowship and communal identity.

Organization and the spread of Christianity

As did other new cults, Christianity spread first to the major urban centers along the trade routes of the Empire. Paul and the earliest missionaries often found their first converts among the local Jews and "God fearers" when they arrived in a new city. That often caused conflict with local Jewish leaders. Such conflict sometimes aroused the hostility of Roman authorities.

During the first century C.E., individual Christian communities established a local system of clergy and leaders—deacons and deaconesses (servants), presbyters (elders), and bishops (overseers)—who ministered to the needs of their congregations, established policies, and regulated activities. Later, missionaries were sent out under the direction of these larger centers and established churches in the smaller surrounding communities. The urban bishops were the ones who coordinated this expansion and naturally came to exercise great influence and authority.

By the end of the second century, the bishops of the major cities were recognized as the heads of whole networks of churches in their regions. Furthermore, because of the strong sense of Christian brotherhood, the bishops and various churches regularly corresponded with each other to provide mutual support in the face of difficulties. In this way, they also ensured that local practices and beliefs conformed to the authoritative accepted teachings of Jesus and his disciples.

It is significant that Jesus's immediate disciples or the Apostle Paul had founded the earliest Christian churches. These early foundations were seen as direct historical links with the words and deeds of Jesus himself through the apostolic succession of their bishops. Churches founded in the generation after Paul and the disciples naturally looked to the apostolic churches for guidance and authoritative teachings. They wished to confirm that they were proceeding in accordance with the words and spirit of Christ's teachings, which they considered imperative for obtaining salvation. Therefore, the bishops of the apostolic churches, especially in the four major cities of Rome, Jerusalem, Alexandria, and Antioch, achieved great respect and authority. Often they were able to impose their will on the lesser churches, so that Christianity reached a degree of organizational and doctrinal unity matched by no other religion in the ancient Mediterranean world.

This emerging universal (Catholic) organization was challenged in the mid-second century by the Marcionite Christians, followers of Marcion, the wealthy son of an Eastern bishop. Marcion taught that the stern creator god of the Hebrew Bible (Old Testament) was not the same as the better, merciful god of the New Testament. He rejected the human incarnation of Christ. He saw Jesus as a manifestation of the merciful god in human form, not flesh. Marcion also emphasized an ascetic faith as the path to salvation. Persecution under pagan emperors and Constantine in the third and fourth centuries weakened the Marcionite Christian Church. Marcionites survived, however, for hundreds of years in the East until Manichaeism (pp. 550–1) absorbed many of them.

Diverse appeal of Christianity

Another factor that helped the spread of early Christianity was its openness and appeal to all classes and both sexes. Women were not excluded from or segregated within it. In fact, Paul and the early missionaries never would have succeeded without the heavy financial and moral support of numerous women such as those commemorated in the Book of Acts and the Pauline letters. In the early Church, deacons and deaconesses shared in ministering to the congregations. Moreover, the simple ceremonies and the grace-giving rites of baptism and communion posed no expensive obstacles to the poor. Indeed, Christ's teachings praised the poor and the humble and made their lot more bearable by encouraging the practice of charity toward them in the present and promising them a better life in the future.

On the other hand, basing Christianity on written works—such as the Jewish Scriptures, the four Gospels, and the sophisticated Pauline letters—gave it an appeal to the educated upper class as well. Converts from this class provided the trained thinkers and writers who established a tradition of Christian apologetics aimed at counteracting popular misconceptions about Christians and official hostility toward them. Justin Martyr, who went from Flavia Neapolis (Nablus) in Palestine to establish a Christian school in Rome, addressed just such a defense of Christianity to Antoninus Pius and Marcus Aurelius.

Persecution of Christians

The Christians needed to defend themselves from attack for two reasons. Their rigid monotheistic rejection of other gods and their refusal to participate in traditional activities with their pagan neighbors were an offense to those around them and bred personal hostility toward them. This hostility was fed by the normal human fear of the unfamiliar. Accordingly, people were quick to blame Christians for all manner of misfortunes that befell them individually or collectively. Frequently, they denounced Christians to Roman officials for their "crimes." Moreover, Roman authorities had always been suspicious of secret societies and feared that they were plotting against the state. This fear seemed borne out in the Christians' case. They refused to propitiate the gods who were believed to protect the state and would not perform the required ceremonies before the image of the emperor.

During the first two centuries, most of the persecutions and resultant martyrdoms were the consequences of purely local personal and political tensions. By the beginning of the second century, Christianity had become widespread in the eastern provinces, and local agitation against it was frequent. Pliny the Younger faced such a situation when he was governor of Bithynia-Pontus. Emperor Trajan wrote Pliny that there should be no organized hunt for Christians or acceptance of anonymous accusations. He insisted, however, that those fairly accused and convicted of being Christians be executed unless they renounced their faith and sacrificed to the gods. Hadrian insisted that accusations against Christians had to stand up under strict legal procedures or be dismissed. Although he disliked them, Marcus Aurelius himself did not actively promote the persecution of Christians. Neither did he punish governors who yielded to popular pressure and condemned Christians to torture and death (p. 469). The result of the individual martyrdoms in the first and second centuries was to strengthen the resolve of the faithful and impress thoughtful non-Christians. The latter were often moved to convert by the heroic examples of martyrs.

ROMAN ARCHITECTURE IN THE FIRST TWO CENTURIES C.E.

Architecture was a very creative aspect of Roman imperial culture in the first two centuries C.E. Augustus had used the resources of the state for building projects far more than ever before. His example was followed and enlarged upon by most succeeding emperors during this period. With the resources thus made available, architects found no end of opportunities to use their creative talents.

Imperial palaces

Each emperor had to have his own splendid residence on the Palatine, or at least he had to add to that of his predecessor. Nero, of course, took advantage of the fire of 64 to construct his extravagant Golden House, an architectural achievement of the first order. It covered an area twice as large as that of the Vatican today (p. 432). Vespasian destroyed Nero's palace and built a smaller one on the Palatine to symbolize the beginning of a new order. Vespasian's sons, especially Domitian, continued to enlarge this new palace until it, too, became a huge complex, the Domus August[i]ana, that destroyed or buried many older buildings beneath its foundations. Its remains are visible on the Palatine today.

FIGURE 26.1   The Colosseum (Coliseum), or Flavian Amphitheater.

Emperor Hadrian was an innovative architect and designed a splendid villa near Tibur (Tivoli), about eighteen miles east of Rome. It surpassed Nero's Golden House in complexity of design, and much of it remains. What is most striking about the whole complex is the imaginative combination of different geometric shapes—curves, octagons, rectangles, and squares—to create new visual effects.

Flavian and Trajanic public buildings

Augustus' Julio-Claudian successors did not contribute greatly to the public architecture of Rome. The Flavians, on the other hand, introduced a dynamic era of public construction (plan, p. 390). Vespasian completed a temple of the Deified Claudius and began the great complex named the Temple of Peace (in commemoration of the end of the Jewish revolt), also called the Forum of Vespasian, near the Forum of Augustus and the original Forum. The actual temple faced a great colonnaded square and was flanked by rectangular halls that housed a library and, perhaps, some administrative functions.

Vespasian also began the monumental task of building the Colosseum (Coliseum), the Flavian Amphitheater as it was originally called. It arose on the site of Nero's demolished Golden House and received the name *Colosseum* from the nearby colossal bronze statue originally intended for the vestibule of the Golden House (p. 432). The Colosseum's remains stand today as a symbol of Roman imperial architecture, a massive structure showing a sophisticated blend of decorative styles and impressive engineering.

Titus continued work on the Colosseum and started to build the baths named for him over another part of the Golden House. Titus also began a temple to his father at the northwestern end of the old Forum and the arch that still bears his name at the top of the Via Sacra (Sacred Way) leading to the Forum (p. 441). Domitian completed the Colosseum and his brother's projects and built a new stadium, with seats for 30,000 in the Campus Martius. It remained one of the city's most famous structures for centuries. The length of the arena was about 750 feet, and its shape and size are preserved by the modern Piazza Navona. Between Vespasian's forum and those of Augustus and Julius Caesar, Domitian constructed a narrow forum with a temple of Minerva at its northeast end. It is called the Forum Transitorium or the Forum of Nerva, who dedicated it after Domitian's death.

Before being assassinated, Domitian had also begun to construct what came to be called the Forum of Trajan and the Markets of Trajan, who extensively redesigned them. Trajan's forum is the largest of the imperial fora, and its remains are still impressive. It was to the northwest of Augustus' forum, and its southern corner bordered the northern corner of Caesar's in order to complete Caesar's original plan of providing a connection from the republican Forum to the Campus Martius. The base of the Quirinal Hill had to be cut back to make room for its enormous design. The main feature was a great basilica to house law courts. Behind the basilica, two libraries (one Latin and one Greek, as was customary) faced each other. In the midst of the courtyard between them stood one of Rome's most remarkable monuments, the column of Trajan. After Trajan's death, Hadrian built a magnificent temple to the Deified Trajan and Trajan's wife, Plotina, on the open side of this courtyard so that the whole area had an architectural balance.

Across a street running along the outside of the forum's northeast wall was a complex known today as the Market(s) of Trajan. It ran several stories up the side of the Quirinal. Instead of housing markets, it probably contained the offices of those who handled the daily business of the Empire.

Hadrian's public buildings

In Rome, Hadrian was primarily concerned with rebuilding and restoring what already existed, but he was responsible for the construction of three unique projects that epitomize the way that Roman imperial architecture combined disparate forms and styles into structures that are both massive and interesting. The first was the largest temple in Rome—the Temple of Venus Felix and Roma Aeterna—between the Colosseum and the Temple of Peace (Forum of Vespasian). It was really two temples back to back. In the back of each was a seated statue, one of Venus and one of Roma. This arrangement took advantage of a convenient Latin pun: Venus is the goddess of love, *amor* in Latin, which is the name of Rome, *Roma*, spelled backward. Only its foundations remain, however. The emperor Maxentius rebuilt the temple with back-to-back apses in the early fourth century.

Hadrian's most famous building is the Pantheon, Temple of All the Gods. A Christian church since 609, it is the best-preserved ancient building in Rome today. It is the perfect example of the imaginative combination of shapes and forms that distinguishes Roman imperial architecture. The front presents the columned and pedimented facade of a Classical Greek temple. This facade may preserve the lines and dedicatory

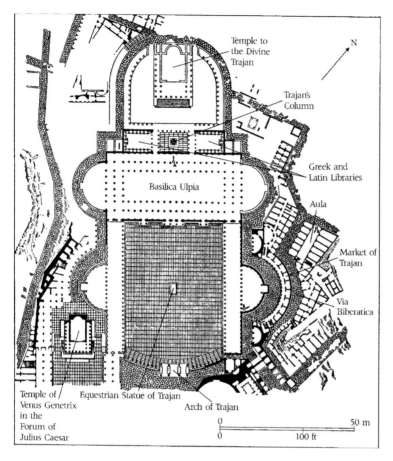

Temple to
the Divine
Trajan

N

Trajan's
Column

Greek and
Latin Libraries

Basilica Ulpia

Aula

Market of
Trajan

Via
Biberatica

Temple of
Venus Genetrix
in the
Forum of
Julius Caesar

Equestrian Statue of Trajan

Arch of Trajan

0   50 m

0   100 ft

FIGURE 26.2   Plan of Trajan's Forum, with Basilica Ulpia, Rome.

inscription of the original Pantheon, built by Augustus' colleague Marcus Agrippa, but it and the rest are almost completely the work of Hadrian's builders.

The conventional facade joins a huge domed cylinder that is the temple proper. Thus, the rectilinear is uniquely combined with the curvilinear. This theme is carried out further in the rectangular receding coffers sunk in the curved ceiling of the dome, in the marble squares and circles of the floor, and in the alternating rectangular and curved niches around the wall of the drum. Moreover, the globe and the cylinder are combined because the diameter of the drum is the same as the distance from the floor to the top of the dome, so that if the curve of the dome were extended, it would be tangent with the floor and wall of the drum. Finally, the whole building is lighted by a round opening, the *oculus* (eye), about thirty feet in diameter in the top of the dome. This hole is open to the weather, but because of its great height, most moisture evaporates before it reaches the floor during a rain.

FIGURE 26.3 Front view of Hadrian's Pantheon, with an inscription from Agrippa's earlier building.

The dome exemplifies how Roman engineers took advantage of the properties of concrete, whose use the Romans greatly advanced. To reduce the dome's weight, progressively less dense material was used in the concrete as the dome rose, and the dome was made thinner as it neared the top. The recessed coffers reduced the weight still further and created a grid of structural ribs. Once the concrete set, the dome was a solid, jointless mass of exceptional stability, as its survival for 1900 years testifies.

Across the Tiber, there arose another architectural marvel of the age—Hadrian's tomb—a colossal round mausoleum over 200 feet in diameter. It eventually held the bodies of Hadrian, his successors through Caracalla, and a number of their family members. In the Middle Ages that massive structure long served as a fortress and was known as the Castel Sant' Angelo, a name it still bears. After Hadrian, the pace of building in second-century Rome slackened considerably.

ARCHITECTURE IN THE PROVINCES

A fine example of imperial architecture and planning in a smaller town is Thamugadi (Timgad), a colony established by Trajan for veterans in North Africa. It was laid out on a grid of broad, intersecting main streets and side streets. The main streets were colonnaded, and other amenities, including a large Greek-style theater, baths, and a well-appointed forum, were provided. By 200 C.E., 12,000 to 15,000 people dwelt there in comfort and security.

SCULPTURE

The Roman tradition of realistic portraits and statues continued through the second century C.E., as can be seen in the busts of the various emperors. The best example is the bronze statue of Marcus Aurelius mounted on a horse, the single bronze equestrian statue to have survived from antiquity (p. 472). Panels of sculptured relief in the tradition of Augustus' Ara Pacis (p. 392) constituted one of the most common forms of official art. In the courtyard behind the Basilica Ulpia, however, Trajan set up a completely new kind of relief to commemorate his Dacian wars. It is a column about twelve feet in diameter and exactly one hundred Roman feet (about ninety-seven English feet) high. Around this column winds a spiral relief depicting the wars themselves. The vast and complex logistical, engineering, and military aspects of the wars are portrayed in a realistically detailed narrative that leads dramatically to the death of King Decebalus. There are some 2500 separate figures, but through it all, Trajan is a unifying presence appearing over fifty times. The width of the spiral and size of the figures increase as they move upward to compensate for the greater viewing distance from the ground. A bronze statue of Trajan surmounted the top until it was replaced by one of St. Peter in 1588. The large pedestal on which the column rests was Trajan's mausoleum.

Marcus Aurelius imitated Trajan's column with one of his own in the Campus Martius. Its dimensions are the same, and it has a spiral relief depicting the Second Marcomannic War (172–175). Artistically, however, this relief is very different from Trajan's. The realistic details of scenery are omitted, there is no attempt at three-dimensional spatial relationships, and there is no unified, dramatic narrative sequence. There is constant motion and striving, almost chaos. Through it all, however, Marcus Aurelius stands out. He is not merely part of the action. He repeatedly faces outward and dominates the viewer's attention to become a solid, powerful presence in the midst of all the confused action. The details of mundane reality are sacrificed to present the viewer directly with the essence of the emperor's role in events. This style approaches the "otherworldly" art of the late Empire and the Middle Ages.

FIGURE 26.4   City of Thamugadi (Timgad).

PAINTING

Most of what is known of Roman painting in the first two centuries C.E. comes from the wall paintings found at Pompeii, Herculaneum, and other sites buried by the eruption of Vesuvius in 79 during Titus' reign. These frescoes are the work of artists and craftsmen adapting or copying on plaster the works of great masters or following standardized decorative scenes according to the tastes of their customers. Pleasant or romantic landscapes, still lifes, and scenes from famous myths or epics abound.

Decorators set off these scenes by painting the surrounding wall in an architectural style. From roughly 14 to 62, the Third (Egyptianizing) Style was most popular. Instead of creating the illusion of depth, the painters used painted architectural forms to provide a flat frame within which the picture could be featured. After 62, the Fourth (Ornamental) Style prevailed: perspective is heavily used to give the illusion of infinite depth behind the wall, and there is great flamboyance in the design of the architectural forms. They often resemble stage sets, are weighed down with intricate detail to the point of looking like baroque fantasies, and probably show the influence of Nero's tastes, which can be seen in the surviving decorations from his Golden House.

MOSAICS, COINS, AND MEDALLIONS

Numerous mosaics from the first two centuries C.E. are found all over the Empire, especially in the villas of North Africa. They are very valuable documents for social and economic life. They also exhibit remarkable taste and workmanship. The coins and medallions of this period are among the finest in history. The art of medal engraving was stimulated by Hadrian's issue of a series of bronze medallions. They reveal a love of symbolism and allegory and reached a level of skill and technique comparable to that of the most beautiful coinages in the ancient world.

SOCIAL DEVELOPMENTS

As already seen, the composition of the Roman upper class changed over the first two centuries because emperors recruited administrators from the local Italian and provincial elites as loyal counterweights to the old republican senatorial families of Rome. Members of those families were understandably resentful. After the purges of Nero and Domitian, however, most of the old republican noble families had disappeared.

Upper-class women

In the early Empire, there was a concerted attempt to "put women back in their place." This attempt was reinforced by widespread Roman exposure to Classical Greek literature and philosophy, which tended to view women with a certain amount of anxiety, hostility, and insistence on their inherent inferiority. This view is paramount in the sixth satire of Juvenal (p. 484). Earlier, Augustus' marriage legislation had tried to make women conform to the ideal of virtuous wife and mother. Still, women of the

FIGURE 26.5   Frescoed walls (ca. 60–79 C.E.) of a room from the house of the Vettii, rich wine merchants of Pompeii.

imperial family and upper classes carried on the late Republic's tradition of actively involved women who strove to pursue their own and their families' agendas. Augustus' ex-wife Scribonia and his last wife, Livia, are prime examples. Mothers and wives of emperors were often depicted on coins and deified or otherwise honored to advertise their family connections and exalt their sons and husbands. Inscriptions and statues honored women throughout the provinces for their civic benefactions and numerous other women for accomplishments as athletes, musicians, and physicians.

Despite old biases and hostility, the legal rights of women improved in step with social reality. In 126, Hadrian liberalized women's right to make wills. Marcus Aurelius made it legal for mothers, not just fathers, to inherit from children.

The lower classes

Unfortunately, the poor and the powerless, male and female, in any society seldom see dramatic improvements in their overall conditions. Still, the lot of lower-class citizens, freedpersons, provincials, and slaves improved somewhat over the first two centuries C.E. in comparison with the first century B.C.E. The general internal peace and prosperity of the period fostered traditional upper-class patronage and euergetism. Life became a little more secure and less desperate for the great mass of people. Almost all of the emperors tried to alleviate real hardship. They made great efforts to secure a stable grain supply for Rome in order to sustain those who received free grain and keep the price affordable for the rest. The urban poor also benefited from the emperors' efforts to improve flood control, housing conditions, and the water supply and to upgrade public sanitation through the construction of public latrines and baths. In many of the great provincial cities, wealthy local benefactors undertook similar projects.

At least in Italy, children outside of Rome benefited from private charitable endowments and the *alimenta* of Trajan and his successors, but girls always received less per capita than boys. In the provinces, the emperors' attempts to provide efficient and honest administration must have kept the peasantry from being exploited so mercilessly as they often had been. It would be naive, however, to think that all imperial officials acted as scrupulously as they were supposed to.

Some well-educated Greek slaves and freed slaves in the imperial household had impressive careers. Narcissus, Callistus, Polybius, and Pallas are notable under Claudius (p. 423). The freedwoman Claudia Acte was an important figure in the Emperor Claudius' household. She became Seneca's confidante as well as Nero's mistress. She acquired great wealth in land and slaves and remained loyal to Nero even after he married Poppaea Sabina.

One of the most interesting freedwomen in Roman history is Antonia Caenis. She was Antonia the Younger's confidential secretary. Surviving Caligula's reign, she served both Claudius and Nero. She became the mistress of the rising young officer Vespasian until he married. Still, she continued to advance his career in court circles. They resumed their relationship after his wife died. She lived with him in the palace until she died.

Some freedpersons from less exalted households also became very wealthy. Others practiced middle-class trades and professions, and still others existed at the poverty level. All remained second-class citizens despite being eligible for honorific posts such as *Augustalis* (p. 358).

It is difficult to know the effect of humane legislation by Hadrian and Antoninus Pius on the treatment of slaves (p. 464 and 467). Manumissions were still frequent, as the innumerable funerary inscriptions of freedpersons prove. Augustus' attempt to reduce manumissions by taxing them and limiting the number of slaves that a master could free in his will had a limited effect. Regardless of more enlightened attitudes on the part of some, slaves were still subject to torture as witnesses, and if a slave killed a master, all of his slaves could be punished by death.

Middle-class prosperity and urban growth

Under the general peace and stability within the Empire during the first two centuries C.E., the wealth of the Empire rose dramatically. People of moderate means or possessed of talent, enterprise, and good luck prospered to an extent never known before (and only again in recent times). Increased incomes gave rise to an unprecedented urge to travel, which was further encouraged by the construction of a huge network of excellent roads. Greater prosperity was reflected in the rebuilding of old cities, the colonization of new sites, and the growth of important settlements around major military camps on the frontiers. A traveler in Asia Minor, North Africa, Spain, or Gaul would see familiar-looking temples, theaters, libraries, baths, and fine homes everywhere.

ECONOMIC TRENDS

The growth of Rome and other cities continued to stimulate imperial agriculture, industry, and commerce, but Italy declined as a center of production in relation to the provinces as the products of farm and shop moved freely over land and sea. Foreign trade steadily expanded.

Agriculture

In the eastern provinces, the establishment of peace and better administration after the end of Rome's civil wars ultimately promoted the revival of agriculture, which continued to be dominated by smallholders. Agriculture in the western provinces expanded to supply the huge Roman market. On the other hand, provincial competition hurt small, marginal producers in Italy. Their decline led to the creation of far-flung holdings known as *latifundia* (p. 176). Smallholders gave up their land to large operators and became tenant farmers, *coloni*, in return for a fixed share of their crops. *Latifundia* began to appear even in the great grain-growing regions of North Africa, Sicily, and Gaul.

Mining and manufacturing

The creation of stable frontiers and the construction of great roads, harbors, and canals throughout the Empire also opened up new sources of raw materials and encouraged the spread of manufacturing. The production of lead ingots and pig iron was of major importance in Britain. Tin, copper, and silver continued to be important in Spain. The gold mines of the new province of Dacia were vigorously exploited.

In the East, the old manufacturing centers flourished. The workshops of Egypt and Syria produced papyrus, blown glass, textiles, purple dye, and leather goods. Asia Minor supplied marble, pottery, parchment, carpets, and cloth.

In the West, the Italian producers of glass, pottery, and bronze wares sent their products far and wide during the first century. Then they went into decline as provincial centers, especially in Gaul and the Rhineland, took over their export markets during the second. In the first century, Lugdunum (Lyons) in Gaul became the center of the western glass industry, although the second century saw Colonia Agrippina (Cologne) in Germany replace it. *Terra sigillata*, the famous red dinnerware with raised decorations from Arretium in Italy (p. 386), was successfully imitated by Gallic potters on a vast scale for western European markets. Even the famous bronze workers of Capua lost their western markets to Gaul's skilled craftsmen.

Imperial commerce

Once provincial farmers and craftsmen made products comparable to those of Italy, their proximity to local markets gave them an unbeatable advantage over Italian exporters. Also, compared with products from the interior of Italy, provincial products originating near the seacoast or on waterways often had better access to the lucrative markets of Rome and coastal Italian cities. For example, despite the wonderful network of imperial roads, it was still cheaper to ship an amphora of wine from Arelate (Arles) or Narbo in southern Gaul to Rome by sea than to transport one overland to Rome from only fifty miles away in Italy.

The same factors, however, sharply limited the potential for manufacturing and commerce in the provinces beyond the points achieved by the second century C.E. Only producers with easy access to water transport could profitably export. Moreover, the slowness of transportation and the lack of refrigeration or modern preservation techniques meant that only spoilage-resistant agricultural products or salted and pickled foods could be shipped long distances. Only expensive manufactured goods whose production was limited by the geographic location of raw materials or highly specialized craftsmen could be profitably exported over significant distances. Therefore, the market for such goods was limited to the well-to-do. The mass of people either had to do without or settle for inferior locally manufactured imitations. As a result, most manufacturing tended to remain small and localized, and large-scale commerce was limited.

Foreign commerce

Because of the greater distances involved, commerce beyond the imperial frontiers was limited to high-value goods. Still, the increase that did occur in imperial prosperity stimulated the demand for foreign luxuries and the exploration of foreign trade routes. Traders traveled north along the coast of Germany and to the Baltic islands in search of amber and furs for Roman markets. Over 4000 Roman coins have been found on the Swedish island of Gotland alone. During the first century, the Parthians had forced diversion of the Chinese silk trade south to India, whence it proceeded by ship to Red Sea ports. By the end of the century, however, Greek and Syrian merchants were making regular contact with silk caravans from China at Bactra (Balkh in north-central Afghanistan) and later, under Hadrian or Antoninus, a little farther east at Tashkurgan (Stone Tower).

By the beginning of the first century, Greek merchants had penetrated overland through Bactra to the Punjab. Since the time of Augustus, merchant fleets had also sailed between southern Arabia and western India for perfumes, gems, spices, and cotton cloth (p. 373). Finds of Roman coins and pieces of *terra sigillata* pottery indicate that in the early first century Roman goods were transshipped across the southern tip of India from places like Muziris (Cranganore) on the west side to places like Arikamedu near Pondicherry (ancient Poduke?) on the east side (map, p. 375). By the second half of the century, some sailors had braved the dangerous passage around the southern tip to Tabrobane (Ceylon, Sri Lanka) and eventually made their way up to the Bay of Bengal and perhaps to Indochina as far east as Hanoi. In 166, a group even paid court to the Chinese Emperor Huan-ti at Loyang, far up the Hwang-ho (Yellow River), to talk about setting up regular trade by sea with the West. In the long run, however, little was accomplished.

There was also trade with non-Roman Africa. During the first century, merchants traded along the Somali coast for frankincense. During the second, they may have gone as far south as Zanzibar and Mozambique in search of ivory. Explorers even penetrated inland to the sources of the Nile in lakes Victoria and Albert. From the sub-Saharan regions through Fezzan in North Africa, there was a brisk trade in exotic animals for the innumerable games at Rome and many other cities.

INHERENT ECONOMIC AND FISCAL WEAKNESS OF THE ROMAN EMPIRE

Despite the real economic growth of the first two centuries C.E., serious underlying weaknesses are visible as early as the time of Nero. They limited the Empire's economic potential and contributed to a long-term decline beginning in the third century (pp. 542–4). For example, foreign luxuries were often purchased with silver and gold coins. The elder Pliny complained that under Nero the Indian trade alone drew off 60 million sesterces a year, whereas the rest of the Eastern trade took another 40 million. In the second century, the deficit may have been reduced by the export of some manufactured goods, such as bronze and tin goods, dinnerware, blown glass, woolen cloth, and even rewoven silk. Nevertheless, the most prized Roman products were the Empire's fine coins, and the constant drain of precious metal eventually helped to undermine the stability of the monetary and fiscal systems.

Structural problems

Except for copper, brass, and bronze coins used for small change, the monetary system was based on the circulation of coins whose value was fixed largely by their actual content of precious metal. Credit, necessary to expand business, was severely limited by the amount of coinage in circulation. If coins were debased to sustain or increase the amount in circulation, prices eventually rose so that no long-term advantage was gained.

By the time of Nero, the productivity of the Spanish gold and silver mines was declining. That decline, the monetary drain caused by foreign trade, and Nero's own huge spending led his officials to reduce the metallic content of both gold and silver coins (pp. 542–5). Vespasian kept the weight of the Neronian denarius, but he significantly reduced the proportion of silver to about 85 percent. Titus further reduced it to 80 percent. Domitian tried to restore the Augustan level of 98 percent. Ultimately, he had to settle for 91 percent, just under the Neronian standard. Trajan's new silver *denarii* contained slightly less silver, 89 to 90 percent. The profit to the treasury from minting these coins was increased, but there was no inflationary impact on prices. They remained quite stable for the next fifty years. Indeed, the purchasing power of silver relative to gold increased when Trajan expanded the supply of gold by opening up the gold mines of Dacia to Roman exploitation. Then, under Marcus Aurelius, the output of gold and silver mines fell sharply, while plague and war put severe new strains on the economy. In spite of the large surplus that Antoninus Pius had reportedly left behind in the treasury, Marcus Aurelius found himself obliged both to sell the palace jewels and treasures and to debase the silver currency by raising its copper content to approximately 34 percent in order to finance the Danubian campaigns.

A greater problem lay in the very structure of Greco-Roman civilization. Its values, level of technological development, and economic goals were not conducive to producing the kind of dynamic growth in economic activity and productive technology that has allowed the modern world (so far) to meet challenges that the Roman Empire eventually could not overcome. The Greeks had an impressive record of achievement in theoretical science (natural philosophy) and mathematics. In the Hellenistic period, Archimedes (ca. 287–212 B.C.E.), Hero of Alexandria (?–ca. 150 B.C.E.), and others even invented many mechanical contrivances, such as the endless chain, the compound pulley, the lifting crane, and the reaction turbine. Still, people never systematically attempted to put these inventions to practical use to save labor, increase productive capacity, and build an industrial economy capable of bearing the financial load of a highly centralized bureaucratic state.

Some have seen the reason for this state of affairs in the heavy use of slave or dependent labor and the aristocratic contempt for ordinary work. Furthermore, formal ancient education reflected and perpetuated the attitudes of those who had little to do directly with economic production. The heavy emphasis in elite education on grammar, rhetoric, and abstract philosophy to the exclusion of practical science and technology was designed to produce jurists, administrators, orators, and cultured gentlemen. Except in medicine, mathematics, and astronomy, what would be considered scientific or technical training was mostly the passing along of practical knowledge in handbooks or orally from master craftsman to apprentice. Therefore, innovation occurred and spread slowly. Moreover, there was little incentive for innovation. There was no concept of intellectual property and patents, which would have allowed individuals to profit from new discoveries. The result was inefficient communications and transportation, poor productive techniques, and lack of labor-saving machinery in comparison with the modern Western world since the nineteenth century. Consequently, the Empire could not meet its greatly increased military needs and maintain a healthy civilian economy at the same time during the mounting crises after the second century. As a result, the third century produced a period of serious disruption.

SUGGESTED READING

Anderson, G. *The Second Sophistic: A Cultural Phenomenon in the Roman Empire*. London and New York: Routledge, 1993.

Clauss, M. *The Roman Cult of Mithras: The God and his Mysteries*. Translated by R. Gordon. New York: Routledge, 2000.

Fantham, E. *Roman Literary Culture From Cicero to Apuleius*. Baltimore: The Johns Hopkins University Press, 1996.

Mattern, S. P. *Prince of Medicine: Galen in the Roman World*. Oxford and New York: Oxford University Press, 2013.

CHAPTER 27

Conflicts and Crises under Commodus and the Severi, 180 to 235 C.E.

The third century C.E. in Roman history really began with the death of Marcus Aurelius in 180 and lasted a little more than hundred years until the accession of Diocletian in 284/285. It falls into two almost equal parts. The first extends from the death of Marcus Aurelius in 180 to the assassination of Severus Alexander in 235. During that time, the frontiers of the Empire remained well defended, although under pressure. Only two serious internal political crises arose: from 193 to early 197 and from 217 to 221. The century's second part stretches from 235 to the ultimate victory of Diocletian in 285. Frequent civil wars and assassinations saw the rapid rise and fall of twenty-six emperors or pretenders, constant breakthroughs on the borders, and the near breakup of the Empire under those two stresses and a devastating plague.

Despite the differences between the first and second parts of the third century, several political trends give it unity throughout. The city of Rome itself remained of great symbolic significance, but actual power shifted to the frontier provinces. Their defense demanded ever more attention. The growing importance of defense and the provinces is clearly illustrated by the fact that almost all of the third-century emperors were generals of provincial birth. Many came from the Danubian provinces, where the problems of defense were often acute and where many of the Empire's best soldiers were recruited.

The growing importance of the provinces and the parallel decline of Roman and Italian primacy also led to increasing regionalism, sectionalism, and disunity. Often the armies and inhabitants of one province or region would support their own claimant to the throne or oppose a challenger from another part. At times, some areas even broke away under their own emperors.

Defense and personal safety became the overriding concerns of emperors. Their office increasingly lost the characteristics of a civilian magistracy that it had retained since the days of Augustus. The Principate was becoming an absolute monarchy resting on raw military power and the trappings of divine kingship along Near Eastern and Hellenistic lines. Also, as the emperors tried to mobilize all the state's resources to meet its defensive needs, the bulk of its people sank into the status of suffering subjects instead of satisfied citizens. The wealthy and influential few, mainly senators and equestrians, were neutralized and co-opted by grants of greater social and legal privileges and lucrative posts in the imperial bureaucracy. The lower classes, however, paid harsher penalties than others for crimes and were subject to greater oppression in the name of the state. In better times, more benevolent or less desperate emperors had afforded them a measure of protection and dignity.

SOURCES FOR ROMAN HISTORY, 180 TO 285 C.E.

The lack of reliable written accounts makes the period from 180 to 285, especially after 235, difficult for historians. Cassius Dio's later and most valuable books (except 79 and 80), which covered his own times, are preserved only in epitomes and fragments. Valuable information about the period from 180 to 238 is contained in the eight extant books of Herodian's contemporary *History of the Empire after Marcus* in Greek and the *Historia Augusta*, probably from the late fourth century, in Latin. Unfortunately, Herodian's moralizing rhetoric sometimes reduces his reliability, and the biographies of emperors starting half-way through Elagabalus' reign (218–222) in the *Historia Augusta* are more romantic fiction than history. Minor relevant historical works from the fourth century include biographies like Aurelius Victor's *Caesares* and the anonymous *Epitome de Caesaribus* and brief histories of Rome like those of Eutropius and Rufius Festus (pp. 632–3). In the late fifth or early sixth century, Zosimus, a pagan Greek, covered events from 270 to 410 in an account called the *New History*. Unfortunately, the first of its six books is missing the section on Diocletian.

Sources written in Syriac, a dialect of Aramaic that was spoken in a region extending from Asia Minor to the Arabian peninsula, are increasingly important for the period. They include such secular writings as the *Letter of Mara bar Serapion* and several chronicles. Syriac Christian writings such as the *Oration of Meliton the Philosopher before Antoninus Caesar*, the *Acts of Thomas*, and several martyrologies are particularly valuable.

Greek and Latin Christian writers also became more numerous and important during the third century. They supply much information on the history and doctrinal controversies of the expanding Christian Church and on secular affairs as well. Among the Latin Christian authors, the most notable in this period are Tertullian and St. Cyprian (p. 559). Tertullian's works reveal much about the social life of the period. St. Cyprian's works are particularly valuable for the history of the persecution of Christians that occurred in the 250s. They also cover the Donatist controversy over Christians who denied their religion during the persecution and then wanted to be taken back by the faithful afterward. Also valuable for this period are St. Jerome's *De Viris Illustribus* (*On Famous Men*) and his translation and extension of Eusebius' *Chronicle* (p. 565).

Of the contemporary Greek Church Fathers, Clement of Alexandria and Origen stand out (p. 560). They document the growth of Christian theology and provide unusual glimpses into the pagan Greek mysteries that they combated. Eusebius of Caesarea in Palestine (ca. 260–ca. 340) produced two historical works that are valuable in reconstructing the third century. The original Greek version of his chronicle of events from Abraham to 327/328 C.E. is lost, but its substance is preserved in an Armenian translation and in Jerome's extended version. Fortunately, his *Ecclesiastical History*, an invaluable general account of the growth of the early Church in the Empire, is intact.

Justinian's codification and summary of the Civil Law (p. 675) preserves numerous fragments of third-century legal works. Together with coins, papyri, inscriptions, and archaeological material, they constitute the bulk of information about life in the third century. In particular, avid interest in local archaeology throughout countries once embraced by the Roman Empire has produced a better understanding of defensive policies and the social and economic conditions of the provinces.

COMMODUS (180 TO 192 C.E.)

Marcus Aurelius had done everything that he could to prepare his son and heir, Commodus, for his role as emperor and ensure a smooth transition of power. Commodus had been given the best teachers available, had been proclaimed a Caesar at age five, and had received a grant of *imperium*, a consulship, and the title *Augustus* at fifteen. From then on he was joint ruler with his father.

Aurelius had reasonably expected that after he died, his experienced advisors would continue to guide his young heir along the path that he had set. Unfortunately, sometimes the advisors disagreed. This dissonance eventually contributed to divisions and jealousies among members of the imperial family, military officers, and powerful senators. The consequences for Commodus' reign were disastrous. Some advisors, like T. Claudius Pompeianus, second husband of Commodus' sister Lucilla, wanted Commodus to finish his father's great war with the Quadi and the Marcomanni. Others, whether out of conviction or desire to advance in the new emperor's favor or both, advised him to negotiate a settlement and return to Rome. A negotiated settlement had much to recommend itself: the war had already placed a great strain on imperial resources. The Roman army had been weakened by plague. Although Aurelius' plans for a frontier based on the Elbe River and the Carpathian Mountains did have some strategic advantages over the longer Rhine–Danube line, it would have greatly extended the Empire's lines of supply through territory that would take a long time and many troops to pacify adequately.

Commodus sided with those who advised negotiation. Still, he kept up the military pressure for several months after Aurelius' death in order to obtain a peace in accordance with well-established Roman precedents. The Quadi, Marcomanni, and Iazyges agreed to surrender Roman deserters and captives, create a demilitarized zone along the Danube, furnish troops to the Roman army, and help feed that army with annual contributions of grain. This settlement was reasonable and produced stability along the Danube for many years.

A young emperor's problems

A newcomer who had great influence with Commodus was the palace chamberlain (*cubicularius*), a Bithynian Greek freedman, Saoterus. Not since Claudius and Nero had imperial freedmen enjoyed such public prominence as Commodus gave Saoterus. He seems to have generated the kind of resentment among the upper classes, particularly the senators, that the freedmen of those earlier emperors had incurred. For his part, Commodus was like the young emperors Caligula, Nero, and Domitian in that they, too, had also assumed the position of *princeps* without serious prior experience in working with senators. Commodus failed to appreciate how important it was to maintain the goodwill of these wealthy and influential men, who bitterly resented affronts to their *dignitas*. He did not understand that emperors needed at least to appear to share power with the senatorial elite if they wished to remain secure on their thrones.

Military men of senatorial rank were another problem. Marcus Aurelius had promoted a number of talented new men to the senate and major military commands during his long wars. They were eager for an opportunity to earn greater glory. Many were unhappy with Commodus' decision to abandon his father's expansionistic policy, which would have given them that chance.

The situation was made worse when Commodus' marriage failed to produce an heir. It tempted other people with some connection to the imperial family to try for the throne. They believed that they could gain support from those who disliked Commodus and also satisfy those who supported dynastic succession. Thus, several factors combined to create a deadly atmosphere of intrigue, fear, and suspicion that left an indelible mark on the surviving sources for Commodus' reign. These sources are undoubtedly biased and sensationalistic, but they still reflect serious underlying problems.

Lucilla: plots, power plays, and executions

As early as 182, a number of senators conspired with Commodus' sister Lucilla (Annia Aurelia Galeria Lucilla) to assassinate him. Her second husband, T. Claudius Pompeianus, whom she could not tolerate, was not one of them. Her daughter (by her first husband, Lucius Verus [pp. 469–70]) and two of her lovers were. One of those two was Quintianus. He was Claudius Pompeianus' nephew or son by a previous marriage and was engaged to her daughter. The other was Ummidius Quadratus. He was a relative of Marcus Aurelius by adoption and stepson of one of Commodus' other sisters. Quintianus bungled the assassination when he paused to proclaim that the senate was sending the dagger in his hand. Commodus' bodyguard grabbed him, and the plot failed.

All of the conspirators were arrested and executed, even Lucilla after she was briefly exiled on the Isle of Capri. Soon, suspicion also fell on Commodus' wife, Bruttia

Crispina, daughter of one of Aurelius' old advisors. Accused of adultery, she, too, was executed after a short exile on Capri. The innocent Claudius Pompeianus prudently retired from public life to avoid any suspicion of wanting to be emperor. Ironically, two members of Ummidius' household became close members of Commodus' court: the freedman Eclectus eventually became Commodus' chamberlain, and the freedwoman Marcia soon became his concubine.

Right after the failed coup of 182, the joint praetorian prefects, P. Taruttienus Paternus and Sextus Tigidius Perennis, along with the freedman M. Aurelius Cleander, caused the murder of Saoterus. Cleander replaced him. When Paternus was promoted to the senate, Perennis became sole praetorian prefect and promptly engineered Paternus' execution on the charge that he was plotting to place his son-in-law on the throne. For the next two years, Perennis was the dominant figure at court.

A number of senators who had been close friends of Marcus Aurelius were executed on charges of being associates of Paternus and seeking to overthrow Commodus. Perennis also removed senatorial generals from their commands and replaced them with equestrian legates. Two of those who were removed seized chances later to become emperor, Helvius Pertinax (a protégé of Claudius Pompeianus) and Septimius Severus. Didius Julianus, a relative of Paternus' son-in-law, also made a bid. In the meantime, morale in the armies declined and gave rise to a series of provincial mutinies (sometimes called the Deserters' War), which seems to have spawned another attempt at assassination.

In 185, Perennis himself succumbed to a group of palace freedmen under the leadership of Cleander as chamberlain. The freedwoman Marcia also participated. Allegedly, Cleander and Marcia appointed imperial administrators in return for large bribes and controlled affairs in general. A series of praetorian prefects rose and fell until Cleander took an unprecedented step for a freedman and had himself appointed as an equal to the regular joint prefects in 188.

Cleander met his fate two years later in a plot that may have been orchestrated by Helvius Pertinax in conjunction with a group of men connected to the province of Africa, where Pertinax had served as proconsul. Pertinax was now urban prefect and commanded the Urban Cohorts. The man who soon replaced Cleander as praetorian prefect, Q. Aemilius Laetus, was also from Africa. Laetus, in turn, appointed his fellow African provincial, the future Emperor Septimius Severus, as governor of the strategic Danubian province of Panonnia. Severus, moreover, had served as Pertinax's legate in Syria. Severus' brother was appointed to govern the Danubian province of Lower Moesia. Another African provincial, Decimus Clodius Albinus, received the important command of the armies in Britain.

Provincial administration and defense under Commodus

Commodus apparently left the routine running of the Empire to his favorites. It was in their best interest to see that the system functioned smoothly even when they were pursuing their own personal agenda. Under Perennis, there were serious incursions from the North of Britain into the Roman province. Even the governor was killed.

A new governor retrieved the situation and enabled Commodus to be proclaimed Britannicus in 184. Apparently, however, the new governor's harsh discipline soon provoked a rebellion in the legions. Perennis fell to Cleander before he could take any action. Ironically, Cleander called on Pertinax, whom Perennis had earlier cashiered. Pertinax revived his career by restoring order among the legions in Britain.

It is clear that Commodus' treaty with tribes across the Danube did not lead to Roman neglect in that quarter. Under Perennis, operations occurred beyond Dacia, probably against Sarmatian tribes. In 188, preparations were underway for a sequel to Aurelius' two German wars. Probably they were directed at an uprising of the Quadi. Either they were sufficient by themselves to restore peace or they were dropped because of another conspiracy against Commodus.

In North Africa, Roman commanders conducted operations against the Mauri (Moors) and extended or enlarged Roman defenses in Mauretania and Numidia. In the East, imperial governors faithfully maintained the network of fortifications and roads that protected Rome's provinces. Throughout the Empire, disaster relief and benefactions, all in the Emperor's name, of course, were provided to various cities and gratefully acknowledged with laudatory inscriptions.

Commodus' quest for popular adoration

Although Commodus ignored the sensibilities of the senate, he carefully cultivated popularity among the masses at Rome. In 186, he established a fleet to carry food supplies from the province of Africa to Rome on a regular basis. That kept supplies plentiful, prices low, and the common people of Rome happy. During his twelve-year reign, he made eight *congiaria* (donations of money) to the citizens and entertained them frequently with lavish shows of chariot races, gladiatorial combats, and beast hunts in the arena.

Commodus sought to win popularity with the spectators of these spectacles by taking part himself. Demonstrating his skill with javelin and bow, he killed hundreds of wild beasts in the arena. He trained and fought left-handed as the kind of light-armed gladiator called a *secutor* (pursuer). In the last year of his life, he even set up an inscription boasting of 620 victories in gladiatorial combat, more than any other left-handed fighter.

Commodus' association with divinity

That inscription was on the base of the colossal statue in front of the Colosseum. Commodus had his head placed atop the statue and added the club and lion skin of Hercules. Numerous coins and portrait busts depicting Commodus as Hercules also appeared. Hercules was one of the most popular gods in the ancient world. He was a mortal who had achieved divinity by his great deeds on behalf of humanity. Rulers since Alexander the Great had sought to be identified in the popular mind with this divine hero. Commodus, toward the end of his life, even celebrated himself on coins as HERCULES COMMODUS.

In his last year, Commodus also associated himself in statues and on coins with various other deities such as Jupiter, Mithras, Sol (the Sun), Cybele, Serapis, and Isis. Clearly, he was aiming to become some kind of divine absolute ruler. He had his clothes embroidered with gold and used various titles associated with deities. He even turned Rome into a colony whose name, Commodiana, came from his own. Therefore, he would not be just the ruler of the city but literally its venerated founder and creator.

The assassination of Commodus, December 31, 192 c.e.

Commodus' actions finally alienated so many people that there was no one left to protect him. His attempts to buy popularity exacerbated the fiscal crisis evident since his father's wars. It forced him to debase the coinage in order to cover expenses. By 186, the weight of the *denarius* had fallen 8.5 percent and its silver content from 79.07 fineness (percent of precious metal) to 74.25. Inflation was the unhappy result. Even worse, during his last two years, his need for more and more money as well as his fear of conspiracy fueled an alarming increase in the executions of prominent persons and the confiscation of their property. On top of that, a disastrous fire swept through Rome in 192.

It is alleged that at the end of 192, Commodus was planning to move permanently into the gladiatorial barracks next to the Colosseum, kill the two new consuls on January 1, and, dressed as a gladiator, become sole consul in their place. This story may have been circulated to justify his assassination. At any rate, the Praetorian Prefect Laetus, the freedman Eclectus, who had replaced Cleander as chamberlain, and Commodus' concubine Marcia believed that it was no longer safe to let Commodus continue. Marcia attempted the actual murder by poisoning his dinner on December 31. Apparently, the effects of too much wine during the day's end-of-year celebrations caused him to vomit most of the poison. While he was recovering in his bath, his wrestling partner, Narcissus, another freedman who had joined the plot, strangled him.

PERTINAX (JANUARY 1 TO MARCH 28, 193 c.e.)

It is not difficult to see the hand of Helvius Pertinax at work behind the scenes: during the past two years, his friends had been placed in strategic commands. Now, Laetus and Eclectus informed him immediately after the deed was done and accompanied him to the camp of the Praetorian Guard. With their help, Pertinax received the acclamation of the guardsmen after he had promised each one 12,000 sesterces. Then, while it was still very dark, he called a meeting of the senate to confirm his accession. In the meantime, Claudius Pompeianus, Pertinax's old benefactor, arrived in Rome. He could not have come from his villa sixty miles away so soon after Commodus' assassination unless he had been notified of the plot in advance. Pertinax tactfully offered to step aside in his favor, and he, equally tactfully, refused, thereby giving the blessing that Pertinax had probably desired.

The senate gratefully confirmed Pertinax and vociferously damned Commodus' memory. Yet, Pertinax ensured his body a decent burial despite calls for throwing it into the Tiber. Pertinax attempted to restore order and refill the treasury. He reduced taxes in general, granted clear title and ten years' remission of taxes to new occupiers of war-torn and plague-depopulated land, and put up for sale the luxuries that Commodus had accumulated in his palace. He even restored the coinage to the weight and fineness of Vespasian's day.

Unfortunately, he made two serious mistakes. Selling off high offices to raise needed money alienated many senators who had been offended by the practice under Commodus. Also, like Galba after Nero, Pertinax alienated the Praetorian Guard, whose support had been only grudging. He failed to indulge the guardsmen and their prefect Laetus as much as they had expected. After two unsuccessful coups, a group of guardsmen marched on the palace and murdered him only eighty-seven days after he had taken office.

DIDIUS JULIANUS (MARCH 28 TO JUNE 1, 193 c.e.)

The oft-repeated ancient story that the guardsmen then held an auction and gave the throne to M. Didius Julianus is a highly exaggerated oversimplification. Laetus probably had chosen Julianus before the murder of Pertinax. After it, in the guardsmen's absence from the praetorian camp, Pertinax's father-in-law offered the guardsmen 20,000 sesterces each for their support. Julianus arrived and secured their backing by pointing out the danger to them of choosing a man whose son-in-law they had just murdered and by promising each man 25,000 sesterces.

Confirmed by a helpless senate, Julianus still faced opposition. Hostile crowds finally thronged into the Circus and called for the governor of Syria, Pescennius Niger, to seize the throne. Clodius Albinus in Britain and Septimius Severus on the Danube also claimed the purple. Septimius raced to Rome first. Julianus initially resisted and then negotiated with Severus. Deserted by the praetorians, whose shifty prefect Laetus he had removed, Julianus was murdered by a guardsman on his sixty-sixth day as emperor.

THE ACCESSION OF SEPTIMIUS SEVERUS (193 TO 211 c.e.)

L. Septimius Severus was a native of Africa and spoke Latin with a Punic accent. He was born in 146 at Lepcis (Leptis) Magna, a town not far from modern Tripoli (ancient Oea). He is proof of the growing importance of the provinces. He had enjoyed an active career, was well educated, and loved the company of poets and philosophers. Apparently, his first wife had died childless. His second was a rich and intelligent Syrian woman named Julia Domna, who bore him two sons—Septimius Bassianus (Caracalla) and Septimius Geta.

Severus moved swiftly to consolidate his power. He seized the various treasuries, restocked the depleted granaries of the city, and avenged the murder of Pertinax, whose name he assumed. He increased the pay of his own troops to make sure of their continued loyalty and disbanded the Italian Praetorian Guard. He then replaced it with

15,000 of his best legionary soldiers, largely from Illyria and Thrace. The change in the composition of the Guard helped to remove the special privileges of Italy in the choosing of emperors and in the government of the Empire.

The war against Pescennius Niger, 193 to 194 C.E.

Severus thereupon set about dealing with one rival at a time. He temporarily acknowledged Clodius Albinus in Britain as his adopted successor with the title of Caesar. That would secure his rear as he advanced east against Niger. Meanwhile, Niger had won major support in the provinces of Asia and Egypt. He had also seized Byzantium as a base from which he could threaten Severus' Danubian provinces. In a swift and savage campaign, Severus defeated Niger and captured Antioch. Niger was overtaken and killed as he attempted to escape to the Parthians across the Euphrates. Byzantium, however, fell in late 195 only after a protracted siege. It was virtually destroyed and was reduced to a dependency of neighboring Perinthus until it was rebuilt a few years later.

First War against Parthia, 194 to 195 C.E.

After Niger's defeat and death, Severus attacked Parthia. King Vologeses IV had not only offered assistance to Niger but had tampered with the loyalty and allegiance of the king of Osrhoene, a Roman client in northwestern Mesopotamia (map, p. 369). In 194 and 195, Severus overran Osrhoene (most of which he turned into a Roman province), northern Mesopotamia, and Adiabene (northern Assyria). Here the campaign came to an abrupt end.

The war against Clodius Albinus, 195 to 197 C.E.

At the other end of the Empire, Albinus had amassed an army in Britain for a conflict with Severus. Albinus had been growing suspicious of the emperor's sincerity in acknowledging him as Caesar and successor. Supported by a large following in the senate, he decided to make a bid for supreme power. To enforce his claim, he crossed over into Gaul and set up headquarters at Lugdunum (Lyons). He received considerable support in Gaul and Spain as well as Britain. Septimius drew his forces mainly from the Danubian provinces and Syria.

Severus headed west after the fall of Byzantium secured his rear. Other loyal officers had gone earlier to secure Rome, Italy, and the northern provinces. Severus stopped to reinforce the loyalty of armies along the way and then spent time in building up popular support at Rome and asserting control over the senate and public affairs. He finally collected his forces in Pannonia in early 197 and marched on Gaul. Near Lugdunum, the two enemies fought a furious battle that ended in the defeat and suicide of Albinus. Severus allowed his victorious troops to sack and burn the city of Lugdunum and carried out a ruthless extermination of the adherents of Albinus in the provinces and in the Roman senate.

NEW SOURCES OF IMPERIAL AUTHORITY
AND LEGITIMACY

Although Severus had arrived in Rome at the head of an army in 193, he had tried to conciliate the senate and cooperate in order to legitimize his claim to the throne against his rivals. He had already taken the name of *Pertinax* so that he could pose as the avenger of the previously slain senatorial appointee. In Rome, he had donned civilian dress and had sworn to the senators that he would never execute a senator without a trial by peers. He also had promised not to encourage the use of informers.

Severus had little chance to prove himself. Many in the senate either distrusted him or, because he had been born a provincial of only equestrian rank, disliked him. Although Clodius Albinus had come from Africa, he was of the hereditary nobility. Therefore, he had been much more acceptable to the senate. In particular, he may have had the support of those who had backed Didius Julianus. The latter's mother came from Albinus' hometown. Senators who promoted the fortunes of Albinus had inevitably provoked Severus' wrath. Therefore, after he had secured the East against Pescennius Niger and Parthia, Severus dropped the policy of conciliation with the senate and formally relied on the army as his principal source of authority in establishing himself and his family as a new dynasty at Rome.

In the past, the army had been used to force the senate, which was still the recognized source of legitimate authority, to authorize the appointment of a new emperor. Septimius Severus, however, went a long way to making the army the recognized source of authority instead. For example, in 195 he had the army in Mesopotamia declare Albinus a public enemy in order to legitimize the war against him. In the same year, he also had the army ratify his adoption into the family of Marcus Aurelius, the Antonines, and proclaim the deification of his "brother" Commodus. (Because the senate itself had condemned the memory of Commodus, he even forced it to revoke its previous action.) In 195 or 196, he also had the army proclaim his elder son, Septimius Bassianus (Caracalla), as Caesar in place of Clodius Albinus and bestow the name *Marcus Aurelius Antoninus* upon him in order to emphasize the family's new Antonine pedigree.

This pedigree legitimized the claim of Severus and his sons to the throne through dynastic succession. It also allowed Septimius to claim the support of divinity for himself and his family. He was now the "son" and "brother" of deified emperors. While publicizing numerous portents foretelling his accession to the throne, Severus officially reinforced his claims to divine sanction through coins, inscriptions, and the imperial cult. In the military camps, the statues of Severus and other members of his family were worshiped as the *domus divina* (Divine House). Severus unofficially came to be called *dominus* (lord), a title with increasingly divine overtones. On one coin, his younger son, Geta, is depicted as the sun god crowned with rays, giving a benediction, and identified as *Son of Severus the Unconquered, Pius Augustus*, a designation that recalls the Unconquered Sun, an increasingly popular deity. Severus' wife, Julia Domna, is portrayed as the Great Mother Cybele on some coins and on others as seated on the throne of Juno. She was hailed as Mother of the Augusti, Mother of the Senate, or Mother of the Fatherland (*Mater Patriae*). Severus is also referred to in inscriptions as a *numen praesens* (present spirit), and dedications were made to him as a *numen*, clear indications of his divinity.

SYSTEMATIC REFORM

Having defeated Albinus and clearly established new bases of imperial authority and legitimacy, Septimius Severus initiated the most comprehensive series of changes in the Roman government since the reign of Augustus. Up to his time, many changes had occurred, but they had been subtle and evolutionary. What Septimius did was often in line with changes that had been gradually occurring. Still, he was the first to give them formal expression. Also, he was revolutionary in ruthlessly following their implications to create a clearly new system that gave an entirely different spirit to the Principate.

Major downgrading of the senate

Severus took his revenge on the senate by revoking its right to try its own members. He condemned twenty-nine of them for treason in supporting Albinus. He also appointed many new members, particularly from Africa and the East, who would be loyal to him. Italian senators became a minority. Moreover, he favored *equites* with a military background over senators in administrative appointments as deputy governors in senatorial provinces and as temporary replacements when regular senatorial governors became ill or died. When he added three new legions to the army, he put equestrian prefects instead of senatorial legates in command. He also abolished the senatorially staffed standing jury courts (*quaestiones perpetuae*). He placed cases formerly heard by them under the jurisdiction of the city prefect (*praefectus urbi*) within a hundred-mile radius of Rome and the praetorian prefect (*praefectus praetorio*) everywhere else.

As the result of a process of evolution dating back to Augustus, the senate had become simply a sounding board of policies formulated by the *princeps* and his Imperial Council, which had now become the true successor of the old republican senate. Since its inception, the Council had grown in membership and now included not only many of the leading senators and equestrians, but also the best legal minds of the age— Papinian and, later, Ulpian and Paul (p. 557).

The powers of the praetorian prefect were greatly increased: he was in charge of the grain supply and was commander-in-chief of all armed forces stationed in Italy. He was also vice-president of the Imperial Council, now the supreme court of the Empire and its highest policy-making body. From 197 to 205, Severus' senior prefect was C. Fulvius Plautianus, a kinsman from Lepcis Magna. He was a man of extreme ambition, arrogance, and cruelty, who wielded almost autocratic power because of his overpowering personality and his influence upon the emperor.

Fiscal reforms

The confiscations of property belonging to political enemies in both East and West were so enormous that Septimius created the *res privata principis* (the private property of the *princeps*). It was a new treasury department separate and distinct from the *fiscus* (the regular imperial treasury) and from the *patrimonium Caesaris*. The new treasury, administered by a procurator, gave the emperor stronger control over both the fiscal administration of the Empire and the army. Soldiers' annual base pay was raised from 300 to 400 *denarii* per man. Popular with the soldiers, this increase was also necessary in order to compensate for the inflation that had raged since the reign of Commodus. The resulting need for more coins forced Severus to reduce the silver content of the *denarius* to about 56 percent by the end of his reign. Although that ultimately increased inflationary pressure, it temporarily produced a revival of economic prosperity and a fairly respectable surplus in the treasury.

Legal developments

Several legal developments under Severus were already implicit in those under Hadrian, especially in the jurist Julianus' revision of the *Perpetual Edict* (p. 463). The major Severan reform was the already mentioned abolition of the regular standing jury courts and the transfer of their cases to the jurisdiction of the urban prefect and the praetorian prefect. Under the Severi, the practical division of the Roman citizen body into the more privileged honorable orders (*honestiores*) and less privileged humble people (*humiliores*), which had always existed to one degree or another, became even more pronounced. The *honestiores* included senators, *equites*, all local municipal magistrates, and soldiers of all ranks; the *humiliores* included people who did not have enough wealth to hold local offices, freedmen, and the various poor citizens of all types. The emperors sanctioned different treatment of the two classes. A privileged person might be exiled or cleanly executed, an underprivileged one sentenced to hard labor in the mines or thrown to the beasts for the same crime. Furthermore, *honestiores* could much more easily appeal to the emperor than could *humiliores*.

Provincial administration

In general, the provincial policy of Septimius Severus was a corollary to that of Hadrian and the Antonines. They had begun to make the status of the provinces equal to that of Italy. Severus continued this policy mainly because of political and dynastic motives. Disbanding the Italian Praetorian Guard, stationing a newly created legion in Italy, and appointing Near Eastern and African senators were mainly measures to consolidate his regime. Although he spent money liberally in Rome and Italy on public works, on the feeding and amusement of the Roman populace, and on the resumption of the public alimentary and educational program (which Commodus had suspended), he spent equally vast amounts in Africa and Syria. Thus, the Severan regime saw the consummation of earlier policies leading to a balance, equalization, and fusion of the various geographical and cultural elements of the Greco-Roman world under the leadership of the emperors.

At the same time, Severus had to prevent the concentration of power in the hands of provincial governors who might prove as dangerous as Pescennius Niger and Clodius

Albinus. He followed the policy of Augustus, Trajan, and Hadrian and partitioned large legion-filled provinces. He divided Syria and Britain each into two separate provinces and detached Numidia from Africa to create smaller provinces and correspondingly weaker provincial governors.

Military reforms

Owing his power entirely to the soldiers and genuinely wishing to provide adequate defense, Septimius Severus made significant improvements to the army. He not only increased its size from thirty to thirty-three legions but also made army life as attractive as possible. He allowed junior officers to organize social clubs. The members all contributed money for drinks, entertainment, and financial insurance during service and after discharge. Severus legalized marriages between soldiers defending the Empire's frontiers and native women living near forts and encampments. Thus he abolished the anomaly of long-standing but not officially countenanced marriages. The Praetorian Guard, though no longer composed solely of Italians, western provincials, and Macedonians, continued to be an elite corps drilled in the best Roman tradition and renowned as a training school for future army officers.

In his reorganization of the army, Severus began to replace more senatorial commanders with *equites*. They were often ex-centurions promoted from the ranks. The commanders of his three new legions were no longer senatorial *legati* but equestrian prefects with the rank of *legatus*. Some of them even became provincial governors. Severus democratized the army by making it possible for a common soldier of ability and initiative to pass from centurion on to the rank of tribune, prefect, and *legatus*. He might eventually reach the high office of praetorian prefect, if not emperor. Even ordinary veterans became a privileged class rewarded with good jobs in civilian posts after discharge. While raising the pay of the legionaries, he also permanently leased lands from the imperial estate to certain auxiliary units. They thus became permanent peasant militias in their sectors of the frontier.

IMPERIAL WARS AND DEFENSE, 197 TO 201/202 C.E.

Severus paid careful attention to military affairs because he was primarily a military man. While he let the praetorian prefect Plautianus virtually run the government, he preferred the role of imperial warrior. He gloried in conquest and supervising the frontier defenses.

The Second Parthian War, 197 to 198 C.E.

While Severus had been fighting Albinus, Vologeses IV had attacked Osrhoene (map, p. 369). After purging the senate in the early summer of 197, Septimius immediately set out for Syria and renewed war against Parthia. In conscious imitation of Trajan, he swept down Mesopotamia and sacked the Parthian capital, Ctesiphon (near modern Bagdad). He did not pursue the fleeing Parthian king but returned to Syria. From there, he rearranged the borders of the province of Osrhoene and recreated Trajan's short-lived province of Mesopotamia from Adiabene. The great fortress city of Nisibis was its capital. Thus he greatly strengthened the eastern frontier for the immediate future. Still, he had unwittingly helped pave the way for the rise of a much greater threat twenty years later, the aggressive Sassanid Persian dynasty.

Hatra, Syria, Arabia, Palestine, and Egypt, 198/199 to 201/202 C.E.

Although Severus failed to capture the wealthy city of Hatra, he did obtain an anti-Parthian alliance with it. Then he added part of southern Syria to the province of Arabia. He divided the rest into Syria Coele (roughly modern Syria), with its capital at Antioch, in the north and the much smaller Syria Phoenice (modern Lebanon), with its capital at Tyre, in the south (maps, p. 369 and 375). He vigorously upgraded the fortifications and military roads on the desert frontier of Arabia. Syria Coele was then extended eastward to include the strategic city of Dura-Europus, which guarded the crossing of the middle Euphrates. Severus also incorporated the military forces of the formerly independent caravan city of Palmyra into the Roman army and placed it under the control of the governor of Syria Phoenice.

Late in 199, Septimius Severus entered Egypt. On the way, he had stopped in Palestine. He was favorably received there, and he granted certain unspecified privileges that gratified the Jewish population. Egypt was of special interest to him for a number of reasons. Its security as Rome's major source of grain was vital to every emperor. In particular, Severus needed to make sure of Egypt's loyalty in view of its earlier support of Pescennius Niger. At Alexandria, he closed the tomb of Alexander the Great. Pescennius Niger had appealed to that magical name by claiming to be a second Alexander. Severus spent some months on legal and administrative affairs. Most notably, he finally granted Alexandria and other Egyptian cities the right to have their own municipal councils like those of cities elsewhere. Also, he permitted Egyptians to become senators at Rome for the first time. The very first one was a friend of Plautianus, who was becoming more and more powerful. Severus also took a great interest in the Egyptian priests' books of sacred lore and magic, which he then confiscated in order to prevent anyone else from obtaining their power.

Africa, 202 to 203 C.E.

After a brief return to Antioch, Severus set out for Rome. He remained there barely long enough to distribute donatives and *congiaria*; celebrate the wedding of Caracalla to Plautianus' daughter, Fulvia Plautilla; and celebrate the tenth anniversary of his accession (April 9, 202) with the most elaborate games and spectacles imaginable. Then he returned to the province of Africa Proconsularis and his hometown of Lepcis Magna. He dispensed benefactions to it and other African cities and towns. If he had not done so earlier, he also made Numidia into a fully separate province from Africa Proconsularis.

Militarily, Severus made further provisions for safeguarding the frontiers of Numidia and Mauretania well into the Sahara. In early 203, he launched a major campaign deep into desert regions south of Africa Proconsularis. This campaign created a much deeper frontier to protect the rich cities of the Mediterranean coast.

ROMAN INTERLUDE, 203 TO 207 c.e.

In the summer of 203, Severus returned to Rome for the longest stay of his reign. In that year was dedicated his great triumphal arch in the Forum, commemorating his victory in the First Parthian War. This monument, which still stands today, symbolizes the dominant role that Severus wished to play as emperor. It rests on the spot where he claimed to have had a vision that foretold his becoming emperor. This arch used to face the now-vanished one that commemorated Augustus' diplomatic retrieval of Roman military standards and captives from the Parthians more than 200 years earlier. It symbolically towers over the Comitium (the ancient meeting place of the *comitia curiata*) and the senate house and is flanked by the remains of the Temple of Concord. Thus the arch both expresses Severus' wish for harmony with the senate and the Roman populace and makes clear that it was to be on the terms of Rome's military monarch, who had even surpassed Augustus by defeating the hated Parthians.

The rest of Severus' time in Rome revealed problems in the imperial family and court that did not bode well for the future of the Severan dynasty. Severus' two sons, as rivals for the throne, hated each other. They also both hated the all-powerful praetorian prefect Plautianus, to whom Severus had been loyally devoted. Plautianus had frozen their mother out of Septimius' confidences, and Caracalla hated Plautianus' daughter Plautilla, the wife who had been thrust upon him at fourteen. Certain revelations in 204 had undermined Severus' confidence in Plautianus. By 205, Caracalla, now eighteen, felt confident enough to procure Plautianus' assassination and to divorce Plautilla. Then followed a purge of Plautianus' supporters in the senate. The appointment of the experienced commander Q. Maecius Laetus and the distinguished jurist Papinian as joint prefects of the Praetorian Guard did not disperse the atmosphere of suspicion and fear.

THE WAR IN BRITAIN, 208 TO 211 c.e.

Severus, accompanied by Julia Domna and their sons, Caracalla and Geta, spent the last years of his reign in Britain. An expedition into the heart of Scotland failed to bring the natives to battle. They resorted instead to guerrilla tactics and inflicted heavy losses on the Roman army.

Despite the losses and the apparent failure of the whole campaign, Septimius achieved important results. The display of Roman power and the thorough reconstruction of Hadrian's Wall effectively discouraged future invasions of England from the north. Britain enjoyed almost a century of peace. Severus, however, was not to see Rome again. He died at Eburacum (York) in 211. According to Dio, he advised Caracalla and Geta on his deathbed to "agree with each other, enrich the soldiers, and despise everyone else" (Book 76/77.15.2). Probably these words are rhetorical inventions, but they are significant in their emphasis on favoring the military and their contrast with the failure of his heirs to work together.

CARACALLA (211 TO 217 C.E.)

With Septimius dead, Caracalla and Geta together ascended the throne. Their attempt at joint rule proved hopeless because of their long-standing mutual jealousy. Each lived in mortal dread of the other. Soon Caracalla treacherously lured Geta to their mother's apartment and murdered him, supposedly in his mother's very arms (see Box 27.1). Caracalla carried out a pitiless extermination of Geta's supposed friends and supporters, among them Papinian, the jurist and praetorian prefect. To silence the murmurs of the soldiers over Geta's killing, Caracalla increased their basic pay from 400 to 600 *denarii*, an expenditure that exhausted the treasury and compelled him to raise more revenue. He doubled the tax on inheritances and the manumission of slaves and continued to reduce the weight and fineness of coins. He issued a new coin, called the *Antoninianus*, supposedly a double *denarius* but actually not double in weight. He also earned the undying hatred of many nobles by continuing his father's policy of downgrading the importance of the senate while favoring the soldiers and the provincials.

27.1 DAMNATIO MEMORIAE

On some occasions when a prominent politician had been declared an enemy of the state by the senate and then killed, the Romans further subjected him to what is referred to by modern scholars as *damnatio memoriae* (the condemnation of his memory). Caracalla, with impressive thoroughness, made sure that such memory sanctions were applied to his brother Geta after his death.

Damnatio memoriae took different forms over the course of Roman history. It could include a ban on the condemned man's name being given to any of his descendants, the destruction of his house, and the confiscation of his property. Emperors could suffer the indignity of having their decrees revoked. More striking to us now are the visible efforts to mutilate all physical reminders of the condemned: simple removal was not enough. Geta's name has been chiseled out of numerous inscriptions from across the whole of the Empire, and his portrait busts, statues, and painted images were intentionally damaged with hammers and other implements. Our sources report that Caracalla melted down coins that Geta had minted. On a few surviving coins that originally bore his image, Geta's face has been scratched off.

Caracalla, the new emperor's commonly used nickname, came from a long Gallic cape that he used to wear. He was a fairly good soldier and strategist and had some shrewd political instincts. The most historic act of his reign was the promulgation of the *Constitutio Antoniniana* in 212 to extend citizenship to all free inhabitants of the Empire. This action was in keeping with his father's policy of reducing the privileged position of Italy and the old senatorial elite. By this legislation, Caracalla obliterated all distinction between

CRISES UNDER COMMODUS AND THE SEVERI

Italians and provincials, between conquerors and conquered, between urban and rural dwellers, and between those who possessed Greco-Roman culture and those who did not. There may also have been some hoped-for advantages in terms of a unified legal system, increased availability of recruits for the Roman army, uniform liability for paying taxes, and even a shared state religion, all difficult matters to decide.

Another manifestation of Caracalla's shrewdness was his proposal of marriage to the daughter of Artabanus V of Parthia. If he was serious, he may have hoped to unite the two great powers against the less civilized tribes beyond the frontiers. It is difficult, however, to see how either the Roman or Persian aristocracy would have tolerated such an arrangement. He may only have been looking for an excuse to go to war.

German and Parthian wars

Attempts at diplomacy notwithstanding, Caracalla spent the major part of his reign fighting wars. He proved himself a real soldier emperor. In 213, he proceeded to the Raetian border to attack the Alemanni. They were a formidable but newly organized confederacy of mixed resident and displaced Germanic tribes. They had migrated westward and settled along the right bank of the upper Rhine. After decisively defeating them at the river Main, Caracalla built and restored forts, repaired roads and bridges, and extended a 105-mile stone wall from six to nine feet high and four feet thick along the Raetian frontier. The latter successfully withstood numerous assaults for the next twenty years.

After similarly strengthening the defenses in Pannonia and along the lower Danube, Caracalla proceeded to the East. He brutally suppressed an uprising in Alexandria and resumed war against Parthia since his proposal to unite the two empires by marriage had been rejected. In 216, he marched across Adiabene (northern Assyria) and invaded Media. After sacking several fortified places, he withdrew to winter quarters at Edessa (Urfa) in Osrhoene. There he made preparations to mount a more vigorous offensive the following spring. He did not live to witness the consummation of his plans. On April 8, 217, while traveling from Edessa to Carrhae to worship at the Temple of the Moon, he was stabbed to death at the instigation of the praetorian prefect M. Opellius Macrinus (map, p. 369).

MACRINUS (217 TO 218 c.e.)

As ringleader of the plot against Caracalla, Macrinus secured the acclamation of the army and ascended the throne. He was a Mauretanian by birth, an *eques* in rank, and the first *princeps* without prior membership in the senate to reach the throne. To affiliate himself with the Severan dynasty, he adopted the name of Severus, bestowed that of Antoninus upon his young son Diadumenianus, and even ordered the senate to proclaim Caracalla a god. Realizing that he needed some military prestige to hold the loyalty of the army, he continued the war with Parthia but proved to be a poor general. After a few minor successes and two major defeats, he lost the respect of the army by agreeing to surrender his prisoners and to pay Parthia a large indemnity. This inglorious settlement, together with his unwise decision to reduce the pay for new recruits and the opposition of Severus' family, ultimately cost him his life and throne.

POWERFUL SYRIAN EMPRESSES

Through marriage to Julia Domna, Septimius Severus had been connected to a family of remarkable Syrian women. They actively sought a leading role in imperial politics. Julia Domna, and her sister, Julia Maesa, were well educated, shrewd, and tough. Their father was the high priest of the sun god Elagabalus (Heliogabalus) at the Arabian city of Emesa (Homs, p. 379) in Syria. He probably was descended from its old royal house. Women of the family were accustomed to power and influence. Domna had enjoyed great importance at the beginning of Severus' reign but had been outmaneuvered for a time by the ambitious praetorian prefect Plautianus. She had then devoted herself to creating a circle of influential intellectuals. She was able to recover her former strength after the fall of Plautianus. Indeed, she had probably contributed to it through Caracalla. In 208, she had accompanied Severus to Britain. After his death, she had tried to promote the interests of her more even-tempered son, Geta. Failing to prevent his murder, she had made the best of it with Caracalla. She accompanied Caracalla to Antioch on his Parthian expedition in 215 and died there soon after his assassination. Macrinus then forced her sister, Maesa, to retire to Syria.

FIGURE 27.1 Empress Julia Domna, wife of Septimius Severus.

In Syria, Maesa plotted to restore her family's imperial fortunes. She had gone back to Emesa with her two daughters, Julia Soaemias and Julia Mamaea. There, Varius Avitus, the fourteen-year-old son of Soaemias, had inherited the high priesthood of the sun god Elagabalus, and he himself came to be known by that name as emperor.

ELAGABALUS (218 TO 222 c.e.)

Knowing how the army cherished the memory of Caracalla, Maesa concocted the rumor that Elagabalus was the natural son of Caracalla and, therefore, was a real Severus. She presented him to the legions of Syria. Persuaded by the offer of a large donative, they saluted him as emperor under Caracalla's royal name, *Marcus Aurelius Antoninus*. Macrinus, deserted by most of his troops and defeated in battle, fled. He was later hunted down and killed.

A year later, wearing a purple silk robe, rouge on his cheeks, a necklace of pearls, and a bejeweled crown, Elagabalus arrived in Rome. He had brought from Emesa a conical black stone—the cult image of the god Elagabalus—which he enshrined in an ornate temple on the Palatine and worshiped with un-Roman sexual practices (which probably have been exaggerated in the retelling by hostile and sensationalistic sources) and outlandish rites to the accompaniment of drums, cymbals, and anthems sung by Syrian women. What shocked the Roman public even more than any of these strange rites was his endeavor to make that Syrian sun god the supreme deity of the Roman State.

In order to devote more time to his priestly duties and (in Roman eyes) scandalous ceremonies, Elagabalus entrusted most of the business of government to his grandmother. He also appointed his favorites to the highest public offices—a professional dancer, for example, as praetorian prefect; a charioteer as head of the night watch (*vigiles*); and a barber as prefect of the grain supply (*annona*). Maesa realized that the un-Roman conduct of Elagabalus would lead to his downfall and the ruin of the Severan family. She tactfully suggested that he ought to adopt Gessius Bassianus Alexianus, her grandson by Julia Mamaea, as Caesar and heir to the throne. When Elagabalus saw that Alexianus, whom he adopted under the name of *Marcus Aurelius Severus Alexander*, was preferred by the senate and the people, he regretted his decision and twice attempted to get rid of the boy.

Maesa and Mamaea appealed to the Praetorian Guard. The guardsmen were happy to hunt down Elagabalus and his mother, Soaemias. They seized the two in their hiding place—a latrine—cut off their heads, and dragged the corpses through the streets to the Aemilian bridge. There they tied weights to them and hurled them into the Tiber.

SEVERUS ALEXANDER (222 TO 235 c.e.)

The accession of Severus Alexander was greeted with rejoicing. Although he was studious, talented, and industrious, he was only fourteen, and his capable mother, Mamaea, held the reins of power. She was virtually, even to the end of his reign, the empress of Rome.

The reign of Alexander marked the revival of the prestige, if not the power, of the senate. Mamaea enlisted its support in order to strengthen the arm of the civil government in controlling the unruly and mutinous armies. She accordingly set up a council of sixteen prominent senators to exercise at least a nominal regency, though actually, perhaps, to serve only in an advisory capacity. Among the sixteen senators were the imperial biographer Marius Maximus and the historian Cassius Dio (p. 556). Senators also probably held a majority in the enlarged Imperial Council. The president of both councils was the praetorian prefect. He was normally of equestrian rank but was now elevated, while in office, to senatorial rank. Accordingly, he could sit as a judge in trials involving senators without impairing the dignity of the defendants. At this time, the praetorian prefect was the distinguished jurist Domitius Ulpianus. Thus the new regime not only enhanced the dignity of the senate but also enlarged the powers of the praetorian prefect at the expense of the old executive offices. Under Severus Alexander, the tribunes of the *plebs* and *aediles* ceased to be appointed.

Social and economic policy

The government seems to have tried to win the goodwill and support of the civilian population by providing honest and efficient administration. It reduced taxes and authorized the construction of new baths, aqueducts, libraries, and roads. It subsidized teachers and scholars and lent money without interest to enable poor people to purchase farms. One major reform was the provision of primary-school education all over the Empire, even in the villages of Egypt. Another was the legalization, under government supervision and control, of all guilds or colleges (*collegia*) having to do with the supply of foodstuffs and essential services to the city of Rome. Under this category fell wine and oil merchants, bakers, and shoemakers. In return, the guilds enjoyed special tax favors and exemptions and the benefit of legal counsel at public expense.

The military problem

The fatal weakness of Alexander's regime was its failure to control the armies. In 228, the Praetorian Guard mutinied. The praetorian prefect, Domitius Ulpianus, was murdered in the emperor's palace itself because he was too strict. The soldiers in Mesopotamia mutinied and murdered their commander. Another excellent disciplinarian, the historian Cassius Dio, would have suffered the same fate had not Alexander whisked him off to his homeland of Bithynia.

Never had the need for disciplined armies been greater. Rome's recent wars with Parthia had so weakened the decrepit Arsacid regime that it was overthrown between 224 and 227 by the aggressive Sassanid dynasty of Ardashir (Artaxerxes) I (224–241 C.E.) and his son Shapur (Sapor) I (241–272 C.E.). They sought to reestablish the old Persian Empire of the Achaemenid dynasty (ca. 560–330 B.C.E.). By 331, Ardashir had already overrun Mesopotamia and was threatening the provinces of Syria and Cappadocia. After a futile diplomatic effort, Alexander himself had to go to the East. He planned and executed a massive three-pronged attack that should have ensured a decisive victory. Because of poor generalship and excessive caution, it resulted only in heavy losses on both sides. It produced nothing more than a stalemate at best. Alexander returned to Rome to celebrate a splendid but dubious triumph in 233.

Meanwhile, the Alemanni and other German tribes had broken through the Roman defenses and were pouring into Gaul and Raetia. Accompanied by his mother, Alexander hurried north in 234. After some early successes, he followed his mother's suggestion and bought peace from the Germans with a subsidy. His men were disgusted. They would have preferred to use some of that money for themselves. They mutinied in 235 under the leadership of the Thracian Gaius Iulius Verus Maximinus (Maximinus Thrax), commander of the Pannonian legions. Alexander and his mother were both killed.

Thus, the mutineers terminated the Severan dynasty. They also ushered in almost a half century of civil wars. Those wars were usually connected with such problems as Severus Alexander had faced on the frontiers of the Empire.

SUGGESTED READING

Birley, A. R. *Septimius Severus the African Emperor.* 2nd ed. New Haven and London: Yale University Press, 1988.

Hekster, O. *Commodus: An Emperor at the Crossroads.* Amsterdam: J.C. Gieben, 2002.

Icks, M. *The Crimes of Elagabalus: The Life and Legacy of Rome's Decadent Boy Emperor.* Cambridge, MA: Harvard University Press, 2012.

CHAPTER 28

The third-century anarchy, 235 to 285 C.E.

After the murder of Severus Alexander in 235, chaos threatened to engulf the Roman Empire. The frontiers were under repeated attack. The office of emperor became a football tossed back and forth among a bewildering number of usurpers. Whole regions broke away under their own emperors. The Empire seemed about to disintegrate completely. Many painful, long-term adjustments had to be made before order could be restored and the Empire preserved for the future.

REASONS FOR THE CRISIS

Many interrelated factors combined to create this crisis. A number of them had existed for some time and had been the reasons for Septimius Severus' efforts to make fundamental changes in the imperial system. Others were more recent. The combination was almost lethal.

The failure of the Severan dynasty

One of the major factors was the failure of the Severi to produce another emperor of Septimius Severus' stature. Under increasing stresses and strains, there was no one person powerful enough to maintain firm control over the whole in the face of regional needs and interests. Therefore, the crisis was intensified by numerous civil wars between regionally backed rivals for the throne.

Internal tensions

Severus had grasped the essential need to eliminate the dominant positions of the senate and of Italy in order to create a stronger, truly united Empire in accordance with geopolitical reality. Unfortunately, the integration that he had promoted had not yet been completed. Many traditionally minded senators and Italians were determined to protect their prestige and privileges. They worked to undermine emperors of equestrian and provincial origin, whom they had had no hand in making. Because they did not have the military power to protect their nominees, all that they succeeded in doing was creating more chaos.

Interregional jealousies were just as bad. The legions and inhabitants of one province or group of provinces often believed that an emperor who came from another part of the Empire was not paying enough attention to their problems. Therefore, they often rebelled and set up an emperor who would look after their needs. For example, the Pannonian legions, to whom the northern frontiers were a special concern, had mutinied against the Syrian Severus Alexander because, in their eyes, he had shown weakness in dealing with the invading Germans.

Defensive system and increased pressure on the frontiers

By the time of the Severi, the Romans had created an elaborate system of defense that went back to the Flavian emperors, was formalized by Hadrian, and was elaborated by his successors. It depended on broad frontier zones that took advantage of natural defenses, such as mountain ranges, deserts, major rivers, and large bodies of water, whenever possible. These zones were anchored in the rear by large concentrations of troops. The troops manned fixed installations, such as walls, palisades, ditches, and large fortified camps or towns close to major supply and communications routes, such as navigable rivers and carefully constructed military highways. The frontier armies also maintained an extensive network of forward forts and observation posts to protect trade and settlers and to monitor the activities of native peoples. The larger forces stationed in the rear could be warned quickly and mobilized against rebellions and raids.

The Romans did not usually conceive of these frontiers as fixed limits to their *imperium*: the frontiers were fluid and marked the temporary limits of their actual control and administration. As time and circumstances permitted or required, the frontier could be moved forward, as when Antoninus Pius built a new wall beyond Hadrian's in Britain, when Marcus Aurelius unsuccessfully tried to incorporate large new territories beyond the Danube, or when Septimius Severus successfully pushed forward the frontiers in the East and North Africa.

The problem is that, as the Romans moved farther and farther from the Mediterranean core of the Empire, the harder it was to maintain the system, and the more it came under external pressure that it could not handle. So long as the level of attacks on the frontiers remained relatively low or infrequent, this system could work. Local units could handle small-scale incursions. If a major threat occurred in one sector, units could be called up temporarily from others to mount a major campaign.

The Romans had largely subdued and pacified the nearer, more settled Germanic tribes along the Rhine–Danube frontier. Consequently, the Empire was exposed to heavier and more frequent attacks from larger, more unsettled, and more warlike tribes migrating from northern and eastern Europe. Moreover, the Romans had also helped to bring down the Parthian Empire by expanding eastward. Now, they had to face the more vigorous belligerence of the new Sassanid Persian dynasty that took over from the Parthian Arsacids. Throughout much of the period, in effect, Roman emperors confronted every military strategist's nightmare, major simultaneous wars on two fronts.

Meeting an emergency on one front by summoning troops from another merely invited a dangerous attack on the second. Knowing that, men were reluctant to leave the fronts entrusted to their care and fight on another. Also, many had become closely attached to their sectors of the frontier since Septimius Severus had permitted Roman soldiers to contract permanent marriages and allowed non-Roman auxiliaries to take up farming near their posts. Therefore, they often raised up their local commanders as emperors in the hope of securing greater imperial concern for their region.

Shortage of manpower and money

In many ways, the Roman Empire was trapped. The only way in which the defensive system could have been made to work in the face of mounting pressure on all fronts would have been to increase dramatically the size of the army. In particular, the army needed more well trained, well paid, and well equipped legionary troops. The crucial point is that under the conditions then prevailing, the Roman Empire could produce neither enough men nor enough wealth to support such an increase. The productive capacity of ancient agriculture and industry was low, and the transportation and communications systems were cumbersome (pp. 505–6). Medical knowledge and effective therapies were very limited. In the best of times, therefore, poor nutrition and disease kept the natural increase of the population low. By the middle of the third century C.E., another great plague was raging (p. 533). It was difficult to find large numbers of additional soldiers within the Empire unless they were removed from the productive sector of the economy. Removing them made it more difficult to generate the taxes to equip and pay them. It was possible to recruit auxiliary troops from neighboring peoples. Yet, they were not so well trained or equipped as Roman legionaries, and more money still had to be found to pay them, even at lower rates.

As Augustus had long ago realized in better times, the Empire could not easily raise and support even twenty-eight legions. Both he and Tiberius had left the number at about twenty-five after the loss of Varus' three legions in 9 C.E. (p. 367). The number of permanent legions had not reached thirty until Marcus Aurelius. Septimius Severus had raised it to thirty-three. That number is 32 percent larger than under Tiberius. By allowing Roman soldiers to marry and auxiliaries to settle as farmers, Septimius may have attracted more men to serve, promoted the birth of future Roman soldiers, and eased the burden of supplying frontier forces. Still, when he and then Caracalla made service more attractive and sought the loyalty of the troops by significantly raising their rate of pay, they greatly increased the burden to the treasury beyond the cost of three additional legions. The treasury could not support these increases, particularly on top of Septimius' numerous expensive civilian and military building projects. Neither the money raised from confiscating the estates of wealthy senators nor the booty captured in the Second Parthian War sufficed. Afterward, Rome's wars were seldom profitable. In fact, without the troops to defeat attackers, emperors often bought them off with subsidies, which left the Empire even less to spend on active defense. Raising taxes was unpopular with everyone and made it more difficult for small producers to survive.

The fiscal problems were made even worse by a declining supply of precious metals from the Empire's mines. By 170, the Romans did not have sufficient technology to exploit fully the remaining ores in many of its mines. Therefore, Septimius, Caracalla, and most of their successors during the third century resorted to further and further debasement of the coinage. That eventually ignited a truly disastrous inflationary spiral that nearly ruined everyone.

THE EMPERORS OF TROUBLED TIMES

Through fifty years of crisis, emperors rose and fell with such frequency that any account seems little more than a blur of names, battles, and dates. Bewilderment is compounded by the scanty, biased, and frequently fictitious ancient accounts. Nevertheless, recent research has shown that many of the emperors were neither the fools nor the tyrants that biased ancient authors depict. Many of them valiantly tried to stem the chaos, but their reigns demonstrate how the problems just outlined were making it impossible for them to do so and destroyed them in the process. It is a wonder that the Empire survived at all.

THE NIGHTMARE BEGINS, 235 TO 253 c.e.

Having led the mutiny against Severus Alexander in 235, Maximinus Thrax (the Thracian) became emperor. During his brief reign (235–238), he was very successful against the Germanic tribes across the Danube. He seemed on the verge of completing Marcus Aurelius' grand scheme of conquest. He was popular with his soldiers because he doubled their pay when they made him emperor, and he led them to victory. Unfortunately, the leaders of the senate scorned him because he had come up through the ranks as an ordinary soldier. Their view is reflected in the sources that depict him as an ignorant peasant.

Maximinus' civilian support was weakened when he significantly debased the coinage and vigorously enforced the collection of taxes to finance his military pay raises and campaigns against the Germans. His tax collectors particularly offended the wealthy North African landowners who had become powerful in the senate since the time of Septimius Severus. They raised up a revolt in 238 and proclaimed the rich but elderly M. Antonius Gordianus as the Emperor Gordian I. His son of the same name became the joint ruler Gordian II. The result was a disastrous civil war that aborted Maximinus' successful operations on the Danubian frontier and left both Gordians dead in that same year.

The senate appointed two of its members, M. Pupienus Maximus and D. Calvinus Balbinus, in place of the Gordians. The Praetorian Guard pressured the senate to make Gordian III, the thirteen-year-old nephew of Gordian II, emperor designate with the title of *Caesar*. Maximinus' failure to take the strategic city of Aquileia led to his death at the hands of his soldiers. They accepted the senatorial appointees.

Senatorial attempts to restore a sound currency did not leave enough money for sufficient donatives to the praetorian guardsmen, who promptly killed Pupienus and Balbinus after fewer than sixty days. Gordian III now became the reigning emperor (238–244) with the powerful support of his father-in-law, the praetorian prefect C. Furius Timistheus.

Another debasement of the coinage provided cash. Timistheus ably organized a massive campaign in 242 to stabilize the frontier on the lower Danube and check the advance of the Sassanid Persians under the mighty Shapur (Sapor) I in the East. Between 243 and 244, Timistheus and Gordian III broke the Persian siege of Antioch, recovered the province of Mesopotamia, and marched deep into Persian territory. They were on the point of taking the Persian capital of Ctesiphon when Timistheus died. Then Gordian himself died, apparently after falling from his horse in battle. Another tradition, however, says that the new praetorian prefect, Philip, an Arab sheik from what is now Jordan, took advantage of a threatened food shortage and engineered a mutiny, which resulted in the death of Gordian.

The army acclaimed Philip, often called Philip the Arab, as the new emperor (244–249). He was able to reach a settlement with Shapur. The Persians recognized Roman control over the provinces of Lesser Armenia and Mesopotamia and may have freed recently captured Romans. The cost to Rome, however, was high—10,000 pounds of gold that the Empire could ill afford and weakened the monetary system further. At least it bought Philip time to return to the Danube. There he had enough military success to permit him to go to Rome in 247.

Philip courted the goodwill of the senate and conscientiously attended to governing. At the same time, he prepared a magnificent—and costly—celebration of Rome's one-thousandth anniversary. He hoped to enhance his own stature in the eyes of all. Sadly, events were beyond his control. While he was celebrating in Rome, an invasion of the Goths and Carpi caused the Danubian legions to acclaim their general as emperor in Philip's place. That move prompted the rise of two other pretenders in the East. When Philip sent the senator C. Messius Quintus Decius to restore order on the Danube, the latter's success merely prompted the soldiers there to make him emperor. Another civil war resulted. In 249, Philip was defeated and slain near Verona in a battle that wasted scarce manpower and left Decius the dubious prize of being emperor (249–251).

Pagan Latin writers generally favor Decius because he was a respected consular senator. Christian writers, not surprisingly, condemn him for instituting Rome's first empire-wide, systematic persecution of Christians. In his view, Christians belonged to a subversive organization that refused to recognize the state religion and obstructed the defense of the Empire by preaching peace. Ironically, in 251, while he was preoccupied with these concerns, the Goths poured across the Danube. Decius hurried from Rome and fell into a trap on boggy ground at Abrittus, near Adamclisi in the Dobrudja (a region south of the Danube, along the Black Sea). The Romans lost both Decius and thousands of men in one of the biggest military disasters in their history.

Decius' ineffectual and, perhaps purposefully, unhelpful subordinate commander C. Vibius Trebonianus Gallus received the acclamation of the remaining troops. At the start of his brief reign (251–253), Gallus made a disadvantageous treaty with the Goths. They returned home with all of their plunder, their high-ranking Roman prisoners, and the guarantee of an annual tribute that further drained the imperial coffers. Again, troubles on the Danube inspired Persian aggression in Syria. An outbreak of plague made it difficult for Gallus to respond. When he did, the Danubian troops rebelled and raised up their commander, Aemilius Aemilianus, in 253. Gallus was killed by his own men. The soldiers in Raetia soon declared for an old and respected senator named P. Licinius Valerianus (Valerian). As he marched to seize Italy, Aemilianus was murdered. The senate gladly accepted Valerian and his son, P. Licinius Egnatius Gallienus, as co-emperors.

THE AGE OF GALLIENUS, 253 TO 268 C.E.

The period encompassed by the reigns of Valerian (253–260) and Gallienus (253–268) is often called the Age of Gallienus. It witnessed the culmination of the destructive trends originating in the past and laid the groundwork for future recovery. It began in catastrophe. New invaders were breaking through the shattered and weakly defended frontiers along the Rhine and the Danube. In the Near East, the Persians had invaded the provinces of Mesopotamia, Syria, and Cappadocia. Scarcely a province escaped the havoc wrought by invasion: the widespread destruction of property, the sacking and burning of cities, and the massacre and enslavement of citizens.

Pirates infested the seas as in the days before Pompey; bands of robbers and thieves raided the countryside; earthquakes rocked both Italy and Asia Minor. At the height of the devastating invasions, a plague broke out in Egypt. It infected the entire Empire for more than fifteen years. The death toll was staggering. Two-thirds of the population of Alexandria perished. During the worst of the epidemic, as many as 5000 a day died in Rome alone. The high death toll created a shortage of rural and urban labor. Production fell sharply. Worse still, the plague severely depleted the ranks of the army. The impact of all these blows, occurring simultaneously or in rapid succession, aggravated the problems that broke the resistance and shattered the unity of the Empire.

The breakdown of imperial defense increased the localist spirit of the troops on the frontiers. This localist spirit, together with the constant desire for more pay as the shortage of goods and declining value of coins drove up prices, increased the number of locally supported usurpers. During the reign of Gallienus alone, eighteen usurpers made vain attempts to seize the throne.

Developments in the East

In 253, the Persian Shapur (Sapor) I invaded Mesopotamia and Syria while the Goths were plundering the coasts of Asia Minor. In 256, Valerian himself led an expeditionary force to the East. He accomplished little except to take out his frustrations by persecuting some Christians. Finally, out of desperation and in the midst of a plague in 260, he sent his disease-weakened legions against the main Persian army at Edessa. He fell into the hands of Shapur and died a pathetic captive. His humiliation is still commemorated on a huge rock-carved relief that Shapur commissioned.

The remnants of Valerian's army managed to counterattack when Shapur invaded Asia Minor. They actually captured his baggage train and harem and forced him to withdraw toward the Euphrates. There he was badly mauled by Odenathus, the Roman client sheik of the rich and powerful caravan city of Palmyra. That disastrous encounter left Shapur politically and militarily crippled for a long time.

Palmyra

Palmyra was an oasis in the Syrian Desert. It lay astride the main caravan routes from the Mediterranean to central Asia and to the Persian Gulf. Piled high in its marketplace were such goods from China, India, Persia, and Arabia as textiles, spices, perfumes, jewelry, and precious stones. By the second century, it had become one of the major cities of the Near East. It boasted fine wide streets and highways, shady porticoes, stately arches, and magnificent public buildings.

Since the time of Trajan, Palmyra had been an important recruiting ground for the Roman army. The famous Palmyrene cohorts of mounted archers and armored cavalry had rendered invaluable service all over the Empire. Later on, the Severi, who gave Palmyra the rank of titular colony and admitted some of its leading citizens into the senate, allowed these units, though officially part of the Roman army, to serve as a semi-independent Palmyrene army in Syria and along the Parthian (Persian) frontier. That was the army with which Odenathus humbled Shapur on the western banks of the Euphrates.

The services that Odenathus had performed for Rome on his own initiative were not lost on Gallienus, now sole emperor. He showed his gratitude by rewarding Odenathus with flattering high-sounding titles and by making him commander of all the Roman forces in the Near East. Odenathus returned the favors. First, he helped to destroy a pair of pretenders who had tried to take advantage of the crisis in the East while Gallienus was occupied in the West. He then invaded Persia in 266. After besieging Ctesiphon, he turned back to face the Goths. They had invaded Asia Minor by land and sea, had laid waste the rich cities of Chalcedon and Nicomedia, and had destroyed the great temple of Artemis (Diana) at Ephesus. Odenathus failed to overtake them, however. They had already sailed away on the Black Sea with their loot and captives. Shortly after that, an unknown assassin stabbed him to death. His capable widow, Zenobia, assumed power in Palmyra and held it until the reign of Aurelian (p. 538).

Losses in the West

Meanwhile, Gallienus, constantly at war since 254, had been busy clearing the Alemanni and the Franks out of Gaul and the Rhineland. He beat back their attempts to cross the Rhine and strengthened Roman fortifications. Farther south, the Marcomanni and the Alemanni had been hammering away at the Danubian defenses. They had broken through and pushed down into Italy. The Marcomanni had penetrated as far as Ravenna in 254; the Alemanni had reached Mediolanum (Milan) four years later. Gallienus first halted the Marcomanni by concluding an alliance with them and granting them land south of the Danube in Upper Pannonia. Then, in 258 and 259, he crushed the Alemanni near Milan. During the next year, he had to suppress two dangerous rebellions in Pannonia. Legions there, irked by his continued absence on the Rhine, had thrown their support first to one pretender, then to another.

The situation in the Rhineland rapidly deteriorated during his brief absence. The Alemanni crossed the upper Rhine and invaded the Rhône valley and the Auvergne. The Franks surged over the lower Rhine and overran Gaul, Spain, and even Mauretania (Morocco). The Saxons and the Jutes, who dwelt along the coasts of Germany and Denmark, began roving the seas and raiding the shorelands of Britain and Gaul. That was not all. In 259, the legions on the Rhine, in fear and desperation, mutinied. They renounced their allegiance to their absent emperor in favor of Postumus, the general whom Gallienus had left in command of the Rhineland. The armies of Spain and Britain later followed suit.

Hampered by the German and Gothic invasions of the Danubian provinces as well as by the rebellions of other pretenders to the throne, Gallienus could do no more than compel Postumus to confine himself to the western provinces. Left alone, Postumus drove the Franks and the Alemanni out of Gaul, energetically defended the frontiers, issued his own coinage, and established an efficient administration. Gallienus himself could not have done better.

The last battles of Gallienus, 268 c.e.

The Goths were encouraged by their success in Asia Minor during 266. Joined by the Heruli in 267, they began the largest invasion of the third century. A great armada of ships put to sea. A massive land army invaded the Balkans and the Aegean area, ravaged Greece, and sacked the cities of Sparta, Argos, and Athens. The Athenian rhetorician and statesman Dexippus counterattacked with a hastily recruited local army. In 268, the invaders passed north through Epirus and Macedonia and finally arrived in Moesia. There, Gallienus intercepted them and destroyed thousands of them in the bloodiest battle of the third century. This victory might have been the end of the Gothic peril had not Gallienus been compelled to break off pursuit. He had to hasten back to Italy to suppress the rebellion of Aureolus, the cavalry general to whom he had entrusted the defense of Italy against Postumus. Gallienus defeated Aureolus in battle near Mediolanum (Milan), only to be assassinated by his own staff officers. They all were Illyrians who may have felt that Gallienus had not devoted enough energy to the defense of the Danubian lands.

THE REFORMS OF GALLIENUS

Before his death, Gallienus had laid the foundation of future recovery and prepared the way for the reforms of Diocletian and Constantine. His purpose was to strengthen the central government by restoring discipline in the armies. That helped to prevent the rise of usurpers and made it easier to defend the Empire against increased attacks on the frontiers.

Administrative

The most significant of Gallienus' reforms was to regularize the exclusion of senators from direct command of legions. He replaced them with equestrian prefects, many of whom were now coming up from the ranks. One purpose of this reform may have been to prevent rebellions and attempts by ambitious senatorial commanders to usurp power. It also aimed at the restoration of military discipline and efficiency by providing an adequate supply of professional officers willing to endure the hardships of army life on the frontiers and capable of enforcing strict military discipline. The reform not only completed the process of professionalizing the army but also dealt a heavy blow to the prestige of the senate.

Equestrians also gradually replaced senatorial governors in most of the imperial and occasionally even in the senatorial provinces. Therefore, civil and military powers at the provincial level generally remained linked. In the most devastated provinces, Gallienus even combined fiscal responsibilities with civil and military powers in the hands of experienced equestrian officers. With those combined responsibilities, they could deal effectively with crises.

Military

While he promoted from the ranks to provide experienced senior officers, Gallienus also made some major tactical and strategic changes. They were not part of any grand, preconceived system but were practical responses to sometimes temporary situations and were not always permanent. A major and permanent tactical change, however, was to place greater emphasis on cavalry units to increase the mobility of the Roman army and meet the challenges posed by the notoriously effective Persian and Alemannic horsemen.

The new cavalry corps consisted of Moorish bareback-riding javelin men; Dalmatian horsemen; Osrhoenian and Palmyrene mounted archers; and cataphracts (*cataphractarii*), heavily armored (both horse and rider) cavalry of the Persian type. Gallienus regarded this cavalry corps so highly that in 263 he placed it on a par with the Praetorian Guard. Its commander, the *magister equitum*, soon rivaled and later eclipsed the praetorian prefect. Though only of equestrian rank, he became the most powerful man in the Empire next to the emperor. Claudius Gothicus, Aurelian, and Probus were later to use this command as the springboard to the emperor's throne.

Temporarily, Gallienus strategically abandoned the eastern and western extremities of the Empire to regional dynasts. He concentrated mostly on saving the Empire's central core: Egypt, western Asia Minor, Greece, the Balkans, Italy, and North Africa. Although he distrusted Postumus and never recognized his authority as legitimate, Gallienus left him in de facto control of the westernmost provinces and responsible for defending the Rhine. Gallienus maintained nominal suzerainty over Odenathus and Zenobia in Syria and Mesopotamia but left them on their own to deal with Persia. His immediate need was to defend the Alpine and Danubian frontiers. He maintained and strengthened fortifications and infantry units as a first line of defense in the frontier zones themselves. Behind the frontiers, he also fortified numerous cities capable of resisting and absorbing attackers who broke through the first line of defense.

Finally, in response to various large incursions, Gallienus stationed large cavalry detachments (*vexillationes*) at strategically located major cities in the rear. From these secure, well-supplied positions, they could move swiftly in any direction to meet emergencies in their sectors. Such bases were located at Mediolanum (Milan), Verona, and Aquileia to protect Italy and defend the Alpine frontier; at Poetovio in Noricum and Aquincum (Budapest) and Sirmium in Lower Pannonia to protect the middle Danube; at Lychnidus in Macedonia and Byzantium in Thrace to protect the Balkans, Greece, and the Aegean (map, pp. 378–9). Once the core of the Empire had been secured and the frontiers stabilized, the *vexillationes* would be shifted elsewhere.

The constant need for an emperor to be in personal charge of imperial defenses from bases like Mediolanum reduced the political importance of the city of Rome and the senate. Emperors had to establish mints, arms factories, and their own residences in major military centers. Where the emperor was, there Rome was also. In the fourth century, Mediolanum in the West and Byzantium in the East would displace Rome as principal imperial residences.

AN ASSESSMENT OF GALLIENUS

Of all his imperial predecessors, Gallienus seems to have resembled Hadrian most closely. He had the same keen intellect, indefatigable energy, and crucial capacity for swift decision. Gallienus shared Hadrian's love of poetry and the arts, as well as his admiration for Greek culture, literature, and philosophy. He also shrewdly abandoned his father's distracting persecution of Christians. He established a policy of toleration that lasted for forty years, a period known as the Little Peace of the Church.

INITIAL RECOVERY UNDER ILLYRIAN SOLDIER EMPERORS, 268 TO 275 C.E.

Gallienus was shamefully assassinated by the Illyrian officers whose careers he had previously promoted. Nevertheless, they vigorously carried on his work of rescuing the Roman Empire. The first, Claudius II (268–270), earned his *cognomen*, Gothicus, by thoroughly crushing the Goths before he died of the plague. He was briefly succeeded by his brother, but L. Domitius Aurelianus, Aurelian, soon seized power (270–275). Aurelian had been Claudius Gothicus' *magister equitum* and was known as *Manus ad Ferrum* (Hand on Steel) for his harsh discipline. He earned another title, *Restitutor Orbis* (Restorer of the World), by regaining most of the ground that Rome had lost in the previous decade. He twice had to drive invaders out of Italy and was in danger of losing Rome before he was able to drive them back to Germany and secure the northern frontier.

Aurelian's reforms

Aurelian returned to Rome to suppress a serious revolt of mint officials who were aggrieved at the emperor's efforts to check their profiteering from debased coins. He immediately closed the mint for a time as a preliminary step toward his projected reform of the coinage. In order to protect Rome from future assault and capture by invaders, he began the construction of a brick wall around the city in 271. The wall was twelve miles long, twenty feet high, and twelve feet thick. It had eighteen gates protected by round towers and had square towers projecting out every one hundred feet. Convinced of the impossibility of permanently holding Dacia, with its irreparably broken defenses, Aurelian withdrew all the garrisons and most of the civilians from the province. The withdrawal not only shortened the frontier defense line of the Empire but also released troops for service elsewhere. The evacuated civilians were resettled in the ravaged and depopulated provinces of Pannonia, Moesia, and Thrace, and Dacia was abandoned to the Goths.

Zenobia and the reconquest of the East, 272 to 273 C.E.

With Italy and the Danubian provinces temporarily safe from attack, Aurelian was free to attempt the reconquest of the East. The enemy whom he had to conquer was not the Persian king, but Zenobia, the energetic and capable queen of Palmyra. She not only maintained a court of pomp and splendor, but also gathered about her scholars, poets, and artists. Her chief advisor was Cassius Longinus (213? to 273), a celebrated Athenian rhetorician, polymath, and philosophical writer.

Zenobia took advantage of Claudius Gothicus' death, plus Aurelian's usurpation and subsequent preoccupation in Italy and on the Danube. She extended Palmyra's dominion to include Egypt and Asia Minor as far north as Bithynia. She had even concluded an alliance with the Persians but received little help from them. Sometime in the second half of 271, Zenobia and her son assumed, respectively, the titles Augusta and Augustus and claimed the imperial purple.

Aurelian sent his *magister equitum*, M. Aurelius Probus, to Egypt and immediately advanced through Asia Minor himself (map, p. 379). He overcame Palmyrene forces at Tyana and Antioch on the Orontes and proceeded to Emesa. There, the Romans won a resounding victory and then set out to besiege Palmyra. Well prepared for a siege, Palmyra stubbornly resisted. It finally capitulated when the queen attempted to flee to Persia for help. Brought before Aurelian, the captured Zenobia saved her life by accusing Longinus and her other advisors and friends of inspiring her aggressions. Longinus had to die. What happened to Zenobia's son is unknown, but Aurelian was very lenient with the people and city of Palmyra. He stationed a small garrison there and at once set out for Europe.

He had gone so far as the Danube when word came in early 273 that Palmyra had risen in rebellion and massacred the garrison. Aurelian's return was swift, his vengeance terrible. Not even women or children escaped his wrath. He had Palmyra's treasures carted away, tore down the walls, and reduced the once proud and powerful city to a small desert town. Soon after, he suppressed a rebellion in Alexandria with similar ruthlessness.

The reconquest of Gaul, 273 to 274 C.E.

Aurelian then set out to reconquer Gaul. After the murder of Postumus in 268, the Gallic succession passed first to Victorinus and then to Tetricus, a harmless old senator who could neither keep out the German invaders nor maintain authority over his own army officers. His opposition to Aurelian was halfhearted and ineffectual. In 274, when his subordinates finally compelled him to fight, he deserted his troops and surrendered to Aurelian.

Aurelian's triumph and the fate of Zenobia

Now Aurelian was able to return to Rome and celebrate a magnificent triumph as Restorer of the World (*Restitutor Orbis*). Tetricus and, according to most accounts, Zenobia were paraded in Aurelian's triumphal procession. Afterward, Aurelian, with unusual leniency, appointed Tetricus chief inspector of Lucania (*corrector Lucaniae*) in southern Italy. Stories of Zenobia's fate vary. She may have died or been executed shortly after Aurelian's triumph. In another version, Aurelian presented Zenobia with a villa at Tibur (Tivoli), where she ended her days as the wife of a Roman senator.

Economic reforms

In 274, Aurelian grappled with another gigantic task: the restoration of internal stability. The most pressing problem was the regulation of the coinage. It had depreciated so much since 267 that people had to use *denarii* and *antoniniani* (double *denarii*) by the sackful (3125 *antoniniani* to the sack). Aurelian reduced the official valuation of the *antoninianus* from eight sesterces (two *denarii*) to one sesterce in order to bring it in line with the eightfold rise in the price level after 267. Whether that change actually halted inflation is debatable. He increased the number of provincial mints and permanently abolished the senatorial mint at Rome. Thus, he reduced Rome's municipal autonomy and the prerogatives of the senate.

To relieve the distress that had resulted in Rome from the rise of food prices, Aurelian placed the bread-making industry under the direct control of the state, which sold wheat for milling to the bakers' guild (*collegium*) and fixed the price of bread. He suspended the monthly grain dole and arranged instead for the daily distribution of two pounds of bread to all eligible citizens. For the same citizens, he instituted regular distributions of pork, oil, salt, and, possibly, wine. Following the example of Alexander Severus, Aurelian placed all guilds (*collegia*) engaged in the transport and processing of food and other necessities under state control. They thereby became agencies of the government.

THE NIGHTMARE RESUMES, 275 TO 285 C.E.

A corrupt secretary trying to save himself from punishment spread a false rumor that Aurelian had marked a number of officers for execution. It prompted them to assassinate the emperor. When they learned the truth, they let the senate nominate its own leader, M. Claudius Tacitus (275–276), as the next emperor. New invasions already threatened the Empire. Tacitus, then in his mid-seventies, even won some victories against the Goths and Alans who had invaded Asia Minor. His six-month reign marked only a fleeting resurgence of senatorial power before he was assassinated by his own soldiers.

A confrontation ensued between the praetorian prefect, Florianus, and the *magister equitum*, M. Aurelius Probus. It ended with Florianus being murdered by his own men and Probus becoming emperor (276–282). Initially, Probus tried to clear invaders out of the provinces. He also attempted to turn those whom he defeated into manpower for Rome. Although he killed tens of thousands of Franks and Alemanni, who had overrun Gaul, he recruited 16,000 of them as Roman soldiers. That practice would become more and more common in the future. To lessen the impact of the new soldiers as a group, Probus assigned them in small units to various provinces. In 278, he settled 100,000 Scythians and Germanic Bastarnae on abandoned land in Thrace after the Goths had driven them from southern Russia. In 279, he subdued the troublesome Isaurian tribesmen of southern Asia Minor and established colonies of veterans there to keep the peace and breed young recruits for the Roman legions. The Isaurians became one of the best sources of Roman soldiers for the next two centuries.

During these same two years, Probus also cleared Raetia and Pannonia of invading German tribes. His generals liberated Egypt from a Sudanese tribe known as the Blemmyes. In 280, his departure for an attack on Persia sparked a rebellion in Gaul that demanded his attention. When he tried to resume the expedition against Persia in 282, he fell victim to yet another mutiny.

The sources say that the soldiers turned on Probus because he worked them too hard on land reclamation and public works projects. A more compelling reason may well have been the troops' reluctance to be drawn away from their posts for another war in a far-off land that had been the graveyard of many a Roman general and army. In Raetia, the troops were already putting up the praetorian prefect Marcus Aurelius Carus as emperor, and Probus' troops declared for him.

Carus and his sons, Carinus and Numerian (282 to 285 c.e.)

Carus was another Illyrian. He, too, was a professional soldier and a fairly competent general. He did not even bother to seek senatorial confirmation of his position as emperor. Upon his accession, he conferred the rank of Caesar on his two sons, Carinus and Numerian (Numerianus). Later in 282, leaving Carinus to defend Italy and Gaul, Carus set out for the East with Numerian. Early in 283, he defeated the Quadi and the Sarmatians, who had come over the Danube. Then, he marched against the Persians. He crossed the Euphrates, took Seleucia, and then crossed the Tigris to capture Ctesiphon (map, p. 387). This series of successes came to an abrupt halt in 284 with his mysterious death, attributed by the ancient sources to a bolt of lightning. It is far more likely that Carus fell victim to foul play at the hands of Arrius Aper, the praetorian prefect and father-in-law of Numerian. Later, Aper secretly arranged Numerian's assassination, probably because the troops were reluctant to continue farther into Persia.

The army in the East acclaimed Diocles, commander of the emperor's bodyguard at the time, as Numerian's successor. The first act of the new emperor (who is better known as Diocletian [Gaius Aurelius Valerius Diocletianus, 284–305]) was to run Aper through with his sword. Carinus, who had acquired the rank of Augustus in the West, refused to acknowledge Diocletian as his colleague and marched east in 285. The two foes clashed in Moesia in the valley of the Margus (Morava). In the fierce battle that ensued, the superior army of Carinus had almost achieved victory. Then, Carinus himself received a dagger's thrust through the heart by a military tribune whose wife Carinus had seduced. His victorious but leaderless soldiers accepted Diocletian as their emperor. Diocletian, however, dated his reign from his initial acclamation in 284. He would finally bring an end to the political nightmare of the third century and would do much to set the future course of Roman history.

SUGGESTED READING

Hekster, O. *Rome and Its Empire, AD 193–284. Debates and Documents in Ancient History.* Edinburgh: Edinburgh University Press, 2008.

Potter, D. S. *The Roman Empire at Bay, AD 180–395.* 2nd ed. *Routledge History of the Ancient World.* London and New York: Routledge, 2014.

CHAPTER 29

Changes in Roman life and culture during the third century

Historians used to portray the third century as a catastrophic decline from the economic, social, and cultural heights of the first and second centuries C.E. The accumulation of new evidence and analysis over last fifty years paints a different picture. The heights of the earlier centuries have been overemphasized. Changes in so vast an entity as the Roman Empire in the third century varied enormously in pace and scale with local conditions. What might be true of one area might not hold in another. For example, there was often a contrast between the Greek East and the Latin West. The political and military crises of the third century may have accelerated some trends or retarded others. In either case, there were striking continuities as well as significant breaks with the past.

ECONOMIC LIFE

In modern terms, the Roman Empire had an underdeveloped economy. It had reached its limited potential during the relative peace and stability between Augustus' victory in the civil wars of the late Republic and the death of Antoninus Pius in 161. Beginning with Marcus Aurelius, invasions, civil wars, and plague disrupted production and trade in significant parts of the Empire. The increase in the size of the army and the civil bureaucracy to cope with these crises created heavy demands for money and manpower. These demands were very difficult to meet with an economy capable of producing only small surpluses per capita under the best of conditions. Increased demand without a concomitant increase in productivity created serious inflationary pressure.

The inflationary spiral

As seen in the previous two chapters, emperors, when faced with growing expenses for defense and a declining supply of precious metals, increased the number of coins by making them lighter and adding less gold and silver in proportion to base metal. By the 250s, the debasement of the coinage had become so bad that the continued increase in the number of debased coins in circulation caused inflation to spiral ever higher. Between 267 and 274, for example, prices had increased as much as 700 percent.

Fortunately, people could often avoid using cash. Barter could be used in many local exchanges of goods and services. Some taxes had always been paid in kind. Still, the poll tax and other taxes had to be paid in cash. Rapid inflation made it difficult to save up enough to satisfy the tax collector, particularly when inflation was increasing the amount of extortion in which tax collectors had habitually engaged. Therefore, ordinary people had less money to spend in the marketplace.

The great landowners were strong enough to resist the tax collectors and supply their wants from their own vast holdings. Members of the curial class, those of middling wealth who made up the bulk of municipal councils (*curiae*), were responsible for collecting local taxes. They could shift some of their tax burdens onto the lower classes or seek refuge by joining either the bureaucracy or the army. Soldiers were in a good position to demand raises and bonuses, which were often the objects of their mutinies and rebellions. On the average, however, their wages no more than kept pace with inflation. They often resorted to extortion or force against civilians to obtain what they could not buy.

Inflation, combined with the disruptive effects of military and political turmoil and destructive plagues from 235 to 285, had many negative economic consequences. The public and private alimentary and educational trust funds, one of the Principate's finest achievements, were wiped out. Credit, never a very highly developed aspect of the economy, became almost unobtainable. Poverty, always extensive, became even worse.

Decline of trade and commerce

The volume of trade and commerce, both internal and international, declined severely in many parts of the Empire during the third century, particularly after 235. In the absence of any improvement in ships or seamanship, this decline is underscored by the smaller number of third-century commercial shipwrecks found in the Mediterranean. Progressively debased coins, high inflation, and the decline in trade probably hurt banking, which principally involved money changing.

The coastal raids of the Saxons and Jutes and the virtual collapse of the Rhine–Danube frontier severely disrupted trade in the northwestern provinces. In the East, the disintegration of the Parthian Empire after Septimius Severus and the collapse of the Han Empire in China at the same time disrupted the overland trade with the Far East and India. The sea routes to India across the Arabian Sea seem to have been abandoned early in the third century, too. The need for importing large amounts of grain at Rome kept trade flowing between North Africa and Italy. Yet, even that trade suffered temporarily in the third century.

Disruption of agriculture

The decline of trade and commerce accompanied the disruption of agriculture. A major component of trade was the transportation of basic agricultural commodities such as grain, wine, and olive oil. If the markets for these products declined or if the producing areas ceased to produce, trade between the two declined or ceased, too. For example, when the Roman market for olive oil shrank in the late second century as plague ravaged the city's population, the rich olive-producing region of the Guadalquivir valley in Spain declined.

Agriculture in provinces along the unstable northern frontiers was particularly hard hit. Farmers suffered from invaders and impoverished Romans-turned-brigands. They often faced even more damage from Roman armies sent to drive off the attackers or fighting each other in civil war. It made little difference to the farmers whether their crops, animals, and supplies were stolen, requisitioned, or destroyed in the fighting. They were left destitute in the end.

Often an army just passing through a district en route to some other destination could spell disaster. Ancient armies on the march needed enormous amounts of local provisions. The emperor or his high commanders and the exalted personages of their retinues were a scourge. They had to receive lavish hospitality commensurate with their high station even if the locals were reduced to beggary.

If a farmer escaped the previous calamities, he still faced extraordinary taxes and requisitions. They were imposed to support unexpected wars elsewhere or to pay the expenses associated with the accession of the latest new emperor or local usurper. As a result of all of those pressures, much land, particularly of marginal quality or on unstable frontiers, went out of production.

Increase of great estates

In many cases, particularly in those parts of the West where agriculture still prospered, the number of *latifundia*, large holdings of estates farmed by *coloni* (tenants), increased. *Coloni* paid a percentage of their production to their landlords, many of whose villas were now fortified. The hereditary senatorial magnates and provincial elites or new men from the army and bureaucracy were the only ones with the resources to buy extra land or take over what others had abandoned. Often small farmers willingly surrendered their land to larger neighbors and became *coloni* in return. They needed the protection that powerful landlords—with their social connections, fortified villas, and private retainers—could provide against tax collectors, military recruiters, brigands, and outside attackers.

Like medieval manors, the landlords' estates were largely self-sufficient. They produced most of what was needed for local consumption. Tenants, paying their rents in kind, supplied the landlords with raw materials, food, and textiles. Resident artisans provided most of the items needed for everyday use. Only specialized products, such as iron and luxuries for the landlord, had to be bought from outside.

Mining and manufacturing

The widespread decline in other areas of economic activity is paralleled by declines in mining and manufacturing. The inability to produce enough gold and silver to keep up with the demand for coins contributed heavily to the monetary chaos and inflation of the third century. The decline of trade and agricultural prosperity in many regions reduced the demand for manufactured goods such as tools and equipment; high-quality pottery and cloth; building materials, furniture, and decorative artwork; and carts, wagons, boats, and ships. The decline was so bad in the third century that when demand revived in the fourth, there was a shortage of people with the skills required to meet it.

SOCIAL TRENDS

In the third century, the Roman Empire was, as it always had been, a vast multiethnic, multicultural conglomeration of peoples on three continents. By Caracalla's *Constitutio Antoniniana* of 212, all of those who were of free status shared a common citizenship (pp. 522–3). In many ways, that was the logical culmination of a process that had begun with the first extension of Roman citizenship in Italy during the Republic. The progressive elimination of the distinction between Romans and non-Romans had been a hallmark of Rome's successful expansion for hundreds of years.

Social role of the army

During the third century, the army had made it possible for provincials of non-Italian origin to rise to the top of the imperial hierarchy. Septimius Severus, a native of the province of Africa, is a perfect example. Maximinus, the Thracian whom the Pannonian legions had made emperor after Severus Alexander, had been appointed to several equestrian military offices by Septimius. The Emperor Philip the Arab came from an Arabian family that Septimius had favored. Philip himself had been promoted to the equestrian office of praetorian prefect in 243. The emperors Claudius Gothicus and Aurelian had been talented equestrian military officers from Balkan provinces. They were the first in a series of emperors generally identified as Illyrians that culminated with Diocletian and Constantine.

It was a long-standing Roman policy to post soldiers far from their home provinces. Under Septimius Severus, for example, there were Arabs serving in Gaul and Goths serving in Arabia. After completing their terms of service, soldiers frequently retired where they had been stationed. That trend was encouraged by Septimius Severus' abolition of the prohibition against soldiers' marrying. Although native soldiers from the provinces had learned Latin and become Romanized, they also brought some of their own traditions and customs to the areas where they settled.

Greater public recognition of important women

During the Republic and the first two centuries C.E., the women of elite families and emperors' households had always been important. They were vehicles for building useful marital alliances. Many played significant, even if informal, roles in politics. Scandal and censure by horrified males was mostly their reward. For dynastic and propaganda purposes, the mothers and wives of emperors were positively portrayed in traditional female roles on coins, in inscriptions, and via honorific statues. In the third century, however, Septimius Severus and his family produced a change. They came from Syria and North Africa, where there was a tradition of placing greater public emphasis on important women. Women of prominent families received more public recognition as patrons of their communities in Roman Africa than anywhere else in the Empire. It probably seemed natural, therefore, to an emperor of Punic descent from North Africa to give great public prominence to the role played by his Syrian wife, Julia Domna.

No Roman woman, not even Livia, had ever before received the variety of honors bestowed upon Julia Domna. She was depicted on coins as Cybele or seated on the throne of Juno with titles such as *Mother of the Camps and Senate* or *Mother of the Fatherland*. Statues and inscriptions honoring her were set up everywhere. At Aphrodisias, in western Asia Minor, she even was hailed as the goddess Demeter and given a temple. Under Caracalla, she functioned almost as a prime minister or secretary of state with her own Praetorian Guard. She carried on much of the imperial correspondence in Latin and Greek all over the Empire. Julia Maesa and Julia Mamaea achieved even greater public prominence under Elagabalus and Severus Alexander (pp. 524–5).

Salonina, wife of Emperor Gallienus (253–268), did not gain the prominence of Domna, Maesa, and Mamaea, but she figured heavily in dynastic propaganda on the coins of Gallienus' reign. Her portrait appears on literally hundreds of issues from the period, particularly on those minted at Milan. That was Gallienus' main residence. Salonina often maintained the imperial presence among the troops there while Gallienus was off fighting elsewhere. She also supported Gallienus' cultural agenda and was noted for accompanying him to hear the philosopher Plotinus lecture. Under the soldier-emperors who followed Gallienus, the women of the imperial Court became less visible again, but the stage was set for the emergence of women who would play dominant roles in the imperial Court, particularly in the eastern half of the Empire during the fourth, fifth, and sixth centuries.

At Carthage in 203, a young aristocratic woman named Vibia Perpetua and a pregnant slave named Felicitas achieved an entirely different kind of public prominence. These two women were among the early martyrs of the Christian Church. Their deaths are portrayed in *The Passion of Perpetua and Felicitas*. Most of it is presented as Perpetua's own account of her experiences between being arrested and marched off to face death in the gladiatorial arena. In the depiction of her confrontations with her father and the Roman governor and in her various dreams, Perpetua completely over-turns the existing male-dominated social and political order. She, ordinarily a power-less woman, feels empowered by her sufferings and impending death. She is called a *domina* (mistress) and appears victorious over her normal masters. Perpetua, Felicitas, and their fellow martyrs are portrayed turning suffering and death into joy and eter-nal life. Shown unbowed and in control to the very end, Perpetua guides the sword of the trembling gladiator to her own throat. Whatever the facts may be, *The Passion of Perpetua and Felicitas*—along with similar tales of martyrs, often female—became a popular and powerful tool for converting others, particularly women, to a faith that promised the power to overcome suffering and powerlessness.

Decline of cities

The problems and changes of the third century caused suffering, anxiety, and a sense of powerlessness for many people. Urban dwellers were hard hit in many areas. Numerous factors caused cities to shrink and decline: natural disasters such as plagues and the large earthquakes that hit much of the Empire between 242 and 262, economic contraction, and attacks during invasions or civil wars. To survive, cities had to erect fortresses and walls that characterized cities in Europe and the Mediterranean world for centuries thereafter.

A sign of shrinkage is that walls sometimes enclosed only a fourth of a city's for-mer area, although there are cases where extensive habitations remained outside the walls. Inside the walls, public buildings and monuments often decayed. Even Rome, which was becoming the capital of the Empire in name only, began to recede from the high tide that it had reached in the first and second centuries. A few cities like Milan, Verona, Aquileia, Sirmium, and Antioch thrived as major defensive centers. Many cities regained lost ground slowly, if at all. Cities in the East, however, did not fare so badly as those in the West.

The plight of the curial class

The decline of trade, manufacturing, and agriculture and the shrinking of cities paral-leled the progressive weakening of the curial class (*curiales*). It comprised the merchants, businessmen, and medium-sized landowners who served as local municipal magistrates and decurions, members of the municipal *curia* (council). In the past, the *curiales* appro-priated municipal funds for public works, baths, temples, entertainments, and welfare. Through traditional euergetism, they often supplemented those appropriations with their own private wealth to gain reputations as benefactors of their communities. They also served as collectors of imperial taxes and provided for the feeding and bedding of troops in transit and for changes of horses for the imperial post (*cursus publicus*).

As the government and the army made more and more demands on communities in the form of requisitions and taxes, the *curiales* had less and less to spend on private benefactions. Unable to pressure the great senatorial landlords, they pressed harder on those below them to relieve their own financial burdens. Service as a decurion or magistrate had once been a highly sought honor. Now it became more and more a burden to be avoided. Many *curiales* sought escape by gaining positions in the imperial bureaucracy, becoming soldiers, or subordinating themselves to some great landowner as his tenants (*coloni*).

The urban poor

Only in Rome and a few other favored cities did the urban poor find any significant relief. In those cities, usually major imperial residences, the emperor tried to maintain his traditional role as patron and benefactor. There, the poor received food and entertainment on an incongruously generous scale. Most cities had to depend on local revenues and benefactors to support such generosity. Their poor could no longer be fed and entertained. Life became desperate for many. Crime, prostitution, the selling of children, military service, and flight to the countryside or even beyond the imperial frontiers were among the few options for survival. Those who professed Christianity, however, found relief through the growing charitable activities of the local churches. They encouraged more fortunate members to share what they had with the poor. Not coincidentally, the number of urban Christians increased significantly.

Slaves and coloni

Slavery remained a major feature of Roman social and economic life in the third and subsequent centuries. That is clear from the amount of attention devoted to issues involving slaves in the imperial law codes. By the second half of the third century, however, the supply of cheap unskilled slaves for agricultural labor probably was shrinking. Emperors who were successful in defeating attackers preferred to enroll captives in the Roman army or settle them on deserted lands. Therefore, large landowners increasingly welcomed those who wished to farm a portion of their land as *coloni*.

The expansion of upper-class landowners

As so often in times of great economic stress, the ranks of the very rich increased at the expense of those even greater numbers who were sinking lower and lower on the socioeconomic scale. Some of the old senatorial families in the West would reach princely levels of wealth, status, and power. Below them was a growing class of large, if not truly grand, landowners. Their ranks were swollen by an influx of numerous newcomers. Often, they had risen from a lower station through the army and imperial bureaucracy to positions where they had the power to enrich themselves. Among the military men were former non-Roman auxiliaries and soldiers from key frontier provinces like Illyricum, Pannonia, and Thrace.

The newcomers had conservatively invested their gains in land. When they retired, they imitated those of hereditary wealth by devoting the bulk of their attention to creating great holdings in the country. Their wealth enabled them to enjoy the luxuries that still came by way of foreign and domestic commerce, and they acquired more land whenever they could.

Increasing stratification and regimentation

The militarization of the government in the third century was reflected in the increasing stratification and regimentation of society in general. A primary example is the increasing official acceptance of harsher penalties for *humiliores* than those for *honestiores* (p. 518). As the great landowners rose higher, there was pressure to reduce the *curiales* to lower status and to tie the *coloni* to their landlords.

THIRD-CENTURY CULTURAL LIFE

The disruptions of the third century severely reduced the resources and leisure available for maintaining the cultural life of the old Greco-Roman elites. That was especially true in the hard-hit West, although some areas did better than others. In the East, where the urban and economic declines were generally less severe, the Greek-speaking urban elites more vigorously carried on the traditions of their class. Everywhere, however, the old elites' control of the cultural agenda was weakened. Long-scorned native and popular influences began to make themselves felt at all levels. Nowhere was that more true than in the matter of religion.

RELIGION

The Roman Empire continued to exhibit much religious diversity during the third century. In particular, the people of the countryside, the *pagani*, continued to worship their traditional gods. On the other hand, the religious changes that were already visible in the cities, army camps, and administrative centers of the Empire during the first and second centuries (pp. 489–90) accelerated in the third.

Those trends were aided by Caracalla's grant of universal citizenship in 212. It gave legitimacy to people and traditions that the old Roman and Greek elites had not sanctioned. One of the grant's stated purposes was to allow all people to conduct religious sacrifices in common. It also enabled those who did not share the religious traditions of the old elites to gain power more easily as officials and even emperors.

Moreover, the disasters of the second half of the third century made many people question the power and value of both the old gods and the ration-alistic philosophies of happier times. More and more people were drawn to deities, religions, beliefs, and occult practices that had more universal appeal or promised to empower those who felt powerless. That was particularly true in the cities and army camps. There mystery religions, magicians, and charlatans who claimed to have power over the forces of evil continued to gain adherents.

Religion and the state

Various emperors tried to enlist religious support for the state by claiming the personal favor of some divinity who would protect it. Decius, who mounted the first general persecution of the Christians (250), was trying to regain the favor of the traditional anthropomorphic deities, to whom Rome's success in better days had been attributed. He wanted to restore what the Romans called the *pax deorum* (Peace of the Gods), which the old public priesthoods and festivals were supposed to preserve. Many traditionalists in the Roman senate welcomed and participated in this movement. Pagan senators at Rome remained a bastion of the traditional state religion for at least another 150 years.

Autocracy and monotheistic religions

During the third century, the tendency toward absolute monarchy in earthly government paralleled the growing popularity of various religions with claims of universality and some kind of supreme deity. Emperors sought religious sanctions for their sole authority over the universal empire that they were trying to preserve. It was no longer easy to believe in the divine nature of the emperors themselves, who rose and fell with bewildering rapidity. None of the emperors after the Severi was deified. Still, people could accept the idea of an autocratically governed universal empire sanctioned by some kind of overarching supreme deity. The rise of the universal cosmopolitan state had precipitated the decline of the old national and local polytheism. It encouraged the acceptance of more universalistic Eastern religions and mystery cults. They were focused on some extraordinarily powerful deity, often paired with his/her consort, son, or helper (pp. 490–2). The idea of a supreme universal deity was also reflected in the rapidly spreading philosophy of Neoplatonism. It stressed the quest for knowledge of the divine One. The One was at the center of the universe. All else depended on it (pp. 554–5).

The trends toward autocracy and monotheism visibly manifested themselves at Rome. There Emperor Aurelian erected a resplendent temple to Sol Invictus, the Unconquered Sun. He even established a college of pontiffs of senatorial rank to superintend the worship of this supreme god of the universe. Sol Invictus became the divine protector of the Roman Empire. Aurelian appeared on his new coins with a radiate crown representing the rays of the sun.

Isism and Mithraism

The mystery cult of Isis did not continue to gain strength as it had in the first and second centuries C.E. (pp. 490–1). Mithras, however, attracted the helpful interest of Commodus and the Severi. His cult grew, and he eventually became identified with Sol Invictus as *Deus Sol Invictus Mithras* (The God Mithras the Unconquered Sun). Had the Roman emperors remained devoted to Sol Invictus after the reign of Aurelian, Mithraism might have become more deeply entrenched in the population. Its all-male base, however, was too small to survive the emperors' conversion to Christianity in the fourth century.

Manichaeism

One of the most potent forces in the second half of the third century and for the next 200 years was Manichaeism. It is the religion named for the Persian prophet Mani.

He was a friend of the Sassanid Persian king Shapur (Sapor) I and started preaching with royal support in 242. A little over thirty years later, however, Mani was executed by Shapur's grandson Bahram (Vahram, Varahan, Varanes) I under the influence of a conservative religious reaction.

Mani combined elements of Greek philosophy, Babylonian astrology, various Eastern mystery cults, Gnosticism, and Christianity. He counted Buddha, Zoroaster, and Jesus all as prophets. Zoroastrian dualism provided the fundamental starting point of Manichaean belief. Originally, the universe was divided between Two Principles or Roots, the Light and the Dark. The realm of Light contained everything good; the Dark, everything bad. At some time, the forces of the Dark invaded the Light. The ensuing struggle produced this world from the bodies of the forces of Darkness, who had swallowed part of Light's realm.

Mani taught that Jesus had revealed this miserable state of affairs to Adam and showed him how he could gradually free the particles of Light from the prison of his physical body, which was composed of Darkness. In that way, Adam would be able to restore the original perfect state. Unfortunately, the agents of Darkness created Eve to entice him from his task. Adam then scattered the particles of Light still further by begetting children. Jesus, however, using the moon and the sun, set up a mechanism to distill the souls of the dead and reconstruct the Perfect Man. Eventually, according to Mani, the world will end with Jesus' second coming. A great fire will refine its remains for 1468 years until all heavenly material is freed and the Realm of Light is completely restored. There was, however, no survival of the individual personality and no personal victory over the forces of evil in this world or over death in the next. Christianity promised both. Therefore, some have argued, many found Christianity more appealing. Also, the Manichees never enjoyed the advantage of converting a Roman emperor and lost the support of the Persian emperors, whereas Christianity eventually became the religion of Rome's rulers.

Judaism and Christianity

Judaism maintained itself among the Jewish population dispersed throughout the Empire. It remained a legally recognized ancestral religion. Therefore, there was no official persecution, although local outbreaks of violence against Jews did occur. Christianity, because it had assumed an identity quite distinct from its Jewish origins, had lost any claim to special protection as an ancestral religion. Always liable to individual legal prosecution for refusing to worship the gods of the state, Christians became subject to systematic imperial persecution in the mid-third century as Decius and Valerian sought unity through religious means (p. 532). Early Christian writers support the oft-repeated popular view that great numbers of Christians suffered martyrdom through horrible forms of execution at the hands of Roman persecutors. The actual number, however, was quite modest, probably under a thousand. Still, the impact of the martyrs was enormous. Christian authors endlessly retold or replicated stories of martyrdom to demonstrate the power of Christianity to triumph over pain and suffering.

The blood that martyrs spilled in fact and fiction nourished the spirits of the urban middle and working classes. Facing an increasingly uncertain future, the excluded and marginalized members of society were largely cut off from the upper-class civic life and institutions of the cities in which they lived. They often found refuge in the tightly knit, yet accepting, communities of Christians. Therefore, during the period of toleration known as the *Little Peace of the Church* after Valerian's death (260–302), the numbers of Christians continued to grow geometrically. Christianity became more firmly rooted than ever in the cities of the Empire's core. It also spread deeply into the smaller cities and towns of the peripheral provinces. The soldier-emperors from remote rural villages in the Danubian provinces were too busy defending the frontiers or putting down usurpers to notice or care until Diocletian began to rebuild the Roman state.

Two factors prevented Christianity from becoming just another Hellenized Eastern mystery cult. The first is that Christians accepted as the foundation for and proof of their faith in Jesus as the Messiah the Holy Book of the Jews (the Christian Old Testament), which has a completely different spirit from the mystery cults. The second is the unity fostered by the idea of apostolic succession (pp. 492–3). Doctrinal and institutional unity must not be exaggerated in this period. Still, the emerging Christian Church was more united, particularly on a regional basis, than other religions. That situation helped to check the spread of beliefs and practices too radically divergent from the spirit of the Old Testament and the early Christian writings canonized by the beginning of the third century as the New Testament. Those writings were largely the work of men whose background was still more Jewish than Gentile. This Christian religious system appears already worked out in all its major details between 180 and 190 in the works of Irenaeus, bishop of Lyons, particularly his *Five Books against Heresies* and the *Demonstration of Apostolic Preaching*.

The Christian Church in the West

By 200, the Christian Church in the West had already matured to its familiar form. Irenaeus, a Greek who had come from Asia Minor, was the last major Christian writer in the West to use Greek. After him, Latin became the standard language of the Western Church for both theology and daily use. The form and order of Sunday worship and the celebration of the Eucharist had assumed their standard outlines. Already, the bishop of Rome was recognized as having primacy over other bishops and churches. He even received deference from the bishop of Carthage, the second largest Western bishopric and home of an important school of Christian thinkers.

In the mid-third century, disputes between Rome and Carthage arose over the question of treating apostates who wanted to return to the Church and over the validity of baptism by heretics. The Roman bishops tended to be liberal on both counts. The Carthaginians, led by Cyprian (p. 559), favored the more strict view of the Roman priest Novatian; however, the threat of persecution from without prevented a serious breach. Eventually, the issue erupted into the Donatist schism of the fourth century (pp. 586–7), but in the third, Carthaginian bishops generally remained loyal to the bishop of Rome. The Church at Rome rejected the Eastern practice of commemorating Christ's death on the date of the Jewish Passover and established the observance of Easter Sunday. It also compiled the version of the New Testament generally accepted as canonical.

The Christian Church in the East

On the whole, the state of the Church in the East was much more fluid than in the West during the third century. Gnostic Christian sects flourished, particularly in Egypt. They espoused elaborate cosmologies and dualistic views similar to those of many Greek philosophies and dualistic religions such as Zoroastrianism and Manichaeism. They saw the divine, immortal soul as being trapped in the evil, mortal body and believed that Jesus brought knowledge (*gnosis*) of these matters. Acceptance of the truth of this knowledge would free the soul from its mortal prison and allow it to return to the pure heavenly realm, where it naturally belonged.

The bishops of Rome and Alexandria maintained a close relationship in an effort to control the Gnostic Christians. Nevertheless, Greek-speaking Alexandria was much more open to the influence of Greek philosophical thought than the Latin-speaking West. By the end of the second century, Alexandria began to produce important Christian thinkers. The intellectual influence of Greek philosophy there stirred up many theological disputes (pp. 638–9).

Around 170 C.E., Tatian, a disciple of Justin Martyr, founded a Syriac-speaking Christian Church in the client kingdoms and borderlands east of the Roman province of Syria. Its basic testament was Tatian's Syriac harmony (unified version) of the Four Gospels. It became known as the *Diatessaron* (*Four-in-One*). The conversion of King Abgar of Edessa gave great impetus to the Syriac Church. It remained strong and orthodox for many centuries.

It did produce one major heretic, however, Bardaisan (Bardesanes). He was a highly educated Aramaean trained in astronomy and astrology. Becoming a Christian about 180, he combined many of the ideas that he had picked up earlier with his new faith. This synthesis of Christian and non-Christian ideas was the basis of many of the views espoused in the third century by both the Persian prophet Mani (p. 550) and Christianized Mesopotamian Gnostics known as *Mandaeans*, who survive in modern Iraq.

In Asia Minor, whose churches were the earliest outside Palestine, Christians were numerous. They tended to remain on good terms with their pagan neighbors. In the mid-third century, an internal dispute arose over the question of readmitting to the Church those who had lapsed during the Decian persecution. A number of Christians in Asia Minor adopted the strict position of Novatian. His followers had become a schismatic sect and had extended to all major sins his view on the inability of the Church to grant absolution. The Novatians, therefore, were very puritanical. They tried to lead completely sinless lives, called themselves *Cathari* (Pure Ones), and insisted on the rebaptism of converts from other Christian churches.

In the late second century, a popular Christian movement had been introduced by Montanus, a convert in Phrygia. He began prophesying in the belief that the second coming of Jesus was near. Church leaders declared Montanus a heretic. If the validity of his prophetic movement had been granted, the doctrines of the Church would have been thrown into chaos by the constant occurrence of new revelations among those claiming divine inspiration. The vital unity of the Church would have been destroyed before it had had a chance to consolidate its position in the Empire.

The only other controversy of note involving the churches of Asia Minor was the refusal to bow to Rome over the question of when to celebrate Easter.

Magic and superstition

Magic and superstition continued to be popular with people of all classes. A collection of works under the supposed authorship of Hermes Trismegistus (Thrice-Greatest) that dealt with astrology, alchemy, magic, and theurgy (the art of summoning and controlling divine powers) was very popular. Theurgy became a subject of great interest in the late third century as people sought more and more for a means of controlling an increasingly chaotic world.

SCIENCE AND PHILOSOPHY

The temper of the times was not conducive to objective scientific thought. The last creative, rigorously systematic philosopher of antiquity was Plotinus (205–270), a Greek from Egypt. He had studied at Alexandria under a mysterious philosopher named Ammonius Saccas. He also joined the expedition of Gordian III to Persia (243) in order to study the wisdom of Persia and India. When Gordian was killed the next year, Plotinus went to Rome, where he joined a group of ascetic philosophers and set up a school.

Starting with Plato's philosophy, Plotinus created a systematic explanation of the universe and produced a new school of thought called *Neoplatonism*. This system is expounded in a magnum opus known as the *Enneads* (*Groups of Nine*) in six sections of nine books each. It is heavily influenced by the mystical Pythagorean elements in Plato. For Plotinus, everything is derived from the One. It is a single, immaterial, impersonal, eternal force. From the One, reality spreads out in a series of concentric circles. The utmost circle is matter, the lowest level of reality. Each level of reality depends on the next highest: Matter depends on Nature, which depends on the World-Soul, which depends on the World-Mind, which depends on the One. A person contains all of these levels of being in microcosm. By focusing the power of the intellect, an individual can attain a level of being equal to that of the World-Mind. At that point, one may be able to achieve such a complete unity of self that an ecstatic union with the One itself is achieved.

Obviously, Plotinus' goal was shared by contemporary religions. It was philosophical, however, because it was reached entirely through contemplative intellect, not through magic, ritual, or an intermediary divine savior. Such rigorously intellectual mysticism, however, was far beyond most of Plotinus' contemporaries. Neoplatonism soon was overlaid with the magical musings of people like Iamblichus (p. 635).

The *Enneads* was actually published by Plotinus' pupil and assistant Porphyry (232/233–ca. 305). Porphyry did the most to popularize Plotinus' ideas. He saw them as the bulwark of pagan philosophy and religion against the Christians, who threatened the old ways. He wrote a massive fifteen-book defense of tradition against the Christians. It set the stage for his own pupil Iamblichus' even more vehement effort to rally the forces of paganism and block the spread of Christianity in the fourth century.

EDUCATION AND THE WORLD OF LETTERS

During the second century C.E., the city of Rome ceased to be the Empire's center of literary activity. A writer no longer had to go there and write for its elite to gain a significant audience and reputation. By the third century, authors from many different parts of the Empire were writing to satisfy the needs of diverse audiences in many different fields and genres. State and philanthropic support for education in literature and rhetoric was still strong in the first half of the third century, but it suffered heavily in the crisis of the second half.

Paideia

Even with support from the state and private benefactors, education remained an expensive luxury reserved for the wealthy and well-to-do. Most teachers and professors demanded fees on top of their public salaries. Advanced education usually meant the expense of sending students away from home in late adolescence to teachers of rhetoric and philosophy in major cities like Rome, Carthage, Athens, Antioch, and Alexandria. Women, therefore, were still generally excluded. To a large extent, the system defined the upper-class men whom it taught and set them apart from ordinary men. Educated aristocrats from diverse provinces all over the Empire often had more in common with each other than with the lower-class inhabitants of their hometowns, whose native language they might not share. In the eastern provinces, the local notables all spoke Greek and studied a canon of Classical authors beginning with Homer and ending with the Attic orators. They learned many by heart and, as a result, used a uniform dialect of Attic Greek that allowed them to recognize one another instantly.

In the West, elite boys first acquired a basic knowledge of Greek and a thorough grounding in the Latin classics of the late Republic and early Principate: Catullus, Cicero, Caesar, Vergil, Horace, Livy, and Tacitus. Then they capped their studies with a stint at one of the major educational centers in Greece so that they could deal as equals with the local leaders of the eastern provinces. In Greek terms, they had acquired the distinctive form of education, *paideia*, that marked them out as sharers in a common elite culture and code of gentlemanly conduct. It allowed them to blunt the invidious distinctions between the rulers and the ruled and to maintain a civil discourse based on mutual understanding and respect that facilitated the smooth functioning of imperial rule.

The system's heavy emphasis on literature and rhetoric produced innumerable people who could turn a quick hexameter verse or make a fine-sounding speech. Hundreds of competent but second-rate examples exist, particularly in the Greek East. Many of the emperors were products of this system. They shared the literary interests of the educated upper class, on whom they depended to run the Empire. Septimius Severus was well educated in literature and law and wrote his autobiography (now lost) in Greek. His wife, Julia Domna, was very interested in philosophy and religion and patronized pagan sophists (p. 524). Severus Alexander had an intellectual circle that included historians, orators, and jurists. Carus' son Numerian was highly regarded as a poet. Gordian I and Gallienus were also poets. The latter took an interest in Plotinus' philosophy as well. He even had plans to set up a Neoplatonic state headed by Plotinus in Campania.

Introduction of the codex book

Along with the spread of education arose a greater need for a less expensive and less cumbersome form of book than the old *volumen* (roll). The need was met in the third century by the widespread use of the parchment codex, a form that had been available for more than a century but that had not caught on until now. It comprised individual leaves of parchment bound together in a stack along the left-hand edge in the manner of wooden-backed wax writing tablets. It was much more useful for taking notes and writing out individual exercises. Because it was cheaper and more convenient, it made books written in codex form accessible to a wider public. That feature made it particularly attractive to Christian writers.

Biography and history under the Severi

Julia Domna's role as patroness has been exaggerated in the past to include almost every literary and intellectual figure of note in Rome at the time. The only known important member of her circle whose work has survived is Philostratus (b. ca. 170), a Greek sophist. He wrote a collection of biographies of previous sophists. At Domna's request, he also composed a biography of the first-century C.E. Cappadocian mystic and miracle worker Apollonius of Tyana, whom he presented as a pagan equivalent of Christ. Probably not long after Philostratus, Diogenes Laertius, another Greek author, produced a collection of biographies of ancient philosophers that is useful in reconstructing the history of Greek philosophy.

Under Severus Alexander in 229, the Greek historian Cassius Dio produced his history of Rome from its founding. Although not an historian of the first rank, Dio used many good sources that are now lost, and he preserves much valuable information. A few years later, Herodian produced his less reliable but still important Greek narrative of events from 180 to 238. Marius Maximus, a contemporary of Dio and Herodian, wrote a continuation of Suetonius with Latin biographies of the emperors from Nerva to Elagabalus. These accounts often included spicy fiction with the facts but also contained much of value. Although they are now lost, they provided the basic framework for the biographies in the first and best part of the notorious *Historia Augusta* (p. 634).

Roman scholarship and legal science

The Severan and early post-Severan period saw the production of many commentaries on Classical Latin authors and learned treatises on technical subjects. They were aimed at teachers, students, and officials, who all needed to master basic information quickly. Some users came from non-Roman backgrounds and needed easy guides to Roman culture. Others just found that the material to be mastered was increasingly difficult to understand with the passage of time and too voluminous to be managed in its original form.

Some authors catered to people's desire to learn more about the diverse places and peoples that made up the Empire. Under the Severi, Claudius Aelianus (Aelian), a Roman writing in Greek, preserved much curious information on animal and human life in his *De Natura Animalium* and *Varia Historia*. Gaius Julius Solinus covered the whole Empire in a wide-ranging Latin compendium called *Collectanea Rerum Memorabilium*. First, he traced Rome's rise from its foundation to the creation of Augustus' Principate. Then, after treating the Italian and Greek core of the Empire, he worked counter clockwise to cover Germany, Gaul, Britain, Spain, Africa, Arabia, Asia Minor, India, and Parthia. It is a compilation of information culled from previous works like Pliny the Elder's *Natural History* on plants, animals, people, and customs. He is the first person known to have called the body of water that linked together many parts of the Empire the Mediterranean Sea (*Mare Mediterraneum*, "Sea in the Middle of the Land").

Roman civil law, *ius civile*, was the glue that bound together the diverse peoples and places that made up the Empire. Previous officials and emperors had modified Roman law to fit new conditions and peoples as the Empire expanded. Over the years, a huge number of individual laws, edicts, and decisions had been issued. There was a great need to organize and explain them for ease of use. Three major jurists from different parts of the Empire took up the task under the Severi. Papinian (Aemilius Papinianus), probably a North African, became Septimius' praetorian prefect in 203 and was executed in 212 after criticizing Caracalla. His legal commentaries in fifty-six books were so useful that later German kings used them as guides for establishing their own courts. Ulpian (Domitius Ulpianus) was a Phoenician from Tyre and praetorian prefect to Severus Alexander from 222 to 228, when he was murdered by disgruntled praetorian guardsmen. Among his numerous works are eighty-one books commenting on the praetor's edict. Paul (Julius Paulus) succeeded Ulpian as praetorian prefect (228–235). His 319 books of commentaries surpassed both of his predecessors' combined. Later in the third century, Herennius Modestinus analyzed the differences between similar-seeming cases. Near the end of the century, the *Codex Gregorianus* collected the rescripts of emperors from the previous two centuries.

Poetry and Greek romances

The third century was primarily an age of prose, not poetry. Significantly, the best poetry reflects the interests of aristocratic landowners more concerned with their rural worlds than philosophy or great contemporary issues. A late compilation called *The Latin Anthology* preserves a number of examples.

The best Latin poet of the age was Marcus Aurelius Olympicus Nemesianus (late third century). Nemesianus was from Carthage and was close to Emperor Carus and his son Numerian. He had hoped to write an epic on Numerian in the grand style of Vergil's *Aeneid*. The deaths of Numerian and his father, however, ended that project. What remain are four fine pastoral poems in the manner of Vergil's *Eclogues* and an unfinished didactic poem on hunting, the *Cynegetica*, in the tradition of Vergil's *Georgics*.

Typical Greek writings of the age are popular prose romances. They usually involve a virtuous heroine and steadfast hero who are separated by some mischance after falling in love. They experience all manner of hair-raising adventures, disasters, and narrow escapes until they are happily reunited in marriage at last. This genre originated at least as early as the first century C.E. Five representatives have survived: Achilles Tatius' *Leucippe and Cleitophon* is now dated to the mid-second century. *Chaereas and Callirhoe* by Chariton of Aphrodisias is probably from around 180. Heliodorus of Phoenician Emesa probably wrote his *Aethiopica or Theagenes and Charicleia* around 220. Longus (of Lesbos?) and Xenophon of Ephesus, respectively, seem to have written *Daphnis and Chloe* and the *Ephesiaca* or *Anthia and Habrocames* at some time in the third century.

The style of these works and the quality of production evident from surviving papyrus fragments indicate that they were aimed at the urban elites of the Greek East. They reflect the values of a privileged class that had the resources to withstand life's misfortunes without really suffering. They also seem to promote standards of male and female behavior designed to confirm the elite position of the upper class within the social hierarchy. Those standards reinforced the stable family structure and harmonious social relations that helped the upper class to perpetuate its elite position.

Secular literature after the Severi

The mid-third century saw a steep decline in literary production. Little of note except in philosophy survives. Two relatives of the sophist Philostratus, a father and grandson each confusingly named Philostratus, wrote three volumes entitled *Eikones* (*Images*). In the sophistic style of rhetoric, they describe over eighty works of art. An even more important sophist than Longinus (p. 538) in the post-Severan period was the Athenian Dexippus, who had helped to drive off the Goths and Heruli from Athens in 268 (p. 535). He wrote a history of Alexander's successors, a chronological summary of history down to 270, and a history of the Gothic wars from 238 to 275. Unfortunately, all three are largely lost, but quotations found in later authors like Zosimus (p. 707) show that he was a worthy historian who modeled himself on Thucydides.

Christian literature

During the third century, Christian literature came into its own. It usually did not have the same audience and purpose as secular works. It was also more creative because it had something new to say. Writings such as the Church's official accounts of various martyrdoms and the less formal passion narratives were aimed at people from the bottom of the social hierarchy ("passion," from the Latin *passio*, means "suffering"). The first in Latin appears around 180. It recounts the deeds of the martyrs of Scillum in North Africa, *Acta Martyrum Scillitanorum*. *The Passion of Perpetua and Felicitas* follows in ca. 203. Many others appeared throughout the century.

These accounts of suffering and death were subversive of the prevailing political and social order. In them, Roman authorities were delegitimized as they, often unwillingly, imposed violent and unjust punishments on innocent sufferers. Christians defined themselves through these narratives as a community of sufferers. They rejected the bonds of the dominant social order reaffirmed by the happy endings of Greek romances. Wives, husbands, children, parents, and friends were abandoned in the joyous pursuit of a martyr's death. Others saw that death as an ignoble defeat and punishment, but Christians viewed it as a glorious triumph. Through suffering, they rejected this world and entered the glorious life with Jesus in heaven: "Whoever comes to me and does not hate father and mother, wife and children, brothers and sisters, yes, even life itself, cannot be my disciple" (Luke 14:25–26). For Christians, death was the happy ending.

The Christian rejection of prevailing norms also appears in the works of Tertullian (ca. 160–ca. 240), a North African from Carthage. Son of a centurion in the Roman army and trained as a lawyer, he was the first of the Latin Church Fathers and a master of the art of defending the faith (apologetics). He became one of the founders of Western Christian thought. Over thirty of his works survive on such subjects as martyrdom, the soul, baptism, the resurrection of the flesh, marriage, and the proper behavior of women, whom he regarded with puritanical distrust. He was a brilliant pleader full of aggressive zeal in proclaiming a new Christian vision of the world. Eventually, however, he became an adherent of the Montanist heresy (p. 553).

Not all Christian apologists were as hostile to the pagan world as were Tertullian and the writers of passions and martyrologies. For example, although he, too, was a lawyer from North Africa, Tertullian's contemporary Minucius Felix was more upper class in origin. He shows how Christianity was beginning to penetrate the social elite, to whom he tried to appeal on their own terms in his elegant dialogue, the *Octavius*.

Occupying the middle ground is St. Cyprian (ca. 200–258), another Carthaginian and a younger contemporary of Tertullian. A well-educated member of the upper class, he was a famous teacher of rhetoric. After converting to Christianity and giving all of his goods to the poor in 246, he was appointed bishop of Carthage in 248. He admired Tertullian's rigorous morality and wrote on many of the same subjects. Yet, he was more refined and less strident. He conducted his duties as bishop like an upper-class Roman magistrate striving for equity and justice. In his writings, he introduced legal language and concepts that helped to shape the Catholic Church in the West. Although he had courageously protected his flock during Decius' persecution, he was ultimately martyred under Valerian. The *Life of Cyprian*, by his deacon Pontius, is the earliest known Christian biography.

The only Christian Latin poet of note in the third century probably was Commodian (ca. 250). He wrote at Carthage and mirrored Tertullian in his zeal and harshness.

Unlike most other poets whose work survives from antiquity, he uses accent rather than long and short syllables to produce his hexameter verses, which give voice to the hopes, and prejudices, of the lower classes.

Christians who wrote in Greek had produced the earliest apologetic works and accounts of martyrs. Many such Greek writers were active in the third century. They were usually well-educated members of the urban Greek upper class. Their writings furthered Christianity's appeal to that class in ways that reflected its traditions. Titus Flavius Clemens, Clement of Alexandria (ca. 150–ca. 215), for example, was born a pagan, most likely at Athens. He was steeped in Platonic philosophy and Classical literature before he was converted and went to study with an unknown Christian teacher in Egypt. He eventually became head of a Christian school and an influential apologist. In such surviving works as his *Exhortation to the Greeks*, he argues with grace and serenity that Christianity is superior to paganism.

Origen, Origenes Adamantius (ca. 185–ca. 255), was the son of a martyr and gave catechetical instruction to Christian converts at Alexandria. He also may have studied with the Platonist Ammonius Saccas, Plotinus' renowned teacher (p. 554). He had a famous personal library, wrote voluminously on textual and interpretive problems in the Bible, and systematically explained Christian beliefs in *On First Principles*. He countered the now-lost anti-Christian writings of the earlier (ca. 180) Platonist philosopher Celsus in *Against Celsus*.

In many ways, Origen was the founder of systematic theology. He made logic, dialectic, natural science, geometry, and astronomy standard parts of the Christian curriculum. With such training, the Alexandrian Church Fathers skillfully used Greek philosophy against their pagan critics and gave a more intellectual cast to Christian thought. It, in turn, gained greater respect among the pagan intellectual elite of the Empire.

The influence of Platonic thought, however, caused Origen to develop two controversial views: that this world resulted from evil and was not a perfect creation before the Fall; that the three divine persons who make up the Christian Trinity (God the Father, God the Son [Jesus Christ], and God the Holy Spirit) are not totally one and the same. With the first, Origen encouraged ideas linked with Christian Gnosticism. With the second, he set the stage for the divisive conflicts over the Trinity in the fourth century under Constantine (p. 587).

After a dispute with the bishop of Alexandria, Origen settled at Caesarea in Palestine and opened a school there. Tortured horribly during Decius' persecution, he died a little later at Tyre. His influence remained very strong in Palestine through students like Pamphilus, who inherited his library. Origen's friend Sextus Julius Africanus was a learned Christian from Jerusalem. He eventually went to Rome on an embassy to Elagabalus and later set up a library in the Pantheon for Severus Alexander. His *Chronographies* was the first attempt to rationalize biblical and Church history with secular history. It formed the basis of Eusebius' later *Chronicle* (p. 565).

Less is known about the influential writer Methodius, one of Origen's detractors. He wrote *On the Resurrection* to counter Origen's denial of a bodily resurrection of the flesh. He also countered the Gnostics in his *On the Freedom of the Will*. Although those works are now fragmentary, his popular *Symposium of the Ten Virgins*, in which the Christian heroine Thecla gives a prize oration on virginity, is complete (p. 621).

The tales of Christian martyrs and the apologetic and theological writings of the Latin and Greek Church Fathers are a major accomplishment. They helped to spread Christianity among all classes during the third century. They made it strong enough to withstand the greatest persecution of all, which was soon to come.

ART AND ARCHITECTURE

Despite all the troubles of the age, considerable art was produced for emperors and wealthy magnates. The influence of native traditions from all over the Empire mirrors the increasingly diverse origins of the imperial elite. Old styles, themes, and symbols were often creatively adapted to new times.

Sculpture

Portrait sculpture on coins maintained a high standard of realism as vehicles of official propaganda. Portrait sculpture in the round also continued the vigorous Roman tradition of such art. From the Severi to Valerian, sculptors strove for psychological realism in order to emphasize the true character of the subject. Under Gallienus, there was a preference for more idealized portraiture in the Classical Greek style. After that, the influence of Neoplatonism caused a shift to a more schematized, geometric style that gave a transcendent quality to the subjects, a style that prefigured the Middle Ages.

There were not many opportunities to produce monumental public relief sculptures through the difficult times of the third century. On the other hand, relief sculpture became a striking feature of the elaborately decorated private stone sarcophagi that wealthy Christians and pagans began to use as the new religious influences of the age caused the practice of bodily burial to replace cremation. Some feature groupings of Classical figures around a philosopher or poet, who symbolize the triumph of wisdom over death. Others feature a heroic figure in the midst of a chaotic battle to symbolize the triumph of good over evil. Christians depicted the Good Shepherd or Old Testament stories of God's deliverance. Despite the unclassical lack of balance in many of these scenes, the individual figures are very skillfully carved and are thoroughly in the tradition of Greco-Roman realism.

Painting and mosaics

Painting and mosaic art continued to flourish throughout the third century. Painting is represented mainly by murals preserved on the excavated walls of homes, public buildings, tombs, synagogues, temples, and churches from around the Empire. Excellent mosaics also adorned many of these buildings, particularly their floors. The level of technical skill remained very high, and the scenes represented are valuable in reconstructing the life of the times.

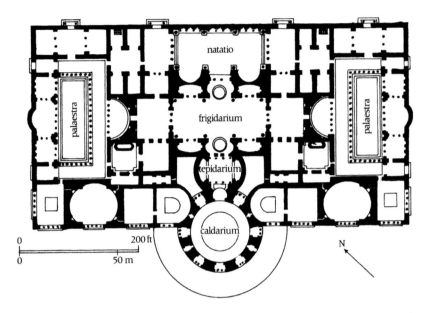

FIGURE 29.1 Plan of the Baths of Caracalla, Rome. (From Roman Art, second edition, Nancy and Andrew Ramage, Prentice Hall, 1996)

Architecture

Despite the Empire's serious economic problems, the building activity under the Severi was more than had been seen for many years. At Rome, the Arch of Septimius Severus still stands in the Forum (p. 521). Massive new additions were made to the imperial residence on the southeastern corner of the Palatine Hill. Below it, Septimius erected the Septizodium (or Septizonium), a huge marble façade resembling the architectural backdrop to the stage of a theater. About 275 feet long and three stories high, it was divided into seven bays, one for each of the planetary deities. The program of statuary and decoration probably honored members of the imperial family as well as the seven deities. It was meant to impress people passing by on the Appian Way, which it screened off from the Palatine. Caracalla built a huge new complex of baths and a new camp for the imperial bodyguards, both of which are now in ruins. In North Africa, Septimius' hometown, Lepcis (Leptis) Magna, received a whole complex of monumental buildings. Their remains today provide a striking example of imperial architecture and urban planning. All of these remains, moreover, show solid Roman craftsmanship.

During the anarchy between the Severi and Diocletian, there was not much opportunity for public architecture other than defensive works, such as Aurelian's partially preserved twelve-mile-long wall around Rome and fortifications in the provinces. Christian churches in various cities, however, had begun to accumulate enough wealth to erect some significant buildings. There is little that can be known about these churches now. Many were destroyed in the persecutions early in the following century or were replaced by more impressive structures after the persecutions ended.

SUMMARY AND PROSPECT

As do all ages, the third century of the Roman Empire had one foot in the past and the other in the future. The massive inflation of the latter half of the century was rooted in the basic nature of the ancient economy and technological limits of the time (pp. 505–6). In the West, many cities and the once-prosperous curial class declined. Small landowners, unable to withstand the pressure of Roman tax collectors, military requisitions, raids on the frontiers, and pressures from rich neighbors, were often reduced to dependent *coloni* foreshadowing medieval serfs. On the other hand, the wealthy became ever richer as they amassed huge amounts of land and paid more attention to their great villas in the country. In the East, the cities and small farmers fared better and were poised for revived prosperity in the next century. In either case, the bulk of the population lived in the countryside, as it always had, and followed the traditional rhythms of life in a peasant economy that functioned largely apart from the inflation-ravaged commercial economy.

The free inhabitants of the Empire acquired citizenship, and military service brought "barbarians" and people from different parts of the Empire into greater contact with each other (pp. 612–3). Still, the provincial upper classes were mainly the ones who found greater opportunities for advancement in the army and government. Similarly, a few women of the privileged classes achieved greater public prominence, but most women saw little improvement in their conditions. Women and the lower classes, however, increasingly found refuge among the growing ranks of the Christian Church. It was much more inclusive then than was the aristocratically dominated secular society.

Christianity and other popular mystery religions gave greater expression to the cultural traditions of those who could not afford to acquire the educated polish of upper-class *paideia*. In fact, Christianity often represented a challenge to all that the privileged classes held dear. Nevertheless, as Christianity began to penetrate the upper classes, the upper classes, in turn, began to shape Christian institutions, thought, literature, and art along familiar lines. By the beginning of the fourth century and the conversion of the Emperor Constantine, Christianity was becoming as much a force for spreading Classical culture to the previously excluded as it was a challenge to that culture.

SUGGESTED READING

Swain, S., Stephen Harrison, and Jas Elsner (ed.). *Severan Culture*. Cambridge: Cambridge University Press, 2007.

Langford, J. *Maternal Megalomania: Julia Domna and the Imperial Politics of Motherhood*. Baltimore: John Hopkins University Press, 2013.

CHAPTER 30

Diocletian

Creating the fourth-century Empire, 285 to 305 C.E.

In Roman history, the fourth century C.E. is often reckoned from the acclamation of Diocletian as emperor in 284 to the death of Theodosius in 395. The real turning point between the third and the fourth centuries, however, is the death of Carinus in 285. Only then did the unprecedented barrage of political, military, and natural disasters characterizing the third century begin to lose intensity in the face of Diocletian's subsequent actions.

The gigantic mobilization required to meet Rome's difficulties over the third century had furthered the trend toward an absolute military monarchy that can already be seen with Commodus and Septimius Severus. Under Diocletian, the Principate gave way completely to the Dominate. The term comes from *dominus*, "lord and master," which was synonymous with an absolute monarch and was now used in public documents to refer to the emperor. Diocletian instituted sweeping military, administrative, and fiscal reforms to ensure the survival of the Roman Empire united under his command as the senior of four ruling partners, tetrarchs, who formed the Tetrarchy.

SOURCES FOR ROMAN HISTORY DURING THE FOURTH CENTURY C.E.

The latter part of the fourth century C.E. is one of the best documented periods in Roman history. Unfortunately few major pagan or Christian writers cover Diocletian's

crucial reign at the century's start. The pagan Greek historian Zosimus (p. 707) portrayed Diocletian very favorably in his *New History* (ca. 500 C.E.), but the sections that
cover Diocletian's reign in detail are missing. On the other hand, the rest of the narrative, which is very biased against Constantine and the Christians, is complete. The
excellent *History* (or *Res Gestae*) written in Latin by the pagan historian Ammianus
Marcellinus is missing the part that covers Diocletian, Constantine, and Constantine's
sons up to 353, but it is extant for the period from 353 to 378 (p. 634). Quintus Aurelius
Symmachus, a staunch pagan upholder of senatorial tradition at Rome, has left a major
body of letters. They provide valuable insights into the world of well-connected Roman
aristocrats (pp. 633–4). The works of the Neoplatonist Iamblichus and Eunapius' *Lives
of the Philosophers and Sophists* also shed much light on the time and its people (p. 635).

The letters and poems of Ausonius, a Gallo-Roman aristocrat and rhetorician, illustrate the life of the increasingly Christian elite of the western provinces
(pp. 634–5). Themistius, a pagan philosopher and rhetorician, and other skilled orators
produced numerous panegyrics on Constantine and members of his dynasty (p. 636).
The voluminous letters and speeches of the great pagan Greek rhetorician Libanius
of Antioch shed light on many personalities and events during the second half of
the fourth century (p. 636). The letters and essays of Julian the Apostate, the former
Christian who tried to restore the primacy of paganism when he became emperor, are
very helpful for his lifetime (p. 635).

Historical writings of secondary importance include the biography of Diocletian
at the close of the *Historia Augusta* and several fourth-century *breviaria*, brief historical
surveys of Roman history, the last parts of which are of real value since they record
events of the authors' own time (p. 634). A number of interesting fourth-century technical treatises and handbooks on grammar, rhetoric, geography, medicine, and military
affairs have also survived.

The surviving works of Christian thinkers and churchmen from the fourth century
are very extensive. They are full of quotations from otherwise lost documents, such as
imperial statutes and edicts, proceedings of Church councils, imperial correspondence,
and letters written by bishops and other ecclesiastical officials. Their biases are obviously
counter to those of strongly pagan authors and often involve partisan or theological
controversies within the Church as well. One of the best, but most biased, Christian
writers is Lactantius (ca. 240–ca. 325). Aside from his doctrinal works, important for
understanding the evolution of Christian thought, his Latin tract *On the Deaths of the
Persecutors* presents a hostile view of the policies and personalities of Diocletian and
those with whom he shared power (p. 637). The works of the Greek bishop Eusebius of
Caesarea are important despite their obvious favoritism: versions of his *Chronicle* and his
Ecclesiastical History mentioned earlier (p. 638), his *Life of Constantine* (unfinished), and
the *Praise of Constantine* (with the *Tricennalian Oration*, which celebrates Constantine's
thirtieth anniversary as emperor) are invaluable. Other Greek histories of the Church
are those of Theodoret, Sozomen, and Socrates, which end in 408, 425, and 439, respectively (p. 707). Many other great churchmen writing in both Greek and Latin provide
a wealth of material for all aspects of history in the latter half of the fourth century
through their histories, biographies, letters, sermons, and doctrinal writings (pp. 637–8).

Other sources include inscriptions, papyri, coins, archaeological materials, and especially imperial statutes (*constitutiones*[1]). The latter are preserved in numerous documents: inscriptions, papyri, various juristic and literary works, the *Theodosian Code* (published in 438 during the reign of Theodosius II, 408–450), and the *Justinian Code* (first published in 529 during the reign of Justinian I, 527–565). The three most important inscriptional texts are Diocletian's famous *Edict on Maximum Prices*, his *Currency Edict*, and the great Paikuli inscription of Narses I of Persia (293–302), who recounted his triumphs and the acts of homage paid him by Roman envoys and the vassal kings of Asia.

An important document is the Laterculus of Verona. It lists the provinces created under Diocletian's reorganization of the Empire. Another major document is the *Notitia Dignitatum* (*List of Offices*), an apparently official, illustrated register of military units and their postings throughout the provinces. As it stands, it comes from the western half of the Empire after the division that prevailed from 395 onward, but the information on the East is earlier. Because it reflects the ideal of stated policy, it does not necessarily represent actual practice. It must be used with caution when trying to determine what was really happening at any particular moment.

The archaeological evidence for the fourth century is enormous. Diocletian and his co-emperors, then Constantine and Constantine's heirs, spent prodigiously on building in Rome, Constantinople, and other important cities where emperors frequently resided, such as Trier, Milan, Sirmium, Nicomedia, and Antioch. Fortifications, camps, guard stations, and signal posts were constructed all over the Empire. The elite spent huge sums on building and expanding rural villas as they focused more and more on a self-sufficient life in the countryside. Christians built shrines, monasteries, and major urban churches with great fervor after persecution ended early in the century and official support began.

THE RISE OF DIOCLETIAN

The humbleness of Diocletian's origins has been exaggerated by hostile or overly dramatic sources. One of a series of talented, well-trained officers from the Danubian provinces, he probably came from a relatively well-to-do provincial family. He had been a cavalryman under Gallienus, a *dux*, or cavalry commander, in Moesia, and a commandant of the imperial mounted bodyguard. His excellent military record is nevertheless overshadowed by his career as an organizer, administrator, and statesman. He inspired excellent advisors and generals to assist him loyally in restoring stability to the Empire.

The chief military and political problems facing Diocletian were the strengthening of the power and authority of the central government, the defense of the frontiers, the recovery of the rebellious and seceding provinces, and the removal of those conditions that favored constant attempts to seize the throne. Diocletian's first act was to find a loyal representative who could take over the defense of the West and permit him to concentrate his energies on the protection of the threatened Danubian and eastern frontiers. Such a loyal representative would convince the western legions of his concern for western problems and would lessen the danger of revolt. His choice fell upon

Maximian, an old comrade in arms, whom he elevated to the rank of Caesar and sent to Gaul.

In Gaul, Maximian quickly crushed a rebellion of desperate peasants (the Bacaudae) and drove out the Germans into the region east of the Rhine. In recognition of these victories, Diocletian raised Maximian to the rank of Augustus in 286. Maximian was to rule jointly with Diocletian and to be second only in personal prestige and informal authority.

Maximian had not been so successful at sea. To clear the English Channel and the North Sea of the Frankish and Saxon pirates who had been raiding the shores of Gaul and Britain, he established a naval base at Gesoriacum (Bononia, Boulogne) on the coast of Gaul and placed Marcus Aurelius Carausius in command of the Roman fleet. Carausius, a native of the German lowlands and an experienced and daring sailor, overcame the pirates within a few weeks. Then, he ambitiously enlarged his fleet with captured pirate ships and men, seized Gesoriacum and Britain, and conferred upon himself the title of Augustus. Diocletian was too occupied to do more than protest and Maximian's fleet was wrecked at sea. Carausius maintained undisturbed sway over Britain for seven years as Emperor of the North.

In the East, however, Diocletian successfully displayed Roman might on the Danube and the Euphrates. Between 286 and 291, he repelled invasions and strengthened frontier defenses. In 287, successful negotiations with the Persian King Bahram (Vahram, Varahan, Varanes) II (276–293) obtained Persian renunciation of claims to Roman Mesopotamia and recognition of Rome's ally Tiridates "III" (261–317) as the legitimate king of Armenia.

THE TETRARCHY: A NEW FORM OF IMPERIAL RULE, 293 TO 312 C.E.

In order to strengthen imperial control of the armies and forestall usurpers such as Carausius, Diocletian resolved in 293 to create the four-man ruling committee known as the *Tetrarchy*. Two Caesars were to be appointed to serve as junior emperors and successors to two Augusti. One would serve under Diocletian, the Augustus in the East, the other under Maximian, the Augustus in the West. Diocletian selected Gaius Galerius, another Danubian officer and a brilliant strategist, as his Caesar. Maximian's choice was yet another Danubian, C. Flavius Julius Constantius, commonly called *Chlorus* or "Pale Face," who proved himself an excellent general, a prudent statesman, and the worthy father of the future Constantine the Great.

The Tetrarchy was held together by the personality and authority of Diocletian, the senior Augustus. It was doubly strengthened by adoption and marriage. Each Caesar was the adopted heir and son-in-law of his Augustus. Diocletian's daughter, Valeria, married the Caesar Galerius. Maximian's daughter (or stepdaughter) Theodora was already married to the Caesar Constantius. Also, Maximian's son, Maxentius, married Galerius' daughter, Valeria Maximilla.

On the death or abdication of an Augustus, his Caesar, as his adopted son and heir, supposedly would take his place. The new Augustus would, in turn, select a new

Caesar. The Tetrarchy was indivisible in operation and power: laws were promulgated in the names of all four rulers, and triumphs gained by any one of them were acclaimed in the name of all. On the other hand, each member of the Tetrarchy had his own separate court and bodyguard and had the right to strike coins bearing his own image and titulature.

Each Augustus and Caesar oversaw those provinces and frontiers that he could conveniently and adequately defend from his own headquarters. Maximian protected the upper Rhine and upper Danube from Mediolanum (Milan) and Aquileia in Italy. Constantius shielded the middle and lower Rhine, Gaul, and later Britain from Augusta Treverorum (Trèves, Trier) in Gaul. Galerius seems initially to have guarded the Euphrates frontier, Palestine, and Egypt from Antioch in Syria (293–296) and then the lower Danube and the Balkans from Thessalonica (Salonica, Thessaloniki, Saloniki) in Macedonia and Serdica in Thrace (299–311). For most of his first ten years, Diocletian oversaw the middle and lower Danube and Asia Minor from his bases at Sirmium on the Save River and Nicomedia on the Sea of Marmara (Marmora, Propontis); from 299 to 302, he looked after affairs in Asia Minor, the Levant, and Egypt from Antioch and then from Nicomedia (302–305).

The Tetrarchy in action

While Diocletian held the reins of power, the Tetrarchy fully justified his expectations. Each of the four rulers set about restoring peace and unity in his own part of the Empire. Constantius weakened Carausius by capturing the port of Gesoriacum (Bononia, Boulogne) and defeating his German allies. In 293, a treacherous rival assassinated Carausius, and, in 296, Constantius successfully reestablished Roman rule in Britain. Returning to the Continent, he strengthened the fortifications along the Rhine frontier and established a long period of peace after a spectacular victory over the Alemanni in 298.

The activities of Diocletian and Galerius in the East are poorly documented, but recent research supports the following outline. Between 293 and 296, Diocletian waged a series of successful campaigns against the tribes along the lower Danube. He restored Roman defenses in the area while events in Persia and Egypt occupied Galerius' attention. In Persia, a new king, Narses (293–302), overthrew Bahram II and began to subvert the treaty of 287. He also promoted the religious beliefs of the Manichees (pp. 550–1), whose missionary activities raised Roman suspicions. At the same time, Egypt was being disturbed by the raids of the Blemmyes from the Sudan. They could no longer be left unchecked. Galerius probably spent all of 294 and the first few months of 295 in Egypt in order to drive out the Blemmyes and strengthen Egypt's defenses.

Meanwhile, Narses was causing increasing alarm on the Euphrates frontier. By the fall of 296, hostilities could no longer be avoided. Narses had driven Tiridates III out of Armenia and was poised to strike at Roman territory. Diocletian brought reinforcements from the Danube and guarded the Euphrates. Galerius rushed off to intercept Narses. The latter won an initial victory. Galerius, with significant help from his wife, Valeria, obtained enough reinforcements and resources to turn the tables in the following year. He captured the king's harem, regained control of Mesopotamia, and seized the strategic fortress of Nisibis as well as the Persian capital of Ctesiphon (map, p. 379).

While Galerius was fighting Narses, tax increases precipitated a serious revolt in Egypt under the leadership of Domitius Domitianus and Aurelius Achilleus.[2] Diocletian brought an army from Syria in mid-297 and besieged Alexandria for eight months. After subduing the whole of Egypt during the rest of 298, he returned to join the victorious Galerius at Nisibis for the final peace negotiations with Narses.

Narses had to accept harsh peace terms in order to get back his wives and children. He agreed to surrender Mesopotamia, which now extended to the west bank of the upper Tigris, and five small provinces east of the Tigris. He acknowledged Greater Armenia and the kingdom of Iberia south of the Caucasus as Roman protectorates. He also agreed that merchants traveling between the Roman and Persian empires must pass through the Roman customs center at Nisibis. The victory of Galerius was so complete that the Persians did not risk war with Rome for another fifty years.

The creation of the Tetrarchy had been fully justified. Constantius was victorious in the West and Galerius had secured the East. Strong defenses existed around the Empire: in Britain, along the Rhine, Danube, and Euphrates rivers; in Mesopotamia; and in Egypt. Captured invaders had become settlers who helped to repopulate and defend lands adjacent to the frontiers. That four-headed, seemingly decentralized, but actually united, power gave Rome twenty years of stable rule.

DIOCLETIAN'S OTHER INITIATIVES

In addition to establishing the Tetrarchy and consolidating the military defenses of the Empire, Diocletian brought to fulfillment growing changes in almost every department of the government. These changes were not the innovations of a radical but rather the continuation and strengthening of the trends that had been developing in the shift toward absolute monarchy.

Exalting the emperor

Diocletian went much further than previous emperors in attempts to exalt the emperor above ordinary mortals. He surrounded himself with an aura of such power, pomp, and sanctity that any attempt to overthrow him would appear not only treasonous but also sacrilegious. Diocletian assumed the title of *Jovius* as Jupiter's earthly representative sent to restore the Roman Empire. He bestowed on his colleague, Maximian, the name of *Herculius* as the earthly analog of Hercules, son and helper of Jupiter. Together they demanded the reverence and adoration due to gods for the Jovian and Herculian dynasties that they had founded. Everything about them was sacred and holy: their palaces, courts, and bedchambers. Their portraits radiated a nimbus or halo, an outer illumination flowing from an inner divinity.

Diocletian adopted an elaborate court ceremonial and etiquette, not unlike that prescribed at the royal court of Persia. He became less accessible and seldom appeared in

FIGURE 30.1 The dioceses and provinces of the Roman Empire in 314 C.E.

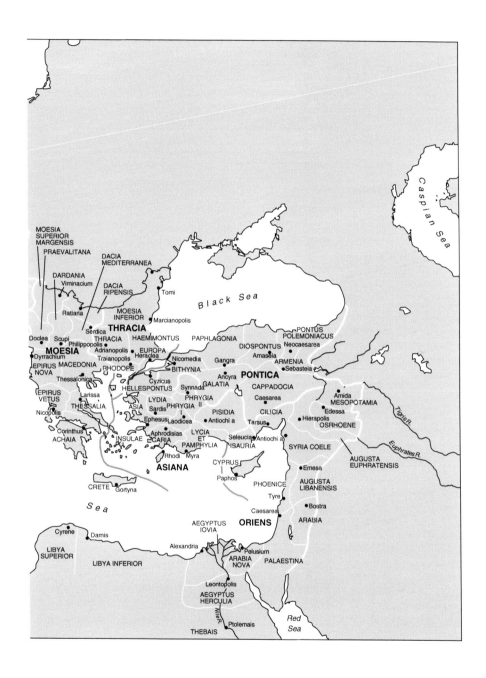

MOESIA
SUPERIOR
MARGENSIS

PRAEVALITANA

DACIA
MEDITERRANEA

DARDANIA
Viminacium

DACIA
RIPENSIS

Tomi

Ratiaria

MOESIA
INFERIOR

Marcianopolis

Black Sea

Serdica

THRACIA

Doclea Scupi

THRACIA

HAEMIMONTUS

PAPHLAGONIA

PONTUS
POLEMONIACUS

Philippopolis

Adrianopolis

DIOSPONTUS

Neocaesarea

MOESIA

Dyrrachium

Traianopolis

EUROPA

Heraclea

Amaseia

ARMENIA

EPIRUS
NOVA

MACEDONIA

Nicomedia

Gangra

Sebasteia

RHODOPE

BITHYNIA

Thessalonica

Cyzicus

Ancyra

PONTICA

Amida

EPIRUS
VETUS

Larissa

HELLESPONTUS

Synnada

GALATIA

CAPPADOCIA

MESOPOTAMIA

THESSALIA

ASIA

LYDIA

PHRYGIA
I

Caesarea

Edessa

Nicopolis

Sardis

PHRYGIA
II

Hierapolis

OSRHOENE

Ephesus

Laodicea

PISIDIA

Corinthus

Aphrodisias

Antiochi a

Tarsus

CILICIA

ACHAIA

INSULAE

CARIA

LYCIA
ET
PAMPHYLIA

Antiochi a)

Seleucia

SYRIA COELE

AUGUSTA
EUPHRATENSIS

ASIANA

Rhodi Myra

NISAURIA

CRETE

Gortyna

CYPRUS

Paphos

PHOENICE

Emesa

AUGUSTA
LIBANENSIS

Sea

Tyre

Caesarea

Bostra

ARABIA

Cyrene

Damis

AEGYPTUS
IOVIA

ORIENS

LIBYA
SUPERIOR

Alexandria

Pelusium

LIBYA INFERIOR

ARABIA
NOVA

PALAESTINA

Leontopolis

AEGYPTUS
HERCULIA

*Red
Sea*

Ptolemais

THEBAIS

*Caspian
Sea*

Tigris R.

Euphrates R.

Nile R.

public. When he did, he wore the diadem and carried the scepter. He arrayed himself in purple and gold and sparkled with jewels. Those to whom he condescended to grant an audience had to kneel and kiss the hem of his robe. This act of adoration was incumbent also upon members of the Imperial Council (*consilium*), which acquired the name of *Sacred Consistory* (*sacrum consistorium*) from the necessity to remain standing (*consistere*) while in the imperial presence.

Provincial administration

To increase the control of the emperor and prevent ambitious governors from amassing too much power, Diocletian completely reorganized the administrative system. Following a trend initiated by Septimius Severus, he completed the abolition of Italy's privileged status and divided it into a dozen provinces. In addition, by subdividing the old provinces, he increased the total number of provinces from about 40 to about 105 (map, pp. 570–1). He also deprived most governors of their former military functions.

The new provinces were grouped into twelve administrative districts known as *dioceses*. Each diocese was subject to a vicar (*vicarius*) of equestrian rank. He supervised all governors, even those of senatorial rank except the three senior senatorial governors: the proconsuls of Africa, Asia, and Achaea. Like all governors (except those of Isauria in Asia Minor and Mauretania in North Africa), the vicars were civilian officials whose main function was the administration of justice and supervision of tax collection. The dioceses, in turn, were grouped into four prefectures: Gaul and Italy in the West, Illyricum and the Orient in the East. A praetorian prefect supervised the vicars in each prefecture and reported directly to the tetrarch who resided at the headquarters of that prefecture.

Diocletian assigned command over the armies and garrisons stationed in the provinces to professional military men known as dukes (*duces*). To ensure close supervision and the mutual restraint of ambitious impulses, he made the dukes dependent on the governors and other civilian officials for military supplies and provisions. In some dioceses, several dukes might serve under the command of a higher officer known as a *comes* (companion, count).

Military reforms

During the third century, Rome's system of frontier defense had essentially collapsed. In the latter part of the century, Gallienus and his capable Illyrian successors surrendered control of the Empire's eastern and western periphery and concentrated on holding its central core. After they checked the attacks of outsiders against the core, they regained effective control over the periphery. Diocletian represents the culmination of this process. Having regained political and military control within the territory of the Empire, Diocletian instituted military reforms to restore frontier defenses.

Although not all of the details are clear, Diocletian's reforms represent the reestablishment of Rome's traditional defensive strategy. Tactical and organizational changes plus a huge increase in manpower simply made it more effective. First of all, Diocletian increased the size of Roman military forces (infantry, cavalry, and naval, both regular and auxiliary) by as much as 100,000 men to a total of around 500,000. He probably kept the official manpower of individual legions at around 5500. Tactically, however, he spread out the legions and the other forces in numerous smaller detachments. Some manned small, heavily constructed forts and guard posts along roads and supply routes in frontier zones. Others served as easily mobilized forces billeted in strategically located fortified cities and towns within the frontier provinces. In this way, the army could guarantee the safe acquisition, transportation, and storage of supplies. It could also protect communications in general, sound the alarm when any sector of the frontier was attacked, and quickly bring up mobile forces as needed.

There is no major shift in Roman defensive strategy here. The fortified roads were built in forward areas to provide protective zones for the provinces proper. That fits a pattern going all the way back to Augustus. Units stationed in the rear performed the same function as those once stationed in large legionary camps. It was easier, however, to supply them by stationing smaller detachments in various cities and towns. Furthermore, the dispersal of provincial troops in small units made it more difficult for provincial commanders to win over large numbers of troops quickly for a rebellion.

The tetrarchs commanded armies large enough to meet major emergencies along the most vulnerable frontiers. Each of the four controlled a different prefecture from his strategically located headquarters. Constantius kept an eye on the Rhine from Trier; from Milan, Maxentius could defend the *Agri Decumates*, the dangerous triangle formed by the upper reaches of the Rhine and Danube rivers; Galerius guarded the rest of the Danube from Sirmium; and Diocletian protected the eastern frontiers from Nicomedia in Bithynia. With each tetrarch were highly mobile troops, especially cavalry. They constituted his *comitatus* (personal escort) and formed the nucleus of the large field armies that would be assembled from smaller provincial units where and when they were needed.

Recruiting enough soldiers for Diocletian's expanded army was a real problem. Conscription had fallen into disfavor, and the government could not afford to call too many men away from most occupations in any case. Diocletian employed conscription cautiously, enforced hereditary military obligations, utilized voluntary enlistment, and hired foreign mercenaries.

To make sure that imperial armies were adequately armed and equipped, Diocletian instituted or expanded a system of state-owned workshops (*fabricae*) that produced directly for the military. Those located near sources of iron ore in Asia Minor specialized in armor or weapons. Some were located in strategic western cities such as Sirmium, Salona, and Ticinum. A number of shops produced cloth or leather, which other shops turned into clothing, headwear, and footwear (p. 608).

The reform of the coinage, 286 to 293 C.E.

Diocletian attempted to end the frightful monetary chaos and inflation of the late third century by reforming the Roman coinage. His system of silver and gold coinage, though not a long-term success itself, served as a model for his successors. In 286, he began to replace the old *aureus* with a new gold coin at the rate of sixty to the standard Roman pound of 327.45 grams (12 Roman ounces, 11.536 ounces avoirdupois [English/U.S.]). By 301 at the latest, this gold coin was known as the *solidus* (pl. *solidi*). In 293, Diocletian introduced a silver coin, the *argenteus*, at ninety-six to the pound and roughly equivalent to the old *denarius* of Nero's time. To answer the need for small change, he struck three denominations: a new copper *denarius* of less value than the old silver one, a silver-washed copper piece worth two new *denarii*, and a more heavily silvered bronze *nummus* worth five new *denarii*. Despite these changes, Diocletian was unable to mint enough good gold and silver coins to satisfy the government's needs, and the new copper *denarius* and the two *billon* (silver-coated base metal) coins were issued in huge numbers that only added to inflation.

The Edict on Maximum Prices, 301 c.e.

Unfortunately, Diocletian's administrative and military reforms also added fuel to the inflationary fires of the time. When he increased the number of provinces from about 40 to about 105 and created separate military commanders and civilian governors for each, he increased the number of highly salaried provincial officials fivefold. On top of that, he added the four praetorian prefects and twelve *vicarii* and all their staffs. The creation of various new imperial residences for the four tetrarchs, the building of frontier forts and roads, and monumental building programs in Rome entailed even more expense. Between 150 and 300, the basic rate of military pay had increased sixfold. By increasing the number of soldiers by somewhere between one-fourth and one-third and by giving donatives at regular intervals throughout the year, Diocletian raised the government's cost for manpower and supplies even more.

Diocletian made the situation even worse in early 301 by issuing his famous *Edict on Maximum Prices*, one of the most valuable Roman economic documents available. It has been reconstructed from numerous fragmentary Greek and Latin inscriptions largely in the eastern part of the Empire but more recently also in Italy. It set a ceiling on the prices of over a thousand different items from wheat, barley, rice, poultry, vegetables, fruits, fish, and wines of every variety and origin to clothing, bed linen, ink, parchment, and craftsmen's wages.

In a remarkable preamble to the edict, Diocletian sharply condemned speculators and profiteers who robbed the helpless public. He was particularly concerned about the purchasing power of soldiers, who had little other than money to exchange in the marketplace. The penalty for those who overcharged was death. With the prices for goods and services fixed and the value of money falling, it became unprofitable to sell goods at the official prices. Therefore, people either refused to produce goods, sold them illegally on black markets, or simply relied on barter, which had always played a strong role in the everyday economy, particularly for the countryside. In the face of economic realities, the edict had to be relaxed to encourage production and the availability of goods for sale in markets. The edict had become largely a dead letter by the end of Diocletian's reign.

Tax reform

In order to meet the increased needs of the government and reduce the effects of infla-tion on the imperial budget, Diocletian instituted a thorough rationalization of the tax system. He made it more efficient and dependable. He did away with many taxes. His new system relied on two basic types of taxes that had traditionally been used through-out the ancient Mediterranean world, the land tax and the poll (head) tax. It was also traditional that many taxes were paid in kind, that is, in the form of agricultural prod-ucts (such as grain, oil, wine, and meat) or manufactured goods (such as cloth, leather, tools, building materials, and arms). They provided the *annona*, by which the emperors fed, clothed, and equipped the armies; paid the soldiers and government officials; and sustained the poorer residents of Rome. What Diocletian tried to do was regularize these traditional practices on an empire-wide basis.

Under his system, agricultural labor and land were taxed according to certain stand-ard units. The system for assessing labor is usually referred to as *capitatio* and that for land as *iugatio*. They are derived, respectively, from *caput* (pl. *capita*), "head," and *iugum* (pl. *iuga*), "yoke" (the amount of land that could be plowed in a day with a yoke of oxen). Theoretically, all of the land throughout the Empire was divided into *iuga*, which varied in size with the types of crops grown and the quality of the soil. All agricultural labor, human and animal, was reckoned in *capita*, with women and young teenagers being counted at half the value of men and with draft animals proportion-ally lower. The property owner was then assessed at so many *capita* and so many *iuga*. Every five years until 312 and then every fifteen thereafter, a new assessment, called an *indictio* (indiction), would be made. Thus, the term *indictio* came also to be used for the period of time that the assessment was in force. For each year during an indiction, the government would calculate how much food, material, and labor it would need and divide those amounts by the total number of units to find out how much would have to be collected per unit from each property owner.

On paper, this system looks like the soul of simplicity and fairness. In practice, how-ever, it was not. Surviving documents show that sometimes taxes in kind were con-verted to taxes in gold *solidi*. There was also great variation in the terminology actually used and even in the meaning of the same term. In some cases, *caput* may refer to the labor equivalent of one adult male. In other cases, *caput* may be interchangeable with *iugum* and represent the amount of labor needed per *iugum*. Figures from one estate indicate that such a *caput* may be equivalent to the labor of twelve and one-half adult males. In southern Italy, land was assessed in units of fifty Roman *iugera* called *millenae* (sing. *millena*), and in North Africa, the *centuria* of 200 *iugera* was the standard unit. If, as has been argued, the standard *iugum* equaled twelve and one-half Roman *iugera*, then the *millena* and *centuria* can easily be divided into four and sixteen *iuga*, respectively, but certainty is impossible.

Moreover, it is not reasonable to expect complete consistency in so vast an empire as Rome's, with its strong regional differences and traditions. Insofar as Diocletian did not include provisions for taxing merchants and craftsmen, his system was unfair to the owners of agricultural land. Also, although rural landowners were supposed to be taxed in proportion to what they owned, there were many inequities and injustices in the way in which assessments were actually made and taxes collected. It was always easier for the wealthy landowners, who were responsible for collecting the taxes at the local level, to shift a disproportionate share of the tax burden onto the poor through dishonesty and extortion.

The great virtue of Diocletian's system was that it gave taxpayers relief from the totally unexpected and unregulated ad hoc requisitions characteristic of the late third century. It also provided the government with a dependable source of supply that did not rely on the government's own worthless money.

THE PERSECUTION OF CHRISTIANS

The end of Diocletian's career saw renewed systematic persecution of Christians, which brought his reign to a tragic and bloody close. Why Diocletian broke the religious truce begun forty years earlier under Gallienus has been the subject of much speculation. Some scholars have seen his persecution based on religious principle: Diocletian, the self-proclaimed representative of Jupiter, sought to restore the old Roman faith and moral code. The circumstances under which the persecution began give some support to this view. They also show that Diocletian was politically concerned about ensuring conformity and uniformity among the population in order to strengthen the state in pursuit of security. Enemies of Christianity, like the Caesar Galerius and Hierocles, author of the *Lover of Truth*, were quick to brand the Christians as subversives and evil influences on the Empire.

The incident that sparked the persecution occurred in 299 at a public sacrifice. When the diviners inspected the entrails of the slaughtered animals in order to determine the will of the gods, they reported that the presence of hostile influences had frustrated and defeated the purpose of the sacrifice. Diocletian angrily gave orders that all persons in the imperial palace offer sacrifice to the traditional gods of the state or, upon refusal to do so, be beaten. The edict even applied to his wife, Prisca, who is alleged to have been a Christian or Christian sympathizer. Next, he permitted Galerius to post orders that all officers and men in the army be required to offer sacrifice on pain of dismissal from service.

In 303, Diocletian drafted an edict that ordered the destruction of Christian churches and the surrender and burning of Christians' sacred books. It also prohibited Christian worship and restricted the rights of prosecution and defense formerly enjoyed by Christians in courts of law. One evening in the winter of 303, without having waited for the official proclamation of the aforementioned edict, the imperial police suddenly entered, ransacked, and demolished the Christian cathedral that stood opposite the emperor's palace in Nicomedia. The edict was posted throughout the city the next day. An enraged Christian who tore down one of the posters was arrested and burned at the stake.

Within the next fifteen days, two fires of unknown origin broke out in the imperial palace in Nicomedia. Numerous Christian suspects were imprisoned, tortured, and killed. At the same time, revolts ascribed to Christians in Syria and Cappadocia, though easily suppressed, led to the proclamation of two more edicts. One ordered the imprisonment of Christian clergy. The other sought to relieve the overcrowding of the prisons: it offered liberty to all who would consent to make a sacrifice to the gods of the state and condemned to death those who refused.

After his visit to Rome, where he had just celebrated the twentieth anniversary of his accession, Diocletian became very ill and ceased to attend to public affairs. According to Eusebius, Galerius seized the opportunity to draft and publish a fourth edict, which required all Christians to offer the customary sacrifices under pain of death or hard labor in the mines. None of the four edicts, except perhaps the first, was enforced everywhere with equal severity. In Gaul and Britain, Constantius limited himself to merely pulling down a few churches, whereas Galerius and Maximian were far more zealous in their domains. When Diocletian abdicated in 305, the persecution was at its height and would not end until 311.

THE ABDICATION

On May 1, 305, in the presence of the assembled troops at Nicomedia, Diocletian formally abdicated. With tears in his eyes, he took leave of his soldiers. He told them that he was too old and sick, probably from a stroke, to carry on the heavy tasks of government. On the same day at Milan, in fulfillment of a promise previously extracted by Diocletian, Maximian also resigned. Diocletian nominated Constantius Chlorus and Galerius as the new Augusti, with seniority for Constantius, who received as his special provinces Gaul, Britain, Spain, and Mauretania. Galerius took the Balkans and most of Asia Minor. Galerius, in turn, nominated his nephew Maximinus Daia as his Caesar in the East and ruler over the provinces in the rest of Asia Minor, Syria, and Egypt. Constantius accepted Galerius' friend Flavius Valerius Severus as his Caesar in the Herculian dynasty. Severus was to rule over Italy, Roman Africa, and Pannonia.

After their abdication, the two ex-Augusti went into retirement. Maximian, fuming over his enforced abdication, went to Lucania (or Campania) to await the first opportunity to snatch back his share of the Empire. Diocletian retired to an enormous fortress palace on the Dalmatian Coast outside of Solin (Salona, Salonae) at Split (Spalatum, Spalato). He spent the last eight years of his life there in the manner of a good Roman gentleman. He tended his estate and intervened directly in events only once (p. 582). Whatever influence he may have kept at the seat of power disappeared in 311 with the death of his son-in-law, Galerius. Indeed, even Galerius shortly before he died issued an edict that called for an end to Diocletian's policy of persecuting Christians and proclaimed official toleration of their religion (p. 583). Diocletian himself died from either illness or suicide probably in December of 312.

PRISCA AND VALERIA

Diocletian's wife, Prisca, and his daughter, Valeria, were still deeply involved in imperial politics. After Diocletian had retired to Split, Prisca went to live with Valeria and her husband, Galerius, in Thessalonica (Salonica, Thessaloniki, Saloniki). Valeria had received many high honors in her role as Diocletian's daughter and Galerius' wife. Just as Julia Domna before her, she had been named Mother of the Armies. After the defeat of Narses, she was the first woman ever to be granted a laurel crown of victory by the senate. The Pannonian province of Valeria was even named after her.

When Galerius died, the western Caesar, Licinius, succeeded him (p. 583). The eastern Caesar, Galerius' nephew Maximinus Daia, unwillingly had to stay put. Licinius was left in charge of the politically important Prisca and Valeria. They did not feel safe with him. He probably feared that they would attract the attention of potential challengers for his throne. Prisca and Valeria fled to the disgruntled Daia. His daughter was betrothed to Galerius' adopted illegitimate son Candidianus, whom the childless Valeria had helped raise. Daia gave them refuge precisely because he wanted to challenge Licinius. When, however, Valeria refused to marry him, he banished them to house arrest in Syria.

They escaped when Daia perished after Licinius defeated him in 313. At that point, the two women seem to have joined Candidianus, whom Licinius initially treated well at his court in Nicomedia after Daia's death. Then, Licinius began to fear Candidianus as a rival and had him executed along with another possible pretender. Prisca and Valeria fled to Thessalonica, where they were hunted down and beheaded in 315.

PROBLEMS LEFT BY DIOCLETIAN

Ultimately, many of Diocletian's reforms and policies did not work. He had created a huge administrative and military machine that surpassed the ability of the economy to support it and impeded communication between the center and the periphery. It encouraged corruption and reduced citizens of all ranks to subjects. Their response to an oppressive system was frequent disobedience. A new system of coinage and attempts to control prices only led to more inflation, shortages, and black markets. Diocletian's persecution unnecessarily alienated the Christian community. Moreover, the Tetrarchy was held together only by the dynamism of Diocletian himself. Once he was removed, his successors began struggling amongst themselves for personal dominance. Another series of civil wars erupted and threatened to destroy the empire that he had rescued from total collapse.

NOTES

1 The *constitutiones principum* (statutes of the emperors), which had the validity of laws, included (1) *edicta*, or edicts (official proclamations of the emperor as a Roman magistrate, which were valid during his term of office for the whole Empire); (2) *decreta*, or decrees (court decisions of the emperor having the force of law); (3) *rescripta*, or rescripts (written responses to written inquiries on specific points of law). Although the *constitutiones* were originally valid only during the principate of their author, they later remained in force as sources of public and private law unless revoked by a later imperial constitution.

2 Manichaeism may have provided some link between their revolt and Narses' hostile actions. At least Diocletian may have thought so by the time he outlawed Manichaeism in 302.

SUGGESTED READING

Leadbetter, B. *Galerius and the Will of Diocletian*. London and New York: Routledge, 2009.

Rees, R. *Diocletian and the Tetrarchy*. Edinburgh: Edinburgh University Press, 2004.

CHAPTER 31

Constantine the Great and Christianity, 306 to 337 C.E.

Diocletian had lived to see the disintegration of the Tetrarchy and the recognition of a religion that he himself had persecuted. He saw his own great fame fade into obscurity before the blazing light of Constantine's rising sun and died in the belief that he had worked in vain. In principle, however, after gaining control of the Empire, Constantine continued many of the social, economic, military, and administrative policies established by Diocletian.

Constantine the Great, as he came to be called by Christian writers, was the son of Constantius Chlorus, Maximian's Caesar and eventual successor as Augustus in the West. His mother was named Helena, but her origin and the details of Constantine's early years are hard to discern. The existing information is scanty and distorted by the biases of his Christian boosters and pagan detractors. For example, the former call Helena a virtuous Christian wife and mother, but the latter call her only a concubine of low birth and questionable morals.

Although certainty is impossible, the best evidence indicates that Constantine was born in 272 or 273, probably in or near Naissus (Nĭs or Nish) in what was then the Balkan province of Moesia, later Dardania, and now Serbia. By 289, his father had set aside his mother in favor of a politically advantageous marriage to Theodora, the (step) daughter of Maximian, who was then Diocletian's Caesar in the West. Subsequently, Constantine was sent to Diocletian's court in the East, where he received excellent training in the arts of politics and war.

Constantius may have had little choice in these matters: his own military success marked him as a potential rival for power. Demonstrating his loyalty by accepting Maximian's (step)daughter in marriage and sending his son to live under the watchful eye of Diocletian may have been a way to guarantee the safety of himself and his family. Constantine never seems to have held his father's actions against him, and he rejoined his father soon after Diocletian and Maximian abdicated.

THE RISE OF CONSTANTINE, 306 TO 312 C.E.

By 306, Constantine had already distinguished himself militarily during Galerius' victorious Persian campaigns of 298 and was becoming a popular figure with the troops. Although Constantius was nominally the senior Augustus after 305, Galerius was the actual master of the Empire. He still basked in the glories of his Persian victories. The two Caesars, his nephew Maximinus Daia in the East and his old friend Flavius Valerius Severus in the West, were both devoted to him. The presence of the young Constantine at what was now Galerius' court also gave Galerius a popular advocate with the army and leverage with Constantius.

Galerius' leading role in the last persecution of the Christians engendered a strong bias against him in the later sources, which are largely Christian and favor the Christian hero Constantine. Here, for example, is a summary of Lactantius' story about how Constantine rejoined his father (*On the Deaths of the Persecutors*, 24.5ff.):

When Constantius asked Galerius to let Constantine help him battle the Picts, who had invaded Britain from Scotland in 306, Galerius was unwilling to let him go. One day, however, when Galerius was in a good mood after dinner, he gave Constantine a pass to use the imperial posting system (*cursus publicus*) to go wherever he wanted. Taking no chances, Constantine left in the middle of the night to rejoin his father. As he had feared, Galerius changed his mind the next morning and sent pursuers. Constantine foiled his enemies by killing or laming the remaining post horses after each change of mounts.

The truth is probably more prosaic. In fact, it can be shown that instead of reaching Constantius on his deathbed in Eburacum (York), as the story goes on to claim, Constantine joined him at the port of Gesoriacum (Bononia, Boulogne) on the English Channel. From there, they set sail for Britain and successfully defeated the Picts before Constantius died at Eburacum on July 25, 306. Contrary to the principles of the Tetrarchy, the army immediately proclaimed Constantine as the new Augustus at the head of the Herculian side of the Tetrarchy.

That title, however, now rightly belonged to Constantius' Caesar, Severus. Constantine seems to have tried to protect himself and his position by being both accommodating and opportunistic. For the moment, he accepted the title of Caesar from Galerius and did not contest Severus' elevation to the position of Augustus in the Herculian dynasty. Galerius rewarded him by sharing the consulship with him in 307. During that year, however, Constantine had an opportunity to obtain recognition as an Augustus from another source.

The usurpation of Maxentius, 306 C.E.

Maximian's son Maxentius had been incensed at receiving nothing when Severus and Constantine were made Augustus and Caesar in the West. Questioning the status of Constantine's mother, he argued that he, as the legitimate son of an ex-Augustus, had a better right to the throne. At Rome, the Praetorian Guard and population in general backed him because they resented the loss of privileges that Diocletian, Galerius, and Severus had gradually removed as they sought to increase the revenues of the state. Therefore, Maxentius declared himself Augustus. Maximian repudiated his retirement, reclaimed the title of Augustus, and backed Maxentius.

Complex maneuvers

Severus failed to dislodge Maxentius from Rome in the spring of 307 and soon after withdrew to Ravenna. Ultimately, he surrendered to Maximian and abdicated, but that did not save his life. In the fall of 307, Maximian visited Constantine in Gaul. Constantine had prudently concentrated on building up the defenses and loyalties of his own provinces. He had avoided direct involvement in the conflicts of the others. Now, he threw in his lot with Maximian and Maxentius against Galerius in return for their recognizing him as an Augustus. He divorced his first wife and married Maximian's daughter Fausta. Constantius had originally betrothed Constantine to her fourteen years earlier, but no marriage had yet resulted. Now, it would have been dangerous to leave Fausta free for Maximian and Maxentius to use in attracting some other ally. Also, as the daughter of the former Augustus of the Herculian dynasty, she strengthened Constantine's dynastic position even further.

In April of 308, Maximian turned against Maxentius but failed to drive him from Rome. Maximian fled to Constantine, who gave him refuge. Galerius tried to stabilize the situation in November of that year by summoning a meeting with Diocletian at Carnuntum on the Danube in Upper Pannonia (map, p. 378). Diocletian refused to resume power. Maximian was forced to retire again, and Maxentius was condemned as a usurper. Galerius obtained approval of his old comrade Licinius to replace Severus as Augustus in the West.

Constantine and Maximinus Daia (Galerius's Caesar) did not attend and refused to accept subordinate positions as "sons of the Augusti." In late 309 or early 310, Galerius yielded and accepted them as full-fledged Augusti. Later, in 310, Maximian tried to raise a revolt against Constantine in Gaul. He apparently committed suicide after Constantine captured him.

Abandoning the Tetrarchy

By 310, it probably was apparent to Constantine that the tetrarchic system of Diocletian would never work and that he had the opportunity to consolidate the whole Empire under his own leadership. Galerius was dying of cancer, Maximinus Daia and Licinius hated each other, and Maxentius' position in Rome and Italy was rapidly deteriorating.

At that point, Constantine repudiated the Herculian dynasty as the basis of his claim to rule and sought a new sanction by announcing his descent from the renowned Claudius Gothicus. In place of Hercules, he adopted as his patron deity the Unconquered Sun (Sol Invictus), who was identified in Gaul, it seems, with Apollo. Sol had also been the protector of Claudius Gothicus and Aurelian. Constantine's claim of descent from Claudius Gothicus would enable him to assert not only his right to the throne by inheritance but also his right to undivided rule over the whole Empire. Fortified by this new sanction, Constantine declared Maxentius a usurper and a tyrant, but he postponed further action to await more favorable circumstances after the death of Galerius.

The Edict of Religious Toleration, 311 C.E.

After the abdication of Diocletian, the persecution of the Christians had continued in Galerius' dioceses (Illyricum, Thrace, and Asia Minor) and particularly in those of Maximinus Daia (Syria and Egypt). Finally, near death in 311, Galerius became convinced of the futility of the Christian persecutions. As senior Augustus, he issued his famous Edict of Toleration that granted Christians all over the Empire freedom of worship and the right to reopen their churches, if only they would pray for him and the state and do nothing to disturb public order. He explained his change of policy by stating that it was better for the Empire if people practiced some religion than none at all. A few days after the proclamation of this edict, Galerius died.

Predictably, after the death of Galerius, Maximinus Daia at once overran and seized the Asiatic provinces of Galerius and threatened Licinius' control over the Balkans. In anticipation of war with Maxentius, Constantine had made an alliance with Licinius and betrothed to him his half-sister Constantia, who was then in her late teens. Meanwhile, Daia had made a secret agreement to cooperate with Maxentius.

Constantine's invasion of Italy, 312 C.E.

Constantine launched his long-awaited invasion of Italy in the spring of 312. He set out from Gaul with an army of nearly 40,000 men and crossed the Alps. Near Turin, he met and defeated a large force of armored cavalry dispatched by Maxentius. Quickly seizing northern Italy, he advanced against Rome. Maxentius had originally intended to defend the city behind the almost impregnable walls of Aurelian because Constantine's army probably was not equipped either to take the city by storm or to conduct a long siege. Nevertheless, either belief in signs sent by the gods or fear of a popular uprising caused Maxentius to change his plan. Instead, he went out to meet Constantine in open battle.

The Battle of the Milvian Bridge, 312 C.E.

Maxentius had ordered the Milvian Bridge to be destroyed as a defensive measure in accordance with his earlier strategy. Now, he led out his army over the Tiber on a hastily constructed pontoon bridge. It comprised two sections held together with chains, which could be quickly cut apart to prevent pursuit by the enemy. Maxentius advanced along the Flaminian Way as far as Saxa Rubra, "Red Rocks" (about ten miles north of Rome), where Constantine had encamped the night before.

Lactantius says that on the night before the battle a vision appeared to Constantine and bade him place upon the shields of his soldiers the Christogram (☧), a monogram consisting of an X with a vertical line drawn down through it and looped at the top to represent *chi* and *rho*, the first two letters of Christ's name in Greek, ΧΡΙΣΤΟΣ. With less plausibility, Eusebius asserts that Constantine told him years later that sometime before the battle, he saw a miraculous sign across the face of the sun: a flaming cross and beneath it the Greek words ἐν τούτῳ νίκα or, as handed down in the more familiar Latin form, *in hoc signo vinces* (in this sign you shall conquer). Whatever vision Constantine may have had (if he had one at all), when he went forth into battle, he soon drove the enemy back to the Milvian Bridge and won a total victory.

The next day, Constantine entered Rome in triumph. In the forefront of the procession, a soldier carried the head of Maxentius on a spear. The jubilant throng hailed Constantine as liberator. The senate damned the memory of Maxentius, declared his acts null and void, and proclaimed Constantine senior Augustus of the entire Empire.

A VICTORY FOR CHRISTIANITY

Although the senate undoubtedly hailed the elevation of Constantine as the triumph of *libertas*, the true victor would turn out to be the Christian Church. Constantine's arch of triumph includes a representation of the Unconquered Sun and bears an inscription that claims that he achieved victory by the intervention of an unnamed divine power (*instinctu divinitatis*) and by his own greatness of mind (*mentis magnitudine*). Nevertheless, a victory statue of Constantine held a cross in its right hand. That publicly recognized the valuable support of the Christians, which he had cultivated by his tolerant policies in the provinces under his control.

Although Constantine eventually came to ascribe his victory wholly to the intervention of Christ, he did not become an exclusive believer in Christianity upon his victory at the Milvian Bridge. On the other hand, he clearly was a believer before his baptism at the end of his life. Exactly when his full conversion took place cannot be said. The interactions of political considerations and personal developments made it a complex, gradual process. He was obviously too keen a statesman to attempt to impugn or suppress immediately the religious beliefs of 80 to 90 percent of his subjects, not to mention the senate, imperial bureaucracy, and army. Also, one victory, however brilliant and decisive, could not in one day completely change his old beliefs.

As emperor, Constantine continued to hold the ancient Roman office of *pontifex maximus*. A set of gold medallions struck in 315 represents a blending of typical Roman and Christian symbolism: it shows the emperor with the Christogram on his helmet, the Roman she-wolf on his shield, and a cruciform-headed scepter in his hand. Constantine continued to strike coins in honor of Mars, Jupiter, and even Hercules until 318; and coins in honor of the Sun until 323. Thus Constantine's reign was a link between the pagan Empire that was passing and the Christian Empire that was to come.

As senior Augustus, Constantine ordered Maximinus Daia to discontinue his persecution of the Christians in the East. Daia only grudgingly obeyed. In 313, Constantine instructed his proconsul in Africa to restore to the churches all confiscated property; to furnish Caecilianus, the newly elected bishop of Carthage, funds for distribution among the orthodox bishops and clergy in Africa, Numidia, and Mauretania; and to exempt them from all municipal civic duties or liturgies (public services provided to the community at private expense). That done, Constantine left Rome for Milan (Mediolanum) to attend a conference with Licinius.

The conference of Milan, 313 C.E.

At the conference of 313 in Milan, the long-expected marriage of Licinius and Constantia took place. The two emperors also reached a general agreement regarding complete freedom of religion and the recognition of the Christian Church or, rather, granting each separate local church legal status as a "person."[1]

The publication of a so-called Edict of Milan is open to some doubt, although the agreements reached included not only Galerius' documented Edict of Toleration from 311 but also all of Constantine's rescripts concerning the restitution of the churches' property and their exemption from public burdens. Licinius enforced these agreements not just in his own domains in Europe but even in the East, which he soon liberated from Maximinus Daia.

The end of Maximinus Daia, 313 C.E.

Maximinus Daia was undoubtedly a man of some principle, military competence, and statesmanship, but he is understandably vilified by Christian writers. Despite the publication of Galerius' Edict of Toleration, Daia had still sporadically persecuted the Christians in his dominions or subjected them to humiliating indignities. Constantine's order in 313 to desist was obeyed, but with neither alacrity nor enthusiasm.

After the defeat and death of his ally Maxentius, Daia stood alone against the combined forces of Constantine and Licinius. Constantine's departure for Gaul to repel a Frankish invasion of the Rhineland presented Daia with an excellent opportunity to attack Licinius. In the dead of winter, Daia crossed the Bosphorus (Bosporus) and captured Byzantium. Licinius rushed from Milan with a smaller but better-trained army. The two forces met near Adrianople (Adrianopolis). Defeated in battle, Daia disguised himself as a slave and escaped. Licinius pursued him into Asia Minor, where Daia fell ill and died. Licinius, with the East now in his hands, granted the Christians complete religious freedom. As he had agreed at the conference of Milan, he also restored to them their confiscated churches and properties.

CONSTANTINE AND LICINIUS: THE EMPIRE DIVIDED, 313 TO 324 C.E.

Once again the Empire was divided between two rival and distrustful brothers-in-law, as it had been in the days of Marcus Antonius and Octavian. In 315, Constantine tried to reinforce his position. He gave his half-sister Anastasia in marriage to a senator named Bassianus, the brother of a high-ranking officer under Licinius. When Constantine asked Licinius to agree in making Bassianus a Caesar in charge of Italy, Licinius used Bassianus' brother to suborn Bassianus' help in assassinating Constantine. When Constantine discovered the plot, he had Bassianus executed. War with Licinius soon followed in 316.

Licinius was defeated with heavy losses in Pannonia but fought to a draw in Thrace. Because neither wished the inconclusive struggle to continue, they arranged a truce: Licinius agreed to abandon his claim to any territory in Europe but Thrace; Constantine agreed to waive his claim as senior Augustus to the right of legislating for Licinius' part of the Empire.

The peaceful compromise was neither destined nor intended to last. After a few years of apparent harmony and cooperation, relations between the two emperors slowly deteriorated. Constantine did not really want peace. Licinius' eventual reversal of the policies agreed upon in Milan presented Constantine a ready-made, though specious, pretext for the war that gave him the whole Empire.

Unlike Licinius, Constantine had drawn closer to Christianity ever since the Battle of the Milvian Bridge. The benefits that Constantine bestowed upon the Church at that time were in thanks to the Christians' deity for the heavenly aid that he believed he had been given in battle. In turn, he recognized the Christian Church on earth and made it an effective partner of the state.

Constantine certainly had to take into account the predominance of pagans in the population, army, and bureaucracy. Still, he authorized measures that went far beyond the agreements reached in Milan and granted Christians ever more privileges and immunities. An important feature of his religious policy was to permit the pope (bishop of Rome) and the orthodox clergy to determine correct doctrine and discipline within the Church. In a constitution published in 318, Constantine recognized the legality of decisions handed down by bishops' courts. He also allowed the bishops to enforce their decisions by the authority of the state. In a rescript of 321, he not only legalized bequests by Roman citizens to the Christian Church but assigned to it the property of martyrs dying intestate. In the same year, he proclaimed Sunday a public holiday and day of rest for people working in law courts and state-run manufacturing operations.[2] Symbolic, too, of Constantine's growing personal acceptance of Christianity was that after the Battle of the Milvian Bridge, he adopted the *labarum*, a standard consisting of a long-handled cross with a *chi-rho* monogram at the top.

The Donatist Schism

Constantine's personal experiences and Christian mentors such as Bishop Hosius of Corduba had convinced him of the power of the Christians' deity. He also saw the benefits that the state could derive from being united with the strong, effective organization that the Christian Church identifying itself as universal (Catholic) had become. Therefore, Constantine took a serious view of a schism that was rending the Church in Africa and destroying unity in the state. The schism derived its name from Donatus, the fanatical leader of a radical group of dissident clergymen. This group had protested strongly against the election of Caecilianus as metropolitan bishop of

Carthage. They claimed that he was too ready to grant pardon and restore to clerical office those who had betrayed the faith during Diocletian's persecution and had surrendered the Holy Scriptures for burning. The Donatists championed Donatus himself, who had endured six years of prison and torture without breaking. Contrary to the will of the pope in Rome, they held their own election and installed Donatus as bishop of Carthage.

The African dispute rose to a crescendo of fanaticism when Constantine denied the Donatists a share in the benefactions that he had recently granted the African clergy and congregations loyal to the pope. Two church councils summoned by Constantine in 313 and 314 ruled against the Donatists. They appealed to the emperor to judge their case himself. At last, he agreed. After much deliberation, he reaffirmed the decisions of the councils and ordered the military suppression of the Donatists and the confiscation of their churches. In 321, realizing that persecution only heightened their fanaticism and increased the turmoil in Africa, Constantine ordered the persecutions to cease. He scornfully left the Donatists "to the judgment of God." His first attempt to restore peace and unity in the Church had failed dismally.

The Arian heresy

Similar religious problems confronted Licinius, but he handled them differently, yet no more successfully. At first, he faithfully observed the decisions reached in Milan, but, when a Christian controversy arose in Egypt and threatened to disrupt the peace and unity of his realm, he resorted again to systematic persecutions of the Christians. The dispute centered on Arius, a priest associated with a group in Egypt that also opposed leniency toward Christians who had betrayed their faith during Diocletian's persecution. He held views about the nature of Christ that his opponents could use to discredit him as a heretic. He argued that Christ was not "of the same substance" (*homoousios*) as God the Father but "of different substance" (*heteroousios*): since Christ was the Son of the Father, he must, therefore, have been subsequent and posterior; although he was begotten before all worlds, there must have been a time when he was not.

Arius' view was not substantially different from the occasional utterances of some great Church Fathers of the early third century (e.g., Origen, St. Dionysius of Alexandria, and Tertullian in his old age). Bishop Alexander of Alexandria, however, argued that the Son was of the same substance with the Father, and that all three persons of the Trinity (God the Father, God the Son [Jesus Christ], and God the Holy Spirit) were one in time, substance, and power, representing the three aspects of the Almighty Power of the universe.

Alexander, whose position eventually prevailed as the orthodox view, excommunicated Arius and touched off a raging controversy that even drew in Licinius' wife, Constantine's half-sister Constantia. Never really sympathetic toward Christians, Licinius now saw in their controversies a disruptive element all the more dangerous because of his impending power struggle with Constantine (on whose behalf he perhaps suspected they were saying their prayers). Accordingly, in 320, he renewed the persecution of the Christians.

The defeat and death of Licinius, 324 c.e.

Although renewed Christian persecutions provided Constantine with a moral issue in his ultimate war against Licinius, he found a more immediate cause in the Gothic invasion of Moesia and Thrace in 323. To repel the invasion, Constantine had no other recourse but to trespass upon the Thracian domains of Licinius. Licinius made an angry protest; Constantine rejected it. Both sides at once mobilized.

In the middle of 324, Constantine attacked and defeated Licinius' forces. Licinius surrendered. An appeal by Constantia elicited an oath from Constantine to spare his life. Licinius was exiled to Thessalonica (variously known as Salonica, Thessaloniki, Saloniki). Six months later, however, Constantine broke his word and had him put to death on a charge of treason. Constantine was now sole emperor, something that Roman Empire had not seen in almost forty years. The new slogan of the Empire came to be "one rule, one world, and one creed."

CONSTANTIA AND HER SISTERS

Constantine was still insecure enough about a year later to execute the young son that Constantia had borne Licinius. Somehow, Constantine's relationship with her survived despite the bloodshed. Neither Constantia nor Anastasia seems to have remarried after the executions of their husbands. Their sister, Eutropia, was luckier. She was married to the respected senator Virius Nepotianus. She was the only one of Constantine's half-siblings to survive the purges after his death (pp. 596–7). Her son, however, also named Nepotianus, did not survive even a month as emperor in 350 before he was killed by the usurper Magnentius (pp. 596–7).

Both Anastasia and Constantia were honored members of Constantine's court. Constantia took an active interest in theological debates and religious politics. She corresponded with Bishop Eusebius of Caesarea, the Church historian and admiring biographer of Constantine. She even attended the Council of Nicaea called to deal with the controversy concerning Arius and helped his defenders. Constantine greatly mourned her death about five years later.

THE COUNCIL OF NICAEA, 325 c.e.

Military victory had suddenly reunited the Empire politically, but did not so quickly and decisively restore the religious unity that Constantine had striven to bring about. In all his efforts to promote religious unity, Constantine labored under one distinct handicap: he failed to see the religious importance of the controversy between Arius and the bishop of Alexandria. Because his chief aim was to achieve unity within the state, it made little difference to Constantine whether the Father, Son, and Holy Spirit represented a single, indivisible godhead or were three separate deities. He was a doer, not an intellectual. Accordingly, writing to Arius and Bishop Alexander, he urged them to get down to fundamentals: they should abandon their battle of words over what he considered abstruse and unimportant points of theology. His letter naturally failed to end the controversy.

Still hoping for an amicable solution to the problem, Constantine summoned an ecumenical council at Nicaea in Bithynia, to which bishops from all over the Empire might travel at state expense and at which he himself would also be present. The council opened on May 20, 325, with some 300 bishops, virtually all eastern, present. In his brief opening address, Constantine avowed his own devotion to God and exhorted the assembled bishops to work together to restore the unity of the Church. All else, he declared, was secondary and relatively unimportant. Reserving for himself only the right to intervene from time to time to expedite debate and deliberation, he then turned the council over to them.

The Council of Nicaea defined the doctrine and completed the organization of the Catholic Church. Its decisions not only were relevant to the problems of 325 but also affected Christianity for all time. It formulated the Nicene Creed, which, except for some minor modifications adopted at the Council of Constantinople in 381, has remained the creed of most Christian churches to this day. It declared Christ *homoousios* (of the same substance with the Father), proclaimed the Trinity indivisible, excommunicated Arius, and ordered the burning of his books. Easter was fixed to fall on the first Sunday after the first full moon following the spring equinox. Twenty canons (rules) also were formulated for the regulation of Church discipline and government throughout Christendom.

The negative consequences of the Council of Nicaea were momentous. First of all, it made compromise on the issue of Christ's nature more difficult and split the Church into two hostile camps for years. It also bedeviled imperial politics, since some emperors were Arian and others upheld the Nicene Creed. While enjoying official favor under Constantius II (337–361) and Valens (364–378), Arians were able to spread their version of Christianity across the Danube to many of the Germanic tribes who eventually took over much of the western half of the Empire. It had remained staunchly orthodox in upholding the Nicene Creed. Consequently, sectarian hostility between the orthodox population of old Roman territories and the new German overlords hindered unity in the face of worse invasions later.

Ironically, the problem would have been less severe if the Germans had remained pagans. They could have been forgiven their ignorance and more easily converted. The Arian Germans already considered themselves true Christians and resented their rejection by those Christians who called themselves *orthodox*.

The Council of Nicaea also deeply influenced future relations between Christianity and the state during the remainder of Roman and subsequent Byzantine history. The formal role that Constantine played by convening the council reinforced the already close association that had developed between the head of state and the emerging Catholic Church during the Donatist Schism. Constantine's actions at the Council of Nicaea provided the model for the Caesaropapism of later centuries, when the emperors dominated the Church and manipulated it for purposes of state. Constantine himself claimed to be *Isapostolos* (Equal of the Apostles) and the elected servant of God. He later tried to enforce universal orthodoxy by banning such Christian sects as the Novatians, Valentinians, and Marcionites, whom he called heretics.

CONSTANTINE'S SECULAR POLICIES

In adopting Christianity and abandoning the Tetrarchy, Constantine had radically broken with Diocletian. Still, he mainly followed Diocletian's lead in other spheres, making changes that were more incremental than radical.

Monetary and fiscal changes

Constantine's officials created a stable gold *solidus* minted at seventy-two to the Roman pound by making about a 16 percent reduction in the weight of Diocletian's *solidus* (*aureus*: minted at sixty to the pound). They replaced the *argenteus* with a new silver coin, the *miliarense* (denoting a thousandth part of the gold pound). Silver remained in short supply, however, and the overproduction of base-metal coins continued to fuel inflation in terms of the ratio of base-metal coins to gold (p. 506). Fiscally, Constantine supplemented Diocletian's taxes in kind with taxes in cash like Rome's first tax on business, the *collatio lustralis* or *chrysargyron* (p. 617).

Military developments

The idea that Constantine abandoned a strong perimeter defense and substituted a policy of defense in depth (let the invaders in and pick them off after they have spread out) for one of preclusive security (keep invaders out) has been largely discredited. This understanding of his policy was based on two mistaken assumptions: first, that the Romans shared the modern idea of borders as fixed lines that clearly demarcated Roman territory from non-Roman; second, that Constantine withdrew the best troops from the frontier rearward to fortified positions and service in a mobile field army. Supposedly, he left only a weak peasant militia to sound the alarm when invaders appeared. As it has been mentioned already, Romans did not think in terms of fixed borders. The walls, roads, and rivers that are often viewed as boundaries were really part of a system of broad frontier zones. Within the frontier zones, they served to display Roman power, observe and control the movement of people, ensure military communication, and provide for the transportation of troops and supplies.

Both Diocletian and Constantine essentially kept the traditional Roman system of frontier defense. They did, however, disperse small detachments of soldiers in the cities and towns of frontier provinces to break up large concentrations of troops or oversee and protect the collection and storage of supplies as taxes in kind. Therefore, the troops responsible for guarding the frontier became more interspersed among the civilian population of frontier provinces. Over a long period of time, the distinction between soldier and civilian in the frontier zones became blurred. That blurring became common in the late fourth century and throughout the fifth as emperors settled invaders on vacant land in return for military service.

Constantine's major military innovations were to increase the size of the mobile forces attached to the imperial court (*comitatus*), to accelerate the enrollment of Germans in imperial armies, and to appoint them to the highest governmental offices.

To the regular troops of the *comitatus* (the *comitatenses*) Constantine added a new elite corps composed of some infantry, but mainly of cavalry and known as the *protectores*. He also replaced the old Praetorian Guard, which he disbanded in 312, with a personal bodyguard of crack troops. Most of them were Franks. To this bodyguard, he gave the distinctive name of *Palace Schools* (*scholae palatinae*).

Another important military development was the reorganization of the high command and the complete separation of military commands and civil functions. Constantine gave the operational military functions of the praetorian prefects to two supreme commanders known as *master of the infantry* (*magister peditum*) and *master of the cavalry* (*magister equitum*). Similarly, he abrogated the authority of the provincial governors over the dukes and counts, who commanded the frontier garrisons.

Administrative and political developments

Though stripped of their operational military functions, the praetorian prefects were still very powerful dignitaries. Each exercised the powers of a deputy emperor in one of Diocletian's four great prefectures: Gaul, Italy, Illyricum, and the East. After 331, all judicial decisions handed down by them were final and were not subject to appeal even to the emperor. They supervised the administration of the imperial posting system (*cursus publicus*), the erection of public buildings, the collection and storage of taxes, the control of craft and merchant guilds, the regulation of market prices, and the conduct of higher education. Even more important, their executive control over the recruiting and enrollment of soldiers, the construction of military installations, and the provision of supplies acted as a powerful brake on ambitious army commanders.

High officials like the master of the infantry and the master of the cavalry were members of a vastly expanded imperial court (*comitatus*). Constantine kept Diocletian's policy of surrounding the emperor with an elaborate court ceremonial to promote an aura of sacredness. He increased the number of personal attendants, many of whom, in Persian style, were eunuchs and became powerful by controlling personal access to the emperor. The most important were the chamberlain or keeper of the sacred bedchamber (*praepositus sacri cubiculi*) and the chief of the domestic staff (*castrensis*).

The highest administrators and important palace officials (*palatini*) made up the Sacred Consistory, the Imperial Council. The most powerful was the master of offices (*magister officiorum*). He controlled the newly formed Agents of Affairs (*agentes in rebus*), who carried dispatches, gathered intelligence, and controlled the movement of troops. He also oversaw the imperial bodyguards, arsenals, and arms production. He even controlled appointments with the emperor, received ambassadors, and thus influenced foreign policy.

Constantine and his successors still held the office of consul on occasion, retained the title *pontifex maximus*, and advertised their *tribunica potestas* in the tradition of Augustus. Nevertheless, the old magistracies continued to decline. Praetors had lost their judicial functions under Septimius Severus. Quaestors no longer had senatorial revenues to handle after the militarization of all provinces during the third century. By 300, the old praetors and quaestors had been reduced to one each. Their only duty was to conduct the games and entertainments during festivals in Rome. Constantine, however, created a new quaestor, the quaestor of the sacred palace. He was in charge of records, charters, and administrative directives as well as the drafting of laws.

Two consuls continued to be appointed, one at Rome and one at Constantine's new eastern capital, Constantinople, but their office was merely honorary. The last real function of the consuls, as presidents of the senate, had already been transferred at some point to the urban prefect. His court heard the civil suits of all senators and the criminal suits of senators domiciled in Rome. The consuls' other previous functions now belonged to a vicar of the praetorian prefect for Italy.

Under the presidency of the urban prefect, the Roman senate became only the municipal council of Rome. It no longer ratified the appointment of emperors, and its advisory function had been taken over by the Sacred Consistory. The emperor now merely informed the senate of his decisions, for which courtesy he received fulsome thanks.

In keeping with a long-standing trend, Constantine finally abolished the distinction between senators and equestrians. Because the need for competent officials was great, offices previously restricted to one class or the other were now open to both. *Equites* who were appointed to senatorial offices became senators. Therefore, the number of senators swelled to about 2500. Ironically, this change increased the prestige of the senators as a class, while the senate itself declined as an institution. Now senators became a part of the highest strata of imperial government, especially in the less urbanized West, where the great senatorial landowners were in a position to monopolize the highest posts. Constantine even revived the term *patricius* (patrician) as an official honor for senators who had performed particularly important services.

THE FOUNDING OF CONSTANTINOPLE, 324 TO 330 C.E.

Since the time of Hadrian, the city of Rome and peninsular Italy had gradually lost their earlier dominance within the Empire. Citizenship, privileges, wealth, and political power had steadily spread outward to the provinces. Provincials came to make up the bulk of the soldiery, the bureaucracy, and the senatorial class and finally occupied the throne itself. Although the city of Rome still had much symbolic value for its possessor, it was no longer strategically well placed in relation to the constantly threatened frontiers. Milan eventually supplanted it as the strategic imperial residence in the West. Constantine realized, as had Diocletian, that the Empire had to be defended and administered from strategically located imperial residences in both the East and the West. Also, Rome's loss of privileges and Constantine's increasing favor toward the Christian Church alienated old pagan families that still dominated Rome. Therefore, the idea of a new Rome strategically located in the East and free from the deeply rooted pagan traditions of the old Rome greatly appealed to Constantine. His choice for his Eastern residence was the old, decaying Greek city of Byzantium. He began to transform it in 324 and gave the city its new name *Constantinople* (City of Constantine).

This choice was a stroke of genius. Constantinople, now the Turkish city of Istanbul, is located where the Black Sea flows through the straits known as the Bosphorus (Bosporus) into the Sea of Marmara (Marmora). Here Europe meets Asia. Through the city passed roads linking the Near East and Asia Minor with the Balkans and Western Europe. Those roads gave easy access to two of the main battlefronts of the Empire, the lower Danube and the Euphrates. Situated on a promontory protected on two sides by the sea and by strong land fortifications on the third, Constantinople occupied an almost impregnable position. It was not be taken by storm for more than 1000 years. It also enjoyed an excellent deep-water harbor (later called the Golden Horn). A great chain quickly and easily closed its entrance against attack by sea. Ideally located for trade, it captured the commerce of the world from the East and the West, the North and the South: furs from the North; silk from the Orient; spices from India and Arabia; fine wines and olive oil from Asia Minor and the Mediterranean; grain, precious stones, and exotic animals from Egypt and Africa.

In every way, save religion, Constantine made the new imperial city an exact equivalent of Rome. Rome was still the capital, but a capital no longer limited to one place. Rome was now almost an idea conveyed by replicating its essential features in Constantinople. The New Rome, as it was also called, had to share or duplicate old Rome's essentials: part of the senate (mostly senators from the eastern provinces); one of the two annual consuls; a *Populus Romanus*, privileged and exempt from taxation; and, above all, a *plebs* who received free entertainment and food.

To beautify the new city, Constantine ransacked ancient temples and shrines—even Delphi, from which he removed the tripod and the statue of Apollo. His confiscations, which some accounts (probably exaggerated) place at 60,000 pounds of gold, made it possible for him to build in Constantinople an enormous imperial palace, a huge hippodrome, a university, public schools and libraries, and magnificent Christian churches—Holy Peace (*Hagia Eirene*), Holy Wisdom (*Hagia Sophia*), and Holy Apostles. After dedicating the new city on May 11, 330, Constantine resided there most of his remaining life.

THE DEATH OF CONSTANTINE THE GREAT, 337 C.E.

Domestic tragedy marred what Constantine could otherwise have considered a glorious reign. In 326, he had his eldest son, Crispus, a youth with a brilliant military future, put to death on a trumped-up charge of raping his stepmother, the Empress Fausta. It appears that she had engineered the story to remove him as a possible rival of her own three sons—Constantine II, Constantius II, and Constans. In the same year, the empress herself died, scalded in a hot bath, supposedly after the emperor's mother, Helena had revealed that Fausta had committed adultery with a slave.

In 337, while preparing to lead an army against Persia in retaliation for unprovoked aggression against the Roman protectorate of Armenia, Constantine fell ill. A visit to the hot springs of Helenopolis failed to help. On the way back to Constantinople, near Nicomedia, he felt the relentless approach of death. He asked Bishop Eusebius of Nicomedia, who had vigorously defended Arius at Nicaea, to administer the sacrament of baptism. (It was not uncommon to put off baptism until late in life in order to die in a blameless state.) While still arrayed in the white robes of a Christian neophyte, Constantine died. His tomb was the mausoleum connected with the Church of the Holy Apostles.

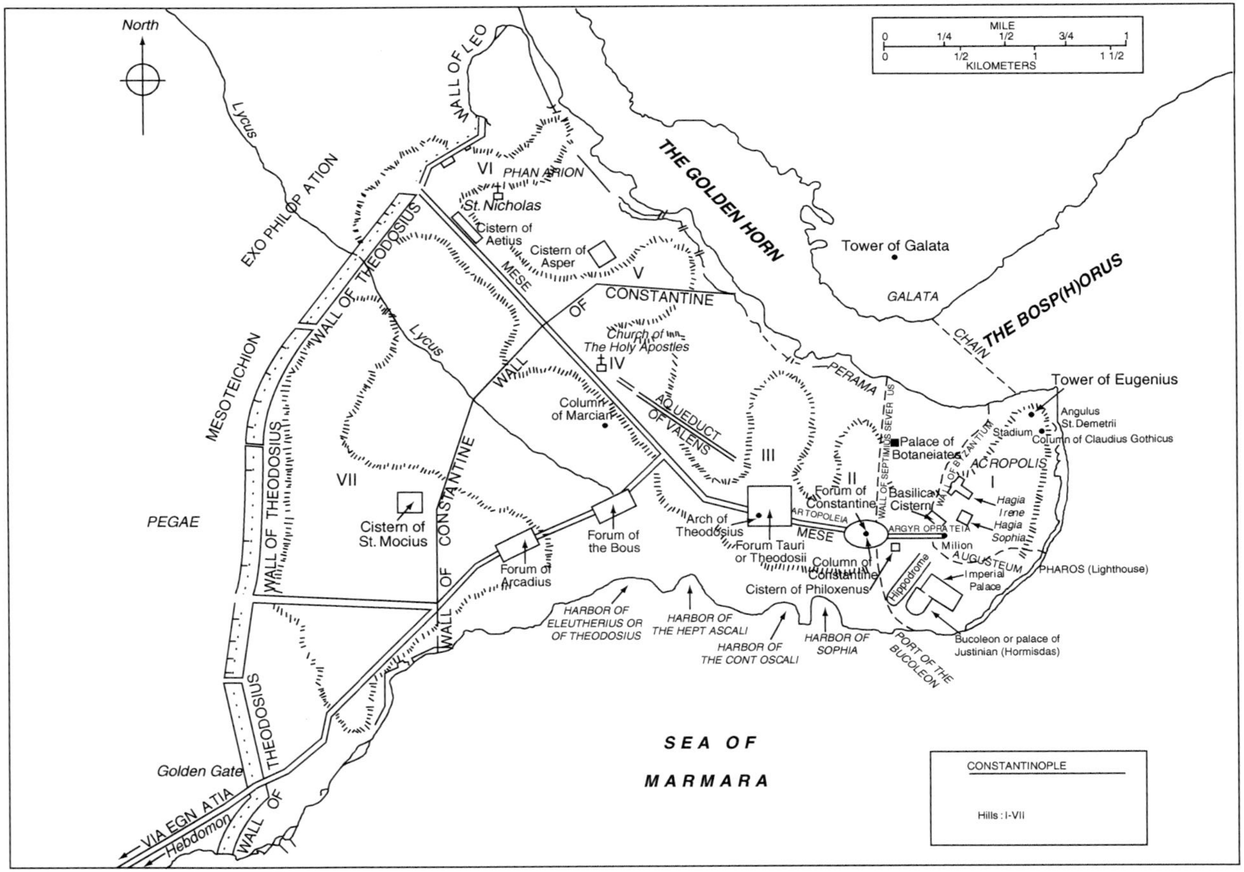

FIGURE 31.1 Constantinople (Hills: I–VH)

OVERVIEW

It would be difficult to overstate the significance of Constantine's reign. He had ruthlessly eliminated all political rivals and reunited the Roman Empire under one ruler. He had taken Christianity, a small, persecuted sect, and given it the impetus that made it one of the major religions of the world. Indeed, he greatly influenced the formulation of its most widely accepted creed and institutional structure. Finally, by following up and skillfully modifying Diocletian's reforms and by his splendid choice of a new residence, Constantine laid the foundations of the Byzantine Empire, which was to last 1000 years and have an incalculable impact upon Europe and the Near East.

NOTES

1 In much the same sense, modern business and nonprofit corporations are legally "persons." They can own property, make contracts, and sue or be sued in court.
2 The proclamation could have been interpreted by a Christian as instituting "the Lord's Day" and by a pagan as celebrating "the holy day of the Sun."

SUGGESTED READING

Drake, H. A. *Constantine and the Bishops. The Politics of Intolerance.* Baltimore: John Hopkins University Press, 2000.
Van Dam, R. *The Roman Revolution of Constantine.* Cambridge: Cambridge University Press, 2007.

CHAPTER 32

From Constantine's dynasty to Theodosius the Great, 337 to 395 C.E.

Diocletian and Constantine had helped to save the Roman Empire from the chaos that had threatened to engulf it in the last half of the third century. They had single-mindedly mobilized Rome's diminishing resources for the supreme effort of self-preservation. As a result, the Empire survived intact for the rest of the fourth century, despite many destructive problems: bloody feuding among Constantine's heirs, two serious military defeats, distracting struggles among Christians and between Christians and pagans, and the increasing need to man the armies with Germanic recruits or mercenaries.

MURDER AND CIVIL WAR

Although Constantine believed that he had provided for the safe transfer of his soul from the earthly to the heavenly realm, he could not provide for the safe transfer of power within the earthly realm. After his death, bloody rivalries and power struggles soon erupted. His two half-brothers and most of their sons were butchered by troops acting on false rumors that the half-brothers had murdered Constantine. Only two young nephews of Constantine survived, the half-brothers Gallus and Julian.

The false rumors allegedly originated with Constantius II (337–361), second son of Constantine and Fausta. Previously appointed as Caesars, Constantius II and his two brothers, Constantine II (337–340) and Constans (337–350), assumed the rank of Augusti and divided the Empire among themselves. Constantine II, the oldest brother, received the western half of the Empire. Under his supervision, Constans, the youngest brother, governed Africa, Italy, and Illyricum. Constantius II held the East. In 340, a quarrel led Constantine II to attack Constans in Italy. Constantine II was killed, and Constans took over the West. Constans vigorously defended the British and German frontiers, but his harshness as a commander and his inability to relieve inflation made him unpopular. In 350, Magnentius, a high-ranking officer of British and Frankish ancestry, overthrew and executed Constans. Meanwhile, Constantius II had been defending the East against the Persian King Shapur (Sapor) II (309–379). He disengaged himself from the Persians and defeated Magnentius in a series of battles beginning in 351. Magnentius finally committed suicide in 353 and left Constantius II as sole emperor.

Constantius' search for a partner

Soon after moving west, Constantius II realized that he needed a loyal subordinate to hold the East. Even Constantine had relied on his sons to help him hold together the vast Empire, whose unity was constantly threatened by external forces and internal pressures. Yet, close ties of blood did not guarantee harmony between or among those who shared power. Consider, for example, Constantine executing his son Crispus, the murder of Constantine's half-brothers and nephews, and the civil war between Constantine II and Constans. Still, it was too dangerous not to have someone share the burdens of power, and family ties were usually the most reliable.

In 351, after much hesitation, Constantius II chose Gallus, one of his two surviving cousins, as Caesar and put him in charge of the East. Constantius gave his sister Constantina (sometimes called Constantia) to Gallus in marriage to bind the Caesar more closely to the Augustus. Ironically, Constantina may have encouraged Gallus to aim higher. Moreover, Gallus' success against the Persians, his hot temper, and his actions against powerful interests at Antioch aroused the jealousy and suspicion of Constantius. Therefore, Constantius recalled Gallus to Italy in 354. Gallus sent Constantina to intercede for him with her brother, but she died on the way. The mausoleum that she had previously provided for herself at Rome still stands, and her magnificent porphyry sarcophagus now rests in the Vatican Museums. Gallus was arrested and beheaded. His younger half-brother, Julian, came under suspicion, too. With some help from Constantius' wife Eusebia, however, he was spared.

By the next year, 355, it became clear that Constantius needed another partner. While he was fighting restless tribes along the Danube, Gaul was thrown into turmoil by a combination of military rebellion and Germanic invasion. Eusebia and others urged him to appoint the twenty-three-year-old Julian as Caesar. Julian did not have Constantius' complete trust. He was a totally inexperienced young man who had spent all but his last four years under close house arrest in an atmosphere of suspicion and intrigue. Constantius, however, was finally persuaded by those who favored Julian. Having been made a Caesar, Julian received Constantius' other sister, Helena, for a wife.

Julian had the advantage of a congenial personality and a sharp intellect well trained by his tutors in rhetoric, history, and philosophy. Without repeating Gallus' political mistakes, he became a popular commander and administrator and methodically restored Roman defenses all along the Rhine between 357 and 359.

By 359, court intrigue and the death of the Empress Eusebia began to weaken Julian's position and arouse Constantius' jealous suspicions. Using a threat from Persia as an excuse, Constantius demanded many of Julian's troops. The troops refused to go. In February of 360, they proclaimed Julian emperor, ostensibly against his will. Then, Helena died childless. For the next year, while Constantius was securing the eastern frontier, Julian negotiated for a peaceful settlement with him. Constantius adamantly refused all offers of joint rule and set out to attack Julian in 361. Julian had already seized the initiative by marching east first. Before their two armies could clash, Constantius suddenly became ill and died. There was no son to succeed Constantius. He and Eusebia had been childless. His new wife, Faustina, would produce a posthumous daughter, Constantia. She would eventually unite the dynasty of Constantine the Great briefly with that of Valentinian I (p. 601). The Empire, however, needed a proven leader immediately. Julian became sole emperor without a struggle.

THE EMPIRE UNDER CONSTANTIUS II

Although not one of history's more pleasing characters, Constantius II had not been a bad emperor. In many ways, he was a Tiberius to Constantine's Augustus. Insecure and indecisive, he was often unduly influenced by unscrupulous members of his court and resorted to deviousness to secure his ends. To the best of his limited abilities, however, he had dutifully followed the path marked out by his father. "One Empire" and "one Church" were the foundations of his policies, as they had been for his father. The former helps to explain his role in the cold-blooded actions of 337, his subsequent refusal to recognize either Magnentius or Julian as co-emperors, and his willingness to resort to civil war in each case. Constantius II never neglected the arduous duties of protecting the frontiers. Most of his reign was spent in the military camp, not the sumptuous accommodations of the new capital. He was not so bold a general as his father or his rival Julian, but he did maintain the Empire's territorial integrity.

As an administrator, Constantius II continued the centralizing tendencies of Diocletian and Constantine. At the same time, his legislation shows an honest attempt to mitigate the abuses of bureaucratic power that the system fostered. Finally, he zealously encouraged the union of the Christian Church and Roman State that Constantine had begun. He reaffirmed Constantine's earlier ban against pagan sacrifices and ordered the closing of all pagan temples in 356. Theologically, Constantius II espoused a moderate Arian position and promoted doctrinal unity from that perspective. In 359, he summoned two regional councils of bishops—in the West at Ariminum (Rimini) on the Adriatic coast of Italy and in the East at Seleucia on the Calycadnus in Cilicia. Both councils eventually accepted a creed that declared Christ to be "like the Father," and this creed was confirmed by a general council at Constantinople in the following year. Had Constantius lived longer and defeated Julian, he might have been able to make the compromise stick, but his death in 361 quickly threw religious matters into turmoil once more.

JULIAN THE APOSTATE EMPEROR (361 TO 363 C.E.)

As was the case with all of his relatives, Julian had been raised a Christian. His secondary education had been supervised by Bishop George of Cappadocia. He had even taken lower orders as a lector in the Church. George, however, had a fine library of Classical literature and Greek philosophy, especially Neoplatonist philosophy. Julian found the spirit of Hellenism in these works more attractive than the Christianity espoused by those who had murdered his family and forced him to endure years of lonely exile. When released from exile, Julian had gone to Pergamum to study rhetoric and then to Athens and the study of philosophy. Sometime in the course of these studies, he became convinced that paganism was the path of true religion and secretly converted. Soon after he entered Constantinople in 361, however, Julian openly proclaimed his devotion to the old ways by rescinding laws hostile to paganism.

Officially, Julian merely proclaimed religious toleration for all; in practice, he used all the subtle powers of his office to advance paganism at the expense of the Church. While he hoped that toleration would produce the unedifying spectacle of uncompromising adherents of the Nicene Creed fighting with Arians, he worked to create a Neoplatonic syncretism of pagan cults with the sun god as the Universal One. He even tried to give this unified Neoplatonic paganism an ethical emphasis and organizational structure modeled on those of the Church that he had renounced. To Christians, Julian was a demonic agent of Satan, an impression reinforced by his emphasis on magic, divination, omens, theurgy, and elaborate sacrifices, which even many of his friends thought excessive. Nevertheless, the sudden and dramatic turn that his fortunes had taken since 354 had convinced Julian that the gods were on his side, and he forged ahead. He decreed an end to imperial financial support for Christian churches and rescinded privileges previously granted to the Christian clergy. He also forbade Christians to teach the classic works of Greco-Roman literature and philosophy, a move that was intended to marginalize Christians in terms of the dominant culture.

The Persian War

Convinced of his own destiny, Julian did not want to wait to prove his prowess. He quickly prepared to invade Persia in order to gain permanent security for the neighboring provinces and glory for himself as another Alexander the Great. While he was using Antioch as a base for preparations in 362, Julian promoted his pagan revival among the inhabitants of this great city, one of the most staunchly Christian in the whole Empire.

At best, the Antiochenes ignored him; at worst, they laughed at him. For the first time since his meteoric rise, Julian met failure, and it shook his self-confidence.

Confidence returned with the success of his initial invasion of Persia (March, 363). He was tempted to push on into the interior, although he had not brought the main Persian army to battle and had no clear strategic objective. He crossed the Tigris to Ctesiphon but failed to take it. Retreating north in the deadly heat of summer and low on supplies, the Roman army was now constantly harassed by the main force of King Shapur II. While riding off without his breastplate to rally the troops in a sudden attack on the rear guard, Julian received a mortal spear wound in the side. He lingered into the night before dying (June 26, 363). Some say that the spear was hurled by a Christian in his own ranks. In the days following, the Persians taunted the retreating Romans with this idea to undermine morale. In the confusion of battle, however, no one had been able to tell who threw the spear, and certainty can never be attained.

The early death of Julian was a major turning point in Roman history. Had he enjoyed a long reign like Diocletian's or Constantine's, his policies would have had a great effect. Certainly, he would not have been able to eliminate Christianity, as he fervently wished. Still with official support, the kind of theologically and institutionally unified paganism that he advocated could have become a strong counter force to the Christian Church. It might have jeopardized the whole Empire by splitting it between two large, antagonistic, and well- organized religious camps.

JOVIAN (JUNE 363 TO FEBRUARY 364 c.e.)

Julian had no heir, and, as did his hero Alexander, he refused to designate a successor while he talked on his deathbed with friends. Upon his death, Julian's generals, the legionary commanders, and cavalry officers met to choose a successor. Their first choice was Julian's close advisor Saturninus Secundus Salutius, praetorian prefect of the East, a moderate pagan and a popular individual in general. Old and unambitious, however, he refused. After considerable further debate, the officers finally settled on a Christian officer ironically named Jovian.

The Romans struggled on. They reached a crossing point on the east bank of the Tigris, but rough water held them back. Shapur, who still feared a pitched battle, offered to negotiate. Jovian, irresolute, insecure, and perhaps anxious to confirm his claim to the throne at home, accepted very disadvantageous terms. They included the surrender of Nisibis, the almost impregnable stronghold that was the anchor of Roman defenses in Mesopotamia; abandonment of Roman provinces beyond the Tigris; cessation of the Roman protectorate over Armenia; and payment of an annual subsidy to Persia to defray the expenses of defending the Caucasus. In return, Shapur granted peace for thirty years.

Jovian died after reigning only eight months. His one major act after negotiating the treaty with Shapur was to rescind Julian's anti-Christian legislation. Though pro-Christian, he did not pursue repressive policies toward pagans. Julian's pagan friends and supporters did not suffer for their earlier allegiance, and all were free to worship as they wished.

VALENTINIAN I (364 TO 375 C.E.) AND
VALENS (364 TO 378 C.E.)

With the death of Jovian, the chief military officers and civilian officials chose Valentinian (Flavius Valentinianus) as the next emperor. He was an experienced Christian Pannonian officer, though only of secondary rank. His backers also insisted that he choose a co-emperor, so that equal imperial attention could be given to problems in the East and West. Valentinian chose his brother Valens and left him in charge of the East while he oversaw the West from Milan. Julian's old Gallic legions, pagans, and many who favored the house of Constantine the Great—including Constantius II's widow, Faustina—supported Procopius, a relative of Julian's mother. He attempted to usurp the throne in late 365 but was suppressed and executed in early 366. Faustina disappeared from history.

As military men, Valentinian and Valens energetically defended the Empire. Unfortunately, Valentinian died in 375 after suffering a stroke during angry negotiations with the Quadi. He left his share of the imperial title to his sixteen-year-old son Gratian. A year before, Valentinian had reinforced Gratian's imperial legitimacy by marrying him to Constantius' posthumous twelve-year-old daughter, Constantia.

In the East, Valens fought back the Goths in Thrace from 365 to 369. He turned his attention to Persia in 371. He had managed only to restore Roman control over Armenia before he needed to rush back to face a rising tide of Goths on the Danube.

The Battle of Adrianople, August 9, 378 C.E.

Fleeing the terrifying raids of the Huns (pp. 657–8), thousands of Goths begged Valens for permission to resettle in Roman territory. Welcoming such an increase in manpower for Rome, Valens agreed, on the condition that they surrender their arms. The Romans were not prepared to handle such a vast influx of refugees. Corrupt officials mercilessly exploited their plight. The Romans sold them bad food, even dog meat, at high prices or in exchange for other Goths, whom they sold into slavery. Abused and frustrated, the Goths rose up in mass revolt in 377. An incompetent Roman commander soon lost control of the situation. Other Goths and even some Huns crossed into the Empire to join the fight against the Romans.

Valens, who had marched off against the Persians again, had to bring his army all the way back to Thrace. He arrived in the summer of 378 to take charge of the situation. Impatient and not wanting to share the laurels of victory with his young nephew Gratian, Valens sought battle without waiting for Gratian's reinforcements.

After a morning's march, he met the Gothic army on August 9, 378, near Adrianople (Adrianopolis) in Thrace (map, p. 571). The Goths offered to negotiate to gain enough time for their cavalry to arrive. The Roman soldiers stood waiting in the sun on a hot, dusty plain. By afternoon, smoke from brush fires set by the Goths and the lack of a midday meal compounded the Romans' discomfort. Suddenly, in the midst of negotiations, some Romans in the front line broke ranks. A battle erupted. Gothic horsemen arrived just in time to drive off the cavalry protecting the Romans infantry's flanks.

After that, the Romans did not have a chance. Out of an army of 30,000, two-thirds of the troops, scores of officers, and the foolish emperor himself perished. The Balkans were the Goths' for the taking.

The policies of Valentinian I and Valens

Except for the disaster at Adrianople, the joint reign of Valentinian I and Valens had been militarily successful. They had strengthened the Roman army by recruiting mercenaries from the warlike tribes along Rome's frontiers. Then they had successfully defended those frontiers until Valens' foolish haste at Adrianople. In civil matters, however, they had been much less successful. Men of the camp, they had little sympathy for the civilian upper class and vice versa. They tended, therefore, to choose as their civil administrators less educated and more opportunistic men of their own social class.

By their legislation, the two did try to protect the poor, ensure justice, and prevent fiscal abuse. For example, Valentinian created an empire-wide office of *defensor civitatis*, an ombudsman, whose duty was to protect citizens from arbitrary officials. Nevertheless, the good intentions of the co-emperors were frequently thwarted by ruthless and rapacious officials like those who so fatefully abused the Goths. Honest officials had little chance against the influence of the corrupt. For example, when Theodosius, a general who had put down a revolt by Firmus in Africa, uncovered official wrongdoing in that province, powerful men at the western court turned against him, and he was executed in 376 (p. 615).

On matters of religion, both emperors were tolerant of pagans and banned only sacrifices and the attendant practices of magic and divination. In the West, Valentinian was an orthodox adherent of the Nicene Creed (p. 589), but he kept out of theological disputes and allowed the religious authorities to work out their own problems. He did, however, forbid unscrupulous clerics from taking advantage of widows and unmarried women to obtain lucrative gifts. In the East, Valens adhered to the official moderate Arianism established by Constantius II in 359. Unfortunately, he tried to impose it forcibly and caused clerical discontent, popular unrest, and persecution of dissenters.

GRATIAN (375 TO 383 c.e.) AND THEODOSIUS THE GREAT (379 TO 395 c.e.)

When Valens died, the young Gratian was at a disadvantage. He had received a good education and was guided by competent advisors. As a young man, however, he was in a precarious position despite his marital connection to the dynasty of Constantine. To ensure the loyalty of Illyricum after the debacle at Adrianople, the troops of Illyricum had proclaimed Gratian's four-year-old half-brother Valentinian II as co-emperor. Gratian accepted their move. Yet, he gave Valentinian II no further territory and left him with his mother (Justina, Gratian's own stepmother [p. 615]) and a Frankish general named Merobaudes as regents. Gratian himself created a second colleague in 379 by recalling from exile the son of the Theodosius who had been unjustly executed three years previously after suppressing Firmus' revolt.

The son was named Theodosius, also. His first task was to confront the Visigoths, a group of Goths who had been plundering the Balkans since the defeat of Valens. Theodosius pursued them for three years without inflicting a decisive defeat. Unwilling to prolong the costly conflict, he agreed to let the Visigoths settle within the Empire as autonomous federate allies with their own kings. In return, they agreed to fight for Rome under their own national commanders. The settlement of foreign tribesmen after capture in war or after terms of military service in Roman armies had been a common occurrence. Nevertheless, to grant anyone autonomous status within imperial territory was a radical departure from previous policy. At the time, there was little else that Theodosius could have done. Unfortunately, his innovative settlement to meet the needs of the moment set a precedent that would tempt other invaders to press for similar treatment later on and thus further undermine the integrity of the Empire.

Magnus Maximus overthrows Gratian, 383 C.E.

In the West, Gratian's education gained him the respect that the upper classes had denied his father. He put his own, more refined friends in place of the rougher Pannonian advisors whom his father had provided. He became more interested in the pursuit of game on royal estates than of the enemy on the frontiers. He also was intensely interested in promoting orthodox Christianity. After issuing an edict of general religious toleration upon the death of Valentinian I, he had soon rescinded it. Probably he did so under the influence of the talented and zealous Bishop Ambrose of Milan. In 382, Gratian renounced the title *pontifex maximus*, removed the Altar of Victory from the senate house at Rome, and confiscated the endowments of the Vestal Virgins and ancient priestly colleges. A senatorial embassy led by Symmachus (see pp. 633–4) went to Milan to petition for a reversal of these measures but was rebuffed: the senators were not even admitted into the Emperor's presence. Symmachus was no more successful two years later, after the death of Gratian, when he wrote to Valentinian II about the issue. Pope Damasus and Ambrose successfully opposed his efforts.

Absorbed in other interests, Gratian fatally neglected his troops. His position also may have been weakened by the fact that he and Constantia had not produced an heir in nine years of marriage. In 383, very shortly after Constantia had died (in childbirth?), soldiers in Britain proclaimed Magnus Maximus, their commander, as emperor. Maximus then seized Gaul, captured Gratian, whom the army had promptly abandoned, and had him executed before he and his new wife had been able to have any children. Meanwhile, Theodosius faced hostility from the Persians and another group of Goths, the Ostrogoths. Not risking the complications of a civil war, he accepted Maximus as his colleague in charge of Britain, Gaul, and Spain. Valentinian II, under the sole regency of his mother, kept Illyricum and received Italy, Dacia, and Macedonia as well.

In 387, however, after Theodosius had defeated the Ostrogoths and reached a settlement with Persia, Maximus tried to seize Italy. Theodosius gave refuge to young Valentinian II, married the boy's sister Galla, and marched west. After two defeats, Maximus' own troops surrendered him to Theodosius in 388. Theodosius'

Frankish master of the soldiers, Arbogast, recovered Gaul from Maximus' son Victor. Subsequently, Valentinian II was placed in charge of the West under the guidance of Arbogast.

The revolt of Arbogast

Arbogast was one of many Germans to reach high rank under Theodosius, who relied heavily on Germanic tribes to make up for the chronic shortage of military manpower. In 392, Arbogast quarreled with the young Valentinian. Now twenty, the latter was eager to assert his own independence as a ruler. He failed in his confrontation with Arbogast and was found hanged soon after; whether by his own or another's hand is not clear. Arbogast, however, had little to gain under the circumstances. He did not dare to proclaim himself, a "barbarian," as emperor. Only after his overtures expressing loyalty to Theodosius were rebuffed did he set up a puppet in the West, the rhetorician Eugenius, head of the secretarial office and a tolerant Christian, if not a secret pagan.

To gain support from powerful pagan senators in Rome, Eugenius sanctioned a revival of the traditional public cults. His attempts to come to terms with Theodosius failed. Theodosius reluctantly prepared to invade the West again. On September 6, 394, the two armies finally met at the Frigidus River near Aquileia. After an initial repulse, Theodosius gained the victory with timely aid from a storm and the defection of some enemy troops. Eugenius was killed, and Arbogast committed suicide, whereupon Theodosius became sole emperor of the reunited Empire.

THE DEATH OF THEODOSIUS AND THE DIVISION OF THE EMPIRE, 395 C.E.

Theodosius' health had been failing for some time, although he was only forty-eight. He died at Milan in early 395, five months after his victory. Some say that by leaving the West to his ten-year-old son Honorius and the East to his seventeen- or eighteen-year-old son Arcadius, Theodosius permanently split the Empire, whose unity he had so recently preserved. Still, Theodosius was probably convinced of the strategic necessity of having an equal representative of imperial authority in both the East and the West. It was the illegitimacy of Eugenius' rule in the West that Theodosius could not countenance, not the division of authority, which had long become an accepted principle. He had shown no predisposition to challenge the legitimate western emperors Gratian and Valentinian II, and it is clear that he intended his dynasty to be the vehicle for continued unity between East and West.

Much more difficult for Theodosius were the expenses of civil wars and the defense of frontiers. The taxes and manpower required were more than the economy and population could safely bear. The situation was also made worse by Theodosius' return to an elaborate court and the inauguration of a costly building program to increase the splendor of Constantinople. The operation of an already vast bureaucracy needed to meet the increased military, administrative, and fiscal burdens of the times produced ever more problems as numerous officials corruptly sought their own interests at the expense of everyone else.

It was primarily because of his religious activities that later, Christian ages called Theodosius "Great." A pious orthodox Christian, he increasingly supported those who accepted the Nicene Creed, which he reinforced by summoning the First Council of Constantinople in 381. In his efforts, he was encouraged by the zealous Bishop Ambrose of Milan. At first, he applied his orthodox piety only to Christians themselves. Then, late in his reign, edicts of 391 and 392 legally banned the outward expression of pagan worship. Theodosius did not reverse the long-standing official Roman policy of religious freedom for the Jews. Yet, he was often unable to protect them from the ethnic and religious bigotry of their neighbors. By withholding communion, Ambrose even forced Theodosius to rescind an order that a Jewish synagogue in Callinicum be rebuilt at the town's expense after a mob of fanatical monks had destroyed it.

Paganism certainly did not disappear in the face of Theodosius' official hostility. Still, without governmental sanction and financial support, its public manifestations gradually decayed. Many representatives of old families kept hoping for a restoration of the old religious order. Their political and social prominence had been reinforced by their control of time-honored priesthoods, cults, and ceremonies. Their hopes were momentarily raised when Arbogast and Eugenius sought their support by sanctioning a revival of public pagan cults. Those hopes were quickly chilled by Theodosius' victory at the Frigidus River and were doomed in the long run by the general transformation taking place.

SUGGESTED READING

Cameron, A. *The Later Roman Empire, AD 284–430*. Cambridge, MA: Harvard University Press, 1993.

McEvoy, M. A. *Child Emperor Rule in the Late Roman West, AD 367–455. Oxford Classical Monographs*. Oxford and New York: Oxford University Press, 2013.

CHAPTER 33

The evolving world of Late Antiquity in the fourth century C.E.

The restored Empire of Diocletian and Constantine was still recognizably Roman. Nevertheless, such changes had taken place in the Roman world by the beginning of the fourth century that scholars generally identify it as the beginning of a new period of ancient history, called Late Antiquity. In the more stable atmosphere created under Diocletian and Constantine, economic, social, and cultural changes in the fourth century were more evolutionary and less revolutionary than they had threatened to become in the latter part of the third. Furthermore, the pace and scope of change, as always, were uneven.

ECONOMIC CONDITIONS

A lack of silver undermined Constantine's attempt to revive the silver coinage (p. 590). Hyperinflation from too many copper and billon coins continued throughout the fourth century. In 334, the ratio of the *denarius* (now only a unit of account based on copper or bronze *nummi*) to gold was 300,000 to the Roman pound. By Constantine's death in 337, it was 20 million to the pound, and 330 million by 357! Constantine did, however, manage to stabilize the gold coinage with his new *solidi*, not only by minting them at seventy-two per pound, but also by measures designed to release hoarded gold. The long-term stability of gold, however, rested on increased measures to recover gold coins through taxation and forced purchases from moneychangers and the rich.

The production of gold mines was also steadier as a result of increased security and political stability. Silver supplies were inadequate because the available ores were of low quality or difficult to mine.

In effect, the Roman government created a two-tiered system, a stable one based on gold and an unstable one based on copper. The gold system benefited the government and the wealthy. The stable purchasing power of gold enabled the government to retain the loyalty of the armies by regular cash donatives. Gold was also used to pay officials, to buy and subsidize food and entertainments for the urban *plebs* of Rome and Constantinople, and to provide annual subsidies and diplomatic payoffs to ensure peaceful frontiers. The rich were the only ones with enough income to acquire gold in sufficient quantities to protect themselves against inflation. The lower ranks of the curial class and the poor saw their copper and billon currency continually lose its purchasing power and had to avoid using money as much as possible. Under such conditions, the rich continued to get richer as the rest got poorer.

Agriculture

The economic advantage enjoyed by wealthy senatorial landowners and emperors meant the continued amassing of vast landholdings in a few hands. Nevertheless, the total amount of land under cultivation shrank in some areas. Particularly in the less developed and less defensible parts of the West, the invasions and civil wars of the third century had caused much hardship. The large landowners who had been able to protect themselves or find refuge elsewhere were able to buy or take over the lands of the less fortunate when more favorable conditions returned. They shrewdly spread their holdings over many provinces, particularly in relatively productive and protected areas.

In the East, land remained more in the hands of smaller independent proprietors, particularly in Asia Minor, Syria–Palestine, and Egypt. Those areas had not suffered so badly during the third century. A senate at Constantinople had only recently been created from the ranks of moderately wealthy local aristocrats (p. 613). They had not been able to emulate the wealth of the old western senatorial families. Also, the proximity of more large and relatively prosperous cities gave eastern farmers access to urban markets where they could find good prices.

Trade and industry

On the whole, markets were more regional than empire-wide during the fourth and subsequent centuries. Still, the situation was not so bleak as once imagined. It is true that the great landowners tried to be as self-sufficient as possible. They maintained their own staff of craftsmen to produce many of the articles needed to run their domestic and other operations. To make up for what they did not produce themselves, they often exchanged different products with each other. Yet, markets and independent tradesmen and craftsmen did not disappear. The great proprietors often made handsome profits by selling in bulk to wholesale traders, to municipal governments, and even to the army and the imperial government.

Some of these profits were exchanged in urban markets for specialty items that could not be made on country estates. Essential commodities like metals, marble, papyrus, spices, salt, and slaves had to be purchased via major trade networks. As the fourth century progressed, some taxes in kind were commuted to payment in gold, and troops were paid more in gold than in rations. Therefore, the buying and selling of goods increased.

In the East, large cities and towns had always been more numerous and were generally more able to recover from the third century (p. 612). Demand from private purchasers was enough to support a large number and variety of independent craftsmen and shopkeepers. Itinerant merchants made the rounds of smaller villages that could not support specialized craftsmen. The trade in luxuries from beyond the Empire revived in the fourth century. The state tried to control foreign trade through a few official gateways such as Clysma (Suez) in Egypt, Hieron on the Bosphorus (Bosporus), Nisibis in Mesopotamia, and Carnuntum on the Danube. Exports of strategic material were forbidden, and a duty of 12.5 percent was collected on imports. In comparison, the levy on goods transported internally was only 2 to 2.5 percent. Internal trade in western Europe and the Mediterranean was as free as it had been in the glory days of the second century or would be until the creation of the modern European Economic Community. The high cost of transportation, however, and the limited private market still kept private trade and industry restricted to a few basic commodities, luxuries, and specialized craft goods.

The economic influence of the state

The state's increased military expenditures from Diocletian onward made the state a greater economic force than ever, particularly in the East. The great sums expended on building up the defenses of the eastern frontier helped to stimulate the economic prosperity of the region in general. All over the Empire, the state played a larger role in the production and distribution of goods during the fourth century through taxes in kind, the establishment of large state-run workshops (*fabricae*), and heavy utilization of the *cursus publicus*, the state's transport system that moved messages, officials, and military materials across the Empire. Approximately forty *fabricae* turned out all of the arms and armor needed by the army. Others turned wool and linen into some of the uniforms and clothing worn by soldiers and government officials. State-owned dye-works produced their own dyes and dyed the cloth. The *fabricae* were originally under the praetorian prefect and then the master of the offices. The count of the sacred largesses oversaw other operations. Hereditary groups of workers supplied the labor. They received rations, fuel, and raw materials from in-kind taxes and had to meet annual production quotas. The state also had its own mines and quarries. Some employed convicts for labor. At others, labor was requisitioned from local landowners as needed.

Because transport by water was much more efficient than by land, the state tried to ship large cargoes, such as grain, stone, timber, and military supplies, by water as much as possible. Seaborne goods were carried by state-mandated guilds of shippers (*navicularii*). They were wealthy individuals who financed ships dedicated to government service. They were paid half the commercial rate but received valuable reductions in taxes, freedom from curial duties, and protection against loss from shipwreck. They could also carry deck passengers and consignments of small high-value items for extra revenue. Similar guilds of barge operators on the Tiber between Rome and Portus brought grain and firewood to Rome. The state also ran its own boats on major rivers like the Rhine and the Po.

The state-run *cursus publicus* provided enormously expensive transportation over land. It operated two levels of service: the express post (*cursus velox*) supplied light transportation from saddle horses to four-wheeled carriages pulled by eight or ten mules for fast couriers, small loads of valuables, and authorized travelers. The wagon post (*cursus clabularis*) carried heavy freight such as food, clothing, building materials, arms, and military baggage.

There were way stations every ten or twelve miles on the trunk roads: *mansiones* provided travelers' services as well as fresh animals; *mutationes* provided changes of animals only. Both were staffed by public slaves who repaired equipment and took care of the animals. They were given rations of state food and clothing. The state acquired animals through an annual levy. Local landowners provided fodder as a tax in kind. Provincial governors had to maintain the buildings out of provincial taxes.

The praetorian prefect and master of the offices issued warrants to use the *cursus publicus*. Provincial governors received only two, one for sending messages to superiors and one for local matters. Important senators, bishops, and dignitaries often obtained warrants, too. Inspectors from the Agents of Affairs (*agentes in rebus*) watched out for unauthorized users.

The growing economic influence of the Church

The Christian Church became a major economic influence. Constantine first allowed churches to inherit property. By the end of the century, churches had acquired vast landholdings. Many wealthy Christians piously donated their land and wealth to their local churches or founded monasteries and church-run charities. Bishops, who often came from the class of wealthy aristocratic landowners, operated these holdings just as any secular owner. Taking on the traditional aristocratic role of public benefactors, the bishops distributed food, clothing, and money to the needy from the Church's own resources.

The Church also replaced aristocratic benefactors and municipal councils as the biggest local builders of the fourth century. The building of magnificent public buildings gave way to the building of magnificent churches as more and more wealth flowed into the Church and away from secular benefactions. Other buildings included hospitals, orphanages, homes for the elderly, shrines to martyrs, and even baths.

Pilgrimages to shrines like that of St. Martin at Tours or St. Felix at Nola, to the Holy Land, and to the abodes of renowned holy men brought prosperity to those places and stopping points along the way. Pilgrims needed food, accommodations, and transportation. They bought souvenirs, amulets, holy water, and pictures or statuettes. Saints' feast days provided the opportunity to hold lively market fairs.

THE SOCIAL CONTEXT

The fourth century saw continuing demographic change, increasing social stratification and regimentation, the declining status of the curial class, and a growing public role for upper-class women. The eastern and western halves of the Empire experienced these changes differently, however. Demographically, for example, the western provinces in the fourth century do not seem to have recovered all of the population lost during the third. The East was growing in population by the end of the fourth, a factor that helped the eastern sector's economy recover, too.

The urban scene

Some cities did not recover from the shocks of the third century (p. 547). Still, local circumstances stimulated the growth of others, perhaps at the expense of neighboring communities. For example, as imperial residences or other strategic centers on the great military highways, western cities like Augusta Treverorum (Trier), Arelate (Arles), Mediolanum (Milan), Ravenna, Aquileia, Vindobona (Vienna), and Sirmium were able to prosper from the stimulus of public expenditures. In Thrace, Constantinople, the Empire's new eastern capital, grew into a great city. Other eastern cities benefited from greater expenditures on frontier defenses against Persia. The continued export of grain from North Africa also provided a solid economic base for cities like Carthage, Hippo Regius, and Thamugadi (Timgad).

In Italy, Rome largely recovered from the disasters of the third century. The emperors maintained and even expanded benefactions of food and entertainment. They also financed new construction and the restoration of old buildings, which provided employment. The last great period of secular public building in Rome occurred during the reigns of Diocletian and Constantine (pp. 645–7). Constantine and his Christian successors lavished enormous resources on the building of Christian churches (pp. 647–8). The great nobles also built extravagant private mansions for themselves that rivaled imperial palaces. By 367, therefore, Rome's population seems to have approached 1 million again.

It used to be thought that the great landowners had abandoned the cities to reside on their great rural estates, particularly in the West. New research indicates that this view is too stark. While wealthy aristocrats did spend time visiting their rural properties, they also maintained their city residences and still participated in urban life.

In Rome and many other western cities, local leadership began to shift to Christian bishops. Often these bishops were connected with or patronized by important families. Bishops could have great influence over a Christian emperor, as did the powerful St. Ambrose, bishop of Milan. The growing economic importance of their churches increased their influence and patronage at the expense of secular officials. Indeed, their charitable activities created large groups of loyal dependents. In the late third century, the bishop of Rome was already supporting between 1500 and 2000 widows, orphans, and poor men. No comparable figures for western cities are available from the fourth century, but the fourth-century bishops of Antioch in Syria supported 3000 needy widows and virgins alone.

In the East, the secular municipal councils still played an important and active role in the lives of their cities. Although members of eastern elites were individually less wealthy than in the West, they were more numerous. If some wealthy decurions were drawn away to imperial service, the Church, or the senate in Constantinople, enough remained to keep up the traditional competition for patronage and prestige that gave Greco-Roman urban life its vitality.

Now the competition often centered on the ability to gain the favor of the emperor or his representatives. They had the vast wealth and power to provide the benefits that urban elites could not supply by themselves. Whereas the elites of Rome and Italy had previously drained off the wealth of the East to the West, the emperors based in the East spent their revenues there. Constantinople, splendidly founded by Constantine and nourished by later fourth-century emperors, grew into one of the great cities of the world. It became an economic engine that pulled other major eastern cities in its train. Alexandria, for example, always prosperous, prospered even more as it supplied grain to the new imperial city and turned imported materials from Africa, India, and the Far East into luxuries for the imperial Court. The prosperity of the major cities then rippled through the smaller surrounding cities and towns into the countryside.

The political role of cities

If a monarchy is not to be a tyranny, rule depends upon the consent, or at least the acquiescent awe, of the governed. In many ways, the politics of the Empire were an elaborate form of theater. Cities were the stage and their large lower-class populations the audience whose applause and approval validated the emperor's legitimate power. In major administrative centers, imperial subsidies augmented the local funds expended on the distribution of food and popular entertainments such as theatrical performances, beast hunts (often involving public executions), chariot races, and athletic games. Imperial processions marking the visit of the emperor were elaborately theatrical. Diocletian sprinkled gold dust in his hair on such occasions to create a soft halo of reflected light.

When bread, circuses, and other spectacles failed to keep the masses happy, however, a grimmer drama often played out. Religious tensions, conflicts between the infamous circus factions (pp. 677–8), food shortages, higher taxes, and other sources of discontent often led to violence and riots. They might undermine an emperor's authority if not properly handled with theatrical displays of rage, clemency, or some combination of the two. Two incidents in the reign of Theodosius are illustrative.

In 387, rioting tax protesters at Antioch insulted Theodosius' name and dragged the toppled statues of him and his wife through the streets. Theodosius sent in troops, executed many rioters, and ordered harsh penalties for the city and its leaders. Then he kept the populace in a state of suspense and anxiety while he listened to lengthy appeals for clemency from the local pagan notables and Christian leaders. Dramatically yielding to the Christians' entreaties just in time for Easter, Theodosius solidified his support among the single most powerful group in Antioch and reinforced their growing dominance in the city's affairs.

The second incident occurred three years later, in 390, at Thessalonica, the city most closely linked to Theodosius' rise to power. After rioters had lynched a local Gothic military commander, Theodosius and his military advisors ordered the execution of the culprits. In carrying out their orders, the Gothic soldiers instituted a vengeful massacre that sent shudders throughout the Empire. After his point had been made, Theodosius again donned the mask of Christian piety by performing a minor act of penance before St. Ambrose at the cathedral in Milan. It then became the setting for another great theatrical show of imperial pomp in celebrating with Honorius and Valentinian II the concord of his dynasty. By such displays, Theodosius maintained his authority in the cities that constituted the essence of the Empire.

The growing "barbarian" presence

Demographically, the intermingling of the Roman and "barbarian" populations along the frontiers proceeded. In fact, the distinction between so-called "barbarians" and Romans was largely an artificial one. It reflects the attitudes of the educated upper classes toward those who did not have the level of education, refinement, and social pedigree that they considered to be hallmarks of civilized life. Upper-class authors left most of the literary records that have shaped the modern view of uncouth barbarian hordes destroying the Roman Empire. From their narrow perspective, it might have been true. In terms of Roman society at large, assimilation between the Roman and non-Roman populations in the frontier zones had been going on for a long time. The fourth century saw only an intensification of an ongoing process in both the East and the West.

In the East, Egypt, and North Africa, the situations along the frontiers were very fluid. Trade and the movements of nomadic tribes produced a constant flow of goods, people, and influences. Whereas Christianity spread Roman influence in Persia, Manichaeism spread Persian influence in the Roman Empire. The mutual capture of each other's soldiers and towns as a result of frequent warfare further mingled the populations. Both used nomadic Arabic tribes (often identified as Saracens) as proxies against each other. Many of the Saracen tribes bordering Rome's eastern provinces were ruled by Roman-appointed tribal chiefs (*phylarchs*).

Archaeological evidence shows that along the northern frontiers there was little difference in the material cultures of the Romans and non-Romans. Romans had adopted the local style of dress, which was more suited to northern climes, utilized wood more extensively for construction, drank beer, bought Germanic slaves, and may have adopted such non-Roman innovations as coulters and asymmetrical plowshares for agriculture. The non-Roman upper class adopted villa-style agriculture, drank imported Roman wine, ate off imported Roman tableware, and eagerly sought other high-status Roman goods such as silver plate, gold coins, spices, and jewelry.

By the end of the fourth century, even Germanic tribes that were relative new-comers on the Roman frontier had been undergoing heavy Romanization for over a century. The Franks, Vandals, Burgundians, and Alemanni in the West and the Goths (also called *Tervingi* and *Scythians* in the sources) in the East had all occupied territories along the frontier since the mid-third century. Constantius II had supported efforts of the Arian bishop Ulfila to convert the Goths to Christianity. When they petitioned for admittance to the Roman Empire as *laeti* in 376 to escape the terrifying Huns, the Romans had already used some of them as auxiliaries in the Persian campaigns of Gordian III in 242 and Julian in 363. Valens, therefore, had hoped to welcome them as a permanent source of valuable military manpower. The dynamic, long-standing—but not always pretty—Roman process of integrating new ethnic and cultural groups into the state and society was still at work.

Under Valens, Valentinian, Gratian, and Theodosius, strongly Romanized Germans were everywhere. They provided more and more of the forces that accompanied the emperor (the *comitatenses*). They also occupied the most important military offices. These Germanic generals were usually the sons of men who had fought in Rome's armies and settled on Roman lands. They fought and thought as members of Rome's military elite. They loyally served their emperors or advanced their own personal careers within the imperial system. The civilian aristocratic literati who labeled such men "barbarians" had no objection to them doing Rome's fighting. They were jealous that a new class of Romans was achieving the political power and social prestige that they considered their birthright. The contemptuous aristocrats conveniently forgot the origins of their own families.

The ruling class

Diocletian had greatly increased the size of the Empire's ruling class. His administrative and military reforms dramatically enlarged the number of high-ranking bureaucrats and officers. Local notables were now directly responsible for meeting the local tax levies. Ironically, this broadening of the ruling class had the effect of increasing the height and steepness of the hierarchical pyramid that had always characterized Roman society.

Under Diocletian, the senatorial class at the top of the Roman social pyramid consisted of 500 or 600 families. A man of that class held the rank of *clarissimus* (most renowned). The men who held administrative posts under Diocletian often rose from the ranks of the army and were granted equestrian titles of various degrees. The highest was *eminentissimus* (most eminent), the lowest *egregius* (outstanding).

During the fourth century, the tendency was to cheapen the value of these ranks by letting people have titles of higher rank without higher achievement. Ever-higher ranks had to be created to distinguish those at the top of the pyramid from those lower down. Constantine, for example, watered down the rank of *clarissimus* by appointing many holders of equestrian rank to it or by increasing the number of offices that bestowed such rank. For the highest-ranking senators, he revived the title *patricius* (patrician). Constantius II created a completely separate senate at Constantinople. It had 300 members drawn largely from new families. By the time of Theodosius, it reached 2000 members. The senate at Rome had increased in a corresponding manner. Already, therefore, Valentinian I had begun to distinguish a senator who had held the office of consul or been made *patricius* by calling him *illustris* (illustrious). Below the *illustris* now were the *spectabilis* (notable) and *comes* (companion, count). In the next century, the *gloriosus* overtopped the *illustris*.

Rank, of course, does not always equal status. Many of the men who reached high senatorial rank under the fourth-century emperors were of relatively low social status. Emperors promoted loyal and talented men from nonsenatorial families to offices that bestowed senatorial rank. They gave outright grants to those who had earned their favor. Other men, particularly from the curial class (p. 547), obtained senatorial rank through bribery and influence. Therefore, the senatorial class in the fourth century was characterized by great social, geographic, and ethnic diversity. It included men who originated from every class and province and not a few foreign tribes and nations. A number of Persians, Germans, and Sarmatians, for example, had become generals in Roman armies and thereby achieved senatorial rank. Slaves, peasants, and higher civil servants all made their way into the senatorial class. Some made it through service in the army and imperial ministries, others via successful careers as doctors, advocates, architects, and professors.

There were strong reasons for wanting to achieve senatorial rank in the fourth century. For most of it, senators were free of extraordinary taxes and did not have to supply corvée labor or perform curial duties. By the end of the fourth century, however, those privileges had been legally denied to all senators except those of the highest rank (the *illustres*). Nevertheless, senatorial rank gave a man useful influence. It enabled him, regardless of the law, to avoid performing curial duties or paying his taxes. Above all, it freed him from the humiliation of being flogged by public officials. Legally, the curial class was free from such demeaning treatment, but high-ranking officials increasingly violated the law as they sought to assert their own or the state's authority. They would not dare, however, to establish the precedent of abusing a man of equal rank. Some men even hoped to pursue high political office and join those families who already enjoyed elite social status from generations of power and privilege.

Opportunities were especially available in the East because Constantinople and its senate were new foundations. They, in contrast to Rome and its senate, had no noble families who had controlled them for generations. Therefore it was easier for men of obscure origin to found great families. For example, Flavius Philippus, son of a sausage manufacturer, went from a simple notary to become a consul in 348. He founded a family that included a praetorian prefect, two consuls, and the Emperor Anthemius. The Pannonian peasant Gratian became a high-ranking military officer and father of the emperors Valens and Valentinian I.

Members of new senatorial families (or those aspiring to be) improved their social status through the pursuit of land, education, friendship, and marriage. To be accepted by the best families, one had to acquire the cultural accoutrements of upper-class *paideia* through rigorous training in rhetoric and the ancient classics. Landed wealth and education opened the way to influential friendships (often formed at school) and intermarriage. They, in turn, linked large landowning families together in ever-growing networks of wealth and influence. By the end of the fourth century, these elite families had attached their networks firmly to the highest-ranking offices and often managed to ensnare the emperor himself.

For example, Justina, mother of the Emperor Valentinian II and stepmother of Emperor Gratian, came from a prominent Roman family. As a young girl, she had become the second wife of Gratian's father, Valentinian I. He was a son of the peasant-born Pannonian officer Gratian mentioned earlier. Justina brought up her stepson and son in the traditions of the landed nobles. They favored those nobles with imperial appointments at the expense of the rough Pannonian officers preferred by their father. When Gratian needed someone to take over the East after the death of his uncle, the co-emperor Valens, at Adrianople, he chose Theodosius, who came from a prominent landowning family in Spain. The name of Theodosius' first wife, Aelia Flaccilla, even recalls the Hispano-Roman family to which Aelius Hadrianus, Emperor Hadrian, belonged.

Theodosius' father (p. 602) had been well connected with prominent senatorial families at court. His friends even included the great Q. Aurelius Symmachus (see below and pp. 633–4). After the death of Valentinian, he had fallen victim to a powerful faction of Pannonian officers at court, whom Gratian later purged. Upon coming to power, Theodosius himself appointed many senatorial aristocrats from Gaul and Spain to positions at court. Eventually, he took Justina's daughter Galla, sister of Valentinian II, as his second wife.

By the end of Theodosius' reign, the networks of aristocratic power and patronage had produced higher and higher concentrations of wealth and power in the hands of a few fabulously rich families, particularly in the West. For example, about twenty great families in six large clans owned most of the land in Gaul and Italy. Some of them like the Acilii Glabriones, Anicii, Caeionii, Petronii Probi, and Valerii traced their lines back to the Republic and the Principate. Others like the Aurelii Symmachi were more recent arrivals. Still, Q. Aurelius Symmachus, consul at Rome in 391 and famous champion of traditional paganism, had nineteen houses or estates in Italy, Sicily, and North Africa and could spend 2000 pounds of gold on his son's praetorian games. One of his close relatives, probably his sister, was married to one of the Anicii. His daughter married Nicomachus Flavianus, son of the very influential Virius Nicomachus Flavianus, twice praetorian prefect and consul in 394. Symmachus' son married a granddaughter of that same man, and one of his son's great-granddaughters married another of the Anicii.

The father of the famous noblewoman and, later, Christian saint Melania the Younger was a Valerius. Her mother came from the Caeionii. Melania inherited their vast properties from all over the western provinces. Rents from these properties provided her an annual income of 120,000 *solidi* (ca. 1700 Roman pounds of gold [see p. 115 for weights]). Melania's cousin Petronius Probus had immense holdings all around the Empire. Among the rich senators, one who ranked in the middle by wealth could expect an annual income just of gold in the range of 1000 to 1500 Roman pounds.

The aristocrats who dominated the eastern court were not so wealthy or so closely intermarried as those in the West. As already noted, the senate at Constantinople was too new to be dominated by a handful of families. Power and wealth were distributed among a number of major cities and their notables, the large local landowners whose families had dominated them for generations. Antioch alone had ten such families. To one of them belonged the famous rhetorician Libanius, friend of Julian the Apostate and zealous supporter of paganism (p. 636).

The middle classes

Beneath the small number of great senatorial landowners and officeholders—the *honorati* (literally, honored with public office)—there was a broad middle class often distinguished as *honestiores* (more honorable). Soldiers comprised the largest single group in the class. Although military life could be hard and dangerous, the prospect of regular pay, food, clothing, and shelter plus a nice bonus along with a grant of land upon retirement could be very attractive to men in the less-developed provinces.

After the soldiers, the second largest bloc among the *honestiores* was the *curiales*, the men of property who comprised the decurions of the local municipal councils (*curiae*). Their position continued to deteriorate in the fourth century. As the demands of the government and exactions of corrupt imperial officials increased, being a decurion could easily mean financial ruin. The local decurions were personally liable for any shortfall in the imperial tax receipts from their territory. They were also subject to heavy requisitions of labor and supplies to support the *cursus publicus* and nearby troops.

The class as a whole became poorer in both status and wealth. Local magnates like Libanius were able to obtain high offices and senatorial rank, which conferred immunity from curial obligations. Some, by the sheer weight of their wealth and influence, could with impunity refuse to perform their curial duties. Others gave their property to the Church in return for clerical appointments. Since the time of Constantine, such appointments procured exemption from curial burdens. Repeated decrees to prevent the desertion of decurions show the extent of the problem. As those who had the resources escaped, their places had to be filled by men of lower wealth and status. Diocletian decreed that anyone who owned at least twenty-five *iugera* (about sixteen acres) of land—even the illiterate, illegitimate, or slave born—belonged to his local *curia*. By 376, the status of *curiales* was so low that they became legally subject to flogging. To that extent, they were now no better than slaves and lowest-ranking citizens, the *humiliores*.

Still, despite their increasing problems and justified complaints, many *curiales* were upwardly mobile during the fourth century. Although their status was supposed to be hereditary, the constant need for educated personnel to run the machinery of government and provide vital services presented opportunities for advancement to those with the proper education. Many decurions, even of restricted means, did everything they could to ensure that their sons (rarely their daughters) received such an education. Doctors, advocates, and professors were in high demand and received good incomes. Successful advocates in the imperial courts could look forward to obtaining high-ranking offices. Professors of rhetoric, literature, law, and philosophy sought imperial appointments to salaried chairs. Major cities like Rome, Constantinople, Athens, Alexandria, and Berytus (Beirut) had many such chairs. Important smaller cities, such as provincial capitals, all had at least two. Any city of consequence had at least one publicly salaried doctor. Carthage, for example, had five. There were also private doctors and teachers who could make good incomes on private fees. Those with public salaries could receive extra fees and gifts.

The clergy of the Christian Church became paid professionals and attracted the educated sons of decurions. Famous bishops (later saints) like Augustine of Hippo, Athanasius of Alexandria, Eusebius of Caesarea, Basil of Caesarea, Gregory of Nyssa,

Gregory of Nazianzus, and Synesius of Cyrene all came from the curial class. For example, Augustine's father was only a minor decurion from the African town of Thagaste. He struggled to pay for Augustine's education, but he had connections. After he died, Augustine was able to continue higher studies at Carthage with the help of a wealthier family friend. As bishops, these men achieved tremendous power and influence by controlling the resources, wealth, and income of their churches (p. 609). Being born into the curial class, therefore, could still be a ticket to success.

The lower classes

The lower classes, *humiliores* (more humble), had less chance to improve their lot than the *curiales*. In the cities, they were generally the merchants, shopkeepers, craftsmen, and wage laborers. The tax on businesses, the *collatio lustralis* or *chrysargyron* (gold and silver tax) instituted by Constantine, weighed heavily on craftsmen and small businessmen. It was payable every five years in gold or silver on the total worth of the business. Assessments were subjective and left much room for official abuse. It was difficult for small operators to save the gold or silver required. Tax collectors used beatings and torture to extract what they demanded. Poor workers were lucky to earn between one twenty-fourth and one forty-eighth of a *solidus* per day. Often, they could not survive without handouts from the emperor and wealthy benefactors or, increasingly, the highly effective charity of the Church.

The vast majority of the *humiliores* and of the Empire's population were rural peasants. The numbers of independent proprietors continued to shrink in the fourth century, and more became *coloni* (tenants) on the great estates (pp. 544–5). In both East and West, laws were made to bind both peasant proprietors and *coloni* to their lands in order to ensure production and the collection of taxes. They were, however, difficult to enforce. The demand for labor was so high that landlords were willing to protect fugitives, who could, therefore, bargain for favorable terms of tenancy.

The persistence of slavery

Slaves in the home, workshop, and field remained a major part of Roman life in the fourth and later centuries. Sometimes slaves on great estates became tenants as the practical difference between *coloni* and slaves became blurred. Supplies of new slaves were not so cheap and plentiful as in the days of imperial conquest, but Roman victories on the frontiers still resulted in large numbers of captives. Those who were not settled as *laeti* or made to serve in Roman armies right away were enslaved. Kidnappings, the sale of children by the poor, and slave-breeding also kept up the numbers. An idea of the scale of slave ownership by the rich can be found in the 8000 slaves freed by Melania the Younger when she adopted the life of a Christian ascetic (p. 620). Nor was Christianity a force against slavery. Melania was not making a moral statement about slavery in granting her slaves freedom. Rather, she was freeing herself from property. In view of the increasingly harsh treatment of free citizens from all but the highest rank, there is no reason to believe that the treatment of slaves improved significantly either. Slavery remained as the brutally logical consequence of a social system that emphasized hierarchical power relationships right through the Middle Ages.

PRIVATE LIFE

The roles of men and women and the nature of marriage and the family were complex in the fourth century C.E. as a result of changing laws, certain medical theories, and the growing influence of Christian ideas and attitudes.

Men and women in the eyes of the law

Under Diocletian, men still had an advantage over women in terms of legal rights and privileges. Christian emperors issued laws that restricted a wife's ability to divorce a husband. Constantine even ruled out a husband's drinking, gambling, and philandering as valid causes for divorce. The only permitted grounds for divorcing a husband were murder, sorcery, or desecrating tombs. If a wife sought divorce and could not prove one of those charges, Constantine called her "presumptuous" and required that she forfeit everything she owned down to her last hairpin and suffer deportation to an island. A man could not divorce a woman except for adultery, sorcery, or pimping, but if he sent away a wife for any other reason, he had only to give back her dowry and could not remarry. If he did remarry, his first wife could confiscate the second wife's dowry. Notice how the man's second marriage is not voided and the second wife pays for his transgression!

Julian returned to earlier laws, which gave women greater freedom in obtaining a divorce. Still, the double standard for sexual behavior remained. Women who had sex outside of marriage or formal concubinage continued to be condemned. Yet, even under Christian emperors, the law allowed married men to have sex with slaves, prostitutes, and unmarried women of low status. Women who worked in certain occupations, actresses and waitresses, for example, were still considered to be no better than prostitutes. The assumption always was that any unchaperoned woman who had public contact with men was sexually available. Therefore, a man was not guilty of unlawful intercourse (*stuprum*) with such a woman.

On the other hand, Constantine blamed even a respectable woman if a man abducted her. If she connived in the abduction to force her father to consent to a marriage that he opposed, she had robbed him of his rights (having been abducted, she was no longer a suitable bride for any but her abductor). If she had truly been abducted, she had not screamed loudly enough for help from her family. If she had been where her family could not have come to her aid, she should not have been there.

On the prevailing assumption that women were weak and needed protection, they were normally excused any ignorance of the law. Constantine ruled, however, that women could not be allowed to profit from ignorance of the law either. Legally, women were excluded from being guardians and standing surety for another's debts. In 373, however, widowed mothers and grandmothers were allowed to become guardians of their children and grandchildren if they promised not to remarry.

The chaste life

During the fourth century, many factors combined to cause both men and women to advocate and adopt a life that emphasized sexual continence, celibacy, virginity, and asceticism. For Christian women, the powerful image of the Virgin Mary encouraged them to accept the superiority of virgin or celibate status. For Christian men, the story of Eve and the serpent causing man's fall from grace in the Garden of Eden reinforced the negative view of women that had often prevailed in the pagan world of Greece and Rome. The dangers represented by the "daughters of Eve" could be avoided if men lived chaste and celibate lives. If a man and a woman did choose to marry, the leaders of the Church could not advocate dissolution of a "union sanctioned by God." They could, however, hope that the couple would give up sexual relations after the birth of a child or two, as the Gallic Bishop Sidonius Apollinaris urged a young friend and his wife to do.

The Christian emphasis on chastity and celibacy meshed with secular medical theories and pagan beliefs. Many educated men became convinced to do everything possible to conserve and retain their sperm and expend it only rarely for the sole purpose of obtaining legitimate children. According to Galen and many doctors after him, men needed to retain their sperm as much as possible because it contained their vital spirit, *pneuma*, and was essential for their strength and health. Therefore, many men had begun to practice rigorous continence and even gave up sexual activity after obtaining children. Galen and other medical writers like Soranus and Oribasius believed, in contrast with Aristotle, that women also produced *pneuma*-laden sperm that was expended during intercourse. Therefore, many women wished to avoid sexual activity as much as possible, too.

Retaining the *pneuma* allowed it to be concentrated and refined into purely psychic *pneuma*, which strengthened the soul and brought one closer to the divine as one became a more spiritual being. That seems to be the long-standing motivation behind the self-castration of the priests of the Great Mother (Cybele) and the requirement that her priestesses be virgins. These ideas also seem to be inherent in the words ascribed to Jesus in Matthew 19:12, "For there are eunuchs who have been so from birth, and there are eunuchs who have been made eunuchs by others, and there are eunuchs who have made themselves eunuchs for the sake of the kingdom of heaven. Let anyone accept this who can." In the same vein, St. Paul reinforced the idea that a life of continent celibacy is spiritually superior for Christians (1 Corinthians 7:8 and 25–39). Ideas like those probably influenced Constantine to abolish the Augustan penalties for men who did not marry. That in turn, may have decreased some of the pressure on women to be married.

Women in the Church

Of course, the theories and ideology concerning virginity were articulated primarily by men. Fourth-century Church Fathers like saints Ambrose, Jerome, John Chrysostom, Basil of Caesarea (the Great), and Gregory of Nazianzus preached and wrote to persuade women to choose virginity and the celibate life. Bishops in major cities kept legions of widows on their charity rolls. These women performed valuable services as members of Christian religious communities or as deaconesses in churches. Many women of wealthy and illustrious families dedicated their fortunes as well as their bodies to the service of God. Attempts were made to ensure that wealthy heiresses and widows did not deny their children and other close kin their rightful shares of family fortunes. Still, nothing could stop them from using their own money for good works after taking a religious vow of celibacy. Indeed, such women were eagerly cultivated by bishops and influential churchmen, who sometimes became suspected of impure motives.

St. Jerome had such a large following of pious noblewomen in Rome that suspicions finally forced him to leave and resettle in Palestine. Some of the women followed him there, among them Fabiola, a rich widow who sold her property and used the proceeds to finance a hospital, monasteries, and a trip to Palestine. Similarly, the wealthy widow Paula and her daughter Eustochium left Rome in 385 for Palestine. They founded monasteries in Bethlehem and helped take care of the cantankerous Jerome until they died. Widowed at twenty-two, Melania the Elder, grandmother of Melania the Younger, went to Egypt to visit Christian hermits in the desert. Then she went to Palestine and lived there for over twenty-five years after founding a monastery in Jerusalem. She was a friend of Jerome's erstwhile friend and later rival Rufinus (p. 704).

In the late third and early forth centuries, Melania the Younger was married at age twelve or thirteen to her paternal cousin Valerius Pinianus (Pinian). Their two children died as infants, and at age twenty, she persuaded Pinian to join her in a life devoted to continence and Christian charity. They supported the work of Paulinus at Nola in Italy. Then, in 410, they went to the province of Africa to escape the advancing Visigoths (pp. 655–6). There they met St. Augustine and founded some monasteries. Later, they visited the hermit monks of Egypt. They finally settled in Palestine, where they built more monasteries and became acquainted with Jerome. The sale of properties in Britain, Spain, Gaul, Italy, Sicily, and North Africa supported all of these activities. At Constantinople, the young widow Olympias founded a community of women who performed works of charity. She also used her great wealth to support bishops Nectarius and John Chrysostom at Constantinople, as well as numerous other churchmen there and in other cities.

The Church Fathers of the fourth century also had to take women seriously not only as providers of services and monetary support but also as spiritual and intellectual beings. In the Bible, woman was viewed as God's creation, and it was asserted that God's son, Savior of the human race, had been born of Mary, a mortal woman. Fourth-century Christian thinkers generally agreed with Plato and against Aristotle that the soul was not sexed. Women, though physically inferior, were men's equals in soul and potential for virtue. Although the Church Fathers were adamant about not letting women be public teachers and preachers, they often formed intellectual friendships with women that seem amazing in retrospect. Because Christianity rested on a body of scriptures, upper-class Christian women frequently received a thorough grounding in the Bible and other important Christian texts. Jerome discussed many theological issues with his friends Marcella and Paula. Paula and her daughters, like Jerome, had learned Hebrew, and Jerome even dedicated some of his biblical commentaries to Paula. St. Augustine addressed a book on widowhood to a great noblewoman, Anicia Juliana. John Chrysostom carried on a vigorous correspondence with his friend Olympias at Constantinople. She is also the subject of a significant early Christian biography.

Olympias' biography is an example of Christian writers' increased attention to women. The biography of St. Melania (Melania the Younger) appeared in both Greek and Latin and was widely read. Gregory of Nyssa wrote a loving biography of his sister Macrina as a model of the Christian virgin. In it, he compares her to Thecla, one of the most famous female figures in works of the fourth-century Church Fathers. Thecla's first appearance in Christian literature may be as early as the second century C.E. in the apocryphal work known as the *Acts of Paul and Thecla*. As a young girl, she supposedly heard St. Paul teaching at Iconium in Asia Minor, was converted, and immediately took a vow of chastity. Her horrified mother and fiancé unsuccessfully tried to force her to relent and then had her and Paul arrested. After a series of miraculous escapes from horrible punishments, she accompanied Paul briefly and then settled in Selcucia as a holy woman teaching and healing for many years. In the third century, Methodius, author of the *Symposium of the Ten Virgins*, actually designated her as a disciple of Paul and portrayed her as giving the prizewinning speech in a rhetorical contest on virginity. Whether she had really existed is of little consequence. Christians of the fourth century believed that she had. Just about every major Christian author of the period praised her as the paragon of Christian womanhood.

Elite pagan women

Just as educated upper-class Christian women achieved prominence in fourth-century Christian intellectual circles, so did women of the educated pagan elite in the secular world. The most notable in the fourth century are Sosipatra of Pergamum (ca. 315–375) and Hypatia of Alexandria (ca. 355–415). Sosipatra's wealthy father gave her an expensive education in mystical religious and Neoplatonic lore because she was thought to have clairvoyant powers. She married a famous Neoplatonic follower of Iamblichus (p. 635), Eustathius of Cappadocia. After his death, she established herself as a highly sought after teacher at Pergamum. Coincidentally, her son Antoninus became a famed pagan priest and theurge at Canopus. In nearby Alexandria, Hypatia studied mathematics, astronomy, and Neoplatonic philosophy with her father, Theon. She collaborated with Theon on many of his mathematical and astronomical works. As a renowned teacher and scholar in her own right, she produced her own work in those fields, too (p. 636). Among her many well-to-do male students was the famous fifth-century Church Father and bishop of Ptolemais, Synesius of Cyrene (p. 708).

Marriage, the family, and children

The fourth century saw some significant developments in ideas and attitudes concerning marriage, the family, and children, particularly as Christianity became a powerful force in Roman life. Influential Christians like St. Augustine, Basil of Caesarea, and John Chrysostom tried to eliminate the double standard enshrined in Roman custom and law by defining adultery as the infidelity of either husband or wife. In general, they had little success. Men did not want to lose their sexual freedom; wives often found it convenient to let them have it in order to avoid ill temper or an unwanted pregnancy. Constantine, however, did rule that married men could not have concubines.

Both pagan and Christian moralists condemned contraception. One of the main purposes of ancient marriage was the production of legitimate children. Contraception in both pagan and Christian eyes was for prostitutes, and using it in marriage was considered to reduce nuptial relations to a sordid transaction for the gratification of lust. To Christian writers like John Chrysostom, contraception was even equivalent to murder because it took away life from the child who would have been born. For the moralist, therefore, the only way to avoid pregnancy in marriage was abstinence.

Despite the moralists, however, contraception was neither illegal nor even officially condemned by any council of the Church until 572. Various forms of contraception were available. They ranged from practicing intercourse in ways that would avoid fertilization to charms, spells, and amulets. Some, such as suppositories made from wool dipped in olive oil or vinegar, worked fairly well and safely. A number of herbs and drugs could be useful. Others were often dangerous poisons. The latter frequently resulted in an abortion if a woman were already pregnant.

Roman law, as well as pagan and Christian moralists, condemned abortion and infanticide. Disagreement arose over what constituted abortion. Hippocratic medical writers did not think that conception was complete before the end of the first three months of pregnancy. Therefore, they considered terminating a pregnancy in the first trimester to be contraception, not abortion. Christian writers, however, were opposed to the termination of a pregnancy at any stage. A law of 374 agreed with the Church in considering infanticide a capital crime. Still, there was no law against the widespread practice of exposure, the parental abandonment of infants whom passersby might or might not rescue, as chance would have it.

The fourth century saw considerable disagreement over who might be permitted to marry and have children. All agreed that incestuous marriages should be forbidden, but the definition of incest in the Greek-speaking East traditionally was less strict than in the Latin West. For the Romans, "degree of kinship," which determined incest, was measured by "acts of generation." A parent and child or brother and sister were the products of two acts of generation and were in the second degree of kinship. An aunt and nephew or uncle and niece were in the third degree as products of three acts of generation, which produced two siblings and the child of one. First cousins were in the fourth degree through four acts of generation, which produced two siblings and a child of each. Except for the special law passed as a favor to Emperor Claudius that allowed a man to marry his brother's daughter, Roman law had forbidden marriage within the third degree. Moreover, Roman custom frowned heavily upon marriages in the fourth degree.

During the fourth century, both Roman law and the Church were imposing tighter restrictions. The Church banned all marriages within the fourth degree. In 295,

Diocletian had reiterated the prohibition on marriage within the third degree (except for the exemption noted earlier) and also banned marriage between all ascendants and descendants in the same direct line or between a man and his former stepmother, step-daughter, mother-in-law, or daughter-in-law. In 355, a brother's former wife and the sister of a former wife were excluded. Sometime later, Theodosius I outlawed marriage between first cousins. In the Greek East, however, marriages in the third and fourth degrees or even between half-siblings had been a common practice to keep property within the family. As a result, there were constant petitions from eastern subjects for exemption from the law and constant opposition from the Church Fathers to practices they thought immoral.

Except for the rare archaic form of Roman marriage known as *confarreatio* (p. 57), a pagan marriage ceremony was basically a civil act that served the interests of the state and the families concerned. It involved a public declaration by both bride and groom (or their fathers) that a marriage should be made, and this was usually symbolized by the giving of rings and the joining of right hands. It would be preceded by appropriate sacrifices and the observance of *auspicia* on the day of the wedding, but it does not seem that the Romans observed anything like a modern wedding ceremony presided over by a priest and fraught with religious meaning. Its celebration was mainly secular, with much feasting and entertainment among those who could afford it.

For Christians in the fourth century, marriage took on greater and greater spiritual meaning as a divine institution, not just a civic or familial duty. To the traditional customs, which also included veiling and, in the East, crowning the bride, Christians added the consent of a bishop, prayer, and often Holy Communion. Jesus was depicted as actually joining the couple. Attempts to eliminate the feasting and entertainment were not successful, however.

Because the Christian model of marriage was the love of Jesus for the Church, mutual consent and conjugal love received greater emphasis in Christian thought on marriage. Although heretical extremists might reject marriage in favor of holding women in common or rejecting sex entirely, orthodox thinkers declared that God approved sex with pure motives within marriage and that marriage was no hindrance to salvation. It was a sacrament worthy of praise for those who remained faithful to each other. In emphasizing mutual respect and love, the Christian ideal emphasized the equal spiritual worth of men and women. Nevertheless, because the male leaders of the Church viewed women as being weaker and less able to resist sin than men, they still advocated the subordination of wives to husbands. On the other hand, when a pagan man married a Christian woman, they adamantly rejected the traditional notion that a woman should follow her husband's lead in religion.

Clearly, the more spiritual view of marriage among Christians raised problems for non-Christians. The fourth-century Church Fathers disapproved of marriage between Christians and Jews or pagans. Under civil law, marriages between Christians and Jews could even be punished by death.

The high mortality rate, particularly for women of childbearing age, meant that many families might include the children of two or more wives. Fathers often died before their children were grown, so that a stepfather and children from the new marriage were not unusual in a household. The orphaned children of relatives might also be present. A further complication might be the presence of a child born to the husband by a slave or concubine.

Among the upper classes, there were not only numerous household slaves but also clients, relatives like a widowed mother or unmarried sister, and long-term house guests. The result was a household far more complex than the simple nuclear family. The opportunities for significant interactions between diverse individuals in such an environment were extensive. For example, many upper-class Roman mothers used slave wet nurses to care for their young children. Strong affective bonds often developed between nurses and their charges as witnessed by numerous inscriptions.

There is plenty of evidence from grave inscriptions and literary sources that parents often had much love and affection for their children in previous centuries. Nevertheless, affective bonds between parents and children and the value of children as human beings seem to have received more stress during the fourth century. That is also reflected in Christian sources. It has been argued, for example, that the use of wet nurses reduced the affective bonds between mother and child. Significantly, the fourth-century Church Fathers condemned the practice for that reason.

Christian writers also condemned the exposure of infants. Bishops established funds for widowed mothers, set up homes for abandoned babies, and urged families to adopt orphans. Constantine, perhaps motivated as much by a concern for manpower as by sentiment, reinstituted the *alimenta* for the whole Empire to help poor parents so that they would not be driven to infanticide or selling their children. Interestingly, he provided for boys and girls equally instead of favoring boys. He also ruled that parents who had abandoned a child could not reclaim it later from a person who took it in. (He also, however, gave the finder the option of raising the child as free or slave.)

Children's legal rights were reinforced in relation to their parents. For example, although the age of adulthood was twenty-five, Constantine ruled that boys could take over their savings or inheritances at twenty and girls at eighteen. The need for Christians to be able to read the Scriptures spurred churches to set up grammar schools open to all boys and girls. Thus, the status of children as well as women was not revolutionized during the fourth century but seems to have become greater than in earlier centuries.

OVERVIEW

Clearly, the fourth century was an improvement over the third. The economy revived even if it did not reach the heights of the first and second centuries. The overproduction of copper and billon coins made them virtually worthless, but the stable gold *solidus* was economically beneficial, particularly to the government and the wealthy. The upper classes, especially in the West, amassed far-flung agricultural properties. Small farmers, burdened by the government's need for more taxes, often became tenants, *coloni*, of large landowners. The latter still bought and sold in urban-based markets. In general, markets tended to be regional, but international trade revived. Not all cities regained what they had lost in the third century. Nevertheless, expenditures by the state and the growing Christian Church stimulated the growth of a significant number of cities around the Empire.

Wealthy landowners did not abandon the cities to live only on their rural properties. Many of them, including heavily Romanized "barbarians," were people whom the emperors had promoted in imperial service. While they became richer, the middle-class *curiales* and the poor sank in wealth and status. Increasingly, the Church tried to provide relief to the poor, but their lives always remained precarious.

Women's rights were still more restricted than men's in Roman law. Christian thinkers recognized women as the spiritual equal of men, but still did not let them have the most prestigious roles in the Church. They encouraged women to read and study Christian texts and be models of chaste virtue and benevolent piety. A number of women, however, became prominent intellectually, religiously, and, as will be seen, politically. Both Christians and pagans stressed a more ascetic lifestyle that limited sex to the begetting of children. They also took measures to protect the lives of those children and provide equally for the welfare and basic schooling of both boys and girls.

SUGGESTED READING

Cameron, A. *The Last Pagans of Rome*. Oxford and New York: Oxford University Press, 2011.

Harper, K. *Slavery in the Late Roman World, AD 275–425*. Cambridge and New York: Cambridge University Press, 2011.

Kaster, R. A. *Guardians of Language: The Grammarian and Society in Late Antiquity*. Berkeley, Los Angeles, and London: University of California Press, 1997.

Humphries, M. *Early Christianity*. New York: Routledge, 2006.

CHAPTER 34

Christianity and Classical culture in the fourth century

The fourth century is one of the most culturally rich periods in Roman history. A revival of Classical Greco-Roman traditions followed the disruptions of the previous fifty years. There was also a creative interaction with the diverse traditions of native cultures that had been overshadowed in the period when Rome and Italy had dominated the life of the Empire. Christianity, having been freed from persecution and even enjoying imperial favor, became a major factor in that process.

CHRISTIANITY AND THE EXPANSION OF CLASSICAL CULTURE

Eusebius in his Greek *Ecclesiastical History* and Rufinus, who translated it into Latin, loudly proclaimed the total victory of Christianity over the old gods of Classical pagan culture between Constantine and Theodosius. For obvious reasons, that became the accepted position of the Christian Church, and it is still widely repeated. St. Augustine, however, rightly rejected this smug triumphalism. As Augustine himself was living proof, Christianity and Classical pagan culture interacted and influenced each other in countless ways (see Box 34.1). The worldviews of pagan and Christian thinkers had begun to converge under the influence of Neoplatonism (p. 554).

34.1 THE CODEX CALENDAR OF 354 c.e.

An elegant example of the interaction between Christianity and classical pagan culture was created in the year 354 c.e. by the most famous Latin calligrapher of the day, Furius Dionysius Filocalus. He created a richly illustrated book (codex) that was then presented as a gift to a wealthy aristocrat named Valentinus. The original was lost by the early medieval period, but several copies survive.

The codex, created by one Christian for another, presents a blend of pagan and Christian material that appears to reflect the relatively peaceful coexistence of these two major religious groups in Rome at the time the book was created, and it reinforces the idea of parallels between Christian and imperial institutions. The book's centerpiece is a month-by-month calendar of festivals, games, and other events celebrated in the city – the official Calendar of Rome for 354 c.e. This includes only pagan holidays and anniversaries, as these were the most important items in the communal calendar. The other sections of the codex preserve information important for every Roman aristocrat of the day: a brief history of the city; chronological lists of emperors, consuls, city prefects, martyrs, and bishops; a list of dates for the Easter holiday up to the year 411 and another recording imperial birthdays. The codex also includes astrological plans, important to both pagans and Christians in the mid-fourth century c.e.

In the end, Christianity did more to spread Classical culture to those previously excluded from it than to destroy it. Although Classical culture had spread far and wide over the Roman Empire, it had done so like a net, not a blanket. It had been restricted largely to those who had acquired traditional *paideia*, the educated Latin- and Greek-speaking elites of the Empire's cities. The Mediterranean Sea lanes and Rome's famous roads were the threads that tied together the urban knots into a strong net of imperial control. Often, neither Latin nor Greek was the native language of the poorly educated peasants of the countryside and lower classes of the cities. They constituted a large mass of "inner barbarians" who were excluded from the dominant culture of the urban elites.

Christianity had grown precisely because of its appeal to the excluded populations of the Empire. Christians believed that God had sent Jesus to save the souls of the poor and the humble just as much as those of the rich and powerful. The Christian Church actively sought to include the excluded through its missionary activities, charitable works, inexpensive rituals, and communal worship. Unfortunately, as Christians grew in power after Constantine, zealots and builders of personal empires also forcibly converted people who had not succumbed to gentler methods of persuasion.

Ironically, the original language of the Church was the premier language of the Empire's educated classes—Greek. St. Paul, the writers of the Gospels, and the other authors of the New Testament all spoke and wrote Greek. Even the Jewish Scriptures used by Paul and other Hellenized Jews, who constituted many of Christianity's early converts, was the Greek translation of the Hebrew Bible known as the *Septuagint*. One had to have a certain level of elite education to be able to read and study the texts that were the basis of Christian doctrine if one were to become an authoritative Christian leader. Translations, culminating with the great Vulgate Bible of St. Jerome (ca. 385), eventually made these texts available in Latin, the dominant language of the elites in the West.

Therefore, Christianity gave the formerly excluded populations access to elite culture through the Greek and Latin of its fundamental texts, teachings, and preachings. That may explain in part the attractiveness of Christianity to Constantine. He and his third-century predecessors had come from rough frontier provinces along the Danube. To the civilian population of the Mediterranean provinces, they and the rest of the Roman army were hardly different from the attackers whom they were supposed to fight. In the process of converting to Christianity and settling in Constantinople, Constantine sought to shed his uncouth military image and appear as a champion of the more civilized, civilian elements in Roman society. In the West, he promoted the recovery of the landed aristocracy, and in the East he gave the notables of the Greek cities extensive access to power in his new regime. Under Constantine and his Christian successors, political success lay open not just to military officers but once more to the cultivated men of civilian virtues.

The traditional *paideia* of civilian elites fostered a common code of cultured civility. That civility allowed them to create a system in which those religious issues that did divide them did not lead to constant conflict and intolerance. Pagan and Christian symbols were combined in ways that were acceptable to many in both camps. Constantine, for example, kept the title *pontifex maximus*, which indicated the emperor's care of religious matters. After Gratian ceased to use it, it became a title of the bishop of Rome. Images of the old pagan deities in exquisite Neoclassical style were used to represent the power, peace, and prosperity of the restored order, which was also protected by the Christians' God. His cross now appeared on such things as the foreheads of statues honoring Rome's first emperor, Augustus, and his wife Livia outside the city hall of Ephesus and on the milestones along Roman roads.

Appealing to the educated urban elites, Christian apologists argued that their religion was the guarantor of civilization against the "barbarism" that seemed to be pressing in from all sides. As the "sublime philosophy," Christian revelation was called the ultimate source of truth for the best teachings of the Classical philosophers. It was the firm foundation of the high ethical standards imparted by traditional *paideia*. Only the Christian God, they said, had saved the tottering edifice of the Roman Empire from collapsing during the shocks of the third century; through Christ, the solid steel of true philosophy could reinforce it for the future. In visual art aimed at elite audiences (frescoes, mosaics, elaborately carved sarcophagi, and expensively crafted small objects), Jesus is no longer the simple carpenter's son of the Gospels who preaches to equally humble disciples and people of the countryside. He is now the Divine Schoolmaster dressed in a philosopher's robe, seated on a professor's *cathedra* (official chair), holding a book, and lecturing to similarly dressed well-bred men of philosophic visage. The classical figure of the cultured man seated in his study and holding a scroll of some famous author is transformed into a similarly seated Christian saint or evangelist with a book open before him.

Talented and ambitious men had acquired elite *paideia* in order to become part of the restored Empire's new ruling class in the fourth century. Many had come from Christian homes or had converted to Christianity. Accordingly, they often ended up as leaders of the growing Church, which had intertwined itself tightly with the dominant culture of the restored Empire. By continuing to include the "inner barbarians," Church leaders also could mobilize an impressive number of supporters and become powerful forces in their local communities and even imperial politics. Through thousands of sermons, hymns, pastoral letters, inspirational writings, and devotional books in Greek and Latin, they inculcated into their flocks the languages and many other attributes of their own Classical educations. Thus, Greek penetrated even more deeply into the populations of the eastern provinces, and Latin replaced the languages of the countryside in the western.

In the cities, learned bishops exposed their congregations to sermons that displayed the highest standards of Greco-Roman rhetoric. The logic and metaphysical speculation of the Greek philosophical schools informed the theological debates surrounding the Trinity, the nature of Christ, and the status of the Virgin Mary. By incorporating the legal and administrative system of Rome into the Church's institutional structure, these bishops reinforced the political and social values of the old Greek and Roman elites at the grassroots level. For Christians as well as pagans, therefore, education in the Greek and Latin Classics remained the key to cultural literacy and success in both secular and ecclesiastical careers (see Box 34.2).

34.2 THE CLASSICAL EDUCATION OF SAINT JEROME

Saint Jerome (see p. 703) played a central role in the creation of the Latin version of the Bible (the Vulgate), but he was also a man steeped in the classical tradition. Born about the year 347 C.E. to a wealthy Christian family in the province of Dalmatia, Jerome (Hieronymus, in Greek) received his early childhood education in his hometown of Stridon. At around the age of eleven or twelve, he and his close friend, Bonosus (who would grow up to become a famous hermit), were sent to Rome to further their education. It was here, under the tutelage of Aelius Donatus, the most important grammarian of the day, that Jerome laid the foundations of his own Latin style and honed his skills at interpretation and exegesis—all on pagan texts. Donatus' influence on readers of Latin literature extended for centuries, well into the medieval period. This came directly through his own widely popular treatises on grammar and style, as well as through his commentaries on Terence and Vergil, authors central to the education of young students. Donatus also influenced readers indirectly through Jerome's revision of older Latin translations of the Christian Bible into its canonical form and his original translation of certain books of the Old Testament into Latin directly from the original Hebrew and Aramaic, or from Greek intermediaries.

Monks, holy men, and Christian paideia

Of course, Christians who came from humble origins did not have the resources to attain the highest levels of elite *paideia*. For them, Christian baptism and revelation provided an alternative route to the virtue and wisdom claimed by the educated elites. Through such claims, the poor and uneducated people of low status in society could assert their worth as moral and intellectual equals, nay, even superiors, to the culturally dominant upper classes. By ostentatiously rejecting the trappings of cultured life that the upper-classes held dear, ordinary Christians could, paradoxically, claim to have beaten their "betters" in what traditionally mattered most, moral excellence and wisdom.

That attitude was manifest to the extreme in the great growth of Christian asceticism (from the Greek *asketikos*, characterized by rigorous training) during the fourth century. Great numbers of Christian men and women sought to live alone as monks (from the Greek *monachos*, solitary) and hermits (from the Greek *eremites*, dweller in the desert [*eremos, eremia*]) or anchorites (from the Greek *anachorites*, one who has withdrawn to the countryside). As already noted in the earlier discussion of virginity and celibacy (p. 619), during the fourth century, there was a growing interest in the ascetic rejection of the body and physical world in favor of spirituality. The ideal of the solitary holy or wise person living a pure life apart from the world became especially attractive to Christians: Jesus is said to have told people to give up their worldly goods in order to enter the kingdom of heaven. This ideal had had its counterpart for centuries in that of the pagan philosopher who dressed in a simple cloak and gave up the pursuit of worldly fame and riches for that of goodness, beauty, and truth. If Christianity was the sublime philosophy, then Christians who gave up the comforts of a civilized community and struggled to pursue holy wisdom in their desert cells became the sublime philosophers.

Those who took up such an arduous task became popular heroes. People saw in them superhuman concentrations of wisdom and spiritual power similar to those of the old pagan oracles and miracle workers. Many sought their advice and their healing power. Others, who hoped to emulate their example, set up camp nearby. Soon the surrounding desert became as crowded and busy as the society that they had left behind. If one wished to remain free of the distractions of human society, it was necessary to strike out farther into the desert.

Early Christian monasticism is illustrated by St. Anthony, the son of a moderately well-to-do Coptic farmer near Thebes in Upper Egypt. He took literally Jesus' reported challenge to give up everything and follow him. Anthony became a hermit on the outskirts of his village around 270. By 285, he had moved his cell much farther into the desert proper, away from the nearest habitation. Even there, however, he attracted others, and by 305 he had organized them into a loose community called a *laura*. The monks remained completely autonomous. They met together for common worship once a week but were not bound by formal rules or institutions. This movement gained further momentum from a highly fictionalized Greek biography of St. Anthony. Ascribed to St. Athanasius of Alexandria, it achieved wide popularity and quickly appeared in the West via Latin translations.

Soon some monks began to live together and share a common life under fixed regulations and the directions of a leader. They came to be known as *cenobites* from the Greek words meaning common life (*koinos bios*). Their leaders were eventually called *abbots* from the Aramaic word for father (*abba*). In 326, St. Pachomius founded the first known such community at Tabennisi, near Thebes in Egypt. He enforced strict discipline and physical labor under the abbot's direction.

Both eremitic and cenobitic monasticism spread rapidly among men and women in the East. In 360, St. Basil of Caesarea (Cabira, Niksar) in Pontus set up a new form of cenobitic monastery. His rules were more elaborate and humane than those of Pachomius. He prescribed more study and communal labor rather than excessive asceticism. Basil's rule was widely imitated and became the model for Greek monasticism.

Monasticism did not spread so rapidly or become so popular in the West as in the East. St. Martin of Tours pioneered the movement in Gaul at Poitiers about 360, but only two or three other Gallic monasteries existed by 400. It was also around 400 when St. Ambrose brought monasticism to Italy and St. Augustine introduced it into North Africa.

Ostensibly cut off from the outside world, those who followed the ascetic life were kept in touch with what was going on through many letters and visitors. They also had to go to neighboring villages and towns to get their grain ground and exchange produce or handicrafts for the bare necessities that even they occasionally needed. Many monks hired themselves out as seasonal laborers to acquire the meager rations of grain needed to sustain them. In the East, the ascetics who settled on marginal lands, particularly in the Egyptian, Syrian, and Judean deserts, helped to pioneer the settlement of those areas for the region's expanding population. In the West, monasteries more often were associated with the activities of urban bishops and were founded as communities in or near their cities. The ascetic rejection of the civilized ideals embodied in the traditional pagan concept of *paideia* took particularly striking forms in Syria. Asceticism had already been popularized there by Gnostic sects (p. 533), Manichees (pp. 550–1), and Marcionite Christians (p. 493). In the mid-fourth century, the Syriac Christian writer Ephrem of Nisibis popularized an extreme brand of asceticism that inspired truly bizarre behavior in many Syrian holy men. Some lived for years on small platforms atop columns as stylites (from *stylos*: column in Greek), some literally became wild men who dressed in a few skins and ate grass and roots as "grazers," and others immobilized themselves in chains under the most deprived circumstances.

Not all of them were so uneducated as stereotypical, pious biographies indicate. A number were educated people of a fairly privileged background. They had decided to abandon their previous ways of life for an ascetic one as the path to true wisdom and virtue. On the one hand, they ostensibly rejected the trappings of the cultured life that *paideia* fostered. On the other, as writers, orators, and thinkers, they used the skills that it had inculcated to promote the ascetic ideal and advocate their own positions on theological issues.

Many monks and holy men in the East became embroiled in the religious and theological disputes of neighboring cities and towns. They often engaged in fanatical actions against Jews, pagans, and Christians whose views differed from theirs. For example, in

386, bands of Syrian monks attacked the temples of local villages. In 388, one group destroyed the house of worship used by Valentinian Christians (who were labeled heretics because their founder, Valentinus, held certain Gnostic beliefs) and even burned down the Jewish synagogue at Callinicum (p. 605). In 391, under the urging of Bishop Theophilus at Alexandria, a mob of monks tore down the Serapeum, the great temple of Serapis that had been at the heart of the city's pagan identity for centuries.

In these and many other episodes, powerful Christian bishops and zealous monks made Christianity the dominant religion of the Empire. Often they had the tacit consent of Theodosius, who could not risk openly attacking shrines and practices dear to many of his subjects. Christian leaders were satisfied, however, with banishing the pagan gods and sacrifices from public life. As yet, they made no concerted moves against educated and influential pagans, with whom they shared much else in common and who continued to express themselves in art and literature in traditional ways. In fact, both Christians and pagans contributed to a fourth-century cultural flowering that was pollinated from many sources in the Empire's diverse landscape.

THE EDUCATED WORLD OF LETTERS

The return of stability under Diocletian and Constantine and their expansion of the imperial bureaucracy created a heavy demand for education. Many leading families throughout the Empire felt the need to reestablish continuity with Rome's glorious past after the disruptions of the previous half-century. Members of the newly risen ruling elite needed to become better acquainted with the core culture of the Empire and acquire the refinements appropriate to their new status. For example, even Germans who achieved military and political importance in imperial service sought the education of Roman aristocrats. Therefore, generous public salaries were once more provided to teachers of rhetoric and philosophy, and students flocked back to their schools from all corners of the Empire.

Minor secular Latin literature in the fourth century

Recovering and reconstructing the elite culture of the Latin West was particularly difficult. It had not been so deeply rooted outside of Italy as elite Greek culture had been in the Greek-speaking cities of the East. Therefore, during the first half of the fourth century, demand for basic textbooks, reference works, commentaries, and technical handbooks was particularly great in the Latin West. Besides grammar and rhetoric, topics like medical and veterinary science, military science, agriculture, practical mathematics, and geography all found their fourth-century muses. Geographical subjects were particularly popular among Latin writers. Latin was still the language of administration throughout the Empire, and the elite needed to have an idea of the vast and diverse regions under their control. One of the geographical works is a treatise of unknown authorship written in about 360 and entitled *Expositio Totius Mundi et Gentium* (*A Description of the Whole World and of Nations*). What it says about non-Roman peoples is often fantastical. The descriptions of Roman provinces and their cities are cursory but give a sense of the Empire's extent and the principal products available in each part.

Furthermore, pious Christians from the Latin West who made pilgrimages to the holy shrines of the Greek East wanted to know what to expect along the way. Various maps, handbooks, and travelers' accounts called itineraries survive from the fourth century. Pilgrimages are the subjects of two interesting itineraries. One is a trip by an anonymous author to Jerusalem in 333, the *Itinerarium Hierosolymitanum*, which starts in Burdigala (Bordeaux) and returns to Milan via Rome. The other is the *Itinerarium Egeriae* (or *Peregrinatio Aetheriae*) by an aristocratic woman named Egeria (or Aetheria). Probably from Spain, she traveled on her own to Sinai, Palestine, and Mesopotamia in the late fourth century.

There was also a great demand for brief summaries of Roman history among the numerous officials and emperors who came from provinces not steeped in the traditions of Rome. The North African Aurelius Victor sketched the lives of the emperors through Constantius II in his *Liber de Caesaribus*. Shortly after the death of Theodosius (395), someone summarized Victor in the *Epitome de Caesaribus* and extended his account to 395. Another unknown writer also included Victor in a collection known as the *Tripartite History* to create a complete summary of Roman history by including the *Origo Gentis Romanae* (*Origin of the Roman Nation*), which covered the mythological past from Saturn to Romulus, and the *De Viris Illustribus Urbis Romanae* (*Concerning the Illustrious Men of the City of Rome*), sketches of famous men from the Alban kings to Mark Antony.

Two minor historians were members of the Emperor Valens' court. One was Eutropius, who had served in Julian's Persian campaign. He wrote the *Breviarium ab Urbe Condita* (*Summary from the Founding of the City*), which covered everything from Romulus to the death of Jovian (364) in ten short books. Clearly written and concise, it became very popular, was translated into Greek, and was often used in schools. Rufius (or Rufus) Festus wrote a similar summary that competed for the attention of Valens, to whom he dedicated it. Called the *Breviarium Rerum Gestarum Populi Romani* (*Summary of the Deeds of the Roman People*), it, too, extended from Romulus to 364 C.E., but it gave greater stress to wars of conquest.

The revival of the great tradition of Latin literature

The work of reconstruction and recovery during the first half of the fourth century led to a reflourishing of Latin literature among the great senatorial landowners during the second half of the century. Not all of them were pagan, but they wanted to link themselves firmly to the great traditions of Rome's glorious past. They wanted to reinforce their power and influence in the Latin West by fostering a sense of community and renewal, a true *Reparatio Saeculi* (Restoration of the World) as even Christian emperors advertised on their coins. One of the central figures in this group was Quintus Aurelius Symmachus (ca. 340–ca. 402). His family took a special interest in preserving copies of Livy's history, and he became the most famous Roman orator of his day. Holding many high offices, he fought St. Ambrose over removing the Altar of Victory from the senate (p. 603).

Ten books of letters survive along with fragments of his speeches. They present a vivid picture of the life of the wealthy senatorial class in fourth-century Rome.

Ambrosius Theodosius Macrobius, who straddles the fourth and fifth centuries, presents a similar picture. As a young man, he was acquainted with the circle of Symmachus. His major work, the *Saturnalia*, purports to be the learned conversations of Symmachus and his friends at a banquet held during the Saturnalian festival. Their discussions about the festival, Roman antiquities, grammar, and literary criticism preserve a wealth of ancient scholarship otherwise lost. Macrobius also wrote a commentary on the "Dream of Scipio" from Cicero's *Republic*. The idealized view of the Roman statesman and the Platonized Stoicism that underlay Cicero's thought at that point were attractive to the Neoplatonic antiquarian pagans of Macrobius' day.

It was probably in the same circle depicted by Macrobius that the strange biographical pastiche of fact and fancy known as the *Historia Augusta* was composed. It covers the emperors from Hadrian to the accession of Diocletian. It was written allegedly by six different authors in the reigns of Diocletian and Constantine. Computerized stylistic analysis, however, confirms the theory that it was really written by one person. That such a hoax could be perpetrated at all, however, indicates the existence of a bold and confident spirit at the time.

The more serious history of Ammianus Marcellinus (ca. 330–ca. 400) reveals a similar spirit, although its substance contrasts markedly with that of the *Historia Augusta*. The last great Roman historian, Marcellinus boldly took up the mantle of Livy and Tacitus by carrying the history of Rome from where Tacitus left off in 96 C.E. to the Battle of Adrianople in 378. Born probably a pagan at Antioch, he was a native speaker of Greek, but he retired to Rome after a successful military career and wrote in Latin. He used good sources and exercised a well-balanced judgment even though he had a definite agenda of his own. He seems to have hoped that a tolerant and enlightened pagan would provide the leadership necessary to block what he saw as a tyrannical partnership between the emperor and the Christian Church. Devoting over one-third of the work to the lifetime of Emperor Julian, he showed approval for the idea of a revived paganism. Nevertheless, he was critical of Julian's overzealous hostility to Christianity. He also censured the moral failings of the great senatorial aristocrats.

Julius Obsequens sought to bolster the pagan cause in the little treatise *De Prodigiis* (*On Prodigies*). He summarized the prodigies recorded by Livy from 196 to 12 B.C.E. and showed how the Romans had avoided the calamities that they portended. He wanted to emphasize, therefore, that the old reliable rites should not be abandoned in favor of the Christianity that condemned them.

Any well-educated person was expected to be able to turn out a competent poem. Some fourth-century authors produced work that, if not equal to those of the Golden Age, at least measured up to the Silver. The most prolific and well-known poet of the fourth century is the Christian Decimus Magnus Ausonius (ca. 310–ca. 394). A member of the provincial aristocracy from Burdigala (Bordeaux) in Gaul, he received a rigorous education in the Classics. He then became a professor of rhetoric in his hometown, which had become a thriving educational center. His connections led to a successful political career at court and the coveted honor of a consulship in 379. Much of Ausonius' poetry reveals the life and outlook typical of his class. His longest work, the *Mosella*, is an *epyllion* (little epic) celebrating the delights of the Moselle River valley with its lovely landscapes and prosperous estates. Although he was a Christian, Ausonius delighted in the recovery and preservation of Rome's Classical heritage, which he skillfully reworked in carrying on a centuries-old literary tradition. What mattered most was whether something furthered the image of Rome's lasting greatness, not whether it was pagan or Christian.

Hellenism in the fourth century

During the fourth century, the educated upper classes of the Greek-speaking East were firmly attached to Hellenism, the elite Greek culture fostered by traditional *paideia*. In the schools that flourished once more, Hellenism became closely linked with Neoplatonic philosophy, which blurred even further the distinctions – rarely very clear in earlier centuries – among magic, religion, rhetoric, science, and philosophy. Of the vast body of writings by fourth-century Neoplatonic teachers and scholars, however, only a fraction survives.

Iamblichus (ca. 250–ca. 325) stands out as one of the most influential men of the century. Born at Chalcis in southern Syria, where he received his early education, he ultimately studied Neoplatonic philosophy under Plotinus' successor Porphyry. He then used Neoplatonism, particularly its Pythagorean elements, to support the ritualistic magic and superstitions of traditional paganism. Establishing his own school at Apamea in Syria, he spent his life trying to counteract the growth of Christianity and restore paganism. He created a vast synthesis of mystery religions and pagan cults centered on Mithras and buttressed with elaborate symbolism, sacrifices, and magical spells. He became a renowned theurge. His followers claimed that he caused spirits to appear, glowed as he prayed, and levitated from the ground.

Iamblichus' writings, several of which survive, and the work of his students, inspired Emperor Julian to abandon the Christianity of Constantine's dynasty and put the full weight of the imperial office behind revitalizing paganism in opposition to Christianity. When Julian became emperor, Iamblichus' former student Eustathius, husband of the famed Sosipatra (p. 621), joined his circle at court. Except for a letter from Eustathius to Julian, the only writings to survive from that circle are the essays and letters of Julian himself.

The contemporaries to whom Julian wrote and often referred would not be so well known if it were not for Eunapius of Sardis (ca. 354–ca. 420). Eunapius was a relative and student of one of Julian's former teachers. He shared Julian's hatred of Christianity and zeal for pagan Hellenism. His *Lives of Philosophers and Sophists* are full of fascinating details that reveal the social, political, and intellectual life of the educated class. They also contain many absurd tales of mystical powers, magic, and miracles as Eunapius tries to create the pagan counterparts to the pious biographies of Christian saints. Unfortunately, Eunapius' *Universal History*, which continued the work of Dexippus (p. 558) from 270 to 404, is lost. Although it was heavily biased in favor of Julian, it was based on much good information and was a valuable source to later historians.

Science and mathematics

Like many of the Neoplatonic philosophers and sophists, Eunapius also had scientific interests. One of his interests was in medicine, which he shared with his friend Julian's doctor, Oribasius of Pergamum (ca. 320–ca. 400). Oribasius produced a collection of extracts from the great second-century physician Galen and an even more ambitious collection of excerpts in seventy or seventy-two books from medical writers as early as 500 B.C.E. Although the first is lost, most of the latter survives in whole or in summaries that he made for Eustathius and Eunapius.

Alexandria flourished again in the fourth century as a center of medicine and science. With public support, Magnus of Nisibis founded a thriving school of medicine there. He was a close contemporary of Theon of Alexandria (ca. 335–ca. 400), a famous Neoplatonic teacher of mathematics and astronomy, and father of Hypatia (ca. 355–415 [p. 621]). Several of Theon's scientific essays and commentaries survive. Hypatia gained an even greater reputation than her father in mathematics and astrology, which in her teaching she combined with an interest in Hermetic and Orphic religious ideas. As a result, she was very popular and attracted many students. Her influence with the imperial prefect of Egypt so frightened the partisans of the violent and aggressive Bishop Cyril of Alexandria that they ambushed her one night, dragged her into a church courtyard, stripped her, and hacked her to death with potsherds.

The Sophists

Of the many men who concentrated on the teaching of rhetoric in the fourth century, only three are still represented by extant works: Himerius of Bithynia (ca. 310–ca. 390), Themistius of Paphlagonia (ca. 317–ca. 388), and Libanius of Antioch (314–ca. 393). Of the three, Libanius is the most important. Without his writings, our knowledge of the fourth century would be far poorer than it is now. He was the most famous literary figure in the Greek-speaking East. From all of Greco-Roman Antiquity, only Aristotle and Plutarch are comparable to him in the sheer volume of surviving work. His speeches, rhetorical exercises, and approximately 1600 letters take up twelve volumes of standard Classical text and span the years from 349 to 393. They are gold mines of social, political, and cultural history because Libanius was one of the central figures of his time and place. His vast correspondence linked him with emperors, prefects, governors, and many other prominent men of his day, such as Themistius, Himerius, and even the Jewish Patriarch Gamaliel.

A vigorous defender of pagan Hellenism, Libanius attracted talented and ambitious young men of the eastern provinces to his school in Antioch. Although he eagerly supported Julian's attempt to restore Hellenic paganism to cultural and religious dominance, he advocated tolerance toward Christians. Indeed, a number of leading Eastern Christians, such as St. John Chrysostom, St. Basil, and St. Gregory of Nazianzus (pp. 638–9), were his students and friends. Julian's death almost drove Libanius to suicide. He lived in constant fear of reprisals under the militantly Christian Emperor Valens. Still, his courage revived after Valens' death at the Battle of Adrianople. He became influential again under Theodosius, who appointed him honorary praetorian prefect in 383.

CHRISTIAN LITERATURE OF THE FOURTH CENTURY

Christian writers of the fourth century basically came from the same social and intellectual milieu as their pagan counterparts. In fact, they had often studied together at the same schools and exhibited the same Neoplatonic influences and rhetorical styles. Many Christian writers had not even become Christians until they were adults when Christianity began to penetrate the upper classes in greater numbers under Christian emperors.

Christian Latin authors

A good example of an upper-class convert in the Latin-speaking West is Arnobius (ca. 250–ca. 327). He had been a pagan rhetorician at Sicca Veneria in the North African province of Numidia. He suddenly converted to Christianity around 295 and became a powerful critic of pagan beliefs in his *Adversus Nationes* (*Against the Nations*). One of the greatest Latin Church Fathers, however, was Arnobius' student and fellow North African, Lactantius (Lucius Caecilius Firmianus Lactantius [ca. 250–ca. 325]). He taught rhetoric at Diocletian's court in Nicomedia. After converting to Christianity, he surpassed even Tertullian as the Christian Cicero. He argued that Christianity had absorbed and confirmed what was best in the old pagan world and would usher in an even better one through God's salvation. In the *De Mortibus Persecutorum* (*On the Deaths of the Persecutors*), Lactantius' stress on the triumph of Christianity and the glorification of Constantine became the hallmark of much subsequent Christian historiography. Two of Lactantius' greatest successors in style and substance are St. Jerome and St. Augustine near the end of the fourth century and in the early fifth (pp. 703–4).

Hilary of Poitiers (Hilarius Pictaviensis [ca. 315–367]) started out as a well-to-do pagan in Gaul. He converted to Christianity and ended up as bishop of Poitiers around 350. He strongly opposed the Arian heresy in his *De Trinitate* (*On the Trinity*) and is the first known author of Latin hymns.

An even greater writer of hymns from Gaul was St. Ambrose (339–340 to 397), who became bishop of Milan. He came from a wealthy Christian family related to the great pagan traditionalist Symmachus at Rome. Ambrose himself was sent to Rome, where his family connections allowed him to pursue the finest education and a major political career. As governor of northern Italy, he was so successful that the people insisted on making him bishop of Milan in 374. Despite his initial reluctance, he became a zealous voice for orthodoxy against Arianism. He also used his powerful bishopric to overshadow popes, browbeat emperors, and oppose Symmachus over the issue of restoring the Altar of Victory to the Senate House (pp. 633–4). Too numerous to list here, his hymns, sermons, essays, and letters are invaluable for understanding the history of his time.

Another great Christian hymnist was Prudentius (ca. 348 to after 405), an advocate from Spain in the imperial administration at Ravenna. His two collections of hymns, *Hymns for Every Day* and *The Martyrs' Crowns*, have had a great influence on western Christian hymnology. He also supported the removal of the Altar of Victory from the senate house in his essay *Against Symmachus*.

The writing of hymns in the fourth century paralleled the growth of Christian poetry in general, which reflected Classical models. The Christian poet Proba (ca. 310–380) provides a good example. She was a convert from the high aristocracy. Her knowledge of Vergil was so thorough that she was able to weave together different lines and partial lines from his works into a type of poem called a *cento* to express Christian ideas. Unfortunately, her epic on the civil war between Magnentius and Constantius II is lost.

Christian writers in the Greek East

With the victory of Constantine and the building of Constantinople as a primarily Christian city, ecclesiastical writers raised their rhetorical trumpets throughout the Greek-speaking East. The man who contributed most to the paean of the Church triumphant in the fourth century was Bishop Eusebius of Caesarea in Palestine (ca. 260–ca. 340). He was a learned student of Pamphilus, the student to whom Origen had bequeathed his library (p. 560). He had sought a compromise between Arians and anti-Arians at the Council of Nicaea (pp. 588–9). An ardent admirer of Constantine, he lauded the emperor and his sons in his *Praise of Constantine* and unfinished *Life of Constantine*. He also produced several apologetic works refuting attacks on Christianity and arguing for the truth of Christian beliefs.

Eusebius is remembered primarily as the first Christian historian. His *Chronicle*, preserved in Armenian and Latin translations, summarized the history of the world from Abraham to 327/328 C.E. His *Ecclesiastical History* is an innovative work that detailed the growth of what he considered the true Church from Christ's birth to 324. In it, he abandoned the exclusively rhetorical approach used by most ancient historians and relied on extensive direct quotations from documents and his other sources to support his narrative.

Rhetoric, however, still shaped much of Eusebius' work, as it did that of many other Greek Church Fathers. For example, St. Athanasius (ca. 295–373), bishop of Alexandria, had received a good Classical education in grammar and rhetoric. He utilized it against pagans and heretics in a vociferous defense of orthodoxy. As a deacon at the Council of Nicaea (325), he had played a major role in rejecting Eusebius' attempt to reach a compromise position on the Trinity in the Arian controversy. Three years later, he was made bishop of Alexandria. Bitter political and theological conflicts there caused his exile five times. Twice he spent his exile in the West, where he introduced monasticism. He has left behind a large body of apologetic, dogmatic, ascetic, and historical writings along with numerous letters, which are all essential for understanding the crucial religious dispute of the century.

St. Basil of Caesarea in Cappadocia (330–379) and his fellow Cappadocian St. Gregory of Nazianzus (329–389) studied at Athens and probably with Libanius at Antioch. Basil is famous as the author of two sets of regulations, *Long Rules* and *Short Rules*, that formalized the monastic practices of the Eastern Orthodox Church (p. 631). He also wrote a very influential work entitled *An Address to Young Men*. In it, he discussed ways of adapting the traditional Classical curriculum to the needs of Christians. Made bishop of Caesarea in 370, he has left an impressive body of sermons, essays, and letters. The latter, numbering over 350, provide a fascinating look into his life and times.

Basil and Gregory of Nazianzus were both staunch defenders of orthodoxy against Arianism. Gregory has left forty-five excellent orations on topics ranging from the Trinity and love for the poor to eulogies. His lively letters also provide many details of interest to the historian. More astonishing are the 17,000 lines of poetry that employ all of the forms of Classical verse on a myriad of theological, moral, and personal topics.

St. Gregory of Nyssa (ca. 330–395) was the younger brother of Basil, who made him bishop of Nyssa in 371 or 372. He combined deep philosophical learning with genuine pastoral care and faith in the ability of people to develop their inner spirituality. His *Against Eunomius* offers one of the best defenses of orthodoxy against Arianism. His dialogue *On the Soul and Its Resurrection* rivals Plato's *Phaedo*. One of his most interesting works is a biography of his sister Macrina, whom he presents as the ideal of Christian womanhood (p. 621).

John Chrysostom (ca. 354–407), whose last name means "Golden-Mouthed," was the greatest orator among the fourth-century Greek Church Fathers. Born to a leading family at Antioch, Chrysostom studied first with the great Libanius, who would have chosen him as a successor had he not converted to Christianity under the influence of his second teacher, Meletius, bishop of Antioch. After six years as a monk in the Syrian Desert, Chrysostom was ordained a deacon at Antioch and preached his first sermon in 386. In 387, he made his mark in twenty-one sermons *On the Statues*. By them, he counseled and comforted his parishioners while Theodosius threatened harsh punishment for the destruction of his statues during riots over increased taxes that year (p. 611). His skill won him great admiration. For the next ten years, he was the greatest preacher in the greatest church at Antioch.

In 397, Chrysostom became bishop of Constantinople. His preaching made him an instant celebrity but aroused the enmity of other bishops, high officials, and the Empress Eudoxia (p. 663). Other bishops did not like the increased prominence of the bishop of Constantinople. The Empress Eudoxia and many members of the court resented his moral crusade against vice, luxury, and corruption. They also resented the great popularity that he gained from his charitable work with the poor, sick, and oppressed. Eudoxia eventually obtained his exile to Armenia, where he died. Almost a thousand of his impressive and moving sermons survive.

Many Greek-speaking Christian authors adopted the pagan forms of biography and the novel to write hundreds of hagiographies (lives of saints) and martyrologies (accounts of martyrdoms). Their fictions often overpower facts, but they still have historical importance by providing insight into the values and ideals being communicated. The most famous such work is the *Life of St. Anthony* (p. 630).

FOURTH-CENTURY ART AND ARCHITECTURE

The establishment of the Tetrarchy under Diocletian and his colleagues ushered in a new era in Roman art and architecture. New styles developed alongside the

Greco-Roman Classical traditions. They served the needs of imperial propaganda and, from the time of Constantine, the rapidly expanding Christian population and Church. In an increasingly spiritual and religious age, the hieratic traditions of Near Eastern art became more and more prominent in the arts of painting, mosaic, and sculpture. That tradition de-emphasized worldly full-bodied, three-dimensional naturalism. It strove for a flatter, transcendent, spiritual quality. Human figures were often posed in a rigidly frontal manner in order to focus on the full face. Facial features were frequently rendered schematically to de-emphasize the mortal person in favor of some greater reality, particularly through the treatment of the eyes as the "windows of the soul." The rest of the body was hidden under simple drapery. The use of flat, perspectiveless presentations emphasized detachment from the world by making figures "float" on the surface of a relief, fresco, or mosaic. The importance of a figure like the emperor or Jesus was emphasized by making it bigger than the surrounding figures and reducing humbler folk to small, schematized, even crude figures.

FIGURE 34.1 Figures at St. Mark's in Venice are thought to represent Diocletian and the other three tetrarchs.

Imperial portraiture and relief

In the official art of the emperors, many of those stylistic devices are often used to focus on the emperors' extraordinary power, the permanence of their rule, and the subordination of themselves as individuals to higher things.

A perfect illustration is a group portrait of the four tetrarchs that probably once stood in Constantinople but is now built into an outside corner of St. Mark's Cathedral in Venice. It is made out of dark-purple Egyptian porphyry, an extremely hard, durable stone reserved for imperial use. The four are divided into two pairs with arms clasped around each other's shoulders to indicate the loyalty of each Caesar to his Augustus. Aside from a beard to indicate the older Augustus in each pair, the four are indistinguishable from each other to symbolize their unity and the primacy of their office over themselves as individuals. Their solid, squared-off shapes give the impression of the firmness and uniformity of their rule, while their wide-open eyes, deeply drilled pupils, and furrowed brows show their vigilance, commitment, and care. Similar features can be seen in imperial portraits on fourth-century coins.

Depictions of Constantine underscore his supremacy as a ruler. That is strikingly evident in the eight-and-one-half-foot-high head from a colossal marble statue of the seated Emperor Constantine. It was originally placed in the apse of the great Basilica of Maxentius and Constantine (p. 647). Enough fragments of the rest remain to show that it reached to a height of thirty feet and had the same heavy, square proportions that give the tetrarchs' statues their powerful effect. The left hand probably held an orb to symbolize the emperor's worldwide rule, whereas the right arm was held straight out from the side and bent ninety degrees upward at the elbow, with the index finger pointing to the heavenly source of that rule.

As that statue was meant to dwarf everyone in the presence of the divinely appointed, all-powerful emperor, so were the depictions of Constantine on the famous friezes that adorned his triumphal arch in Rome. One panel shows an enthroned Constantine in a pose much like that of his colossal statue. He towers over ranks of poor citizens reaching out to receive donations of money that officials, as depicted in four small panels above the crowd, were giving out in his name.

The continuation of the Classical style

Despite the very un-Classical elements found in fourth-century imperial sculpture and portraiture, much of the Classical tradition survived. For example, the portrait of C. Caecilius Saturninus Dogmatius, who rose to praetorian prefect under Constantine, clearly shows the traditions of realism in Roman portraiture (p. 643, Figure 34.3). Another larger-than-lifesize head of Constantine (above) maintains the squared-off look of the tetrarchs and the upraised look of the eyes, but the modeling of the chin, mouth, and nose is very Classical, reminiscent of the Augustus from Prima Porta (p. 393). Indeed, the slight tilt of the neck and the prominence of the ears enhance that resemblance.

Those parallels reinforced the idea that the age of Rome's greatness had been restored (*Reparatio Saeculi* [p. 633]). Constantine further linked himself with the great age of the Empire at its height by reusing reliefs and sculptures from the monuments of Trajan,

Hadrian, and Marcus Aurelius. Therefore, the Classical and newer, hieratic styles were found side by side on his triumphal arch.

Constantine's own hieratic friezes probably had been executed by sculptors who were used to carving the reliefs that decorated late third-century sarcophagi (p. 561). The wealthy new ruling elite of the fourth century linked itself to Rome's glorious past through the Classical style of these elaborate funerary monuments just as it did through the revived study of Classical history, rhetoric, and literature. Even as Christian members of the new elite took over much from Classical literature, rhetoric, and philosophy to express their new faith, so they adopted Classical symbols, motifs, and styles in the visual arts for their sarcophagi.

The richly carved marble sarcophagus of the Roman aristocrat Junius Bassus (p. 644, Figure 34.4) who was urban prefect when he died in 359, spectacularly portrays Christian subjects in high Classical style. The front is divided into ten equal bays, five on top and five below. Each bay is framed by Corinthian columns, which support a straight entablature across the top row and alternating arches and pediments across the bottom. The scenes depicted in the bays are from the Old and New Testaments. Yet, the sculpting of the figures and clothes in each scene is clearly in the same tradition as the Parthenon frieze in Athens or the Ara Pacis of Augustus (p. 392). In the center of the top row, Jesus sits enthroned like a Roman emperor between Saints Peter and Paul. The two bays to his right depict Abraham preparing to sacrifice Isaac and St. Peter

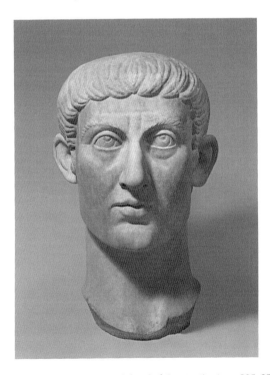

FIGURE 34.2 Large portrait head of Constantine I, ca. 325–370 C.E.

24121 - ROMA - Caio Celio Saturnino, detto Dogmazio - Museo Laterano - Ripr. Int. - Anderson - Ron

FIGURE 34.3   C. Caecilius Saturninus Dogmatius, 326–333 c.e. Gregorian Profane Museum.

being arrested. The two to the left of Jesus show him facing charges before Pontius Pilate. Below, the central scene presents Jesus riding on a donkey to Jerusalem. To his right are Job on a dung heap and the naked Adam and Eve flanking the serpent and the Tree of Knowledge. To his left are Daniel being brought into the lion's den and St. Paul being led to execution.

Many other works of art produced for wealthy Christians and pagans reflect the Classical revival of the fourth century. The fact that a work of art depicted a purely pagan scene did not mean that it belonged to a pagan any more than the owner of a copy of the *Iliad* or the *Aeneid* had to be a pagan. A great silver dish commemorating Theodosius' tenth anniversary as emperor in 388 combines elements of the hieratic and Classical styles, while it also combines Christian and pagan motifs. It depicts Theodosius flanked by his son Arcadius and the western Emperor Valentinian II. They are all presented in the standard frontal hieratic, though not excessively rigid, pose, and each, like a Christian saint, has a nimbus projecting a divine aura around his head. Theodosius' seniority in status and age is indicated by his greater size, and

FIGURE 34.4 Marble sarcophagus of Junius Bassus.

the armed guards are simply placed on different levels without any use of perspective to convey depth.

On the other hand, the three enthroned figures are depicted within a Classical architectural framework that closely resembles the entrance to Diocletian's palace at Split (Spalatum, Spalato [pp. 646–7]). In the space below the enthroned figures, a fluidly curved partially draped Mother Earth figure reclines amid stalks of ripened grain in a scene reminiscent of the Ara Pacis of Augustus (p. 392).

More purely Classical is a scene from the panel of a carved ivory diptych on p. 646. Such diptychs became popular among the wealthy elite to commemorate important events like marriages and consulships. This one seems to commemorate a marriage between two families associated with support of traditional paganism at Rome, the Symmachi and Nicomachi. The modeling of the figures and clothing is very Classical, and there is an attempt to portray depth, although the decorations on the altar are rather flatly incised instead of being carved in the round. Because a pagan sacrifice is depicted, the person who ordered it probably was making a religious statement, but it clearly became appreciated as a work of art to survive during the centuries after all members of the elite had embraced Christianity.

Mosaics and wall paintings

The great traditions of decorating the homes of the wealthy and well-to-do with mosaics and wall paintings continued in the fourth century. Many superb examples have been found all around the Empire. The painting of walls in an architectural style in the fourth century is indicated by the surviving interior walls of houses at Ephesus. Figured wall painting is known mainly from tombs whose owners probably were not rich enough to afford mosaics. Frontality, the lack of perspective, and the upraised eyes seen in other media are apparent in both pagan and Christian tomb paintings. Christians also increasingly decorated their churches with mosaics and wall paintings. Unlike

FIGURE 34.5 Ceremonial silver dish depicting Theodosius I (The Great), Valentinian II, and Arcadius (end of the fourth century).

pagan temples, which served primarily to house cult statues and dedicatory offerings, Christian churches were houses of worship, where congregational activities took place inside. Therefore, once they were secure and increasingly wealthy after Constantine's rise to power, Christians began to build elaborate churches and decorate them in the tradition of fine homes and public buildings such as baths.

Minor arts

Minor arts flourished in the fourth century. Ivory carvers produced not only commemorative ivory diptychs but also small, elegant, round lidded boxes, hair combs, and jewelry. Gem carvers and goldsmiths fashioned rings and jewelry of all kinds for the rich and powerful. Glassblowers and molders mass-produced bowls, cups, pitchers, and vases in many colors, shapes, and sizes for larger numbers of people. An interesting art that developed in the fourth century was the striking depiction of minor scenes and portraits by engraving glass with gold leaf, often on the bottoms of bowls or dishes or on round medallions.

Architecture

Diocletian and the tetrarchs revived the Severan policy of constructing massive public buildings and palaces to celebrate their power and the restored Empire. Diocletian's baths in Rome were the biggest ever constructed. Today, Michelangelo's great church

FIGURE 34.6 Ivory diptych of the Symmachi, 388–401 C.E.

of Santa Maria degli Angeli occupies only the central hall, whereas much of the rest is occupied by the Museo Nazionale Romano delle Terme. The only other Diocletianic building of note in Rome is the small senate house that he built on the site of earlier senate houses in the Forum.

Diocletian poured much money into construction at Nicomedia, his imperial residence in the East, and at his great fortified retirement palace on the Dalmatian Coast at Split (Spalatum, Spalato). The latter was laid out like a great military camp surrounded by thick walls between square towers. In the middle of the three landward walls were gates fortified with projecting octagonal towers. They entered onto colonnaded streets corresponding to the *cardo* and *decumanus* of Roman camps and planned towns. The walls enclosed almost eight acres containing not only the living quarters along the seaward wall but also barracks, exercise grounds, a temple, and an octagonal mausoleum.

Maximian expanded Milan (Mediolanum) for his imperial residence, and Galerius built up Thessalonica for his. Little survives at Milan, but part of Galerius' complex survives at Thessalonica. His triumphal arch with its marble reliefs was really a foursided gateway. There, the colonnaded road leading to his palace from his mausoleum intersected with a colonnaded section of the Via Egnatia, the main military road from Italy to the East. The palace has totally disappeared, but the round, domed mausoleum, which is reminiscent of the Pantheon, survives as the church of St. George. In Rome, Constantine restored monuments such as the Circus Maximus and built new ones such as the triumphal arch that bears his name. He also finished the huge basilica begun by Maxentius. Three of its six massive side vaults still soar 114 feet into the air. Originally, a vaulted clerestory rose another 40 feet above them. It covered an area approximately 350 feet by 220 feet and housed the colossal seated statue of Constantine (p. 642, Figure 2) in an apse projecting off the back. Both he and his mother, Helena, also built large baths for the people of Rome.

Constantine continued the tradition of round or polygonal buildings like the mausolea of Augustus, Hadrian, Diocletian, and Galerius. His mother was buried in the round mausoleum originally built for himself near the Via Casilina. The octagonal baptistry built for his original cathedral of St. John Lateran still survives. The round mausoleum of his daughter Constantina (Constantia) was built about ten years after his death and is now the church of Santa Costanza.

Constantine spent much money on construction and reconstruction in Italy, North Africa, and along the Rhine frontier in Gaul. Of course, his greatest concentrated program of public construction was at Constantinople. Unfortunately, nothing of it remains there. It has all been replaced by centuries of later building. The remains of his work in Gaul, however, are significant for the development of medieval Western architecture. The crenelated walls and round towers of his great fortified camp at Divitia (Deutz) across the Rhine from Cologne (Colonia Agrippina) even look like the bailey of a medieval castle. The buildings that he built for his imperial residence at Augusta Treverorum (Trier, Trèves) in Gaul foreshadowed the Romanesque architecture of early medieval Europe. Their style is discernible from the ruins of his great baths and from the large audience hall of his palace, which still survives as a Lutheran church.

Constantine's most notable contribution to architecture was his program of building impressive Christian churches all over the Empire, not just in Constantinople. The amount of money, men, and material mobilized for this effort was enormous. Constantine himself gave personal attention to the choice of architects and designs. At Rome alone, he sponsored the building of two major churches inside the walls and at least a half dozen at the sites of major martyr cults outside the walls. The first of Constantine's churches was the great cathedral of St. John Lateran, built inside the walls on the site of the former Lateran palace. St. Peter's Basilica was the last and greatest of Constantine's Roman churches. It was located across the Tiber on the slope of the

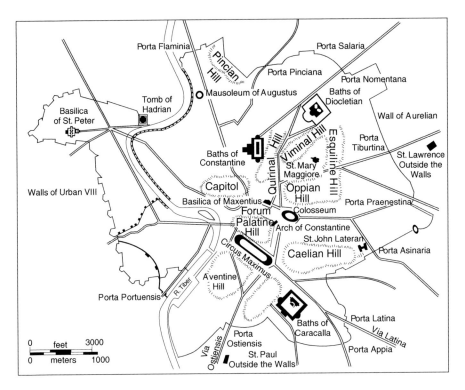

FIGURE 34.7 Christian Rome.

Vatican Hill where an ancient tradition said St. Peter was buried. Begun around 332, it took over sixty years to complete. Although it was razed to make way for the present St. Peter's in the late fifteenth century, pictures and descriptions survive.

At Antioch, Constantine began a great octagonal church surmounted by a gilded dome. It was located on an island in the middle of the Orontes River. Subsidiary buildings and courtyards surrounded it, and it was connected to the imperial palace. Many other cities, like Tyre and Nicomedia, received major churches, but Jerusalem and the Holy Land, of all places besides Rome and its vicinity, benefited most from Constantine's church-building activities. Constantine's mother, Helena, went to Jerusalem on a pilgrimage in 326 to identify the sites associated with Christ's birth, crucifixion, resurrection, and ascension. Constantine then supported the building of major churches at these sites. By 333, in amazingly short order, four basilica churches had been completed.

Pagan temples, particularly in the countryside, continued to be built or rebuilt throughout the fourth century despite the lack of imperial patronage. The revived prosperity of cities in the East prompted the restoration of many temples and other public buildings as well as the construction of some new ones. Valens, for example, gave Antioch a new forum, and a proconsul restored a temple dedicated to Hadrian at Ephesus. Large lavishly decorated villa complexes sprouted up all over the Empire.

After the reign of Julian, however, the pace of building slowed for the rest of the fourth century. Unfortunately, Theodosius' strictures against paganism led to the destruction of a significant portion of the Empire's architectural heritage because of the zealous destruction of pagan temples by increasingly militant Christians. Nevertheless, the eventual conversion of some major pagan temples such as the Pantheon at Rome and the Parthenon at Athens to Christian churches preserved a few great monuments of Classical architecture. They symbolize the way in which Christianity and Classical culture creatively interacted during the late Empire despite the tensions that also existed. Although Christianity became more dominant and more intolerant from Theodosius onward, it could not eliminate or escape the cultural context that shaped it.

SUGGESTED READING

Elsner, J. *Imperial Rome and Christian Triumph: The Art of the Roman Empire A.D. 100–450. Oxford History of Art*. Oxford: Oxford University Press, 1998.

Grubbs, J. E. *Law and Family in Late Antiquity: The Emperor Constantine's Marriage Legislation*. Oxford and New York: Clarendon Press, 1995.

MacMullen, R. *The Second Church: Popular Christianity A.D. 200–400*. Atlanta: Society of Biblical Literature, 2009.

Watts, E. J. *The Final Pagan Generation. Transformation of the Classical Heritage, 53*. Oakland: University of California Press, 2015.

CHAPTER 35

Germanic takeover in the West and Imperial survival in the East, 395 to 518 C.E.

The Roman Empire was radically transformed during the fifth century, which effectively extends from 395 to 518. Theodosius the Great had recognized that simultaneous pressure from Persian kings in the East and migrating German tribes in the West required a continual imperial presence on both fronts. That and a desire for imperial unity necessitated sharing the imperial office between two or more colleagues dynastically linked by marriage, blood, or both. Therefore, Theodosius made one of his two sons emperor in the East and the other emperor in the West when he died in 395.

Unfortunately, this arrangement was not sufficient to meet all of the Empire's challenges. The rapid rise and fall of emperors, usurpers, power brokers, and tribal kings make the fifth century even more chaotic and difficult to study than the third. After all is said and done, however, the eastern emperors managed to preserve their half of the Empire intact, while the western emperors gradually lost power until they finally disappeared. Local Germanic kings holding imperial titles that legitimized their rule over "Roman" territory preserved the shadow, but not the substance, of the Roman Empire in the West.

SOURCES FOR ROMAN HISTORY FROM 395 TO 518 C.E.

With the notable exception of Ammianus Marcellinus and far less so of the fourth-century epitomators, the sources for the first twenty-five years of this period are much the same as for the fourth century (pp. 564–6). Zosimus and Orosius, however, end their histories in 410 and 417, respectively. After them, there are no general narrative sources of even their limited breadth on which to rely. The more narrowly focused, though useful, ecclesiastical histories of Theodoret, Sozomen, and Socrates end in 408, 425, and 439, respectively. Evagrius began his *Ecclesiastical History* with the Council of Ephesus (431) and carried it down to 594. Its attempt to be impartial is sometimes marred by credulity. It and the other ecclesiastical histories have one great virtue, however: they often quote official documents, a practice that secular historians usually avoided. The letters and essays of Synesius of Cyrene provide valuable contemporary evidence for the early fifth century (p. 708).

From 439 onward, there are some thin chronicles. Prosper of Aquitaine continued Jerome's *Chronicle* from 378 to 455. Chronicles of the Byzantine scholar John Malalas and the learned Spanish Bishop Isidore of Seville (Hispalis) both cover the fifth century. Another Spanish bishop, Hydatius, continued Jerome to 468. Gennadius of Massilia continued Jerome's *De Viris Illustribus* to ca. 500. Medieval Byzantine compilers like Photius and Constantine Porphyrogenitus preserve many valuable fragments from lost works. For example, Porphyrogenitus' compilation of diplomatic sources preserves Priscus of Panium's fascinating account of an embassy to Attila the Hun. Isidore of Seville gives a sympathetic view of Germanic invaders in his *History of the Goths, Vandals, and Suevi*. Also important for the non-Roman side of events is Jordanes. He was of Gothic lineage and served as a secretary (*notarius*) to an Ostrogothic military commander. He became a monk or cleric and wrote two brief historical works. His variously titled summary of Roman history (or, simply, *Romana*) includes the unsettled tribes of northern Europe. His *Getica* (or *On the Origin and Deeds of the Goths*) is based on the lost twelve-volume *History of the Goths* by Cassiodorus (p. 705). Cassiodorus' extant *Chronica* covers world history from Adam to 519. The British monk Gildas covers the Anglo-Saxon invasions of Britain in his *De Excidio et Conquestu Britanniae* (*On the Destruction and Conquest of Britain*).

Important documentary evidence is supplied by the various compilations of Roman law beginning with the *Code* of Theodosius II, which was published in 438. It contains many laws issued during the previous forty years. Subsequent collections of new laws, *novellae*, issued by Valentinian III and Theodosius II also contain valuable explanations for their issuance. Summaries of other laws issued by Theodosius II are contained in Justinian's *Code*. The *Notitia Dignitatum* (p. 566) gives important insights into the administrative structure and military dispositions of the time. Other useful contemporary writings are the poems of Rutilius Namatianus and Claudian and the poems and letters of Sidonius Apollinaris (p. 702). The numerous biographies of saints, churchmen, and upper-class individuals that begin to appear in this period also help. What they lack in breadth they make up in detail about social, economic, and cultural conditions.

The amount of archaeological, epigraphical, and numismatic evidence is rapidly expanding and constantly adding new insights into this crucial period of Roman history.

FIGURE 35.1 Germanic kingdoms about 562 C.E.

WESTERN WEAKNESSES AND EASTERN STRENGTHS

Various problems and weaknesses contributed to the undermining of Roman power more in the West than in the East. The West faced a greater number of external threats along more permeable frontiers and could no longer depend on surplus revenues from the East. The East could pursue war and diplomacy more effectively with the central-ized Persian Empire on the long eastern frontier. The West was exposed to the more volatile tribal peoples on a frontier that stretched along the Rhine and the Danube for 1000 miles. The East, however, had to guard only the last 500 miles of the Danube. The East could use its surplus wealth to buy off attacking tribes and induce them to go elsewhere, usually west. The East also had a more deeply rooted unity in the culture of more densely populated, urbanized Greek-speaking provinces. Latin culture had not achieved comparable penetration in a number of western areas that were less densely populated and urbanized.

Weak child emperors and strong Imperial women

Upon Theodosius' death in 395, Arcadius (395–408), then seventeen or eighteen, obtained sole authority in the East. The ten-year-old Honorius (395–423), who had been summoned to Milan when Theodosius fell ill, was left as the western emperor. Their accessions illustrate the unfortunate pattern of child heirs that weakened the whole dynasty of Theodosius in both East and West. When Arcadius died in 408, his successor was his seven-year-old son, Theodosius II (408–450). Honorius was succeeded in 423 by his five-year-old nephew Valentinian III (423–455). Theodosius' sons and grandsons could not rule independently. They depended on older advisors and regents and were unable to break away from them after reaching maturity. As powerful individuals vied for influence and dominance at court, the general welfare was often sacrificed to personal interests. Moreover, the women of the dynasty were the more capable and interesting characters: Galla Placidia, half-sister of Honorius and Arcadius and mother of Valentinian III; Placidia's daughter, Honoria; Galla Placidia the Younger, daughter of Valentinian III; Empress Eudoxia, wife of Arcadius; Pulcheria, sister of Theodosius II; the latter's wife, Eudocia; and their daughter, Eudoxia, wife of Valentinian III. Holding the keys to succession through birth and inheritance, they became public players in the political arena and were particularly successful in the East.

Under the youthful successors of Theodosius, the nominal unity of the Empire was maintained by having one of the two annual consuls nominated at Rome and the other at Constantinople. The facade of unity was reinforced by the public display of the emperors' statues together and the publication of imperial laws with the names of both in the headings. Frequently, however, laws issued by one were not reciprocally issued by the other, and the administration of the East and the West went in separate ways despite instances of cooperation in times of military or dynastic crisis.

Germanic commanders in Imperial service

One of the outstanding features at the beginning of this period was the prominence of Germanic generals in the high imperial commands. The trend had become significant under Gratian. Practical reasons can explain it. The foremost probably was the sheer need for military manpower. Recruiting warlike bands of Germanic peoples became an attractive way to fill that need. Theodosius resorted to it by making the Visigoths federate allies after Adrianople. Although Theodosius had risen to power as a military leader, he was also a cultured aristocrat. He preferred to emphasize the civilian role of the emperor as head of state and to rely for military protection on "barbarian" generals whose loyalties were primarily to him, their patron. Thus, able chieftains and warlords gained the opportunity to win imperial favor and advance in rank. That was particularly true in the West, where the need for military manpower was greater than the Roman population could supply. Therefore, western emperors had to depend more heavily on Germanic mercenaries and federates.

Internal rivalries and shifting alliances

Unfortunately, the high positions achieved by Germanic officers often aroused the jealousy and hostility of high-ranking Roman military and civilian officials. Such positions also gave their Germanic holders a chance to pursue both personal and tribal animosities in the arena of imperial politics. Internal Roman rivalries and power struggles aggravated the situation. Rival Roman emperors and factions often granted imperial titles and conceded territory to one Germanic leader or another in return for help against fellow Romans. While the Romans were thus distracted by internal conflict, other tribes seized the opportunity to cross into Roman territory unopposed. When the Romans could not dislodge them, peace was bought with further titles and territorial concessions granted to them as federate allies. In the midst of it all, alliances and coalitions between Roman emperors or powerful commanders and various tribes or tribal kings were made, unmade, and remade with such abandon that it is nearly impossible to follow their course. Accordingly, as the following careers of Stilicho and Alaric under Honorius illustrate, all of these situations could prove dangerous to the peace and safety of the Empire, particularly in the West.

STILICHO AND ALARIC, 395 TO 410 C.E.

Stilicho, son of a Vandal who had served in the Roman army, became one of the *protectores*, officer candidates who formed part of the emperor's bodyguard. He soon caught the eye of Theodosius and married the latter's niece, Serena. Stilicho had risen to the supreme military command as *magister utriusque militiae*, master of both cavalry and infantry, when Theodosius marched west against Arbogast. Finally, before dying, Theodosius entrusted Stilicho with protecting the young heirs to the throne.

Stilicho, however, hoped to elevate his own son to the purple. He soon came into conflict with Rufinus, the corrupt and powerful praetorian prefect of the eastern Emperor Arcadius. The immediate question at issue was control of the strategically important prefecture of Illyricum. Gratian had transferred it from the West to Theodosius in the East to aid him after the Battle of Adrianople. Stilicho claimed that Theodosius had intended to transfer it back to the West, but Rufinus persuaded Arcadius to reject Stilicho's position.

In the spring of 395, Stilicho arrived in Illyricum with a large body of troops. He claimed to be returning them to Constantinople, whence they had come with Theodosius in 393. While Stilicho was in Illyricum, he captured the Visigothic king Alaric, who had recently ravaged Macedonia and Thrace before heading west. Rufinus feared that Stilicho would gain the credit for destroying the Visigothic menace and thereby would strengthen his claim to Illyricum. Rufinus persuaded Arcadius to order Stilicho to send the eastern legions immediately to Constantinople and return west. Stilicho obeyed. He also let Alaric go free. That move put the latter in his debt for the future and would earn Arcadius the displeasure of the defenseless Romans of the Illyrian prefecture.

The eastern troops returned under the command of Gainas, an Ostrogoth with whom Stilicho plotted the assassination of Rufinus. On November 27, 395, Rufinus appeared along with Arcadius to review the troops at Constantinople. Gainas and his accomplices crowded around Rufinus with friendly gestures and flattering talk. Then, with the trap closed tight, they cut him down.

Alaric and the downfall of Stilicho

For the next ten years, Alaric and Stilicho alternately fought and cooperated as each sought to increase his power at the expense of Honorius and Arcadius. Arcadius tried to undercut Stilicho by making Alaric a *magister utriusque militiae*, master of both cavalry and infantry, for Illyricum and stirring up trouble for Honorius. Alaric invaded Italy in 401 while Stilicho was fighting German tribes across the Alps. Stilicho had to strip the northern defenses to drive off Alaric. Subsequently, a mass of Ostrogoths and other Germans swept into Italy in 405. On the last day of 406, large numbers of Vandals, Suevi, Alans, and other tribes crossed the frozen Rhine into Gaul. They precipitated the usurpation of power in the westernmost provinces by a provincial commander in Britain, a man named Constantine, no relation to the earlier emperor of that name.

When Stilicho broke off his long-delayed invasion of Illyricum to put down this new Constantine, Alaric invaded Noricum and demanded 4000 pounds of gold as a subsidy plus military employment for his men. Stilicho persuaded a reluctant Roman senate to acquiesce. This action gave jealous Roman officials at court ammunition to attack him with charges of treasonable collusion with Alaric. They also rumored that he planned to set up his son as a third emperor in the Illyrian prefecture. Palace plotters turned Honorius against Stilicho and brought about the arrest and execution of Stilicho and his son in August of 408.

Alaric attacks Rome

Internal power struggles merely made relations between Honorius and Alaric worse. Honorius now refused to honor the agreement with Alaric. The latter immediately invaded Italy and besieged Rome while Honorius cowered in the safety of Ravenna's swamps. Lacking aid from Honorius, the Roman senate negotiated with Alaric. He agreed to lift the siege in return for a huge payment. This ransom was approved through communication with Honorius, who also agreed to hand over hostages as a token of good faith. Again, however, Honorius did not live up to his promises, and in late 409 Alaric marched on Rome once more. Negotiations resulted in the city's being spared. With senatorial approval, the urban prefect, Priscus Attalus, was declared emperor and agreed to cooperate with Alaric. Alaric himself was given Stilicho's old post as supreme *magister utriusque militiae*, while his brother-in-law, Athaulf (Adolph), became count of the domestics. Other important posts were filled by friends of Attalus, all of whom belonged to the circle of powerful pagan senators that had been headed by the late Quintus Aurelius Symmachus, who had clashed with St. Ambrose about the Altar of Victory (p. 655).

A terrified Honorius offered to negotiate for a joint rule, but Attalus refused. Just as Honorius was about to flee Ravenna for Constantinople, 4000 troops arrived from the East and gave him the resolve to stay. Differences arose between Attalus and Alaric about using non-Romans to fight Romans. Alaric decided to revoke his support of Attalus and come to terms with Honorius. Unfortunately, Sarus, a Visigothic rival of Alaric, intervened on behalf of Honorius and destroyed any chance of peace. Alaric then besieged Rome again and did not spare it this time (August 24, 410). For the first time in 800 years, foreign invaders sacked Rome. For two or three days, Alaric allowed his men to plunder, loot, and burn. Although contemporary sources exaggerated the physical damage to the city, much valuable loot and many captives, including Honorius' half-sister, Galla Placidia, were carried off.

Alaric did not long enjoy what he had seized. After marching south and having a fleet wrecked before he could get to Sicily, he died at Consentia (Cosenza). His followers diverted the nearby Busentus River, buried him in its exposed bed, and then turned the river back into its natural course so that his final resting place could never be desecrated.

THE VISIGOTHIC MIGRATION AND SETTLEMENT AFTER ALARIC

The Visigoths elected Alaric's brother-in-law, Athaulf, as their new king. After spending almost a year in raiding Italy, they crossed the Alps into Gaul in 412 and supported a rebellion there. Later, they switched support to Honorius' efforts to regain control of the province. Honorius, who had not learned his lesson before, refused to reward them afterward. Athaulf promptly seized Narbo, the capital of Narbonese Gaul, along with other important towns. He then married Honorius' captive half-sister, Galla Placidia. She shrewdly cooperated in his attempt (ultimately futile) to gain recognition and cooperation from Honorius. Honorius sent out his supreme commander, Constantius, who had long wanted Placidia for himself, to dislodge the Visigoths. They fled to Spain, where Athaulf was assassinated (415).

After a few days of turmoil, Wallia was elected to succeed Athaulf. He failed in an attempt to lead his people to Africa. Faced with starvation because of a Roman blockade, he negotiated with Constantius. In return for food, Wallia agreed to return the widowed Placidia, become allied with Rome, and attack Vandals and Alans who had invaded other parts of Spain. His success against them frightened Constantius. He recalled the Visigoths to Gaul (where he could more easily oversee them) and settled them in southern Aquitania (Aquitaine).

The Visigoths settled as federate allies governed by their own kings and bound to serve Rome militarily. Lands of Roman owners were partially divided among the Visigoths, whereas the Romans retained the rest of their property and remained subject to Honorius without any Visigothic control. The Visigoths wanted an independent kingdom, however, and eventually Wallia's successor, Theoderic I, forced the Romans to grant him sovereignty over Aquitania.

THE VANDALS, ALANS, AND SUEVI

After the Vandals, Alans, and Suevi had crossed the frozen Rhine in 406, they raided and plundered their way south into Aquitania. They remained there until 409 when the usurper Constantine drove them across the Pyrenees to Spain. After a Roman blockade of supplies denied them food, they agreed to settle as Roman federates in return for land. Then, the Romans persuaded Wallia and the Visigoths to attack these unwelcome guests. Eventually, only the Asding branch of the Vandals, which absorbed the remnants of the other tribes, remained free under the leadership of King Gunderic. In 428, Gunderic was succeeded by his able and ambitious brother Gaiseric.

GALLA PLACIDIA, VALENTINIAN III (423 TO 455 c.e.), AND AETIUS

Constantius had finally succeeded in marrying Placidia (417) and producing an heir, Theodosius' grandson Valentinian III. After the death of Constantius (421), Placidia and Honorius became estranged, and followers loyal to each rioted against one another. In 423, Placidia and her children took refuge at Constantinople with Theodosius II, who had succeeded his father, Arcadius. The childless Honorius died a few months later. No immediate successor was available in the West. Consequently, a high-ranking court official, John, was proclaimed emperor at Ravenna. Theodosius II supplied a large force to reconquer the West for the five-year-old Valentinian III. To tie the western branch of the Theodosian dynasty more firmly to the eastern, a betrothal was arranged between Valentinian III and the infant daughter of Theodosius II. She was named Eudoxia after her famous paternal grandmother, the Empress Eudoxia (p. 663).

Instead of fighting outsiders, the Romans now fought among themselves. Placidia, who served as regent for Valentinian III, was also supported by Boniface, count of Africa. A talented officer named Aetius supported John, the rival emperor at Ravenna. He raised an army of Huns, with whom he had spent his youth as a hostage. They arrived too late to save John from his enemies but secured favorable terms for Aetius as count and master of the cavalry to defend the Gallic provinces against the Franks and Visigoths (425). Aetius was able to force Placidia to appoint him master of cavalry and infantry in 429. In the meantime, Boniface had revolted in Africa and called in Gaiseric's Vandals, who began to seize North Africa for themselves in 429. Nevertheless, Boniface became reconciled with Placidia, and she replaced Aetius with him. Aetius called in the Huns again and secured restoration to power with the rank of *patricius* (p. 613) in 434.

ATTILA AND THE HUNS, 443 TO 454 c.e.

The Germanic tribes had invaded the Roman Empire partly because of pressure from the Huns (p. 601). Pastoral nomads, the Huns may have originated on the steppes of what is now Kazakhstan. Depicted in the sources (mostly hostile) as short, dark, and wiry, they were excellent horsemen, fierce fighters, and inured to hardship by a nomadic life. They terrified the more settled Germans in their path. By the time of Theodosius the Great, they had halted in the old Roman province of Dacia and exacted tribute from the Germanic tribes living in southern Russia: the Ostrogoths, Heruli, and Alans. Sometimes, they raided Roman territory; sometimes, they served in Roman armies. Under Attila, who became king in 443, they continued to harass the Balkans and demand increasingly larger subsidies. About 450, Attila suddenly turned his attention to the West in an attempt to create a vast European empire of his own. Honoria, sister of Valentinian III, had called on Attila to help her gain a position of power in the West for herself. At the same time, the Vandal Gaiseric was encouraging the Huns to attack his Visigothic enemies in Gaul.

Attila was overextended when he attacked Gaul in 451 and was already in retreat when Aetius, King Theoderic of the Visigoths, and other Germans, such as the Burgundians and Franks, fought him to a draw on the Mauriac Plain. Aetius, however, allowed the Huns, who had been very useful to him in the past, to escape. Attila then attacked Italy to demand the hand of Honoria. The diplomacy of Pope Leo, the timely outbreak of a plague among the Huns, and the arrival of an army from the East induced Attila to withdraw in 453 without Honoria. In 454, before he could attack again, he died while consummating his marriage to the sister of a Burgundian king. Without Attila's forceful leadership, his empire quickly broke up under the attacks of the eastern Germanic tribes that he had dominated.

THE BURGUNDIANS

The Burgundians had followed the wake of the Vandals, Alans, and Suevi. In 407, they crossed into Gaul from the east bank of the Rhine. They had settled near Worms and cooperated with a Roman usurper. Subsequently, Honorius recognized them as federates. Later, Aetius enlisted their enemies the Huns to attack them for not supplying promised troops to the Roman army. In 443, however, he settled them in southeastern Gaul in what is now Savoy between Lake Geneva, the Rhône River, and the Graian Alps (map, p. 652). They, in turn, fought for him when he had to battle Attila in 451. After the deaths of Aetius and Valentinian III, the Burgundians extended their domain down the Rhône to where it is joined by the Druentia (Durance). Officially, their kings remained federate allies of Rome because they valued the prestige derived from imperial titles. In fact, however, they were autonomous rulers who served the emperor at their own discretion, not his.

THE FRANKS

Just as the Burgundians had taken advantage of the disturbed conditions in Gaul during 407 to carve out territory there for themselves, so did the Franks. There were two groups of Franks: Ripuarians and Salians. The Ripuarians had been settled along the middle Rhine on the German side for some time. They now crossed over and established themselves on the left bank as well. They, too, used their arms to serve Rome and were among those who fought Attila in 451.

More numerous and important were the Salian Franks. They had been expanding southward from the shores of the North Sea near the mouth of the Rhine. They had already crossed the lower Rhine and seized control of Toxandria, between the Mosa (Meuse) and the Scaldis (Scheldt) rivers, before 350. The Emperor Julian had halted their expansion and made them federates of Rome. Later, they were able to take advantage of the problems in Gaul after 406 to expand farther south to the Samara (Somme). As federates again, they aided Aetius against Attila's Huns in 451 and remained loyal until 486. At that point, Clovis (Chlodovechus), king of the Franks and founder of the Merovingian dynasty, overthrew the last vestiges of Roman power in Gaul and extended his rule to the Liger (Loire), which was the border of the Visigothic kingdom (map, p. 652).

ANGLES, SAXONS, AND JUTES

While these events took place on the Continent, Germanic tribes along the North Sea—the Angles, Saxons, and Jutes—began to raid Britain. In 408, the Saxons made a devastating raid that undermined British loyalty to the usurper Constantine, who was operating in Gaul by that time. Eventually, Roman political and military authority was reestablished, but the western emperors could never really spare the resources to provide adequate security. By 428, Angles, Saxons, and Jutes were making permanent settlements along the English coast. Around 442, the Roman garrison left Britain and never returned. Therefore, the Germanic invaders steadily gained ground in the whole area north to the Tweed and west to the Severn (map, p. 652).

THE VANDALS IN AFRICA

By 431, only Cirta and Carthage held out against Gaiseric in Africa, despite the reconciliation of Count Boniface and Galla Placidia. A grant of federate status in Numidia bought only temporary peace in 435. Gaiseric seized Carthage in 439 and then began to raid Sicily and other islands. In 442, Valentinian III recognized the Vandals as an independent kingdom.

THE END OF IMPERIAL POWER IN
THE WEST, 454 TO 500 c.e.

For twenty years, Aetius had been the power behind the throne. He preserved what was left of the western Empire by skillfully playing off the Huns and Germanic tribes against each other. He was also able to betroth a son, probably Gaudentius, to one of Valentinian III's daughters, the younger Galla Placidia. Understandably, however, neither the elder Placidia nor Valentinian III appreciated being dominated by Aetius. After all, he had once supported the usurper John against them and thwarted their earlier attempts to get rid of him. It was easy, therefore, for Petronius Maximus, head of an old and powerful senatorial family at Rome, and the chamberlain Heraclius to enlist Valentinian III in a scheme to assassinate Aetius. The plot succeeded on September 21, 454. With his own hand, the foolish Valentinian III slew the one man really capable of defending his throne. Chaos ensued.

Valentinian sought the support of Olybrius, a senator from the powerful family of the Anicii (p. 615), by promising the younger Placidia to him in marriage. Maximus expected to become patrician in place of Aetius. Instead, he found himself blocked by Heraclius. Maximus then arranged with friends of the murdered Aetius to assassinate both Heraclius and Valentinian III (March 16, 455). Because Valentinian III had no male heirs, a struggle for the throne followed. Maximus' money obtained the support of the soldiers against both Maximian, a friend of Aetius, and Majorian (Julius Valerianus Majorianus), a high-ranking officer eager for the purple. To strengthen his position, Maximus forced Valentinian III's widow, Eudoxia (daughter of Theodosius II), to marry him and Valentinian's elder daughter, Eudocia, to marry his son Palladius. Eudocia, however, previously had been pledged to Huneric, son of the Vandal king Gaiseric, a match that Gaiseric wanted badly. Therefore, perhaps even with the cooperation of Eudoxia, Gaiseric invaded Italy and sacked Rome (June 3, 455). He carried off Eudoxia and both of Valentinian III's daughters (the younger Placidia and Eudocia) back to Africa. Soon thereafter, Huneric married Eudocia, who had been conveniently widowed when angry Romans slew Maximus and Palladius as they tried to flee the advancing Vandals.

The collapse of central authority, 455 to 476 C.E.

By the time Gaiseric sacked Rome in 455, the western emperor retained authority in only Italy, the islands of the western Mediterranean, and the parts of Spain and Gaul where powerful Roman aristocrats still held sway. By 476, even those places had generally fallen under German overlords. In that year, the eastern Emperor Zeno accepted reality and acknowledged the Vandals' possession of Roman Africa, Lilybaeum in Sicily, Sardinia, Corsica, and the Balearic Isles. Meanwhile, East–West rivalries, internal factionalism, and ambitious Germanic generals and kings were also destroying imperial rule in Italy itself.

Majorian and the ascendancy of Ricimer, 457 to 472 C.E.

After the angry Roman populace had killed the usurper Petronius Maximus as he fled the Vandal advance in 455, there was a year and a half of chaos. The Visigothic king Theoderic II and Gallo-Roman aristocrats supported one of Aetius' former subordinates, the praetorian prefect Avitus. The eastern emperor recognized Avitus, but Gaiseric and the Roman senators and soldiers opposed him. They favored Majorian.

Majorian also obtained the backing of Ricimer, grandson of the former Visigothic king Wallia. Ricimer recently had been appointed *magister utriusque militiae* under Avitus. As a Visigoth and an Arian Christian, however, Ricimer could never be accepted as an emperor himself. Therefore, he worked assiduously to be the power behind the throne for the next sixteen years. On April 1, 457, he succeeded in getting the eastern Emperor Leo I to make him a patrician and confirm Majorian as western emperor (457–461). Although Majorian succeeded in punishing his Visigothic and Gallo-Roman opponents, he suffered the same fate as many other emperors for failing to recapture Africa. The Roman populace would not long support an emperor who could not guarantee the vital flow of grain from Africa. Therefore, Ricimer stripped him of office and executed him (August 21, 461).

After three months, Ricimer persuaded the Roman senate to elect Libius Severus as emperor (461–465). The eastern emperor, Leo, would not concur, and Severus died amid suspicions of being poisoned by Ricimer. Leo eventually appointed a Greek named Anthemius as western emperor (467–472 [p. 666]). He also arranged a marriage between Ricimer and Anthemius' daughter. Leo even obtained the release of Valentinian III's widow (Eudoxia) and her daughter Placidia the Younger from Gaiseric. Then, he turned on Gaiseric with a vast three-pronged attack against Vandal North Africa in 468. Intrigues and jealousies among the constituent forces caused the expedition to fail. Gaiseric was left more firmly entrenched than ever.

As western emperor, Anthemius also enjoyed little success. He was unable to stop Euric, king of the Visigoths, from seizing more territory in Spain and Gaul. As a Greek, moreover, Anthemius was merely tolerated by the Romans in preference to the "barbarian" Ricimer. In 472, Ricimer overthrew Anthemius and raised up Olybrius. Gaiseric also supported Olybrius, who seems finally to have married the younger Galla Placidia while she was still at the Vandal court. Ricimer soon died. Olybrius reigned for only a few months in 472 before he died, too.

Gundobad, Orestes, and Romulus Augustulus

After the deaths of both Ricimer and Olybrius, the situation became even more chaotic. Leo and the *magister utriusque militiae* Gundobad, Ricimer's Burgundian nephew, struggled to appoint their candidates to the western throne. Gundobad succeeded in elevating Glycerius (473–474), who commanded the corps of officer candidates known as the *domestics*. Gundobad, however, left to become king of the Burgundians. Leo then appointed his own relative Julius Nepos, master of the soldiers in Dalmatia, to the western throne. Nepos marched on Rome in 474 and supplanted Glycerius as emperor in the West.

To replace Gundobad, Nepos chose as the new Germanic commander in Italy a certain Orestes, who had been a secretary (*notarius*) to Attila the Hun. Orestes then replaced Nepos with Romulus, his own twelve-year-old son. Romulus not only had the name of Rome's legendary founder, but he also received the nickname *Augustulus* (little Augustus), which mocked his title *Augustus*, the name of Rome's first emperor. Romulus Augustulus, nominally the last western Roman emperor, was never recognized in the East. Nepos returned to Dalmatia and remained the official Roman emperor of the West until his murder in 480.

Odovacer (Odoacer), the Ostrogoths, and Theoderic the Amal (476 to 493 c.e.)

Trying not to alienate powerful Roman landowners, Orestes refused to grant German mercenaries land in Italy. They overthrew him and Romulus Augustulus in 476. Then, they proclaimed one of their officers, Odovacer, as their king. He, however, obtained the support of the eastern Emperor Zeno and the Roman nobility by accepting Zeno's appointment as *patricius* (patrician). Zeno, nevertheless, did not trust Odovacer and wanted to get rid of him.

In the meantime, the Ostrogoths had been plundering Illyricum, Dacia, and Thrace right up to the gates of Constantinople (p. 666). By 483, they had been united under a dynamic king named Theoderic. He is called Theoderic the Amal because he first rose as leader of the Amal clan. In 488, Zeno hit upon the idea of enlisting Theoderic the Amal to overthrow Odovacer and govern Italy as his representative. Persuaded by a subsidy of gold, Theoderic invaded Italy in 489. After four years, Odovacer surrendered in February of 493. A few weeks later, Theoderic slew Odovacer with his own hand on the pretext that Odovacer had been plotting against him. Officially, Theoderic ruled Italy as *patricius* appointed by Zeno. His position as a subordinate representative of the eastern emperor was confirmed and refined by Zeno's successor, Anastasius, in 497. For all practical purposes, however, Italy had now become the newest Germanic successor state of the western Empire (map, p. 652).

By 500, therefore, the localization of imperial power in the West under Germanic kings was complete. Anglo-Saxon chiefs held sway in most of Britain, with the Romano-Celtic Britons confined to the far-western enclaves of Cornwall, Wales, and Cumberland. The Franks, under Clovis, held the old German provinces along the Rhine and Gaul south to the Loire. Soon, they would take much of Aquitania from the Visigoths, who would continue to rule a good portion of Spain for 200 years. The Burgundians would rule along the Rhône until they were conquered by successors of Clovis in 534. The Vandals, under the family of Gaiseric, would rule North Africa and the islands west of Sicily. The Ostrogoths, under Theoderic the Amal and his family, would rule Italy until the Emperor Justinian's ultimately unsuccessful reconquest of the West (pp. 679–91).

THE THEODOSIAN DYNASTY IN THE EAST, 395 TO 450 C.E.

Arcadius (395–408), Theodosius the Great's seventeen- or eighteen-year-old heir in the East, had been dominated by the praetorian prefect Rufinus until Gainas the Ostrogoth assassinated Rufinus in November of 395 (p. 655). Gainas then aimed for the same power in the East as Stilicho enjoyed in the West. Many aristocrats and average citizens at Constantinople bitterly resented the power of the Germans in the army. On July 12 of 400, a major riot broke out in the city, and large numbers of German soldiers were massacred. Gainas himself fled for his life. His overthrow did not spell the end of powerful Germanic generals in the East. After that, however, they never became so numerous or entrenched as they became in the West.

Arcadius' wife, Eudoxia (grandmother of Valentinian III's wife of the same name), and the aristocratic praetorian prefect Aurelian led the anti-German faction at the eastern court. Eudoxia was determined that nothing would threaten the Theodosian dynasty. She made sure that the throne would pass to Theodosius II, her son by Arcadius. Her elevation to the rank of Augusta in 400 had been part of the attempt to rally public support for the dynasty against Gainas. Her forceful and highly public political activity brought her into conflict with the eloquent, popular, and austere bishop of Constantinople, St. John Chrysostom (Golden-Mouthed). Influenced by Christian asceticism, he had a very narrow view of women's proper place and behavior.

Chrysostom's harsh public criticisms of Eudoxia threatened to undermine the popularity of the dynasty. She cooperated with his rivals and jealous detractors within the Church to depose and silence him (p. 639). Shortly thereafter, she suffered a fatal miscarriage. She had, however, already stamped her powerful influence on her eldest daughter, the nine-year-old Pulcheria, who grew to be a worthy successor.

Pulcheria, Eudocia, and Theodosius II (408 to 450 c.e.)

When Arcadius died, Pulcheria's brother, Theodosius II, was only seven and her two sisters even younger. The youth of all four tempted ambitious individuals to build up positions of power and influence in order to supplant the Theodosian dynasty. The very able and well-connected praetorian prefect Anthemius might have raised his own family to the purple in the East if it had not been for the strong and precocious Pulcheria. Indeed, Anthemius' grandson and namesake eventually became the ill-fated Emperor Anthemius (467–472) in the West after both branches of the Theodosian dynasty perished.

By publicly swearing a vow of perpetual virginity at fourteen and by persuading her younger sisters to do likewise, Pulcheria prevented the elder Anthemius and his allies from establishing claims to the throne through marriage and inheritance. In 414, after age or intrigue had removed Anthemius, Pulcheria became an Augusta and regent for Theodosius II. She took control of Theodosius' education to keep him from morally and politically corrupt influences and under her control. In the highly religious atmosphere of Constantinople, the dynasty's reputation for piety was a powerful factor in its favor. Pulcheria's formal regency may have ended officially when Theodosius came of age, probably on his fifteenth birthday. Nevertheless, she remained of paramount influence at court for several more years.

Powerful men in the senate of Constantinople opposed her. Many of them still championed traditional Hellenism, which radical Christians opposed. The Hellenists eventually undercut Pulcheria's influence by finding Theodosius a wife in 421. Later romantic legend has Pulcheria initiate the marriage. Contemporary sources paint a different picture. Influential aristocrats and intellectuals connected with Anthemius and his friends contrived to find a wife for Theodosius II. The bride they chose was Athenais, daughter of the pagan philosopher Leontius, for whom they had obtained the chair of rhetoric at Athens. Although Athenais had to convert to Christianity and take the name Eudocia, her becoming empress was a great comfort to the Hellenists. Her brothers, her uncle, and their friends rapidly advanced to the highest offices.

Eudocia and her supporters helped to inspire two of Theodosius' greatest accomplishments. In 425, he created a real university at Constantinople to compete with those of Alexandria and Athens. There were lecture rooms in the Capitol, and ten endowed chairs each in Greek and Latin grammar along with five in Greek rhetoric, three in

Latin rhetoric, two in law, and one in philosophy. Four years later, Theodosius inaugurated his most famous work, the *Theodosian Code*. All the laws issued by emperors from Constantine to himself were collected and compiled into a single reference work. After nine years and the labor of sixteen jurists, it was jointly issued by Theodosius II and Valentinian III on February 15, 438.

Naturally, Pulcheria resented her loss of influence and sought to eclipse her rival. Pulcheria emphasized her virgin piety to gain the support of the populace and powerful bishops like Cyril of Alexandria. They all feared a resurgence of paganism. Eudocia, who bore two daughters, Eudoxia (wife of Valentinian III) and Flavilla (d. 430), was hampered by her failure to bear a son. The Council of Ephesus in 431, which declared the Virgin Mary to be *Theotokos* (Mother of God), represents a triumph for the maneuverings of the virgin Pulcheria and her allies. They wanted to promote Mary's greater glory for their own various purposes (p. 665).

Theodosius' chamberlain, the eunuch Chrysaphius, temporarily outmaneuvered both women. Pulcheria withdrew to the suburbs of Constantinople in 441. Eudocia's downfall on suspicion of adultery followed in 443. Eudocia, who had become a friend of the famous Christian ascetic Melania the Younger (p. 620), spent the rest of her life doing pious works in Jerusalem. Pulcheria, however, would eventually reassert herself.

PERSIANS AND HUNS, 408 TO 450 C.E.

After the Persian treaty of 387 with Theodosius I, relations with the Persian Empire had become stable, even friendly. The Persian King Yazdgard (Yazdigird, Yezdegerd) I (399–420) was tolerant of Christians. About 409, the praetorian prefect Anthemius even obtained the king's help in settling disputes among Persia's Christian bishops. Subsequently, Yazdgard gave legal recognition to the bishop of Ctesiphon as head of the Church in Persia. There is even a credible story that the dying Arcadius asked Yazdgard to protect the young Theodosius II from Roman usurpers. Unfortunately, relations with Yazdgard soured in the last year of his reign when a fanatical Christian bishop demolished a fire altar belonging to Persia's official Zoroastrian religion. Yazdgard's son and successor Bahram V (Vahram, 420–439) instituted a persecution that produced a stream of Christian refugees begging for help. Persuaded by the pious Pulcheria, Theodosius II imprudently attacked Persia in 421.

The war did not go well. In 422, Huns took advantage of the situation to invade Thrace. Pulcheria's policies were disgraced. Her aristocratic opponents, who had regained ascendancy through the marriage of Theodosius to Eudocia, negotiated a peace that many sources claim as a great victory for Theodosius. At the same time, a subsidy of 350 pounds of gold a year induced the Huns to keep the peace.

The Huns, particularly under Attila, knew a good thing when they saw it. Whenever the East's forces were distracted on another front, they attacked Thrace. Constantinople itself was impregnable, thanks to the earlier actions of Anthemius. He had ordered the construction of a massive western wall from the Propontis (Sea of Marmara/Marmora) to the Golden Horn, strengthened the navy, and provided for a secure food supply. Nevertheless, the treasury was saddled with increasingly ruinous subsidies to get rid of the Huns. During a Persian attack in 441 and 442, for example, Attila extorted an immediate payment of 6000 pounds of gold and an annual tribute of 2100. The wealthy aristocrats' resentment of taxes needed to pay these sums contributed to the downfall of the eunuch Chrysaphius after he bungled an assassination attempt against Attila.

CHRISTIAN CONTROVERSIES AND IMPERIAL POLITICS

In the late Roman Empire, Christian theological disputes always had great political significance. Nestorius, bishop of Constantinople (428–431), claimed that Christ had two separate natures, human and divine, in one person but not commingled. Therefore, he opposed calling Mary *Theotokos* (Mother of God). He thus threatened to lower the status of the Virgin Mary, with whom the virgin Pulcheria had associated herself in the minds of common people. After Pulcheria and her allies, particularly the contentious and unscrupulous Cyril of Alexandria, defeated Nestorius at the First Council of Ephesus (431), the latter was exiled (p. 709). Many of Nestorius' persecuted followers were welcomed in Persia, where they spread the Nestorian sect of Christianity. Another theological dispute helped to undermine Pulcheria's enemy Chrysaphius in 450. He supported the influential monk Eutyches, who held the Monophysite view that the human and divine had been combined into a single (*monos*) nature (*physis*) in Christ. Eutyches' trial for heresy in 448 and the disgraceful politicking that led to his restoration at the Second Council of Ephesus in 449 ultimately hurt his patron Chrysaphius and helped Pulcheria.

GERMAN AND ISAURIAN GENERALS

The final nail in Chrysaphius' coffin was the problem of ambitious Germanic generals. After the downfall of Gainas, Anthemius had kept Germanic officers out of high military commands. When Pulcheria eclipsed him, she revived the dynasty's traditional practice of utilizing powerful Germanic generals. That led to the rise of Aspar, part Goth, part Alan, which displeased senatorial leaders at Constantinople. After thrusting aside Pulcheria, Chrysaphius tried to check Aspar by recruiting warlike mountain tribesmen from the province of Isauria on the south coast of Asia Minor. Their chief Tarasicodissa, who took the Greek name *Zeno*, soon realized that he was more powerful than Chrysaphius. When Chrysaphius refused to do his bidding, Zeno helped to procure his downfall in 450, and Pulcheria resumed her dominance in the court of Theodosius II. A little later in the same year, the emperor fell from his horse during a hunting party and died.

PULCHERIA AND MARCIAN (450 TO 457 C.E.)

Backed by Aspar, Pulcheria firmly controlled political and religious affairs. Still, he, a "barbarian," and she, a woman, could never be accepted as holders of the throne themselves. They chose, therefore, to elevate one of Aspar's close subordinates, the tribune Marcian. As a Roman from Illyricum or Thrace, he was acceptable to the leading senators. A pro forma marriage with Pulcheria gave Marcian a dynastic claim and protected her politically crucial virginity. To forestall scandal among the pious, they issued a commemorative gold *solidus* depicting Jesus standing between the couple and sponsoring the marriage of his virgin "bride" to the new emperor.

Reversing the policies of Chrysaphius, Marcian and Pulcheria refused to continue payments to Attila. He was too involved in the West to retaliate before he died. His death and the breakup of his empire allowed them to resettle Germanic federates, particularly Ostrogoths, in abandoned territories along the Danube. Without having to pay the Huns anymore, they also tried to accommodate the senatorial class by reducing taxes, alleviating the expenses of holding offices, and trying to halt the sale of offices, too. The marriage of Marcian's daughter by his first wife to Anthemius, grandson of the late praetorian prefect Anthemius (p. 663), also pleased the senate. When Pulcheria died in 453, she had overcome all obstacles to her control of dynastic power. Paradoxically, however, her reliance on her own virgin status for authority and her success in coming between Theodosius II and her rival Eudocia before they could produce a son meant that the dynasty could no longer continue in the East and would pass away altogether with the death of Valentinian III two years later in the West (p. 660).

LEO I (457 TO 474 C.E.)

When Marcian died, most senators probably would have preferred to elect his son-in-law, the younger Anthemius, as his successor. Instead, Aspar forced them to elect one of his officers as Leo I. Leo, however, did not want to be Aspar's puppet. He surrounded himself with Isaurian bodyguards and married his daughter Ariadne to Zeno. They worked to weaken Aspar.

In foreign policy, Leo asserted his independence by installing the younger Anthemius as emperor in the West and by mounting a massive joint expedition to North Africa against Gaiseric the Vandal in 467 (p. 661). The failure of that expedition weakened Zeno, so that Aspar and his two sons intrigued against him more boldly. In 471, Leo and Zeno lured them into the palace, where the emperor's eunuchs ambushed them. Aspar and one son were killed. The other son was captured and allowed to live.

The Ostrogothic general Theoderic Strabo used Aspar's murder as an excuse to demand appointment in his place and lands in Thrace for his Ostrogoths. They now elected him their king. Leo rebuffed Strabo, who then ravaged Thrace as far as Constantinople itself. In 473, they reached a compromise. Strabo received Aspar's old post, and the Ostrogoths received a subsidy of 2000 pounds of gold a year.

LEO II (473 TO 474 C.E.) AND ZENO (474 TO 491 C.E.)

In 473, Leo I named Leo II, Zeno's son by Ariadne, his colleague and destined successor. Leo I died some months later in early 474. In turn, Leo II took his father, Zeno, as co-emperor. He died before the end of the year and thus left Zeno in sole possession of the throne. Zeno was resented because he was an Isaurian outsider. He soon had to face a serious revolt led by Theoderic Strabo and the widow of Leo I, Verina, another strong eastern empress. In 476, Zeno temporarily succeeded in defeating his domestic enemies. He still had to deal with Theoderic Strabo, whom he tried to fight with the rival Ostrogothic leader Theoderic the Amal. Zeno adopted Theoderic the Amal, made him master of the soldiers, and sent him to fight Strabo in Thrace. The Amal, however, turned the tables on Zeno and tried to play Strabo against him. More domestic plots involving Verina followed and were not completely suppressed until 488. Meanwhile, Theoderic Strabo had died. In 488, Zeno was also able to come to a satisfactory agreement with Theoderic the Amal, now king of all the Ostrogoths, whom he authorized to overthrow Odovacer in Italy (p. 662). Zeno had finally rid himself of serious foes and was free from plots for the remaining three years of his life.

RELIGIOUS CONTROVERSIES CONTINUED

Theological disputes bedeviled the East from Theodosius II to the Arab conquest of Syria and Egypt two centuries later. They originated in questions raised about the nature of Christ in the Arian heresy (p. 587). They were exacerbated by the jeal-ousies of rival bishops (patriarchs) vying for preeminence with each other at Rome, Constantinople, Alexandria, Jerusalem, and Antioch.

Cyril, bishop of Alexandria (d. 444), had been a powerful and violent ally of Pulcheria against Nestorius, bishop of Constantinople. Nestorius was an ally of Cyril's archrival, John, bishop of Antioch (d. 441/442), who believed that Christ had distinct, but united, human and divine natures. Cyril supported the Monophysites, who argued that Christ's two natures had been fully combined into a single nature. After the First Council of Ephesus in 431, Pulcheria had used her renewed influence to force John and Cyril to accept a compromise in 433 to preserve the unity of the Church. The resultant Formula of Union stated that there had been a "union of two natures" result-ing in "one Christ, one son, one Lord." Many Alexandrians had refused to accept the compromise. In 444, they elected the extreme Monophysite Dioscorus their bishop. He immediately persecuted Cyril's old followers and instituted another attack on the views taught at Antioch. Dioscorus' powerful ally at Constantinople was Chrysaphius' friend Eutyches, who was convicted of heresy at Constantinople in 448. His restoration through Dioscorus' blatant manipulation at the Second Council of Ephesus in 449 gave Alexandria primacy over religious affairs in the East and provoked further disorder and disharmony in the Church.

Emperor Marcian and Pulcheria could not ignore the political dangers of this situ-ation. In cooperation with Pope Leo I, they brought about the Fourth Ecumenical Council, held at Chalcedon in 451, to try to settle the issue of Christ's nature. Chalcedon condemned Eutyches for heresy once more, deposed Dioscorus, and adopted a theo-logical position based on the Formula of Union from 433 and the views of Pope Leo I as set forth in *The Tome of Leo*—namely, that Christ is completely human and completely divine:

> [He is] one and the same Christ, son, lord, only begotten, recognized as of (in) two natures without mixture, change, division or separation, the distinction of

nature having in no way been taken away by union, but rather with the individual character of each nature being preserved and concurring into one person and one substance, not partitioned or divided into two persons but one and the same son and only begotten: God, word, lord Jesus Christ.

This Chalcedonian formula still prevails in the Greek and other eastern Orthodox churches as well as the Roman Catholic Church and many other Christian denominations in the West, but it was widely unpopular in Syria, Palestine, and Egypt, where the Monophysites had extensive appeal.

Disorder between Monophysites and Chalcedonians over control of major bishoprics multiplied after Marcian's death in 457. Finally, in 482, Zeno and Acacius, bishop of Constantinople, tried to end the disruptive religious controversy by issuing a decree of union, the *Henotikon*. It asserted the orthodoxy of the view set forth at Nicaea in 325 and Constantinople in 381 (p. 605), condemned the views of Nestorius and Eutyches, and anathematized anyone who had deviated at Chalcedon or would at any future council. The *Henotikon* did not pacify the extreme Monophysites and Chalcedonians. Also, Pope Felix III (Felix II)[1] refused to ratify a document that ignored *The Tome of Leo*. Zeno and Acacius, whom he had excommunicated, ignored him.

The *Henotikon* was flexible enough that Monophysite patriarchs (bishops) could assent to it and thereby keep their positions. As a result, Alexandria, Jerusalem, and Antioch all had Monophysite patriarchs under Zeno. The problem did not really disappear, however. It continued to cause difficulties in later reigns and had serious consequences for eastern unity in the face of Islam. Muslim views on the oneness of God were more compatible with the Monophysite position than with that of the orthodox Chalcedonians, who dominated Constantinople. Significantly, the Monophysite sects of Coptic and Jacobite Christians still survive in Egypt and Syria today.

ANASTASIUS (491 TO 518 C.E.)

Reflecting the importance of women in imperial politics, Ariadne, daughter of Leo I, held the key to the future after the death of her husband Zeno in 491. The senate at Constantinople asked her to choose his successor. She did so by marrying the moderate Monophysite Anastasius, a pious and respected usher (*silentiarius*) of the Sacred Consistory (Imperial Council).

Internal and external conflicts plagued Anastasius' reign. Isaurians, disappointed that Zeno's brother had been passed over in favor of Anastasius, eventually revolted and took seven years to be suppressed. Between 502 and 506, Anastasius fought King Kawad (Kavadh, Kavades, Cawades, Qawad) I (483–531) of Persia to a draw. He then effected a lasting peace that enabled him to check the devastating raids of the Bulgars. They had united the remnants of Attila's Huns and were attacking Illyricum and Thrace after the Ostrogoths departed. Anastasius' first response was to build the Long Wall (probably in 497), a defensive bulwark about forty miles west of Constantinople from the Propontis (Sea of Marmara/Marmora) to the Black Sea.

Since Anastasius was a Monophysite in religion, Euphemius, the Chalcedonian bishop of Constantinople, had refused to permit his coronation until he signed a pledge to support orthodoxy. For twenty years, Anastasius kept his pledge by upholding Zeno's *Henotikon*. Religious extremists, however, brought his efforts to naught. By 511, the Chalcedonians had taken over the bishoprics of Antioch and Jerusalem, and Anastasius began to intervene on behalf of the Monophysites so that they would not become alienated and hostile. That, however, led to a dangerous rebellion by Vitalian, the pro-Chalcedonian count of the federates in Thrace, between 511 and 515.

Reforms

The most successful part of Anastasius' reign entailed his fiscal reforms. In 498, he abolished the gold and silver tax (*chrysargyron*) on urban craftsmen and shopkeepers. Whatever revenue was lost from this measure was made up by setting aside an equivalent amount of income from the private imperial estates. In 513, he even began to phase out the *capitatio*, which was a severe burden on the peasantry (p. 575).

This latter move was probably made possible by the increased revenues resulting from his scrupulous and systematic fiscal management, which eliminated fraud and waste. He limited bureaucratic "fees" and made certain that soldiers received their proper pay. He demanded a careful accounting of military rations to prevent their theft. He also made the procurement of supplies more efficient. After switching much of the land tax from payment in kind to payment in gold, the government acquired only the supplies that it actually needed.

Anastasius further tightened the system of tax collecting by appointing *vindices* (protectors [sing. *vindex*]) to oversee provincial officials and municipal councilors, *curiales*. The *vindices* saw to it that taxes were collected honestly and that the wealthy did not receive preferential treatment. Finally, Anastasius introduced a series of copper coins useful for small daily transactions. Previously, there had been nothing between the gold *solidus* and the almost worthless copper *nummus* (*nummia* in Greek). The new coins were based on a well-made bronze *follis* (literally, a "bag," pl. *folles*) valued at forty *nummi*, with fractional denominations thereof valued at twenty, ten, and five *nummi*. Their quality and convenience were greatly appreciated by the people. They were also profitable to the treasury because they cost less to produce than the value of the gold *solidi* that the treasury received in exchange.

All of these reforms increased the imperial revenues while they actually reduced the burden of taxation. By being prudent and scrupulous in normal operations, Anastasius could, without straining the imperial finances, be generous to cities and provinces that suffered damage from wars or natural disasters. When he died in 518, he left a surplus of 320,000 pounds of gold in the treasury, a precious legacy to his immediate successors.

OVERVIEW AND PROSPECT

The death of Theodosius the Great in 395 ushered in a confusing and chaotic century for the Roman Empire. By the end, the western half had disintegrated into a number of unstable Germanic kingdoms. The East, however, despite dynastic upheavals and divisive religious controversy, had survived intact: Germanic kingmakers had been purged, the Ostrogoths had been lured off to Italy, a stable peace had been worked out with Persia, and the state's finances had become unusually sound. For the moment, the future of the Empire in the East appeared to offer the hope of stability if the problem of finding a successor to Anastasius could be handled quickly.

NOTE

1   The confusion over the numbering of this Pope arises from whether or not one counts the antipope Felix II (ruled 355–356 C.E.).

SUGGESTED READING

Heather, P. *The Goths*. Oxford and Cambridge, MA: Blackwell, 1996.
Kelly, C. (ed.). *Theodosius II: Rethinking the Roman Empire in Late Antiquity. Cambridge Classical Studies*. Cambridge and New York: Cambridge University Press, 2013.

CHAPTER 36

Justin, Justinian, and the impossible dream of universal Empire, 518 to 602 C.E.

The death of Anastasius without a direct heir in 518 produced another crisis of succession, but most people seemed anxious to avoid a destructive struggle. The new emperor, Justin (518–527), gained the crown through intrigues that are not entirely clear. He was an Illyrian of fairly humble origin and limited education who had become the count of the Excubitors (*comes excubitorum*), the emperor's personal bodyguards. Having risen to high rank, he had promoted his family's fortunes by bringing his nephews to Constantinople and obtaining for them every advantage of education and rank. Already in his sixty-sixth year, Justin groomed his favorite nephew, Justinian, for succession by closely associating him with his reign right from the start.

SOURCES FOR THE PERIOD OF JUSTIN AND JUSTINIAN

The sources for Justin's reign are limited. In *On the Ceremonies of the Byzantine Court*, Constantine Porphyrogenitus preserves the official account of Justin's election and coronation. About twenty-five of his laws appear in Justinian's *Code*, and his letters on religious matters are extant. The principal narrative sources are the contemporary account of the Byzantine chronicler John Malalas, the chronicle of Isidore of Seville

(Hispalis) (p. 706), and the ecclesiastical histories of Evagrius (pp. 707–8) and John of Ephesus. Evagrius wrote in Greek from the Chalcedonian point of view; John of Ephesus, in Syriac from the Monophysite.

Justinian's reign (527–565), on the other hand, is one of the best documented in ancient history. Procopius of Caesarea records, often as an eyewitness, military and diplomatic history in his *Persian War, Gothic War,* and *Vandalic War* up to 552. Writing immediately after Justinian's death, Agathias covers the events from 552 to 558 in his *Histories* (p. 708), and large fragments of a continuation to 582 by Menander the Protector are preserved in the *Historical Excerpts* of Constantine Porphyrogenitus. The Latin poet Corippus describes military action in Africa from 546 to 548 and the early reign of Justin II (pp. 702–3).

For internal affairs, John the Lydian's *On the Magistracies of the Roman People* and Procopius' *On Buildings* are very useful. Procopius' *Secret History* is full of scurrilous gossip and scandal designed to present Justinian and his wife, Theodora, in the worst possible light. It does, however, give insights into the working of the bureaucracy, whose abuses are blamed on the emperor himself. The most important sources for internal affairs are, of course, the laws preserved in Justinian's law code, the *Codex Iustinianus*. The laws are quite complete up to 534 when the second edition of the *Code* was published. Of his subsequent laws, 180, mostly dated between 534 to 544, are preserved in other collections. Saints' lives and ecclesiastical documents in great number from this period are also valuable sources of information.

For Italy in this period, the philosophical writings of Boethius, a Roman noble who had a significant political career in Ostrogothic Italy, are very important, as are the writings of Cassiodorus and Jordanes (p. 705). Of paramount importance are the writings of Pope Gregory the Great (540–604), guardian of papal power in the political and ecclesiastical struggles of the period (p. 715). Venantius Fortunatus wrote informative saints' lives and panegyrics in prose and poetry relating to the kingdom of the Franks. Most important for the Franks is the *History of the Franks* by Gregory of Tours (538–594 [p. 705]). Isidore of Seville documents events in Visigothic Spain, and through the excellent *Ecclesiastical History of the English People* (*Historia Ecclesiastica Gentis Anglorum*), the learned and venerable British monk Bede (672 or 673–735) preserves much valuable material on events at the outer edge of the western provinces that Justinian hoped to recover.

THE REIGN OF JUSTIN (518 TO 527 c.e.)

Justin's first acts as emperor were to execute his two closest rivals and reverse the pro-Monophysite policies of Anastasius. As natives of Latin-speaking Illyricum, Justin and Justinian sided with Rome in favoring the Chalcedonians (pp. 674–5). Justin immediately convened a council of bishops in Constantinople and instituted a brutal purge of Monophysite bishops and their supporters, but he failed to unseat Bishop Timothy IV at Alexandria. Having weakened the Monophysites, he then turned on the powerful orthodox military commander Vitalian and had him assassinated while he was consul in 520. Justinian succeeded to Vitalian's offices.

Militarily, Justin's reign was a success against "barbarian" tribes, but not the Persians. His nephew Germanus, regional commander in Thrace, prevailed on the Thracian frontier for ten years. The Tzani, a fierce tribe on the borders of Colchis and Armenia, were pacified and Christianized. That cut off Persian access to the Black Sea. Late in his reign, Justin intervened in the religious affairs of Iberia, a Persian client state in the Caucasus, and rejected the proposal of Kawad (Kavad) I that Justin adopt Chosroes (Kosroes, Khusro, Khusrau) I (531–579), Kawad's favorite son, to secure his succession to the Persian throne. It was a clever ploy that would have given Chosroes claim to the Roman throne. Justin's insulting reply triggered a Persian attack. Before any decisive battles took place, Justin died after designating Justinian as his successor (August 1, 527).

JUSTINIAN (527 TO 565 c.e.)

In the prime of life and a native speaker of Latin inspired by the history of Rome's great accomplishments, Justinian yearned to recover the West and restore the territorial integrity of the Empire. A passionate believer in Chalcedonian orthodoxy as the true, universal Christian faith, he also hoped to root out paganism and heresy in the united realm and spread the "true faith" to other realms. Those two goals were tightly linked. His devotion to them bordered on the fanatical. By championing orthodoxy, Justinian hoped to earn divine favor for achieving his secular goals. With success in the secular realm, he hoped to be able to enforce his version of the true faith on God's behalf. In the process, he increased the emperor's control over administration, defense, finance, religion, and commerce and created the model of Byzantine autocracy.

Justinian's faith was buttressed by serious theological study, which also seems to have reinforced a penchant for system, order, and equity in secular affairs. This passion for order and system also reflects a man who wanted to be in control of everything. There is not a great difference between a conscientious, talented administrator pursuing lofty goals with systematic efficiency and an autocrat who demands uniform obedience for the good of the state in whose name he rules. Justinian's desire for religious orthodoxy led to the systematic persecution of nonbelievers and heretics. He also loved elaborate ceremonials and rules of etiquette designed to exalt him far above his most distinguished subjects. Even senators had to abase themselves by prostration in the presence of either the emperor or empress, now called *Lord* and *Mistress*. High officials and members of the court referred to themselves as their slaves. Finally, jealous of his authority, Justinian was reluctant to take advice from most others except the empress and was too willing to listen to charges of disloyalty against those who were trying to serve him best.

THEODORA (508–548 c.e.)

Justinian's empress was the beautiful, intelligent, witty, self-confident, and bold Theodora. She carried on the tradition of effective female leadership established in the eastern court by Eudoxia and Pulcheria. Her importance to Justinian's reign is difficult to overestimate. She acted with great independence, and Justinian publicly acknowledged her as a partner in counsel. He gave her the palace of Hormisdas in Constantinople and great rural estates. Income from the estates allowed her to maintain a large number of loyal followers ready to do her bidding. She was a powerful friend, whose patronage could advance the careers of some, and a formidable foe, whose enmity could destroy those of others. She was even bold enough to act in contradiction to Justinian's policies when it seemed best to her.

Theodora's power and her undeniably humble origin naturally aroused the jealousy and resentment of senatorial aristocrats. As a result, many scandalous rumors were circulated concerning her past and her activities as empress. Because so much about her comes from obviously hostile and biased sources, it is difficult to separate fact from fiction. That her birth was too humble to be acceptable for marriage to the heir to the imperial throne probably accounts for the adamant refusal of Euphemia, Justin's wife, to agree to let Justinian marry her. Procopius, however, in his *Secret History*, probably goes too far with the story that she was the daughter of a bear-keeper from the circus and had a sordid career, first as a child actress, then as the most profligate of prostitutes.

No doubt, Theodora's early life was not perfect, but much of Procopius' pornographic portrait probably was inspired by a few simple facts. Her father probably was the bear-keeper for a circus faction known as the Greens (p. 678). She may well have become an actress, although the coincidence that Justin abrogated the law forbidding senators to marry actresses about the time that Justinian married Theodora may be the only basis for the story. It does seem that she had borne a daughter to a lover prior to her relationship with Justinian, but that and her interest in saving impoverished young girls from the all-too-common fate of enforced prostitution may be the only facts behind the lurid tales of her youth as told by her enemies.

Protection of women

Theodora deserves much praise for her attempt to protect women from abuse and secure better rights for them. She actively worked for laws to prohibit the sale of and traffic in young girls for prostitution. She even paid her own money to free those already held captive. To provide for their refuge and rehabilitation, she converted a palace across the Bosp(h)orus into a home called *Metanoia*, Repentance. She also protected women from harsh and arbitrary divorce on charges of adultery—charges that husbands often trumped up to get rid of unwanted wives.

RELIGIOUS POLICIES OF THEODORA AND JUSTINIAN

Another group that benefited from Theodora's concern was the Monophysites. Theodora favored their views, whereas Justinian sided with the Chalcedonians. As a champion of Chalcedonian orthodoxy, Justinian opposed all whom he viewed as heretics. Against the Manichees and Montanists, he employed harsh measures at the start. In the case of the more widespread Monophysite heresy, he hoped to find a theological formula that would reconcile Chalcedonians and moderate Monophysites. In that way, extreme Monophysites could be isolated and then eliminated by harsh actions if necessary. All efforts to find a theological compromise acceptable to the majority on both sides failed.

Justinian acted on many other religious matters during his long reign. With his fanatical passion for systematization and good order, he passed numerous laws regulating internal affairs of the Church. He also pursued strong measures against pagans and other non- Christians, whom he thought it his duty to convert or eliminate. In 529, he ordered all pagans to be instructed in the Christian faith and to be baptized or lose their property and be exiled. He even closed the Platonic Academy in Athens and executed some prominent pagan aristocrats at Constantinople. Moreover, Justinian enacted laws against Jews and Samaritans that denied them honorable status, restricted their civil liberties, and forced them to bequeath their property to orthodox Christians only. Later, he even dictated the rules for worship in Jewish synagogues, and in 562, he persecuted pagans with renewed vigor.

LEGAL REFORMS

Justinian's legal reforms were more praiseworthy and more successful than his religious policies. The disorganized mass that Roman law had become after centuries of growth and change needed rationalization and systematization. On February 13, 528, Justinian appointed a commission to collect all previous codified and uncodified imperial edicts; update, edit, and simplify them; and codify them into the *Codex Iustinianus*. This task was completed by Justinian's quaestor, Tribonian, and the other commissioners on April 7, 529.

In December of 530, Justinian set Tribonian to codify the legal commentaries of the Classical jurists in the *Digest*, which was completed in three years. It was then time to update the *Code* to include the large legislative output of Justinian up to that time. This second edition, which survives today, appeared on November 16, 534. A year earlier the *Institutes* had been published as a textbook to simplify the study of law.

ADMINISTRATIVE REFORMS

In the administration of the Empire, Justinian built on Anastasius' legacy as he earnestly tried to eliminate corruption and increase efficiency. One of Justinian's most beneficial reforms was the elimination of *suffragia*, payments for offices, which were then recouped by graft and corruption. He also issued standard rules for provincial governors and strengthened the powers of the civic defenders, *defensores civitatis*, who were supposed to act as ombudsmen for the provincials. He streamlined provincial administration by abolishing the vicars, who had been in charge of dioceses since the time of Diocletian (p. 572). In provinces where there were no serious external threats, Justinian combined the office of civil governor and military commander once more. He also gave Christian bishops powers to oversee public officials and provide for the general welfare.

In the capital, Justinian bolstered the office of prefect of the watch (*praefectus vigilum*) and gave him a new title, praetor of the *plebs* (*praetor plebis*). He took measures to provide for the populace's security and supply food for the armies. He also created a new office, that of *quaesitor*, investigator. This official made sure that visitors to Constantinople left upon completion of their business, returned illegal immigrants to their homes, and found work for unemployed legitimate residents.

JOHN THE CAPPADOCIAN

Justinian's praetorian prefect, John the Cappadocian, carried out these administrative reforms. As with so many reforms, however, they sometimes worked better in theory than in practice. With the abolition of the office of vicar, lawless bands could escape capture by moving from one provincial jurisdiction to another within the same diocese. The corruption and abuse of power that thrive in large bureaucratic organizations, especially in societies where some people are viewed as superior and others as inferior, could not be completely eliminated. In fact, with the abolition of the middle-level vicars, the reforms probably did as much to enhance the power of John the Cappadocian as they did to eliminate corruption.

John's success in securing revenues for Justinian aroused the hatred of those who had to pay more taxes. It also excited the jealousy of those who resented the power and favors that he received from the emperor. No doubt, he was ambitious, often ruthless in his methods, and eager to maximize his own financial rewards. Still, one must discount considerably the monstrous picture painted of him by sources like Procopius and John the Lydian. The former was a jealous courtier, and the latter another praetorian perfect. They represented wealthy aristocrats and officials who had evaded taxes or enjoyed profits from corruption and had felt the sting of John's strong fiscal administration most severely. Justinian needed John the Cappadocian to maximize revenues because the aggressive policies and ambitious programs that Justin and he followed quickly exhausted the surplus that Anastasius had built up.

THE FIRST PERSIAN WAR, 527 TO 532 C.E.

When Justinian became sole emperor upon Justin's death in 527, he inherited the latter's war with Persia, which was going badly. He had no desire to conquer Persian territory and hoped simply to put enough military pressure on the Persians to force them to accept a long-term peace that would free him to reconquer the West. The war see-sawed back and forth until the death of the Persian king, Kawad, in September of 531. The new king, Chosroes, wanted to be free to meet any challenges to his succession. Therefore, he entered into serious negotiations with Justinian's ambassadors. Finally, in the spring of 532, a treaty of Eternal Peace was signed. The Persians accepted the prewar boundaries, and Justinian paid Chosroes 11,000 pounds of gold as the price for Chosroes' agreement not to demand an annual subsidy for defending the Caucasus.

THE NIKA REBELLION OF THE BLUE AND GREEN CIRCUS FACTIONS, 532 c.e.

In the middle of the negotiations with Chosroes, Justinian almost lost his throne in an uprising involving the circus factions that controlled the chariot races at Constantinople. Chariot races were very popular everywhere (see Box 36.1). Ever since Augustus, emperors had often relied on the goodwill of the masses as a counterweight to the jealousy of the senatorial aristocracy. Consequently, emperors usually were generous patrons of the races. As Roman culture spread through the Empire in the first two centuries c.e., each provincial city of any significance had its own circus for chariot racing and had its own versions of the Red, White, Blue, and Green circus factions that had originated during the time of the late Republic (p. 325). Constantine, of course, replicated the races and factions at Constantinople.

36.1 THE POPULARITY OF CHARIOT RACING

Charioteers were the rock stars of the Roman world: their sport was the most popular entertainment throughout the Empire over many, many centuries. Races among two- or four-horse chariots were held at a specially built track called a circus. The Circus Maximus, Rome's premier racing venue, could seat approximately 150,000, making it about one-third larger than the largest stadium in the modern world, Rungrado First of May Stadium in Pyongyang, North Korea (114,000 people). The largest sports stadium in the United States—ranking second largest in the world—is Michigan Stadium at the University of Michigan in Ann Arbor, Michigan, which seats just over 107,600.

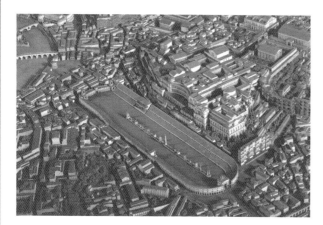

FIGURE 36.1   Circus Maximus, Rome.

The sport offered not only high-speed excitement and the opportunity for betting, but also the possibility that the emperor or the local dignitary hosting the races would distribute some sort of gift to the assembled crowd. In addition, there was always a chance of real violence. Crashes, called *naufragia* ("shipwrecks"), were common, and once one occurred, workers had only about one minute to clear the wreckage before the remaining racers came around the track again. When the most famous driver of his day died in a wreck at the Circus in Rome, Pliny the Elder, writing in the middle of the first century C.E., reports that a deranged fan threw himself onto the charioteer's funeral pyre and died. Fans did what they could to improve their preferred faction's chances of winning: numerous curse tablets, bidding spirits and demons to attack the horses and drivers of rival groups, have been found at circuses throughout the Roman world.

By Justinian's day, however, the Reds and the Whites had been completely overshadowed by the Blues and the Greens at Constantinople. These two factions had acquired such widespread followings and organizational strength that they were a significant element in the political life of the capital. Emperors and powerful senators sought to manipulate the two factions for their own political and religious ends. Emperor Anastasius, for example, had favored the Greens, who became associated with his Monophysite views. The orthodox Justin and Justinian, therefore, had catered to the Blues by putting some in governmental posts, supplying them with money for their activities, and protecting them from punishment for their disorders and crimes.

Neither faction, however, was strongly committed to any one theological doctrine. Once Justinian had secured his own power, he urged the city prefect, Eudaemon, to curb the lawless behavior of both the Blues and the Greens. On January 13, 532, Justinian refused to commute the sentences of two men, one Blue and one Green, who had survived a bungled hanging. The two factions decided to cooperate to force the men's release. They adopted *nika* ("conquer" in Greek) as their watchword, which gave the subsequent popular uprising its name.

That evening, rioters set fire to a number of public buildings, including the entrance hall of the Great Palace and the Church of Holy Wisdom, *Hagia Sophia*. Renewal of the chariot races the next day failed to divert their attention. They set fires at the northern end of the Hippodrome, the circus where the races were held. The ranks of the original rioters were now swollen by those who had suffered from Justinian's fiscal policies. There were, for example, numerous small farmers who had abandoned their land in the face of heavy taxes and had migrated to Constantinople. Powerful senators who resented both Justinian's autocratic ways and his fiscal maneuvers encouraged them. They were now demanding removal of three key ministers: Eudaemon, prefect of the city; Tribonian, Justinian's quaestor; and John the Cappadocian. Justinian reluctantly complied.

No matter what Justinian did, however, he could neither calm nor crush the howling mobs. When they proclaimed Anastasius' reluctant nephew Hypatius emperor in his stead, Justinian decided to flee. At the crucial moment, however, the dauntless Theodora, who had known deprivation once, argued that death in defense of the throne was far better than exile. Justinian ordered his loyal eunuch Narses to sow dissension between the Blues and the Greens with bribes and reminders of Anastasius' former favoritism toward the Greens. Then, the general Belisarius and another commander made a surprise attack on the tightly packed mob in the Hippodrome. The subsequent slaughter broke the back of the revolt. The unfortunate Hypatius and his brother were executed, suspect senators were exiled, and the circus factions ceased to be a problem. Justinian was then able to consolidate his autocratic rule, which had fueled resistance in the first place.

THE REBUILDING OF CONSTANTINOPLE

Just as Nero, an earlier promoter of imperial autocracy, had used the great fire of 64 to rebuild Rome on a magnificent scale suitable for the capital of an exalted emperor, so Justinian rebuilt Constantinople after the conflagrations of the Nika Rebellion. In autocratic fashion, Justinian also took the opportunity to renovate his palaces entirely and decorate them with splendid mosaics glorifying his reign. In keeping with Justinian's desire for divine favor to support his rule, churches received special attention. Constantine's Church of Holy Peace, *Hagia Eirene*, was rebuilt on a scale second only to that of his neighboring *Hagia Sophia*, Holy Wisdom. His earthquake-damaged Church of the Holy Apostles was replaced at this time, too.

Hagia Sophia was Justinian's most ambitious project and took five years to build. To make it a monument worthy of both Holy Wisdom and Justinian's reign, thousands of pounds of gold were spent on its construction and furnishings. The pulpit was covered with gold and jewels, the altar was solid gold, and the bishop's throne was constructed of thousands of pounds of gilded silver. One source places the total cost at 320,000 pounds of gold. Even if it were exaggerated by a factor of ten, the cost would still be staggering. Perhaps Justinian would have been wiser to put off such huge domestic expenses until he had completed his great scheme of reconquering the West.

He launched that campaign right after the Nika Rebellion and the signing of the peace treaty with Chosroes. His failure to devote enough resources to operations in the West after his initial success almost ruined the whole enterprise and caused serious long-term problems in both the East and the West.

RECONQUEST OF THE NORTH AFRICAN PROVINCES, 533 TO 534 C.E.

By 532, conditions in the Vandals' kingdom of North Africa were favorable to Justinian's hopes of reconquest. The previous Vandal king, Hilderic, had been a descendant of Theodosius the Great. His mother was Valentinian III's daughter Eudocia, who had married Gaiseric's son Huneric (p. 660). Clearly hoping to be more than a Vandal king, Huneric had stopped persecuting the orthodox Roman Catholics in his realm and had entered into a treaty with Justinian. Unsuccessful against Moorish raiders, however, he had been deposed by his cousin Gelimer. Invoking the treaty with Hilderic, Justinian considered attacking North Africa. Recalling earlier emperors' disastrous attacks on the Vandal kingdom, many advisors protested. A bishop's assurance of divine favor encouraged Justinian to proceed, albeit cautiously. In 533, his favorite general, Belisarius, sailed for North Africa with between 15,000 and 20,000 soldiers. Accompanying Belisarius was his able and fearless wife, Antonina. She was a close friend of Theodora and a real power in politics at court.

Victory was deceptively easy. Gelimer was incompetent and distracted by revolts. Belisarius swooped down on North Africa without opposition. They were helped by the Catholic population, who resented the Arian Vandals. Within a year, North Africa was reconquered. In 534, it and Sardinia were formally organized into the separate praetorian prefecture of Africa. Unfortunately, the unexpected ease and speed with which the African operation proceeded were a disaster in disguise. They would encourage Justinian to seize opportunities for reconquering western territories, which proved extremely difficult and costly to retain after the initial victories.

ITALY IS INVADED, 536 TO 540 C.E.

Soon after the recovery of the North African provinces, an attractive opportunity arose to restore Roman power in Italy. From his capital at Ravenna, Theoderic the Amal had provided an enlightened Ostrogothic regime for Italy throughout most of his long reign (471–526). He greatly admired Roman culture and institutions. Although he was an Arian, he had tried not to provoke his orthodox Roman subjects. For all classes in Italy, therefore, life had gone on much as before, and they had enjoyed relative peace and prosperity. The only major difference was that taxes were now paid to Theoderic, who held the political and military power. Unfortunately, neither the orthodox Roman aristocracy nor Theoderic's fellow Ostrogoths always appreciated his policies. Yet, he had managed to prevail over both until his death in 526.

Theoderic's ten-year-old grandson, Athalaric, succeeded to the Ostrogothic throne. His mother, Theoderic's daughter Amalasuntha, acted as regent. She continued Theoderic's policies and gave Athalaric a Classical education. A powerful anti-Roman faction among the Ostrogoths, however, insisted that Athalaric be raised as a German warrior. They ultimately prevailed, and Amalasuntha entered into negotiations with Justinian for asylum. The intemperate behavior fostered by Athalaric's peers, moreover, led to his alcoholic death in 534.

FIGURE 36.2 Hagia Sophia, with the four minarets added by the Turks.

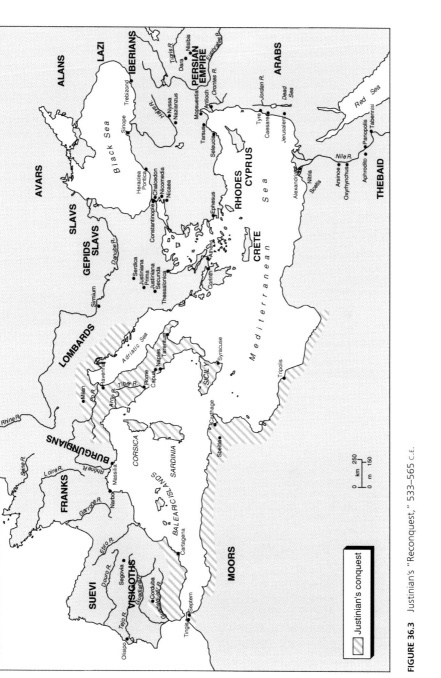

FIGURE 36.3 Justinian's "Reconquest," 533–565 C.E.

Amalasuntha then offered the throne to her cousin Theodahad, with the proviso that she be his guide. Once securely enthroned, however, Theodahad ordered her imprisoned and executed (535). Empress Theodora may even have secretly maneuvered him into doing so in order to give Justinian the chance to act as Amalasuntha's avenger.

At any rate, Theodahad's actions gave Justinian a convenient pretext to intervene. First, he seized Sicily and Illyricum and then opened negotiations with Theodahad. Ultimately, Theodahad promised to hand over Italy to Justinian in exchange for luxurious exile on rich eastern estates. Then, a Gothic army momentarily recovered Illyricum. Theodahad reneged on his promise, and Justinian ordered the invasion of Italy. Belisarius and Antonina finally arrived in Italy with fewer than 10,000 men in June of 536. They made good progress because the feckless Theodahad scarcely opposed them and the Catholic population of Italy generally supported their cause. Naples, however, had to be taken by a long siege and clever stratagem before they could march on Rome.

Vitigis and the siege of Rome, 537 to 539 c.e.

In the meantime, the Ostrogoths had replaced the fainthearted Theodahad with Vitigis (Vitiges, Witigis), a successful general unrelated to the Amal royal clan. To legitimize the change of rulers, Vitigis forcibly married Amalasuntha's daughter Matasuntha. Although he negotiated unsuccessfully with Justinian and called on the Franks for aid, the majority of Romans, led by Pope Silverius and the senate, brought about the surrender of Rome to Belisarius. Vitigis then mounted a siege that Belisarius, always with Antonina's help, stoutly resisted for over a year.

Rival commanders

Belisarius was unable to break the siege when John, the ambitious nephew of the Vitalian assassinated under Justin (p. 672), brought reinforcements to Italy. John soon became insubordinate, however, and hampered Belisarius' success. The problem was compounded when Narses brought more reinforcements and also refused to take orders from Belisarius. Justinian finally recalled Narses and clearly designated Belisarius as the supreme commander.

The capture of Ravenna, 540 (spring) c.e.

Firmly in command and aided by an attack by the double-dealing Franks against the Ostrogoths, Belisarius methodically attacked the Ostrogoths' stronghold in the North. He was kept supplied by sea while war-induced famine worked enormous hardship on both the Ostrogothic garrisons and the civilian population. From Ravenna, Vitigis vainly summoned the Lombards from beyond the Danube and secretly encouraged Chosroes to divert the Romans by starting another war on the Persian front. Learning of the latter move, Justinian offered generous terms to Vitigis, who readily agreed. Belisarius, however, resented losing five years of hard work on the eve of total victory and refused to sign the treaty on Justinian's behalf. Fearing bad faith on Justinian's part, the Ostrogoths ceased dealing with him.

Changing tack, once they recognized Belisarius' dislike for Justinian's policy, they proposed to accept Belisarius as a new western emperor. He pretended to accept the offer and was received into Ravenna with an armed escort. He then treacherously seized Vitigis and Matasuntha, many Ostrogothic nobles, and the royal treasury. He took them all back to Constantinople in May of 540. Vitigis was kept there until he died in 542.

Justinian was not wholly pleased by Belisarius' unauthorized actions and did not give him a triumph, as he had after the Vandalic War. Despite the superficially spectacular results, the situation in Italy was left worse than Justinian's terms would have made it. The Ostrogoths north of the Po refused to surrender to anyone after Belisarius' duplicity was revealed. Bound by no treaty, they created the problem that Justinian had hoped to avoid—major wars on two fronts.

TROUBLES IN NORTH AFRICA

Justinian's haste to invade Italy before securing adequate control of North Africa had already produced an example of that strategic difficulty on a smaller scale. Moorish tribes had begun devastating raids right after Belisarius' departure. It took two years to repel them, but they were still restive. No sooner had the Moors been repulsed than about two-thirds of the Roman army in North Africa mutinied for various reasons. Slowness in collecting taxes in the new province caused long delays in paying the soldiers. Many soldiers resented the harsh discipline of their new commander, Solomon. Non-Roman auxiliaries felt that they had been poorly rewarded with booty. Men who had married Vandal women were aggrieved that Justinian would not allow the women to inherit their fathers' and former husbands' estates, which he confiscated instead. Also, many of the Romans' Germanic allies were Arian Christians, who resented Justinian's suppression of Arianism among the conquered Vandals.

The mutineers besieged Carthage. It was rescued only when Belisarius interrupted his invasion of Italy and returned from Sicily. Belisarius, however, soon had to return to Sicily. Justinian placed his own capable cousin, Germanus, in charge of restoring order in North Africa. Germanus defeated the rebels decisively in the spring of 537 and consolidated control until Solomon received command again in 539. For the time being at least, those actions reduced Justinian's worries in North Africa.

THE SECOND PERSIAN WAR, 540 TO 562 C.E.

By 539, Justinian's biggest worry was the threat of renewed war with Persia. The situation on the eastern frontier was already unstable. Armenia had always been a point of contention between the Romans and Persians. A revolt had broken out there because of Roman fiscal exactions. Unable to defeat the Romans, the rebels had appealed for help from the Persian king, Chosroes. With additional encouragement from Vitigis in Italy, Chosroes opened the war in 540. It was not officially ended until 562.

In Chosroes, the successor of Kawad (p. 676), Sassanid Persia had an energetic and able leader comparable to the Roman Empire's Justinian. Chosroes continued administrative and land reforms begun by his father, he made the army more efficient, and he took great interest in literature, philosophy, and religion. In every way, he hoped to increase the glory and greatness of the Sassanid Persian Empire.

Justinian's successes in Africa and Italy had aroused fear and envy in Chosroes. He scarcely needed the pleas of either Ostrogoths or Armenians to prompt his breaking of the Eternal Peace of 532 and renewing war on Justinian's eastern flank in 540. In the meantime, fortunately for the Romans, Justinian had carefully rebuilt or strengthened frontier fortresses and the walls of cities in Mesopotamia and Syria. Chosroes' main goals, therefore, were not so much to capture Roman territory as to make a show of strength by successfully besieging some major strongholds in Syria. Chosroes wanted plunder or money from those whom he besieged or threatened. He hoped to force Justinian to pay tribute in return for peace on the frontier. Justinian would have agreed to pay the 5000 pounds of gold demanded immediately plus an annual subsidy of 500 pounds if Chosroes had not unsuccessfully besieged the great fortress of Dara during negotiations.

In 541, however, Chosroes scored a major coup. He seized the Roman client kingdom of Lazica, ancient Colchis, at the eastern end of the Black Sea. Chosroes garrisoned its fortress city of Petra to secure his control of the kingdom. Then, he returned to Persian territory. He had to face Belisarius, who had arrived to take command and had captured a major Persian stronghold. In 542, when Chosroes failed in attacking a Roman fortress, he and Belisarius made a temporary truce.

RESUMPTION OF WAR IN ITALY, 541 TO 543 c.e.

Justinian probably was anxious to secure some kind of truce, however imperfect. He needed the incomparable Belisarius back in Italy. The new Ostrogothic king, Ildebad, had been determined to continue the war in Italy. Bad Roman policies made it easy for him to do so in 541. First, with the departure of Belisarius in the previous year, military command in Italy was left fragmented among his former subordinates. Second, the harsh fiscal policies of imperial administrators were alienating both the soldiers and the very people whom Justinian claimed to be freeing from tyranny. Murder, however, ended Ildebad's success within months.

Ildebad's cousin Totila became king shortly thereafter. In the following year, he took the offensive against the divided Roman commanders. He quickly recovered most of southern Italy except Naples, which fell in the spring of 543 only after a lengthy siege. Totila increased the ranks of his army by recruiting slaves and wisely refrained from plundering the countryside for supplies. Instead, he collected the regular taxes and rents, which provided regular income without ruining the territory. His humane treatment of captured cities and towns also advanced his cause.

TROUBLES EVERYWHERE

In 542, the Romans had been forced to battle not only the Ostrogoths and Persians but a far more deadly enemy as well—plague. The initial outbreak was enormously destructive. Its appearance in Syria had already contributed to Chosroes' willingness to sign the truce with Belisarius. Up to 300,000 people may have died in Constantinople alone. Justinian himself became ill but survived. Those who did survive became immune. Subsequent attacks appeared with diminishing severity during the next twenty years, until a general immunity had built up in the Empire's population.

The truce of 542 with Chosroes was not highly effective. Immediately afterward, Chosroes demolished a Roman fortress. In 543, he was preparing an invasion of Roman Armenia but was thwarted by another outbreak of plague and the revolt of a son. On the other hand, the Romans successfully invaded Persarmenia near the headwaters of the Euphrates. Finally, in 545, Chosroes, after failing to take Edessa in 544, consented to a meaningful five-year truce. In return, Justinian paid him 2000 pounds of gold, but the agreement did not extend to the conflict over Lazica. The truce was subsequently renewed for another five years on similar terms in 551.

INTERNAL CONFLICTS AND ADMINISTRATION

As soon as Justinian had regained firm control after the Nika Rebellion, he had reappointed John the Cappadocian as praetorian prefect. Nevertheless, John remained the object of machinations by his enemies, particularly Theodora. She resented his influence with her husband and may honestly have thought that he had ambitions for the throne himself. Antonina, Belisarius' wife, helped Theodora against John because she wanted Belisarius to be supreme in Justinian's favor. In 541, Theodora finally secured John's banishment from the capital and his forced ordination into the Church. After Theodora's death, however, Justinian freed John and allowed him to return to Constantinople, but only as a priest.

After John, Justinian adjusted the administrative system to provide a middle level of authority over groups of provinces once more. He also continued to issue laws designed to improve administrative procedures and control abuses. In the financial sphere, John's role was assumed by Peter Barsymes, first count of the sacred largess and praetorian prefect in 543. Procopius portrays Peter Barsymes negatively, too, but laws inspired by him show that he was concerned to protect both revenue and small taxpayers by fair procedures. That would not have appealed to the wealthy and powerful, who often tried to shift taxes onto the weaker citizens and exploit them.

BELISARIUS RETURNS TO FACE TOTILA
IN ITALY, 544 TO 549 C.E.

After the initial truce with Chosroes in 542, Justinian had reassigned Belisarius to take charge of the war against the Ostrogoths in Italy. No doubt Belisarius' preparations were hindered by the outbreak of plague at Constantinople in 543. He and Antonina did not arrive at Ravenna until 544. Also, he desperately lacked manpower. Plague and lack of funds due to the war with Persia and Justinian's expensive building program probably hindered recruitment. He brought only 4000 men with him. Moreover, many of the soldiers originally sent to Italy had deserted because they had not been paid for years. Belisarius finally persuaded Justinian to divert some troops from the East now that there was a truce with Chosroes, but they were not adequate.

Totila besieged Rome in 545. Belisarius, faced with disobedient subordinates, had to abandon efforts to relieve it. Totila eventually captured it with the help of treachery at the end of 546. In 547, Belisarius retook the depopulated and devastated city. Still, he was not able to mount a major offensive even after Justinian sent him 6000 assorted troops in 548.

Clearly, Belisarius was Justinian's best general, but even he could not successfully prosecute a war without adequate forces. Therefore, he sent Antonina to Constantinople in the hope that she might obtain more men through her influence with Theodora. Unfortunately, Theodora had died on June 28, 548, just before Antonina arrived. Justinian was preoccupied with finding enough men to prosecute the war in Lazica, which had been exempted from the truce with Chosroes in 545. Seeing her husband in a hopeless situation, Antonina then asked that he be recalled: it was futile to remain. Belisarius returned to Constantinople in early 549. He was reappointed chief military commander for the East but remained inactive in Constantinople for many years.

THE LAZIC WAR, 549 TO 557 C.E.

Chosroes was determined to preserve his unprecedented access to the Black Sea by consolidating his hold on Lazica (Colchis). Justinian was just as determined to prevent Rome's ancient enemy from retaining this strategic naval advantage. The Lazi had soon begun to dislike Persian oppression even more than the Roman kind. They asked for Roman help, and Justinian sent 7000 men to retake Lazica in 549. The city of Petra was recaptured in 551, but the war was a stalemate after that.

PEACE IN THE EAST

In 557, Chosroes and Justinian signed a five-year truce that included Lazica. They finally worked out a fifty-year peace in 562. In return for evacuating his positions in Lazica, Chosroes received an annual subsidy of 30,000 gold pieces. He also agreed to guard the Central Caucasus against outside attackers. Other provisions regulated commercial, military, and diplomatic relations between the Persian and Roman empires. They also set up rules for arbitrating personal disputes between Persians and Romans on the frontier to prevent wider conflicts. In a separate agreement, Chosroes promised to tolerate the Christians in his empire so long as they did not seek converts.

DISASTER IN ITALY, 549 TO 551 C.E.

After Belisarius' departure in 549, things went from bad to worse in Italy. The ease with which Belisarius had initially reconquered both North Africa and Italy had deceived Justinian and caused him to discount the seriousness of subsequent problems in the West. Also, he needed large amounts of money to expend on buildings or art to glorify God and the Empire and to mount campaigns against Chosroes in the East or to buy him off with subsidies. Therefore, Justinian was even more willing to believe that Belisarius and others in the West wanted more than they needed. Already undermanned, therefore, Roman armies in both Italy and North Africa suffered mutinies and betrayals by troops angry over the lack of pay.

Just such a situation caused some Isaurian soldiers to betray Rome in 550 to Totila again after Belisarius left. That finally spurred Justinian to take more vigorous action. He rejected Totila's offers to renegotiate. Totila then promptly invaded Sicily, which previously had been spared. At last, Justinian placed his cousin Germanus in charge of the war. Using private as well as public money, Germanus prepared a proper expedition to recover Italy.

THE RECOVERY OF ITALY, 552 TO 562 c.e.

Germanus had shrewdly married Vitigis' widow, Matasuntha. As Amalasuntha's daughter, she was the granddaughter of Theoderic. By marrying her, Germanus hoped to divide Ostrogothic loyalties. Unfortunately, he died before he could depart for Italy. In his place, Justinian appointed the popular and capable Narses, who had clashed with Belisarius earlier (pp. 678–9). Narses arrived in Italy with at least 25,000 men, almost half being Lombards, Heruli, Gepids, and Huns. He promptly defeated Totila in a set battle in 552, and Totila was killed in flight.

In the same year, Narses won another great battle against the Ostrogoths. After that, Ostrogothic resistance was confined to a number of fortified cities. Narses systematically reduced them, but he soon had to face a large army of Franks and their Alemannic subjects. They swept into Italy from the north in 553 to reap what Narses had sown. Narses kept to the fortified towns, whereas the Franks dissipated their energies in plundering much of the rest of Italy. Finally, in 554, Narses annihilated them at a great battle outside of Capua. Italy south of the Po was free at last from warfare, but it was not until 562 that Narses finished taking Ostrogothic strongholds between the Po and the Alps.

The Pragmatic Sanction, 554 c.e.

In 554, Justinian issued what is known as his *Pragmatic Sanction* to restore order and provide proper imperial administration to Italy. It restored rights and property to prisoners and exiles, slaves to their masters, and *coloni* (tenants) to their landlords. Gothic landowners of long standing, however, retained their property. Justinian also forbade the kind of fiscal and administrative abuses that had caused so much discontent after the initial reconquest, and he provided for the proper provisioning of troops without undue burdens on the people.

WARS ON OTHER FRONTS, 544 TO 561 c.e.

While Justinian was confronting simultaneous wars or uneasy truces on the eastern frontier and in Italy, he was not free of trouble elsewhere. Remarkably, he even continued to pursue reconquering other parts of the West before he had adequate control of North Africa and Italy. In 544, the Moors revolted once more in North Africa. They were aided by the Roman general in charge of Numidia, who wished to rule Africa independently, and by troops who had not been paid. This revolt was not crushed until 547. The Moors then remained subdued (except for a brief rebellion in 563) for the remainder of Justinian's reign.

After 550, Justinian seems to have devoted greater energy to the West. He not only committed adequate resources to prosecute the war in Italy but also rather treacherously took advantage of a dynastic struggle among the Visigoths. By backing a Visigothic pretender named Athanagild, Justinian was able to recapture part of southern Spain along both the Atlantic and Mediterranean coasts. The Visigoths then accepted Athanagild as king, but the Romans refused to hand over the captured territory to him. Instead, they organized it into the province of Baetica, which included such important cities as New Carthage, Malaca, and Corduba.

In the Balkans, various frontier tribes had periodically raided Thrace and Illyricum since 529. Three tribes combined for a massive invasion in 559. One group penetrated Macedonia and Greece as far south as Thermopylae, another attacked the Thracian Chersonese (Gallipoli Peninsula), and another drove through Thrace right up to the walls of Constantinople.

Belisarius, who had long learned to do much with little, took charge again in this emergency. With a makeshift army of his 300 loyal bodyguards and some hastily recruited, poorly armed civilians, he set a clever ambush for the 2000 Huns who confidently rode up to attack his small force before Constantinople. Without any losses, his men killed 400 Huns, while the rest retreated in panic. At Thermopylae and at the entrance to the Chersonese, Roman defenses held. The invaders went back across the Danube after Justinian promised them an annual subsidy. A similar offer in 561 dissuaded the Avars, another group of central Asian invaders. The Balkans then remained calm for the rest of Justinian's reign.

Invading tribes could be persuaded to accept subsidies because it was impossible for them to remain in the Balkans for very long after an initial breakthrough. Between 540 and 549, Justinian had expended much effort on building and repairing defenses and forts at hundreds of places along the Danube and throughout the Balkan peninsula. Perhaps that is why he did not feel able also to commit adequate resources to Italy during this period. At any rate, his expenditures in the Balkans proved their worth. Raiders could sweep through the open country, but the Romans could hold the well-supplied fortified places with a few men and harass the enemy when they scattered to plunder. Roman forces could also wait to attack them in the rear after they had exhausted available food and were returning encumbered with spoils.

JUSTINIAN'S LEGACY AND HIS SUCCESSORS, 565 TO 602 C.E.

Justinian was one of the most important emperors in Roman history. He stood at the crossroads of antiquity. His failures demonstrated that the empire of Old Rome was gone forever. Nevertheless, Justinian left a legacy that shaped the Byzantine Empire of the New Rome at Constantinople for centuries to come.

Law and administration

Justinian's policy of codifying and revising the corpus of Roman law was a great success. It is what one recalls first about his reign (p. 689). The elimination of outdated and contradictory laws and the systematic presentation of those retained provided a uniform and efficient body of law such as is necessary for the well-being of any large, complex state. It still provides the model for the legal systems in most European nations.

Justinian's attempt to provide more efficient and honest administration by increasing salaries, combining functions to lessen the number of officials, and centralizing authority at Constantinople was not always successful. No system is immune to corruption. Justinian remained flexible, however, corrected mistakes and abuses when he could, and definitely improved upon what had existed before. During his reign, imperial administrators better served the interests of both the ordinary person and the state as a whole.

Byzantine autocracy

Justinian's legal and administrative reforms contributed to the creation of a fully autocratic monarchy, which was characteristic of the succeeding Byzantine Empire. The office of emperor had grown more and more autocratic since the time of Augustus—sometimes faster, as under Caligula, Nero, Domitian, Septimius Severus, or Diocletian; sometimes more slowly, as under Vespasian, Antoninus Pius, Tacitus, Probus, or Gratian. The personalities of the individual emperors had affected the pace, but in the long run, the need for a powerful, efficient, central authority to deal with increasingly large and complex problems pushed the emperors in the direction of autocracy. Justinian's policies were the culmination of that process. The Byzantine autocracy had all the unpleasant faults of any highly centralized, bureaucratically administered monarchy. That fact resulted in the pejorative meaning of the word *Byzantine* when applied to the complex politics of large organizations. Nevertheless, for centuries, Justinian's successors and their ministers were able to maintain armies and organize resources enough to preserve Greco-Roman civilization in the East from being overwhelmed by a constant stream of outside attackers.

Long stable reign

Perhaps Justinian's greatest success was in living so long and sparing his subjects the civil wars and disorders that would have accompanied shorter reigns. A well-disciplined man of Spartan habits, he enjoyed a sound constitution. It enabled him to survive the plague that killed countless thousands. He also seems to have been safe from plots. Only two conspiracies after the Nika Rebellion are noteworthy, and they were revealed before he was in any serious danger.

Unfortunately, two men connected with Belisarius were involved in one of these plots. That raised suspicions against him. He was forced to dismiss his armed retainers and was disgraced. Contrary to legend, however, he did not end his life as a blind beggar. Justinian restored him to favor after less than a year, and they passed the rest of their days together. Belisarius died in March of 565, and Justinian followed a few months later on November 14, 565.

Religious persecution

Despite notable accomplishments, Justinian's reign was, on balance, a failure. One of his biggest failures was in the sphere of religion. His policy of seeking divine favor by uniting the Empire under the orthodox version of Christianity as defined at Chalcedon was a disaster. It only created deep animosities toward the imperial government among inhabitants who espoused different faiths or other versions of Christianity. Persecution of the Jews and Monophysite Christians in Egypt and the Levant so embittered many of them that they welcomed the Muslim conquerors who seized those lands seventy-five years after Justinian's death. Similarly, the Arian Christians of North Africa resented the continued attempts to impose a hostile orthodoxy. Again, the resultant divisiveness made it easier for the Muslim conquerors in the mid-seventh century. Likewise, the devastating Ostrogothic rebellion after the initial reconquest of Italy was fueled by the Arian Ostrogoths' resistance to the imposition of orthodoxy.

Bankruptcy of the Empire

By the time Justinian died, the imperial treasury had been exhausted by the expenses of his grandiose building projects, his impetuous wars, and the ruinous subsidies that he agreed to pay some enemies in order to be free to fight others. The desperate state of the treasury subsequently contributed to his successor's decision to risk war with Persia rather than continue subsidies. Ironically, that war dragged on for twenty years and weakened the Empire even further.

Mishandling of succession

Justinian compounded problems by his poor handling of the arrangements for providing a successor. He had two choices: Justin, an able general and son of his cousin Germanus, and another Justin, a nephew whom Theodora had greatly favored. Although the latter had no conspicuous abilities, Justinian had advanced him to high rank. Nevertheless, Justinian had not clearly indicated who was to succeed. Unfortunately, the less able Justin was well placed to seize the throne and immediately executed his rival when Justinian died. As Justin II (565–578), he had pretensions that bordered on megalomania. He pursued a disastrous foreign policy with Persia and eventually revived his predecessor's internally disruptive religious persecutions. On the other hand, his fiscal frugality so overcompensated for Justinian's excessive spending that he undermined imperial security. Finally, he became so mentally unbalanced that he could not rule. In

574, Empress Sophia persuaded him to appoint as Caesar a man named Tiberius, count of the Excubitors. In 578, the latter smoothly succeeded Justin as Emperor Tiberius II (578–582). Nevertheless, too much damage had already been done.

Tiberius II and his successor Maurice (582–602) achieved some success on the Persian frontier, but Maurice's attempt to regain control of the Balkans from Slavic invaders without adequate pay for his troops led to his assassination and disastrous political instability just as the first wave of Arabic Muslim conquests was about to crash upon the provinces of the East. The smaller state that eventually survived was no longer the eastern Roman Empire that had evolved between Constantine and Theodosius I, but had clearly become what is now called *Byzantine Greece*.

Reconquest of the West

Even Justinian's reconquest of the North African provinces, Italy, and part of Spain must be counted as a failure—his biggest. To pursue these unprovoked wars, he had to weaken frontier defenses. Their weakened state invited external attacks from Persia and various aggressive tribes. The net result was to overstrain the resources of the Empire and undermined it for the future.

Furthermore, the reconquered provinces did not repay the costs of their conquest and subsequent defense. The North African provinces suffered periodic revolts and constant raids from the surrounding Moors. By the time Italy finally had been pacified, the long years of warfare had devastated its cities and permanently impaired its prosperity. The imperial province in Spain was under constant pressure from the surrounding Visigoths, from whom it had been treacherously seized.

After all of the trouble and expense of reconquering these western provinces, they began to be lost right after Justinian's death. In 568, the Lombards and their allies invaded northern Italy. By 572, they held everything between the Po and the Alps. By 590, much of the rest of Italy had also been lost. About sixty years after Justinian's death, the Visigoths wrested back the territories in Spain. By 709, the Muslims had also swept away the remnants of imperial power in North Africa.

FINAL JUDGMENT

Justinian wasted his considerable talents in trying to recapture the West and impose an empire-wide religious orthodoxy. If he had concentrated on strengthening the Roman Empire that he had inherited in the East and if he had not sown internal bitterness and discord with his religious policies, the Roman Empire of the East might not have suffered severe losses in the seventh century. Moreover, the Germanic successors to imperial power in the West might have been better able to resist subsequent conquerors, who did more extensive damage to Roman civilization in Europe. The historical conditions that had made possible the universal Roman Empire of the first two centuries C.E. no longer existed. The resources needed to maintain it under changed circumstances had not been there to prevent the loss of the West in the first place. They were not available under Justinian. His effort to revive the dead had only weakened the living.

SUGGESTED READING

Cameron, A. *The Mediterranean World in Late Antiquity 395–700 AD*. 2nd ed. *Routledge History of the Ancient World*. London and New York: Routledge, 2012.

Hughes, I. *Belisarius: The Last Roman General*. Yardley, PA: Westholme Publishing, 2009.

Potter, D. *Theodora: Actress, Empress, Saint. Women in Antiquity*. New York: Oxford University Press, 2015.

CHAPTER 37

The transformation of the late antique Roman world, 395 to 600 C.E.

The restored Roman Empire of the fourth century had disintegrated during the fifth and sixth. Since the time of Montesquieu and Edward Gibbon, many modern thinkers have attempted to explain Rome's fall. It is an impossible task. The process of disintegration took place over a huge area for a long time. It was extremely complex in detail. The factors involved are so numerous, their interactions so involved, and the evidence so limited in comparison that a definitive analysis is impossible. At the general level, however, it is clear that given its geographic, economic, social, political, and cultural characteristics, the Roman Empire was unable to sustain the frequent and simultaneous blows of "barbarian" migrations and invasions in the West and war with the Sassanid Persians in the East. Without those or similar external factors, the Roman Empire as a political entity might have continued indefinitely, despite its weaknesses.

During the fifth and sixth centuries, many of the internal characteristics that identified the Empire in Late Antiquity as still Roman in the Classical sense underwent major transformations. As always, changes did not occur at a uniform pace or even in the same way everywhere within the Empire's vast territories. By the early seventh century, however, the cumulative effects had created a world that was quite different from that of the fourth and was recognizably medieval despite significant continuities with the Classical Roman past.

THE ECONOMY

In general, the economy of the late antique Roman world declined in the fifth and sixth centuries, sooner and more steeply in the West than in the East and more in some ways than in others. Despite overall economic decline, there were major shifts in wealth that enriched some even while others saw their wealth reduced or destroyed altogether. In the West, Germanic kings and their loyal warriors were enriched at the expense of Roman landowners. The latter often lost anywhere from one-third to all of their property to their new overlords. In the East, wealth poured into the new capital at Constantinople to the benefit of the eastern emperor and a growing class of imperial functionaries. Everywhere, Christian churches, monasteries, and shrines received countless donations of land, money, gold, silver, jewels, and other precious goods from those who piously sought divine favor or shrewdly hoped to acquire influence in an increasingly powerful institution.

Economic fragmentation and declining trade

Although reduced in volume, long-distance trade in luxury goods continued to follow traditional patterns between the eastern and western Mediterranean. Those who had retained their wealth or were newly rich were willing to pay for high-status goods at prices that attracted suppliers no matter what the risks and hardships. In the East, regional trade and production remained steady until the Arabic Muslim conquest in the early seventh century.

In general, however, the collapse of the Roman state in the West fragmented the economy of the Roman world and caused major changes in the production and distribution of goods. The Roman armies and the system of taxation and supply to maintain them had been powerful forces promoting the production and transportation of a wide range of goods in large quantities over considerable distances. Roman administrative centers and major military posts had stimulated the development of profitable urban markets. The state's system of military roads and transport had subsidized commercial shipments. The government's demands for taxes and supplies had spurred the higher levels of organization and production that had sustained a larger and more sophisticated private sector than would have been possible otherwise. By the end of the fifth century, this system had disappeared in the western provinces.

Decline of monetization and the monetary system

During the fifth century, the only stable coinage was based on gold. Silver disappeared into private hands as hoarded coins or the elaborate silver plates and utensils that adorned churches and wealthy homes. The increasingly debased bronze or copper coins were so worthless that they had to be sealed up by the hundreds or even thousands in a leather bag (*follis*) and exchanged by weight. In the West, the Germanic successor kings tried at first to maintain imperial-style fiscal and monetary systems. Gradually, they surrendered the control of taxation and the right to coin money to local magnates and towns. By the early seventh century, coins ceased to circulate widely.

In the East, at the end of the fifth century, Emperor Anastasius successfully reformed the coinage of the eastern provinces (p. 699). His good-looking, well-made new bronze coin, the *follis* (so named because it was worth a bagful of the old coins) and its fractions, held their value. Justinian continued to improve them until the wars of the 540s. Then, war debts and the need for bronze to make arms forced him to debase the bronze coins once more.

As a result, inflation wracked the economy of the eastern Empire. Tiberius II (578–582) and Maurice (582–602) stabilized the coinage temporarily, but the assassination of Maurice and subsequent chaos, the wars with Persia, and attacks by the Arabs threw the monetary system of the East into turmoil. Inflation raged, most imperial mints ceased to function, and uniform, regular denominations of coins for daily use could not be maintained.

Agricultural trends

As trade and the Roman monetary system that supported it declined in the fifth and sixth centuries, the amount of cultivated lands in Roman territory declined, too. Contrary to older views, soil exhaustion was probably not a general problem. Often good or potentially good land was simply abandoned because of population loss or lack of security. In some fortunate or protected areas, particularly in the East, agriculture flourished and even expanded well into the sixth century. Justinian's wars in the West caused enormous destruction. Even in the East, their huge expenses were overburdening the small proprietors, and the concentration of land in the hands of a wealthy few became more pronounced than it had been in that part of the Empire.

SOCIAL AND DEMOGRAPHIC CHANGES

The economic trends of the fifth and sixth centuries accompanied major social and demographic changes. Although the population of the Empire had always been overwhelmingly rural, it became more so. At the same time, the total population declined. By the end of the sixth century, the late antique social world had given way to one that would characterize the medieval world for centuries.

The end of the Classical city

Although the urban population of the Roman Empire as a whole was probably never much more than 10 percent, the Classical Greco-Roman city gave Roman civilization its unique character. The Classical city had a number of easily recognizable features: citizen rights and civic institutions; an identifiable architectural style; standard public buildings and monuments like shrines, temples, baths, theaters, amphitheaters, circuses, markets, libraries, fora, honorific statues, commemorative arches, and inscriptions of all kinds; public works such as aqueducts, fountains, latrines, sewers, and well-paved streets. Maintaining and spreading the distinctive form of the Classical city had provided the social, cultural, and administrative glue that had held together

Rome's far-flung empire. During the fifth and sixth centuries, the cities of the Roman Empire were abandoned, destroyed, or transformed into something quite different in every way from what they had been before. Those that remained inhabited shrank to shadows of their former selves; their economic function became much more limited, primarily as local or regional market towns; the Classical style and construction of buildings gave way to local vernaculars; ecclesiastical institutions replaced civic; and the amenities disappeared.

The decline of Roman cities was both a function of and a contributor to the other changes taking place in the late antique Roman world. Attacks by invaders and usurpers weakened them so that they were more vulnerable to attack. The decline of trade and agriculture undermined them economically so that there was even less of a market for trade goods and agricultural products. The inability or unwillingness of urban elites to perform increasingly burdensome civic duties weakened civic institutions still further.

Like lights successively going out on a cascading power grid, Roman cities declined in a progression that began on the fringes of the less heavily urbanized West and culminated in the older, more heavily urbanized East. Cities along the northwestern frontier in Britain, northern Gaul, and Germany rapidly declined at an early date. Between 400 and 500, urban life disappeared in these areas. Many sites were abandoned altogether, but some places, such as London, York, and Augusta Treverorum, survived mainly as the locations of major churches and ecclesiastical residences.

Even Rome had practically collapsed by 550. During Justinian's Gothic War, its population may have been reduced to 20,000, and Procopius reports that at one point it was abandoned. After 600, Rome seems to have been primarily a site of monasteries and churches inhabited by clerics and a few Byzantine officials.

In Roman North Africa, Carthage decayed badly after Justinian's reconquest. Many of the occupied areas were abandoned in the seventh century. Burials, which used to be forbidden within the walls of the city, began to intrude upon ruined structures. After it fell to the Arabs in 698, it was abandoned altogether. By the time of the Arab Conquest, Lepcis (Leptis) Magna, on the coast between Carthage and Cyrene, had shrunk from a city covering 320 acres at its height to only 70.

In general, the cities of the East fared much better than those of the West in the fifth and sixth centuries. The cities of the northern Balkans, however, went into decline when the Huns and Ostrogoths invaded in the second half of the fifth century. Greek cities like Athens, Corinth, Argos, and Sparta declined precipitously after the Slavic attacks in the 580s. Athens remained inhabited, but the others were eventually abandoned.

The cities of Asia Minor and the Levant show new building activity accompanying growing wealth and population until the Persian and Arab invasions of the seventh century. Thereafter, rapid decline set in. The Sassanid Persians sacked Antioch in 611, Damascus in 613, and Jerusalem in 614. Between the Persian sack of 616 and the Arab attack of 654/655, the great city of Ephesus shrank to little more than a fortress. The Muslim capture of Alexandria in 642 ended its role as the supplier of grain to Constantinople and caused it to decay.

Constantinople itself had reached its apogee as a Classical city under Justinian. While Rome was shrinking, Constantinople had grown in population to about half a million. During the seventh century, however, as it lost control of the cities from which it drew its wealth, it too began to contract. Preoccupied with its own internal political intrigues and religious factionalism, it had lost the spirit and resources of a Classical city.

Changing patterns of rural settlement

The amount of archaeological information available for the countryside in Late Antiquity is not so great as that for cities, nor is it easy to interpret. Nevertheless, evidence for the transition to later patterns of settlement in the fifth and sixth centuries is beginning to come to light in some places. In the East, the pattern of village-farming life tended to endure in agricultural areas that were still prosperous. In the western provinces, rural life was in a state of flux. In many areas, life on the villa estates of great landowners began to resemble more that of medieval manorialism than that of the rural world in the high Empire.

In Italy, the shift from the Classical pattern of dispersed settlement in open land to the medieval pattern of hilltop villages often occurred. Archaeological surveys in South Etruria indicate a drastic drop in population and the creation of fortified hilltop settlements to protect the area from invading Lombards. A similar trend is evident in the upper valley of the Volturnus River. Although much more work needs to be done to confirm the details and to investigate other parts of Italy, it is safe to say that the transformation from the Classical to the medieval countryside was well underway by 600 C.E.

Attempts to improve the position of women and children in society

In the fifth and sixth centuries, there were attempts at improving conditions for women and children. How much these attempts actually affected the daily lives of most is hard to assess. Still, that efforts were even made is significant.

Emperors could not make up their minds on whether to permit divorce by mutual consent or not. There was always a fear that liberalized divorce would break up families too easily and harm the interests of the children in family property. Theodosius II allowed women to divorce unilaterally because of outrageous infidelity or abuse. Anastasius allowed divorce by mutual consent. In 542, Justinian added impotence to the list of grounds allowing a woman to seek divorce, but he banned consensual divorce and disallowed wife beating as grounds for divorce. (He did, however, institute heavy fines in an attempt to stop husbands from beating their wives.) A year after Justinian's death, Justin II returned to the more lenient position that men and women should be allowed to dissolve unhappy marriages by mutual consent without formal grounds. Working within a long legal tradition, Christian emperors, even in their most strict legislation, never adopted the teachings of churchmen like Basil of Caesarea,

Augustine, or Jerome that a woman could never divorce her husband and that neither could remarry until the other's death.

Justinian's legislation made a concerted effort to improve conditions for lower-class women, particularly prostitutes or those equated with prostitutes. There is good reason to believe that the powerful influence of Theodora had something to do with it (p. 674). In 535, Justinian made it a crime to force or trick girls into prostitution. Justinian also tried to protect all women from *raptus*, which encompassed seduction, abduction, and rape. Contrary to previous law (p. 618), a man who had intercourse with a woman of any class was unable to avoid a charge of *stuprum* (unlawful intercourse) unless she was his wife. Justinian also put the blame for *raptus* squarely on the man committing the deed. The penalty was execution. A woman's relatives or master could summarily kill her *raptor* if they caught him in the act. If the victim were a slave or freedwoman, the executed man's heirs could receive his property. A freeborn victim got to keep the executed man's property plus that of any accomplices, and she was free to marry without stigma. If she were in an adulterous relationship with a seducer, a woman could, if the family wished, be divorced and prosecuted with the man, but she could also simply be given a whipping and sent to a convent for two years. After that, she could return to her husband if he would have her.

Justinian tried to protect the property rights of children in their mother's family by asserting that consanguinity should be reckoned through females as well as males. He also decreed that a child could not be enslaved to pay off a parent's debts, a long-standing evil in the ancient world. Finally, he declared that no foundling could be raised as a slave. An unintended consequence, however, might have been a greater reluctance of people to take in exposed infants. On the other hand, the organized efforts of the Church to provide for such infants may have filled any gap.

Romans and Germans

Germanic rule seriously affected western Roman aristocrats. In Gaul, when the Visigoths and Burgundians were settled in Aquitania and Savoy in 418 and 443, the Roman inhabitants had to surrender one-third of their arable land, cattle, *coloni*, and slaves to the newcomers. Later they had to give up another third. Both the Visigoths and the Burgundians governed the old Roman inhabitants under special, Roman-based codes of law. That not only tended to segregate the Romans and Germans but made disputes between them more complicated. The Visigoths also forbade intermarriage between Romans and themselves.

In Italy, Odovacer took only one-third of each Roman's possessions for his men, and Theoderic the Amal merely reassigned those thirds to his Ostrogothic followers when he took over in 493. He allowed many landowners simply to pay one-third of their rents as taxes to the king instead of losing the land itself. Theoderic also tried to preserve the Roman administrative system intact and did not segregate the old Roman inhabitants. They could even serve as military officers.

The Vandals under Gaiseric in North Africa confiscated all the property of the Roman inhabitants and probably reduced to serfs those who did not flee. In northern

Gaul, the Franks were completely different. After their initial conquests, they left the Roman inhabitants in possession of all of their property.

General relations between old inhabitants of the West and newcomers were frequently strained. The Germanic tribesmen were not used to settled ways and orderly government, despite the earnest attempts of some of their kings to preserve continuity. Germanic officials were just as corrupt as the previous Roman ones. Lawlessness and violence were common everywhere.

Moreover, there was the added problem of the religious differences between the Arian Germans and the orthodox Catholic Romans. Ethnic antagonisms and religious differences tended to become intertwined. The situation was especially acute in the Vandal kingdom, where the kings were particularly fanatical Arians. Huneric banished about 5000 Catholic clergy to the desert and used Catholic bishops for forced labor on Corsica.

The Burgundians, Visigoths, and Ostrogoths were more tolerant and tried to cooperate with the Catholic hierarchy. Unfortunately, King Theoderic of the Ostrogoths found that orthodox clergy cooperated with his enemies. The Burgundian king Gundobad (474–516), former supreme commander at Rome (p. 661), had a better relationship and even allowed his children to be converted to Catholicism. His tolerance had a direct impact on the pagan Franks. Clovis, founder of the Merovingian dynasty of Frankish kings, married Gundobad's daughter Clotilda. She persuaded Clovis to be baptized as an orthodox Roman Catholic. After that, the Franks converted directly from paganism to Clovis' new faith. Thus, the foundation was laid for historically significant relations between the Franks and the Church at Rome.

RELIGION

From Justinian onward, Christians and their controversies increasingly dominated religious life. Justinian's attempts to root out paganism did not completely succeed but dealt it serious blows. Jews found the state increasingly hostile.

Pagan survivals

Although the public cults and rituals of paganism declined rapidly after Theodosius' attacks at the end of the fourth century, pagan intellectuals lived relatively undisturbed. Theodosius had not instituted the ancient equivalent of the Inquisition. Only the outward practices of paganism, not belief itself, were attacked. Pagan books freely circulated, and pagan thought still dominated the schools of law, rhetoric, and philosophy, where pagans and Christians freely mingled. During the fifth and early sixth centuries, many high imperial officials, who were usually trained in the schools, continued to be pagans, both openly and secretly. Even after the brutal murder of the pagan scholar Hypatia by the partisans of Cyril in 415 (p. 636), Alexandria remained a center of Neoplatonic thought with an Aristotelian twist. Athens continued as another center of Neoplatonism and even increased its intellectual prestige.

Justinian was the one who initiated what might be called an inquisition to eradicate pagan thought. He encouraged civil and ecclesiastical officials to investigate reports of continued pagan practice and forbade anyone except baptized Christians to teach. When the leaders of the schools at Athens refused to conform, Justinian confiscated the schools' endowments (529). Some of the scholars fled to the court of Chosroes I in Persia but soon found life uncongenial there. Chosroes did them one great service, however: in his treaty of 532 with Justinian, he stipulated that they be allowed to return to the Empire and live in peaceful retirement.

Justinian also sought to root out the paganism that had persisted among the simple folk of the countryside. He sent out aggressive officials to close out-of-the-way shrines that had escaped previous attempts at closure. He supported wide-ranging missionary activities to convert the unconverted. The task was made easier because there had already occurred a certain synthesis of Christian and pagan practices. The former simple services of the Primitive Church had now given way to more elaborate ceremonies that included the use of incense, lights, flowers, and sacred utensils. A myriad of saints and martyrs had taken over the competing functions of many pagan deities and heroes. It is no mere coincidence that the Parthenon at Athens, home of Athena the Virgin (*Parthenos*), became a church of the Virgin Mary; that the celebration of the Nativity came to coincide with the date of Mithras' birth and the season connected with pagan celebrations of the winter solstice; or that sleeping in a church of Saints Cosmas and Damian could now produce the cures that used to be found in a temple of Castor and Pollux. Nor would the distinction between theurgy and the celebration of the Eucharist be clear to the unsubtle mind.

Christian heretics and Jews

Many developments in late imperial Christianity involved heresies and schisms such as Arianism (p. 587), Monophysitism (p. 665), and Donatism (pp. 586–7). They have been discussed in chapters on the political events with which they were intimately bound because they had aroused popular passions. Other heresies have been noted in connection with religious developments during the third century (pp. 553–4).

In the early fifth century, the Pelagian heresy is worthy of note. It raised fundamental questions about sin and salvation that have exercised Christian thinkers ever since, although it did not touch off any great popular conflict at the time. The Church taught that saving grace could be obtained through only two sacraments, baptism and penance: baptism, which could not be repeated, would wash away the taint of Adam's original sin and any personal sins incurred in this life up to the moment of baptism; penance could eliminate those committed thereafter. As a result, in the fourth century, many who espoused Christianity put off baptism until the last possible moment in order to die sinless in a state of grace. After baptism in childhood or early adulthood became more common in the fifth century, penance was relied on as the means of wiping out sins committed before death. Therefore, many people paid little attention to the strict Christian moral code. They lived just as sinfully as non-Christians. Indeed, there was even less need to show restraint because they knew that all could be wiped away by baptism or penance.

Among those who were troubled by this unedifying state of affairs was a Welsh layman named Morgan, later known as Pelagius. He denied the doctrine that Adam's original sin derived from his nature and was transmitted to posterity. Therefore, he argued, it was possible to gain salvation through one's own efforts in leading a righteous life. Pelagius' views were originally accepted in the East, but St. Augustine (pp. 703–4) led an attack on them in the West at a council in 416. Eventually, after numerous intervening councils, they were condemned at the Third Ecumenical Council at Ephesus in 431.

Justinian, in his zeal to achieve "one Church and one Empire," was anxious to root out heretics as much as pagans. He barred heretics from the professions of law and teaching, forbade them the right to inherit property, and would not let them bear witness in court against orthodox persons. He even instituted the death penalty for Manichees and relapsed heretics.

Justinian was no friend of the Jewish population either. For centuries, the Greek and Jewish communities in the cities of the East had been at odds over the rights and duties of citizenship. At times they even rioted against each other. With the Greek population becoming more and more Christian, however, the explosive element of religious hatred made things worse. At Alexandria, for example, riots between Christians and Jews gave the newly elected bishop Cyril an opportunity to solidify his leadership of the Alexandrian church. He increased its power in the city by conducting a virtual pogrom against the Jewish population. It was Hypatia's support of the imperial prefect's efforts to curb Cyril's violence that led to her murder in 415 (p. 636).

Justinian abandoned the secular toleration that the Roman government had traditionally maintained toward Jews. Although he did not forbid orthodox Jews to practice their religion, he subjected them and Samaritans to the same civil disabilities as heretics. These policies resulted in two serious revolts of Jews and Samaritans in Palestine in 529 and about 550. They produced much bloodshed and no relief for the oppressed.

THE NEW CULTURAL SPIRIT

The tree planted during the cultural revival of the fourth century continued to grow in the fifth and sixth, but as cities declined, it increasingly required the special environment of a church, cloister, or ruler's court to flower. On the stock of elite pagan rhetoric, philosophy, literature, and art, Christianity had grafted the traditions of those formerly on the social and geographical fringes of the Roman world. The pagan stock still produced new shoots, but they were completely overshadowed by the luxuriant growth of the new graft, which transformed the cultural landscape of the age. It was a landscape dominated by theological debate, experiencing holy mysteries, discovering allegories, and a sense that, in the face of change, what was useful from the past needed to be collected before it was lost.

LATIN POETRY

Despite the internal conflicts and disruptive invasions of the fifth century in the West, pagan and Christian Latin poetry flourished.

Claudian (ca. 370 to ca. 404 c.e.) and Namatianus (d. after 416 c.e.)

Two poets who represent the old pagan stock in Latin literature are Claudius Claudianus and Rutilius Namatianus. Claudian was a pagan Greek from Alexandria and became the court poet of Honorius and Stilicho. He wrote in Latin and produced highly polished classicizing poems in praise of his two patrons and members of their families. Rutilius Namatianus was a wealthy pagan from Gaul, a member of the old Gallo-Roman elite. He left Rome in 416 to attend to his Gallic estates, which German raiders had badly damaged. He described his journey in the long elegiac poem *De Reditu Suo (On His Return)* that gives a moving tribute to the city of Rome and keenly observes the country through which he passes, but he crudely condemns the "barbarian" Stilicho, Judaism, monasticism, and all else that he saw as destroying paganism and the Empire.

Paulinus of Nola (353–431 c.e.)

A famous younger Christian contemporary is Paulinus of Nola (Meropius Pontius Paulinus). A wealthy Gallo-Roman, he was a prized pupil of Ausonius (pp. 634–5). Consul at Rome (378) and then governor of Campania, he married a wealthy woman from Spain. They eventually settled in the Campanian town of Nola. There, they devoted themselves to the cult of St. Felix of Nola. Each year for the saint's feast day, Paulinus composed one of his *Natalicia*, poetic sermons that use rural themes and everyday experiences to communicate Christian ideas to the pagan peasants. Paulinus' large correspondence links him not only with Ausonius, but also with many of the leading Christian figures of his day like St. Ambrose, St. Augustine, St. Jerome, Melania the Elder, and Melania the Younger.

Sidonius Apollinaris (ca. 430 to ca. 480 c.e.)

Like Paulinus, Bishop Sidonius Apollinaris of Clermont (Augustonemetum) near Gergovia (p. 719), had given up a prominent public career for the Church. He saw Classical culture and Christianity as allies against uncouth invaders. The twenty-four poems of his *Carmina* include occasional poems reflecting his social world and others in praise of the emperors Avitus (his father-in-law), Majorian, and Anthemius (pp. 660–1). Of great historical value are the nine books of letters that he published as bishop.

Dracontius (ca. 455–ca. 505 c.e.) and Corippus (fl. 540–570 c.e.)

Blossius Aemilius Dracontius and Flavius Cresconius Corippus were products of the late Roman literary culture of North Africa. Dracontius, a wealthy landowner from Carthage, wrote a number of poems on both pagan and Christian themes. His long poem *The Tragedy of Orestes* and two short epics (epyllia) *On the Rape of Helen* and *Medea* show his deep engagement with Classical mythology. His *On the Praises of God* celebrates the benevolence of God toward the pious. He also invokes Christian themes in the *Satisfactio*, a poem in which he asks pardon for offending a Vandal king.

Corippus had held some imperial offices before he left North Africa for the court at Constantinople. There, he continued the Latin Classical tradition with Vergilian-style historical epics: one about John, general in the Moorish War, and the other a celebration of Emperor Justin II.

Fortunatus (ca. 530 to 600 C.E.)

The last significant poet of the sixth century was Venantius Honorius Clementianus Fortunatus (p. 672). Born near Treviso in northeastern Italy, he received a solid Classical education at Ravenna. As a young man, he traveled across Germany and Gaul and eventually settled at Poitiers. There he became a bishop and close friend of both Gregory of Tours (p. 705) and the influential Merovingian queen Radegunda. Eleven books of his poems survive. They include panegyrics on various Merovingian kings, epitaphs, consolations, religious poems and hymns, and verse biographies of Radegunda and St. Martin of Tours.

LATIN PROSE

The greatest Latin authors of the fifth and sixth centuries wrote in prose. Their works included history, biography, philosophy, theology, sermons, and letters. They are rich sources for the history of Rome in the West during these centuries.

St. Jerome (ca. 347 to ca. 420 C.E.) and St. Augustine (354 to 430 C.E.)

The two greatest masters of late Latin prose were St. Jerome and St. Augustine. Educated at the height of the fourth century (see p. 629), they wrote in the early fifth and reflected high Classical standards. As Paulinus of Nola advocated, however, they applied their skill on behalf of propagating the faith. Yet, steeped as they were in the Classical tradition, they were devastated by the sack of Rome in 410.

Jerome (Sophronius Eusebius Hieronymus) was born at Stridon in Dalmatia and educated at Rome. As a young man, he traveled and studied in the Greek East. After learning Greek, he returned to Rome and rose to prominence as secretary to Pope Damasus I. Damasus asked him to undertake his most enduring work, the Latin translation of the Bible, commonly known as the *Vulgate*. For that task, he learned Hebrew in order to read the Hebrew Scriptures. Jerome was also a prolific commentator on the Bible and a harsh polemicist in theological debates. He carried on many of his disputes through a vast correspondence with people like St. Augustine. These letters and his historical works (p. 509) make him a major witness to his age.

Augustine (Aurelius Augustinus), bishop of Hippo Regius in Africa Proconsularis, is the greatest example of the complex blend of pagan learning and Christian faith, at least in the West. Born of a pagan father and a Christian mother at Thagaste, about one hundred miles south of Hippo, he studied rhetoric at Carthage. Then, he went to Rome to make his mark. There, he became acquainted with Symmachus and his circle. Through them, he gained appointment to a professorship of rhetoric at Milan. He was greatly influenced in thought and style by Cicero. He was also a Manichee before he became an orthodox Christian. His conversion took place at Milan through association with St. Ambrose, who was part of an influential circle of Christian Neoplatonists.

Augustine's voluminous letters, sermons, and commentaries show the influence of pagan Classical literature and philosophy everywhere. Two works stand out—his *Confessions* and his magnum opus, the *Civitas Dei* (*City of God*). The former traces his intellectual and spiritual development from a callow student smitten with Cicero to a Manichee, to a Neoplatonist, and finally to a baptized Christian. The latter work was stimulated by Alaric's sack of Rome in 410 and the flood of upper-class pagan refugees to Africa. Their presence threatened to undermine the recently won supremacy of orthodox Catholicism in his region.

In his best Latin rhetorical style, Augustine met them on their own terms. He made a systematic critique of the ancient myths and historical views on which they based their paganism. His refutation of Neoplatonism was philosophically rigorous. Even in arguing for his radically Christian view of reality, however, he argued on the basis of shared concepts, such as Divine Providence and the quintessentially Classical sociopolitical concept of the *civitas*, a community of citizens. For Augustine, the Christian is a citizen of God's perfect heavenly community and longs for it while he or she dwells as a resident alien in this earthly community. Yet, Augustine does not reject the earthly city. As part of God's creation, it is good, though not perfect. The good Christian, while enjoying its virtues, can work to eliminate its faults. There is no puritanical rejection of the Classical *civitas* that pagans loved. It is simply augmented by the vision of another that is even better.

Rufinus (345 to 410 C.E.)

Rufinus of Aquileia had been a friend of Jerome and was primarily a translator of Greek works, particularly Origen's (p. 560), which otherwise would be lost. Jerome's eventual doubts about the orthodoxy of Origen offended Rufinus and triggered a nasty dispute. Rufinus also translated Eusebius' *Ecclesiastical History* into Latin and extended it to the death of Theodosius I.

Orosius (ca. 390 to after 417 C.E.) and Salvian (ca. 400 to ca. 480 C.E.)

Augustine's younger friend Paulus Orosius, a priest from Spain, wrote theological treatises and a seven-volume history of man, the *Historia adversus Paganos*. He wrote it for Augustine to use in writing the *City of God*. Orosius argued that God had created the Roman Empire in order to spread Christianity and that Romano-Christian culture would eventually absorb the Germanic invaders. Salvian of Marseilles, however, declared in his *De Gubernatione Dei* (*On the Governance of God*) that God had sent the invaders to punish sinful Christians.

Gregory of Tours (538 to 594 C.E.)

Gregory, bishop of Tours (Limonum) in Merovingian Gaul, was a prolific writer of verse and prose. His poems are lost. Of his prose works, the most important is his *History of the Franks*. It begins with Adam but concentrates on the murderous doings of the Merovingian Franks. To Gregory, their bloody crimes are earthly episodes in the struggle between good and evil, which eventually will be won by good, represented on earth by the Church.

Martianus Capella (fl. ca. 435 C.E.)

A pagan resident of Carthage, Martianus Capella is another representative of the vibrant Latin culture of late Roman Africa. He wrote between the sack of Rome (410) and that of Carthage (439) and sought to sum up the essence of Classical culture in an encyclopedic work entitled *On the Marriage of Mercury and Philology*. Heavy with allegory, it reflects the religious-mystical world of Late Antiquity. It also establishes the model for the medieval educational curriculum based on the seven liberal arts: the *trivium* of grammar, dialectic, and rhetoric plus the *quadrivium* of geometry, arithmetic, astronomy, and music.

Boethius (ca. 480 to 524 C.E.)

Boethius is one of the great preservers of the Classical tradition in the sixth-century West. He was a philosopher from the Anicii family (p. 615) and had enjoyed the patronage of King Theoderic in Ostrogothic Italy. He was later executed on suspicion of treason. Attempting to sum up the best of ancient thought, he wrote on mathematics, music, Aristotle, and Cicero and had started the monumental task of translating all of Plato and Aristotle into Latin. He also wrote defenses of the orthodox view of the Trinity. His most popular work is the *Consolation of Philosophy*, written to comfort himself in jail. There, in a dialogue with the allegorical figure Philosophy, he espouses many pagan philosophical views that show how blurred the distinction could be between Neoplatonic paganism and Christianity.

Cassiodorus (487 to 583 C.E.)

Of a distinguished Italian family related to Boethius, Cassiodorus was one of the last holders of major Roman offices in the West. He became a consul, master of offices, and praetorian prefect. He published two historical works, the *Chronica*, which is a world history from Adam to 519, and the lost *History of the Goths*, which was used by Jordanes in his work on the Goths (p. 651). Cassiodorus also published the *Variae* which contains 468 official letters written while he was a high official in Ostrogothic Italy. Upon retirement, he founded a monastery in Bruttium, where he promoted the study and preservation of literature and useful knowledge that would enable the Romans and Germanic newcomers in Italy to forge a new nation. His treatise *Educational Principles of Divine and Secular Literature* was widely used as a guide to reading in the Middle Ages.

Isidore of Seville (Hispalis) (ca. 570 to 636 c.e.)

Bishop Isidore of Seville is most famous as an encyclopedist. He also wrote an important historical account of the Goths, Vandals, and Suevi as well as a *Chronica* and *De Viris Illustribus*. Succeeding his brother as bishop of Seville in 600, he worked hard to promote orthodox Catholicism in alliance with the Visigothic throne, but he also embraced ancient learning. He summarized rational explanations of natural phenomena in his *De Natura Rerum*, dedicated to King Sisebut in 613. In 620, the king commissioned an even greater encyclopedia, the *Etymology* or *Origins*. Unfinished when Isidore died, it was edited into twenty books. Through etymology, he tries to get back to and preserve the original meaning of the words that embody the skills, techniques, and tools essential for maintaining civilization.

CLASSICIZING GREEK POETS

The rigorous *paideia* maintained in the Greek cities continued to produce writers who could mimic the ancient Classics with ease. Much of their work has an artificial air. Sometimes, however, there is real merit.

Quintus of Smyrna (fl. ca. 350 c.e.) and Nonnus (fl. ca. 400 c.e.)

Quintus of Smyrna wrote a sequel to the *Iliad*, often called *Posthomerica*. It fills the gap between the *Iliad* and the *Odyssey* by recounting such things as the death of Achilles and the building of the Trojan horse. Less traditional in subject is Nonnus, a Christian from the Egyptian Thebaid who flourished around 400. A master of Greek epic verse, he paraphrased the Gospel of John in meter. His magnum opus, however, is an amazing epic in forty-eight books on the life and loves of the god Dionysus, the *Dionysiaca*. Thoroughly pagan in spirit, it weaves together mythological traditions from Egypt, India, and the Near East and revels in lush sensuality.

Minor Greek poets of Late Antiquity

A collection known as the *Greek Anthology* preserves a large number of clever epigrams in Classical style from a collection called *The Cycle*, authored by a number of high-ranking officials at Justinian's court. One of them, Paul the Silentiary, composed an excellent epic description of Justinian's great church Hagia Sophia for its second consecration in 562 (p. 711). He also wrote love poetry that has been much imitated by later writers.

Finally, a poem that has inspired countless retellings is Musaeus' romantic *Hero and Leander*, which tells how the young Leander is smitten by the beautiful Hero when he sees her at a religious festival. He convinces her of his love and swims across the Hellespont each night to join her secretly in her family's lofty tower by the shore. One night, overpowered by a storm, he drowns. When Hero spies his body washed up below, she hurls herself from the tower to join him in death.

THE LATE GREEK HISTORIANS

History is the premier Greek genre in the fifth and sixth centuries and is represented by several important authors.

Olympiodorus (fl. 410 to 425 c.e.) and Zosimus (fl. 490 to 520 c.e.)

A pagan Greek from Egyptian Thebes, Olympiodorus wrote a detailed account of the western Roman Empire for the period from 407 to 425. Significant fragments preserved in writers like Zosimus show that he was a serious and thoughtful historian. Zosimus was an official of the imperial treasury in the late fifth and early sixth centuries. His *New History* is an account of the Roman Empire from Augustus to Alaric's sack of Rome in 410. It is particularly valuable for the third, fourth, and early fifth centuries in the East. Zosimus used now-lost sources like Dexippus (p. 558), Eunapius (p. 635), and Olympiodorus. Zosimus was outspokenly anti-Christian and constantly blamed Rome's troubles on neglect of the old gods.

Socrates (ca. 380 to 450 c.e.)

The most significant church historian of the mid-fifth century was Socrates Scholasticus. His *Church History* continues Eusebius from 306 to 439. He was not a cleric, but an advocate at Constantinople. A well-read student of philosophy, theology, and logic, he respected Hellenism and brought a balanced sense of judgment to his work. That quality and his careful citation of sources make him particularly valuable.

Sozomen (ca. 400 to 460 c.e.) and Theodoret (393 to ca. 460 c.e.)

Another layman writing ecclesiastical history in Constantinople was Sozomen. He drew heavily on Socrates Scholasticus for his *Church History* and covered almost the same period (325–425). The Syrian bishop Theodoret of Cyrus (393–ca. 460) wrote another *Church History* covering virtually the same period as Socrates and Sozomen (323–428). As a bishop and theologian deeply involved in the controversy between Nestorius and Cyril over the nature of Christ (p. 667), Theodoret had an interesting perspective on the history of doctrinal issues. His *History of the Monks of Syria*, which includes three women as subjects, is an important source for the ascetic movement in the East.

Evagrius (ca. 535 to 600 c.e.)

A later church historian from Syria was the well-connected advocate Evagrius at Antioch. He admired Eusebius, Socrates, Sozomen, and Theodoret. He continued their work in his *Church History* from 428 to his own time. He carefully quoted his sources but was too credulous at times. He was hostile to the Monophysites and attacked the anti-Christian views of Zosimus. Pessimistic about people's ability to control events, he ascribed many things to God.

Procopius (ca. 500 to 565 c.e.) and Agathias (ca. 530 to ca. 582 c.e.)

The outstanding figure of late Greek secular historiography is Procopius. An advisor to the great Belisarius, he chronicled the age of Justinian (p. 672). The last secular Greek historian of the sixth century was Agathias. A lawyer and an official at Constantinople, he was also one of the love poets at court. He edited *The Cycle*, which contained many of his own poems. After Procopius died, Agathias decided to write his own militarily oriented *History*. His interest in the Franks and Persians and his use of Persian sources make him valuable. Unfortunately, when he died he had written only five books. They cover the campaigns of Narses in Italy and the end of the Lazic War.

PHILOSOPHY

Alexandria and Athens remained centers for Neoplatonic pagan philosophers. The distinction, however, between Neoplatonism and Christianity became more and more blurred. Philosophers and theologians shared the same intellectual world.

Synesius of Cyrene (ca. 370 to ca. 414 c.e.)

A good example of someone in whom Neoplatonism and Christianity tended to merge is Synesius, an aristocrat from Cyrene in the province of Libya. After studying with the pagan philosopher Hypatia in Alexandria, he successfully represented Libya at Constantinople in a plea for a reduction of its taxes. Later, he organized local efforts to defend Libya from the attacks of Berber tribes. Christians in Libya were so impressed with his leadership abilities that they insisted on electing him bishop of the important city of Ptolemais in 410. Synesius agreed only on the condition that he would give up neither his wife, who was a Christian, nor some of his most cherished philosophical beliefs. In return, he accepted basic Christian doctrines like the Resurrection. He wrote some typical rhetorical/philosophical essays on subjects like kingship and the decline of humanistic learning in the face of Christian asceticism and peasant superstition. He also wrote hymns that show his poetic talent and an important collection of 156 letters that provide a valuable look at life in his part of the late Roman world.

Proclus (ca. 410 to 485 c.e.) and Simplicius (ca. 490 to 560 c.e.)

There were no major original thinkers in the fifth and sixth centuries, but Proclus, who headed the Academy in Athens, was a significant synthesizer. He wrote commentaries on some of Plato's dialogues and compiled encyclopedic works on physics, Platonic theology, and astronomy. Living a very ascetic, monkish life and even writing Neoplatonic hymns, he, too, illustrates the shared religious-mystical views of the day. Another important commentator was Simplicius. He studied at both Alexandria and Athens in the sixth century and wrote extensively on Aristotle. After Justinian officially ended the teaching of philosophy in Athens, Simplicius somehow kept on working. There is even a hint that he established a new school at Carrhae (Harran) in Persian territory.

THEOLOGY

By this time, it was very difficult to separate philosophy and Christian theology. The Platonists and Aristotelians, for example, presented questions that Christian theologians had to confront and ideas that they could use. Many of them were relevant to the Christological debates over the nature of Christ that dominated Greek theology in the fifth and sixth centuries.

John Philoponus (ca. 490 to ca. 470 c.e.)

The great rival of the Neoplatonists was John Philoponus, a Monophysite Christian and an Aristotelian. He was the principal philosopher at Alexandria. It is understandable that, as a Christian, he would attack Proclus' belief that the world had no beginning.

Cyril (ca. 375 to 444 c.e.), Nestorius (ca. 381 to 451 c.e.), and John of Antioch (d. 441 or 442 c.e.)

The fifth- and sixth-century Christological debates began with the dispute between Bishop Cyril of Alexandria and Bishop Nestorius of Constantinople over granting Mary the title *Theotokos*, "Mother of God" (p. 665). Nestorius, no original theologian himself, came from Antioch, where some theologians taught that Christ was the true union by association of two personal subjects, one human and one divine. Cyril, ally of Pulcheria, wanted to assert the supremacy of his bishopric over Antioch and Constantinople. He speciously accused Nestorius of teaching the heresy that Christ comprised two separate persons (p. 667). Bishop John of Antioch naturally allied with Nestorius against Cyril. After Nestorius was condemned at the Council of Ephesus (431), John and Cyril reached a compromise called the Formula of Union (p. 667). Some of Nestorius' supporters, however, did take what is called the *Dyophysite* (two separate natures) position to the heretical extreme that Christ was two persons and established a separate Nestorian church that Nestorius himself never supported.

Pseudo-Dionysius, ca. 500 c.e.

Works spawned by the bitter Christological debates of the fifth and sixth centuries fell into obscurity once the politics that drove them were settled by the Arab Conquest. On the other hand, one of the most influential theological works from this period is a collection of spurious writings by an author purporting to be a first-century Athenian

FIGURE 37.1   Bishop Abraham, sixth- or seventh-century icon from Middle Egypt.

Christian named Dionysius and once thought to be St. Paul's convert Dionysius the Areopagite. He is now called *Pseudo-Dionysius* and was really writing around 500. He was trying to reconcile Christianity and Neoplatonic philosophy. The ideas expressed are heavily influenced by the teachings of Proclus. They teach the Neoplatonic idea that God cannot be known directly and interacts with people through a series of nine angelic emanations. Contemplation and prayer, however, can free the soul for ecstatic union with God.

ART AND ARCHITECTURE

After 395, little new ground was broken in architecture until the time of Justinian. Except at Constantinople, there was little building activity beyond defensive works and churches. From the time of Constantine onward, great works of art from pagan temples were carried off to decorate the buildings of the New Rome. Despite official attempts to preserve the great monuments of the past, many old pagan temples were used as quarries for the building of Christian churches. Early Christian churches generally adopted the style of the Roman basilica, a simple rectangular building with arched windows, a semicircular apse at one end, and a pitched wooden roof. Eventually, side aisles were added, and then in Justinian's Church of the Holy Apostles at Constantinople, two short wings or transepts were added near one end to produce a plan in the shape of a cross.

Hagia Sophia

Justinian's Church of Hagia Sophia (Holy Wisdom) set a whole new style of church architecture. The best available architects, Anthemius of Tralles and Isidore of Miletus, were in charge of building a new Hagia Sophia to replace the one destroyed in the Nika Rebellion (pp. 677–9). Anthemius, who had specialized in domed churches, conceived the novel plan of combining a domed roof with a floor plan in the shape of a Greek cross. It was about 250 feet by 225 feet with a dome above the 100-foot square where the arms intersected.

The outside, as became typical of Byzantine churches, was plain, but the interior was richly decorated. Different-colored marbles from around the Empire were used for pillars and floors and to sheathe the walls. The domed ceiling was covered with pure gold, and huge mosaics decorated the church throughout.

The new Hagia Sophia was dedicated on December 26, 537. Unfortunately, however, Anthemius and Isidore had miscalculated the stresses in its innovative design, and the dome eventually collapsed in 558. Isidore the Younger built a new dome over twenty feet higher to provide more vertical thrust. It was finished in 562 and has endured to this day.

Decorative arts

Under the patronage of the Church, emperors, kings, and the wealthy few, the decorative arts reached new heights during the fifth and sixth centuries. There were gold and silver plates with finely chased reliefs; goblets, chalices, crosses, and crowns encrusted with gemstones; exquisitely carved ivory plaques and containers; richly embroidered tapestries and robes; elaborately designed rings and jewelry; fancy reliquaries; beautifully decorated books; and lavishly wrought icons, wall paintings, and mosaics. All were marks of piety and status.

Icons received particular attention during the fifth and sixth centuries. An icon is the image (*eikon* in Greek) of a particularly holy person, object, or scene. Icons were often painted on wooden panels with egg tempera or molten wax (encaustic). Their use stems from the cultural traditions of Egypt and the Near East, which influenced the Hellenistic and Roman practice of creating similar portraits of gods, emperors, kings, officials, and renowned men of letters. These Classical and pre-Classical predecessors often influenced the pose, grouping, and symbolism found in Christian icons. For example, the popular icon of the seated Virgin holding the infant Jesus child on her lap has its parallel in similar Egyptian depictions of Isis and Horus, her son.

By the fifth century, the popularity of icons increased as people began to believe in their ability to ward off evil. During the next century, it was common to bow and genuflect before icons. A cult of icons emerged, supported by theological speculation of a Neoplatonic bent about the relationship of an image to what is being imaged.

Icons employed the same flat, perspective-less, otherworldly style popular in wall paintings and mosaics during the fourth century (pp. 639–40). Their otherworldly

FIGURE 37.2 Deesis mosaic, 12th–13th century, showing Emperor Commenos II, Virgin Mary, Jesus Christ, and Empress Irene, Hagia Sophia, 532–37, by Isidore of Miletus and Anthemius of Tralles, Istanbul, Turkey. © Manuel Cohen/Art Resource, NY.

FIGURE 37.3 Mosaic depicting Justinian and attendants and Saint Maximian. San Vitale, Ravenna, Italy.

quality was enhanced by powerful symbols, rich color, and a skillful handling of light. The combination of color and light is particularly impressive in the mosaics of the period. Subtle patterns created by richly colored bits of glass and stone make them glow with inner life. Many stunning examples can still be found at Ravenna in churches like San Vitale and Sant'Apollinare in Classe from the time of Justinian.

To enter these sanctuaries is to enter a completely different world from that of the first Roman emperor 600 years earlier. The pieces of the mosaic that constituted Roman culture had been rearranged into a very different pattern. Still, something of its substance remained, and memories of the old pattern endured.

FIGURE 37.4   Mosaic of Theodora with attendants, San Vitale, Ravenna, Italy.

SUGGESTED READING

Mitchell, S. *A History of the Later Roman Empire AD 284–641: The Transformation of the Ancient World. Blackwell History of the Ancient World*. Malden and Oxford: Blackwell Publishing, 2007.

Wickham. C. *Framing the Early Middle Ages: Europe and the Mediterranean, 400–800*. Oxford: Oxford University Press, 2005.

CHAPTER 38

The Church and the legacy of Rome

The social, political, and cultural values promoted by Christian empresses, emperors, clergymen, and male and female lay leaders, artists, and writers played a powerful role in the transformation of the late antique Roman world into the medieval West and the Byzantine Empire. It should be clear by now, however, that Christianity and its ecclesiastical institutions were not alien imports to that world, but organically grew out of it. Christianity is deeply rooted in Judaism, and the Judaism of the first century C.E. had been permeated by the culture of the Hellenistic Greek world that Rome inherited. The Jewish people had lived in that world for 300 years before the Roman annexation of Judea. The early Christian missionary Paul was a highly Hellenized, Greek-speaking Jew who claimed Roman citizenship. He did much to spread Christianity beyond the Jewish community in the first century C.E. and shape Christian theology. The new religion that he spread grew by converting the pagan population of the Roman world. For 300 years, many of the great leaders and thinkers among Christians were converts who had been steeped in Classical literature, rhetoric, and philosophy. The Christian desire not to be of the world while in it was impossible for any human being, even the most rigorous ascetic, to attain fully. Christianity, then, must be seen as part of the systemic evolution of the Roman world. It was as much an effect of that world's gradual transformation as it was a cause.

TRANSMITTING THE ROMAN CLASSICAL LEGACY

Even as Christianity was helping to transform Classical Roman civilization, it was spreading the legacy of that civilization far beyond its traditional boundaries. Ireland (Hibernia) had been known to Greek and Roman mariners and geographers since at least the late seventh century B.C.E. The famous Roman general Agricola had even contemplated invading it from Britain under the Flavians. Nevertheless, active contact with the Greeks and Romans had been minimal, and their cultural influence had been commensurate. By the fifth century C.E., however, contact with the Celts in Britain had brought Christianity to some of those living in the south of Ireland. Prosper of Aquitaine wrote that in 431 Pope Celestine I sent a deacon named Palladius to believers in Ireland. A few years later, a British bishop named Patricius (Patrick) came to missionize pagans in northern Ireland. He had once been taken there as a slave before escaping back to Britain. In thirty years, he had created a flourishing Church, which was based in rural monasteries because Ireland was devoid of cities.

Although they were independent of the urban-based episcopal system led by the bishop of Rome, the Irish monks were deeply immersed in the Latin Christian tradition. They produced an extensive Latin literature of poetry, letters, sermons, saints' lives, biblical commentaries, and inspirational tales. Safe from the Germanic migrations that swamped the Roman West, the Irish developed a strong scholarly tradition. Irish missionaries like Columba (ca. 521–ca. 597) and Columbanus (d. 615) transferred it to northern Britain and Gaul in the sixth and seventh centuries. Some of the earliest manuscripts of late Latin authors and the Latin Bible are preserved in Irish manuscripts.

By 595, Britain had been lost to the Roman Empire for at least 150 years. The pagan Saxons had driven the Christianized Celtic population to the western parts of the island, and Irish missionaries had reevangelized mainly the North along the Scottish border. At that point, however, Pope Gregory the Great saw an opportunity to convert the Saxons to Christianity through the Roman Catholic Church. The Saxon king Ethelbert of Kent had married Clovis' great-granddaughter Bertha, a Roman Catholic. Gregory called upon a Benedictine monk who came to be known as St. Augustine of Canterbury (not to be confused with the earlier St. Augustine of Hippo). He was to lead missionaries to Ethelbert's court at Canterbury in hopes of converting his kingdom. After a two-year delay, the missionaries finally arrived at Canterbury. They quickly succeeded in converting Ethelbert, and Gregory made Augustine the first archbishop of Canterbury. After that, he rapidly evangelized neighboring Anglo-Saxon kingdoms. The Celtic Christians of the West and North, however, differed with the Roman Church over the date to celebrate Easter (the Paschal controversy), the appropriate tonsure for monks, and the independence of bishops. Many of these issues were finally resolved at the Council of Whitby (663–664), and Celtic Christianity was effectively united with the Church of Rome.

In East Africa, Arabia, and the Far East, Christian sects that have been labeled heretical did the most to transmit the Greco-Roman legacy beyond the traditional bounds of the Roman world. The Ethiopian kingdom centered at Axum (Axumis, Auxume) and the kingdoms of Nubia had enjoyed considerable commercial and diplomatic contact with the Empire for a long time. Their conversion to Christianity linked them even more closely to the cultural and intellectual world of Late Antiquity. Nubia, extending up the Nile between Aswan and Ethiopia, comprised three kingdoms that were eventually united by the kingdom of Nobatia. In 542, Empress Theodora sent Monophysite missionaries to convert the region. As a result, Nubian Christians aligned with the Monophysite Copts in Egypt, along with whom they were cut off from the Orthodox Church at Constantinople by the Arab Conquest. The cultural heritage of this wealthy kingdom has only recently received serious attention.

South of Nubia, the Ethiopian royal family at Axum had been converted to Christianity by the mid-fourth century, apparently through the efforts of two brothers. One of them, Frumentius, supposedly was consecrated the first bishop of Axum by Athanasius of Alexandria. After the Council of Chalcedon in 451, Ethiopian Christians sympathized with the Monophysites and received a number of influential Monophysite refugees from Syria and Egypt. They founded so many churches and monasteries that Cosmas Indicopleustes, a sixth-century merchant in the Indian trade, asserted that Ethiopia was thoroughly Christianized.

A rich body of Christian writings appeared in the ancient Ethiopic language, Ge'ez. The Septuagint and New Testament, the *Life of St. Anthony*, the monastic rules of Pachomius, and many other Greek texts were translated into Ge'ez. The only complete text of the apocryphal book of Enoch exists in an Ethiopian translation. Many other Ethiopian translations of important Greek, Arabic, and Coptic originals are still awaiting proper scholarly attention.

In 523, King Kaleb of Ethiopia (514–542), in alliance with Justin I, sent an expedition across the Red Sea to South Arabia to rescue Christians who were being persecuted by an ally of Persia. Syriac Christians had been particularly active in spreading Christianity to the Arabian Peninsula. They were so successful that Islamic traditions mention a Christian cemetery and an icon of Mary and Jesus at Mecca and claim that Mohammed conversed with monks and other Christian Arabs. Indeed, Syriac Christians communicated Greek logic, rhetoric, and science along with Christian mysticism and even theology to the Arabs.

In the Far East, Syriac Monophysite and Nestorian missionaries spread Christianity to India and China. The so-called "Thomas Christians" in India today are descended from the early Indian converts. A Nestorian missionary named Mar Sergis was working in Lint'ao (Lintan) 300 miles west of the Chinese capital at Xi'an (Sian) by 578. A-lo-pen was preaching Nestorian Christianity in Xi'an itself by 635 and placed Christian Scriptures in the library of the Emperor T'ai-Tsung. He probably helped to translate the still-extant *Treatise on Jesus the Messiah* into Chinese. The story of his career and a list of thirty-five Chinese Christian books are preserved in the *Treatise of Veneration*. Many later writings, artifacts, and ruins of the early Chinese Christians have survived and show the interaction of Christianity and Buddhism along the ancient Silk Road. Buddhism survived later official persecution in China, but Christianity did not.

In the Caucasus region, Armenia had become the first officially Christian nation when Gregory the Illuminator (ca. 240–332) converted King Tiridates III. The Armenian bishop Mashtots (361/362–440) and Sahak, the Syriac bishop of Samosata (Samsat), invented the first alphabet for Armenian. They turned it into a literary language by initiating the translation of the Bible and other early Christian texts, which provided the foundation for later original work by Armenian scholars and theologians. Works by many important Greek authors whose originals are lost survive in Armenian translations. After Chalcedon, the Armenians, too, became Monophysites and spread that version of Christianity to other peoples of the Caucasus.

THE IMPERIAL CHURCH

As Christian missionaries spread Rome's cultural legacy beyond the traditional boundaries of the Classical world, the Church also preserved Rome's imperialistic spirit. In the East, where Constantinople maintained the imperial political and military apparatus, the Byzantine rulers and Orthodox patriarchs (bishops) became so firmly united in the cause of Empire that the term *Caesaropapism* has often been used to describe the relationship between the Church and the secular state. In the West, where the secular apparatus of the senate and the Caesars disappeared, the bishops of Rome (popes) erected an ecclesiastical structure in its place.

The rise of ecclesiastical power

While the power of the Roman emperors and their officials in the West declined during the fifth and sixth centuries, Christian ecclesiastics gained increasing control over civic and secular affairs. During the first three centuries C.E., Christians had created an ecclesiastical administrative structure outside of, but parallel to, the secular administrative system. It had spread through the network of cities that were the basis of Roman imperial control. By the fourth century, many cities had churches headed by an official whose title was the Greek word for overseer, *episkopos*. From the Latin transliteration, *episcopus*, are derived *episcopal* and related words in English. Germans corrupted the pronunciation *episcopus* into *Bischof*, which came into English as *bishop* through the Anglo-Saxon dialect of German.

The bishop's church was called a *cathedral* (from the Greek word for his throne, *kathedra*). From it, he might control other churches and Christian institutions such as hospitals, orphanages, old-age homes, and homeless shelters in his city and its surrounding territory, which constituted his "see" (from the Latin *sedes*, "seat"). Other churches and institutions within the see might be independent dioceses and parishes with their own endowments and clergy, but a bishop and his cathedral church would certainly have the most prestige in comparison.

Christian bishops in individual Roman provinces had created provincial councils called *synods* (congresses) modeled on the secular provincial councils made up of leading representatives from municipal *curiae* (p. 366). Bishops usually met once or twice a year to discuss common issues in the provincial capital (*metropolis*, mother city). The bishop of the *metropolis* presided. Therefore, the metropolitan bishop came to exercise influence over the bishops in other churches of the province. The Council of

Nicaea formalized the authority of metropolitan bishops in 325. It also recognized the extraprovincial primacy of sees in great cities like Alexandria, Antioch, Rome, and Carthage. As a result, a hierarchy of bishops reflecting the administrative hierarchy of cities in the Roman imperial system had emerged. Thus, the administrative organization of Christian churches mirrored that of the Roman government.

When Constantine sought to enlist this organization in the effort to restore peace and stability to the Roman world under his leadership, it became even more like the administrative apparatus of the Roman Empire. In 314, Constantine summoned bishops from the western provinces to the largest synod yet held. It met at Arelate (Arles) to deal with the Donatist controversy in North Africa (pp. 586–7). In 325, he summoned the Council of Nicaea, which was the first ecumenical council because bishops from the whole Empire were invited, although virtually all who came were eastern (pp. 589–9). The next six ecumenical councils, which are the only other ones accepted as such by both the Greek Orthodox and Roman Catholic churches, were also summoned by emperors.

Clearly, bishops were now very important people. The ecclesiastical and imperial hierarchies had been joined at the top. Bishop Hosius of Corduba (ca. 257–ca. 357) was one of Constantine's major advisors. After the establishment of the eastern court at Constantinople, resident and visiting bishops, whom subsequent emperors frequently consulted, constituted a perpetual (endemic) council. As Constantine and his Christian successors bestowed money, power, and privileges upon the Church and its clergy, aristocrats saw an opportunity to acquire leadership and prestige through the control of important episcopal sees. In Constantine's restored Empire, the Church became a new vehicle of civilian power for the traditional aristocracy of a world that had become increasingly dominated by upstarts and "barbarians" through the military.

Christian congregations gave a bishop a well-organized group of supporters whom he could mobilize against secular and ecclesiastical rivals through effective preaching. He also had significant wealth at his disposal. imperial donations and private bequests to churches and Christian charitable foundations had placed large amounts of money and property in episcopal hands. Constantine himself had set a precedent by granting to the churches of Rome estates with incomes totaling over 400 pounds of gold a year. Leaving something to the Church in one's will became customary for Christians of all classes. Moreover, the Church had to pay only the regular taxes on its lands, which were free from extraordinary imposts and the burden of corvées.

As a result, bishops of large churches enjoyed impressive incomes. John Chrysostom said that the church at Antioch had revenues equal to those just below the wealthiest citizens. In the first half of the sixth century, the church at Ravenna enjoyed annual rents of 12,000 *solidi*, and at the beginning of the seventh century, the bishop of Alexandria had 8000 pounds of gold in his treasury. Such resources allowed the bishops of major sees to exercise patronage and maintain staffs or retinues greater than those of secular aristocrats and even rivaling those of imperial officials.

According to one document, the bishop of Ravenna annually received 3000 *solidi*, 880 fowls, 266 chickens, 8800 eggs, 3760 pounds of pork, and 3450 pounds of honey as well as an unspecified number of geese and quantity of milk. That income fed his household and provided gifts and banquets for the people whom he cultivated in maintaining the dignity of his office. At the great church in Constantinople, Justinian tried to limit the ordained staff to 525, not to mention additional personnel like grave-diggers, funeral attendants, and parabalans (stretcher-bearers for the sick and infirm). At Constantinople alone, the funeral attendants numbered 950 under Justinian. At Alexandria in the early fifth century, Cyril had a force of 500 rugged parabalans at his disposal as he tried to overawe imperial prefects and other rivals in the violence that led to the murder of Hypatia (p. 636).

It is no wonder that emperors and imperial officials were willing to grant as much respect to bishops as they did to wealthy secular aristocrats, renowned pagan orators and philosophers, or charismatic holy men. They needed the cooperation of these powerful men to maintain control at the local level. Bishops, therefore, could exercise greater freedom of speech, *parrhesia*, than many in dealing with imperial authorities. They also had greater opportunities to catch the ear of a Christian emperor. Bishops could use this influence on behalf of their cities to obtain relief from taxes, assuage the wrath of an angry emperor, or secure imperial gifts and benefactions.

The resources and respect commanded by a bishop could allow him to assume the leadership of his entire community when the secular powers failed. In 451, for example, Bishop Anianus of Orleans (Cenabum, Aurelianum [d. 453]) successfully organized the defense of his city against the Huns. The great Gallo-Roman aristocrat Sidonius Apollinaris (p. 702) had risen all the way to consul and prefect of Rome when he turned to the Church and around 445 became bishop of Clermont (Augustonemetum) near Gergovia. He organized resistance to the Visigoths and was imprisoned when they were victorious. They soon reinstated him, however, and acknowledged his leadership of the local Roman population. In 540, Megas, bishop of Beroea (Aleppo) in Syria, vainly tried to save his city from the Persians in the face of apathetic Roman authorities.

In the East, the prominent metropolitan bishops of Alexandria, Antioch, and Constantinople had perpetuated the intercity rivalries of the old civic elites. These rivalries frequently manifested themselves in bitter doctrinal disputes as each bishop tried to assert the dominance of his city's theological position. The Arab conquests of the seventh century put an end to that situation by leaving Constantinople as the largest surviving Christian see of the Greek East. After that, the interests of church and state in the Byzantine Empire became indissolubly linked.

THE RISE OF ROME

In the West, the abandonment of Rome for Milan as the emperors' principal residence in the mid-third century had long prepared the way for the separate authority of the pope, bishop of Rome. When Alaric and the Visigoths besieged the city in 408, Pope Innocent I stepped into the political vacuum and tried to save the city. Pope Leo I intervened to save Rome from Attila the Hun in 450 and managed to negotiate with the Vandals in 455 to lessen the fury of their sack. Under Julius I (337–352), the Council of Serdica (343) tried to settle the dispute between Athanasius and his Arian opponents (p. 638). It declared that Rome, as the apostolic see of St. Peter, could hear appeals from other bishops. Carthage was the only real rival of Rome in the West, but it did not have an apostolic connection. Therefore, Roman bishops increasingly held primacy in the West and claimed it in the East. In 381, the First Council of Constantinople (Second Ecumenical Council) proclaimed Constantinople as the "New Rome," second in primacy only to "Old Rome."

The emperors Gratian and Valentinian III issued decrees in support of the popes in ca. 378 and 445. After the western line of emperors ended in the late fifth century, Pope Gelasius I (492–496) virtually declared himself joint ruler in a letter to the eastern Emperor Anastasius. He used the image of "two swords" that governed the world: the spiritual authority of the bishop of Rome as *Vicar of Christ* and the temporal power of the emperor. After the adversities following Justinian's death, Pope Gregory the Great (590–604) set out to conquer the West for Rome once more, not with new legions, but with loyal missionary bishops. They would enlist the armies of heretic and pagan nations in the cause by converting their kings and queens to Rome's faith. Rome in the West would now be the Church.

SUGGESTED READING

Brown, P. *The Rise of Western Christendom: Triumph and Diversity, A.D. 200–1000.* Rev. ed. Malden, MA and Oxford: Wiley-Blackwell, 2013.
Jenkyns, R., (ed.). *The Legacy of Rome: A New Appraisal.* Oxford: Oxford University Press, 1992.

Index

Note: This index also functions as a glossary of many Latin terms encountered in the text. It is not designed to be a complete concordance of proper names and places mentioned. Almost all individuals are listed, but only the major cities and provinces are included. Most Romans, especially before the fourth century c.e. and except emperors (who are usually included under their conventional names in English), have their primary entries under the names of their *gentes*: e.g., Julius for Caesar, Tullius for Cicero.

For given names the following conventional abbreviations are employed: A. for Aulus, Ap. for Appius, C. for Gaius (originally spelled Caius), Cn. for Gnaeus (originally spelled Cnaeus), D. for Decimus, L. for Lucius, M. for Marcus, M'. for Manius, Mam. for Mamercus, P. for Publius, Q. for Quintus, Sex. for Sextus, Sp. for Spurius, T. for Titus, and Ti. for Tiberius.

For convenience, Church councils, important battles, and major wars are listed alphabetically under the headings "Council of," "Battle of," and "War(s)."

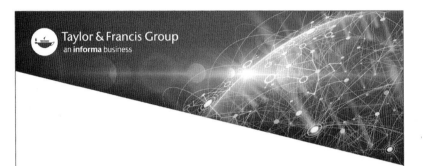